Digital Organizations
Leadership Disrupted

Ganesh Shermon

First Printing: 2017

ISBN **978 - 1- 365- 59421- 2**

LULU Publishing, Raleigh, NC.

www.lulu.com

Lulu Publishing Services Rev. date: January 1st, 2017

Chapters

Preface

Chapter 1   Business of Digital Organizations

Chapter 2   Case for the Digital Intellect

Chapter 3   Cultural Manifestation Patterns

Chapter 4   Influence of Digital Organizations

Chapter 5   Built by Leadership disrupted

Chapter 6   Organization Model Interfaces

Chapter 7   Linking The Digital Organizational Dots

Chapter 8   Emergence of a Digital Culture

Chapter 9   Leading an Intellectual Company

Chapter 10   Digital Building Blocks

Chapter 11   The Intellectual Company – Discover

Chapter 12   Leadership Disrupted

Epilogue   People Factor - A Digital Mind Set

Annexure 1   *Measuring Digital Organizations in an Intellectual Company*

Annexure 2   *Conceptual Understanding of Organizational Models, Leadership disrupted Styles and Four Types of Cultures*

Preface

Discover the Intellectual Company! When we think of organizations we think of an amorphous, large, complex perhaps global, institutions that have built in mechanisms for vision, strategy, structure, roles, goals, policy processes, people, technology, systems, clients, products and activities. True, but organizations are also symbols of its people who aspired, nurtured and struggled away to make it work; not to forget its collection of stories, rituals, episodes, values, experiences that can be broadly summarized and called as culture. Organizations are also a collection of emotions, feelings, trust, values, beliefs, struggles and successes. Binding force in an organization is always and will be its leadership (People/Practices). For leaders who take up this responsibility to glue, a vision and values to customers and products or technology with change or people with their dreams and aspirations, have a significant role in making or breaking organizations. Leaders build or destroy organizations while leaving behind an indelible mark – a legacy from which organizations take a very long time to succeed or recover from its impact. Sometimes organizations never do! Through their personal values! And the ethics that their organizations display today and in times to come. Organizations are indeed products of a leader's imagination. It takes the shape of that dream. And in that dream, good or bad, lies its destiny. This book is an outcome of an attempt to understand organizations as they link and align with culture and leadership in a digital business model. This books attempts to weave together a case for alignment between organization, culture and leadership by linking dots in understanding the business of digital organizations while establishing a case for the digital intellect. The book assumes that leaders display behaviors through an understanding and comprehension of their business realities, challenges and opportunities, manifested as everyday decisions. The book is built on the premise that organizations have their leadership disrupted owing to digital influences in technology, knowledge, millennial mindset, people attitudes, skills, behaviors, rapid changes in customer needs, speed and agility, flexible structures, dynamic - creative designs, unique people actions (expectations and deliverance), talent issues, business climate, HR programs, work values and business ethics (all displayed as culture). The book concludes by defining an organization model – operating core, new forms of leadership – Teacher – Learner - Scientist, the emergence of a digital culture (Evolving), the presence of an Intellectual Company, including digital building blocks and the intellectual people factor - A Digital Mind Set.

May I please place on record my gratitude and appreciation to individuals, organizations, leaders and followers, my firm, each and every one of them, who without hesitation supported the research work in all possible ways. They were truly the inspirers of the document produced herein. I owe an enormous debt of gratitude to past and present colleagues from KPMG, its CEOs, partners, consultants and clients.

And my gratitude and obligation goes to, my friends, inspirers, mentors and guides, who took me at face value when I spoke of my desire to write a book on a complex subject and agreed to support my research. Each of them kept at it through these many years guiding, directing, channeling, following up and pushing to get on with it. They set targets, subtle, meaningful and worthy to complete.

A writer is only as good as his clients, corporate entities, teachers, trainers, content sources, mentors, guides and, editors. It has been a privilege to have so many supporting this book. Hundreds, from multiple domains, countries, ethnicity, culture specialists, thought leaders contributed to this book by graciously, generously spending the time to be interviewed, by sharing their ideas, or by pointing me to people, research material and, case studies. Of special mention would be some terrific contribution, great inspiration with interviews, case studies, research content, books, blogs, thought papers, authors, futurists, organizational material from Adam Grant, Adrian Gore, Aditya Puri, Alessandro Di Fiore, Allan Freed, Allain Gosselin, Allen Webb, Allen J. Morrison, Allan Alter, Anh Nguyen Phillips, Andres Hervas-Drane, Andy Manko, Andrall E. Pearson, Andrew Mayo, Andrew McAfee, Andrew Shimberg, Andrew Arcuri, Anshuman Singh, Anthony Bourdain, Anthony Goldbloom, A Lakhani, Arvind Mahajan, Ashish Gupta, Armina Kapadia, Arun Sundararajan, Austin O. Oparanma, Brad Karsh, Bharath Ramakrishnan, Bill Owens, Bobby Parikh, Ben Van Deputt, Benn Konsynski, Bert Spector, Bernd Schmitt, Belal A. Kaifi, Bhrigu Joshi, Bill Briggs, Bruno Aziza, Bukowitz Wendi, Caroline Webb, Carolyn Dewar, Carlos Dominguez, Claudia Saran, Claudio Fernández-Aráoz, Charles Swindoll, Christi Joseph Paul, Christine Barton, Christine Bader, Christian Schm, Chris Egan, Chris Townley, Christoph Zott, Christopher A. Bartlett, Claudio Feser, Claudia Joyce, Clifford Geertz, Colin Price, Courtney Templin, Cristina San Jose, Dan Pink, Daftuar C N, Darius Ghandhi, Darren Faint, Dave Ulrich, David Kiron, David M. Schweiger, David Mathison, David Maxfield, David Knight, David Teece, Deidra J. Schleicher, Deepa Shekar, Detlef Pollack, Donald J Boldwell, Don Valentine, Davis Dyer, Donald F. Van Eynde, Donna Morris, Dorian Pyle, Doug Palmer, Douglas Iverster, Derek Dean, Didier Bonnet, Dragonetti, Nicola C, Edgar Schein, Edward Hallowell, Elena Corsi, Elisa Farri, Eli Pariser, Emily Jane Fox, Emily Lawson, Erik Brynjolfsson, Eric Matson, Eric Clemons, Eric Steven Raymond, Erik Rorth, Fei-Fei Li, Ferzaan Engineer, Fr. E Abraham, Fr. E H McGrath, Fr. J A Arroyo, Fr. Ozzie Mascarenhas, Frances Frei, Frank Felden, Fred Luthans, Frederick Dalzell Gary P. Pisano, Gavin Wright, Gerald C. (Jerry) Kane, George Collins, George Westerman, George Gilder, Glenn Finch, Gregory Moorhead, Gyan Chandra, H. James Wilson, Hal B. Gregersen, Harvey Mackay, Harold Lasswell, Hema Thakkar, Henry Mintzberg, Henry David Thoreau, Henry Jenkins III, Hewlett, S. A., Hortense de la Boutetiere, Howard Gardner, Hornstein, Andreas, Jac Fitz-enz, Jack Welsh, Jacques de Villiers, Jacob Morgan (Chess Media), Jacques Bughin, James Brian Quinn, James Guthrie, Janette Batten, Jay I. Sinha, James Manyika, James Heskett, Jaana Remes, James Krohe, Jr, James Champy, Jamie Hawkins, Janardhana Reddy, JC Herz, J Jay Scanlan, J. Stewart Black, Jeff Fromm, Jeffrey Schmidt, Jennifer Alsever, Jerry Rao, Jerry O'Dwyer, Jeremy Howard, Jeffrey Sonnenfeld, Jeffrey R. Immelt, Jeffrey Dunn, Jeetu Singh, Joseph Grenny, Jon Younger, Josh Bersin, J Martin Hayes, Jim Austin, Jimmy Diamantakis, Jim Rohn, Jim Nordstrom, Jonathan Woetzel, Jonathan Davidson, John Hagel III, John Ratey, John D'Arcy, Dr. John Halamka, John D. Sterman, John Brownstein, John Kotter, John Seely Brown, John Girardi, John Van Maanen (MIT), Jorge Lopez, Jon Kaplan, Julian Birkinshaw, Julia Kirby, Kathleen M. Sutcliffe, Karl Sveiby, K Kumar, Khari Johnson, Kelsey Robinson, Ken Richardson, Kenneth Boulding, Keith Rosen, Kevin Crowston, Krishnakumar Natarajan (Mindtree KK), Kris Dunn, Laura Croucher, Laura Nash, Laura Wining, Leif Edvinsson, Leigh Weiss, Linda S. Gottfredson, Linda Garneau, Ling Lau, Liz Gryger, Lowell Bryan, Loren Gary, Lorrie Lykins, Lynda Gratton, M S Banga, Ma. Evelina Ascalon, Marc Beaujean, Marc de Jong, Marcus Shingles, Margaret Rouse, Marise Ph. Born, Mark Kramer, Mark Smith, Mark Spears, Mark Williamson, Martin Mocker, Martin Gill, Martin Harrysson, Mary-Ann Russon, Maryam M. Kaifi, McMahan G C, McWilliams, A, Melanie Reuter, Michael Schrage, Michael Fitzgerald, Dr. Michael Haydock, Michelle A. Barton, Michael Beer, Michael Porter, Michael S. Bernstein, Mike Malone, Mike Miller, Mike Rhodin, Monideepa Tarafdar, Moses Abramovitz, Mohamed-Hédi Charki, Mohamed Zain, Mohd Rizal Razalli, Mohd Hasan Selamat, M S Krishnan, Narendra Mulani, Natrajan Ramkrishna, Nathan Bennett, Nathan Marston, Natasha Buckley, Nathaniel Branden, Nick Bontis, Nick Beim, Nicolai J. Foss, Nile M. Khanfar, Nina Kruschwitz, Nitin Nohria, Noel Tichy, Nola Weinstein, Norman Lee Johnson, Norton D.P, Ofir Turel, Oliver Bossert, Oulton, Nicholas, Dr P Bala Subramainam, Pamela Kirk Prentice, Paolo Gaudiano, Paul A. David, Paul Michelman, Patrick Sullivan, Paul Willmott, Patti Schaar, Pavan Bhosle, Per Krusell, Peter Aceto, Peter Outridge, Peter J.

Carroll, Phil Ryan, Peter Weill, Pierre Lévy, Pradeep Khandwalla, Prasad Kurian, R Pettinger, Pierre Nanterme, Prahalad C.K, Pradeep Udhas, R H Davenport, R Sridhar, Rajiv Chandran, Rajesh Gupta, Ralph Landau, Ranjit Bawa, Randy Boissonnault, Raphael Amit, Ramon Casadesus-Masanell, Rebecca Shockley, Renee Boucher Ferguson, Richard Boulton, Richard Petty, Richard Rekhy, Rich Grange, Ricky W. Griffin, Richard Hagberg, Richard Helm, Rick Lamanna, Rik Kirkland, Rinju Sarah Mathew, Rita Johnston, Robert Reich, Robert J. Alio, Robert G. Smith, Romie F. Littrell, Roos G, Roos J, R S S Mani, R Sridhar, Robert Bolton, Robert Kaplan, Robert Lambertucci, Roger Roberts, Rosabeth Moss Kanter, Rusli Abdullah, Russell Eisenstat, Russell Parera, Ryszard Barnat, Samuel Tilden, Sanjay Lalbhai, Sarah Zimmerman for Suzy Kaseem, Sarita Kumari, Sarah Tattersall's, Satty Bhens, Sean Silverthorne, Selena Rezvani, Sharad Sarin, Shahar Markovitch, Sherbin, L, Siegwart Lindenberg, Srinath Sridharan, Stacey Madge, Stanley D. Truskie, Stephanie L. Woerner, Stephanie Russell-Kraft, Steve Case, Stephen A. Miles, Stephen Robbins, Stephen Gregg, Sumantra Ghoshal, Sumberg, K, Susan Lund, Susita Asree, Tangly Catlin, Terry Leap, Terence McKenna, Theodore Kinni, Timothy Taylor, Thomas W. Malone, Thomas G. Apel, Thomas A. Hickok, Thomas Stewart, Thomas Gumsheimer, Tom Saar, Tom Tierney, Traub, James, Vasant Dhar, Veronika Belokhvostova, Verna Allee, Vijay Gurbaxani, Victor L. Brown, Vidya Santhanam, Vinayak Kamath, Wayne Brockbank, Wageeh A. Nafei, Wilton Henriques, Winston Brill, William Mishler, Williams Ruth, Wright, P M.

Research for this book required an understanding of a wide variety of corporations attempting to build stakeholder value through capturing contributions made by organizational intellectuals. Case content from some corporate sector players need special mention, a grateful acknowledgment and thank you. Airbnb, Air Canada, AON, Abbot, Accenture, ADP, Acquire Media Corp., Acrolinx GMBH, Adobe, Atos, A T Kearney, Atex, Attensity, Attivio, AlphaGo, Andersen, Amazon, American Express, Apple, Applied Materials, Arvind Inc. Astra Zeneca, AT & T, Aviso, Bank of America, Bayer, BASF, BCE Inc, BCG, BDO, Best Buy, Bell Canada, Berkshire Hathaway, Betterment, Big Think, Bitly, Bitcoin, Blackstone, Bleachers Report, Bloomberg, Blue Fountain Media, BMO, BNP Paribas, Boeing, Bose, Boston Scientific, Boston University, bOX, British Airways, Bunge, Business Manager, BuzzFeed, Cadburys, Cargill, Carnegie Mellon, Castrol, Chevron, Cisco, Citibank, CIBC, CNN, Coca Cola, Cognizant, Connotate Inc., Cornerstone on Demand, Columbia University, Continuous. Ai., Cornell University, Costco, Conagra, Coursera, CSC, CultureIQ, Culture Amp, CVS, Cxense ASA, Danaher, Degreed, Dell, Deloitte, Deutsche Lufthansa AG, DNN Corp, Disney, Discovery, Dollarama, Duke University, Eaton Corp, eBay, EMC, Emory University, Enterra, Enterprise, Ericsson, Etsy Inc., EY, Facebook, FEDEX, Fitbit, Fortune, Forbes, Floqq, Fujitsu, Fuze, GE, GenPact, General Dynamics, General Assembly, Georgia Tech University, Glint, Google, Goldman Sachs, Grand Thornton, Granyon, Grovo, GSK, Harvard University, Halogen, HCL, HDFC Bank, Hertz, HP, Hitachi, hiQ Labs, Home Depot, HourlyNerd, Hudson Bay, Hudson Interactive, Huemor Huffington Post, IBM, ICICI Bank, IDBI, Ignite Visibility, Indiana University, Infosys, Infor, Instagram, InstaCart, Intel, Intrepid Learning, Jabil Circuit, J P Morgan, J & J, KPMG, KKR, Kenexa, Korn Ferry, Kentico Software, Krux Digital, Lumesse', Loblaw, Linked In, L'Oréal, Lyft, 3 M, Magnolia, MasterCard, McMaster University, McGill University, McCain Foods, MediaPass, Mercer, MIT Sloan School of Management, Michigan State University - MI, Microsoft, Micron tech, Morgan Grenfell, NetSuite, Netflix, Novartis, Nutanix, McKinsey, McDonald, MSU, MindTree, Namely, National Geographic, Net Suite, NEST, Nike, Nordstrom, Northwestern University, NewYork University - Stern School, Office Depot, OpenText, OpenSesame, Oracle, Paylocity, PayPal, Pandora, Pathgather, Penn State University, Pepsi, Pfizer, Periscope, P & G, Placed Inc., Pluralsight, Purdue University, PwC, Queens University, Qualcomm, Quartz, Quintiles, Rapid & LLC, RBC, RBS, Reckitt Benckiser, Reuters, Rogers Communications, SAB Miller, SAP, Sanofi, Samsung, Shopper Drug Mart, SHRM, Salesforce, Scotia Bank, SEOP,

SEO Brand, SilkRoad, Slack Technologies, SnapChat, Southwest Airlines, Splunk, Spotify, Standard Chartered, Stanford, Starbucks, SONY, Suncor Energy, Staples, SumTotal, Syngenta, T Mobile, Taco Bell, Taleo, Target, Targa Resources, Tata TCS, Thermo Fisher Scientific, Temple University, Tesla, T D Bank, Texas Instruments, The Economist, Teradata, ThinkAnalytics, Tim Hortons, TINYPulse, Transnet, Twitter, Tumbler, Uber, Udemy, Ultimate Software, Unilever, UCLA, UC Berkley, University of Chicago – Booth School, University of Illinois – Urbana Champaign, University of Pennsylvania – Wharton School, University of Maryland, University of Michigan - Ann Arbor, University of Minnesota, University of North Carolina, University of Texas - Austin, University of Texas - A & M, University of Toronto, University of Virginia, University of Western Ontario, Darden, UPS, Verizon, Vimeo, Visa, Vista Print, Walgreens, Washington Post, Workday, Workopolis, Wellington Asset Management Company, Walmart, Wendy's, Wells Fargo, Western Digital, Wharton, Whirlpool Corporation, Verizon, Vodeclic, Wealthfront, Webtrends, Wingify, WIPRO, Wisetail, Yale University, YELP, You Tube, XEROX, Xyleme, Zenzar, Zumobi.

More than One - Research Assistance - For Anavir Shermon –(www.anavirshermon.com) engagement with this book commenced soon after I started writing it based on my research. A Senior in Industrial & Operations Engineering at the University of Michigan, Ann Arbor, his experience lay in the domain of Operations, Corporate Strategy & Structure, Continuous Improvement, Lean, and Engineering Economics with a keen focus in Game Theory. Thanks to his experience as robotics mechanical co lead role through FIRST Robotics, learnings and some very exciting work in a Research Assistant role to Professor Roman Kapuscinski (Chair of Technology & Operations, Ross School of Business, University of Michigan), on a Behavioral Science Project, to Professor Amy Nguyen-Chyung (Assistant Professor of Strategy, Ross School of Business, University of Michigan), on an Entrepreneurship & Strategy project and to Professor Mariel Lavieri (Associate Professor, Department of Industrial & Operations Engineering, University of Michigan, his active engagement with editing this book over the last 18 months was substantive. His contribution to the book involved compiling research material, articulating multiple research hypothesis, data management, statistical analysis, compiling & analyzing public domain reports on digital businesses, building case studies, analysis of industry history & development, analysis of digital companies' competitive and comparative advantages, data mining, critiquing, validating, and conducting literature reviews. Many of my clients had asked me if I had any tools or materials that could help them in designing a digital culture. Anavir, helped build organizational surveys pertaining to "*Measuring Digital HR in an Intellectual Company, Measuring Intellectual & Human Capital, Building and Sustaining a Digital Culture and Digital Business Alignment Inventory*" etc. In addition, Anavir did background secondary research on work in progress at US Universities in relation to digital businesses. He helped in building graphics, case studies, obtaining leadership style feedback, identifying digital trends in relation to changing digital business models, organization structures, strategic building blocks in HR, disruptive elements in people management, obtaining digital companies best practices and culture stories. This was followed with work in all other areas including administering questionnaires, interpreting the reports, performing general due diligence, compiling stories on leadership styles apart from editing, patiently identifying, revising, placing all of the graphics for the book by analyzing and incorporating these into respective chapters. Not to forget how Anavir saved me from making many an error, more complex/unreadable, while editing and making this book significantly more simple and easier to read. To me, his greatest contribution was to think and act as a Millennial, which he is, in contrast to me, a Baby Boomer. Anavir provided sharper interpretations, shooting out hypothesis, differentiations, anecdotal references and critical insights into the "Leadership Disrupted".

To us, this book at one level is nothing but a significant compilation of some amazing research, citations, verbatim reproductions, white papers, blogs, frontiers, thought work, interviews, analytics, focus groups and original research contribution by thinkers from Hackett Group, ASTD, Aberdeen

Human Capital, MIT Sloan School of Management, MIT SMR, American Management Association, A T Kearney, Conference Board, McKinsey Consulting, BCG - Boston Consulting Group, HBWSK, EY, HBR, KPMG LLP, Bersin by Deloitte, Deloitte Inc. PwC and every attempt has been made to acknowledge their contributions closer to the text and in the preface. If there have been any inadvertent misses please accept my sincere apologies. **"Business Manager"** journal and Editor Anil Kaushik need special mention for continuously supporting new ideas through my publications of papers in his journal. **MindTree Inc**. is showcased as a Best Practice Global Digital Enterprise.

Krishnakumar Natarajan (KK) is profiled as a symbol of an ideal CEO. **No Noise, Just Voice!**

Dedicating this book to KPMG LLP, its CEOs has been a no brainer. As a CEO at KPMG, Richard Rekhy, became an embodiment of change – leading from the front with energy and a forceful style, determination, single minded dedication to make changes, working with an inherited legacy structure – federated organizational model. Richard simply wanted to fast forward growth and make things happen in the shortest possible time. Working on and changing moving parts is never easy. Having known Richard for over 18 years, have seen in him concern for clients, their business needs and wants with a philosophy that he has practiced through his life and a twitter handle that boldly states, "Think Straight Talk Straight" telling it, as it is. Richard led KPMG, from the front, focused on himself, his priorities, his goals, his end state objectives and knew what he had to do, how to do and make an impact, challenging the traditions of Big 4 practices, that is today seen as a symbol of what every professional service firm's partner/leader should benchmark - aspire to be or not to be and to do or not to do – no matter what may be the cost and consequence. With no regrets or apologies Richard continues to seek new horizons. Reminds me of a quote, **"When they go low. We go high"**.

For my family, Kavita Shermon, my wife, a Business Owner, (www.riverforestconnections.com & www.rforc.com , www.RiverForestEStore.com with very little time, who simply stood by supporting, (editorial, documentation, critique, specialist) despite multiple time zone business obligations (Read – Tough, Demanding, Particular, Precise, Clear, Unforgiving of mistakes) and son, Anavir Shermon, Michigan Engineering, University of Michigan, Ann Arbor, MI, multi-tasking between his University assignments, research role responsibilities and given his research and editorial obligations towards this book, decided to stay away from Canada, to help him contribute meaningfully, his claim that I am pretending to rewrite the declaration of independence? Of course, not to forget some terrific editorial comments, critiquing, simplifying language, design, customer service and marketing support from LULU Publishing, Raleigh, NC. A big thank you.

To all of you do we dedicate this work, nothing shattering this earth, but done with all earnestness, as a symbol of gratitude for lifelong learning. That, without each and every one of you and your work, my dream of authoring a longitudinal research based book on what I call as **"Leadership Disrupted"** would simply not have happened.

We call it the "Digital Organizations – Leadership Disrupted".

Dr. Ganesh Shermon
Oakville, ON. Canada
GRShermon@ICLOUD.Com

Chapter 1

Business of Digital Organizations

HOW! Digital HR! We are often asked is there a method or a way to influence or build the desired organizational culture. Is there something called a right or a wrong culture? Would organizations seek to alter its cultural path consciously and is it possible to do so? Our answer to that is a resounding YES. What "you got" is what "you get" and "what you have". Right or Wrong - Good or bad! And this is not about whether organizations are actually right or bad. It is what people perceive it to be in those organizations. One is not declaring that there a standard formula, and if executed effectively, organizations would have a new or a desirable, favorable culture. NO, such a recipe does not exist. But with equal resolute can also state that if organizations were to understand, appreciate their As Is culture, with all of its facets, aspects, players, issues, challenges, goals in regard to their existing culture, it is indeed possible to influence such an As Is culture to a To Be desired state culture. It is possible to influence cultures where there is an honest attempt to understand the gaps in what the leadership believes is a gap between existing and desirable culture (In their opinion or based on opinions received from its people, customers – whatever may be the appropriate process they have followed to gather reliable data) with an aim to build a desired outcome (Could be Ethics, Resources, Compliance, Economic, Structural, Strategic, Processes, National – Global, Work Environments, Policy Perspectives, Rewards, Customer Relationships, Product Qualities, Nature of Business and there are many such variables to be covered in this outcome definition). These actions would or may mean and necessitate influencing strategy, structure, technology, leadership, rewards, people, values, purpose, policies, programs, rituals, attitudes, behaviors and To Be processes. It does not mean that such organizations can wish away its past, its history, stories, rituals or challenges, leadership disrupted practices or reputational image dimensions, but it can surely attempt to alter its course by responding and answering questions with a "YES, we will continue", "NO, we will discontinue", "May be, we will continue", "May be we will continue along with doing the following additional things", "Do More, Do Less", and so on…. This book will cover many case studies, client experiences and research content where researchers, management consultants and organizational scientists have helped transform/ alter / modify / influence / change corporate cultures. Every large company that has attempted transformation or have transformed, successfully or otherwise have in a small or big way influenced its culture. At the substantive level, large scale change management programs are always about changing cultures. At some level in this book, we will close by saying, "It is all about **Intellect,** All about PeoPle, Stupid! APPS!" Pun intended!

The world of 2020! Awesome to look forward!! But, as I write, BNN reports, "George Clemenceau, the premier of France in WW1, once famously stated that "War is too serious a matter to be left to the military" (often misquoted as "to be left to the generals"). 100 years later, on another battleground, the global economy, the Central Banks are battling to get people and businesses to spend", today's world economy is changing rapidly. Not because of external factors alone. But owing to an implosion too. World events like the Eurozone debt crisis for Europe, the shrinking of manufacturing growth in China for Chinese currency, the downgrading of the North American economy for US debt, US economy is stalling, declining earnings, yet with very record high valuations, TINA, fall in Canadian dollar for Balance of trade, BREXIT for UK, (Economist writes, The Bank of England had not changed base rates in seven years, but when it finally moved, it did so with a bang. In response to the low growth it expects in the wake of Brexit, it cut rates by a quarter point, to 0.25%, expanded its quantitative easing scheme and introduced a new funding scheme for banks. The move came on August 4th—three prime ministers, two disappointing European football championships and one referendum since the last wiggle in the rate), US election rhetoric, Oil price crisis for Saudi Arabia cost cuts, have had a worldwide impact on business, sentiment and confidence. PwC projects, "The UK's vote to leave the EU shocked currency and stock markets, and has led to an environment of economic and political uncertainty. Against this backdrop, we have revised our main scenario projections for UK real GDP growth to 1.6% and 0.6% in 2016 and 2017 respectively, down from 1.9% and 2.3%. This revised estimate assumes that the Bank of England embarks on some monetary loosening due to the expected reduction in aggregate demand, and in an attempt to stabilize financial markets. We're also assuming that fiscal policy is supportive of growth. But Brexit will be on the minds of policymakers outside the UK, and indeed the EU, as well. The Swiss central bank has already intervened in the foreign exchange markets and the US dollar appreciated slightly following the referendum - though it hasn't reached the levels it was at earlier this year. Therefore, we are still expecting the Fed to raise interest rates, although probably not until December or later". In such unstable times, companies are increasingly facing the heat of shareholder demanding performance despite a volatile business environment.

Organizational Struggle – Organizations, may desire, hope or even pray, but seldom get time to adapt themselves to a rapidly changing business landscape. Thus, in the existing scenario, the impact of culture, smart talent, leadership as they inevitably engage with disruptions through technology cannot be overemphasized. Organizations need leadership disrupted which can make sense amidst this ambiguity, find patterns in the chaos and take charge to meet the desired end state of performance and value realization. Business leaders, on the other hand, also need to address not only these challenges to skilfully manoeuvre their respective organizations to the next level but would need to be wary of the fact that in this battle for supremacy they are also on a headless chicken run against their competition. The days of marathons are over for many companies and business models; it is all about frequent bursts of 100 meters' dash only. And every leader wishes they could be an Usain Bolt. Increasingly there is a new generation of corporate life, which have become more dependent on the machine and its application. Their orientation to work life has become computer-centric, sometimes meaningless, cynical and self-defeating. Their orientation has been to move on and on into cyberspace, move into the knowledge-based business and hope to keep their psychic space intact.

Demographic SHIFTS of the 20th-century patterns have been influenced by choices made by double income families, population control in China, an emergence of BRICA countries, greater emphasis on governance at the political level, the changing profile of workforce and their expectations. There is an increasing reality of older, mature competencies, more tenured employees staying in the work place longer. A significant majority are now reaching to dangerously closer to their age of retirement exposing organizations to wide gaps in skills and competencies and are now presenting a real and present danger to business continuity in some critical workforce segments. The possibility of this imminent exit and its implications are now becoming a true reality of organizational policy makers. Extrapolate. Exasperate. Enervate. Or be extravagant. This is not an exaggeration! The 20th-Century corporations cannot possibly prepare to enter the 21st Century without envisioning the coming 100—not to mention the 1,000 – years of management is obvious. To our mind, many 21st century corporations no longer can think the way they thought in the year 2000 or 2002, (Y2K, dot-com, or BPO or ATM banking for example).

BUT again, there is a CHOICE! Between reinventing, altered understanding of the business model, forward integrating from the here-and-now to predicting only a slightly altered future, leaping over logical barriers to prophesies a transformed tomorrow- for the corporation, for the CEO, for the manager, for the young and bright talent…indeed, for each and every activity of the company, **smart**

talent is at the core! At one end, smart talent will remain the substantive need of the customer, and at the other the core digital product offering of your company.

We KNOW! Organizations are products of the ways that people imagine, think, act and interact in differing situations, exploit the opportunities provided to them and actively engage and manage themselves given business dynamics. People in turn become products of experiences, interactions, connections, interfaces, feedback and collaborations in such organizations. Experiences and connections are made possible by the processes deployed by organizations. And best of processes are those that are practiced seamlessly enabled by technology that facilitates behaviors as it happens for people segments across time zones, geographies, languages, values, and cultures.

1. *The nature of an organization is what exemplifies it, describes its character, and makes its shape recognizable. It encompasses the choices that will be made about future products and services, as well as future customers and markets.*
2. *In business today, strategy traditionally answers the question "How can we compete in the market, and maintain an advantage?"*
3. *Strategic organizations provide the vision, direction, and the purpose of growth for any organization.*
4. *Strategic focus is not about small goals, micromanagement of business strategies or delivering poor customer satisfaction.*
5. *Rather, it provides an all-encompassing umbrella under which businesses and leadership devise appropriate strategies, goals to create value.*
6. *Strategic leadership provides clarity regarding to two strategic issues; what should be the plan of action by providing the vision, direction, and creating the context for growth;*
7. *Plan on how to execute the plan by sketching out a road map for the organization that will allow it to unleash its potential, by crafting the corporation's portfolio,*
8. *Help determine what businesses should be there, what are the performance requirements of the business, and what type of alliances make sense.*

Being = Vision X Culture X Strategy X Commitment - "An organization that seeks to change its nature and be something different focuses on four requisites: **vision, culture, strategy, and commitment.** These four issues are interactive rather than additive. If one is missing, the multiplicative power is severely diminished. The first requirement is a clear vision of what the organization must become. The vision must be basic, honest, positive, and inspiring. It can't be hyperbole. It must be backed with evidence of why it is imperative. The reasoning must be not only commercial but also humanistic. You win the hands and minds with commercial reasoning. You win the hearts with humanistic reasoning. The second requirement is culture. Great companies are built on great cultures. Culture is the powerful, driving life force of an organization. It is the corporate blood that carries the nutrients throughout the system to nourish, support, and revivify. The next requirement is strategy. There has to be a grand plan to carry out the vision. The strategy focuses on the internal tactics that will be deployed to deal with the external market factors. Externally, the state of technology; competition; global, national, and regional economies; government policy and regulations; and community support influence a corporate strategy. Strategies that ignore external forces ultimately drive a company to inappropriate and belated actions. When the strategy or the culture gets out of sync with the market- place, the company suffers. Someone once said that success is the first step on the road to failure. What that means is that success often breeds arrogance, the "you can't argue with success" cliché. Writes, Jac Fitz – enz, in, "The ROI of Human Capital" 2009. "Arrogance is a slippery slide that quickly propels anyone on it to the bottom. The final and critical requirement is commitment. Without commitment, everything else is just words. So it is in many organizations-inspiring words on plaques, promises of a new culture, grand strategies in impressive folders. Then the first bump in the road overturns the shiny new vehicle. Every- one at the top of the organization must demonstrate every day that there is commitment behind the words" he says.

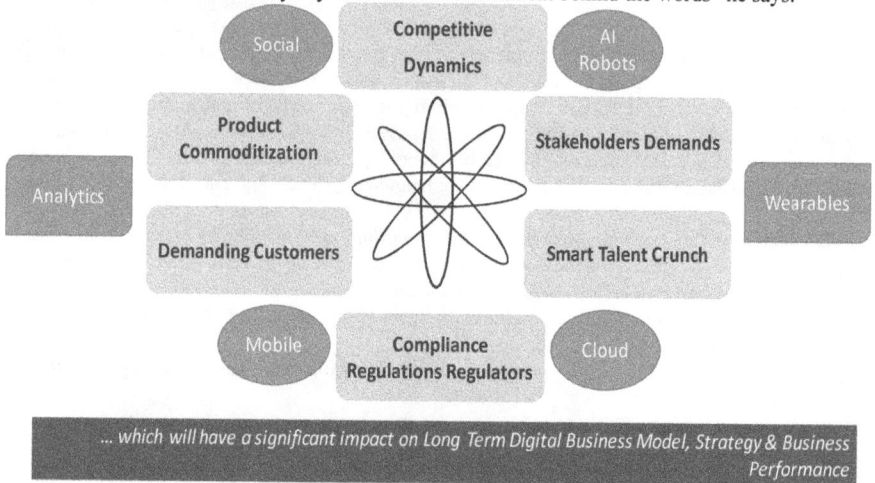

Social

Competitive
Dynamics

AI
Robots

Product
Commoditization

Stakeholders Demands

Analytics

Wearables

Demanding Customers

Smart Talent Crunch

Mobile

Compliance
Regulations Regulators

Cloud

... which will have a significant impact on Long Term Digital Business Model, Strategy & Business Performance

Figure 1 – Market Forces Influenced by Digital Changes – Global Impact

Today, we are faced with the unenviable situation characterized by:

Business GAP – This is a gap between Business Intent & Achievement. In fact, traditional definitions of what is a business gap are now only hypothetical given that changes affecting business performance are far more dynamic. For example, Financial parameters are no longer the single window panacea for organizational performance measurement, although some short-term Street Guru's may disagree! Why would then many companies have a PE multiple or a Market Cap not truly reflective of their financial performance? Business managers are looking for substantive ways to authorize organizational issues that can deterministically guarantee performance. But this obviously is never to be. What is promised to the Board and the shareholders is not necessarily the possibility that the CEO is mandated to accomplish and report. (Refer - Market Forces Influenced by Digital Changes – Global Impact)

Whose talent is it, anyway? Talent Gap - Broadening the talent horizons

Traditional answers to talent management questions – how to source, supply, hire, develop, engage and retain the best people – are too narrow. Instead, to create the capabilities they need to win, organizations should consider business acquisitions, joint ventures or alliances as alternative sources of supply of talent. This may mean looking to the crowd, to alumni or other businesses for ideas or inspiration. It also may mean taking the flexibility of your workforce to a whole new level through the greater use of contingent workers, for example. Finally, it is worth reiterating the need to look at talent management practices through the eyes of the next generation of employees. How should it feel to be hired, on-boarded, nurtured and rewarded by your organization? Many organizations – particularly those of a global nature – also suffer from a lack of clarity concerning who actually 'owns the talent'. This can make it difficult, if not impossible, to enable the best people to make the internal career or job moves that genuinely drive personal development and engagement.

Effective and forward-thinking talent management calls, therefore, not only for the clarification of this ownership but also for talent management to be on the agenda at the most senior levels.

Uncertain ENVIRONMENT – Don't do it if you can't do it! Forecasting is a dangerous business, says Rita Johnston. The Meteorological Office only claims 80 per cent accuracy for UK weather forecasts, for a maximum of eight days. Apparently safe predictions from established trends, such as the Victorian forecast that the streets of London would be knee-deep in manure (due to the proliferation of private horse-drawn carriages), were overtaken by unforeseen innovations (in this case the combustion engine), whereas apparently wild flights of fancy (such as Arthur C Clarke's space predictions) have come to pass. Historically, an accepted method of forecasting the future has been to look at current trends and to project them, incrementally, ahead. For many years Alvin Toffler (1980), JOHN Naisbitt (1982), Marshall McLuhan (1980), EDWARD De Bono (2000), Charles Handy (1994) and others have warned us that the pace of change is now increasing not arithmetically but logarithmically and so our forecasts have had to take this into account by projecting trends exponentially rather than incrementally. But an "Analytics Specialist – Data Scientists – Big Data Analyst" will tell you just the opposite. Today the degree of accuracy with which one can project the future is higher than before. Big Data analysts can predict to an accuracy level upwards of 90%. State of uncertainty about future requirements of Knowledge, Skills, and Competencies continues to haunt business executives. These analytical techniques establish optimum levels of control, analytical process of establishing objectives and drawing up alternative programs can be assisted by building hierarchical programs. As business pressure changes, as new ways of working emerges new portfolio of assets come into reckoning a need is felt for new knowledge, skills and capabilities to manage such assets. This is despite the early entry of the information era with on line availability of data and information available to process as knowledge. Why have high performing manufacturing companies discounted for their future earnings despite their potential to do well commercially? Why are companies in the knowledge industry positioned more competitively for the 21st century?

Generations DISCONTINUITY - Generation Xers enjoy work but are more concerned about navigating the work/life balance. They are the first generation to grow up with computers and the internet as part of their lives. Constant familiarity in the networked world has had a profound impact on their approach to problem-solving and collaboration. They follow a close pattern with the Baby Boomers in working on knowledge based activities that require depth, quality, and consistency. This group values individual & collective time, at times quite mutually exclusive. From a retention perspective, this group seeks identity with an organizational learning program and recognition systems that identify and differentiates the know how folks from known fewer masses. CEO's from this generation have acquired the capability to manage a combination of enterprises that straddle both the old and the new economy quite adeptly. Globe & Mail quotes the Amway Global story. For Amway, Generation Y is its fastest rising demographic.

Contradictions GALORE - Millennials Have Least Analytical Acumen, AMA Study Suggests, says, Phil Ryan, "nearly one in five Millennials (19%) are perceived to be lacking analytical skills when compared with other generations in the workplace, according to a study sponsored by American Management Association (AMA). The survey looked at how prepared organizations are to compete in an age of Big Data and involved nearly 800 respondents from more than 50 industries. Participants were asked to assess the analytical skills of their employees by age group. With a combined 58% rated as advanced or expert, the Gen X cohort's analytical strength was rated highest, followed by Baby Boomers with 41% and Millennials with 35%. Despite their familiarity with technology, Millennials aren't seen as having equal analytics savvy," said AMA Senior Vice President Robert G. Smith. "But what's really at issue here is an analytical mindset, which includes both quantitative and qualitative ability more than any specific number-crunching skill. In other words, employees need to know what to look for, what questions to ask, and how to make inferences and draw conclusions based on data in order to drive the organization forward. According to Smith, organizations are taking a hard look at the skills and competencies they will need over the next decade. "Companies will be stepping up development and training, and analytical skills will be high on the list of priorities. What they're seeking is strength in data analysis and critical thinking across the whole organization, not just among a select number of experts as in the past. Management realizes it is imperative to build the right skills…across all age groups in an organization."

Multi-Generation Workplace Behaviours				
Work Aspect	Generation-Y (16-30 years)	Generation-X (31-46 years)	Boomers (47-65 years)	Traditionalists (66-86 years)
Networks Communication	• They are quicker to respond to texts or "ping" their social media network. • They don't need face-to-face encounters to build on relationships • Generation Y is not very comfortable using e-mail as a dominant mode of communication • They are constantly balancing the costs of working somewhere against the personal benefits they derive, being entrepreneurial including a match in values.	• They have disproportionate preference for communication over e-mails. • They are slightly reluctant to communicate Face-to-face or over phone • Prefer systemic solution to problem solving • Have the ability to strategically leveraging peoples' differences to achieve competitive advantage/ better business results.	• Boomers typically rely on face-to face meeting or phone calls. • They value face to face encounters as a medium of building rapport and relationships. • Believe that native values would make things happen in connecting with people • Worked on the notion of learning based contribution, occurrence based delivery and task based performance.	• Traditionalists don't see the utility of social media as a work place tool. They have preference for face-to-face meetings • They tend to view knowledge as power and they sometimes hoard it to stay in control. • Lack of transparency around compensation, rewards and career decisions. • Do not actively engage. Believe in formal structural processes, hierarchical styles, distant from rank & file
Managing and Feedback	•Millennials/Generation Y prefers regular communication and feedback regardless of how it is delivered. •They rely on constant feedback, review processes, style monitoring mechanisms and coaching. They prefer real time feedback.	• Generation –X understand the importance of feedback and often integrate both qualitative and quantitative aspects. • They seek feedback on an intermittent basis and as a source of intrinsic motivation.	• They prefer to provide feedback on a need to know basis. • Feedback provided is related to end term performance results. • Focus of feedback is more on present performance rather than improvement focus.	• Traditionalists often tend to rationalise the need for feed back. • They view coaching and mentoring as a need based intervention.

Figure 2 – High Level Characteristics of Multi-Generational Workforce

Arrival of MILLENNIALS - Millennials have gone from representing just over 10 per cent of its global sales force in 2005 to nearly a third now. Gen Y now makes up a third of new Canadian memberships. Amway has seen Gen Y shoot up 21 per cent in recruiting and 19 per cent in sales generated. The demographic trend is also reflected at cosmetics giant Mary Kay Cosmetics Inc., where just over 20 per cent of the 38,000-strong Canadian sales force is Gen Y, while half of the U.S. sales force is under 35. Significant changes have been noticed amongst the generational divide and tend to have real implications for how employers and employees work together in a global mobility context. For example, Baby boomers put a heavy focus on work as an anchor in their lives. Managing lives around work is central to the way they have lived. Baby boomers worked on the notion of learning based contribution, occurrence based delivery and task based performance. They demonstrated a high degree of consistency in performing high quality repetitive tasks that required concentration, focus and single mindedness to closure or achievement. Baby boomers who have reached leadership positions are likely to lead mature organizations in business or functional roles with very little difficulty. They possess an intrinsic capability to handle complex brick and mortar economy companies with ease. Retaining this generation does not rest with the organization. The high degrees of self-motivation in this band of employees who have seen many economic down turns have a built in resilience to bounce back and manage their careers. (Refer - High Level Characteristics of Multi-Generational Workforce).

Based on an EY Global Insights Case study, MIT SMRs, Laura Wining investigates GE'S big bet on data and analytics, "To stanch the brain drain over the past few years, many companies have been forced to hire back retiring workers to serve as consultants — an unsustainable practice. Brennan says that the industry needs a way to capture and codify the departing knowledge. "But there's also got to be a refresh so that you can attract new talent and arm them with tools, technology, and the capability to get their work done efficiently," he says. "The tools that a 26- or 28-year-old PhD in petroleum engineering wants to use are fundamentally different than ones preferred by somebody who's leaving the workforce," he adds, noting that Millennials expect that cutting-edge analytics and tools will be available in the workplace. "When I entered the workforce, I had better tools at work than I'd ever had access to at home, but most of the employees we bring into GE have access to better technology than we allow them here, and we've been playing catch-up. The same thing is happening with our customers," says Dan Brennan, executive director for the Industrial Internet for GE Oil & Gas".

"GE's ad campaign aimed at Millennials emphasizes its new digital direction" continues, Laura Wining. "The campaign was designed to recruit Millennials to join GE as Industrial Internet developers and remind them — using GE's new watchwords, "The digital company. That's also an industrial company." — of GE's massive digital transformation effort. GE has bet big on the Industrial Internet — the convergence of industrial machines, data, and the Internet (also referred to as the Internet of Things) — committing $1 billion to put sensors on gas turbines, jet engines, and other machines; connect them to the cloud; and analyze the resulting flow of data to identify ways to improve machine productivity and reliability. "GE has made significant investment in the Industrial Internet," says Matthias Heilmann, Chief Digital Officer of GE Oil & Gas Digital Solutions. "It signals this is real, this is our future."

Reward Mechanisms for Millennials - "In the Best Way to Pay for Generation Y rate six types of rewards as at least as important as compensation. Few companies in today's knowledge-intensive economy would deny that they compete on the caliber of their people. With this richer understanding of the two generations that now dominate the workforce, the challenge becomes clear. Companies whose employment offers align best with the shared values of Boomers and Gen Ys will enjoy a major talent advantage". In HBR 2009 "How Gen Y & Boomers Will Reshape Your Agenda" Sylvia Ann Hewlett Laura Sherwin and Karen Sumberg write further, "If we were designing a workplace from scratch today, or consulting to a big employer, we would insist on crucial elements.

In order, they are:

- *High-quality colleagues*
- *Flexible work arrangements*
- *Prospects for advancement*
- *Recognition from one's company or boss*
- *A steady rate of advancement and promotion*
- *Access to new experiences and challenges*"

Consumerism - In the context of an ageing population in some geographies and younger generational "employee critical mass" at another geographical location there are seemingly apparent contradictions to the way in which talent has to be managed. Corporate programs articulated in a US HQ may not always be relevant to a young Chinese worker in Beijing or a software programmer in Bangalore, India. In just over 10 years, approximately 75 per cent of the North American workforce will be comprised of members of Generation Y & the Millennials. This presents significant challenges; with political, business and non-profit leaders facing numerous issues from energy and environmental conversations to indigenous engagement and educational quality and attainment. How will this generation prepare to work independently and take on leadership roles at all levels of society? Asks, Randy Boissonnault, President of Xennex Consulting. A large workforce number of this 75% will comprise of workforce from other parts of the world who would have migrated to US or Canada.

Multi-Generation Workplace Behaviours				
Work Aspect	**Generation-Y** (16-30 years)	**Generation-X** (31-46 years)	**Boomers** (47-65 years)	**Traditionalists** (66-86 years)
Getting Work Done	• They rely on technology, internet and social platforms to get their work done. • Millennials want more control of the work they do. Including determining the way things should get done • Millennials may tend to see work/life flexibility as a necessity rather than a perk. • Career paths would not be linear, would be flexible, lateral, make horizontal growth that are knowledge intensive, real visibly supervising an intellectual mind.	• Gen Xers are independent, enjoy Informality, are entrepreneurial, and seek emotional maturity • Enjoy work but are more concerned about navigating the work/life balance • Constant familiarity in the networked world has had a profound impact on their approach to problem-solving and collaboration • Competition for skills and talent is increasing. More importantly, this competition for skills is expected to intensify and become even more competitive when the Baby Boomers begin to retire	• Boomers are procedure and rules oriented while getting the work done. • They possess a strong commitment to team work and collaboration to get work done. • Prefer working on knowledge based activities that requires depth, quality and consistency. • "intellect hierarchies", positions of leaders and managers held by those with a knowhow, know-what and the know-why	• They strictly rely on work ethics to get things done. • This generation is highly dedicated but at the same time risk averse. • High degrees of self-motivation in this band of employees who have seen many economic down turns have a built in resilience to bounce back and manage their careers.
Getting Ahead	• They have a strong learning orientation. • Flexible workdays, part time decisions would become common with employees determining work goals, work content and work methodologies depending upon the technological infrastructure available for effective performance. • They seek opportunities to grow and develop through knowledge enhancement and development.	• Gen Xers are willing to develop their skill sets and take on challenges and are perceived as very adaptive to job instability in the post-downsizing environment. • They want to build a repertoire of skills and experiences they can take with them if they need to, and they want their career path laid out in front of them • CEO's from this generation have acquired capability to manage a combination of enterprises that straddle both old / new economy	• They have a higher priority for work over personal life. • They tend to work hard to reach to the next level of career progression. • They put in stretched hours at work to achieve their career aspirations. • Baby boomers put a heavy focus on work as an anchor in their lives	• Traditionalists view better position as a career advancement opportunity. • leadership positions are likely to lead mature organizations in business or functional roles with very little difficulty. They possess an intrinsic capability to handle complex brick and mortar economy companies with ease.

Figure 3 – High Level Characteristics of Multi-Generational Workforce

Diversity - It is but a reality that workforces around the world are fast becoming more diverse across a number of unique and personalized dimensions (age, cultural preferences, ethnicity, Color, psychological profiles, learning abilities, sexual combinations, identity clarity, work glass ceiling, global experience acceptance, leadership – personal styles, employment choice, life preferences, personal attitudes, ethnicity, sexual orientation, etc.). Organizations are now strategically leveraging peoples' differences to achieve competitive advantage/ better business results. There is a concerted effort to ensure that programs are established to attract and retain employees who bring in varying perspectives, point of view and perhaps contradictions, to enable them to deal with business exigencies and talent trends as they encounter. Many trend analysts from firms like EY, Deloitte, Accenture see the need to recognize the impact increased employee diversity could have on the organization. To be effective, they say, diversity strategies should to some extent reflect the customer base and geographies of the organization. Alignment with corporate strategy on diversity directions needs to be attained. Diversity's Definition Has Changed, says Selena Rezvani in, "Five Trends Driving Workplace Diversity In 2015" Forbes issue, "In addition to creating a workplace inclusive of race, gender, and sexual orientation (to name a few), many organizations are seeking value in something even simpler, diversity of thought. In some industries that are known for being insular – think law or high-tech companies – seeking out talent with different thinking and problem solving backgrounds in critical. Deloitte research underscores that diverse thinkers help guard against groupthink, a dynamic observed firsthand last year with a large corporate client. Partnering with the company just after they had experienced a major product failure, the CEO lamented that the failure resulted from too much blind agreement internally – something Deloitte's study calls "expert overconfidence." Future-thinking companies see the danger in this lack of diversity and often question their own hiring and retention practices—and even their everyday operating norms. **It's Less About Being a Good Corporate Citizen:** The business case for diversity has never been more front and center than it is now…and why not? Basic economic theory suggests that consumers will correct for a company's lack of diversity by simply not spending money there—making slow-to-change organizations extinct. The same can be said of employees, who are constantly balancing the costs of working somewhere against the personal benefits they derive, including a match in values. Gains in employee engagement, effort and retention alone make for a compelling diversity proposition. Add to that customers who evangelize your diversity philosophy and products—and feel you have insight into who they actually are, and the diversity ROI is hard to ignore. These companies also achieved a proper balance between formal and informal forms of communication. A few common methods of communication adopted by these companies included small meetings, face to face interaction, one-on-one discussion, breakfast gatherings, all staff meetings, video conferencing and informal employee dialogue sessions, use of newsletters, videos, telephone hotlines, fax, memoranda, e-mail and bulletin boards; and brochures and guides to educate employees about the downsizing process, employee rights and tips for surviving the situation. Many organizations encouraged employees to voice their ideas, concerns or suggestions regarding the diversity in digitization process. According to many best practice organizations, employee inputs contributed considerably to the success of their change activities as they frequently gave valuable ideas regarding the restructuring, increase in production, and assistance required by employees during this large scale diversity driven change program.

Technology Will Move from Burden to Benefit: Global ORGANIZATION analytics expert and thought leader Josh Bersin found in his research that the average large company has more than 10 different HR applications (including diversity data), taking considerable effort to bridge and synthesize that data into meaning. Luckily, startups are building new "diversity technology" that drives more precise, actionable change. Gap Jumpers came up with software that allows for blind interviewing and testing via the computer, helping to sidestep the risk of biased hiring decisions. **Unitive** helps employers write more inclusive job descriptions and creates accountability during interviews, for example calling out if a hiring manager disregards criteria they initially said was very important to them in a hire. Not surprisingly, those companies seen as most mature in terms of HR also spend the most on Organization —and foresee their largest future HR investment being in technology".

PwC says - Only Technology Matters - Technology enabled business environment and Intellect, as a basic unit is inevitable. The organizations are likely to be driven, managed and determined by those who possess the intellect to forecast, foresee and lead the corporate unit. The organization would be densely networked with singular and multiple variables (people groups, technology, vendors, customers etc.) and linked with the environment. Technology has become an integral part of lives that deal with corporate priorities. All forms of stakeholders.

Deloitte's Bersin - HR Technology is Scaling - "The HR technology market, which is now more than $15 billion in software alone, is exploding with growth and innovation," says Josh Bersin, principal, Bersin by Deloitte. "One of the most disruptive changes is the trend toward automating HR practices and integrating systems, making them so easy to use that people think of them as part of their daily life. By embedding and automating people practices into applications employees use every day, 'systems of record' are becoming 'systems of engagement.' At the same time, these cloud based talent platforms give leaders the real-time information they need to adapt to changing business and labor conditions. The big vendors (SAP, ORACLE, WORKDAY) now make up 60% or more of the market" and are growing their share (and acquiring others) while dozens of other companies

(CornerstoneOnDemand, SumTotal Systems, PeopleFluent, Halogen Software, Ultimate Software, Silkroad, Saba, Infor, and others) make up the rest. Solutions in this market are radically redesigning their user interfaces, bringing substantive digital linkage, sophisticated integration and invest heavily in object-based design, embedded analytics, and ease of use in every way. Communication was found to be a primary success factor of effective transformational scaling. According to a survey conducted in major US companies, 79% of the respondents revealed that they mostly used letters and memorandums from senior managers to communicate information regarding transformation including restructuring or downsizing to employees – post digital actions. However, only 29% of the respondents agreed that this type of communication was effective. The survey report suggested that face-to-face communication (such as briefings by managers and small group meetings) was a more appropriate technique for dealing with a subject as traumatic (to employees) as downsizing. According to best practice companies, employees expected senior leaders to communicate openly and honestly about the circumstances the company was facing while facing technological onslaught (which led to downsizing).

EY POV - Platforms Integrated – An EY research on HCM trends states, "Technological progress has enabled how systems contain more and more functionality that in turn bring people, technology and performance together. From wage-related HRIS or Payroll and benefit systems, (ADP, Ceridian) which only needed to calculate wages, systems are growing to a fully integrated, unified, best of breed HCM Platform solutions (Workday, Oracle Fusion, Success Factors, CoD, UltiPro, SalesForce, SABA, ADP, Adrenalin etc.) that are comprehensive and thorough tools supporting strategic decisions. The information contained in systems is expanding from wage-related to talent management to competency-related employee data.

KPMG on Analytics Mobility - A trend is that ROI, Analytics and linkages to financial and non-financial information are more and more joined in order to determine the efficiency and effectiveness of the function. In order to increase productivity, reduce operating costs, and free HR staff to focus more on strategic and value adding tasks, people function is increasingly offering self-service through respectively designed portals to managers and employees. A few top of the line HCM platform solutions provide a single source of truth as a promise to clients who wish to demonstrate openness and transparency to their employees in the way talent is attracted, developed, deployed, retained and managed in their enterprise". There is a need to "redesign workplace to help knowledge people work in an integrated and connected architecture. Information sharing is not limited to users within organizations. By means of mobility, smart phone or IPADs, portals and recruitment self-services, potential employees can be reached and supplied with relevant information. Managers can use similar services to approve requests of a transactional nature or perform value adding transformational tasks such as provide on line feedback, coaching, testing, hiring, interviews or learning, 360 feedback or E training".

Need for Flexibility, Personalization & Customization - For many professions, work is no longer defined by the office location, nor by the hours of the day, nor by the specific tool used by the trade. Many employees have home-based offices and may perform their tasks before or after the actual workday. Flexible workdays, part time decisions would become common with employees determining work goals, work content and work methodologies depending upon the technological infrastructure available for effective performance. Obviously what flows from this would be greater the technology infrastructure the better is likely to be individual output and contribution. Career paths would not be linear, would turn grossly flexible, lateral and would make horizontal growth that are knowledge intensive, real and visibly supervising an intellectual mind. Career paths would create comparable performance yardstick, meaningful measures and performance evaluation would insist customized evaluation process and tailor made compensation reward program.

Need for an Altered Maslow "Need" Hierarchy – Individualism - Expectations and preferences of employees are becoming more diverse. Employees want more room to express their individualism, and they are expecting that HR services and programs should be flexible enough to accommodate their individual preferences. Monogrammed shirts with your name, as a brand is no longer the prerogative of the C Suite executives. Young executives are wearing made to order work wear that demonstrate their individualism. My work has to be fun, my life has to be fun and I want to do a job that's fun. Generation Millennial often have varying concerns: because of their deep know how with technology, they believe they can work flexibly anytime, anyplace, and that they should be evaluated on work product, not on how, when, or where they got it done. The real revolution is a decrease in career ambition in favor of more family time, less travel and less personal pressure. However, this group consists of a large mass that lack consistency in their outlook towards work life. While their expectations from employer's match with generic trends their work ethic to support such an expectation falls way behind. Guess WIFI connectivity, Smart Watch, Facebook membership, WhatsApp and Battery are likely to be on top of these needs too!!

Need for Frequent Rewards – "Young are no longer saving as their parents did. Their debt is on the rise. In a North American context, Melanie Reuter, director of research for the Real Estate Investment Network, says, "They will be the first generation that is not going to be better off than their parents were," Her interpretation. 'But, because millennials are such a large group, representing about 27 per cent of the population', says Reuter, it's imperative that businesses gauge this group's behavior and respond accordingly. "If you don't pay attention to what this generation wants, regardless if you agree or not, you won't have a business soon because they are such a large cohort that they do have spending power." Nearly half of millennials (41 per cent) prefer to be rewarded or recognized for their work at least monthly, if not more frequently, whereas only 30 per cent of non-millennials would like that level of frequency'.

Need to be Open & Transparent - Employers should increase transparency around compensation, rewards and career decisions. They should create a meaningful rewards structure that regularly acknowledges both large and small contributions made by employees. Debbie Amery of PwC, "Compensation and rewards have to be individually charted depending on the intellect brought in by the employee along with the time frame for its delivery. The company should have reward programs on a group basis for knowledge workers. The Performance Appraisal system must have built in rewards for system creators".

Need for Global Influences & Mobility - KPMG research focuses on how enterprises driven by globalization and trade agreements, both employees and employers are now expecting greater mobility within and across the organization. They have seen trends such as increased recruiting at a global level, greater number of international mobility, choices and how employees face a vast array of options with respect to geographic, political, and social-conditions attributes of their employment. Both employers and employees now expect greater mobility within and across organizations. In today's world, employees are willing and often seeking to broaden their range of employment and career opportunities by making request transfers to a different city, region, country, or continent. In the Country, full labor mobility across the continent is now the norm.

Need for Intellectual Hierarchies - Corporate hierarchies now turn into "intellect hierarchies", positions of leaders and managers held by those with a knowhow, know-what and the know-why, rather than an upgraded position in the hierarchy with fancy titles made available through a corporate career plan. Dan Schawbel the Founder of Millennial Branding states, "One specific technological trend that has a direct relevance to where, when, and how people work is the emergence of mobile communication and productivity tools. The problem is that most workers grow impatient with their current roles (including titles, identity, branding) and think that the only solution is to move to another company. In a new study in partnership with American Express, we found that 73 per cent of managers are very willing or extremely willing to support employees who want to move within the corporation and 48 per cent of millennial employees are interested in making these moves. Employees need to look left and right not just up if they want to be successful. At the higher levels in an organization, you need to have a firm grasp on how different groups operate or you won't be able to manage them properly".

Need to Internalize Impact of Labor Force - An often forgotten reality that is unlikely to ever go away is the presence and impact of labor force and their trade unions. The nature of labor unions can differ by geography and industry but their role, values and purpose at a broad level continues to go on and on. In some geography they have managed to adapt, work their way constructively with their employers to obtain a fair status for their constituents and in other geographies the degree of militancy and unreasonableness continues unchanged. Of greater degree of frustration is the trend of governments managing business enterprises and unable to deal with trade unions to make their support productivity and performance. Tim Wright from Talent Cultures says, "Competition for talent is fierce because talent is a leading factor in a company's competitive advantage. Recruiting, developing and retaining talent are the tools that build competitive advantage. Talent management starts with recruiting. Stronger recruiting efforts contribute to greater talent acquisition. Employee engagement adds to developing and retaining talent. It demonstrates the company's appreciation of their value to the company — as it builds their value to the company. What company does not look for every possible way to gain advantage over their competition?" Consulting major KPMG Human Capital Practice report of 2012 (Shermon 2012) seeks to focus on the need for HR strategists to tailor their strategies to reflect their own organized labor circumstance, that organizational strategy should not neglect organized labor, even in jurisdictions where it is not an immediate risk and how HR strategy should paint a long-term picture of the nature and risks of organized labor in their operating jurisdictions, and possibly even those of their suppliers.

Need to Dispel Myths about Millennials – Change is complex: it does not come in a tidy package, with infallible steps to success. It takes unexpected diversions and displays the frustrating complexity that is the hallmark of human behaviour. There is considerable evidence to start indicating the multiple types of behavioral perceptions on Millennials. From smart, innovative, entrepreneurial, freedom loving, getting things done generation to lazy, selfish, whimsical, convenient values and so on. "Our survey asked U.S. Millennials and non-Millennials which words best describe the Millennial generation. While Millennials' perceptions of themselves are generally favorable, non-Millennials tend to view them far less kindly, often referring to them as "spoiled," "lazy," or "entitled." As the pace of change increases, capacity to change (individual/institutional) effectively becomes critical. Long-term success will require a capacity to change: the ability to create and react to change in a continuous and strategic way. Companies that develop these skills will outlive their competitors: they will use change as the source for innovation and long-term growth, and as a new way of thinking. These perceptions may be coloring how executives view the Millennial consumer, preventing companies from understanding and fully addressing the product and service needs of this generation— and establishing strong brand relationships. We found a generation engaged in consuming and influencing, one that embraces business and government and believes that such institutions can bring about global change, one that is generally optimistic, and one that has often-unexpected attitudes and behaviors". In, a BCG Research Report of 2012, "The Millennial Consumer Debunking Stereotypes" authors Christine Barton (BCG), Jeff Fromm (Share Like Buy), Chris Egan (Service Management Group), continue, "Those companies that truly "get" the Millennials and engage with them appropriately have an opportunity to differentiate themselves in the marketplace and forge long-term relationships with their customers. Our research did confirm one stereotype: U.S. Millennials are extremely comfortable with technology". In fact, there is a school of thought from psychologists on a Freudian relook at the development of personalities in the context of this digital age. If an entire generation is growing up in the social world how have their personalities evolved in comparison to baby boomers and gen X where on line virtual reality world, simply did not exist. "They are "digital natives," meaning that they've largely grown up with technology and social media, using these new tools as a natural, integral part of life and work. Millennials consider themselves fast adopters of new technologies and applications, and they are far more likely than non-Millennials to be the very first or among the first to try a new technology." Due to the loss of experienced workers, companies incurred expenditure on overtime pay and employment of temporary and contract workers. It was reported that about half of the companies that downsized their workforce ended up recruiting new or former staff within a few years after downsizing because of insufficient workers or lack of experienced people. Today many companies are frequently rehired former employees until it absorbed the 'shock' of downsizing. It was also reported that in some cases, they even paid recruitment firms twice the salaries of laid-off workers to bring them back. A manager commented, "It seemed like they would fire someone and [the worker] would be right back at their desk the next day." Justifying the above, leaders said, "It does not happen that much, but who better to bring back than someone who knows the ropes?" Very few people bought this argument, and the rationale behind downsizing and then rehiring former employees/recruiting new staff began to be questioned by the media as well as the regulatory authorities in various parts of the world.

Inspector Gadget - "They also tend to own multiple devices such as smartphones, tablets, and gaming systems. More U.S. Millennials than non-Millennials reported using MP3 players (72 percent versus 44 percent), gaming platforms (67 percent versus 41 percent), and smartphones (59 percent versus 33 percent), while more non-Millennials reported using desktop computers at home (80 percent versus 63 percent) and basic cell phones (66 percent versus 46 percent). As a result, U.S. Millennials are much more likely to multitask while online, constantly moving across platforms—mobile, social, PC, and gaming. Both groups spend roughly the same amount of time online, but Millennials are more likely to use the Internet as a platform", Facebook as a communication tool, Internet of Things as a Network Connectivity Tool, Pinterest as self-help tool, Twitter as a 140 Character point of view, or Instagram as reflection of our projection, "to broadcast their thoughts and experiences and to contribute user-generated content. They are far more engaged in activities such as rating products and services (60 percent versus 46 percent of non-Millennials) and uploading videos, images, and blog entries to the Web (60 percent versus 29 percent). It's no surprise that U.S. Millennials spend less time reading printed books and watching TV. Only 26 percent watch TV for 20 hours or more per week (compared with 49 percent of non-Millennials), and when they do watch, they're more likely to do so on their computers through services such as Hulu (42 percent versus 18 percent)."

Need for Millennials to Move On – Welcome Founders - During the early 21st century, many companies began offering flexible work arrangements to their employees in an attempt to avoid the negative impact of corporate renewal programs, restructuring, transformation and downsizing. Such an arrangement was reported to be beneficial for both employees as well as the organization. A flexible working arrangement resulted in increased morale and productivity; decreased absenteeism and employee turnover, reduced stress on employees; increased ability to recruit and retain superior quality employees improved service to clients in various time zones; and better use of office equipment and space. This type of arrangement also gave more time to pursue their education, hobbies, and professional development, and handle personal responsibilities. All Hail 'The Founders' in at long last, a name for the generation after Millennials in "The Atlantic" – David Sims, Dec 2,

2015, "With civilization in flames and popular culture disrupted beyond recognition, the world is looking to a new generation to rebuild it. Enter "The Founders." According to a new nationwide survey conducted by MTV, the children of the new millennium will rescue the world from the sins of the past, and befitting this worthy mission, they get maybe the most self-important name imaginable. Yes, the spirit of MTV's new project is well-meaning and intended to capture the diversity of the country's youngsters. But the report goes a step further to paint a bleak picture of the present, and saddles the next generation with the task of "founding the new world." No pressure, kids. (Refer - Leadership Disrupted - Digital Business Model – What Employees Want). Most Millennials Reject the Term 'Millennial'. The name "The Founders" comes from the kids themselves, according to MTV's survey of more than 1,000 respondents born after the year 2000. America is still reckoning with Millennials (loosely classified as those born from the mid-1980s to the late-'90s) one think piece at a time, but according to this survey, their fate is already sealed. As the children of indulgent baby boomers, Millennials are classified as "dreamers" who live to disrupt and challenge established norms. The Founders, by contrast, are "pragmatists" who will navigate a tougher world defined by 9/11, the financial crisis, and gender fluidity. Previous generations had to worry about getting into college and finding a job, but the next one is tasked with cleaning up their mess. One thing "The Founders" have in common with other generations? They're reacting to those who came before. The terms "Baby Boomer," "Generation X-er," and "Millennial" have all become pejoratives, though the MTV survey's description of the latter is particularly rough. Millennials' celebrity icon? Miley Cyrus, who "pushed back against Disney's model" of fame. Their defining movie? High School Musical, which "disrupted the model of cliques" (a phenomenon previously unseen on screen, apparently). What's more, Millennials are defined by the video game The Sims, building houses "within the templates" of society. The Founders, meanwhile, live in the world of Minecraft, where regular laws of physics don't apply and all the building has to be done by hand. The implication being that they're going to make a different society, cube by pixilated cube. Their pop-culture heroes are YouTube stars and Vine comedians, ordinary folk finding fame in the democratic moray of the world wide web". In many organizations where transformation was successfully implemented and yielded positive results, it was found that senior leaders had been actively involved in the change process. Though the methods used varied from organization to organization, the active involvement of senior employees helped achieve change goals and objectives with little loss in quality or quantity of service. The presence and accessibility of senior leaders had a positive impact on employees - those who were downsized as well as the survivors. According to a best practice company source, "Managers at all levels need to be held accountable for - and need to be committed to - managing their millennial employees in a humane, objective, and appropriate manner. While HR is perceived to have provided appropriate service, it is the managers' behavior that will have the most impact." In many companies, consistent and committed leadership helped employees overcome organizational change caused by changes.

Need to Manage Generational Conflict – The concept of contingent employment also became highly popular and the number of organizations adopting this concept increased substantially during the early 21st century. According to the Bureau of Labor Statistics (BLS), US, contingent – unique employees were those who had no explicit or implicit contract and expected their jobs to last no more than the assignment. They were hired directly by the company or through an external staffing agency on a contract basis for a specific work for a limited period of time. Here is a flip. "Why perpetuate this annoying idea that Millennials are somehow exceptional and require special consideration and treatment? Because it's true. The argument that Millennials and the generation following them should be integrated into the workforce like all generations before them is illogical—if we take emotion out of it, this becomes clear. While some may be immovable in their disagreement with the notion that the Millennial generation is unique, there's no argument that their circumstances indeed are. The dominant factor setting Millennials apart, of course, is technology and their relationship with it". Lorrie Lykins, in AMA 2013 continues further to make a business case for Millennials. in OMG: "The

Time to Invest in Millennials Is Now, the author says, Generational conflict—friction between two generations in the workplace—is a well-worn story. Even in the current era of three or even four generations in the workplace, making the dynamic more complicated, it's nothing new. And if the past informs the future, we know that after some jostling and adjusting, the new kids figure out who's in charge (that would be the older folks), settle in, and everyone gets back to work. So the Millennial generation (those born between 1977 and 1997) should be no exception, right? Not so much. Millennials, who will account for 40% of the U.S. workforce by 2020, require more than their predecessors did in terms of investment in development on the part of their employers. Sure, Baby Boomers (born between 1946 and 1964) encountered new technologies in the smoke-filled workplace of the 1980s. It came in the forms of the IBM Selectric III, word processors, and dot matrix printers. Technology didn't dominate our lives. Stress was also a factor, but not relentlessly so".

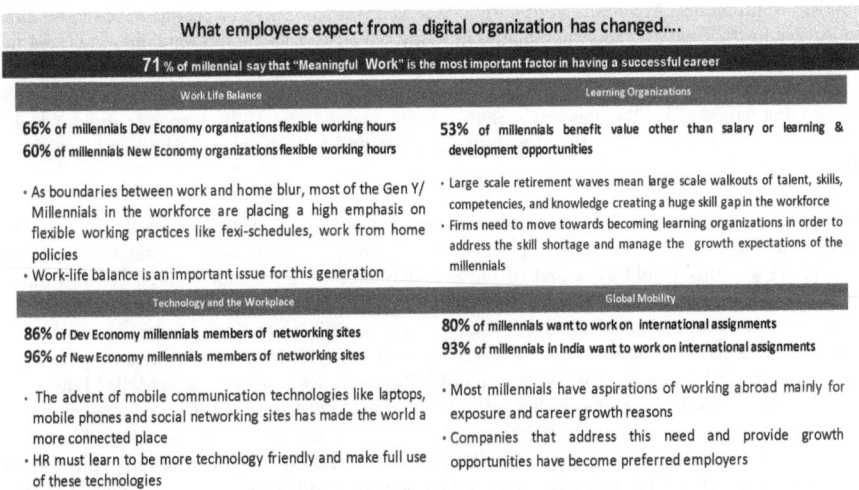

What employees expect from a digital organization has changed....	
71 % of millennial say that "Meaningful Work" is the most important factor in having a successful career	
Work Life Balance	Learning Organizations
66% of millennials Dev Economy organizations flexible working hours 60% of millennials New Economy organizations flexible working hours	53% of millennials benefit value other than salary or learning & development opportunities
· As boundaries between work and home blur, most of the Gen Y/ Millennials in the workforce are placing a high emphasis on flexible working practices like fexi-schedules, work from home policies · Work-life balance is an important issue for this generation	· Large scale retirement waves mean large scale walkouts of talent, skills, competencies, and knowledge creating a huge skill gap in the workforce · Firms need to move towards becoming learning organizations in order to address the skill shortage and manage the growth expectations of the millennials
Technology and the Workplace	Global Mobility
86% of Dev Economy millennials members of networking sites 96% of New Economy millennials members of networking sites	80% of millennials want to work on international assignments 93% of millennials in India want to work on international assignments
· The advent of mobile communication technologies like laptops, mobile phones and social networking sites has made the world a more connected place · HR must learn to be more technology friendly and make full use of these technologies	· Most millennials have aspirations of working abroad mainly for exposure and career growth reasons · Companies that address this need and provide growth opportunities have become preferred employers

Figure 4 - Leadership Disrupted - Digital Business Model – What Employees Want

Need to Manage Depleting Skills & Competencies - Companies did not have to pay unemployment taxes, retirement or health benefits for contingent employees. Though these employees appeared on the payroll, they were not covered by the employee handbook (which includes the rights and duties of employers and employees and employment rules and regulations). In many cases, the salaries paid to them were less than these given to regular employees performing similar jobs. Thus, these employees offered flexibility without long-term commitments and enabled organizations to downsize them, when not required, without much difficulty or guilt. Analysts commented that in many cases HR managers opted for contingent employees as they offered the least resistance when downsized. So short term commercial gains overtook concern for competency building and training. But as we write, competition for skills and talent is increasing. More importantly, this competition for skills is expected to intensify and become even more competitive when the Baby Boomers begin to retire (2012). Another issue is a mismatch between the skills and education young people are acquiring in their postsecondary educations and what's needed in the work force. The search for talent has become increasingly competitive over the past several years. Talent plays a significant role in leading organizations. A talent mindset is the deep-seated belief that having better talent at all levels is how you out perform your competitors. It is gained by identifying talent who fit in effectively with an organizational knowledge needs built around a capability profile that sustains its competitiveness and is definitely not driven by hiring a critical mass to meet with a quarter to quarter wall street analysts thirst for valuation information.

Need to be Non – Aligned - However, analysts also commented that while contingent employment had its advantages, it posed many problems in the long run. In the initial years, when contingent employment was introduced, such employees were asked to perform non-critical jobs that had no relation to an organization's core business. But during the early 2000s, contingent employees were employed in core areas of organizations. This resulted in increased costs as they had to be framed for the job. Not only was training time consuming, its costs were recurring in nature as contingent employees stayed only for their specified contract period and were soon replaced by a new batch of contingent employees. Productivity suffered considerably during the period when contingent employees were being trained. The fact that such employees were not very loyal to the organization also led to problems. Alignment with corporate strategy on diversity directions needs to be attained. Relationships that are of a reporting nature in today's scenario where accountability is vested in jobs will turn into responsibility vested in people and their relationships. Jobs by themselves, unless it is deeply entrenched with the overall business strategy, would turn meaningless given the dynamic set of change that would affect the business scenario on day to day basis. If the corporate strategy is driving the diversity objectives, then HR's structure, programs, and policies need to be put in place to support the corporate direction.

Need to Sponsor Multi Culturalism - The organizational population will turn increasingly diverse in social and cultural milieu, perspectives, viewpoints and behavior, competing and at times conflicting and this would be a part of the everyday workplace. Cultural diversity (also known as multiculturalism) is a group of diverse individuals from different cultures or societies. Usually cultural diversity takes into account language, religion, race, sexual orientation, gender, age and ethnicity. Companies started to embrace corporate diversity in the early 2000s. This was due to many trends in demographics and a changing workforce. KPMG Research deals with these aspects. "Education and tolerance in the recent years have allowed gays, lesbians, and trans-identified employees to be open about their sexual orientation in the work place without the fear of persecution. Tolerance and accessibility has also allowed people with disabilities to be employed alongside fully able individuals. For a multinational entity, with customers and employees in different regions and countries, a global perspective on diversity needs to be adopted".

Need to Ensure Human Resources Empowerment - Analysts also found that most contingent employees preferred their flexible work arrangements and were not even lured by the carrot (carrot and stick theory of motivation) of permanent employment offered for outstanding performance. In the words of Paul Cash, Senior Vice President, Team America (a leasing company), "It used to be that you worked as a temp to position yourself for a full-time job. That carrot is not there anymore for substantial numbers of temps who prefer their temporary status. They do not understand your rules, and if they are only going to be on board for a month, they may never understand." With such an attitude to remain outside the ambit of company rules and regulations, contingent employees reportedly failed to develop a sense of loyalty toward the organization. Consequently, they failed to completely commit themselves to the goals of the organization. Brad Karsh & Courtney Templin authors of Manager 3.0, state "Millennials are not better or worse," Karsh said. "They are just different, and will need to adapt to management. One of the key things to remember, he said, is that millennials are highly collaborative. They grew up enrolled by their parents in sports and many other activities with a team ethos. "They don't like the word 'boss,'" he noted in an interview".

"Experience is what you get when you didn't get what you wanted. And experience is often the most valuable thing you have to offer" Says Peter Aceto president and chief executive officer of ING Direct".

Based on **Accenture (http://bit.ly/2b1jfqj) - A Point of View on Trends in HR – 2014 Report**

- **Trends Reshaping the Future of HR -** *Accenture's ongoing research, "The Future of HR," has identified 10 key trends that are reshaping the HR function: Including cloud adaptability, mobility, social alignment, big data, apps, employee experience and so on*
- **Mobility - Tapping Skills, Capabilities, Technique Expertise Anywhere, Anytime, Anyway -** *With widening skill gaps, some residing in countries far away, HR will need to quickly access critical skills on demand, when and where they're needed.*
- **Intellect - Managing Your People as a Workforce of One – Collective Individuality -** *HR will need to treat each employee individually, (as if they are one-person intellectual bargaining category) with customized HR and talent-management solutions.*
- **Staffing - The Rise of the Extended Workforce included Retired, Changed Role Profiles - Revists -** *HR's mission and mandate will evolve to enable it to maximize the extended workforce's strategic value. This new lot will need to be brought into the workforce*
- **Disruptions in Tech - Digital Radically Disrupts HR -** *A range of technologies, comfort zone processes are transforming how people understand, appreciate and carry out their work, and how people managers support employees.*
- **Territorial - Reconfiguring the Global Talent Landscape -** *HR will transform to adapt to a more global world, match talent with tasks in various locations, and support mobile workforces across geographic barriers.*
- **External Connects - Social Media and Multiplicity Devices Drives the Democratization of Work** *Knowledge – Learning – Intellectually smart workers will harness social media to collaborate, connect, mutually learn, radically disrupting organizational structures, role dynamics, shared responsibilities, hierarchies and job titles.*
- **Talent Management Meets the Science of Human Behavior -** *Scientific insights and analytics will provide HR with new tools to drive workforce performance.*
- **Business Model - HR Drives the Agile – Disruptive Organization -** *HR will play a critical role in enabling companies to adapt to changing business conditions.*
- **Compliance - HR Must Navigate Risk and Privacy in a More Complex World -** *HR will need to adopt risk-management force multiplier strategies covering everything from confidential data to the turnover of talent.*
- **Employee Experience - HR Expands Its Reach to Deliver Seamless Employee Experiences -** *HR will evolve from a stand-alone function to one that spans disciplines, integrates business and boundaries to deliver cross-functional, holistic employee experiences highlighting need for feedback, self-discovery and identity.*

Need for Generation Millennial Determining Digital Revolution - According to some analysts, the employment arrangement was not beneficial to changing baby boomers or Gen X employee profiles. Under the terms of the contract, they were not eligible for health, retirement, or overtime benefits. Discrimination against contingent employees at the workplace was reported in many organizations. The increasing number of contingent employees in an organization was found to have a negative effect on the morale of regular employees. Their presence made the company's regular employees apprehensive about their job security. In many cases regular employees were afraid to ask for a raise or other benefits as they feared they might lose their jobs. But for millennials this was ok. "Millennials have grown up in the digital age. They show greater familiarity than previous

27

generations with communication, media, and digital technologies. Because they are more "wired," this gives Millennials a competitive advantage and makes them an asset when it comes to working with new technologies. Tolbzie (2008), however, also points out that, "they are also sometimes called the "Trophy Generation" or "Trophy Kids" based on the emerging trend in sports and competition to reward everyone for participation, rather than for winning" (p.12). Because of this experience they have been said to reject in-house competition and politics. Furthermore, because many watched their parents be adversely affected by the dot-com bubble burst and high rates of divorce and layoffs, millennials are thought to be skeptical of long-term commitments, and are said to desire greater flexibility in their career. (Refer - Leadership Disrupted - Digital Business Model - Composition of Workforce). In A Multi-Generational Workforce: Managing and Understanding Millennials, researchers, Belal A. Kaifi, Wageeh A. Nafei, Nile M. Khanfar & Maryam M. Kaifi (International Journal of Business and Management Vol. 7, No. 24; 2012) further say, "One research study described millennials as "opinionated" and they "[expect] to be heard" (Hartman & McCambridge, 2011, p. 24). So if these are their traits as individuals, what are their traits as leaders? A study conducted by Gibson, Green, and Murphy (2010) identified the differences in management values between the generations, showed that the top five values for managers of Gen Y were: family security, health, freedom, self-respect, and true friendship (p. 39)". Stuck with large number of employees in coordinating roles and an unclear estimation of future growth, the bureaucratic institutions are neither equipped with people nor scalable processes in pockets where the business volumes have far outstripped the designed process capacity. For example, one large bank found in its credit card business that the volumes that it handled in last five years was greater than the total business handled in the first fourteen years of existence. Controls and checks, which guarantee process integrity, have hence been by passed just to keep pace with the volumes. "This study also concluded that the management styles and values of the generations were more alike than different. A study by Hartman and McCambridge (2011) revealed that academic and business researchers concluded that the development and use of effective communication strategies is a critical skill set for all managers. These skills have been directly linked to both individual effectiveness (e.g., opportunities for promotion, special assignments, team effectiveness) and to organizational effectiveness and bottom line performance. Their study focused on university students of the millennial generation, which showed that although Millennials have been characterized as being technologically sophisticated and capable of multitasking, they are deficient in oral, written, and interpersonal communication skills. Thus, it becomes imperative to understand more about this generation who will be leading organizations of the future".

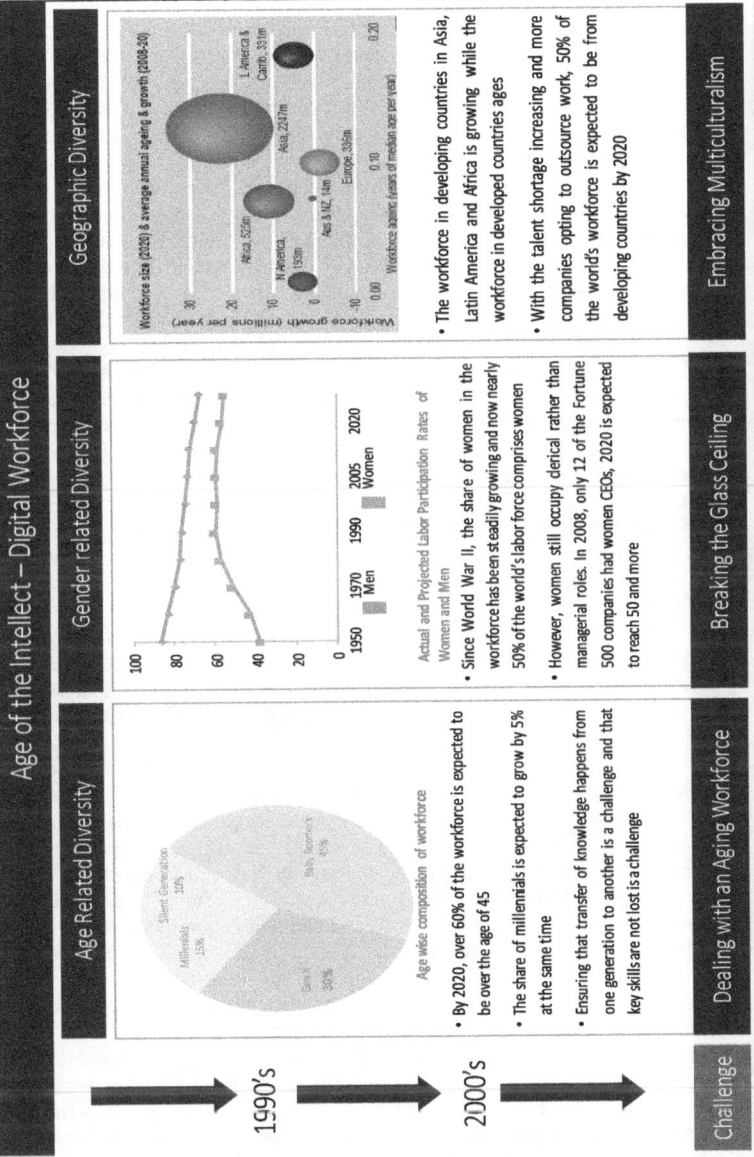

Figure 5 - Leadership Disrupted - Digital Business Model - Composition of Workforce

The Leadership Disrupted – Easy to Deal, Speed, Flexibility, Courage, Character, Perpetuity, Freedom, Savvy, Multi-Tasking, Work Ethic, Know-How, Intellectual Arrogance, Socially

Conscious, Change Friendly, Individual & Team, I & We, Tech Dependent are some words you would associate with these Millennials. Freedom loving smart talent. Because of their deep know how with technology, they believe they can work flexibly anytime, anyplace, and that they should be evaluated on work product, not on how, when, or where they got it done. The real revolution is a decrease in career ambition in favor of more family time, less travel and less personal pressure. Demographic profile analysis of the target employees has changed irretrievably. It is essential to build a generic profile of the employee (Gen X, Baby boomers etc) before designing an alternative program for millennials. Considerations such as likely age-group, class of the worker, number of family dependents, sole bread-winner for the family, average salary, education levels, qualification, skill levels, memberships with trade unions, etc play a very important role and need to be defined upfront. However, this millennials group consists of a large mass that may appear to lack consistency in their outlook towards work life. So in a way policies would need to be more flexible. We are still trying to see patterns amongst millennials. While their expectations from employer's match with generic trends their work ethic to support such an expectation falls way behind. For example, this generation would sail through college without studying for a single day, or would not think twice if there is a commercial opportunity which could mean a speed of response that may include many sacrifices. They have perhaps a distaste for what they perceive as menial work given their love for technology. They may just avoid "difficult people" instead of engaging with them constructively. But as we have seen, these are more myths than reality. Members of this generation are described as preferring collective action, working in teams, wanting work that really matters to them, and being civic-minded, eco-aware, confident, conventional, optimistic, and socially conscious. And they don't come with the baggage of the past, arrogance of their positions, or their extended identity through qualifications, wealth and connections of the traditionalists or the baby boomers.

A rigid organization, collective and conventional as they may, which replicates the entire outfit in every branch, is the first hurdle. This structure is similar to that of the Government where at the lowest level the district administration represents the Government to the common citizen and performs all the (or most of the) functions that the Government performs. The structure may be suitable for disbursing actions and raising money but does not pay attention to crucial factors such as the spread between the cost of lending and borrowing. The risk due to this has resulted in huge non-performing assets. This multi-layer structure is also accompanied by an incremental authority system, with no clear definition of the associated enhanced competencies needed for exercising this authority. A sound performance management, work role analysis and information management system can eliminate these layers. "Flexible work arrangements and the opportunity to give back to society trump the sheer size of the pay package, and Millennials truly have some unique factors. For example - **Portrait of Gen Y** - To satisfy your Gen Y employees as they become a large proportion of the labor pool, you'll need to address what makes them tick. Here are five facets of their inner workings. **Ambition** - 84% profess to be very ambitious - These are go-getters: About as many Gen Ys who call themselves very ambitious say they are willing to go the extra mile for their company's success. **Loyalty vs. Quest** - 45% expect to work for their current employer for their entire career - Gen Y employees fully hope to remain faithful to a workplace, but the clear majority say they also want work to bring a range of new experiences and challenges. They may be more susceptible to wanderlust than they realize. **Multicultural Ease** - 78% are comfortable working with people from different ethnicities and cultures - Gen Ys are clearly at ease with diversity, whereas only 27% of Boomers have such a comfort level. Even when it comes to networking, Gen Ys excel at diversity: More than a quarter network primarily with people of a different ethnicity. **Healing the Planet** - 86% say it's important that their work make a positive impact on the world, Gen Y workers want an employer who shares their eco-awareness and social consciousness, even down to the details of office energy use. Nearly one quarter say it's very important to work in a green, environmentally conscious workplace, **Networking by Nature,** 48% say having a network of friends at work is very important, working in teams is a top motivator for Gen Y employees. They love to connect with others and enjoy working in offices that are open and conducive to socializing. They want people, even bosses, to be readily accessible." writes, "In, How Gen Y & Boomers Will Reshape Your Agenda, Hewlett, S. A., Sherbin, L., & Sumberg, K, 2009". **Work-profile change** - It is likely that the work/ job profile of the retained employees is going to significantly change. Performance standards might be raised significantly and meeting the same might be essential. Further, an employee who was earlier considered productive in light of other unproductive employees, in the absence of the same might not be so. Another possibility that exists is that the employee might be transferred to another department, stream, SBU, etc where she is placed in an entirely new work climate. Finally, the employee may also have to take-on additional responsibilities to address the new profile. Social impact initiatives are also helping create talent beacons in the market as employees become more socially conscious. "Sound HR and business strategies should consider the expectations of talent and consumer pools as a whole, and with a particular focus on Millennials. There has been a convergence between "social impact" and "innovation," largely driven by Millennials, who account for $1 trillion of current US consumer spending. As widely reported, Millennials' decision-making processes are often influenced by a desire to have a larger purpose in life. This has made corporate social responsibility (CSR) an imperative and not an option in", 2016 Deloitte study of the Social Impact Practices", authors Marcus Shingles, Bill Briggs, & Jerry O'Dwyer write. They further add, Millennials respond with increased trust and loyalty, and are more likelyto buy those companies' products.8 Even more pointedly, in a recent survey of Millennials, more than 50 percent of 13- to 25-year-old respondents said they would refuse to work for an irresponsible corporation"

On balance this generation seeks more from minimal/but well thought through effort given their knowledge of technological processes, social collaboration, playing with Xbox, Pokémon, UTube, Jabber, Chatter, Slack, Yammer, Facebook @ Work, Jive, Confluence, HipChat, Podio, posting pictures on Instagram or exploring music through Spotify, wide networks, device friendly, but find it difficult to work hard (prefer to work smart) but seek advanced knowledge or work based skills to advance their careers or employability. Maximization of returns based on their current usage of knowledge is their competitive spirit for the present. And employees with these traits present a management challenge. Retention of this segment is a tough one. And it does not start with retention. It starts with attracting only the right kind to hire for leadership roles and the masses for short term contribution. Planning to retain large masses of Millennial without a planned process to develop their capabilities would lead to substantive grief. "Gen Ys are usually the offspring of Boomers—and a famously doted-upon set of children. Perhaps that's why these two generations seek each other out in the workplace. Boomers delight in taking Ys under their wing: 65% say that members of the younger cohort look to them for advice and guidance. Generation Y's motto, meanwhile, seems to be "Trust those over 50." Most Ys (58%) say they look to Boomers, rather than Xers, for professional advice, and over three-quarters say they enjoy working with Boomers. The fact that 42% of Ys go to Boomers for mentoring is also remarkable, given the layers that typically separate them in a corporate hierarchy", concludes Hewlett, Sylvia Ann.

"This is the Leadership Disrupted".

What is intellect? *The part or faculty of the human soul by which it knows, it recognizes, it absorbs, it senses, it thinks, it analyzes, as distinguished from the power to act, behave, feel and to will;* sometimes, the capacity for absorption and beyond, higher forms of knowledge, intelligence, as distinguished from the power to perceive objects, aspects, environment, material, symbols, artifacts in their relations; the power to judge, decode, decipher and comprehend; the thinking faculty; the understanding, the closing and finale.

Intelligence is 'the faculty of adapting oneself to circumstances' said Francis Binet and Henri Simon, the authors of the first IQ test (Wolf 1973). Intelligence is the operation of gathering information, an ability to comprehend; to understand and profit from experience or new information about specific and timely events; "they awaited news of the outcome". That which makes the human mind determine a course or choice of action, after sifting through alternatives, after evaluating risks or after predicting an outcome and that which has the power to create, destroy, add, delete, enhance or subsume. Are Organizations Intelligent? Is an organizational intellect a collection of individual intellect?

Digital Business - *Enterprises must strengthen/discover in some situations their digital business models — how they engage their customers digitally to create value, how they energize their staff, how would they connect with their vendors, how do they bring in new stakeholders, how do they ask their R & D to think disruption via mechanisms such as robotics, applications, ASPs, portals, tech engines, websites, cloud hosting, social networks, wearables, analytics, collaboration and mobile devices. Dynamic business-to-business trading hub where multiple buyers and sellers come together and conduct transactions. (Examples - Extends customer reach and enhances customer service. Provides virtual procurement and virtual supply functionality. Preserves proprietary processes and procedures, relationships, pricing, and pre-negotiated contracts. Aggregates buying power among independent companies, divisions, and partners. Provides meaningful tools to facilitate dynamic trade and marketplace interaction).* **Digital business** *is the creation of new* **business** *designs by blurring the* **digital,** *and physical worlds and that which converges strategy to execution to feedback value chain with a technology delivery vehicle. It promises to usher in an unprecedented convergence of people, business and things that disrupts existing business models – even those born of the Internet and e-business eras and includes the interaction and negotiations between, business, wall street, behavioral psychology and things. It is when things start to negotiate amongst themselves, or when customers become both buyers and sellers in the same medium, as well as people and business that we start to see how we have entered an entirely new and disruptive world. In the past, people were a proxy for things in business. In the future, things will be an agent for themselves and will thus shift that way a business views its opportunities. Digital technology drives improvement at the traditional business process and business model levels. However, the differentiating fight will be for "business moments" – the third level of digital reinvention created by the need to compete with increased speed and agility. Technologies such as the Internet of Things and 3D printing will enable new digital business processes, models and moments. Refer -* **Jorge Lopez is a vice president and distinguished analyst at Gartner** *(Modified from Forbes 2014).*

Digital Tracing - In an excerpt from their book, *Changing Fortunes: Remaking the Industrial Corporation (2003)*, HBS Dean and Professor Nitin Nohria and co-authors Davis Dyer and Frederick Dalzell discuss how General Motors and Kodak are attempting to adapt to the new age economy. To succeed in becoming a hybrid company, business leaders must pay attention to the following principles:

1   *This is a difficult path to follow if the core business is losing money. The distractions of managing a failing business complicate the challenges of succeeding in a new one. Therefore, pursue the hybrid alternative before the core business deteriorates to crisis proportions.*

2   *Start by introducing services that complement existing products and combine them into solutions.*

3   *As services grow to size-able proportions, treat them as an independent business rather than as an adjunct to the industrial core.*

4   *While it is important to have internally differentiated management practices to respond to differences among the industrial and post-industrial businesses, provide linking mechanisms to integrate them"*

Need to Converge with Intellectual Capital Movement - Concepts dealt with in this book are an attempt to pull together the developments over historical intervals the Intellectual Capital movement but more importantly to trace the emergence of human capital definitions, measurement tools and techniques. With this as the background the book will establish the need for a comprehensive human capital in the context of three variables, culture, leadership disrupted and Organizational Management and an understanding that is leading to the discovery of an Intellectual Company.

Need to understand Digital Business Models - At a simplistic level software organization, consulting, advisory firms, research, new product development, design and generic knowledge based value-adding companies (advertising, experience services, financial services, communication, entertainment, education, multi-product conglomerate corporations) are treated as knowledge firms given their role in development of raw data, creation of unknown into known and the utilization of people as the primary state of creators. Digital companies would need to ask, How can Digital Organizations enable the firm to achieve its short term and long term goals? How can Digital Organizations be effectively deployed to capture, analyze and deliver information to support organization's decision making? What is the required architecture to support integration of the various technology components with applicable customer, product, technology, people and process components? To what extent can the existing Digital Organizations investments be utilized to meet the future needs? What are the incremental investments in Digital Organizations that a firm has to make? What are the Digital Organizations options for effective management of movable and immovable assets? What is the appropriate governance structure for management of Digital Organizations? What should be the priority and phasing for deployment of various technology initiatives? How can technology help in implementation of information security? What are the options for network segmentation to meet the firm's information management requirements?

Need to understand changing managerial styles - Thus, leaders while influencing culture display managerial styles in the organization and may be expected to demonstrate behaviours different from their usual set of expected behaviours. In other words, there may be a need to re-define or adjust the existing leadership styles, competency framework and opportunities to display a variety of managerial skills. Cultural Leadership framework provides the "To-Be" state of the leadership disrupted behaviours and acts as a guiding light for leaders.

Cultural Intellectualization - Digital Businesses face four foundational challenges for Transformation. Leaders may not be able to sustain the intellectualization effort without investing to change the fundamental mindset of people. In other words, leaders in the organization may need to create the culture of optimization. In many cases, leaders may need to manage a parallel cultural transformation, with focus on optimization, as they lead efforts to create an optimized organization.

Role of Leadership

Redefining the role of business executives in leading the business as promoters, investors, change agents and business managers

Building Culture & Values

Inculcating vision values as the business DNA in its growth journey

Organization Models, Restructuring & Transformation

Aligning organization structure to business strategy building the evolution roadmap

Business Model & Performance Management Framework

Deploying business strategy through the organization and employee performance management system

Figure 6 – Digital Businesses face four foundational challenges for Transformation...

Need for Adoption of Cultures - People, who work in such organizations, must receive an opportunity to gain acceptance while they change the ways they think, feel and act in relation to the problems, issues or challenges on hand. The growth of learning capabilities and self-renewal attitudes brings in team congruence, candor and transparency in communication. There is a role played by culture, organizational models and Leadership disrupted in Creating an Intellectual Company. Technology would need to adopt cultural practices. For example, The enterprise's **Business Strategy**, Operating Model, Geographic Expanse, Type of Business, Industry Specifics, Regulatory Compliance Requirements – Factors that influence technology deployment in the enterprise, **Applications** that assist in processing, storage and distribution of the business information and supporting operational and administrative needs, **Technology** that supports and helps manage the applications, The **Information** produced and used by the Business, Key Decision Makers, Operations Personnel, Regulators, Customers, Suppliers, General Public and **Governance** and **Organization** that enable **Delivery** of IT services.

Need to sustain change - Creating and sustaining an Intellectual Company may require extraordinary leadership commitment. The above avenues of intellectualization may be explored and leveraged only with the right leadership disrupted alignment, a cultural mindset and a business model that focuses on realizing short and long term value. Leaders may be expected to lead organizations in a way very different from the way they may have been traditionally leading the organizations.

Need for a Good FIT within Organizational Cultures - Successful organizations, typically a competing organization or a Performing Enterprise, will also seek a good internal fit, with their culture properly matched to their technology. As stated, routine technologies provide stability and work well when linked with a culture that emphasizes centralized decision making and limited individual initiative. Non routine technologies, on the other hand, require adaptability and are best when matched with cultures that encourage individual initiative and downplay control. Voluntary School s tend to ask for steady cultures where identifiable sets of members and member behaviors are asked, understood and appreciated. Intellectual Company models continue to be difficult to identify and map.

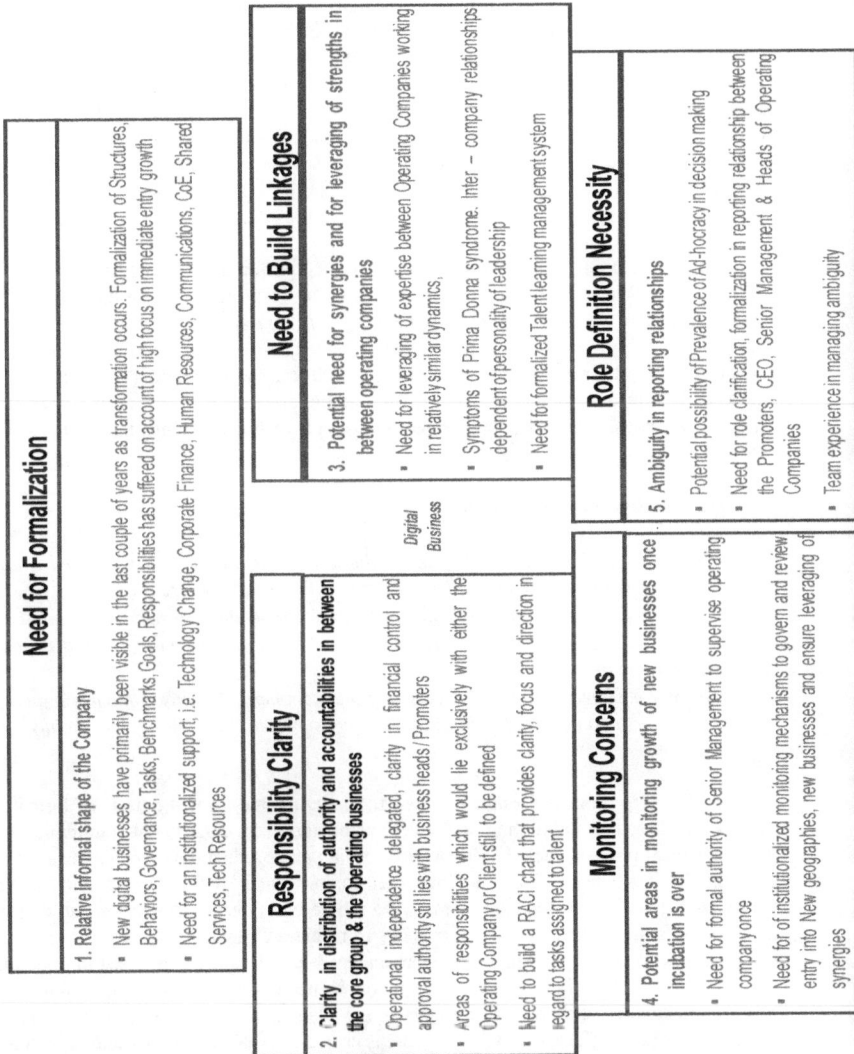

Need for Formalization

1. Relative Informal shape of the Company

- New digital businesses have primarily been visible in the last couple of years as transformation occurs. Formalization of Structures, Behaviors, Governance, Tasks, Benchmarks, Goals, Responsibilities has suffered on account of high focus on immediate entry growth

- Need for an institutionalized support; i.e. Technology Change, Corporate Finance, Human Resources, Communications, CoE, Shared Services, Tech Resources

Need to Build Linkages

3. Potential need for synergies and for leveraging of strengths in between operating companies

- Need for leveraging of expertise between Operating Companies working in relatively similar dynamics,

- Symptoms of Prima Donna syndrome. Inter – company relationships dependent of personality of leadership

- Need for formalized Talent learning management system

Responsibility Clarity

2. Clarity in distribution of authority and accountabilities in between the core group & the Operating businesses

- Operational independence delegated, clarity in financial control and approval authority still lies with business heads/ Promoters

- Areas of responsibilities which would lie exclusively with either the Operating Company or Client still to be defined

- Need to build a RACI chart that provides clarity, focus and direction in regard to tasks assigned to talent

Digital Business

Monitoring Concerns

4. Potential areas in monitoring growth of new businesses once incubation is over

- Need for formal authority of Senior Management to supervise operating company once

- Need for of institutionalized monitoring mechanisms to govern and review entry into New geographies, new businesses and ensure leveraging of synergies

Role Definition Necessity

5. Ambiguity in reporting relationships

- Potential possibility of Prevalence of Ad-hocracy in decision making

- Need for role clarification, formalization in reporting relationship between the Promoters, CEO, Senior Management & Heads of Operating Companies

- Team experience in managing ambiguity

Figure 7 – Transforming Digital Business Models sometimes give rise to need for compelling organization and people related challenges

Need to Manage Contradictions - What is blatantly evident is presence of many leaders in given line functions whose titles distinctly connotes leadership disrupted but whose behavior borders on petty mindedness, turf creation, showing poor sensitivities, wining at every issue with a gross inability to courageously put deadlines, chase goals forward and lead the team by example. These leaders are those who typically would articulate the right thing be it business goals, performance objectives, key tasks and benchmarks, quoting examples of other well run organizations, espouse latest management theories. In practice they are nothing but tyrants to seek power of pleasure and privilege to command and control people. When not in the current role they are perhaps spending a lot of time to prove their leadership by demonstrating how other units or functions are not doing their jobs. Organizations in our experience are grossly perceptive of such leaders and over time turn wary. Organizational counseling efforts are critical to up front leaders who continue to practice styles that worked in the past and educate them of the new realities. In our judgement these are classical cases of basic feedback and developmental systems not available in the corporation.

Need for Starting with Competencies and Capabilities - Competencies have undergone a radical change. While at one point in time leading an institution was an expected top management competency, today this supplemented by learning, teaching and spiritualizing the CEO role. Leading is no more the only condition for leadership effectiveness. Causes for Human Attrition & Exits are inexplicable despite managerial assumptions on hiring and retaining people have significantly improved. People are no longer staying for traditionally understood reasons like job satisfaction, content, challenges, compensation, careers etc. employees are leaving their jobs for various other reasons.

Consequently, there are issues:

- *Cost of acquisition of the Human Resource in both knowledge based and traditional outfits have lost its logical codes. -- Skyrocketing cost structure to hire the best*
- *Only Capital, when utilized effectively, is appreciable when turned on, nurtured and developed*
- *Culture definition has encountered considerable refinement though not at its maximization of Human Worth*
- *Motive for Human Resource Accounting and commercial forms of human capital measurement - more for a commercial gain or a basic measurement of qualification, defined as talent in the company*

Need for Org System Design – Organization structures form the heart of formalization. These structures are based upon building on the core competence. Its consequent communication as a part of the management process, included innovation, design and product development as a cutting edge for a competitive advantage, building an integrated supply chain with a single window service focus, moving from pyramids to teams, self-managed where possible. In addition, a flat, delayered, flexible and dynamic structural relationships, moving from hierarchies to competencies and on to networks and an attitude to get on with it. "Managers engaged in redesign should keep in mind the importance of balancing both. And in order to do that, he or she needs a model-an intellectual tool for sorting out those complex interests while reconfiguring the elements of the organization. This isn't just a theoretical exercise. The selection of a model is critical; in reality, it will guide the designer's analysis and action. Here's why. Problem solving in any organizational situation, including design, involves the collection, analysis and interpretation of information to identify specific problems and appropriate responses. When asked to "draw a picture of an organization," most managers usually respond the same way: They sketch some version of the traditional, pyramid-shaped structure that has characterized hierarchical organizations for centuries. It is a perspective based on a snapshot in time; it focuses on a stable configuration of jobs and work units as the most critical factor in an

36

organization. Certainly, that view provides some helpful ways to conceptualize the enterprise. But in the long run, it's a seriously limited model, one that excludes such critical factors as leadership, external influences, informal behavior, and power relationships". Construction of a structure in a going concern implies an evolution to be absorbed in one change. Drawing the structure is not as important as getting the information and execution process streamlined. The ongoing task of systems, styles, shared values, superordinate goal congruence is significantly more complex. "The traditional model captures only a fraction of what's really going on within any complex organization. Over the past two decades, there's been a growing tendency to replace the traditional static model with one that views the organization as a system". The philosophy of building critical mass, achieving client – product integration, developing profitable client relationships, sustaining and growing revenues, building distinctive competitive advantage, perhaps, is the single line of strategic thinking which pervades our corporate today. "This new perspective stems from repeated observations that social organisms display many of the same characteristics as mechanical and natural systems. In particular, some theorists argue that organizations are better understood if they are thought of as dynamic and "open" social systems", writes David Nadler in his 1996 book, "Competing by Design". And would need to check whether each proposition and strategic initiative has sufficient attention within the design; and where the design appears to give too little attention, consider alterations or other changes that will correct the flaw.. He continues, "Think of any organization, as an institutional priority, with which you're familiar-your own, for example. Is the competitive environment it competes in today the same as it was ten or even five years ago? Has the nature of competition been altered by new competitors, different technologies, or government deregulation or disruptions? Is the organization structured and managed as it was in the past? Do its employees use the same skills, knowledge, and management techniques as they used to? Have customer demands changed in terms of value, quality, delivery, and service? Clearly, every component of the organization, along with the external environment in which it operates, is subject to constant change. And each change has the potential of launching a serious ripple effect. Despite the evident importance of people, managers often complain that the designs they adopt are thwarted by people problems.".

Need for Org Design Principles - The classical theorists developed a set of principles of organization, but the suggestion that they were universally applicable is no longer tenable. The principles were in any case often inconsistent. There are, however, a number of guidelines which should be taken into account when designing or modifying organization structures, although their application will depend on the circumstances.

- *Equity - Allocation of work.* The work that needs to be done has to be defined and allocated to the appropriate job-holders or departments. Related activities should be grouped together to avoid unnecessary overlap and duplication of work. Matters requiring a decision should be dealt with as near to the point of action as possible. Managers should not try to do too much themselves. Neither should they exercise too close supervision.
- *Depth of Supervision - Levels in the structure.* Too many levels of management and supervision inhibit communication and create extra work (and jobs). The aim should be to reduce the number of levels to a minimum. Reducing the number of levels to create flatter structures does, however, impose a much more stringent requirement to improve teamwork, delegation and methods of integrating activities when spans of control are much wider and middle managers with a coordinating role no longer exist. The process of reducing the number of layers is facilitated by the use of information technology to speed up information flows and help decision-making.
- *Stress Levels - Span of control.* There are limits to the number of people anyone can manage or supervise well, but these vary considerably between different jobs. Most people can work

with a far greater span of control than they think they can, as long as they are prepared to delegate more effectively, to avoid getting involved in too much detail and to develop good teamwork among the individuals reporting to them. In fact, wide spans of control are beneficial in that they can enforce delegation and better teamwork and free the higher-level manager to spend more time on policy-making and planning. Limited spans of control encourage managers to interfere too much with the work going on beneath them and therefore constrain the scope that should be given to their subordinates to grow with their jobs.

- *Accountability - One person, one boss.* Generally speaking, individuals should report only to one boss. This avoids conflicting orders being given to one person. If managers bypass immediate subordinates when issuing instructions, it can cause confusion and undermines authority.
- *Art of Letting Go - Decentralization.* Authority to make decisions should be delegated as close to the action as possible. Duplication of the function and hence potentially higher costs, across product segments within each LOB is the constraint on not letting go.
- *Effectiveness - Optimize the structure.* Design the ideal organization by all means, but also remember that it may have to be modified to fit in the particular skills and abilities of key individuals.
- *Integration – Align to organizational needs.* While it is possible to centralize the entire customer management for the organization from a business stand-point, to ensure greater control on customer management within each product and obtain higher customer centricity, it is critical to manage it within each product segment. The organization structure has to be developed or amended to meet the needs of its situation. In today's conditions of turbulence and change this inevitably means a tendency towards more decentralized and flexible structures, with greater responsibility given to individuals and an extension of the use of taskforces and project teams to deal with opportunities or threats. This implies an informal, non-bureaucratic, organic approach to organization design (i.e., the form of the organization will follow its function, not the other way around). M Armstrong – Handbook of Management Techniques.

Need for Digital Design Thinking – Organizations, particularly those at the cutting edge of technology, has possibly been an exception, in a sense, that they have been significantly more dynamic in their techno- structural interventions than what one would be expect of industries in low technology areas. "The Design should flatten the organization wherever possible, enable the redeployment of resources to digital organizational aspects, strive for simplicity and focus on key customers, build mobility, configured core business processes, integrate with technology and enable greater integration of special markets into the core business", espouses Mark Smith, National Leader – Financial Services at KPMG Canada. "As a longer term goal, work toward shared information systems, cloud enabled processes, strategic functions to report to Corporate but generic and shared services to be distributed as required. At a cultural level, create speed to market, move decision-making out to organization units facing customers, support doing things once, doing them one simplified way, move decision-making to those closest to the work and drive a culture of trust and interdependence. In addition, effective designs should help foster more innovation, enhance external focus, create fewer levels, facilitate greater delegation, increase span of control/provide challenging work, deepen consumer understanding, minimize headcount and costs, support growth targets and increase organizational speed". Leverage Shared Service Centers will continue to dominate cost management, although this will veer more towards near shore centers. All operational HR services and related management responsibilities will be bundled in Shared Service Centers, including policy implementation and advice as well as compliance reporting and KPI tracking functions. Leverage outsourcing / offshoring to the greatest extent possible without cannibalizing SSC scale effects. Depending on the maturity of the product or policy being supported, the service delivery will be tiered in three levels: Tier 0 offering employee and manager self-services; Tier 1 offering product and policy advice in a service center; and Tier 2 offering specialist advice on complex product and policy questions. As an earlier, Global Head of the People and Change Practice at KPMG, now Industry Head for Financial Services, Mark Smith has seen it all. He says, "Engage in Business Strategy discussions (including crowd funding, crowd sourcing, crowd engagement) to help determine required capabilities. Also represent employee interests and provide an understanding of the impact of new business strategies, digital disruptions and actions on employees. By emphasizing the need to create a consistent cultural face and identity through common values and principles"; Mark identifies multiple perspectives, for example

- *For external stakeholders who form relationships with the entire organization and not just with a certain businesses or divisions of a large multi business company*
- *For employees and potential employees, the firm's overall culture is what attracts and inspires. Think of Coke-Cola or HP with their diversified businesses but single overall corporate image*

And to shape programs to help implement the organizations strategic goals

- *The CEO and leadership teams have short term and long terms strategic goals (example: Innovation, Globalization, Customer Service), some of which will require HR professionals to build the capabilities in the organization in order to realize them*
- *Corporate HR draw upon centers of expertise, embedded HR professionals within the businesses and line managers to accomplish strategic goals through the HR service.*

Arbitrate between centers of excellence and embedded HR

- *Centers of excellence like standardization and consistency while embedded HR functions like flexibility to adapt HR practices to the needs of the business.*
- *Establish Centers of Expertise for specialist HR expert services. For those HR services that are required for DB to achieve or maintain a competitive advantage in the market place, Centers of Expertise will be established to design and develop new HR products and services and for offering specialist expert advice to HR and the business. They will also be managing expert HR vendors. CoEs may be organized as local or virtual teams*
- Standardize processes and supporting systems globally. Processes must be standardized globally across businesses; any exceptions must be supported by a clear business case. Regional or local variations are solely driven by regulatory requirements or the limited scale of small local HR-teams. The infrastructure supporting these processes will be globally aligned and based on consistent and 90% standard software solutions
- *Corporate HR can balance the needs of both groups while keeping the multiple stakeholders in mind with the objective to create value for each stakeholder, concludes Smith".*

Need for Dynamic Disharmony – Disruptions in the Journey – "Sensing is a valuable capability for leaders, who must react to the force of events. Dynamic disharmony between a business and its market is the ideal in the face of constant change. When things are going well, sometimes what is needed is radical change. Radical changes would leave people wondering if more foresight might have prevented the upheaval. Change or die is the imperative that has driven ambitious people throughout history while knowing when and how to act are the tricky parts of any change effort", write Nohria and Champy in Arc of Ambition, 2000, (Perseus Books). They continue, "era by era, innovators have tirelessly pursued and achieved countless transformations. Changes in how we live, work, play and procreate. Transformations take many forms, each a learning experience. Changes in how we make money, peace and war. Changes in how we communicate, run organizations, govern society, envision the universe, explain the meaning of life. Over and over, new generations mobilize new resources to invent industries, cure diseases rebuild cities, remedy injustices, and make everything generally better. A defeat calls for reorganization, not retirement and a leader must be ever alert to the world outside organizational walls".

Need for Aligned Organizational Models - Effectiveness requires that an organization's culture, strategy, environment, and technology be aligned. The stronger the organization's culture, the more important it is that the culture fit properly with these variables. The successful organization will achieve a good external fit-its culture will be shaped to its strategy and environment. Market-driven strategies, for instance in competing and performing enterprise models, are more appropriate in dynamic environments and will require a culture that emphasizes individual initiative, risk taking, high integration, tolerance of conflict, and high horizontal communication. In contrast, product-driven strategies focus on efficiency, work best in stable environments, and are more likely to be successful when the organization's culture is high in control and minimizes risk and conflict.

De Risk of focused efforts

3. The group intends to target significant portion of the customer wallet risking thinning of limited resources

- Resource & target stretch
- Priority to ensure that structure supports de risk issues
- Strong Retail Mindset evident
- Need for more hands on problem solving focus at the operating level
- Need to identify Governance measures on effort

Strategic Direction

1. Need for crystallization of the Group's Values, Vision Statement and Long Term Mission

- The Organization is still in the process of crystallization of the same
- Great foundation, baby steps, significant aggression
- Need for focus in defining business purpose, goals, culture alignment, team actions, redefend business model and techno interfaces to strategy

Digital
Business

Reporting Ambiguity

5. Need for clear demarcation of Accountabilities and Responsibilities of the Company Management vis-à-vis Businesses and Functions

- Informal Dual reporting of the Business & Product Heads of products, geographies, matrix and staff
- Individual resistance from functional heads s to submit to review by on account o personality fixation and perceived lack of specific team working in a integrated business context
- Global – Local Integration of Markets & Processes

Simplification

2. Need for defined standards, benchmarks, policies and processes

- Relatively new organization model focused on growth with a focus on digital trends
- Priority on entry into new businesses
- Continues to grow and is experiencing pangs of stress while growing
- Aligned team necessary

Intellectual Talent Resourcing

4. Attracting and retaining the 'Right' Talent could prove to be a potential roadblock in view of lack of standardized processes

- Need for defined compensation and long term reward policies
- Need for career management system need for proper succession planning
- Need for Performance Management System which in turn could create distrust due to lack of transparency
- Ability to build competencies, aptitude and factors that help identify intellectual factors, special intellect and value creating actions

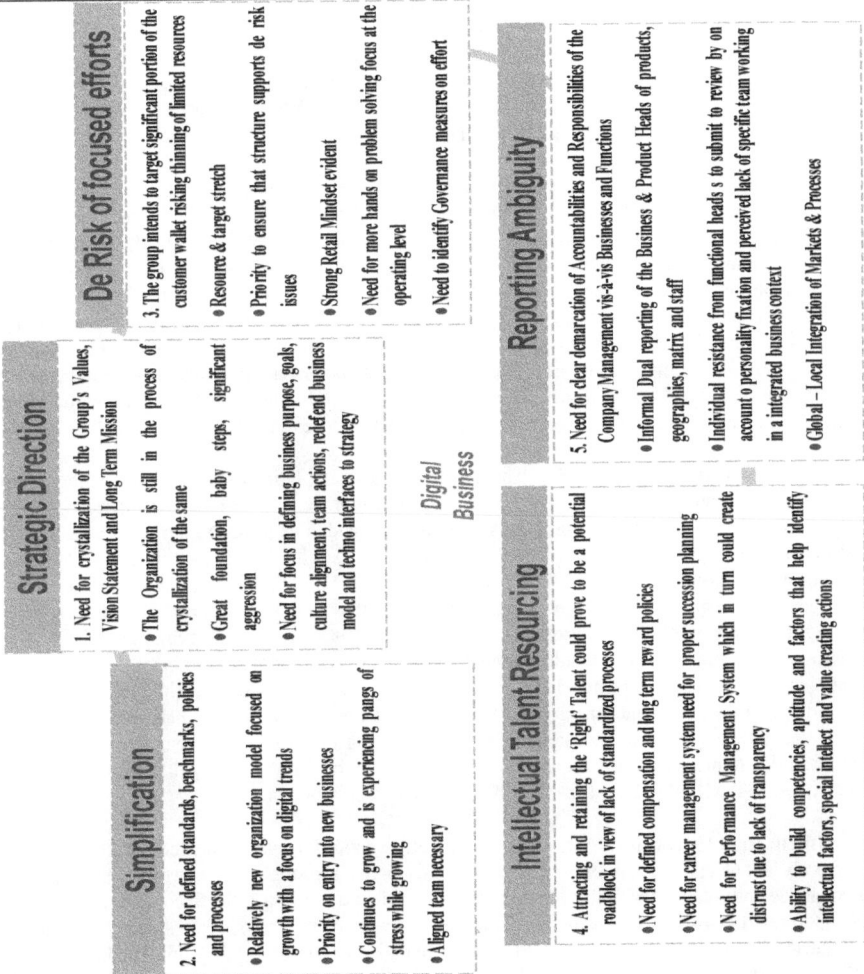

Figure 8 – Transforming Digital Business Models sometimes give rise to some compelling organization and people related challenges

Need to converge Leadership disrupted Styles with Culture, Organizational Models in a Digital Business context. Leadership disrupted in turn becomes key for impacting organizational culture in the context of specific types of organizational model. The role of the leader primarily focuses on creating key organizational systems and process that provide strategic contribution. They position themselves to add value by defining organizational priorities in the organizational model that they work in (Example - Competing Organization Models and Market Forces) and by sensing conditions and events in the business environment that affect strategy. Flatter and more lateral organizational structures and a decrease in the number of layers call for leadership from everyone.

Leaders operate effectively when someone or the same set of individuals lead by challenging the group and helping it set priorities and pressing for excellence in performance. The leader sets direction for the organization and builds mechanism to allow people to understand what that direction is and to measure their progress. It is particularly difficult for managers in their traditional hierarchical organization (Mechanistic or Institutional Model) to give best heroic leaders. Refer - People issues are abundantly evident across the globe)

Need for Capital - Capital takes different forms. A firm's assets are known as its capital, which may include fixed capital (machinery, buildings, and so on) and working capital (stocks of raw materials and part-finished products, as well as money, that are used up quickly in the production process). Financial capital includes money, bonds and shares. Human capital is the economic wealth or potential contained in a person, some of it endowed at birth, the rest the product of training and education, if only in the university of life. And Capital is something owned which provides ongoing services. In the national accounts, or to firms, capital is made up of durable investment goods, normally summed in units of money. Broadly: land plus physical structures plus equipment. Human Capital can be defined as that which when deployed by an individual enables the individual/people to earn a living, and a summation of all that is put together is the capital.

Need for Intellectual Models - The accounting models, human resource accounting, historical benchmarks, balance sheet analysis, the one-off endeavors e.g. to measure qualification and state human capital worth, and other quick fix solutions have landed us in several problem areas preventing efforts at investing in the creation of a scientific model. As we have seen, there is a lack of substantive Theory & Research work in this field and Human Asset Valuation has so far ignored as being too complex to be mapped, documented and tested for validity. We take comfort in simplistic solutions of managing people on hygiene or motivating needs. There has been some degree of distraction owing to traditional approaches – As a result, financial calculations turn more predominant than human worth, apart from excessive dependence on the performance management systems, without adequate research on individual data on what makes people and organizations perform. Yet there is an opportunity to value qualitative factors of the creation of intellect, in a quantifiable manner and to remove these uncertainties in measuring the organization's human wealth and identifying the Business Einstein we need a model that first defines the "wealth" element in a human being.

Intellectual Outcomes - And this book is neither about IQ related intellect or intelligence nor is it merely about capital (Intellectual/Human). This book is more about outcomes from intellectual knowledge and intellectual ability; in an organizational context; in a collective context; that which can be interpreted beyond, when we say "she reads extensively to improve her mind"; "she has a keen intellect", "he can learn", "her ability to perform in a given situation", "they think and act" , "the team discovered this molecule", "this digital product was through an AI application", (all in the context of building an intellectual company) and the capacity for rational thought or inference or discrimination; including as we are told that people are endowed with reason and capable of distinguishing good from evil or a person who uses the mind creatively, constructively or destructively. Intellect manifests itself in people whose value is to be measured as an individual or as a collective human capital group. But it is not good enough to know the definition as much as to know where does it lead us empirically. There are needs to be fulfilled.

Welcome to the Knowledge Organization, writes, K E Sveiby, "In Knowledge Organizations knowledge flows are more important than financial flows. People are revenue creators, not cost items. Their true output is a better performance among their customers. It is a world in which the customer relation is no longer one-way market driven, but partnerships in which solutions are co-created and knowledge flows both ways. Such organizations are not easy places to manage, because the power balance has shifted. Knowledge workers know more about the technical field than their bosses, have a better feel for the market and are closer to the customers". The individuals in the knowledge-based organization are networked with other individuals and other knowledge source and this eliminates the limitation of knowledge available with an individual. Thus, the knowledge-based organizations create a seamless joint between individuals and other knowledge sources. Thus, an individual truly becomes boundary less. Knowledge environments are established by building enablers for people, process and technology to integrate with knowledge systems. Knowledge Management systems are technologies that support Knowledge Management in organizations, specifically - knowledge generation, codification, and transfer. The use of KM in organizations is now widely recognized and expected to be an important part of organizational practices in the future. They are environments where the staff value the approbation of their professional peers more than the approval of their leaders. These expectations are not driven by a asking how do you stay in control when the primary production factor - creativity of the staff - flourishes best in chaos? How do we help staff feel entitled to availability of knowledge? How do you exercise power when your level in the organization's hierarchy is irrelevant and your primary power tool, control of the information flow, is usurped by the internet and collegial networks? How do you know that you are on the right track, a path when the management information system does not report knowledge flows and the financial results are hopelessly out-of-date by the time they reach you? In such a world manager' power base is their relative level of Knowledge". In, Knowledge Management Framework in a technology Environment, *Mohd Hasan Selamat, Rusli Abdullah and Christi Joseph Paul in* IJCSNS, 2006 publication, write, "The IT society we live in today is becoming a knowledge society. An organization's knowledge is professional intellect, such as the technical know-how, know what, concepts, and even the knowledge architecture used. Clearly, the quest to move beyond information management and into the realm of knowledge management is a complex undertaking involving the development of structures that allows the company to recognize, create, transform and distribute knowledge (Davenport, et al., 1998; Quinn, et al., 1996; Drucker, 2000).

Shifting Knowledge - Managing this kind of organization is not going to be easy as individual's growth in this organization means reduction of the power of control and increase of accountability. This implies that any individual wanting to have leadership disrupted role in this type of organizations will have to be willing to let go of control. This means, the individual will have to be exceptionally skillful handling relationships along with being an expert in his or her area of work. "Their role shifts from supervising subordinates to supporting colleagues. Their management information system reports competence utilization, value added, knowledge flows, customer image and staff attitudes. This information is available for everyone on the central network. The managers no longer manage people or even knowledge, but the space in which knowledge is created. This space is both the intangible culture and the tangible environment, such as the office. The culture encourages knowledge sharing so people are recognized publicly and rewarded for sharing. Top management recognizes trust as the bandwidth of sharing and have made investments in trust building one of their top priorities. Hoarding of knowledge and information as a means of career advancement is actively discouraged and the best knowledge workers are paid more than their bosses". In "HRD in Knowledge Based Industry" / Hari Iyer Et all, in Personnel Today; 1997 the authors write, "The intelligent people prefer to agree rather than obey. Hierarchies are out. Authorities in these organizations does not come automatically with title; it has to be earned. The authority is not based on being able to do one's job better but on the ability to help others to do their job better, by developing their skills, by liaising with the rest of the organization, by continual encouragement and leading by example. The organization of consent puts a premium on competence. There is no place for the incompetent and there are few hiding places in these organizations. "The open culture is further encouraged by the lay-out of the office, the décor, seating, space between people, ergonomics and sustainable environments. It is possible to focus on health and robustness while working. The top managers no longer hide on the top

43

floor, but have their desks on the same floors as the knowledge workers, because they recognize the value of the informal information networks. The corner rooms, now conference rooms, are used intensively for knowledge creation; they are no longer empty symbols of power occupied by bosses who are seldom there. The coffee machine, not for watercooler gossip, is now recognized as a generator of creative encounters, so it is in the center and not tucked away in a corner".

"Can you deal with such a world? I believe you can and you have no choice - Aren't you already there!" asks Karl Sveiby.

Culture Frameworks – This section provides a framework on cultures as they relate to this thesis and also details Edgar Schein's 3 cultures model. The section also provides for assessment of additional aspects to defining cultures including emerging cultures and how do they relate to Schein's model of cultures. Consequently, understanding culture has become a basic foundation for study of organizational practices and the method that a leader or the CEO wishes to choose to manage his/her organization. And the reasons to do so are many.

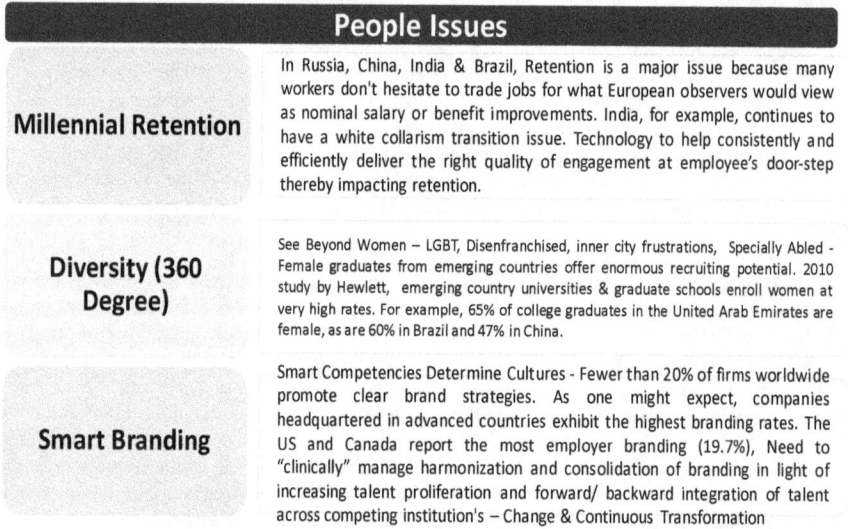

People Issues	
Millennial Retention	In Russia, China, India & Brazil, Retention is a major issue because many workers don't hesitate to trade jobs for what European observers would view as nominal salary or benefit improvements. India, for example, continues to have a white collarism transition issue. Technology to help consistently and efficiently deliver the right quality of engagement at employee's door-step thereby impacting retention.
Diversity (360 Degree)	See Beyond Women – LGBT, Disenfranchised, inner city frustrations, Specially Abled - Female graduates from emerging countries offer enormous recruiting potential. 2010 study by Hewlett, emerging country universities & graduate schools enroll women at very high rates. For example, 65% of college graduates in the United Arab Emirates are female, as are 60% in Brazil and 47% in China.
Smart Branding	Smart Competencies Determine Cultures - Fewer than 20% of firms worldwide promote clear brand strategies. As one might expect, companies headquartered in advanced countries exhibit the highest branding rates. The US and Canada report the most employer branding (19.7%), Need to "clinically" manage harmonization and consolidation of branding in light of increasing talent proliferation and forward/ backward integration of talent across competing institution's – Change & Continuous Transformation

Figure 9 – People issues are abundantly evident across the globe

People Issues

Intellectual Talent Scarcity	Workforce Plan revealed that 57% of BRICA employers have difficulties in filling job positions. This percentage is the highest among countries (for Brazil) in the Americas and ranks third in the world. The environment is currently challenged by a skills shortage and the majority of the workforce is unskilled to semi -skilled. This poses a major challenge when dealing with any form of change intervention from a management and leadership perspective.
Performance Dissonance	66% of the companies aiming at People Strategic Management, 67% aiming at Evaluation of Results and 75% at Talent Management considered the company objectives in the assessment of results of the investment in employees' education. Employees need to learn to adapt adapt operations to highly variable market conditions.
Work Force Alignment	People Management practices at BRICA companies in relation to their developed countries. Indicate strong control being exerted by BRICA HQ over their subsidiaries, attempting to impose their own organizational culture on the host country. Cultural backgrounds need to be well understood within the environment as staff may resist certain behavioural changes which may be in conflict with their traditions and values.

Figure 9 A – People issues are abundantly evident across the globe

Leadership disrupted Styles – This section detail leadership disrupted theory to a considerable degree to provide the basis for the researcher to attempt identifying additional leadership disrupted styles that may emerge in the course of the study. Given the above detailing of leadership theories and its development, the Researcher has proposed leadership definitions and questions in the context of an **"Digital Culture"** defined by addressing questions in respect of Organization and Management Models.

Five sets of questions on **"leadership disrupted"** have been addressed with a broad definition of what do these questions focus upon in the context of the Digital Culture.

- *Does a digital culture influence organization history, tradition, vision, purpose, values, management style, structure, roles, communication and performance ethic in a digital business context?*
- *Does a Leader drive the organization to help build/alter/change/influence a sustainable culture?*
- *Do Digital HR focus upon in terms of knowledge, skills, attitudes, behaviors, technology?*
- *Does a Leader act when confronted with challenges that pertain to purpose, vision, values, ethics, purpose, relationships and collaboration?*
- *Does a leader deploy people policies, programs, performance measures, rewards and other HR programs?*
- *What Organizational models appear to be effective in a digital business context?*

Leaders should display ownership for their work & be accountable

Leader need to have not just the right skills but the right values as well

Creating a Leadership Pipeline

Leaders should not only be technically sound but also acceptable by the other employees

Leaders are people who lead not by just by speech but also by action

Leaders should work in teams & see beyond their functions

What do you look for in a Leader?

Leaders are people who can walk the talk

Increase in Organizational Performance – Profitability and Growth

Leaders should be acquainted with the culture around them

Leaders should be able to manage large size teams

Leaders should be able to take up ownership and responsibility

Leaders should be able to manage and assess people

Leaders should be capable of identifying tech trends and customer practices

Structured and transparent framework to identify and nurture high performing employees

...Identifying Factors Likely to have a significant impact to fast forward this change process

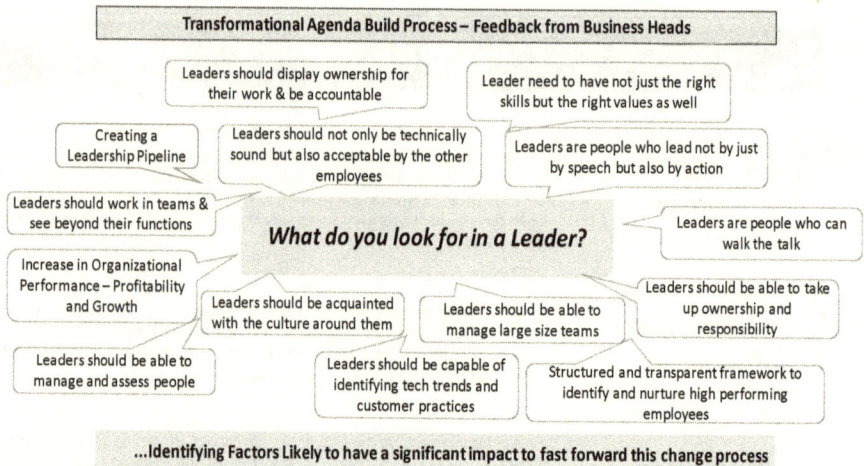

Figure 10 – Building a Transformational Agenda - Measuring the Pulse of an Organization – Business Heads

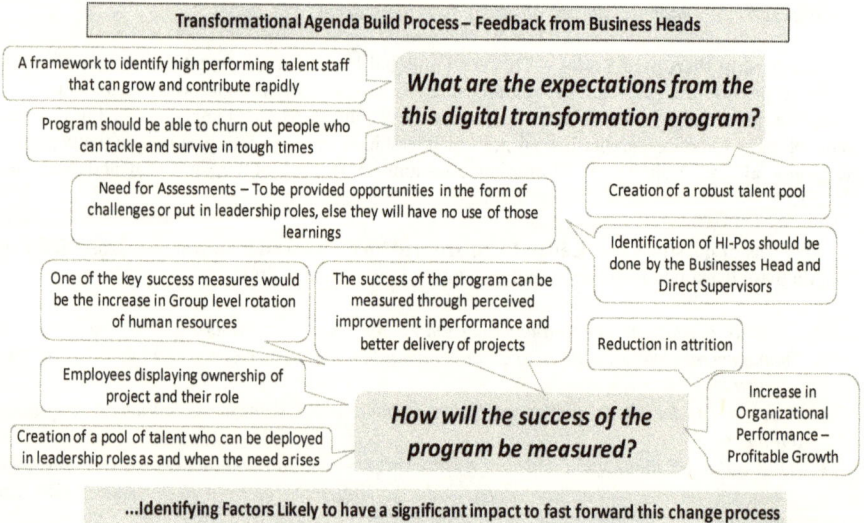

A framework to identify high performing talent staff that can grow and contribute rapidly

What are the expectations from the this digital transformation program?

Program should be able to churn out people who can tackle and survive in tough times

Need for Assessments – To be provided opportunities in the form of challenges or put in leadership roles, else they will have no use of those learnings

Creation of a robust talent pool

Identification of HI-Pos should be done by the Businesses Head and Direct Supervisors

One of the key success measures would be the increase in Group level rotation of human resources

The success of the program can be measured through perceived improvement in performance and better delivery of projects

Reduction in attrition

Employees displaying ownership of project and their role

How will the success of the program be measured?

Increase in Organizational Performance – Profitable Growth

Creation of a pool of talent who can be deployed in leadership roles as and when the need arises

...Identifying Factors Likely to have a significant impact to fast forward this change process

Figure 10 A – Building a Transformational Agenda - Measuring the Pulse of an Organization – Business Heads

Accenture (http://bit.ly/2b1jfqj) helped us identify core HR questions - In thinking about how their organizations need to change, HR executives should ask:

1. *Is HR becoming more of a People Management function as against a HR policy, process, technology function?*
2. *How well do we support day-to-day talent decisions that enable business strategy?*
3. *Are we able to provide the business with actionable insights that drive competitiveness?*
4. *Are we taking full advantage of newer technologies to connect with talent, internally and externally?*
5. *How well are we using technology to succeed in the age of "digital HR"?*
6. *Are we incorporating evolving technologies into our HR organization's plans for the future?*
7. *Does our culture support identifying and building a leadership pipeline?*
8. *Have we positioned the HR Function in the Board speaking of people needs.*
9. *Do our HR systems provide a "consumer grade" user experience that meets employee expectations?*
10. *Do we provide mobile devices and HR tools to users and business managers—or even let them use their own devices for work?*
11. *Are we using social media networking internally to let our employees collaborate and communicate?*
12. *Can we track internal social media activity to help improve our processes and performance?*
13. *Can we leverage employee experience with consumer technologies to drive adoption of HR tools?*
14. *Does our technology work across functions, or does it enforce traditional silos?*
15. *Can we easily inventory skills across the global organization and match that against future business needs?*
16. *How does development, compensation and performance management work together to engage and retain our high performers?*
17. *Do our systems support an individualized, "workforce of one" approach?*
18. *Are we able to clearly align learning, development, employee goals, compensation and performance management with overall corporate goals and strategy?*
19. *Do we spend too much time and money maintaining standalone HR systems?*
20. *Are we using analytics effectively to monitor HR performance and drive improvements?*
21. *Can we use employee segmentation to deliver increasingly tailored HR services to groups and individuals in the workforce?*
22. *Are we able to "look ahead" to identify employees who are at risk of leaving, or to predict team and individual performance?*
23. *Are we using workforce data to provide a clear picture of HR performance to senior management?*
24. *How can analytics help us be more proactive in planning programs and identifying potential improvements in HR?*
25. *Do we have an opportunity to expand the universe of data being used in analytics to answer key workforce questions with increased speed and accuracy?*
26. *Can we use real-time transactional data to create consistent global reports?*
27. *Are we leveraging the growing amount of information available in the talent marketplace?*
28. *How quickly and effectively can our recruiters sift through candidate data to find high-value prospects?*

47

29. How can we improve our ability to use social media to proactively reach and engage talent?
30. How can we tap into our employees' connections to augment our recruiting efforts?
31. Are we using technology to improve onboarding and drive engagement, productivity and retention?
32. Is Employee Experience an eventual people management goal?

Organization and Management Models – This section detail organization & management models and the theoretical material available in literature to understand organizational types and their characteristics. Additional analysis has been included to elaborate on characteristics of organizations. To enable building the organizational model it is necessary to delve a little into the make-up of the human mind, the evolutions, mental make-up that form the learning and personality disposition and the consequent need for structures and organizations. (Refer - Building a Transformational Agenda - Measuring the Pulse of an Organization – Business Heads).

Articulated assumptions for the study - We have attempted to bring in the relevance of Leadership on culture and their context to the Organizational Models. This has meant looking at some fundamental thought positioning, some of which are mentioned below:

1. *Leaders drive organizations to perform in ways they believe would support their goal orientation. This impacts culture.*
2. *In doing so the Leaders influence and impact the organizational culture in a business context.*
3. *The leaders in turn also assume a concrete degree of clarity on the organizational purpose, its business philosophy and shareholder expectation. An all-encompassing culture and values operate in the environment.*
4. *Consequently, organizations work in a context influenced by its culture in which the said philosophy operates. The culture is defined in this organizational context and is also influenced by the leader.*
5. *Effectively, for example, in an organizational context of Competing Organization, influenced by an operator culture and led by a teacher may not be compatible given incongruent nature of this relationship, with each bringing its own nuances. So alternate models would need to be studied.*
6. *We would need to establish the appropriate connection that links up each of these factors, being leadership, culture and organizational and management models, relevantly.*
7. *And bring to bear that leadership influence over culture is limited unless the organizational model/context is considered.*
8. *Staff seek an business environment in which they can learn and contribute.*
9. *Technology has changed the way employees seek careers choices and opportunities to engage and contribute.*
10. *Devices, wearables, networks, Wi Fi, data, social media, APPS form an integral part of an organization. External world is fast integrating with the internal world.*

The method followed included a scenario and case based analysis. Various scenarios were structured to identify dominant characteristics in organizational and management models, culture and leadership as it influences each other. Scenarios (Some Factors Covered included, Vision, Values, Business Model, Structures, HR Policies, Leadership, People, Talent, KPIs/ Measures, Goal Orientation, Influence, Presence, Role, Perception, Action, Outcome, Shareholder Value, Governance, Compliance, Rewards, Product/Customers) provided below were used for validation and interviewing.

1. *Scenario 1: History and Tradition of the Organization*

2. *Scenario 2: Structure and Hierarchy Influence, Management Style, the Role of the CEO in building organization vision*

3. *Scenario 3: The Role of the CEO - Board in regard to vision, values, strategy processes technology and people actions and leader's influence in the existence of specific types of cultures*

4. *Scenario 4: Leadership disrupted Style as practiced by the management groups*

5. *Scenario 5: CEO focus on performance, climate, communication, and HRM practices, on monetary reward programs and influence over high performers, and management attention on retaining high performers.*

6. *Scenario 6: Role of the leader in building work processes, in managing people strategy issues, and organizational emphasis on competing and performing in a complex environment.*

7. *Scenario 7: Board - Leader's emphasis on building future leaders through mentoring, coaching and teaching, emphasis on team work*

8. *Scenario 8: Role of the CEO in enabling organization to restructure and right size.*

9. *Scenario 9: Role of the CEO in preparing the organization to change as required.*

10. *Scenario 10: Organizational - Leader's role in sponsoring innovation, new ideas, take risks and implementing experiments and*

11. *Scenario 11: Organizational/CEO's role in enabling inters dependencies between functions, businesses, technologies and the organization as a whole.*

12. *Scenario 12: Leader as a person – Vision, values, beliefs and the dream*

13. *Scenario13: Leader's emphasis on the Individual and the Intellect, and a role in building individual and organizational knowledge*

14. *Scenario 14: CEO's role in emphasizing on culture aspects pertaining to empowerment, delegation, individual contribution, accountability and*

15. *Scenario 15. CEO's role in actively participating in attracting, retaining and rewarding star talent and performers*

16. *Scenario 16: Leader's role in helping the organization retain an open mind to an unknown futuristic business environment.*

17. *Scenario 17: Leaders determine Business Models that helps organizations create value*

18. *Scenario 18: Technology choices become evident as organizations gain greater clarity on their value to employees and customers.*

19. *Scenario 19: Leaders cannot stop social collaboration processes that have been set in motion*

20. *Scenario 20: Leaders cannot stop Millennials from doing what they want to do!*

Chapter 2

Case for the Digital Intellect

Organizations seldom get time to adapt themselves to the rapidly changing business landscape. Thus, in the existing scenario, the impact of culture, smart talent and leadership cannot be overemphasized. Organizations need leadership which can make sense amidst this ambiguity, find patterns in the chaos and take charge to meet the desired end. Business leaders, on the other hand, need to address these challenges and skilfully manoeuvre their respective organizations to the next level. Increasingly there is a new generation of corporate life, which have become more dependent on the machine and its application. Their orientation to work life has become computer centric, sometimes meaningless, cynical and self-defeating. Their orientation has been to move on and on into cyberspace, move into the knowledge based business and hope to keep their psychic space intact.

This chapter focuses on the following:

A. *What is Intellect, Intelligence and Intellectual Company*
B. *Defining a Digital Business Model – Alternate Models,*
C. *Human Capital – Definitions, Inclusions, Exclusions, Skills, Competencies and Value including intellectual capital value*
D. *Intellectual Company Value – Integrated view of intellect on human capital activity, ability to value invisible assets, systemic capability to manage knowledge*
E. *Digital Tech Performance Challenges and Maturity*
F. *Bundle of competencies - A Human Capital Primer*
G. *Intellectual Capital – Definitions, Context, Capital Augmentation, Forms of Intellect (Corporate), Goodwill, Know How Company*
H. *Intellectual Capital – Literature Survey*
I. *Strategic Assessment of Intellectual Capital Application Base*
J. *Digital Business – Four Levels Maturity, Three Levels of Cultural Mindsets, Global Digital Collaboration*
K. *Digital Business – Four Levels Maturity, Three Levels of Cultural Mindsets, Global Digital Collaboration*
L. *Business Case for Digital HR in an Intellectual Company*
M. *Point of View - Intellect and Intellectual Capital as the Human Capital is surely the challenge of the new economic enterprises*
N. *A Five Point Charter towards building an Intellectual Company.*
O. *Study Dynamics*

The new generation employees consist of the machine dependent process workers (today with neural networks, machine deep learning based, AI, Robotics in a mobile enabled, cloud hosted, analytics friendly, socially adaptable, wearables) who possess the capability to generate, institutionalize, internalize and synthesize information, data and knowledge for commercial purposes. They are specialists with a purpose, sometimes very specific to the changing needs. While the organization and the business environment border on high integration with the knowledge processors, the individuals considerably encounter performance stresses given stretching demands on their work output, speed and alignment with the ever increasing learning base. Organization which has traditionally used this resource as a body available for use, in the context of an information era cares and concern for the well-being of an intellectual worker is inevitable.

A. What is Intellect, Intelligence and Intellectual Company

"The Intellectual Company" *personifies the human being and makes the human mind – intellect as the foundation of value for a corporation. An institution that brings together knowledge and wisdom through a collective process for application of mind including effective use of technology to enable such application to be driven by the intellect.*

What is intellect? *The part or faculty of the human soul by which it knows, it recognizes, it absorbs, it senses, it thinks, it analyzes, as distinguished from the power to act, behave, feel and to will;* sometimes, the capacity for absorption and beyond, higher forms of knowledge, intelligence, as distinguished from the power to perceive objects, aspects, environment, material, symbols, artifacts in their relations; the power to judge, decode, decipher and comprehend; the thinking faculty; the understanding, the closing and finale

"What is Intelligence" is 'the faculty of adapting oneself to circumstances' said Francis Binet and Henri Simon, the authors of the first IQ test (Wolf 1973). Intelligence is the operation of gathering information, an ability to comprehend; to understand and profit from experience or new information about specific and timely events; "they awaited news of the outcome". That which makes the human mind determine a course or choice of action, after sifting through alternatives, after evaluating risks or after predicting an outcome and that which has the power to create, destroy, add, delete, enhance or subsume. When must people think of intelligence they will probably think of IQ (intelligence quotient), which is someone's score on an intelligence test. The key function of intelligence, he said, is to enable anticipation of change, and thus constructive action to utilize or nullify it. Bukowitz Wendi and Williams Ruth in How to use The Knowledge Management Field Book – FT Press (1999) write, "Mindscaping taps into the intelligence that operates below the level of consciousness. Margulies believes that this non-linguistic intelligence is deeper and richer than the limited aspect of our intelligence we bring to bear on most problem solving. 'Mindscaping asks people to approach their problem from an odd angle. Many don't believe that it will get them from point A to point B. But after putting themselves in an initially uncomfortable situation, almost everyone ends up at point D, farther than they thought they could go toward reaching innovative solutions". 'One of the essential functions of knowing is to bring about foresight,' said Piaget. Ultimately, modularity, functionality, adaptability and intelligence are useless unless the organization design is geared to deliver products and services on a dynamic, adaptive basis.

What is Applied Intelligence? The importance of the concept, both socially and scientifically, persists undiminished including a value judgment on the people who can think and do. The execution of business strategy is often hampered by a lack of reliable information. In today's turbulent and unpredictable conditions, it's more important than ever to gain continuous market insight and have the agility to react quickly. In fact, organizations driven by the need to foster a learning and knowledge intensive culture are seeking ways to identify and nurture human intelligence. Intelligence that can predict and work towards an uncertain future including the need to commercially value intellect to sponsor a better market capitalization and financial gain. Wendi and Ruth provide an example, "Resumix provides advanced automated staffing and skills management solutions that help organizations source and identify the most qualified people to accomplish strategic corporate objectives. The company uses a combination of integrated artificial intelligence technology, image processing, client/server architecture and database technology to incorporate both hard and soft information about applicants or employees in its analysis of skill sets. 'Most organizations use the system to manage a very specific slice of knowledge management. They have a position that needs to be filled and want to find the best person to fill it,' says Dr Kathy Brush, Vice President of Marketing. 'However, we are beginning to see some organizations wake up to the power of using the system across the full spectrum of knowledge management which includes aligning the human resource retention strategy with the overall business strategy.' Building Business Intelligence into your organization is a starting point in applying intelligence. There are a number of reasons why business intelligence projects fail. The most common is ownership of business intelligence being limited to specialists within an organization instead of being embedded in processes. Individual departments produce reports from poor quality information (which includes duplication) leading to a lack of trust in the data. Also, business intelligence is often not linked to the performance management strategy, so KPIs are poorly defined and become irrelevant over time. Indeed, it may, for various reasons, actually be increasing in importance. IQ testers say they can measure but do they state what is it that they are measuring? They say those measured differences reflect genetic differences at least as much as 'environmental' differences, but how valid have their concepts and methods for demonstrating that actually been? Challenges Ken Richardson! In our context a renewed strategy for creating significant and lasting customer value, generating intense loyalty to share the wallet, sustain competitive advantage and building on past successful strategies is a starting step in understanding smart – intelligent organization. There is overwhelming evidence to demonstrate the recurring gap between strategies, human competencies, structured relationships all in for a given environment. In order to create truly valuable business intelligence, organizations should clearly define who owns, uses, and produces information and how it is presented. Such tight ownership and control should help give consistent, accurate reports and allow fair, "like for like" comparisons of performance. The compelling need to relate intellect, as it can be understood, at both a psychological and a cognitive level is nevertheless gaining importance.

What is Social Intelligence? Social Intelligence, if such a thing exists, is the historical creation of a particular culture, analogous to the notion of childhood.' To support this idea, they review evidence indicating that what counts as intelligence varies widely across cultures, changes over time in the same culture, is defined differently for children of different ages, and changes with the changing social experiences of individuals. Rather similarly, Sternberg says that 'intelligence is invented.... it is not any one thing.... Rather it is a complex mixture of ingredients... The invention is a societal one.' Another approach to explain and characterize human social intelligence has been to look to another primate for enlightenment. That many other species exist as social groups, presenting to the individual a particularly complex and structured social environment, has long been recognized. Accordingly, authors such as Nicholas Humphrey have stressed the role of the social world, especially in primates, as the seat of intelligence. This has been called the 'social function of intellect' hypothesis, and suggest that the need to reconcile individual needs with the social cohesion of the group requires a new order of individual smartness of primates in general, and humans in particular. Humphrey, for example, suggests that the range of technological skills the long period of dependency in offspring, and the complex kinship structures found in primate groups requires extensive powers of social foresight and understanding. Multi-stakeholder planning ought to include stakeholders who are external to the organization, but who have a stake in helping achieve the organization's goals. Together with internal participants, external stakeholders can help identify, refine and rank goals for improving relationships, partnerships, and networks. J. H. Crook and others point to the constant need to read others' intentions, feeling and states of mind. At least one study has indicated a relation between social complexity (albeit using only the crude index of group size) and individual intelligence in primate groups. Richard Byrne says that this is leading us to a real understanding of primate intelligence. Ken Richardson in articulating these views has surely investigated the genesis of social collaboration and application of intelligence in the digital business world by demonstrating human social intelligence has emerged as a dauntingly powerful force from the interactive relations between a cultural level of social life and the cognitive regulations of individuals.

Collective - Symbiotic intelligence (http://bit.ly/2bfsaow) "is shared or group intelligence that emerges from the collaboration, collective efforts, and competition of many individuals and appears in consensus decision making. The term appears in sociobiology, political science and in context of mass peer review and crowdsourcing applications. It may involve consensus, social capital and formalisms such as voting systems, social media and other means of quantifying mass activity. Collective IQ is a measure of collective intelligence, although it is often used interchangeably with the term collective intelligence. Collective intelligence has also been attributed to bacteria and animals. One way to understand the various artifacts of organizational - collective intelligence is to view them as existing on a spectrum of refinement ranging from relatively raw data, to information, then to organizational knowledge, and finally to organizational wisdom. Data are raw facts and numbers that alone are meaningless without a context for interpretation.

Universality - It can be understood as an emergent property from the synergies among: 1) data-information – Learning – Intellect - knowledge; 2) software-hardware; and 3) experts (those with new insights as well as recognized authorities) that continually learns from feedback to produce just-in-time knowledge for better decisions than these three elements acting alone. Or more narrowly as an emergent property between people and ways of processing information. This notion of collective intelligence is referred to as Symbiotic intelligence by Norman Lee Johnson. The concept is used in sociology, business, computer science and mass communications: it also appears in science fiction. Pierre Lévy defines collective intelligence as, "It is a form of universally distributed intelligence, constantly enhanced, coordinated in real time, and resulting in the effective mobilization of skills. I'll add the following indispensable characteristic to this definition: The basis and goal of collective intelligence is mutual recognition and enrichment of individuals rather than the cult of fetishized or hypostatized communities." According to researchers Lévy and Kerckhove, it refers to capacity of networked ICTs (Information communication technologies) to enhance the collective pool of social knowledge by simultaneously expanding the extent of human interactions.

Power of WE - Collective intelligence strongly contributes to the shift of knowledge and power from the individual to the collective. According to Eric S. Raymond (1998) and JC Herz (2005), open source intelligence will eventually generate superior outcomes to knowledge generated by proprietary software developed within corporations (Flew 2008). *Ann Macintosh of the Artificial Intelligence Applications Institute (University of Edinburgh)* identifies some of the specific business factors, including: Marketplaces are increasingly competitive and the rate of innovation is rising; Reductions in staffing create a need to replace informal knowledge with formal methods; Competitive pressures reduce the size of the work force that holds valuable business knowledge; The amount of time available to experience and acquire knowledge has diminished; Early retirements and increasing mobility of the work force lead to loss of knowledge; There is a need to manage increasing complexity, as small operating companies are trans-national sourcing operations and Changes in strategic direction may result in the loss of knowledge in a specific area.

Alternate Source - Media theorist Henry Jenkins sees collective intelligence as an 'alternative source of media power', related to convergence culture. He draws attention to education and the way people are learning to participate in knowledge cultures outside formal learning settings. Henry Jenkins criticizes schools which promote 'autonomous problem solvers and self-contained learners' while remaining hostile to learning through the means of collective intelligence. Both Pierre Lévy (2007) and Henry Jenkins (2008) support the claim that collective intelligence is important for democratization, as it is interlinked with knowledge-based culture and sustained by collective idea sharing, and thus contributes to a better understanding of diverse society. Similar to the *g factor* for general individual intelligence, a new scientific understanding of collective intelligence aims to extract a general collective intelligence factor **c factor** for groups indicating a group's ability to perform a wide range of tasks. Cross discipline science of intelligence includes, **Cognitive science.** Insights from how we learn and know will certainly improve tools and techniques for gathering and transferring knowledge., **Expert intelligence systems, handy robots, artificial intelligence, machine thinking and smart thinking system.** AI and related technologies have acquired an undeserved reputation of having failed to meet their own — and the marketplace's — high expectations. In fact, these technologies continue to be applied widely, and the lessons practitioners have learned are directly applicable to knowledge management. This is in addition to **Computer-supported collaborative work (groupware).** In Europe, *knowledge management* is almost synonymous with *groupware* and therefore with Lotus Notes of yesterday or share point portals today. Sharing and collaboration are clearly vital to organizational knowledge management — with or without supporting technology. Definition, operationalization and statistical methods are derived from *g*. Similarly, as *g* is highly interrelated with the concept of IQ, this measurement of collective intelligence can be interpreted as intelligence quotient for groups (Group-IQ) even though the score is not a quotient per se. Causes for *c* and predictive validity are investigated as well". (http://bit.ly/2bfsaow).

WE versus I - Once information has been used by a person or group, then it becomes the basis for creating knowledge through the **process of knowing for us.** In order to have knowledge, one must first experience knowing. Scientists Humberto Maturana and Francisco Varela offer one explanation of the process of knowing. "Knowing for "We" is effective action, that is, operating effectively in the domain of existence of living beings. When people are able to act effectively in a particular circumstance we are inclined to believe it is because of something which they know. If people have knowledge, the they are able to pose a question or raise an expectation that defines those actions which can be effective in a given situation. "Intelligence does not arise only in individual brains; it also arises in groups of individuals. This is collective intelligence: groups of individuals acting collectively in ways that seem intelligent. In recent years, a new kind of collective intelligence has emerged: interconnected groups of people and computers, collectively doing intelligent things. Today these groups are engaged in tasks that range from writing software to predicting the results of presidential elections. This volume reports on the latest research in the study of collective intelligence, laying out a shared set of research challenges from a variety of disciplinary and methodological perspectives. Taken together, these essays—by leading researchers from such fields as computer science, biology, economics, and psychology—lay the foundation for a new multidisciplinary field" write, in Handbook of Collective Intelligence, edited by Thomas W. Malone and Michael S. Bernstein. http://bit.ly/2b79EgH

Means not End - Decision support systems. According to Daniel J. Power, "Researchers working on Decision Support Systems have brought together insights from the fields of cognitive sciences, management sciences, computer sciences, operations research, and systems engineering in order to produce both computerized artifacts for helping knowledge workers in their performance of cognitive tasks, and to integrate such artifacts within the decision-making processes of modern organizations." But in practice the emphasis has been on quantitative analysis rather than qualitative analysis and on tools for managers rather than everyone in the organization. **Semantic networks.** Semantic networks are formed from ideas and typed relationships among them — sort of "hypertext without the content," but with far more systematic structure according to meaning. Often applied in such arcane tasks as textual analysis, semantic nets are now in use in mainstream professional applications, including medicine, to represent domain knowledge in an explicit way that can be shared.

Knowledge Mapping - Continue, Malone and Bernstein, "For instance, it is sometimes defined in terms of specific processes, such as: "Intelligence is a very general mental capability that, among other things, involves the ability to reason, plan, solve problems, think abstractly, comprehend complex ideas, learn quickly and learn from experience" (Gottfredson, 1997). Another common way of defining intelligence is in terms of goals and the environment, such as: "the ability to adapt effectively to the environment" (Encyclopedia Britannica, 2006), or "the ability to solve problems, or to create products, that are valued within one or more cultural settings (Gardner, 1993). Intelligence as process for creating knowledge has been well-described by numerous writers, including Americans Chris Argyris, David Kolb, and Peter Senge, and Europeans Charles Handy, Ronnie Lessem, and Reg Revans. One of the most thought-provoking writers in this area is the Japanese scholar Ikujiro Nonanka. Throughout much of the works of these scholars one is able to find several important themes that links knowledge – intelligence nurtured and built by continuous learning. First, knowledge often derives from a cyclical – regulated process of learning through experience, internalized as wisdom, in other words, an action-learning – execution - feedback cycle (open systems model). Secondly, this action-learning cycle or wheel of learning spins around in continuous process that includes: (1) theories of how things work, (2) experiences that test the validity of ideas, (3) observing and reflecting behaviors that are used to define meaning found in experiences, and (4) questioning and experimenting with new ideas – similar to Kolb on learning styles inventory. The most common operational definition of intelligence in psychology is as a statistical factor which measures a person's ability to perform well on a wide range of very different cognitive tasks (Spearman, 1904). This factor, often called "general intelligence" or "g," is essentially what is measured by IQ tests. There is even controversy about whether it would be legitimate to call behavior intelligent, no matter how intelligent it seemed, if it were done by a computer rather than a person (e.g., Searle, 1999).

Collective Intelligence - Every time people engage in the process of "knowing" they are defining their view of the world to focus on the usefulness of particular actions at certain times. While information may be necessary for the certain knowledge, it is not sufficient. When people who "know" something take either effective action, or ineffective action, they gain a new level of experience that shapes their future capacity for knowing other things. So the process of knowing is a way of experimenting with information to see if it works for you. Once you discover whether something works, you must then decide whether that discovery is consistent with what you already believe is true. In view of all this complexity, our definition of collective intelligence, as given above, is a simple one: *groups of individuals acting collectively (collaboratively?) in ways that seem intelligent.* Several aspects of this definition are noteworthy: (1) The definition does not try to define "intelligence" since there are so many ways to define it. This definition is, therefore, compatible with all of the above definitions of intelligence. (2) By using the word "acting", the definition requires intelligence to be manifested in some kind of behavior. By this definition, for instance, the knowledge represented in a collection like Wikipedia would not, itself, be considered intelligent, but the group of people who created the collection could be. (3) The definition requires that, in order to analyze something as collective intelligence, one must identify some *group* of *individuals* that are involved. In some cases, this may be straightforward, such as noting the individual humans in an organization, but in other cases, it may be useful to draw these boundaries in unusual ways. Learning and knowledge creation are subjective processes that depend on how one view self, others, and the way the world works. Another useful explanation of the process of learning through experience that has developed with roots in the biological sciences can be found in the work of biologists Maturna and Varela. By summarizing the process of learning, as these scientists appear to understand it, we may begin to make the important distinction between the various artifacts of organizational intelligence even clearer. For instance, one could analyze the operation of a single human brain as collective intelligence, if one regards the whole brain as a group of individual neurons or brain regions. Or one could analyze the collective intelligence of a whole economy by noting that the economy is a collection of many different organizations and people. (4) The definition requires that the individuals act *collectively*, that is, that there be some relationships among their activities. We certainly do *not* intend this to mean that they must all share the same goals or always cooperate. We merely mean that their activities are not completely independent, that there are some interdependencies among them (e.g., Malone & Crowston, 1994). Knowledge mapping describes what knowledge an organization has, who has it and how it flows (or doesn't) through the enterprise. Knowledge mapping can show what changes are needed in organizational and personal behavior, business processes and enabling technologies so knowledge can be applied to improve results. It is valuable in pointing out improvements to existing processes and identifying people who have been acting as barriers to knowledge proliferation, whether inadvertently or on purpose. Knowledge mapping can also can clarify what information various people really need and locate the best sources for it. It can reveal, for example, the best practices that fieldworkers have developed but have kept to themselves and a few colleagues. Most importantly, knowledge mapping can answer a crucial question: Is your organization socially ready to become a knowledge organization?

For instance, different actors in a market buy and sell things to each other, even though they may each have very different individual goals. But their goals would need mapping to help cater to their needs as they return to shop. And different problem solvers in an open innovation community like InnoCentive's compete to develop the best solutions to a problem. (5) Finally, by using the word "seem," the definition makes clear that what is considered intelligent depends on the perspective of the observer. For instance, to evaluate whether an entity is acting intelligently an observer may need to make assumptions about what the entity's goals are. IQ tests, for example, do not measure intelligence well if the goal of the person taking the test is to annoy the person giving the test! Or an observer may choose to analyze how intelligently a group of Twitter user's filters information even if none of the individual users have that goal".

Intellectual Outcomes – All of these discussions are neither about IQ related intellect - intelligence nor is it merely about capital (Intellectual/Human/Smart Special). This book is more about outcomes from intellectual knowledge and intellectual ability; in an organizational context; in a collective context; that which can be interpreted beyond, when we say "she reads extensively to improve her mind"; "she has a keen intellect", "he can learn", "her ability to perform in a given situation", "they think and act" , "the team discovered this molecule", "this digital product was through an AI application", (all in the context of building an intellectual company) and the capacity for rational thought or inference or discrimination; including as we are told that people are endowed with reason and capable of distinguishing good from evil or a person who uses the mind creatively, constructively or destructively. Intellect manifests itself in people whose value is to be measured as an individual or as a collective human capital group. But it is not good enough to know the definition as much as to know where does it lead us empirically.

According to Merriam-Webster's dictionary, intelligence is described as the ability to apply knowledge to manipulate one's environment or to think abstractly as measured by objective criteria. This use of knowledge and learning by people needs measurement. A working definition of an Intellect could be, a domain instinct, expertise, repository within an individual, active and dormant, utilized and unutilized to create, destroy, analyze, substitute known and unknown sources of content, actions, behavior, learnt or available through acquisition, education, experience and inheritance. (Shermon, SAICAB 1998).

B. Defining a Digital Business Model

Digital Business Model - Companies create value, and incur risk, by assembling unique combinations of assets. It is this portfolio that is called the business model, and it determines a company's economic success. Capital takes different forms. A firm's assets are known as its capital, which may include fixed capital (machinery, buildings, and so on) and working capital (stocks of raw materials and part-finished products, as well as money, that are used up quickly in the production process). Financial capital includes money, bonds and shares. Human capital is the economic wealth or potential contained in a person, some of it endowed at birth, the rest the product of training and education, if only in the university of life and Intellectual Capital includes intangible, goodwill, human capital and so on. And Capital is something owned which provides ongoing services. In the national accounts, or to firms, capital is made up of durable investment goods, normally summed in units of money. Broadly: land plus physical structures plus equipment.

"A World-class Restaurant At One-third The Price", writes, Sean Silverthorne In HBSWK 2013, "Ristorante D'O, a high-end gourmand eatery located near Milan, Italy, has a unique business model among Michelin starred restaurants. It sells meals at prices almost a third less than competitors—and has an 18-month waiting list. Its secret?" Think about how you visualize your organization. Do you picture groups of neatly lined-up boxes with solid lines, reporting structures, and audit trails? Do you think the New World of work will look nothing like this? (This is creating a hybrid that is specific to assets derived from knowledge:
Intellectual or Knowledge-based Asset: Anything valued without physical dimensions that is embedded in people or derived from the processes, systems, and culture associated with an organization -brands, individual knowledge, intellectual property, licenses, and forms of organizational knowledge (e.g., databases, process know-how, relationships). The organization is probably already silently morphing into more of a hybrid organization. The upper ranks of your company may still operate in a traditional hierarchical fashion, but natural dynamic teams are forming as midlevel managers tackle the dynamics of the New Economy. Going forward, the new virtual organization will consist of a series of interconnected hub-and-spoke combinations that represent leaders, departments, internal divisions, external customer bases, and business partners "A series of smart, waste-reducing choices regarding menu, meal design, service process, layout, and reservation process. "The deeper issue in the case," write authors Gary P. Pisano, Alessandro Di Fiore, Elena Corsi, and Elisa Farri, "concerns how businesses based on the creative talent of an individual (like Chef Oldani) can grow, without losing what makes them special." Purchase the case, "Chef Davide Oldani and Ristorante D'O."

Digital Transparent Business Models are transparent to all. They can crash quickly, because switching costs in the digital world are often lower than in the physical world. The three components of your digital business model — content, experience and platform — work together to create a compelling customer value proposition. This comparison takes place through the process known as reflection as a means to experimentation with business options. When people pause to discover the meaning of their experiences in relation to their beliefs we say that they have engaged in the process of reflection. Reflecting is a means of discovering what one really knows (or doesn't know). When businesses discover that either they know or don't know something, then they have learned through the benefit of their experience and application of assumptions. Raphael and Zott (Raphael Amit and Christoph Zott in MIT SMR 2012, "Creating Value Through Business Model Innovation") as, *"We define a company's business model as a system of interconnected and interdependent activities that determines the way the company "does business" with its customers, partners and vendors. In other words, a business model is a bundle of specific activities — an activity system — conducted to satisfy the perceived needs of the market, along with the specification of which parties (a company or its partners) conduct which activities, and how these activities are linked to each other".* "The customer experience embodies what it's like to be a digital customer of your organization, whether buying digital or physical products. Amazon's customer experience includes the website and the digitized business processes touching the customer, like the shopping cart and payment options, as well as messaging, such as delivery alerts and email acknowledgments." "Networked, friendly & egalitarian". These three adjectives could well describe the workplace of the future. Not to forget "connected"! For, just like the 'how' and 'why' of work, the 'where' will change too. "The softer aspects of the workplace will also be influenced by the touch of technology. And "think Social". That may not be most accurate forecast ever written, but a little wishful thinking never did any harm. It has already become clear that is the all-perspective force driving change in the workplace. How can organizations make it worthwhile for people to share information? The business case presents a formal declaration of the reasons for moving the organization from the current state, the As-Is, into the envisioned state, the To-Be. It sets out both the financial justification of the new design and the qualitative arguments to demonstrate that the As-Is is not a desirable alternative in the long term. The business case provides an indication to the client that the investment and upheaval that the change will cause is warranted by the quantitative and qualitative results of the To-Be state.

The way we work, the way we interact with each other, even the physical parameters of the workplace are in the midst of a metamorphosis. "The experience also includes Amazon's well-developed customer-created content: customer product ratings and reviews, as well as sophisticated tools like search, a detailed history of purchases and tailored recommendations. An Amazon platform allows for Amazon Seller Central to engage actively with Amazon to widen their own customer base. Corporate information specialists are well aware that the opportunity now exists for them to dust off their image as mousy introverts and become key players in the brazen digital age. The platform consists of a coherent set of digitized business process, data and infrastructure. The platform has internal and external components and may both deliver digital content to the customer as well as managing physical product delivery to the customer. Amazon's internal platforms include customer data and all the business processes that don't touch the customer, such as customer analytics, human resources, finance and merchandising. External platforms include the phones, devices, wearables, tablets or computers that consumers use to research and purchase the products, along with telecommunications networks and Amazon's partnerships with delivery companies like UPS or "Shoppers who become Sellers", that deliver physical products and generate text messages on delivery; all of these external platforms neatly integrate with Amazon's internal platforms". Amazon platforms now use both buyers and sellers as being interchangeable. Digital Market Place follows a basic value chain track - Assess the Market; Focus on a Specific Market Category; Leverage Industry Expertise and Relationships; Invest Capital Upfront to Acquire a Market Base; Find Creative Ways to Attract Initial Buyers/Sellers. Build Content and Community; Identify Market Models and

Mechanisms; Select the Appropriate Enabling Tools and Technology; Select a Revenue Model that is Fair to Both Buyers and Sellers; Be Among the First to Market.

Digital Business Influences HR – Includes selecting the Appropriate Enabling Tools and Technology means choosing the right technology to support a digital marketplace. Key benefits that enabling tools can provide are as follows; Reduce time to market, Greater staff interaction, Lower transaction costs, Minimal initial investment – scalable and Protects long term investments (People, Customer, Products, Technology). In a KPMG 2012 EIU survey, a worldwide study, reports, "HR needs to eliminate the jargon off its specialization (the same challenge IT continues to face) and begin to link its work more explicitly to business value. The right business language helps to open the door, but it is also important to provide a robust business case for projects. It entails thinking more carefully about the specific business outcomes of the actions that HR recommends. What is the impact on customer service, or the reduction in costs, or the increase in staff loyalty, or other metrics that are more specifically relevant to the line managers and departments being supported? Importantly, it is also about taking a fuller perspective of the whole business, including both internal factors as well as external business conditions, and creating HR strategies to t. In turn, this requires a far deeper grasp of the organization's core business model and strategy and the implications this holds for the rest of the business – to date, something that far too few HR practitioners have mastered". This survey included interviews with BP in Bombay where the Head of Retail business spoke of the need to connect customers beyond loyalty programs or petro cards. Fashion for feature richness in auto preferences can be notoriously fickle, and most auto producers believe that they face high costs due to short life cycles, greater degree of customization, coupled with highly uncertain demand. It designed an information system that enabled fast communication between the retailers and production, and a production system that could quickly respond. The information system ensured that everyone in the organization, from retailers and agents to subcontractors, knew what had been sold and could easily determine what was needed to replace stocks. Auto manufacturers rely on small shops dedicated to the sale of its items in minimal inventories, there are only short time lags between production and the final consumer. By integrating Sales and Design into the production process, manufacturers could supply merchandise within days, and introduce new products cheaply and quickly. This required careful integration of traditionally separate functions like stock and assembling systems. It developed the concept of strategic center, where retailers, agents, designers, purchasing and factories were linked not by formal long term contracts but by information sharing and a sense of common purpose. The strategic center achieved common goals without bureaucracy, a combination many other organizations had sought and failed to achieve. Company success has been built on developing multiple capabilities to achieve multiple advantages. "To put this in context, a business that fundamentally focuses on providing low-cost goods will require a fundamentally different HR strategy than one that is focused on delivering leading-edge innovation. In a Business Model a technology-enabled HR function will allow professionals to avoid being immersed in the minutiae of record-keeping, transactions and life-cycle processes. But it will also likely reduce the number of HR staff that companies require. These slimmed-down departments will then be able to focus on providing more strategic, higher-order services."

Digital Business Economies - Just as a military organization constantly assesses the availability of trained manpower, equipment, ammunition, intelligence, and logistics relative to requirements as a measure of mission readiness, organizations must assess the status of the digital assets and their interaction with other knowledge economic value, as their indicators of strategic readiness. Raphael and Zott, "To achieve economies of scale with digital business models requires the development and reuse of digitized platforms across the enterprise. Without such shared platforms, the IT units in companies implement a new solution in response to every business need, creating a spaghetti-like arrangement of systems that do meet specific customer needs but are expensive and fragile — and don't scale enterprise-wide. Worse still, the customer experience suffers as the customer gets a fragmented product-based experience rather than a unified multi product experience. In MIT SMR 2013 issue, "Peter Weill and Stephanie L. Woerner in "Optimizing Your Digital Business Model" asks, "What does it take to create the strongest possible online presence? They ask (Additional Business Model Questions have also been added):

- *How have the basic principles towards building a business model changed?*
- *What characteristics appear to determine value realization in a business model?*
- *Which of the business models have survived multiple cycles of recession or economic upturns and downturns?*
- *What intellectual capital factors (Social, Structural, Financial, Intellectual, Human) resources/factors/strategic priorities appear to have dominated in each of the successful or not so successful business models?*
- *What are our business models today, and how have they changed over the last 10 years?*
- *How do our business models compare with those of our traditional and nontraditional competitors?*
- *What appears to key factors that are pushing digital companies seeking to alter their business models?*
- *How can we adjust our overall business model to include more revenue from the models that are most highly valued today (such as IP landlord and innovative manufacturer)?*
- *What options exist with these business models to manage optimization for realizing shareholder value?*
- *How unique is your business model in comparison with market and competitive forces?*
- *What resources become available to this business model?*
- *What business models that we believe will be most highly valued in the future?*
- *To make any change in our business model, what competencies do we need to further develop, and what strategic experiments can we do today to test new business models for tomorrow?"*

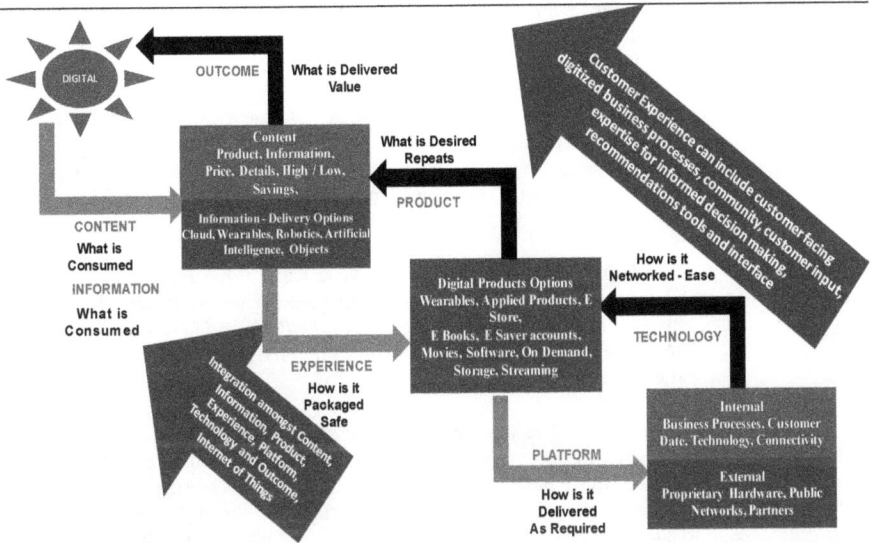

Figure 11 - Adapted & Modified from Digital Business Model - In MIT SMR 2013 issue, "Peter Weill and Stephanie L. Woerner in "Optimizing Your Digital Business Model" asks, what does it take to create the strongest possible online presence?

"Peter Weill and Stephanie L. Woerner business model framework is based on defining the types of assets a company sells and the rights it grants customers to use those assets. define four asset types and four ways companies manage asset rights to generate revenue.

Weill and Woerner Digital Business Model Asset Types:

"Financial Fiscal assets, which include cash as well as securities like stocks, bonds and insurance policies that give their owners rights to potential future cash flows;

Physical Material assets, which include durable items such as computers, as well as nondurable items such as food;

Intangible Goodwill assets, which include intellectual property such as patents and copyrights, as well as other intangible assets like knowledge, goodwill and brand value;

Human Capital - People assets, which include people's time and effort. People of course cannot be legally bought and sold, but their time and knowledge can be "rented out" for a fee".

Peter Weill, Thomas W. Malone and Thomas G. Apel, Digital Business Model companies manage asset rights to generate revenue are as:

Originators - Creators, which sell ownership , copyrights, royalties, of products they have created by transforming or assembling raw materials or components Ford, 3M and Intel are examples of this type of company;

Logisticians - Distributors – Supply Chain such as Wal-Mart or Amazon.com's retail business, which sell ownership of products, channels, they bought but did not substantially change, except by transporting, repackaging or marketing;

Attorneys - Owners - Landlords, which sell only the right to use assets – tenure for tenor, for a specified period of time; Marriott, Hertz, Accenture and Citigroup are examples of the landlord model. We included in this category companies that employ licenses or subscriptions to sell limited rights to use their intellectual property (IP) assets — companies such as Microsoft and The New York Times;

Arbitrators – Negotiators - Brokers, which receive a fee – value for matching buyers and sellers without ever taking ownership or custody of the product; examples include Charles Schwab, eBay and realtors". Adaptation Refer - *Digital Business Model - Peter Weill, Thomas W. Malone and Thomas G. Apel, in MIT SMR 2011, "New research suggests that the stock market particularly values business models based on innovation and intellectual property".*

"In these new business models every white collar professional will need to be a mini-CEO. That's what the white collar worker will need to be successful in the hyper-competitive, fluid corporation of tomorrow. For continued relevance in the changing environment, the new worker would need to value add constantly. The future will have three types of staff on its rolls: The professional core with high qualifications, essential to the organization. The contractual fringe that may include skilled individuals and small organizations. The flexible labor force that flits from one job to another, and cannot be expected to demonstrate high degree of loyalty". Michael Porter and Mark Kramer write, "The more tightly corporate philanthropy is aligned with a company's unique strategy—increasing skills, technology, or infrastructure on which the firm is especially reliant, say, or increasing demand within a specialized segment where the company is strongest—the more disproportionately the company will benefit through enhancing the context". "And there will be no rules, no prototypes in this workplace governing the X employees. "Innovative manufacturers — which we define as those who invest more than their industry average in research and development — are the top performers in the market. Apple is an example of an innovative manufacturer. Apple's business model in 2008 was 86% manufacturer, 7% contractor and 7% IP landlord, and the results — products like the iPhone, iPhone apps, iPad, MacBook Air, iTunes — have paid big dividends. This is a powerful combination from an investor perspective. Disney has dramatically shifted its business model over the last 20 years from renting physical assets like theme parks (65% of revenue in 1984 but only 30% in 2009) to licensing intellectual property (15% of revenue in 1984 but 63% in 2009), with clear investor buy-in for this strategic shift. Disney stock outperformed the S&P 500 stock index over the last five years and beat that index by more than 20% in the two-year period ending December 31, 2010" write *Peter Weill, Thomas W. Malone and Thomas G. Apel,* "we see that the company's shift in business models over time has played directly into the sentiment of investors. Disney has reduced revenues from one of the least valued business models, physical landlord, while increasing its reliance on one of the most valued business models, IP landlord. And Disney has also retained innovative manufacturing, the more highly valued part of the manufacturing business model". As information technology enables collaborative work across organizations, there is a clear need for further research employing network level outcomes. For example, Benetton's ability to create mass fashion at low cost gave the organization a significant advantage over its competitors. For the young people it provided unrivaled value for money. Benetton was the first truly global textile organization. Mass production itself was a strategic innovation. Traditionally, retailers aiming at mass markets have built large outlets to exploit scale and scope economies. Benetton's innovation was to develop and adapt for the mass youth market small outlets that traditionally sold high - priced merchandise to a limited clientele. Benetton's small outlets were, and still are operated by partners, reflecting the firms strategic network philosophy, that help create an image of exclusivity. But digital sales, on line outlets, e stores were launched at early stages of the internet. At Benetton, the original and fundamental idea was to provide fashion at a price and quality accessible to young people - a mass -fashion market, which went against prevailing conventional wisdom. Fashion, it was always assumed, had to be expensive, while most of what was accessible to the young at low prices was staid, tatty, or out of date and boring. To achieve its goal, Benetton had to employ techniques that reduced the costs of the garments it sold while producing clothes which appealed to young people. The ability to act quickly and at low cost, which is essential in a fashion oriented business. Ability to manage variety at a low cost. Variety to Benetton is evident not in its range of goods but in the markets it serves. Benetton was the first textile producer - retailer to become truly international, with a large network of retailers catering to young people in different parts of the world. Benetton's ability to create mass fashion at low cost gave the organization a significant advantage over its competitors. For the young people it provided unrivaled value for money. Benetton was the first truly global textile organization. Mass production itself was a strategic innovation.

Asset Rights		Weill, Malone, Apel - Digital Business Model Asset Type				Share of Total Revenue of US Listed Firms
		Financial	Physical	Intangible	Human	
	Creator	0%	Manufacturer 57%	0%	N/A	57%
	Distributor	Financial Trader <1%	Wholesale - Retail 14%	0%	N/A	14%
	Landlord	Financial Landlord 8%	Physical Landlord 10%	IP Landlord 2%	Contractor 8%	28%
	Broker	Financial Broker <1%	Physical Broker <1%	0%	"+/-" 0%	1%
	Share of Total Revenue of US Listed Firms	9%	81%	2%	8%	100%

The authors explain that the Business Model Framework defines the typs of assets a company sells and the rights it grants customers to use those assets. This is an illustrative and not a legal business model based on companes listed in the US Exchanges and comparing those with revenus generated through one or more of the business models

Figure 12 – Digital Business Model - Peter Weill, Thomas W. Malone and Thomas G. Apel, in MIT SMR 2011, "New research suggests that the stock market particularly values business models based on innovation and intellectual property"

Creating Value Through Innovation, is Raphael & Zott's POV

"We suggest that managers ask themselves the following six key questions as they consider business model innovation", continue, Raphael Amit and Christoph Zott in MIT SMR 2012, "Creating Value Through Business Model Innovation:

1. *What perceived needs can be satisfied through the new model design?*
2. *What novel activities are needed to satisfy these perceived needs? (business model content innovation)*

3. *How could the required activities be linked to each other in novel ways? (business model structure innovation)*
4. *Who should perform each of the activities that are part of the business model? Should it be the company? A partner? The customer? What novel governance arrangements could enable this structure? (business model governance innovation)*
5. *How is value created through the novel business model for each of the participants*
6. *What revenue model fits with the company's business model to appropriate part of the total value it helps create?"*

"To illustrate how managers might productively and proactively use these questions, consider the business model of McGraw-Hill's book publishing business. In the U.S., general and trade books (including consumer titles and celebrity author books) represent about 55% of industry revenues, while academic and professional books generate the remainder. Until recently, only in business-to-business and academic text segments have websites been a true marketing platform for digital content. While e-readers such as the Kindle and the iPad are now rapidly gaining popularity, the time-consuming and expensive book publishing process had not changed in a material manner in many decades, say Raphael and Zott. Interestingly this is a function of the publishing industry, authors and readers. Today large publishing houses are focusing on generating over 50% of their revenues from the electronic formats. This is apart from an opportunity to converge books with audio, video, video on demand and other communication formats. "However, Google, Amazon and other competing information and content providers have stimulated a growing customer interest in electronic formats. Publishers in the U.S. and Europe are searching for solutions to meet the emergent demand for creating and delivering digital content on portable devices while preserving and enhancing value".

Catlin, Scanlon and Willmott Business Model Drives Innovation - "Raising your Digital Quotient", is the theme that Tangly Catlin, Jay Scanlan, and Paul Willmott write in McKinsey Quarterly 2015, "Axel Springer used its digital business model as the dominant organizing principle in its recent reorganization—an approach that promotes the emergence of the distinct culture, performance-management system, and governance that growing digital businesses require. In the meantime, Axel Springer's strong legacy businesses can adapt and evolve to master the new digital landscape separately". Similar to when Liz Claiborne used on an on line merchandizing process for placing garment order from a remote factory in India. Marks & Spencer, (M&S) UK. retailer, has also demonstrated an extraordinary capacity to innovate collectively. Limited in growth potential in its traditional market by high market share and threatened by the trend to small boutiques by firms such as Benetton and Next, it moved from being a clothing store to dominating one segment of the food trade as well. It has captured the number one position as the innovator of fresh prepared foods. Identifying and then satisfying this newly created segment. Its shelves are filled with fresh foods ranging from simple salads to complete meals, many of which could be described as gourmets. To achieve its purpose, it had had to organize supply chains completely different from those of the traditional food industry. Value added actions - It had to pioneer new packaging, new processing, and new ideas of customer service with great attention to quality. All this has required change because handling fresh, prepared food requires far higher standards than required in handling clothes or fresh unprepared and frozen foods. These standards have subsequently migrated to other parts of the organization to improve the service delivery of stores handling both fresh food and clothes. There must be a recognition that something of potential worth has been discovered and that there is a freedom to follow up, Marks and Spencer's demonstrates the lasting value of such freedom. It discovered an interesting feature reputedly by accident when it sold out its fresh fruits every Friday afternoon. The first reaction of the mangers was that they had failed to serve their customers, but the customers reaction was different. They became convinced that the food of the following day would be really fresh, so more of them came to buy. Instead of admonishing and imposing the old system, the business moved to a policy of deliberately limiting stocks to reinforce the message that freshness was ensured. The nature of necessary experiments varied greatly according to where a business stood in its path toward rejuvenation and frame-breaking change. "When Starbucks rolled out a new point-of-sale system, for example, managers videotaped transactions and interviewed employees to fine-tune the checkout process. That check out feedback at Starbucks allowed the company to trim ten seconds off any mobile or card-based transaction, allowing employees to process sales more quickly and saving customers 900,000 hours of time in line each year". Raphael Amit and Christoph Zott in MIT SMR 2012, "Creating Value Through Business Model Innovation", write "Business model innovation can occur in a number of ways: By adding novel activities, for example, through forward or backward integration; we refer to this form of business model innovation as new activity system "content." By linking activities in novel ways; we refer to this form of business model innovation as new activity system "structure." By changing one or more parties that perform any of the activities; we refer to this form of business model innovation as new activity system "governance." Content, structure and governance are the three design elements that characterize a company's business model. Change one or more of these elements enough and you've changed the model".

Kane, Palmer, Phillips et all Business Model Influences Digital Enterprises – Cultural challenges in digital organizations deal with how can we effectively work through cultural differences, engaging the organization through targeted global communications or designing and managing a cost effective, complex training program. Creating a productive, high performance global project team, maintaining project team and executive commitment and focus while designing roles, org structures, and performance systems to support and sustain the changes. "Most companies, however, are constrained by a lack of resources, a lack of talent, and the pull of other priorities, leaving executives to manage digital initiatives that either take the form of projects or are limited to activities within a given division, function, or channel. Despite this, some companies are transcending these constraints, achieving digital capabilities that cut across the enterprise". In, July 2016 MIT SMR issue research, "Aligning the Organization for its Digital Future", Ge Kane, Doug Palmer, Anh Nguyen Phillips, David Kiron and Natasha Buckley, write, "Preparing for a digital future is no easy task. It means developing digital capabilities in which a company's activities, people, culture, and structure are in sync and aligned toward a set of organizational goals. Our research found that nearly 90% of digitally maturing organizations — companies in which digital technology has transformed processes, talent engagement, and business models — are *integrating their digital strategy with the company's overall strategy. Managers in these digitally maturing companies are much more likely to believe that they are adequately preparing for the industry disruptions they anticipate arising from digital trends"*. This is confirmed by Raphael and Zott, "An innovative business model can either create a new market or allow a company to create and exploit new opportunities in existing markets". The reason for developing a business case is to identify the financial justification for the potential benefits arising as part of the case for change, in order to provide an objective support to the investment in the costs of the change. These potential benefits and costs may be tangible or intangible and they may be easily quantifiable or purely qualitative. "Dell, for example, implemented a customer-driven, build-to-order business model that replaced the traditional build-to-stock model of selling computers through retail stores". "A key finding indicates that digitally maturing organizations have organizational cultures that share common features. These features consistently appear in digitally maturing companies across different industries. The main characteristics of Digital HR include: an expanded appetite for risk, rapid experimentation, heavy investment in talent, and recruiting and developing leaders who excel at "soft" skills. Leading a digital company does not require technologists at the helm". "Canon Corporation provides a good example of what an entrepreneurial organization can achieve. Famous as a leading producer of cameras, Canon decided to explore the possibilities of entering the photocopier business. Many years of patient building of new capabilities was needed before it could make significant inroads into the market dominated by Xerox/HP and several players like Brother, Samsung and Panasonic. Each business has been provided with powers to translate corporate policies and the job of corporate is to keep track of the cash flow every quarter. There was a time when there was at least one (or even more) businesses which had to be paid from profits made by others. But now each business is profitable. Imaginative reconceptualization of the means to manage access to customers and the purpose and design of the machine itself. Though many of Canon's successes were seemingly bold and imaginative leaps, close inspection of what was actually done shows that rapid progress at any one time was usually the result of combining separate capabilities that were built earlier. A team was set up resolve the critical problems surrounding maintenance of the photocopier drum, which was the source of 90 percent of the problems. The answer, which seems in hindsight to be almost trivial, was a disposable drum that the user could replace without the assistance of a skilled technician. Because team-based approach had already been put in place as a dominant value in the organization, this solution was not only identified but put into practice in a surprisingly short time. This was but one of many innovations that helped put canon into a winning position in the photocopier market. And digital is changing the way work is done. In an interview with John Hagel III (Deloitte), Gerald C. (Jerry) Kane an associate professor of information systems at the Carroll School of Management at Boston College and the MIT Sloan Management Review guest editor for the Digital Business Initiative asks in the MIT SMR 2016, "Do you have a clear and shared 10- to 20-year view of how **digital is going to transform your business**"?

Digital Business Technology Trends - In BCG (BCG Perspectives) March 2016 research document, Thomas Gumsheimer, Frank Felden, and Christian Schmid in "Recasting IT for the Digital Age" and in "Autonomic platforms" Ranjit Bawa, Jacques de Villiers, & George Collins of Deloitte 2016,, predict digital trends, "Across industries, digital technologies are shattering established business paradigms and advancing rapidly as businesses, governments, and nonprofit organizations find more and more ways to leverage them. The following is a small sample of digital technologies that are either already developed or on the threshold of viability.

- *Augmented-Reality and Virtual-Reality Applications. Augmented-reality applications integrate digital information—including images, sound, video, graphics, and GPS data—with the real-world environment. Virtual-reality applications deliver a complete virtual experience and are transforming a wide range of products, services, and processes across industries. For example, Lowe's has created a home-improvement simulator, called the Holoroom, that allows the company's customers to virtually construct, view, and plan home improvements before making a purchase - BCG.*

- *Applications infrastructure (shared applications such as e-mail, collaboration, internet capability, mobile computing).*

- *Communications management (broadband networks, intranets). Vendor-Provided Middleware - integrator is Becoming a Standard. We can offer fairly complete middleware tools to connect to other systems. While data integration continues to be a major challenge all offer turnkey integration tools to help connect their HR software to everyone else's. The reason this has happened is that there is so much "replacement" going on. Any new vendor has to gracefully coexist with many other systems. This used to be the IT department's problem. Now, with cloud as the predominant delivery model, it's the vendor's problem. So the vendors have built or OEM'd integration tools.*

- **Blockchain.** *This cryptographically secure distributed-ledger protocol, perhaps best known as the technology that underpins Bitcoin, has attracted significant attention from venture capital firms and investors. Established financial-industry players are also showing considerable interest: more than 40 investment banks have joined the innovation firm R3, which leads an industry-wide consortium that focuses on the technology. These companies believe that blockchain technology could change the financial-market paradigm by accelerating banking processes at relatively low cost - BCG.*

- **Gamification** *is entering the talent staff management world. In selection where simple games can be used to test cognitive and social capabilities. In recruitment where candidates are able to experience what life is like in an organization by participating in a simulation. In performance management by introducing leader boards, points and badges related to specific desired behavior. In training, where games and simulations are often far more effective than traditional classroom training.*

- **Cloud-Based ERP Systems.** *These systems offer companies far greater speed and flexibility than legacy ERP systems. They are often based on in-memory technology that enables fast transactions and a real-time experience, and they look and feel like apps. They are provided on-premises or via the cloud through usage-based license models. SAP's cloud-based ERP package, SAP S/4HANA, for example, offers both data-analytics capabilities that are a thousand times faster than those of its predecessor and a variety of new features and capabilities.*

- **WATCH for Wearable Computing and The Internet of Things.** *Start Up Style Tech Savvy vendors like us will dominate. We will see increased tracking of our work habits and actions. Not only is the content market being rationalized, but new forms of content are emerging. Much research shows that "spaced repetition" is one of the best ways to learn certain topics (math, language, other topics which require memorization). There are now a variety of free tools that create decks of questions and answers which are delivered to you like a Twitter stream.*

- **Channel management** *(Web sites, call centers) and Facility management (large-scale mainframes, server farms, LANs)*

- **Cobots.** *Collaborative robots are capable of learning and can work side-by-side with humans. Robots made by Denmark-based Universal Robots, for example, can perform a variety of jobs, from sorting eggs to sorting blood samples. Programming these robots requires no coding skills, only the ability to use a touch-screen user interface. By connecting "Cobots" with machine learning, it might be possible to develop increasingly powerful robots in the future— for example, robots that can train themselves - BCG.*

- **Data Security -** *In the post-Snowden world everyone's becoming more careful about digital security. The HR industry hasn't yet had a data breach as serious as the Sony hack of late last year, a TARGET attack, but even attacks like this not aimed explicitly at employee data are a wakeup call to talent managers and HR executives.*

- **IT Integration management** *(IS planning, service-level agreements, supplier negotiations) and Architecture and standards (for data, communication, technology, and so on). For inbound interfaces standard processes is followed like file format in which vendor and* *customer will supply the requisite data at the scheduled frequency. For outbound interfaces the drivers will focus towards reducing the number of outbound interfaces on the basis of target systems data commonality and, accordingly, will provide the necessary data in a single common flat file format.*

- **Continuous Delivery and DevOps.** *These approaches close the gap between development and operations, enabling companies to release software reliably at any time, independent of fixed-release schedules. Continuous delivery also fosters a zero-defect mentality while fully automating the delivery pipeline. Best-in-class practitioners of continuous delivery become capable of continuous deployment: some companies release software more than 100 times per day - BCG. Applications now focus on an innovative and high-quality user experience. The application is extensible and configurable via the metadata framework, which is essential to support complex customer requirements, but the workflow capabilities are relatively complex. Integration in the cloud is delivered though a third-party solution, middleware and prepackaged integrations are delivered as well, but custom integrations via the APIs require significant technical expertise. The business intelligence capabilities feature graphical content and reporting tools but more analytical content and advanced capabilities (e.g., predictive intelligence, in-memory are differentiated.*

- **IT education** *(training, management education) and IT R&D (emerging technologies). Identify solutions offers many value-adds (productivity tools, standardized and preconfigured components, accelerators, templates, and methodologies) enhancing a conventional out-of-the-box Oracle EBS R12 solution, differentiating it from a more standard offering thus streamlining processes and reducing the need for customizations, whilst providing for improved automation and control*

- **Data Lakes.** *These repositories can store both structured and unstructured data. Their underlying technology—Hadoop, for example—supports a high degree of physical distribution of data, ensuring scalability, stability, and availability. Data lakes, which store copies of the source data, allow analysts to explore the data using any type of analytics—such as real-time or complex algorithms—that they choose. This is an improvement over traditional data warehouses, which can support only the type of analytics that is based on the warehouse's data model - BCG.* **Data management** *(centralized data warehouses), Security and risk (security policies, disaster planning, firewalls)*

- **Drones.** *Unmanned aerial vehicles equipped with high-resolution cameras allow utilities and oil and gas companies to inspect onshore and offshore facilities, such as power grids and oil rigs, in all types of weather and without shutting down a facility to ensure the safety of human inspectors. Eventually, drones may be capable of performing repairs and routine tasks throughout these companies' maintenance cycles as well - BCG.*

- **Cloudy perspective:** *Cloud solutions will likely play a part in any organization's autonomic platform initiatives. Increasingly, virtualized environments are being deployed in the cloud: In 2014, 20 percent of virtual machines were delivered through public infrastructure-as-a-service (IaaS) providers.15 However, don't confuse the means with the end. Ultimately, cloud offerings represent a deployment option, which may or may not be appropriate based on the workload in question. Price per requisite performance (factoring in long-term implications for ongoing growth, maintenance, and dependencies) should drive your decision of whether to deploy a public, private, or hybrid cloud option or embrace an on-premises option based on more traditional technologies. Deloitte 2016*

- **Hybrid Integration Services and iPaaS.** *These services greatly simplify the challenge of connecting applications to a cloud environment and reduce the cost of doing so. Encapsulated services, or wrappers, connect any application or resource, ensuring that the benefits of the cloud, such as load balancing, can be assessed anytime, anywhere. Hybrid cloud environments preserve investments in legacy systems through their ability to access existing mission-critical data and work flow processes. New cloud services can speed the time to market for new products and help companies seize new market opportunities. Cloud Platform is hosted on a robust, reliable and highly secured infrastructure residing at its data center. A logical data center topology for an appropriate hosting environment - BCG.*

- **The Internet of Things.** *Applications based on the Internet of Things are not new, but they continue to evolve and can be used in many diverse situations. These applications, which allow connected devices to gather and share data, also facilitate dynamic responses to product demand, real-time optimization of maintenance in manufacturing, and remote monitoring of individuals' health, including the related notification of the appropriate parties in the event of an emergency. Amazon's Dash Replenishment Service, for example, enables connected devices to order consumer goods, such as toner for printers, when supplies are running low - BCG.*

- **Hosting** – *Multi-tenant hosting environment and provides the following services, Maintenance and support of the hosting environments, High availability and redundancies built in data link, switches, routers, firewall, load balancer levels and clustering for Production environment, Disaster Recovery (DR). Access to DR site will be provided to SPoCs, Multi-level data backups, MPLS connectivity with Amazon data center and Amazon delivery center and Internet connectivity. The hosting environment consists of servers, network components, applications, storage and connectivity. The DR site is located at a distant location from the Primary site. The data is kept synchronized at the DR site using continuous replication so that the DR site may be leveraged to support critical processes in case of any disaster at the primary site.*

- **API economy:** *In some modern IT architectures, large systems are being broken down into more manageable pieces known as microservices. These sub-components exist to be reused in new and interesting ways over time. For example, organizations may be able to realize autonomic platforms' full potential more quickly by deconstructing applications into application programming interfaces (APIs)— services that can be invoked by other internal or external systems. These modular, loosely coupled services, which take advantage of self-configuration, self-deployment, and self-healing capabilities much more easily than do behemoth systems with hard-wired dependencies, help reduce complex remediation and the amount of replatforming required for legacy systems to participate in autonomic platforms. Deloitte 2016*

- **Systems Requirements** - *Access a cloud solution – Installation of recent versions of Google Chrome internet browsers or Internet Explorer 9 (IE9) onwards on user desktops, Internet access over https to the domain name. Ensure internet network connectivity to their employees to access Solution. TCS expects with a minimum 2TB internet connectivity. Facilitate access to email server to send notifications from domain name. Configuration of site WAN/LAN, operating systems, application systems, interfaces, connectivity and any other software on desktop/laptop will be responsibility. For example, Forrester indicates, "Workday has a good user experience that continues to improve with more mobile capabilities and responsive* *design. The configurability and flexibility of the application is a key strength, including the business processes, object definitions, and business rules. The integration capabilities are embedded in the architecture (no third-party tools required) and consist of prebuilt integrations, a non-technical interface builder, and the more technical Workday Integration Studio. For BI, Workday has embedded reporting tools and real-time analytics. Its big data and predictive intelligence capabilities are a work in progress, however".*

- ***Multidimensional Master-Data-Management Tools.*** *Once these devices are fully developed, they will allow companies to better respond to the increasingly complex data-management demands that digitization is generating. The benefits will include an enhanced ability to manage data holistically among business functions and across industries, data domains, and organizational structures. Product companies are making major investments to rollout an innovative user experience for employees, candidates and other users, but the current interface is not as compelling. The strategic configuration layer has some non-technical capabilities available to customers, but some application components (e.g., benefits) can only be configured by the client interfaces. It has made significant strides in improving integration capabilities and now offers a developer website which publishes its standards-based APIs. These solutions have a good selection of standard reports, ad hoc reporting, and dashboards. Many master data management solutions are currently using advanced big data technologies, and it is moving toward providing benchmarks and predictive capabilities - BCG.*

- ***Robotic-Process Automation.*** *Robots have been able to replicate muscle-power-driven tasks for years. With the advent of robotic-process automation, the technology now extends into knowledge-related and back-office work, such as tasks traditionally performed by call center employees, doctors, and lawyers. The next step of robotics' evolution could produce a code-free virtual workforce that replicates human actions and can automate any software-based process. Robotic Process Automation (RPA) is fast emerging as the key lever to drive productivity for Business Process Services (BPS) delivery. While automation has been part of the strategy of enterprises for years, the broad-based emergence of RPA in the past two to three years offers a new and powerful tool. This has created a compelling avenue to pursue the next wave of productivity and quality gains for the enterprise. (Everest 2016).*

- ***Robotics:*** *While much of the broader robotics dialogue focuses on advanced robotics—drones, v autonomous transportation, and exoskeletons—progress is also being made in the realm of virtualized workforces. RPA, cognitive agents, and other autonomic solutions are advancing in both IT operations and business process outsourcing. Their promise encompasses more than efficiency gains in mundane tasks such as entering data. Indeed, the most exciting opportunities can be found in higher-order, higher-value applications, such as virtual infrastructure engineers that can proactively monitor, triage, and heal the stack, or virtual loan specialists that help customers fill out mortgage applications. Deloitte 2016*

- ***Global In-house Centers (GICs)*** *are an integral part of the business process services delivery for enterprises and, therefore, have an opportunity to be at the forefront of the RPA movement. Given that continuous productivity improvement is table stakes for every GIC, and RPA offers an attractive means to drive significant improvements, many realize that adoption of RPA in GICs is no longer a matter of "if" but "when". Further, automation provides a unique opportunity to eliminate low-value work and generate higher-value activities and roles. (Everest 2016).*

- **Self-Learning Machines.** *The algorithms that these machines employ provide more precise results than those that can be achieved with traditional big data. They also reveal correlations that are hidden from traditional big-data applications and can explore data even with very limited knowledge of the context. This technology has already become available to a broad audience through services such as Amazon Machine Learning, which is capable of delivering billions of forecasts per day. The ability to build anything we can design, by manipulating molecules under direct computer control, will be a disruption to the system. A transformative, disruptive, discontinuous disrupt to ecological, economic, political, and social systems — on a local, national, and global scale - BCG.*

- **Containers:** *Though the hype around the container movement is largely justified, we remain in the early days of adoption. IDC analyst Al Gillen estimates that fewer than one-tenth of 1 percent of enterprise applications are currently running in containers. What's more, it could be 10 years before the technology reaches mainstream adoption and captures more than 40 percent of the market.12 Consider adopting a twofold strategy for exploration. First, look at open-source and start-up options to push emerging features and standards. Then, tap established vendors as they evolve their platforms and offerings to seamlessly operate in the coming container-driven reality. Deloitte 2016*

- **3-D Printing.** *The potential applications of this technology continue to expand exponentially, and demand for printers is soaring: Gartner expects more than 490,000 units to be shipped in 2016. This technology helps companies reduce downtime and cost considerably by allowing them to print parts at their various facilities on an as-needed basis instead of storing available component parts in centralized locations. Amazon, for example, recently filed a patent for mobile 3-D-printing delivery trucks, in which products would be printed upon order in locations close to customers, speeding time to delivery and sparing the company storage and inventory costs. As the variety of printing materials continues to expand—printers can now handle glass, carbon, textile fibers, and biological material—3-D printing's possibilities will continue to grow - BCG"*

- **Nana Tech Not just new products** — *a new means of production; Manufacturing systems that make more manufacturing systems — exponential proliferation; Vastly accelerated product improvement — cheap rapid prototyping; Affects all industries and economic sectors — general-purpose technology; Inexpensive raw materials, potentially negligible capital cost — economic discontinuity; Portable, desktop-size factories — social disruption; Impacts will cross borders — global transformation. A collaborative project to study the facts and implications of advanced nanotechnology — a website for researchers worldwide to work together, helping to build an understanding of the technologies, their effects, and what to do about them. http://on.bcg.com/2b6XUvo*

Delivering the Digital Goods: In smaller projects, or in projects involving advising on a transaction, *e.g. implementation of an IT system*, rather than on an issue, *e.g. cost reduction in a company*, a single business case may be produced. The number and types of business cases that could be presented depends on the size of the assignment and on the number of points at which a client is required to make a decision. This would include outcomes such as, The identification, quantification, validation of the design opportunities, the financial payback with quantifiable potential benefits and costs of the proposed changes and the assumptions, constraints, risks and timing of cash flows. "Business models built with consideration only of how they work in isolation of those of other players will often exhibit poor performance. How well iTunes works as a channel for digital content distribution depends not only on the intrinsic operation of the model but also on how it interacts with p2p. Clearly, the extent to which two business models interact is not exogenously given but a result of choices made by the designers. Conversely, managers must also ponder how aggressive their business models are toward those of other players and ask whether or not complementarities are exploited. While this point might seem obvious, the academic and practitioner communities have so far offered little insight on how to think about interaction between business models". In iTunes vs. Peer-to-Peer, Sean Silverthorne (Professor Ramon Casadesus-Masanell and collaborator Andres Hervas-Drane discuss their recent research on competition in digital distribution) in HBSWK 2007, "At a broad level, in designing new business models, managers must carefully consider how robust a given design is to models of other industry participants with which they interact. Our paper makes a first step towards a general theory. At a more concrete level, given that p2p file sharing networks are likely to improve in performance as Internet infrastructure develops, the content industry must make tough choices regarding their revenue models. Moves towards monetizing products not subject to costless replication and distribution, such as live concerts and merchandising (for music) and product placements (for movies and network shows), will become essential for the financial health of media companies. ITunes demonstrates that to compete effectively against free p2p networks, online digital distribution must deliver experiences to consumers that cannot be easily matched by decentralized, self-sustained peer-to-peer networks. In designing new models, managers must consider how robust a given design is to models of other industry participants with which they interact. Managers must also ponder how aggressive their business models are toward those of other players and ask whether or not complementarities are exploited. The "scarce" resource in digital goods distribution through p2p networks is not content, but bandwidth. As a consequence, ISPs will have a more visible role in shaping industry structure". Digital Interventions included, "Assessing existing cultures and develop a culture plan to leverage differences and reduce barriers. Assessing and addressing impacts to all stakeholders and develop regional specific communications and involvement plans and engaging regional change agents to push ownership to the sites. Developing an end-user training strategy and plan leveraging e-learning and Web-based technology, capability transfer plans to push ownership to the business as quickly as possible. Preparing global executive action plans and executive playbooks and developing workforce transition plans to move the organizations to the desired end-state across all countries".

Hagel III Deloitte Human Capital Tech Talent - And Hagel responds, "A lot of individual executives have actually thought about this and have a point of view, but they're completely diverse in terms of their view of where and how the market's going to evolve. And so, have they aligned around a shared view of the 10- to 20-year future? Another key question, in terms of talent, is: Have you been applying digital technology to accelerate learning and performance improvement in the work environment on a day-to-day basis? With the mounting performance pressure and the accelerated pace of change that digital technology is bringing about, our view is that the learning that's going to be most powerful is not by accessing what other people already know. It's driving new knowledge creation through practice in the workplace itself, rather than in a training room, by addressing challenges and business situations that have never been confronted before. And that's a very different approach to learning. And digital technology, we think, can be very powerful in the work environment. But it's rarely being used for that purpose". "But that seems to point also to **culture.** Culture has a substantive role in building a business model. For example, top management meetings. Meeting with the CEO/CFO to assess the potential cost savings in the business and scope the project (i.e. the size of the team and skill base required to identify and quantify the potential savings). This discussion should allow the project manager (obtaining participation and commitment from members) to develop an understanding of: The scope of the project for example, will it cover all of the business or will some areas be excluded? The performance improvement targets the client has set or would like to achieve and the basis on which these targets have been set. (gain trust and common understanding).

The basis on which the client would like to measure the success of the project. Generally, success will be measured in financial terms such as costs reduced, revenue increased etc., however the client might also be interested in measuring the success of the project using non-financial measures. If so, these should be identified now to help ensure the business case team collects the necessary information/statistics that will allow performance to be measured on an on-going basis as part of the business case. (Win alignment). Any activity based costing exercises, Business Process Re-engineering exercises or any other similar exercises that the business has undertaken which could provide the project with useful information on activities, activity costs and process maps. This type of information can provide both the analysis team and the business case team with information that can make identification of opportunities easier.

Digital Business Model Characteristics - Are there **certain competencies, characteristics, features, signals of companies that you see are more digitally successful or not?** A credible business case that quantifies the opportunities identified by the project team during, the feasibility of the business model or, in the case of a Business Transformation context, the Scoping and Mobilization phase. The purpose of this business case is to attract the client to invest in designing and implementing the actions to result in the opportunities that have been identified. Hagel responds, "I'd say most large company cultures are shaped by what we call the "scalable efficiency" model of business. The whole focus on scalable efficiency is predictability, reliability, and everybody's supposed to know exactly what to do and when to do it. In that kind of culture, acknowledging that you don't know something is a sign of great weakness and puts you at risk of getting fired. We see a shift from "scalable efficiency" to "scalable learning" as the core Institutional Corporate model, enabled by digital technology. A key foundation of scalable learning is a culture where actually it's not only okay, but it's expected that you're not going to know and that you will ask for help. That's a huge shift. And it goes to the leadership question. Leadership in the future, I believe, is actually around being able to frame the right questions, the highest-impact questions, where the leader is actually saying, "I have no clue, but this is a really important question. And if we could figure it out, we would do amazing things." That's a completely different model of "digital leadership".

Benn Konsynski's at Emory - Business Model Impacts Digital Trends and Culture – Early agreement of the baseline (for example, generally base profit figure from which any additional profits generated will be attributed to the project) or aspects pertaining to changes in processes, structure, roles, relocations, downsizing is an absolute imperative. Obtaining buy-in from stakeholders to the financial or human calculations produced by the business case team is needed before embarking on Communication. Provision of timely support to the project manager that allows early identification of opportunities. This support will assist the project manager to ensure that the main project team do not misdirect their efforts at inefficiencies that are not going to yield significant potential benefits while ignoring others that may produce substantial potential benefits. Constant communication with the analysis team helps ensure: the analysis team have access to the latest cost information on the area they are reviewing; the business case team are kept up to date on statistics, volumes, assumptions supporting opportunities identified by the analysis team. Any early identification of cost reduction or revenue enhancement opportunities (quick hits) by the project team are included as potential benefits achieved by the project. The objective is to ensure we do not include in our work any improvements that the transformation project has already identified. However, it is possible they have included cost reduction targets in their budget but have not identified how to achieve the targets. If so these targets should be discussed with the Financial Director (or similar) with the view to understanding how they intend to achieve these targets and agreement sought that if our project identifies the means to achieve these targets, they will be measured as potential benefits generated by the project. This task is extremely important and the confirmation of the baseline is needed as early as possible in order to avoid later disputes with the client over the extent to which performance improvements were a result of this project and how much is due to other projects already commissioned or general operational cost reduction within the organization.

Model Influencers - In broad terms, a business model sets out to quantify the costs (easy) and the benefits (not so easy) of an investment decision as it has the case of internet of things – a model that requires to help organizations capture value as technology, networks, intelligence commerce and things converge through an integrated architecture. This has not always been the norm, and in the past the focus has often been on managing the cost, instead of understanding the benefit. "Internet of Things, personal area technologies, core predictive analytics and other current pursuits are profound, and a basis for social and economic innovation, and worthy focus. It is the nexus of these changes that make radically new things possible. So, I'd rather start from the standpoint of rethinking business and rethinking commerce and challenging patterns of social interactions and then work back into how those capabilities are made available or enriched by the digital trends". In a conversation with Gerald C. (Jerry) Kane, for MIT Sloan Management Review's Social Business Big Idea Initiative (and a one-time student of Benn Konsynski's at Emory), Konsynski describes how both the McCormick spice company and UPS are shaping their futures, and what companies, whether large or small, old or new, can do to keep ahead. "Let's start with the big picture: analytics, mobile, wearable, cloud computing. What do you think the big digital trends are going to be in the next couple of years? Well, the first thing that comes to mind is — all those things you mentioned are, to me, attrition warfare. It's where we're at going forward. I think the exciting things are going to be the leapfrog things that will leap further into the horizon for us. It is interdiction warfare that is more interesting. It is the acceleration that is more exciting than the velocity — how change is changing. A part of that means I start to work backward, not forward — the future is best seen with a running start. I'll go backward to better see the future possibilities — standing starts are poor means of seeing the future. The elements that you're talking about are sort of the evolution of the, quote, "normal" today, and that would be in the social digitization of our historic practices". These are substantive change based investments and would have a direct impact on the business model. The current norm is to position the project as an investment, taking into account costs and benefits, hence the increasing prominence of the business case as a decision-support tool. The need for a formal business case is also driven by increases in scope, potential impact and cost of a project. As the project scope extends to include market-facing processes and structures, the probability increases of gains being made in turn-over, profitability and market share. This moves the game to a new level. Instead of the paradigm of "I am going to spend $1m to save $2m", it moves to "I am going to spend $3m to improve my value proposition, increase my turnover by 10 percent, increase my margins by 5 percent, get to a more dominant position in the market, retain my best people and save $2m." In the latter approach, the business case becomes indispensable.

Benn Konsynski's at Emory - New capabilities make new business models possible. McCormick & Company, a Fortune 1000 spice and flavor manufacturer, has over 126 years of history of knowledge of flavors and food, continues Benn Konsynski. "They've established something called FlavorPrint, which represents a flavor of a spice or dish as a point in a 50-dimensional space. If I'm an expert on spices and flavors, and if I can represent a flavor for a spice, I can do it for a dish. If I can do it for a dish, I can do it for a meal. If I can do it for a meal, I can map your preferences, your own FlavorPrints. If I can do it for you, I can do it for your household. If I can do it for your household, I can do it for your neighborhood. So I'm McCormick, and I look at a $4 billion industry, some half of which is industrial spice — where I play a significant role. Major food manufacturers come seeking insight about flavoring their offerings as they advance new product flavors to new market demographics. Witness the product proliferation of the recent decades in drinks and spices and flavors in meals, ingredients and variations. We're even running experiments in contests in the market. We're gamifying flavors, and crowdsourcing product/flavor configurations. If I can do that, if I can get the right kind of personal profile and preference data, I can target even to a store level. A store in one neighborhood might have a different flavor preference than a store in another neighborhood. The exact same SKU may be hotter in your neighborhood than in somebody else's neighborhood. In the end, we are augmenting the traditional retail market and employing a same-day delivery structure to target your household. The consumer interest is in having the product to your house that you want in your house at the time you want it".

Value Networks in Business Models – "But value chain thinking is rooted in an industrial age production line model that gradually has been superseded by the new enterprise model of the value network or value web. A major strategic challenge today is reconfiguring a business from value chain organization to the more fluid structure of the value network. In the fast-moving world of e-commerce there is increasing buzz about e-webs and business webs. But business webs are just one type of value network. Virtually any organization can be understood as a value network. For example, Research by Jim Austin of the Harvard Business School documents how companies' collaborations with nonprofits yield important benefits in:

- *Strategy enrichment:* Generating business opportunities and promoting a positive and trusted image with customers (particularly important for retail service organizations), regulators, and legislators
- *Human resource management:* Attracting and retaining higher-quality employees; strengthening employee motivation and morale; developing leadership capabilities
- *Culture building:* Shaping and reinforcing the core values that elicit desired employee behavior
- *Business generation:* Enhancing a company's reputation, building goodwill, expanding networks of relationships, increasing access to key consumers, and providing a venue for testing innovations

Yes, any organization, including government agencies and non-profits. Although interest in business webs is fueling development of new types of analysis, these value network perspectives can help explain the dynamics of non-profits, economic clusters and national economies as well. Earlier issues of the Journal of Business Strategy have explored this shift by featuring new thinking about value clusters, value webs and Value Networks, and our understanding is continuing to grow. However, most approaches to analyzing and reconfiguring value networks have not taken into account the role of knowledge and intangible value exchange as the foundation for these emerging networked enterprises. Even with the widespread interest in the knowledge economy, intellectual capital and intangibles, these generally have not found their way into our business models. As a result, efforts to understand value networks often confuse rather than help. The key to reconfiguring business models for the knowledge economy lies in understanding the new currencies of value. Kaplan and Norton, write, "The partnership between Timberland, the outdoor boot and apparel outfitter, and City Year, an urban youth service corps, provides an excellent example of such a strategic collaborative relationship. It took several years for this relationship to evolve from the philanthropic stage—giving money and in-kind donations (Timberland boots to City Year corps members); to the transactional stage—joint events, such as cause-related marketing, event sponsorships, licensing, and paid service arrangements; to the integrative stage—the company and the community organization have become an integrated joint venture that is central to both organizations' strategies. Value creation becomes a joint process, rather than two separate processes, for one for the company and one for the community organization. (one for the community organization). A value network generates economic value through complex dynamic exchanges between one or more enterprises, customers, suppliers, strategic partners and the community". These networks engage in more than just transactions around goods, services and revenue. The two other currencies are knowledge value and intangible value or benefits. I call these currencies because all three serve as a medium of exchange, which is the basic definition of currency. All three are important in a value network". Continues, Verna Allee in "Reconfiguring the Value Network", in Journal of Business Strategy, volume 21 - N 4 - 2000, writes, "The key business question in the knowledge economy is, "How is value created?" The traditional answer to that question is – "through the value chain." **Goods, Services and Revenue (GSR)** - Exchanges for services or goods, including all transactions involving contracts and invoices, return receipt of orders, request for proposals, confirmations or payment. Knowledge products or services that generate revenue or are expected as part of service (such as reports or package inserts) are part of the flow of goods, services and revenue. **Knowledge** - Exchanges of strategic information, planning knowledge, process knowledge, technical know-how, collaborative design, policy development, etc., which flow around and support the core product and service value chain. **Intangible benefits** - Exchanges of value and benefits that go beyond the actual service and that are not accounted for in traditional financial measures, such as a sense of community, customer loyalty, image enhancement or co-branding opportunities. These value exchanges lie at the heart of a value network. Further, every exchange of value is supported by some mechanism or medium that enables the transaction to take place. For example, if two people want to exchange messages about a meeting they may use the mechanism of e-mail or voice mail to support the exchange". Georgia-Pacific and The Nature Conservancy (TNC) provide an example of a relationship that has evolved from confrontation to collaboration. TNC wanted to preserve land, untouched, and Georgia-Pacific wanted to use land intensively to harvest trees. The two organizations found common ground to jointly manage unique forested wetlands in ways that preserved biodiversity while also permitting commercial development. Other such integrative relationships include Starbucks and CARE; Bayer North America and the Bidwell Training Center in Pittsburgh; Reading is Fun and Visa, International; The College Fund (the largest minority educational assistance organization in the United States) and Merck; The National Science Resource Center (for improving the teaching of science in elementary and high school education) and Hewlett-Packard; Time to Read and Time Warner. Successful collaborations generally occur when the community partner complements the company's core business or strategy.

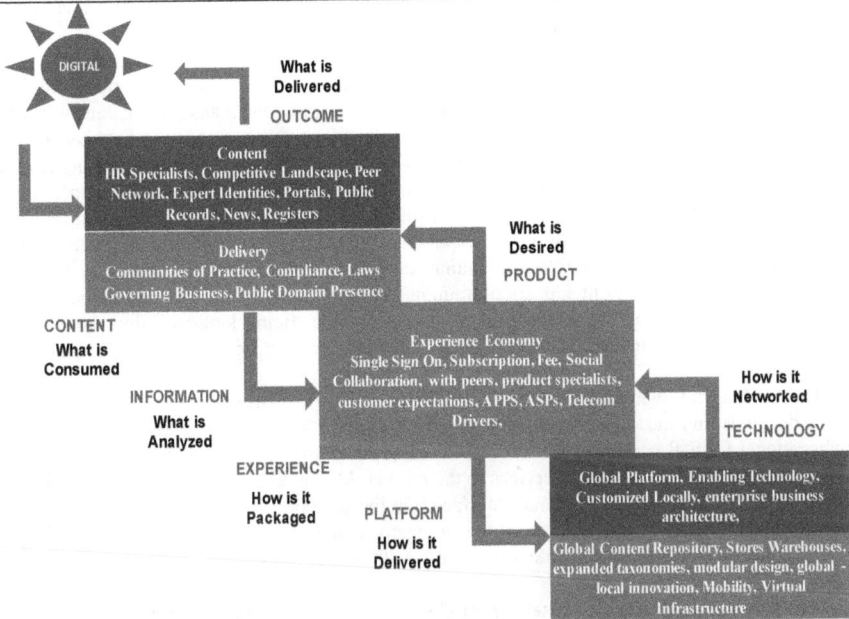

Figure 13 - Adapted and Modified from Digital Business Model - In MIT SMR 2013 issue, "Peter Weill and Stephanie L. Woerner in "Optimizing Your Digital Business Model" asks, what does it take to create the strongest possible online presence?

C. Human Capital – Definitions, Inclusions, Exclusions, Skills, Competencies and Value including intellectual capital value

Human Capital can be defined as that which when deployed by an individual enables the individual/people to earn a living, and a summation of all that is put together is the capital. Investing in education, training, and health care can increase human capital, for example. Economists increasingly argue that the accumulation of human as well as physical capital (plant and machinery) is a crucial ingredient of economic growth, par-ticularly in the emerging economy. Even so, this conclusion is largely a matter of theory and faith, rather than the result of detailed empirical analysis. Labor economists have attempted to bridge the gap in research by using measures about education, experience, age and training as human capital control variables in many of their research work.

For economist Theodore Schultz, 'Human capital' "refers to all those human capacities, developed by education, that can be used productively -- the capacity to deal in abstractions, to recognize and adhere to rules, to use language at a high level. Human capital, like other forms of capital, accumulates over generations; it is a thing that parents 'give' to their children through their upbringing, and that children then successfully deploy in school, allowing them to bequeath more human capital to their own children." -- Traub (2000) - Traub, James. The New York Times January 16, 2000. Human capital is the attributes of a person that are productive in some economic context. Often refers to formal educational attainment, with the implication that education is investment whose returns are in the form of wage, salary, or other compensation. These are normally measured and conceived of as private returns to the individual but can also be social returns.

Alex Tabarrok in The Economist writes, "Economists have continued to work in solving the tricky problem of how to measure **human capital** in an attempt to understand and value an intelligent company, even within the same country over time, let alone for comparisons between countries. Levels of spending on, say, education are not necessarily a good indicator of how much human capital an education system is creating; indeed, some economists argue that higher education spending may be a consequence of a country becoming wealthy rather than a cause". But that education does have a linear correlation to development of human capability, but whether it is capital is the issue. Never the less, even modest estimates of the stock of human capital in most countries suggests that it would pay to greatly increase investment in education, training, learning systems, technologies including medical sciences that would extend the working lives of most people. Being longevity does help economic growth. The non-economic benefits would be worth having, too. (Improvised Economist Definition).

Human Capital enables all the skills, expertise and competencies of the company to react to market demands and customer needs including leadership and management issues and capabilities. Organizational Capital comprises the capabilities of a company, its infrastructure and organizational processes to produce products and services to the market. Market Capital represents the capabilities of a company to interact with the external interface like the customer, partners, and suppliers and other stakeholders. Innovation Capital refers to a company's ability to innovate, improve and develop unutilized potential as well as generate long-term wealth - http://bit.ly/2aapCaQ

Human Capital Dominates Intellectual Capital Value – "Global capital markets have opened up the supply side, while widespread excess industry capacity has reduced the demand side. The recent reversals in some sectors notwithstanding, most companies are awash in capital. Of them, many cannot even generate sufficient high- quality capital-budget projects to use the available resources — and therefore go on merger-and-acquisition expeditions. Recognizing that the company's scarce resource is knowledgeable people means a shift in the whole concept of value management within the corporation. One of the most basic issues is how the value that the company creates should be distributed. Most companies operate under the assumption that shareholders, as contributors of capital, have the primary claim. But recruiting difficulties that large traditional companies face, employees' eroding sense of loyalty and cynicism over the growing gap between the compensation of those at the top and those on the front lines all indicate that value distribution must change". Christopher A. Bartlett and Sumantra Ghoshal in SMR Winter 2002, Building Competitive Advantage Through People, further continue, "Human Capital, not financial, capital must be the starting point and ongoing foundation of a successful strategy. For the vast majority of companies, that assumption simply is no longer true. Without denying the need for prudent use of financial resources, we believe that, for most companies today, capital is not the resource that constrains growth. The rapid spread of stock options as a form of compensation shows that companies have begun to recognize that the owners of the scarce resources are no longer only the shareholders but also the employees".

Nick Bontis and others also indicate that Human capital is also a primary component of the intellectual capital construct (Bontis, 1996, 1998, 1999, 2001a, b, 2002a, b; Bontis et al., 1999; Edvinsson and Malone, 1997; Edvinsson, 2002; Stewart, 1997, 2001; Sveiby, 1997; Bontis and Girardi, 2000). Human capital is more than above meaning and Intellectual Capital measurement techniques do not provide a comprehensive perspective or a deeper appreciation of HC measures and validity. It pertains to what people know that enables them to come together to make a company successful. While it would be inaccurate to say that it is more important than process or structural or customer capital, it is fair to say that without human capital nothing else would be worth much for long. In other words, the absence of human capital will sink a company faster than the absence of any other kind of capital. Furthermore, human capital enables the leverage of all of the other types of capital. Without it, there is no company; with it, there is always a chance of success. The distinction between human and structural capital is fundamental to managing knowledge. "Human Capital matters because it is the source of innovation and renewal, whether from brainstorms in a lab or new leads in a sales rep's little black book. But smart individuals don't necessarily make for smart enterprises" - Thomas Stewart.

Digital Convergence to Human Capital - "Technology was getting dull earlier this decade, says David Yoffie (Harvard Business School expert in technology strategy). But the sudden arrival of digital convergence has turned the tech world upside down. What are the right bets to place? And what factors appear to influence this digital world?" Writes, In Developing a Strategy for Digital Convergence, - Sean Silverthorne in HBSWK 2006.

Digital Business *does not mean altering traditional technology services to add a feature like cloud, or mobility or hosting and addressing it as a digital business or asking your business managers to alter project income codes to fake it as Digital Revenues. Continues, Yoffie,*

"In, fact, technology company managers must deal with a number of factors that many other industry executives don't, including:

- *Building a digital business culture necessitates moving away from an excessive cost centric business outsourcing model (Avoidance of Bodyshopping Strategies).*
- *Digital convergence has arrived, creating entirely new products, services, and collaboration opportunities.*
- *The technology industry is tilting to horizontal. Players need to learn to complement each other as well as compete.*
- *Network effects create strong market advantages for companies that can capitalize on them.*
- *The tech company's most valuable assets in the form of human capital walk out the door every day.*
- *Tech companies largely rely on components from other vendors, meaning that complementary assets must be managed adroitly. Case in point, the relationship between Apple & Samsung, Microsoft and Intel.*
- *Tech companies contend with high, upfront fixed costs, attrition, lack of talent and low marginal costs.*
- *They deal with the effect of standards in locking in customers and raising switching costs.*
- *Bersin by Deloitte Continues, "Mobility will dominate all new business technology as Millennials expect to be able to utilize mobile devices and mobile apps to work anytime, anywhere.*
- *Gamification will be built into more business systems to engage Millennial employees.*
- *Greater emphasis on learning management will increase as Millennials demand more on the job training for advancement opportunities.*
- *HRMS will play a big role in "big data"*

D. Intellectual Company Value *– Integrated view of intellect on human capital activity, ability to value invisible assets, systemic capability to manage knowledge*

81

How is data, information, knowledge, learning, training, especially the integrated view of intellect on human capital activity, aggregated to become information and eventually intelligence in a digital context

Return on Investment – "Concepts shows how data, information, knowledge, learning, training, especially the integrated view of intellect on human capital activity, are aggregated to become information and eventually intelligence. It describes the variables, the combinations, the contexts, and the applications". Jac Fitz-enz (1970) did some - http://www.hci.org/presenter/dr-jac-fitz-enz critical and pioneering work through the Saratoga Institute, California, HRM measurement, Human Value Management and ROI of Human Capital. Price Waterhouse now and Arthur Andersen involvement at earlier stages meant looking at business perspectives on human capital valuation. Of some significant work done over the last 30 years through the Saratoga Institute, Jac-Fitz-Enz (http://bit.ly/2a9KDxS)recent work on ROI of **Human Capital** is critical for a number of specific works on human capital beyond the generic work done on HC along with Intellectual Capital research. It provides explicit examples of the connections among the corporate, business unit, and human resources levels. In our context this work enables us to focus on aspects that deal with the making of the intelligence and consequent impact of the intellect in an organizational context.

Opportunity to value invisible assets by developing a hierarchy of human values, value sets and study how these aid or impede firms' achievement of their business goals.

Intangibles Dominate Human Capital – "In collaboration with Benjamin Tonna, Itami developed a hierarchy of human values as well as several instruments for measuring and describing the value sets of individuals and corporations and with firms to identify their values, analyze how those values aid or impede firms' achievement of their business goals, and change the values, if necessary, to make them more supportive of the firms' business goals, objectives, targets and strategies". Itami (1980) drawing upon Sveiby (http://www.sveiby.com/articles/icmmovement.htm) published **"Mobilizing Invisible Assets"** a ground breaking work on the value of invisible assets to the corporation. "Not published in English until 1987, it was slow to be found by people involved in intellectual assets and therefore slow to be seen as noteworthy contribution to the field. Nevertheless, readers of Itami's work uniformly conunent (permissive discrimination) on its prescience and the clarity of its insights into intangible assets and their importance to the corporation. In 1981 Hall established a company to commercialize research on human values. For more than 25 years Hall studied human values." Kaplan and Norton provide an example, "Take the example of a Consumer Bank and its strategy map that defines seven strategic themes, one of which is "Cross-sell the Product Line." The human resources executive at Consumer Bank owns the process for developing the *human capital* required to support the strategy. Human resources and line executives, at a planning workshop, identified the "financial planner" as the job most important to the cross-selling process. The workshop further identified four competencies as fundamental to this job—solution selling skills, relationship management, product line knowledge, and professional certification. Similar work with Consumer Bank's information technology executive led to specific objectives for the *information capital* (networks, data, and knowledge) to support the strategy. Information technology and line executives identified four technology priorities—a financial self-planning model, a customer profitability system, an integrated customer file, and Web-enabled access by customers".

The emergence of the Intelligent enterprise, the digital company, the pursuit beyond the age of smart machine and development of intrinsic and systemic capability to manage knowledge – based intellect.

Of significance to our work on **Intellectual Company** is the work of James Brian Quinn of the Amos Tuck School of business. His work titled **"The Intelligent Enterprise"** quite ably demonstrated the emergence of an enterprise powered by the intellect, driven by the mind and performed by a collective energy. "The enterprise attempted strategies, structures, and processes that were not in sync with what the industry standards established yet were very successful and enterprising to state the least. It meant that the capacity to manage knowledge-based intellect is the critical skill of this era (Quinn, 1992). Hudson in 1993 looked at the human capital issues pertaining to native or inherited intellect, education and capability criterion. Work at Celemi focused on competence, efficiency and stability in the context of human capital measurement. Wright et al. (1994) a resource based school of thought demonstrated that competitive positioning and a sustainable advantage is derived when a pool of Human Capital deployed to drive corporate performance beyond strategic orientation ordained by the top management". In an interview with John Hagel III (Deloitte), Gerald C. (Jerry) Kane at the Carroll School of Management at Boston College and the MIT Sloan Management Review guest editor for the Digital Business Initiative says in the MIT SMR 2016, "Everywhere we look, companies are "going digital" — adding mobile apps, making customer service available online, solving problems via Twitter. But **Deloitte Center for the Edge** co-founder John Hagel III considers this window dressing, and fears many executives aren't recognizing **how business is changing at a fundamental level"**.

E. Digital Tech Performance Challenges and Maturity

Performance Pressure in Tech Intellect Value - Upon reflection, some managers may discover that it is their own world view which is inhibiting their own effectiveness. Inevitably, those managers who have regarded management to be an acquired skill, which exists largely external to themselves may still be trying to reconcile these two opposing views. Similarly, other managers have made the simultaneous realization that it often is their own thinking that limits their performance. "I think there's a tendency to look at digital technology and think about it more as an opportunity, a choice," Hagel (DTT) told MIT Sloan Management Review. "The mounting performance pressure in our shifting business landscape turns this from an opportunity and choice into an imperative. The longer you wait, the more marginalized you're going to become." The irony, Hagel notes, is that same digital technology that's creating all this pressure also creates a very different approach to transformation that can help large companies to really become very different entities over time. "I'm an optimist," he adds. "I actually view this 'dark side' and mounting performance pressure from an optimistic view, in the sense that the old approaches are just not sustainable, and some senior executives have seen the need for fundamental change driven by this technology. The big issue for them is how to get that change to happen in a large traditional organization."

In the hard systems approach improvement are seen as stemming from the achievement of four fundamental goals: (I) reduction of uncertainty levels through rationalization, (2) prediction of future states of the systems, (3) preparation for these predicted future states, and (4) control of all relevant forms of performance through negative feedback mechanisms, to assure efficiency. "Part of it is just what I call the **"dark side"** of **digital technology"**, says Hagel, "which is mounting performance pressure, in part enabled and precipitated by the digital technology. In a world of mounting pressure, there's a natural human instinct to stick to what you know. Don't go out of your comfort zone because things are really scary out there. And so there's a tendency to just hold on and just squeeze harder on what you're currently doing. The excuse that I got from executives all over is, "Well, we're prisoners of Wall Street." Investors just want quarterly performance and a little bit more money to the bottom line, and that's what we're focused on: short-term efficiency improvements. Those are probably the two big factors, when I talk to executives, as to why they're not thinking more ambitiously or creatively about what this technology enables." The purpose of work was separated from the worker's purpose. In today's turbulent environments, extraordinary situations arise frequently, overlapping and often compounding each other in real time. There is little opportunity to take matters "upstairs" and work out new orders, and even less time to rehearse the performance altering decisions made in coursing streams of work. "And I think that the other piece is the curse of success. Large companies that have created enormous wealth and generated incredible market positions on a global basis — who's going to argue that what they're doing today is wrong? I think they lose the creativity and become complacent and assume that somehow, whatever's going on today is a blip or an aberration, and we'll get back to where we were and things will be back to normal. Generalizations are always risky, but most of the executives I talk to are still very much focused on digital largely as a way to do "more of the same," just more efficiently, quickly, cost effectively. But I don't see a lot of evidence of fundamentally stepping back and rethinking, at a basic level, "What business are we really in?"

F. Bundle of competencies - A Human Capital Primer

What makes a person valuable to the organization is the consummate acumen for enterprise and execution i.e. the generation of ideas and the speed of implementation.

Competencies Influences Value - "In the computer software field, with which I am (K Kumar) most familiar, we classified competencies under five major heads - domain, technology, project management, initiative and leadership. A software project attempts to computerize applications such as production scheduling in a manufacturing organization, trade settlement in a stock exchange or recoveries for an insurance company. An analyst developing the requirements for the system must have expertise in the specific business area such as manufacturing, securities trading or insurance". K Kumar states in his paper, Role of Human Intelligence, "An employee has a bundle of competencies, each of which needs to be valued, and referred by S Mahaligam (2001) in "An article on Human Capital" in Praxis, Business Line. "We call this business knowledge the domain expertise, he says. A software designer must be knowledgeable about the technology that provides the platform for the system and makes it work. Similarly, project management is an essential area of expertise for a person leading a part or whole of a project, to ensure that resources are marshaled to yield effective results in the required time. Besides these, what makes a person valuable to the organization is the consummate acumen for enterprise and execution i.e. the generation of ideas and the speed of implementation. These come under the umbrella of initiative". http://bit.ly/2aD6vDK

Value of talented people is best realized when organizational competency processes helps recognize employee intellect and contribution

Talent Values - The main argument of Robert Reich is the need for a **competency theory** of the firm that recognizes the "value of talented people" to an organizational system - This Competency Theory was later absorbed by Sveiby - It can be viewed as a mix of human capital, structural capital and customer capital. Human capital generates innovation--whether of new products and services, or has improving business processes. Structural capital is the knowledge that belongs to the organization as a whole in terms of technologies, inventions, data, publications, strategy and culture, structures and systems, organizational routines and procedures and customer capital is the value perception, networks, relationships, product loyalty and price competitiveness that customers perceive and act upon in relation to a company or its product. Additional work involved acknowledging intellectual capital has the prospective to progress the effectiveness of both resources and labour markets (Bukh et al., 1999; OECD, 1999) - http://robertreich.org.

An alternate view on competency as that which predominantly focuses on knowledge, skills as against behavior and differentiating management of knowledge from management of intelligence.

"Competence" - Roos Et all, define competence as being essentially about knowledge and skills, and by knowledge they mean specifically the "technical or academic knowledge of things," related to education, something that "has to be taught." **"Skills"** they see as its practical counterpart. This approach is reflected in many of the measures used by the pioneering Scandinavian companies. The delineation between the terms **"knowledge management"** and **"intellectual capital"** also seems unclear at times. In our view, a company concerned with intellectual capital controls knowledge management. And **Knowledge management**, as a function, describes the act of managing the object, intellectual capital (Petty and Guthrie, 2000; Guthrie and Petty, 1999)".

Opportunity to classify areas for understanding and appreciating intellectual capital in the context of education, work, experience, innovation and unique factors.

Measuring Competence - Karl Sveiby looks at classification of the area of work, growth (number of years in the profession), level of education, competence index (Example **Level * Performance = Competence Index, Years in the Profession * Seniority * Level of Education,)** competence turnover, renewal/innovation (competence enhancing customers, diversity, training and education, efficiency and utilization (proportion of professionals in the company), leverage effect of employees to pull revenues, value added per employee, value added per professional, profit per professional/employee, stability – average age, seniority, pay position and professional turnover rate. Karl Sveiby and Hudson have come close to the concept of Strategic Human Capital articulated in this paper. Refer: **Measuring Competence, ©Karl Erik Sveiby 1996, 2001**

Evidence - In our view, however, **competence** is more complex than this. The most useful knowledge comes though experience, and what a person knows a lot about may be little to do with their formal education. For example, if I have a degree in substance manufacturing, but how much I can tell you a decade later is a definite questionable situation on academic learning.

- *Attitude. This, say Roos et al., depends mostly on personality traits and can be changed very little. It is influenced by "motivation, behavior and conduct." The Human Capital Monitor argues that these are strongly dependent on the environment in which people work.*
- *Intellectual agility. This is used to cover innovation, flexibility, and adaptability—traits seen at a group or organizational level as much as in individuals.*

Again strategic approaches in its measurement including aspects pertaining to competence, attitude and intellectual agility but measures it through an appreciation of how was it gained and how has it been applied.

Thomas H. Davenport, sees competencies as owned and invested by the individual, and the task of the organization as to harness it, keep it, and grow it while it is available. Davenport builds his approach on the increased level of control that people have taken of their own lives, their ability to build upon their competencies, and the norm of people staying with an employer only for as long as their conditions are satisfied. Europeans may question this very US attitude to employment, but it does not invalidate the basic concepts.

Davenport breaks it into three elements:

- *Ability. This is subdivided into knowledge—"the intellectual context in which a person performs"; skill—"the means of performing tasks"; and talent. By the latter he means a specific aptitude, such as being a very good surgeon or a teacher*
- *Behavior. This is the way in which the task is performed, and embraces attitudes and personal traits*
- *Effort. By this is meant application of the ability. It relates to motivation and commitment, but has overtones of productivity.*

These categories concern the individual's competencies. Promotion *of* fear prevents risk-taking and discourages initiative. Perhaps worst *of* all, structural policy barriers -rigid chain *of* command, overuse of prescribed protocols, denigrating raise and compensation systems, to name a few -act to stimulate organizational ignorance: the learning *of* counterproductive behaviors rather than optimization *of* performance. An organization brings individuals together, however, and makes something greater than their own independent contribution. The way in which people collaborate toward common goals is also part of human capital. (Andrew Mayo, The Human Value of Enterprise).

Roos, Roos, Edvinsson, and Dragonetti divides human capital as follows: (Andrew Mayo, The Human Value of Enterprise)

While some progress was made through a small number of specialists to seek more empirical data on the human capital dimension, significant emphasis financially was invested in the Intellectual Capital measurement techniques and of which human capital continued to be one of the parts.

Wright, P M, McMahan G C, McWilliams, A (1994) "Human Resources and sustained competitive advantage a resource based perspective, "International Journal of Human Resource Management, Volume 5, Number 2, pp 310 - 26

Consequently, researchers attempted to bring value orientation to measuring Intellectual Capital as they applied to human capital:

- *To align the company's HR competencies with the business goals*
- *To ensure necessary skills in the organization to maintain competitive advantage and business performance over the long-term*
- *To know what company's skills and knowledge consists of*
- *To manage and measure the company's most important asset - the intangible assets*
- *Understanding work level intellect at the human capital level*

G. *Intellectual Capital – Definitions, Context, Capital Augmentation, Forms of Intellect (Corporate), Goodwill, Know How Company*

The Context of Capital (www.economics.about.com) - is used here to demonstrate the possibility of capital deepening, an opportunity to increase capital intensity (amount of capital to per unit of labor input) normally in a macro context where it is measured by something analogous to the capital stock available per labor hour spent. In a micro context, it could mean the amount of capital available for a worker to use, but this use is rare. Capital deepening is a macroeconomic concept, of a faster-growing magnitude of capital in production than in labor. And if we were to see it in the context of growth in labor contribution then we have multiple multipliers to enhance the deepening capability. Industrialization involved capital deepening - that is, more and more expensive equipment with a lesser corresponding rise in wage expenses. Capital deepening of a certain input (e.g. a certain kind of capital input, a recent key example being computer equipment) can be measured in the following way. Estimate the growth of the services provided by this input, per unit of labor input, in year T and in year T+1. The growth rate of that ratio is one common measure of the rate of capital deepening. - Oulton, Nicholas. 2002. "Productivity versus welfare: or GDP versus Weitzman's NDP." Bank of England.

The Economist defines Capital as the Money or wealth put to economic use, the life-blood of capitalism. "Economists describe capital as one of the four essential ingredients of economic activity, the factors of production, along with land, labour and enterprise. Production processes that use a lot of capital relative to labour are capital intensive; those that use comparatively little capital are labour intensive". http://faculty.sfhs.com/lesleymuller/AP_Euro/IR/cap_labor_defs.pdf

Capital takes different forms,

- *The new assets are traditionally thought to be intangible and not measurable*
- *Defined digital assets are value centric*
- *Assets beyond physical space*
- *The market is rewarding companies based on what type of assets they leverage*
- *Opportunity to exploit borrowed resources for personalized investment (mortgage funds for investment real estate)*
- *Business design reflects how a company assembles tangible and intangible assets*
- *Therefore, a company's asset portfolio is its key determinant of economic success*
- *Companies must adjust their asset portfolios to alter risk and reward*
- *New digital tools are necessary to adjust asset portfolios based on market signals*
- *Negotiable instrument*
- *Emphasis on People & their value is significant*
- *Knowledge Economy is weightless*
- *Intellect is possible to be valued*
- *Cash is Queen*

Capital Augmenting - Refer econport, "And this in turn leads us to capital augmenting. One of the ways in which an effectiveness variable could be included in a production function is through the Solow model. If effectiveness A is multiplied by capital K but not by labor L, then we say the effectiveness variable is capital augmenting. For example, in the model of output (Y where $Y=(AK)aL1$-a) the effectiveness variable A is capital-augmenting but in the model ($Y=AKaL1$-a) it is not. The Solow model is meant to describe the production function of an entire economy to enable all variables to be treated as aggregates. The date or time is denoted t. Output or production is denoted Y(t). Capital is K(t). Labor time is denoted L(t). Labor's effectiveness, or knowledge, is A(t). The production function is denoted F() and is assumed to have constant returns to scale. At each time t, the production function is: $(Y = F (K, AL)$ which can be written: $(Y(t) = F(K(t), A(t)L(t)) - AL)$ is effective labor. Effectively the model deals with production, labor productivity and effectiveness and the knowledge and includes labor augmenting and capital augmenting". Refer - Hornstein, Andreas, and Per Krusell. 1996. "Can technology improvements cause productivity slowdowns?" NBER Macroeconomics Annual 1996 - MIT Press. pp 214-215. Hulten, 2000

Digital Culture Productivity- Prof. John D. Sterman provides an example. "Let's take project management as an example. Let's say you're designing a new product or managing a large-scale construction or software development project. There's a combinatorial complexity issue; For example, in developing a new aircraft you might have several million different parts that all have to be designed to function without interfering with one another and that can be assembled in a sensible and efficient sequence. Managing the coordination of so many elements is a problem of combinatorial complexity. There's a number of modeling tools to help, such as PERT, Gantt charts, critical path methods, CAD/CAM tools and so on. But there's a dimension of project management that doesn't relate to how many different parts there are, how many lines of code there are in your software, but depend on dynamic complexity. Suppose for example the customer changes the specifications after the project has begun. Such changes occur often in large projects because the customers need change, the available technology changes, and so on. As you respond to the change you might find that now you're running behind schedule. So you might add re- sources, for example, hire more programmers. In the long run, adding programmers should boost the rate of coding. and speed the completion of the project. But, what may happen is that the project could fall further behind. Why? As you add programmers you're diluting the experience base of your team, you're increasing the coordination and training burden for the members of the team, you're going to have more meetings, you're going to have longer meetings. With less experienced people you're going to lower the productivity of the experienced folks on your team as they help with training and answering the questions of the inexperienced people. You're going to see a higher error rate coming from the inexperienced people. Productivity may actually drop, forcing people to work longer hours. Longer hours might then increase fatigue and bum-out and lead to a still higher error rate and still lower productivity in a vicious cycle. If this goes on long enough, if the experienced people are frustrated by not being able to get their work done, by being tired, by having to train all these inexperienced people, by having to go to more meetings, by having to redo work that they already thought they'd done, then some of them might quit. If they do, then you've got to hire still more inexperienced people, closing the reinforcing feedback and leading to still lower productivity. These are problems of dynamic complexity. They arise from the multiple feedback loops that are created by the decision processes of each individual on a team. While these decision rules are usually locally sensible, the result, as they interact with the decisions of others, is to worsen the situation. system dynamics modeling is designed to help understand that dynamic complexity". In the Digital HR, technology can indeed influence productivity. In, "Sales Gets a Machine-Learning Makeover", H. James Wilson, Narendra Mulani, Allan Alter, MIT SMR 2016, provide examples of value addition, "Gainsight, a company that offers software to manage sales and customer service more effectively, helped the online questionnaire service Survey Monkey create automated alerts to ensure that all team members were up to date on renewals, invoicing, and upsell opportunities. Using Gainsight's technology, Survey Monkey cut the process time to send an invoice by about a third. Another company called Anaplan is helping Hewlett-Packard reduce the time spent gathering sales data from a month to three days, effectively a 10-fold improvement. Instead of churning through month-old data, sales teams can make decisions with fresh, up-to-date analysis, allowing sales staff to spend time on higher-value tasks. Similarly, a machine-learning company called Aviso, working with an enterprise cloud company called Nutanix, can compress a 12-hour task of compiling sales reports into four minutes. That's a 100-fold improvement".

Another example would be a capital utilization variable as measured telecommunication or the utilities usage. An example: in the context of a railroad, automatic railroad signaling, track-switching, and car-coupling devices are capital augmenting.

From Moses Abramovitz and Paul A. David, 1996. "Convergence and Deferred Catch-up: productivity leadership and the waning of American exceptionalism." In Mosaic of Economic Growth, edited by Ralph Landau, Timothy Taylor, and Gavin Wright. - Source: Romer, 1996, p 7. Source:

Romer, 1996, p 7; Solow, 1956; that is: Solow, Robert. "A contribution to the theory of economic growth." Quarterly Journal of Economics - Feb. 1956 and (www.economics.about.com).

Intellect – Types and Options - Let us look at what makes organizations derive capital value. Essentially through multiple formats:

1. *Unique Intellect: No other firm has exactly the same set of knowledge, skills, abilities, innovations, codified knowledge, patents, trade - marks, copy rights, IP and trade secrets. They are unique and difficult to duplicate and may require considerable time & resource to do so.*
2. *Differentiable Intellect: includes assets such as manufacturing, distribution which while similar is different in some ways from those of competitors. They differ in size, shape, complexity, production rate and cost structure. Complementary business assets (innovations) are important to knowledge firms for generating & maintaining profits.*
3. *Generic Intellect: Includes those not differentiable, such as cash, fixed assets, real estate, fixed capital and tangible assets. All of the assets are found in a balance sheet.*
4. *Disposable Shared Intellect: Includes those forms of assets that can be hired, leased, shared or obtained by paying a sharing fee in perpetuity. For example, cloud computing, information shared on the cloud, or wide area, Self Help, virtual data warehouses hardware sharing, Data as a Shared Service, Meta Block Housing, global knowledge caves, Private Personal Data Management, SaaS, Platform as a Service, IaaS, Product as a Software (PRaaS) and finally Service as a Software. SEaaS. Information capital, consisting of systems, databases, libraries, and networks, makes information and knowledge available to the organization. Information capital, like human capital, has value only in the context of the strategy.*

Intellect is Beyond Intellect - John Kenneth Galbraith (1969) first published the term **intellectual capital** in 1969. He believed that intellectual capital meant more than just "**intellect as pure intellect**" but rather incorporated a degree of "intellectual action". In that sense, intellectual capital is not only a static intangible asset per se, but an ideological process; a means to an end and there is much to support the assertion that IC is instrumental in the determination of enterprise value and national economic performance – "Journal of Intellectual Capital" (Burton-Jones, 1999; Boisot, 1999; Mouritsen, 1998) but indisputably the intellectual capital association is grounded in the need for application (Roos et al., 1997; Larsen et al., 1999; Mouritsen, 1998). Intellectual capital research has primarily evolved from the desires of practitioners (Bontis, 1996; Brooking, 1996; Darling, 1996; Edvinsson and Sullivan, 1996; Saint-Onge, 1996). This had surely led to an absence of pure research from the academic world but has gained an interest from the academia since the involvement of faculty from some of the North American Universities and many of the ideas, concepts being solemnized today can be traced back several years - Tobin's "q" and Flamholtz work being a few examples. (Chung and Pruitt, 1994) Further development of intellectual capital as an academic emphasis has seen researchers begin to investigate ideas relating to the influence of micro-level (i.e. organization-specific) conceptualizations of the value of intellectual capital on the behaviour of the capital and labour markets (Bassi and McMurrer, 1999; Holland, 1999; Lev and Mintz, 1999; DCTU, 1999; Westphalen, 1999; Leadbeater, 1999; Canibano et al., 1999a; Bukh et al., 1999; OECD, 1999). Petty and Guthrie, 2000 state in their literature survey work that Brennan and Connell (2000) undertook a wide-ranging examination of a number of topical empirical research studies on different aspects of intellectual capital that were obtainable at the OECD Symposium. The studies covered included: Andriessen et al. (1999); Backhuijs et al. (1999); Brennan (1999); Bukh et al. (1999); Canibano et al. (1999b); Danish Agency for Trade and Industry (1998; 1999); Guthrie et al. (1999); Hoogendoorn et al. (1999); Johanson (1999); Johanson et al. (1999a); Miller et al. (1999).

Goodwill is Intellect - The need to recognize **intellectual capital** is best described by Robert Reich "Members of the accounting profession, not otherwise known for their public displays of emotion, have fretted openly about how to inform potential investors of the true worth of enterprises whose value rests in the brains of employees". Reich has used the term 'goodwill' to signify the indistinct sector in the corporate balance sheets between the company's tangible assets and the value of its talented people. But as intellectual capital continues to overtake physical capital as the key asset of the corporation, shareholders find themselves on shakier and shakier ground." It is up to symbolic analysts (Reich, 1991) who are equipped to identify and solve intellectual capital issues that will sustain the knowledge advantage for their own organizations.

Know – How is Intellect - Sveiby (1986) concurrently published "The Know-How Company" on managing intangible assets. Sveiby as the founding father of the very early "Swedish Movement" in knowledge management and intellectual capital. In 1986, he published his first book (written in Swedish) in which he explored how to manage the rapidly growing field of knowledge companies-organizations that have no traditional production, only the knowledge and creativity of their employees. In 1990, he published Kunskapsledning (written in Swedish again), the world's first book dealing with "knowledge management". Sveiby was the first to recognize the need to measure human capital, and he pioneered accounting practices for these intangible assets, testing them in his own company. In 1989, the results of the Konrad working group in the book "The Invisible Balance Sheet", was written proposing a theory for measuring knowledge capital by dividing it into three categories: **"customer capital, individual capital, and structural capital"**. The approach was adopted by a large number of Swedish-listed companies and, in 1993, the Swedish Council of Service Industries adopted it as their criterion proposal for annual reports, the first ever standard in this field. One of the many people inspired by Sveiby's concepts was Leif Edvinsson. Edvinsson went on to re-label these intangible assets as "intellectual capital" when he shaped Skandia's first annual report enhancement on intellectual capital in 1995. Sveiby uses the heading "professional competence" for human capital. This he defines as a combination of educational attainment levels and years of experience. He then breaks it down, as for the other components of intellectual capital, into aspects of growth/renewal, efficiency, and stability, defining his overall framework for measuring intellectual capital components. **"The Intellectual Company"** complements the **"The Know- How Company"** articulated by Sveiby.

The **measurement concepts of intellectual capital** differ about the dimensions, but writers generally conceive of intellectual capital as comprehensively composed of (a) human capital e.g. knowledge in people's heads, the employee competence, (b) structural capital e.g. knowledge that doesn't go home at night, and (c) customer capital e.g. relationships with customers in form of price advantage, loyalties, brands, and image.

Few authors (Brennan and Connell (2000) (Guthrie and Petty, 1999a, 1999b; Petty and Guthrie, 2000; Guthrie et al., 1999, Literature Review, 2000) (being an exception), however, have traced the sequence of events involved in development of intellectual capital and its application at both research and organizational contexts. Patrick Sullivan enumerated the basic research and developments in the context of Intellectual Capital.

If the obvious answer is "Yes" to the fact that we know "What" to do, then the consequent question will be "How"? We will first attempt to demonstrate a value perspective on how an individuals' **intellect**, his/her knowledge/learning, a combination of the three, that helps add/create/deplete value.

H. Intellectual Capital – Thought Work

We have therefore done a detailed literature survey of the intellectual capital models to demonstrate a need for a measure that looks at Human Capital from a holistic value creation standpoint. More importantly we will demonstrate that a laundry list of ratios, indices, measures do not provide a holistic view of all aspects that pertain to the **Intellect.**

We will demonstrate that the measures attempted through Intellectual Capital measurement route cannot be meaningfully pulled together by organizational leaders to act upon the learning from such measures. Also that the outcome from the measures tells you a current state but with no meaningful recipe or work steps on what to do with the ratios. Apart from the fact that these measures are quite arbitrary and are driven by considerations that are meant to be practical and application oriented rather than the empirical need to validate each of the variables and measures.

Richard Petty, James Guthrie in **"Intellectual Capital Literature Review"** write "One of the most workable definitions of intellectual capital in our opinion is that offered by the Organization for Economic Co-operation and Development (OECD, 1999) which describes intellectual capital as "the economic value of multiple categories of intangible assets of a company:

- *Organizational ("Structural, Social, Financial, Physical") capital;*
- *Human, People, Capability capital.*
- *Intellectual, Smart Tech Capital*

"More precisely, structural capital refers to things like proprietary software systems, distribution networks, and supply chains. **Human Capital** includes human resources within the organization (i.e. staff resources) and resources external to the organization, namely customers and suppliers. Often, the term **"intellectual capital"** is treated as being synonymous with **"intangible assets".** The definition offered by the OECD, however, makes an appropriate distinction by locating intellectual capital as a subset of, rather than the same as, the overall intangible asset base of a business. As such, there are items of an intangible nature that do not logically form part of a company's intellectual capital. A firm's reputation is one such item. Reputation may be a by-product (or a result) of the judicious use of a firm's intellectual capital, but it is not part of intellectual capital per se. Historically, the distinction between intangible assets and intellectual capital has been vague at best. Intangibles have been referred to as "goodwill" (APC, 1970; ASB, 1997; IASC, 1998), and intellectual capital as part of this goodwill. Recently, a number of contemporary classification schemes have refined the distinction by specifically dividing intellectual capital into the categories of external **(customer-related) capital, internal (structural) capital, and human capital** (e.g. Sveiby, 1997; Roos et al., 1997; Stewart, 1997; Edvinsson and Stenfelt, 1999; Edvinsson and Malone, 1997). From a utilitarian point of view, the distinction has proved a winner by facilitating the preparation of "intellectual capital accounts" (typically included in the traditional annual report) which are employed differently in making decisions regarding organizational value that are more encompassing than decisions made previously (Guthrie and Petty, 1999a; ICAEW, 1998; Sveiby, 1998).

Sveiby continues, "In the summer of 1989, Sullivan began his research into **"commercializing innovation".** The focus of Sullivan's work has been the extraction of value from IC. As one of the founders of the ICM gathering, Sullivan has encouraged companies and individuals involved with value extraction to share information and to jointly develop decision processes, methods, and systems that produce practical results. This analysis is one of the outcomes of that approach. He has been closely associated with the ICM model of a knowledge firm, which was formulated at the first gathering meeting using much of his thinking as its basis. In fall 1990 Sveiby published **"Knowledge Management"** and between fall 1990 and January 1991 Thomas Stewart published on Intellectual Capital and Brainpower. Stewart's provocative paper **"Intellectual Capital"** as a cover article in Fortune began substantive interest amongst commercial enterprises and consulting firms. Stewart began his association with intellectual capital when, as a feature writer for Fortune magazine, he wrote a brief article in 1991 about new ideas in business. That led to a longer story, which became "Brainpower," published in 1992. Stewart's interest in knowledge management led him to write **"Intellectual Capital,"** which appeared in 1994. Now a member of the board of editors of Fortune magazine, Stewart published a book, Intellectual Capital - The New Wealth of Organizations (Doubleday) in 1997 and later The Wealth of Knowledge by Doubleday again".

In fall 1991, Skandia organized the first corporate IC function, names Edvinsson VP and in 1992 **James Brian Quinn** of Amos Tuck School of Business produced a first of its kind work titled, **"The Intelligent Enterprise"**. This to my mind demonstrated a paradigm shift to what this paper on Strategic Human Capital Measurement will attempt to provide a perspective. That in Intellectual Company intelligence is measured quite differently and consequently ought to be valued quite radically.

ICM Movement by SVEIBY - St. Onge (1993) then established the concept of **Customer Capital.** The father of the thought on customer capital, Hubert St. Onge is considered to be one of the most creative thinkers in the field of learning and knowledge management. St. Onge, credited with contribution to the learning programs for the Canadian International Bank of Commerce, was interested in how to translate learning into both human and structural capital. He began by exploring the relationship between human and structural capital and the firm's financial capital. He realized that in command to be commercially successful in the long term, the first two capitals must focus on customer-related interests. In so doing, the firm created a stock of capital around its customers, which St. Onge dubbed later as customer capital. (St. Onge defines structural capital in largely the similar way that this paper defines intellectual assets; see definition later in this appendix.) The St. Onge replica shows that long-term profits are created at the confluence between human, structural, and customer capital.

New Generation Measures - W Hudson (1993) worked on **Intellectual Capital** with a particular reference to **human capital measures**. Hudson in 1993 through his publication, **"Intellectual Capital: How to build it, enhance it, use it"** John Wiley, NY, demonstrated the need to study, genetic inheritance, education, experience and attitudes as important considerations in understanding, valuing and measuring Human Capital. Nick Bontis (1994) and his work of the last 15 years including an intensive case perspective on **intellectual and human capital measurement** have been substantive. Bontis can be credited with the act of bringing empirical research methodology and validation techniques to his work on **Intellectual Capital.** Bontis of Strategic Management Department at McMaster University belongs to the new generation IC Movement and has done significant work bringing the research and the practitioners together in understanding the primary role of human capital in an endeavor to measure and value intellectual capital. Of significance is his work in the measures and models, particularly in regard to financial services industry, country specific studies in Malaysia, Australia and Canada. (Bontis 1994, 1996, 1998, 1999, 2000). Sullivan, Petrash, Edvinsson (1994) then decided to host a gathering of IC managers. Petrash joined Dow in 1986 and after a series of jobs was asked to create an intellectual asset management function to identify innovations or ideas that might have been overlooked by the corporation and bring them to commercialization if possible. Petrash developed an intellectual asset vision and implementation model, including approaches and tools to enable the company to maximize the value of its existing portfolio of intellectual assets. The success of this work led Dow to expand his responsibilities;

Petrash was Dow's Director of Intellectual Capital/Knowledge Management. Since 1998 he has been a partner with PwC specializing in consulting on intellectual assets with an emphasis on tax". http://www.sveiby.com/articles/icmmovement.htm

Asset Utilization Models - Lev (1996) created the Intangibles Research at New York University. As a professor at the Stern School of Management at New York University, Lev first began his research into valuing intangibles in the early 1990s and focused his energy in understanding utilization of assets, balance sheet presentation and influence of such assets on firm's financials. Lev's work focused on quantifying the value of intangibles and correlating those values with financial measures observable in the capital. The resultant questions - "Shouldn't then, a measure of the organization's wealth include the wealth of its human resources?" and "Shouldn't our planning process enable us to project the organizational capabilities in terms of the human resource wealth thus measured?" "Shouldn't there be a measure that integrates knowledge, data, information all pertaining to the individual compiled together with a historical perspective, current scenario and future potential?"

Balance Sheet/ Profit & Loss/ Income & Expense Emphasis - Teece's, Technology Theories (1986) - http://www.sveiby.com/articles/icmmovement.htm thereafter published a paper on extracting value from innovation. Teece's 1986 article **"Profiting from Technological Innovation"** brought together much of the work done by academic researchers and economists leading toward a resource-based theory of strategy. This article was instrumental in demonstrating the economist's view of technology commercialization and contained several ideas that were key to a management capability for extracting value from innovation. The work acknowledged sources of value in technological innovation, the mechanisms for converting value to profits, and the steps necessary for commercializing innovation. These efforts were followed by Alfred Rappaport's (1986) work titled creating shareholder value, Sveiby (1988) publication of "The New Annual Report" introducing **"knowledge capital"** including the 1989 "The Invisible Balance Sheet".

Skandia Hidden Values - Edvinsson and Malone (1997) based on their experience and work decided to publish **"Intellectual Capital"** a work at Skandia that later became a benchmark for industrial organizations. As Corporate Director of Intellectual Capital at Skandia AFS, a Swedish insurance company, Edvinsson was responsible for creating ways to describe what Skandia called "the hidden values" and develop an intellectual capital management model for the firm. As one of the best-known spokespersons for intellectual capital management, Edvinsson built upon the concept pioneered by Sveiby of reporting on external capital. Skandia has now issued some six intellectual supplements to its annual financial reports, outlining the firm's intellectual capital and the ways in which this hidden value, of commercial significance and benefit to stakeholders, is used for specific and strategic contribution to customers and shareholders. Thereafter in April 1997 Stewart book, **"Intellectual Capital"**, was published followed by the June 1997 Hoover Institution conference on measuring intellectual capital, the 1998 Richard Boulton, Libert and Samek Study covering over 10,000 corporations as a part of this identity creation program.

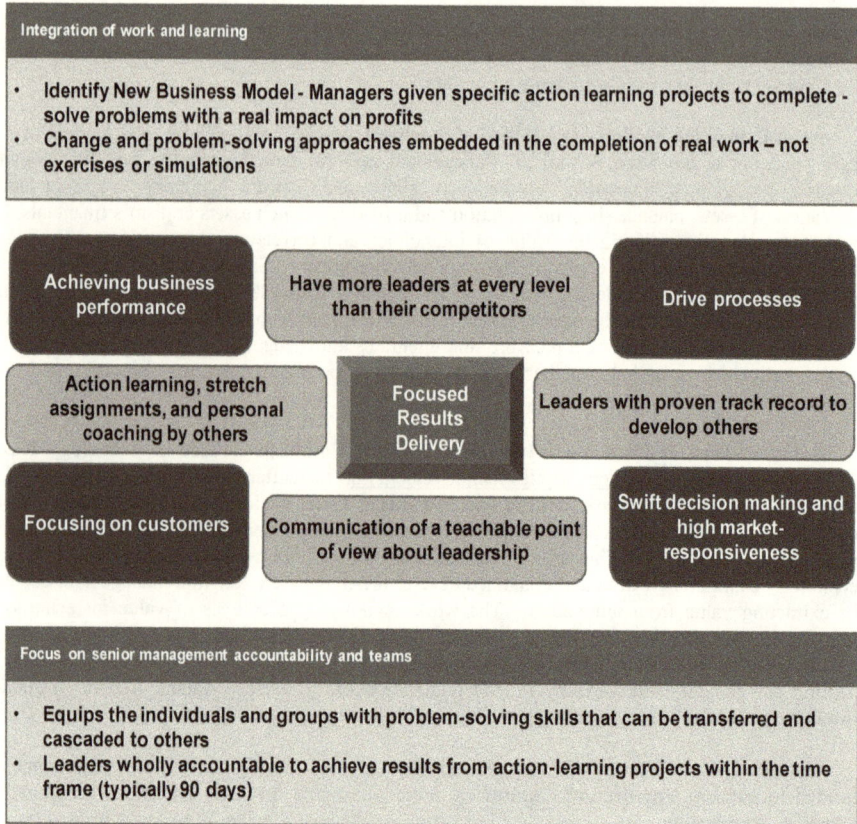

Integration of work and learning
• Identify New Business Model - Managers given specific action learning projects to complete - solve problems with a real impact on profits • Change and problem-solving approaches embedded in the completion of real work – not exercises or simulations

Achieving business performance	Have more leaders at every level than their competitors	Drive processes
Action learning, stretch assignments, and personal coaching by others	Focused Results Delivery	Leaders with proven track record to develop others
Focusing on customers	Communication of a teachable point of view about leadership	Swift decision making and high market-responsiveness

Focus on senior management accountability and teams
• Equips the individuals and groups with problem-solving skills that can be transferred and cascaded to others • Leaders wholly accountable to achieve results from action-learning projects within the time frame (typically 90 days)

Figure 14 - Learning Oriented Transformation – Program Sample

Andersen research on how do organizations create or destroy value – **"Cracking the Value Code"**. - http://bit.ly/2aslcdS Boulton defined the need for companies to create value, and incur risk, by assembling unique combinations of assets and declared that it is this portfolio that is called the business model, and it determines a company's economic success. This is where learning dominates the transformation process. See figure - *Learning Oriented Transformation – Program Sample*.

Knowledge – Intellect Interface - The delineation between the terms **"knowledge management"** and **"intellectual capital"** also seems unclear at times. In our view, knowledge learning management is about the management of the intellectual capital controlled by a company. Knowledge management, as a function, describes the act of managing the object, intellectual capital (Petty and Guthrie, 2000; Guthrie and Petty, 1999). A hurdle associated with this increased complexity of classification is that traditional accounting practice does not provide for the identification and measurement of these "new" intangibles in organizations, especially knowledge-based organizations (Guthrie et al., 1999; IFAC, 1998; SMAC, 1998). Continues Guthrie, "New" intangibles such as staff competencies, customer relationships, models, and computer and administrative systems receive no recognition in the traditional financial and management reporting model. Interestingly, even traditional intangibles like brand equity, patents, and goodwill are reported in the financial statements only when they meet stringent recognition criteria, otherwise they have, until recently, also been omitted from the financial statements (see IFAC, 1998; IASC, 1998). The limitations of the existing financial reporting system for capital markets and other stakeholders have motivated an evolving dialogue on finding new ways to measure and report on a company's intellectual capital. The product of this dialogue is a plethora of new measurement approaches that all have the aim, to a greater or lesser extent, of synthesising the financial and non-financial value-generating aspects of the company into one external report. Principal among the new reporting models are the intangible asset monitor (Sveiby, 1988; 1997; Celemi, 1998); the balanced scorecard (Kaplan and Norton, 1992; 1996); the Skandia value scheme (Edvinsson and Malone, 1997; Edvinsson, 1997); and the intellectual capital accounts (DATI, 1998)". http://bit.ly/2ai9G56

I. The Intellectual Company

"**The Intellectual Company**" in our assumption personifies the human being and makes the human mind as the foundation of the corporation. Our assumption borders on a singular dependence on the human being and the human mind to make organizations of the future effective. All other organizational factors are presumed to be secondary.

Intellect is Core - Intellect seen in its purest form is propaedeutic in its conceptual state. It is primarily elementary and forms the core of the enterprise. Individuals seek freedom of expression, in an environment where learning, teaching and understanding is available and is in a position to adapt, contribute and improve as they learn. The intellectual company deals below the surface of overt relationships, seeks psychological contract built on trust, collaboration and mutuality of purpose and provides an environment that offers respect and dignity to the individual. The Corporation has an undebatable, unalterable dictate on the faith in the human mind, the spirit and power of the intellect. Business Process facets of the corporation described above through the knowledge organization succeeds the management of the enterprise.

Organization – Culture Relationship – There is a view to establish a relationship is echoed by Ghoshal and Bartlett. "The implications are profound for **Human Capital Movement.** Top management must begin renegotiating both implicit and explicit contracts with key stakeholders, particularly with employees. Unless those who contribute their human and intellectual capital are given the opportunity to enjoy the fruits of the value creation they are driving, they will go where they have that opportunity — typically to newer, less tradition-bound companies. Just as there is value in attracting and developing individuals who hold specialized knowledge, there is value in the social networks that enable sharing of that knowledge. Indeed, unless a company actively links, leverages and embeds the pockets of individual-based knowledge and expertise, it risks underutilizing it or, worse, losing it. As companies seek the best ways to convert individual expertise into embedded intellectual capital, the classic response is to give the task to the chief information officer along with the faddish title of "chief knowledge officer".

Big Data Management and Technology Relationship – "More Data is Big Data - At heart, analytics provides insight by analyzing large amounts of data—and generally speaking, the bigger the data pool, the better the information gleaned through analytics. Having analytics tools built into an integrated talent management system can make it easier to pull data from across HR processes and factor in things like employee engagement, cost of employment, retention, and so on. But information from other internal sources, such as finance and operations, can also be useful. So too can external data about competitors' recruiting and compensation practices and customer expectations. All of this is driving interest in the use of big data in HR. Today, a growing volume of information is not captured in traditional databases. Instead, it is found in emails, social media, blogs and other unstructured forms. Big data systems make it possible to include this unstructured data in HR analytics to encompass a broad range of issues. For example, if a company is thinking about opening a new R&D facility in a new region, big data could help it compare employment costs and skills availability in different locations - http://bit.ly/2b1jfqi ".

Ease of Adoption - Standardization of processes is a starting point, for benchmarking many times leads to an evaluation of a solution as a delivery model because the resulting simplification and efficiencies make transition to a newer system easier and faster. Bersin by Deloitte in 2015 predictions, say, "In 2015, the HR software market will likely continue its shift from a focus on "systems of record" to a focus on "systems of engagement." HR tools are now workforce productivity systems—and, if people cannot easily learn to use them, then they will be underused and often unsuccessful. Make sure you test the products with users and ask your vendor to explain its design process to make sure it has a significant investment in the user experience of its products. While vendor support and service are still critical to success, ease of use and ease of adoption by employees—not just HR—are now keys to selecting the highest value HR technology platforms". Theodore Kinni in MIT SMR March 2016 blog on, "What's happening this week at the intersection of management and technology" writes of "Boosting big data ROI - Aggressive adoptions of new technology can be a double-edged sword. Early adopters can get a jump on the competition and capture a lion's share of the rewards... as long as they can successfully integrate it into their companies — a substantial risk given the unknowns that often accompany new technology. Big data is no exception, reports Jacques Bughin, director of McKinsey's Brussels office, in a McKinsey Quarterly article. Bughin bases his conclusions on his firm's latest study of investments in big data among 714 companies of varying sizes, across industries and geographies. Growth in first-time adoption of digital technologies and market growth has been fueled by general economic progress. It revealed that data analytics delivered value-added productivity benefits — especially in competitive intelligence, marketing, and operations and the supply chain — and increased operating profits in the range of 6%. But, warns Bughin, it also revealed investing in the analytics needed to manipulate big data isn't enough. In addition, companies have to invest early — the first movers in the survey captured a full 25% of the rewards of big data. They have to invest in skills as well as technology — 40% of the profit improvement among the companies in the survey came from coordinating investments in tech and the people needed to put it to work. For example, Gartner (2013) states, "Increasing familiarity with the Business Process model (adoption) throughout the enterprise, especially as some lagging functional areas become familiar with the success of BP in other functional areas within their enterprise. There are many challenges when offering services across continental Europe, and they will continue to impede adoption for the forecast period. Challenges include optimizing cost savings in an already weak economy, supporting language requirements, addressing labor law and trade union issues, and countering the absence of labor arbitrage benefits. Therefore, Gartner forecasts Western Europe almost flat, at negative 0.3% in euros (although positive 2.5% in U.S. dollars), resulting in a five-year CAGR of 3.1% in euros (3.6% in U.S. dollars)." And, they have to hire lots of experts — 15% of operating profit increases are linked to building a department staffed with a broad range of data and analytics talent that can be deployed across the organization. "Where big data analytics may create local fiefdoms, online social networks create distributed pockets of autonomous connection, affiliation, and even affection," explains Clemons. The challenge of digital transformation: Pretty much everyone agrees that digitization is an essential ingredient of corporate transformation and success. Wharton's Eric Clemons reminds us that the devil is in the details".

Systems Thinking has its roots in Intelligence - Organizations with dominant systems thinking have possibly made people orientation second to the systemic orientation. The information era brings in the inevitability of systems, data management and systemic approaches to management problem solving. While the 90's saw the systems dominance to make business performance advanced and electronic the 21st century possibly has a modified version of the system story. A situation where system creators no longer turn subservient to what they have created but have actually built adequate flexibility and innovation modules to grab the attention of every individual who is working with the system and see the potential to add value and make a difference to the system. The suggestion may sound preposterous to organizations that have spent millions of dollars to make their data and process systems beyond the tinkering capability of the individual. After all the logical fear could be the unleashing of anarchy with every working individual tampering with the system as they are working. Well, perhaps, it is this or may something significantly more meaningful. Organizations in preparedness of tomorrow, the model organization, as well as those that are right there today have created working the system to manage a corporation of today for tomorrow. Do we as a consequence have adequate checks, balances and flexibility built into a system to make it versatile, high performing and dynamic?

Optimization of Assets – Intellectual Capital Movement - Concepts attempted in this book are an attempt to pull together the developments over historical intervals the Intellectual Capital movement but more importantly to trace the emergence of human capital definitions, measurement tools and techniques. With this as the background the book will establish the need for a comprehensive human capital understanding leading to the discovery of an Intellectual Company.

Boulton et all work related to understanding organizations and classifying their assets into 3 types dealt earlier. **Unique Assets:** No other firm has exactly the same set of knowledge, skills, abilities, innovations, codified knowledge, patents, trade-marks, copy rights and trade secrets. They are unique and difficult to duplicate and may require considerable time & resource to do so. **Differentiable Assets:** includes assets such as manufacturing, distribution which while similar is different in some ways from those of competitors. They differ in size, shape, complexity, production rate and cost structure. Complementary business assets (innovations) are important to knowledge firms for generating & maintaining profits. **Generic Assets:** Includes those not differentiable, such as cash, fixed assets, fixed capital and tangible assets. All of the assets are found in a balance sheet. Significantly Technical know-how, Customer Capital, Human Capital, Non-compete agreements, Goodwill, Brand, Trademark, Patent and of the like formed the heart of their intangibles argument. http://bit.ly/2aslcdS

This book is based on the fact that all assets (tangible & intangible) can be broadly valued by one or more of the valuation techniques (cost, economic value, intellectual differentiators) and the level of subjectivity varies across types of assets being measured as well as the method of valuation being employed. This also included:

- *The new assets are traditionally thought to be intangible and not measurable*
- *The market is rewarding companies based on what type of assets they leverage*
- *Business design reflects how a company assembles tangible and intangible assets*
- *Therefore, a company's asset portfolio is its key determinant of economic success*
- *Companies must adjust their asset portfolios to alter risk and reward*
- *New digital tools are necessary to adjust asset portfolios based on market signals*
- *Emphasis on People & their value significant*
- *Knowledge Economy is weightless*
- *Technology enables value (Intangibles to Dominate)*

Richard Boulton also addressed critical questions: http://bit.ly/29W7DFt & http://bit.ly/2aslcdS

1. Where in the company is its value created?
2. What is a digital business model that impacts value?
3. Does the company create value through its intellectual capital, its differentiable tangible assets, or its generic tangible assets?
4. What portion of the value created does each kind of asset produce?
5. What percentage of the company's resources is allocated to unique assets, differentiated assets or generic assets?
6. What percentage of company's value is a result of its unique assets, differentiated assets or generic assets?
7. How would I like my company to create value?
8. Should my company reallocate the resources it devoted to unique assets, differentiated assets or to generic assets?
9. How does digital value establish customer loyalty?
10. What factors influence employee engagement and culture in a digital enterprise.

Intellectual capital continues to include structural, customer and human capital although there has been an abundance of alternate approaches and additional factors to include in the measurement and understanding of IC. These additional dimensions continue to be researched and new learnings are becoming available.

Sveiby in http://bit.ly/2a9sFPY writes, "Roos et al. (1997) argued that "IC could be allied to other disciplines such as corporate strategy and the construction of measurement tools. But the emphasis continued to be financial and intellectual capital dominated to be measured alongside traditional, quantifiable, financial data (Johanson et al., 1999). A number of modern-day taxonomy of schemes has sophisticated the peculiarity by expressly isolating intellectual capital into the categories of **external (customer-related) capital, internal (structural) capital, and human capital** (Sveiby, 1997; Roos et al., 1997; Stewart, 1997; Edvinsson and Stenfelt, 1999; Edvinsson and Malone, 1997).

Multiplicity of Options for the Intellectual Company - An abundance of new measurement approaches that all have the aim, to a greater or lesser extent, of synthesizing the financial and non-financial value-generating aspects of the company into one external report. Principal among the new reporting models are the intangible asset monitor (Guthrie and Petty, 2000) (Sveiby, 1988; 1997; Celemi, 1998); the balanced scorecard (Kaplan and Norton, 1992; 1996); the Skandia value scheme (Edvinsson and Malone, 1997; Edvinsson, 1997); and the intellectual capital accounts (DATI, 1998). Brennan and Connell (2000) provide an appealing structure for comparing more than a few alternatives. Several of the frameworks have the similar three but expansive classification categories - human, customer and structural capital. However, these classification schemes are presented differently in each of the models. Edvinsson & Malone (1997) provide a number of methods for measuring IC that fall out of Skandia's IC addendum (Skandia, 1994, 1997 etc.). Bontis (1998) uses Likert-type scales to tap into the interrelationships of IC sub-phenomena. Covin and Stivers (1998) use a survey methodology to examine the state of the field in Canada and the US. Bontis, Dragonetti, Jacobsen and Roos (1999) evaluate and contrast the IC framework with VBM (Value Based Management), VR (Value Realization), EVA (economic value added), BSC (balanced score-card) and HRA (human resource accounting)".

An interesting turn in the study of these dimensions pertained to labor productivity and new methods of value realization methods identified by consulting firms – for example, VBM, VR, BSC, EVA, HRA

Intellectual Application - Sveiby in http://bit.ly/2a9sFPY writes, "The first work on application driven **Intellectual Capital** originated in Japan. This was through the work of Hiroyuki Itarni, who studied the effect of invisible assets on the management of Japanese corporations. The second was the Work of a distinct set of economists seeking a different view of the theory of the firm. The economists continued upon their work to seek realization of market determinants and influencers beyond what was physically visible. The economists emphasized the emergence of labour contribution beyond traditional productivity dimensions. The views of these economists (Penrose, Rumelt, Wemerfelt, and others) were coalesced by David Teece of UC Berkeley in a seminal 1986 article on technology commercialization. (Sullivan 2000) Finally, the work of Jac Fitz-enz, Nick Bontis, Andrew Mayo amongst other academic researchers and Karl-Erik Sveiby in Sweden, published originally in Swedish, addressed the human capital element of intellectual capital and, in so doing, provided a rich, diverse and alluring view of the potential for valuing the business venture based upon the education, experience and work level/professional competencies, demonstrated capabilities and knowledge of its employees. Concurrently consulting organizations created their off the desk models on intangible asset valuation, all of which was experienced by the economy through the Dot Com boom and fall. (Andersen 2001) and (Refer- Patrick Sullivan - A brief history of the ICM movement - Patrick H. Sullivan (2000); Value-driven Intellectual Capital; How to convert Intangible Corporate Assets into Market Value" http://www.sveiby.com/articles/icmmovement.htm

Literature review provides us the work done by several researchers in regard to **Intellectual Capital,** and in particular aspects pertaining to financial, structural process, renewal, development and human capital. **Intellectual Company** to our perspective continues to be over and beyond what generic IC measurement approaches have attempted. More importantly each of the authors, researchers have confined their measurement to evaluating a series of ratios that they judgmentally consider as important measures for each of the stated areas, e it structural, process etc.

J. Strategic Assessment of Intellectual Capital Application Base

Innovations in Intellectual Capital dimensions with a specific emphasis on Human Capital included an 8 dimension frameworks, called SAICAB – Strategic Assessment of Intellectual Capital Application Base.

SAICAB Factors - Our serious attempt will be to define critical intellectual measurement factors, demonstrate that these factors comprehensively cover all aspects of an individual in an organizational context, provide a method to value each of the SAICAB eight factors (combination of subjective and objective judgment), combine the scores of the eight factors and define steps for its usage and application. We will then make a case for building an intellectual company with valuable human capital by bringing together a consistent method for valuing/measuring human capital. While our work deals at the individual level we need to take cognizance of the fact that **"Strategic Assessment of Human Capital Application - SAICAB"** is in an organizational context and aligning individual effectiveness measures with that of organizational context is an imperative.

It is here we believe a window is available to conceptually package **Intellectual Company** into concrete and conceptual blocks and derive measures as a subset of each of these blocks. Professional intellect is derived from genetic inheritance at one level but at a substantive level through series of learning and knowledge experiences that demonstrates the value of individuals to the institution. At an organizational fitment or performance evaluation level if we were to estimate individuals we would attempt to

(1) study the certifications, work skills, employability factors and background of the individual from a digital knowledge perspective, a

(2) Seasoning and Mastery demonstrated through summary of work or other related/relevant experience that could be considered as appropriate for a digital position. We would then evaluate if the person brings in an

(3) attitudinal disposition, perhaps, learning capability, and the willingness to learn and apply on the job. Together with this would be our fitment process to evaluate

(4) social Collaboration skills and competencies that the individual possesses or brings to the table as a member of the team//function or the organization. As we move into decision-making levels or specific positions we may consider whether the person is in possession of some

(5) unique capabilities, tech contributions, innovations, original work or in our parlance special intellect. In addition, we would evaluate before decision the

(6) performance track record, analytics, consistencies, relevance, application orientation, metrics measured and achieved,

(7) potential, futuristic variables to grow in the organization and any, assessment capabilities, projections, performance consistency, readiness for additional roles, versatility

(8) Learning, teaching/training, distributing capabilities or training needs fulfilled or that he/she may possess.

As the individual settles down on the job we commence evaluating his/her performance, potential for growth, development of competencies, further inputs in advancing educational qualifications, quality of experience received, application of learning on the job and training and development needs. In effect these eight factors continue to be the fundamental criteria on the basis of which individuals are hired, retained or fired. Surely the summation of the value of these eight factors should provide us a value of the individual. If, of course, we are in a position and with a desire to find ways to measure each of the eight factors and the progress/retreat that the person may experience in each of these eight factors while being on the job.

SAICAB Eight Business Factors (A to H)

A. *Certification Factor – CF*
B. *Seasoning Factor – SF*
C. *Special Intellect Factor – SIF*
D. *Social Factor – SF*
E. *Value Factor – VF*
F. *Digital Competency Factor –DCF*
G. *Leadership Succession Factor – LSF*
H. *Learning Mastery Factor – LF*

SAICAB – Strategic Assessment of Intellectual Capital Application Base integrates individual intellect with that of the organization through eight factors as below:

Eight Organizational Factors

1. ***Knowledge Analytic*** *- Organized pool of Information, data and collected material both physically and mentally*

2. **Domain Experience** - *Process of gaining Knowledge, Competencies and Skill through activities, methods, and processes, in varying environments which has in-built feedback*
3. **Special Intellect** - *Ability to apply the special power of the mind, to create a fundamental pool of information, experience and output*
4. **Distinctive Competency** - *Having the necessary ability, authority, skill and knowledge to behaviorally perform organizational roles or act in situations that warrant successful demonstration of experience*
5. **Digital** - *Process of preparing oneself for effectively executing a (organizational) role*
6. **360 Degree Learning** - *Pool of Information acquired through continuous effort that has no reference point to start or terminate including social.*
7. **Cohort Mentoring** - *The ability to impart a situational advise in order to develop a competency, through examples and practice*
8. **Intellectual Credit Risk** - *An Opportunity cost of Investment in IC or the potential to use the intellect* & **Intellectual Security** - *Securing oneself from obsolescence in a Knowledge economy and use it to advance competitiveness*

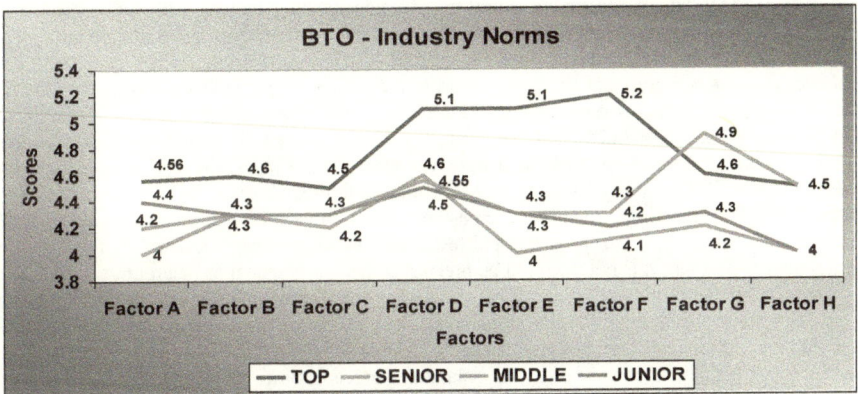

Figure 15 - SAICAB – Establishing Factor Comparisons – Individual Factors with those of the Organization - Building the Organization – Intellectual Company Capital Factors

K. **Digital Business – Four Levels Maturity, Three Levels of Cultural Mindsets, Global Digital Collaboration**

Criticality of Digital Maturity – "Companies can have four levels of digital maturity: high digital and transformation management intensity, low digital and transformation management intensity, or a mix of the two. Companies in the lower left are Digital Beginners. These businesses do very little with advanced digital capabilities, although they may be mature with more traditional applications such as ERP or electronic commerce. Although companies may be Digital Beginners by choice, more often than not they are in this quadrant by accident. They may be unaware of the opportunities, or may be starting some small investments without effective transformation management in place". George Westerman, Didier Bonnet and Andrew McAfee in "The Advantages of Digital Maturity", MIT SMR 2012, further continues…

"The Four Levels of Digital Maturity - Organizations in the top left are Digital Fashionistas. These companies have implemented or experimented with many sexy digital applications. Some of these initiatives may create value, but many do not. While they may look good together, these digital applications are not implemented with the vision of gaining synergies among the items. Digital Fashionistas are motivated to bring on digitally powered change, but their digital transformation strategy is not founded on real knowledge of how to maximize business benefits. Companies lacking enterprise-level governance may find they are in this quadrant at the corporate level, even if digital efforts are more mature in some business units. Companies in the bottom right are Digital Conservatives. They favor prudence over innovation. Digital Conservatives understand the need for a strong unifying vision as well as for governance and corporate culture to ensure investments are managed well. However, they are typically skeptical of the value of new digital trends, sometimes to their detriment. Though aiming to spend wisely, their careful approach may cause them to miss valuable opportunities upon which their more stylish competitors will pounce. Businesses in the top right quadrant are Digirati. They truly understand how to drive value with digital transformation. They combine a transformative vision, careful governance and engagement, with sufficient investment in new opportunities".

Business Model on Maturity - Early on, in understanding maturity, we had indicated that a business model may be used to persuade stakeholders to undertake the transformation, i.e. the business case is used to build a "case for change". This business case will typically be broadly defined, and not be very detailed. It will convey the value of change to the client, with the aim of building support for their commitment to change. The scope of this deliverable depends on the client, the nature of the engagement and the client's potential design. It should include a conceptual framework and high-level estimates of costs and benefits. At this stage, the level of analysis is limited due to the lack of details regarding the design, and has a limited accuracy level. A good business case is guided by the following principles: The business case cannot reflect on precise, validated numbers. The client's business case projects and estimates these numbers forward, guided by sound assumptions. As such, it is not meant to be precise. Instead, it is meant to be accurate within an order of magnitude. Assumptions need to be made that are reasonable, objective and conservative. Optimism, ambition and similar emotions should not influence the assumptions. All assumptions should be reviewed and approved by the client. The benefits need to be defined in terms of the key performance indicators, as defined by the balanced scorecard. Since these measures are defined from strategic objectives, and will ultimately be used to evaluate the success of the project, they are the same measures to be used in the business case.

Maturity Drives Competitive Advantage - "Through vision and engagement, they develop a digital culture that can envision further changes and implement them wisely. By investing (post business model evaluation) and carefully coordinating digital initiatives, they continuously advance their digital competitive advantage. Companies take different paths to digital maturity", say Westerman, Bonnet and McAfee. They continue, "Nike started by developing digital intensity in silos. Then it added elements of transformation management intensity to link the silos and launch new capabilities. Indian paint manufacturer Asian Paints went the other way, creating vision, governance and IT capabilities to become a more unified company. Then it repeatedly built on its capabilities to transform its customer engagement, internal operations and business models. Both companies are reaping huge benefits".

IT Capability Maturity - Transformation teams may add value by helping to translate business requirements into technology design requirements. IT improvement opportunities may involve considering new systems, modifying existing systems, considering new IT governance approaches, or considering alternative sourcing options. The client's goals for these improvement efforts may be focused on IT performance, reliability, and security. In a transformational context, the business performance goals are the ultimate objective, not the technology itself. Information systems contain many specialized components, which must work seamlessly together. To manage project complexity, it is helpful to group related system components. These layers of related components are sometimes called a logical view. An example is the grouping of databases, data definitions, and storage systems as "data layer" or the grouping of screens, formatting, and interface tools as a "presentation layer.". "An IT organization can rely on a framework called the IT Capability Maturity Framework (IT-CMF) to answer these questions. The framework provides a structured and comprehensive set of 32 capabilities linked to the ways in which IT drives value. Individual capabilities are supported by an objective set of criteria to assess or demonstrate maturity and metrics to measure the contribution to business value. These capabilities fall into nine groups that address the different ways that technology drives value to the business". Andrew Arcuri and Richard Helm in BCG Research of July 2015 - "Getting Fit for Transformation - The Importance of a Fit IT Function - Getting Fit for Transformation - The Other Technology Strategy Every IT Leader Needs" write further, "*IT-Enabled Business Innovation:* Value through executing product, service, process, and IT innovations, *Agile IT Architecture:* Value through achieving system flexibility and integration capability to enable efficient business change, *Business and IT Operational Integration:* Value through strong business and IT collaboration, *Business and IT Strategic Alignment:* Value through an integrated business and IT strategy and roadmap, *High-Performance Organization:* Value through an effective and efficient organization to deliver IT services, *Portfolio, Program, and Project Delivery:* Value through well-governed portfolio- prioritization and program-delivery processes, *Service Delivery:* Value through standard, simple services with cost and quality differentiated on the basis of business needs, *Sourcing Management:* Value through a strategic sourcing capability that enables access to scale, efficiency, and market innovation, *Cost Management:* Value through transparent, relevant, and business-oriented forecasting and allocation" form these parameters.

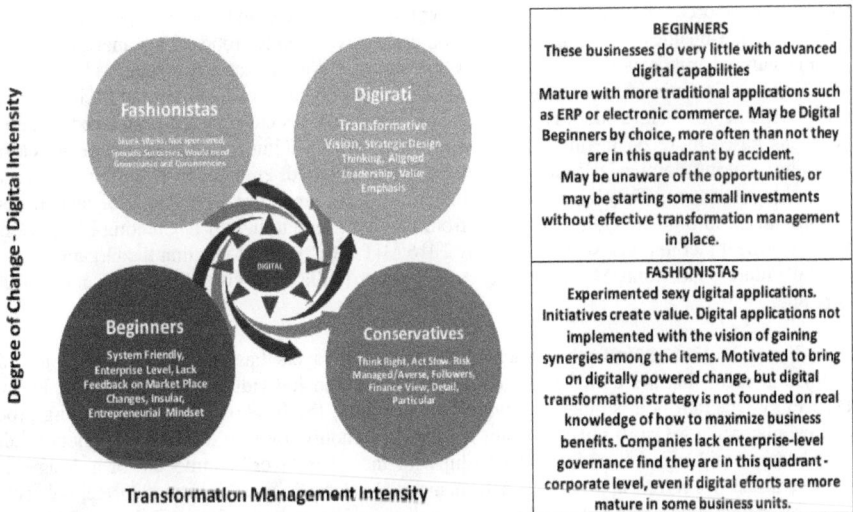

Figure 16 – Advantages of Digital Maturity - George Westerman, Didier Bonnet and Andrew McAfee in "The Advantages of Digital Maturity", MIT SMR 2012.

Three Digital Cultural Mindsets – Building upon the benefits need to be projected and estimated in terms of anticipated performance improvements, as measured by the KPI's, off the baseline values. The latter refers to the "as-is" performance levels. Measurable, but the majority should be. These may often contain some stated benefits that are either un-quantified or intangible. These should be kept to a minimum. The development of a change agenda relies on a number of important inputs. These include the following: The **Key Performance Indicators (KPI's), Measures** as defined by the Balanced Scorecard, are necessary to ensure that the correct business parameters will be measured. These will be strategically aligned, and if they are chosen correctly, a good performance improvement in those measures will help ensure that the project outcome is a success. **Base Values**, attached to each KPI, as is state of change expectation, are necessary to establish the "as-is" performance level. This will serve as a reference point in performance management going forward, and will be the basis on which the benefit of the project, and of the chosen "to-be" design, will be quantified. The **Scope** of the change. Through liaison with the client, consensus needs to be reached on the exact question that the change needs to answer, and on "what success looks like." Much of this requirement will already be addressed in the Project Charter, but it remains important to revisit and help minimize the expectation gap. Different member firm clients want different benefits from a transformation, and one needs to help ensure that the feasibility of reaching the desired outcome is being addressed in the stakeholder analysis in culture building. Furthermore, there needs to be agreement on the various design alternatives to be considered, as well as the assumptions and the variables to be used in modeling the outcomes. Finally, it is important to understand the format in which the client firm wishes to communicate, as it should determine the format in which the business case is presented. The best approach is to refer to the management reports, financials and annual reports, and to ask the client about their preferences. **Data and information** relating to the client business. This is related to the base values, but is a broader set of information that describes the business and its activities. An audited set of financial statements and more current management reports are always a good start, but cast the net much wider to include annual reports, press reports and analyst reports. The inputs may vary in terms of magnitude and complexity, depending on the purpose of the business case, needs to be comprehensively understood. "Our analysis found three distinct cultural mindsets that relate closely to stages of digital maturity. (Refer - Digital Cultural Mindset) The first mindset is common among early-stage digital organizations and is characterized by a low appetite for risk, a hierarchical leadership disrupted structure, work performed in silos, and decisions based more on instinct than on data. Conversely, cultural mindsets that relate closely to digitally maturing companies value experimentation and speed, embrace risk, and create distributed leadership structures. They also foster collaboration and are more likely to use data in decision making. In the middle are cultures en route from the first group to the third. Creating Effective Digital HR is a critical fact in this research". In, July 2016 MIT SMR issue, "Aligning the Organization for its Digital Future", Ge Kane, Doug Palmer, Anh Nguyen Phillips, David Kiron and Natasha Buckley, continue,

"**Three Distinct Mindsets** – Each of these logical layers has specialized design techniques, behavioral focus that are aimed at the configuration of their individual components. For example, a Data Flow Diagram is a popular technique for illustrating the flow of information among processes and people, while a Data Entity Diagram is a tool commonly used by database designers to identify key database tables and their interrelationships for the "data layer" component of a design. Digital designers take a layered approach to help manage the complicity of information technology. Since specific change components may require specialized skills and techniques, it is common to define both an overall approach and then to assign specific "solution layers" to a specialized team. "Digitally maturing companies are constantly cultivating the characteristics mentioned above. Nearly 80% of digitally maturing entities surveyed are actively engaged in initiatives that will bolster risk taking, agility, and collaboration. On the part of their early-stage peers, the number falls to 23%. Developing a digital culture may require significant shifts in corporate behavior, according to Google's Gingras. "If you look at the history of corporate culture, you see that it's about improving efficiency, increasing margins, and eliminating risk," he says. "But none of this works in the world of the Internet, where things change so incredibly fast." As a result, digitally maturing companies surveyed place a strong emphasis on innovation and are over twice as likely to be investing in innovation than are early-stage entities — 87% versus 38%. More than 80% of digitally maturing companies plan to develop new core business lines in the next three to five years in response to digital trends. Only about half of early-stage companies have similar plans. At CVS, for example, innovation and experiments are the pulse of the company. "We invest in innovations with a small 'i,' such as what you can do to improve the customer experience tomorrow, and also in innovations with a capital 'I' that are more transformational," says Tilzer. "We think of the impact of these innovations in three time zones: this year, in one to three years, and then beyond three years."

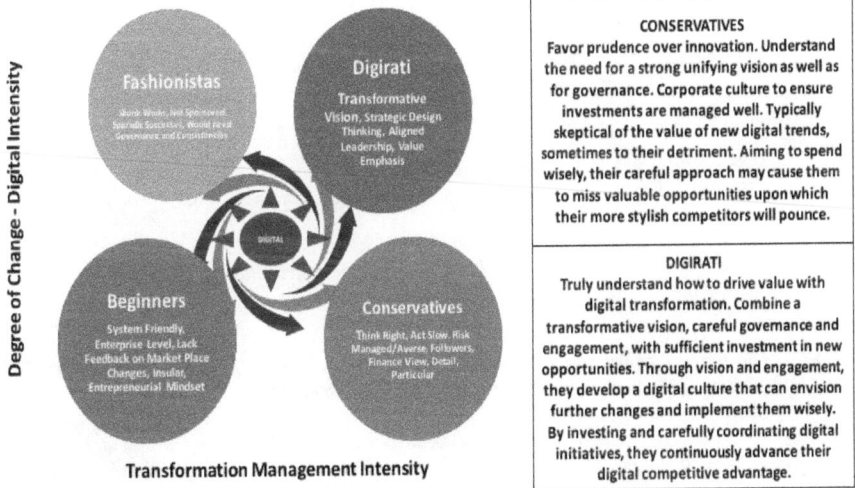

Figure 16 A – Advantages of Digital Maturity - George Westerman, Didier Bonnet and Andrew McAfee in "The Advantages of Digital Maturity", MIT SMR 2012.

Three Stage Big Data Digital Culture – "What we found is that there are six cultural stages, kind of like the five stages of grief, except that this one is a positive one because the higher you go the better shape you are in, say the authors in, "The Big Deal About a Big Data Culture (and Innovation) - 2012 SMR Bruno Aziza (SiSense), interviewed by Renee Boucher Ferguson and discussed the multiple stages of Culture in a Big Data environment. The Cost-Benefit Analysis adds to the big data perspective and is what the business case is all about, from an analytical perspective. This is where the costs of the project are analysed, and where benefits are analysed, categorized and quantified. If a compelling cost-benefit rationale cannot be developed, it is unlikely that any decision-maker will move forward with a project. This is a hurdle that must be breached. The first activity is to start collating all the information and parameters that will be required to develop the CBA worksheet. There are some standards that are met at this stage;

Benchmarking	Compare the current process against external, leading practice process to identify improvement opportunities
Eliminate Bureaucracy	Remove unnecessary tasks and steps that do not add value to the process (e.g., administrative tasks, paperwork)
Eliminate Duplicate Steps	Integrate activities and/or improve collaboration
Process Cycle Time Reduction	Reduce cycle time by streamlining operations
Automation	Automate process steps to improve speed, efficiency, and quality
Standardization and Quality Management	Create standardized process with limited exceptions
Activity Based Costing	Identify and trace all material costs incurred in producing the process outputs (e.g., product, services).
Process Flowcharting	Provide qualitative and quantitative information about the process

- *"The first stage we call **Increased Visibility.** This is when people are looking at data and they're not able to realize what the data is telling them. They see a picture and they say, Well, is this a picture of somebody robbing the bank or somebody that's protecting the safe? They see the context but they don't understand the details. Process improvement begins with the definition of clear objectives and business requirements. For a performance improvement engagement, these objectives should be aligned with the business strategy. There are various drivers for initiating a process improvement opportunity: reducing cycle or processing time; merging multiple processes; creating processes around new technologies; adapting to new regulatory environments; changes to support sourcing options. The client's goals for these improvement efforts may be focused on quality, reliability, or revenue. Any changes to the process may impact the organization, technology, and risk management. The design effort should consider this impact and work closely with the integrated design team to help ensure a proper balance.*

- **The second stage we call Move Beyond Gut Feel.** *It's the ability to understand the data and its details and apply judgment to it in a way that tactically, you're able to react to information faster than anybody else. In these first two stages, the types of problems you're trying to solve are backwards looking analysis. With respect to technology, you're basically building infrastructure so you understand where your data comes from and what happened yesterday. This may require substantive benchmarking. To help validate the design approach or to help identify design alternatives, it is useful to benchmark the current process against other* *locations/functions within the organization or to gather information about similar processes externally. The purpose is to understand what "they" are doing and to use this combined experience and knowledge to help improve the design. Comparing the current process against leading practices is a useful tool for identifying alternatives. Benchmarking provides a way to discover and understand methods that can be applied to your process to help support improvement. Key Activities - Measure the current process and identify quantitative data to describe the current state (e.g., effort, cost, time); Keep the measurement data as simple as possible, with a focus on the KPIs for the design requirements; Gather qualitative data (e.g., process map, high-level descriptions) and similar quantitative metrics on external processes from internal or external sources; Leverage industry standards and the experiences of the engagement team to identify leading practices; Use surveys or feedback through industry organizations; Analyze the differences and identify how the current state may be adapted to achieve the desired results; Develop alternative designs that can be reviewed and approved by the Stakeholders.*

- ***The third stage is Plan for Success*** *and it is essentially saying, here is what success means? Here is what we can say, based on what we know, what we think we should be able to achieve. And that informs our strategy, It's really only when you have that kind of handle on the world, if you will, that you're now able to do the next set of stages. If the primary objective is to change the business to plan for success, then the other areas should adapt as required. In determining the preferred design approach, a number of questions and considerations need to be addressed: What are the organization's strategic goals? What degree of process centralization is desirable? What are the customer's expectations and needs? What outsourcing opportunities exist? Define preliminary process boundaries; Develop a high-level process overview (e.g., flowchart, block diagram); Document operating assumptions; Obtain feedback from end users and management teams; Establish process improvement objectives; Design processes that help support the delivery of corporate strategy and objectives. One goal of process design is to develop a method for performing a series of steps in the most cost-, time-, and quality-effective manner. This section provides some high-level guidance on techniques for achieving these objectives. It is up to the professional to seek additional information or training on the related topics.*

- ***Stage four is Execute on Strategy.*** *So basically we can now align our strategy to our knowledge, our understanding of the world from a complete standpoint, and our ability to adjust based on success or failure on certain actions. Very few companies are at this stage. Generally, the following tips should be considered when applying any of these techniques: Begin with a thorough understanding of the current process in order to obtain qualitative and quantitative information. Clearly document and validate the objectives for the improvement effort, and determine whether the objective is focused on time reduction, cost reduction, quality, or overall improvement. Work closely with subject-matter professionals (SMPs) in the technology, risk/control, and process areas to understand the full impact of the current process and any proposed changes.*

- ***Stage 5 – Power to Compete -*** *Now there are a few more organizations that continue climbing. What happens next is what we call the **Power to Compete, or stage five.** It's only when you have visibility, when you're able to understand your full context and define a strategy that you can execute on, and you understand the levers, that you can truly then stretch your organization to a point where you are able to compete. But when we mean compete, this is not just making deals. We mean compete like taking strategic market share from the market you're* in, or adjacent markets. Bureaucracy is likely to be a big spoiler and would need to be managed. Identify points where bureaucracy is causing unacceptable delays or effort. Bureaucracy may take the form of paperwork, a multi-step approval process, or over-delegation. The engagement team should work to evaluate and minimize all delays, documentation, reviews, and approvals where appropriate. Eliminating bureaucracy requires support from executive leadership. Every step in the process should be justified from a financial, risk/control, and time perspective. Reduce documentation requirements by improving record retention processes (e.g., Does this information already exist somewhere else within the organization?) Is information sent to teams that do not need or use the information? Eliminate unnecessary copies; Are there approval requirements from parties that do not have the authority or necessity to approve the activity? Are there duplicated approval steps? How often is the step rejected? What is the cost of performing the inspection or approval step versus the risk to the organization if it is not performed? Calculate the resource cost of each activity (e.g., HR, facilities, technology, third-party, transportation); What is the cost of performing rework or process failure? Are there unnecessary written requirements (e.g., formal signatures, notary)? Is the step providing a value-added output, or is it being conducted just to support informational purposes? Reduce the length and complexity of memos and other correspondence (e.g., make them more direct, better formatted); Does the step add value to the process? Is the step required by the customer or the organization? Can some of the data be eliminated? Is a data gathering task necessary or valuable to the process?

- **Stage Six** - Process cycle time reduction would be a supportive step. The engagement team should focus on steps with long cycles and those activities that sit on the critical path for the process. The critical path activities are those activities where a delay might impact the entire process (e.g., the following steps cannot be accomplished without completion of the current step). Process flowcharting provides a valuable tool for identifying the "time-delay" steps. The other techniques in this section may also help to reduce cycle time. Measuring improvements in cycle time can help document performance improvement. Consider geographic locations, time differences, and local business customs; Can activity dependencies or sequences be adapted? Create priority processing for critical tasks to reduce unnecessary delays or interruptions. Eliminate unused data; Can a backup process reduce rework or wait time? Identify areas where the sequence of steps have a linear flow and the inputs and outputs of the steps are mutually exclusive. Consider performing these steps in parallel.

- *Stage Seven is achieving a Culture of Performance, which is more of the North Star rather than a place where you end up". The following symptoms may identify an opportunity for design improvements: Client decision making delays effective reaction to market conditions; The organization does not respond innovatively to a changing customer or competitive environment; Changes to business strategy, mergers, acquisitions, or movement into new markets occur; Changes to performance values, goals, or the management system arise; Corporate growth takes place either organically or through mergers and acquisitions; New technology or process reengineering is introduced; Cost reduction, revenue enhancement, or performance improvement exercises; Executive management wishes to increase control and power base. sult of process integration where two similar processes were combined without fully analyzing points for elimination. This process requires an understanding of each of the steps beyond a high-level perception of what a title implies. Even if two steps are named differently, the underlying activities may still be very closely related. Is the same activity being performed at different times by different parties? Combine activities where necessary; Can improved information sharing reduce a duplicated step? Consider using technology to improve collaboration capabilities; Can the order of the tasks be adjusted to eliminate duplicate steps down the line? Is information gathered at one point that can be shared to avoid research at a future step? Is it useful to centralize the process information through a collaboration tool to help ensure that all parties have access?*

Artificial Intelligence and IBM Watson – Automation opportunities should be validated by technology SMPs. Although automation offers opportunities for reducing time and effort, the overall effectiveness of the automation will depend on the accuracy of the information that is input into the system and the ability of the users to analyze the outputs. Automation will not provide a "quick fix" for poorly designed processes. Conduct meetings with technology professionals to identify automation opportunities; Consider automating repetitive operations that may be performed more accurately and quickly through technology assisted means; Identify process steps for which automated operations procedures already exist; Consider implementing the automated steps in a phased approach to allow for proper training to be delivered; Consider running manual steps and automated steps in parallel during a pilot exercise and measure to see if the expected results are achieved. Applications for the Watson's underlying cognitive computing technology are almost endless. Because the device can perform text mining and complex analytics on huge volumes of unstructured data, it can support a search engine or an expert system with capabilities far superior to any previously existing. In May 2016, Baker Hostetler, a century-old Ohio-based law firm, signed a contract for a legal expert system based on Watson to work with its 50-human bankruptcy team. ROSS can mine data from about a billion text documents, analyze the information and provide precise responses to complicated questions in less than three seconds. Natural language processing allows the system to translate legalese to respond to the lawyers' questions. ROSS' creators are adding more legal modules; similar expert systems are transforming medical research.

Speed Breaker - "The exact moment when computers got better than people at human tasks arrived in 2011, according to data scientist Jeremy Howard, at an otherwise inconsequential machine-learning competition in Germany. Contest participants were asked to design an algorithm that could recognize street signs, many of which were a bit blurry or dark. Humans correctly identified them 98.5 percent of the time. At 99.4 percent, the winning algorithm did even better. Or maybe the moment came earlier that year, when IBM's Watson computer defeated the two leading human Jeopardy! players on the planet. Whenever or wherever it was, it's increasingly clear that the comparative advantage of humans over software has been steadily eroding. Machines and their learning-based algorithms have leapt forward in pattern-matching ability and in the nuances of interpreting and communicating complex information. The long-standing debate about computers as complements or substitutes for human labor has been renewed. The matter is more than academic." Some of the categories that are impacted by the machine learning - automation evolutions include, **Economic conditions**: What are the current economic indicators relating to inflation, cost of finance, currency exchange rates, tax rates, trade barriers, development incentives, and so forth. **The industry**: Obtain an understanding of the high-level issues in the client's industry, if that is not already in place. Know what the client's market share is, what the industry growth rate is, who the main competitors are, where the growth is going to come from. An understanding of these will make it easier to detect any miscalculations in the CBA during review. **Life cycle and forecast horizon**: Every CBA has a finite period within which feasibility needs to be established. Two realities are considered here: (1) Every business model or future state option has a finite life-span, after which time the model will no longer be relevant or efficient, having been overtaken by newer models or made redundant by new technologies. (2) Since the CBA relies on projected information, the projections become less reliable as the timeline extends. With cognisance to these two constraints, choose a forecast horizon carefully, and liaise with the client to ensure consensus. **Working Capital**: This estimates cash, inventory and receivables to support the new business model. It is as much an investment as capital expenditure, but normally recovered at a higher rate, should a project be abandoned. **Basic Sales and Cost Forecasts**: These are primary data inputs to the calculation, and should be readily available from the client's financial department for use in the "Case for Change". "Many of the jobs that had once seemed the sole province of humans—including those of pathologists, petroleum geologists, and law clerks—are now being performed by computers. And so it must be asked: can software substitute for the responsibilities of senior managers in their roles at the top of today's biggest corporations? In some activities, particularly when it comes to finding answers to problems, software already surpasses even the best managers. Knowing whether to assert your own expertise or to step out of the way is fast becoming a critical executive skill. Yet senior managers are far from obsolete". In, **Artificial intelligence** meets the C-suite - Rik Kirkland, Jeremy Howard, Erik Brynjolfsson, Andrew McAfee, Jeremy Howard and Anthony Goldbloom in McKinsey Quarterly, round table, continue.

Machine Acceleration - "As **machine learning** progresses at a rapid pace, top executives will be called on to create the innovative new organizational forms needed to crowdsource the far-flung human talent that's coming online around the globe. (Andrew McAfee). Those executives will have to emphasize their creative abilities, their leadership skills, and their strategic thinking. **The First Machine Age** was about power systems and the ability to move large amounts of mass. **The Second Machine Age** is much more about automating and augmenting mental power and cognitive work. Humans were largely complements for the machines of the First Machine Age. In the Second Machine Age, it's not so clear whether humans will be complements or machines will largely substitute for humans; we see examples of both. That potentially has some very different effects on employment, on incomes, on wages, and on the types of companies that are going to be successful (Erik Brynjolfsson). A digital brain can now drive a car down a street and not hit anything or hurt anyone—that's a high-stakes exercise in pattern matching involving lots of different kinds of data and a constantly changing environment. (Andrew McAfee). I don't think this means that everything those leaders do right now becomes irrelevant. I've still never seen a piece of technology that could negotiate effectively. Or motivate and lead a team. Or figure out what's going on in a rich social situation or what motivates people and how you get them to move in the direction you want. These are human abilities. They're going to stick around. But if the people currently running large enterprises think there's nothing about the technology revolution that's going to affect them, I think they would be naïve". In addition to understanding which design element is "dominant" or "primary," it is also important to understand to what extent each element can interact with the others. For example, new processes require that people are trained across new skills, and new technologies may require supporting maintenance and operations processes. It is important to understand the interdependencies between the four elements to allow for changes in the impacted areas.

Targeting Differentiation - But these changes are treated as a transformation intervention. Achieving an integrated design requires a multidisciplinary team. Whenever possible, the transformation leader should build a team with complementary experience and skills across each of the design elements. Following are some key points for leading an effective design team: Involve resources with experience in the client's industry and regulatory environment; Have clear communication and documentation of the business objectives and design requirements; Hold design meetings on a frequent basis to help ensure that the different design areas work together to best achieve the business requirements; Discuss and track changes, issues, and improvement opportunities throughout the design process. "So the role of a senior manager in a deeply data-driven world is going to shift. I think the job is going to be to figure out, "Where do I actually add value and where should I get out of the way and go where the data take me?" That's going to mean a very deep rethinking of the idea of the managerial "gut," or intuition (Andrew McAfee). Top executives get where they are because they are really, really good at what they do. And these executives trust the people around them because they are also good at what they do and because of their domain expertise.

Unfortunately, this now saddles executives with a real difficulty, which is how to become data driven when your entire culture is built, by definition, on domain expertise. Everybody who is a domain expert, everybody who is running an organization or serves on a senior-executive team, really believes in their capability and for good reason—it got them there. But in a sense, you are suffering from survivor bias, right? You got there because you're successful, and you're successful because you got there. You are going to underestimate, fundamentally, the importance of data. The only way to understand data is to look at these data-driven companies like Facebook and Netflix and Amazon and Google and say, "OK, you know, I can see that's a different way of running an organization." It is certainly not the case that domain expertise is suddenly redundant. But data expertise is at least as important and will become exponentially more important. So this is the trick. Data will tell you what's really going on, whereas domain expertise will always bias you toward the status quo, and that makes it very hard to keep up with these disruptions (Anthony Goldbloom)".

Digital Viability - As the focus shifts to option selection and validation, and the viability question of such innovations becomes more focussed and accurate, this data will be obtained from the conceptual and detailed designs. Future Cost of Abandonment: Not all projects are successful, and some organizations are more sophisticated in how they view and evaluate the continue/discontinue decision of projects that run into trouble. In general, it is a good practice to allow for a contingency in the event of a project failure, to allow for assets to be disposed of, and resources to be redeployed. Required Rate of Return / Hurdle Rate: Usually, this will be dictated by the financial department of the client firm. The required Rate of Return is typically the client weighted average cost of capital, plus a risk premium. The latter will be determined by the project's specific risk in relation to the firm's general risk. Sensitivity Testing: Any CBA needs to be equipped to deal with changes in variables. A typical question in a client's mind may be: "What will the impact on the NPV be if the prime lending rate increases by x percent, and our currency weakens by y percent?" At what point does the project become no longer feasible? Hence it is important to have economic and business variable be entered into the CBA worksheet as variables, to allow for sensitivity testing and scenario planning to be done. Mandatory Contingencies: In many instances, a member firm client will have a few unique contingencies that will need to be built into the CBA worksheet. The next step is to help the client to quantify the investment costs of changing. The costs will typically include the once-off cost of transition (travel and expenses, professional fees, hardware, software, and training), as well as the ongoing costs of the client's business activities. This should include all costs incurred by the new business model. It is important to note the year in which the costs will be incurred, and to follow basic accounting principles to distinguish between capital costs and operating costs. The aim here is to establish a realistic monthly budget, projected forward to the forecast horizon.

Digital Intelligence - Once the costs are quantified, in building intelligent networks, products or solutions, the focus shifts to benefit identification, and estimating the value of those benefits. This is a more complex task, and requires greater skill. Benefits may arise mostly from cost reductions or increases in revenue, yet there could be other benefits as well, depending upon the environment, and the scope of the transformation: Less rework and resource waste; Faster billing and collections, and improved cash flow. This may be taken as a one-time benefit or as an ongoing reduction in interest expense; Improved customer retention. Studies have shown that the cost to attract new customers (advertising, sales, etc.) is high; therefore retaining current customers can be a significant benefit; Reduced forms and materials. These savings should be relatively easy to substantiate. Reduced staffing. These savings are typically the most controversial and may require the most extensive analysis. The cost of redeployment or severance may be significant. Improved utilization of equipment or other assets. In some industries, especially capital intensive ones, with a rapid rate of obsolescence, gains made in asset utilization can be a significant benefit. Benefits can be expressed in reduced replacement cost, or reduced capital and maintenance requirements. The following are good principles to follow in the identification and quantification of benefits: Benefits may be quantitative or qualitative, tangible or intangible. Be sure to understand the types of benefits and how they directly relate to the objective of the project; When identifying benefits, try to progress beyond mere cost reduction and cost containment. Most of the broader-scope transformation projects have the ability to create opportunities for revenue growth and margin gains, which have a far greater benefit potential than cost reduction. Once the obvious cost-savings have been dealt with, shift the focus of the project team to identifying the benefits arising from new products, better products, more products, strategic pricing, value selling, revenue management, customer segmentation and targeting, distribution channels, customer acquisition, retention, loyalty and alliances.

"The company's Digital Innovation Lab experiments with technology to pave the way for bold efforts in the future, such as a partnership with IBM Watson to use artificial intelligence to help consumers identify their health risks. But the lab also addresses pain points that customers have today. But innovations such as IBM Watson, the Google self-driving car, and new flexible robots are redrawing the boundaries about what kinds of work can be automated. For instance, computers can now write corporate earnings previews and sports stories. Pharmacy automation has moved from identifying dangerous drug interactions to actually filling pill bottles, improving safety and freeing employees for other tasks" MIT SMR 2015, "Revamping Your Business Through Digital Transformation" George Westerman and Didier Bonnet write, ScriptSynch, for example, is an app that lets customers manage the timing and delivery of prescription refills, while the CVS Express app allows customers to place orders online and have the merchandise brought to their cars. We've already seen the power of specialized AI in the form of IBM's Watson, which trounced the best human players at Jeopardy! and Google DeepMind's AlphaGo, which recently defeated one of the world's top Go players, Lee Sedol, four games to one. While these specialized AIs can't pass a Turing test, they can process and manipulate enormous quantities of data at a rate our biological brains can't match". Typically, a client situation will have a dominant "leverage point" for the performance improvement project; this leverage point is usually the driving reason behind the business change, and it is where design begins, with the other design elements adapting to the changing design element. For example, the growth of Web browser technology helped enable the emergence of online – net – app – virtual banking as a possible new business need. Many financial institutions started the design process by adapting their IT to work with popular Web browsers. As the new technology was tested, business process, risk management, and organizational elements needed to adapt. In this case, an IT change was the initial leverage point, while the changes to other business elements were secondary. Generally, the design process begins with designing the primary leverage element, then adapting the secondary elements, and finally integrating and harmonizing the overall design. This process may be repeated until a working design can be tested and is deemed effective.

"Herein lies the parallel to management: Within the next five years, I expect that forward-thinking organizations will be using specialized AIs to build a complex and comprehensive corporate "knowledge graph. Columbia University's Bernd Schmitt thinks that within 20 years, robots will be doing some of the analytical decision making now done by human managers. He points to the computer IBM Watson, which is already developing the capability for legal and medical analysis. "Frankly, I don't think the job of a manager is more complicated than that of a doctor or a lawyer write, Bernd Schmitt, "Are You Ready for Robot Colleagues? MIT SMR 2016, "Is the convergence between artificial and human intelligence, which once seemed like just a gleam in the eyes of computer scientists and science fiction authors, almost upon us? And if robots become as clever as we are, how will the role of managers change? But just look at IBM Watson. In 2011 it outperformed humans on the TV game show Jeopardy! and today it's doing very, very well with legal documents and with medical diagnoses, and it's outperforming human resource managers. This is a super computer — in this case not a robot in human form, but a system — that can do as well as humans or better. And that's the direction of technological singularity".

Digital Cultural Mindset

Maturity Hierarchy

1. Early Cluster	2. Developing Cluster		3. Maturity Cluster				4. Seasoned			
Digital Factors	**Commencement Behaviors**	1	2	3	4	5	6	7	8	**Desirable Behaviors**
Agility Nimble Skilled	Slow - Deliberative	1		2		3			4	Nimble - Quick to Act
Speed of Response	Uptight Stubborn		1	2			3	4		Appropriate
Risk Appetite Favored	Cautious Careful	1			2	3			4	Bold - Exploratory
Compliance Mindset	Risk Averse		1	2		3		4		Achievement Driven
Decision Making	Instinctive Impulsive		1	2	3		3	4		Analytical Driven
Analytical Fact Finding	Data Driven Analytics			1	2	3			4	Evidence - Knowledge
Leader Structure	Hierarchical Structural	1		2			3		4	Distributed Leveraged
Design Thinking	Fundamental Hypothsis	1			2	3		4		Digital Connections
Passion for Work	Work to Live		1			2	3		4	Live to Work
Values Aligned	Commercial Profitability			1	2		3	4		Ethical Forces
Work Style	Independent - Siloed	1			2	3		4		Collaborative
Competencies	Basic Preliminary	1			2	3	4		4	Mastery Distinctive

Figure 17 – Digital Cultural Mindset - "Modified from "Three distinct cultural mindsets generated by a hierarchical cluster analysis relate closely to the stages of digital maturity"- Gerald C Kane, Doug Palmer, Anh Nguyen Phillips, David Kiron, Natasha Buckley et all, in MIT SMR 2016 in Aligning The Organization For Its Digital Future

Leadership disrupted Ignorance in the Digital World - "Although executives are generally knowledgeable about changes in global competitiveness, many are ignorant about specific markets. For example, an international study by BT Group PLC found that 55% of Western business executives didn't even know that the Indian currency is the rupee". Claudio Fernández-Aráoz in SMR 2007, "Making People Decisions in the New Global Environment", continues, "many executives are likewise unaware about the huge investments in communication technologies in India that, combined with its intellectual capital, make it not only a cheap place to outsource work but also a source of extremely powerful research for the entire world. I recently had the personal experience of outsourcing to India a huge piece of extremely complex research". **Intangible Benefits** - *During the course of brainstorming and evaluating benefits, be aware that the team will probably identify benefits that are quantifiable but cannot be translated into a tangible payback. These may include improving response time to customer inquiries, reducing the number of contacts required to complete a transaction, and improving the timeliness and accuracy of information. If the impact of the improvement is significant for customers or the organization, these quantifiable benefits may be used to augment tangible benefits. Know that intangible benefits that cannot be quantified, such as improved employee morale, will also be found. Document and describe these benefits. Be aware that* *the team should not seek an* exhaustive list of such benefits, but rather should identify those that most closely address the organization's vision and business objectives. In other cases, tangible benefits cannot be estimated. Involve the client sponsor in helping the team to decide what benefits to investigate. The client sponsor can frequently make assumptions about customer retention rates and revenue increases that the team is uncomfortable making. This is an excellent reason to keep the sponsor involved in the design effort on an ongoing basis. Be able to differentiate between a feature of a design and its benefits. A feature can lead to a benefit but isn't one on its own. For example, the fact that a design makes it possible to use only one screen to deal with a call center query, instead of three screens, is a feature of the solution. The associated benefits could be improved productivity, less waiting time, etc.

Global Digital Collaboration - The following are general guidelines to bear in mind throughout the development of a collaborative commercial model: Maintain regular communications with the essential members of the client leadership team and other leading project stakeholders (while current assessments are being conducted), to help ensure they are not caught off guard by last minute, surprise conclusions. "Previews" of this nature prepares these audience members for issues they will face, and can serve as a forum to identify political obstacles or other potential problems before they arise. Development of a business case requires the focus of at least one analytical individual, typically an individual who understands financial analysis and fundamental financial practices and policies. It should be someone who can interpret and understand how performance improvements may translate into benefits and identify resources requirements that translate into costs. This individual should understand the client's financial, historical and business performance, and required financial justification criteria. A financial analyst may help project team members understand "where the money is" from a potential benefits perspective. This person supports other team members, who are performing the specific analytical tasks that translate operational and technical opportunities into quantitative financial benefits. The business case analyst also owns the final business case development, including any required payback calculations. This would mean to, identify all costs associated with the project, even if they are not obvious (e.g. maintenance costs when purchasing new equipment, training costs when hiring new employees, etc.). The client needs to understand and agree on all benefits, because ultimately they will be accountable for delivery of the identified benefit. This is a critical success factor. Projects approved because of expected financial results will be expected to deliver results. The business case is a powerful mobilizing process for any change initiative. It helps to ensure not only identification and agreement to improvement, but that specific individuals "sign up" for the delivery of the benefits associated with the change.

"The project required access to proprietary and public databases as well as careful investigation and judgment about the career histories and backgrounds of thousands of individuals. After describing the work to a few Western colleagues, I asked them for their estimates about the costs of conducting that research in India. The lowest estimate was 200% greater than the actual cost, and the highest estimates were 2,000% greater and upwards! Indeed, many executives in the United States and Western Europe don't realize that sophisticated brains in India are incredibly cheap and productive, providing a fast and economical means of performing work requiring substantial intellectual capabilities" says Claudio Fernández-Aráoz sought feedback from his North American colleagues. As Arun Seth, chairman of BT India, asserts, "Indian businesses have shown remarkable agility and speed at adopting new collaborative tools and technologies quicker, in many cases, then in the U.S. or Europe. Western organizations need to start collaborating in and with BRICA businesses or be left behind."

Social Collaboration Tools - A collaboration tool helps people to collaborate. The purpose of a collaboration tool is to support a group of two or more individuals to accomplish a common goal or objective they have set themselves. Collaboration tools can be either of non-technological nature such as paper, flipchart, post-it notes or whiteboard, purely based on computer systems such as Memex or, which is more common these days, enabled through complex and often web-based collaborative software like Wiki or SharePoint that perfectly integrate in an agile work environment and make us more efficient. Leaders offer team collaboration products that are rated highly by G2 Crowd users and have substantial scale, market share, and global support and service resources. Collaboration tools allow groups to have real-time discussions and to shape an idea or thought together. Trends in terms of collaboration target on helping to maintain the "main idea" within big organizations and make connections visible. Also the idea of bringing people who are not working in a company on a regular basis into the organization and make use of their knowledge. Online collaboration tools are web-based applications that offer basic services such as instant messaging for groups, mechanisms for file sharing and collaborative search engines (CSE) to find information distributed within the system of the organization, community or team. Wiki. Additionally, the functionality is sometimes further expanded by providing for example integrated online calendars, shared online-whiteboards to organize tasks and ideas or internet teleconferencing integrations. "**Leaders include:** Slack, Jabber, Chatter, Facebook at Work, Podio, and Yammer. High Performers provide products that are highly rated by their users, but have not yet achieved the market share and scale of the vendors in the Leader category. **High Performers include:** Wrike, Confluence, HipChat, Paymo, Samepage, Flowdock, Guru, eXo Platform, Jive, Redbooth, iMeet Central (formerly Central Desktop), and Campfire. Contenders have significant Market Presence and resources, but their products have received below average user Satisfaction ratings or have not yet received a sufficient number of reviews to validate their products. **Contenders include:** WebEx Social. Niche products do not have the Market Presence of the Leaders. They may have been rated positively on customer Satisfaction, but have not yet received enough reviews to validate their success. **Niche products include:** VMware Socialcast, IBM Connections, Bitrix24, Zimbra, Zyncro, and BOLSTE". (http://bit.ly/2aOZUK0)

   "**The Kiel Approach to Collaborative Systems**" states that there are three viewpoints of collaboration - **communication, coordination and collaboration.** These categories are often used to structure the variety of collaboration tools available. **Communication collaboration tools** allow to exchange information between individuals. **Coordination tools** are defined as "the deliberate and orderly alignment or adjustment of partners' actions to achieve jointly determined goals". **Collaboration tools** supporting this are the ones who allow you to set up group activities, schedules and deliverables. The variety of available online collaboration tools is overwhelming. Their focus ranges from simple to complex, inexpensive to expensive, locally installed to remotely hosted and from commercial to open source. **For example:** Voicemail, Instant messaging, VoIP / video call, Voice over IP, Time-tracking software, Spreadsheets, Video conferencing, Group Skype, Telepresence, Video on Demand, Teleconference, E-Mail, mailing lists and newsgroups, Email, Group calendar, Online calendar, Workflow management, Hypertext, Shared whiteboards, Whiteboarding, Video communication systems, Chat, Decision support system, Multiplayer game.

   Zoom In Zoom Out - "One of the things that we've ended up focusing heavily on is an approach to strategy that is very prevalent within Silicon Valley and the high-tech community, but very alien to large, traditional companies. It's what they call the "zoom-out/zoom-in approach" to strategy — they focus on two time horizons, and they do it in parallel. One key question is: What is our relevant market or industry going to look like 10 to 20 years from now? And what are the implications for the kind of company we need to become in order to be successful in that market or industry?" In an interview with John Hagel III (Deloitte), Gerald C. (Jerry) Kane an associate professor of information systems at the Carroll School of Management at Boston College and the MIT Sloan Management Review guest editor for the Digital Business Initiative asks in the MIT SMR 2016, continue, "That's the "zoom out" part. They "zoom in" to a totally different time horizon, which is 6 to 12 months. And I give them Bill Gates in the early days of Microsoft as an example of a much higher-level view of the future. His zoom-out, 10- to 20-year view of the computer industry could be summarized in two sentences: One, computing is moving from centralized mainframes out to the desktop. Two, if you want to be a leader in the computer industry, you need to be a leader on the desktop. Not a lot of detail, but enough detail so that when he got a call from IBM one day asking him to develop an operating system for new desktop computers, he took that phone call that day, versus the 10 others that would have been distractions".

Collaborating Roles - Developing role profiles and supporting processes. This technique involves defining roles and responsibilities, including client decisions on the design of key operational elements of the organization (e.g., workflow, job design, support processes, performance measurement). In addition, this technique looks at performance measures, communication channels, and HR policies, including the reward structure. Developing a new reward structure may require the assistance of SMPs. Additional work could begin on defining competencies and resource plans. This is particularly important if there is a need to recruit externally. It may be necessary to outsource areas that are not core competencies, so an understanding of which areas require outsourcing would be needed at this stage. In determining the preferred design approach, a number of questions need to be addressed: How does the current architecture support the current business strategy? What components drive value and competitive advantage (e.g., knowledge management, security, collaboration)? What degree of centralization is desirable? What is the capacity to change the existing architecture, based upon past experiences and management capability? What restrictions are imposed or opportunities available within the tax arenas that may impact the design? What are the customer's expectations and needs? How must the architecture fit into the larger organization (e.g., interfaces to third parties)? What sourcing opportunities exist? Help a client select the appropriate design process for its situation; Help a client communicate requirements to design specialists; Participate in design teams to help integrate process, organization, or risk management considerations within the IT design; Execute specific design techniques through standardized methods (e.g., security, continuity, business systems controls, IS governance, strategy).

Zoom In / Out Questions – "And on that time horizon, the key questions are: What are the two or three business initiatives — no more — that would have the greatest impact in accelerating our movement towards that longer-term destination? Do we have a critical mass of resources against those two or three business initiatives today? And how would we measure success? What are the relevant performance metrics that would tell us whether we are, in fact, accelerating our movement? Those are totally different. The time horizon in traditional companies is the one- to five-year plan. And that's totally irrelevant in the zoom-out/zoom-in. They spend almost no time on one to five years. Isn't it hard to predict the future accurately on the 10- to 20-year timeframe? Some of the pushback I get from executives is, "You're talking about a detailed blueprint 10 to 20 years from now. I have no clue what that looks like!" It's challenging, there's no question about it. I don't want to pretend it's an easy task. I think that part of the art is focusing on what are the fundamental forces that are reshaping the business landscape and taking a high-level view".

L. Business Case for Digital HR in an Intellectual Company

What is the Strategic Business Case for Digital HR? - Why is intellect determining business value realization in a global context? At a simplistic level software organization, consulting, advisory firms, study, new product development, design and generic knowledge based value-adding companies (advertising, financial services, communication, entertainment, education, multi-product conglomerate corporations) are treated as knowledge firms given their role in development of raw data, creation of unknown into known and the utilization of people as the primary state of creators. Knowledge thrives in cultures where intellect and learning is respected. Intellect is found in intelligent companies. Intelligent companies attract intellectual talent. And such talent can only be attracted and retained by organizations that has a culture that supports learning, intellectual contribution and acquisition of knowledge.

A strategic justification for the transformation project will be the differentiator. And this has to be beyond a business case. While the Business Case (we have seen before) is usually argued in terms of: Benefits to the client; Costs to the client; Risks the project will be exposed to. For the strategic case to be sound the benefits will outweigh the costs once the risks have been taken into account. If strategic clarity is wanting, then the project will probably not go ahead. The benefits and costs will in most cases be financial, but there will be cases where these are harder to quantify, most often when it is strategically defined. Vision led transformation are always difficult to quantify. For example, the costs of designing a 'user friendly' application may be easy to quantify (extra development time etc.), but the benefits may be less quantifiable (it is hard to measure if users are able to more effectively use the application). Other Intangible benefits may also be accrued; for example, users may get more pleasure from using the application. The Strategic Model Quantifies the Benefits and Value Added by our services and should create a tangible needs awareness from transformation leaders, while Assessing "The Environment for change", begin business case development model. The benefit is what creates the need and helps identify the problem or improvement to be made, I.e. the change we plan to make need to prove that the change adds quantifiable value and the client only has a need for our service because of the quantifiable benefit received from the change. Under this method, detailed quantifiable data will be collected and input into a discounted cash flow model to determine the net present value of the benefits and costs associated with a client engagement. A Client Value Analysis (benefits strategic models) will be calculated with respect to four dimensions of data. The four types are described below: External: Detailed Shareholder Value and Market Valuation information. Strategic: Actual and projected Revenue Growth and Market Share. Tactical: effect of New Products/Services and Competitive Responses. Operational: Quantifies the implementation of Process Improvements and/or Cost Reductions. The use of Business Case Modeling not only quantifies benefits; it also provides a means to create client awareness of value-added services. It is imperative that we continuously communicate the timing of benefits and results with the client. Use the results of the Business Case to create a Shared Vision of how our services will benefit the client.

Quality- A good quality strategic case deliverable will take into account: A consideration of the benefits to the business over time; A calculation of risks (weighted on impact and probability) which may obstruct the successful completion of the project; Careful consideration of all actual, and potential, costs to the business over time; and Use of the time value of money (e.g. net present value techniques) to ensure the project will deliver positive financial gains in the future.

Completeness - The deliverable is complete when it: Has reached a high level of quality; Has been communicated to, and accepted by, the client (it may form part of a job arrangement letter, or be part of the project proposal); Details the projects objectives, costs, benefits, stakeholders, dependent projects etc.; and It is considered that real value can be generated for both the transformation objective and output goals.

Value - The benefits of delivering to a strategy are: Both parties can be confident that the project will be of benefit; and The risks and costs are understood at an early stage; If the strategy were not delivered then there is a risk that: The project would not benefit transformational journey - The costs would be greater than expected; and Unforeseen risks may disrupt (and hence add cost to) the project.

Important in any strategy is the completion of the value proposition. This outlines the benefits and costs expected throughout and at the end of the project. Most go/no-go decisions will be rooted in the value proposition.

Digital Waves - "**The first wave** was focused on creating the infrastructure of the online world; it was dominated by companies like AOL, Cisco, and Microsoft. The **second wave** was driven by software as a service; it was — and still is — dominated by companies like Google, Uber, Workday and Facebook. **The third wave,** says Case, will be "an era when the term '**Internet-enabled'** will start to sound as ludicrous as the term 'electricity-enabled.'" In this phase, the Internet of Things will become the Internet of Everything". Steve Case in "Surfing the Internet's Next Big Wave", MIT SMR 2016, writes, "How to beat the Ubers of tomorrow: The book that every tech titan eventually gets around to penning has been a long time coming from Steve Case. "I am writing this book today," explains the co-founder of AOL (through which half of the traffic on the Internet once flowed) and the co-architect of its jaw-dropping merger with Time Warner, "because we are living at a pivotal point in history, and I want to offer whatever perspective I can to ensure a bright future." The perspective that Case offers in **The Third Wave** (with a bow to futurist Alvin Toffler) will be particularly interesting to the leaders of large companies that are well-established in their industries. He contends that we are entering a new phase of Internet growth". Strategic Benefits and costs continue to be categorized into several areas including: "Financial; Technical; Strategic; and Environmental". Not all of these can be directly measured in financial terms. However, it is important that each benefit or cost is derived and that a person in the project team or client team is made responsible for the benefit. A secondary benefit may arise from the first. For example, a new system may result in shortened reporting periods that in turn allow for better cash flow. Our project team can only be responsible for the shortened reporting periods. The secondary cash flow benefit is the responsibility of the client and we should not be held responsible. It is not necessary for all benefits to be received during the project's lifetime. Many projects have an expected payback longer than the project's life.

Robots – Here I come - In HBR.org, Michael Schrage points out that once you've got a robot on the job, your job is just beginning. "Brilliant, hard-working machines will require job reviews every bit as much as lazy and toxic humans," says Schrage, a research fellow at MIT Sloan School's Center for Digital Business and author of The Innovator's Hypothesis. "Effective executives understand the productivity and customer loyalty future depends as much on motivating and managing their machines as inspiring their people." So who's going to be held accountable for the actions of, oh, a chatbot named Tay? Let's just say, as Schrage does, "Empowering smart machines to — pun intended — live up to their potential may well become the essential new 21st-century leadership skill." Enhancing knowledge management initiatives: Social intranets, and their ways and means (wikis, blogs, microblogging, tagging, and bookmarking tools, file-sharing, etc.) are powerful enablers of knowledge management. But many large organizations are still struggling to realize their full potential. (For one thing, breaching siloes is easier said than done, as Gillian Tett recently showed in her book, The Silo Effect.)"

Revenue Implications - Once the costs and benefits have been quantified (i.e. this is merged in a worksheet tool, in the format of an Income Statement and Cash Flow Statement projection). The net revenue flow and cash flow implications should be available. In differentiating between Profit and Loss on the one hand, and cash flow on the other, do note the following: Interest on borrowings (e.g. where the transformation was financed) is an expense and, therefore, affects profit, loss, and cash flow. However, the repayment of the capital portion of the loan is not an expense and does not have an effect on profit/loss. It does impact on cash flow. And Tax is only payable when there is a profit situation (this is valid in most countries). However, if there is a loss situation and it changes to a profit situation in later years, cumulative losses are offset against profit until such time as all cumulative losses have been offset. A situation could arise where tax expenses are shown but no tax is actually paid. One of the better ways of evaluating the merit of a design option, or deciding whether to proceed with a design or not, is to calculate the Net Present Value (NPV) of that option. If the NPV is positive, i.e. the present value of positive revenue exceeds the present value of revenue outflows, the option is usually considered to be favourable. When several options are under consideration, a comparative NPV is usually a good basis for consideration. The NPV is calculated as follows: Forecast the cash flows generated over the period of analysis, i.e. the forecast horizon; Determine the Required Rate of Return (also called the hurdle rate) for this project. The financial department of the client firm should be able to provide this. This should reflect both the risk-free cost of capital, and the risk premium specific to the project; Use the hurdle rate to discount the future cash flows of each option; Calculate net present value (NPV) by subtracting the dollar amount of the investment from PV; Choose the option with the greater NPV (provided it is greater than zero). The benefits of using NPV include: You can make better investment decisions using NPV than if you do not use it; The decision (whether or not to implement a recommendation) takes into consideration the opportunity cost of capital (the return available on the open market), as well as the risk of the opportunity. The limitations of NPV include: Sometimes short term payback wins over long term benefits, when it should not. Sometimes the biggest benefits are not quantifiable in financial terms, and hence do not influence the NPV calculation. This can be mitigated by supplementing the NPV with qualitative descriptions of the intangible benefits.

Managing Robots – Continuing further, But Steve Case makes a point for the smart human to Michael Schrage, "Robots need to be managed, too: Won't it be nice to replace all those pesky humans at work? Well, maybe not. Robotics can appear to be a managerial panacea — lower costs, less backtalk, etc. But a couple of timely, new articles point out that they will come with their own set of challenges. In the first, which appeared in Tech Crunch, Dmitry Slepov calls out the current infatuation with robots and reminds us that they've been hard at work doing complex tasks, like semiconductor manufacturing, for decades. The problem, warns Slepov, who is managing director of Tibbo Technology, "[is that] after watching numerous videos showing cool automation in action, it would be easy for you to get the wrong idea about how much effort it takes to automate anything." Then, he proceeds to enumerate the many steps — and expenses — involved in putting robots to work after you buy one. Suffice it to say that the typical employee onboarding process looks like a breeze in comparison".

Asset Appreciation - "**First,** intellectual capital is a firm's only appreciable asset. Most other assets (building, plant, equipment, machinery…) begin to depreciate the day they are acquired. Intellectual capital must grow if a firm is to prosper. A manager's job is to make knowledge productive, to turn intellectual capital into customer value. **Second,** knowledge work is increasing, not decreasing". Dave Ulrich in SMR Winter 1998 http://bit.ly/2apaCWs paper on **"Intellectual Capital = Competence x Commitment"** continues, "James Brian Quinn has observed that the service economy is growing directly in service industries such as retail, investments, information, and food and indirectly in traditional manufacturing industries like autos, durable goods, and equipment. As the service economy grows, the importance of intellectual capital increases. Service generally comes from relationships founded on the competence and commitment of individuals. **Third,** employees with the most intellectual capital have essentially become volunteers, because the best employees are likely to find work opportunities in a number of firms. This does not mean that employees work for free, but that they have choices about where they work and, therefore, essentially volunteer in a particular firm. Volunteers are committed because of their emotional bond to a firm; they are less interested in economic return than in the meaning of their work. Employees with this mind-set can easily leave for another firm. **Fourth,** many managers ignore or depreciate intellectual capital. In the aftermath of downsizing, increased global competition, customers' higher requirements, fewer management layers, increased obligations, and pressures exacted from almost every other modern management practice, employees' work lives have not always changed for the better".

Dave Ulrich continues with this illustration. "In a recent workshop with sixty high-potential managers from a successful global company, we discussed careers. Of these managers (mostly in their thirties and early forties), 50 percent did not think that they would stay with the company long enough to retire, not because of lack of opportunity but because of the enormous stress and high demands. Within this group, 90 percent personally knew someone who had voluntarily left the company in the past six months because of the increased workload. When a group member shared these issues with an executive, he was told that a job at the company was a good one, there were backups for anyone who did not want to work hard, and discussions of work-life balance were not useful for business results". Concludes Ulrich, "**Fifth,** employees with the most intellectual capital are often the least appreciated".

Employee Attitudes to Customer Satisfaction - There is another perspective, the author continues in the SMR research. "Some studies have correlated front-line employees' attitudes to a firm with customers' attitudes to the same firm. For example, our opinion of McDonald's, Sears, or Ford relates to the service we get at the local establishment. At a time when companies are investing millions to train executives to think strategically and act globally, our impressions are likely to come from employees who serve us when we buy food, clothes, or cars. In many firms, these employees are transient and not committed or competent to answer our questions or meet our needs. As a result, the overall image of the organization falls. Sixth, current investments in intellectual capital are misfocused. Under the name "corporate citizenship," many senior executives talk about work-family issues. This seems to imply that after you have done all the real business, then you spend time on employees' citizenship concerns. Intellectual capital is the most important business issue. Douglas Iverster, president and COO of Coca-Cola, said, "People are our defining assets." He added that in leveraging human and intellectual capital, he staked his career on creating a learning culture throughout his company".

Building upon this Competence X Commitment formula our proposition for Intellectual Capital includes the 8 SAICAB factors in addition to its application that includes establishment of a culture in an organizational context led by leaders.

"While many agree that intellectual capital matters, few can explicitly quantify it". Dave Ulrich in SMR Winter 1998   http://bit.ly/2apaCWs paper on **"Intellectual Capital = Competence x Commitment"** asks, "What Is **Intellectual Capital**? This lack of definition leaves the concept relevant, timely, and important —but vague. While there has been research on the concept, I propose a simple, yet measurable and useful definition: **intellectual capital = competence X commitment"**.

"This equation", says Ulrich, "suggests that within a unit, employees' overall competence should rise but that competence alone does not secure intellectual capital. Firms with high competence but low commitment have talented employees who can't get things done. Firms with high commitment but low competence have less talented employees who get things done quickly. Both are dangerous. Intellectual capital requires both competence and commitment. Because the equation multiplies rather than adds, a low score on either competence or commitment significantly reduces overall intellectual capital. Or an employee might document his or her growth in intellectual capital by assessing the increase of knowledge, skill, or ability within a time frame and by evaluating commitment to the organization's goals and purposes. Such personal assessments can be accumulated into a collective assessment of the intellectual capital within a unit". **Thus becoming an Intellectual Company"**.

Leveraging Digital Technologies – *"The business case for Digital technologies for Human Capital Management (HCM) is clear – better employee experience, reduction of manual effort, adoption of leading practices, simplification, employee empowerment, and talent insights. The explosion of cloud based talent management platforms has also meant lower investments in IT assets, and seamless platform upgrades"* writes Bharath Ramakrishnan, a Leader at Tata's Center for Excellence in Digital HCM Solutions.

He continues, *"The attraction with Digital technologies for HCM is that - if designed and implemented well, they enable the following:*

- *Re-imagination of HR processes*
- *Rich user experience across a variety of devices*
- *Automated transaction processing*
- *Obtain feedback and deliver quick actions*
- *Facilitate employee collaboration*
- *Ability to configure platform for leading practices meeting employee aspirations*
- *Instant actionable insights based on role with links to business outcomes*

A number of HR processes are seeing significant changes in practice. While some are a natural progress of re-evaluation of feedback & outcomes (such as moving away from forced ranking based performance management), the majority have been strongly influenced and powered by Digital technology.

Some of the areas where this influence has been far reaching include:

- **Collaboration:** *Enterprise collaboration platforms with forums, knowledge repositories, conversations tools and other features have made team work in global organizations of today more rewarding and result-oriented.*
- **Well-being:** *The fast evolving area of employee well-being allows a holistic approach to health, safety and motivation.*
- **Recognition:** *Social platforms enable instant recognition from a variety of stakeholders. Incorporation of game elements such as points, badges and leader-boards can be energizing for employees.*
- **Social Recruiting:** *Business networking and social platforms are emerging as a key source for recruitment. The trend is getting stronger and the tools for social recruiting are maturing and becoming more capable.*
- **Corporate Social Responsibility:** *Digital platforms are increasingly being adopted for team based community initiatives – a trend expected to get stronger.*
- **Learning Platforms:** *A variety of learning methods which are immersive for employees are now available including social learning, virtual classrooms, video based learning and eLearning. The authoring tools and learning platforms allow for creation of content which is rich and engaging. Collaborative learning includes, Social Learning – Course communities with Blogs, Wikis, uploads, events, chats, polls, Course and Faculty Feedback and Reviews, Mentor based learning and multi-mode learning processes includes Course Management, eLearning, Offline Learning, Mobile Learning, External Learning*
- **Employee Surveys:** *Feedback from employees on a variety of areas can be obtained, analyzed and actioned much quicker today.*
- **Performance Management:** *The transition from term based force ranking systems to continuous feedback is being driven by Digital technologies.*

- **Talent Science:** *Analytics, recommendation engines leverage advances in machine learning and other disciplines for a variety of people predictions such as retention risk, organization capability and others.*

The above is a summary which is only illustrative of the possibilities for re-imaging HR practices.

Cloud HCM platforms today incorporate leading practices, offer a variety of configuration options, and are faster to implement than legacy ERPs. However, HR transformation initiatives require planning, deep domain & technical expertise, creative inputs and careful governance. To draw an analogy – the Cloud HCM platforms are like airplanes which an airline company can procure. The airline company needs to align the purchase to organization vision/strategy, customer segment, interior design, personalization options, routes, service differentiators, customer feedback monitoring and actions. HR transformation initiatives cannot be viewed in isolation – they offer an excellent opportunity to re-imagine and implement simplified & rewarding HR processes.

The nature of work is changing, and both processes and systems need to facilitate that. Some of the changes which workplaces will see include – more diverse & global employee population, new methods of time tracking, wearables providing a variety of data inputs, need for multi-disciplinary teams to collaborate, the rise of robots, employee flexibility, purpose driven work, advances in computing & mobile devices, connected devices, and several other changes. In the emerging workplace of tomorrow, HR teams will play a critical role to enable organizational effectiveness, and HCM platforms as part of the larger Digital ecosystem will play a critical role in building people capability, meeting employee aspirations, building employee engagement, and improving business outcomes. HR transformation needs design thinking, effective communication, dialogue and change management. Leveraging Digital technologies can help HR improve the employee experience, productivity and provide better talent insights. It is however, an excellent opportunity to re-imagine HR practices for competitive advantage. The most successful adopters of Digital technologies for HR have re-imagined their practices to motivate, empower, and unleash the potential of their employees.

The true promise of Digital technologies is the ability to design and implement creative & progressive HR processes".

Digital Aikido - At the neck breaking speed with which the Digital world has re-shaped our reality, the rules of the game have had to evolve at an equal pace in order to keep up with this transformation. Consumers, employees, governments, communities and businesses all seem to have developed a new set of expectation that is deeply influenced by Digitization. The distribution of power, which is primarily the power of information, is more equitably distributed with information being widely and freely accessible to everyone. This phenomenon has thereby shaken the traditional structures of power and control. What really matters now is how this powerhouse of information or data is harnessed, curated and applied to create value. _This is not any different for businesses. The sole purpose of business has and will always be to 'create value'. With this set at its nucleus, how can any organization survive the impact of the disruptive force of digitization engulfing it? Does it adapt and flourish or resist and perish? The answer albeit a no brainer is not an easy one – it's greatly a matter of skill and will, says Armina Kapadia, Head of Strategy at Essar Algoma Steel Canada.

"I reflect on the concept of 'Aikido', a form of martial arts to explain this skill", she continues. "The term AIKI refers to the principle or tactic of blending with an attacker's movements (read as 'digitization') for the purpose of redirecting the momentum of the opponent's attack with minimal effort and in the process protecting it from injury. The principles of AIKI is therefore to understanding *the rhythm and intent of the opponent to find the optimal position and timing to apply a counter-technique.*

Therefore, from a purely literal interpretation, Aikido is the "Way of combining forces" – in this context, the two forces being that of the business and its unique organizational capabilities on one hand and the force of the digital wave on the other hand, which when combined together will become a strategic and unique capability of the business.

This capability can be better explained as digital products, services and customer experiences conducted through digital connections among systems, people, places and things, throughout the value chain of the business. Digital capability should not be confused as the IT strategy or capability of an organization. Implementation of cloud computing, mobile applications, social media, remote sensors etc. are not digital capability. A digital strategy is not a set of isolated projects or automation efforts to introduce technology for certain aspects of the business but it is one that has a defined design and plan of action of integrating the real and virtual worlds with an aim to stay competitive and offer an enhanced product or service to the end-user. The customer is the direct beneficiary of the digital strategy. An example of a digital solution could be the ability to convert data from online sales into individually targeted offers for each customer in order to generate more sales. Unearthing the genome of a digital culture is key in understanding how organizations can adapt and re-build their workplace practices and structures to succeed in the digital age. Let's take a quick peep into some of these key cultural traits.

Aikido Disruptively innovative: *Technologies such as 3D printing, artificial intelligence, advanced robotics, wearables, alternative energy, biotechnology, digital medicine can leave existing systems in a state of shock and want for a timely reaction. This technological renaissance calls to redefine every element of an organisational make-up: its value creation strategy, structure, processes, leadership disrupted styles, skills and of course the overall culture of the future.*

Driven by data: *Data is the foundation of digital transformation. Conversion of information into insights through data analytics has become a strategic discipline that is scalable, offers reliable diagnosis and predictable outcomes. Analytics are being used by businesses to derive intelligence for improving internal efficiency, improving customer service and strengthening the corporate brand. The strategic use of data requires redefined governance models, strong data infrastructures, processes, platforms and skillsets that are able to appreciate and use such analytics to the advantage of business and the community's larger good.*

Customer centricity: *The age of the customer is in full swing. Customers are in control of the information and experience available to them. Similarly, businesses have voluminous data and analytics on customer needs, expectations, buying patterns and behaviours at every single touch point which allows them to tailor their offerings and promote personalisation of products and services. This level of value add signifies a culture of service that is capable of anticipating and reacting to customer needs in real time and to a high level of accuracy.*

Aikido Agility: *Operating and delivering services in real time means suggests that systems are able to innovate around the business moment and offer a solution or service that can be consumed at a given point in time. This level of service is affordable only if it is quick, of high quality and low cost. The Digital system is capable of producing fast insights that capture business moments and situations in order to convert them into revenue and value for the customer.*

Imagine this, Burberry Group Plc, for example, has a vision to build a digital model whereby when you as a customer put on a Burberry coat, the store systems will know you are wearing it, will provide an image of you wearing the coat, and identify other options for color, trim, and even accessories — all while you are still trying on the coat. It will provide information about the coat itself, its manufacturer, and other information such as its pricing. It will feel as if the store is anticipating your needs from the moment you walk in. (See - Agility Matters in the Digital Industrial Economy – Wall Street Journal, June 2014)

Tolerance for mistakes: Experimenting and making iterations is seen as an inevitable part of delivering in a digital era. With the pace at which changes take place, established positions and assumptions do not hold their ground for a long time. Trial and error therefore becomes part and parcel of the investment philosophy for organisations.

Aikido Collaborative: A digital strategy cuts through functions, departments and skillsets to generate holistic and integrated solutions that offer value to customers. To make sense of data a systems thinking is critical. There is need to go beyond the silo mentality and find answers that ensure the untapped potential inherent to the business value chain is maximised and utilized. This requires seamless collaboration across the board to share business knowledge, skills and insights.

Ethics: With the power captive in technology and information, comes responsibility. This responsibility is to ensure data security, privacy, safety, quality, adherence to regulatory aspects and the social impacts of using technology. Digitization also fosters transparency in an organisation as it reveals and provides insights from every part of the business, right from its operations to how revenue is generated and service delivered. Hence the responsibility to use it discretely and judiciously is key to businesses. In, "Social impact of exponential technologies".

Aikido Catalyst for social good: Technological innovations and its accessibility to the masses has blurred the meaning of "have" and "have nots" in the world. Technology transcends borders and boundaries. For example, innovations such as 3D printing can provide for affordable housing and basic amenities to the underprivileged classes.   Similarly, digital medicine can democratize prevention, diagnosis and treatment. It is almost now a caveat that an organisation's success depends on how quickly and painlessly they adopt a digital culture. There is simply no escape from this fact. Digital is the only way to the future. This albeit needs careful and systematic manoeuvring of business expectations, new standards of operations and re-tooling the talent landscape through the most optimal structure, sourcing and engagement strategies for the millennials and deploying a leadership disrupted style that is conducive to building the desired digital culture.

Networks versus hierarchical structures: The need for agility requires responsibility to be closer to the point of decision making. The traditional hierarchal or bureaucratic structures slow down approval processes required for making quick changes and decisions. Millennials would rather prefer to work in teams and communities of mutual interest and passion. Hierarchical or pyramid structures are no longer the best way to organise work and decision flows. Information flows through autonomous and interconnected teams.   Moreover, data is the lifeblood of digital and is accessible to everyone. It lends significant power to make decisions. Hence the concept of self-empowered teams and organisations leads itself to flatter structures where power and authority can be distributed horizontally.

Aikido Engaging the Digital workforce: The digital generation namely the Millennials have grown up with broadband, smartphones, laptops and social media and are therefore wired very differently than their baby boomer counterparts in the workplace. Since this group of talent has it *unique set of career aspirations, attitudes and expectations of work, the strategies needed to engage millennials requires a whole different approach. Below are some characteristics and corresponding engagement strategies for Millennials.*

- *Ambitious: They expect rapid progression, and have an ambition to move quickly. Timely and frequent feedback and encouragement to improve performance and growth is desired.*
- *Development and work/life balance is their first choice benefit. Flexi work structures and focus on career development opportunities are beneficial. With the extensive use of technology means that the line between work and home has become increasingly blurred.*
- *With the inherent sense of freedom and connectedness with networks of like-minded groups, there may be a fragile sense of loyalty to employers. Parting with an employer is not a difficult decision. Hence, engagement and retention strategies are ever so more important for organisations.*
- *Self-confidence: Being immensely confident individuals, they want to believe their work is purposeful and well aligned to a worthwhile mission. Tailored recognition and reward strategies helps restore their sense of confidence.*
- *Socially minded: Their drive to increase social good and work towards philanthropic causes is very pronounced and real.*

The leadership required to drive and support transformation to a digital culture is one that is prepared to challenge traditional ways and receive change with open arms. They are innovative and disruptive, socially conscious and bold. They are change champions, are able to lead multi-generational workforces and diversity in its true sense. Moreover, an extra dose of humility may only serve them useful for times when they need to accept reverse mentoring from the millennial workforce, concludes Armina. Get ready. Set. Go. - "The best way to predict the future is to create it". - Peter Drucker.

M. Point of View - Intellect and Intellectual Capital as the Human Capital is surely the challenge of the new economic enterprises

In effect, it is evident that with over 20 different types of methodologies, many building upon one another, quite a few frameworks have been experimented with, but not quite established in the Intellectual Capital Measurement scenario. Surely the absence of empirical evidence is glaring. And empirical works presented (Example – OECD Conference, Teece, Bontis, et. al) continue to experiment and explore new and innovative methodologies without the possibility of a prescriptive model emerging as a standard or a tool to follow.

While each of the models brings in an element of human capital measure none of them appear to be comprehensive enough to cover the labor potential aspects that HR schools of thought would like to see. For example, the implications on account of learning and training capability, value realized through performance on the job, potential demonstrated through special intellect or unique, research and original thinking, competencies and skill profiles essential to perform a job effectively. Or the traditional HC measures dealing with education, experience and productivity. Just as the resource-based models suggest the need to provide for deprecation to HC factors have also not been comprehensively addressed.

The commercial writers have surely not presented any working measurement model that can be understood and applied with a reasonable sense of clarity and definitiveness, needless to mention they lack empirical validity or the statistical rigor necessary to prove causal relationships.

This is apparent from the ever-increasing literature and application oriented models that are emerging particularly from business consultants and practicing managers who are seeking to establish commonplace causal relationship between intangible assets and market capitalization, albeit for influencing the share market. While literature survey does show significant thinking at the conceptual level, definitions, assumptions, approaches etc, there appears to be little agreement amongst the writers on a defined model for measurement. That there are but a few from the academic world working on IC measurement is strikingly clear. In fact, the need for economists to delve into this area of research is a crying need for the development and progress that is necessary to build upon an important area of the 21st century. That the works of academic researchers have confined their contribution primarily at the conceptual level demonstrates a level of cynicism that perhaps exists at the universities on the commercial concepts that are being deployed to measure IC. In any event human capital measurement tools have been least developed from a valuation perspective, more not so, from a labor understanding and utilization perspective. Essentially questions to be addressed deal with causal relationship between firm performance and intellectual capital, drivers that can influence creation, development, deployment and utilization of IC resources and finally establishing a standard or a benchmark or some indices by which the measurement tends to follow a pattern that is internally consistent, reliable over time and valid to prove an hypothesis in varying situations.

There is a case to bring together learning from multiple fields namely, economics, finance and managerial learning's from management and marketing. It may be wise to focus on the IC movement by dividing the 4 areas, namely, structural, customer, organizational and human capital dimensions into such 4 areas of independent research as against the current trend to combine all four into one combined valuation technique and thereby unable to do justice to any one of them comprehensively.

Finally comes the quality of being an inspiration to others: Is a person a thought leader? The ability to apply a new technology in ways unanticipated is one example of displaying thought leadership.

Intellect and Intellectual Capital as the Human Capital is surely the challenge of the new economic enterprises and has still some way to go.

Richard Petty, James Guthrie in **"Intellectual capital literature review"** writes "Intellectual capital is implicated in recent economic, managerial, technological, and sociological developments in a manner previously unknown and largely unforeseen. Leaving a consideration of methods aside, there is also the issue of what topics are most relevant and interesting to researchers. The best way to delimit the topics is to identify some questions that are open to investigation:

- *What motivates firms to want to measure their intellectual capital? For instance, do firms intend that measuring IC will enable them to predict future performance better? Alternatively, do firms view the measurement of IC as something that will assist them operationally by augmenting decisions related to staffing or supplier or customer relationships? Is it the case that management believes the labor and capital markets will view the company more favorably if it reports on its IC? Perhaps managers simply think that the firm needs to report on its IC in order to be viewed as an innovator rather than a follower.*
- *What are the current, and anticipated, effects of reporting intellectual capital? Is reporting IC likely to favorably impact productivity? Improve efficiency? Deliver external kudos? Enhance corporate spirit? Establish a more relevant corporate identity?*
- *Is generating information on intellectual capital feasible from a cost/benefit perspective?*
- *Within an organization, who is best positioned to measure and manage intellectual capital?*

- *How might current methods of measuring intellectual capital be improved? How feasible is it to develop further the various reporting frameworks for intangible assets that are currently in use such as the IAM (Sveiby, 1997) or the balanced scorecard (Kaplan and Norton, 1992)?*
- *What is the extent of demand for intellectual capital reporting at the market and firm levels?*
- *Is information on intellectual capital transparent, robust, reliable, and verifiable (i.e. auditable and suited to inclusion in external reports)?*
- *In what manner are current gaps in information a barrier to the better internal management of intellectual assets and improved enterprise decision making?*
- *What specific difficulties are associated with the development of an IC reporting system and how might they best be overcome*
- *Where should IC information be presented/reproduced? (Annual report? Press release/promotional material?)" - http://bit.ly/2a8IsOV*

N. SIX Point Charter towards building Digital HR?

Charter 1 - What's your organizational business model. Do you have an Organizational purpose and strategy that binds employees to your vision? Is that vision shared?

Laura Croucher, Country Head of People & Change Practice with KPMG Canada, speaks of the need for leaders to drive inspiration by walking the talk. To her organizational purpose is about leaders who drive a message not only through a powerfully established variety of channels but also those who convey messages that have a strong and consistent story line spread over time, geographies and cultures. For Laura, employees bind, share and perform, when they see an unadulterated environment in which people can engage without the trials and tribulations of justifying their everyday existence. Laura again is a proponent of the freedom ethic. Leaders fail at critical intervals to demonstrate that their chase for revenue targets is built around a strong strategy, supportive processes, performing culture, world class products and services and finally meaningful metrics that would help their people work towards achievement of their vision. For many of Laura's clients her value adding questions have been simple and straight. Have you established a culture of change and performance that can sustain over time enhancing shareholder value? Are your people sufficiently trained, competent and ready to roll out to new engagements as when required? Are you using sufficient big data, analytics to challenge people? For Laura answers to these are but a starting point to build a freedom loving intellectual enterprise.

Charter 2 - Do you have a target operating model that necessitates building an integrated digital Organization?

Leaders who have been mandated to take responsibility for their organizations think of the many things done soon after taking over as the CEO and now to focus on establishing an ethos for people – client - vendor management triangle. Establishing role holders for various hierarchical – demographic levels of the employees and business partners dedicated to various generational segments. Some leaders demonstrate the need to help understand what drives a 22-year-old professional accountant or a consultant to perform and stretch differentiated from that of what inspires a 50-year-old partner (rich and famous) to build world class solutions and client relationships. If money and fame cannot stretch you what else can!

The old adage that one size fits all was the first hurdle this leader dismantled. Her leadership style to lead from the front demonstrated to her direct reports the changed style that appeared to work in a large global consulting world which works fundamentally on the basis of long term client relationships and satisfaction. She set an uncompromising tone at the top. To support diversity overtly, establish integrity in practice, ensure shared values or dynamic connect with smart people lost in projects a 1000 miles away or to share messages of what vision is she aspiring to reach in 5 years' time, every aspect of partnership management and its intricacies that makes the consulting world so complex and challenging was demystified to that lonely intellectual worker.

Charter 3 - Do you have a culture that trusts people and a company that conveys its message of values. mutual respect, knowledge, intellect, competence and collaboration to its people?

"Often you discover that the employees you are slamming are perhaps working more rationally than you are", says, Frances Frei in the Conference Review issue of summer 2010 (Conference Board, Canada). Frei says how, Leaders often deride their employees on how lazy, uncommitted, distracted, risks averse and lacking focus. And the same leader is in trouble when asked why a smart, motivated, well intentioned employee should work against the system. Leaders refer to this as the "need for active engagement" as the Canadian way! People have to be dealt with as complete individuals and have to be managed beyond the contract. He speaks of the need for leaders to not just be well intentioned and passionate but show such overt behaviours consistently in all of their actions. Consultation must be continuous since change itself is continuous. To some leaders, the challenge lies in the leader's courage to bring the devil into the board room and discuss transparently aspects of the culture that facilitates or hinders trust. Tough, they say, trust is not easy to implement unless you believe in it yourself and willing to go the extra mile. They laugh at the joke, Trust in God but for all others bring data! Kris Dunn, VP (People) of DAXKO, a US based technology company, says, ask people to bring documentation where consistent bad behavior breaking trust is evident. In his view human nature exists, and HR pros get to see the downside in employee relations issues that involve anger, ambition, lust, lies etc. Charles Swindoll writes, "Courage is not limited to the battlefield or the Indianapolis 500 or bravely catching a thief in your house. The real tests of courage are much quieter. They are the inner tests, like remaining faithful when nobody's looking, like enduring pain when the room is empty, like standing alone when you're misunderstood."

Charter 4 - Do you offer an inclusive environment that provides absolute and non-negotiable respect for your people? Is each of your business led by leaders who not only bring in passion and intellect but have a generous dose of emotional connect?

As Peter Aceto, and concurred by other leaders says, "Your willingness to show vulnerability, emotion and weakness, yet being human and connected is of course ingratiating to your team. But what are your intentions? This must be crystal clear. If you were undergoing a transformation, if you were asking your teams to push the envelope and take giant leaps of change, would they do it? Why would they believe you? Why would they follow you?"

Hal B. Gregersen, Allen J. Morrison and J. Stewart Black in the 1998 SMR issue, through Developing Leaders for the Global Frontier spoke of the need for navigating through unchartered waters while they adapt and manage an unknown future.

Respect for the individual is also manifested in the form of dignified work. Each employee is entitled to fair, courteous and respectful treatment by his or her supervisors, subordinates and peers." James Krohe, Jr, in the Conference Review, (2010) has a simple rule. "If you love your people let them free. Winning back disengaged employees will require changing the nature of work itself. Leaders who seek compliance as a form of getting things did have consistently proven how terrible a way it is to seek engagement". Dan Pink, author of "A whole new mind" says "management, as we traditionally think of it is a great way to get compliance". Pink, says, "By surrendering many of the decisions about the means of work to the people who do it, new management models promise to liberate the craftsman inside every clerk and thus liberate big business". Down with the bosses - Up with the self-directed intellectual worker.

Charter 5 – Leadership Disrupted - What are your critical culture building questions that you would like answered to help smart, intelligent staff contribute to your corporation?

1. Does your management encourage or discourage innovation and risk taking or do they dominantly display a compliance mindset?
2. What is the price you pay in the organization for failure?
3. And for which your culture should be receptive to new ideas and programs.
4. Are your leaders committed to your effectiveness?
5. This could also mean are your leaders spending adequate time to build individual capabilities to be effective?
6. Are your leaders doing their job to help you realize your value?
7. If you were offered a role to structure your leaders time how different would it be from what it is today?
8. Does it reward employees for coming up with new ideas and challenging old ways of doing things or punish those who challenge established norms and practices?
9. How receptive is your institution towards those who think and act out of box? Perhaps outliers?
10. Do mavericks fit in or do they get pushed out?
11. Is rapid changing in circumstances the norm in your organization or does management vigorously protect the status quo?
12. Does the organization truly value excellence or is the mentality simply "just ship it"?
13. Does management pay attention to the wellbeing of its employees or is it completely focused on task performance and profits?
14. Does a high level of employee participation characterize the culture or does senior management make most decisions?

Charter 6 - Digital HR – How would you build an Agenda for Transformation to help build a Digital Culture?

1. What "organizational capabilities" do you need to build to support your desired growth? Do you believe that you are managing a strategically focused organization?
2. Do you have the right organization and business structure to be able to efficiently market, manufacture and deliver its products (and services) to the target customers?
3. Do you believe that you have a dynamic (open) organizational culture to scan its business environment, understand its dynamic nuances and adapt itself for growth in a continually changing World?
4. Is your leadership concerned at the lack of pace to make change happen given its aggressive growth objectives?
5. Is the organization reaching a state of inertia reflecting in depleting margins, shareholder value and dissipating customer satisfaction or is the organization is gaining greater degree of competitiveness, value realization and profitability and wishes to consolidate?
6. Has the organization over time gained a degree of complexity that makes it difficult for it to be agile, nimble, responsive & sensitive? Does the organization wish to retain simplicity & nimbleness like when it was small?

7. Does your organization have efficient internal processes and systems to effectively market, manufacture and deliver its products (and services) to its customers?
8. Is the leadership concerned with Single view of the truth?
9. Is a large physical asset base a strength or a weakness? Is size and scale a problem or a benefit?
10. Does the company market a bundle of complex product - service offerings, develop complex products, and develop unique processes to meet changing market demands including unique business model processes?
11. Is there a degree of Complexity deeply rooted and embedded in an organization in the way we do things?
12. Is there an absence of cross-functional /cross business/cross segment involvement & requires senior level sponsorship to drive decisions across multiple areas?
13. Has the company stacked new processes, governance models, technologies, and operating principles on top of old?
14. Complexity is a proxy for costs and is it a compounding problem? Have you attempted simplifying processes and the way you get things done? Has technology helped make change happen?
15. Organizations can only do what is within their control– reduce costs, but, lack of technology, KPIs & metrics, a scorecard blocks sustainable cost reduction or value enhancement as it feeds upon itself – Are things within control being done?
16. Are your Headcount optimizations supported by process or system simplification? are you chasing headcount reduction without a strategic end state?
17. Headcount optimization sever informal process ownership, human process integration and reduce the ability to plug gaps - The resulting instability exacerbates complexity, especially when limited resources are left to fix the problem? Do you have a history of such experiences in your company?
18. Companies often define their operating platform in relation to their business strategy, when operating strategies are not aligned with business strategies to define operating requirements, simplification is eluded
19. Do all Systems & Processes talk to one another? Do you have sufficient Analytics to make appropriate business calls?
20. Where do you see the organization, in a few years from now? Do you have a People agenda supported by an empowered HR Leadership disrupted?

O. Study Dynamics

What influences Companies those are most competitively poised for survival, growth & prosperity in the 21st century? The endeavor in this book is to "Study the influence of leadership on cultures in the context of specific organizational models in digital organizations – through a case analysis method to endeavor to correlate the learning for purposeful organizational performance and architecture".

Between 2000 to 2016, in a 15 -year period, we attempted work related experience mapping and a research study organized through formal, secondary, observation and anecdotal research. We selected a set of companies performing business – employee - customer facing roles relating to Management Consulting, Devices, Software, Information Technology, Business Services, BPO, Telecommunications, FMCG, High Tech Manufacturing, Advertising and financial services. The industry segment chosen was to demonstrate the greater relevance of the individual and the quality of mind on the end product and profitability of the corporation. The study meant to seek and identify organizations in preparedness towards the new millennium through its cultural and leadership disrupted influences. The study would attempt to establish a relationship between the leadership disrupted style prevalent in the company and its influence on the culture.

Chapter 3

Cultural Manifestation Patterns

This chapter establishes the fact that cultures form the foundation of an organization in the context of its history, practices, values, beliefs etc. Given that this book is about linking Culture, Leadership disrupted and Organizational Models to understand Digital HR, the chapter focuses on the following:

A. *Identifying a Digital Culture - A company's key to success is in its heart and soul.*

B. *Cultural Differentiators - Key behaviors that make the DNA of an exceptional organization culture*

C. *Retain Core Culture - Challenges for organization during this journey of expansion in terms of retaining its core culture?*

D. *Shape Culture - Often the values of the founder are instilled in the organization and shape its culture going forward.*

E. *Culture is Beyond History Now – It's now a function of talent brought in. A company's culture begins with its founders – what they believe in, what they value and how they work*

F. *Culture is Social - After setting up the core values from inception, how important is it to ensure that the social teams have aligned.*

G. *Digital Values - How can we build the powerful dynamics of a value driven culture that existed more vehemently in the inception stage.*

H. *The Digital Culture Study – Scenarios, Purpose, Goals, Emphasis - culture assessment model (Scenario based case analysis) 8 comparable organizational models, 8 leadership disrupted models providing the Digital Companies 8 alternatives to choose 4 organizational types and 8 alternatives to choose 4 leadership disrupted types. The 16 alternatives would help connect leadership influence on organizational culture in the intellectual company.*

I. *Culture Literature Survey - As we trace history we see substantive work highlights of which are provided below to start with.*

J. *Appreciating Culture in the context of an Intellectual Company - The culture of an organization is an amalgamation of the practices, values and beliefs of the people in an organization.*

K. *Business Case to Study Culture - Why study organizational culture in the context of an Digital Intellectual Company?*

L. *Culture Operates at Various Levels - The Visible Artifacts to the Deeply Rooted Unconscious*

M. *Cultural Influences - How do Cultures manifest and influence patterning?*

N. *Cultural Understanding – Defining*

O. *Schein and Classification of Definitions of Organizational Culture*

P. *Values & Ethics - And the need for Value based Ethical Features of organizational culture can also be articulated together with an understanding of pressures and influences.*

Q. *In which case Why Assess Culture? Fundamentally to close the gap between the real and ideal culture, to explore the possibility of an Intellectual Culture*

R. *Alternate Culture Analysis - To provide a framework for different types of cultures compared to Schein an alternative Culture Analysis. This is to enable us to evaluate and study the varying dimensions and definitions of each of the cultures.*

S. *New Types of Cultures - Some additional and not so conventional Types of Culture have also been covered to provide a perspective*

T. *Intellectual Capital = Competence x Commitment*

Organizations substantially exist. So do cultures. And Leaders. As organizations grow so do cultures. Structures bind them together. Rewards drives behaviors. Yet growth in organization and development of a culture does not mean similarities or incongruent aspects of the culture. As organizations grows so do its people and more particularly so do its leaders. As time passes these leaders in turn begin to influence the organization culture. While it is possible that home grown leaders influence culture in a particular way so do direct mid-level hires who do their own influences. Effectively organizations, structures, behaviors, cultures and leaders co-exist.

Any study would have to necessarily connect the way organizations, cultures and leaders influence one another. Essentially that is the purpose. And the focus is to identify cultures that exist, impact or is desirable in Digital Companies. To identify how does a leader influence culture in the context of specific types of organization and management models? The leader performs his/her role and while doing so is influencing and managing the culture. But is inevitably operating within a defined or a pre-determined organizational type (Structure) – this could be a study focused on a knowledge company, an altruistic Voluntary School, a Knowledge Bureaucracy, a Professional Organization, a Adhocracy or a legendary institution that has passed through tough times. But the assumption here continues to be new age digital institutions.

Businesses that are now digital with a focus on culture, leadership and organizational models, for example ask:

- *Does a digital culture influence organization history, tradition, vision, purpose, values, management style, structure, roles, communication and performance ethic in a digital business context?*
- *Does a Leader drive the organization to help build/alter/change/influence a sustainable culture?*
- *Do Digital HR focus upon in terms of knowledge, skills, attitudes, behaviors, technology?*
- *Does a Leader act when confronted with challenges that pertain to purpose, vision, values, ethics, purpose, relationships and collaboration?*
- *Does a leader deploy people policies, programs, performance measures, rewards and other HR programs?*

And in all of this the **leader is performing to a situation and style** that could vary from being an autocrat to a charismatic professional to that of a bureaucratic manager or simply a technocrat. To this we add the dimension of a culture that is either influencing the leader or is being influenced by the leader and that culture could vary from that of being operator like, engineering oriented. Or the human environment and all of it understood as we see cultural manifestation in what we observe, cognitively, intuitively, consciously or otherwise forms people and their behaviors. Effectively the leader is now operating in a culture that is driven by the type of an organization and is acting in a particular leadership disrupted style as he/she has deemed it appropriate. We are seeing the possibility of an evolving digital culture in digital organization.

This means that, for the purpose of this study, one has to research to a certain degree of depth aspects related to digital institutions, culture, organization, management models and leadership in the context of specific organizations and their leaders. To this, our attempt in providing linkages between the multiple culture related factors and should as well prove certain types of hypothesis detailing certain assumptions on how does the leader influence culture in the context of a management model.

A. Identifying a Digital Culture - A company's key to success is in its heart and soul.

New World - "Everybody in the world is thinking about the next 10 percent. How do you think about a 10x improvement in an industry? Our role is how do you apply a technology to that—to fundamentally transform that industry? Think about the implications to this. If you are successful, there's no competition, because you're creating something that has never been created before. You've got an opportunity to really define a market. Second, it really inspires people to think big about the aspirations of the company and how they could do something that really does change the overall trajectory of an industry. And third, you get the best people who want to solve the biggest, toughest problems in the world. And so, by nature, people want to start to work on those problems, and even if there's just a halo effect of working at Google, that's a real benefit for us". But next steps are possible only if there is an acceptance of problems and issues in the current environment. There can be many reasons for inefficient and ineffective processes. Barriers between functions may cause managers to limit their activities to their own "silo." "Inadequate systems support may slow down service delivery. Unclear accountabilities make it difficult to see where or how to start a change effort. And finally, since the AS IS function has not traditionally been a well-measured function, tracking (and therefore improving) customer satisfaction and process performance has been based on anecdotal evidence at best. A comprehensive process redesign can be a powerful enabler of the function as it addresses the many pressures for change within the organization: strategic pressures – globalization; mergers and acquisitions; cost reduction; building organizational capabilities; misalignment of strategy, technology, process, and organization; organizational pressures – unclear roles/responsibilities, increased need for communication and/or flexibility; process pressures – redundant activities, high costs, fragmented functions, no documentation; and technology pressures – inadequate/inappropriate systems, too many manual processes". In an interview conducted with Jon Kaplan, vice president of US sales and operations at Google by Barr Seitz published in the McKinsey Quarterly, continues, "there are product managers who can create amazing, incredible products. An example of this is our contact-lens project, Iris, which applies technology to the contact lens—the contact lens is connected to the Internet and it monitors your glucose. We were able to launch this as a product and then, in partnership with our business organization, struck a deal with Novartis to license it. That's a great example for somebody who has a very tangible product. I think it's now permeated the entire organization to say, "What does a 10x relationship change with our clients look like?" On How Google supports its culture, Jon Kaplan states, "We are, as you could imagine, highly analytical about our culture. One of the key ways that we measure how Google is changing over time is called Googlegeist, which is our internal survey that we give to all of our employees once a year, in January. It covers every aspect of what a great culture would include: innovation and autonomy, forward thinking, teamwork. All the things that are important to the DNA of the culture. This is a very comprehensive study. We look at this and analyze it every single year, and then we actually take every piece of feedback—the big buckets of feedback, where we need to improve—and, over the course of the rest of the year, all of our programs are designed to address the areas of our Googlegeist feedback that have not performed very well".

Thinking Digital - Values – Some Characteristics

- *We live our life just one way; Just as we were ordained to behave; the right way! In doing what is right or wrong, organizations, leaders, structures or processes do not exercise a choice, just excuses.*
- *Promoters owe more than what they think to the communities in which they serve*
- *Organizations are products of its leaders*

- *Culture is not just about past; it is also about every-day living as they impact tomorrow's history*
- *Organizational leaders determine what their customers would receive as a product or a service*
- *Ethics is not a matter of choice – Not an option, it is an obligation*
- *Compliance is not about rule of law; it is about the way things should get done in a civilized society*
- *Courage is not limited to the battlefield or an argument won or putting down someone because you have a majority vote or bravely catching a thief in your house. The real tests of courage are much quieter. They are the inner tests. That which only you know.*
- *Values are about remaining faithful when nobody's looking, like not falling for the mighty and powerful, like not showing off what you are not, like not preaching what you don't practice, like restraining your temptation to fall in line, like enduring pain when the room is empty, like standing alone when you're misunderstood."*
- *It's the curse of old people (leaders who over stay their need) that they realize that they control nothing.*
- *When we are wrong and surrender, we are honest; When we are in doubt and surrender, we are wise; But when we are right and surrender, we value relations.*
- *In a court of law, it's not good enough to know that you have committed a crime. We have to prove it.*
- *Absence of evidence is not the evidence of absence.*

Things Change – For strategic thinkers like Kaplan, when a company starts, its core strength is a group of 4-5 executives who are ready to give in their best and pave the future of the company. These leaders bring together all the elements that can hold an organization together. They are committed, aligned and are seeking to do things as one team. They create a sense of belongingness, a feeling of oneness within the company that binds everyone together like a family, and are willing to live through joys and struggles of a family. Eventually, these individuals lay the foundation of a culture, values, beliefs, norms, attitudes, do's and don'ts, that the company becomes synonymous with. Their personal and professional value system – heart - becomes reflective of the organization's value system. However, as the company grows, new people come in and with them, they bring new outlook. This leads to the creation of a diluted – altered culture as a result of an amalgamation of values, of people history stories, rituals, actions towards staff, customers, vendors, that seep in to the organization with time. This diluted – altered culture becomes a collection of values which determines the evolution of the organization in the long run. The emotional connect at this stage becomes tough to retain as individual growth and ambition finds place. There is an example of a Big 4 consulting firm who would conduct an evaluation of their vendors every 3 months and would do a select and deselect process every few months. This institution has never been known to build an honest relationship with their vendors. For digital organizations vendors are as much a part of their eco system that helps them to succeed as any other internal full time or contractual staff.

Family is the Soul - Take the example of the joint family system which once brimmed of happiness and chatter, it has lost much of its glory owing to technological advancement, changing gender roles and better employment opportunities, which compel people to move out from the comfort of their homes. One cannot help reminiscing of those days, when everyone was connected through shared values leading to a harmonious co-existence. However, much of it is lost as terms like tolerance; adjustment and compromise have all been refined.

B. Cultural Differentiators - 5 key behaviors that make the DNA of an exceptional organization culture? Do you think these key elements are easier to witness in a smaller set up (company during inception stage)?

- *Respect & Dignity for the Individual, Diversity & alignment with values.*
- *Transmit Fun & Joy at the Place to Work.*
- *Competent Leaders lead from the Front aligning people to his/her vision & strategy*
- *Extraordinary desire & practice to do the right thing - Honest, upright work place*
- *Provides people space to contribute – A canvas to paint*

Social Work Place - The best of work places do not have rules. They only have a vision; for themselves and for their companies! They practice that vision by believing, trusting, enabling & doing. This is where things happen because people act on what they believe is right, and perform together out of alignment. It is aligned when people tell you stories about their company, its people that can be quoted & show excitement at any news about their company. They would introduce their company to people they care for & known as their own. They would have friends at work who go beyond work. These people take their company home every day, not just work. After all people seek identity, pride & belonging wherever they may be & whatever they may be doing. Work environments in which people have dignity, beliefs, and those that binds people to a common cause, in whatever profit motive context may it be, there is only an environment of joy, not rules. You are ruling!

"The companies that survive longest are the ones that work out what they uniquely can give to the world—not just growth or money but their excellence, their respect for others, or their ability to make people happy. Some call those things a soul". - Charles Handy

Social is for Real - There is a strong line of research in goal theory, for example, supporting the role of objective-setting, a key element of most performance-pay schemes, as a powerful motivator in its own right. Clear, participative objective-setting has been shown to correlate with improved motivation and performance in situations as diverse as Canadian forests and London building sites. Goal setting helps to direct attention, mobilize effort and increase persistence and a number of research studies, such as French and Marsden's, demonstrate how performance-related pay can be associated with improved goal setting. Who is to say whether a pay scheme influences effort and behavior because of the money on offer, or because of the objectives and target achievements which have to be satisfied? "Enduring Pro-Social Management Models", Goal-framing theory provides a useful new way of looking at the challenges companies face in aligning behavior around goals". Julian Birkinshaw, Nicolai J. Foss and Siegwart Lindenberg in "Combining Purpose with Profits", MIT, SMR 2014, continues, our research found many companies with a clear sense of purpose, typically expressed as a set of pro-social goals such as putting employees first or investing in local communities. But, in the majority of cases, there was no discernible impact on the way employees actually behaved. Sometimes the pro-social goal was just a set of words — in effect, a veneer on top of a gain-driven company". This overlap of motivational and other contextual variables also makes effective research studies very difficult to conduct, particularly in respect of individual performance pay schemes.

"Sometimes the pro-social goal had been genuine at some point in the company's history, but over time, its meaning atrophied as other goals became more salient (Birkinshaw, Foss and Lindenberg). However, we also found a small number of highly successful companies whose pro-social goals seemed genuine. It is surely no coincidence that the research on team and collective reward schemes, is generally more positive than for individual schemes, when the results of these schemes, for example in a gainsharing plan, where the payment directly relates to the value of gain to the organization, are much easier to measure.In talking to employees at multiple levels and in looking at the way they behaved and the things they valued, we could see evidence that these companies' pro-social goals were influencing employee motivation and behavior" - http://bit.ly/29VNuf0 . Financial rewards alone cannot extract those employee behaviors that really add value, which create the mindset required for an employee to voluntarily commit to fully contribute to competitive success.

C. Retain Core Culture - What are some of the challenges for organization during this journey of expansion in terms of retaining its core culture? Do you think often times these key elements which held the company together tends to get diluted eventually as the company grows?

- *Change in Leadership, Organizational &/or Business Model impacts culture.*
- *Economic downturn impacts culture & sometimes sub cultures are formed. (New Coalitions, Power Centers, Political Regrouping, Risk Aversion).*
- *Mindless expansion without much thought on quality of process, people, technology & organization. (Losing consistency in quality, inculcation of poor practices, High Performance Arrogance, Living for the Day)*
- *Breakdown in Communication in old fashioned hierarchy conscious organizations – People depend & communicate only on the basis of old boys' network, batch mates, frat clubs, cohorts, self-interest, corrupt practices*
- *Inability to become a Global Enterprise despite global presence*

Retain what is real - Every organization has its own unique culture even though they may not have consciously tried to create it. Rather it will have been probably created unconsciously, based on the values of the top management or the founders or core people who build and/or direct that organization. Over time individuals (particularly the organization's leaders) attempt to change the culture of their organizations to fit their own preferences or changing marketplace conditions. This culture then influences the decision-making processes, it affects styles of management and what everyone determines as success. When an organization is created it becomes its own world and its culture becomes the foundation on which the organization will exist in the world. People's actions in organizations are not always 'their own' but are largely influenced by the socialization processes of the specific culture to which they belong.

Shared Vision for Real - One of the key problems specific to team bonus schemes is the 'social loafing' or 'free rider' phenomenon, of recalcitrant individuals earning bonus through the efforts of their higher performing and harder working colleagues. "When asked about different aspects of their transitions, executives rank business-related activities among the most important to the transition's overall outcome. The largest share say it was very or extremely important to create a shared vision and alignment around their strategic direction across the organization". McKinsey Consultants, Hortense de la Boutetiere, Carolyn Dewar and specialist Rajiv Chandran in McKinsey Quarterly, continue, "creating a shared vision on business priorities continues to be critical. This is also among the most difficult aspects to carry out: just 30 percent of all respondents (and 39 percent of those reporting successful transitions) say it was easy to create a shared vision in their new role. Indeed, executives reporting the most successful transitions stand out from the rest in how they built buy-in and communicated a vision to their teams and their organizations. These respondents are nearly twice as likely as others to say their organizations understood their initial priorities well—and were much more effective at communicating which initiatives would not continue, given those priorities. The most successful executives also say that 69 percent of their direct reports actively supported their initial strategic directions, compared with 60 percent of direct reports for their peers." But this is not without its share of problems. Studies have shown that the traditional job-for-life contract has been broken by economic and social forces. There is considerable debate as to the effects of this breakdown. Some see it as having a disastrous effect on employee morale, trust and commitment. Writers cite countless studies showing that staff regard money very much as a secondary motivator, and that the use of money as an incentive to perform actually weakens the more important intrinsic motivators such as responsibility, work interest and social belonging.

D. Shape Culture - Often the values of the founder are instilled in the organization and shape its culture going forward. How can an organization retain a distinctive personality in times ahead?

- *Distinguish Ownership (Promoters, Family, Friends,* Professional) & Management (Leaders who lead the operations of the enterprise)
- *Organizational stories, rituals, sagas, form the best connecting pin to retain inherited cultures*
- *Sufficient* use of digital connections – Social Media usage, blogs. Devices, mobility, analytics, networks, wearables, AI, cloud, collaboration, Email, Newsletters, Town Halls, Events
- *Choose leadership that is aligned to the culture of the enterprise*
- *Demonstrate linkage* to individual & organizational values
- *Show consistency in actions – Inconsistency is NOT the hallmark of enlightened leadership!*
- *Link Performance & Rewards/Reprimand in a way that reinforces appropriate behaviors*
- *Respecting the law of the land – Not with* a compliance mindset but with a desire to do the right thing.
- *Establish a formalized process for Succession*
- *Build Corporate Governance into the DNA of the enterprise.*

Reshape History - People of varying backgrounds often have different belief and value systems which give rise to dissimilar attitudes. Beliefs and values form a basis of attitudes towards technology. Therefore, varying backgrounds and belief systems contribute to an individual's attitude towards a technology. Belief systems also contribute to attitudes towards innovation adoption rate. In, "Finding the speed to innovate", Satty Bhens, Ling Lau and Shahar Markovitch in their McKinsey Quarterly, state, "Be clear about the change, and set high aspirations - Senior leaders should create a compelling vision of where the organization needs to go, provide resources for a change program, lay out a road map, and put in place clear measures of success. A change program should articulate a new operating model for how teams work together, including who has decision rights and what process checks are needed. A road map should include the assignment of people with specific responsibilities, a plan for building capabilities, and the identification and sequencing of architecture and tool changes. Goals should be bold but specific—for instance, reducing time to market from months to days, or rolling out releases in seconds, not hours. One logistics company set a high bar—to transform its entire technology delivery process within a year—and communicated it widely".

E. Culture is Beyond History Now - A company's culture begins with its founders – what they believe in, what they value and how they work. Is it also when these individuals leave behind their past and work together to create something new, try new approaches to culture. As the company matures and expands, how important is it for leaders to reflect on their core values time and again?

- *Founders Values forms the core of the corporate values*
- *Founders management style influences other members of the pyramid*

- *Organizational cultures initially are created by the founders of organizations and subsequently are maintained by the founders' chosen leaders.*
- *Founders form organizations based on personal beliefs about how to interact with the environment and about the natures of reality, people, activities, and relationships.*
- *They make presumptions about what should or should not be, what works or does not work, and what constitutes appropriate or inappropriate organizational activity.*
- *More difficult for founders to leave behind their past and sometimes are the cause for the downfall of the enterprise*
- *Over time, shared realities evolve into consensually validated organizational cultures that become the "correct" ways of solving organizational problems related to survival and adaptation to the external environment and to integration of the internal processes required to ensure survival and adaptation.*
- *Best of founder oriented organizations have an old fashioned character – These organizations are jargon free, have no quick fix techniques being deployed, have no surveys to tell them about employee engagement and do things in a thought through, as if it is in a pre-ordained way.*
- *They act on issues after substantive deliberation. Their people know that too. It takes time in this organization, but when done, it is done well.*
- *They make distinctive difference between theory & practice, they reflect on risks, cost & consequences; they belabor & agonize over impact of their decisions on values, culture, long term implications.*
- *Their outlook towards future is about holding on to a strong present, preparing for a stable future and building a foundation that holds on a many do's and many don'ts in behaviors.*
- *People in such companies feel that they are led by responsible leaders and in whose hands their life is safe!*

F. Culture is Social - *After setting up the core values from inception, how important is it to ensure that the social team you have in place not only buys into the core values of the company, but ideally can provide their further enhancements of ideas and values to the evolution of your early culture?*

Social Trust - Where there is trust, involvement and a commitment to fairness, the social schemes work. In companies where employees feel they lack a sense of belong as a team and are not treated with respect, or where, what they think and feel is quite inconsequential, you know that the place has a distinctive stench. Chilled out work places, thrive on trust, team spirit and have people who stand by what they consider as a commitment to one another. These are environments where, whether at an individual, group or at an Institutional Corporate level, if a commitment has been made then it is expected that they are honored. No matter what may be in store in an unknown future? Do you remember an industrialist who recently said, "A promise is a promise that I/we had/have made to my customer, and I will do it". Culture in organizational terms is broadly the social/behavioral manifestation and experiencing of a whole range of issues such as:

Team working is best influenced by:

- *the way work is organized and experienced*
- *how authority exercised and distributed*
- *how people are and feel rewarded, organized and controlled*
- *the values and work orientation of staff*

- *the degree of formalization, standardization and control through systems there is/should be*
- *the value placed on planning, analysis, logic, fairness*
- *how much initiative, risk-taking, scope for individuality and expression is given*
- *rules and expectations about such things as informality in interpersonal relations, dress, personal eccentricity*
- *differential status*
- *emphasis given to rules, procedures, specifications of performance and results, team or individual working*

G. ***Digital Values - How can we build the powerful dynamics of a value driven culture that existed more vehemently in the inception stage (Sense of belongingness, spirit of togetherness, of oneness, family camaraderie, ownership, personality/person driven culture) in a larger set up? Do you think many of these elements tend to erode as the company grows in size over the years?***

- **Conservative Values**
  - o Conservative traditional values are an individual's values that believe in following **'rules' or Conservative ways** of doing things. It is the value of adhering and **upholding old practices and society norms** in high esteem.
- **Structural Values**
  - o When an individual would act according to recognized roles, duties & responsibilities, that individual is said to be high on his **hierarchal** values. He/she believes in differentiation and divisions based on some criteria and demonstrate **respect for the chair and authority.**
- **Influencing Power values**
  - o Influencing values are those in which an individual desire to **gain personal Influencing, authority & status** and has the capability to assert himself. The individual wants the ability or capacity to perform or act effectively and has the ability or authority to do so.
- **Commercialized Materialistic Values**
  - o Commercialized values pertain to achieving agreed goals & completing practical tasks. The theory or attitude is that **physical well-being and worldly possessions constitute the greatest good** and highest value in life. The individual tends to have a great or excessive regard for **worldly concerns.**
- **Performance Meritocratic Values**
  - o Performance values encompass **building 'expert' status & extensive technical competence.** A system in which advancement is based on individual ability or achievement and focuses on **quality, perfection, excellence, driving for high value with hard working disposition**
- **Environment Community Values**
  - o Environment values are values that aid in **bettering social contacts, improving team membership** and getting on well with others. It involves the **attitudes and proclivity** towards the people, the nation, **different cultural groups, ethnic groups, occupational groups, and social units**
- **Self-Sustaining Values**
  - o Self-Sustaining values constitute **acting independently, taking risks** and showing constant initiative. The values of individuals to **organize, operate, and assume the risk** for a business venture and profits.

- **Welfare Values**
  - o Welfare values refer to the values of **putting the needs of others first** and behaving ethically. The individuals value of being **Welfare able, cooperative, contributive, benevolent and serendipitous.**
- **Eliciting Digital Values**
  - *Definitely lead from the front. There is no confusion on who calls the shots*
  - *A power-orientated culture and characterized by a strong emphasis on hierarchy and orientation to the person*
  - *An additional degree of dependence of hierarchies or the lack of it – degree of freedoms is driven by individual orientation rather than a formal process*
  - *This is generally a family type environment headed by a leader who is regarded as a caring parent and one who knows what is best for all*
  - *In this culture, people not only respect the individuals who are in charge but look to them for both guidance and approval as well*
  - *These cultures are also characterized by traditions, rituals, dogmas, customs, and associations that bind together the personnel and makes it difficult for outsiders to become members*
  - *Other characteristic of the family culture includes the emphasis given to intuitive rather than rational knowledge*
  - *Tend to respect competence more than other forms of enterprises. Families understand the value of how competent people help them increase their shareholder value*
  - *Development of people is more important than their deployment or use, and personal knowledge of others is more important than empirical knowledge*
  - *In addition, people in cultures tend to be motivated more by praise and appreciation, proximity to the owners, power & social recognition in the community than by money*

H. The Digital Study

The sample and subsequent study intently evaluated several companies from the sectors as defined in, namely Professional Services Firms, Information technology, high tech manufacturing companies, FMCG, Telecommunications, Management Consulting, Advertising, financial services. The target profile would consist of CEO's, select top management cadre and HR Managers. Given the inherent difficulty in obtaining time and commitment of CEO's and their top management of high performing/visible companies an appropriate data collection technique was used as the study progresses. It was decided that corrective actions would be taken on an on-going basis to exhaustively collect data.

Accordingly, the study evaluated several companies consisting of financial services, new product organizations, FMCG, management consulting and information technology. We used a culture assessment model (Scenario based case analysis) as a backdrop to the study model outlined below. 8 comparable organizational models and 8 leadership disrupted models providing the digital companies 8 alternatives to choose 4 organizational types and 8 alternatives to choose 4 leadership disrupted types were also finalized. The 16 alternatives helped connect leadership influence on organizational culture in the intellectual company. Various scenarios were structured to identify dominant characteristics in organizational and management models, culture and leadership as it influences each other.

These scenarios provide a set of individual and organizational assumptions in regard to leadership, cultures and organizational models.

Scenario 1: History and Tradition of a Digital Organization

Scenario 2: Structure and Hierarchy Influence, Management Style, the Role of the CEO in building an organizational vision – and in a transformational context

Scenario 3: Role of the CEO in regard to strategy processes technology and people actions and leader's influence in the existence of specific types of cultures

Scenario 4: Digital Leadership disrupted Style as practiced by the management groups

Scenario 5: CEO focus on performance, climate, communication, and HRM practices, on monetary reward programs and influence over high performers, and management attention on retaining high performers.

Scenario 6: Role of the leader in building work processes, in managing people strategy issues, and organizational emphasis on competing and performing in a complex environment.

Scenario 7: Leader's emphasis on building future leaders through mentoring, coaching and teaching, emphasis on team work

Scenario 8: Role of the CEO in enabling digital organizations to restructure and right size.

Scenario 9: Role of the CEO in preparing the digital organizations to change as required.

Scenario 10: Leader's role in sponsoring innovation, new ideas, take risks and implementing experiments and

Scenario 11: CEO's role in enabling inters dependencies between functions, businesses, infrastructure, digital technologies, IT – systems, telecom and the organization as a whole.

Scenario 12: The Leader as a person – Vision, values, beliefs and the dream

Scenario 13: Leader's emphasis on the Individual and the Intellect, and a role in building individual and organizational knowledge

Scenario 14: CEO's role in emphasizing on culture aspects pertaining to empowerment, delegation, individual contribution, accountability and

Scenario 15: CEO's role in actively participating in attracting, retaining and rewarding star talent and performers

Scenario 16: Leader's role in helping the organization retain an open mind to an unknown competitive tech environment.

Scenario 17: Leaders determine Business Models that helps organizations create value

Scenario 18: Technology choices become evident as organizations gain greater clarity on their value to employees and customers.

Scenario 19: Leaders cannot stop social collaboration processes that have been set in motion

Scenario 20: Leaders cannot stop Millennials from doing what they want to do!

Thereafter specific scenario based definitions for Organizational and Management Models and Leadership disrupted Model were constructed driven by conceptual outlines and definitions for what did each of them mean. This in turn enabled the survey feedback and content analysis as one of the additional methods apart from scenario to test for leadership and its influence on organizational culture in the intellectual company.

Observable

BEHAVIOURS

VALUES

BASIC ASSUMPTIONS
"paradigms"

Hidden

Easier to Change

What you see
- Symbols, norms, behaviours
- Work processes
- Leader behaviour
- Communication
- What gets noticed
- What gets measured
- What gets rewarded –
  formally and informally

What you believe in / your
guiding principles

How you think about things
(mind sets)

Harder to Change

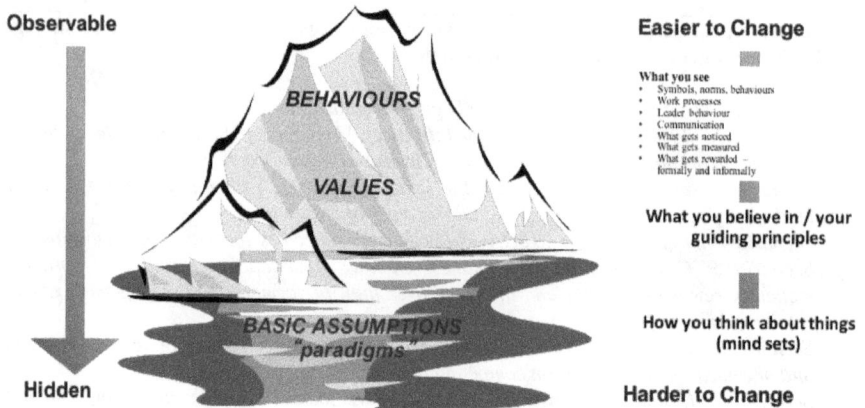

Figure 18 – Factors Influencing Culture

I. **Culture Literature Survey** - As we trace history we see substantive work highlights of which are provided below to start with.

- *1911, Frederick Winslow Taylor's The Principles of Scientific Management launched the scientific management movement with its emphasis on time and motion studies and breaking jobs into small, repetitive tasks in an attempt to find "the one best way" to do each job. Expert engineers and supervisors designed each task and ensured it was done correctly. Piece-rate pay systems were designed to increase motivation and to prevent "soldering," or slacking off. Simple, repetitive tasks minimized the skills required to do the job. Taylor's methods quickly swept the country and the world as the way to organize work.*
- *1922, The great German sociologist Max Weber introduced the concept of "bureaucracy" as the best, most efficient way to organize people. A strong hierarchy of authority, extensive division of labor, Impersonal rules, and rigid procedures would create a well-oiled human machine called the organization. Scientific management as the way to organize work and bureaucracy as the way to organize people were the prevailing paradigms for organizations in the early 1900s. These approaches possessed many desirable features, but also contained serious flaws that led to unintended consequences. In a sense, much of the study, theory, and practice since the late 1920s have focused on the shortcomings of these two paradigms and how to overcome the limitations.*
- *1926, Mary Parker Follett, a management theorist and astute observer of labor-management relations, wrote an article on "The Giving of orders" advocating Participative leadership and joint problem solving by labor and management. Much of her career was devoted to finding ways to reduce adversarial relationships between workers and management. Her papers were collected and published as a book in 1941.*
- *1927 to 1932, the famous Hawthorne studies were conducted at the Hawthorne plant of western Electric Company. Reports on these studies by Mayo in 1933 and 1945, by Roethlisberger and Dickson in 1939 and by Homans in 1950 profoundly and irreversibly affected people's beliefs about organizational behavior. The study demonstrated the primacy of social factors on productivity and morale. People came to work as whole people; their feeling alienated and dispirited. Group norms had more powerful effects on productivity than economic incentives. People were not cogs; organizations were not machines.*

- *1938, The Function of the Executive by Chester I. Barnard presented insights from his experience as president of the New Jersey Bell Telephone Company. Barnard viewed organization as social systems that must be effective (achieve goals) and efficient (satisfy the needs of employees). His acceptance theories of authority proposed that authority derive from the willingness of subordinates to comply with directions rather than from position power.*
- *1939, Study by Lewin, Lippitt, and White demonstrated the superiority of democratic leadership compared to authoritarian leadership an laissez-faire leadership in terms of the effects on group climate and group performance. Democratic leadership seemed to bring out the best in the groups; authoritarian leadership caused dependency, apathy, aggressiveness, and poor performance.*
- *1940s Group dynamics- the scientific study of groups using experimental study methods- was launched by Kurt Lewin and his student. Some early experiments were conducted in the late 1930s.*
- *1940 to 1960s The Hawthorne studies spawned the human relation's movement that was in full flower from the 1930s to the 1960s. The human relations movement advocated Participative management, greater attention to workers' social needs, training in interpersonal skills for supervisors, and a general "humanizing" of the workplace.*
- *1946 and 1947, these years witnessed the beginnings of the laboratory training movement, a direct precursor of OD. Improved interpersonal relation, increased self-understanding, and awareness of group dynamics were lessons learned in laboratory training. Humanistic and democratic values suffused the movement.*
- *1948, Ken Benne and Paul Sheets, pioneers in laboratory training, proposed that the leadership functions of a group should be shared between the leader and group members and showed how that could be done.*
- *1948, Lester Coch and John R. P. French's article, "Overcoming Resistance to Change," reported that resistance to change could be minimized by communicating the need for change and allowing the people affected by the change to participate in planning it. http://psychology.msu.edu/SyllabusRecordFiles/PSY%20992%20Fall%2015.pdf*
- *1950, Ludwig Von Bertalanffy introduced general systems theory concepts and showed their application to physics and biology.*
- *1951, Carl Rogers's Client-Centered Therapy demonstrated the efficacy of non-directive psychotherapy, which holds that individuals have within themselves the capacity to assume responsibility for their behavior and mental health when provided with a supportive, caring social climate. Rogers focus on effective interpersonal communications was applicable to superior-subordinate relations.*
- *1951, Eric Trist and Ken Bamforth of the Tavistock Clinic published the results of their work in British coal mines. This article introduced the concept of organizations as socio technical systems, which postulates that organizations are comprised of a social system and a technological system and that changes in one system will produce changes in the other system.*
- *1954, Motivation and Personality by Abraham Maslow presented a new view of human motivation. Maslow suggested that human motivation is arranged in a hierarchy of needs from lower-level needs such as physiological and survival needs to higher-level needs such as esteem and self-actualization. The theory postulated that when lower-level needs are satisfied, higher-level needs become dominant.*
- *1957, Chris Argyris's Personality and Organization was the first of several books in which he stated that there is an inherent conflict between the needs of organizations and the needs of mature, healthy adults.*
- *1960, Douglas McGregor wrote The Human Side of Enterprise in which he described his famous Theory X and Theory Y assumptions. Those who subscribe to Theory X assume that*

145

people are lazy, lack ambition, dislike responsibility, are self-centered, indifferent to the organization's needs, resist change, and need to be led. Those who subscribe to Theory Y assume that people have the potential to develop, to assume responsibility, and to pursue organizational goals if given the chance and the social environment to do so. The task of management is to change organizational structures, management practices, and human resource practices to allow individual potential to be released. In addition to presenting theory X and Y, this book popularized Maslow's motivation theory, and introduced the concepts of need hierarchy and self-actualization to practicing managers.

- *1961, Burns and Stalker described two very different forms of organization structure-mechanistic and organic. In an environment of slow change, a mechanistic corporate structure may be appropriate; in an environment of high change, an organic organization form is preferred. Organic structures encourage decentralized decision making and authority, open communications, and greater individual autonomy.*

- *1961, Rensis Likert's New Patterns of Management presented data and theory showing the overwhelming superiority of a democratic leadership style in which the leader is group oriented, goal oriented, and shares decision making with the work group. This leadership style was compared to an authoritarian, one-on-one leadership style.*

- *1966, The Social Psychology of Organizations by Daniel Katz and Robert L. Khan Presented the first comprehensive exposition of organizations as open systems.*

- *1969, The Addison-Wesley Publishing Company "OD six-pack," a set of six little books on OD by prominent practitioners, summarized the state of organization development a decade or so after its inception. These six books presented the theory, practice, and values of the field.*

- *1977, The consensus form recent studies, for example Aries De Geus (1997), Fitz-Enz (1997), Ulrich (1997), is that the successful organization for the new millennium needs organization leaders with excellent capabilities in people management skills and understanding of behavioral issues. And strategic specialists with capabilities of designing and promoting organization programs to create effective work practices and an environment of continuous learning.*

- *1977, Ulrich states that the new organizations will see the strategic role of management as focussed on delivering four generic outcomes: strategic execution, administrative efficiency, employee contribution and capacity for change. In addition, the centrality of people to sustained competitive advantage will require the input of strategic HR factors into business strategy formulation.*

- *1980, Geert Hofstede has defined "culture" as "the collective programming of the mind that distinguishes the members of one group or category of people from others". In 1980 he published his book "Culture's Consequences: International Differences in Work-Related Values". As the title suggests, this book was entirely devoted to the study of culture at the national level, in which values played a major role. The book's main innovation was its use of the concept (paradigm) of dimensions of culture: basic problems to which different national societies have over time developed different answers.*

- *1992, Khandwalla - Perspectives on Organizational Cultures. Substantive study by Khandwalla is desirable to study to compare cultures*

- *1992, John Kotter and James Heskett at Harvard produced four major findings, highlighted in their book Corporate Culture and Performance. These are: Corporate culture can have significant impact on long-term financial performance, Culture probably will become an even more important factor in determining corporate success or failure in the future, Cultures that inhibit long-term financial strength are common and develop easily, even in companies full of reasonable and bright people, Corporate culture can be managed and changed.*

- *1982, Deal and Kennedy, People, keeping in mind pursuit of some specific purposes create organizations. Organizations have a formal structure to achieve their objectives. They have formally identified roles, tasks, goals and responsibilities.*
- *1982, Edgar Schein - "Organizational culture is the pattern of basic assumptions that a given group has invented, discovered, or developed in learning to cope with its problems of external adaptation, internal integration. And that have worked well enough to be considered valid and, therefore, to be taught to new members as the correct way to perceive, think, and feel in relation to those problems".*
- *2003, Tichy - Dr. Tichy's approach to "Change Agenting" has itself been a journey of sorts. From his earliest management book, The Transformational Leader: The Key to Global Competitiveness (with Mary Anne Devanna, John Wiley & Sons) in 1986, through 1993's Control Your Destiny or Someone Else Will: How Jack Welch Is Making General Electric the World's Most Competitive Company (with Stratford Sherman, Currency Doubleday), he concentrated on processes by which leaders manage change. But in his recent book, The Leadership Engine: How Winning Companies Build Leaders at Every Level (with Eli Cohen, HarperBusiness, 1997), and his newest, The Cycle of Leadership: How Great Leaders Teach Their Companies to Win (with Nancy Cardwell, HarperBusiness, 2002), he has trained his sights on the mechanics of teaching leadership. His most controversial admonition: Teaching must be interactive — the boss has got to learn as much as the staff, a construct Dr. Tichy calls a "virtuous teaching cycle." (http://bit.ly/29VOrnC Strategy + Business = Randall Rothenburg) - "People cannot be expected to learn one expertise and just apply it routinely in a job. Your expertise is in steadily renewing your knowledge base and extending it to new areas. That lifelong cycle of learning really is the foundation of the new information organization and economy." - George Gilder*
- *2004, Shermon, Ganesh, "Competency Based HRM", the culture of an organization or an institution is an amalgamation, a summation of the values, beliefs, experiences and assumptions of the people and the processes in an organization. (Add to it organization and management type and nature). It is not linear and is largely octopus like. It can be experienced in the implicit rules and expectations of behavior in an organization where, even though the rules, policy frameworks are not formally written down employees know what is expected of them. In fact more often than not culture cannot be found in written documents. Management (Leadership) whose decisions on policy, strategy and implementation usually help facilitates the culture of the organization and usually set it too. The organizational culture usually has norms, artifacts, and actions, stories and sagas that support the organizational actions and goals*
- *2012, Ulrich - Dave Ulrich's professional focus has addressed questions on how organizations add value to customers and investors through both leadership and strategic human resource practices. In the human resource area, he and his colleagues have worked to redefine and upgrade HR. With his colleagues Wayne Brockbank and Jon Younger, Ulrich has articulated how the modern HR organization can be organized into shared services, centers of expertise, and business partners. He has also co-directed research on over 40,000 respondents about the competencies required for successful HR professionals; in addition, he has helped shape thinking on how to transform HR practices so that they are aligned to customer needs and integrated around organization capabilities. In the leadership area, Norm Smallwood and Ulrich have worked to focus on the outcomes of effective leadership; they have also shown how leadership will increase customer share by creating a leadership brand within the company. Their work also illustrates that investing in leadership will increase shareholder value. Their work also synthesizes the thicket of leadership competency models into a unified*

view of leadership. Their current work attempts to look at leadership through the eyes and expectations of investors - http://bit.ly/2a1lUxK

- *2015, Ulrich & Allen Freed – Calculating the Market Value of Leadership – Refer HBR - http://bit.ly/1BZcNDo . In recent years, investors have learned that defining the market value of a firm cannot just be based on finances. GAAP and FASB standards require financial reporting of earnings, cash flow, and profitability – all measures that investors have traditionally examined. But recently, these financial outcomes have been found to predict only about 50% of a firm's market value. Another challenge is that this financial information has become widely known and shared, meaning that the investor insights it affords are hardly unique. To gain more insights into a specific firm, investors have shown more interest in intangibles like strategy, brand, innovation, systems integration, collaboration, and so on. Investors have also worked to track and measure these intangibles, even if more subjective. We believe that a next step for investors is to analyze the predictors and drivers of these intangible factors — which means focusing on leadership. What we need is a leadership capital index, similar to a financial confidence index (such as Moody's or Standard & Poor's). It would move beyond casual and piecemeal observations of leaders to more thorough assessment of leadership.*

J. Appreciating Culture in the context of an Intellectual Company - The culture of an organization is an amalgamation of the practices, values and beliefs of the people in an organization

Simply Culture Tracings - Culture happens as time passes and as actions impact behavior. It can be felt in the implicit rules and expectations of behavior in an organization where, even though the rules are not formally written down employees know what is expected of them. Management whose decisions on policy help establish the culture of the organization usually sets it. The organizational culture has values and beliefs, sometimes rituals that support the organizational goals. Over time established actions, consequent behavior and counter behavior become commonly understood as culture.

Consequently, understanding culture has become a basic foundation for study of organizational practices and the method that a leader or the CEO wishes to choose to manage his/her organization. And the reasons to do so are many.

Culture Demystified - *The culture of an organization or an institution is an amalgamation, a summation of the values, beliefs, experiences and assumptions of the people and the processes in an organization. (Add to it organization and management type and nature). It is not linear and is largely octopus like. It can be experienced in the implicit rules and expectations of behavior in an organization where, even though the rules, policy frameworks are not formally written down employees know what is expected of them. In fact, more often than not culture cannot be found in written documents. Management (Leadership) whose decisions on policy, strategy and implementation usually help facilitates the culture of the organization and usually set it too. The organizational culture usually has norms, artifacts, and actions, stories and sagas that support the organizational actions and goals. (Shermon 2004). Organizational culture may be thought of as the manner in which an organization solves problems to achieve its specific goals and to maintain itself over time. Moreover, it is holistic, historically determined, socially constructed and difficult to change (Hofstede etal.,1990) A collective programming of the mind which distinguishes one category of people from another. (Hofstede 1980). Hofstede (1991) has demonstrated that managers in different countries differ in the strength of their attitudes and values regarding various issues. He has used this information to argue that national Cultures differ along five dimensions: Power Distance,*

Individualism/ Collectivism, Masculinity/Femininity, Uncertainty Avoidance, Confucian Dynamism. The Societal or National Culture within which an organization is physically situated. The Vision, Management style and personality of an organization's founder or other dominant leader. The type of business an organization conducts and the nature of its business environment. Power distance is the extent to which the less powerful members of organizations within a country expect and accept that power is distributed unequally. Individualism/Collectivism pertains to the extent to which individual independence or social cohesion dominate. Characteristics of High masculinity societies - Men supposed to be assertive, tough and focused on material success. Women supposed to be more modest, tender and concerned with quality of life.

Characteristics of High femininity societies - Social gender roles overlap. Both men and women supposed to be modest, tender and concerned with the quality of life. Uncertainty Avoidance - Uncertainty avoidance is defined as the extent to which the members of a culture feel threatened by uncertain or unknown situations. Confucian Dynamism. Confucian dynamism refers to the degree to which long-termism or short-termism is the dominant orientation in life, and is linked to the Confucian concept of 'virtue' which Hofstede contracts with a Western preoccupation with 'truth'. Hofstede.

For example:

- *People seek identity, identity is an important component of culture*
- *Organizations work in a context or a situation, so do its people*
- *Culture implies existence of awareness, existence, rituals, conflicts, confrontation, relationships, feelings, emotions, satisfaction*
- *Cultures exists at an individual, institutional regional, national, global level.*
- *Where cultures exist, sub cultures exist too*
- *Awareness or Unawareness of the existing and desired ways of working in a context influences cultures, as it impacts people*
- *Stakeholders ask for direction, a set of goals and tasks. Unclear vision, lack of clarity in the future necessitates studying culture*
- *Lack of Leadership to influence, foresee and shape a desired culture needs management attention*
- *Absence of a desire to understand and evolve cultures through managerial actions*
- *Culture implies collaboration possibilities, formalization and some level of structural stability in the group - shared, deep-rooted & stable*
- *The other element that culture implies is patterning or integration of the elements into a larger paradigm*
- *Culture formation is therefore, a striving toward patterning and integration*
- *The culture of an organization is defined as a set of shared assumptions. (Schein, 1992). Over time the notion of cultures has been expanded to include amongst others the following:*
- *Observed behavioral regularities when people interact, the language they use, the customs and traditions that evolve, and the rituals that are employed (Jones et all, 1988) groups norms (Kilmann and Saxton, 1983);*
- *Espoused values (Deal and Kennedy, 1982);*
- *The broad policies and ideological principles that underlie a group's actions towards their stakeholders (Ouchi, 1981);*
- *The ropes or rules of the game that a new comer must learn to become accepted in the organization (Ritti and Funkhouser, 1982);*

- *The feelings conveyed between participants (Schneider, 1990);*
- *Embedded Skills (Peters and Waterman, 1982)*
- *Mental models and habits or ways of thinking (Douglas 1986)*
- *Shared meanings and understandings (Smircich, 1983). Metaphorical and symbolic ideas that somehow surface or become exposed in the material artifacts of an organization. (Gagliardi, 1990: Morgan, 1986, Schultz, 1991).*
- *Leader is a dealer in hope (Napoleon Bonaparte).*
- *Expression of a Nation's Character (Somerset Maugham)*

Culture Extends Beyond the Superficial - These concepts were developed from the works of Hacberg Consulting Group, (HCG), "An organization's culture is not just the espoused or an articulated list of values developed at an offsite, similar to a vision workshop or a strategic planning seminar, by the leadership disrupted team and framed on the wall in the office, customer site and factory lobby. These are ideals, norms, rituals, practices, history, tradition, collection of stories, if you will! Perhaps at best hope. What the organization aspires to be and what values one hope to endorse, may be different from the values, beliefs, and norms expressed in the organizational actual practices and behavior. It is critical that we find out who we really are as well as striving for who we want to be. Awakening the emperor to the fact that he/she has no clothes is often a risky and delicate first step in closing the gap between the real and the ideal. Or the financial controller, who brings the bad news of poor bottom line when the SBU Heads should have actually been called, accounted for and dispensed with. Cultural assessment can provide measurable data about the real organizational values and norms that can be used to get management's attention. It can dispel some of management's illusions about what really matters in the organization and will tell them how far off the mark things really are. Management may find that it is not practicing what it preaches. However, telling the CEO the truth about the organization he/she has built, can often be dangerous to your career progress. Delivering such a message takes skill as a coach and a willingness to take risks and confront conflict". Refer - http://bit.ly/2akvhwy

Culture & Schein - The culture of an organization is an amalgamation of the values and beliefs of the people in an organization. It can be felt in the implicit rules and expectations of behavior in an organization where, even though the rules are not formally written down employees know what is expected of them. It is usually set by management whose decisions on policy usually set up the culture of the organization. The organizational culture usually has values and beliefs that support the organizational goals. Schein 1992.

Basic Assumptions, Values and Norms Drive Practices and Behaviors

Culture is Changing - "The culture of an organization operates at both a conscious and unconscious level. Often the people who see the culture more clearly are those from the outside--the new hires, the consultants or vendors. When coaching or advising senior management, remember that culture comprises the deeply rooted but often unconscious beliefs, values and norms shared by the members of the organization. Those not living inside the culture can often see it more objectively. Culture drives the organization and its actions. It is somewhat like "the operating system" of the organization. It guides how employees think, act and feel. It is dynamic and fluid, and it is never static. A culture may be effective at one time, under a given set of circumstances and ineffective at another time. There is no generically good culture. There are however, generic patterns of health and pathology". Refer - http://bit.ly/2akvhwy

Cultures Collide (Artifacts, Space, Symbols, Material)- A constraint with broad impact is the historic organization culture and accompanying capabilities. All managers are aware that their corporate culture can limit their choice of organization design. Compare Procter & Gamble and Unilever. Both companies compete head-on in many markets around the world. Unilever, because of its history of dual UK and Dutch nationality, small home market and decentralized structure, developed cultural norms and skills about co-ordinating across borders that are completely different to those of P&.G. These differences caused Unilever in the mid-1990s to organize geographically just at the moment when P&G was deciding to reinforce its global product divisions. The differences in culture and skills made it quite rational for two companies with similar market strategies to choose different structural solutions. "There are various material products or artifacts created by organizations which are symbolic elements of their cultural traditions, beliefs, and value patterns. In Bank A many of its artifacts reflected its strong commitment to its personnel, while similar types of artifacts in Bank B reflected quite different values. In Bank A, for example, the employees eating facility in the main office was quite plush and decorated like a fine restaurant, expensive wood paneling, numerous plants throughout the room, cushioned booths, and so forth. In Bank B, by contrast, the same type of facility in the main office was much more like a traditional cafeteria, relatively spartan in nature, simple chairs and tables, and a small refrigerator in one of the corners. This distinction is a reflection of the values and orientations of each bank, the importance of a comfortable physical setting for Bank A (people orientation) compared to the "lean and mean", competitive aura of Bank B (task orientation). The differences in physical setting were further reflected in the branches. Bank A was so particular about the quality of the physical setting of the branches that it established its own subsidiary corporation to oversee and control any construction or upgrading of facilities. Bank B's policy was that its branches avoid expensive embellishments and take on a simple, functional appearance. Interestingly, these policies were in direct contrast to the populations served by these banks, the largely blue-collar population of Bank A and the professional, white-collar clientele served by Bank B". Anthony F. Buono, James L. Bowditch, John W. Lewis, III, in "When Cultures Collide: The Anatomy of a Merger" continue further, "Another Material symbol of the different cultures is reflected by the location and nature of the offices of the two CEOs. The office of Bank A's CEO was located in a prime corner of the third floor of the main office building, isolated from the day-to-day workings of the organization. Richly decorated, the office was framed by a panoramic window looking out over the city. The office of Bank B's CEO, in contrast, was much simpler in nature, with two glass enclosed walls facing inside the bank overlooking the teller cages and officer's platform. The offices, in effect, were physical symbols of the style of each CEO (see McCaskey, 1979), the external focus and preference for delegation of Bank A's CEO, and the more internally focused concern for detail style of Bank B's CEO". Most managers have a strong sense of what will work in their particular environment. If a company has always had problems in persuading shared services to be genuinely responsive to other units' needs, they will be skeptical about extending the role of shared service units in future. It product units and customer units have consistently fought over product development and pricing strategies; it will be necessary for any new organization to pay close attention to how these friction points will be handled. If the relationship between the management teams in Germany and France has always been friendly and co-operative, important co-ordination benefits may be easily achievable without changing boundaries or responsibilities.

Rites **Patterns** **Norms** ~~Stories~~ *Myths*

The beliefs & values held in common &
taken for granted within an organization*

Attitudes *Artifacts*

Legends **Values**

An excuse not to make much
needed business changes !

Organization
Personality

Assumptions *Purpose* Behaviour

Rituals

The unwritten rules about
how to survive "get on"

Style **Symbols** Actions Beliefs

...or most commonly, 'The way we do things round here'

Figure 19 – Culture – What is it?

K. Why study organizational culture in the context of an Digital Intellectual Company?

Wasted Intellect in the Traditional Corporate World - "The lack of strategic direction and dysfunctional activities undertaken at enormous cost in terms of wasted human resources and money by organizations should provide sobering lessons in terms of organizational learning and business performance. Never before have so many employees had formal business education and management qualifications and not provided a significant direction and contribution for individual growth. How then could the past decade show evidence of so many managers clearly having little strategic appreciation of how to manage an organization in order to achieve long-term sustainable competitive advantage?" Refer – J Martin Hayes - http://bit.ly/2ahfjjU

Need for New Forms to Nurture Intellect - A number of recent studies have provided a wealth of evidence and analysis on the efforts of organizations to manage not only change, but to develop the type of organization and leaders which can operate successfully in a future of continuous change. (Fitz-Enz, 1997; Flannery et al., 1997; Kaplan and Norton, 1996; Pfeffer, 1994, 1997; Price Waterhouse, (PwC) *1996)*. Much of the study has not been produced in university business schools, but comes from business Consultancy groups. Such groups being Prince Waterhouse and the Hay Group and privately-funded study institutes such as the Saratoga Institute (Fitz-Enz), with its relationships with Andersen Consulting and the Nolan Norton Institute, the study arm of KPMG, which sponsored the study resulting in the "Balanced scorecard" (Kaplan and Norton, 1996).

Fast Changing Personality in Intellect - Basically, organizational culture is the personality of the organization. Culture is comprised of the assumptions, values, norms and tangible signs (artifacts) of organization members and their behaviors. Members of an organization soon come to sense, feel and experience the particular culture of an organization. Culture is one of those terms that are difficult to express distinctly, but everyone knows it when they sense it. For example, the culture of a large, for-profit corporation, driven by performance and competition is quite different than that of a hospital, driven by its voluntary nature and that that is quite different from that of a university, with its focus on the intellect and knowledge. You can tell the culture of an organization by looking at the arrangement of furniture, what they brag about, what members wear, etc. -- similar to what you can use to get a feeling about someone's personality. Refer - http://bit.ly/1P5nMmp

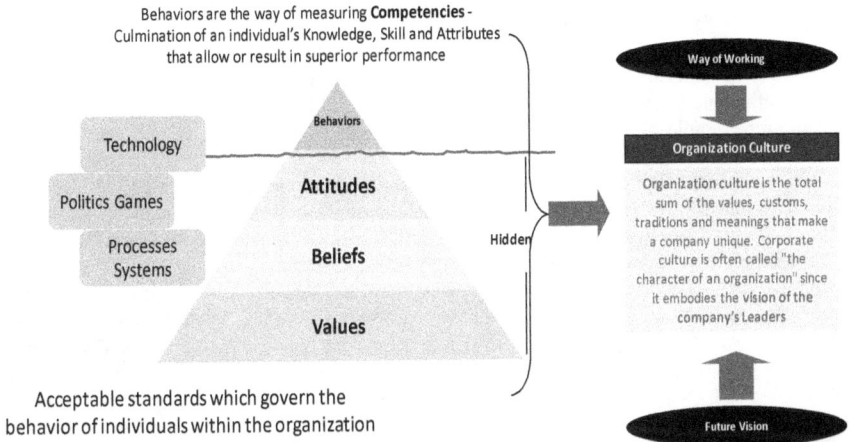

Figure 20 – Culture – A Perspective

Culture is Significantly More Evolving - "Corporate culture can be looked at as a system, a mechanism that works to a plan and process at a systemic level. Inputs include review, feedback from, e.g., society, social companions, relationships, professions, laws, stories, heroes, values on competition, process or service, etc. The process is based on our assumptions, experiences, background, personality, values and norms, e.g., our values on money, resources, relationships, emotional connects, time, facilities, space and people. Outputs or effects of our culture are, e.g., organizational behaviors, technologies, strategies, image, products, services, appearance, etc. The concept of culture is particularly important when attempting to manage organization-wide change. Practitioners are coming to realize that, despite the best-laid plans, organized to a pre-programmed method, organizational change must include not only changing structures and processes, but also changing the corporate culture as well".

Cult Revitalization - "There's been a great deal of literature generated over the past decade about the concept of organizational culture" -- particularly in regard to learning how to influence, impact or change organizational culture. Organizational revitalization and change efforts are rumored to fail the vast majority of the time, yes rumored. Usually, that failure is credited to lack of understanding, an experiential appreciation about the strong role of culture, thick and thin and the role it plays in organizations. That's one of the reasons that many strategic planners now place as much emphasis on identifying strategic values as they do in defining mission and vision, not just commercial goals and objectives". http://bit.ly/1P5nMmp

L. Culture Operates at Various Levels - The Visible Artifacts to the Deeply Rooted Unconscious

Multiple Levels of Culture - "Culture can be viewed at several levels. Some aspects of culture are visible and tangible and others are intangible and unconscious. Basic assumptions that guide the organization are deeply rooted and often taken for granted. Avoidance of conflict is a value that is an excellent example of an unconscious norm that may have a major influence on the organization but is frequently unconscious". Refer HCG research on Corporate Culture: Telling the CEO the Baby is Ugly"- http://bit.ly/2akvhwv - "For an insider, this is difficult or impossible to see, particularly if the individual has "grown up" in the organizational culture. Recently hired employees, the external consultant and the executive coach is frequently in the best position to identify these unconscious assumptions or values. Espoused or secondary values are at a more conscious level; these are the values that people in the organization discuss, promote and try to live by. All employees of Hewlett Packard, for example, are required to become familiar with the values embodied in the "HP Way.""

Cultural Fit - "Do any 'specialist cultures', units with cultures that need to be different from sister units and the layers above, have sufficient protection from the influence of the dominant culture? The purpose of the specialist cultures test is to identify parts of the organization that need more independence than the design currently allows. Normally the design can be adjusted to accommodate the autonomy needs of the unit without making too big a compromise on some other dimension, such as co-ordination. Sometimes, however, adequate solutions prove impossible to develop, in which case the proposed design must be rejected. The risk to the specialist culture eliminates that design option from further consideration: it is a "knock-out" factor. Judgments about which units require specialist cultures and whether a unit is likely to be dominated require careful thought. However, they need to be made, and the test insures that managers give the issue the scrutiny it warrants. "In addition to the importance of assessing strategic fit and conducting careful financial due diligence, the following steps are representative of the approach to M&A integration that Hewlett-Packard has developed. Conduct human capital due diligence — obtain structured external (for example, independent) assessments of the top management team. Depending on the size of the companies involved, the assessment might involve the C-level plus one, two or three levels of the organizational chart". In, "6 Steps to (Re)Building a Top Management Team - SMR 2008, Stephen A. Miles and Nathan Bennett recommend the need to Reduce Role Ambiguity. "They write on the Elements of the Hewlett-Packard M&A Playbook (http://bit.ly/2a3X52o). This approach is quite similar to Pfizer – Warner Lambert Merger. The pharma major's focus to build upon the brands and facilities of Warner Lambert helped Pfizer build upon WL cultural best practices, people management practices and structural efficiencies. "Invest to develop ways to identify and objectively assess the tacit elements of the companies involved. This might include key elements of each company's culture, history, and any "sacred cows" that would be risky to confront too soon. Additionally, this should involve understanding the acquired company's "real" practices (as opposed to what written documentation or the organizational chart suggests). For example, how do decisions really get made? Where do power and influence really lie? Who are the leaders that are sitting in positions not automatically part of the management team? Identify the members of the top management team, (leader's ability and willingness to influence change) and involve them in the development of an on-boarding plan (Socialization as a method to influence networks) to provide a structured approach to their roles in the integration with milestones to gauge progress. Develop and implement a system to capture employee input, and use the findings to track progress on issues of concern for them".

M. How does Culture manifest and influence patterning?

Visible Leadership disrupted Influence - Leaders influence the way culture manifests itself. Terry Leap in SMR 2008 article, "When Bad People Rise to the Top" writes, "Bad CEOs possess the work ethic and intellectual wherewithal to succeed, but they allow their personalities and lack of emotional maturity to sabotage their work, their organizations and their careers. Some CEOs instigate trouble with colleagues, investors, clients and board members. Tales of inept and abusive individuals have become part of the folklore in some organizations. These often ruthless and remorseless CEOs flaunt their power through tirades and sarcasm, aggressive questioning about arcane matters, predatory smiles and contemptuous glares. Others are arch manipulators who control or distort information sent to investors, board members and key executives. The worst of these CEOs condone major frauds and massive misappropriations".

Culture Stability implies some level of structural stability in the group - shared, deep-rooted & stable. The other element that culture implies is patterning or integration of the elements into a larger paradigm.

Visible Internal Cultural factors - In reality, what management pays attention to and intrinsic rewards (work, life, satisfaction, quality, home, health, and welfare) is often the strongest indicator of the organization's culture. Refer HCG research on Corporate Culture: Telling the CEO the Baby is Ugly"- http://bit.ly/2akvhwy -"This is often quite different than the values it verbalizes or the ideals it strives for. Think for a minute about the organization in which you work.

Culture formation is therefore, a striving toward patterning and integration. Culture is best understood as we study into various organizational, business and operational elements that determine formation of culture.

Factors That Influences a Digital Culture:

- *A mission – vision – purpose statement*
- *Who are we identity*
- *Social Networks*
- *Self Service Freedom*
- *Tech Enablement/Dependence*
- *Why do we exist*
- *Whom do we serve*
- *Values, concerns and business ethics*
- *Terms of employment*
- *Forms of organization*
- *Importance of network relationships*
- *Approach to decision making*
- *Location or pattern of authority limits, delegation powers, authority matrix*
- *Communication practices*
- *Sharing of information*
- *Criteria for Assessment*
- *Delegation of authority*
- *Emphasis on teamwork*
- *Focus on Quality*
- *Degree of Specialization*
- *Tolerance of diversity*
- *Speed of Action*
- *Method of Control*
- *Extent of mutual trust*
- *Commitment to learning and development*
- *Openness to outsiders*
- *Sensitivity to value and feelings*

Culture Networks - In addition, there are focused determinants that influence patterning as they impact culture and the way work organizes to deliver results. Illustratively some of them are company history and traditions, Corporate vision and mission; Culture associated with its business sector. And culture of its headquarters' nation, Culture of its leadership team or professional groups, Culture of its key networks/ relationships, External attitudes and expectations, Form of organization and method of operation, Homogeneity of beliefs and values etc.

And, critical add on requirements supporting above being:

- *The organizational structure of reporting and relationships*
- *Company policy*
- *Personnel practices*
- *Work flow and work loads*
- *Job design*
- *Management and supervisory styles.*
- *Leadership disrupted and its commitment to impact change.*
- *Thus for studying Dimensions of Culture – External and Internal Integration is the next step.*
- *External and internal integration forms the 2 dimensions of a culture.*

Visible External Cultural Factors - External environment deals with Vision and Mission, Goals and objectives, (http://bit.ly/1HFnsVx) means to achieve goals, measuring results, effecting change if any. Internal integration includes common language, accepted norms of behavior, generically done activities, existing groups and coalitions, group boundaries for inclusion or exclusion, distributing power and status, developing norms, allocating reward and punishment, explaining the unexplainable situations as they exist in organizations. Concurrently culture provides consistency, validity on one's way of understanding actions of colleagues, set of roles that have established over time, order and structure and creates an internal way of life. It also determines the conditions for internal effectiveness, the nature and use of power, sets expectations and priorities, let people know how close they can get to one another, and provides framework for addressing, managing and resolving conflicts. Yet there are things which can affect the organizational culture on an individual or personal level.

Evidence in Culture:

- *Sheer perception*
- *Personal disposition*
- *Levels of trust*
- *Risk taking*
- *Personal goals and ambition*
- *Nature of work and the environment*
- *Pre conceived notions,*
- *Nature of experience encountered*
- *Pre-determined assumptions*
- *Stress*
- *Fears and anxieties*
- *Social interaction*
- *Expectations*
- *Factions and politics*

An attempt has been made to bring together a definition in regard to culture.

N. Cultural Understanding – Defining

The culture of an organization or an institution is an amalgamation, a summation of the values, beliefs, experiences and assumptions of the people and the processes in an organization. (Add to it organization and management type and nature). It is not linear and is largely octopus like. It can be experienced in the implicit rules and expectations of behavior in an organization where, even though the rules, policy frameworks are not formally written down employees know what is expected of them. In fact, more often than not culture cannot be found in written documents. Management (Leadership) whose decisions on policy, strategy and implementation usually help facilitates the culture of the organization and usually set it too. The organizational culture usually has norms, artifacts, and actions, stories and sagas that support the organizational actions and goals. A collective programming of the mind which distinguishes one category of people from another. (Hofstede 1980)

Schein Defines - To Edgar Schein (1982) - http://bit.ly/1HFnsVx, "Organizational culture is the pattern of basic assumptions that a given group has invented, discovered, or developed in learning to cope with its problems of external adaptation, internal integration. And that have worked well enough to be considered valid and, therefore, to be taught to new members as the correct way to perceive, think, and feel in relation to those problems".

Holistic - Organizational culture may be thought of as the manner in which an organization solves problems to achieve its specific goals and to maintain itself over time. Moreover, it is holistic, historically determined, socially constructed and difficult to change **(Hofstede ET al., 1990)**.

O. Schein - Classifications and Definitions of Organizational Culture

Omnipresence may be said of "culture". If it is everywhere, and pervades every aspect of our existence, then how can it be subject to analysis, Schein (1992) offers at least a partial solution. R S S Mani (http://bit.ly/2a6pG7U) provides an expert view, "It has been observed with respect to the concept of "power" that its omnipresence makes it difficult to usefully apply in specific situations (Pfeffer, 1981).

Schein divides organizational culture into three levels:

Levels of Culture - At the surface are **"artifacts"**, those aspects (such as dress) which can be easily discerned, yet are hard to understand; Beneath artifacts are **"espoused values"** which are conscious strategies, goals and philosophies; And **"basic assumptions"**.

Underlying Assumptions - Schein (1982) The core, or essence, of culture is represented by the basic underlying assumptions and values, which are difficult to discern because they exist at a largely unconscious level, yet provide the key to understanding why things happen the way they do. These basic assumptions form around deeper dimensions of human existence such as the nature of humans; human relationships and activity; reality; and truth.

Elements can be studied - Schein (1992) himself acknowledges that, even with rigorous study, we can only make statements about elements of culture, not culture in its entirety. The approach, which Schein recommends for inquiring about culture, is an iterative, clinical approach, similar to a therapeutic relationship between a psychologist and a patient. Schein's disciplined approach to culture stands in contrast to the almost flippant way in which culture is referred to in some of the popular management literature". Refer - http://bit.ly/2a6pG7U

Essentially culture is an all pervasive collective behavior. (Schein 1982) And tacit assumptions are those that are subtle, unconscious, difficult to surface, cannot confront or debate, taken- for-granted, theories-in-use, unknown signals, assumed practices, informal understandings. Yet tacit assumptions surface when challenged or when put to personal and dignity risk. Or when there is challenging position on identity. Dimensions of **"tacit assumptions"** being humanity's relationship to nature, nature of reality and truth, nature of human performance, nature of human activity, nature of human relationships. Tacit assumptions become visible when a person articulates his/her perception. **"Values"** are cognitive sub-structure of culture and determine what people think ought to be done. Commonly espoused and original ideas stated by a leader & accepted as values to reduce uncertainty in critical areas of the group's functioning and form as a guide as a way of dealing with intrinsically uncontrollable or difficult events. And beyond, reasonable understanding of what might appear to be culture lies a whole new meaning that has emerged as important elements, being artifacts, espoused values and basic assumptions.

Artifacts are visible and superficial manifestations, product of human action, has an aim, a physical presence and sub categories of artifacts include, symbols, behavior patterns, language, technology, rules, systems, procedures and programs. The sources of organizational culture depend on the societal or national culture within which an organization is physically situated, the vision, management style and personality of an organization's founder or other dominant leader and the type of business an organization conducts and the nature of the business environment.

Observed Artifacts, they exist Schein (1982) and "become what is understood as an acceptable and done thing. And in many ways do not follow a pattern beyond what organizational members believe and practice. Some of the most visible expressions of the culture are called artifacts. These include the architecture and decor, the clothing people wear, the organizational processes and structures, and the rituals, symbols and celebrations. Other concrete manifestation of culture is found in commonly used language and jargon, logos, brochures, company slogans, as well as status symbols such as cars, window offices, titles, and of course value statements and priorities. An outsider can often spot these artifacts easily upon entering an organization".

- *For insiders, however, these artifacts have often become part of the background.*
- *Espoused values (Deal and Kennedy, 1982) could be adaptability, autonomy, cooperation, creativity, equality, and honesty, rationality. Empathy is another visible identification for culturally permissive organizations.*
- *Basic assumptions are mental maps - cognitive stability and are dealt with when a solution to a problem works repeatedly, it gets taken for granted.*

For example:

- *The boss is right. All our employees need to be pushed. Our people will sacrifice for the company*
- *We are all in it together*
- *We are the best*
- *Reinforcement achieved through sharing*
- *A need to understand, learn, contribute and get accepted*

- *Makes a culture vulnerable to environmental vagaries or unpredictable scenarios*
- *Those in this organization we value, as they form the intellect and as we are a thinking company.*
- *Makes the culture emerge strong in familiar environments and thin in unknown contexts.*
- *And strongly influence reason, communication, interpersonal relationships, and decision-making....*

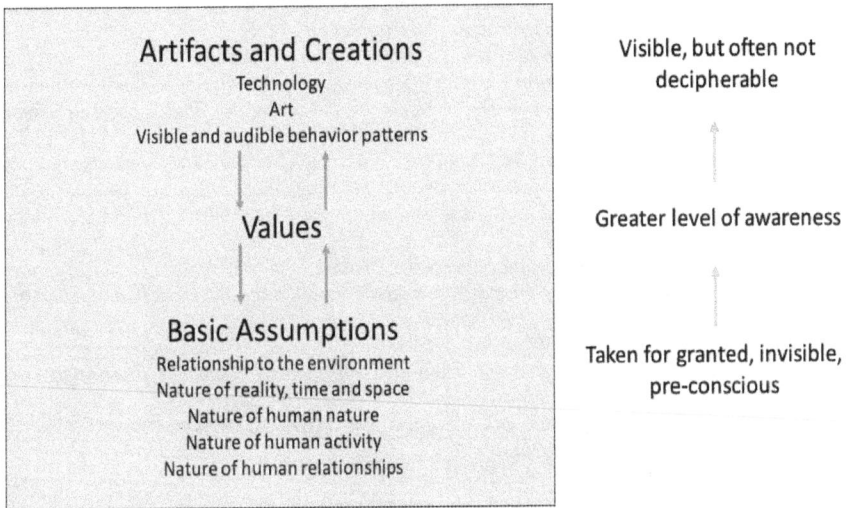

Figure 21 - Levels of Culture (Schein 1982)

While the above indicates where we identify and nurture towards a unified culture, there are also some characteristics that differ, quite strongly in very many situations.

Characteristics of Culture - Culture implies the existence of certain dimensions or characteristics that are closely associated and interdependent. Language spoken within the context, the usage of content for justifying a position or personal point of view, examples quoted to prove right and wrong all demonstrate inter relatedness. But most authors make no effort to specify these characteristics. Rather, they talk of culture as some abstract "milieu." Culture has since time come to be understood as complex yet within our grasp of attempting definitions and scoping its usage. If culture exists, and we argue that it does, it should have distinct dimensions that can be defined, reasonably understood, available for interpretation and measured. Culture provides an opportunity for a dialogue in an institutional context. Toward that end, we propose that there are ten characteristics that when mixed and matched tap the essence of an organization's culture. While the whole of organizational culture maybe somewhat different from the summation of its parts, the following represent the key characteristics along which cultures differ.

1. *Individual Freedom and Autonomy. The degree, of approachability, defined borders, values time, responsibility, freedom, and Independence that individual either has or has chosen to retain/give up for a purpose or otherwise.*

2. **Risk Approach and tolerance.** *The degree, to which people identify with their self, define their territory, enable their appreciation of encroaching upon boundaries and are encouraged to be aggressive, innovative, and risk seeking.*
3. **Goals and Path driven direction.** *The degree, to which the organization or the individual defines an end objective, establishes policies, creates individual or group goals and performance expectations and enables systems to monitor and manage performance.*
4. **Combined Integration.** *The degree to which units within the organization are governed by common purpose, are encouraged to operate in a coordinated manner and share consequent risk and reward commensurate with their tasks and challenges.*
5. **Management Inclination, mutuality and support.** *The degree to which a management provides opportunity to contribute, nurtures an enabling environment, handles power and politics, defines vision, clears communication, provides development and assistance, and support as essential to their subordinates.*
6. **Structural Chain of Command and Control.** *The degree to which an organization provides appropriate configurations, defines roles, demarcates competencies, attempts to manage through a number of rules and regulations and the amount of direct supervision that are used to oversee and control employee behavior.*
7. **Self-Diagnosis, Identity and Group Synergies.** *The degree to which members identify with self, their peers and groups, the organization as a whole rather than particularly or exclusively with their work groups or fields of professional expertise.*
8. **Motivational Tools of Reward system.** *The degree to which reward allocations (i.e., salary increases, promotions) are based on employee performance criteria in contrast to seniority, favoritism, and so on.*
9. **Conflict happening, management and tolerance.** *The degree to which employees are encouraged to air conflicts and criticisms openly.*
10. **Communication patterns hierarchical trends.** *The degree to which organizational communications are restricted to the formal hierarchy of authority.*

Structural/Behavioral - These ten characteristics include both structural and behavioral dimensions. For example, management support is a measure of leadership disrupted behavior. Most of these dimensions, however, are closely intertwined with an organization's design. To illustrate, the more routine an organization's technology and the more centralized its decision-making process, the less individual initiative employees in that organization will have. Similarly, functional structures create cultures with more formal communication patterns than do simple or matrix structures. Close analysis would also reveal that integration is essentially an indicator of horizontal interdependence.

More than just a collection of experience - What this means is that organizational cultures are not just reflections of their members'' attitudes and personalities but also involves members who are implicitly or explicitly involved in the institutional experience. A large part of an organization's culture can be directly traced to structurally related variables (Roles, goals, tasks, jobs, positons, geography, supervisory, policies, programs, technologies). In addition, a significant amount of variable that are business process (Commercial, Customer satisfaction, vendor management, supplier relationships) related are involved in influencing, impacting and resolving culture variables. Several connected and unconnected organizational factors turn relevant when a study of culture is undertaken.

Wilton Henriques Culture Characteristics

1. *"In an increasing digital world, with progressively reducing human contact, it is paramount that an Organization's fabric or culture shines transparently through its leadership behavior and processes, so that irrespective of whether it's stakeholders see its leaders or not, they*

know what to expect. In a digital world, the human voice can never reach the distance covered by the voice of a value driven culture.......a culture where performance is as much valued as its enablers of ethics, integrity, trust and respect for all its stakeholders.

2. *In Human Capital courses, there is always a subject on Organizational Behavior. But, in reality, Organizations cannot and do not behave. It's the behavior of the Senior Leadership and Top Management that that makes up the Organizational Behavior. Culture is what all the Organization's stakeholders come to anticipate as the expected response, on a consistent basis, especially in situations of conflict, or when the chips are down. Organizations are always the product of its Leadership, for which building trust is of paramount importance.*

3. *It's breach of this trust....trust that an Organization's stakeholders expect from the Leadership that causes a breakdown of culture. Culture becomes the first casualty, when Leadership does deals.....versus promoters, self-interests, external influences etc, which compromise the Organization's cultural characteristics. Breach of trust is an age old phenomenon and has been around since the Garden of Eden. It's the Leadership obligation and accountability to guard the Organization's culture with all its might. More than ever, in Digital culture, Leadership must visibly display that it has the necessary back bone for this guardianship.*

4. *More than ever, in a digital world, the strength of an Organization's Values and Culture, will be judged by how much its stakeholders trust its leadership to deliver consistently on its promises.....of performance and ethical behavior in all its dealings. Does the Organization have a set of Positive Behavioral Indicators and Negative Behavioral Indicators as well as business and HR processes, by which it assesses and takes decisions with respect to its relationships - with its business partners, customers, employees and other stakeholders. Are the positive behaviors encouraged and rewarded and the negative ones frowned upon and discouraged?*

5. *To create and sustain a Culture based on consistent Values, Integrity, Trust, and ethics, visibility of Leadership actions and behaviors is essential for credibility. Otherwise, it's like winking at a girl in the dark.....You know what you're doing (or think you do), but she doesn't.*

6. *Values are about remaining faithful when nobody's looking. Leadership is all about authenticity and character. As Leadership, will your actions and decisions every day pass the " newspaper " test ? .... If your actions and decisions were to be published on the front page of the most popular newspaper, along with your photograph, would you feel proud enough to share the story with your loved ones at home? It's amazing how this simple test or reflection can keep us grounded as leaders". – Wilton Henriques – Member of the Board at Avantha and an Evangelist for Cultural Change based on Values.*

Archetypes are very seldom found in isolation. In practice, most organizations (except for the very small) have some features of each other and conclusions may be drawn, too. Whichever the dominant culture, the main concerns are:

- *Relationships between people, hierarchies, authority, reporting, attention to task and interaction during work;*
- *Standards, of behavior, attitudes and performance; of integrity, honesty and openness; of mutual respect and regard;*

- *Values and shared values, the basis on which these are established, and the gaining and maintenance of commitment; the creation of a strength and identity of purpose;*
- *A management and organization style that is suitable both to productive and effective work, and also to underpinning the standards and values that ensure this can take place;*
- *Expectations and aspirations, ensuring that what the organization offers is clearly understood at the outset by all who come to work in it and reconciling these with those of the people concerned.*
- *Being positive and dynamic rather than negative, emergent and inert;*
- *Working within the pressures and constraints present in particular situations, locations and types of work; and devising means by which these tow can be reconciled with organizational purposes; aims and objectives;*
- *Establishing universal interest in the success and future of the organization; reconciling and harmonizing the divergence of interests, personal and professional aims and objectives within the organization's overall purposes;*
- *Establishing strength of identity between staff and organization; a common bond; pride and positive feelings in belonging to the organization; and a team, group and organization spirit.*
- *Understanding Interventions through archetypes, typical patterns for a better understanding of how culture works*
- *These archetypes are very seldom found isolation. In practice, most organizations (except for the very small) have features of each. Some conclusions may be drawn, however. Whichever the dominant culture, the main concerns are:*
- *A management and organization style that is suitable both to productive and effective work, and also to underpinning the standards and values that ensure this can take place;*
- *And archetypes are followed with Norms as the rules, practices and as they are understood and followed*

Visible → Invisible

BEHAVIOR PATTERNS
- Employees respond quickly to customer requests
- Managers involve lower-level employees in decision making
- Managers work long hours

SHARED VALUES
- The customer is king
- Employees make a difference
- Quality over quantity…whatever it takes

BASIC ASSUMPTIONS
- It is right to give people what they pay for…The people who pay are why we are here
- Everyone has the power to, wants to and has something to contribute
- Putting out less than a perfect product is unethical

Hard to Change → Extremely Hard to Change

Figure 22 – Manifestation of Culture

It is all about Norms. "Norms may be written or may evolve as unwritten understandings over time. Most newly organizing activities find it effective to start out with an initial set of norms (standards, benchmarks) with the understanding that these will need to be reviewed and modified frequently. Some organizations decide to review norms at the beginning or end of each meeting. The establishment and adherence to norms helps build discipline, trust between members, and supports a safe environment". Donald J Boldwell writes, "Norms are the rules (Refer – High Performance Teams - http://bit.ly/2ahkrVj)that the organization agrees to follow as it conducts its work. While norms may touch on any aspect of behavior the following are most commonly included: Meetings will start on time. (Some include a penalty for being late. This may involve a small standard contribution to the team recreation fund, the requirement to take notes at the next meeting, or as one innovative team determined, the requirement to sing a few lines of the song of the team's choosing.) A designated scribe will take minutes and publish them for all. An agenda is published in advance and an initial step in team meetings is to agree on the amount of time allowed for discussion of each topic. Decision-making is by consensus. Consensus hopes for unanimous support. Individual team members may not fully agree with a team decision, but will fully support it.

Does Silence Mean Consent? Since all team members are expected to contribute their views on issues and concerns, when the member achieves consensus, those remaining silent are understood to be supporters of the decision. Absence may also mean consent when the organization agrees that absent members will be given notice of decisions and the opportunity to express concerns prior to the decision becoming final. Members agree to hold themselves and each other accountable for meeting commitments made to fellow team members. High Performance cultures usually includes the following norms: No Zingers are put-downs or cheap shots directed at fellow members. Zingers, while common in some cultures, show a lack of respect for team members and cause individual team members who receive zingers to mentally withdraw from team participation.

Celebrate Success. High Performance cultures take time-out to recognize small steps or progress towards milestones or objectives. This act of recognizing small victories is essential in the development of team confidence and commitment. High performance cultures go beyond achievement or power. They have individuals who are teams and teams who behave as if they are leaders and so on. They are empowered, competent and drive towards result orientation. And they rise above politics and petty games. And have the grace to retrace, to regret or feel good or bad about things. Any team member for recognition can identify individual contributions as well as overall team results by the entire team. Celebrations may take different forms but most often might involve a simple team cheer.

No Rank/All Peers. While it is best to start out with an elected or designated team leader, High Performance Teams strive to achieve a state where leadership migrates from one team member to another to take advantage of the skill or abilities of different team members as the topic or situation changes. A critical success factor in the development of High Performance cultures is the concept that all team members are equal in decision making and that every team member is valued and has a contribution to make. It is the responsibility and obligation of every team member to identify the skills and talents of all other team members and to encourage each team member to employ those talents in the team's progress toward objectives.

Have Fun. Working on a High Performance organization can and should be fun. But the team needs to recognize the importance of play in developing team spirit and morale. Deadly serious teams can create a Titanic mentality that will significantly lower chances for success. Humor and fun, so long as it is not at the expense of others, can help build energy and improve the organization ability to succeed. Time out needs to be taken for fun. This can be in the form of team building activities, brainteaser problem solving or new learning such as juggling, or drawing, poetry or song writing.

Quality Reviews. The organization needs to consciously set time aside to monitor the quality of its work and progress towards goals. These quality checks can be as short as a minute or two where one member asks the others, "what did we learn? How could we improve our performance, based on what we have observed over the last few hours or days?"

P. Values & Ethics - And the need for Value based Ethical Features of organizational culture can also be articulated together with an understanding of pressures and influences.

The effects of rites, rituals, routines, habits, badges and status symbols all lie in the value that the organization places on them and the regard in which they are held by the members of staff. There is no point in offering anything, or in undertaking any form of cultural activity if a negligible or negative response is received. In general, therefore, these forms of culture development both anticipate people's expectations and seek to reinforce them and to meet them.

Dysfunctional aspects of culture are a reality as we study culture. Culture is a liability when the shared values do not agree with those that will further the organization's effectiveness. This acts as a hindrance when the organization's environment is turbulent. And Culture is a Barrier to change. Consistency in behavior is acceptable in a stable environment, but is a roadblock in turbulent environment. Companies have had difficulty in adapting to upheavals in their environment due to their strong cultures that are driven by shared historical experiences and attitudes, Traditions and customs, Social, political and religious values, Education and process of socialization, Degree of homogeneity or presence, Perception and Knowledge base. Barrier to diversity is driven by strong cultures enforce conformity, limit the range of values and styles that can vitalize the functioning of an organization, insulate organizations from getting a fresh outlook to its problems and opportunities and act as an obstacle to mergers and takeovers. Cultural influences in turn deal with physical environment, economic and social infrastructure, built-environment, life-style pace and quality, language, communication and interaction, media and communication infrastructure, behavior patterns, customs and habits. Culture as a consequence does provide for leadership influence and there are ways that leader can create and maintain the desired culture. These include, being a **"role model"** or example for the staff by actually behaving in the way that s/he wants them to behave. And rewarding appropriate behavior in some way, communicating to staff what behavior is desired in as many ways as possible, providing training in order to highlight the activities that support the sort of climate that the manager is trying to encourage.

Continues Donald J Bodwell in http://bit.ly/2ahkrVj , **"High Performance cultures is created** with a mission or purpose in mind. This purpose or mission should be expressed in the form of a written charter. Over time cultures develop their own set of norms. Norms are rules or guides for team behavior and decision making. The idea of using culture to solve problems and achieve results is based, in part, on a concept that the collective brainpower of an organization far exceeds the ability of any manager. Therefore, to a large degree, cultures are self-directed". Organizational Strategy & Design deal with Flexible and adaptive organizational structure that promotes high performance and is compatible with business segment operating models including deriving alignment of strategic organizational goals with the business segment and individual roles & responsibilities and alignment of strategic goals to business segment goals and metrics, as well as individual metrics. Clear objectives with robust measurement tools and feedback processes. Leadership alignment of roles & responsibilities with organizational structure and culture with business segment and organizational goals. Performance value drivers to be inherent within cultural values and organizational goals e.g. empowerment, talent development, learning, knowledge sharing etc. Organizational leaders to live the cultural values and use them as a non-negotiable reference point in decision making. Culture and Values may include, clear brand strategy for external and internal communications of company values, some identify and manage those aspects of organizational change necessary to implement the transition to a high performing culture , Cultural aspirations and values widely known and embraced across the business and staff have a clear sense of the organizational vision and mission. "High Performance cultures are also empowered. People are motivated by the challenge of achieving dramatic results within a short time-frame. It is quite normal for people in these cultures to thrash and churn during the early stages of development. This will usually appear chaotic to outsiders and members alike. It is also normal for 75 percent of the real work of an organization to be accomplished during the last 25 percent of the time allotted. Members are expected to learn as they work together. Often the scope of work of a team touches or involves the activities of many people beyond the team itself-this external group can be referred to as the community of interest that must be included in the team's communication loop. All members experience a shortage of resources. This phenomenon must be understood, expected, and available resources defined for the organization from its inception." Jennifer Pellet's "Realizing the High Performance Enterprise", published in the February 2006 in *Chief Executive Magazine*: Mention high performance enterprise and the usual suspects come to mind. Microsoft, for its culture of innovation; Walmart, for its revolutionary distribution system; Toyota, for its production system; and Dell, for continually streamlining its supply chain. High performance means something different to each of the above companies, yet all four of them consistently deliver exceptional results in specific functions, and even in overall performance. How do they achieve those results? What common characteristics are shared by these high performers? What are the critical factors required for consistent high performance? What are the common drivers of high performance? Over the last 25 years, numerous researchers have attempted to answer these questions.

For this would reflect in the pressures and influences on organization culture for which Leadership is an important factor

Evaluation Stage - Organizational culture at its evaluation stage encounters known and unknown, unobservable pressures. The particular attitudes, values and ethics of the nature, geography in which business is to be conducted and from where the organization staff is to be drawn will create external pressures. In many parts of the world this includes religious, social and influential pressures. No science of any kind can be divorced from ethical considerations. Science is a human learning process which arises in certain subcultures in human society and not in others, and a subculture as we seen is a group of people defined by acceptance of certain common values, that is, an ethic which permits extensive communication between them. Kenneth Boulding indicates- "Other forms of prejudice may also have to be taken into account; for example, some people do not readily accept direction from women or members of particular racial or ethnic groups. At times these pressures are mandated, as we would see under legal pressures. Local working practices, rituals and customs, especially those relating to hours of work, peer working norms, physical setting of work groups, festival working, holidays enjoyed, working spouses, and ways of working, have also to be considered". In some parts, activities close down for several hours in the middle of the day; in others, people start and finish early, for example. Afternoon nap in some situations is a practice and is not frowned upon. And the leader has a role in influencing what activities are pursued or not.

Religious and communal pressures are a reality as the New World order develops. In some cases, also, strong pressure is placed on people to accept the invitation to dine out with colleagues and groups drawn from the rest of the organization. While this may be presented as an invitation it may actually be an instruction, and rejection of this is likely to be detrimental to the career or prospects of the individual and the general respect in which she is held. In some situations, physical distance affects culture as they deal with proximity to perceived powers, leaders, office location etc. The inability to see and meet others when work is being carried out in a foreign location or one remote from the main organization. This has effects on the structuring and ordering of tasks and activities, relationships between the staff at the location, and making processes, and the attitudes and approaches to local problems and issues. Those at the location, and especially the person with overall responsibility and control, are likely to experience feelings of isolation from time to time and may need to be supported if the overall effectiveness of that part of the organization is to be sustained.

Psychological distance has an equivalent degree of impact in several cases. It is likely to exist as a feature of physical distance even if there is a full range of physical, electronic and telecommunications available. At best it may even be that using equipment perhaps is more important than face to face meeting. Psychological distance is also certain to be present to a greater or lesser extent between the organization and the local community at least at the outset, and it is also likely that this will never quite be removed. The organizations own culture and the interaction of its prevailing attitudes, values and beliefs with those of the locality have also to be considered. Strong prevailing practices and standards may have to be reconciled and harmonized between organization and community. This is best achieved if a high level mutual understanding, respect and interest is developed quickly, and if high overall standards of probity and integrity are also established.

Life styles – Way of living has caused undue hardship to people living over time together and as income levels change so do their disposition to their old society. Standards of living and the wider expectations of the community should be considered from the point of view that there is no point in offering high levels of material reward if these are not valued by the people of the location. There is no point in offering promotion and advancement prospects if people do not want to move from the area. The organization's success in a particular location therefore involves understanding its expectations, and presenting and harmonizing its own objectives and interests in ways compatible to all.

Triggers - As we move from archetypes, patterns, norms, beliefs and artifacts, values, then form the core of our understanding on how does culture get embedded, reputation, ethics and image impacting areas must be seen from all points of view. The organization may go into a given location for commercial advantage but with preconceived ideas or prejudices (which may either be positive or negative). The organization may bring with it a particular reputation (again, positive or negative) and, again, either about itself or the sector which it represents or within which it operates. There may be wider questions of prejudice, fear and anxiety to be overcome as the organization tries to live up to (or live down to) it reputation. Areas that have had bad experiences of multi-national activities in the past, for example, may be anxious about the next influx. People believe and live by the image we have created by our actions in the organization. That this is an important consideration is seldom realized as leader's act upon their decision-making compulsions and bottom line pressures. The activities of stock markets, and the price and values of shares all bring pressure from time to time. This becomes acute when questions of confidence or possible takeovers and mergers- and therefore changes came up.

Enablers - All organizations have to work within the laws of their locations. These exert pressure on planning, logistics, travel, transportation, production methods, waste disposal, health and safety, marketing and selling, contractual arrangements, staff management, human resources, industrial relations and the equality (or otherwise) of opportunity and access, community relations, organizational and professional insurance, and the reporting of results. Pressures are compounded when the organization operates in many countries and under diverse legal codes. Balances have to be found in these cases to ensure that, as far as possible, everyone that works for the organization does so on terms that transcend the varying legal constraints. Law of the land is an inevitable follows me syndrome. It is made to appear that there is no choice and we shall do so. Organizations are therefore obliged to set absolute standards which more than meet particular legal minimal. Moreover, the phrase 'We comply with the law' invariably gives the message that 'The only reason that we set these standards is because we have to', and that the organization has therefore been pressured into these standards rather than achieving them because it believes that they are right. It calls into question not just the organization's attitude to the law, but also its wider general attitudes, values and standards.

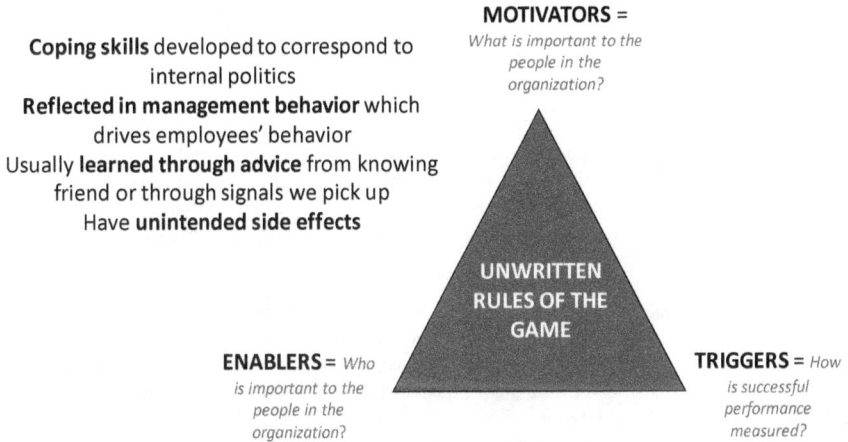

Coping skills developed to correspond to internal politics
Reflected in management behavior which drives employees' behavior
Usually **learned through advice** from knowing friend or through signals we pick up
Have **unintended side effects**

MOTIVATORS =
What is important to the people in the organization?

UNWRITTEN RULES OF THE GAME

ENABLERS = *Who is important to the people in the organization?*

TRIGGERS = *How is successful performance measured?*

Figure 23 - Organizational Emphasis on Culture

Stressors - Value challenging pressures arise from the nature of work carried out and from the standards and customs of the communities in which the organization operates. There are also general ethical pressures on many activities concerned that are covered by the law; examples of these pressures are given in box enclosed. Again, the ideal response of any organization is to put itself beyond reproach so that these pressures are accommodated and leave the way clear to developing productive and harmonious relationships with all concerned.

Values and Ethics, is it a value, art or science? It is a subject about which there has been and still is an immense amount of difference of opinion despite the time and labor which have been devoted to its study. In the business environment, managers are also often cornered, sometimes compelled into situations, which require ethical decision-making. There is possibly no single way to explain conceptually or realistically the imponderables that work role professional encounter while performing a job. It is also eminently possible for counter points of view and perspective to emerge whenever a debate ensues. Nevertheless, organizations have to reckon with clarity and precision on the stand and conviction that they wish to demonstrate as far as ethics and values are concerned. A recent 2016 Deloitte study of the Social impact practices", authors Marcus Shingles, Bill Briggs, & Jerry O'Dwyer write, "of the Fortune 500 found that 11 percent of organizations had made minimal investment in social impact programs; another 53 percent had invested modestly in programs focused on charitable donations and volunteer work. The study found that only 33 percent of companies could be considered "impact integrators": organizations that have made driving the types of change we're describing here central to their business strategies and goals. For example, they ask, why not, "financial services industry, explore new ways for blockchain to democratize banking, enable micro-transactions, and simplify philanthropic donations. The consumer food industry could potentially leverage biotechnology to change the health benefits profile and affordability of their products. The entertainment industry might partner with educational leaders to leverage advances in augmented and virtual reality to revolutionize learning and education. By supporting the maker movement and exploring new ways to leverage 3D printing, manufacturers could help provide affordable housing and basic necessities to the world's underserved populations. Hospitals and the health care industry have opportunities to use digital medicine to reinvent and democratize prevention, diagnosis, and treatment. Applying advanced technology can expedite the journey and amplify the effect. From using artificial intelligence and cloud computing to run advanced analytics studies of clean water to deploying drones to deliver food and medicine to villages isolated after natural disasters,6 real progress is being made, to exponential effect".

Drivers-Shapers - Experts in human behavior argue that ethics and values are learned as a natural part of human development, derived from school, religion and other influences. Some authorities say that ethics as the innate notion of right and wrong and cannot be taught to an adult. This means that an individual has to been shaped as honest and upstanding (or devious and venal) long before he or she sets foot in a corporate sector. Countries and the corporate that form an integral part of the economy try hard to avoid dealing with value based issues that they are confronted with on a day to day basis unless forced to do so. This has an economic, survival instinct on the one hand and a unexplainable hesitation to deal with the soft aspects of resolving an ethical dilemma, on the other hand. Several types of "professional" excuses are abundant when a potential value conflict surfaces while getting things done. Or for that matter when consumerism and corporate values clash the reality of conflicts are inevitable. Over time these practices become precedence and the fundamental value of dealing with ethics upfront loses its importance. After all we have done it before and it has worked why not now? To the individual manager value based conflicts tend to be largely personal, seldom corporate in nature or intensity. It turns corporate only when the espoused value is real and happening in the company. In performing these value based roles managers see its application on a commercial basis if that is what they have been trained to do so. Alternatively conflicts emerge when the decision-maker is unable to cope with commercial conflicts as differentiated with those of personal conflicts.

Coalitions-Trackers - Managers are people whose identities are composed of a network of roles, which are clusters of rights and duties within an socio-economic function. All organizations are in important respects social networks and need to be addressed and analyzed as such. The actions (attitudes and behaviors) of actors in organizations can be best explained in terms of their position in networks of relationships. Networks constrain actions, and in turn are shaped by them. Part of being a good manager is being aware of the moral dimensions of one's roles in the context of the networks and the organizations that they represent. Managers can unwittingly engage in a wide range of role-related acts that are regarded as ethically questionable. A larger question before us is whether managers get to see this dissonance between what is being perceived as unethical to what is being practiced – Refer - http://bit.ly/2aj5EdI

Motivators - A survey of HBR subscribers reveals that the biggest issue is not defining sexual harassment but recognizing it when it occurs. An issue debated as way back as in 1981. Or as late as in 1990 did the US government enact the "1990 Americans with Disabilities Act" that limits the use of medical tests by employers. Because of this tests designed to reveal a physical or mental impairment are permitted only under special circumstances. (The ADA is a civil rights law that prohibits discrimination against individuals with disabilities in all areas of public life, including jobs, schools, transportation, and all public and private places that are open to the general public). The Canadian Human Rights Act is a statute passed by the Parliament of Canada in 1977 with the express goal of extending the law to ensure equal opportunity to individuals who may be victims of discriminatory practices based on a set of prohibited grounds such as sex, disability, or religion.

Values and - or Ethics? This is followed by **Value Based Ethics** that is concerned primarily with the relationship of goals and techniques as applied to execution of the stated goals towards an intended output/result through a set of means and processes to specific human ends. And it impacts culture. And can also be defined as an attempt to ascertain the responsibilities and ethical obligations of professionals. Here the focus is on people rather than issues, and the primary question deals with how an individual with how individuals should conduct themselves in fulfilling the ethical requirements of their business lives. Peter Drucker argues that business professionals are no different than other professionals in that they should abide by what technically in the academic discipline of ethics is referred to as the "principle of non-maleficent". It studies the impact of acts on the good of the individual, the firm, the business community, and the society as a whole. Crossing horizons of definitiveness is real in any pursuit of a meaningful debate on ethics. In fact, it is essential for reaching a sense of conclusion, if possible. While it does not concentrate on the obligations, neither mandatory nor insisted, which a person has as a private individual and a citizen, these creep into the socio-economic system which governs business itself as businessmen are not people who are far removed from any ordinary citizen.

Laura Nash (1981) deals with the issue stating "Ethics without the sermon". The twelve issues dealt by Laura Nash addresses the basic question: "Is my business decision also an ethical decision?" Nash provides a framework that demonstrates the importance of critical thinking in business ethics where the goal is a corporate practice that does not foster unnecessary social harm. She emphasizes that her program works in a concrete setting; that it is not utopian, philosophical abstraction. Refer – www.rforc.com

Responsibility and Obligation – This is in regard to ethics that goes with establishing culture. This means that, through value based ethics we are able to closely study the special obligations, which a person and a citizen accept when he/she becomes a part of the world of commerce. Obligations in any event necessitate a reciprocal behavioral pattern in sync with individual values and beliefs viewed concurrently with those of the firm. Ethical congruence is the alignment of an organization's stated values, the decisions of its leaders, the behaviors that are encouraged by its systems and the values of its employees. The leader's responsibility is to give employees guidance: what values we expect/require employees to demonstrate, in what priority and how "absolute" those priorities are. Before a business can reach ethical congruence it must be clear on what it truly values. There must be a clear definition and articulation of values, beliefs, core philosophies, norms and ideals that the organization chooses to follow, practice over good and bad times and wishes to stand by them under any circumstance. Once stated, agreed, articulated, this core operational and execution/implementation philosophy has to be tested for compatibility and acceptability with business vision, mission, core strategy and tactics, short and long term goals and objectives and expected behavioral outcomes.

Courage to Act - Together with courage for the execution roles played by leaders in institutionalizing ethics

We would like to draw a parallel to what Donald F. Van Eynde (1998) calls as the Case for courage in Organizations. "Managerial courage is defined as the willingness to do what is right in the face of risk". Value based ethics deals with courage to act upon what we believe in and the willingness to sacrifice for the purpose. Risk here means a real or perceived danger to oneself or one's reputation or one's career. And includes such actions as confronting the status quo, embracing change in the face of resistance and opposing a popular but unhealthy idea. It means doing what is right, and what needs to be done. The determining factors are values and the other is the situation of power and position that the incumbent has to cope with to do what he believes in. Refer – www.riverforestconnections.com

In effect, for cultures,

- *There is no "right" or wrong about an organization's culture*
- *"It" exists and is observed, commented upon, criticized, or praised*
- *Culture is what the leader and his people choose to adopt*
- *What one sees, hears and feels when encountering a new group*
- *The visible products such as the architecture of its physical environment, language, technology and products, easy to observe - difficult to decipher.*

Q. In which case, Why Assess Culture? Fundamentally to close the gap between the real and ideal culture, to explore the possibility of an Intellectual Culture and to establish an organization form and architecture for managing performance.

Assess Culture Gap - Gartner in February 2006, identified the following, from "Setting ambitious targets. Consistently and continuously achieves those objectives and sets the bar at increasingly higher levels; Displays a strong sense of purpose through shared values both inside (among employees) and outside the organization (among customers, suppliers, and other stakeholders); Maintains a strategic focus and alignment so that employees know how they are contributing to the results of the organization; Has the ability to adapt to changing circumstances quickly; Has a common and shared business model throughout every part of the organization where processes are being continuously improved. These characteristics can only be achieved if there is only one version of the truth. There is strong focus on reliable data. Processes have common data measures and benchmarks. For example, terms such as "employee" and "revenue" have standard and common definitions. Gartner research has shown that the quality of 25% of all data used for management information is poor enough to cause problems as it may be incomplete, contain factual errors or is unfit for its intended purpose to an understanding that high performance organizations have an excellent grasp on information management." "If the organization wants to maximize its ability to attain its strategic objectives, it must understand if the prevailing culture supports and drives the actions necessary to achieve its strategic goals. This is performance oriented. Cultural assessment can enable a company to analyze the gap between the current and desired culture". "Why would a company be interested in assessing its culture? Continues the author Rich Grange, in (http://bit.ly/2akvhwy). Developing a picture of the ideal and then taking a realistic look at the gaps is vital information that can be used to design interventions to close the gaps and bring specific elements of culture into line. It is in this appreciation that there are aspects of culture (Processes, Policies, Structure, Roles, Delegation, Power) that enables organizations to determine interventions. If the competitive environment is changing fast, your organizational culture may also need to change. However, one may only need to change some of its practices and secondary values while keeping a few precious and non-negotiable core values intact. Often an objective assessment tool can zero in on a limited number of elements of culture that need to change, rather than embarking on the futile attempt to change the entire culture. Value and Goal Alignment across Subcultures, Divisions and Geographic Regions have become essential in understanding cultural impact on organizations".

Assess Dominant Culture – many companies, continue, Grange, (http://bit.ly/2akvhwy) there is a strong dominant culture that is pervasive throughout the organization and across business units or even regions. (Dominant as differentiated with multiple sub cultures in each of the geographic units). This kind of organization is said to possess a high level of cultural integration (Rare but possible. However, often the culture in large organizations is not singular or uniform. Organizations can vary widely in terms of the degree of cultural integration and the strength of the subcultures that coexist. Multiple cultures or Subcultures may share certain characteristics, norms, values and beliefs or be totally different. These subcultures can function cooperatively or be in conflict with each other. In general, subcultures can differ by function, (engineering vs. marketing), by their place in the hierarchy, (management vs. administrators, assistants) by division, by site, or by geographic region and country.

Assess Homogeneity - It may be both undesirable and unrealistic to try to homogenize the organization across all of its parts. Still, a thoughtful assessment of the culture can facilitate the alignment of values and strategic goals across subcultures and geographic areas. It is very important for global companies to tolerate and support a certain amount of cultural differentiation. Yet there may be a core of values, a subset of four or five deeply held principles that management thinks should cut across subcultures, divisions, and international settings. In addition, Individual-Organization Fit has been seen as a context to leadership relevance to organizational performance and architecture.

Assess Impact of Growth - Corporations that are growing fast must hire a large number of new employees. It is critical that these new hires are a good fit with the current culture. If an individual is out of synch with the culture, the organization's cultural antibodies will often attack. However, there must also be a good fit with the culture that you are trying to create. It is now possible to make hiring decisions based on quantitative assessment of the compatibility between the candidate's personality, values and behaviors and both the current and desired culture.

Assess Integration - Culture can be a serious barrier to performance. As part of a company's essence, it is normally slow to change. This can create performance problems for companies with cultures that are not open to innovation and adaptability. Constructive Contribution - alignment forms the bed rock to ensure cultural integration. the actual value added within which the people of the organization operate. This aspect is said to part of the culture when results are valued more than mere hard work, and when performance is considered more important than political connections being recognized and rewarded. Individuals are also expected to take personal responsibility for their actions and there is usually a tolerance of unusual styles of behaviors of the people who actually perform the work. "Cultural differences will become a critical issue in units that are either being combined or are forming new interrelationships with other units. Essentially, people will be required to deal with new people who are comfortable with their current ways of thinking and behaving, and who are politically vested in the status quo. The extent to which these differences are managed and resolved could ultimately determine the success of an acquisition. During acquisitions, people often operate on barely sufficient information about their counterparts in the other firm and the other firm itself. In the absence of concrete information, it is easy for people to speculate and develop inaccurate, and often negative, stereotypes about their counterparts". In Sharing Knowledge, 1999, Managing cultural integration - David M. Schweiger, Allain Gosselin, and Robert Lambertucci, write, "The net effect is potential inter unit and interpersonal conflict and even hostility (i.e. the proverbial "culture clash"). High Performers manage and govern innovation effectively. They identify innovations that will have the greatest effect on performance, and make innovation part of leadership agendas. When this occurs the likelihood that units are effectively combined and value is realized is greatly diminished. In fact, a recent study (Chatterjee, Lubatkin, Schweiger, & Weber, 1992) demonstrated that cultural differences among members of combining top-management teams may adversely affect the post-closing performance of acquiring firms. (It is important to note, however, that in cases where people are unimportant to the success of acquisitions, or can be easily replaced, this may be less of an issue.) It has been suggested (Blake & Mouton, 1984; Marks, 1988; Schweiger et al., 1992; Schweiger, Ritchie, & Csiszar, 1991) that mechanisms for increasing learning and understanding between members of combining organizations can be very effective in resolving conflicts, improving decision making, developing teams, and facilitating employee adaptation".

Assess Drivers – Hagberg Consulting Group on challenges in CEO communication on cultures write, "Reward systems, forms of recognition, may also prove to be a powerful mechanism for promoting co-operation. Mechanisms for increasing learning include forms of information exchange (e.g. show and tells, literature), task and socially focused off sites, intergroup mirroring and conflict resolution, and so forth. For the learning process to be effective, individuals must first be given an opportunity to learn about their counterparts, both as individuals and as employees. Such learning creates a basis by which inaccurate stereotypes, imagined differences, and thus unfounded sources of conflict are eliminated; substantive similarities and differences are better understood; and substantive differences are tolerated, utilized, or resolved. (Validation of cultural stereotypes is an essential part of this difficult communication. Often leaders are blind to the realities of what exists in their organizational setting because they seem to live in it on an everyday basis.) While cultural differences, politics, and conflict cannot be completely eliminated, they may be either minimized or effectively channeled. Culture clash is always a critical concern. A conscious effort needs to be made to create a new culture different from the ones already existing, and not to force individuals to adopt the culture of the other group. A new logo, a new uniform for employees, a challenging corporate mission emphasizing excellence, and the creation of tens of problem-solving committees all over the company are examples of actions taken to help employees acknowledge the beginning of a new company. Also, in order to limit the development of an "us vs them" mentality, several events were organized to help each group better understand the other group. Open-door visits are organized for the families of employees. Numerous formal and informal meetings were scheduled, particularly with senior staff, with the objective of putting both groups face to face and helping them verbalize their assumptions about the other group. An outside facilitator was used to help the staff. Finally, a unique "core" company-value-training program is launched for all staff, supervisory, and management personnel. The cornerstones of the mandatory programs are based on the company mission and values, the performance management program, and open communication".

Assess Adaptability - Today the pace of change is so rapid, particularly in the high tech industries. Only organizations that can adapt to this fast changing environment can survive. However, as Built to Last, by Jim Collins and Jerry Porris has demonstrated, enduring great companies are usually built on both a solid foundation of timeless core values, but also on the adaptability of their behavioral practices, secondary values, structures and other cultural artifacts. The secret to a company that will last is its ability to manage both continuity and change. (Culture outlasts Strategy). Such companies are capable of responding with nimbleness to the environmental drivers that necessitate change in strategy and practices. These drivers include: rapid technological change, changes in industries and markets, deregulation, aggressive competition, the global economy, increased organizational complexity, new business models. (External factor analysis in cultural audits). Getting a profile of the current culture can enable organizations to thoughtfully bring the elements of the culture into alignment and move forward towards an ideal. Organizations develop cultures whether they try to or not. If the intention is to appraise individual-organization fit, align culture with its strategic goals, understand subcultures, assess mergers and acquisitions partners, or to make organizational changes in practices or values, understanding your culture in an objective manner can give the CEO a business advantage and spare CEO enormous time and money. Not understanding culture in today's business world can be fatal." – (http://bit.ly/2akvhwy)

R. Alternate Culture Analysis - To provide a framework for different types of cultures compared to Schein an alternative Culture Analysis. This is to enable us to evaluate and study the varying dimensions and definitions of each of the cultures.

Power culture

This is where the key relationship exists between the person who wields power and influence, and those who work for them. It depends on the figure at the center that is the source of power. Everyone else draws their strength, influence and confidence from this center and requires its continued support to ensure prosperity and operational viability. The relationship is normally terminated when there is a loss of confidence on the part of the person at the center of power with those who work for her. Individuals generate power cultures when they attract those who have faith in them and who wish to be involved with them. The main problem that a power culture must face is that of size. As it grows and diversifies, it becomes difficult for the person at the center to sustain continued high levels of influence. There is also the problem of permanence, of what happens when the person at the center of power passes out of the organization. In situations where she has generated the ideas, energy, identity and strength of the situation, a void is let when she leaves or dies. The structural form of the power culture may be seen as like a spider's web, or wheel. The main relationship between the subordinates is with the center. The key relationship is with the center or source of power, hence no joining lines between the 'spokes'. The key issue is the continuation of confidence and reciprocity between the two.

Analytics Can Shift the Power Structure. Most chief executive would readily nod assent to the frequently heard statement that staff are a company's greatest asset. Yet, the people within an organization do not always experience decision and policies reflecting this in everyday life. They are much more likely to see the company being driven by efficiency and minimizing costs. Creating an organization that enables the realization of these business and people strategies is a challenging task; the majority of the challenge is actually in unlearning our current assumptions about people and the way they need to be managed. While it is fashionable to predict that the future organization will be a loosely bound adhocracy on the lines of some small electronic firms, or large research and development labs or strategic management consulting firms, it is unlikely that this will be the singular organization form that a large proportion of tomorrow's firms which will provide a bulk of revenues for tomorrow, will adopt. "Interestingly, Analytical Innovators are also much more likely than other groups to say that analytics has started to shift the power structure within their organizations. (The problem is that people do not fit the strict financial definition of an "asset." They cannot be transacted at will; their contribution is individual and variable (and subject to motivation and environment), and they cannot be valued according to traditional financial principles. And yet, organizations today are as much concerned about the "war for talent" as any other business issue. Why is this so? It is very simple. The valuation of companies has changed progressively since about 1990, putting a much higher value on "intangible assets" such as knowledge, competence, brands, and systems. These assets are also known as the "intellectual capital" of the organization. And it is people, and alone-the "human capital"-who build the value.) Whereas 59% of Analytical Innovators agree somewhat or strongly that there is such a power shift in their organizations, just 7% of Level 1 say the same thing. Consistent with our other findings, the more an organization uses analytics to build competitive advantage and to innovate, the more likely it is to say analytics has shifted its power dynamics". David Kiron, Pamela Kirk Prentice and Renee Boucher Ferguson in "Innovating with Analytics", MIT SMR 2012 issue, continue, "At PayPal, for example, business analysts — at least a select group of them — are increasingly viewed as 'thought partners' who provide not only answers to what to change in the organization, but also how to implement that change. Quantifying impact and leveraging analytics in general are increasingly mandated components of every new PayPal initiative across finance, operations and products, according to Veronika Belokhvostova, director of global business analytics at PayPal".

People/person culture

People/person culture exists for the people in it: for example, where a group has decided that it is in its own overriding interest to band or form together and produce an organization for its own benefit. This may be found in certain study groups; university departments; family firms; and companies started by groups of friends where the first coming together is generated by the people involved rather than the matter in hand. The key relationship is therefore between people, and what binds them is their intrinsic common interest. Hierarchy and structure may evolve, but these too will be driven by this intrinsic common interest. The key relationship is between the people; what binds them is their intrinsic common interest. Hierarchy and structure may evolve incidentally; they too will be driven by this intrinsic common interest

Analytics Can Shift Power Struture					
Shifting Preferences	1st Quartile	2nd Quartile	3rd Quartile	4th Quartile	Outlier
To What Extent Do U Agree with, "Analytics Has Shifted The Power Structure Within My Organization?					
Digital Life Cycle	Start Up	Growth	Transforming	Evolved	Challenged
Somewhat Agree					
					35%
				36%	
			27%		
Strongly Agree		1%			24%
	6%			13%	
		4%	6%		
	1%				
Analytical Innovators	Level 1	Level 2	Level 3	Level 4	Level 5

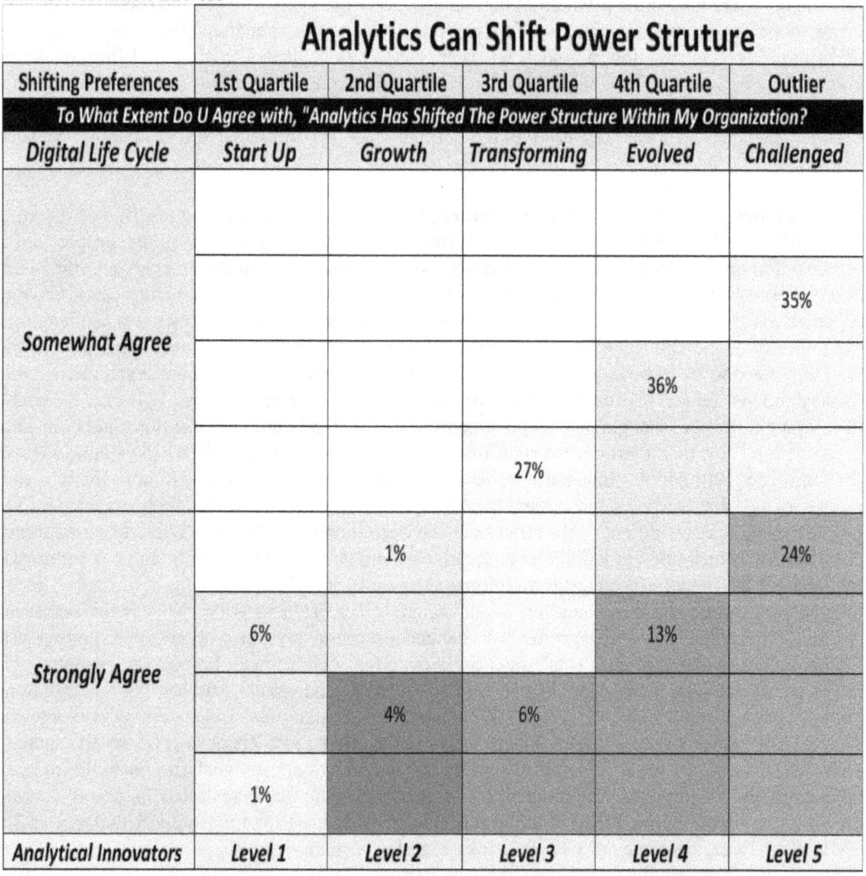

Figure 24 – Adapted from "Analytics Can Shift Power Structure" (David Kiron, Pamela Kirk Prentice and Renee Boucher Ferguson in "Innovating with Analytics", MIT SMR 2012)

Task culture

Task cultures are to be found in project teams, marketing groups and marketing-oriented organizations. The emphases are on getting the job completed, keeping customers and clients satisfied, and responding to and identifying new market opportunities. Such cultures are flexible, adaptable and dynamic. They accommodate the movements of staff necessary to ensure effective project and development teams and continued innovation; and concurrent human activities such as task forces, project responsibility and short term contracts. They are driven by customer satisfaction. They operate most effectively in prosperous, dynamic and confident environments and markets.

They may also generate opportunities and niche activities in these and create new openings. Their success lies in their continued ability to operate in this way. The key relationship here is with the tasks. The form of organization is therefore fluid and elastic. The structure is often also described as a MATRIX, or GRID; none of these gives a full configuration- the essence is the dynamics of the form, and the structure necessary to ensure this.

Role culture

Role cultures are found where organizations have gained a combination of size, permanence and departmentalization, and where the ordering of activities and preservation of knowledge, experience and stability, are both important and present. The key relationship is based on authority and the superior-subordinate style of relationships. The key purposes are order, stability, permanence and efficiency. Role cultures operate most effectively where the wider environment is steady and a degree of permanence is envisaging. Other forms may also be identified.

Focal elements

This is where the organization identifies one key element as its cultural base. These are to be found in such areas as safety and learning cultures, whereby the particular point- safety or learning, for example, is placed at the center of the organization's commitment to standards. This is whereby everything is designed, built, structured and organized so that accidents and disasters cannot happen. Examples of learning cultures are to be found across all sectors and are instigated by companies as integral to continuous change and improvement, drives for flexibility and dynamism, the development of potential, quality and organization behavior transformation. The key relationship is based on authority and the superior-subordinate style of relationships. The key purpose is order, stability, permanence and efficiency.

Tribes (Tribal Culture)

This is where organizations create a tribal concept. This is usually accompanied by strong visions from the top. Its purpose is to unleash strong creative forces and generate high levels of enthusiasm, ethics, energy and fun. This is the stated position above all in some groups. It is also to be found in some people cultures. It may also be found as a feature of other creative and dynamic pockets of organizations. Regular brainstorming groups also produce this among themselves, especially where their activities are successful.

Pioneering culture

Pioneering cultures are the extension of the process of constant improvement and innovation into constantly questioning the ways in which things are done, continuously seeing new markets, projects and opportunities. It involves attention to processes and practices, technology, organizational form and structure, communication, knowledge, customers an staff. The objective is the equivalent of 'getting the response in first', anticipating and responding to changes in customer needs, first time right, quality emphasis, improving the organization as a whole, developing and enhancing productive and staff quality. This is a part of the thrust of business process re-engineering, digital products and services, internet of things and total quality management.

Entrepreneurial culture

This is where the thrust of the organization is aimed directly at creating and fostering new initiatives, generating new business ideas and ventures, and then often selling them on, either in the form of franchises or sales of assets to other organizations. These grew up where opportunities were identified and acted upon by individuals who then either withdrew from the company that they had founded or else took on experts and managers in order to sustain the fledgling business. Other more general examples are to be found in computer software, games and entertainment; and also in the supply of components to manufacturers and assemblers. Entrepreneurial cultures are based on the creativity, dynamism, vision, energy and enthusiasm of the entrepreneur, who may nevertheless lack the organizational and behavioral expertise necessary to sustain a permanent and continuing enterprise.

Intrapreneurial culture

Intrapreneurial and enterprising individuals who work within organizations rather than creating their own are hired by organizations as change and development agents. They gravitate to those places that give the space and direction needed for their qualities of creativity, dynamism, vision and energy. They act as internal pioneers, constantly questioning the status quo, seeking ways of improving products, services, processes, quality an satisfaction, and enhancing the effectiveness of the organization as a whole. The most successful intrapreneurial cultures are those that combine an overall clarity of vision and purpose with the ability to enable high-quality individuals to operate with the freedom and space that they need.

S. New Types of Cultures - Some additional and not so conventional Types of Culture have also been covered to provide a perspective

There are different types of culture just like there are different types of personality. **Author Jeffrey Sonnenfeld (Web Study) identified the following types of cultures. (http://bit.ly/2ajbLip)**

Academy Culture

Employees are highly skilled and tend to stay in the organization, while working their way up the ranks. The organization provides a stable environment in which employees can development and exercise their skills. Examples are universities, hospitals, large corporations, etc. - http://bit.ly/1P5nMmp

Employees are "free agents" who have highly prized skills. They are in high demand and can rather easily get jobs elsewhere. This type of culture exists in fast-paced, high-risk organizations, such as investment banking, advertising, etc.

Club Culture

The most important requirement for employees in this culture is to fit into the group. Usually employees start at the bottom and stay with the organization. The organization promotes from within and highly values seniority. Examples are the military, some law firms, etc.

Fortress Culture

Employees don't know if they'll be laid off or not. These organizations often undergo massive reorganization. There are many opportunities for those with timely, specialized skills. Examples are savings and loans, large car companies, etc.

The Working Culture

This is a culture for that there is no significant incremental performance need or opportunity that would require it to become a team. The members interact primarily to share information, best practices, or perspectives and to make decisions to help each individual perform within his or her area of responsibility. http://bit.ly/2aDfWmP Such an example would be a KPMG Foundation, or Pfizer Study and Development Team or the Narottam Lalbhai Study Center or ATIRA the center for textile study at Ahmedabad, Gujarat. The scientists ring in specialized experience and would rather work by themselves.

Pseudo-Performance Culture

This is a group for which there could be a significant, incremental performance need or opportunity, but it has not focused on collective performance and is not really trying to achieve it. It has no interest in shaping a common purpose or set of performance goals, even though it may call itself a culture. Pseudo Performance Cultures are the weakest of all groups in terms of performance impact. For example, A Human Capital Group at a consulting firm that has strong political moorings would fall into this category. The CHROs office used to be a politically motivated organization with poor ethics and values that symbolized in its inter actions with people, process or clients. Appearing (appearances)to be performance driven had been more important to this group than truly building value and a lasting proposition.

Potential Performance Culture

This is a group for which there is no significant incremental performance need, and that really is trying to improve its performance impact. Typically, however, it requires more clarity about purpose, goals or work-products and more discipline in hammering out a common working approach. It has not yet established collective accountability.

Knowledge Cultures

This is a small number of people with complementary skills who are equally committed to a common purpose, goals and working approach for which the hold themselves mutually accountable. Business Consulting Practice at KPMG or EY is significantly a knowledge driven culture where competencies are placed and combined together to deliver a solution to a client problem.

Linking Competencies and Culture

Competencies and culture determine high performance. High Performance is generally defined as performance results that exceed normal standards of measurement (for indicators like cost, speed, accuracy, quality, and control). This basic definition of high performance is satisfactory for defining "what" high performance is generically, but it does not offer insights as to "how" and "why" some companies consistently accomplish tasks at higher standards than others. Moreover, it does not offer insights into the process of measuring relative performance across industries to determine "who" gets to be called a high performer. A unique study deals with the specific context of a relationship between competencies and psychometrics. In the paper, Organizational culture as a moderator of the personality-managerial competency relationship: A study of primary care managers in Southern Thailand. Nirachon Chuttipattana, Faridahwati Mohd. Shamsudin. Leadership in Health Services Volume: 24 Issue: 2 2011 the authors, "examine the moderating or contingent effect of organizational culture on the relationship between the personality and managerial competencies of primary care managers in Thailand. A survey involving distribution of questionnaires to 358 rural primary care managers in southern Thailand was conducted. Self-reported measures on personality, managerial competency and organizational culture constructs, adopted from previous research, were employed. Exploratory factor analysis, confirmatory factor analysis, and hierarchical multiple regressions were used for data analysis. Humanistic, prescriptive, and leadership culture moderated significantly the relationship between conscientiousness and specific dimensions of managerial competency, i.e. partnership, collaboration, and visionary leadership. In particular, the study found that managers seemed to be demonstrating the highest level of such competencies when they scored high on conscientiousness and worked in an environment that emphasizes a high humanistic culture, high leadership culture, and low prescriptive culture." Some research outcomes indicate that high-performing workgroups are comprised by knowledge workers who work in environments in which they 1) are valued, 2) can do their best thinking, and 3) have the freedom to seize opportunities. Such workgroups are adaptable, knowledgeable, and resourceful. "The findings may be generalizable to any people working in primary care who have a responsibility to engage people in their own care and may also examine links between strength of organizational culture and economic success. Further research could be done in other countries to see whether this conclusion is in fact correct. It would also be useful to research whether the findings apply to other health and social areas. Specific personality traits have an influence on managerial competency within certain organizational cultures. A humanistic and leadership culture should be fostered in primary health care units. Focusing on developing conscientiousness in managers should not be overlooked. Relevant training development programs may be important. This study argues that the effects of personality on managerial competency are moderated by organizational culture. To be enduring high performers, companies had to be adaptable, and to do that, they had to have the right balance between control and creativity. The findings will be useful to policy makers and those responsible in human development, particularly, health care managers".

Driving Customer Function Business Competency - The objective in this transformation for customers is to integrate the target company's marketing plans, operations, processes, technology and people into those of the core competency company by means of the following key steps: collection and assimilation of content, customer and behavioral data; analysis and hypothesis development and understanding of 'As is'; business case development and formulation of marketing blueprint for the future; implementation and prioritization of activities in relation to products, markets, customer expectation and technology interface. At the end of the implementation the newly integrated organization will have: established its understanding of key accounts and its implications on behaviors (and grading of customers) with responsibilities assigned; revised plan for product development and withdrawal as they relate to product – market strategies; steps for considering customer service and support operations (e.g. branches and call centres) and clear responsibilities assigned for any required territory transitions. Business performance involvement is a critical outcome from any competency mapping process. In the research, "Influence of leadership competency and organizational culture on responsiveness and performance of firms", Susita Asree, Mohamed Zain, Mohd Rizal Razalli (2010), in the International Journal of Contemporary Hospitality Management Volume: 22 Issue: 4 2010, "investigate the operations strategy of service firms (hotels and value realization) in order to determine whether the infrastructural aspects of their operational practices, i.e. leadership competency and organizational culture, would affect their responsiveness (as a cumulative capability) to their employees and customers and eventually their performance (increase in revenue). The approach takes the form of an empirical analysis of data (using structural equation modeling) obtained via a questionnaire survey involving 88 hotels of various ratings in Malaysia. The findings indicate that leadership competency and organizational culture (short versus long term) have positive relationships with responsiveness. In addition, responsiveness has a positive relationship with hotel revenue. These findings imply that leadership competency and organizational culture are important factors for hotels to be responsive to their customers, and in turn responsiveness to customers would improve hotel revenue Implications include the fact that managers need not only to improve their leadership disrupted competency but also to instill an organizational culture that is supportive of their employees. (It would be unfair to accuse all organizations of paying much more attention to the short term than the long term, but the reality is that it is easy for short-term pressures to dominate resourcing decisions. People whose role is to focus on the future may be given a lower priority when it comes to restructuring resources. "Shareholder value" is still linked in many minds with current profitability. It is true that it provides dividends for shareholders and owners, but the future of a share reflects the collective judgment of investors about the future of a company. What they are looking for is the prospect of the revenue streams to come, and historical profits may or may not be a guide to that). These operations practices would make their hotel more responsive to customer needs, which in turn would help to improve their hotel performance. There are differences between this study and prior studies. Leadership disrupted competency was examined in the context of service operations practices where evidence was provided that leadership competency would affect cumulative capability of responsiveness of service firms. Organizational culture was viewed in the context of operations practices, where the finding implies that organizational culture practices, such as attentive listening to staff, giving reward and recognition for their performance, and taking care of their welfare, would lead to a positive effect on the ability of a hotel to be responsive toward their customer needs".

High Performance Cultures

This is group that meets all the conditions of real teams, and has members who are also deeply committed to each other's personal growth and success. That commitment usually transcends the team. The high performance team significantly outperforms all other like teams, and outperforms all reasonable expectations given its membership. Unilever is perhaps one of the finest examples of being an everlasting performance driven organization, where end and means equally matter no matter what may be the consequences. Unilever PLC would rather take a short-term loss to build a long term sustainable business.

Refer http://bit.ly/2aoNE2Z & http://bit.ly/29W11Dv for further details on above mentioned cultures.

Khandwalla (1992) Perspectives on Organizational Cultures. Substantive research by Khandwalla is desirable to study to compare cultures

The Mechanistic Corporation Culture exhibits the values of bureaucracy and feudalism. (Burns and Stalker 1961). Organization work is conceived as a system of narrow specialists, as among craft guilds. Authority is thought of as flowing from the top and information and instructions follow formally through prescribed channels.

The Organic Culture (Burns and Stalker 1961) is a contrast to the mechanistic culture with formal hierarchies of authority, departmental boundaries, rules and regulations frowned upon quite severely. There is an emphasis on getting tasks accomplished, ensure transparent flow of information, build equity in processes, ease of communication strongly advocated.

The Authoritarian Culture (Likert 1967) is power centric towards the superior with reinforcement mechanisms created to follow orders. The actions are directive with limited scope for dissent and command and control forms the basis of management.

The Participative Culture believes in the human nature to cooperate to participate in decisions than to have them imposed upon them. Group problem solving, collaboration instead of conflict are some practices.

The Management Systems (Churchman 1968, McClelland and King 1972, Daniels and Yeates 1988) Culture depends on the technical nature of work and consequent engineering emphasis to management. Actions involve analysis, study for more effective ways to handle issues, processes are streamlined and established, standardization is encouraged and overall effort to bring in method to management actions is key to this culture.

The Entrepreneurial Culture (Peterson 1982) defines spirit to growth, individual initiative, risk taking roles, vision and the willingness to work through building capability and attitude towards the organization.

The Paternalistic Culture (Dayal 1977) identifies with the promoter who often is also the owner of sorts given their early start up history. The organization follows with the family trail, their beliefs, values and practices and imbibes many as its own. The organization values loyalty and in return provides security and stability to its employees on the job.

The Altruistic Culture (Greenleaf 1977) revolves around an institutional format with its basic beliefs in favor of good for the society and the larger environment. Selfless service, the desire to contribute to a larger well, make individual and institutional contribution substantive in both intellectual and wealth generation focus drive the organization.

Digital Transformational Culture – Good to Great investigated what it is that transforms consistently good companies to great companies, and what distinguishes those companies that make the transition from similar companies that do not, using a methodology best known for its matching pairs analysis/comparison. This was a massive 5-year research project to empirically discover answers to these questions. The methodology of the project is considered to by some to be of high standards, or at least a "break through" in the design of such studies. The results of the good to great research were a framework of concepts that shows the transformation from good to great as a process of extensive buildup followed by breakthrough, broken into three broad stages: disciplined people, disciplined thought, and disciplined action. Wrapping around the entire framework is a concept called the flywheel, which captures the gestalt of the entire process of going from good to great. "The findings did not reveal different types of Digital HR as one had expected, but instead demonstrated that a singular set of cultural characteristics typify digitally mature companies. There are not different roads to digital maturity, but one clear path that all companies can follow across company size or industry — at least in terms of effective digital culture. This finding provides a powerful road-map for executives trying to increase the digital maturity of their companies. These results, however, have two important caveats. First, the responses used to categorize the company culture came from executives and employees alike, who were asked to describe how the company actually is operating — not what it aspires to. The implication is that any attempt to make one's company more risk tolerant, more agile, with more distributed leadership, etc. must involve more than simple lip service from management on these issues. Many companies talk extensively about making their company more agile and amenable to failure, but the companies that are actually able to bring about these changes are far fewer in number. While the characteristics of effective digital culture are simple and clear, bringing them about is not necessarily easy. Second, respondents at more mature companies are also more likely to report that their companies plan to engage in initiatives to further develop the cultural characteristics of digitally mature companies. Companies that are further ahead with respect to digital maturity are doubling down on these efforts to move their companies even further down this road. Missing strategic opportunities from integration is a starting point for problem definition. They are also actively recruiting employees who can fit into this digital culture. On the other hand, companies that are further behind are less likely to be considering these types of initiatives to develop a digital-friendly culture. And employees at these companies are also more likely to report actively seeking to leave their companies — many within the next year". (The pace of restructuring in organizations always seems to be on the increase, through acquisitions, mergers and disposals, or simply reorganization. However, the rate of failure in restructuring is well documented: for example, research by KPMG in 1999 showed that 53 percent of the mergers studied failed to bring added shareholder value. Although a commercial firm may pay a significant premium for the intangible assets of another company, much of this value is often lost through the pursuit of cost-driven "synergies." Lawyers and accountants focus on liabilities and numbers; meanwhile, the really valuable assets like expertise, experience, customer relationships, and knowledge may be lost in the process.) Gerald (Jerry) C. Kane in MIT SMR 2016 blog on "One Weird Trick" to Digital Transformation, continue, *"The culture of digital companies could be broken out into three distinct groups that were almost a direct parallel to the early, developing, and maturing groupings.* We ended up getting nearly an identical result using an entirely different statistical method that didn't incorporate any of the self-reported measures of digital maturity measures in its analysis. This result provides very powerful confirmation that our three-level model of early, developing, and maturing digital companies is the right way to talk about digital maturity". This is where successes and failures are created.

Beyond Tech Culture – "It shows that technology is only part of the story of digital transformation. This analysis also did not account for the types of digital initiatives in which a company engaged and invested in. For companies struggling with identifying which parts of their business to make more digital first, developing a more digital culture could be a compelling place to start. Every person brings a different combination of capabilities and contributes to the organization in a unique way. When one joins or another leaves, there is an impact on human capital "stock" that is more than a mere adjustment in headcount. Each individual employee lends the organization their "personal human capital" in exchange for value in various forms: salaries, challenge, development, and so on. Digitally mature companies are seeking to widen their advantage, and companies that are behind may need to move aggressively in order to keep up. So for companies that want to start down the road to digital maturity, the "one weird trick" that will help is developing an effective digital culture. The cultural characteristics we identified — appetite for risk, leadership disrupted structure, work style, agility, and decision-making style — are by no means all your company needs to successfully compete in a digital world, but you cannot compete without them".

Digital Culture - Having provided a comparative analysis of the theories on various types of cultures we provide an outline for Edgar Schein's 3 cultures model and its relevance to this study. In addition, in the next chapter, we have introduced a 4th culture as an emerging characteristic of cultures called **"Evolving"** or the **"Digital Culture"**.

T. Intellectual Capital = Competence x Commitment

In conclusion, Dave Ulrich in SMR Winter 1998 paper on **"Intellectual Capital = Competence x Commitment"** asks, "One trap in creating intellectual capital is to focus only on competence. Just having more competent employees who are not committed to doing good work is like trying to win a team sport with an all-star team. While the individual players may be talented, they do not perform as a team. Building commitment involves engaging employees' emotional energy and attention. It is reflected in how employees relate to each other and feel about a firm. In many cases, the competitive pressures that require more employee commitment actually reduce it. Competition demands more of employees; they must be more global, more customer responsive, more flexible, more learning-oriented, more team driven, more productive, and so on. These demands require committed employees who give their emotional, intellectual, and physical energy to the firm's success. Unfortunately, many managers do not deal with increased employee demands effectively. (They continue to expect more and more of employees, creating not commitment but stress and burnout. Employees may become depressed and experience various symptoms, for example, employee burnout. Imagine a competition that requires you to work very hard for a long time. Then imagine your feelings when you win an award. What if you could not celebrate your success but must quietly accept the award and then immediately prepare for the next round of competition? Does that sound like fun? Too many work settings have taken the fun out of winning. Establishing, striving for, and accomplishing goals should be energizing, exciting, and worthy of celebration. Some companies have maintained a culture of fun. Southwest Airlines requires that employees be very serious about airline rules and regulations but also go out of their way to help passengers enjoy flying on Southwest. Flight attendants sing, dance, climb into overhead bins, and entertain passengers while performing their required duties. Sam Walton's hula on Wall Street after exceeding goals was fun for employees and also showed that he would go to great (and humorous) lengths for his employees if they delivered results. (The restructuring of organizational boundaries continues all the time, through acquisitions, disposals, mergers, and alliances. Many plans and aspirations fail to be realized, and value is not only lost to shareholders but to other stakeholders as well. The desire for synergy is too often expressed in cost terms alone, when it is value-adding synergy that is more often than not the real goal). Defining a work culture can encourage employees. Harley-Davidson employees frequently wear Harley T-shirts and Levis to work. They ride their bikes to rallies and join customers in the Harley experience. Hallmark encourages creative department staffers not only to innovate with their card designs but to decorate their workstations to show their creativity and personality. Intellectual capital comes from employees' competence and commitment. Both must exist together for intellectual capital to grow. Leaders interested in investing, leveraging, and expanding intellectual capital should raise standards, set high expectations, and demand more of employees. They must also provide resources to help employees meet high demands. Employees will become engaged and flourish, and the organization's intellectual capital will become its defining asset." There is a strong cultural element to performance and productivity. Writes Ulrich, "Like teenagers, employees may also feel that the demands on them exceed their resources or ability to cope. A lack of commitment does not come from the demands (because competitiveness requires that employee demands must be high) but from the imbalance of demands and resources. By listening to employees and having exit interviews, surveys, and employee activities, a company can find evidence of employee depression and lack of commitment. Too often the focus is on cost savings, and meanwhile opportunities to create much greater value from new revenue synergies are missed. To reduce depression and increase commitment, the company needs to appropriately balance demands and resources, so aspirations (demands) slightly exceed resources. Once demands and resources are balanced, employees can contribute. The learning from each such event is absolutely critical. This is a risky activity with immense opportunity for things to go wrong. It is an area fraught with politics, reputation protection, and power games. There may be many interpretations of what went well and what did not. However, as much learning as possible needs to be captured and put into the explicit knowledge memory. If the next team involved is able to access such a memory it could save many mistakes, although this is not guaranteed in the excitement of the moment. In the value-creating organization, it should be normal procedure. **They are committed to improve and competent enough to make the right improvements. Their intellectual capital increases".**

Chapter 4

Influence of Digital Organizations

Why do so many organizations fail to learn? According to Schein, (1992) - organizational learning failures may be caused, not by resistance to change, human nature, or poor leadership, but by the lack of communication among three "cultures." The culture of operators evolves locally in an organization or unit and is based on human interaction. Operators may use their learning ability to thwart management's efforts to improve productivity. The engineering culture represents the design elements of the technology underlying the organization and how the technology is to be used. Engineers, whose reference group is outside the organization, share common educational, work, and job experiences. They are preoccupied with designing humans out of systems rather than into them. The executive culture revolves around maintaining an organization's financial health and deals with boards, investors, and capital markets. As executives, whose reference group is also outside the organization, are promoted, they become more impersonal, seeing people more as a cost than as a capital investment. Refer - http://bit.ly/29SI9Jm

A. *Three cultures of management - Operator, Engineering and Executive Culture*
B. *Digital Culture, In respect of organizations and leadership*
C. *Organizational Questions in respect of Digital Culture*
D. *Measuring Intellect*
E. *Role of the Leader in Transmitting Culture*
F. *Leadership impact on organizational cultures influenced by negative actions*

Each culture must learn how to learn and to analyze its own culture. To Schein, Organizational learning, development, and planned change cannot be understood without considering culture as the primary source of resistance to change. "This ability to perceive the limitations of one's own culture and to develop the culture adaptively is the essence and ultimate challenge of leadership - Denison".

Productivity and Learning Ability - The complexity and competitiveness of today's business environment requires that companies continuously raise the bar on their effectiveness. Top performance increasingly demands excellence in all areas, including leadership, productivity, and adaptation to change, process improvement, and capability enhancement (knowledge, skills, abilities, and competencies). "In general, the boundaries of productivity move outward when engineers and managers innovate and implement more effective and efficient ways of producing goods and delivering services and when designers and engineers create new and better products and services". For teams to succeed, every employee must understand how their everyday activities relate and are important to the overall mission of the organization. Management has a responsibility to keep two-way communication flowing and recognize the team's day-to-day achievements. Employees in turn are more invested in the company. They feel a sense of ownership because their teams are directly involved in the decision-making process - Productivity increases! "The labor-productivity frontier has grown four times over since 1964, and there are many good reasons to expect it will advance. As machine learning takes holds, for example, deep-learning algorithms may substitute for people in some jobs that were previously their sole province. It's hard to know how this will play out, though history suggests we could be pleasantly surprised by the productivity benefits from redeploying people to new areas, as was the case in the shift from agriculture to manufacturing. Simultaneously, a range of technological changes in manufacturing, such as advanced robotics, large-scale factory digitization, and 3-D printing, are enabling shorter supply chains and greater proximity to innovative supply ecosystems'", write in "A productivity perspective on the future of growth", Say, James Manyika and Jonathan Woetzel are directors of the McKinsey Global Institute, where Jaana Remes is a partner write in McKinsey Quarterly, "Beyond Boundaries - Pushing out the labor-productivity frontier is also important". Preoccupation with managing change, and failing to lead, to create a vision, and provide united direction. Delaying decisions about the future shape of the business, causing uncertainty and missing opportunities that arise from the period when people expect change. The makeup of "tribes who drive productivity, performance and are focused on value creation" must be understood and mapped. Where are the networks of loyalty in the acquired organization? After power struggles, key senior people resign. Other people follow in their wake. Information and knowledge are closely guarded from the new parent. This will happen if suspicion, distrust, and insecurity prevail. In a positive atmosphere, people are keen to learn from each other and exchange for mutual benefit. Building this atmosphere must be a priority for any integrating manager.

When organizations attempt to redesign or reinvent themselves, says Schein, the cultures collide and failure occurs. Executives and engineers are task focused and assume that people are the problem. Executives band together and depersonalize their employees. Executives and engineers can't agree on how to make organizations work better while keeping costs down. Enough mutual understanding must be created among the cultures to evolve solutions that all groups can commit to. First, says the author, we must recognize the concept of culture. Next we must acknowledge that engineers or executives alone cannot solve problems, but must work together. Third, we must conduct cross-cultural dialogues.

The bottom line for leaders is that If they do not become conscious of the cultures in which they are embedded, those cultures will manage them. Cultural understanding is desirable for all of us, but it is essential to leaders if they are to lead". Refer – Denison Consulting - http://bit.ly/2a4bfAC

A. The Three cultures of management by Edgar Schein (1992) Refer - http://bit.ly/2a1xR6P - Operator, Engineering and Executive Culture

The Operator Culture

Human Interaction - The culture of operators has been defined as that which involves a strong human interaction, team working and passion to work to a vision. This culture is the most difficult to describe because it evolves locally in organizations and within operational units. Thus one can identify an operator culture in the manufacturing plant, in the chemical complex, in the appliance manufacturing plant, in the cockpit, and in the office, but it is not clear what elements make this culture broader than the local unit. Operators are found in organizations where human interaction receives higher importance than mechanical processes. To get at this issue we must consider that the operations in different industries reflect the broad technological trends in those industries. At some fundamental level, how one does a thing in a given industry reflects the core technologies that created that industry. And as those core technologies themselves evolve the nature of operations changes. For example, as Zuboff (1988) has persuasively argued, information technology has made manual labor obsolete in many industries and replaced it with conceptual tasks. In a textile plant the worker no longer walks around the looms and bleaching machines, observing, smelling, touching and manipulating. Instead he or she sits in a central control room and infers the conditions in the plant from the various indexes that come up on the computer screen. This process of focus based on automation does not take away the interactive nature of the operator role.

Collaborative - The operator culture is based on human interaction and most line units learn those high levels of communication, trust and teamwork as essential to getting the work done efficiently. Operators also learn that no matter how clearly the rules are specified of what is supposed to be done under different operational conditions, the world is to some degree unpredictable and one must be prepared to use one's own innovative skills to deal with them. If the operations are complex as in a nuclear plant, operators learn that they are highly interdependent and that they must work together as a team especially when unanticipated events have to be dealt with. Rules and hierarchy often get in the way under unpredicted conditions. Operators become highly sensitive to the degree to which the production process is a system of interdependent functions all of which must work together in order to be efficient and effective. These points apply to all kinds of "production processes" whether we are talking about a manufacturing, purchasing, sales function, a clerical group, a cockpit, or a service unit.

Productivity - The tragedy of most organizations is that the operators know that to get the job done effectively they must adhere to the assumptions stated above, but neither the incentive system no the day to day management system may support those assumptions. Operators thus learn to subvert what they know to be true and "work to rule," or use their learning ability to thwart management's efforts to improve productivity. In order to understand why this happens we must examine how two other major cultures operate in organizations.

The Engineering Culture

Balanced - In all organizations there is a group that represents the basic design elements of the technology underlying the work of the organization and has the knowledge of how that technology is to be utilized. This occupational community cuts across nations and industries and can best be labeled the "engineering culture" Kunda, (1992). He visualizes how culture works as an alternative organizing principle to rational legal bureaucratic authority. The high tech man resembles poet modern man and the compliant Soviet man, Hollander, (1966), a rationally shaped citizen whose loose assemblage of superficial values is company oriented and whose behavior is easily changed. Kunda shows how carefully a moral map is imprinted with the just the necessary shading of ambiguity around trivial decisions to provide a sense of choice and freedom. Because of High Technology no lay off rule, burned out employee's stay on, aware that they have failed according to known and well accepted standards. Striving to balance self-esteem and loyalty when that are failing, failures are seen by colleagues as tragic heroes rather than miscreants. In a company driven by the engineering culture, an employee mentioned that in the parking lot of this organization are signs that say "Maximum Speed Limit – 10.5 Miles Per Hour." Though this culture is most visible in traditional engineering functions one can see it in operation equally in the designers and implementers of all kinds of technologies – information technology, market study, financial systems, and so on. The shared assumption of this community is based on common education, work experience, and the requirements of their job. We project that in natural law-based organization a kind of creative inspiration could be found in any job. Engineers, for example, could have fully elaborated product and process ideas compose themselves in their awareness; and because those ideas flow from the level of natural law that is always economical and always holistic, those product and process ideas will be most efficient, free from problems, most aesthetically pleasing, and healthiest for people and the natural environment.

Reinforced Education - Engineers and technocrats of all persuasions are attracted to engineering in the first place because it is abstract and impersonal. Their education reinforces the view that problems have abstract solutions and those solutions can, in principle, be implemented in the real world with products and systems that are free of human foibles and errors. Engineers in the broadest sense, are designers of products and systems that have utility, elegance, permanence, efficiency, safety, and maybe, as in the case of architecture, even aesthetic appeal, but they are basically designed to require standard responses from their human operators, or, ideally, to have no human operators at all.

- *Engineers are proactively optimistic that they can and should master nature*
- *Engineers are stimulated by puzzles and problems and are pragmatic perfectionists who prefer people free solutions*
- *The ideal world is one of elegant machines and processes working in perfect precision and harmony without human intervention*
- *Engineers prefer linear, simple cause and effect, quantitative thinking.*

Complex System - In the design of complex systems such as jet aircraft or nuclear plants, the engineer prefers a technical routine to insure safety rather than relying on a human team to manage the contingencies that might arise. Engineers recognize the human factor and design for it, but their preference is to make things as automatic as possible. Safety is built into the designs themselves. An Egyptian Airlines pilot when asked whether he preferred the Russian or U.S. planes, immediately that he preferred the U.S. planes and gave as his reason that the Russian planes have only one or two back-up systems, while the U.S. planes have three back-up systems. Two engineers were overheard as saying to each other during a landing at the Seattle airport that the cockpit crew was totally unnecessary. The plane could easily be flown and landed by computer. Both the operators and the engineers often find themselves out of alignment with a third critical culture, the culture of executives.

The Executive Culture

Corporate by Nature - The third culture of management to be explored is the "executive culture," the set of shared tacit assumptions that CEO's and their immediate subordinates share

---

worldwide. This executive worldview is built around the necessity to maintain the financial health of the organization and is fed by the pre-occupations of boards, of investors, and of the capital markets. Whatever other pre-occupations executives may have, they cannot get away from having to worry about and manage the financial issues of the survival and growth of their organization (Donaldson & Lorsch, 1983). The essence of this executive culture is below.

What Schein has identified as the executive culture applied particularly to CEO's who have risen through the ranks and have been promoted to their jobs. Founders of organizations or family members who have been appointed to these levels exhibit different kinds of assumptions and often can maintain a broader focus (Schein, 1983). It is especially the promoted CEO who adopts the exclusively financial point of view because of the nature of the executive career. As managers rise higher and higher in the hierarchy, as their level of responsibility and accountability grows, they not only have to become more pre-occupied with financial matters, but they also discover that it becomes harder and harder to observe and influence the basic work of the organization. Other managers who think like they do, thus making it not only possible but likely that their thought patterns and world view will increasingly diverge from the world view of the operators. Second, as they rise, the units they manage grow larger and larger until it becomes impossible to know everyone personally who works for them. At some point they recognize that they cannot manage all the people directly and, therefore, have to develop systems, routines, and rules to manage "the organization."

Human Capital Resources - People increasingly come to be viewed as "human resources" and are treated as a cost rather than a capital investment. In a roundtable moderated by Allen Webb, editor in chief of McKinsey Quarterly, Claudio Feser says, "If you visualize the self as a kind of container, you have two opportunities. One is to put more good things into the container—by learning new strategies and skills, for example—and another is to change and expand the container itself. Now, for some people, amplifying the container is easier than it is for others. Does this have to do with intellectual ability? With culture? With humility or education? What has it to do with? Failures are important for learning. It seems there is a part of leadership that is immutable—having a sense of who you are and acting authentically, in accordance with it—and another part that's more contextual, such as skills and knowledge. However, what seems to be common to both of those parts is that they are developed over time and with practice. They are developed by learning from mistakes and successes. Having a growth and learning mind-set is crucial. Not only at the individual level, though." These are cultural aspects to people and their mind sets towards development. "Leaders are also formed in a context. By organizing companies and building corporate cultures that promote challenge and debate, company leaders create Learning Companies that accelerate the speed at which they and others grow." With change?

The executive culture thus has in common with the engineering culture a predilection to see people as impersonal resources that generate problems rather than solutions. Or, another way to put this point is to note that both the executive culture and the engineering culture view people and relationships as means to the end of efficiency and productivity, not as ends in themselves. If one must have human operators, so be it, but let's minimize their possible impact on the operations and their cost to the enterprise.

The Operator Culture

- *The action of any organization is ultimately the action of people.*
- *The success of the enterprise therefore depends on people's knowledge, skill, learning ability and commitment.*

- *The knowledge and skill required are "local" and are based on the organization's core technology*
- *No matter how carefully engineered the production process is or how carefully rules and routines are specified, operators will have to deal with Unpredictable contingencies*
- *Therefore, operators have to have the capacity to learn and to deal with Surprises*
- *Most operations involve inter-dependencies between separate elements of the process hence operators must be able to work as a collaborative team in which communication, openness, mutual trust and commitment are highly valued.*
- *Operators work in teams as deemed necessary as the nature of their work involves mutual co-existence.*

The Engineering Culture (Global Community)

- *Pro-actively optimistic, nature can and should be mastered: "that which is Possible should be done"*
- *Based on science and available technology*
- *Stimulated by puzzles and problems to be overcome*
- *Pragmatic, oriented towards useful products and outcomes*
- *Perfectionist, oriented toward elegance, simplicity, precision: "keep it neat and simple"*
- *Preference for "people free" solutions, for working with "things"*
- *The ideal world is one of elegant machines and processes working in perfect Precision and harmony without human intervention*
- *Safety oriented, over design for safety: "U.S. Built planes have three back-up systems"*
- *Preference for linear, simple cause and effect, quantitative thinking*
- *absolutes view of reality*
- *Attractive to people whose careers are oriented in "technical/functional Competence." and "pure challenge"*

The Executive Culture (Global Community)

Financial Focus

- *Absolute focus on finances – without financial survival and growth there are no returns to shareholders or to society.*
- *Executives focus on financial survival and growth to ensure returns to shareholders and to society.*
- *Financial survival is equivalent to perpetual war with one's competitors*
- *The economic environment is perpetually competitive and potentially hostile: "in a war one cannot trust anyone"*
- *Therefore, the CEO must be "the lone hero," isolated and alone, yet appearing to be omniscient, in total control, and feeling indispensable: "I'm ok".*
- *Organization and management are intrinsically hierarchical: the hierarchy Is the measure of status and success and the primary means of maintaining control*
- *We have to be team, but accountability has to be individual; "you are all Competing for my job"*
- *People have to be empowered, one must delegate, and one must trust people, Yet the more one does, the more one loses control. Because control is paramount, empowerment must be tempered and limited.*

- *Therefore, the willingness to experiment and take risks extends only to those things that permit one to stay in control.*
- *Because the organization is very large it becomes depersonalized and Abstract, and, therefore, has to be run by rules, routines (systems), and rituals ("machine bureaucracy")*
- *Personal relationships are a means to the end of motivation and control, they Are not ends in themselves (the inherent value of relationships and community is lost as one rises in the hierarchy)*
- *The attraction of the job is the challenge, the high level of responsibility, and the sense of accomplishment (not the relationships)*

Self-image: the embattled lone hero

- *The economic environment is perpetually competitive and potentially hostile: "in a war one cannot trust anyone"*
- *Therefore, the CEO must be "the lone hero," isolated and alone, yet appearing to be omniscient, in total control, and feeling indispensable: "I'm ok"*
- *O.K., After all I'm here: they are not ok., They have not made it to the top"*
- *One cannot get reliable data from below because subordinates will tell one what they think one wants to hear: therefore, as a CEO one must trust one's own Judgement more and more (i.e. Lack of accurate feedback increases own sense of Rightness and omniscience)*
- *One has to shout to be heard at all, and then the message has to be simple and of high amplitude*
- *Executives cannot get reliable data from subordinates so they must trust their own judgement.*
- *Individuals willing to do whatever to get things done all by themselves*

Hierarchical and individualistic focus

- *Organization and management are intrinsically hierarchical: the hierarchy Is the measure of status and success and the primary means of maintaining control*
- *We have to be team, but accountability has to be individual; "You are all competing for my job"*
- *People have to be empowered, one must delegate, and one must trust people, Yet the more one does, the more one loses control. Because control is paramount, empowerment must be tempered and limited.*
- *Therefore, the willingness to experiment and take risks extends only to those things that permit one to stay in control of their role, tasks and goals.*
- *Leaders who believe that their organizational title makes the difference, rather than their contribution to their institution.*

Task and control focus

- *Because the organization is very large it becomes depersonalized and Abstract, and, therefore, has to be run by rules, routines (systems), and rituals ("machine bureaucracy")*
- *Personal relationships are a means to the end of motivation and control, they Are not ends in themselves (the inherent value of relationships and community is lost as one rises in the hierarchy)*

- *The attraction of the job is the challenge, the high level of responsibility, And the sense of accomplishment (not the relationships)*
- *The ideal world is one in which the organization performs like a well-oiled Machine, needing only occasional maintenance and repair*
- *Though people are necessary, they are a necessary evil not an intrinsic Value; people are a resource like other resources to be acquired and managed, not ends in themselves*
- *The well-oiled machine organization does not need whole people, only the activities that are contracted for*
- *People need to be configured and structured to obtain their best of performance. It is desirable that they are led, directed and managed.* Three Cultures by Edgar Schein. http://bit.ly/2a2qdx4

B. Digital Culture, In respect of organizations and leadership disrupted

Interestingly at an early stage of our research we discovered the presence of a **"Digital Culture"** defined by addressing 5 questions in respect of defined organizations and 5 questions in respect of its leadership. A set of definitions and explanatory aspects of the **"Digital Culture"** was attempted and studied. We propose to utilize these definitions as the base of the scenario based case analysis as well as to help combine types of cultures that prevail in an organization to that of its leadership, their style and its impact on the organization and management model.

Digital Cultural Analysis

Cultural analysis is broken down into five component parts and four influences:

Digital Culture Mapping influences

- *Driven by 4 influences that enables evolution of culture to be gradual, systematic, flexible, adaptive and appropriate.*
- *Identity ensures applicability of cultural context and evolution to be appropriate and relevant to an organizational situation.*
- *Responsive focuses on agility and speed of absorption and review capability to understand, appreciate and apply in situations.*
- *Internalize measures the degree to which evolution of the culture has been accepted and assimilated by the group and its membership. It also provides a concurrent understanding on how do other inter linking factors read with one another through the process of evolution.*
- *Driven by leadership and processes that are consciously influenced and managed by players who are actively pursuing creation of a desired culture and adept on focusing on evolution.*

C. Organizational Questions in respect of Digital Culture.

Key questions addressed are:

1. *What is the organization history, tradition, management style, structure, and communication and performance ethic?*
2. *What Drives the Organization?*
3. *What is the Organizational Focus?*
4. *How does the Organization Act?*

5. What is the long term organizational orientation?

What are the organization history, tradition, management style, structure, and communication and performance ethic?

The organization values history and tradition. The organization is built upon stories that lasts over time and that is believed and revered by people as important learning of the past. In the organization time is not an important consideration, as it is perceived to be relative to the tasks and is managed appropriately as long as basic human processes are followed. . The organization emphasizes an appropriate management style that foster learning. The organization focuses on learning environments that involves brings together intellect, knowledge, systemic processes, personal mastery and role models. The climate is conducive and non-threatening to share successes and failures and is not a performance consideration. The organization believes in creating effective structures and hierarchies that provides clarity to roles, responsibilities, tasks and actions. The organization has effective communication channels, with and without boundaries, people enjoy communicating in relation to business and tasks to be accomplished. A leadership and management that pays attention to high performance lead the organization. The organization believes in swift and effective communication, work long hours to conclude tasks, people live at work, identify with winning and use all resources at one's disposal to accomplish tasks. The organization emphasizes an appropriate management style that foster learning. The organization emphasizes learning environments that involves brings together intellect, knowledge, systemic processes, personal mastery and role models.

What Drives the Organization?

The organization is driven by orientation to people, their actions, beliefs in the value of human good and concerns and by organizational energy to learn, self-develop, perpetuate individualization as they grow to compete. It is managed by structural effectiveness, procedural clarity, defined end states and eventual success of people and the systems that lasts over time. And supported by the need for internal and external energy to perform and focus on results. There is a conscious endeavor to support a cause that extends beyond commercial perspective in many situations. And the will to promote and perpetuate intellect as it determines individual and organizational means and tasks and denies organizational members the time, space and opportunity to learn as things evolve. Preplanning is an important business consideration and decision making a critical management tool. Taken up by the successes, stories, rituals and processes that have proved in time that it works and should be followed. Driven by business bottom line, financial focus and the need to achieve tasks and goals established to be accomplished.

Jobs make very different demands upon their holders. These demands seldom follow a meaningful and predictable pattern from which one- draw conclusions for managing tomorrow. Job role demands and choices make jobholders exercise options before embarking upon an activity relevant to business process. "Employees are unlikely to react spontaneously—or in an emotionally intelligent way—if they feel the weight of a lengthy and detailed rule book. Which brings us to an understanding of the "why." As everyone knows, a range of motives drives human beings: from the purely selfish (fear and greed) to the more creative, altruistic, and personally fulfilling (problem solving, artistic excellence, service to others). Great customer service companies are invariably good at allowing people to discover their motivations themselves. After all, these companies know that most frontline employees actually want to help customers and to gain their goodwill". They go on, "Get meaning into people's work", write, Marc Beaujean a principal in McKinsey's Brussels office; Jonathan Davidson a director in the Toronto office, where Stacey Madge is an associate principal". Technology has the power to provide extensive statistics such as the time an individual spends logged on to a system, number of keystrokes and volume of output; but does this information provide a meaningful measure of job performance? "The appointment of general managers is done on the basis of the best person available. Then we find that results are not what we expected, or the person suddenly quits. The issue here is how important customer relationships are. If we lose customers, we may save cost, but that is little benefit if the revenue goes with it. So there is a vital analysis of key (= loyal, profitable, high-potential) customers and whether they are strongly linked to individuals in the acquired firm. The question here is what we mean by "best." Market-oriented research and development. At Dunlop, claims a writer, 'We let R&D people do their own thing. There was little direction.' Researchers recall as long ago as 1957 the frustration of not being able to persuade British Leyland to make minor adaptations in its vehicles to meet operating conditions. Africa. The failure of BL's marketing function to provide a lead for research and development weakened it against more market-conscious competition, he believes. Edwards upgraded the research and development facilities of BL, creating BL Technology Ltd, 'a central technical facility, but one largely directed by the operating companies towards meaningful market-related work.' Having the best track record of bottom-line results in the previous culture does not guarantee a continuing record if (a) a local merging of cultures has to take place; and (b) the individual finds him- or herself subject to the demands of an alien culture. High emotional intelligence and sensitivity may, for a while, be more necessary characteristics than a successful business record. "Employees deliver exceptional customer service—and perform well at moments of truth—only if they know clearly what they are supposed to do and why. (The "what" part addresses their intellectual selves, the "why" the subconscious feelings that motivate them to work.) Like any other good story, the answers to these questions ought to be clear, compelling, and resonant. Efforts to help employees understand the "what" can be complex, but they are more successful when the material is presented as simply as possible. Companies should use general statements of values and principles, repeat them regularly, and avoid the extensive protocols that undermine empowerment. "The trick is to allow these employees to express this urge while simultaneously restraining their selfish motives, which experience suggests are incompatible with good behavior at moments of truth.

Demonstrating emotional maturity - There were two components to this factor. First, less-effective managers have difficulty maintaining their composure under stress, and allow their immediate personal needs to distort the way they see themselves as managers. Second, they're also turf- and status-conscious. They see little value in mingling with people in "lower" levels, or in pitching in to perform menial or nontraditional tasks during a crunch. Highly effective managers project a combination of urgency, passion, composure, and confidence during tough times. They're not afraid to work collegially with anyone (regardless of department or level), or doing whatever is needed to get the job done. People will work hard when they are given the freedom to do the job the way they think it should be done, (an emotive connect) when they treat customers the way they like to be treated," observed Jim Nordstrom, the former co-president of Nordstrom. "When you take away their incentive and start giving them rules, boom, you've killed their creativity." the authors continue, Raising the skill and the will of leaders involves the same degree of self-discovery that frontline employees should experience; the difference is that leaders focus less on the emotions needed to serve customers than on the emotions required to help frontline staff perform well. The necessary skills include identifying opportunities to improve the customer experience and the company's performance, coaching and having tough conversations with employees, and facilitating frontline, store-based training—particularly by creating an environment where employees can learn from "positive deviants." (This term, coined by Richard Tanner Pascale and Jerry Sternin, refers to employees who excel in an imperfect system.)"

What is the Organizational Focus?

There is a substantive focus on making people productive through internal drivers without clarity on final goals and tasks. They identify with organizational vision and values. They have a work and off work identity that they cherish including people productivity through learning drivers on what can be done should be done. Enterprise success is viewed on a holistic basis and dependent on people expertise.

Apart from an organizational vision, values, philosophy and performance that provides the linkages. Focus through driving synergies of the people and process systems that integrate organizational goals to an end objective with a desire on delivery through advancement of learning, knowledge, skills but lacks need for attitudes and appropriate behavior to make things happen. Emphasis on building internal architectures, organic growth opportunities, systems and processes that drives individual and team performance, resents acquisitions, mergers that takes it away from its current state of equilibrium. Focus on driving results through structure, style, roles, and benchmarks as it impacts organizational effectiveness making performance the only end objective.

A number of targets for managing human capital may need to be reset as a result of cultural revamp. The change itself is almost certain to lead to a refocusing of the organization's overall strategy. This may affect the cause-and-effect chains, and therefore the measures we use. We may need to create a new cultural vision and template. Although the more powerful partner has a natural tendency to dominate, the combination of cultures can be used to create something new. "Rigorous data monitoring helps teams quickly refine or jettison new initiatives, so that such companies fail often and succeed early. Nordstrom's Innovation Lab, for example, launches customer-facing initiatives in a series of one-week experiments. To build an app that helps customers shop for sunglasses, the innovation team set up temporary camp in the retailer's flagship Seattle store. There, it mocked up paper prototypes and had shoppers tap through them as you would a live version. Customers shared feedback on the features they found most helpful and pointed out problematic or unintuitive elements in the prototype. Coders used that information to make real-time adjustments and then released a new live version of the app for customers to test-drive on the spot. After a week of continual tweaking and re-releasing, it was ready for the store's sales associates". These are the value-creating people, for whom we will have paid part of our intangible asset premium. Hence it is important to identify who and where they are as part of the due diligence exercise. Attention needs to be given as a priority to the value-creating teams in different functions. In the rush to make short-term savings from administration and operations, it may become too late—exit value. People lack direction, so they do what they feel will best enhance their own position. Providing a clear vision of where the new organization is going is much more important than unraveling the details of integration. It is particularly important that customers see people pulling in the same direction. Vacillation on this leaves people in a vacuum. There is often considerable uncertainty as to where accountabilities lie— these should be clarified along with the direction. In McKinsey Quarterly 2015, "Raising your Digital Quotient", Tangly Catlin, Jay Scanlan, and Paul Willmott say, "At the heart of agile cultures is the test-and-learn mind-set and product-development method, which can usefully be applied, or translated, to nearly any project or process that incumbents undertake. Instead of awaiting perfect conditions for a big-bang product launch or deferring market feedback until then, digital leaders learn, track, and react by putting something into the market quickly. (Cultural Integration is typically done by setting up functional and market based project teams, made up of members from each constituent company, coordinated by an integration director. They reflect the traditional silos of the organization. The value-creating organization would want coordinating teams linked not to functions or departments, but to stake-holder interests. There will also be one concerned with overall intellectual capital, and subsets of this such as a team responsible for knowledge assets. This is the heart of integration: the transfer of intangible asset value in terms of capabilities, knowledge, and methodologies.) Then they gauge interest, collect consumer reactions, and pursue constant improvements. Teamwork and collaboration are important in any context, digital or otherwise. Wharton's Adam Grant says the single strongest predictor of a group's effectiveness is the amount of help colleagues extend to each other in their reciprocal working arrangements. But collaborative cultures take on even greater importance as companies look to boost their DQ, since many lack the established digital backbone needed to unify traditionally siloed parts of the organization, from customer service to fulfillment to supply-chain management to financial reporting".

How does the Organization Act?

Action through policies, rewards, interactive processes, job design making people an important consideration in organizational issue and through making knowledge an important performance parameter. There is action through making systems the critical consideration for organizational effectiveness with an orientation measured by appropriates planning, measured steps, building consensus and reasonable task orientation.

Action through making people subservient to systems and external stimuli. Popular prevalence of merciless meritocracy and rewards to processes and systems that goes beyond human dependence. Action orientation is expected to be more an outcome given smooth working methods and competitive pressures built within the organizational framework. Substantive action to demonstrate what finally matters in the organization, the stakes involved and reward and punishment that follows post action.

The value-creating organization will have an overriding priority not to lose value-creating assets. It is very easy to do this with the cost focus of traditional management accounting, and without any real understanding of how and where value is created. "You have to look at the **cultural integration as part of the acquisition process** and ask, what is it that you need to preserve to make the deal successful and what are you expecting will change? We don't tend to be loud and proud about things, but we do have a fantastic track record of making successful acquisitions, and I think it's because we invest a lot of time in this area. We're doing something right in terms of bringing people in and allowing them the opportunity to really do their best work and make an impact. I think that's critical. Are there employees who have gotten lost or been left behind in this transformation or have you made a concerted effort to make sure they have the skills to deal with what's new and different?" Donna Morris (Adobe), interviewed by Gerald (Jerry) C. Kane in MIT SMR 2016, "Adobe Reinvents its Customer Experience" continue. "Engaged employees ensure personalized customer experience". "Being a public company, we're focused on ensuring shareholder success, so we've had to bring people along. We're also a company that treats people with the utmost respect, but if they're not able to make the journey, they go somewhere else. (What is proved time and time again is that inexperienced integrators always make mistakes. Overwhelmed with the volume of tasks to be done, often under pressure to make savings quickly, fired up with the excitement of something new and different from everyday work—all these factors can work together to cause the initial objectives to fail. A very experienced integration director on her early experiences in acquisition says: "Never put a person in charge of an integration who is out to make a name for him- or herself." In other words, wisdom and experience will serve you best). Moving forward and not being stuck in the past is an imperative. Our company is all about creating rich experiences, and people feel a connection with that. We're not as customer-facing as Facebook or Apple, but people connect with Adobe very often in their everyday life. If they've read a magazine, or been online, or watched a movie, or exchanged a PDF document, they've interacted with Adobe, and that element of working for a company that's actively engaged in so many aspects of our everyday life is definitely of interest to candidates.

Mobility is going to continue to disrupt and transform the way we engage with technology. Using video, not only for collaborating but also as a learning platform, will continue to evolve and change.

What is the Long Term Organizational Orientation?

Long term organization growth, meaning profits, shareholder value meant people growth. Long-term competitive advantage through focus on performance empowerment. Orientation to building an enterprise that works through economics cycles without a major emphasis on revitalization or renewal. Competitive advantage seen as dominance and measures that sustain organizational competitiveness.

Goals to build sustainable business models that can seamlessly move from one situation to another without a strong immediate task and performance pressure. Sustainability only based on enhanced intellectual capital, innovation and newness of things done within and without the organization. Need to make teams work together to achieve group goals that achieves today's performance and tomorrow's systems. Destination treated as an end in itself and pursuit of the goals set as non-negotiable and that it should be accepted and achieved by all internal stakeholders.

"Companies must also nurture digital talent with the right incentives and clear career paths. Here, some incumbents may have more advantages than they realize, since these young people seem eager to help iconic brands in fashion apparel, luxury cars, newsmagazines, and other categories to reach digital audiences. When that's done well, companies establish a virtuous cycle: the nurturing of good talent attracts more of it, allowing organizations to build quickly on the initial foundation to secure a stable of digital leaders. That critical mass, in turn, serves to draw in similar candidates in the future." In McKinsey Quarterly 2015, "Raising your Digital Quotient", Tangly Catlin, Jay Scanlan, and Paul Willmott continue, "High-DQ companies sometimes feel the need for a digital leader on the executive team who combines business and marketing savvy with technological expertise. (Trying to get all details of the new company and its organization agreed before initiating action and change—this uncertainty potentially loses customers and employees. Declaring completion too soon, and failing to follow through and track changes. Hiring talent and integrating them with the organization role is not over just because the project plans are complete). But while executive leadership is important, the most critical thing is midlevel talent: the "boots on the ground" who can make or break digital initiatives and are ultimately responsible for bringing products, services, and offers to market. In today's environment, finding that talent isn't easy. To facilitate the search, companies should recognize that, in many instances, digital competency matters more than sector knowledge, at least in the early stages of a digital transformation. Only 35 percent of digital talent in the companies we analyzed had digital experience outside them. High-DQ companies are also creative about training and nurturing talent. A number of years ago, for example, P&G launched an employee swap with Google to shore up P&G's search engine–optimization skills, while the Internet giant gained a deeper knowledge of marketing. Such opportunities build competency while expanding the methods and possibilities open to companies that take advantage of them".

D. Measuring Intellect

Dave Ulrich & Allan Freed write in HBR 2015 article - "Calculating the Market Value of Leadership" say, "Organizational refers to the systems these leaders create to manage leadership throughout the organization and the application of organization systems to specific business conditions. Using these two domains, previous leadership and human capital work may be synthesized into a leadership capital index that investors can use to inform their valuation decisions. Each domain consists of five factors:

Individual

1   *Personal proficiency: To what extent do leaders demonstrate the personal qualities to be an effective leader (e.g. intellectual, emotional, social, physical, and ethical behaviors)?*

2   *Strategist: To what extent do leaders articulate a point of view about the future and accordingly adjust the firm's strategic positioning?*

3   *Executor: To what extent do leaders make things happen and deliver as promised?*

4   *People manager: To what extent do leaders build competence, commitment, and contribution of their people today and tomorrow?*

5   *Leadership disrupted differentiator: To what extent do leaders behave consistent with customer expectations?*

Organizational

1   *Culture capability: To what extent do leaders create a customer-focused culture throughout the organization?*

2   *Talent management: To what extent do leaders manage the flow of talent into, through, and out of the organization?*

3   *Performance accountability: to what extent do leaders create performance management practices that reinforce the right behaviors?*

4   *Information: To what extent do leaders manage information flow throughout the organization (e.g., from top to bottom, bottom to top, and side to side)?*

5   *Work practices: To what extent do leaders establish organization and governance that deal with the increasing pace of change in today's business setting?"*

E. Role of the Leader in Transmitting Culture

Leader is Pivotal - One of the critical factors in understanding a corporate culture is the degree to which it is leader-centric. Ask yourself, how central is our leader to the style of this organization? If you are the leader yourself, the culture of your company is likely to reflect your personality, including your neurosis. So if the CEO avoids conflict and tends to sweep it under the carpet, don't be surprised if you see avoidance of conflict played out in the organization. The behavior that is modeled by the leader and the management team profoundly shapes the culture and practices of the organization. What management emphasizes rewards and punishes can tell you what is really important. The behavior of members of the senior team, their reactions in a crises and what they talk routinely talk about, all sets the tone of the culture. If the culture is already firmly established when the CEO assumed leadership and he/she simply inherited a strong set of traditions, then he/she may play the role of the guardian of the old culture. On the other hand, CEOs such as Lou Gerstner at IBM, Lee Iacocca at Chrysler, Sandy Weil/John Reed at Citicorp were brought in to be change agents charged with dramatically transforming the organizational culture including the Continuing issues of CEO and the LEADER in influencing and changing Culture. Refer - http://bit.ly/2aoP8uc

Leader Leads Change - R S S Mani in http://bit.ly/2a6pG7U writes, "Again CEO/Leader is expected to manage organizations through a process of change. And changing an organization is messy, complicated business. A study by Kotter and Heskett (1992) indicated that culture change becomes tougher as organizations become more established and successful. The very bases for a company's earlier success can be hindrances to needed changes under new and different scenarios from those that existed previously".

Prevailing models provide uncertain guideposts. For example, it is standard fare within the leadership disrupted literature (Bennis, 1994) to depict the need for a "vision" of a desired future state of the enterprise. R S S Mani in http://bit.ly/2a6pG7U continues, "What if elements of a vision clash with each other? What if a leader, for example, decides to embrace a total quality management culture built upon trust among all parties and, at the same time, embarks upon a series of layoffs which are likely to engender distrust among those same parties? The conventional wisdom in response is to acknowledge that there will be sadness and losses and a murky period which goes under the heading of "the neutral zone"; but, in the end, there will be "new beginnings" (Bridges, 1981). How long does the neutral zone last? Existing study provides no solid answers. How long will leaders with a vision wait for the culture to change in positive ways? Study supports the idea that culture change is a multi-year effort (Schein, 1992).

Leadership disrupted Contingency - If we broaden our conceptualization of culture change to include both intended consequences (planned change) and unintended consequences (unplanned change), then it is at least possible to be confident that downsizing is a catalyst for culture change. Organizational theorists from Lewin (1951) forward, including Chris Argyris (1992) have insisted upon the need for a destabilizing element in any change process. The existing status quo is conceptualized as a dynamic in which forces resisting change and forces pushing for change have found a balance. In order to shift the balance (in the favor of change), the situation needs to be "unfrozen". In other words, people have to be rocked out of their comfortable existence, so they will be alerted to the need for change". Some leadership approaches take a universal perspective; other uses a contingency perspective. Leaders, in their pursuit of assuming significant roles, must navigate through different leadership passages. Transition from one level to the next corresponds to the natural evolution of the work hierarchy. Each level mandates employees to demonstrate specific leadership competencies for them to move to the next level. It is advisable that leaders may go through leadership competency assessment while making a transition to the subsequent level. Furthermore, it is also advisable that such transitions may be supported with the creation of individual development plans for selected leaders.

F. Leadership disrupted impact on organizational cultures influenced by negative actions

Studying leadership impact on cultures is relevant to the study given the inter relatedness that is being proposed and here is a negative context – downsizing and restructuring. Shermon (2000) qualifies as a destabilizer of status quo ante even under circumstances where departures are voluntary. Hickok (1995), for example, documented symptoms of survivor illness at an Air force installation that had, up to the point of the study, experienced only voluntary departures. The literature is replete with examples of burnout, depression, anger, and betrayal as common responses by survivors of layoffs, restructuring and change Noer (1993); Brockner, (1992). Not all responses are negative: there are reports of people getting "charged up", finding new excitement in their work, being challenged by the prospect of "doing more with less" or saving the organization (Noer, 1993). Hickok (1995) found that "implementers" of layoffs (i.e., those "pulling the strings") had more positive reactions than did "implementees" (i.e., those who were having the layoffs "done to them").

In any event, it should be acknowledged that cultural change has altered the rule of the employment "game". The way these changes have tended to be theoretically euphemized is by indicating that the "psychological contract" between employers and employees has been violated Rousseau, (1995). No longer can the leader offer job security. The "new" psychological contract being marketed is conditional employment, with the availability of training and development opportunities to help keep employees "employable", even if not at this particular company (e.g., Tichy and Sherman, 1994; Waterman, Waterman, and Collard, 1994).

From a broader cultural perspective, cultural change can be seen as the embodiment of the **"creative destruction"** inherent in capitalism. As Schumpeter (1950) wrote about capitalism, restructuring and consequent cultural change might not be pretty to watch and people will get hurt for sure, but this is the way the market takes care of itself. There is no entitlement to a job any more than there is entitlement for a corporation to exist. People, as well as organizations, need to gear up to compete in the marketplace. Bridges (1994) and others warn anyone within hearing distance that only the foolish will let their fates be decided by those they work for; the wise ones will think and act like entrepreneurs, or the leaders even if they fall under the label "employees".

The symbolic aspects of culture change driven by a leader associated with organizations should not be overlooked. The very act of change creates an appearance of leadership that is taking charge. In the instance of the United States government, for example, when leaders make the claim that by eliminating hundreds of thousands of federal jobs they have reduced the cost of government or when Congress converges as one team to eliminate Osama Bin Laden or to handle Hurricane Sandy. The symbolism associated with the change may weigh more heavily in people's minds than the costs, which may include contracting out at a much higher price for services previously provided in-house.

The political aspects of culture change associated with downsizing are also quite dramatic. Change represents a power shift in the direction of top management and shareholders. One way of conceptualizing the change is via expectancy theory (Vroom, 1964). The unsaid message is that management is not afraid to decide who "has a future" with this organization and who does not. The message is "if you want to continue to work here, you will have to work harder, be more responsive, be more of a team player, etc.

There are **"Theory X" and/or "Theory Y" dynamics** (McGregor, 1960) at work with change as well, depending upon the circumstances. The underlying theme of Theory X thinking, emulated by the leader, is that workers cannot be trusted to put forth effort on their own. They need to be externally motivated by the threat of punishment in order to put out their best efforts. Of all the change driven practices, the one most closely associated with Theory X is the practice of giving people no termination notice. In spite of what would seem the obvious inhumanity of walking people who have worked for an organization for twenty or more years straight to the door, this remains a common corporate change management practice. The assumption that would seem to underlie the practice is that people will use notice time to undermine the organization or at least to be unproductive. That is a leader's call.

From a **Theory Y perspective,** for the leader, cultural change and behavior modification may be seen as a way to free up workers to do the good work they care to do. The analysis that precedes change is designed with the intent of reducing unnecessary or low value work, minimizing bureaucratic controls, and eliminating unneeded communications layers. Cultural change intent, from a Theory Y perspective, is to enable workers to be challenged by interesting work and to have the opportunity to produce extraordinary results that are aligned with the organization's mission and goals.

In **Leadership in high-performance Organizational Cultures** (published by Quorum Books 2000), Stanley D. Truskie suggests, "there is a direct link between leadership, organizational culture, and performance." According to his study and analysis, the most effective leader has an impact on "forming the culture of an organization, which further can have an enhancing effect of improving the level, ensuring the consistency, and sustaining the organization's continuing performance improvement." Truskie believes that many leaders are preoccupied with identifying and then manifesting an "ideal" style of leadership when, in fact, no such style exists. That is to say, even the most effective leaders have significant human imperfections; however, they are aware of these imperfections and make every effort to ensure that these imperfections do not have a negative impact on their respective organizations.

Exceptional leaders have an organizational leadership disrupted strategy: "a guiding plan that creates an internal environment; a culture that is healthy, balanced, and adaptive." The ultimate organizational objective is to achieve superior, long-term performance. Truskie's own objective is to formulate a model that enables any organization to achieve that objective by developing the effective leaders it needs. Truskie introduces what he has named the L4 Strategy. This concept provides a framework and some principles to help clarify and guide one's thinking in addressing important and complex leadership issues and challenges. With meticulous care, reiterating key points along the way, Truskie explains how the L4 Strategy gives clarity and direction to establishing organization direction, and, to developing organizational effectiveness. There are four "cultural patterns" which, according to Truskie, the effective leader must set or re-set in proper balance within her or his organization: The Cooperation Culture, The Inspiration Culture, The Achievement Culture, and The Consistent Culture.

On Change - Here is a key point: Because the needs of a given organization change, sometimes dramatically and often unexpectedly, the effective leader must be prepared to adjust the balance of the four "cultural patterns." When there are only moderate out-of-balance conditions, "rebalance initiatives" are needed. But when the conditions are severe, time is of the essence; therefore, counterbalance initiatives are needed. The L4 leader's presence and style are critical to the success of either sets of initiatives. Truskie correctly notes that leadership must not be limited to that provided only by a CEO. Apparently agreeing with Noel Tichy's analysis in, Truskie stresses the importance of developing leadership throughout the organization. Ideally, an organization will thus have a combination of leaders who, individually and in collaboration, implement both a directional leadership strategy and an organizational leadership strategy.

On numerous occasions, Truskie cautions that there is no one "ideal" style, nor an infallible "model", nor any single combination of leadership traits, characteristics and behaviors that are most appropriate to all organizations in all phases of their development.

Leadership disrupted in Organizational Cultures is Truskie's explanation of the potential, beneficial implications of the L4 Strategy with specific relevance to creating and then sustaining a high-performance organizational culture. Leaders as well as those whom they lead must constantly monitor the balance of four aforementioned cultural patterns. Imbalances are inevitable. Although Truskie does not discuss it, he would probably agree that an early-warning system of some kind is highly desirable. The model he provides suggests various ways by which to recognize and then respond effectively to symptoms of such imbalances.

Influence of Digital HR - "To help companies better prepare for their digital futures, we delved into how digitally maturing organizations strengthen their cultures and develop the talent that drives them", say, Gerald C Kane, Doug Palmer, Anh Nguyen Phillips, David Kiron, Natasha Buckley et all, in MIT SMR 2016 in Aligning The Organization For Its Digital Future, "Their research conclusions include, "**Creating an effective digital culture is an intentional effort:** Digitally maturing companies are constantly cultivating their cultures. Nearly 80% of respondents from digitally maturing companies say their companies are actively engaged in efforts to bolster risk taking, agility, and collaboration. Only 23% of companies at the early stages of digital development are doing so. 1. **Senior-level talent appears more committed to digitally maturing enterprises:** Companies that give their senior vice presidents, vice presidents, and director-level leaders the resources and opportunities to develop themselves in a digital environment are more likely to retain their talent. In contrast, approximately 30% of such leaders who lack such opportunities are planning to find new jobs in less than one year. 2. **Digitally maturing organizations invest in their own talent:** More than 75% of digitally maturing organizations surveyed provide their employees with resources and opportunities to develop their digital acumen, compared to only 14% of early-stage companies. Success appears to breed success — 71% of digitally maturing companies say they are able to attract new talent based on their use of digital, while only 10% of their early-stage peers can do so. 3. **Soft skills trump technology knowledge in driving digital transformation:** When asked about the most important skill for leaders to succeed in a digital environment, only 18% of respondents listed technological skills as most important. Instead, they highlighted managerial attributes such as having a transformative vision (22%), being a forward thinker (20%), having a change-oriented mindset (18%), or other leadership and collaborative skills (22%). A similar emphasis on organizational skills above technical ones for succeeding in digital environments was also reported for employees. 4. **Digital congruence is the crux:** To navigate the complexity of digital business, companies should consider embracing what we call digital congruence — culture, people, structure, and tasks aligned with each other, company strategy, and the challenges of a constantly changing digital landscape. For example, a conservative and hierarchical organization populated with energetic entrepreneurs may not be able to harness their drive and energy. (Trying to be fair to both partners and give equal treatment—as we observed earlier, will not work out practically. Applying a universal integration process to all units regardless of differences in size or difficulty—the integration in the homebase of a multinational will always require more extensive attention than in smaller units). Similarly, an organization with a flat and nimble structure may still struggle if its culture fears risk. When culture, people, structure, and tasks are firing in sync, however, businesses can move forward successfully and confidently."

Chapter 5

Built by Leadership Disrupted

This Chapter focuses on building upon the leadership connection to culture as well as the organization. Thereafter we introduced a set of Leadership disrupted Styles in the context of the Digital Culture and also provided appropriate definitions to enable construction of the Scenario based case analysis.

A. *Leadership – Definitions & Early Thoughts*
B. *Leadership Studies by Iowa, Michigan, Likert, Blake & Mouton, Vroom, Khandwalla*
C. *Leadership Theories of Traits, Transformation, Contingency, Situational, Path Goal, Decision Tree, Vertical Dyad Linkage, Managerial Grid, Group and Exchange*
D. *Social, Collaborative Group Learning, Group and Exchange Based Leadership Approaches*
E. *Analytical Perspectives on Leadership*
F. *Digital Culture Leadership that promotes full human development*
G. *Leadership Power Dimensions*
H. *Comparative Study Critique*
I. Transformational Leadership disrupted
J. *Leadership disrupted Definitions in the context of the Digital Culture*

Defining leadership, assessing leadership and developing leadership may prove to be the most important business differentiators of current times. Hard aspects of the business such as strategy, structure, technology and processes may be imitated without much difficulty, but the real value and differentiation is created in something which cannot be imitated: "The Digital Leadership". Thus, in a nutshell, leadership has clearly emerged as a source of competitive advantage for organizations of current times. Effective organization cultures are positive and designed rather than emergent. They must be capable of gaining commitment to purpose, the ways in which this is pursued and the standards adopted by everyone. Leadership Cultures are a summary and reflection of the aims, objectives and values held by the institution. Where one of these is apparent, different groups and individuals form their own aims and objectives and adopt their own values; and where these are at variance with overall purpose, or negative in some way, they are dysfunctional and may become destructive. The reverse of this- the organization's commitment to its people – is also essential. A strong sense of identity towards the organization and its purposes and values is required, and this happens when these are clear and positive direction from its leadership. (Shermon 2012 – KPMG)

A. Leadership – Definitions & Early Thoughts

Leadership has probably been written about, formally studied, and informally discussed more than any other single topic. Many writers and managerial practitioners have propounded a series of definitions and sometimes myths. Leaders are born, leaders are heroic, a leader's performance is measured by results, leaders maintain stability in an organization etc. We have over time reached some set of conclusions although not exhaustive.

In the early 20th century one prevailing orthodoxy held that organizations cannot operate democratically because, especially during crisis, organizations need firm leaders and obedient subordinates (Bell, 1950; Michaels, 1959). Leadership was seen a stable characteristic of individual people: either one had leadership traits or one did not. During the 1920's and 1930's this orthodoxy was challenged in many ways: Weber (1947) portrayed leadership as a kind of a activity that bureaucracies depersonalize and that followers might judge illegitimate.

The person in the role of leader who fulfils expectations and achieves group goals provides rewards for others that are reciprocated in the form of status, esteem, and heightened influence. Because leadership embodies a two-way influence relationship, recipients of influence assertions may respond by asserting influence in return. The very sustenance of the relationship depends upon some yielding to influence on both sides.

It is critical to understand whether socially sensitive intellectual leaders possess and share certain characteristics?

- *They seek knowledge intensive content in their work*
- *They like to supervise and work with "smart" peers*
- *They identify themselves as change agents*
- *They have a comfort to be socially visible*
- *They are courageous, speak their mind*
- *They believe in people*
- *They are value-driven*
- *They are lifelong learners*
- *They have the ability to deal with complexity, ambiguity and uncertainty.*
- *They are visionaries.*

- *They have a string technology affiliation*

In addition to attribution, charismatic and transformational theories, social learning, affiliation, productivity emphasis and a substitute approach have emerged to meet the challenge of understanding the complexities and alternatives of leadership.

Robert J. Alio (Alio, 1999) identified three central tasks based on his analysis of high performing organizations:

- *Reinforcing Values: To identify and communicate the values and establish the purpose of the enterprise.*
- *Developing Vision: To envision the end state and help the organization define strategy.*
- *Building Community: The ability to forge a community of individuals who will work together to realize their individual and collective potential.*

Connecting Leadership to Organizational Factors & Culture			
Vision			
Organizing Arrangements, Social Factors Physical Setting, Technology			
Goals - Objectives	Culture	Space configuration	Tools & equipment
Strategies - Purpose	Management Style	Physical ambience	Plant Machinery
Structure - design	Communication	Interior design	Technology - Devices - Wearables
Policies Processes	360 Degree Interaction	Architectural design	Systems
Admin Systems	Informal patterns	Financial Structuring	Job Design - Redesign
Reward systems	Individual Attributes	Customer Relationships	Workflow
Ownership - Promoters	Networks	Transport Logistics	Tech Processes
Values - Beliefs - Perception	Social Connect	Connectivity WIFI	Tech Systems - Socio Tech Systems
Binding Contracts	Leadership	Bandwidth	Digital

Figure 25 - Connecting Leadership Disrupted to Organizational Factors & Culture

A Definition of Leadership and the theories that govern leadership in the context of organizational culture. A detailed analysis of the various theories is attempted below by us and finally based on Khandwalla 1992 study work on **"Excellence in Organizational Design"** an analytical appreciation of the leadership and organization work is provided.

Leadership disrupted is both a process and a property. As a process, leadership involves the use of non-coercive influence. As a property, leadership is the set of characteristics attributed to someone who is perceived to use influence successfully. Leadership is the process of influencing a group of followers, adding value, and helping the community adapt to change. Leaders drive the organizational members towards achievement of the organizational goals by influencing people who are responsible for the tasks.

Goal Congruence - From an organizational viewpoint, leadership is vital because it has such a powerful influence on individual and group behavior. Moreover, because the goal toward which the group directs it efforts towards a desired goal of the leader, it may align with organizational goals. Leadership involves neither force nor coercion. A manager who relies on force to direct subordinates' behaviors is not exercising leadership.

Traits - There are several distinct theoretical bases for leadership. At first, leaders were felt to be born, not made. This so-called "great man" theory of leadership implied that some individuals are born with certain traits that allow them to emerge out of any situation or period of history to become leaders. This evolved into what is now known as the trait theory of leadership. The trait approach is concerned mainly with identifying the personality traits of the leader. Dissatisfied with this approach, and stimulated by study such as the Ohio State studies, authors switched their emphasis from the individual leader to the group being led. In the group approach, leadership is viewed more in terms of the leader's behavior and how such behavior affects and is affected by the group of followers. The situational approach was initially called Zeitgeist (a German word meaning "spirit of the times"); the leader is viewed as a product of the times and the situation. The person with the particular qualities or traits that a situation requires will emerge as the leader. Such a view has much historical support as a theoretical basis for leadership and serves as the basis for situational (Hershey and Blanchard) – and now, contingency- theories of leadership.

Essentially.

- *Management and leadership are distinct elements. Management involves formal position power, whereas leadership relies on social influence processes.*
- *Some leadership approaches focus on traits, whereas other focus on behaviors.*
- *Some leadership approaches take a universal perspective; other uses a contingency perspective.*
- *The Leadership Grid evaluates leader behavior along two dimensions, concern for production and concern for people. It suggests that effective leadership styles include high levels of both behaviors.*
- *The Contingency theory of Leadership suggests that a leader's effectiveness depend on the situation.*

B. Leadership Studies by Hawthorne, Iowa, Michigan, Likert, Blake & Mouton, Vroom, Khandwalla

Learning – Social Roles: Emphasis on social roles, supervisory styles, freedom systems, are now pronounced in today's leadership and talent management thinking. Millennials comfort with social presence is an interesting outcome from this research.

Hawthorne studies (Mayo 1946, Roethlisberger; and Dickson 1939) claimed to show that productivity rises when supervisors act friendly towards their subordinates. Barnard (1938) said that authority originates in the subordinates who obey orders rather than in the superiors who issue orders. Of these challenges only the one from Hawthorne studies became orthodoxy, as one short-lived school of thought called human relations. By the 1950's numerous synthesis was taking place. Coch and French (1948) and Lewin (1953) were espousing democratic leadership. Bales (1953), Cartwright and Zander (1953) and Gibb (1954) were viewing leadership as an activity performed collectively by groups rather than individually by group members. Bales (1953, 1958) was distinguishing leader's social roles from their task roles, and Cattell and Stice (1954) and Stogdill (1948) were considering the different personality attributes of distinct types of leaders. By the late 1950's the Ohio State Studies were identifying two dimensions of leadership behavior: (1). Consideration, by which a supervisor displays friendship, mutual respect. Trust and warmth and (2) initiating structure, by which a supervisor organizes subordinate's activities (Fleishman et all, 1955. Stogdill and Coons, 1957). In effect, what were initially seen as conflicting views being reinterpreted as independent dimensions of a complex phenomenon?

The Iowa, Ohio State, and Michigan studies are three of the historically most important leadership studies for the study of organizational behavior. Unfortunately, they are still heavily depended upon, and leadership study has not surged ahead from this relatively auspicious beginning. Before analyzing the current status of leadership study, it is important to look at the theoretical development that has occurred through the years.

Historical contributions to the study of organizational behavior had indirect or direct implications for leadership style. For example, the Hawthorne studies (see above) were interpreted in terms of their implications for supervisory style. Also relevant is the classic work done by Douglas McGregor, 1960, in which his Theory X represents the old, authoritarian style of leadership and his Theory Y represents the enlightened, humanistic style. And indeed the Theory Z focused on participate management. The studies discussed are directly concerned with style. The Iowa studies analyzed the impact of autocratic, democratic and laissez faire styles, and the studies conducted by the Michigan group found the employee-centered supervisor to be more effective than the production-centered supervisor. The Ohio State studies identified consideration (a supportive type of style) and initiating structure (a directive type of style) as being the major functions of leadership. The trait, group and social learning theories have indirect implications for style, and the human relations and task directed styles play an important role in Fiedler's contingency theory. The path-goal conceptualization depends heavily upon directive, supportive, Participative and achievement oriented styles of leadership.

The Iowa Leadership Studies (Pettinger, 1986)

Learning – Virtual Teams: To us virtual teams benefit from research by Kurt Lewin, Lippitt, Group Dynamics. Today teams work using remote access, flexible work locations, home offices, using technologies such as face time, Instant Messaging, Skype or Vonage (VoIP) methods to connect.

Group Dynamics - A series of pioneering leadership studies conducted in the late 1930s by Ronald Lippitt and Ralph K. White (Luthans, 1989) under the general direction of Kurt Lewin at the University of Iowa have had a lasting impact. Lewin is recognized as the father of group dynamics and as an important cognitive theorist. In the initial studies hobby clubs for ten-year-old boys were formed. Each club was submitted to three different styles of leadership- authoritarian, democratic and laissez faire. The authoritarian leader was very directive and allowed no participation. This leader tended to give individual attention when praising and criticizing but tried to be friendly or impersonal rather than openly hostile. The democratic leader encouraged group discussion and decision making. He tried to be "objective" in his praise or criticism and to be one of the group in spirit. The laissez faire leader gave complete freedom to the group; he essentially provided no leadership.

Choice of Styles - Under experimental conditions, the three leadership styles were manipulated to show their effects on variables such as satisfaction and frustration/aggression. Some of the results were clear-cut and others were not. One definite finding was the boys' overwhelming preference for the democratic leader. In individual interviews, nineteen of the twenty boys stated they liked the democratic leader better than the authoritarian leader. The boys also chose the laissez faire leader over the autocratic one in seven out of ten cases. For most of the boys, even confusion and disorder were preferable to strictness and rigidity.

Pattern Maintenance - Unfortunately, the effects that styles of leadership had on productivity were not directly examined. The experiments were designed primarily to examine patterns of aggressive behavior. However, an important by-product was the insight that was gained into the productive behavior of a group. For example, the authors (Ronald Lippitt and Ralph K. White) found that a research group of boys subjected to the autocratic leader reacted in one of two ways: either aggressively or apathetically. Both the aggressive and apathetic behaviors were deemed to be reactions to the frustration caused by the autocratic leader. The authors also pointed out that the apathetic groups exhibited outbursts of aggression when the autocratic leader left the room or when a transition was made to a freer leadership atmosphere. The laissez faire leadership climate actually produced the greatest number of aggressive acts from the group. The democratically led group fell between the one extremely aggressive group and the four apathetic groups under the autocratic leaders.

Effect on Groups - Sweeping generalizations on the basis of the Lippitt and White studies are dangerous. Preadolescent boys making masks and carving soap are a long way from adults working in a complex, formal organization. Furthermore, from the viewpoint of modern behavioral science study methodology, many of the variables were not controlled. Nevertheless, these leadership studies have extremely important historical significance. They were the pioneering attempts to determine, experimentally, what effect styles of leadership have on a group. Like the Hawthorne studies, the Iowa studies are too often automatically discounted or at least de-emphasized because they were experimentally crude. The values of the studies were that they were the first to analyze leadership from the standpoint of scientific methodology, and, more important, they showed that different styles of leadership can produce different, complex reactions from the same or similar groups.

The Ohio State Leadership Studies (Luthans, 1989)

Learning - Search for Effectiveness - The Ohio State studies started with the premise that no satisfactory definition of leadership existed. They also recognized that previous work had too often assumed that leadership was synonymous with good leadership. The Ohio State group was determined to study leadership; regardless of definition or of whether it was effective or ineffective.

In 1945, the Bureau of Business study at Ohio State University initiated a series of studies on leadership. An interdisciplinary team of authors from Psychology, sociology, and economics developed and used the **Leader Behavior Description Questionnaire** (LBDQ) to analyze leadership in numerous types of groups and situations. Studies were made of Air Force commanders and members of bomber crews; officers, non-commissioned personnel, and civilian administrators in the Navy Department; manufacturing supervisors; executives of regional cooperatives; college administrators; teachers, principals, and school superintendents; and leaders of various student and civilian groups.

Leader Behavior Description Questionnaire - LBDQ - In the first step, the LBDQ was administered in a wide variety of situations. In order to examine how the leader was described, the answers to the questionnaire were then subjected to factor analysis. The outcome was amazingly consistent. The same two dimensions of leadership continually emerged from the questionnaire data. They were consideration and initiating structure. These two factors were found in a wide variety of studies encompassing many kinds of leadership positions and contexts. The authors carefully emphasize that the studies show only how leaders carry out their leadership position. Initiating structure and consideration are very similar to the time-honoured military commander's functions of the mission and concern with the welfare of the troops. In simple terms, the Ohio State factors are task or goal orientation (initiating structure) and recognition of individual needs and relationships (consideration). The two dimensions are separate and distinct from each other.

Task Versus People - The Ohio State studies certainly have value for the study of leadership. They were the first to point out and emphasize the importance of both task and human dimensions in assessing leadership. This two-dimensional approach lessened the gap between the strict task orientation of the scientific management movement and the human relations emphasis, which had been popular up to that time. However, on the other side of the coin, the rust for empirical data on leadership led to a great dependence on questionnaires in the Ohio State studies to generate data about leadership behaviors, and this may not have been justified.

Validity Question - For example, Schriesheim and Kerr concluded after a review of the existing literature "the Ohio State scales cannot be considered sufficiently valid to warrant their continued uncritical usage in leadership study". In addition to the validity question is the almost unchallenged belief that these indirect questionnaire methods are in fact measuring leadership behaviors instead of simply measuring the questionnaire respondent's behavior and/or perceptions of, and attitudes toward, leadership. A multiple measure approach, especially observation techniques, seems needed for the future. The discussion later in the chapter will further explain this need for a behavioral emphasis in leadership studies in its accompanying observation measurement techniques.

Multiple Measures Required - In addition to the validity question is the almost unchallenged belief that these indirect questionnaire methods are in fact measuring leadership behaviors instead of simply measuring the questionnaire respondent's behavior and/or perceptions of, and attitudes toward, leadership. Schriesheim and Kerr, 1987, concluded after a review of the existing literature "the Ohio State scales cannot be considered sufficiently valid to warrant their continued uncritical usage in leadership study". A multiple measure approach, especially observation techniques, seems needed for the future. The discussion later will further explain this need for a behavioral emphasis in leadership studies in its accompanying observation measurement techniques. Refer detailed notes on OB - Pettinger & Luthans

The Early Michigan Leadership Studies

Learning – Task – People Orientation: There are several distinct theoretical bases for leadership. At first, leaders were born, not made. This so-called "great man or one knows it all" theory of leadership implied that some individuals are born with certain traits, skills, capabilities and competencies that allow them to emerge out of any situation, experience, encounter or period of history to become leaders.

Productivity - At about the same time that the Ohio State studies were being conducted, a group of authors from the Survey Study Center at the University of Michigan began their studies of leadership. In the original study at the Prudential Insurance Company, twelve high-low productivity pairs were selected for examination. Each pair represented a high producing section and a low producing section, with other variables, such as type of work, conditions, and methods, being the same in each pair. Non directive interviews were conducted within the 24 section supervisors and 419 clerical workers. Results showed that supervisors of high producing sections were significantly more likely to be general rather than close in their supervisory styles and be employee-centered (have a genuine concern for their people). The low producing section supervisors had essentially opposite characteristics and techniques. They were found to be close, production-centered supervisors. Another important, but sometimes overlooked, finding was that employee satisfaction was not directly related to productivity.

Likert System 4 - The general, employee-centered supervisor, described above, became the standard-bearer for the traditional human relation approach to leadership. The results of the prudential studies were always cited when human relation advocates were challenged to prove their theories. The studies have been followed up with hundreds of similar studies in a wide variety of industrial, hospitals, governmental and other organizations. Thousands of employees, performing unskilled to highly professional and scientific tasks, have been analyzed. Rensis Likert, the one-time director of the Institute for Social Study of the University of Michigan, presented the results of the years of similar study in his books and became best known for his "System 4" leadership style.

Leaders Behaviors - This evolved into what is now known as the trait theory of leadership. The trait approach is concerned mainly with identifying the personality traits of the leader. Dissatisfied with this approach, and stimulated by study such as the Ohio State studies, authors switched their emphasis from the individual leader to the group being led. In the group approach, leadership is viewed more in terms of the leader's behavior and how such behavior affects and is affected by the group of followers.

Situation - Finally, some additional theories, in addition to the leader and the group, the situation began to receive increased attention in leadership theory. The situational approach was initially called Zeitgeist (a German word meaning "spirit of the times"); the leader is viewed as a product of the times and the situation. The person with the particular qualities or traits that a situation requires will emerge as the leader. Such a view has much historical support as a theoretical basis for leadership and serves as the basis for situational – and now, contingency- theories of leadership.

Expectancy - More recently, some of the expectancy concepts of motivation began to be adapted to leadership. Called the path-goal theory of leadership, this modern approach is a step toward synthesizing motivational and leadership concepts. The leadership substitutes approach recognizes the limitations of existing theories and suggests that environmental factors may take the place of, or "substitute" for, leader traits, behaviors, or processes. Finally, analogous to developments throughout the field of organizational behavior, a behaviorally oriented social learning approach to leadership has been proposed. This comprehensive theory emphasizes the reciprocal determinism among the leader (including his or her cognition), the environmental situation (including followers and macro variables), and the behavior itself. The following will examine in detail these major theoretical bases of leadership.

Analysis of Likert's (Likert, 1961) Approach.

System 4 - One of the major criticisms of Likert's work concerns its over dependence on survey questionnaire measures for gathering data to develop the theory and application of system 4 management. Sole dependence on Likert scale questionnaire responses is not enough. There is increasing criticism of data gathered only by questionnaires and interviews. Multiple measures of behaviorally oriented variables in organizations are needed. More use of archival information (existing records kept by every organization for other uses, for example, government reports, personnel records, and performance data) and data gathered through observation are needed.

Ethical - Although ethical standards must always be maintained, subject awareness must be minimized to increase the reliability and validity of data that are gathered for study purposes. Both questionnaires and interviews have a great deal of subject awareness or intrusiveness. Archival analysis and some naturalistic observational techniques minimize subject awareness and are called unobtrusive measures. Not only Likert's work but also much of the other study reported is based upon indirect questionnaire measures. What is needed is to supplement these measures with other measures such as observations and archival data.

Multiple Measures - As earlier pointed out, the use of multiple measures increases tremendously the chance of getting better, more accurate, and more valid data. Another problem inherent in Likert's scheme besides the real and potential measurement problems is the implication of the universality of the system 4 approach. Likert points out that "difference in the kind of work, in the traditions of the industry, and in the skills and values of the employees of a particular company will require quite different procedures and ways to apply appropriately the basic principles of system 4 management". But he still implies that system 4 will always be more effective than system 1. Proponents of situational/contingency leadership theories and their study findings would, of course counter this generalization.

C. Leadership Theories of Traits, Transformation, Contingency, Situational, Path Goal, Decision Tree, Vertical Dyad Linkage, Managerial Grid, Group and Exchange

Learning – Skills/Attributed determine behavior: The basic theory and mechanism is that the concerned leader, regardless of her position in a given organization, receives thoughtful evaluations and suggestions for improvement from everyone with whom she comes in contact with: superiors, colleagues, customers, vendors and subordinates and uses it in a symbolic way. This attitude to listen, learn, internalize is through behaviors, traits and attitudes developed. They deploy such a learning to effect organizational performance.

Traits - The scientific analysis of leadership started off by concentrating on leaders themselves. The vital question that this theoretical approach attempted to answer was what characteristics or traits make a person a leader? The earliest trait theories, which can be traced back to the ancient, Greek and Romans, concluded a person is born, not made. The "great man" theory of leadership said that a person is born either with or without the necessary traits for leadership. Famous figures in history- for example, Napoleon – were said to have had the "natural" leadership abilities to rise out of any situation and become great leaders.

Universality - Eventually, the "great man" theory gave way to a more realistic trait approach to leadership disrupted. Under the influence of the behaviorist school of psychological thought, authors accepted the fact that leadership traits are not completely inborn but can also be acquired through learning and experience. Attention turned to the search for universal traits possessed by leaders. The results of this voluminous study effort were generally very disappointing. Only intelligence seemed to hold up with any degree of consistency. When these findings are combined with those of studies on physical traits, the conclusion seems to be that leaders are bigger and brighter than those being led, but not too much so.

Causal Conditions - When the trait approach is applied to organizational leadership, the result is even cloudier. One of the biggest problems is that all managers think they know what the qualities of a successful leader are. Obviously, almost any adjective can be used to describe a successful leader. Recognizing these semantic limitations and realizing that there is not cause-and-effect relationship between observed traits and successful leadership, there is some evidence to suggest that empathy or interpersonal sensitivity and self-confidence are desirable leadership traits.

Skills - In general, study findings do not agree on which traits are generally found in leaders or even on which ones are important than others. Similar to the trait theories of personality, the trait approach to leadership has provided some descriptive insight but has little analytical or predictive value. The trait approach is still alive, but now the emphasis has shifted away from personality traits and toward job-related skills. Katz has identified the technical, conceptual, and human skills needed for effective management. Yukl includes skills such as creativity, organization, persuasiveness, diplomacy and tactfulness, knowledge of the task, and the ability to speak well. These skills are important and can be used both to select leaders and in training and development.

Biblical Learning - The guiding principles enunciated above can be extended for biblical work ethics in the secular world. This section examines other biblical principles that are relevant for leadership development. Managers and industry leaders share many things in common with church leaders. Hence, lessons for managers can be drawn from the relationships between church leaders and members of the congregation. The Book of Hebrews exhorts everyone to "Obey your leaders and submit to their authority. They keep watch over you as men who must give an account. Obey them so that their work will be a joy, not a burden, for that would be of no advantage to you" (Hebrew 13;17). There are, however, distinct differences between church leaders and managers in the secular world that must be recognized. For a start, both operate in different organizational settings where objectives are also dissimilar. Outside of the church, it is also possible for a church leader to function as a manager in the secular world. It is within this context that biblical work ethics can be transferred outside of the church to be practiced by a church leader-cum-manager. It is generally recognized that a Christian functions as a church leader because of God's calling and not by choice. When God touches the inner heart of a person to call them to lead the church, they know it is a privilege and that the undertaking carries with it tremendous responsibilities (Lee, 1997). Consequently, there are two key areas that a church leader has to fulfil or strive to fulfil. These two areas concern the leader's role and qualifications within which leadership lessons can be drawn to achieve managerial efficacy in the secular work.

Contingency Theories of Leadership

In some instances, the symbolic nature of leadership is as important as its substance. Recently some writers have argued that the true meaning of leadership lies in its symbolic nature as opposed to its substance. In other words, the actual decisions and actions taken by leaders matter very little: more important is the symbolic aura that the leader's behaviour conveys. In the widely used technique to assess the leadership competencies through 360-degree mechanism many prolific leaders have been perceived to be more symbolic than substantive. The same employee might also be asked to evaluate her co-workers as well as her department manager. Many organizations simultaneously deploy assessment centres and 360-degree mechanism to assess their organizational leadership – Shermon 2012 - KPMG.

Social Skills - After the trait approach proved to fall short of being an adequate overall theory of leadership, attention turned to the situational aspects of leadership. Social psychologists began the search for situational variables that impact on leadership roles, skills, and behavior and on followers' performance and satisfaction. Numerous situational variables were identified, but no overall theory pulled it all together until Fred Fiedler proposed a widely recognized situation-based model for leadership effectiveness. A brief review of his study techniques and findings is necessary to fully understand his contingency theory of leadership effectiveness.

Least Preferred Co-worker. Fiedler, 1967, developed a unique operational technique to measure leadership style. Measurement is obtained from scores that indicate the least preferred co-worker (LPC). This LPC approach calculates the degree to which leaders favorably perceive their worst coworkers and relates to leadership style in the following manner:

- *The human relations or "lenient" style is associated with the leader who gives a relatively favorable description of the least preferred co-worker.*
- *The task-directed, or "hard-nosed", style is associated with the leader who gives a very unfavorable description of the least preferred co-worker.*

Fiedler's Findings. Through the years the performance of both laboratory groups and numerous real groups (basketball teams, fraternity members, surveying teams, bomber crews, infantry squads, open-hearth steel employees, and farm supply service employees) was correlated with the leadership styles described above. The results were somewhat encouraging, but no simple relationships between leadership style as determined by the leaders' LPC score and group performance were developed. Eventually, Fiedler concluded that more attention would have to be given to situational variables. He became convinced that leadership style in combination with the situation determines group performance.

Fiedler's Contingency Model of Leadership Effectiveness – Refer Fiedler and http://bit.ly/2a5dkj7

To test the hypothesis, he had formulated from previous study findings, Fiedler developed what he called a contingency model of leadership effectiveness. This model contained the relationship between leadership style and the favorableness of the situation. Fiedler described situational favorableness in terms of three empirically derived dimensions:

- *The leader-member-team relationship, driven by mutual relationship is a network which is the most critical variable in determining the situations favorableness.*
- *The degree of task, action, outcome structure, which is the second most important input into the favorableness of the situation.*
- *The leader's position and role oriented authority and power obtained through formal – streamlined authority, which is the third most critical dimension of the situation.*

Path – Goal Theory - Despite a relative degree of acceptance of the contingency and path-goal theories of leadership and the great (at least relative to areas in organizational behavior) amount of study that has been conducted, few would disagree today that leadership is still in trouble. Leadership is currently being attacked on all fronts- in terms of theories relating to it, study methods for studying it, and applications. There are a number of modified and new approaches that have emerged. For example, just as the expectancy notions of motivation evolved into the **path-goal theory of leadership,** so has the attribution approach been used to analyze leadership. There are also a number of new theoretical formulations such as charismatic and transformational leadership. **Charismatic leadership** is a throwback, an opportunity to the old conception of leaders, as is perceived by folks, as being those who "by the force, persuasion and commitment demonstrated through their personal abilities are capable of having profound and extraordinary effects on followers. Although the charismatic concept of charisma goes as far back as the ancient Greeks and is cited in the Bible, its modern development is attributed to the work of Robert House. This theoretical approach to leadership has only preliminary study findings and a recent behavioral framework contrasting non-charismatic and charismatic leaders. Identifying charismatic characteristics, personality factors of leaders can become very important as organizations attempt to transform their traditional ways of being led, managed and driven to change and meet the challenge of dramatic change. It is this transformation process that has led to another new theoretical development of leadership.

Attribution - Path-Goal Leadership Theory - The other widely recognized modern theoretical development for leadership studies, besides the contingency approach, is the path-goal theory derived from the expectancy framework of motivation theory. This is a healthy development because leadership is closely related to work motivation on the one hand and power on the other. Any theory that attempts to synthesize the various concepts seems to be a step in the right direction.

Although Georgopoulos and his colleagues at the University of Michigan's Institute for Social Study used path-goal concepts and terminology many years ago in analyzing the impact of leadership on performance, the modern development is usually attributed to Martin Evans and Robert House, (Luthans, 1989) who wrote separate papers on the subject. In essence, the path-goal theory attempts to explain the impact that leader behavior has on subordinate motivation, satisfaction, and performance. The House version of the theory incorporates four major types or styles of leadership disrupted. Briefly summarized, these are:

- *Directive leadership disrupted: This style is similar to that of the Lippitt and White authoritarian leader. Subordinates know exactly what is expected of them, and the leader gives specific directions. There is no participation by subordinates.*
- *Supportive leadership disrupted: The leader is friendly and approachable and shows a genuine concern for subordinates*
- *Participative leadership disrupted: The leader asks for and uses suggestions from subordinates but still makes the decisions.*
- *Achievement-oriented leadership disrupted: The leader sets challenging goals for subordinates and shows confidence that they will attain these goals and perform well.*

Critical Review of Path Goal

The more recent reviews of the study on the path-goal theory are not as supportive as the above. For example, it should be noted that only a couple of hypotheses have really been drawn from the theory, which means that it may be incapable of generating meaningful predictions. Another note of pessimism offered by these reviewers is that only one of the two hypotheses has received consistent empirical support. Study has generally substantiated the hypothesis that the higher the task structure (repetitiveness) of the jobs performed by subordinates the higher the relationship between supportive leader behavior/style and subordinate satisfaction. On the other hand, the second hypothesis- that the higher the task structure, the lower the correlation between instrumental (directive) leader behavior and subordinate satisfaction-has received, at best, mixed study support. Schriesheim and DeNisi then report results of their own study, which indicates that the path-goal theory is capable of producing meaningful and testable predictions beyond the two task structure hypotheses. Also, a recent comprehensive review of forty-eight studies demonstrated that the mixed results of the individual studies, when cumulated were transformed into support for continued testing of path-goal theory. Overall, the **path-goal theory,** like the other theories presented in this chapter and others, seem to need more study, but it certainly warrants further attention in the coming years. One recent analysis concluded that leaders will be perceived most favorably by their subordinates, and succeed in exerting most influence over them, when they behave in ways that closely match (1) the needs and values of subordinates and (2) the requirements of a specific work situation. In other words, the path-goal theory, like the expectancy theory in work motivation, may help better explain the complexities of the leadership disrupted process.

Political Leadership disrupted - As Luthans writes James MacGregor Burns identified two types of political leadership: transactional and transformational. The more traditional transactional leadership involves an exchange relationship between leaders and followers, but transformational leadership is based more on leaders' shifting the values, beliefs, and needs of their followers. Bass applied these ideas to managing modern organizations, and there have been some recent theoretical development and analysis.

Transformational Leader - On the basis of interviews with top executives of major companies, Tichy and Devanna 1986 – **Transformational Leader,** stress that modern corporate leaders must use a transformational approach to cope with change and use innovation and entrepreneurship. The effective transformational leaders share the following characteristics:

- *They identify themselves as change agents*
- *They are courageous*
- *They believe in people*
- *They are value-driven*
- *They are lifelong learners*

They have the ability to deal with complexity, ambiguity and uncertainty. They are visionaries.

Transformational leadership disrupted aims at transforming people and organizations in the literal sense. The leaders appeal to the employee's need for meaning and higher work purpose. Their leadership transcends daily affairs without compromising ethics and values. People do not just follow the passionate and energetic leader but they place trust in him, believe in his vision for the future and internalize his values to achieve that vision. They leaders often help unlock human potential and support employees realize meaningful goals.

Servant leadership disrupted , as opposed to the traditional view of leadership, assumes the leader to be the steward and servant of her followers (in our context, the employees of the organization). It postulates that the leader first serves the followers and over the course of time evolves into a steward. Servant leadership is more about the leader focussing on helping followers do their jobs and help reach them beyond their self; rather than the leader directing and controlling the followers in their actions.

Level-5 leadership describes the highest level in the hierarchy of leadership. It views leadership in terms of institutionalizing systems, processes and structures within the organizations. In contrast to charismatic leaders, level 5 leaders display extreme humility and strong will simultaneously. Their modesty tends to belie their iron will and capability to make tough decisions for the greater good of the organization. The leaders, post defining roles and responsibilities for various individuals, essentially provide supporting structure and processes to their followers.

Dispersed leadership distinguishes the idea of the leader and the leadership. It postulates that successful leadership of change does not come from the top of the organization; instead it comes from within the organization. The theory shifts the emphasis away from the concept of heroic leader. It further says that leaders are emergent rather than appointed basis the influence they exercise over their colleagues in the organization and encourages developing communities of interdependent leaders across organization. One thing that makes leadership all the more elusive and complicated are the followers. Generalizations of leadership have failed due to the diversity of situations in which leadership is applied. However, in addition to these, certain transitory factors such as the time available for task completion, specific outcome required, urgency of the task, emotional state of the follower (and of the leader), would play a significant role in the final manifestation of leadership behaviour. For example, if a leader needs to bring about change in the followers' motivation levels, she is more likely to use transformational leadership; but if time is short and task completion is necessary, then a transactional leadership style might prove more effective. KPMG 2012

Emphasis on Social Learning - In addition to attribution, charismatic and transformational theories, social learning and a substitute approach have emerged to meet the challenge of understanding the complexities and alternatives of leadership. Various theoretical and practical aspects of leadership are available in literature. The classic study studies on leadership set the stage for the theoretical development of leadership. The trait theories concentrate on the leaders themselves but, with the possible exception of intelligence and empathy/interpersonal sensitivity and self-confidence, really do not come up with any agreed upon traits of leaders. In recent times the trait approach has surfaced in terms of managerial skills and abilities identified for selection and training/ development purpose.

Critical Analysis of the Contingency Model. Although there is probably not as much criticism of Fiedler's work as there is, for example, of Herzberg's motivation theory, a growing number of leadership authors does not wholly agree with Fiedler's interpretations or conclusions. For example, initially some analysts raised some criticisms of the procedures and statistical analysis of the studies used to support the validity of the model. Schriesheim (Luthans 1989) and his colleagues have been especially critical of the reliability and validity of the LPC instrument. Fiedler and his colleagues have answered these criticisms of LPC to their satisfaction, but the fact remains that this questionnaire measure (and others such as those developed at Ohio State and Michigan – (Luthans 1989)) do have problems and may be a major reason why leadership understanding and predictability has not progressed as fast as it was once thought it would. As Korman took care to point out. The need for better measurement in leadership theory is a matter of prime necessity. Measurement and theory go hand-in-hand and the development of one without the other is a waste of time for all concerned…. The point is not that adequate measurement is "nice". It is necessary, crucial, etc. Without it, we have nothing. It may well be that there has been an over dependence on the LPC type of measure for leadership theory and study.

The Vroom Yetton (Vroom, 1973) model was first developed several years ago and has since been modified. The model contains five leadership styles, seven situation dimensions, fourteen problem types, and seven decision rules. The leadership styles consist of variations on autocratic, consultative, and group styles, and the situational dimensions are of two general types:

- *The way in which problems affect the quality and acceptance of a decision and*
- *The way in which the problems affect the degree of participation. The seven situational dimensions are stated in the form of "yes"- "no" questions and the answers can quickly diagnose the situation for the leader.*

Decision Tree - Vroom and Yetton uses a decision tree to relate the situation to the appropriate leadership style. The seven situational questions are listed at the top. Starting at the left, the manager would answer each question above the box in the decision tree until it led to the appropriate style. In this way the manager could determine the appropriate style on the basis of the given situation. Vroom and Yetton also point out that the fourteen problem types (the combinations of the seven situational variables, listed as 1 through 14 in the decision tree) could actually have more than one acceptable leadership style. In order to be acceptable, the style must meet the criteria of seven decision rules that protect quality and acceptance. If more than one style remains after the test of both quality and acceptance (and many do), the third most important aspect of a decision- the amount of time- is used to determine the single style that ought to be used in the given situation. The styles shown at the ends of the various branches on the decision tree reflect the single best style that should be used in light of the way the situation was diagnosed by answers to the questions at the top.

Chance Probability - Although the potential problem that support of the Vroom-Yetton model may be attributed to chance alone may be discounted, there may be a problem with the dependence on the self-report data. For example, managers going through training and development programs are simply asked to recall a problem they have encountered and to indicate which of the five styles in the model they used to solve the problem. In addition, managers are given standardized problem cases and are asked which style from the model could best be used to solve each case. Such methods, of course, have a number of internal validity problems (experimenter effect and social desirability effect) and external validity problems (the use of standardized cases in a training situation may not generalize to the real world). In addition to the validity problems of the model, it may also have limited utility for two major reasons:

"First, it is not as parsimonious as other models of leader decision process choice and

Secondly, it deals with only one aspect of leader behavior, that of selecting different decision processes for different problem situations."

Vroom answers this criticism by reanalyzing his data and concludes that the relative complexity of his model is justified for predictive purposes. Also, a revision of the model by Vroom and Jago that replaces the yes-no with five-point scales and adds new attributes dealing with time, information, and motivation contains recent study that indicates greater accuracy of prediction.

Overall the **Vroom-Yetton model** has much surface logic, and it does give precise answers to practicing managers. However, as in the case of the other approaches, more study is needed. On the positive side, its attempt to bridge the gap from theory to practice may be a step in the right direction, and it can serve as a prototype for the actual practice of contingency management. The Vroom-Yetton model is a fitting conclusion to the discussion on leadership. The progression has been from theory to styles to specific prescriptions. Several studies have tested this model. Vroom and his colleagues have done most of this study, and they do provide some evidence that the model is valid. However, more recent critiques that have closely examined the methodology used in these studies have led to questions about the validity of the model.

The Vertical Dyad Linkage Model (Robbins, 1990) Relevant to the exchange view of leadership is the vertical dyad linkage (VDL) approach, sometimes called leader-member exchange (LMX). The VDL theory says that leaders treat individual subordinates differently. In particular, leaders and subordinates develop dyadic (two-person) relationships that affect the behavior of both leaders and subordinates. For example, subordinates who are committed and who expend a lot of effort for the unit are rewarded with more of the leader's positional resources (for example, information, confidence, and concern) than those who do not display these behaviors.

Over time, the leader will develop an "in-group" of subordinates and an "out-group" of subordinates and treat them accordingly. Thus, for the same leader, study has shown that in-group subordinates report fewer difficulties in dealing with the leader and perceive the leader as being more responsive to their needs than out-group subordinates do. Also, leaders spend more time "leading" members of the in-group (that is, they do not depend on formal authority to influence them), and they tend to "supervise" those in the out-group (that is, they depend on formal roles and authority to influence them). Fred Luthans (1992) - http://bit.ly/2a1CyO4

Finally, there is evidence that subordinates in the in-group (those who report a high quality relationship with their leader) assume greater job responsibility, contribute more to their units, and are rated as higher performers than those reporting a low-quality relationship. This VDL theory has been around for some time now, and although it is not without criticism, in general the study continues to be relatively supportive and seems to have considerable potential for predicting important dimensions of the leader-subordinate exchange.

Situational Leadership (Hersey and Blanchard, 1977) and Managerial Grid (Blake and Mouton, 1966) and Fred Luthans (2010) - http://bit.ly/2a1CyO4

Although they recognize that there may be other important situational variables, Hersey and Blanchard focus only on this maturity level of subordinates in their model. The key for leadership effectiveness in this model is to match up the situation with the appropriate style. The following summarizes the four basic styles.

- *Telling style. This is a high-task, low-relationship style and is effective when followers are at a very low level of maturity.*
- *Selling style. This is a high-task, high-relationship style and is effective when followers are on the low side of maturity*
- *Participating style. This is a low-task, high-relationship style and is effective when followers are on the high side of maturity*
- *Delegating style. This is a low-task, low-relationship style and is effective when followers are at a very high level of maturity*

The theoretical rationale is generally criticized as being "weak, because **Hersey and Blanchard (Life Cycle and Situational Approach)** have neglected to provide a coherent, explicit rationale for the hypothesized relationships." They also, by their own admission, highly oversimplify the situation by giving only surface recognition to follower maturity. Also, as in the grid approach, there is a noted absence of any empirical tests of the model. One review of all facets of the approach was particularly critical of the instrument that Hersey and Blanchard used to measure leader effectiveness. Overall is true of the other style approaches, this situational approach seems to be of some value in training and development work in that it can point out the need for flexibility and take into consideration the different variables affecting leaders, but until more supporting study is conducted, this type of approach has limited utility for identifying leadership effectiveness.

Managerial Grid Style and Systems 4

One very popular approach to identifying leadership styles of practicing managers is Robert R. Blake and Jane S. Mouton's managerial grid. This shows that two dimensions of the grid are concern for people along the vertical axis and concern for production along the horizontal axis. These two dimensions are of course equivalent to the consideration and initiating structure functions identified by the Ohio State studies and the employee centered and production centered styles used in the Michigan studies. Leadership style.

Schermerhorn (1996) suggests that leadership is the process of inspiring others to work hard to accomplish important tasks. Leadership is also one of the four functions that constitute the managerial process:

- *Planning sets the direction and objectives;*
- *Organizing brings the resources together to turn plans into action;*
- *Leading builds, the commitment and enthusiasm needed for people to apply their talents fully to help accomplish plans; and*
- *Controlling makes sure things turn out right.*

9 by 9 Style - An important development in behavioral studies was the development of the leadership grid used as framework for portraying types of leadership behavior and their various potential combinations (Blake and Mouton, 1994). The grids consist of two dimensions – concern for production and concern for people. These two dimensions are integrated to form the 9-by-9-leadership grid. Other managerial traits portrayed in the 9-by-9-leadership grid include:

- *Grid 1,9 Country Club Management: thoughtful attention to needs of people for satisfying relationships leads to comfortable, friendly organization atmosphere and work tempo.*
- *Grid 1,1 Impoverished Management: exertion of minimum effort to get required work done is appropriate to sustain organization membership.*
- *Grid 5,5 Organization Man Management: adequate organization performance is possible through balancing the necessity to get out work with maintaining morale of people at a satisfactory level.*
- *Grid 9,1 Authority-Obedience: efficiency in operations results from arranging conditions of work in such a way that human elements interfere to a minimum degree. Grid 9,9 Team Management: work accomplishment is from committed people; interdependence through a "common stake" in organization purpose leads to relationships of trust and respect (Blake and Mouton, 1994 and Fred Luthans (2010) http://bit.ly/2a5hRlv).*

Task Orientation - The five basic styles identified in the grid represent varying combinations of concern for people and production. The 1,1 manager has minimum concern for people and production; this style is sometimes called the "impoverished" style. The opposite is the 9.9 manager. This individual has maximum concern for both people and production. The implication is that the 9,1 is the best style of leadership, and Blake and Mouton have stated in no uncertain terms: "There should be no question about which leadership style is the most effective. It's that of the manager whom we call, in the terminology of the Managerial Grid, a (9,9) "Team builder." Blake and Mouton provided empirical evidence that their interactive notion of leadership style (that is, concern for people interacting with concern for production) has more predictive validity than additive situational approaches. The (5,5) manager is the "Middle-of-the-Road", and the other two styles represent the extreme concerns for people (1,9) "Country Club" manager) and production (9,1) "Task" manager). A manager's position on the grid can be determined by a questionnaire developed by Blake and Mouton and can play an important role in organization development (OD).

Employee Centricity - The general, employee-centered supervisor, became the standard-bearer for the traditional human relation's approach to leadership. The results of the prudential studies were always cited when human relation's advocates were challenged to prove their theories. The studies have been followed up with hundreds of similar studies in a wide variety of industrial, hospitals, governmental and other organizations. Thousands of employees, performing unskilled to highly professional and scientific tasks, have been analyzed. Rensis Likert, the one-time director of the

Institute for Social Study of the University of Michigan, presented the results of the years of similar study in his books and became best known for his "System 4" leadership style.

D. Social, Collaborative Group Learning, Group and Exchange Based Leadership Approaches

Learning – Social: A multi-cultural social environment is challenging with different values, sometimes clashing head-on, but it can also be a wonderful learning opportunity if we can only understand those differences and tap that energy.

Social Independence - Any of the other theoretical approaches, standing alone, seem too limiting. For example, the one-sided, cognitively based trait theories suggest that leaders are causal determinants that influence subordinates independent of subordinates' behaviors or the situation. The contingency theories are a step in the right direction, but even they for the most part have a unidirectional conception of interaction, in which leaders and situations somehow combine to determine leadership behavior. Even those leadership theories that claim to take a bi-directional approach (either in the exchange sense between the leader and the subordinate/group or in the contingency sense between the leader and the situation) actually retain a unidirectional view of leadership behavior. In these theories, the causal input into the leader's behavior is the result of the interdependent exchange, but the behavior itself is ignored as a leadership determinant.

Social Learning - Obviously, the focus of a social learning approach, and what distinguishes it from the other approaches, is the role of leadership behavior and the continuous, reciprocal interaction between all the variables. With this as the focus of attention, the alternative study methods and application, techniques for leadership naturally follow. As Kerlinger noted, "observations must be used when the variables of study studies are interactive and interpersonal in nature. Thus, there is a need for observational measures of leadership behaviors in naturalistic settings. The study foundation for a Leader Observation System (LOS) has been completed. Now the LOS is being used to analyze various leadership situations and relevant variables. This LOS approach may be an effective supplement, if not an alternative, to the more traditional questionnaire methods used in leadership study.

Social Networking - As far as leadership application for the social learning approach is concerned, the four terms contingency S-O-B-C (situation-organism-behavior-consequence) model can be used by leaders to perform a functional analysis. Unlike the more limited A-B-C (antecedent-behavior-consequence0 functional analysis can be either overt (observable) as in the operant view, or convert (unobservable), as recognized in the social learning view, and, of course, recognition is given to the role of cognitive mediating processes by the insertion of the O. The successful application of this S-O-B-C functional analysis to human resources management "depends upon the leader's ability to bring into awareness the over or convert antecedent cues and contingent consequences that regulate the leader's and subordinate's performance behavior. More specifically, in this leadership application, the subordinates are actively involved in the process, and together with the leader they concentrate on their own and one another's behaviors, the environmental contingencies (both antecedent and consequent), and their mediating cognition.

Social Supervisory - The leader becomes acquainted with the macro and micro variables that control his or her own behavior. The leader works with the subordinate to discover the personalized set of behavioral contingencies that regulate the subordinate's behavior. The leader and the subordinate jointly attempt to discover ways in which they can manage their individual behavior to produce more mutually reinforcing and organizationally productive outcomes. In such an approach, the leader and the subordinate have a negotiable, interactive relationship and are consciously aware of how they can modify (influence) each other's behavior by giving or holding back desired rewards. Although work has been done on the theoretical development of a social learning approach to leadership, study and application are just getting under way. Only time will tell whether it will hold up a s viable, approach to leadership. However, because of its growing importance as a theoretical foundation for the fields of psychology and organizational behavior as a whole and because it recognizes the interactive nature of all the variables of previous theories, a social learning approach to leadership would seem to have potential for the future.

Social Exchange - "The group theories of leadership have their roots in social psychology. Classic exchange theory, in particular, serves as an important basis for this approach. This means simply that the leader provides more benefits/rewards than burdens/costs for followers. There must be a positive exchange between the leaders and followers in order for group goals to be accomplished". Fred Luthans (2010). Chester Barnard applied such analysis to managers and subordinates in an organizational setting more than a half-century ago. More recently, this social exchange view of leadership (Barnard) has been summarized as follows:

"The person in the role of leader who fulfils expectations and achieves group goals provides rewards for others that are reciprocated in the form of status, esteem, and heightened influence. Because leadership embodies a two-way influence relationship, recipients of influence assertions may respond by asserting influence in return. The very sustenance of the relationship depends upon some yielding to influence on both sides".

Social psychological - The above quote emphasizes that leadership is an exchange process between the leader and followers and also involves the sociological concept of role expectations. Social psychological study can be used to support the exchange and role concepts applied to leadership. In addition, the original Ohio State studies and follow-up studies through the years, especially the dimension of giving consideration to followers, give support to the group perspective of leadership. A thorough review of study indicated that leaders who take into account and support their followers have a positive impact on attitudes, satisfaction, and performance.

Degree of Social Consciousness - For many organizations today change is problematic. About 80 percent of major organizational change initiatives are said to fail. A fully alert state of consciousness provides the greatest freedom and potential for creative change. The conscious organization takes on the qualities of spontaneous evolution and self-organization (Wheatley, 1992; Ray, 1993) which science has observed in the systems of the natural world. In such an organization, as in nature, evolutionary change is spontaneous, continual, and without resistance.

E. Analytical Perspectives on Leadership

Luthans (2010) writes, "We presented and analyzed various theoretical and practical aspects of leadership. The classic study studies on leadership set the stage for the theoretical development of leadership. The trait theories concentrate on the leaders themselves but, with the possible exception of intelligence and empathy/interpersonal sensitivity and self-confidence, really do not come up with any agreed upon traits of leaders. In recent times the trait approach has surfaced in terms of managerial skills and abilities identified for selection and training/ development purpose. http://bit.ly/2aDmfXG

Contingency Model - The group and exchange theories emphasize the importance of followers, and although the vertical dyad linkage (VDL) model is still quite popular and is generating considerable study, the group/exchange theories in general are recognized to be only partial theories.

Today, the widely recognized theories of leadership are situational based. In particular, Fiedler's contingency model makes a significant contribution to leadership theory and potentially to the practice of human resource management. The path-goal approach is also an important contribution to leadership theory. It incorporates expectancy motivation concepts. Both the Fiedler and the path-goal approaches have generated a growing body of study on leadership dimensions, but there are still problems. A social learning approach that incorporates the leader, the situation, and the behavior itself is proposed as an alternative theory. This approach emphasizes the importance of behavior and the continuous, interacting nature of all the variables in leadership. Finally, it is now recognized that certain subordinate, task and organizational characteristics may substitute for or neutralize the impact that leader behavior has on subordinate performance and satisfaction.

Managerial Grid - There are many style implications in both the classic leadership studies and the modern theories. Blake and Mouton's managerial grid, Hersey and Blanchard's situational model, and Likert's four systems focus Tannenbaum and Schmidt focused on Boss or Subordinate centered attention directly on leadership styles. Each of these is of value in relation to the actual practice of human resources management. The grid is valuable mainly because it allows managers to describe their styles. Hersey and Blanchard's approach shows how group being led, and Likert's work has implications for organizational effectiveness. Likert's recognition of intervening variables and their time lag affects has significant implications for practice. Finally, the Vroom-Yetton model attempts to prescribe exactly what style to use in a given situation. All these approaches to style need more and better study in order to make meaningful contributions to the actual practice of human resources management in the future" http://bit.ly/2aDmfXG .

Leadership Continuum - Expectancy - Leona Edward writes in http://bit.ly/2amyCaV "More than the titles we are attempting to understand the underlying meaning of the leadership style and its impact and influence over culture. The verbal descriptions and the relationship between authority and freedom give a rough representation of characteristics of the various styles of leadership. One thing is certain: leadership style can make a difference. For example, a recent survey found that senior executives view their companies' leadership styles as pragmatic rather than conceptual and conservative rather than risk taking. Importantly, these same executives felt that to meet their current and future challenges, the styles should be the other way around. For ease of presentation, the styles listed may be substituted for the expressions "boss-centered" and "subordinate-centered" used by Tannenbaum and Schmidt in their classic leadership continuum". Or alternatively as Monitor, Disseminator, Spokesman, Leader, Liaison, Negotiator, Problem Solver and Figurehead as defined by Henry Mintzberg. Or that of Victor Vroom's expectancy theory. Vroom and Yetton attempted to provide a specific, normative model (how decisions "ought" to be made in given situations) that a leader could actually use in making effective decisions.

Talent Drives Leadership disrupted - Gerald C Kane in MIT SMR 2015 in "The Talent Imperative in Digital Business" write, "First, employees report to a surprisingly high degree (80%) that they preferred for work for digital leaders. This result is not limited to Millennial employees, either; the percentage of employees who express preference for working for a digitally enabled company remains consistently above 70% for all age groups. Second, fewer than half of all respondents indicated that they were satisfied with their organization's digital efforts. As might be expected, this result is strongly correlated with the organization's digital maturity — employees are least satisfied with those organizations that are digital laggards. Taken together, these results mean that your organization's efforts at digitization have a surprising outcome: It may influence your ability to attract and retain talent. Does this mean that employees will just quit their jobs because their companies are not digitally advanced enough? Probably not. Yet even if employees consider your company's digital maturity as only one factor among many when making employment decisions, the implications can be significant. Some of this desire to work for digital leaders may result from the fact that digital sophistication is associated with future competitive advantage. Between 85–90% of respondents indicated that digital technologies are disrupting their industry, changing the way they work, and will be important for their business in coming years. Employees recognize that as the world becomes more digitized, companies who understand and can navigate this digital environment will be better poised to compete and survive in this future environment. It is only natural that employees will prefer to work for companies that they believe have strong growth prospects for the future, and digital maturity is an important part of that future growth. Recognizing the talent implications of digital business is one thing, but what can you do to make your company more digital-friendly? One approach is to hire the requisite talent from technology or digitally mature companies to lead your own digital efforts. Many companies are doing just that, and — according to David Mathison of the CDO club — an increasing number of these technology executives hired in as chief digital officers are eventually becoming CEOs of those companies".

Here and Now Generational Needs - *"I want it fast, and I want it* **now."** U.S. Millennials are all about instant gratification. They put a premium on speed, ease, efficiency, and convenience in all their transactions. For example, Millennials shop for groceries at convenience stores twice as often as non-Millennials. They also value getting through the line quickly in so-called fast-casual restaurants (upscale fast-food chains without table service, such as Chipotle) (81 percent versus 71 percent) and care relatively less about "friendly" service. This preference for efficiency is even reflected in how they participate in causes. Of Millennials who make direct donations (34 percent), almost half donate through their mobile devices (15 percent), compared with only 5 percent of non-Millennials. To meet the expectations of this generation, companies will need to rethink their existing customer-service models. These consumers are always in a hurry, and it's critical to determine how you can get them to spend time developing a relationship with your brand". In, a BCG Research Report of 2012, "The Millennial Consumer Debunking Stereotypes" authors Christine Barton (BCG), Jeff Fromm (Share Like Buy), Chris Egan (Service Management Group), continue, *"I trust my friends more than 'corporate mouthpieces'."* "For this generation, the definition of "expert"—a person with the credibility to recommend brands, products, and services—has shied from someone with professional or academic credentials to potentially anyone with firsthand experience, ideally a peer or close friend. U.S. Millennials also tend to seek multiple sources of information, especially from non-corporate channels, and they're likely to consult their friends before making purchase decisions. For example, more Millennials than non-Millennials reported using a mobile device to read user reviews and to research products while shopping (50 percent versus 21 percent)".

F. Digital Culture Leadership that promotes full human development

"Failure gets punished. But you can create experimentation platforms where you can try out things, test things, with very low risk — if it fails, it's not going to bring the company down. That's a huge enabler of accelerated learning in the work environment". In an interview with John Hagel III (Deloitte), Gerald C. (Jerry) Kane of MIT Sloan Management Review asks in the MIT SMR 2016 issue, "Do you know any companies that are being **successful with digital as an ongoing learning platform"?** Hagel responds, "One is Intuit in the financial services software business. They've been very focused on how to use digital technology to create experimentation platforms for workers throughout their company. The whole notion is, how do you reduce the risk of failure? Because if you're going to learn faster, you're going to fail a lot. And one of the things holding workers back is the fear of failure. A company called LiveOps, which outsources call center operations for larger companies — they have 20,000 people who work for them, and they've done some interesting things. One is they gave each one of their workers a real-time performance dashboard that fed back to them how they were doing on multiple dimensions of performance, which is something they borrowed from World of Warcraft. Most companies who do that would have used it as an instrument of punishment: You're falling behind these three metrics; you've got six months to get your act together or you're out of here. What LiveOps did was, they actually invited workers to ask for help, and they created an online digital discussion forum where workers could come in and say, for example, "I'm having trouble handling this kind of customer call. Anybody have any ideas?" Then they started to watch, recognize, and reward the workers who were emerging as helpers and advice givers. So they've created a powerful peer-to-peer learning environment for their workers". In a conscious organization, the primary task of leaders will be to promote the full development of all the individual members. This is the epitome of transformational leadership – to lead others to lead them (Manz and Sims, 1993)." Transformational Leadership (Shermon 2012 – KPMG) is the process of leading for change rather than for stability. In particular, transformational leadership is the set of abilities that allow the leader to recognize the need for change, to create a vision to guide that change, and to execute the change effectively. The leader becomes acquainted with the macro and micro variables that control his or her own behavior. The leader works with the subordinate to discover the personalized set of behavioral contingencies that regulate the subordinate's behavior. The leader and the subordinate jointly attempt to discover ways in which they can manage their individual behavior to produce more mutually reinforcing and organizationally productive outcomes. In such an approach, the leader and the subordinate have a negotiable, interactive relationship and are consciously aware of how they can modify (influence) each other's behavior by giving or holding back desired rewards. "While each conscious organization will function in a unique manner that firs its circumstances, what will be common to all conscious organizations will be that they engage in practices to harmonize the individual with the cosmos. A few important study studies indicate that followers/subordinates may actually affect leaders as much as leaders affect followers/subordinates. For example, one study found that when subordinates were not performing very well, the leaders tended to emphasize initiating structure, but when subordinates were doing a good job, leaders increased their emphasis on consideration. In a laboratory study it was found that group productivity had a greater impact on leadership style than leadership style had on group leaders may adjust their supportive behavior in response to the level of group cohesion and arousal already present".

Follower - "In other words, such studies seem to indicate that subordinates affect leaders and their behaviors as much as leaders and their behaviors affect subordinates. Some practicing managers, such as the vice president of Saga Corporation, feel that subordinates lack followership skills, and there is growing evidence that the newer generation of managers is increasingly reluctant to accept a followership role. Moreover, it is probably not wise to ignore followership. Most managers feel that subordinates have an obligation to follow and support their leader. As the CEO of Commerce Union Corporation noted, "Part of a subordinate's responsibility is to make the boss look good." Refer – Ryszard Barnat - http://bit.ly/2akTTp2

G. Leadership Power Dimensions

Analyzing Power, authority and responsibility in the context of Leadership and its impact of styles and behavior

It has been observed that power performs a significant role in leader behavior and influences the leader's style significantly. It is therefore important to study the various aspects of power and attempt its context when evaluating the appropriate leadership style of leaders.

Capacity Maximization - Power refers to a capacity which the leader has over the behavior of an employee so that the employee will do something he or she would not otherwise do. Bases of power refer to what the manager has that give him powers. The leaders' power bases are what they control that enable them to manipulate the behavior of others. Pfeffer (1981, 1992) suggest that there are four types of power bases:

- **Coercive power** – *the coercive power base is dependent on fear. The manager has coercive power over employees if they can dismiss, suspend or demote them.*
- **Reward power** – *the opposite of coercive power is the power to reward. Material rewards would include salary and wage increase, commissions and fringe benefits.*
- **Persuasive power** – *if a person can decide who is to be hired, manipulate the mass media, control the allocation of status symbols or influence a group's norms, they have persuasive power.*
- **Knowledge power** – *when an individual controls unique information and when that information is needed to make a decision, that individual has knowledge-based power.*

The types of power bases are, however, dependent on the sources of power. Sources of power reveal where managers get their power base. The four sources of power identified by Pfeffer (1981, 1992) are:

- **Position power** – *position power resides in the position regardless of the person holding the job.*
- **Personal power** – *personal power resides in the person regardless of his or her position in the organization, for example, if that person has charisma.*
- **Expert power** – *those who have expertise in terms of specialized information can use it to manipulate others.*
- **Opportunity power** – *being in the right place at the right time can give the opportunity to exert power.*

Authority is power that has been legitimized within a specific social context. Only when power is part of an official organizational role does it become authority. Authority includes the legitimate right to use resources to accomplish expected outcomes (Luthans, 1992; Schermerhorn, 1996).

Responsibility – Authority Gap - Responsibility is an obligation to do something with the expectation that some act or output will result. Authority is closely linked to responsibility because a manager responsible for accomplishing certain results must have the authority to use resources to achieve those results. The relationship between responsibility and authority must be one of parity, that is, the authority over resources must be sufficient to enable the manager to meet the output expectations of others. There are, however, some important differences between authority and responsibility. Responsibility cannot be delegated down to others but authority can (Kelly, 1980).

Individual Ownership - Managers are usually quite willing to hold individuals responsible for specific tasks but are reluctant to delegate sufficient authority for them to do their jobs well. In effect, managers try to rid themselves of responsibility for results but yet are unwilling to give away their cherished authority over resources (Moorhead and Griffin, 1995).

H. Comparative Study Critique

Connecting Leadership to Cultures and Organizational Models - Falling back on the work done by Khandwalla (1992) we now turn to some comparative Study Analysis of select works to provide a perspective towards building our proposition on connecting leadership to organizational models and culture. This work has been specifically brought in here to bring together the relevance of going beyond understanding leadership for its merit but connecting leadership in the context of organizations. This critique as a consequence deals with leadership impact in varying situations including, strategic planning, globalization, cultural change, people strategy, innovation corporate excellence, transformation and organizational leadership. The author hopes to get closer to the aspect of bringing relevance and appropriateness of studying core fundamental theories in regard to culture, leadership and organization and also studying cross comparison studies to make the connection amongst these three variables legitimate.

Efficacy of Effective Human Relations (Rensis Likert – Khandwalla 1992)

Human Relations Programs - Humans lead organizations, and the quality of their leadership can make or mar organizational excellence. The study is by Likert of the leadership style of 31 U.S. organizations. The going concept of effective leadership in the fifties when Likert did his study was that of a great man or a ferocious taskmaster. Likert showed that employee-oriented leadership that works to develop a team through participatory decision-making might give better results than one that is excessively task oriented. That of Bowers's follows Likert's study and Seashore, in which the concept of human relations oriented leadership, is further elaborated. But human relations may not be enough. For surpassing achievement, leaders of organizations need to 'turn on' their staffs for extraordinary efforts. Bennis and Nanus did a study of 90 U.S. leaders of organizations who led by vision, positioning, and trust. Singh and Bhandarkar have reported a detailed study of five Indian 'transformational' leaders who changed the culture of their respective organizations and fairly dramatically improved their performance. Finally, Woycke's study reports the contrasts between charismatic leaders and non-charismatic leaders of Third World governments.

Relationships Oriented Leadership - In the fifties, Rensis Likert emerged as a study-oriented spokesman for the efficacy of good human relations in organizational settings. He provided considerable data to try and show that employee-oriented supervision, cohesive groups, and good communications at work are associated with high group productivity. In one of the studies conducted at the Institute for Social Study at Michigan University, U.S., data were collected from 31 geographically separated departments of a company. These departments performed essentially the same functions. The extent to which their managers were employee oriented and used group discussion methods to solve problems and make decisions (human relations oriented leadership) was measured through a questionnaire. This measure of the manager's human relation's orientation was correlated with the productivity of the department. What is more, it was correlated with the desire for greater responsibility on the part of their subordinates. It was also found that the group of departments with human relations oriented leadership, high loyalty of the subordinates to the department, etc., had the best productivity record. Similar results were found in a study of Voluntary School s; their rated effectiveness was correlated with how participative were they in the Voluntary School..

Influence of Leadership Style on the Organization (Bowers and Seashore – Khandwalla 1992))

Leadership Influence - In a study of 40 agencies of an American life insurance company, were interested in studying how the style of the leader of the organization influences the performance of the organization. Bowers and Seashore developed several measures of performance for these agencies. Then they tried to relate them to few dimensions of leadership:

- *The extent to which the leader extends support to his subordinates;*

- *The degree to which he facilitates interactions between them, through, for example, group decision making;*
- *The extent to which the leader facilitates the work of his subordinates through planning, scheduling of work, etc.; and*
- *The degree to which the leader emphasis the achievement of organizational goals. Bowers and Seashore found that all these dimensions of leadership were correlated with decrease in business costs, that is, with efficiency. Since Bowers and Seashore were measuring the human relations style of leadership (emphasis both on employee needs and organizational requirements), their study suggests that human relations oriented leadership tends to improve organizational efficiency.*

Social Participation - Studies in India seem to buttress this finding. J.B.P. Sinha, for example, found that in work groups with what he called the NT (nurturing-task) type of leadership, the performance tended to be better as compared to work groups with authoritarian leadership. Participatory leadership also performed better. Singh, Warrier, and Das found that the participatory, democratic leadership style was the best in a study of 24 groups. In a study of some textile mills, the Padakis found that a progressive sort of paternalism was more in evidence in two high performance mills than in two low performance mills.

Influence of Leaders towards Corporate Excellence (Bennis and Nanus – Khandwalla 1992)

Corporate Excellence - Bennis and Nanus interviewed 90 American leaders – 60 'successful' corporate chief executives and 30 'outstanding' leaders from the public sector. While no performance data were provided, the assumption seemed to be that these were leaders of excellent American organizations and they had contributed to the excellence of the organizations they led. Bennis and Nanus found that these leaders tended to be transformational leaders, that is, they got the commitment of their staff to effective organizational action, converted followers into leaders, and leaders into agents of change. They passionately articulated a vision of organizational excellence and thereby provided a focus for the organization, glue that welded its different stakeholders together. They effectively communicated their vision not just through information but also through graphic metaphors, analogies, gestures, drawings, symbolic acts, that made their vision and values come alive to others. They created trust by highlighting the direction of change for the organization and by exhibiting their dedication to it. Without being egotistic these leaders had positive self-regard and the self-confidence that comes with it, and they knew well their strengths and weaknesses, and to match their strengths and skills with their jobs. Their positive self-regard turned on their followers and made them confident of achieving high success.

I. Transformational Leadership

Transformational Leadership (Singh and Bhandarkar – Khandwalla 1992)

Traits - They intensively studied five Indian transformational leaders who had effected substantial changes in the operating cultures of their organizations as well as in their performance. A number of managers in each organization rated what the culture of the organization was before the leader took charge and what it was some years after he took charge. They also rated their leader. These leaders apparently changed the organizational culture towards more open vertical and horizontal communications, participative target setting, teamwork, role clarity, meritocracy, decentralization, Innovativeness, risk taking, results orientation, dynamism, concern for tasks as well as people, etc. Overall, the eleven most widely noted traits of the five leaders were:

The leader empowered his subordinates, that is, made them feel that they were worthwhile and important to the organization.

- *He was willing to take risks to achieve results.*
- *He was clear about the mission, purpose and goal of the organization.*
- *He was a good team builder, capable of generating positive group feeling among the members.*
- *He kept his balance in the face of calamities.*
- *He was a good boundary manager, ably managing the organization's interface with the government, politicians, and heads of other organizations and departments.*
- *He felt care and concern for the individual – for his work as well as his personal problems.*
- *He was quite open and receptive to the new ideas of others.*
- *He was a good planner.*
- *He evoked a sense of confidence and trust.*
- *He was accessible to anyone who wanted to see him.*

The work of Singh and Bhandarkar suggests that the transformational leader in a Third World setting must be an effective human relations leader; he/she must also be good at boundary management, entrepreneurship, planning, and stress management.

Innovative Entrepreneurs (Manimala- Khandwalla 1992)

Out of Box - Here the author's **(Manimala Khandwalla)** interest was in examining how pioneering and innovative (PI) entrepreneurs differ from non-PI entrepreneurs in the decision rules or 'heuristics' they use in running their business. They studied 164 cases of mostly 'successful' entrepreneurship (all cases were Indian barring a few Canadian ones). He developed an index of Innovativeness in which he included not only items of technological innovation (new products and/or manufacturing process) but also innovations in various areas of management such as finance, human resource management, marketing, government relations, organizational structure, etc. They scored each case on this index of Innovativeness, and then compares the decision rules used by those with relatively low scores. Some major differences emerged. For instance, PI ventures tended far more to search continuously and widely for new growth ideas, and preferred to develop their ideas in-house rather than just borrow them.

Resource Maximization - They also preferred more commonly to build up their resources, expertise and capabilities before seeking technical or financial collaboration with other parties. They were also more inclined to enter new markets through new products where there was virtually no competition, and they tended to rely more heavily on quality and reliability of their products as tools of competition. They preferred more often to start small, learn the ropes, and then grow fast, generally by diversifying in areas related to their main business.

Professionalism - As they grew in size they tended more often to professionalism their management and sought to delegate authority but with accountability (e.g. by creating divisions and profit centers). They tended to rely more than the low Innovativeness ventures on expertise. They rewarded competence more, and also stressed more teamwork, trust, and looking after the needs of their staff (paternalism). They took more risks but they reduced them by aggressively seeking relevant information and by pilot testing ideas. They spent more effort to build up a network of influential contacts by serving on various public bodies, helping other firms in distress, inducting influential persons on their boards, taking initiative during a social crisis, etc. Manimala's study indicates alternative sorts of management in competitive domains, one that goes for exclusive niches through innovation, and the other that seeks survival and growth in familiar terrain.

Performing Transformations in a Volatile Business Environment (Hall – Khandwalla 1992)

Business Model Volatility - William Hall (http://bit.ly/2a4lFQO) found it intriguing that in many highly competitive, mature, declining American industries like steel, construction equipment, automotive, and cigarette, there were at least a few companies with excellent profitability well above the average for the industry. How did these enterprises retain excellence when their domain was crumbling? Leading companies in eight industries facing a hostile environment averaged 20% return on equity, versus 13% for the eight industries, and 15% for the 1000 largest U.S. corporations (Fortune 1000 companies). Hall examined the business strategies of the two most successful companies in each of the 8 depressed industries.

Hall found that single-mindedly they followed one of two basic strategies:

- *Achieve the lowest unit costs relative to competitors, coupled with an acceptable product quality, and a pricing policy to gain profitable volume and market share growth (that is, a relatively low price policy based on low unit costs); or,*
- *Achieve the highest product/service/quality differentiated position relative to competition, coupled with both acceptable unit costs and a pricing policy that yielded sufficient margins (that is, a relatively high price policy based on perceptions by customers of premium product quality). The low prices invested heavily in the latest, most efficient technology. The high prices identified niches in which their products commanded premiums.*

Transformational Culture to Diversify (George – Khandwalla 1992)

Diversification Strategy - **Paul George** wanted to see if the type of diversification strategy pursued by a corporation affected its long-term performance. He studied the financial performance of 32 pairs of Indian private sector manufacturing companies. In each pair one had diversified and the other in the same industry had not. He found that the diversifiers tended to outperform the non-diversifiers. George also studied the sort of diversification pursued by the diversifiers. He identified four different types of diversification: related, dominant unrelated (a major business with one or more relatively minor unrelated diversification's), restricted unrelated (two or more unrelated groups of products, but related diversification within each group), and unrestricted unrelated in which no single group of products was dominant. George found that related diversifiers tended to outperform unrelated diversifiers. Dominant unrelated diversifiers showed the best performance while the worst performance was of unrestricted unrelated diversifiers. George's results were broadly similar to the results of Western studies of diversification. What is more, Western study also indicates that diversified companies that decentralize by adopting a divisional form tend to perform better than those that do not divide.

Turnaround Transformational Strategies in the Third World (Khandwalla 1992)

Analytics Driven Turnaround - Khandwalla tried to identify the kind of management needed in Third World conditions to regenerate sick organizations. In this study, ten Indian companies were examined that had been sick but had attempted to turnaround, that is, become healthy again. Half were relatively successful in improving their financial performance; the other half, from roughly comparable industries, were much less successful. Both groups had changes in their top management's and had the support of financial institutions and other stakeholders as part of their turnaround strategies. But the more successful group reported far more numerous attempts at enforcing management control over operations early in the turnaround effort, and many more attempts at quick pay-off projects, quick or immediate reduction in costs, and attempts at increasing sales revenues. Also, they were far more aggressive in mobilizing the staff for turnaround through such devices as sharing the facts about the organization's sickness with them. And getting staff members to participate in decision making, forming task forces to look into problem areas and to recommend solutions and help out in the implementation etc. The more successful management also paid more attention to better coordination of operations by forming coordination committees and setting up forums to review performance and actions in various areas of the organization. Compared to the less successful ones they seemed much more dynamic and also seemed to act on many more fronts simultaneously.

Professional management originated in the West, Khandwalla declares. With its emphasis on expertise, meritocracy, proper management systems and procedures, concern for optimal performance on a number of goals, etc. it has been thought of as a major force for excellence in Third World settings. A number of management institutions have been set up in Third World countries to promote professional management. Three studies follow that examine the relationship between professional management systems and practices and organizational performance. The first is a study by Negandhi and Prasad of 30 companies operating in India, half of which were U.S. subsidiaries practicing American style professional management. The second is a study by Thurne and House of the contribution of long range planning to corporate performance. The third is a study by Enthemkuzhy of the possible contribution of human resource development systems and practices to organizational performance. These studies indicate the practices needed for institutionalized and versatile types of organizational excellence.

Benchmarking Transformations Best Practices (Negandhi and Prasad – Khandwalla 1992)

Global Network Comparisons - Negandhi and Prasad examined 15 pairs of Indian companies. In each pair, one company was under indigenous management while the other, in the same industry, was a subsidiary of an U.S. company, and therefore reflected American management practices. Most of the pairs were chosen from relatively sophisticated technology industries like pharmaceuticals, heavy machinery and engineering, metals, etc. The attempt was to see how differences in national corporate management philosophies affected performance. Negandhi and Prasad developed a measure of progressiveness of management philosophy. Aggregating the top management's concern for serving various stakeholders such as employees, consumers, distributors, suppliers, owners, government, community, did this. They also developed a measure for the progressiveness of organizational practices. Companies that were decentralized and participatively managed had formalized personnel practices (systems of manpower planning, staff selection, training, appraisal, compensation system). And had instituted "professional" management processes (such as long-range planning, budgeting and resource allocation, goal setting, cost and quality control) scored higher on progressiveness of practices than companies that were centralized and authoritarian, did not have formalized personnel management practices and professional management processes.

KPIs and Metrics Used for Transformations - Negandhi and Prasad developed a subjectively assessed measure of excellence that they called managerial effectiveness. Its ingredients included whether or not the organization could attract high level manpower. Whether or not this manpower was properly utilized for policy making and planning, how low were staff turnover and absenteeism, how high was the staff morale and cooperation, how well the organization adapted to external environment, whether executives stressed corporate or departmental objectives, etc. Negandhi and Prasad found that American subsidiaries generally outscored their Indian counterparts on progressiveness of management philosophy, organizational practices, and managerial effectiveness. Furthermore, all three were correlated, so that those companies that had progressive management philosophies also tended to have progressive organizational practices. And including managerial effectiveness, while those that did not have a progressive management philosophy (that is, did not have adequate concern for the various stakeholders) tended to be low on progressive organizational practices and managerial effectiveness.

Strategic Long Range Planning Effectiveness (Thune and House – Khandwalla 1992)

Strategic Contribution to Business Success - Thune and House wished to determine whether formal long-range planning, an important component of organization and management, contributes to corporate performance or not. In their study, a company had a formal planning system if the company specified its corporate strategy and goals for at least three years into the future and developed specific operating procedures and programs for achieving these goals. If neither condition was met, the company was deemed to be a non-planner. Thune and House studied the performance of 17 matched pairs of companies in 6 American industries over a 7-year period. In each pair one was a planner, the other was a non-planner. In each pair, the companies were matched for size, rate of growth, and industry. Thune and House found that though the pairs were initially matched for size and growth rate, the planners significantly outperformed the non-planners. Indeed, the planners surpassed their own performance before they took to planning.

Emphasis on Profitability - Two Third Work-studies tend to support the Thune and House finding that planning contributes to organizational excellence. In a study of state-owned enterprises of the Indian State of Andhra Pradesh, Bhatt found that those enterprises that planned tended to perform better than those that did not. Jorgensen, examining the performance of eleven East African state-owned enterprises, found a strong correlation between profitability and internal planning (internal planning meant that the enterprise made its own plans rather than being saddled by government directives about its future activities).

Global Transformational leadership (Woycke – Khandwalla 1992)

Charismatic Leadership -Woycke's study of 20 Third World leaders, half of whom were 'charismatic – perhaps wily too' (e.g. Modi, Castro, Nasser, Nehru, Sukarno, and Mao Zedong) and half non-charismatic, makes some points that are similar to those made by Bennis and Nanus. Eight traits differentiated the charismatic from the non-charismatic leaders. First, the charismatic leader seemed to have a magnetic or compelling personality. Second, the charismatic leader had a sense of calling, something he just had to do. Third, the charismatic leader identified himself with his mission in life. Fourth, the charismatic leader was an orator who could move the masses. Fifth, the charismatic leader was adept at using symbols and slogans. Sixth, others saw the charismatic leader as a supreme, the ultimate fount of legitimacy. Seventh, the charismatic leader unified followers and sought and got support across contending factions. Eighth, the charismatic leader was able to get loyalty and devotion of his followers. Does the Third World need transformational or charismatic leaders? Both share some traits, but they also differ. The charismatic leader captivates followers; the transformational leader empowers them, turns followers into leaders, leaders into change agents, and thereby reduces their dependence on him/her. The charismatic leader reinforces uncritical hero worship and the herd mentality of dependency prone people; the transformational leader evokes autonomy and self-reliance. While the charismatic leader may have a role to play in unifying bickering factions, he/she can also strand followers in a morass of sentimental dependency. Transformational leadership may be more conducive for individual and organizational excellence in the Third World. Growth, competitive and turnaround strategies as contributors to organizational (especially corporate) performance have received a great deal of attention. Competition in liberalizing Third World economies is growing, although it may not yet have reached the level of intensity in most Western countries. Growth and rehabilitation from sickness remain difficult problems in the Third World contexts plagued by government controls, bottlenecks and scarcities. An American study of competitive strategies is followed by two Indian studies, one of corporate diversification strategies and their relationship with corporate performance, and the other of the sort of management that differentiates successful from less successful turnaround management.

HRM Survey Effectiveness (Enthemkuzhy- Khandwalla 1992)

HRM Impact on Leadership and Culture - Abraham Enthemkuzhy did a survey of human resource development (HRD) practices in 68 Indian organizations. HRD has been a relatively new field of 'people management'. It differs from personnel management in being far more concerned with developing the potentialities and competencies of organizational members than traditional personnel management is. The basic idea is to help people develop their potential so that they can contribute more to organizational excellence. Enthemkuzhy tried to measure various elements of HRD, such as HRD profile (HRD-oriented training, promotion, rewards, etc.). HRD climate (an organizational climate of trust, collaboration, authenticity, etc. in which human growth becomes likely, and the perception of existing personnel practices as developing inducing).

Process Management - Enthemkuzhy constructed an index of growth in company profitability as a measure of organizational performance. He was, however, able to use this measure of performance for only 14 out of the 68 organizations he studied. He found that while HRD profile was not correlated with organizational performance, HRD climate was. Thus, while HRD, as a formal system may not contribute much to organizational performance, the widespread perception of employees that they can grow in the organization may. Or to put it differently: It is not enough to have a good personnel management system; it is important that it is seen by the staff to be useful for their and the organization's growth.

Integrate Synergistically - Although organizational leadership, style of management, strategy, management systems, etc. can contribute to organizational excellence. They may contribute even more when they are properly combined, that is, when the organization is so designed that synergistic combinations keeping in mind the context in which the organization operates multiply their individual strengths. As an example, two airlines may perform equally well even though their organizational designs are diametrically opposite. The first may be effective because it operates on only a few contiguous lucrative routes, and therefore can be tightly managed from the top. The other operates on many routes and competes on a national or international level with other large airlines, and therefore needs to be decentralized and professionally managed, with a sophisticated performance information and control system. Good fit among the components of organizational design and with features of the operating context is a complex but exciting frontier of organizational studies.

Cultural Task and Organizational Fit Analysis (Lawrence and Lorsch – Khandwalla 1992)

Task Fit Environment - Lawrence and Lorsch studied 10 U.S. business unites in the plastics, container, and packaged food industries. They were interested in seeing transformations and whether the fit between the nature of the task environment of the organization and the structure of the organization is a significant influence of organizational performance. Half of the units picked by

Lawrence and Lorsch were considered high performing in their respective industries while the other half were considered relatively low performing.

Structural Differentiation - Lawrence and Lorsch noticed that the extent to which the organization's structure and managerial culture as internally differentiated varied with the extent to which the organization's operating environment was differentiated. That is to say, how different the environments of the unit's production, sales, and R&D departments were from one another influenced the extent to which these three departments differed in their structure and managerial culture from one another. But the extent of structural differentiation did not seem, to be relevant to organizational performance.

Effective Managerial Practices - What seemed to distinguish high performers from low performers was the extent of organizational integration – how well the various departments collaborated. When this collaboration was high even when organizational differentiation was high, the performance was especially good. Large organizations tend irresistibly to get differentiated because of increasing functional and role specialization, long hierarchy, etc. The critical lesson of the Lawrence and Lorsch study is that for organizational excellence the management must pay special attention to practices, systems, and structures that improve coordination and collaboration between parts that otherwise may have the tendency to work at cross purposes.

J. Leadership Definitions in the context of the Digital Culture

Given the above detailing of leadership theories and its development, the Author has proposed leadership definitions and questions in the context of an **"Digital Culture"** defined by addressing 5 questions in respect of Organization and Management Models and 5 questions in respect of its leadership style. Sets of questions have been addressed with a broad definition of what do they focus upon in the context of the **Digital Culture.**

1. *How does the Leader influence the organization history, tradition, management style, structure, and communication and performance ethic?*
2. *How does the Leader drive the organization?*
3. *What does the Leader focus upon?*
4. *How does the Leader act?*
5. *What is the Leader's long-term orientation?*

We can establish and elicit specific leadership styles as a part of the study to enable a unique identification to that particular style.

Leadership disrupted Questions addressed deals with:

How does the Leader influence the organization history, tradition, management style, structure, and communication and performance ethic?

The CEO enables the organization to change, manage people strategies and influence existence of specific cultures. The leader emphasizes culture as an important aspect of organizational building and believes in influencing people to shape cultures. The leader facilitates people practices, HRM activities, organizational climate and its conduciveness to performance. The leader mentors, coaches, teaches, builds other leaders, and enables work processes that make work life easy for organizational members. The leader pays attention to building knowledge and enables the organization to retain an open and invigorating mind to unknown environments. The leader supports innovation as a necessary competitive condition to learn, sponsors risk-taking behavior and drives people to fly into unknown territories. The leader emphasizes teamwork, enables interdependencies between functions, businesses, technologies and the organization as a whole. Spends over 50% of time to manage employee retention and rewarding high performers. The leader provides a vital direction to restructure and right size as situation demands, yet retaining the option to break and build as deemed appropriate. The leader is focused on the vision, practices values, emphasizes individual intellect as they impact organizational goals, actively participates in attracting, retaining, and rewarding talent and leads in times of crisis. The leader acknowledges the presence of a culture and without denying its presence attempts to manage it to the organizational advantage. The leader believes in competing in challenging environments by preparing the organization in advance, sets meaningful goals and targets and competes to conquer. The leader practices what he/she wishes to implement. There first desire to work effectively as followers and thereafter take on a leadership mantle. Some critical issues outlined below are also addressed: How did the organization get to be the way it is? What are the people here like to work with? Why? What are the spotlight measures of performance and the spotlight rewards and punishments? What is done to help a person along once he or she starts work in this organization? What does it take to do well in the organization? How are good people recognized? How does one find out how one is performing in this organization? What are the ways one finds out what is really going on in the organization?

How does the Leader drive the organization?

The leader drives by example and by experimentation. The leader seeks to create a high performing culture. The leader makes his voice and choice adequately known to organizational members and makes no bones about letting known pleasure and displeasure. The leader has a point of view. A driven need to motivate and keep people in the right frame of mind to be productive and happy. And by the need to make people, processes and systems learn from one another, interact to make a meaningful whole and are constantly seeking holistic behavior from organizational systems. They work by encouraging things to be worked out, provide job clarity, coaches and rewards for performance. Seek participation by sharing strategic goals, communicates, shares values, distinctive concern for individual sensitivity, empowerment, delegation, clear accountability and demonstrated by examples. Communicate and keep in touch by institutionalizing policies that provide clarity to goals, tasks and manages a team through maintaining status quo through conflicting circumstance and taking decisions that involve retaining established norms and practices. Driven by the urge to create, make actions intellectually dominant, treats developmental processes a predominant organizational factor and is willing to compromise for nothing other than intellectual superiority in actions. Asks organizational members to think science rather than processes that cannot be proven. A strong sense of engineering sciences, that technology provides solutions to complex organizational problems, quantitative approaches to most problems and believes in logic and rationality as desired attitudes. Enabled by a performance system that overrides all other considerations and makes individual targets an important element achieving results. Driven by the belief that direction, coaching but through collaboration enable for the organization business models that are appropriate and accepted by people and goals that have been worked to individual and organizational advantage.

What does the Leader focus upon?

The Leaders basically focuses on results, figure the drivers and key success factors of the organization, the revenue model, shareholder priority, the means and methods, resources and talent and the ethics of why should it be done. Additionally, enable training and competency development, customer and client understanding problem-solving mechanisms within and without the organization and spend time on essentials. Focus on creating people oriented systems that enable a culture that brings individuals, teams and organizations together. Create a climate to establish through clear policy perspectives and on delivering intellectual and performance value that sponsors native instincts, creative pursuits, feedback and review processes and encourages actions that facilitates results. Keep people and processes aligned on building for the future through Institutional Corporate processes, demanding systems that connect organizational functions and works through structures that are streamlined, regulated and planned. Make happen action on building loyalty through establishing people oriented systems that enable handling tasks that are individually focused. Keen on managing for today adequately. Focus on attracting and nurturing talent, systems and processes that are of utility today and tomorrow, more tomorrow, and is willing to absorb the costs of human and organizational process costs as a necessary condition of managing the human mind. Sharpen their inclination on adding technical and functional values to business situations enables competency development that is vertical and incisive and promotes organizations to drive business through technological excellence. Establish and communicate priorities that are determined quickly, enables efficient systems, dislikes elaborate meetings, followed through decisively and ensures that different parts of the organization are focused on their own deliverables.

Some issues range from: Who are the three or four key people in the leadership of the organization? How did they get to the top? Organizational Effectiveness and Satisfaction issues? What is the one thing the organization doesn't do as well as it should? Where is the organization headed? What is the employee turnover in the organization relative to other comparable organizations? What is the status of Individual in the Organization? What is the prospective boss like? On which key groups or individuals, in addition to one's prospective boss, would one be most dependent to get the job done successfully? What are the biggest hurdles that have to be overcome to do the job well? What important sources of support are potentially available for getting the job done well? Is there a possibility of becoming stereotyped in the organization? What is the status of those who are similarly stereotyped? What are the prospects for the newcomer's acceptance into the culture? Organization's Agenda for the Individual? Why does the organization want to hire the individual? What does it value about the individual? Where are the individuals now who previously held the job for which the individual is being recruited? Why did they more on? Is "bait and switch", "bait and keep", or "bait and eat" the organization's agenda? http://bit.ly/29WHwtx

How does the Leader act?

Action oriented to demonstrate by action that concern for people enables organizations to perform above expectation, towards developing people competencies ensures organizational competitiveness is appropriately managed by right people and makes organizational goals subservient to competency development. Action oriented through appropriateness of actions driven by circumstance, enabling learning to be documented, creates knowledge sharing atmosphere, drives decisions through consensus and takes meaningful time to accomplish tasks. Demonstrates through individualized working, avoiding teams and consequent inefficiencies meets deadlines under all circumstance and seeks the best. Action oriented to make people believe in the overall good establishes concreteness to tasks to be accomplished and to enable easy and smooth management of the organization, streamlines administrative processes, establishes a string back office operations organization and manages customer oriented roles through follow procedure route. Action oriented to demonstrate merit and results supersedes all other performance factors, does not believe in means as an important consideration while acting upon information and manages rewards as a necessary evil in people management processes. Action oriented to provide criteria for success and failures and ensures it is adequately communicated and holds accountability on streamlined systemic norm and through individualized working, avoiding teams and consequent inefficiencies, meets deadlines under all circumstance and seeks the best. How does the organization make use of a person's experience and ideas? If the organization had to stop doing some of the things it now does, what would not be changed? Which outside groups do the organization pay attention to? Why? How? What must the organization do particularly well in order to succeed? How does one go about selling a new idea in this organization? Who are the key individuals and groups one has to persuade?

What is the Leader's long-term orientation?

Long Term strategy to delivering value through people development individualized tasks, creating an environment that is self-exhilarating. Long Term vision to build an organizational that can culturally sustain itself to renew, learn, contribute in varying life cycles and has adequate organizational energy to grow with momentum. Long Term priority to retain competitive advantage by providing profitability through consistent intervals and prefers revenue to growth. Long Term desire to make lasting organizations that can stream through economic and business life cycles and does not have the pressure to retain performance under all circumstance. Long Term responsibility to build organizational wealth, individual intellect, collective wisdom, sustainable business model and overall organizational effectiveness parameters. Long Term authority to make organizational working built on strong fundamentals of bureaucracy, frameworks and management styles. Prefers streamlined processes rather than the opportunity to reinvent the wheel to resolve conflicts. Long term ambition to create a self-propelling organization that has internal renewal capability to prod organizational performance, individual effectiveness and shareholder satisfaction. Long Term approach to make people processes subservient to technological processes and works towards eliminating elaborate actions that involve meetings, group work, communication forums and large-scale explanation to actions. Long Term drive to retain competitive advantage by providing profitability through consistent intervals and prefers revenue to growth.

Some additional critical issues covered would be, what are the important strategies and tactics for getting things done in the organization? What are the most important tacit assumptions that members of the organization share about work, human nature, and human relationships? What does the organization belief system stand for? What is its motto? What does it take to be highly successful in this organization? What kind of person is most respected? What is considered heroic? What is considered serious punishment in this organization? What kinds of mistakes are not forgiven? What company folklore, rituals, symbols, and ceremonies best reveal the essential character of the organization? Can we make believe this organization is a person: How would we describe this person? What are the main rules that everyone has to follow in this organization in the long run? John Luther writes, "Good character is more to be praised than outstanding talent. Most talents are to some extent a gift. Good character, by contrast, is not given to us. We have to build it piece by piece—by thought, choice, courage and determination."

Rajesh Gupta, President and CEO of State Bank of Canada writes on **Building a high performance culture in a digital organization** - *Company culture determines how things are done and how people in a Company behave. Company culture is therefore the root cause which determines competitive advantage of any company. High performance leads to the correct decisions and the right choices being taken at the appropriate time to improve Company viability and ensuring long term growth.*

Digital initiatives lead to both inculcations of better culture and enhanced performance. Empirical discussions reflect that digital initiatives lead to anywhere between 10% - 25% growth in a Company's topline and also contributes to reduction of expenses. Digitalization leads to greater connectivity among people, better sharing of cultures, enhanced coordination and improvement in processes and technology. It leads to new capabilities and capacity building.

Connecting leadership disrupted styles towards building an organizational culture: *The culture of an organization critically depends upon its leadership. It actually works both ways. The leadership too gets affected by the culture of an organization.*

There are basically two types of leaders – transactional leaders and transformational leaders. Transactional leaders are change resistant and they remain largely in their psychological comfort zone protecting the existing policies and procedures. This makes the organization impervious to change and eats away the vitals leading to progressive competitive dystrophy, disorganization and death. Transformational leaders are adaptive to change. They accept change and adopt a collaborative change management strategy. They believe in shared assumptions, values and norms. While transactional leaders are tactical thinkers, transformational leaders are strategic thinkers. Strategic thinking creates a long term vision of growth, cooperation, collaboration and change.

Using social media / networks towards building an organizational culture: *Social media has become the game changer today. Social Media is defined as the medium that helps to connect people, coordinate processes and leads to better communication and interaction among individual and groups. Social media is the use of web based technologies and internet based applications to build an ideological and technological foundations to transform organizational culture. It leads to:*

- *Greater Participation – Participation is inclusive and everybody is involved in the pursuit of organizational goals*
- *Induces openness – removes barriers and leads to transparency in functioning*
- *Induces community feelings – creates a common organizational interest, hobbies and passions*
- *People can share resources and information easily and effectively*

How organizational structures align with leadership disrupted and culture to build an organization: *Organizations invest in their leaders to build up and meet their business goals. Leadership strategy and formulation as part of an organizational structure is fundamental towards:*

- *Leadership disrupted drives business strategy – this leads to development of sustainable, achievable and scalable goals of an organization*
- *Leadership disrupted shapes the organizational culture – this inculcates entrepreneurship, initiative and risk taking capability among staff. It lays down pragmatic parameters for change management, conflict management and goal orientation*
- *Leadership disrupted develops a sustainable talent acquisition and retention system – attracts, develops and promotes talent*
- *Leadership disrupted designs the organizational structure to support strategy – rewards time management, social networking, learning & development and orients managerial control systems towards implementation of strategic initiatives.*

Chapter 6

Organization Model Interfaces

In this chapter we introduce Organization Management Models as an important consideration to study cultures. The chapter provides an understanding on varying types of organizations through 2 sets of models (4 each) and how do these models impact culture. This is an attempt by the Author to connect Organization Type, Culture and Leadership to make the analysis and findings comprehensive and meaningful.

A. *Changing Organizational Models, Descriptions, Possibilities*
B. *Characteristics of an Organizational Model*
C. *Developing a Framework for Defining Organizational Models*
D. *Organization and Management as Conflict Prone Entities*
E. *Alternate Forms of Organizational Models including Patterns of neurotic organizational types*
F. *The CCCC (C4) framework for Organization Modeling*
G. *Creating a set of Organization and Management Models that builds an Intellectual Company*

A. Changing Organizational Models, Descriptions, Possibilities

Effective organizations were defined as those with a performance orientation of doing what is right for business. In doing so, businesses attempted structural models that were appropriate at a point in time. Models included structural (business) interventions (Microsoft), long range planning (University), environment scanning (Shell), management accounting and systems, management by objectives (GE), leadership pipeline, (Unilever) performance planning (P & G), managerial effectiveness (GE) etc. these models continue to be of relevance to organizations experiencing various stages of their life cycles. Its application and usefulness has varied depending on the usage and manner in which they were implemented. While some of the models have outlived their usefulness there are several other concepts and applications that continue to serve their time.

Organizations (Design, Roles, Goals, Tasks, Benchmarks) - Over the last few decades, organizations have been rocked by a series of economic shocks as has been experienced in the developed economies Stewart, (1993) and crisis Iacocca, (1986). The opportunity for academics and authors was to focus on organizations, culture, leadership and performance. Reed and Hughes, (1993) and then led to some open analysis of cultures and they evolved and directed organizations. Deal and Kennedy (1982) People, keeping in mind pursuit of some specific purposes create organizations. Organizations have a formal structure to achieve their objectives. They have formally identified roles, tasks, goals and responsibilities. Khandwalla, (1992) besides the employ and not employ, make or buy, sell or invest types of decisions organizations have to develop strategies, make decisions for acquiring and deploying resources. Yuchtman and Seashore, (1967). The search for new management paradigms is not a recent phenomenon. Over a sustained period of time, many management writers and thinkers have continuously strived for better methods of working to achieve time, cost and quality objectives of an organization. Seymour and Low, (1990). This search led to promising results at the general management level where a proliferation of new management concepts for business is now apparent. Among others, the more promising concepts or buzzwords include business process re-engineering (BPR), benchmarking, project partnering and total quality management (TQM) (Stephenson, 1996; Ahuja et al., 1994; Low, 1992). Collectively, all these have served to contribute to new thinking or re-examine existing management concepts to rationalize how organizations may be managed more effectively.

To enable building the organizational model it is necessary to delve a little into the make-up of the human mind, the evolutions, mental make-up that form the learning and personality disposition and the consequent need for structures and organizations. Wilber (1993; 1996) proposes that conscious awareness is intellectual in human mind and provides an articulate argument through exposing the learning from the study of remnant trail of clues of over tens of thousands of years. He offers a framework for conceptualizing this development of awareness that starts at the Paleolithic age, where the individual has not differentiated them from the environment – a pre personal stage. And moving on to personal when they can differentiate from environment (contemporary human mind) and finally to the transpersonal where self is a part of the seamless universe.

To our perspective there is learning and relevance to Wilber's analogy as to follow this transition of the development to that of the organization, culture and leadership as leaders in various stages of their understanding of themselves and their environments they transit through the various stages. From an organizational analysis point of view, we could classify the scientific management and Taylorian days as being pre personal, human relations and individual consciousness as being personal and the self-actualization and the intellectual and Learning Companies as being transpersonal. At each of these stages leaders play one of the said roles in the context of their organizations. Mahoney (1991,

p. 425) states: "We are literally, more attuned to and engaged with our inner selves than to our external worlds." Recent evidence from western scientific disciplines indicates that the world is seamless. So are the organizations, its cultures and leaders.

Developed Organizations - A developed organization can be conceptualized as an evolving goal without an end in itself and that the goal is to know and be aware of reality as they relate to their performing and competitive environment. This argument combined together with organizational theory study can be safely argued that cultural management of organizations necessitates a new paradigm, if not a discerning discontinuity, to study into factors that influences and invokes these changes. There has been considerable work done in varying degree by Burnes, (1992) and Mink, (1992), Rosabeth Moss Kanter, (1989), Gerloff, (1985), Robbins, (1990), Schein, (1985) to demonstrate case examples of changing cultures in specific organizations. However, there is loss of material in regard to identified organizational models in which specific cultures operate as they have been influenced by leadership and therefore demonstrates a case for a focused study. Yet every organization is a culture. A community who live in close proximity, share resources, interact actively and depend substantially on one another for their co-existence and results. In this process of living together a culture tends to develop of shared beliefs, norms, values, practices, rituals that bind this community together. Deviations from these are often permitted but within acceptable limits. Kroeber and Kluckhohn, (1952)

Organizations are the dominant form of institutions in our society. Robbins, (1990) They are also distinct entities in our environment. We need organizations for collective and individual success; yet organizations operate through their structure, processes, goals, and norms to limit individual initiative. Gerloff, (1985). Organizations have been conceptualized in numerous ways.

Organizational descriptions - Robbins (1990)

- **Rational Entities in Pursuit of Goals.** *Organizations exist to achieve goals, and the behavior of organizational members can be explained as the rational pursuit of those goals.*
- **Coalitions of Powerful Consequences.** *Organizations are made up of groups, each of which seeks to satisfy its own self-interest. These groups use their self-power to influence the distribution of resources within the organization.*
- **Open System.** *Organizations are input – output transformation systems that depend on their environment for survival.*
- **Meaning – Producing Systems.** *Organizations are artificially created entities. Their goals and purposes are symbolically created and maintained by the management.*
- **Loosely Coupled Systems.** *Organizations are made up of relatively independent units that can pursue dissimilar or even conflicting goals.*
- **Political Systems.** *Organizations are composed of internal constituencies that seek control over the decision process in order to enhance their position.*
- **Instruments of Domination.** *Organizations place members into job boxes that constrain what they can do and individuals with who they can interact. Additionally, they are given a boss who has authority over them.*
- **Information Processing Units.** *Organizations interpret their environment, coordinate activities, and facilitate decision making by processing information horizontally and vertically through a structural hierarchy.*
- **Psychic Prisons.** *Organizations constrain members by constructing job descriptions, departments, divisions, and standards of acceptable and unacceptable behaviors. When accepted by members, they become artificial barriers that limit choices.*

- *Social Contracts. Organizations are composed of sets of unwritten agreements whereby members perform certain behaviors in return for compensation. (Robbins 1990)*
B. Characteristics of an Organizational Model

Does Structure Follow Strategy?

Structure is Strategy in Process - Organizations moved vertically from strategy, to structure and process. In the knowledge generation role, content has a distinctive role to play in making corporations effective. In fact, content and process to a considerable extent go logically together. One at the cost of another has long since been way laid. Nevertheless, for corporations into intense knowledge management roles content tends to be an important area, no doubt. At another conceptual plane one could debate on structure and content preceding strategy given that people who contribute through their intellect have done so without either the strategy or the structure in mind. They have simply made a difference through their thought process. Innovative organizations do not have tight rope structures with clearly defined boundaries of roles and responsibilities. Consulting companies (McKinsey, KPMG, PwC, EY, Andersen, Bain and Company, Price Waterhouse Coopers, BCG - Boston Consulting Group) have long since used the Adhocracy Model (Henry Mintzberg) with team based structures constructed on the basis of competence, client needs and delivery schedules. Their industry and functional specialization matrix structure offers them the unique advantage of providing more than a plain vanilla service. Research labs of large pharmaceutical companies (Glaxo – GSK, Sanofi, Merck, SmithKline Beecham, Novartis, Pfizer, Astra Zeneca, Aventis) have depended on a structure that allows flexibility in roles, areas of contribution and the best person is right there doing what he/she knows best.

Digital Skills - For maximum long-term strategic advantage, companies focus their own internal structures, skills and resources on a relatively few basic source of intellectual or service strengths. To create long range distinctiveness for the customer. We are proposing an organization form that will not be a minority contributor but will reflect the form of the majority of the organizations of tomorrow and for which skills, competencies will need to be appropriately determined. "What skills do you think are the most important as we move toward a more digital workforce? We've always looked for individuals who are continual learners — people who demonstrate a lot of learning agility and who are intellectually curious. What is different are the skill sets we're looking for. They're not the same as what we we've looked for historically". Donna Morris (Adobe), interviewed by Gerald (Jerry) C. Kane in MIT SMR 2016, "Adobe Reinvents its Customer Experience" say "Engaged employees ensure personalized customer experience". "Your decision to make that strategic change has also had sort of wide-ranging impact on how you were organized. Is that a fair statement? That's right, exactly. Our organization structure has changed. The capabilities that we look for across the organization, the skills development, and our investment in that development have all changed. Let's look at data scientists". Structures and skills need to provide an element of flexibility to make this implementable. Adhocracy forms are relevant as adjunct to large bureaucratic forms or at certain points in time where high flexibility is required to cope with high environmental certainty or maybe appropriate for certain industries.

Big Data Scientists - "Traditionally, we haven't looked for top-notch data scientists, but because of our transition to the Cloud, we now have really big data teams that give us insights into our subscriber base — how they use our products, whether they are trial users or already subscribers to the Cloud. Adobe has become a company that's rich in data and insights, so today we have jobs that we wouldn't have had five years ago. Mobile is another area where our capabilities have changed. We have mobile developers and also people who are thinking about what's next with video on mobile and how that's going to affect advertising. Also, as an organization continues to grow and become increasingly complex, leaders will have to demonstrate more maturity. We're looking for leaders who come with scale, who have worked for global companies that are larger than we are, and who are used to handling complexity with simplicity. We also want leaders who can roll up their sleeves and make things happen" In, "The Stress Effect in Information and Communication Technologies", MIT SMR 2016, Theodore Kinni writes, Data trumps analytics: "Lately, the transformational effect of machine learning on analytics is big news, with big data taking a backseat. In these stories, the data that will be shoveled into the analytics furnace will be so readily available as to be almost inconsequential. Not so fast, says venture capitalist Nick Beim in a blog post on TechCrunch. Beim, who is writing about startup opportunities, thinks that it will be the other way 'round. Analytics will be a dime a dozen. "One of machine learning's most lasting areas of impact," he writes, "will be to democratize basic intelligence through the commoditization of an increasingly sophisticated set of semantic and analytic services, most of which will be offered for free, enabling step-function changes in software capabilities.". http://www.nickbeim.com - "One of machine learning's most lasting areas of impact will be to democratize basic intelligence through the commoditization of an increasingly sophisticated set of semantic and analytic services, most of which will be offered for free, enabling step-function changes in software capabilities. These services today include image recognition, translation and natural language processing and will ultimately include more advanced forms of interpretation and reasoning".

Rise of Intelligent Services - "Software will become smarter, more anticipatory and more personalized, and we will increasingly be able to access it through whatever interface we prefer – chat, voice, mobile application, web, or others yet to be developed", continues Nick Beim. "Beneficiaries will include technology developers and users of all kinds. This burst of new intelligent services will give rise to a boom in new startups that use them to create new products and services that weren't previously cost effective or possible. Image recognition, for example, will enable new kinds of visual shopping applications. Facial recognition will enable new kinds of authentication and security applications. (Selection is a matter of strategy. There are many excellent books that will advise on how selection decisions should be made. As the study by Capron showed, pre-acquisition goals are frequently about growth in intellectual capital, such as customer base, brands, market share, methodologies, acquiring specialized knowledge or competence, products, technology, or research capability. Equally, it may also be aimed at greater efficiency in asset utilization, eliminating duplicated resources, and sharing facilities and systems. Here the argument will be based on cost synergies. The commonest strategic reason is known as horizontal diversification, extending the reach of existing technology and markets. This frequently means a combination of large organizations that were previously competitors. Cost synergies always prevail in this case). Analytic applications will grow ever more sophisticated in their ability to identify meaningful patterns and predict outcomes. There are, however, a number of successful playbooks to create more durable data partnerships with incumbents. In consumer industries dominated by large platform players, the winning playbook in recent years has been to partner with one or ideally multiple platforms to provide solutions for enterprise customers that the platforms were not planning (or, due to the cross-platform nature of the solutions, were not able) to provide on their own, as companies such as Sprinklr, Hootsuite and Dataminr have done. The benefits to platforms in these partnerships include new revenue streams, new learning about their data capabilities and broader enterprise dependency on their data sets. In concentrated industries dominated not by platforms but by a cluster of more traditional enterprises, the most successful playbook has been to offer data-intensive software or advertising solutions that provide access to incumbents' customer data, as Palantir, IBM Watson, Fair Isaac, AppNexus and Intent Media have done. If a company gets access to the data of a significant share of incumbents, it will be able to create products and services that will be difficult for others to replicate".

Intellectual Differentiators

Commerce - Economic impact of the firm, obviously, is more than internal management approaches alone. Best of organizations have encountered failures for want of strategic differentiators. For example, Michael E. Porter defined five basic forces as the basic state of "barriers to competition" for a firm: *Economies of scale, Product Differentiation, Capital Requirements, Cost disadvantages independent of size, Access to distribution channels and Government Policy.* At any given point in time firms are at varying stages of advantage on this five-stated entry barriers. It makes vulnerability that much more relevant in the context of a going concern. GE has consistently stated dominance, economies of scale and size as their competitive positioning. Well-managed management's meant attaining bottom line targets and growth curves as promised to the shareholders. Citicorp evaluates countries for its human potential. The goal of meeting quarterly budgets has been dealt with before. When balance sheets are squeezed to show profits in an area where there are none firms do push the balance sheet to its precipice. It is while making the balance sheet look good do corporate managements miss the wood from trees. Several short-term strategies to prop up performance make the firm go belly up as the organization does not possess the sustenance power to hang out there with cash flows and customer loyalties for long. Although achievement of the targeted goals has not secured the corporation from destruction and decay as we have seen it happen to large companies.

Perishable Networks - What has attracted the most interest in neural networks is the possibility of learning. Given a specific task to solve, and a class of functions learning means using a set of observations to find which solves the task in some optimal sense. McKinsey Consultants Lowell Bryan, Eric Matson, Leigh Weiss, say, "In any professional setting, networks flourish spontaneously: human nature, including mutual self-interest, leads people to share ideas and work together even when no one requires them to do so. As they connect around shared interests and knowledge, they may build networks that can range in size from fewer than a dozen colleagues and acquaintances to hundreds". Our hypotheses here are that organization seek stability and while organic forms may arise to cope with temporary instability these forms will perish as soon as they have served their utility. (More attention should be paid to competence transfer and exploitation of revenue-based synergies. Rushing to tell the market that something is happening by announcing cost restructuring may not be in the best long-term interest—even though such transformations are very likely to be made eventually. Rationalizing assets transformational interventions does not necessarily lead to cost savings, particularly where the assets rationalized are those of the target company.) Although the chaos in the environment will be significantly greater than what we are seeing today the organization of tomorrow shall seek stability in the middle of this turbulence. While to an outsider who is spared this chaos the pace of change may be rapid to an insider it will appear tranquil. "Research scientists working in related fields, for example, or investment bankers serving clients in the same industry frequently create informal—and often socially based—networks to collaborate".

Deep Learning - Most large corporations have dozens if not hundreds of informal networks, which go by the name of peer groups, communities of practice, or functional councils—or have no title at all. These networks organize and reorganize themselves and extend their reach via cell phones, Blackberries, community Web sites, and other accessories of the digital age. As networks widen and deepen, they can mobilize talent and knowledge across the enterprise. They also help to explain why some intangible-rich companies, such as ExxonMobil and GE, have increased in scale and scope and boast superior performance". For example, in neural networks, Knowledge' is thus represented by the network itself, which is quite literally more than the sum of its individual components.

Intellectual Proximity is to an Advantage

Simplicity Versus Complexity - As organizations grow in size it is but natural for complexity and distances to emerge between front line realities and decision-making power sources. The front line could mean employees, suppliers, governments, society and more importantly and sadly the customer itself. When this distance becomes more than manageable companies commence reeling under pressure of performance. Somewhere along the line of business we have lost touch. A process of renewal, an act involving "involvement" on a continuous basis, needs to be established and new ways of thinking becomes essential. Thinking differently from initial concept to actual implementation should become an organizational rigor where translation of ideas into workable ideas and that in turn into action plans make the organization vibrant and energized at more than one plane. Every flat structure supports this finding".

Knowledge as Intellect - Sustaining a competitive advantage through management of people has become an inevitable management paradigm. While we evaluate the impact of the factors that make the hardware of the firm we do see the inevitability of turbulence. Yet the people factors, the much-publicized area, deserve the final go signal. "As we move towards the chaos of the future," Bob Buckman of Buckman Labs said, " the progress of Buckman Labs relative to other companies will be determined by the growth in the value of knowledge that exists within the company. The acceleration of knowledge transfer is how we will grow this collection of individuals we call into what it can be. Our strategic advantage lies in the leverage of knowledge". Buckman is today worth several times more than the value of the hard assets that is owned by his firm.

Knowledge Bureaucracy - A contradiction of sorts, perhaps but every **"new idea"** has appeared to be a contradiction at its inception and an anachronism at birth. We shall call this anachronism (as it appears today) the Knowledge Bureaucracy driven IT system. We are using the term bureaucracy not in the pejorative sense of the word but to convey the likely proliferation of this systemic form across the enterprise. For the purpose of contrasting with the prevalent organization form today we shall use the professional bureaucracy as being most representative of contemporary organizational designs and would entail a degree of complexity. "Who should lead the company to its complexity sweet spot? As business complexity is a cross-company issue, no individual business unit leader can typically be in charge. Looking at corporate-level leadership, the CFO would be a natural fit if complexity management was mostly about cost reduction. The COO knows the internal process simplification needs of the company but doesn't typically have a say on products. With the CMO (or the head of innovation), it is the other way around. The CIO often owns neither processes nor products but is especially attuned to a company's complexity as it is layered into IT systems year after year. CIOs are also at the heart of the digitization that helps to rethink complexity management". Martin Mocker, Peter Weill and Stephanie L. Woerner in MIT SMR 2014, "Revisiting Complexity in the Digital Age" continue, on the leadership Challenge – "The CEO sits across both product and process but is often too busy. So what about making a group of people responsible for managing complexity, especially as it's a companywide issue? The executive committee comes to mind, but it's also hard to get a larger group like this to be accountable for both changing and running the company".

Dopamine Squirt - "Edward Hallowell and John Ratey from Harvard, for instance, have written about people for whom feeling connected provides something like a "dopamine squirt" the neural effects follow the same pathways used by addictive drugs". In a McKinsey paper, Derek Dean and Caroline Webb, stated, "Recovering from information overload," Nonetheless, evidence is emerging that humans can become quite addicted to multitasking. This effect is familiar too: who hasn't struggled against the urge to check the smart phone when it vibrates, even when we're in the middle of doing something else?"

System Perspective of Organizations

Socio Tech - The organization is a socio – technical system. Every organization has a particular pattern of tasks, technical, human and structural factor. The tasks of the organization refer to goals, targets and sub tasks. The technical component of the organization includes production, information and other technologies. Maintaining a dynamic equilibrium with the external environment and regarding organization as an open system in continual interaction with a changing environment, is very essential. Daftuar, 2000. There is wide spread agreement amongst organizational theorists that a systems perspective offers important insights into the workings of an organization. Ashmos and Huber, (1987). Differentiation and integration brings the forces of systems that oppose each other together. Systems are classified into fundamentally tow alternatives being open and closed. Closed systems thinking revolve around the physical, its correlates and attributes and view the system as all pervasive and self-contained. Closed system is into a self-loop, draws its energy from its own momentum and does not interact or acknowledge the presence of an environment. To this fallacy does a closed system suffer? We contrast open system recognizes the dynamic interaction of the system with its environment.

Essential characteristics of an Open System are:

- *Environment Awareness – Changes in the environment impact the system.*
- *Feedback – Receive information, adjusts, allows and follows a corrective path.*
- *Cyclical Character – Follows events, receives new inputs and repeats the cycle.*
- *Negative Entropy – Demonstrates propensity of the system to run down or disintegrate while in a state of entropy in a closed system but would mean just the opposite in an open system.*
- *Steady State – Power of the input energy received to retain dynamic position results in a steady state of information and consequent processing.*
- *Movement toward Growth and Expansion – Moving from steady state and into growth and expansion as it retains anti entropy situation. Cycles and sub system is a typical reaction.*
- *Balance of Maintenance and Adaptive Activities – Maintenance and adaptive actions ensure sub system balance and ability to adjust to variations.*
- *Equifinality – that the system can reach the same final state by differing initial conditions and by a variety of paths.*

The Life Cycle Perspective

A life cycle refers to a pattern of predictable change. Life cycle metaphor signifies that organizations go through varying stages of its life. The five-stage model (Cameron and Whetton, 1983) is:

- ***Entrepreneurial Stage*** *– Formative stage, impressionable, ambiguous beginnings, resource management priorities, no established culture or norms to start with, very open and loosely coupled systems.*
- ***Collectivity Stage*** *- Continues from the last stage but with vision and mission clarified, informal communication and networking structures and members working hard to demonstrate achievement of goals with limited bottlenecks.*
- ***Formalization and Control Stage*** *- Stabilized, streamlined processes, including, roles, goals, tasks and structure, formalization of actions, conservative decision making postures and systemic solutions are sought.*

245

- **Elaboration of Structure Stage** – *Diversified portfolio of capabilities, complex managerial processes and decentralized decision processes.*
- **Decline Stage** – *Organizational inability to hold together its strengths, apparent confusion in enabling things to happen, resources short fall is evident and overall organizational state of flux.*

Not all organizations pass through the five stages of the life cycle but the state of the cycle influences the organizational culture and leadership to act in ways that may not do otherwise.

C. Developing a Framework for Defining Organizational Models

Through the century organizational scientists have worked on study spanning across societies, continents, environments and industries studying the nature and meaning to what makes organizations and its systems and people work. Robbins, 1990 and Richard Scott, 1978 have classified substantive amount of this study work and consequent findings that have become seminal work into 4 types.

Type 1 theorists in an closed system loop, with mechanical efficiencies, rational outlook, revolves around the period 1900 to 1930 and conceived of organizations as mechanistic devices to achieve goals and achieving efficiencies of the internal functions was of critical importance. Some of the contributors to this phase being:

Fredrick Winslow Taylor and Scientific Management (1911) replacing the rule of thumb method to determine each element of a worker's job and to enhance productivity, scientific selection and training, cooperation of management and labor and more equal division of responsibilities.

Henri Fayol and Principles of Organization (1916) revolved around fourteen principles and is widely used in today's management theories and practice to varying degree of success, being:

- *Division of Labor*
- *Authority*
- *Discipline*
- *Unity of Command*
- *Unity of Direction*
- *Subordination of Individual Interests to the general Interests*
- *Remuneration*
- *Centralization*
- *Scalar Chain*
- *Order*
- *Equity*
- *Stability of tenure of Personnel*
- *Initiative*
- *Esprit de corps*

Max Weber and Bureaucracy (1920) meant articulating an Ideal Type Organization devolved through a bureaucratic structure characterized by division of labor, a clear authority hierarchy, formal selection procedures, detailed rules and regulations and impersonal relationships.

Ralph Davis and Rational Planning (1928) as Type 1 theorist proposed that structure was the logical outcome to organization's objectives and believed in the primary objective of a business firm being economic service. That economic value can only be meaningfully added if members coordinate and effectively work with one another through linkage to job objectives, results and progresses towards flow of authority and relationships.

Type 2 theorists in a closed system loop and a social perspective, theorists recognize the social nature of organizations, the human relation's school and view organizations as being made up of both tasks and people. Type 2 theorist's human counter points to Type 1 machine view. (Robbins, 1990).

Elton Mayo and the Hawthorne Studies (1927) ushered in an era of human focus that would focus on work groups, employee attitudes, manager employee relationships and the fact that wages by itself was not an adequate factor in increasing productivity than were group pressures, acceptance and concomitant security.

Chester Barnard and Cooperative Systems (1938) merged the learning from Phase 1 into cooperative systems composed of tasks and people that have to be maintained at equilibrium. Managers need to organize around the requirements of the tasks and needs of human resources.

Douglas McGregor and Theory X and Theory Y (1960) had two distinctive views of human beings – Positive and Negative and his Theory Y influenced Participative decision making, the creation of responsible, challenging jobs with authority and power, developing people relationships, enabling learning. While it also brought a forced option scenario that had to be eventually rejected as either or perspective did not fit in with organizational reality.

Warren Bennis and the Death of Bureaucracy (1966) meant anti perspectives that stated centralized decision making, impersonal submission to authority, and narrow division of labor was being replaced by decentralized and democratic structures organized around flexible groups. Influence based on authority was replaced by expertise including flexible adhocracies. Henry Mintzberg later took this up in his exposition on nature of managerial roles and organizational structures.

Type 3 theorists looked neither at mechanistic forces nor the humanistic actions that determined organizations but evolved a synthesis that blended both and articulated it as the contingency approach. It was based on a open systems model, rational in approach and driven by a perspective on environment and technology.

Herbert Simon and Principles Backlash (1947) disagreed with type 1 theorists as well as those of the type 2 propagators but could get around to making his point only in the 1960's. For Simon this meant redefining organizations as complex pattern of communication and relationships in a group of human beings. This pattern provides to each member of the group much of the information and many assumptions, goals and attitudes that enter into decision-making including stable and comprehensible expectations.

Katz and Kahn Environmental Perspective (1966) focused on the open systems and related environments to structure need to adapt to changing environments.

Joan Woodward, Charles Perrow, James Thompson and Technology (1960) provided a framework to connect technological relevance to structures, technology in the context of information processed, automation on jobs, role overlap and other boundary spanning activities essentially covered in structures.

The Aston Group and Organization Size (1986) theory speaks of both large and small organizations having to follow established patterns to enable growth and that both flow through similar issues and consequences.

Type 4 theorists essentially in open systems in a social environment, focus on the political nature of the organizations and connect power and politics to organizational functioning.

March and Simon's Cognitive Limits to Rationality (1958) challenged the classical notion of rational or optimum decisions and that decisions are made out of alternatives, those that were good enough in a given situation. The theorists called for a modified model in understanding organizations very different from the rational cooperative systems perspective.

Pfeiffer's Organizations as Political Arena (1978) encompasses power coalitions, inherent conflict over goals and organization design decisions that favor self-interest of those in power. Control in organizations becomes an end in itself rather than a viable and practical set of means towards a more rational goals and result orientation. Knowledge of behavioral decision making has led to substantive study on the modern day organization of the 21st century.

In effect, **Nystrom ET all (1976)** spelled out how blends of interacting processes can keep organizations in dynamic equilibrium. **Wildavsky (1972)** proposed that self-evaluating organizations might employ dual management groups in order to secure dialectics, competing worldviews and action alternatives. All designers hope to effect organizations into becoming more challenging, productive and rational entities that are governed by pre-determined goals, standards and membership norms.

A hope to improve organizations – to make organizations more effective, people oriented, humane, warm, rational, more fun, more involved with their environments and social structures. More profitable, generating wealth to its shareholders and all that it makes to run some world class organizations. Since they form the basic edifice of the commercial enterprise of the world at large even a small and meaningful improvement is a desirable outcome. And the evidence seems overwhelmingly in favor of this desire to change and move on. Today's organizational processes produce dysfunctional consequences March and Simon, 1958, although it is not as easy to measure them accurately. Stakeholders also complain of organizations. Organizations often emulate processes that are fashionable in other types of organizations in name of best practices without realizing the complete value and applicability /relevance and consequently suffer from absence of desired or promised results (Anderson 1978). In effect our summarization of including organization study and winning organizations as an important element of this study stems from the following:

- *Organizations can be greatly improved arises from the investigation of Nystrom and Starbuck in their study of crisis organizations. (Starbuck and Nystrom 1982)*
- *Hedberg (1976) and Nystrom (1976) started thinking of crisis ridden organizations as less abnormal and that organizations in stagnating environments are deviant and are protecting themselves from environments solely by forces outside themselves, in our context being culture and leadership.*
- *Those organizations excel in environments that are as competitive as can be in varying situations (Peters and Waterman (1982).*
- *Competitive success of the new competition has thus led to an increased interest in networks. Internal organizations are restructuring their relationships with stakeholders. (Nitin Nohria, Et all 1992)*

- *And that there are organizations that defy gravity and convert long term mediocrity or worse into long term superiority. And that there are universal characteristics that cause an organization to go from good to great. (Collins 2001)*
- *And that some organizations are indeed coordinated by output measures. (Mintzberg 1983)*
- *That organizational competitive advantage is driven by focus on its core competence and need to imagine the future (Hamel and Prahlad 1994)*
- *That key learning process in organizations is available, possible and can be implemented. (Senge 1990)*
- *That there are differences in the ways rules emerge and are applied in work organizations are explored brilliantly in a sociological classic. (Gouldner 1964)*
- *And that the work place is ever changing. (Charles Handy 1994)*
- *That successful organizations have been built and built to last (Collins and Porras 1994)*
- *Organizations do operate in a political system (Pfeffer 1981)*
- *Organizations provide for itself scope to develop and change (French and Bell 1982)*
- *That there are factors in the organizations that continue to deserve study (Pettinger 1996)*

And in improving organizations resolving, reckoning and understanding conflict is an essential element.

D. Organization and Management as Conflict Prone Entities

Just as we had studied the relevance of power, authority and responsibility in the section on leadership, the author has brought in the dimension of conflict as an inevitable reality of organization and management models. The relevance to cultures and their impact on leadership styles is perhaps be quite warranted. Interpersonal relations in organizations are bound to create occasional conflicts or disagreement between people on substantive or emotional issues. Schermerhorn (1996) observes that managers spend a lot of time dealing with the following forms of conflicts within organizations:

- **Substantive conflicts** – *involve disagreement over such things as goals, the allocation of resources, distribution of rewards, policies and procedures and job assignments.*
- **Emotional conflicts** – *result from feelings of anger, distrust, dislike, fear, and resentment as well as from personality clashes.*
- **Functional conflicts** – *or constructive conflicts stimulate people towards greater work effort, cooperation and creativity.*
- **Dysfunctional conflicts** – *at very low or very high intensities, dysfunctional conflicts or destructive conflicts occur.*
- **Excessive conflicts** *can be distracting and interfere with other more task-relevant activities. Too little conflict may allow for complacency and the loss of creative high-performance edge. In general, there are six situations where conflicts may arise. These six situations or causes are:*
- **Role ambiguities** – *where unclear job expectations and other task uncertainties increase the probability that some people will be working at cross-purpose, at least some of the time.*
- **Resource scarcities** – *where having to share resources with others and/or compete directly for resource allocation makes a situation conflict prone, especially when resources are limited.*
- **Task interdependencies** – *conflicts often occur when individuals or groups must depend on what others do in order to perform well themselves.*
- **Competing objectives** – *when goals, objectives are established at a level of mediocrity and poorly set or reward systems have been inadequately thought through and are poorly designed*

individuals, dyads, triads, teams and groups may come into conflict by working to one another's disadvantage.

- **Structural differentiation** – *where differences in organization structures and in the characteristics of the people staffing them may foster conflicts because of incompatible approaches towards work.*
- **Unresolved prior conflicts** – *unless a conflict is fully resolved, it may remain latent in the situation as a lingering basis for future conflicts to fester over the same or related matters.*

In so far as **conflict management style** in regard to a leader is concerned, people respond to conflicts with different emphasis on co-operatives and assertiveness. Cooperatives are the desire to satisfy another party's needs and concern; assertiveness is the desire to satisfy one's own needs and concern. Conflict management style may involve the following behavior and their attendant characteristics:

- **Avoidance** – *being uncooperative and unassertive; downplaying disagreement, withdrawing from the situation, and/or staying neutral at all costs.*
- **Accommodation** – *being co-operative but unassertive; letting others' wishes rule; smoothing or overlooking differences to maintain harmony.*
- **Competition** – *being uncooperative, demonstrating lack of collaboration but assertive; working against the wishes of the other party, enabling lack of engagement, engaging in win-lose competition, and/or forcing through the exercise of authority.*
- **Compromise** – *being moderately co-operative and assertive; bargaining for "acceptable" solutions in which each party wins a bit and loses a bit.*
- **Collaboration** – *being both co-operative and assertive; trying to satisfy everyone's concerns fully by working through differences; finding and solving problems so that everyone gains.*
- **Reconciliation** *or revolutionary problem solving which tries to reconcile underlying differences, is often the most effective conflict management style.*

Win - Win - For the leader and for the organization, it is a form of win-win conflict where issues are resolved to the mutual benefit of all parties. But this is more easily said than done in organizational context. However, this is typically achieved by confrontation of the issues and the willingness of those involved recognizing that something is wrong and needs attention. Eliminating the underlying causes of the conflict causes win-win conditions. All relevant issues are raised and discussed openly. Win-win methods are clearly the most preferred of the interpersonal styles of conflict management (Moorhead and Griffin, 1995; Robbins et al., 1994).

Consistency Conflicts - R S S Mani in allexperts.com states, for example "Organizations usually have some degree of flexibility about how they reduce personnel expenses. Decisions to inflict pain upon employees as part of the process may very well reflect an effort to "bust" the existing culture. Moorhead & Griffin (1995), in OB write, "People often assume that reality is objective, that we all perceive the same things in the same way. To test this idea, we could ask students at the Universities of Oklahoma and Nebraska to describe the most recent football game between their schools. We probably would hear two quite conflicting stories. These differences would arise primarily because of perception. The fans "saw" the same things but interpreted them in sharply contrasting ways. Factors underlying these differences are perhaps best explained by the perceptual framework. An object-another person, an event, an activity-is the focal point for perception. A stimulus makes the individual aware of the object. Next, the object is recognized for what it is. The meaning of the object then must be interpreted. Finally, interpretation triggers a response. Responses may include overt behavior, changes in attitudes, or both. Continue, Moorhead and Griffin (1995) - http://bit.ly/1FHqeJH,

"Cognitive dissonance affects people in a variety of ways. We frequently encounter situations in which our attitudes conflict with our behaviors or with one another. Dissonance reduction is the way we deal with these feelings of discomfort and tension. In organizational settings, people contemplating leaving the organization may wonder why they continue to stay and work hard. As a result of this dissonance, they may conclude that the company is not so bad after all; that they have no immediate options elsewhere or that they will leave "soon." Decisions to minimize pain may reflect an effort to reinforce the existing culture. Conflict prone practices whether they tend to reinforce (or leave alone) existing culture or to intentionally destabilize the culture as a stable area. For these purposes, methods which are less disruptive and/or give members more of a sense of control are labeled as reinforcing and those practices which are particularly likely to induce pain among members of the work force (particularly those who are asked to leave) are labeled as destabilizing".

Process Conflicts - The primary thrust of organizational level analysis, on conflict managed situations for leaders deals with rationalization, optimization, is to emphasize the need to plan, analyze and implement cultural impact on organizational models carefully and within the framework of organizational purpose (e.g., Cascio, 1993; Greengard, 1993). Another important individual difference is a person's attitude, their past experience in a past restructuring experience. The dispositional view of attitude formation includes affect, cognition, and intention. The situational view considers a person's social context. Cognitive dissonance occurs when one's attitudes conflict with one's behaviors or with one another. Dissonance reduction is used to resolve the inner conflict that results. Attitude change generally is undertaken via organizational change and development activities. (Moorhead and Griffin 2010 - http://bit.ly/1FHqeJH) Cultural Impact on Organizations is framed within the context of improving and streamlining work processes, as exemplified by total quality management and reengineering (e.g., Cameron, 1991). Key assumptions include a mechanistic notion of organizations, in which the parts are examined to improve fit with the whole. Organizational survival is seen as paramount (e.g., the first order of business is for organizations to thrive and be competitive). Key mental shifts involve development of a "customer first" attitude (stated as part of a total quality management approach) and a realignment of importance among stakeholders, with shareholders coming first (largely unstated).

Value Conflicts - In one of the key early works on optimized organizations, Tomasko (1987) identifies corporate cultures based on mistrust (inability to align with a common set of values and beliefs) as a leading cause of confrontation. Some corporate cultures, he contends, rewards winners, not losers; places control at the top of the agenda; and causes people to believe that it is better to hide mistakes than admit them. In consequence, staff groups (such as planning departments) are formed to serve as watchdogs. Managers respond by attempting to gain control over ever more bloated corporate bureaucracies. Individuals also experience the need for affiliation, that is, the need for human companionship while experiencing conflicts. Tomasko's solution is a flatter, leaner organization in which a team environment prevails and peoples trust each other to contribute to common goals.

Performance Conflicts - Cameron et al (1991) conducted the most extensive single study of rationalized organizations to date in terms of number of organizations involved, breadth of investigation, and time span. The authors conducted a four-year longitudinal study of 30 organizations in the automotive industry. Their viewpoint was that restructuring is a necessary and affirmative approach to becoming more competitive and an appropriate response to the disproportionate growth in the white-collar work force over recent decades. And conflicts are as much a reality in such situations. In effect the leader has to do what is right from a business stand point yet cope with and confront conflicts. The successful companies in their study did not only reduce the work force, but also engaged in organizational redesign and systematic efforts at quality improvement. Successful companies engaged in downsizing as a purposeful and proactive strategy. Interestingly, only a handful of companies in their study were found to have improved organizational performance. Refer - Thomas A. Hickok of University of Southern California – Workforce Reductions. http://bit.ly/2a34EZa

Implosion Conflicts - Two studies of conflict provoking change at major U.S. corporations - Xerox (Kearns and Nadler, 1992) and General Electric (GE) (Tichy and Sherman, 1994) deal explicitly with culture change. Tichy and Sherman refer to a revolution at GE; part of that revolution, under Jack Welch, was to eliminate almost 170,000 positions. One of the basic assumptions at GE: "The ultimate test of leadership is enhancing the long-term value of the organization. A major individual need is the need for power, that is, the desire to control one's environment, including financial, material, information, and human resources. People vary greatly along this dimension. Some spend time and energy seeking power; others avoid power if at all possible. People with a high need for power can be successful managers if three conditions are met. First, they must seek power for the betterment of the organization rather than for their own interests. In addition, they must have a fairly low need for affiliation (fulfilling a personal need for power may well alienate others in the workplace)".

Loss of Self-Control - "Finally, they need plenty of self-control so that they can curb their desire for power when it threatens to interfere with effective organizational or interpersonal relationships. For leaders of a publicly held corporation, this means long-term shareholder value". GE turned against the notion of lifetime employment in favor of a stated goal of providing employees with the best training and development opportunities, but only conditional employment. Xerox also resorted to massive layoffs. Like GE, this rationalization was framed within the larger picture of adopting a total quality management culture. Kearns believed that the number one key to success was shifting focus outward to the customer. Kearns, Nadler, Tichy and Sherman lucidly address the process of conflict prone culture change management. They explicitly state what many will not: that part of the intentional aspect of restructuring in the midst of culture change is the infliction of pain on at least some to get the attention of all".

Pacing Conflicts - Thomas A. Hickok writes, "Tichy and Sherman talk of avoiding the "boiled frog phenomenon" in which frogs boil to death while the water slowly changes from cold to boiling. Kearns and Nadler conclude: "You also have to create dissatisfaction with the status quo. Otherwise, why are people going to work hard to disrupt it? And you cannot wait around until everyone feels induced pain from the marketplace, because then it's too late. So you need to have induced pain. You need to throw a few punches here and there". Moorhead and Griffin (2010) http://bit.ly/1FHqeJH suggest that, "Basically, it suggests that through a variety of processes, commitment, rationalization (self-interpretation of behavior), and information saliency (importance) are defined. These processes include the following:

- *Choice: The freedom to choose different behaviors*
- *Revocability: The ability to change behaviors*
- *Publicness: The degree of visibility to others*
- *Explicitness: The ability to be clear and obvious.*
- *Social norms and expectations: The knowledge of what others expect from someone*
- *External priming: The receiving of cues from others*

Social Conflicts - Attributional and enactment processes then combine with social reality construction processes to influence perceptions, attitudes, and behaviors. Inter- national Perspective discusses some ways in which cultural factors may also come to influence how people in different countries perceive their jobs. To date, the social information processing model has gotten mixed

252

support from empirical research. Laboratory experiments and field studies often have found that social information influences task perceptions and attitudes, but they also have shown the importance of job characteristics. The findings suggest that task perceptions may be a joint function of objective task properties and social information. For example, positive social information and a well-de- signed task may produce more favorable responses than either information or task properties alone would produce. Conversely, negative information and a poorly designed task may produce more negative reactions than either social information or job properties would by themselves. In situations where social information and task conditions do not reinforce each other, they may cancel each other out, as when negative social information may diminish the positive effects of a well-designed task. Similarly, positive information may at least partly offset the negative consequences of a poorly designed task. At present, there is considerable debate as to which of the three views-the job characteristics model, the social information processing model, or a model combining both-is correct".

Pain Inducing Conflicts - There are some organizational level analyses that dissent from the litany of praise for rationalization and consequent conflict management consequences. Handy (1990) argues that an organization does not exist only for profits; that is, profits should be viewed as a means to other desired ends rather than as the sole end. His view is that shareholders have taken over too much of the power. They should, instead, be only one element of a hexagonal ring of stakeholders - which also includes employees, the environment, community, and suppliers. Petruno (1996) reflects the concern that Institutional Corporate shareholder activists have gotten too greedy and imposed too large a price on the thousands upon thousands of employees who have lost their jobs; performance increases may be at the expense of hollowed out companies. Hamel and Prahlad (1994) do not question the legitimacy of cultural Impact through CEO perspectives on rationalizing, but argue that time spent on determining core competencies and relating those competencies to the external marketplace is time much better spent than restructuring and reengineering. The latter may shore up your current position, but does little to prepare you to compete in the future.

Security Conflicts - "In a Newsweek cover story, Sloan (1996: 44) argues that "Firing people has gotten to be trendy in corporate America, in the same way that building new plants and being considered a good corporate citizen gave you bragging rights 25 years ago. Now you fire workers — especially white-collar workers — to make your corporate 'bones'". Downs (1995) offers an even harsher critique. Downs decries the prevalence and public acceptance of a "culture of narcissism", "in which corporations have only one objective, profit. He contrasts the view of Hewlett-Packard's David Packard that the secret to successful management was to keep in balance the triangular interests of shareholders, management, and employees. Part of this narcissism is reflected in the increase of senior executive salaries by 1,000 percent between 1980 and 1995, the same period of time in which record layoffs were amassed".

E. *Alternate Forms of Organizational Models including Patterns of neurotic organizational types*

To enable the author to identify organization and management models that would be of relevance to the study a literature survey was conducted to study the popular organization models articulated by writers. Henry Mintzberg (1989) and Pradip Khandwalla (1992), as being some the very best, were amongst those on whom detailed studies were conducted and are mentioned below. Several other authors and their work has been quoted albeit only at relevant intervals and not on an exhaustive basis.

Basic Types of Organizations (Mintzberg 1989)

Analysis of types of organizations deserves a brief exposition to the work of Mintzberg including a classification of 7 types of organizations and their characteristics.

The *Entrepreneurial Organization* is characterized strategically by often-visionary process, broadly deliberate but emergent and flexible in details. The leader positions malleable organization in protected niches and structures in a simple, informal, flexible with little staff or middle hierarchy and its activities revolve around the CEO who controls personally through direct supervision. The business operates in both simple and dynamic environments, provides scope for strong leadership, sometime charismatic or autocratic, is possible to be in either a start-up, crisis or turn around with a context in small organizations and local producers. But the organization is vulnerable, restrictive and has the danger of imbalance towards strategy or operations.

The *Machine Organization* is characterized strategically ostensibly in planning process but in reality is strategic programming, resistance to strategic change, necessary to over lay innovative configuration for revitalization or else revert to entrepreneurial configuration for turnaround. The context is simple and stable environment, usually in large and mature organizations, rationalized work, rationalizing but not automated technical system, with an external control and a closed system. Is common in mass production, mass service, government and businesses of control and safety. Structurally it is a centralized bureaucracy, formal procedures, specialized work, and sharp division of labor, usually functional groupings, and extensive hierarchy. The key is techno structure, charged with standardizing the work, but clearly separated from middle line with an extensive support staff to reduce uncertainty. It is an efficient reliable, precise and consistent organization but has an obsession with control leading to human problem in operating core, coordination problems in administrative center and adaptation problems at strategic apex.

The *Diversified Organization* is characterized by a strategy driven by headquarters managing corporate strategy as portfolio of business, division in turn manage individual business strategies. The context is market diversity, especially of products and services (as opposed to clients or regions) product related diversification encourages intermediate forms, conglomerate diversification being its purest form. It is typically found in large and mature organizations, especially business corporations but also increasingly government and other public spheres like multi universities. The structure of this organization is market based divisions loosely coupled together under central administrative HQ, with divisions that run businesses autonomously, implying more than limited decentralization to divisional managers, who are in turn subjected to performance control systems that standardize their outputs. There is a tendency to drive structures of divisions towards machine configuration as instruments of HQ though tendency of the organization tends to be a closed system. The organizations resolve some problems of integrated functional machine structures spreading risk, moving capital adding and deleting businesses etc. however conglomerate diversification sometimes is costly and discouraging of innovation, improvements in functioning of capital markets and boards may make independent businesses more effective than divisions. Performance control risks tends to drive the organization towards socially irresponsible or unattached/dispassionate behavior.

The *Professional Organization* is characterized by many strategies, largely fragmented but forces to obtain cohesion with strategies made from professional judgement and collective choice and some administrative fiat. The context is complex yet stable, simple technical system and often but not necessarily the service sector. Here the structure is bureaucratic yet decentralized, dependent on training to standardize skills of its, many operating professionals with its key to functioning is creation of system of pigeon holes within which individual professionals work autonomously subject to controls of the profession. There is minimal techno structure and middle line hierarchy meaning wide span of control over professional work, large support staff, more machine like to support the professionals. There are the advantages of democracy and autonomy but there are also problems of coordination between silos, of misuse of professional discretion, of reluctance to innovate, their public response to problems often machine like and dysfunctional and unionization exacerbates the problems and issues.

The *Innovative Organization* is primarily driven by learning or grass root process, largely emergent, evolving through a variety of bottom up processes, shaped rather than directed by management and often has characteristic cycles of convergence and divergence in strategic focus. The context of these organizations operate in a complex and dynamic environment, including high technology, frequent product change due to severe competition and with temporary and large scale projects. They are typically young due to bureaucratic pressure with aging, common in young industries and works out of two types, being, operating adhocracy for contract project work, administrative adhocracy for own project work, the latter often when operating core truncated or automated. The structures are fluid, organic, selectively decentralized and form adheres to adhocracy. There are functional experts deployed in multidisciplinary teams of staff, operators and managers carry out innovative projects, coordination by mutual movements, adjustments as appropriate, encouraged by liaison personnel, integrating managers and matrix structures. While the organization combines more democracy with less bureaucracy and effective at innovation so very essential for competitive advantage, this effectiveness is achieved at the cost of efficiency with human problems of ambiguity and dangers of inappropriate transition to another configuration. In an engaging presentation on The Eight Essentials of Innovation, McKinsey principal Nathan Marston, Marc de Jong and Erik Rorth from McKinsey's in McKinsey Quarterly explain why innovation is increasingly important to driving corporate growth and brings to life the eight essentials of innovation performance. "The Discovery Group, for example, is upending the medical and life-insurance industries in its native South Africa and also has operations in the United Kingdom, the United States, and China, among other locations. Innovation is a standard measure in the company's semiannual divisional scorecards—a process that helps mobilize the organization and affects roughly 1,000 of the company's business leaders. "They are all required to innovate every year," Discovery founder and CEO Adrian Gore says of the company's business leaders. "They have no choice." "Organizational changes may be necessary, not because structural silver bullets exist—we've looked hard for them and don't think they do—but rather to promote collaboration, learning, and experimentation. (Cost savings can be achieved by transfer of competences, particularly to the target but in both directions. This is the sharing of best practice between the two thought processes or innovation circles. Often it actually means "do it our way please," which may cause loss of productivity and confusion for a period. Likewise, innovation and market capabilities can and should be improved through mutual transfer. However, this is dependent on many of the people who hold the key to those competences remaining in the new organization. As above, the transfer of competences of the target to the innovator is the more difficult to achieve, even though a substantial premium may have been paid for them.) Companies must help people to share ideas and knowledge freely, perhaps by locating teams working on different types of innovation in the same place, reviewing the structure of project teams to make sure they always have new blood, ensuring that lessons learned from success and failure are captured and assimilated, and recognizing innovation efforts even when they fall short of success. Internal collaboration and experimentation can take years to establish, particularly in large, mature companies with strong cultures and ways of working that, in other respects, may have served them well. Some companies set up "innovation garages" where small groups can work on important projects unconstrained by the normal working environment while building new ways of working that can be scaled up and absorbed into the larger organization. NASA, for example, has ten field centers. But the space agency relies on the Ames Research Center, in Silicon Valley, to maintain what its former director, Dr. Pete Worden, calls "the character of rebels" to function as "a laboratory that's part of a much larger organization. Big companies do not easily reinvent themselves as leading innovators". We have used the widely accepted measures of creative complexity, dynamic formalization and flexible centralization as the parameters for comparison and description, although it is quite possible that just as a new paradigm is not comprehensible using the old one, we may actually be witness to the evolution of a new set of parameters for evaluation. In addition to these we have used three new measures which will become relevant in the New Millennium Viz. Networking, Organic Flexibility and Change Propensity. "Too many fixed routines and cultural factors can get in the way. For those that do make the attempt, innovation excellence is often built in a multiyear effort that touches most, if not all, parts of the organization. Our experience and research suggest that any company looking to make this journey will maximize its probability of success by closely studying and appropriately assimilating the leading practices of high-performing innovators. Taken together, these form an essential operating system for innovation within a company's organizational structure and culture".

Ideology (Culture) and Missionary Organization has a rich system of values and beliefs that distinguishes it and is rooted in sense of mission associated with charismatic leadership, developed through traditions and sagas and then reinforced through identifications. This organization can be overlaid on conventional configuration, most commonly entrepreneurial, followed by innovative, professional and then machine organizations. Well sometime so strong that evokes its own configuration. These are clear, focused inspiring a distinctive mission, with coordination through standardization of norms (pulling together) reinforced by selection, socialization and indoctrination of members. They could small units, enclaves, loosely organized and highly decentralized but with powerful normative controls, a reformer, converter and cloister forms with threats of isolation on one side and adaptive assimilation on the other. Reflect back in time and history, The core ideology at 3M admonition, "Thou shall not kill a new product idea." Innovation clearly stands central at this organization where 30 percent of current products were not in existence four years ago and 10 percent were not in existence a year ago. People who cannot buy into this ideological statement have no place at 3M. Leaders at this organization look with a "benevolent blind eye" at the pursuit of projects that are not officially sanctioned, because they do not want to stifle innovation. As already mentioned, Disney's core ideology centers on making people happy. It builds on core values that include replacing cynicism with optimism; nurturing wholesome American values, creativity, dreams and imagination; attending fanatically to consistency and detail; and preserving and controlling the Disney magic. For Goldman Sachs, the core ideology revolves around exceptional client service (a commitment to under-promise and over-deliver), integrity and teamwork. For McDonalds, it is quality, value for money, cleanliness and service. If the core ideology is dear to all employees of an organization, not just to those who write the glowing corporate descriptions that grace public relations documents, the company develops an almost cult-like quality. The general opinion is that companies with that quality – that is with a strong organizational culture – outperform other companies by a huge margin. Strong cultures can be recognized by many different factors that reflect ideological unity, from organizational architecture to language to ceremonies to interpersonal style. As an example, IBM in its glory days had a company song: "We are selling IBM, we are selling IBM. What a glorious feeling..."

The *Political Organization* drives through means of power technically illegitimate, often in self-interest, resulting in conflict that pulls individuals or units apart. It expresses itself in political games, some consistent with, some antagonistic to, some that substitute for legitimate systems of power. It is usually over laid on conventional organization, but some time strong enough to create own configuration through conventional notions of concentrated coordination and influences absent, replaced by the play of informal power. Its dimensions of conflict being moderate, intense, confined and pervasive, as well as enduring and brief. They combine into four forms, confrontation, shaky alliance, politicized organization, and complete political arena. They can trace development of forms through life cycle of impetus, development, resolution of the conflict. Politics and political organization serve a series of functional roles in organizations, especially to help bring about necessary change blocked by legitimate systems of influence.

Mintzberg On Structures – Stephen Robbins in Organizational Theory (1990), "Henry Mintzberg work is the most widely used framework on classifying organizations. He argued that there are five basic parts to any organization. The strategic apex is the organization's top management. The middle line comprises the middle managers with line authority. The operational core comprises workers and first line supervisors. The Technical staff is engineers and other technical professions and trades that serve as advisors to the production processes of the organization. The administrative staff is the staff professionals who advise the line managers on non-technical concerns such as human resources, staffing, public relations, government relations, and the like. As the demands on an organization change based on environmental factors, the organization's design can be specially geared to meet the needs.

- *Operating core – the part of an organization that consists of employees who perform the basic work related to the production of products and services;*
- *Strategic apex – the part of an organization that consists of top-level managers who are charged with the overall responsibility for the organization;*
- *Middle line – the part of an organization that consists of managers that connect the operation core to the strategic apex;*
- *Technostructure – the part of an organization that consists of analysts who have the responsibility for implementing forms of standardization in the organization (they develop programs, procedures, and rules);*
- *Support staff – the part of an organization that consists of people who fill the staff units that provide indirect support services for the organization (e.g. administrative functions). Any one of these five parts can dominate an organization and where each dominates a different organizational form emerges. As a result, there are five distinct design configurations and each one is associated with the domination by one of the five basic parts.*

These are: A *simple structure* which arises when the strategic apex is dominant and control is centralized. A *divisional structure* which arises when middle management is in control and there are groups of essentially autonomous units operating within the organization. A *machine bureaucracy* which arises when the analysts in the techno structure are dominant and control is achieved through standardization. A *professional bureaucracy* which arises when the control lies with the operating core and decisions are centralized. An *adhocracy* which arises when the support staff dominates and the control is achieved via mutual adjustment

The **Simple Structure** is *low in complexity, has little formalization, and has authority centralized in a single person*. The simple structure is best described as a flat organization, typical for small businesses, with an organic operating core and almost everyone reporting to a one-person strategic apex where the decision-making power is centralized. Simple Structure focuses on the line core with a small apex, short vertical middle line, and wide operational core. Typical simple structures have little or no administrative or technical support staff. Simple structures can have wide operational cores or narrow depending on the industry and the degree of technology incorporated into the directing, coordinating and control functions.

Advantages of the simple structure are: There are no layers of inconvenient, unmanageable structure. Decision making is fast and its operations are flexible. The costs of maintaining simple structure are low. Accountability is clear. The goals are quite clear as they are closely associated with those of top management (often a single person).

Disadvantages of the simple structure are: The simple structure concentrates power in one person, thus the problems of the abuse of authority, lack of managerial skills or ability to manage may arise. The concentration of power can become a threat to the organization's effectiveness and survival. It is applicable only to small organizations.

The simple structure is most useful when: The organization is in its formative years. The number of employees is small. The cost of administration needs to be low. Informal communication is sufficient.

Machine Bureaucracy has highly routine operating tasks that are grouped into *functional departments, formalized rules and regulations, centralized authority and decision making* which follows the chain of command. machine bureaucracy is characterized with a dominant technical staff with responsibility for formalizing and structuring the operational core's functions.

Advantages of the machine bureaucracy are: Managerial discretion is substituted with rules and regulations. Thus, similar problems will have similar solutions applied. The structure facilitates the generation and transfer of knowledge within the specialist areas. Standardized operations, coupled with high formalization, allow the parameters of major decisions to be centralized. Standardized tasks are usually performed in a highly efficient manner.

Disadvantages of the machine bureaucracy are: Relative inflexibility and unresponsiveness to the changes in environment. Obsessive concern with following the rules, which often leads frustration of non-members. The organizational practices are quite difficult to change.

The machine bureaucracy is most useful when: The organization is large. A stable environment and technology adopted allow for standardized, routine work (e.g. in mass-production firms). There are special safety needs in the organization (e.g. airlines' employees need to follow certain standardized procedures to ensure safety of customers).

The **Divisional Structure** is a *set of autonomous self-contained units, each typically configured as a machine bureaucracy.* The dominant part of the divisional structure lies with the middle management that reports to, and is overseen by, a head office (usually located close to a central business district). The divisional managers usually have a great deal of control over their individual businesses. They hold major strategic and operating decision-making authority in relation to their businesses. A head office usually provides support services to the divisions (e.g. financial and legal) and evaluates the performance of each division (deciding which division receives capital for investment is based on such evaluation). Organizations are usually divisionalized according to one of the below criteria: Product-based divisionalization; Location-based divisionalization (by geographic area); and Customer-based divisionalization.

Advantages of the divisional structure are: The head office does not need to be involved in day-to-day operations of each division; thus, the top management can focus on the long-term, strategic decision making. There is clear accountability and responsibility for the performance of each division (divisional manager is responsible for meeting goals, usually set up in cooperation with the headquarters). Ineffective performance in one division has little effect on the other divisions. Each division can be 'easily' reorganized or even sold, without affecting the whole organization (other divisions). Also, new businesses may be purchased and then 'easily' become part of the whole organization, without affecting other divisions. It can be said that the divisional structure facilitates the spread of risk (problems in one part of the organization / division are not necessarily a threat to the organization as a whole).

Disadvantages of the divisional structure are: Usually, the cooperation between divisions is not good - there is little incentive with this structural design to encourage exchange of knowledge / information between the divisions. The costs may be relatively high, as, usually, the duplication of activities and resources exists within the organization (e.g. each division has its own accounts department). The above-mentioned duplication often reduces efficiency of the organization. Employees are usually unable to transfer from one division to another, especially if the spatial dispersion is high and the divisions operate in diversified markets.

The divisional structure is most useful when: The products and services the organization offer are quite diverse. The organization operates in numerous markets / countries around the globe. The organization is large and becomes difficult to manage as one unit. The environment is neither very complex nor very dynamic.

The **Professional Bureaucracy** is *a decentralized configuration in which highly trained specialists form the operating core but where the benefits of standardization and decentralization are still achieved.* An example of professional bureaucracy is a university, where the majority of key staff has professional expertise. The power in this design rests with the operating core because they have the critical skills that the organization needs and they have the autonomy – provided through decentralization – to apply their expertise. The only other part of the professional bureaucracy that has a large complement of employees is the support staff, but their activities are focused on serving the operating core. This structure has a large administrative staff usually initiated by a need to fill liaison roles with external constituencies.

The advantages of the professional bureaucracy are: Specialized tasks can be performed with the same relative efficiency as in the machine bureaucracy. High levels of expertise can be brought to solve series of unique problems.

The disadvantages of the professional bureaucracy are: There is the tendency for subunit conflicts to develop. It is not always easy to change / adapt the professional bureaucracy to the environment. This is because the specialists are often constrained by the rules of their profession (e.g. doctors may refuse to take certain action if they believe it to be incompatible with the conduct of their profession). It is difficult to coordinate work of various professionals specializing in very diverse fields. It is difficult to set strategic priorities, as there is no clear strategic apex.

The professional bureaucracy is the most useful when: The environment is complex and stable. The operations of the organization require staff with skills that can be learned only in formal education. The problems organizations are very complex and need expertise of staff in various fields (e.g. in hospitals, people often need to see different doctors to determine their health-problem)

The **Adhocracy** is a *decentralized form* which is characterized by:

- *high horizontal differentiation,*
- *low vertical differentiation,*
- *low formalization,*
- *intensive coordination, and*

- *great flexibility and responsiveness.*

Adhocracies are usually staffed by professionals with a high level of expertise. Vertical differentiation is low because organization needs to be able to adapt to changing circumstances (and the many levels of administration would restrict it). Coordination is quite extensive as it is important for tasks to be carried out in the correct sequence. The formalization is low - there are few rules and regulations (and they are mostly loose and unwritten) and the technostructure is almost non-existent. The adhocracy is far more intensively coordinated than the professional bureaucracy (people are hired whom main task is to coordinate the activities of others). Additionally, the traditional distinctions between supervisor and employee and line and staff in adhocracies are somehow blurred (as all organizational members are specialists in their distinctive field). Power flows to anyone in the adhocracy with expertise, regardless of his or her position. Lastly, the adhocracy, a term borrowed by Mintzberg from Alvin Toffler, that describes the final organizational evolution into what appears to be a simple structure, but whose functional operation is based on rapid response to environmental changes. Among the possible forms, that an adhocracy can take is a Matrix structure, introduced by Texas Instruments. In the Matrix structure, project teams are assembled from functional areas. The result is that each member of a matrix team has two supervisors, the project manager and the functional area manager.

The advantages of the adhocracy are: It is probably the best structure for an organization which needs to be highly adaptable to changing environment, and when the organization needs to be innovative and creative. It is effective when specialists from diverse disciplines are required to collaborate to achieve a common goal (e.g. movie production). No other structure offers flexibility needed when tasks are highly-technical, non-programmed and too complex for any one person to handle.

The disadvantages of the adhocracy are: It is considered one of the most inefficient configurations. Authority and responsibilities are not very clear, thus many conflicts between members take place. There are no clear boss-subordinate relationships. Activities cannot be easily separated into independent tasks.

The adhocracy is most useful when: The company's strategy is diverse, complex, and / or high risk. The technology used is non-routine. The environment is dynamic and complex.

Patterns of neurotic organizational types that have been challenged

Dramatic Organization - Dramatic Organizations are characterized by Impulsiveness. Over ambitious, dominating and power hoarding CEO's leads it. Their Personal styles influence organizational functioning. They have a large temptation to diversify into unrelated markets and products. Eventually the organization is merely an extension of the CEO's personality. This organization is typical of simple, functional structures with lines of authority extending directly to the CEO. Many organizational members are happy doing what the CEO desires, conform to acceptable ways of working. The strategic planning process is dependent on gut and how the CEO feels towards a business at a point in time. The organization is definitely not data or information driven.

Suspicious Organization - Suspicious organizations are wary of their environment. They are always alert and ready to fight in any situation that the business may demand. They like to call themselves as fighting fit to face any situation. The companies are heavily into detail. They create elaborate mechanisms to collect and analyze data, information and facts that make the organization work. At the psychological level they work on low level of trust and delegation. Information as an instrument of power is perceived as a part of the organizational culture.

Compulsive Organization - Effectively compulsive organizations are stagnant bureaucracies. Reliant on narrow, archaic strategy their role envisages primarily managing in a steady state. Dogmatic adherence to traditions and norms, Rigid and formal rules and procedures make their work life an everyday affair. Above all they develop elaborate information system to manage and retain control of all the activities. The decision making style is highly centralized. And they are quite trapped in their glorious past.

Depressive Organization - Depressive organizations are worn-out, purposeless enterprises with no sense of mission or direction that is palpable within the company. They drift and appear to almost run-by themselves. People demonstrate behavior that are listless, apathetic, a passive stance and a gross lack of initiative. Many suffer from "decidiphobia" - fear of deciding or committing to any goals. There is a heavy reliance on outside "messiahs" or consultants for solving their internal everyday problems. Poor internal communication and lack of adaptation to reality with time are some of its additional characteristics.

Detached Organization - Detached organizations are basically "Headless" - leadership at the top. Schizoid Chief Executive who does not have a particular frame of reference in managing the enterprise normally leads it. Their view of the world rarely seeks to offer meaning or purpose to their role and activity. It is rudderless - no unifying or directional effort and the culture is rampant with power struggle, politicking abound and the work life can sometimes be quite miserable for high performers.

Here we have provided a detailed write up of the various organization and **management models studied by Pradip Khandwalla (1992) and his summary view of modes of Management as a symbolic representation to Organizational Models is presented below:**

Conservative mode

Definition: The policies and practices that preserve the organization's basic character and history strengths constitute the conservative mode of management.

Ideology: "A bird in hand is worth two in the bush" philosophy pays in the king run.

Policy framework: Cautious problem solving and decision making; aversion to radical options; tendency to choose compromise solutions; importance of traditions and precedents; primary of stability; growth along familiar lines (sticking to the knitting); aversion to pioneering; tendency to wait, watch, and learn from others' experiences before venturing into new activities.

Appropriateness: Not appropriate in turbulent environments with short reaction times. Appropriate in domains with slow or moderate rates of change.

Degenerate form: Extreme risk aversion or sticking to the familiar and the traditional; negativism.

Practices for institutionalizing a healthy mode: Environmental monitoring; use of professional for identifying needed changes and innovations; constructive conservatism ("change with the times"); a policy of growth compatible with the organization's core values.

Entrepreneurial mode

Definition: Policies and practices aiming at rapid growth of the organization's activities through bold, risky ventures constitute the entrepreneurial mode.

Ideology: No risk no gain.

Policy framework: Pioneering; pursuit of grandeur; charismatic individual at the top; opportunistic growth; taking of calculated risks.

Appropriateness: Domains undergoing rapid growth or turbulence.

Degenerate form: Recklessness; Poor implementation of ambitious projects, neglect of management systems; no capable second line of management, neglect of current activities by top management

Practices for institutionalizing a healthy mode: Communication to stakeholders of the vision of growth; extensive decentralization of routine matters. Dynamic managers at the helm, competent professionals at senior and middle levels; global scanning for fresh growth opportunities. Pioneering into new fields and withdrawing from overcrowded fields; development of a network of contacts; search for partnerships/joint ventures; intrapreneurship.

Professional mode

Definition: The use of professionally qualified experts, a scientific and comprehensive approach, and the use of norms, tools and techniques of management science in decision making constitute the professional mode of management.

Ideology: Management is, or can be turned into, a science for optimal results.

Policy framework: Systematic search for growth opportunities formal forecasts; systematic cost-benefit analysis for all decisions; comprehensive strategies for growth, meeting competition, etc.; long range planning; sophisticated performance monitoring; use of sophisticated tools of decision making use of expertise in decision making.

Appropriateness: Complex domains and moderate uncertainty.

Degenerate form: Over staffing of specialist and experts; inter-departmental, line-staff conflicts due to tunnel vision of specialists; unrealistic advice by staff to top managers; excessive emphasis on qualifications at the cost of native managerial ability; analysis paralysis.

Practices for institutionalizing a healthy mode: Participatory decision-making; job rotation of specialists; sensitivity analysis; comprehensive review of past decisions.

Bureaucratic mode

Definition: Decision making strongly influenced by the values of propriety, standardization, specialization and clear accountability in decision making constitutes the bureaucratic mode of management.

Ideology: Efficiency, propriety, and equity results from properly programming and standardizing activities and fixing clear responsibilities.

Policy framework: Considerable division of labor, specialization, standardization, written specification of tasks of managers, their powers, and responsibilities, and the procedures they are to follow. All significant exceptions, or matters not spelt out, have to be referred to higher authorities. Centralization of policy making, tight control. Emphasis on propriety

Appropriateness: Relatively stable domain; public interest or publicly funded activities. Inappropriate for tasks requiring frequent changes and adaptations.

Degenerate form: High mistrust leads to layer upon layer of control that saps initiative and breeds alienation. Displacement of goals and emergence of excessively procedural orientation. The emergence of a rigid, unresponsive system, Deep inter-departmental conflicts gross delays in decision making.

Practices for institutionalizing a healthy mode: Delegation of routine matters; lateral, committee based coordination; motivation through job enrichment, Participative decision making, job rotation; committee decision making for risky decision; periodic review of rules and procedures for current relevance; highlighting of the purpose and mission of the organization; periodic feedback from clients, and its dissemination to rank-and-file; task forces for innovations and changes; periodic infusion of fresh blood at senior and top levels; papers and files should go directly to the level which takes the decision.

Organic mode

Definition: The policies and practices that enable the organization to respond quickly and flexibly to changing organizational tasks in uncertain situations in the organic mode of management.

Ideology: Organizational flexibility is indispensable for getting results in a situation of flux.

Policy framework: Open channels and free flow of communications and information throughout the organization; creation of widespread awareness of organizational purpose, goals, performance, problems, etc. in the rank-and-file. Freedom to managers to choose an operating style that they find suitable and that gets their jobs done; importance of the expert in a given situation for making decisions. Greater emphasis on getting tasks accomplished than on following prescribed procedures; loose, informal, peer groups' control rather than tight budgetary, formal control. Organization's willingness to adapt freely to changing circumstances regardless of rules, regulations. Precedents, or past practices; control and coordination by interaction, sharing of information, and mutual performance feedback.

Appropriateness: Turbulent environments; young organizations; during implementation of new, unfamiliar projects; organizations producing goods or services to specifications of clients; while executing major changes or innovations; in pioneering and innovative organizations.

Degenerate form: Allergy to any kind of standardization or control; willful breaking of all rules; total confusion about roles and functions; aversion to filing or storing information.

Practices for institutionalizing a healthy mode: Use of peer group pressure and emphasis on evolving shared norms; emphasis on making the organizational purpose, goals etc. known to everyone; use of budgets and other formal means of control only as a second line of defense. Encouragement of not just vertical but also lateral communication, and widespread dissemination of important operating information. The inculcation of the view that management principles, policies, precedents, strategies are means to an end, not ends in themselves, are right only in certain circumstances – they can be dumped or changed if the circumstances change.

Authoritarian mode

Definition: Those policies and practices that facilitate the intensive use of hierarchical power for making decisions and seeking compliance of the rank-and-file to these decisions constitute the authoritarian mode of management.

Ideology: Ultimately, power used wisely is the fastest way of resolving conflicts and getting decisions implemented.

Policy framework: High level of centralization of decision-making authority; severe punishment for disobedience; emphasis on disciplined pursuit of a cause or a goal; ensuring legitimacy for those with power.

Appropriateness: Decision making during crises; situations of chaos or gross indiscipline, as during organizational sickness.

Degenerate form: Rule through brutality and terror; arbitrary, whimsical use of power.

Practices for institutionalizing a healthy mode: The institution of grievance procedures and tights of appeal; strong emphasis on disciplined functioning by the subordinates as well as the sense of responsibility of the bosses; a paternal relationship between the bosses and the subordinates; the indoctrination of the staff in a mission or vision of excellence; emphasis on upholding fine traditions.

Participatory mode

Definition: Those policies and practices that facilitate the reaching of consensus decisions by groups consisting of superiors, colleagues and subordinates.

Ideology: Participation improves group performance by improving the quality of decisions, and by increasing the commitment to decisions collectively reached.

Policy framework: Consensus oriented team decision making at various levels of management including top management, power equalization, or at least reduction in power asymmetry as between superiors and their subordinates. Insistence that at meetings, deviants are not only permitted to speak up but encouraged to speak up and heard with interest and respect; emphasis on creating a climate of trust and collaboration.

Appropriateness: In complex environments in which decisions have multiple angles; in situations where collective motivation and commitment are important for implementing decisions; in organizations of equals. Such as cooperative societies, organizations of professionals, etc.

Degenerate form: Decisions delayed through too many committees; excessive politicization within a democratic framework.

Practices for institutionalizing a healthy mode: Use of experts and professionals during group problem solving and decision making; training to leaders for evolving consensus after free and frank discussion; at least a rudimentary democratic structure, such as a works council.

Intuitive mode

Definition: A mode that stresses common sense, experience, intuitive judgement and shrewdness over formal analysis and resort to experts in making decisions is the intuitive mode of management.

Ideology: Good intuitive judgements lead to far better and faster decisions than those based on formal analysis by experts.

Policy framework: Emphasis on hiring or promoting managers who are quick learners and have relevant work experience; emphasis on apprenticeship and learning through hard knocks rather than formal managerial training; emphasis on evolving sound thumb rules for making decisions; use of wise rather that expert counselors.

Appropriateness: In domains which are quick changing but not necessarily very complex, such as in intensely competitive but unsophisticated industries or political arenas or young but unsophisticated industries or industries during their decline stages.

Degenerate form: Excessively bounded rationality of decision-makers that predisposes them to make errors; pathological aversion to any expert or expertise; excessively whimsical or ad hoc decisions, based on shallow diagnoses.

Practices for institutionalizing a healthy mode: Extensive contacting before making decisions; use of experts etc. as a second line of defence; testing managers for judgement and learning ability; management by moving around.

Familial mode

Definition: A mode that emphasizes control by closely related persons at the top and family type relations at work are the familial mode of management.

Ideology: Organizational cohesion is best achieved by treating the staff like family members and it is this cohesion that takes the organization through good as well as bad times and yields excellence in the long run.

Policy framework: All sensitive managerial posts are manned by persons trusted by the bosses, such as relatives, friends, members of their community; recruiting persons for managerial duties when young and carefully grooming the promising and trustworthy ones for managerial positions. A nurturing attitude towards employees, and standing by them in their hour of need; employee-oriented supervision; rewards or loyalty.

Appropriateness: More useful in collectivist than in individualistic cultures; usable where relatively homogeneous people can operate an organization; a large competence differential between superiors and subordinates; smaller organizations.

Degenerate form: Excessive nepotism that drives or keeps away bright individuals; feuds in the ruling family or group, sycophancy, siphoning or misuse of organizational resources for personal gain by members of the ruling group.

Practices for institutionalizing a healthy mode: Manning of important positions in the organization by relatives or other persons trusted by the bosses who are also professionals. Careful grooming of young recruits for later managerial responsibilities; parental treatment of employees; inculcating of family feeling in staff through cultural functions, etc.; stress on traditional social virtues.

Altruistic mode

Definition: Policies and practices that enshrine noble values, trusteeship for the benefit of stakeholders, and some sort of social contribution constitute the altruistic mode of management.

Ideology: A management that evokes the best instincts of its staff members can conquer all hurdles and be a beacon to others.

Policy framework: Commitment to values and ideals; primacy of pure means; concern for all the stakeholders; commitment to a mission; humane management.

Appropriateness: More in not-for-profit than in commercial organizations; also in organizations of professionals; in missionary organizations more in monopolistic than in highly competitive sectors.

Degenerate form: Business as charity rather than business as a source of charity; altruism as an image building gimmick; public posturing at the expense of pressing internal issues.

Practices for institutionalizing a healthy mode: Management by committed professionals rather than by amateur do-gooders. Prioritization of areas of, and extent of, altruism; cross-subsidization of altruistic activities by 'cash cows'. External communication of the values the organization stands for an example setting practice of these values; refraining from paying exploitatively low remuneration to staff.

Politics - Consequently, Organization politics has been dealt with, again connecting with power, authority, responsibility, and conflicts, all with a relevance to the leadership style implication in a cultural and organizational context. **Political Behavior -** A concept, which is closely related to power and authority in organizational settings, is politics or political behavior. Politics are often viewed as synonymous with dirty tricks or back stabbing and as something distasteful, should best be left to others. However, political behavior in organizations, like power, is pervasive. Pfeffer (1992) defines organization politics as activities people perform to acquire, enhance and use power and other resources to obtain their preferred outcomes in a situation where uncertainty or disagreement exists. Political behavior is therefore the general means by which people attempt to obtain and use power. In essence, the goal of such behavior is to get one's own way about things. In reality, organizations are made up of individuals and groups with different values, goals and interests. This make-up sets the scene for potential conflicts over resources. Perhaps the most important factor leading to politics within organizations is the realization that most of the "facts" that are used to allocate limited resources are open to interpretation. It is in this large and ambiguous middle ground of organizational life – where the facts do not speak for themselves – which politics flourish. As most decisions have to be made in a climate of ambiguity, where facts are rarely fully objective and thus are open to interpretation, people within organizations will use whatever influence they can to taint the facts to support their goals and interest, thus creating the activities called "politicking" (Pfeffer, 1981). "The forbearing use of power does not only form a touchstone; but the manner in which an individual enjoys certain advantages over others is a test of a true gentleman. The power which the strong have over the weak, the magistrate over the employed, the educated over the unlettered, the experienced over the confiding, even the clever over the silly; the forbearing and inoffensive use of all this power and authority, or the total abstinence from it, when the case admits it, will show the gentleman in a plain light. The gentleman does not needlessly and unnecessarily remind an offender of a wrong he may have committed against him. He can only forgive; he can forget; and he strives for that nobleness of self and mildness of character which imparts sufficient strength to let the past be put the past." Refer - General Robert E. Lee

F. The CCCC (C4) framework for Organization Modeling

C4 Framework is the model for org modeling. (***Courage Compassion, Capability Competence Configuration Construction, Culture and Change***). The framework provides both the client and the consultant a conceptual model of defining organizations in the context of structure, competence, and culture. Organizations are created to achieve a set of objectives. Based on environmental imperatives and internal capabilities, these objectives are modified over time. In the process of achieving their objectives, organizations orient their structures, business processes and "a way of doing things" that lends a unique organizational personality. We view this orientation on three dimensions and based on the three dimensions, we have defined various organizational models.

While the model does not straightjacket our appreciation of business processes and the internalized strategy, it does provide a definitive frame of reference and a platform for an appropriate organizational intervention.

C4 Model - Essentially the model provides for enabling appropriate linkages between culture, configuration and competence. It purports to define culture with vision, values, rules of behavior, leadership and frames of reference. And evaluates configuration in the context of work design, managing knowledge, creating decision processes, builds authority processes, communication and performance management. In the competence area the model covers knowledge, competency and behavior. The organization and management model as seen in CCCC (C4) attempts the following:

1. *Measures business configuration effectiveness in a three dimensional manner with competence and culture in the two axis.*
2. *Defines culture in the context of thick and thin cultures or strong and weak cultures*
3. *Ensures organizational evaluation is in the context of competency, behavior displayed and knowledge and intellect as demonstrated by members in an organizational setting.*

Dimension 1: Configuration & Construction

Organizational Configuration Covers Work Design and Organization Structure, Organizational Knowledge Management Process, the Decision-Making Process, Authority Process, Performance Management Process & Systems and Organizational Communication Systems. In our assessment, while the practice or type of each of these processes would differ, it may also be observed that the extent of Configuration in organizations would differ. Based on the intensity of occurrence of each of these processes, the system facilitates mapping an organization on a continuum of Tight to Loose Configuration. Tight configuration implies limited mobility, flexibility to facilitate pace of change. In contrast loose configuration provides for greater versatility to the configuration, ability to make and impact changes yet sometime could be loose enough to lack control.

Dimension 2: Competencies & Capabilities

When it speaks of competencies, it covers Knowledge, Skills and Behavior in the organizational roles. While every organization would seek its employees and associates of the highest level of competencies, the business process or the configuration may steer the level of competency requirements. The systemic analysis process maps the organization on a spectrum of highest level of Competency Focus to a level of Competency Defocus.

Focused competency at both individual and organization level provides competitive advantage and de focused competency makes organizational goals and members flirt from one situation to another without concrete closure of issues or decisions. Competency sharpness and focus is essential for organizational competitiveness.

Dimension 3: Context Change & Culture

Culture in an organization is defined by observation. The visible attributes that form the culture are Vision, Values, Symbols, Rituals, Frames of Reference, and Rules of Behavior. While all these attributes may not be formally defined, organization cultures may have a strong character based on various practices while some cultures would yet be in an evolutionary state. Thick cultures are largely visible, reasonably clear to understand and appreciate its presence and would be understood and practiced by members. Thin cultures are relatively weak, at its formative stage and may need greater clarity and communication to enable members and processes to understand or follow. Thick culture is essential; it is real and it matters: Societies, or at least significant subgroups of societies, are distinguished by a fundamental consensus on basic values and beliefs, shared symbols and meanings, and basic social practices and institutions (e.g., family, marriage, authority patterns). Thick culture is fundamental if not primordial: Cultural meanings are historically rooted and deeply embedded in a society's institutions and practices (Geertz 1963). Culture is transmitted from one generation to the next through socialization processes in which the role of family and kinship groups are primary (Elkin 1960; Dawson et al. 1969). Refer - On Culture, Thick and Thin: Chapter13 - Toward a Neo-Cultural Synthesis by William Mishler and Detlef Pollack.

Dimension 4: Courage & Character

In cultures that encourage individual initiative and downplay control, courage continues to be a critical differentiator. Enterprises that deal with human behaviors that focuses on courage and character tend to seek overt actions that symbolizes bold and honest interactions. These organizations tend to ask for steady cultures where identifiable sets of members and member behaviors are asked, understood and appreciated. Intellectual Company models continue to be difficult to identify and map. Leading practices indicate that next of talent managed companies, build a focus on the people issues into the heart of their business and solutions for their customers. Getting change management in the context of courage right increases value for staff, manages risk for customers, and improves the quality of the experience for our people. "The encouraging thing is that every time you meet a situation, though you may think at the time it is an impossibility and you go through the tortures of the damned, once you have met it and lived through it you find that forever after you are freer than you ever were before. Just as the traditional, thick conception of culture is an ideal type that may not be fully manifest in any specific `real world' referent, the concept of thin culture is also an abstraction. Indeed, thick and thin culture should be understood not as separate and discrete concepts but as the idealized end-points of a single conceptual continuum." Refer - William Mishler and Detlef Pollack - Thin culture does not exist independently of thick culture. Rather, thin culture is defined in contradistinction to thick culture. It is an idea that has been cultivated over time by social scientists who on theoretical or empirical grounds, reject one or more of the basic assumptions of the classical conception. Thin culture can be thought of as a product of a series of `saving moves' (Lakatos 1970) by political scientist's eager to retain as much of the culture concept as they can while diluting or discarding various aspects of thick culture which are perceived to be incompatible with theory or inconsistent with observation". http://bit.ly/2aWEAn6

If you can live through that you can live through anything. You gain strength, courage, and confidence by every experience in which you stop to look fear in the face. You are able to say to yourself, `I lived through this horror. I can take the next thing that comes along.' The danger lies in refusing to face the fear, in not daring to come to grips with it. If you fail anywhere along the line, it will take away your confidence. You must make yourself succeed every time. You must do the thing you think you cannot do." Eleanor Roosevelt - You Learn By Living (1960)

Such courageous leaders focus on building a complete new lines of business that has so far been alien to a companies. Their mandate is to think out of BOX, launch initiatives never before seen in the technology world, not conventional innovation, but disruptive re imagination, the courage to break and reassemble, any number of times, any number of things, until he gets his new initiatives right and not be bogged down by internal politics or alien cultures and its successes but by asking tough questions on what a customer would seek 10 or 20 years from now. And build it. For us, such a leader is a Scientist in a Business Manager role. Best of institutions are not blinded by their successes but humbled by what should they be doing more to help their customers remain competitive, profitable and sustainable. Mickey Mantle writes, "Bravery is a complicated thing to describe. You can't say it's three feet long and two feet wide and that it weighs four hundred pounds or that it's colored bright blue or that it sounds like a piano or that it smells like roses. It's a quality, not a thing." - The Quality of Courage

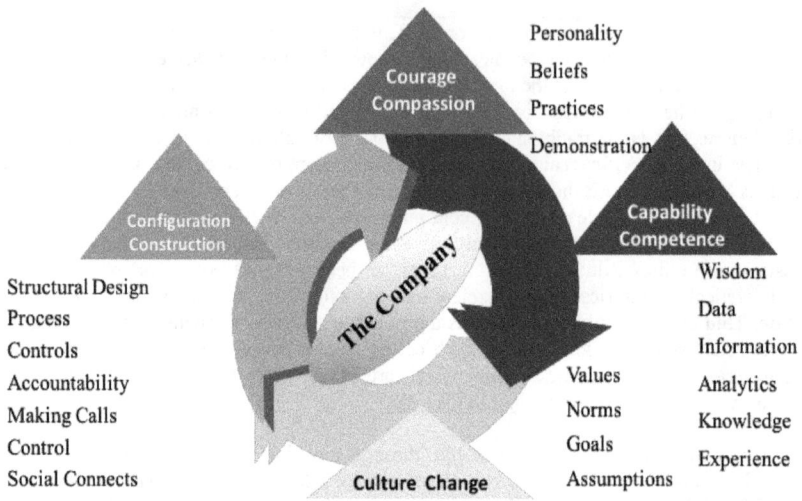

Figure 26 - 4C Model Courage Compassion, Capability Competence Configuration Construction, Culture and Change

Diagnosis & Interventions

While there is no single "Best Organization Model", based on the objective to be achieved, there is one "Best 4C Model" that an organization should strive to be. 4C diagnosis methodology helps map the current position of the organization and examine the appropriateness of the organizations' status on the three dimensions.

The model envisages usage of information, data and knowledge characteristics of the corporation in reaching a well-debated classification of the current and desired organizational fit.

Effectively to enable connecting Organizations meaningfully and to help construct Scenario based case analysis on Culture and leadership disrupted the Author has attempted to define organizations as they demonstrate their values, perspectives and characteristics in the context of culture and leadership. This has been based on comparative analysis of organizational modeling that connects the three factors, namely – Organizations, Culture and Leadership.

G. Creating a set of Organization and Management Models that builds an Intellectual Company

We have identified 8 different types of organization and management models and has attempted to provide an appropriate definition of each of the models. The author has also done a concurrent literature study on each of these proposed models to evaluate and learn from the work of others on its applicability to this study. The purpose is to eventually identify unique organization and management models that can relate to the cultural and leadership learning that is proposed to be connected as a part of this study work.

The 8 sets of Organization and Management Models (Miller and Friesen 1984) relevant to this study to connect leadership disrupted and culture and their definitions are mentioned below:

1. **Competing Organization** – Competitive organizations operate best in volatile and conflict prone environments where survival is driven by superior and competitive performance amongst rival organizations. Competitive organizations chose to be so through their internal positioning and stated objectives and are therefore a desired or planned outcome. Organizations do not become competitive unless they have by choice determined to do so. Competitive organizations nurture cultures that are target and goal conscious, decisive, clear understanding of their strengths, deep appreciation of factors that will enable them to peak performance and are aware of their resources and time lines including obligations to stake holders. Williamson (1963) High Performance, Swift and Effective Communication, concludes tasks, market focused, dominated by systems, high value for money orientation, ambitious, aggressive goal setting, directive and task oriented. Its leadership with respect to a number of concurrent tasks pursues top-level goals of the organization. They are focused, target their rival and go after them. Managerial aspirations with respect to personal goals decline as they seek institutional achievements as against individual glory. Ideology Cooper (1975) of top management tends to become organic in high performance environments, more market oriented, technocratic, and participative and team driven.

Moorhead and Griffin (2010) http://bit.ly/1FHqeJH write, "The need for achievement is most frequently associated with the work of David McClelland. This need arises from an individual's desire to accomplish a goal or task more effectively than in the past. Need for achievement has been studied at both the individual and societal levels. At the individual level, the primary aim of research has been to pinpoint characteristics of high need achievers, the outcomes associated with high need achievement, and methods for increasing the need for achievement.

Intellect Qualifiers - Characteristics of High Need Achievers - High need achievers tend to set moderately difficult goals and to make moderately risky decisions. For example, when people playing ring toss are allowed to stand anywhere they want to, players with a low need for achievement tend to stand either so close to the target that there is no challenge or so far away that they have little chance of hitting the mark. High need achievers stand at a distance that offers challenge but also allows frequent success.

Feedback - High need achievers also want immediate and specific feedback on their performance. They want to know how well they did something as quickly after finishing it as possible. For this reason, high need achievers frequently take jobs in sales, where they get almost immediate feedback from customers, and avoid jobs in areas such as research and development, where tangible progress is slower and feedback comes at longer intervals. Preoccupation with their work is another characteristic of high need achievers. They think about it on their way to work, during lunch, and at home. They find putting their work aside difficult, and they become frustrated when they must stop working on a partly completed project.

N Ach - High need achievers tend to assume personal responsibility for getting things done. They often volunteer for extra duties and find it difficult to delegate part of a job to someone else. Accordingly, they obtain a feeling of accomplishment when they have done more work than their peers without the assistance of others. Developing Management Skills provides 'some insights into the complexities of managing people with a high need for achievement. Consequences of Achievement Although high need achievers tend to be successful, they often do not achieve top management posts. The most common explanation is that high need for achievement helps people advance quickly through the ranks, but the traits associated with the need often conflict with the requirements of high-level management positions. Because of the amount of work, they are expected to do, top executives must be able to delegate tasks to others; they seldom receive immediate feedback; and they often must make decisions that are either more or less risky than a high need achiever would be comfortable with.

Learning Achievement - McClelland estimated that only around 10 percent of the American population has a high need for achievement. Nevertheless, he argued that proper training could greatly boost an individual's need for achievement. The training program developed by McClelland and his associates tries to teach trainees to think like high need achievers, increase personal feedback to trainees about themselves, and develop a group esprit de corps that supports high effort and success. In sum, the trainers work to create a group feeling that will reinforce the characteristics of high need achievers. High need achievers tend to do well as individual entrepreneurs with little or no group reinforcement. (The achievement of the strategic goals set out in the plan. The maintenance and enhancement of the value provided to stake-holders by the constituent companies (called "value capture" by Haspelagh and Jemison, 1991). The enhancement of the combined ability to create future value ("value creation"). All of this requires a real understanding of all the elements of intellectual capital. The acquirer that starts with that is at a considerable advantage; if not, it is unlikely to assess and manage its acquired business successfully. So we need to: Be able to link each strategic goal, through a cause-and-effect chain, with the key elements of intellectual capital that support it. Take each stakeholder in turn, define the key areas of value contribution, and which individuals and teams are critical to that contribution. Compare and contrast the working environment of the two constituents—their cultural norms, processes, values, psychological contracts, and so on—and identify areas of potential dissonance.) Steven Jobs, the cofounder of Apple Computers, and Nolan Bushnell, a pioneer in electronic video games and founder of Atari, are both recognized as high need achievers, and each has done quite well for himself". Let us compare Apple, today, decades after Jobs commenced is first Apple stint and HTC in terms of value realization. "Apple was focused on the production of innovative hardware and software, mostly personal computers. By creating the iPod and the associated iTunes, a legal online music download service, Apple introduced a radical innovation of its business model. Apple was the first computer company to include music distribution as an activity, linking it to the development of the iPod hardware and software. By adding this new activity to its business model, which links the music label owners with end users, Apple transformed music distribution". Say, Raphael Amit and Christoph Zott in MIT SMR 2012, "Creating Value Through Business Model Innovation" Stock Price of APPLE vs HTC. "Recent work on the psychological contract is relevant here. Guest (1996) suggests that a positive psychological contract relates to employee perceptions of fairness, trust and delivery of 'the deal[7]. It is potentially affected by organizational culture, employee expectations/experience and the degree to which employees have any alternative but to grin and bear it. However, Guest found that, although culture and expectations had some effect, it was the presence or absence of high commitment HR practices that had by far the greatest influence on the nature of the psychological contract. In particular, the organization's attempts to: keep employees informed about business issues and performance; fill vacancies from within; make jobs as interesting and variable as possible; deliberately avoid compulsory redundancies and lay-offs; had the strongest links with a positive psychological contract. Making the effort, then, is not just about being nice to people. There is, potentially, a sound commercial pay-off. Hiltrop (1996) supports this view when she argues that employees actively wish to: know more about what is happening in their organizations; understand why their managers make the decisions they do; contribute ideas and participate in decision-making; have autonomy and 'meaningful work experiences'; and generally feel valued and personally recognized." They continue, "Rather than growing by simply bringing

272

innovative new hardware to the market, Apple transformed its business model to encompass an ongoing relationship with its customers. HTC has excelled in many ways, recording many firsts in the smart phone product market space and winning numerous awards for its many technological innovations. Yet HTC's business model has remained centered on hardware design and product innovation. n this way, Apple expanded the locus of its innovation from the product space to the business model — and its revenues, profit and stock price change have reflected that successful business model innovation". See *Creating Value Through Business Model Innovation in Culture Building.*

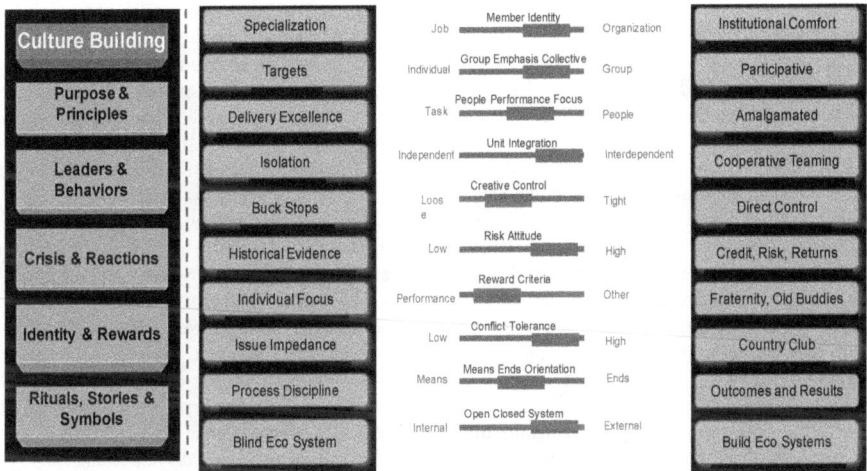

Figure 27 - Creating Value Through Business Model Innovation in Culture Building

Role of Management and Team based organizations follow lateral, freewheeling approach effectively: Employees find opportunities to meet in-groups define problems, understand priorities and solve them together. Reward systems are in place that reflects peer input, mutual learning and intra/inter group and team behavior. Performance based work led business, structures that facilitate self-managed team become necessary. Communication systems and data management archives must improve dynamically facilitating access to customer data on an on line basis. Opportunity by the teams to work through the content and process independent of supervisory control become a basic premise. Khandwalla (1977) Although leadership styles are quite pronounced. The structure of the organization is complex, Sherif (1951) yet meaningfully designed to empower people to decide at the point of impact, cohesive internally. Crotty (1968) in general the organizations are more cohesive, more aggressive and dynamic. Crotty (1968) and Rose (1955) the domain directed activities of the organization involves competitive pricing, persuasive and targeted advertising, vertical integration, diversification and innovation in new products or services. Primary role of management's turn to facilitating lateral communication, learning and contribution. Human resource management systems are created to make self-management teams effective, specialized roles of HR are available to the teams for fulfilling roles which are beyond the team performance like legal, long terms settlement, compensation analysis, specialist training, key talent hiring etc.

"First, it was clear to me that the role of "management" as a coordinator of work would come under increasing pressure. The constant march of robotics and machine learning and the "hollowing out of work" makes management a more and more unclear practice. What is a manager, and what is it that they do? Are we witnessing the end of management? Next, I could see the inevitable shift from a parent-to-child way of looking at the relationship between the manager and their team being questioned and ultimately superseded by an adult-to-adult form. The nexus of this more adult relationship relates to how commitments are made and how information is shared".

Dynamic Formalization antithetic disaggregation: Large organizations of today seek to create formalization through Selection, Role Definitions, Training, Policies and Rituals apart from the pseudo formalization process that occurs through professional training that employees receive as a part of their education. Professional bureaucracies who employ a large number of professionals thrive on these systems of formalization. Human Resource functions in such companies creates and manages a highly formalized environment that guarantees predictability of response. While the New Millennium Organization will be high on selections and training as inputs for formalization of focus and direction of the organization, it will have to give employees a substantial leeway in structuring their roles to maximize the knowledge resources. Overall strategic direction will provide integration along with the guiding vision and the integrating values which will guarantee uniformity of action and intent. We also foresee the emergence of flexible roles and fluid job descriptions that will be strongly influenced by the role incumbent. While in the current scenario, the influence of the incumbent is sought to be curtailed through standardization of responses expected and rigid job descriptions the knowledge Bureaucracy will perhaps thrive on this diversity. The challenges before structure designers is therefore to create role s which are necessary for the organization's unity of direction but still provide the individual with enough indiscretion to make a unique contribution. A more tolerant system of cubby holing individual competencies will be inevitable. Policies will be standardized and shall be assumed as a given in non-task related areas to spare the individual the hassle of using his discretion and simultaneously allowing him the discretion in task related areas. Rituals that are focused around knowledge may emerge in place of the current authority driven rituals. "When technology enables many people to have more information about themselves and others, then it's easier to take a clear and more adult view of the world. Self-assessment, particularly those that enable people to diagnose what they do and how they do it, can help them pinpoint their own productivity issues. They have little need for the watching eyes of the manager. Third, it seemed to me obvious that technology would tip the axis of power from the vertical to the horizontal. Why learn from a manager when peer-to-peer feedback and learning can create such stronger lateral paths of coaching?" Asks, In, Technology and the "End of Management" (MIT SMR 2016), Lynda Gratton (London Business School), writes, "Moreover, technology enabled social networking are capable of creating more robust and realistic maps of influence and power — so no more hiding behind fancy job titles. Finally, the rise of Uber has everyone excited about platforms and how they can create a fertile place for new businesses to be built and act as a conduit for flexible working".

Social Networking and on line connectivity for Deverticalization - The emphasis in today's organization theory is on analysis whereas the trends in the environment point towards a greater congruence and convergence of efforts and initiatives. More than the segmentation of an organization into discrete parts for the sake of analysis, we hypothesize the emergence of a new criteria which measures the organic integrated nature of the organization. This parameter measures the extent to which the constituent parts of an organization are inter linked, interconnected and interdependent. A well-connected and well-oiled organization is like a team of commandos "The Navy Seals" or perhaps like the "The New York Philharmonic" or like the "Chicago Lakers". Communication systems, interaction, coordination and information sharing systems, comprehensive decision analysis and support mechanisms will be the hallmarks of such an organization. While the work organization will depend to a certain extent on the value creation and generation process, an important indicator will be the team effectiveness measure that will measure the effectiveness of the teamwork in a team-based organization.

Social Need for Communication - Com channels intra and inter teams become easy and is now a part of the on-going work process. Jobs utilize functional/technical excellence and expertise available in the corporate set up to its advantage and does not attempt replicating specialization. Members offer space to all contributing and value adding forces in the corporate world. Competing organizations constitute functions, skills and competencies, which are unique and relevant for their own effectiveness, and their learning emphasis is on growing their skills and competencies and not adds on functional specialization available within the system. The organization focuses on affecting individual with different skills together in order to form an effective group. They see the need for intra training to help them gain appreciation of other functions and they in turn to focus on product and service excellence.

2. **Learning Company - Learning Opportunity for the Intellect** - Organizations learn by imitating other behaviors or by accepting other experiences as good for themselves. March and Olsen (1976) describe the learning cycle as stimulus response system in which individual's actions lead to organizational actions which invoke environmental response. Burnes and Stalker (1966) – This organization fosters learning, intellectually stimulating environments, innovative, high internal energy, and adaptability to individuals high, freedom to act, fair play in targets, time to develop, opportunity to apply, experiment, enabling the unknown. Effective learning makes organizations able to cope with problems. Learning takes place when an organization interacts with the environment and by observing the results of their actions. The concept of the Learning Company has been a popular one for quite some time now According to Garrett (1995), the key ideas about the Learning Company were already developed immediately after World War II. It has taken much longer, however, before they were actually applied. The concept came of age under the impact of a rapidly developing world of work and organization. Pedler et al (1991) trace back the history of the concept (and a related one - total quality management) as stemming from earlier approaches set as organization development, individual self-development, action learning, and the excellence movement of the 1970s and 1980s. All of which in turn followed post-war concern of systematic training. The European Commission's (1996) White Paper on Education and Training highlights the impact of the information society on work and organization, the impact of international' organization on the need for competitiveness, and the impact of scientific and technologic knowledge on industry. Growing competition, technological changes, new worry methods, financial constraints, globalization, reorganizations, mergers and the like, give rise to a need for organizations to learn and adapt more quickly to changing circus-stances.

Process to Learn - In the words of McCarthy (1997), 'these processes necessitated continuous improvement both in people and in organizations'. This is a central, if fairly general feature of the Learning Company. There are many more specific definitions of the concept, most of which include notion' about continuous learning, a culture to think out of box, innovation, demonstrate speed and responsiveness, share commitment, team, collaboration in shared vision, openness in communication, shared values, dialogue, the use of IT, empowerment, and so forth. Some of these definitions are of a descriptive nature, others are more normatively orientated.

Culture to Learn http://bit.ly/1r2wfMd "harnesses the full brain power, knowledge, capability, history and experience available to it, in order to evolve continually for the benefit of all its stakeholders Mayo and Lank, (1994). Peddler, Burgoyn and Boydell (1989:2), describe the Learning Company as 'an organization which facilitates the learning, including internalization of all its members and continuously transforms and reinvents itself. As indicated above, this definition contains an individual and an organizational change element Individual learning is necessary but not sufficient for organizations to learn. Interestingly in a more recent publication the same authors define the concept as 'an organization this facilitates the learning of all its members and consciously transforms itself and its context (Peddler et al, 1996:3)".

Intellect Meets Organizational Learning - Apparently, organizations now need to be able to impact upon their environment as well as adapt to the changes taking place/ a concern that had already been raised much earlier by Mintzberg (1979). In fact, Mintzberg showed how (particularly larger) organizations succeed in affecting the circumstances in which they have to operate (for example, their clients, local and government policies, and so forth). Whereas Pedler et al stress the importance of organizational learning, Mumford (1995) finds the Learning Company literature focuses too much on the structural element. In his opinion, individuals (sharp minds – intellect) (and teams) must learn before there can be anything like organizational learning. Another core thinker about the Learning Company, Senge (1990:3), tries to integrate these two approaches. His definition, however, is quite a normative one: "An organization where people continually expand their capacity to create the results they truly desire, where new and expansive patterns of thinking are nurtured, where collective aspiration is set free, and where people are continually learning how to learn together".

He presents his five disciplines for Learning Companies:

1. *Personal mastery, ensuring individual motivation to learn;*
2. *Mental models, creating openness to misconceptions;*
3. *Shared vision, building long-term commitment in people;*
4. *4.Team learning, developing group skills like cooperation, communication and so forth;*
5. *Systems thinking, which constitutes 'the most important discipline', integrating the other four.*

Discipline Consistencies - All the disciplines are to be practiced alongside each other and they have an impact on one another as well. As Hodgkinson (1998) describes, the Learning Company is a process rather than a state, something that all members of an organization have to work on all the time, yet can never be fully realized. Peddler and Aspinwall (1996:182), too, stress that the learning company must remain a particular vision, to be realized in the context of a unique organization. Even though this may be the case, they consider it possible to generalize about organizational learning. People in companies learn from the problems, dilemmas and difficulties they encounter, together with their attempts to overcome them. Companies have much to learn from each other, too, but this can only be achieved if the contrasts are raised and the differences between them made explicit. In other words, there is no such thing as the Learning Company, but a variety of Learning Companies that can benefit from each other's experiences.

3. **Human Organization.** Antony (1970) This organization values history and tradition, builds upon its people strengths, acts through clarity in all its orientation, philosophy to make people productive, high resilience, mutual expectations matched, long lasting relationships, mutual respect in work cultures, work ethic. Human organization co exists with productivity focus subject to a culture that is conducive to combing a conflicting point of view. While they are desirable outcomes the means and methods have still not been conclusively established. More over greater knowledge of human

aspects enables a substantive understanding of the relatedness. There is some overlap of the human organization with that of the Learning Company as both fall into the realm of people orientation and development. However, the fundamental difference in a human organization continues to be excessive people focus, as against task, decision orientation is slow, compromise in difficult situations and poor conflict and competitive positioning.

Human System Needs - The organizational focus on climate and its energy is essential to be understood. In a literature review, Poell et al (1997) concluded that, although there are many definition of the concept of a Learning Company, a number of issues keep recurring. The definitions describe the elements in a human system that makes for an efficient flexible is viable company. Communications are free, open easy. People interact/talk easily and informally y and in a family y like atmosphere all the time. People feel like a young person and would be fortunate to get and continue with this job irrespective of the rewards.

- *Continuous focus on the human interface and on the individual, group and system level;*
- *Single- and double-loop learning processes. Swieringa and Wierdsma (1992) eve conceive of triple-loop learning: not just doing things well, not just doing things better but also doing better things;*
- *Creation and distribution of information and knowledge, cf. Nonaka and Takeuchi (1995);*
- *Inquiry and dialogue in groups (sharing learning experiences);*
- *Increasing the learning capacity of members (learning to learn) cf. Sense (1990);*
- *Integration of work and learning (informal learning, learning on the job);*
- *Shared vision (theory of action) cf. Sense (1990);*
- *Empowerment of individual learners.*

According to the White Paper on Education and Training (European Commission/1996:40)

Vocational training in enterprises is increasingly taking place on the basis of a training plan that the workers themselves and their representatives have been involved in preparing. In the most progressive and most efficient companies, this training is organized less and less around the acquisition of skills for a specific task or even a clearly defined job.

- *Coaching by the manager;*
- *Transformation and innovation;*
- *Learning tied to business objectives but also for personal development.*

Work is performed in multifunctional teams, thinking and doing are integrated into jobs, and workers are empowered to participate in team decision-making processes (Tjepkema, 1993). Poell and Tijmensen (1996) had already concluded that the literature on human learning organiza-tions implicitly proposes a redefinition of the organization of work into team-based struc-tures/ so as to allow for an integration of learning and work. Every work activity can also become a learning activity. Before going on to highlight some criticisms of the Learning Company concept, two actual examples of the way in which a learning company operates may help illustrate the ideas presented here.

4. **The Institution.** Crozier (1964) – This organization has effective Structures, roles and responsibilities, elaborate communication channels, slow to react, defined end states, moderate goal setting, long lasting organization, ability to bounce back high. This organization places a lot of faith and relief on the individual sense of responsibility.

People are well aware of the organization goals, objectives and the strategic direction/mission of the business. The company standards of performance, productivity and growth are higher than those of similar organizations. The organization rewards correctly those who/ what should be rewarded only.

Lastability - Today given the realities of global work force it is critical to structure organizations which can offer combination of high pay and high value at work. As managing teams at the start up stage get over several weakness of the hierarchical approach will emerge. Individuals tend to compete in the hierarchical approach to move up the hierarchy. The employees end up spending their energy and efforts trying to please their boss rather than concentrating on offering service to their stakeholders. The quality of time spent preparing past data, analysis of tons of papers more often post-mortem of yesterday's performance. Displaying work done to the boss, competing with each other to withhold information all of that makes the focus of the individual only on pleasing the boss. There is often a lack of accountability for important organizational goals as everybody is doing work but there is no ownership to the work to be seen in a holistic manner. Putting people at large doing the same things together rather than grouping people who are trying to accomplish the same goals and who are working on the same process is a fast demanded change scenario of the new organization. The alternative is to make the teams responsible for their actions. They are masters of their game. The institution lasts over time. Every enterprise attempts to reach a steady state like an institution as they compete with organizations.

5. **Performing Enterprise** - Khandwalla (1992) – This organization has bottom line paramount, financial focus primary objective, rigors of feedback high, low tolerance for failures, political climate, survival driven beyond values, inability to work in team's evident, non-negotiable goals. Employees enjoy freedom to do their work, to plan and set their work pace, style and methods, but are severally accountable for their goals and targets. Generally, employees here are warm, friendly, forthcoming with a clear agenda on performance orientation. People are proud and happy to be acknowledged as a member of this organization when tasks have been accomplished. Problems are not smoothened out, not avoided but faced. People are permitted to do their own free thing to a remarkable degree. People here come to your help when needed without hesitation as long as there is something in return.

Metrics & KPIs - Members who are driven by achievement of numbers, political and power conscious feel proud of this crowd of men and women. People are expected to use their discretion in their work here. Jobs are well defined/clear and people are aware of their role & responsibilities and all work relates to financial and revenue numbers. Profitability is the only good word. Means are not as important as the end in itself. Ethics tends to be loosely interpreted and guidelines are arranged to suit business needs. Organizational members are trained to break rules although would not accept it openly. Yet leaders know that the rules are broken and they would watch as long as revenue numbers are achieved. There is effort to find better ways of doing things Performance, not personal relationships/considerations are what counts in this organization. Conflict is seen as natural, inevitable, and productive. There is a lot of trust, mutuality and faith in this organization. Things are well systematized and work goes on efficiently perhaps on a clock wise precision, but there are no feelings.

Work Systems Quality - The quality of work at all levels is high. Promotions reflect the stated promotional policy. Superiors rarely listen to Dissident/differing views. High performance organizations have a premium on information, knowledge, learning, capabilities and performance orientation. The individuals working in teams understand the business. They know its strategy, ongoing business performance and with a clear definition of the stakeholders and competitors. High performing individuals see their reward as a function of the success of the business. They are owners in the true sense and share in this performance in ups and downs with clarity that what is key for the business is key for them. They are in a position to influence critical organizational decisions including being in a position to decide on their work, content, method, belief they will work with and actively participate in the decision making process in a highly involved manner. Honda has ventured on the making of a world car betting on a flexible design and they believe only a team can do it. The chief engineer set up skunk works to create the flexible foundation. When all employees add significant value and they act like owners and managers who exercise self-control, seek pleasure in doing more complicated tasks, assignments with stretch, deadlines, which are impossible. They manage and control their own work teams coordinate their work and priorities with other employees, seek feedback learning opportunity and benchmarks on better ways of doing work. They constantly develop new ways to satisfy stakeholders. To add value in real life job situation is no longer the prerogative of top management. There is little opportunity for employees to add value to simple repetitive work. More often than not when individual try to add value and in important situations like self-management, team working, the bureaucracy and the work systems will not let them be.

6. **Intellectual Company.** March and Olsen (1976) – This organization promotes and perpetuates intellect as an end in itself, limited space to learn as organizations evolve, best in class focus, content than process delivery mechanisms, organizational purpose beyond bottom line. Organizations will be built around individuals. The individual will be the foundation of the organization Intellectual nomads is preferable to extremely loyal but average performers. An organization of like-minded individuals will perform better than an organization of diverse individuals. Headcount Management will not be an issue in tomorrow's organization. The organizational culture of tomorrow must focus on individual growth & contribution rather than on their performance.

Mind Drivers it - Change management will become easier in the organization of tomorrow because the intellect seeks change and does not shy away from it. The number of employees working part-time is likely to be larger than the full-time employees Adhocracy will prevail over any other known forms of organizational structures -There are two distinct kinds of organizational people - Thinkers and Doers. Conflict within organizations is inevitable and desirable. Knowledge and Intellect has been dealt with by Watkins and Marsick (1993) emphasize that systems to capture and share individuate learning intellect must be put in place before organizations can benefit.

Interfaces KM /ICM - Nonaka and Takeuchi (199E describe such a system of knowledge creation in companies. They distinguish four types of knowledge conversion among people, which can be combined to form processes in time:

- *Socialization: tacit intrinsic knowledge within an individual, within a team, reproduced as tacit knowledge. People learn from each other by sharing experiences, providing stories, sharing examples, living experiences, imitation/ trial and error, and so forth.*
- *Externalization: tacit intrinsic knowledge made explicit for others to observe, learn and experience from others on the basis of overt sharing. People learn by systematizing and cod tying their implicit knowledge, making visible what is hidden inside them.*
- *Combination: explicit and overt knowledge reproduced as explicit and aware knowledge. People learn using materials and other resources specifically aimed at teaching people.*

- *Internalization: explicit overt knowledge made tacit and covert. People learn by practicing skills, displaying competencies, automating procedures, managing processes, acquainting themselves with tasks by doing them.*

Nonaka and Takeuchi speak about a hypertext, systemic knowledge-based Intellectual Company (smart enterprise) rather than a Learning Company (self-mastery). According to their ideas, this type of company succeeds in combining the efficiency of a bureaucratic – process intensive organization with the innovativeness of an adhocracy organization Mintzberg, (1979). This is achieved by involving all layers of the organization in the right kinds of knowledge conversion at the right time, through codification and commodity orientation of individual tacit knowledge. Grey, (1998). Every member in the company this contributes to the creation, management and proliferation of collective knowledge throughout the organization.

Info Dominates - A critical component of such organizations is a system that continually makes all necessary information available to workers and encourages the sharing of information and ideas. Management strategies must aim at ensuring the availability of information to employees, including the conceptual frameworks to enable them to use that information for organizational ends. Nonaka (1991), that the only reliable source of competitive advantage is the knowledge has argued it that is latent within the organization itself in the memory and potential of employees. The key to unlocking it is to create a sense of identity between employee and organization and to tap into the commitment generated. As with any intellectual, knowledge organization, a high trust climate is essential for this process to occur.

7. **Voluntary School** Hirschman (1970) – This organization, supports a purpose and cause beyond commercial purposes, drives people and process synergies, high resilience to economic up and down turns, long range planning, organizational strategy differentiates businesses and other purposes. Poell et al (1997) presents an alternative concept of the Learning Company, to what we call as the Voluntary School. in response to the criticisms they have raised. It focuses on multifaceted learning and work arrangements (not only group learning in multifunctional teams) and enabling people to handle tensions they encounter in everyday work life (not only developing shared values). These organizations have elaborate management structures, loosely coupled motivational systems that are extrinsic, substantive drivers expected from organizational members to participate in such organizations. The organization works in a slow, steady manner, seeking elaborate and detailed information, covers its tasks through sector, functional and people specialists and participates in completion of long term goals. Goal setting hierarchy is driven by rules, detailed policy framework and delegated responsibility. Accountability tends to be quite dispersed and member's willingness to take decisions at times is painfully slow. Tensions arise because there is always several actors within and outside the organization that want to impact on the way learning and work are organized. In order to create learning and work arrangements in which all of them can participate effectively, it is important to:

- *Deal with the autonomy and empowerment of individual employees;*
- *Provide a clear policy and direction;*
- *Allow participation and learning in-groups, emphasizing shared understanding and reflection; take into account the professional field where new methods and insights are developed.*

Relationships - A Voluntary School should explicitly address the relationship between learning and work and provide people with possibilities to connect the two in multiple ways. Although studies offer some examples of how this could be achieved/ the organizations involved did not really pay much attention to explicitly relating learning to work. There is still significant room for progress in this area.

8. **Mechanistic corporation** Perrow (1972) – Michael, B. (1974) An introduction of organizational design California Management Review. "Mechanistic organizational units are the traditional pyramidal pattern of organizing with functional structures, high degree of specialization, substantive size and governmental orientation. These corporations are largely conglomerate, multi business, geographic organizations, thick internal architectures, long hierarchies, open to change although long in time, stable goals, consistent methods, predictive approaches, systemic and role driven. Roles are procedures are clearly defined and corporate policy for administration is equally clear, valid and rigorous enough to be executed at all times. There is always a policy for nearly every question or an unresolved problem. Communication is channeled and time spans and goal orientations are similar within a unit. These organizations work with a automated, machine like efficiency. Levels arrange authority, influence and information; each higher level has successively more authority, more information and substantive voice in enabling change.

Systemic Mechanical - Decision-making is centralized at the top and it is the top levels that make appreciative judgements to determine what is important in the environment at varying points in time. Top management also determine the way processes would be organized and created for the other levels of the hierarchy on the way they would work, decide, use information and obtain approvals as required. Thus people are conceived of as parts performing specific tasks. These organizations typically work when organizational unit is performing a task that is stable, well defined and likely to be programmable, or when members of the organization prefer well-defined situations. Mechanistic form is efficient and predictable and provides greater clarity to members who have low tolerance for ambiguity and seek secure and stable environment. These forms are less flexible, once a direction and procedures have been set out and difficult to change in the short term". Refer - http://bit.ly/2a26nha

Mechanistic Influence in Machine Learning – "Machine learning is unconstrained by the preset assumptions of statistics. As a result, it can yield insights that human analysts do not see on their own and make predictions with ever-higher degrees of accuracy. More recently, in the 1930s and 1940s, the pioneers of computing (such as Alan Turing, who had a deep and abiding interest in artificial intelligence) began formulating and tinkering with the basic techniques such as neural networks that make today's machine learning possible". Dorian Pyle is a data expert in McKinsey & Cristina San Jose a Principal, state in the McKinsey Quarterly, "Machine learning is based on a number of earlier building blocks, starting with classical statistics. Statistical inference does form an important foundation for the current implementations of artificial intelligence. But it's important to recognize that classical statistical techniques were developed between the 18th and early 20th centuries for much smaller data sets than the ones we now have at our disposal. But those techniques stayed in the laboratory longer than many technologies did and, for the most part, had to await the development and infrastructure of powerful computers, in the late 1970s and early 1980s. That's probably the starting point for the machine-learning adoption curve. New technologies introduced into modern economies—the steam engine, electricity, the electric motor, and computers, for example—seem to take about 80 years to transition from the laboratory to what you might call cultural invisibility. The computer hasn't faded from sight just yet, but it's likely to by 2040. And it probably won't take much longer for machine learning to recede into the background. The people charged with creating the strategic vision may well be (or have been) data scientists. But as they define the problem and the desired outcome of the strategy, they will need guidance from C-level colleagues overseeing other crucial strategic initiatives. More broadly, companies must have two types of people to unleash the potential of machine learning. "Quants" are schooled in its language and methods. "Translators" can bridge the disciplines of data, machine learning, and decision making by reframing the quants' complex results as actionable insights that generalist managers can execute."

Chapter 7

Linking The Digital Organizational Dots

It seems clear that organizations exist less today for the well-being of rank-and file employees than they once did. With the Dow, NASDAQ shattering all records, at periodic intervals, the Sanders popularity, it seems clear that the shareholders, perhaps, have the upper hand in making critical corporate decisions. Building organizational purpose entails understanding what makes the players work with one another and seek to achieve a common purpose, despite seeming difference that only makes organizations more alive and vibrant. Organizations that have evolved this comfort to live with it and reinvent itself over time survive the purpose test. Over time it is understood how character, growth and perpetuity is often the mantra for evolving times rather than employer rankings, best managed awards or management titles. In pursuit of organizational identity, it is ironical that even the intrinsically good get so carried away with defining their purpose based on the way they have been perceived in a particular context, rather than what is truly their self-worth and identity that is perhaps more lasting and enduring.

A. *Purpose of an Organization – For whose benefit does an organization exist?*
B. *What are the basic assumptions among people about working relationships in the organization?*
C. *What are the basic assumptions the organization and the employee make in relation to each other, particularly in the context of a positive or negative cultural situation?*
D. *How does culture affect digital business models?*
E. *Do Organizational Models impact business models?*
F. *Cultural Empowerment in organizations*
G. *Co-Existence of several cultures (sub cultures)*
H. *Emergent or Digital Culture*
I. *Relevance of Leadership disrupted on Organizational Culture in an Organization and Management Model*
J. *Toward a Leadership disrupted Approach to Digital Culture Change*
K. *The Digital Culture Model – Built around 8 Org Models, 8 Leadership disrupted Styles and 4 Organizational Culture*
L. *The Digital Company - Culture as it Impacts Org Formation (Model Details)*

A. Purpose of an Organization - For whose benefit does the organization exist?

Customer - The evidence seems to be that culture change or focus programs are much more difficult and take longer to complete than the corporate-culture school would lead us to expect. This may be because of a fundamental misdiagnosis of the nature of culture. Could it be, for instance, that culture is not so much something that organizations have but rather something that organizations are (Smircich and Calas, 1987)? This view of culture sees it as much more deep-seated and, therefore, less easily changed than is suggested. Mabey and Salaman (1995) also criticize the corporate-culture school (what they describe as 'this prevalent view') because it implies that an organization has a single culture, ignoring the reality of conflicts of interest and power and the effects of inherent organizational inequalities. It seems, therefore, that cultural change will remain difficult and the examples of organizations that appear to have developed the required strong culture will be over-represented by those that are small or have experienced a recent, significant increase in employees and/or are located on green-field sites. Context to cultural change (Examples could be customer focus, reengineering, restructuring, reward systems, social collaboration, family transitions, succession, globalization, downsizing, acquisition – merger) continues to be the single most critical factor for successful cultural transformations.

"Royal Philips creates value by providing locally relevant products to different markets, while keeping the vast majority of its processes standardized on digitized platforms. Once offering just savings accounts, ING Direct has deliberately grown its product and service complexity, increasing its product portfolio to also include payment accounts, credit cards, investment funds, pension plans, brokerage services, mortgages, personal loans and life insurance". Martin Mocker, Peter Weill and Stephanie L. Woerner in MIT SMR 2014, "Revisiting Complexity in the Digital Age" continue, "however, with today's increased digitization, companies can finesse a trade-off; they can increase value-adding complexity in their product offerings while keeping processes for customers and employees simple. Our research suggests that companies operating in this "complexity sweet spot" outperform their competitors on profitability. ING Direct has also shifted from operating exclusively through phone and Internet channels to opening about 30 branch offices across Spain, with the goal of becoming a full-service bank. This growth in product variety has allowed customers to use ING Direct Spain as their primary bank. Today, more than half of ING Direct Spain's 2.4 million customers use multiple ING Direct Spain products. Amazon now offers more than 10 million different products in categories ranging from music to auto parts, providing what it calls "Earth's biggest selection" in an "Everything Store." For almost any product, customers can choose between dozens, if not hundreds, of alternatives from different suppliers. Hipmunk, Inc., a travel website based in San Francisco, California, is another example of a company that uses digitization to simplify the **"customer"** experience. By creatively sorting flights (Hipmunk's "agony" rating is based on a combination of price, duration and number of stopovers), adding visualization and limiting options that are less likely to be chosen (such as a flight with the same price but more stopovers), Hipmunk offers customers a simplified way to make a selection. USAA, a provider of financial products and services based in San Antonio, Texas, has taken the approach of getting value from complex products while simplifying customers' lives a step further. Since its founding in 1922, USAA has grown its product offerings from just auto insurance to more than 100 property and casualty insurance, banking, life insurance and investment management products. More recently, to better meet customer needs, USAA added links between different products to address life events such as buying a house, getting married or dealing with the aftermath of a hurricane. Each life event involves a bundle of linked products such as loans, investments and insurance. One of the company's first multi-product solutions, Auto Circle, targeted the car-buying life event. Previously, customers had to visit different car dealers to get prices, compare those prices and negotiate a purchase, contact the USAA bank for a loan and then ask USAA property and casualty insurance for a quote. The new integrated one-stop-shopping experience guides members through a process to select, buy (at pre negotiated and attractive prices), finance and insure a car in one seamless process. Customers can perform all steps with an easy-to-use app on a mobile device or via USAA's website. The answer is that the digital world offers tools that simplify and narrow the decision-making process. Using search, recommendations, customer reviews, seller ratings and other mechanisms, Amazon has so far been able to provide simple customer-facing processes despite its product complexity. Searching in the physical world is much more complicated. For example, where does a customer find organic cookies — in the organic aisle of a supermarket or in the cookies aisle? Digitization helps with complexity management by effectively delivering on a customer promise of simple but tailored engagement. At the same time, digitization helps internal process simplification despite growing product variety and links. Digitization effectively facilitates the decoupling of product and process complexity, allowing top-performing companies to both delight customers and streamline internal operations. (The HR professional, if involved at the right time, will feel a responsibility to go beyond these needs. Once the digital transformation, merger or acquisition is happening, however, the pressures of communication. reorganization, and harmonization absorb time, and vital issues of managing the asset nature of human capital can be pushed to the background. How often are HR professionals able to highlight why a deal may not work, when the business logic seems technically sound? Machismo and excitement, plus a great deal of optimism, are barriers to customer integration.) While achieving the same result without significant digitization is possible in principle in smaller companies, it used to be close to impossible in large companies".

B. What are the basic assumptions among people about working relationships in the organization?

Commitment & Loyalty - "What is the worth of what have traditionally been termed commitment and loyalty? We just do not know? What is the impact of the feeling that the organization is a community - even a family - with relatively stable long-term working relationships? And how will that play out in terms of cooperation given to others as opposed to "back stabbing" in the intense competition for scarce resources?" Thomas A Hickok of Virginia Tech/Center for Creative Leadership, in Downsizing and Organizational Climate, (http://bit.ly/2a34EZa)responds to his question, "The basic assumptions about working relationships have changed, in ways that cannot yet be well assessed. It appears, at least, that relationships tend to be less "familial" and more competitive than in the past. We can only be sure that things have changed, not how". http://abt.cm/29X9K7D Goethe, "The moment one definitely commits oneself, then providence moves too. All sorts of things occur to help one that would never otherwise occur. A whole stream of events issues from the decision, raising in one's favor all manner of unforeseen incidents and meetings and material assistance which no man could have dreamed would have come his way. Whatever you can do or dream you can, begin it. Boldness has genius, power and magic in it. Begin it now."

C. What are the basic assumptions the organization and the employee make in relation to each other, particularly in the context of a positive or negative cultural situation?

Stability – Freedom - The basic assumptions, says Hickok - Center for Creative Leadership (http://bit.ly/2a34EZa), "by employees and organizations about their employment (contract or otherwise) relationship have changed from long-term and stable, (steady state, permanent, career for life) with organizations expected to make accommodations, demonstrating flexibility to avoid laying people off to more short-term and contingent workforce management. Authors such as William Bridges in Transitions and Noer forecast a happier future (stable/steady/consistent) for those who adapt to the changing times in the new scenario, but that is a difficult forecast to test".

Organizational culture represents a common perception, based on a collection of evidence, experience held by the organization's members. This was made explicit when we defined culture as a system of shared meaning, rituals, norms, experiences, stories, sagas. We should expect, therefore, that individuals with different backgrounds (versatile, unique, rare, different) or at different levels in the organization will tend to describe the organization's culture in similar terms.

Acknowledgement that organizational culture has common properties does not mean, however, that there cannot be subcultures within any given culture. Most large organizations have a dominant culture (Institution Model together with a Division that is Human Organization Model) and numerous sets of subcultures. A common misconception is that an organization has a uniform culture. However, at least as anthropology uses the concept, it is probably more accurate to treat organizations "as if" they had a uniform culture. "All organizations 'have' culture in the sense that they are embedded in specific societal cultures and are part of them." According to this view an organizational culture is a common perception held by the organization's members. Everyone in the organization would have to share this perception. However, realistically, all may not do so to the same degree. As a result, there can be a dominant culture as well as subcultures throughout a typical organization. Some organizational cultures could be labeled "Thick," others "Thin." There seem to be two major factors that determine the strength of an organizational culture: sharedness and intensity. Sharedness refers to the degree to which the organizational members have the same core values. Intensity is the degree or commitment of the organizational members to the core values. The degree of sharedness is affected by to major factors: orientation and rewards. In order for people to share the same cultural values, they must know what these values are.

Micro level - Many organizations begin this process with an orientation program. New employees are told about the organization's philosophy and method of operating. This orientation continues on the job where their boss and coworkers share these values through both word of mouth and day-to-day work habits and example. Sharedness, is also affected by rewards. When organizations give promotions, raises, recognition, and other forms of reward to those who adhere to the core values, these actions help others better understand these values.

Some organizations have been labeled "the best to work for" because the rewards that they give to their people are exemplary and help reinforce commitment to core values. The degree of intensity is a result of the reward structure. When employees realize that they will be rewarded for doing things "the organization's way", their desire to do so increases. Conversely, when they are not rewarded or they feel there is more to be gained by not doing things the organization's way, commitment to core values diminishes. Stephen Gregg, Chairman and CEO of Ethix Corp. writes, "People do not follow uncommitted leaders. Commitment can be displayed in a full range of matters to include the work hours you choose to maintain, how you work to improve your abilities, or what you do for your fellow workers at personal sacrifice."

D. How does culture affect digital business models?

Platforms & Productivity - "In this time of fast-growing enterprise digitization, companies are finding it necessary to build platforms and services to leverage the data they collect and then deliver it to customers if they are going to do business in new and different ways. Embedding data analytics into its workflow and creating actionable insights for doctors from that data is an ambitious goal for WellPoint, and its stumble on the path to it is not unusual; their recovery from that stumble, however, shows great organizational flexibility". (Productivity is the output achieved for a certain input. Where employees directly contribute to a quantifiable delivery output, such as sales and production, measuring productivity is easy. It is more difficult when the role is a supporting one, such as an administrative or design function. Sheer volume of output does not indicate that the output is the right output. Productivity in delivering a service—such as IT support—can be measured by the achievement of stated service levels for the resource that is used. In research and development, the volume measure is the number of new products designed, but the real output is their ultimate added value in sales in the marketplace.) This would necessitate a process for Organic Flexibility and Process Dynamicity - Another important characteristic that will differentiate today's organizations from those of tomorrow will be the placement along the flexibility-rigidity continuum. All organizations have a structure that is relatively permanent and it has several structural appendages that are created either for a temporary period or a specific purpose. Task Forces, Committees or matrix organizations are examples of such appendages. We hypothesize that in the knowledge bureaucracy we may have some loosely held team's functions as permanent appendages. To that extent it will add to the flexibility of the organization it will reduce the rigidity of the structure and make it more organic and "living". Such functions could be the ones that are focused on the important concern areas for the organization, the customer, the environment and itself. We could therefore visualize the emergence of permanent teams at two levels; one at the interfaces - with the environment and the customer and the other at the introspective level; where the organization deals with itself. While the external interfaces are readily apparent, organizations which wish to survive and prosper can ill afford not to introspect and take a long hard look at its own health, coping and survival mechanisms and learning and growing abilities. "Three practices underlie WellPoint's success in this new system: treating the revised project as a cultural change, creating incremental goals, and focusing on the customer. Moving to a Red status may have seemed like an admission of failure, but the executives at WellPoint used it as an opportunity to create new organizational capabilities. Though a waterfall approach has long been used to spec and develop projects, especially in large enterprises, most companies find it difficult to create accurate specifications. Reasons include a lack of people who understand both the business and IT sides of the equation and a lack of history to draw from. For these reasons and others, over 50% of major IT projects fail. And even when they're completed, we find companies are not generating the value that they expected". Michael Fitzgerald in MIT SMR 2014, Preparing Analytics for a Strategic Role" quotes Stephanie Woerner, "WellPoint's effort to update its digital business model by changing the nature of its revenue structure is similar to many of the IT-enabled organizational transformations that we've studied. **Agility** - Agile development works for these projects for a number of reasons because it (1) allows the project to fail fast and for interventions to take place early as the team iterates, (2) creates an environment where business and IT must work together and makes project success a joint responsibility, and (3) focuses on the user. But moving to Agile is a huge cultural change. It's hard to change a culture. Everyone in the organization is affected and they all must buy in. WellPoint targeted ground-up cultural change by bringing in training, adding resources, and hiring people who had experience with the desired change. WellPoint executives committed their time to the project and created metrics that aligned with the desired changes. And progress was celebrated. This leads to the second success factor. By moving to Agile, WellPoint leaders had perfect opportunity to put the focus on incremental goals and successes. **Big goals** (those BHAGs [big, hairy, audacious goals] we've all heard about) can be motivating in the short run because they signal out-of-the-ordinary targets. However, those kinds of goals can be quite demotivating in the long run, if there are no parallel incremental goals, because there is so much opportunity for failure and only one opportunity for success". (Even "hard" productivity measures may not be directly proportional to profitability, cash flow, or added value. For example, a favorite productivity indicator is "revenue per head." This can be growing, and yet profitability and added value can be decreasing because the costs of achieving the revenue are rising faster. In the early stages of a startup this may be fine, since growth is more important than profits. Or we may measure tons or units per head in a factory, encouraging output at the expense of quality.) For a successful digital business model, your enterprise has to have good content, UI, mobility, device friendliness, robotic benefits, smart learning - neural networks, customer experience and digital platforms.

Customer Experience - "If your company doesn't offer a great digital experience, many customers, particularly younger people, will move to industry competitors or do more business with companies like Amazon.com that offer great customer experiences digitally, operate in adjacent industries and are starting to offer services similar to yours. To make this change more difficult, a great digital business model challenges the traditional physical business model that relies on places (such as bank branches, bookstores or department stores) and people (such as sales teams or insurance agents) to delight a customer. A digital business model challenges the physical model in three main areas: **"internal power"**, since who "owns" the customer's experience often changes from product groups to the unit that manages the multi product customer experience; **"business processes"**, which require rethinking to be seamless across channels; and **"customer data"**, which become an enterprise-wide resource rather than remaining hidden in one area", write Weill. For example, the moot question is how can a firm's culture be shaped for best results? Within this perspective culture is transformed into a technical term or a variable that can be brought under managerial control. Culture, here is assumed to act as a control mechanism, to create organizational commitment, to achieve integration within a firm, or to help it adapt to external changes. And certain kinds of culture promise to produce a better performance than others. "Yes, it is a question that is raised many times: What is it about the organization of professionals that allows some firms to adapt to marketplace turmoil and prosper, while others lose share and gradually decline? Why do some firms seem to thrive on change while others melt down? In MIT SMR 2013 issue, "Peter Weill and Stephanie L. Woerner in "Optimizing Your Digital Business Model" continue, "what does it take to create the strongest possible online presence? "Given that, enterprises must strengthen their digital business models — how they engage their customers digitally to create value, via mechanisms such as websites, cloud hosting, social networks, wearables, analytics, collaboration and mobile devices".

Digital Social Responsibility - How the formal and informal culture components come together to define an organization's position on social responsibility will dictate how the organization reacts to social responsibility issues. Depending on where the organization can be classified on the Social Responsibility Continuum as a result of the organizational culture's formal and informal components, all organizational behavior, including decision making, will be influenced for outcomes. For example, a firm whose culture defines it as Social Obligation will react to situations consistently based on the culture's influence. More importantly, the culture will influence organizational decisions even if the social responsibility characteristics of the firm differ from the beliefs of the individual or individuals making the decision.

Do Digital Organizations Have Uniform Cultures? Individuals with different backgrounds or at different levels in the organization will tend to describe the organization's culture in similar terms. There can be subcultures. Most large organizations have a dominant culture and numerous sets of subcultures. A dominant culture expresses the core values that are shared by a majority. An organization's culture is its dominant culture. This macro view of culture that gives an organization its distinct personality. Subcultures tend to develop in large organizations to reflect common problems, situations, or experiences that members face. Defined by department designations and geographical separation. It will include the core values plus additional values unique to members of the subculture. The core values are essentially retained but modified to reflect the subculture. If organizations had no dominant culture and were composed only of numerous subcultures, the value of organizational culture as an independent variable would be significantly lessened. It is the "shared meaning" aspect of culture that makes it such a potent device for guiding and shaping behavior. We cannot ignore the reality that many organizations also have subcultures that can influence the behavior of members.

Digitization – Digital Natives – Customer Voice - "Three trends have converged to raise the stakes for the effectiveness of your enterprise's digital business model. The first is the continued march toward the **"digitization"** of ever-increasing aspects of business — incorporating more of your customers' experience, executing more of your business processes and working together with partners in your value chain. The second trend is the increasing number of **"digital natives"** — your young current and future customers and employees — who expect a brilliant digital experience in all of their interactions with you. The third trend is the dawning of the age of the **"customer voice"**, in which customers have a much stronger impact on enterprises via ratings of their services (such as the customer rating stars on Amazon and customer experience surveys) and via online comments through Twitter and other social media". Refer - *Digital Tech Evolution.*

Digital Tech Evolution

Maturity Hierarchy

Maturity Hierarchy	Cloud	Artificial Intelligence	Analytics	Wearables	Devices	Social	Additive Manufacturing	Virtual Reality	Cognitive Tech - Neural	Security	Mobility	3D - Internet of Things
High Focus												
Moderate Focus												
No Change												
Moderate Focus												
Low Focus												
Not Applicable												
1 year Plan												
2 Year Plan												
Industry Focus	1	2	3	4	5	6	7	8	9	10	11	12
Banking Financials												
FMCG Consumer												
Infrastructure Estate												
Energy - Oil & Gas												
Federal - Provincial												
Media Entertainment												
IT, IT, Digital Services												
Manufacturing												
Technology												
Retail Distribution												
Telecom Networks												
BPO												

Figure 28 – Digital Tech Evolution – Adapted from Digital Strategy — An Industry Take - Gerald C Kane, Doug Palmer, Anh Nguyen Phillips, David Kiron, Natasha Buckley et all, in MIT SMR 2016 in Aligning The Organization For Its Digital Future

Why Digitization Dooms : Roadblocks and Enablers - The world today is witnessing an explosion of digitisation, driven by rapid large scale adoption of smart technologies by people, institutions, businesses, administrations and governments. Organisations are also exploring the ways and means to leverage this digital revolution in order to create innovative products and services, delight their customers, achieve internal efficiencies and improve working environment of the employees", says Hema Thakkar of KPMG.

"All too often digitisation fails. Various statistics reveal that two-thirds of global enterprises are failing to evolve into digital enterprises. While people are increasingly smartly wired, why are some organisations still digitally handicapped? Why do they fail to collectively connect these otherwise wired employees? What are those enablers and roadblocks that make or break digitisation?

Various deep dive analyses reveal the following critical barriers to digital transformation : --

- *Lack of an overarching Vision and Blueprint: Many times, management team - used to conventional ROI and ROCE calculations - is not able to see a strong vision or business case for digitisation beyond efficiency measures and indicators. Digital vision entails a gradual shift of the business focus from low usage to widespread leveraging of existing and emerging digital technologies. The vision also encompasses cultural transformation from analog to digital. Therefore, in a perfectly articulated digital vision, technology is not treated as an "end" in itself but as a potent "means" to realise organisation's vision and business strategy.*
- *A hazy vision leads to a weak blueprint. Lack of direction and absence of understanding of ground realities and operational issues as well as difficulties when going from theory to go-live results in a plan full of loopholes.*
- *Inadequate technological capability: Ineffective infrastructure and inadequate integration of digital technologies – including analytics, database, social, mobile, internet and cloud - slows down the pace of digitisation. However it is a myth that only disruptive, revolutionary IT overhaul ushers in digital transformation. For digitization to succeed, the organisation needs to have a judicious mix of existing tools like email, documentation systems, MIS, allied database management tools, operating systems, virtual platforms and relatively younger and untested technologies such as blogs, cloud computing, wikis and similar next-generation tools. Perfect mix and integration of digital technologies coupled with appropriate upgradation of the existing IT system and platforms promote collective digital collaboration in a holistic manner, without employees making radical shifts in their proven technical habits and behaviours.*
- *Lack of understanding, appreciating and nurturing a digitally capable culture: Digitisation dooms when there is too much focus on technology in isolation. In such a scenario, organisations fail to address deep seated cultural issues, approach-avoidance attitudes towards profound change and lack of rethink on how employees identify themselves with work. Peter Drucker's quote "Culture eats Strategy for Breakfast" emphasises that organisational strategy will only be successfully implemented if it is supported by suitable cultural pillars.*
- *While a new digital culture requires 'enterprise thinking', existing hierarchical and rigid culture is often task oriented, is defined by boundaries and tends to gravitate towards the "status quo" to retain authority rather than improvement focus and agility.*
- *Another key attribute of digital culture is seamless collaboration through cross integrated internal teams who are also empowered to connect to knowledge communities. On the contrary, non-Digital HR bank on stability, long term experience and work planning through hierarchies, which automatically restricts employee empowerment and innovation.*

- *Due to such paradoxical attributes with their pros and cons, culture cannot be changed en-masse. Therefore targeting "wholesale behaviors" for transformation can prove suicidal, as it would lead large scale attrition and demoralisation of the workforce. The solution is to identify the "meta behaviours under existing competencies". These would be required to be changed or replaced with "behaviours under digital competencies" i.e. behaviors required to adopt digitisation, behaviors new digital technologies might foster and behaviors it might inhibit. Such an "evolutionary" process of change is far more long lasting than a disruptive "pull and plug" approach. The reason being that phased and evolutionary digital change assimilates the collective minds of employees with vision and goals of digitisation thoroughly.*

- *Organisations who presume that digitisation is just about adopting perfect digital processes and systems simply fail to understand that digitisation requires everyone to co-create technical, behavioural and cultural digitisation maps for their work areas, and adopt new ways of working. After adopting digital culture, nurturing it regularly through identification of obstacles and suitable course correction to avoid them maintains progress and positive momentum. Digital culture thus starts converging with digital governance.*

- *Faulty Communication: Organisations that digitally mature at a very fast pace have effective program to communicate digitisation vision and strategy. It is to be noted that digital fluency is not the ability to explain the technical know-how, but an ability to articulate the impact and value of digital technologies and digital change.*

- *Resistance from employees and stakeholders: Digitisation often goes against the grain of established ways of working and set management practices. Resistance to digital technologies is a result of the threat they pose to well rooted cultural codes. Resistance indicators can be observed as employees hesitating to adopt a digital blueprint, various divisions collectively escaping the responsibility of championing new processes and leaders' hesitations or apprehensions about embracing new innovations. The remedy is to create a strong sense of "digital purpose" which alleviates interpersonal resistance. Such a shared purpose binds the culture. On the contrary, a low sense of purpose makes it difficult for people to come to agreements, decisions, connect through work and relate with each other.*

- *Leadership Reinforcement of Digitisation: Reinforcement of the vision and implementation plan is critical for the success of digitisation. Leaders not demonstrating and reflecting the deep rooted change agenda in their own work and behaviors script the story of a doomed digitisation. What precisely are the digital culture codes that need reinforcement? Let us take an example of digital pioneers Facebook or Google's innovation centric culture – a critical trait for digitally savvy companies. All the management case studies find that innovation culture is embodied in every aspect of Google and Facebook's daily operations, from customer service to new product development to internal procedures and policies. It is instilled in all employees in the form of innovation-enabling behaviors. Their Managers need to do it, encourage it, reflect it themselves and be in the field themselves, and not just endorse it through the hierarchy.*

- *Thus, culture codes such a seamless team work, employee connectivity, large scale collaboration, networked project teams, customer empathy, responsiveness to internal and external environment need constant reinforcement and recognition by the leadership. Steve Ballmer, CEO of Microsoft once said: "Everything I do is a reinforcement or not, of what we want to have happen culturally. You cannot delegate culture". Leaders should therefore drive digitisation not merely through command and control structure, but through their own visible actions. In day-to-day terms, this means setting up and monitoring new policies for digitisation, aligning rewards/recognitions to these policies, moderating employee behaviours and demonstrating own competencies that will nurture the digital culture without abandoning the old cultural assets. Summing up, "leading by example" by C-suite on virtual and physical platforms to ensure engagement and participation of employees is an absolute necessity.*

Digitisation is no longer a luxury or an IT agenda, but a transformational necessity knocking at the doors of the organisations. In contrast to the organisations that are digital failures, successful digital organisations create a culture that embeds in it a self-sustaining pattern of digital behaviours, thoughts, decisions, value system and beliefs. Digital personality of an organisation does not shape just its internal processes, employee behaviors and culture, but has a deep impact on its customer reach, brand perception and the very tenets of its existence - identity imprint and legacy it continuously creates at each time horizon in the corporate landscape".

Digital Turmoil - "When electronic component distributor Arrow decided it had to be on the Internet, it gave the Arrow.com team terrific new offices, hired young newcomers, and essentially sent a message to mainstay Arrow employees that they were now dinosaurs. But Arrow.com, which could not succeed without strong ties to the rest of the company, so angered Arrow's traditional salesforce that a wall had to be erected between the warring camps". Every organization has its own unique culture or value set. Most organizations don't consciously try to create a certain culture. The culture of the organization is typically created unconsciously, based on the values of the top management or the founders of an organization. In, "What it Takes to Lead Through Turmoil in HBS Working Knowledge, what are the characteristics of companies that successfully transition in times of dramatic change? HBS professor Rosabeth Moss Kanter (Evolve! Succeeding in the Digital Culture of Tomorrow) separates the leaders from the laggards in times of turmoil to Sean Silverthorne (HBSWK 2002), "First there is **Denial** - The laggard sees the change—a disruptive technology, say—as temporary, choosing instead to believe the company is in a fine position when this thing blows over. There is arrogance from past success. In addition, the company seems to need a "perfect certitude" of success before investing in something new, Kanter said. "Companies ask me to talk to them about innovation, and the first thing they ask is, 'Who else is doing it? **Anger and Blame** - Phase two for laggard performers, she continued, is the anger and blame stage. They are moving out of denial, but the corporate response emphasizes stopping "them" rather than innovating. Case in point: The U.S. auto industry. When threatened by superior Japanese imports, domestic automakers at first sought government tariffs rather than building a better car. When Amazon.com bested Barnes & Noble on the Internet, among B&N's responses was to sue Amazon, alleging fraudulent advertising. Then the laggard company enters phase three: **Cosmetic change.** Executives realize they must respond in some way, but the response is often superficial, like putting lipstick on a bulldog, says Kanter. "You've got something that's big and ugly, and you want to improve its appearance, show the world it's really different." The problem, she said, is that "you are not fooling anyone, and you're making the bulldog very angry."

E. Do Organizational Models impact business models?

To answer this question, we need to first differentiate **thick cultures from thin ones.** That different types of organizations have similar or dissimilar perspectives on cultures has to be understood. Of significance is the study work and proposition of Pradip Khandwalla (1977, 1990, 1999, 2001):

Thick & Thin Cultures - Khandwalla continues, Organizations in turn have a thick or a thin culture or otherwise stated as strong or weak cultures. Clifford Geertz, http://bit.ly/1UloEY7 in Interpretation of Cultures, "A thick culture is characterized by the organization's core values being intensely held, clearly ordered, and widely shared. The more members that accept the core values, agree on their order of importance, and are highly committed to them, the stronger the culture is. Organizations that are young or have constant turnover among their members, almost by definition, may have a weak culture, for example, the learning or human organization model because members will not have shared enough experience to create common meanings. This shouldn't be interpreted to imply that all institutions or mechanistic corporations with a stable membership would have strong cultures. The core values must also be intensely held. If the culture is thick, how will it influence the organization's effectiveness?

Differential inevitability - "The downfall of the attempts of governments and leaders to unite mankind is found in this wrong message that we should see everyone as the same. This is the root of the failure of harmony. Because the truth is, we should not all see everyone as the same! We are not the same! We are made of different colours and we have different cultures. We are all different! But the key to this door is to look at these differences, respect these differences, learn from and about these differences, and grow in and with these differences. We are all different. We are not the same. But that's beautiful. And that's okay. In the quest for unity and peace, we cannot blind ourselves and expect to be all the same. Because in this, we all have an underlying belief that everyone should be the same as us at some point. We are not on a journey to become the same or to be the same. But we are on a journey to see that in all of our differences, that is what makes us beautiful as a human race, thick or thin, and if we are ever to grow, we ought to learn and always learn some more." — C. JoyBell C.

Difference in homogeneity - "The answer possibly lies in differential effectiveness" says Geertz "and requires that an organization's culture, strategy, environment, and technology be aligned however unique may it be. The stronger the organization's culture, the more important it is that the culture fit properly with these variables. The successful organization will achieve a good external fit-its culture will be shaped to its strategy and environment. Market-driven strategies, for instance in competing and Performing Enterprise al models, are more appropriate in dynamic environments and will require a culture that emphasizes individual initiative, risk taking, high integration, tolerance of conflict, and high horizontal communication" Also found Geertz material in http://bit.ly/2aidvXT by Sarita Kumari (SIES, Bombay).

Differential Uniqueness - In contrast, product-driven strategies focus on efficiency, work best in stable environments, and are more likely to be successful when the organization's culture is high in control and minimizes risk and conflict. Successful organizations, typically a competing organization or a Performing Enterprise, will also seek a good internal fit, with their culture properly matched to their technology. As stated, routine technologies provide stability and work well when linked with a culture that emphasizes centralized decision making and limited individual initiative. Non routine technologies, on the other hand, require adaptability and are best when matched with cultures that encourage individual initiative and downplay control. Voluntary School s tend to ask for steady cultures where identifiable sets of members and member behaviors are asked, understood and appreciated. Intellectual Company models continue to be difficult to identify and map".

Our Way - Another result of a strong culture (Voluntary School s) is that it increases behavioral consistency. It conveys to employees what behaviors they should engage in. It tells employees things like the acceptability of absenteeism. Some cultures (Human Organization) encourage employees to use their sick days and do little to discourage absenteeism. Not surprisingly, such organizations have much higher absenteeism rates than those organizations where not showing up for work – regardless of reason – is seen as letting your co-workers down. Given that strong cultures increase behavioral consistency, it's only logical to conclude that they can be a powerful means of implicit control and can act as a substitute for formalization.

Form is Supreme - We know how formalization's rules and regulations (Institution Model)) act to regulate employee behavior. High formalization (mechanistic corporation model) in an organization creates predictability, orderliness, and consistency. A strong culture achieves the same end without any need for written documentation. Moreover, a strong culture (sometimes the Institution) may be more potent than any formal structural controls because culture controls the mind and soul as well as the body. It seems entirely appropriate to view formalization and culture as two different roads to a common destination. The stronger and organization's culture, the less management need be concerned with developing formal rules and regulations to guide employee behavior. Those guides will have been internalized in employees when they accept the organization's culture.

Systemic Structural Design Differential – Digitization is systemic power. A feature of digital business is that it is under -managed and under-led. This relates to the areas mentioned above (de-layering and empowerment) but much of it revolves around a proper understanding of power. Digital Power (networked, connected, collaborated, deviced, mobilized, Randomized) as a concept is new but it needs to be thought about. Who has it or who should not have it needs to be thought about. Who has it or who should not have it; what should be added and what should be taken away. Human resourcing is about how people can be successfully managed in an organization to achieve the aims of that organization. To achieve anything yourself, or to work out how you will influence, requires digital power and an understanding of it. Empowerment is itself a derivative of power, referring to the increasing likelihood of action being taken by an individual without further hierarchical reference. So power is central to the debate about HR, and a proper understanding of *leadership* is one of the more benign yet positive aspects of power. "To ramp up digital offerings, some companies create a separate organization and system for implementing their digital strategy, or they acquire a pure-play digital company to speed up the initiative. In and of itself, this can be a good strategy—but only if the digital lab is in step with the rest of the business. Leaders in both traditional and digital camps must designate clear roles and responsibilities, and they must build mutual trust among team members. In practice, having separate digital and traditional organizations can make it difficult to develop standard systems and practices that account for the complexities built into transaction-based legacy IT systems". Oliver Bossert, Martin Harrysson, and Roger Roberts, in McKinsey Quarterly 2015, "Organizing for digital acceleration: Making a two-speed IT operating model work", argue further, "They set up a separate and independent digital organization. "Many organizations have to deal with the problem of trade unions that have, perhaps over many years fought an adversarial struggle with managers who held employees in low esteem. Getting out of the negative bind is not an easy prospect, particularly if individuals come laden with the problem by removing those that do not fit the new culture and cannot change to cope. The problem with trade unionists may be more intractable. Most people can, however, be persuaded to see that change is taking place and will respond positively. Many organizations will find the trade unions tend become legacy systems or cultural residue and are only too ready to embrace these aspects of a desired culture." When legacy systems and new front-end innovations are aligned, staff members in traditional and digital groups can better coordinate their efforts and effectively pursue multichannel marketing strategies. Each side has a role to play in getting things right." Thus, an organization's culture is the set of norms that create powerful precedents for acceptable behavior within the firm. These unwritten "rules of the road" create expectations, some kind of an unwritten ask, around acceptable risk, degree of intervention, change orientation, creativity and innovation, group versus individual effort, customer versus vendor orientation, extra effort, and more. Culture is a powerful force, a meta physical perception, if you will, and can provide an engine to achieve market success or an anchor pulling the firm toward failure. Successful companies tend to be well run and have distinctive cultures that enable them to create and implement strategies that identify them as market leaders. Today's firms often have legacy cultures that are no longer appropriate to today's fast-changing environment. Other firms have the challenge of merging two cultures together to create a successful third. "Perhaps the biggest pitfall, however, occurs when companies try to adopt the same technology platforms that online companies are using and assume this alone will solve their alignment problems. It is not enough just to reorganize around platforms. Companies must reorient themselves and their product-development processes around customer experiences and insights. To enable fast front ends that will complement their transaction-oriented legacy back ends, they can adopt a digital product management model".

F. Cultural Empowerment in organizations

The verb to empower means to enable, to allow or to permit and can be conceived as both self-initiated and initiated by others. Empowerment is the process of enabling workers to set their own work-related goals, make decisions and solve problems within their sphere of responsibility and authority - http://bit.ly/2apoukM Luthans (1992) suggests the following ways in which management can empower employees and reproduced by Littrell.

Management can:

- *Express confidence in employees' abilities, their self-worth and hold high expectations concerning their performance;*
- *Provide staff and opportunity to engage in their learning*
- *Enabling role holders to determine the course of action that they would take when confronted with tough choices*
- *Allow employees to participate in the decision-making process;*
- *Allow employees drive, unencumbered freedom and autonomy in how they perform their jobs;*
- *Set inspirational or managerial goals for employees that would help them take responsibility for their actions;*
- *Use position – referent power in a prudent, thought through and positive way while limiting the use of coercive power.*

Unfortunately, there are many barriers to the empowerment of employees. There is still a widespread belief among managers that to empower subordinates is to lose one's own power. In, Employee Empowerment in China, A Case Study by Romie F. Littrell http://bit.ly/2apoukM writes, "One way to overcome such a perception is to make sure that managers who empower their subordinates are not subsequently blamed for their subordinates' failures nor ignored when their subordinates succeed". Vogt and Murrell (1990) suggest that an individual is empowered through trust, communication, involvement, self-belief and participation that in turn bring about commitment to people, institutions, projects and experiences.

Collective Confluence - Co-existence is inevitable is our perspective. That together with Edgar Schein's three cultures another culture could exist or alternatively two of the four could exist in the same context and situation. Many paradigms or models have recently been constructed to describe organizational culture. One of the most comprehensive and widely known is that by Deal and Kennedy 1994 (McKinsey). Four basic types of cultural profiles they uncovered. Each type is characterized by some combination of two factors: the type of risks that managers assume and the type of feedback that results from their decisions. Most organizations are some hybrid of these cultural profiles; they do not neatly fit into any one of them. However, within the organization there are subcultures that do tend to fit into one of these four profiles. Some organizational cultures may be the direct, or at least indirect, result of actions, substantive positions and views taken by the founders. However, this is not always the case as there are exceptions to timing, data availability and situation. Sometimes founders create weak cultures (tacit or explicit), and if the organization is to survive, a new top manager must be installed who will sow the seeds for the creation, absorption, internalization necessary for a strong culture. There is a clear need for personalities to match cultural needs of an enterprise. Today institutions call it a culture fit. Freud says, "It sounds like a fairy-tale, but not only that; this story of what man by his science and practical inventions has achieved on this earth, where he first appeared as a weakly member of the animal kingdom, and on which each individual of his species must ever again appear as a helpless infant... is a direct fulfilment of all, or of most, of the dearest wishes in his fairy-tales. All these possessions he has acquired through culture. Long ago he formed an ideal conception of omnipotence and omniscience which he embodied in his gods. Whatever seemed unattainable to his desires - or forbidden to him - he attributed to these gods. Tom Tierney of Bain and company report, "In talent-driven organizations, leaders must focus on micromanaging the culture, not micromanaging the stars. Culture is not about a firm's dress code, it is NOT about how you or your partners feel. It is never completely codified in a formal rulebook or policy manual. Culture encompasses beliefs about everything that goes on in a firm. It is a set of invisible guideposts that defines and shapes how people behave. A firm's cultural beliefs guide the decisions that are made and develop the way the firm responds to internal and external threats". One may say, therefore, that these gods were the ideals of his culture. Now he has himself approached very near to realizing this ideal, he has nearly become a god himself. But only, it is true, in the way that ideals are usually realized in the general experience of humanity. Not completely; in some respects, not at all, in others only by halves. Man has become a god by means of artificial limbs, so to speak, quite magnificent when equipped with all his accessory organs; but they do not grow on him and they still give him trouble at times... Future ages will produce further great advances in this realm of culture, probably inconceivable now, and will increase man's likeness to a god still more" - Sigmund Freud, "Civilization and Its Discontents. Every culture, or subculture, is defined by a set of common values, that is, generally agreed upon preferences. Without a core of common values, a culture cannot exist, and we classify society into cultures and subcultures precisely because it is possible to identify groups who have common values" - Kenneth Boulding

Cultural preponderance - A dominant culture expresses the fact that core values that are shared by a majority of the organization's members have a degree of consistency and validity and the likelihood of it being authentic. When we talk about an organization's culture, we are referring, predominantly, to its dominant culture, that which can be perceived, understood and experienced by many organizational members. "The soul takes nothing with her to the next world but her education and her culture. At the beginning of the journey to the next world, one's education and culture can either provide the greatest assistance, or else act as the greatest burden, to the person who has just died." Plato. It is this macro view of culture, an experience that gives an organization its distinct personality. A dominant culture is set of core values shared by a majority of the organization's members. These values create a dominant culture in these organizations that helps guide the day to day behavior of employees.

Sub Cultures for Real - "We have to create culture, don't watch TV, don't read magazines, don't even listen to NPR. Create your own roadshow. The nexus of space and time where you are now is the most immediate sector of your universe, and if you're worrying about Michael Jackson or Bill Clinton or somebody else, then you are disempowered, you're giving it all away to icons, icons which are maintained by an electronic media so that you want to dress like X or have lips like Y. This is shit-brained, this kind of thinking. That is all cultural diversion, and what is real is you and your friends and your associations, your highs, your orgasms, your hopes, your plans, your fears. And we are told 'no', we're unimportant, we're peripheral. 'Get a degree, get a job, get a this, get a that.' And then you're a player, you don't want to even play in that game. You want to reclaim your mind and get it out of the hands of the cultural engineers who want to turn you into a half-baked moron consuming all this trash that's being manufactured out of the bones of a dying world" said, Terence McKenna. Subcultures tend to develop in large organizations to reflect common problems, situations, or experiences that members face. These subcultures can form vertically or horizontally. Important, but often overlooked, are the subcultures in an organization. A subculture is set of values shared by a minority, usually a small minority, of the organization's members. Subcultures typically are a result of problems or experiences that are shared by members of a department or unit. Subcultures can weaken and undermine an organization if they are in conflict with the dominant culture and/or the overall objectives.

Sub Cultural view is functional - continuing Bill Owens espoused, "True leadership lies in guiding others to success. In ensuring that everyone is performing at their best, doing the work they are pledged to do and doing it well". Successful firms, however, find that there is always a degree of uniqueness, a rarity and this is not always the case. "There is a cult of ignorance in the United States, and there has always been. Isaac Asimov said, "The strain of anti-intellectualism has been a constant thread winding its way through our political and cultural life, nurtured by the false notion that democracy means that 'my ignorance is just as good as your knowledge." Most subcultures are formed (natural course) to help the members/leaders of a particular company group, a team, function or a group bonded together with a common cause, deal with the specific, day-to-day problems with which they are confronted. The members may also support many, if not all, of the core values of the dominant culture either because they identify with it or because there is an element of overt group think. When one product division of a conglomerate has a culture unique from that of other divisions of the organization, a vertical subculture may exist. When a specific set of functional specialists – such as accountants, human resources or purchasing personnel – have a set of common shared understandings, a horizontal subculture is formed. Even in terms of organizational structures there is consistency to this view – Horizontal functions and vertical businesses. Of course, any group in an organization can develop a sub culture. For the most part, however, subcultures tend to be defined by departmental designations or geographical separation.

Values link Sub Culture - The marketing function, for example, can have a subculture that is uniquely understood, accepted and shared by members of that function. It will include a set of select core values of the dominant culture, some common understanding plus additional values unique to members of that department. Similarly, an office or unit of the organization that is physically separated from the organization's main operations, geographically, floors, may take on a different personality, simply given its distance and communication networks. Based on the work of Kluckhohn and Strodbeck, Edgar Schein introduced five assumptions of culture. They are based on values and has a relation to the environment, the nature of reality, the nature of time and space, the nature of human nature, the nature of human activity and the nature of human relationships. Culture for an organization could be described with respect to a few parameters. These are: Accountability, Commitment to Core Values, Competitor Awareness, Confronting Conflict, Creativity & Innovation, Customer Driven, Nimbleness, Risk-Taking, Supporting Employee Growth, Teamwork and Trust. Again, the core values are essentially retained but modified to reflect the separated unit's distinct situation. Sub-cultures exist in all organizations and can neither be denied nor ignored. They relate to membership of different groups and vary between these (for example, in the state of openness of dealings between members). Sub-cultures become more destructive when they operate contrary to absolute standards. Refer Deal & Kennedy – McKinsey 1992. *Co-Existence of several cultures (sub cultures)*

G. Khandwalla Perspectives on Organizational Cultures

The Mechanistic Corporation Culture exhibits the values of bureaucracy and feudalism. Burns and Stalker (1961). Organization work is conceived as a system of narrow specialists, as among craft guilds. Authority is thought of as flowing from the top and information and instructions follow formally through prescribed channels.

The Organic Culture. Burns and Stalker (1961) is a contrast to the mechanistic culture with formal hierarchies of authority, departmental boundaries, rules and regulations frowned upon quite severely. There is an emphasis on getting tasks accomplished, ensure transparent flow of information, build equity in processes, ease of communication strongly advocated.

The Authoritarian Culture Likert (1967) is power centric towards the superior with reinforcement mechanisms created to follow orders. The actions are directive with limited scope for dissent and command and control forms the basis of management.

The Participative Culture believes in the human nature to cooperate to participate in decisions than to have them imposed upon them. Group problem solving, collaboration instead of conflict are some practices.

The Management Systems Churchman (1968), McClelland and King (1972), Daniels and Yeates (1988) Culture depends on the technical nature of work and consequent engineering emphasis to management. Actions involve analysis, study for more effective ways to handle issues, processes are streamlined and established, standardization is encouraged and overall effort to bring in method to management actions is key to this culture.

The Entrepreneurial Culture Peterson (1982) defines spirit to growth, individual initiative, risk taking roles, vision and the willingness to work through building capability and attitude towards the organization.

The Paternalistic Culture Dayal (1977) identifies with the promoter who often is also the owner of sorts given their early start up history. The organization follows with the family trail, their beliefs, values and practices and imbibes many as its own. The organization values loyalty and in return provides security and stability to its employees on the job.

The Altruistic Culture Greenleaf (1977) revolves around an institutional format with its basic beliefs in favor of good for the society and the larger environment. Selfless service, the desire to contribute to a larger well, make individual and institutional contribution substantive in both intellectual and wealth generation focus drive the organization.

The Cafeteria Culture, whereby the shared values adopted are those of groups that gather away from the work situations and in such places as the washroom or canteen. Elite's and cliques, whereby strength and primacy is present in some groups at the expense of others. This leads to over mightiness. It affects operations when the elites and cliques are able to command resources, carry out projects and gain prestige at the expense of others; to lobby effectively for resources at the expense of others; and to gain favor at the expense of others. Work regulation, whereby the volume and quality of work is regulated by the group for its own ends rather than those of the organization; when it sets and works to its own targets which are at variance with those of the organization. Informal norming, whereby individuals are pressurized to adopt the attitudes and values of those around them rather than those of the organization. This occurs most when the organizations own norms are not sufficiently strong or structured to remove the local or group pressure. If organizations had no dominant culture and were comprised only of numerous subcultures, the influence of culture on organizational effectiveness would be far more ambiguous. Why? Because there would be no consistency of perceptions or behavior. It is the "shared meaning" aspect of organizational culture that makes it such a potent concept. But we cannot ignore the reality that many organizations also have distinct subcultures.

Designed cultures (for example, need to convert from Performing Enterprise to Competing Organization or from a Human Organization to a Learning Company) mean that the culture is shaped by those responsible for organizational direction and results, and created in the pursuit of this. This involves setting the standards of attitudes, values, behavior and belief that everyone is required to subscribe to as a condition of joining the organization. Policies are produced so that everyone knows where they stand, and these are underpinned by extensive induction and orientation programs and training schemes. Procedures and sanctions are there to ensure that these standards continue to be met. Organizations with very specific cultures are not all things to all people: many, indeed, make a virtue of their particular approach of 'Many are called but few are chosen'. High levels of internalization of shared values are required. *Other perceptions emerge from this.* Feelings of confidence, trust and respect are created. Individual response to the level of organization commitment that is evident in this approach tends to be high.

H. Emergent or Digital Culture

Emergent culture (In our context defined as **Digital Culture** which is significantly more robust than emergent culture defined here in below) is where the culture is formed by the staff (and staff groups) rather than directed by the organization. The result is that people think, believe and act according to the pressures and priorities of their peers and pursue their own agenda. (The Intellectual Company) This is clearly fraught with difficulties and dangers: organizations that allow this happen will succeed only if the aims and objectives of the staff coincide absolutely with their own. It leads to the staff setting their own informal procedures and sanctions, or operating formally in ways that suit their own purposes rather than those of the organization. Individuals and groups, again, are not all things to all people; they may and do reject those who refuse to abide by the norms and values that they have set for themselves.

Digital HR - "Digitally maturing organizations build risk taking into the fabric of how they manage. "We have had to go through a learning exercise in terms of setting expectations," says CVS's Tilzer. "We now talk about experiments as a portfolio and don't focus on things that don't work. By design, every experiment isn't going to pan out and result in something that works in the market. The U.S. Department of Agriculture's Risk Management Agency monitors the cost growth of digital initiatives as an indicator of experimentation. CIO Chad Sheridan believes that if overall development cost growth is too low, then the organization's exposure to risk may be increasing because adequate experimentation and learning aren't taking place. "I'm building failure into my programs," he says. "We plan and budget for the expected downside of our digital investment portfolio to support the expected failure inherent in any program of experiments". The ideal culture is one that serves the organization effectively. It may be summarized as the shared patterns of attitudes, values, beliefs and behavior, covering strategy, operations, decision-making, information flow and systems, managerial and supervisory behavior, the nature of leadership and the general behavior of the staff. It involves setting absolute standards of ensuring that these are achieved. However, an ideal culture would only be possible in a dream. In, July 2016 MIT SMR issue, "Aligning the Organization for its Digital

Future", Gerald C Kane, Doug Palmer, Anh Nguyen Phillips, David Kiron and Natasha Buckley, continue, "Getting an organization to embrace risk goes beyond admonitions that taking risk is acceptable. *People — Deepening the Company's Skills* - As our results show, digitally maturing companies are more than five times more likely to provide employees with the opportunities to develop needed digital skills than are early-stage companies (76% versus 14%). Early-stage companies, by contrast, rely on consultants and contractors. Although this may be an excellent means to support efforts early on, relying solely on outside help should only be a stop-gap measure. The shortage of talent will continue to increase, and employees and executives who don't feel they are gaining digital skills will seek their fortunes elsewhere — sooner rather than later. The talent gap is acute even for developing organizations, and it may continue to grow if organizations can't find ways to develop existing talent or attract new talent. Digitally maturing companies do more than offer training courses. As we pointed out earlier, Salesforce.com combines customized online learning with badges that play a central role in performance evaluation and promotions. However, Hagel at Deloitte's Center for the Edge argues that traditional training courses may be too limited. "With the mounting performance pressure and the accelerated pace of change that digital technology is bringing about, the most powerful form of learning is not accessing what other people already know," he says. "It's driving new knowledge creation through practice in the workplace itself, rather than in a training room. Allied Talent's "tours of duty" are a prime example. A tour of duty is designed to deepen employee skills while engaging employees in creating their career paths. A typical tour lasts for two to four years and is focused on specific goals that support both the corporate mission and the employee's career. Managers are committed to developing employee skills needed to complete the tour and then discuss additional tours of duty based on both the company's needs and the employee's career goals".

I. Relevance of Leadership disrupted on Organizational Culture in an Organization and Management Model

We bring in the relevance of Leadership disrupted on culture and their context to the Organizational Models to this Study. This has meant looking at some fundamental thought positioning in this regard and some of which are mentioned below:

- *Leaders drive organizations to perform in ways they believe would support their goal orientation.*
- *In doing so the Leaders influence and impact the organizational culture*
- *The leaders in turn also assume a concrete degree of clarity on the organizational purpose, its business philosophy and shareholder expectation. An all encompassive culture and values operate in the environment.*
- *Consequently, organizations work in a context influenced by its culture in which the said philosophy operates. The culture is defined in this organizational context and is also influenced by the leader. Effectively, for example, in an organizational context of Competing Organization, influenced by an operator culture and led by a teacher may not be compatible given incongruent nature of this relationship, with each bringing its own nuances.*
- *We would establish the appropriate connection that links up each of these factors, being leadership, culture and organizational and management models, relevantly.*
- *And bring to bear that leadership influence over culture is limited unless the organizational model/context is considered.*

Establish Systems - Leadership in turn becomes key for impacting organizational culture in the context of specific types of organizational model. The role of the leader primarily focuses on creating key organizational systems and process that provide strategic contribution. They position themselves to add value by defining organizational priorities in the organizational model that they work in

(Example Competing Organization Models and Market Forces) and by sensing conditions and events in the business environment that affect strategy. Flatter and more lateral organizational structures and a decrease in the number of layers call for leadership from everyone. Leaders operate effectively when someone or the same set of individuals lead by challenging the group and helping it set priorities and pressing for excellence in performance. The leader sets direction for the organization and builds mechanism to allow people to understand what that direction is and to measure their progress. It is particularly difficult for managers in their traditional hierarchical organization (Mechanistic or Institutional Organizational Model) to give best heroic leaders.

"Leadership is about solving problems". The day soldiers stop bringing you their problems is the day you have stopped leading them. They have either lost confidence that you can help or concluded you do not care. Either case is a failure of leadership" said, Colin Powell. What is blatantly evident is presence of many leaders in given line functions whose titles distinctly connotes leadership but whose behavior borders on petty mindedness, turf creation, showing poor sensitivities, wining at every issue with a gross inability to courageously put deadlines, chase goals forward and lead the team by example. These leaders are those who typically would articulate the right thing be it business goals, performance objectives, key tasks and benchmarks, quoting examples of other well run organizations, espouse latest management theories. In practice they are nothing but tyrants to seek power of pleasure and privilege to command and control people. When not in the current role they are perhaps spending a lot of time to prove their leadership by demonstrating how other units or functions are not doing their jobs.

Organizations in our experience are grossly perceptive of such leaders and over time turn wary. Organizational counseling efforts are critical to up front leaders who continue to practice styles that worked in the past and educate them of the new realities. In our judgement these are classical cases of basic feedback and developmental systems not available in the corporation.

Some of the leadership disrupted styles mentioned above are not rare, but is a diminishing lot. This is of course a contrast to Jack Welch who says, "The idea flow from the human spirit is absolutely unlimited. All you have to do is tap into it". With Jack Welch if you are doing well, you probably have more freedom than most CEO's have in publicly held companies. But the leash gets pulled very tightly when a unit is under performing. "Leaders aren't born, they are made. And they are made just like anything else, through hard work. And that's the price we'll have to pay to achieve that goal, or any goal" - Vince Lombardi. Doug Ivester of Coke stated to be most data driven demanding CEO in the world is at his best leadership challenge. He has to keep pace with benchmarks set by Goizueta. Coke continues to be a standard for keeping to its strengths, articulating goals, current inspiration selling a billion drinks a day, which amounts to 2% of all the world's daily beverage consumption, thereafter to double coke share to double of the worldwide consumption. Leaders continue to make position statements and strike the chord of inspiration. Because change is almost always resisted, it needs a champion. And the more powerful and visible the champion, the more likely the change will be successful.

Digital Innovators - "What we found interesting, even surprising, is that Analytical Innovators are not just those companies we would expect — newer, agile online organizations or huge companies with vast analytics investments. Rather, this group represents variously sized companies across industry sectors and geographies. We also identified interesting characteristics shared by Analytical Innovators. They are more likely to use more of their data. They tend to be more effective at driving the information transformation cycle — capturing, analyzing, aggregating, integrating and disseminating information — and thus embedding analytics in the organization. More of them report a greater need for speed in processing and analyzing data. Perhaps most intriguingly, not only do we see a shift of power with the effective use of analytics, but we also note a marked cultural difference. While many respondents have yet to develop a data-oriented culture, Analytical Innovators as a group tend to score high on those attributes that define such a culture". The relationship between the ideal and the actual culture should be a matter of constant concern because both develop. Specific attention is paid to those gaps in culture that cause problems where, for example, people follow the leads, values and norms of their work or professional group rather than those of the organization. Technological advances and changes may mean that suddenly the ideal hitherto striven for has to be changed in order to accommodate new divisionalization, patterns of work, retraining, regrouping, and so on. David Kiron, Pamela Kirk Prentice and Renee Boucher Ferguson in "Innovating with Analytics", MIT SMR 2012 issue, debate further here, "How a Data-Oriented Culture **Analytical Innovators -** In our survey analysis, we've discovered striking differences between Analytical Innovators and their less analytics-driven counterparts. They tend to be open to new ideas. Customer-facing employees are more likely to have access to data they need. Executives foster analytics-driven decisions, and analytics champions are more likely to exist within these organizations. And more of the companies are able to use analytics to collaborate effectively. One important takeaway is that a data-oriented culture makes it easier for organizations to innovate when decision makers have confidence in where the data comes from, how it is developed and by whom. But another, perhaps more important takeaway is that Analytical Innovators are not just seeing analytics as an important path to value. Instead, they are evolving and changing as organizations as a result of their experience with analytics". Refer - *Managing Information Transformation.*

Managing Knowledge - Intellectual Information and Transformational Cycle					
Shifting Preferences	Level 1	Level 2	Level 3	Level 4	Analytical Innovators
How Effective is Your Organization at the Following analytics - related tasks and activities? (Combines "Somewhat" & "Very Effective" responses)					
Analytical Innovators	20%	40%%	60%%	80%	100%
Abilty to Understand, Isolate and Capturing Information					
Ability to Interpret, thought work while Analyzing Information					
Demonstrated Competence, Experience, Aggregating - Integrating Information					
Developing Skills, Using Insights to Guide Future Strategies, Predictive Capabilities					
Knowledge Focused, Defining Sources, Recipients,Disseminating Information and Insights					
Analytical Innovators, Creators, Change Masters, Out of Box Analysts, Visionaries	20%	40%%	60%%	80%	100%
Analytical Innovators are effective at managing all stages of information transformation cycle, apturing data, analyzing information, aggregating and integrating data, using insights from analytics to guide future strategy disseminating Insights					

Figure 29 – Modified Managing Information Transformation - (David Kiron, Pamela Kirk Prentice and Renee Boucher Ferguson in "Innovating With Analytics", MIT SMR 2012)

Upfront, more ways than one - American Productivity and Quality paper states, "The leader of the organization-most often the CEO-is perhaps the most effective communicator of the importance and necessity of change to the work force. "A true leader has the confidence to stand alone, the courage to make tough decisions, and the compassion to listen to the needs of others. He does not set out to be a leader, but becomes one by the equality of his actions and the integrity of his intent" - Douglas MacArthur. The performance orientation is established at this stage and level. In fact, all best-practice organizations indicated that their CEOs plan and manage organizational change, thus serving as the change agents. "All of the great leaders have had one characteristic in common: it was the willingness to confront unequivocally the major anxiety of their people in their time. This, and not much else, is the essence of leadership" - John Kenneth Galbraith It usually is not enough for the CEO to develop and articulate a vision for the organization. For that vision to be implemented effectively, the CEO must plan and manage the process of change as well. That signals the importance of change throughout the organization and facilitates the congruence between the vision and the change process apart from connecting it to the organizational performance. "It is better to lead from behind and to put others in front, especially when you celebrate victory when nice things occur. You take the front line when there is danger. Then people will appreciate your leadership" - Nelson Mandela.

ICF Kaiser continues, "Of course, large organizations do not have just one leader; leaders are found in a variety of functions and levels, ranging from the CEO to department directors to specially created teams. Since leaders must understand their roles in managing and motivating change, education and development of these leaders becomes essential. All best-practice organizations indicated that formal education and training is an important element of the education programs designed to change their cultures".

Look at history! For example, The Rover Group in the 1990's trained all 3,000 of its managers to ensure they understood the leadership role expected of them. (Refer ICF Kaiser). This program was meant to be a precursor to a plan to bring in new products and services while getting teams to work well with one another. A program of 250 four-day courses, each opened and closed by an executive, was completed in less than three years all for the purpose of meeting common objectives, bring in alignment. At Arizona Public Service, 1,000 leaders attended 17 separate one-week "Focus" sessions to develop an understanding of the corporate strategic plan and sensitivity to cost management. Education alone, however, is not enough skill building has to be a way of life. "Men make history and not the other way around. In periods where there is no leadership, society stands still. Progress occurs when courageous, skillful leaders seize the opportunity to change things for the better" said Harry S. Truman. Organizations that successfully implement significant change reinforce, reward, realign, renew desirable behaviors of leaders and managers with appropriate changes to corporate infrastructure such as role awards, special assignments, identity slots, unique rewards, social teaming, performance appraisal, performance management, and compensation systems. "The challenge of leadership is to be strong, but not rude; be kind, but not weak; be bold, but not bully; be thoughtful, but not lazy; be humble, but not timid; be proud, but not arrogant; have humor, but without folly" said Jim Rohn. Managers and leaders who cannot or will not contribute positively to the change process are encouraged to leave the organization. In 2016, less than 50% of corporate organizations in the top Fortune 1000 have dedicated greater than 3 days of actual learning time off for all of their staff.

Integrity Challenges with Leadership disrupted - In "Liars", How Progressives Exploit Our Fears for Power and Control, author, Glenn Beck asks "why do we accept lies? Glenn Beck, #1 bestselling author and radio host, reveals, "the cold truth behind the ideology of progressivism and how the tenets of this dangerous belief system are eroding the foundation of this country. Politics is no longer about pointing to a shining city on the hill; it's about promising you a shiny new car for your driveway. The candidate who tells the people what they want to hear is usually the one who wins— facts be damned".

"Politicians may be sleazy and spineless, but they're not stupid. And in a digital world, take Donald Trump's example, sleaze hits the ceiling even before they become a substantive politician. They see that the way to win is by first telling people everything that is wrong with the world, and then painting a vision of the life they want—a Utopian vision that they'll create right here on earth, one where no one is ever sick or hungry, jobless, or homeless. They work on the fears of people and nurture it to their personal gain. It is the naïve and believers who continue to fall for this rhetoric. Donald Trump's response, "It is all by Clinton Campaign". Where was Clinton Campaign and Donald Trump in 2005 or 2010 when Trump did what he did? All we have to do is surrender our freedom and someone else's wallet and they'll make it happen. And so they continue to lie, and we continue to believe them, and they keep winning elections. The only way to break the cycle is to understand why Americans fall for the deception over and over again. Glenn Beck reveals the startlingly simple answer: fear. At our most basic level, we're all afraid of something. Progressives from both parties exploit this by first pointing out the things we should be afraid of, and then offering us "solutions" to these fears. Solutions that always require us to give up our freedoms. Solutions that are based on two things: lies, and an unrelenting hunger for power and control. In his signature no-holds-barred way, Beck destroys the false promises of Progressivism and takes us through its history, showing how each "wave" built up on the one before it, ultimately washing up to the beach in the form of Barack Obama, a statesman—and whoever is next".

J. Toward a Leadership disrupted Approach to Digital Culture Change

"A leader is one who knows the way, goes the way, and shows the way". John C. Maxwell. Leadership - How can an organizational leader know how to steer an appropriate course? "If your actions inspire others to dream more, learn more, do more and become more, you are a leader" asks John Quincy Adams. Leadership - This is not an easy task. "It is largely about character, ethics, and values". In the case of the private sector, the market seems to well reward a "tough-nosed" approach to downsizing, and in the case of the public sector, Republicans and Democrats vie for bragging rights over who can eliminate the jobs of the most bureaucrats. "The first responsibility of a leader is to define reality. The last is to say thank you. In between, the leader is a servant" says, Max DePree. In early 1996, a landmark journalistic account of the impact of restructuring impact on U.S. society-at-large (New York Times, 1996) and a Newsweek (1996) cover story lambasting corporate "greed heads" for their excessive profits gained at the expense of many lost jobs reflected more critical coverage than had previously been enjoyed by the corporate community. "My own definition of leadership is this - The capacity and the will to rally men and women to a common purpose and the character which inspires confidence" declares, General Montgomery. AT&T's Robert Allen also was criticized about his pay package of $16 million during 1995, the same year he set about to restructure 50,000 people out of their jobs (Pearl stein, 1996). Overall, however, the media have given quite friendly coverage to downsizing. A leader may have to look beyond external rewards and media coverage to determine how to approach downsizing and related issues. John Wooden writes, "While you, the leader, can teach many things, character is not taught easily to adults who arrive at your desk lacking it. Be cautious about taking on reclamation projects regardless of the talent they may possess. Have the courage to make character count among the qualities you seek in others."

Develop Intellect - "Talent development is an important element of the culture at digitally maturing organizations, which place a decisive emphasis on developing existing talent and recruiting new talent — 76% of respondents from digitally maturing companies say their companies provide resources and opportunities to develop digital acumen. However, only 14% of employees at early-stage companies and 44% at developing companies say that their organizations do. Not surprisingly, 71% of employees at maturing companies say their organization's employees have sufficient knowledge and ability to execute their organization's digital strategy. Only 22% of respondents from early-stage companies make the same claim. Digitally maturing organizations emphasize developing existing talent and recruiting new talent, while early-stage companies are more likely to hire contractors and consultants". Further, Cultivating Digital Talent and Leaders continues to be a priority in this research says Gerald C Kane Et all. Refer - *Digital Life Cycle Development*. In, July 2016 MIT SMR issue, "Aligning the Organization for its Digital Future", Ge Kane, Doug Palmer, Anh Nguyen Phillips, David Kiron and Natasha Buckley, write again, "Digitally maturing companies are also significantly better able to attract new talent based on their use of digital — 71% of respondents from digitally maturing companies say so versus only 10% of those from early-stage organizations, which tend to rely on contractors and consultants to support their digital efforts". This means that the culture is shaped by those responsible for organizational direction and results, and created in the pursuit of this. This involves setting the standards of attitudes, values, behavior and belief that everyone is required to subscribe to as a condition of joining the organization. Policies are produced so that everyone knows where they stand, and these are underpinned by extensive induction and orientation programs and training schemes. Procedures and sanctions are there to ensure that these standards continue to be met. Organizations with very specific cultures are not all things to all people: many, indeed, make a virtue of their particular approach of 'Many are called but few are chosen'. High levels of internalization of shared values are required. Other perceptions emerge from this. Feelings of confidence, trust and respect are created, Individual response to the level of organization commitment that is evident in this approach tends to be high.

Digital Life Cycle Development					
Low to High Quartile Analysis	1st Quartile	2nd Quartile	3rd Quartile	4th Quartile	Outlier
Digital Life Cycle	Start Up	Growth	Transforming	Evolved	Challenged
Human Company	Talent Focus	Retention Thinking	New Talent Profiles	Developed Talent	Poor Attraction
Institution	Policy Focus	Execution Drive	Independent Thinking	Collaborative Build	Structural Conflicts
Competing Enterprise	Builder	Technical Expertise	Benchmark	Best Practices	Lack Digital Thinking
Learning Corporation	Pro Active	Symbiotic Identities	Perceptive	Dynamic Virtual Reality	Pedantic

Figure 30 – Digital Life Cycle Development - Aligning The Organization to its Digital Future

Talent Gap - "As a result, a talent gap is developing for early-stage companies. While these companies need digital talent to help them advance digitally, their lack of progress restricts their ability to bring in that talent. San Francisco-based Salesforce.com Inc. provides the resources and opportunities for its employees to thrive in a digital environment", continue Gerald C Kane Et all. Refer - *Digital Barriers by Maturity Levels* "The cloud-computing company drives continuous learning and skill development through an online platform offering courses that cover its products and particular jobs and roles. When employees complete a course, they receive a badge. But the badges are more than token rewards. The badges also appear in the employee's profile on the company's internal social collaboration site, which helps employees identify people in the company with specific expertise and can be used as part of an employee's performance evaluation. Cancer Treatment Centers of America Inc. is another example. The for-profit hospital network, headquartered in Boca Raton, Florida, offers a mix of in-person, online, and on-demand digital-skills training that fits the schedules and work realities of its busy medical professionals". This is where the culture is formed by the staff (and staff groups) rather than directed by the organization. The result is that people think, believe and act according to the pressures and priorities of their peers and pursue their own agenda. This is clearly fraught with difficulties and dangers: organizations that allow this happen will succeed only if the aims and objectives of the staff coincide absolutely with their own. It leads to the staff setting their own informal procedures and sanctions, or operating formally in ways that suit their own purposes rather than those of the organization. Individuals and groups, again, are not all things to all people; they may and do reject those who refuse to abide by the norms and values that they have set for themselves. According to CIO Kristin Darby, a key component is "at-the-elbow" training. "We will do personal training with physicians anywhere from 6:30 in the morning to 8:00 at night," she says. "We make sure our trainers can be there when it's most appropriate for our doctors." When indispensable employees don't have the time to come to training to develop the necessary skills to operate in an increasingly digital health care environment, the company takes the training to them.

306

When developing employees for success in digital environments, business leaders place a greater emphasis on change skills than on technology knowledge. In an open-ended question, we asked respondents which employee skills were most central to success in a digital workplace. A change-oriented mindset (e.g., willing to embrace change, be flexible, adaptable, and curious) emerged as the most important (38%), followed by digital and technology literacy (27%), and strategic thinking (16%). "Companies are looking for people who have a balance of technical and soft skills," says Restuccia of Burning Glass Technologies. "Today, people with deep technical knowledge are expected to have solid skills in areas such as communication."

	Digital Barriers by Maturity Levels					
Low to High Quartile Analysis	1st Quartile	2nd Quartile	3rd Quartile	4th Quartile	Outlier	Low to High Quartile Analysis
Org Models	Start Up	Growth	Transforming	Evolved	Challenged	Digital Life Cycle
Human Company	Alternate Strategies, Many Players, Multiple thinkers	Understanding What to do - Building Capability	Stretched on Conflicting Priorities _ Dynamics	Sharp Strategic Focus - Markets, Tech, Clients, People driven	No Alternate Strategy - Non Programmed dead ends	Top Barriers by Stages of Stakeholder Maturity Cycle an Organizational Model Context
Institution	Pushing for Focus _ engagement and direction	Enabling Processes - Battling Buraucracy	Independent Thinking - Autonomy Stresses	Sticking to Chosen Path, Inflexible	Diffused focus - Dissipated Energy	
Competing Enterprise	Narrowing Competitive Landscape	Delivering Competing Products & Services	Creative Innovations Beyiond Patterns	Uncertainity Avoidance Dynamic Reactions	Multiple Paths - Turn Tables	
Learning Corporation	Systemic Bureaucracy	Enabling Technical	Disruptive Learnings	Entreneurial Freedom	Systemic Derailment	

Figure 31 – Digital Barriers by Maturity Levels

In a Forrester report, "Recruit And Retain Top Digital Talent, by Martin Gill July 6, 2015, Build Your employer Brand To secure Top Digital Talent" the author identifies, "eBusiness leaders must engage their human resources (HR) colleagues to include the digital credentials of their teams in their firm's employer branding activities. But this isn't a one-off activity. Communicating your digital strategy vision externally can be a great way of attracting candidates.

- *In The Battle for Talent, Networking Is more critical Than ever Before* tools like *algorithmic candidate search are beginning to disrupt recruitment, but many eBusiness professionals nd that the best candidates come from word of mouth and recommendations. Proactively maintaining connections to potential recruits is more important than ever.*

- *Being A Desirable Digital employer means more Than A cool location* - CEO in a *digital hub like New York can certainly help, but leading digital employers must focus more on creating the correct work environment to attract and retain talent. this means providing employees with the tools, environment, and freedom to innovate, learn, and grow".*

Managing talent is one critical sub culture in people management aspects of culture. Sub-cultures exist in all organizations. They relate to membership of different groups and vary between these (for example, in the state of openness of dealings between members). Sub-cultures become more destructive when they operate contrary to absolute standards. Forms of this are as set out below. The canteen culture, whereby the shared values adopted are those of groups that gather away from the work situations and in such places as the washroom or canteen. Elite's and cliques, whereby strength and primacy is present in some groups at the expense of others. This leads to over mightiness. It affects operations when the elites and cliques are able to command resources, carry out projects and gain prestige at the expense of others; to lobby effectively for resources at the expense of others; and to gain favour at the expense of others. Work regulation, whereby the volume and quality of work is regulated by the group for its own ends rather than those of the organization; when it sets and works to its own targets which are at variance with those of the organization. Informal norming, whereby individuals are pressurized to adopt the attitudes and values of those around them rather than those of the organization. This occurs most when the organizations own norms are not sufficiently strong or structured to remove the local or group pressure.

The author Martin Gill continues, "Digital Mastery Demands a new Breed of employee - "The scope and responsibilities of today's digital teams are more complex than ever before. a range of external pressures in influence digital teams, changing the nature of the skills they need to succeed and therefore the kind of talent they must recruit into key roles. successful teams require a complex mix of business acumen, strategic in influence, stakeholder management, and deep technical knowledge. eBusiness teams can't just focus on strategic issues; they must also maintain foundational digital competencies, like search optimization or online merchandizing." However, even if acceptance of managerial responsibility is achieved, change is not easy. If an aggressive management style, backed up by rigorous policing and controls, is simply 'switched off', there is more than a chance that, for a period at least, abuse by employees will be rife. An organization may be able to wait for the changed policies to take effect, but there will be many organizations that financially or politically cannot afford the risk. If the organization works well and is successful and profitable, the manager will rightly be wary of change that may impair rather than improve effectiveness. These two difficulties (employee attitudes to change and the risk of failure) explain why many of the companies that have managed to make significant achievements did so from a position of near disaster. Starting Armageddon in the face can concentrate the attention of managers and employees, which facilitates cultural bread with the past and the ushering in of a new era. For the same reason, many companies operating within a HR framework are on 'Greenfield' sites. They build the desired culture completely form new, even though they behave in their old ways at their other locations! "Senior management can be kidding itself when it comes to corporate culture. A recent study of organizational culture showed a startling disparity between the perceptions of senior management and other employees. "Just as the nature of teams is changing, so are your potential employees. Back before the dot-com boom, a steady job in management consultancy or investment banking was the de facto career path for the average business school graduate. But digital disruption has spawned a new generation of startups, and top digital leaders don't dream of a corner of CEO and a parking spot with their name on it. now, top talent want to make a difference. in this shifting ecosystem, eBusiness leaders face some stark challenges as they try to recruit and retain the best employees. namely:

› *Business education doesn't build digital talent. Digital business leadership demands a heady mix of business and technology skills, and while some visionary academic institutions are evolving, many business schools aren't building tomorrow's digital leaders. a select few are leading by example: institutes like Cornell tech are reinventing the MBA program to teach a blend of business strategy and digital skills, with mixed classes of business and computer science graduates working together. But these institutions are still far from the norm.*

This theme refers to what people consider the major goal of their company. But it also includes the specific realization s of this goal in the form of concrete accomplishments. This theme expresses both the members' past and current intention to head towards this ideal and to bring about the desired results. This theme also comprises specific examples that indicate that the goal has been and is being realized. The goal of building a successful and stable company was considered a major innovation or change. Here organizational members felt that the company could be more successful under stable conditions.

› ***Personal motivation isn't purely monetary.*** *employees' expectations of their employers and their careers are changing, but contrary to popular stereotype, this isn't just an age thing. a recent IBM study showed that the attitudes and desires of Millennials aren't fundamentally different to those of older employees no matter what their age, most employees' primary work motivation is to make a positive impact on their organization. they value collaboration, they want the freedom to work whenever and wherever they want, and they expect access to technologies that help them in the workplace.*

The personal motivation theme strategy comprises innovations that show how the goal of building a successful and stable company has been and is being accomplished. It expresses the means by which the goal is being attained. "Controlled profitable growth while coping with new attitudes and millennial disposition" is the overarching intended strategy. This is usually done through closer monitoring of performance expectation, value alignment or conflicts, efficiency views on work, profitable sales etc… this could be as simple as finding a niche and maintaining and expanding it.

› ***The in-demand technology skills are constantly changing.*** *technology skills are always in demand, and many teams report being under-resourced when it comes to technical skills. But the nature of the skills firms need is constantly changing target. as one eBusiness professional told us, "ten years ago, front-end developers were people who hadn't succeeded at being real developers — now they are the most in demand."*

The theme techno structure refers to structural aspects, tech skills and formal procedures of the company. These provide the conditions that enable the achievement of the major intended goal and the realization of the general strategy. The rules and procedures standardize administrative work and assist in day-to-day activities concerning business models, performance goals, finances, accounting, information, control, and human resource systems.

› ***The recruitment ecosystem has yet to leverage the best of digital.*** *recruitment is on the cusp of digital disruption. Just as business has entered the age of the customer, arguably, recruitment is entering the age of the candidate. Websites like Glassdoor and LinkedIn empower candidates with more information than ever about potential employers, allowing them to reach out directly to people they want to work with, regardless of whether they are hiring or not. What's more, data-driven recruitment tools like Linkedin's "People you Might Want to hire" algorithmic search is only just starting to show potential.".*

This theme comprises management's attitude toward and relation with potential employees. Their special orientation is expressed in formal human resource systems as well as informally in daily activities. This also involves fair treatment of candidates, that is based on an implicit social contract of mutual exchange. Another aspect is independence and responsibility – the notion that the overall goal of building a successful and stable company can only be accomplished if everybody does his or her share in attracting and retaining talent.

Millennials Dominate - "I'm a social creature—both online and offline." Although both generations value personal connections, U.S. Millennials use technology to connect with a greater number of people, more frequently, and in real time. Millennials use social-media platforms more than non-Millennials (79 percent versus 59 percent), and they maintain significantly larger networks: 46 percent have 200 or more "friends" on Facebook, compared with 19 percent of non-Millennials. Millennials feel that they are missing out when they're not up to date with social-media chatter, and they feel validated when the community "likes" their posts. When it comes to making purchases, Millennials are far more likely than non-Millennials to favor brands that have Facebook pages and mobile websites (33 percent versus 17 percent). They overwhelmingly agree (47 percent versus 28 percent) that their lives feel richer when they're connected to people through social media. This desire for connection and shared experience also extends offline. Millennials are much more likely than non-Millennials to engage in group activities—especially with people outside their immediate family. They dine, shop, and travel with friends and coworkers, to whom they look for validation that they've made the right decisions. This can be good news for retailers and restaurants, since groups of consumers tend to spend more money than people who are by themselves. Smart companies are using location-based shopping services such as Foursquare and Shopkick to capitalize on this trend". People express their concern about the work environment either in terms of avoiding any kind of "bottlenecks" or in terms of facilitating work processes. This usually has an effect on employees' satisfaction at work. It is also worth touching on another basic problem. People processes in all its aspects sees *the organization as the purpose*. Everything is done to achieve the corporate mission. Employee development may be laudable and it may be significant, but it is not altruistic – the plans are established and it may be significant, but it is not altruistic – the plans are established and carried out because they benefit the organization. Here again differentiating expectations would decipher additional Millennial understanding. There will be those for whom the emphasis on the common interest between the employer and the employed is unacceptable. There are also those who believe that there are limits to the extent of personal fulfillment that can be achieved in an economic or working environment. One advantage of limited horizons is that the modest aspirant can hope to achieve them within their own sphere of accountability. Since HR is based on questioning and rebuilding the culture and molding every employee plan, it requires involvement at the highest levels of power in the organization. It is very interesting that many well-known adaptation strategies have been the brainchildren of the Chief Executive, examples here could be Google, Facebook, Workday, Mindtree, Twitter, Airbnb and so on. In, a BCG Research Report of 2012, "The Millennial Consumer Debunking Stereotypes" authors Christine Barton (BCG), Jeff Fromm (Share Like Buy), Chris Egan (Service Management Group), continue, "I can make the world a better place." The generation that was taught to recycle in kindergarten wants to be good to the planet and believes that collective action can make a difference. Millennials believe that working for causes is an integral part of life, and they are drawn to big issues. Instead of making one-off charitable donations in cash or in kind, they're more likely to integrate their causes into daily life by buying products that support sustainable farming or "fair trade" principles, or by joining large movements that aim to solve social or environmental problems. Our survey found that Millennials, more than non-Millennials, prefer to actively engage in a cause campaign by encouraging others to support it (30 percent versus 22 percent) or by participating in fundraising events (27 percent versus 16 percent)".

"Maturing digital organizations build skills to realize the strategy. Digitally maturing organizations are four times more likely to provide employees with needed skills than are organizations at lower ends of the spectrum. Consistent with our overall findings, the ability to conceptualize how digital technologies can impact the business is a skill lacking in many companies at the early stages of digital maturity. **Employees want to work for digital leaders.** Across age groups from 22 to 60, the vast majority of respondents want to work for digitally enabled organizations. Employees will be on the lookout for the best digital opportunities, and businesses will have to continually up their digital game to retain and attract them". Refer - *"Strategy, not technology drives digital transformation", Gerald C Kane, Doug Palmer, et all, in MIT SMR 2015.* Many organizations start out with exciting ideas and concepts, but as they grow they lose the culture that made them successful. Other businesses manage to continue growing and keep the culture they created. What separates one type of organization from the other? One of the key factors to keep business culture is to define the culture you want to create from the beginning, and integrate it into how you hire people, how you treat employees, the type of customer service you provide, and the general environment of your organization. As you grow it is important to integrate old employees who understand your values, concepts, and culture with the newer employees who will learn to implement them and bring some of their own culture.

While "moralism" in the study of culture and leadership is best resisted, there are still many leaders who wish to acknowledge a certain responsibility for the "moral" or "spiritual" fabric of the life of their organizations. "The most dangerous leadership myth is that leaders are born-that there is a genetic factor to leadership. That's nonsense; in fact, the opposite is true. Leaders are made rather than born". Warren Bennis. For those persons, the following partisan and unscientific comments are offered. A leader needs to examine just how well the course of downsizing action being proposed fits with the values and beliefs he/she would like to see carried forward. That may require a certain amount of introspection. It may require putting to the side, at least temporarily, the brilliant technical rationale for reductions provided by his/her external management consultants. "The best executive is the one who has sense enough to pick good men to do what he wants done, and self-restraint enough to keep from meddling with them while they do it", said, Theodore Roosevelt

In order to effectively provide a conceptual background to the survey feedback and to facilitate content study, the we have constructed specific definitions pertaining to the following:

K. The Digital Culture Model – Built around 8 Org Models, 8 Leadership disrupted Styles and 4 Organizational Culture

8 types of Organization and Management Models. - OMM
8 types of Leadership disrupted Styles. - LSM
4 types of Organizational Cultures based on Edgar Schein model of 3 cultures. – OCM and the Digital Culture.

The definitions (organization and Leadership disrupted) provided below for critical for the survey feedback and content analysis used while interviewing or studying organizations and their leaders. The definitions enabled us to type organizations and classify them into various categories of organizations or leadership disrupted styles. Thereafter we super imposed the leadership disrupted style on these organizations and studied them for their appropriate culture.

Organizational and Management Model (OMM M1) – Model 1 to connect its relevance to leadership disrupted style as it impacts culture. An appropriate forced rankIng instrument was used to a small sample to obtain respondent ranks - **(Driver, Focus, Action, Long term)**

311

Human Organization

- Driven by orientation to people, their actions, beliefs in the value of human good and concerns
- Focus on making people productive through internal drivers without clarity on final goals and tasks
- Action through policies, rewards, interactive processes, job design making people an important consideration in organizational issues
- Long term organization growth, meaning profits, shareholder value meant people growth

Learning Company

- Driven by organizational energy to learn, self-develop, share learning, build coalitions, drive collaboration through learning, find goals, perpetuate individualization as they grow to compete
- Focus on people productivity through learning drivers, formal processes to learn, learner profile, styles on what can be done should be done
- Action through making knowledge, technology, enablers an important performance parameter
- Long term competitive advantage through focus on performance empowerment

The Institution

- Driven by structural effectiveness, procedural clarity, defined end states and eventual success of people and the systems that lasts over time
- Focus on enterprise success on a holistic basis and dependent on people expertise
- Action through making systems the critical consideration for organizational effectiveness
- Long term orientation to building an enterprise that works through economics cycles without a major emphasis on revitalization or renewal

Competing Organization

- Driven by the need for internal and external energy to perform and focus on results
- Focus on organizational vision, values, philosophy and performance
- Action through making people subservient to systems and external stimuli
- Long Term competitive advantage seen as dominance and measures that sustain organizational competitiveness

Organization and Management Model (OMM M2)- Model 2 to connect its relevance to leadership disrupted style as it impacts culture. An appropriate forced ranking instrument was used to test on the sample to obtain respondent ranks - (Driver, Focus, Action, Long term)

Voluntary School

- Driven by conscious endeavor to support a cause that extends beyond commercial perspective in many situations
- Focus through driving synergies of the people and process systems that integrate organizational goals to an end objective
- Action orientation measured by appropriate planning, measured steps, building consensus and reasonable task orientation

- Long term goals to build sustainable business models that can seamlessly move from one situation to another without a strong immediate task and performance pressure

Intellectual Company

- Driven by the need to promote and perpetuate intellect as it determines individual and organizational means and tasks.
- Focus on delivery through advancement of learning, knowledge, skills but lacks need for attitudes and appropriate behavior to make things happen
- Action driven by merciless meritocracy and rewards to processes and systems that goes beyond human dependence
- Long Term sustainability only based on enhanced intellectual capital, innovation and newness of things done within and without the organization.

Mechanistic corporation

- Driven by the successes, stories, rituals and processes that have proved in time that it works and should be followed
- Focus on building internal architectures, systems and processes that drives individual and team performance
- Action orientation is expected to be more an outcome given smooth working methods and competitive pressures built within the organizational framework.
- Long Term need to make teams work together to achieve group goals that achieves today's performance and tomorrow's systems.

Performing Enterprise

- Driven by business bottom line, financial focus and the need to achieve tasks and goals established to be accomplished
- Focus on driving results through structure, style, roles, benchmarks as it impacts organizational effectiveness
- Action to demonstrate what finally matters in the organization, the stakes involved and reward and punishment that follows post action
- Long Term destination treated as an end in itself and pursuit of the goals set as non-negotiable and that it should be accepted and achieved by all internal stakeholders.

Leadership disrupted Style Model 1 (LSM 1) as it impacts cultural formation in the organization and management model. An appropriate forced ranking instrument was used to test the sample to obtain respondent ranks - (Driver, Focus, Action, Long term)

People Strategist

- Driven need to motivate and keep people in the right frame of mind to be productive and happy
- Focus on creating people oriented systems that enable a culture that brings individuals, teams and organizations together
- Action oriented to demonstrate by action that concern for people enables organizations to perform above expectation

- Long Term orientation to delivering value through people development, individualized tasks, creating an environment that is self-exhilarating

Teacher

- Driven by the need to make people, processes and systems learn from one another, interact to make a meaningful whole and are constantly seeking holistic behavior from organizational systems
- Focus through clear policy perspectives and on delivering intellectual and performance value that sponsors native instincts, creative pursuits, feedback and review processes and encourages actions that facilitates results
- Action oriented towards developing people competencies, ensures organizational competitiveness is appropriately managed by right people and makes organizational goals subservient to competency development
- Long Term vision to build an organizational that can culturally sustain itself to renew, learn, contribute in varying life cycles and has adequate organizational energy to grow with momentum. "The best swordsman in the world doesn't need to fear the second best swordsman in the world; no, the person for him to be afraid of is some ignorant antagonist who has never had a sword in his hand before; he doesn't do the thing he ought to do, and so the expert isn't prepared for him; he does the thing he ought not to do and often it catches the expert out and ends him on the spot." - Mark Twain

Builder

- Driven by encouraging things to be worked out, provides job clarity, coaches and rewards for performance
- Focus on building for the future through Institutional Corporate processes, demanding systems that connect organizational functions and works through structures that are streamlined, regulated and planned
- Action oriented through appropriateness of actions driven by circumstance, enabling learning to be documented, creates knowledge sharing atmosphere, drives decisions through consensus and takes meaningful time to accomplish tasks
- Long Term desire to make lasting organizations that can stream through economic and business life cycles and does not have the pressure to retain performance under all circumstance.

Visionary

- Driven by sharing strategic goals, communicates, shares values, distinctive concern for individual sensitivity and demonstrated by examples
- Focus on collaboration, business models that are appropriate and accepted by people and goals that have been worked to individual and organizational advantage
- Action oriented to make people believe in the overall good, establishes concreteness to tasks to be accomplished
- Long Term priority to build organizational wealth, individual intellect, collective wisdom, sustainable business model and overall organizational effectiveness parameters.

Leadership disrupted Style Model 2 (LSM 2) as it impacts cultures formation in organization and management model. An appropriate forced ranking instrument was used to a small sample obtain respondent ranks - (Driver, Focus, Action, Long term)

Manager

- Driven by institutionalizing policies that provide clarity to goals, tasks and manages a team through maintaining status quo through conflicting circumstance and taking decisions that involve retaining established norms and practices
- Focus on building loyalty through establishing people oriented systems that enable handling tasks that are individually focused
- Action oriented to enable easy and smooth management of the organization, streamlines administrative processes, establishes a string back office operations organization and manages customer oriented roles through follow procedure route.
- Long Term desire to make organizational working built on strong fundamentals of bureaucracy, frameworks and management styles.

Scientist

- Driven by the urge to create, make actions intellectually dominant, treats developmental processes a predominant organizational factor and is willing to compromise for nothing other than intellectual superiority in actions
- Focus on attracting and nurturing talent, systems and processes that are of utility today and tomorrow, more tomorrow, and is willing to absorb the costs of human and organizational process costs as a necessary condition of managing the human mind
- Action oriented to demonstrate merit and results supersedes all other performance factors, does not believe in means as an important consideration while acting upon information and manages rewards as a necessary evil in people management processes
- Long Term desire to create a self-propelling organization that has internal renewal capability to prod organizational performance, individual effectiveness and shareholder satisfaction

Technocrat

- Driven by engineering sciences, that technology provides solutions to complex organizational problems and believes in logic and rationality as desired attitudes
- Focus on adding technical and functional values to business situations enables competency development that is vertical and incisive and promotes organizations to drive business through technological excellence
- Action through individualized working, avoiding teams and consequent inefficiencies, meets deadlines under all circumstance and seeks the best
- Long Term desire to make people processes subservient to technological processes and works towards eliminating elaborate actions that involve meetings, group work, communication forums and large scale explanation to actions

Driver

- Driven by a performance system that overrides all other considerations and makes individual targets an important element achieving results

- Focus on priorities that are determined quickly, followed through decisively and ensures that different parts of the organization are focused on their own deliverables
- Action oriented to provide criteria for success and failures and ensures it is adequately communicated and holds accountability on streamlined systemic norms
- Long Term orientation to retain competitive advantage by providing profitability through consistent intervals and prefers revenue to growth.

A scenario-based analysis was undertaken to study the influence of leadership on the culture of an organization. Each of the scenarios was presented to the study sample and their comments were noted. The scenarios were constructed to provide study material to, for example, a matrix on how do organizational models, culture and leadership integrate with one another.

Example: In organization X defined as a Human Organization, People Strategist is the preferred leadership disrupted style, which in turn influences an executive culture. Or in a Learning Company, the Teacher is a preferred leadership disrupted style and influences both the Executive and Engineering culture. Those all-4 cultures tend to be possible in a Competing Organization that has a Visionary leadership.

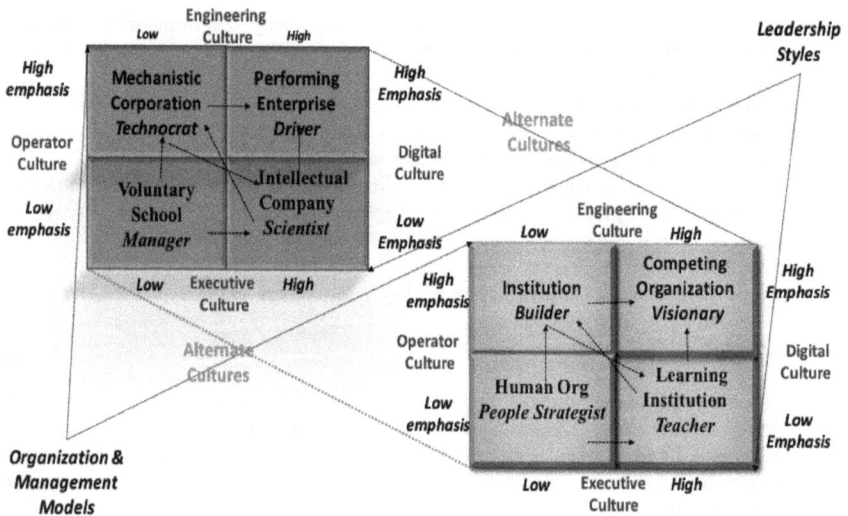

Figure 32 – Defining Digital Culture - Integrating Organizations with Culture & Leadership disrupted

L. The Digital Company - Culture as it Impacts Org Formation (Model Details)

Model 1 focused on four types of organizational models through (Driver, Focus, Action, Long term) being: (Refer - *Defining Digital Culture - Integrating Organizations with Culture & Leadership disrupted*).

1. Human Organization
- Driven by orientation to people, their actions, beliefs in the value of human good and concerns
- Focus on making people productive through internal drivers without clarity on final goals and tasks
- Action through policies, rewards, interactive processes, job design making people an important consideration in organizational issues
- Long term organization growth, meaning profits, shareholder value meant people growth

2. Learning Company
- Driven by organizational energy to learn, self-develop, perpetuate individualization as they grow to compete
- Focus on people productivity through learning drivers on what can be done should be done
- Action through making knowledge an important performance parameter
- Long term competitive advantage through focus on performance empowerment

3. Institution
- Driven by structural effectiveness, procedural clarity, defined end states and eventual success of people and the systems that lasts over time
- Focus on enterprise success on a holistic basis and dependent on people expertise
- Action through making systems the critical consideration for organizational effectiveness
- Long term orientation to building an enterprise that works through economics cycles without a major emphasis on revitalization or renewal

4. Competing Organization
- Driven by the need for internal and external energy to perform and focus on results
- Focus on organizational vision, values, philosophy and performance
- Action through making people subservient to systems and external stimuli
- Long Term competitive advantage seen as dominance and measures that sustain organizational competitiveness

Model 2 focused on yet another four types of organizational models as an effective comparator:

1. Voluntary School
- Driven by conscious endeavor to support a cause that extends beyond commercial perspective in many situations
- Focus through driving synergies of the people and process systems that integrate organizational goals to an end objective
- Action orientation measured by appropriate planning, measured steps, building consensus and reasonable task orientation
- Long term goals to build sustainable business models that can seamlessly move from one situation to another without a strong immediate task and performance pressure

2. Intellectual Company
- Driven by the need to promote and perpetuate intellect as it determines individual and organizational means and tasks.

- Focus on delivery through advancement of learning, knowledge, skills but lacks need for attitudes and appropriate behavior to make things happen
- Action driven by merciless meritocracy and rewards to processes and systems that goes beyond human dependence
- Long Term sustainability only based on enhanced intellectual capital, innovation and newness of things done within and without the organization.

3. Mechanistic corporation
- Driven by the successes, stories, rituals and processes that have proved in time that it works and should be followed
- Focus on building internal architectures, systems and processes that drives individual and team performance
- Action orientation is expected to be more an outcome given smooth working methods and competitive pressures built within the organizational framework.
- Long Term need to make teams work together to achieve group goals that achieves today's performance and tomorrow's systems.

4. Performing Enterprise
- Driven by business bottom line, financial focus and the need to achieve tasks and goals established to be accomplished
- Focus on driving results through structure, style, roles, benchmarks as it impacts organizational effectiveness
- Action to demonstrate what finally matters in the organization, the stakes involved and reward and punishment that follows post action
- Long Term destination treated as an end in itself and pursuit of the goals set as non-negotiable and that it should be accepted and achieved by all internal stakeholders.

Org Scenarios to Test for Leadership and its Influence on Org Culture in the Intellectual Company. Leadership as it impacts cultural formation in the organization

In addition, the research also used an appropriate leadership influence model as it impacts formation of cultures in a pre-defined organization as shown below:

Model 1: The first model defined it as:

1. People Strategist
- **Driven** need to motivate and keep people in the right frame of mind to be productive and happy
- **Focus** on creating people oriented systems that enable a culture that brings individuals, teams and organizations together
- **Action oriented** to demonstrate by action that concern for people enables organizations to perform above expectation
- **Long Term orientation** to delivering value through people development, individualized tasks, creating an environment that is self-exhilarating

2. Teacher
- **Driven** by the need to make people, processes and systems learn from one another, interact to make a meaningful whole and are constantly seeking holistic behavior from organizational systems

- **Focus** through clear policy perspectives and on delivering intellectual and performance value that sponsors native instincts, creative pursuits, feedback and review processes and encourages actions that facilitates results
- **Action** oriented towards developing people competencies, ensures organizational competitiveness is appropriately managed by right people and makes organizational goals subservient to competency development
- **Long Term** vision to build an organizational that can culturally sustain itself to renew, learn, contribute in varying life cycles and has adequate organizational energy to grow with momentum

3. Builder

- Driven by encouraging things to be worked out, provides job clarity, coaches and rewards for performance
- Focus on building for the future through Institutional Corporate processes, demanding systems that connect organizational functions and works through structures that are streamlined, regulated and planned
- Action oriented through appropriateness of actions driven by circumstance, enabling learning to be documented, creates knowledge sharing atmosphere, drives decisions through consensus and takes meaningful time to accomplish tasks
- Long Term desire to make lasting organizations that can stream through economic and business life cycles and does not have the pressure to retain performance under all circumstance.

4. Visionary

- Driven by sharing strategic goals, communicates, shares values, distinctive concern for individual sensitivity and demonstrated by examples
- Focus on collaboration, business models that are appropriate and accepted by people and goals that have been worked to individual and organizational advantage
- Action oriented to make people believe in the overall good, establishes concreteness to tasks to be accomplished
- Long Term priority to build organizational wealth, individual intellect, collective wisdom, sustainable business model and overall organizational effectiveness parameters.

Model 2: And, the second model in leadership defined it as:

1. Manager

- Driven by institutionalizing policies that provide clarity to goals, tasks and manages a team through maintaining status quo through conflicting circumstance and taking decisions that involve retaining established norms and practices
- Focus on building loyalty through establishing people oriented systems that enable handling tasks that are individually focused
- Action oriented to enable easy and smooth management of the organization, streamlines administrative processes, establishes a string back office operations organization and manages customer oriented roles through follow procedure route.
- Long Term desire to make organizational working built on strong fundamentals of bureaucracy, frameworks and management styles.

2. Scientist

- Driven by the urge to create, make actions intellectually dominant, treats developmental processes a predominant organizational factor and is willing to compromise for nothing other than intellectual superiority in actions
- Focus on attracting and nurturing talent, systems and processes that are of utility today and tomorrow, more tomorrow, and is willing to absorb the costs of human and organizational process costs as a necessary condition of managing the human mind
- Action oriented to demonstrate merit and results supersedes all other performance factors, does not believe in means as an important consideration while acting upon information and manages rewards as a necessary evil in people management processes
- Long Term desire to create a self-propelling organization that has internal renewal capability to prod organizational performance, individual effectiveness and shareholder satisfaction

3. Technocrat
- Driven by engineering sciences, that technology provides solutions to complex organizational problems and believes in logic and rationality as desired attitudes
- Focus on adding technical and functional values to business situations enables competency development that is vertical and incisive and promotes organizations to drive business through technological excellence
- Action through individualized working, avoiding teams and consequent inefficiencies, meets deadlines under all circumstance and seeks the best
- Long Term desire to make people processes subservient to technological processes and works towards eliminating elaborate actions that involve meetings, group work, communication forums and large scale explanation to actions

4. Driver
- Driven by a performance system that overrides all other considerations and makes individual targets an important element achieving results
- Focus on priorities that are determined quickly, followed through decisively and ensures that different parts of the organization are focused on their own deliverables
- Action oriented to provide criteria for success and failures and ensures it is adequately communicated and holds accountability on streamlined systemic norms
- Long Term orientation to retain competitive advantage by providing profitability through consistent intervals and prefers revenue to growth.

A scenario-based analysis was undertaken to study the influence of leadership on the culture of an organization. Each of the scenarios was presented to the research sample and their comments were noted. The scenarios were constructed to provide research material to, for example, a matrix on how do organizational models, culture and leadership integrate with one another.

Chapter 8

Emergence of a Digital Culture

Effectively multiple organization and management models have been identified as discerning features of organizations through this study and as they impact organizations. These organization models provide a framework for the study to connect organizational culture to leadership and particularly as they relate to organizations themselves. Organization structure and design involves all of the above and also additional factors such as leadership, culture, power and other human resource dynamics. Organization design involves concepts, clarity, roles, decisions about the configuration of the formal – organic organizational arrangements, including the formal structures, linkages, processes, and systems that make up an organization. The goal of an organization designer is to develop and implement an architecture of organizational arrangements that will, over time, lead to congruence, or good fit, among all the components of the organization: strategy, work flows, people, communication flows, informal organization and the formal organizational arrangements. Organizational capabilities are the unique ways in which each organization structures its work and motivates its people to achieve clearly articulated strategic objectives. These capabilities combine an organization's core competencies – technological innovation, customer focus, low-cost manufacturing of high-quality products – with the ability to sustain and adapt those competencies in the fulfillment of long-term objectives despite changing competition, altered strategies, and the loss of key employees. Good organization architecture requires a balance between the technical requirements, human dynamics and strategic demands of the organization or the business unit. The goal of an organization designer is to develop and implement an architecture of organizational arrangements that will, over time, lead to congruence, or good fit, among all the components of the organization: strategy, work flows, people, communication flows, informal organization and the formal organizational arrangements. Organization's articulation of its strategy, goals and its implication for the organization design. For example – if one of the objectives of the organization is to enhance customer focus, the structure will need to have specific teams to focus on the customer or the study of environmental trends (both macro and industry or sector specific) and its implication for the structure or deregulation in the utilities sector globally. This has led to changes in the business model with breakup of erstwhile integrated monoliths or in some instances diversification of companies like BELL. Another example could be the growth of the internet as an additional business channel either with the suppliers or customer. While pure play digital companies are creating new structures, the challenge is greater for hitherto brick and mortar. In all of the above examples convergence of organizational models with structure and change has been a common thread.

A. *Story of a Digital Organizational Culture*
B. *Define Organization and Management Models*
C. *Discovering Leadership disrupted Styles*
D. *Digital Learnings*
E. *Scenario Analysis*
F. *Role of Leadership disrupted - Creating Cultures – Map to The Intellectual Company*
G. *Is there an IDEAL Organizational and Management Model?*
H. *Trends and Leading Practices*

A. Story of a Digital Organizational Culture

The **Digital organization values history and tradition.** The origins of the organization; the aims and objectives of the first owners and managers, and their philosophy and values; the regard in which these are currently held; the ways in which they have developed. The promoter's business philosophy, the tales of the great grandfathers, stories of what happened on the same issue 20 years back and so on. The organization is built upon stories that lasts over time and that is believed and revered by people as important learning of the past. In the organization time is not an important consideration, as it is perceived to be relative to the tasks and is managed appropriately as long as basic human processes are followed. . Structure and hierarchy influence personal and professional interactions, personal and professional ambitions and aspirations. Hierarchical and divisional relations and interactions influence the nature of performance, attention to achievement and the value placed on achievements; this also applies to functional activities.

The organization emphasizes an appropriate **management style that foster learning**. The organization focuses on learning environments that involves brings together intellect, knowledge, systemic processes, personal mastery and role models. The climate is conducive and non-threatening to share successes and failures and is not a performance consideration. The organization is driven by orientation to people, their actions, beliefs in the value of human good and concerns. Driven by organizational energy to learn, self-develop, perpetuate individualization as they grow to compete. Structural effectiveness, procedural clarity, defined end states and eventual success of people and the systems that lasts over time. There is a desire for internal and external energy to perform and focus on results. Driven by conscious endeavor to support a cause that extends beyond commercial perspective in many situations. Focus on making people productive through internal drivers without clarity on final goals and tasks. They identify with organizational vision and values. They have a work and off work identity that they cherish. Emphasis on people productivity through learning drivers on what can be done should be done. Management style: The stance adopted by the organization in managing and supervising its people; the stance required by the people of managers and supervisors; the general relationships between people and organization and the nature of superior-subordinate relations. The leadership disrupted style and consequent front line management style towards its stakeholders, including employees, the organizational priority towards external forces and the way to deal with such forces. Managerial demands, and the ways in which these are made, influence attitudes and behavior also; Management style influences the general feelings of well-being of everyone else, and sets standards of attitudes and behavior as well as performance

Focus on enterprise success on a holistic basis and dependent on people expertise. Focus on organizational vision, values, philosophy and performance. Action through policies, rewards, interactive processes, job design making people an important consideration in organizational issues. Action through making knowledge an important performance parameter. Action through making systems the critical consideration for organizational effectiveness. Action orientation measured by appropriates planning, measured steps, building consensus and reasonable task orientation. Action through making people subservient to systems and external stimuli. long term organization growth, meaning profits, shareholder value meant people growth. Long term competitive advantage through focus on performance empowerment. Orientation to building an enterprise that works through economics cycles without a major emphasis on revitalization or renewal. Competitive advantage seen as dominance and measures that sustain organizational competitiveness.

CEO Style in a context has been an important factor in studying the Digital culture. This contributed significantly to culture discussions more than any other factor. Leaders influence more directly than any other individual or group in culture. It comprises of their vision, their personal beliefs, values, their disposition towards business processes, the horizons that they wish to achieve, their understanding and dimensioning growth factors and the finally their ambition and goals towards their business purpose. They influence a set of values that helps employees understand which actions are considered acceptable, desirable to the achievement of the goals of the organization.

Leadership provides the **key point of identity for everyone else**, and from which people establish their own perceptions of the organization's general standards. These factors tend to indicate a shift from a current state of corporate culture and leadership to a change not visualized before. Many-unknown variables are emerging into the corporate environment. The emergence of a dominant human mind, economic liberalization bringing in competition and world class as well as world scale actions to the home turf. Added to it is the changing behavioral competencies, measures of performance, strong bottom line orientation and of course the way IT and the Internet/world wide web is changing the basics of running a business enterprise. All of these randomly studied discontinuities necessitate a close scrutiny and investigation of how leaders in business organizations are coping with these radical changes. And, how, their style in turn is impacting the culture. This is the context of the organization culture. Culture is formed from the collection of traditions, values, policies, beliefs and attitudes that prevail throughout the organization and the Digital culture has been no different.

Effectively multiple organization and management models have been identified as discerning features of organizations through this study and as they impact organizations. These organization models provide a framework for the study to connect organizational culture to leadership and particularly as they relate to organizations themselves.

B. Define Organization and Management Models

Human Organization – This is the organization of people contrast with task, a human enterprise with a concern for people, processes, and HRM and people building blocks, as was evident in the samples studied.

The organization also values history and tradition more in the context of people stories and experiences. Their orientation is to enable history to be cherished and continued. These organizations articulate their cultures through people actions. The organization is built upon stories that lasts over time and that is believed and revered by people as important learning of the past. Significant stories revolve around people actions and concerns demonstrated through medical, health, education and social support. The leader is remembered for his/her gesture on a personal occasion of a member. There are strong and deep-rooted beliefs on what can and cannot be done as far as people orientation is concerned. These organizations have detailed socialization programs. In the organization time is not an important consideration, as it is perceived to be relative to the tasks and is managed appropriately as long as basic human processes are followed. The organization is driven by orientation to people, their actions, beliefs in the value of human good and concerns. Focus on making people productive through internal drivers without clarity on final goals and tasks. They identify with organizational vision and values. They have a work and off work identity that they cherish. Action through policies, rewards, interactive processes, job design making people an important consideration in organizational issues. Long term organization growth, meaning profits, shareholder value meant people growth.

Learning Company – This is an organization where people cherish and thrive on learning, knowing and doing.

A **"Learning Company"** grows by sharing collective knowledge gained through experience and reflection (Senge, 1990). The cultivation of consciousness – the capacity to know – builds a foundation for a Learning Company. The organization emphasizes an appropriate management style that foster learning. The organization focuses on learning environments that involves brings together intellect, knowledge, systemic processes, personal mastery and role models. The climate is conducive and non-threatening to share successes and failures and is not a performance consideration. Driven by organizational energy to learn, self-develop; perpetuate individualization as they grow to compete. Focus on people productivity through learning drivers on what can be done should be done. Action through making knowledge an important performance parameter. Long term competitive advantage through focus on performance empowerment. The organizational spirit is in its climate to facilitate helping one another through a process of collaboration and consultative mechanisms. The members believe that their personal competitive advantage is their knowledge and seek to achieve knowledge intensiveness through self-development and personal learning measures. The organizations sponsor innovation and experimentation and demands employees to internalize their learning and convert it into an explicit sharing system. The Learning Company is the foundation of the HR Platform.

This organization embodies potential and competencies beyond the realm of staid corporations. These organizations stand by a set of visions, values, beliefs and actions that are consistent over time and offer the opportunity for managerial members to see their work life as an extension of their life as a whole. Here vision, values and actions does what it is intended to create and keep and is not left to itself as espoused statements and exhortation. People find security not in holding on what they know but in sharing, interacting and letting go what they know in quest of learning more of what they do not know. Learning Companies need a commitment and environment to develop, learn, teach, communicate and train. Imagine an organization where people are only expected to do a job but are never let out to train. Like a tennis player who never has the time to practice. Over time their performance capabilities will substantially diminish as their ability to think and do innovative actions will subjugate and beaten down to a path of obsolescence and personal boredom.

Institutional Corporate – This is an organization where building for a long term sustainable business model is more important than to deliver profits for the next quarter.

The organization believes in creating effective structures and hierarchies that provides clarity to roles, responsibilities, tasks and actions. The knowledge emphasis in the institution is driven by systems that override individual initiative as long as the institutional norms are met. The organization has effective communication channels, with and without boundaries, people enjoy communicating in relation to business and tasks to be accomplished. Driven by structural effectiveness, procedural clarity, defined end states and eventual success of people and the systems that lasts over time. Focus on enterprise success on a holistic basis and dependent on people expertise. Action through making systems the critical consideration for organizational effectiveness. Long term orientation to building an enterprise that works through economics cycles without a major emphasis on revitalization or renewal. Processes in these organizations have become everlasting and are expected to help management tide over their problems by relying on their time-tested processes. Leaders drive institutional interest as an important value and ask members to sacrifice for the sake of the institution and look for rewards and benefits beyond short-term expectation. Considerable degree of conservatism prevails in the culture.

Competing Organization – This is an organization that would drive to beat competition, strive for excellence and build an organizational model that is robust, competitive and bottom line driven.

The organization drives action through its orientation and emphasis to competition, performance and goals focused energies. These organizations ask a price for their actions. Nothing comes for free is the basic belief and they charge for all their actions, intended or otherwise. Their outlook towards commerce is simply driven by shareholder wealth and to a considerable degree personal gains and benefits. A leadership and management that pays attention to high performance lead the organization. The organization believes in swift and effective communication, work long hours to conclude tasks, people live at work, identify with winning and use all resources at one's disposal to accomplish tasks. Driven by the need for internal and external energy to perform and focus on results. Focus on organizational vision, values, philosophy and performance. Action through making people subservient to systems and external stimuli. Long term competitive advantage seen as dominance and measures that sustain organizational competitiveness. Corporate goals focus would be dependent on a performance cycle rather than the traditional quarterly financial reviews. Publicly quoted companies have the obligation of reporting monthly, quarterly results to the investing public. Organizations have long since been lost to this requirement and have trapped themselves into managing the last quarter performance to help show an acceptable balance sheet. Income and expenditures are booked just around the quarter corner to position it for public consumption. Government sectors and government run companies are notorious for maximizing their expense budgets in the last quarter of the year just in case the budget for a similar expense is not approved the next year.

An emerging practice would be to work goal cycles that are not monthly or quarterly or a traditional Roman calendar based instead make it real time and feedback oriented. Organizations should evaluate performance cycles in terms of the work content, targets to be met and the optimum time required to achieve it. The balance sheet/ scorecard as a consequence would reflect a true performance of the tasks completed, tasks on hand and the pending work content. A management accounting/planning/feedback/state of the corporate balance sheet should be the norm for presentation, rather than an accounting balance sheet. Corporations would then be forced to evaluate their performance on a virtual cycle. Strategic prioritization is also in the realm of the intellectual managers of the modern era. It is possible to differentiate prioritization and planning where there is an application of the mind. Formal plans would sustain periodic reviews and dynamic shifts from stated plans and goals set at the beginning of the year. No firm unadulterated plan would survive through the year unchanged. The CEO's priority would be to be in touch with the environment and make changes as and when they are called for. Strategic management would no longer be a one-time formal activity but would on the contrary become yet another specialization wherein consistent shift formalizations are programmed and implemented. Performance appraisals, forced ranking and bell curve should be passé!

Voluntary School - This organization consciously builds non-commercial institutions that still drives performance and goal orientation, but with varying philosophies.

Driven by conscious endeavor to support a cause that extends beyond commercial perspective in many situations. Focus through driving synergies of the people and process systems that integrate organizational goals to an end objective. Action orientation measured by appropriates planning, measured steps, building consensus and reasonable task orientation. Voluntary School s seek to serve a purpose that is enshrined in their business definitions. They exist with a big picture perspective that is established in a context that builds lasting values, beliefs and organizational way of life. These organizations do not wish away the realities of the environment and their obligation towards the society that seek to service. Yet they build institutions that have business bottom line, financial focus, and systems to enable optimum utilization of assets and resources. Long term goals to build sustainable business models that can seamlessly move from one situation to another without a strong immediate task and performance pressure.

Intellectual Company – This is an organization where intellect gains precedence over other forms of organizational contribution. The primary organization driver is the human mind and its use for a commercial purpose.

Driven by the need to promote and perpetuate intellect as it determines individual and organizational means and tasks and denies organizational members the time, space and opportunity to learn as things evolve. Preplanning is an important business consideration and decision making a critical management tool. Focus on delivery through advancement of learning, knowledge, skills but lacks need for attitudes and appropriate behavior to make things happen. Action driven by merciless meritocracy and rewards to processes and systems that goes beyond human dependence. Long Term sustainability only based on enhanced intellectual capital, innovation and newness of things done within and without the organization. Role stresses and work load loop encountered by middle level managers would increase given pressure to perform owing to a push factor from below from managers wanting early and substantive space to contribute and grow. And a pull factor from the top where the top management is demanding on time innovative performance. People do not wish to be told, controlled, directed, guided or led, irrespective of our noble intentions. They would fundamentally like to be left to themselves to show initiative, make new products, redesign, change, create, add value, learn, reflect and make their impact on the company bottom line. They would basically like to be liberated from the corporate bureaucratic shackles. In fact, important shifts and specified emphatic changes are increasing on freedom, autonomy, responsibility, and the influence of employees at all levels are happening across select organizations showing a clear trend.

Mechanistic corporation – These are organizations that are ritualistic and believe that past has provided significant learning and future is an intelligent extrapolation of the past.

Driven by the successes, stories, rituals and processes that have proved in time that it works and should be followed. Focus on building internal architectures, organic growth opportunities, systems and processes that drives individual and team performance, recent acquisitions, mergers that takes it away from its current state of equilibrium. Action orientation is expected to be more an outcome given smooth working methods and competitive pressures built within the organizational framework. Long Term need to make teams work together to achieve group goals that achieves today's performance and tomorrow's systems. Corporate structure and strategy linkages are increasingly turning blurred and lacking in positional clarity owing to closer change dynamics as it impacts the firm. As companies face change and the need to renew itself and get fighting fit, limited time will be available to work close strategy-structure work outs. The organization has a degree of ritualistic fervor that override entrepreneurial initiative and strikes a balance towards established norms, patterns, systems, frames of reference and CEO prerogative.

Performing Enterprise – This organization is focused on end deliverables through means that may be sometimes questionable.

Driven by business bottom line, financial focus and the need to achieve tasks and goals established to be accomplished. Focus on driving results through structure, style, roles, benchmarks as it impacts organizational effectiveness making performance the only end objective. Action to demonstrate what finally matters in the organization, the stakes involved and reward and punishment that follows post action. Long Term destination treated as an end in itself and pursuit of the goals set as non-negotiable and that it should be accepted and achieved by all internal stakeholders. To face competition over time and retaining a winning condition, organizational competencies have to be identified and changed dynamically. This is inevitably realistic identification of what we can do best and having them implemented expeditiously are both equally important. Organizations of tomorrow have to be in touch with their organizational members and their individual competencies to realize what can they do best and at a given point of time. Summation of individual competencies determines the organizational competencies. Making a five-year plan with current state of competencies is a true reflection of a company's suicidal tendency. Knowledge of the business as we ran it yesterday makes no meaning for tomorrow. Competencies would radically shift from one stage of development to another depending upon the stated pre-established position of the organization at a point in time as things shape up. What was evaluated as our source of strength may emerge to be our single largest weakness? There are examples of the buggy whip syndrome where the company has lived on its cash cow of yesterday.

The purpose of using the two models was to evaluate which best represented The Intellectual Company as per the study. It was analyzed eventually that particular leadership styles in a particular cultural context operate effectively in a particular organization and management model. There is uniqueness and specialty about this aspect. This summarizes our position: All 8 leadership styles articulated in this study, all of the 8 organization and management models defined and the 4 cultural alternatives including the one proposed here have been found to be of relevance in a particular context. This has been demonstrated by detailing specific digital companies case studies that indicate how each of them has a certain type of relevance and applicability.

It has been observed that leadership style undergoing a change is dependent on the type of organization and its culture. It has also been seen that varying cultures have influenced CEO's to follow differing leadership styles depending upon their business and commercial cycles. (Example: Sanjay Lalbhai of the Arvind Inc. from the times of prosperity to times of difficulty, the strong desire to hold on to a value based culture despite commercial compulsions and poor value advisors). Now into extraordinary times of success and affirmation of standing by values! It has been observed organization and management models undergoing radical transformation as business compulsions force leadership to relook at their organizational orientation. (Example: Standard Chartered Bank).

This provides a summarized version of the leadership styles broadly analyzed for the purpose of this study project and also indicates the culture and organization and management model as it would be prevalent in that company in relation to its culture and organization and management model. The cases detailed later in this chapter provide a bird's eye view of organizational history, their dreams and aspirations and identifiable indicators in relation to culture, leadership disrupted and organization and management model. Each of the cases has been written with varying perspectives to provide perspective aspects of the organizations studied. Effectively organizations by themselves or for that matter culture and leadership disrupted by themselves strongly need inter connections and linkages to gain a meaningful appreciation of an organization, particularly its culture. It is very desirable to understand these linkages to help understand each of the three aspects of this study, namely, Leadership disrupted, Culture and Organization and Management Model in its totality.

Effectively 8 specific leadership disrupted styles have been identified as discerning features of organizations through this study and as they impact organizations. These leadership disrupted styles provide a framework for the study to connect organizational culture to organization and management models and particularly as they relate to organizations themselves.

C. Discovering Leadership disrupted Styles

People Strategist

The CEO enables the organization to change, manage people strategies and influence existence of specific cultures. The leader emphasizes culture as an important aspect of organizational building and believes in influencing people to shape cultures. The leader focuses on people practices, HRM activities, organizational climate and its conduciveness to performance. Driven need to motivate and keep people in the right frame of mind to be productive and happy. Focus on creating people oriented systems that enable a culture that brings individuals, teams and organizations together. Action oriented to demonstrate by action that concern for people enables organizations to perform above expectation. Long Term orientation to delivering value through people development individualized tasks, creating an environment that is self-exhilarating. Obtaining leadership commitment is a key element. The leadership has been of influence or relevant in this context and have demonstrated commitment to an digital cultural change. Some level of leadership commitment, direction and point of view is often apparent, masterful evidence before a cultural analysis begins. It is not uncommon, for example, for community or organizational leaders to sponsor and effecting initial analysis. It is also frequently true that deeper, perhaps more sensitive, levels of leadership commitment, engagement are necessary to move the organizations beyond contemplation or perspectives. Leaders learn as they learn of an Digital culture. Leaders identify drivers that influence their personal and professional disposition towards influencing culture. Leaders determine to what degree would they influence culture.

Teacher

The leader mentors, coaches, teaches, builds other leaders, and enables work processes that make work life easy for organizational members. The leader pays attention to building knowledge and enables the organization to retain an open and invigorating mind to unknown environments. The leader supports innovation as a necessary competitive condition to learn, sponsors risk-taking behavior and drives people to fly into unknown territories. Driven by the need to make people, processes and systems learn from one another, interact to make a meaningful whole and are constantly seeking holistic behavior from organizational systems. Focus through clear policy perspectives and on delivering intellectual and performance value that sponsors native instincts, creative pursuits, feedback and review processes and encourages actions that facilitates results. Action oriented towards developing people competencies, ensures organizational competitiveness is appropriately managed by right people and makes organizational goals subservient to competency development. Long Term vision to build an organizational that can culturally sustain itself to renew, learn, contribute in varying life cycles and has adequate organizational energy to grow with momentum. Establishing a climate of cheer, enabling building blocks to commence, evaluating need for corrections, improvement, course changes and growth are some of the initiatives taken by the Teacher. With a positive outlook, people look for opportunities rather than obstacles, strengths rather than weaknesses in one another. There is a general recognition that cultural and individual strengths, through teachable points of view, or where there is a convergence of, I meeting we, will make it possible to improve upon current climat and performance conditions.

Builder

The leader emphasizes teamwork, enables interdependencies between functions, businesses, technologies and the organization as a whole. Spends over 50% of time to manage employee retention and rewarding high performers. The leader provides a vital direction to restructure and right size as situation demands, yet retaining the option to break and build as deemed appropriate. Driven by encouraging things to be worked out, provides job clarity, coaches and rewards for performance.

Focus on building for the future through institutional processes, demanding systems that connect organizational functions and works through structures that are streamlined, regulated and planned. Action oriented through appropriateness of actions driven by circumstance, enabling learning to be documented, creates knowledge sharing atmosphere, drives decisions through consensus and takes meaningful time to accomplish tasks. Long Term desire to make lasting organizations that can stream through economic and business life cycles and does not have the pressure to retain performance under all circumstance. Typical builder's efforts adopt a therapeutic model of change. They address problem behavior by focusing attention on the needs, history and skills of the individual. They are personally driven by personal learning and mastery of skills and knowledge and teach skills in managing internal dialogues and belief systems. They adopt aspects of human behavior that seeks joy, pleasure-based approaches, perhaps short or medium term, by focusing on fulfillment for satisfying biological needs while examining their inner feelings, emotive connect and motivations.

Individual focused change initiatives play an important role in culture building projects. It can help people develop social skills needed to work with others. Brings clarity about personal goals and values makes it easier to commit to organizational and community goals and causes Increased awareness about personal strengths and styles. It fosters individual initiative and creativity. Builder initiatives present special challenges to culture change projects. Individual initiative is sometimes viewed as competing with culture change. The most effective building programs engage people in developing their own individual initiative while finding or building supportive environments. The builder provides materials and programs that must frequently be revised to re-establish the link between personal and cultural change. They eventually help build an ability to relate to another through a better understanding of self and learn to find ways to relate to the Digital culture and its impact of self, teams and organizations.

Visionary

The leader is focused on the vision, practices values, emphasizes individual intellect as they impact organizational goals, actively participates in attracting, retaining, and rewarding talent and leads in times of crisis. The leader believes in competing in challenging environments by preparing the organization in advance, sets meaningful goals, makes adaptation to competitive environment possible, and targets and competes to conquer. Driven by sharing strategic goals, communicates, shares values, distinctive concern for individual sensitivity, empowerment, delegation, clear accountability and demonstrated by examples. Focus on collaboration, business models that are appropriate and accepted by people and goals that have been worked to individual and organizational advantage. Action oriented to make people believe in the overall good establishes concreteness to tasks to be accomplished. Long Term priority to build organizational wealth, individual intellect, collective wisdom, sustainable business model and overall organizational effectiveness parameters. In this environment group members share their common experiences with a given problem behavior or experience.

Groups play important roles in supporting individuals through difficult personal changes. The Visionary's integration effort addresses the needs of ongoing social networks such as work teams, families and friends. Unlike support groups, which tend to be time limited, "natural" social networks continue to provide support for years and sometimes for a lifetime. The leader's efforts are designed to increase the quantity and improve the quality of support. Building peer level interface through digital culture adaptation programs that focus on goals tasks values and beliefs. Manages personal motivation and inner energy to succeed given peer comparisons. Acts as a successive hurdle to cope with resistance from self and others and develop appropriate coping mechanisms. Enables competitive spirit into group working situations. Makes the task of the leader simpler given enhanced peer capability to understand for self and for others. Monitoring progress of cultural assimilation through peer focus groups that discusses on learning, contribution, issues, deadlines and things to be done. The leader eventually derives concrete action goals. Visionary leaders establish a clear picture of the current situation, sets specific measurable objectives, commits leaders to a vision for cultural influence. They enable appropriate definitions drive connections between organizational performance framework and culture as it is influenced by the leader, aligns the culture management process to the problem and setting and provide groundwork for the broad-scale introduction and integration of the culture management process.

In a conversation with Gerald C. (Jerry) Kane, for MIT Sloan Management Review's Social Business Big Idea Initiative (and a one-time student of Konsynski's at Emory), Benn Konsynski describes, large organizations — "UPS, say, for example — that have a broad, far horizon; their ecosystem is a lot more than merely picking up packages and delivering. Asset-management and event-planning skills are essential. They have to have extraordinary knowledge and breadth and prediction, forward-looking knowledge, about conditions of an environment. You have an organization in UPS that grows almost the size of its main competitor during the fall, during one season of the year. In the past, we might see that UPS grows the size of its next competitor every holiday season. While that is probably no longer the case, the capacities and capabilities of range of improvisation is only possible with the effective leverage of modern information systems. Culturally adaptive enterprises have to scale up and scale down in a rapid and efficient fashion, and you can only do that if you have effective knowledge of the environment that allows them to grow and shrink. In fact, UPS ran into problems over a year ago and had an amazing suite of tools employed for this recent holiday season. These issues are true in all size of enterprise and market". To ensure a culture that lasts through growth and change, organizations in all industries should take the following steps: Define the culture, understand its inner meaning as it manifests as human behaviors in organizational settings and how it is different from other concepts, valid observations, develop a strategic – operational program plan for implementing that culture. For it to be effective, senior management must implement that culture in all they do including: staffing, resourcing, hiring, benefits, learning, change, compensation, rewards and incentives, creating the environment, and marketing. Make sure employees at all levels of the chain of command and in multiple geographies know what the culture is and that they buy into it and have seasoned employees train new employees and develop a system where new employees learn the written and unwritten parameters of the culture. Constantly evaluate progress and success as you grow and be open to change and inform employees and customers of any changes and how they will benefit. "Success in the 21st century requires any organization to assemble, and reconfigure, resources and capabilities in ways that were not possible in the 20th century commerce arena. Part of the problem is; you don't control all aspects of the ecosystem. So companies have to insulate themselves against risk in that ecosystem. That's not an easy thing to do. You can control the things you own, but it's tough to control the things you don't own or don't have direct contractual information".

Manager

The CEO is effectively a manager of his role and responsibilities. His day starts and closes with review meetings. The CEO manages change, but does not influence it. They manage people strategies and maintain existence of specific cultures. The manager emphasizes tradition as an important aspect of organizational building and believes in influencing systems to shape cultures. The leader focuses on systemic practices, process activities, organizational goals and its connection to performance. Driven by institutionalizing policies that provide clarity to goals, tasks and manages a team through maintaining status quo through conflicting circumstance and taking decisions that involve retaining established norms and practices. Focus on building loyalty through establishing people oriented systems that enable handling tasks that are individually focused. Keen on managing for today adequately. Action oriented to enable easy and smooth management of the organization, streamlines administrative processes, establishes a string back office operations organization and manages customer oriented roles through follow procedure route. Long Term desire to make organizational working built on strong fundamentals of bureaucracy, frameworks and management styles. Prefers streamlined processes rather than the opportunity to reinvent the wheel to resolve conflicts.

Scientist

The leader does his own thing. Coaching, teaching, building other scientists, knowledge managers and enables work processes that make work life intellectually stimulating for organizational members is their priority. The leader pays attention to building knowledge and enables the organization to retain an open and invigorating mind to unknown environments. The leader supports innovation as a necessary competitive condition to learn, sponsors risk-taking behavior and drives people to fly into unknown territories. Driven by the urge to create, make actions intellectually dominant, treats developmental processes a predominant organizational factor and is willing to compromise for nothing other than intellectual superiority in actions. Asks organizational members to think science rather than processes that cannot be proven. Focus on attracting and nurturing talent, systems and processes that are of utility today and tomorrow, more tomorrow, and is willing to absorb the costs of human and organizational process costs as a necessary condition of managing the human mind. Action oriented to demonstrate merit and results supersedes all other performance factors, does not believe in means as an important consideration while acting upon information and manages rewards as a necessary evil in people management processes. Long Term desire to create a self-propelling organization that has internal renewal capability to prod organizational performance, individual effectiveness and shareholder satisfaction.

Technocrat

The leader emphasizes fast paced actions to bring people up the curve. He enables interdependencies between functions, businesses, technologies and the organization as a whole as long as it has a techno commercial perspective. The leader provides a technologically superior direction to restructure and right size as situation demands, yet retaining the option to break and build as deemed appropriate. Driven by engineering sciences, that technology provides solutions to complex organizational problems, quantitative approaches to most problems and believes in logic and rationality as desired attitudes. Focus on adding technical and functional values to business situations enables competency development that is vertical and incisive and promotes organizations to drive business through technological excellence. Action through individualized working, avoiding teams and consequent inefficiencies, meets deadlines under all circumstance and seeks the best. Long Term desire to make people processes subservient to technological processes and works towards eliminating elaborate actions that involve meetings, group work, communication forums and large-scale explanation to actions

Driver

The leader is focused on the vision, practices values, emphasizes individual intellect as they impact organizational goals, actively participates in attracting, retaining, rewarding talent and leads in times of crisis. The leader believes in competing in challenging environments by preparing the organization in advance, sets meaningful goals and targets and competes to conquer. Driven by a performance system that overrides all other considerations and makes individual targets an important element achieving results. Focus on priorities that are determined quickly, enable efficient systems, dislike elaborate meetings, followed through decisively and ensure that different parts of the organization are focused on their own deliverables. Action oriented to provide criteria for success and failures and ensures it is adequately communicated and holds accountability on streamlined systemic norms. Long Term orientation to retain competitive advantage by providing profitability through consistent intervals and prefers revenue to growth.

D. Digital Learnings

Learning 1 - There is a correlation between the leadership disrupted style of the CEO, vision for readiness for the future and the manifested culture in the organization.

Leadership disrupted Style directly has a bearing in the creation, formation, development and sustaining the culture of an organization. This has been evidenced by clear roles that have emerged through the study being Visionary, Builder, People Strategist and the Teacher.

Relationships with the environment; including the ways in which the CEO copes with uncertainty and turbulence; the ways by which the organization seeks to influence the environment; the extent to which it behaves proactively or reactively.

The CEO influences the badges and status symbols: These are the marks of esteem conferred by organizations and its CEO on their people. They are a combination of location (near to or away from the corridors of power of example); possessions (cars, technology, personal department) ; job titles (reflecting a combination of ability, influence and occupation); and position in the hierarchy pecking order.

Admiral James B. Stockdale - "Leadership must be based on goodwill. Goodwill does not mean posturing and, least of all, pandering to the mob. It means obvious and wholehearted commitment to helping followers. We are tired of leaders we fear, tired of leaders we love, and of tired of leaders who let us take liberties with them. What we need for leaders are men of the heart who are so helpful that they, in effect, do away with the need of their jobs. But leaders like that are never out of a job, never out of followers. Strange as it sounds, great leaders gain authority by giving it away."

Leaders Demonstrating" Readiness for a Digital Future" - RDF

Leadership disrupted qualities have been the one of the most often cited factor for a change ready organization. John P. Kotter requires leaders who are motivators, who encourage participation from others, who lead by example and who establish a sense of purpose for the enterprise and its employees. However, the mere presence of leaders is not good enough. Rather, it is important that the corporation have the ability to produce leaders regularly. It is important that in the face of change and retains its core values through well-established succession planning.

Culture is another recurring theme in literature on Change. While researches prescribe a digital culture that is unique to the company and embodies its spirit, they advocate that such a culture has elements that encourage teamwork. The change ready culture will involve employees in decision making and encourage them to take risks and allow them to make mistakes as they learn and gain experience.

Vision, Values and Strategy form another important factor for Change Readiness. An organization ready to change will have to have flexibility to adapt its Vision and Strategy to the changing business requirements. However, what must not change are the values that define the foundations of the business. Further, the vision that gives the enterprise its direction and the strategy that defines the steps in the direction should be known by all.

A *history of successful change* in enterprise transformation in the past helps build confidence that it can be done again. Hence a positive change history is a morale booster and hence a factor for Change Readiness.

The design of *Org Processes* can aid or hinder change. Change requires Org Processes to encourage flexibility in procedures and processes. Change would bring about a realignment of work definitions and work norms. A system riddled with inflexibility will find the transition difficult. As Henk W. Volberda says fast moving markets require institutions to build 'Metaflexibility' which facilitates the continual adjustment of the of the composition of the management's flexibility mix in line with changes in the environment. Meta flexibility includes Operational, Structural, and Strategic flexibility.

A *Performance Management* process that sets challenging goals, review mechanisms, scorecards, outcome measures for its employees and links rewards to performance can be used to drive change.

Teamwork is another desired feature for Change Readiness. A change effort is itself a team effort and not a one person show. Existence and active use of cross-functional teams in a company gives it the ability of effectively using the process for bringing in changes spanning the corporation.

Communication processes are a very important mechanism in ensuring success of a change process. It is of the utmost importance that all employees be fully informed of the change impacting them or their work. Communication should not just be one way but a feedback mechanism is a must to monitor the stress levels caused in the organization by the change process. The existence of a functional two way communication process thus goes a long way in ensuring change readiness of an institution.

Organizational Architecture has to support the above processes. Hence organizational architecture should enable the formation of multifunctional teams and allow the required flexibility to employees. Flexibility in the architecture would permit the enterprise to restructure itself to respond to a market need.

Intellectual Capital represents the organization's knowledge storehouse that can be harnessed and adapted to new situations to crash the learning curve for a change process. This essentially requires that knowledge be generated, captured and reused in an enterprise. According to Stephen A.W. Drew and Peter A.C. Smith organization's memory helps the organization recognize and respond to early signal of change or unanticipated opportunities, thereby improving the organization's change readiness.

Values, Ethics

1. A set of values which provide lasting foundation
2. Shared & internalised values
3. Behaviours consistent with values
4. Communicating – Practising Values across the organization

Vision, Strategy & Business Model

1. A clear Vision for the future – Readiness For Future
2. A strategy aligned with the environment & market realities
3. Strategy converted into a BSC Based Strategy Map, Established goals, tasks, targets, KPI & Benchmarks
4. A economically viable business model
5. Innovations in Business Models Frequent

Flexible Architecture

1. Effective Structure, Roles, Responsibilities, Accountabilities, Delegation of Authority, Responsibility
2. Is each part of the company an excellence centre
3. Flexible boundaries between departments / functions including Head office versus front line roles
4. Prevalence of Teams / effectiveness
5. Knowledge – Data - Strategy – Structure – Intellect Integration

Robust Technology and Processes

1. Implementing Core Business Processes
2. Best in Class Technology
3. Internet of Things
4. Social Compatibility
5. Competency Development, Behavioral Identification, Scoring
6. Performance Management including BSC Scorecard
7. Benchmarking & best practice adoption
8. Social, Mobile, Cloud, Wearables, AI, Analytics, Digital

Figure 33 - Leaders Demonstrating Readiness for a Digital Future – RDF- Eight key levers Digital Culture and transformation of any organization

Learning 2 - The CEO has a role to play in the culture of the company.

The CEO has primary and critical roles to play in the culture of the company. In every company studied it was the CEO who spoke of a culture inherited and culture transformed, the culture desired versus the culture that was existent. Culture is beyond just the CEO.

To Pradeep Udhas, Senior Partner, Global Leader at KPMG LLP, being a leader who needs to have a vision, build upon values and be trustworthy is not new. To him chasing a dream is meaningless when it is a one sided vision. Why are we always chasing after # 1 firm, rather than them following us he asks when wanting to compete with another firm? We have done well, as a firm, but what got us here won't get us there…what is our leadership's answer after 7 years at the helm? His attempt to build a world class firm is built upon 6 fundamental Questions.

1. *Have we built a sustainable competitive advantage?*
2. *Do we have the right growth engine (business model, infrastructure, resources and network)?*
3. *Do we have the appropriate management team in place to meet achieve our goals? Is there a best man / woman for each job?*
4. *Why has there been no innovation in the markets program since it was designed 6 years ago?*
5. *Are we a true partnership? Why then most partners feel that they are rarely consulted on important decisions for the firm and their own business units?*
6. *Why focus all of our competitive energy against one firm? Let us build a firm that encompasses being the best, make knowledge and intellect thrive successfully in our culture, build global alliances, meet client needs and being the best for our people.*

Udhas with additional roles as a Managing Director, Head of Markets and Alliances has a 7 - point philosophy in building a promise to clients.

1. *Always Outthinks and Outdoes Competition*
2. *Decisive and Transparent Governance*
3. *Tigers in the Marketplace*
4. *Energetic - Executes with Speed, Precision and Quality*
5. *Proud of themselves but very collaborative and customer centric*
6. *Best firm to work for*
7. *Demonstrate High Integrity in All Actions*

On Leadership at KPMG, Pradeep Udhas says, "Focus on Global Outlook, Entrepreneurial Spirit and Ability, Commercial Acumen and Investment Foresight, Strategic Thinking, Industry Relations, Stakeholder Relations and People, Culture and Performance should determine the priorities of a leader of a digitally focused professional services firm. For Pradeep concludes, "People come First while we Build KPMG with, "True Partnership culture, Aspiration for people, Collaborative, Common / Shared Vision, Complimentary building blocks of competency and be Values driven".

Transformational Leadership

1. Leadership & Stakeholder Alignment
2. Role of Boards & Executive Management – People Perspective
3. Leaders who create a sense of purpose & Leadership at all levels
4. Leadership behaviours are consistent with values & strategy
5. Social Medias Enabled Branding
6. Employee Friendly attitudes

Adaptive Culture

1. Readiness to Change
2. The Way we Work Digital Factors
3. Non productive & Productive Actions, Processes, Rituals & Wastages
4. Identifying Unique culture which acts as a glue
5. Global Adaptability
6. High Degree of Mobility

Talent Management

1. Intellectual Smart talent
2. Individual & Organizational Competencies
3. Assessment of People & Individual Development Plans
4. Quality of talent / knowledge Dimension
5. Tacit versus Explicit Knowledge & Knowledge Risk Assessment
6. Skill Emphasis, Differentiators,

Change History

1. Factoring a Business Case for Change
2. History of changes experienced including Success rate of previous change efforts – 360 Feedback
3. Extent of Organizational Acceptance Versus Cynicism
4. Ability – Understanding - Willingness to embark on change processes

Figure 33 A - Leaders Demonstrating Readiness for a Digital Future – RDF- Eight key levers Digital Culture and transformation of any organization

The CEO influences routines, rituals and habits: These are the formal, semi-formal and informal ways of working and interaction that people generate for themselves (or which the organization generates for them) to make comfortable the non-operational aspects of working life. They develop around the absolutes- attendance times, work requirements, authority and reporting relationships- and include regular meetings, regular tasks, forms of address between members or the organization and groups, pay days, holidays and some trainee development activities.

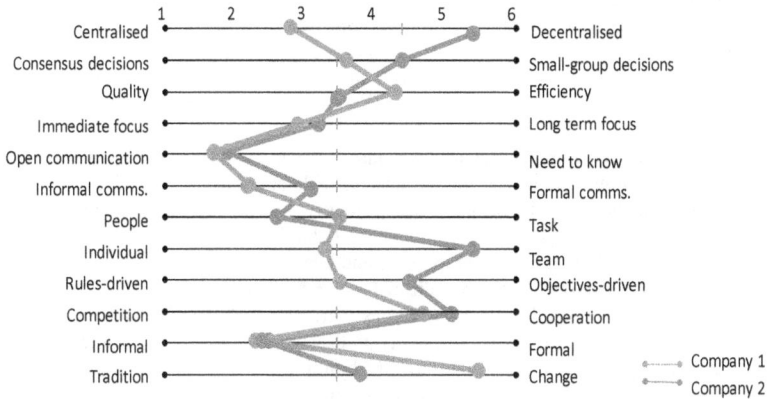

Figure 34 – Competitive Benchmarking - Mapping Digital HR Using Denison – Shermon 2012 - KPMG Research

Learning 3 - The four cultures, Operator, Engineering and Executive & Digital HR exist on a mutually exclusive basis in all the companies. No Company will have one identifiable culture.

The three cultures together with the fourth culture, namely, The Digital Culture, has been identified as those that exist in the organization. More importantly they coexist as can been seen from the visual depicting the sample organization, the organization model, leadership style and the identified culture.

The leaders were observed playing a decisive role in influencing the following factors:

- *Articulating a vision*
- *Enabling shared values*
- *Engaging Teams*
- *Building Alignment*
- *Measuring success*
- *Providing feedback*
- *Implementing promises*
- *Inspiring commitment,*
- *Defining roles*
- *Articulating key performance indicators*
- *Recognizing contributions,*
- *Defining authority limits*
- *Delegating needed resources and*
- *Making sure that plans are followed through to completion*
- *Establishing new standards*
- *Solving Problems*

When one thinks of turbulence, we expect it to be short-lived. I think what we are going through is pretty permanent. It is about the pace of change, and that will only grow exponentially. Now what must companies do? It is extremely difficult. First and foremost, it is crucial to be alive to this change. Companies have to bring in mechanisms that can feel the pulse of customers, suppliers, and most importantly, the technology that could potentially impact them. Second, we have to be extremely focused. We have to pick areas in which we will compete and discard the others. Less is more. It is important to make that switch. (Unilever Past Chairman, M S Banga)

The Tata Group (http://bit.ly/2a5fSdG)has always sought to be a value-driven organization. These values continue to direct the group's growth and businesses. The five core Tata values underpinning the way we do business are: Integrity - we must conduct our business fairly, with honesty and transparency. Everything we do must stand the test of public scrutiny. Understanding - we must be caring, show respect, compassion and humanity for our colleagues and customers around the world and always work for the benefit of India. Excellence - we must constantly strive to achieve the highest possible standards in our day-to-day work and in the quality of the goods and services we provide. Unity - we must work cohesively with our colleagues across the group and with our customers and partners around the world, building strong relationships based on tolerance, understanding and mutual cooperation. Responsibility - we must continue to be responsible, sensitive to the countries, communities and environments in which we work always ensuring that what comes from the people goes back to the people many times over.

Force field analysis is of relevance here. Change in a group or an organization means an alteration in the way things get done in the system. It may mean changes in compensation methods, sales and production levels, leadership styles, or interpersonal functioning, among others. Kurt Lewin's force-field analysis provides a framework for problem-solving and for implementing planned change efforts around a wide range of group and organizational issues. The top and bottom represent opposite ends of a continuum, for example, a team's functioning in terms of its interpersonal climate. The environmental conditions and pressures supportive of more openness in the system are the driving forces represented by the arrows pushing upward which, at the same time, act as barriers to the team's movement backward toward a more closed system. The arrows pushing downward represent the restraining forces that are keeping the system from becoming more open and, at the same time, are driving forces toward a climate of lower interpersonal risk. "We're very intentional with our culture," says Jody Kohner, vice president of employee marketing and engagement. "Culture is not something that happens to us." Being intentional about the culture starts with an emphasis on 'ohana, the Hawaiian cultural value of extended family. "The concept is about an extended group of people that are bound together and responsible for each other," says Kohner. A similarity to force field where there are both positive and represent opposite ends of a continuum of forces. "We reinforce that sense of family from day one through actions, programs, and initiatives." Building trust and empowering career advancement are also intentional elements of Salesforce's culture". Culture must be investigated, perhaps continuously examined and renewed for it to remain vital and supportive of the organization's vision and goals. Leaders must adapt to each wave of change, establish networks, and transform the organization again and again if it is to flourish. Becoming nimbler, instilling accountability, being customer-driven, promoting innovation, agility, developing loyalty, managing personal - professional pressure and work level stress, developing a higher level of trust, respecting the individual, valuing excellence, building teamwork, and confronting conflict. For example, in this context, Sales Force Management supports growth by aligning the Sales Force set up with market requirements. Optimal Sales force size to retain existing business and cover new business potential; increased ability to achieve Sales targets. Optimal territory split according to market potential, Sales targets and Sales Force capacity; improved regional coverage. Improved transparency on Sales Force utilization. Improved Sales Force effectiveness and efficiency due to increased and better prepared Customer face-time. Improved skill-set of Sales Representatives due to systematic development activities. Better information exchange within sales as well as between sales and other departments.

Increased employee motivation. Poor integration strategy including sales force integration is cited as the main reason for failure of M&A transactions. In, Digital HR - Assessing Organizational Readiness for Digital Transformation. In, July 2016 MIT SMR issue, "Aligning the Organization for its Digital Future", Gerald C Kane, Doug Palmer, Anh Nguyen Phillips, David Kiron and Natasha Buckley, continue, "At Salesforce.com — Culture Is Intentional - Salesforce grapples with the cultural challenges that every startup faces when it grows — retaining the values and beliefs that were its essence at its founding. Salesforce preserves its digital culture through calculated efforts. For example, to maintain and enhance its culture, the company asks employees for candid feedback and makes sure that they feel comfortable about being honest. The trust the company builds translates to other values such as empowering employees in their careers. "Silicon Valley is famous for people leaving for other companies," she says. "Our leaders and managers explicitly encourage employees to raise their hands when they want a new challenge. That helps us identify development opportunities and supports a culture of honesty, since there is no retribution for saying what you feel."

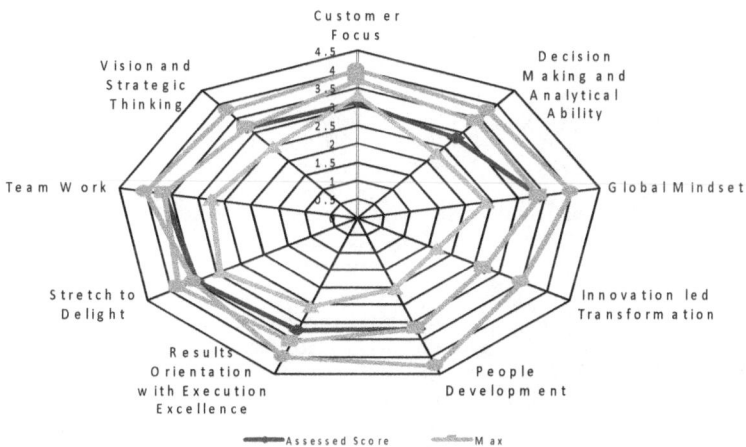

Figure 35 – Digital HR - Assessing Organizational Readiness for Digital Transformation

Learning 4 - The CEO/leaders directly and indirectly influence the existence of any one/all of the three/four cultures in the company by understanding facilitating and hindering factors to Digital HR.

Lao Tsu, "To lead people, walk beside them ... As for the best leaders, the people do not notice their existence. The next best, the people honor and praise. The next, the people fear; and the next, the people hate ... When the best leader's work is done the people say, 'We did it ourselves!" The CEO directly influences the existence of any/all of the four cultures as the CEO has been observed conclusively in practicing one or more of the management styles and in the way that these cultures expect the leader/CEO to behave. The CEO significantly influenced the vision, values, history and tradition. The extent to which the organization's vision, values, histories and traditions are barriers or facilitators of progress; the extent to which the organization values and worships its past histories and traditions; key influences on current activities and beliefs; the position of key interest groups (for example, trade unions). The CEO was observed obtaining decisions on vision, direction, values and the influence on history and tradition.

- As far as organizations are concerned, we have to quickly move from hierarchical to flat and far more flexible. The best way I can describe this is to think of amoebae. Finally, you need something to keep you straight and stable like the rudder of a ship. That is your core value. This is why we should ensure that everyone works under a framework of core values. (Unilever past Chairman, M S Banga)

Organizational Barriers to Digital Culture
- Structural Inertia, Poor Leadership
- Existing forms of using structure, roles and responsibilities
- Resistance from Work groups
- Failure of previous Digital Culture initiatives
- Top Management reluctance to Digital Awareness/Business
- Delayed Strategy Thinking around Digital Business

Individual Barriers to Digital Culture
- Tradition and Set ways
- Loyalty to exiting relationship, Political Coalitions
- Failure to accept the need for Digital Culture
- Insecurity, Nexus of Evil
- Break up of work groups
- Different personal ambitions
- Fear of Loss of Power, skills, income and the unknown
- Redundancy
- Inability to perform as well in the new situation

Factors Impacting Digital Cutures
- Failure to explain the need for Digital Culture
- Failure in proper communication
- Failure to consult, negotiate and offer support
- Lack of involvement in the process
- Failure to build trust and sense of security
- Poor employee relations

Figure 36 - Key Barriers amongst organizations scaling up into Digital and building Digital HR

Leading Bad Practices - "The best practices in organizations are cornerstones of business excellence while poor practices damage the overall organization. It is interesting to note that a poor practice in a single yet critical function impacts all other functions, as also organization's overall performance. Example - A faulty hiring practice leads to organization-wide weak talent base, which in turn leads to an incompetent leadership system – finally resulting in poor business results vis-à-vis competitors" writes Hema Thakkar, Management Consultant with KPMG LLP People & Change Practice.

"One may ask a question", Thakkar continues, "why articulate bad practices ... would it nor breed negativism? Is it not sufficient to understand the best or exemplary practices instead?

The answer to this lies in the fact that deep understanding of "don'ts" and "absent elements" gives a decisive direction to process improvement. These "don'ts" come in many shapes and sizes: either a cultural incapacity, or management incapability, or a faulty workflow design inherent in the process itself! Once the blockages, vulnerabilities, and weaknesses are clearly spelled out, then the Leadership Team is in a better position to put safeguards in place for the smart practice to succeed. One more advantage of listing poor practices is that they transcend the contextual boundaries. A poor practice is bad for the organizational health irrespective of its industry, size, market ranking, or geographical footprint. Therefore a list of poor practices serves as a definitive guidepost of "avoidable circumstances" in any organization, at all the times.'

Compiled below are some research-based "poor or "defunct" practices observed by KPMG while performing a specific role or at client organizations during consulting work. The term "poor practice" is used from a clustered set of faulty processes performed repeatedly. These poor practices are articulated using simple terms highlighting their impact on organizational cultures.

Recruitment, Hiring & On boarding:

- **There is an absence of defined, measurable criteria and competencies to assess potential hires.** *An ambiguous understanding of "required traits" prevails on various selection occasions for various positions. The result is inconsistent hiring decisions and mismatches for critical positions.*

- **Organizations lack tools, techniques, and templates for hiring and selection.** *This may include behavioral tests, interview formats (BEI or Open Ended), situational tests, case studies etc. for identifying the most suitable candidate for various roles. This invariably results in subjective biases in the critical decisions.*

- **Many a time there is a lack of a firm recruitment strategy and a quantifiable hiring plan:** *"whom" to hire (competencies), "from where" (campuses / companies) and "how much" (quantity).*

- **Workforce diversity is missing in its recruitment process.** *The cultural and strategic advantages of diverse workforce – such as innovative ideas, multiple capabilities, inclusive and tolerant culture, multiple dimensions and perspectives, broader skill sets are lost out to the organization.*

- **Some organizations do not have a well-crafted on boarding process based on their vision, values and culture.** *A formal welcome, a generic introduction to the Organization and completion of the administrative formalities constitute joining. Thus, the new employee's initiation in the organizational life is restricted to 'joining' rather than 'systematic familiarization', and he is not instantly aligned to the structure, culture and strategic direction of the organization. As they say "First Impression is the Last Impression"... and the employee invariably carries a hazy impression for a long period after joining.*

Performance Management

- **There is a lack of systematic methodologies -such as a Balanced Scorecard or a rationalized KPA system - to set goals** . *The goals are compiled and force-fitted into a template. Such a loose approach creates multiple, unrelated and overlapping goals, resulting in a diminished*

---

meritocracy, out of turn promotions, subjectivity in talent management, favoritism and a gradual decline of the talent drove the organizational performance culture.

- **Rewards are inadequate, very top driven or opaque.** When inadequate, they are less generous and not well budgeted. Top driven rewards is another unhealthy practice, where the top management is paid hefty rewards while the middle and junior management have to be satisfied with insignificant rewards. Opaque reward system does not allow cross validation or employee grievance handling. All of the above result in misaligned incentives, efforts and results.

- Some organizations **lack formal employee development processes such as job rotations, inter functional mobility, developmental plans, executive education programs aimed to fill skills and competencies gaps.** This leads to unplanned or inadequate employee development.

Communication :

- **Often communication process lacks proper mix of diverse communication channels - such as town-hall, face-to-face meetings, large gatherings, annual day celebrations etc.** Such a restricted and top-down communication then results in employee participation, constructive questioning, discussions and debates take a back-seat. A major setback is the lack of innovative ideas, because no open communication means no reflection !

- **A lack of communicative and consultative approach during key business and people related decision making is another poor practice.** It results in decisions being taken in a presumptive manner, errors of judgment and also a fractured trust among the employees.

- **There is no structured mechanism or a grid for disseminating key messages across the organization.** This leads to inconsistent percolation of the important leadership messages. Too many, much argumentative and uncoordinated cross-functional meetings lacking in collaborative problem solving adds to the confusion and ineffectiveness.

Organizational Climate, Organizational Culture, Work Environment :

- **In many organizations, weak attempts are made to define organizational culture.** There is no clarity regarding the core values that govern culture, cultural drivers or constructs. Since there is an absence of understanding of cultural codes of the organization, learning & development interventions, team building initiatives, OD interventions, talent management processes are not synchronized with one another to strengthen the positive culture.

- **There is too much bureaucracy in the organization. Every** decision is slow, subjected to unnecessary paperwork and has to pass the filters of rules and regulations. Such a sluggish culture hampers the organization's agility to move fast in the competitive marketplace.

- **There is an absence of collaborative culture which fosters team work in the organization.** The functional departments work in silos and hierarchy flourishes. This results in fragmented organization efforts, inter-functional competition, communication gaps and wastage of valuable company time, resources and investments.

- *There is an over-reliance on policy and procedure manuals.* There is a lack of human touch and humane discretion during people decisions leading to a mechanistic work culture.

- *The approach to conflict resolution is competitive i.e. Win – Lose.* Therefore when a strong conflict occurs, communication breaks down, trust and support deteriorate. The result is increased employee stress, decreased productivity and low motivation that limits trust-based collaboration.

- *Sometimes the leadership is too democratic or laissez-faire.* And thus begins a well-intentioned yet misguided "management by consensus" instead of "management by objectives and expertise".

- *Roles, Responsibilities, and Job Descriptions across functions and levels are not clearly defined.* Hence there is responsibility-authority mismatch and lack of ownership.

- *Low priority to employee engagement assessment and planning is one of the worst practices that an organization can follow.* The organization simply does not define the drivers and parameters of employee satisfaction and does not drive employee engagement. The result is highly stressful workplace and more or less disengaged, unhappy employees. This situation is reflected in high absenteeism and a high employee turnover & attrition rate.

- *The framework and practice of 'Work-Life Balance' do not exist.* The culture celebrates highly stretch targets and the management focus is punitive than supportive. This focus may produce short-term results but also inspires negativism and resentment among the employees in the long-term. The employees therefore are highly stressed and burnt out as disequilibrium takes over their life.

- *Unfair labor practices such as undue dismissal, retrenchments or charge sheets are prevalent in the organization.*

- *Unhealthy working conditions and inadequate welfare facilities in the areas of sanitation, health, recreation are prevalent .* A few of them are : Defective or inadequately guarded equipment; hazardous arrangement of machines; shortage of safety devices; faulty, cluttered, congested work lay-out; unhealthy physical parameters at the work stations such as inadequate illumination or ventilation, insufficient arrangement to prevent and treat occupational health hazards and diseases.

These are a few prominent poor practices that deteriorate the organization's performance and reputation permanently. Many of them exist unknowingly, or are defined better on the records but are implemented poorly. Such a snapshot of these practices can be referred by the organizations to avoid the pitfalls while designing their HR architecture", concludes Hema Thakkar.

"Well, first of all, it starts with hiring. We are zealous about hiring. We are looking for a particular type of person, regardless of which job category it is. We are looking for attitudes that are positive and for people who can lend themselves to causes. We want folks who have a good sense of humor and people who are interested in performing as a team and take joy in team results instead of individual accomplishments. "If you start with the type of person you want to hire, presumably you can build a work force that is prepared for the culture you desire..."Another

343

important thing is to spend a lot of time with your people and to communicate with them in a variety of ways. And a large part of it is demeanor. Sometimes we tend to lose sight of the fact that demeanor - the way you appear and the way you act - is a form of communication. We want our people to feel fulfilled and to be happy, and we want our management to radiate the demeanor that we are proud of our people, we are interested in them as individuals and we are interested in them outside the work force, including the good and bad things that happen to them as individuals." Herb Kelleher, Southwest's CEO

Learning 5 - There is a correlation between cultures and the different functions (Marketing, Production, Finance, Personnel, Study, IT) of the company and cultural transformation.

The four cultures of the organization exist irrespective of functional differentiation within an organization. It is possible that in some functions they exist in a little greater degree given the primary disposition of the function. E.g. Production Department does have a strong Operator Culture and R and D has an Engineering Culture, so do their leaders representing a Technocrat or a Scientist.

Defining the culture that supports the organization's vision and business strategy is critical for success. This process requires the leadership team to work through a series of tough choices, which amounts to an efficient reexamination of the organization's purpose, values, vision, strategy and operating priorities. "Our research also suggests that organizational culture is critically important to effectively leveraging digital technologies in the workplace. One of the factors respondents said is most important to effectively leverage digital technologies is the "willingness to experiment and take risks." Gerald C. Kane, Doug Palmer, Anh Nguyen Phillips and David Kiron "Is Your Business Ready for a Digital Future? - MIT SMR 2015, continue on, "Culture and Transformation - They also reported that this trait is among the most lacking in their organizations — something reported by 52% of respondents from early-stage companies and even by 36% in the maturing group. B. Bonin Bough, senior vice president, chief media and e-commerce officer for Mondelez International Inc., the global snack food spinoff of Kraft Foods Inc., spoke of technology companies' ability to tackle this challenge: They've been able to unlock something that's a totally new mindset and approach. Part of it is this notion of iteration, this notion of constantly reinventing the core, constantly cannibalizing what you did before, and the fear that their space moves so fast that they can't sit and wait. We [non-tech companies] have to begin to bring that attitude into our businesses. And so we have to, in a lot of respects, shift culture [and] cultural mindset. For example, Unilever is an effective comparison. Nearly 99% of households would one Unilever product. But in their growth focus there are always issues to deal with. With ambition comes challeng. The company is constantly facing challenges. Some current ones are; Path to Growth - Create an enterprise culture (winning in the market place) by working on leadership & growth/development. More focused brand portfolio - power brands and focusing on relationships with customers (eg Tesco, Walmart, Target, Walgreens, Sainsburys & Asda). "The organizational complexity was compounded by Unilever's wide portfolio of products and by the changes in these products over time. Edible fats, such as margarine, and soap and detergents were the historical origins of Unilever's business, but decades of diversification resulted in other activities. By the 1950s, Unilever manufactured convenience foods, such as frozen foods and soup, ice cream, meat products, and tea and other drinks. It manufactured personal care products, including toothpaste, shampoo, hairsprays, and deodorants. The oils and fats business also led Unilever into specialty chemicals and animal feeds. In Europe, its food business spanned all stages of the industry, from fishing fleets to retail shops. Among its range of ancillary services were shipping, paper, packaging, plastics, and advertising and market research. Unilever also owned a trading company, called the United Africa Company, which began by importing and exporting into West Africa but, beginning in the 1950s, turned to investing heavily in local manufacturing, especially brewing and textiles".(http://hbswk.hbs.edu/item/unilevera-case-study) The relationship between organizational culture, product portfolio, businesses and digital technologies requires a certain mindset, and it may require a shift in your existing mindset before you can leverage digital technologies effectively. For example, Mohamed-Hédi Charki, an associate professor at EDHEC Business School in France, is a researcher studying the impact of a digital collaboration platform in a European cosmetics company. He noted that changing the siloed culture of the company was the biggest challenge associated with the implementation of the company's social collaboration platform. In fact, the CEO believed that the company's siloed culture was a barrier to collaboration and creativity. The company is still coming around and learning to use the tool to communicate and collaborate more effectively".Over the years, ITC http://bit.ly/2a9KKgO has evolved from a single product company to a multi-business corporation. Its businesses are spread over a wide spectrum, ranging from cigarettes and tobacco to hotels, packaging, paper and paperboards and international commodities trading. Each of these businesses is vastly different from the others in its type, the state of its evolution and the basic nature of its activity, all of which influence the choice of the form of governance. The challenge of governance for ITC therefore lies in fashioning a model that addresses the uniqueness of each of its businesses and yet strengthens the unity of purpose of the Company as a whole.

Learning 6 - There is no definite management style(s) of the top management (direct reports and company defined top management excluding the CEO) that influences the culture of the organization?

The direct reports to the CEO invariably were aligned in management style to that of the CEO and where variations were observed there was also a dissonance in their approach to problem solving and decision making.

Darren Faint, a senior professional from the Investment Banking Division, of a Global Canadian Bank describes his personal leadership beliefs and styles in managing a high performing team:

1. *"An effective leader must understand the personalities of their various team players and determine what motivates them to be successful*

   - *Some people require micromanagement and constant supervision. Most other people in a high performing culture know what they need to do and therefore micromanagement can be a hindrance to their performance*

   - *Instead, an effective leader can manage these highly motivated, driven people by supporting them through a simple tap on the shoulder to say "Good job" or becoming involved to help resolve difficult issues*

   - *These people know what is expected of them and what they must do to achieve success – the leader's responsibility is to ensure they don't get in the way of these people but instead to check in on a periodic basis to ensure they have what they need and nothing is in their way*

2. *A leader must understand what the goal or objective is for the team to achieve. In many high performing cultures, it is an annual target that is expected. The leader must fully understand what everyone on the team needs to do to achieve this target and then be able to clearly articulate this target – getting input from the team members is a very effective way to get buy-in*

3. *A leader must understand the various roles on the team – they don't have to know every detail in how to complete a job but must know enough so that they can properly help those team members that may be struggling – a lot of times this support can be achieved by brainstorming out loud and trying to get the team member to think about how they can accomplish their tasks – in many cases the team member knows the answers, the leader just needs to get them thinking – the leader should also be willing to take responsibility for seeking help from others if answers remain unknown – by the leader taking responsibility, it will show their commitment level to the goal*

4. *An effective leader must demonstrate a commitment to the team and demonstrate to the team how they are contributing to the team's goal – too many leaders want to be viewed as a superior and not willing to get their 'hands dirty' – leaders that are involved in the work have a better understanding of what is working and what isn't working*

5. *An effective leader gets to know their team members – from the support staff to the high performing players – this demonstrates that the leader cares about their team members and allows the leader to help when they can see a team member is struggling – if a team member is struggling due to an event in their personal life, an effective leader will recognize this and be able to provide support – this goes a long way to creating high moral in the workplace*

6. *Effective leaders must celebrate successes, even small successes. It doesn't have to be a big celebration, but something simple to motivate team members and help them feel that progress is being made*

7. *At one point in my career, I believed that if you had a team of very strong players, you didn't need a coach or leader. I have learned first-hand that a strong and effective leader will raise the performance of any team, even a team that is composed of very strong players.*

8. *When a leader is effective at managing a high performing team, each team member will not only do their best for themselves but also to ensure their leader is successful*

9. *I believe that the flatter an organization, the more effective the leadership can be. First, leaders in a flatter organizational structure are closer to the work that is being done and can see the impact of their decisions. Too many big corporations today have too many layers and when a decision is made, they have no idea of the unintended consequences of these decisions.*

10. *Organizations that believe and trust in their employees are also critical for success. Many corporations make their employees assume all of the risks involved in daily business transactions but give them very little authority to make decisions.*

Darren Faint concludes, "my leadership style is very much based on the belief that a team effort will always outperform any individual effort. We all have our own specialties and talents. A good leader is able to recognize these talents and put together a team where these talents can be complimented".

The internal relationship balance and the mixture the effectiveness of power, status, hierarchy, authority, responsibility, individualism, group cohesion; the general relationship mixture of task/social/development was observed. Dee Hock says, "Control is not leadership; management is not leadership; leadership is leadership. If you seek to lead, invest at least 50% of your time in leading yourself—your own purpose, ethics, principles, motivation, conduct. Invest at least 20% leading those with authority over you and 15% leading your peers." Founder and CEO Emeritus, Visa.

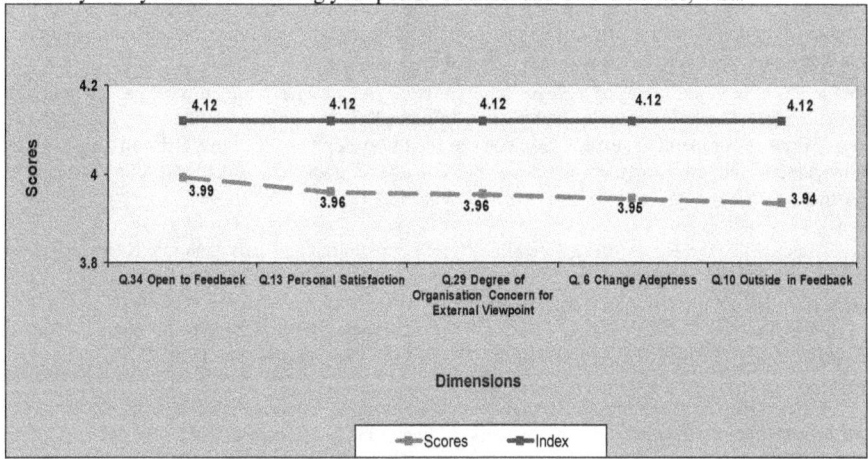

Figure 37 – Select Digital Culture Dimensions – Research Mean and Industry Benchmarks

Learning 7 - There is no difference in leadership disrupted styles that are available in the companies being studied.

Clearly there is no one all-pervasive management style. In this study we identified 8 different styles of leadership disrupted depending upon the organizational model and influenced by the culture that they represented.

Harvey Mackay says, "Don't equate activity with efficiency. You are paying your key people to see the big picture. Don't let them get bogged down in a lot of meaningless meetings and paper shuffling. Announce a Friday afternoon off once in a while. Cancel a Monday morning meeting or two. Tell the cast of characters you'd like them to spend the amount of time normally spent preparing for attending the meeting at their desks, simply thinking about an original idea." The actions of top management also have a major, if not a direct impact on the organization's culture demonstrated through practices, outcomes, feedback and cost and consequences. Employees observe management's behavior, actions speaking louder than words "such as, the time the supervisor was reprimanded or rewarded for doing a good or not a great job on time, just because he was not asked to do it beforehand or the time that so-and-so was fired because she publicly disagreed with the company's position and spoke of her disagreement." These incidents then, over time establish norms that filter down through the organization and convey whether risk taking is desirable; how much freedom managers should give their subordinates; what is appropriate dress; what actions will pay off in terms of pay raises, promotions, and other rewards; and the like.

Learning 8 - Leadership disrupted does not influence and direct the culture of an organization through HRM practices/ processes like hiring, training, performance appraisal, goals, objectives, compensation, rewards and communication. Refer - KPMG EIU Report. The

author was a co-sponsor of this project as a member of the Global Leadership Steercom @ KPMG LLP.

KPMG EIU (Refer Shermon 2012) report states, "The value of the Human Resources (HR) function elicits sharply contradictory views within organizations. On the one hand, in today's competitive global markets, the "war for talent" is understood to be crucial to almost every business. On the other hand, the HR function is often dismissed as non-essential or ineffective. Respondents to the study commissioned by KPMG International, give similarly mixed messages. About eight in ten (81 percent) respondents say that putting in place the most effective talent management strategy will be key to competitive success. Some six in ten (59 percent) believe that HR will grow in strategic importance. But just 17 percent maintain that HR does a good job of demonstrating its value to the business.

Meanwhile, the forces of globalization, talent constraints and new technology are driving rapid change to the HR function. Fifty-five percent of survey respondents believe the metrics that de ne success in HR today will fundamentally change over the next 3 years. *Rethinking Human Resources in a Changing World* examines the nature of the challenges facing the HR function and its future direction. KPMG EIU 2012 report include a few of the following; (Shermon 2012)

Flexibility, the reconfigurable organization is built upon the assumption that there will be change. As routine tasks are automated, more work is becoming project-based and focused around teams, deadlines, and deliverables. People may often participate on multiple teams simultaneously. Networks are actively fostered and valued to allow teams to form and reform around regions, functions, customers, products, processes, and projects. The reconfigurable organization attracts people who have a high tolerance for ambiguity, change, and unpredictability

HR is struggling with the challenges of managing a global, exible workforce. The global workforce has become increasingly integrated across borders while simultaneously growing more virtual and exible. Do not just hire skilled workers; hire "skill able" workers. Successful companies are going after particular kinds of people today These developments have made the retention of key talent and building workforces in new markets the top priorities of HR departments over the last 3 years. Survey respondents expect little change in the next 3 years. Yet only about one in four respondents say that HR at their company excels at core issues such as sourcing and retaining key talent globally; supporting a virtual and exible workforce; and supporting the greater globalization of the business.

Employee Commitment. Much has been written on the new employee contract. In exchange for giving up job security, people want their work contribution to be recognized and rewarded appropriately. In addition, they want to be given the opportunity to learn skills that will be valued in the internal and external marketplace. They also want peers who are trained and capable of performing at high levels. The reconfigurable organization enables its employees to deliver excellence to its customers by providing the right tools, skills, and information. As a result, employees believe in the company's products and services, recommend it as a good place to work, and choose to stay longer with the company.

Managing The Intervention - It is generally cheaper to identify and fix problems during design than during implementation; *Do Not Neglect User Training and Support in Design:* Support requirements, usage standards, and related policies may need to be designed along with the technology. Neglecting these may cause rework as later teams realize a lost opportunity. The design of "good help screens" is a common example. The generation of grouping options can be done in a number of ways, but the following questions should generally be considered: What are the most strategically critical activities around which we should group? What is the best sequence of grouping? (The top-level grouping determines the grouping options farther down.) Which method allows the business to achieve its strategy? Which method fits with the implementation? Which method allows the organization to focus on the new skills needed? Which activities are similar and should sit together? To what extent does the option increase utilization of resources? How does the grouping affect the development of individuals and the organization's capacity to use its human resources? How does grouping affect specialization and economies of scale? How does grouping affect measurement and control issues? How does grouping affect the organization's output? How responsive is each organization form to important competitive demands? What tax and legal restrictions/opportunities are there? Generate linking mechanisms; Determine potential benefits and limitations of each option.

Why is a high-performance workforce a source of competitive advantage? Perhaps the most important reason is because a company's culture cannot be as readily imitated as its products and marketing strategies. Several companies are getting many parts of the human performance agenda right, as the Accenture research initiative uncovered. What, after all, sets high-performing companies such as General Electric, Nokia, Microsoft and Sony apart from their competitors? A variety of things, of course, but these and many other global companies today consistently follow six imperatives that can create a workforce with sustained high-performance levels.

Finding ways to engage with workers will help address the challenges of this global, exible and remote workforce. Insights from interviewees for this report point toward improved employee engagement as the way to address many of these problems. Able to learn is a differentiator. Leading companies hire not just those individuals with the "skill du jour" but those who are good learners—people who will be able to adopt new skills as strategies change. This will involve creative solutions, such as the development of HR policies and approaches that have global application but can be made relevant to local conditions. It will also require new ways to engage meaningfully with a workforce that is less committed to the organization.

Change Readiness - Change is difficult for everyone. Even when people acknowledge that change is necessary and that the end result will be better, the process can be demoralizing and stressful. Often, despite good intentions on the part of managers, people don't understand why change is occurring or why certain decisions have been made. It's not merely a communication problem. People are often told the reasons why a change is occurring. Usually, they're not convinced. It sometimes appears that managers are "rearranging the furniture" rather than making change for sound business reasons. In the reconfigurable organization, employees understand the design assumptions and are involved in the design process. When changes inevitably have to be made again, the mechanisms are in place to have the conversations, debate the options, and move forward with decisions. People may still experience individual negative impact, but the organization is no longer turned upside down by the change. It has developed resilience and collective competence in the process of organizational change.

Technology has already transformed HR and the application of data analytics will foster even more profound change. Sixty-nine percent of companies surveyed say it is more common for the HR function to provide web-based and/or mobile HR platforms (e.g. benefits, payroll) than it was 3 years ago; only 3 percent of respondents have cut back on these technology enhancements. These have already enabled HR to do its basic, administrative work faster and more efficiently. They have also provided employees with more exible and tailored training opportunities while creating a positive culture for communication.

The advent of data analytics – the most commonly cited area by respondents for IT investment in the next 3 years – will lead to the next technological quantum leap for HR. Interviewees explain that the **application of analytics,** if done properly, will enable a more robust understanding of employee-related needs and opportunities. Diverse is good. With business increasingly being played on a global stage, workforce diversity—not only of race and gender but also age, language, thinking style, religion and culture—is critical. Technology-savvy - Companies need employees who understand the strategic value of IT and who not only can envision the new technological future but also can help make it a reality. For example, already 57 percent of respondents say that data analytics is helping to identify future talent gaps.

Technology and economy: twin catalysts for HR transformation. Powerful technologies, emerging in times of heightened financial constraints, present a rare opportunity for HR to enact long-overdue reinvention. Refer - *Strategic Discontinuities - Four key insights/disruptions in People Management.* Looking ahead, HR needs to:

- *develop greater confidence, leadership disrupted and credibility, so that HR heads can deservedly insist on a place in strategic conversations at the highest levels*
- *develop closer partnerships within the company, especially with line managers who will inevitably use technology-driven HR services to play a greater role in employee management*
- *recast its strategy so that it begins from a whole- business perspective and is aligned with the needs of the entire company, not just the HR function.*

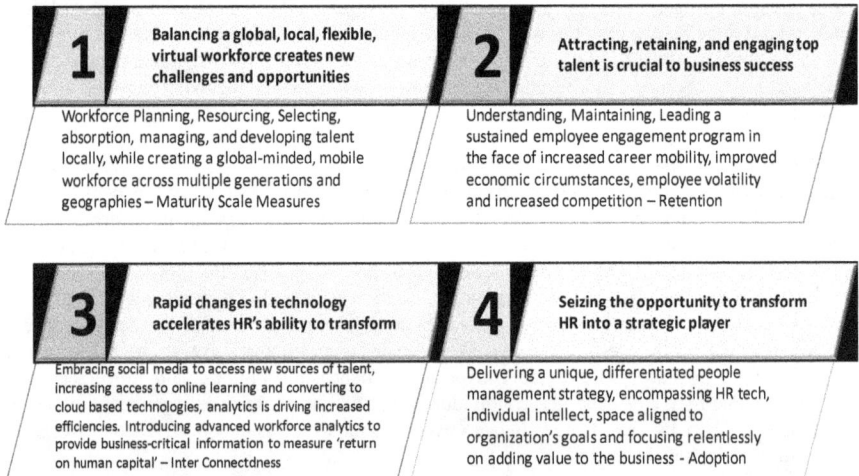

1 Balancing a global, local, flexible, virtual workforce creates new challenges and opportunities

Workforce Planning, Resourcing, Selecting, absorption, managing, and developing talent locally, while creating a global-minded, mobile workforce across multiple generations and geographies – Maturity Scale Measures

2 Attracting, retaining, and engaging top talent is crucial to business success

Understanding, Maintaining, Leading a sustained employee engagement program in the face of increased career mobility, improved economic circumstances, employee volatility and increased competition – Retention

3 Rapid changes in technology accelerates HR's ability to transform

Embracing social media to access new sources of talent, increasing access to online learning and converting to cloud based technologies, analytics is driving increased efficiencies. Introducing advanced workforce analytics to provide business-critical information to measure 'return on human capital' – Inter Connectdness

4 Seizing the opportunity to transform HR into a strategic player

Delivering a unique, differentiated people management strategy, encompassing HR tech, individual intellect, space aligned to organization's goals and focusing relentlessly on adding value to the business - Adoption

Figure 38 – Strategic Discontinuities - Four key insights/disruptions in People Management

Amid current worldwide economic difficulties, the globalization of business continues apace. Companies from developed countries are seeking greener pastures, while those from emerging markets have acquired sufficient scale to start taking on the world. At the same time, cost-conscious businesses are turning to technology to become increasingly exible and virtual. As a result of these forces, HR executives are focusing on the following core challenges as per this KPMG report:

- *balancing the global and the local* – *managing, hiring and identifying talent globally while retaining important local insights*
- *managing a exible and virtual workforce* – *but not at the cost of loyalty and career development*
- *retaining the best talent* – *maintaining employee engagement in the face of a less committed, more exible workforce.*

Sixty-nine percent of survey respondents say that in the last 3 years, their companies have increased the use of mobile or web-based platforms. Nearly half (49 percent) are making greater use of the cloud to power these.

Web-based and mobile apps have enabled many employees to handle their own HR services, including benefits, payroll and performance evaluations. It is also about flexibility. Organizations are increasingly concerned with how "nimble" they are—and need people who can quickly change to meet new strategic demands. Match talent with the right opportunities. A principal reason why many companies have trouble retaining key talent is that they hinder people's mobility within and across the organization—and therefore limit their opportunities to grow. Companies that make it easier for employees to find and take on new opportunities within the organization are better at enhancing overall workforce performance. They also excel at keeping key individuals loyal, motivated and engaged longer than companies with rigid advancement and staffing policies. The shift to mobile and web- based platforms has not always been easy, though. "The story of HR ERPs is a fairly bloody one in most organizations," says Professor Huselid. "They cost a fortune and you see many big companies that can have difficulties just giving the payroll out." Yet the advantages of the HR self-service function are undeniable. Westcott cites the following HR improvements experienced at National Grid.

- *Doing the basics better and more efficiently* – *Moving toward a more self-service model has improved basic HR service efficiency while freeing up HR to focus on delivering more strategic services that add value to the core priorities of the business.*
- *Better training* – *National Grid has moved away from classroom training toward a more interactive, demonstrative approach. "This has been a very positive development and had a very powerful impact," notes Westcott. "It enables employees to learn in more bite-sized chunks and in a much more visual manner."*
- *Creating a positive culture and brand for current employees and potential hires* – *"New technologies are playing an important role in how we connect people in the organization and how we create a culture that is a medium for people," says Westcott? "We are exploring how we use the technology to create a company brand that is attractive to people joining it."*

The next step: data-driven HR

Data analytics is the most commonly cited area (selected by 31 percent of respondents) for planned HR technology investment in the next 3 years finds KPMG report. Analytics will allow HR to not only be involved in managing talent, but to also collect clearer information on its supply chain of talent and where the most demand for particular skills lies. Rather than acting on instinct alone, the HR function will be able to provide a far more granular roadmap of how the organization's people resources need to be reshaped to deliver on the corporate strategy. Many companies try to boost retention simply by throwing more money at key performers as against pushing for analytics. But the fact is that most research on job satisfaction and retention, including the Accenture study, shows that such a tactic may actually undermine the culture and the performance of the organization. What employees really want—besides a competitive compensation package—is the opportunity to grow and develop, both personally and professionally.

- *Data analytics gives HR departments the long-overdue chance to become more empirical, to provide hard evidence for their opinions, thereby gaining much-needed credibility at the highest levels of the business.*
- *Data analytics gives HR departments the long-overdue chance to become more empirical, to provide hard evidence for their opinions, thereby gaining much-needed credibility at the highest levels of the business.*
- *Kate Terrell, vice president, Human Resources, Global Products Organization, at Whirlpool Corporation, a household appliance manufacturer, explains: "When you, arm a business partner of the future with analytics, and they can share the facts with their teams to help drive better decision-making, it allows you to be much more strategic, much more insightful, and potentially, much more laser-focused on where you should be spending your time."*

Collaboration can take a number of forms in the design process: Identifying the current state and the gap between where the organization is today and what needs to change to achieve the strategy. Researching and generating design options, Evaluating and testing proposals, Providing, input and reacting to design alternatives, Detailing and developing design decisions, Creating implementation plans. Participation yields a number of benefits. For example, more Ideas. The more people involved, the more ideas that are generated. In many organizations, people closest to the front lines, who deal firsthand with customers, technology, and process issues, have numerous untapped ideas. Often they can identify quick fixes that will have immediate impact. Commitment to Outcomes. People are more committed to decisions to which they feel they had input. If their suggestions and concerns have been genuinely heard and acknowledged, they will be more amenable to supporting directions with which they may not fully agree. Modeling New Relationships. Most organizational change initiatives have at least one objective focusing on building better working relationships among individuals and organizational units. If the participation process is structured to bring these groups together around the issues of design, new working relationships can be developed away from the heat of high-pressure business issues. Developing High Potentials. Work groups are ideal forums for high-potential employees to learn about other parts of the organization and gain exposure to the organization's senior leadership. The design and refinement process can be used as a development assignment for high performers who are ready to be more broadly involved in the future of the company.

Strikingly though, 81 percent of respondents, says KPMG, see talent management as a key competitive advantage over the coming 3 years. There clearly remains a vast gulf between the perceived importance and the perceived effectiveness of HR today. At the very least, HR has a perception problem. In many cases it may have actually failed to deliver real value. As the shifting challenges of globalization and virtualization combine with the new technological tools available to enable a reshaping of the HR function, executives should take a number of steps to improve the function's contribution and its image.

Make the value of HR more prominent and understood.

Perceptions about HR in the wider company may arise from the very nature of its role. As the HR function works behind the scenes, many in the organization may not be aware of the good things that it is doing. "This is an inevitable part of being a staff support role where HR is the architect and the line managers are owners of the work," says Professor Ulrich in this report.

Today's leading companies recognize that their measurement and development models must operate in real time and support a geographically dispersed workforce. To accomplish that objective, an increasing number of companies are taking advantage of new technology-based performance management tools. In essence, these bring the same type of analytics and tools to human performance management that have been available to supply chain managers for years. HR executives need to make sure the company knows and understands the value they can deliver, in part by insisting on being included in strategic conversations. "However you are organized, HR has to make sure it sits where power sits in an organization. Otherwise you are in a reactive mode and are not making the right proactive contribution," says Mr. Mitchell. This is not a one-way street: it also involves understanding the needs of the whole business better in order to make that contribution. "Learning to listen deeply is one of the skills that HR functions need to develop, not only in terms of the context of their role but in terms of continually improving the organization," says Ms. Van Mazijk. Being heard requires leadership, as well as the ability to provide valuable input. Professor Huselid notes that HR executives "have to be courageous leaders, able to force an argument on what is good business." Although such leadership certainly would help the pro le of HR, its real bene t comes from what it can offer the business. HR executives have to be courageous leaders, able to force an argument on what is good business. KPMG EIU Report.

Think, understand and communicate in the language of business.

HR needs to eliminate the jargon of its specialization (the same challenge IT continues to face) and begin to link its work more explicitly to business value. The right business language helps to open the door, but it is also important to provide a robust business case for projects. It entails thinking more carefully about the specific business outcomes of the actions that HR recommends. What is the impact on customer service, or the reduction in costs, or the increase in staff loyalty, or other metrics that are more specifically relevant to the line managers and departments being supported? Importantly, it is also about taking a fuller perspective of the whole business, including both internal factors as well as external business conditions, and creating HR strategies to align. Using adaptive goal setting could be an example here. A frequent charge levied by employees against their managers is a simple uncertainty about expectations. This lack of clarity hampers the performance not only of the employees but of the entire company. Research has shown a clear increase in shareholder value by companies that can successfully focus their people on the right strategy. In turn, this requires a far deeper grasp of the organization's core business model and strategy and the implications this holds for the rest of the business – to date, something that far too few HR practitioners have mastered. To put this in context, a business that fundamentally focuses on providing low-cost goods will require a fundamentally different HR strategy than one that is focused on delivering leading-edge innovation.

Move from administration to higher-value-added activities.

A technology-enabled HR function will allow professionals to avoid being immersed in the minutiae of record-keeping, transactions and life-cycle processes. But it will also likely reduce the number of HR staff that companies require. These slimmed-down departments will then be able to focus on providing more strategic, higher-order services. Some of HR's traditional administrative work will almost inevitably and another functional home, a shift that 45 percent of respondents expect to occur in the next 3 years. A number of innovative tools and approaches have arisen to address this need. The same performance management tools discussed above, for example, also are helping set and achieve goals by enabling managers to communicate objectives and expectations to their workers in real time via a personalized Web portal. As a result, team members can change direction more quickly to align actions and behavior. There is no compelling reason for HR to manage the transactional administration of payroll, benefits, pensions or mobility (transfer administration), particularly where managed on a contractual outsourcing basis. Of course, HR would remain the architect of these systems. But once the desired model is established, there is no reason why HR needs to pedal the wheels.

Jack Welsh, **"Focus on a few key objectives ...** I only have three things to do. I have to choose the right people, allocate the right number of dollars, and transmit ideas from one division to another with the speed of light. So I'm really in the business of being the gatekeeper and the transmitter of ideas." Leadership significantly influences, directs, guides and monitors the HRM philosophy, policy and practices of the company and the cultures. In all observed companies the HRM Heads were direct reports holding top management status, with a HR strategy, clearly articulated mandate and openly defined policy positions.

In evaluating **HRM effectiveness rites and rituals** were also observed. These are the punctuation marks of organization operations. They include: pay negotiations; internal and external job application means and methods; disciplinary, grievance and dismissal procedures; rewards; individual, group, departmental and divisional publicity; training and development activities; parties and celebrations; key appointments and dismissals; socialization and integration of people into new roles, activities and responsibilities.

Fast-forward to the future

Too often, organizations make plans for *tomorrow* based on the people they have and the situation they are in *today*.

By contrast, organizations need to work with clients to identify the skills and capabilities their organizations will need to win in the future – so they can begin building them into their workforces today.

The process starts by helping them decide where they will need to do business in the future – and what kind of people they will need tomorrow. Strategic workforce planning is, therefore, a key component of an institutions approach to talent management.

This forward-looking focus also helps organizations tune into the needs of their future talent – to see talent management through the eyes of a new set of workers. Specifically, this means taking a cold, hard look at current processes and technologies – and being prepared to radically evolve them to meet the needs of the next generation of employees.

Talent management as a business-critical process

Many organizations are currently failing to pay proper attention to their talent- related risks. With this in mind, it is important to embed talent risks such as succession, skills availability, key person dependencies and retirement cliffs firmly into an organization's enterprise risk management framework. This helps to place these risks on the radar of the right people at the right level. Talent-related decisions must be evaluated for their return on investment – and this intelligence should then be recycled to inform future talent decisions. Most importantly, strategic talent planning should be part of business planning – not a standalone and isolated HR exercise.

Learning 9 - The CEO would not focus on monetary reward program for retention of high performers.

On the contrary the CEO's of all the observed companies was a member of the Compensation and Rewards committee and was actively involved in commissioning in External Salary and remuneration Surveys, was involved in the Key performance target setting, establishing goals, identifying star performers and the managing the program.

It is the issue of people. If people were important yesterday and important today, by God, they will be extremely important tomorrow. Therefore, the priority should be to attract the very best talent. We are going to do it in two ways. One is through remuneration. But the important thing is to make the company an exciting and vibrant place for people to come and work.   (Previous Unilever Inc. chairman)

Speech by the CEO of a Professional Services Firm. "To attract, retain and develop talent are the three key things that the group and our companies need to address. Providing employees with challenging jobs, rewarding them with competitive salaries and investing in their development can do this. This is a different approach from the paternalistic one adopted a couple of decade's back, which was: 'I will take charge of your life.' The formula now is: 'I will make available opportunities that enable you to add value to yourself.' We can provide a framework, a structure and an environment, but whether employees add value to themselves depends on how much they invest in themselves. What we can do is provide a range of challenging jobs, reward good performance, offer competitive remuneration and provide continuous opportunities. People have always been very important to the Tata Group and the human resource function is being given high priority in the restructuring and refocusing exercise presently underway in the organization. That's why the senior management, after a rigorous search, handpicked a new group HR team of three senior professionals. (HR Head) Refer - http://bit.ly/2a5fSdG "

"We are well on our way to closing this year and delivering to our planned targets. Our success to date is testimony to our collective efforts and we should rightly be proud of what we have achieved. In the increasingly competitive environment that we operate in, our ability to sustain and build on the past success requires us to meaningfully distinguish ourselves from the rest - to work with the right clients, bring deep skills to the table, seamlessly blend a number of our service offerings to craft innovative solutions and deliver tangible value in everything we do. Two years ago, we began a process to review our compensation processes. There are a number of objectives that we are seeking to secure: To ensure that our cash rewards are aggressively benchmarked against the market - we hire the best people and we want to reward them suitably. To introduce an element of variability in our compensation structure to more effectively recognize differing levels of performance while at the same time allowing us to drive performance in areas that are core to our business success at any given point in time. To build greater linkages between our performance appraisal processes and our compensation setting processes and in general, to rationalize our overall compensation construct so that it is easier for everyone to understand and administer".

"As part of the process, we introduced a variable, performance linked reward for the Executive Team in FY 2016. We are now extending this arrangement in a relatively less complex manner, to our group of Seniors, Consultants & Senior Consultants and Senior Consultants. Accordingly, we have formulated ASPUR (Active Spurring Performance Through Rewards) as a mechanism to reward specific performance in any given year. ASPUR will, in its proposed form, be based entirely on the performance evaluation of each individual for the year, subject to the overall performance of the Firm as a whole in that year. Subject to the Firm meeting its plan targets, for Fiscal 17, ASPUR will reward performances as follows:

Performance evaluation for the year	Payout Percentage
Meets Expectations	19%
Exceeds Expectations	32%
Demonstrates Excellence	47%

A series of communication meetings have also been planned to provide more information and any clarifications that you may require. Over time, we may vary the parameters within which SPUR will operate, to most effectively respond to your aspirations and to the changing needs of the Firm.

As always, career progression will remain central to our reward strategy. Career progression in turn, is a function of the competencies that each individual develops, and progression to the next higher level of responsibility will be based on a demonstration of the required level of competency by each individual. This is an important distinction that we are making between performance and competency - these are two separate issues and as such must be considered quite independently. As with variable pay, this is a concept that we have already introduced into our overall appraisal system at certain key levels - it is now our intention to extend this concept to all levels of career progression within our Senior Consultant group. To this end, we are reviewing our performance evaluation processes so that they are aligned with this approach, and we will communicate more with you on these aspects over the coming months.

Finally, we are aiming to rationalize our overall compensation framework to provide for a single point of compensation corresponding to each level of responsibility; this will replace the present framework that has multiple compensation points at each level of responsibility. While this has not been fully implemented for Fiscal 2016, the processes that we have outlined above will facilitate such a move and we intend to make effective Fiscal 2017. This single point of compensation will be benchmarked to the market, and as in the past, our endeavor will be to ensure that we have an extremely competitive compensation positioning for all our people.

The year ahead is going to be full of challenges - competition is fierce and the economic environment is not particularly friendly. However, we remain confident in our abilities to produce strong growth in Fiscal 2016. This confidence comes from the fact that we have bright, talented people, a strong client service orientation and a drive to excel. We will need all of that and more, and the individual efforts of each one of you will be vital if we are to make the difference. The formula for sustained, profitable growth is simple - hire the best people, develop deep competencies, continuously challenge and reward the people, and deliver outstanding service to clients. You are central to this equation and we want you to share in the Firm's success - a combination of career progression and ASPUR payouts is designed to ensure just that".

Learning 10 - Top Management's Commitment towards building a Digital Culture.

Top management time of well over 50 % depending upon the season, included, spent their time attracting, mentoring, coaching, training, counseling, performance reviewing and energizing people to join and stay in the organization. All the companies had a well-established socialization and retention program including exit systems etc.

When executives assume, without asking, that they understand the expectations and needs of their people, they risk making poor decisions about such important factors as working environment, employee recognition, incentives and communication methods. To overcome this, you must listen carefully when employees discuss their expectations and needs. Most executives spend 80 percent or more of their time listening to people, but unfortunately half the time they don't really hear what's being said. When an executive treats every employee the same, serious problems arise. Treating everyone the same communicates the message," I don't care enough about you to find out what makes you unique." To remove this block, you must identify and understand the difference among individuals. This does not mean you develop a different set of policies for each employee, but it does mean you recognize and respond to the differences among your people. Executives who view their employees as tools or production units deserve ten years of hard labor as a tool or production unit. On the other hand, those who try to induce in their organizations the intensity and intimacy of their family relationships wins the same sort of satisfaction and security they enjoy at home. Not just for them but for their family relationships win the same sort of satisfaction and security they enjoy at home, not just for themselves but for their employees as well.

Locking employees into a past perception ignores the fact that people change, at times quickly and in major ways. Regardless of deep-seated idiosyncrasies and personality traits, tomorrow's employee may differ as much from today's as today's differs from yesterdays. People acquire new technical knowledge, learn new skills, increase their experience and judgment, improve competence, and evolve interpersonal relationships. Track employee progress a and backsliding with a keen radar. If an employee achieves a major achievement. If an employee seems to have lost something, investigate out why.

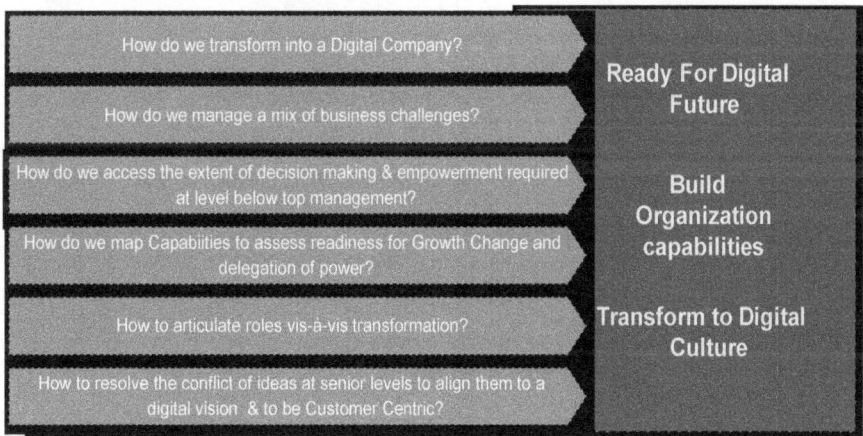

Figure 39 – Select Areas of Focus for Transformation - Digital HR

A shared vision exists when people recognize that they hold similar value systems With a shared vision, members of the culture are enthusiastic about cultural goals and the processes by which they will be achieved. A shared vision implies a sense of inclusion: members of the culture are not being left behind. Given an appropriate consideration, meaning and purpose the employee seek to value and share a vision.

In his masterful work Human Intimacy, Illusion and Reality, Victor L. Brown asserts that the realities of human intimacy include love, trust, openness, sincerity, service, and sacrifices. While the illusions of human intimacy trap us into self-obsession, manipulation, personal gratification, superficiality, and a false belief that violating the realities of human intimacy will not bring damaging consequences. According to Brown, successful human relationships grows from kindness, empathy, and commitment, and he warns that illusions about human relationships arise when people relate to "fragments of human beings," "deny the consequences of human behavior," and "deal in indulgence, not   discipline." https://ojs.lib.byu.edu/spc/index.php/IssuesInReligionAndPsychotherapy/article/viewFile/146/145   - Despite the fact that contemporary society enjoys the virtually unlimited technology to create material comfort, people in our society tend to move from one superficial, unfulfilling relationship to another. Only through deep commitment and hard work can people win lasting pleasure and enduring security. But it does take work to talk to, touch, and in other ways cultivate intimacy with others.

E. Scenario Analysis

This section covers the findings pertaining to the 16 scenarios administered to the respondents. The sample being top management and other managerial cadre were managed in such a way that some of the sample respondents received questions pertaining to the hypotheses, some in regard to scenarios and others on survey feedback and content analysis material for the purposes of constructing the case studies. Scenario and content analysis involved detailing primary and secondary data, cross-verifying findings with third part neutral leaders and comparing with market sources.

Effectively the study comparisons conducted, broadly indicates the following:

- *A Visionary Leader in a Competing Organization influences a Digital culture predominantly.*
- *A Driver in a Performing Enterprise influences a Digital culture.*
- *A Teacher in a Learning Company influences an Executive Culture predominantly.*
- *A Scientist or a Technocrat in a mechanistic corporation influences an Operator Culture.*
- *A People Strategist in an Institution influences an Engineering Culture predominantly.*
- *A Teacher in a Human Organization influences an Engineering Culture.*
- *A Manager in a Voluntary School influences an Operator culture predominantly.*
- *A Builder in an Institution influences an Operator and a Digital Culture.*

It is also important to understand that each if the three aspects pertaining to Culture, leadership and organizational model appears to overlap each other and the exact trigger of what primarily influences another would be desirable to be studied. For the moment that leadership disrupted styles in an organizational context influences culture to a degree has been attempted. This was possible through content analysis of the planned interview, studying the organization case and the CEO's responses. It could equally be valid to see if a leadership style in a particular culture creates what type of an organizational model. Or what type of organizational model's) in a particular type of culture(s) creates specific leadership style(s).

F. Role of Leadership disrupted - Creating Cultures – Map to The Intellectual Company

Various theoretical and practical aspects of leadership are available in literature. The classic study studies on leadership set the stage for the theoretical development of leadership disrupted. The trait theories concentrate on the leaders themselves but, with the possible exception of intelligence and empathy/interpersonal sensitivity and self-confidence, really do not come up with any agreed upon traits of leaders. In recent times the trait approach has surfaced in terms of managerial skills and abilities identified for selection and training/ development purpose.

Historical contributions to the study of organizational behavior had indirect or direct implications for leadership disrupted style. For example, the Hawthorne studies were interpreted in terms of their implications for supervisory style. Also relevant is the classic work done by Douglas McGregor, in which his Theory X represents the old, authoritarian style of leadership and his Theory Y represents the enlightened, humanistic style. And indeed the Theory Z focused on participate management. The studies discussed are directly concerned with style. The Iowa studies analyzed the impact of autocratic, democratic and laissez faire styles, and the studies conducted by the Michigan group found the employee-centered supervisor to be more effective than the production-centered supervisor. The Ohio State studies identified consideration (a supportive type of style) and initiating structure (a directive type of style) as being the major functions of leadership. The trait, group and social learning theories have indirect implications for style, and the human relations and task directed styles play an important role in Fiedler's contingency theory. The path-goal conceptualization depends heavily upon directive, supportive, participate and achievement oriented styles of leadership.

Another major player in the field was Richard Beckhard - http://bit.ly/2a5nlcB . In his 1969 book he described "several assumptions about the nature and functioning of organizations" held by OD practitioners.

Here is his list.

- *The basic building blocks of an organization are groups (teams), structures, designs, functions, roles. Therefore, the basic units of change are groups, not individuals.*
- *An always-relevant change goal is the reduction of inappropriate competition between parts of the organization and the development of a more collaborative condition.*
- *Decision making in healthy organization is located where the information sources are, rather than in a particular role or level of hierarchy.*
- *Organizations, sub units of organization, and individuals continuously manage their affairs against goals. Controls are interim measurements, not the basis of managerial strategy.*
- *One goal of a healthy organization is to develop generally open communication, mutual trust, and confidence between and across levels.*
- *"People support what they help create." People affected by a change must be allowed active participation and a sense of ownership in the planning and conduct of the change.*
- *Robert Tannenbaum, professor at UCLA, and Sheldon Davis, director of organization development at TRW Systems, presented their view of OD values in a 1969 article. They asserted that an important shift in values was occurring and that this shift signaled a more appropriate and accurate view of people in organizations.*

They listed these values in transition as follows: Refer - Robert Tannenbaum

- *Away from a view of people as essentially bad toward view of people as basically good.*
- *Away from avoidance of negative evaluation of individuals toward confirming them as human beings.*

- *Away from a view of individuals as fixed, toward seeing them as being in process.*
- *Away from resisting and fearing individual differences toward accepting and utilizing them.*
- *Away from utilizing an individual primarily with reference to his or her job description toward viewing an individual as a whole person.*
- *Away from walling off the expression of feelings toward making possible both appropriate expression and effective use.*
- *Away from marksmanship and game playing toward authentic behavior.*
- *Away from use of status for maintaining power and personal prestige toward use of status for organizationally relevant purposes.*
- *Away from distrusting people toward trusting them.*
- *Away from avoiding facing others with relevant data toward making appropriate confrontation.*
- *Away from avoidance of risk taking toward willingness to risk.*
- *Away from a view of process work as being unproductive effort toward seeing it as essential to effective task accomplishment.*
- *Away from a primary emphasis on competition toward a much greater emphasis on collaboration.*

For ease of presentation, the styles listed may be substituted for the expressions "boss-centered" and "subordinate-centered" used by Tannenbaum and Schmidt in their classic leadership continuum. The verbal descriptions and the relationship between authority and freedom give a rough representation of characteristics of the various styles of leadership. One thing is certain: leadership style can make a difference. For example, a recent survey found that senior executives view their companies' leadership styles as pragmatic rather than conceptual and conservative rather than risk taking. Importantly, these same executives felt that to meet their current and future challenges, the styles should be the other way around.

G. Is there an IDEAL Organizational and Management Model?

An ideal organization to be one where a person's promotion is unpredictable and depends largely on his own good performance. And where a person can see exactly how his career will progress after certain periods of time, that regards special benefits, such as attractive bonuses, free pension schemes and a company car, as the prime incentives to remain in the job. That concentrates on tempting new employees with interesting work although it is not able to pay as much as other organizations providing less interesting work and where it is emphasized that the 'job comes first', therefore after work pleasure should take secondary importance. And where it is very difficult to carry on work over a weekend period should someone so desire. Where the few changes in tasks that occur allow people to perform one type of work with considerable care and proficiency. And where there is constant pressure to complete a task well in a short period of time and to then become involved with another task. And where there is a general attitude that, even if the working conditions are very poor, much can be compensated by interesting work. Where little that is favorable can be said about the work, itself but where the attitude of management towards its employees' welfare is first class. That gives people jobs that can very likely be done well. That gives people work which is not so difficult that they would, have to rely on luck to do a good job nor so easy that they are bound to succeed. Where it is expected that leisure time will be sacrificed if work pressure is great. Or where it is felt that working late is undesirable because eventually strain will be experienced in normal working hours. That believes that if a person concentrates primarily on working in a warm, close fashion with his co-workers, good work must follow. That regards the successful completion of an employee's assignment as more important than the feelings of that person's co-workers. That expects individuals to help the organization by fulfilling their own personal goals. That expects its employees to strongly identify with the organization rather than think of themselves as individuals apart. Where good working companions and generous holidays are provided to make up for the tedious nature of the work. Where there is more concern with employees' satisfaction with the actual work that they do than with their general conditions of work. Where each employee is solely responsible for most of the work that he performs and where several people are always responsible for, and take the credit for, a particular piece of work.

Would your ideal boss be someone, who gives his employees work that they feel sure of doing well without too much effort or who gives people work requiring quite a lot of struggling to matter? And who insist on finding out how worthwhile his employees see their work but neglects looking into the enjoyment that they get from their work? Who regards the pleasure that his employees get from their work as more important than the actual worthwhile ness of the work. Is he someone who emphasizes the importance of the work group's responsibility for its decisions rather than particular individuals in the group taking the responsibility? Who relies on a particularly efficient individual in a work group to control the group's activities and who expects to be consulted only for very exceptional work problems. Who encourages employees to follow set procedures in their work. Who attempts to provide attractive work for his employees even if it is not of great value to them. Who would not give people work that they could view as of little value even though it may not be highly attractive to them? Who gives his employees general guidelines on which to base their own decision about how to proceed with their work? Who gives clear, very comprehensive instructions on how employees should carry out their work. Who finds that for group morale it is better to try to preserve good co-worker relationships that may be spoiled by letting people keep working at a task to their own satisfaction. Who feels that a certain degree of bad feeling amongst employees is worth tolerating if they are very much involved with their work? Who looks for future employees who will be able to work independently of others. Who looks for future employees who will primarily be good at getting on well with other employees? Who would rather employees consulted him with work difficulties than struggle with them themselves. Who will not interfere with work for which employees have responsibility. Who expects an individual's work rate to remain relatively uninfluenced by his colleagues? Who relies on the group as a whole to produce a given amount of work, expecting the group to influence an individual's quantity of work done? Who views good employee relations as being most important and incompatible with competitiveness? Who insists on individuals trying to achieve a better performance rating than their co-workers. Who gives employees work where they need to write fairly detailed arguments about problems solutions? Who gives employees work that involves very little written reporting or problem discussions? Who feels that working late should be avoided. Who encourages working late in order to meet a deadline.

Digital Cultures in an Intellectual Company

Leadership	Culture	Organization
People Strategist	Operator Culture	Human Company
Teacher	Executive Culture	Institution
Builder	Engineering Culture	Competing Enterprise
Visionary	Digital Culture	Learning Corporation

Figure 40 – Digital HR in an Intellectual Company

H. Trends and Leading Practices

Digital Practice 1 - How Do Leaders Impact Organizational Cultures, structures, designs, roles in a way that works for organizational effectiveness? Edgar Schein - http://www.tnellen.com/ted/tc/schein.html

"Culture Beginnings and the Impact of Founders as Leaders spring from multiple sources:

- Core family philosophy, upbringing, experience, beliefs, values, and assumptions of founders
- Experimentation and consequent learning experiences of group members.
- New beliefs, values, and changing assumptions brought by new members
- Leaders have a point of view and articulate this point of view thorough periodic intervals and at varying locations and groups of people.
- Leaders choose to impact culture conscious of their influence.

The process of culture formation is the process of creating a small group:

Single person (founder) has an idea

- Founder brings in one or more people and creates core group. They share vision and believe in the risk. founding group acts in concert, raises money, work space
- Others are brought in and a history is begun. They influence as they learn, experiment and implement

Founders/Leaders embed and transmit culture by making assumptions that are "taught" to the group. They make out things tried out are leader-imposed teaching and leaders get their ideas implemented through Socialization, Charisma and by acting, by doing, exuding confidence. Do you expect your people to respond to a given situation the same way you would? Even if you say," Of course not," don't be sure. Most of us can't help projecting our own attitudes and approaches on others. Even if you say successfully crawled into another person's head, you have to be constantly on guard against projecting your own ideas onto that person's decision or solution to a problem. Fortunately, if an employee's decision concerns the organization's commitment, competence, or consistency, a strong corporate culture will narrow the range of acceptable courses of action, but many decisions do not concern cultural factors. Some executives push so hard for conformance to a culture model that they thwart innovative, independent thinking, creating "yes" people instead. Such people do not support strong cultures. To remove this block, you must avoid projecting your own skills or styles when you evaluate employees' action. Detach yourself and rely on the tenets of your organization's culture rather than letting your biases determine your judgment".

Varying approaches may be required to address the needs of each engagement. Designing an organizational structure from scratch will require a different approach than helping to design an existing organizational structure. This section provides high-level guidance for the preferred approach techniques. Below are some high-level points to consider when performing an organization design: Keep the number of levels in the organization to a minimum to avoid unrealistic spans of control; Maintain an alignment between knowledge management and the organizational structure for effective communication and collaboration; Involve the client staff in all organization design work in order to achieve the level of client ownership and commitment desired to help ensure long-term sustainability; Use the organization's business strategy to drive its structure; Establish a flexible structure that is consistent with the environmental change demands; Consider creating economies of scale (reduce redundancies) by leveraging a shared services environment; The management structure, culture, and processes should embrace and support the organization design. Leadership must transform before the organization does; Link skills and desired competencies to a comprehensive model that outlines the skill progression required at each organizational level; Provide employees with development tools and training that help them attain the skills and abilities defined in the competency model; Establish clear roles and responsibilities that help the organization to meet its goals and the individuals to realize their full potential.

Digital Practice 2 - What are the Culture-Embedding Mechanisms in the context of leadership disrupted? Primary Embedding Mechanisms

- What leaders pay attention to, measure, and control on a regular basis
- Leaders influence values and ethics
- Leaders reaction to critical incidents and organizational crises
- Leaders allocate scarce resources based on their own observed criteria
- Leaders deliberately role model, teach, and coach
- Leaders allocate rewards and status
- Leaders staff, plan, recruit, select, evaluate, set goals, review, coach, engage, develop, promote, retire, and communicate with organizational members
- They Communicates major beliefs, values and rituals
- What is noticed and consequent comments made casual questions and remarks becomes powerful if leader sees it and is consistent
- Consistency more important than intensity of attention
- Attention on questions that leaders ask
- Attention to agendas for meetings set emotional reactions.
- Important what they do not react to.

Tales of the Field - Ben Van Deputt

Ben, an entrepreneur managing a global business (New Age Optics) out of Burlington, Ontario, Canada speaks of his leadership and culture building experience based on the growth of his business over the last two decades.

"As a young man (17 years +) we - me and a good friend - backpacked extensively for many years through the Swiss Alps, Austria, Italy etc. At an early age I was impressed how small communities thrived without an autocratic leader. My last years at the gymnasium (high school) and later in my university years, I attended an Eastern and Greek philosophy – Plato, in particular course I could helped me explore relationships, actions, core value systems, beliefs, all hands on and through history. I began to appreciate my legacy, my historical orientation, my roots and how would I need to adapt to this global world effectively. The above re-shaped my thinking of leadership at a young age and it has not changed much, only developed, improved, stabilized and explored.

I believe that core values are established at an early age. In the Netherlands, during my Catholic elementary school years grade 1-6, run by friars, I was a good student and I was groomed to become a priest. In my last year at the theological school, I decided that priesthood was not for me.

Gymnasium was my focus in the next 6 years and I eagerly took any elective philosophy class I could and was actively involved in many discussion groups.

This continued into university. My humanitarian and social values were taking shape. Being an engineering student meant mathematics, physics, analysis, problem solving, exploring, discovery and execution – More importantly to be hands on when required. Creating or analyzing forms and shapes or working with imaginary numbers which may not exist. Some Eulerian models captures the concept of sustainability. My discussion talking points as a student then would also include sustainability, (could be about population, ecology, green, energy, financial markets, businesses..............). My management style, structure, and communication and performance ethic has been shaped my early Roman Catholic upbringing, Eastern/Western philosophy and mathematics and is a fusion of the following values; Social and Humanitarian responsibility, "Fairtrade" and Sustainability.

We are all born with common and differing qualities. A few of mine are being curious, awareness, trying to figure out how things work/interact and always loved to create structures, designs, models and artifacts/symbols (Lego). I was 6 when I started elementary school. I had a 3 km walk to get to school. I had a choice, just walking down the streets or taking streets and go partially through a big park. I always preferred the latter. I was always fascinated by the four seasons (in Holland). As a young child I saw that in the fall, small animals were preparing for the winter and storing food away. A big storm in the winter could create havoc - broken tree branches etc. In the spring however, beavers would utilize the dead branches and build a dam. I saw that in nature things always changes and yet, at the same time there is a "constant". Today's successful business must have a philosophy of flexibility and process driven creativity. Elements both, within the company and external always change, yet, there are cycles. "I love what I do, I love being at the helm of my firm". My leadership style is shaped by my vision, awareness and the willingness to adapt and create. Strongly believe that I should continue to strive for perfection (call it improvement) in whatever I do, whether it is playing tennis, managing a business meeting, doing client meetings or resolving an operational engineering problem.

Eastern philosophy is my focus, Awareness, I can hear the air conditioning humming in my office, a car started up outside, I feel the slight touch of my lightweight shirt on my skin, I hear a bird outside at a great distance.....I don't have a single focus, I have multiple focusses; I observe (focus on) myself, my mental state, balance in my life (- awareness -), I observe my team members.....Sustainable organic growth. I have often asked myself, what cultures makes me effective as a leader? I love what I do, I am passionate about my business. It has been and is an ongoing task to shape our culture into one which is vibrant and focused, a culture onto which my vision is superimposed.....My long term organizational orientation towards building culture, change and leadership is best described as my ability to adapt, adjust, imbibe and settle in wherever, in whatever way that is required. Our long term organizational orientation is adaptability and is shaped by; Exploration of trends, what drives the change(s). I.e. our better healthcare results in longevity which results in growing requirements/needs for our aging population, Extrapolate attractive future markets. i.e. the growing demand for live video streaming requires increased network bandwidths, always re-invent to remain competitive and Focus and re-focus on long term survival/success.

Not long ago, job security was what employees were looking for. An employee would work 5 days a week, full time for that same company for 30 years. To me the successful company of the future will be an adaptive one, in which change replaces stability as a key trait. In this type of a company an employee looking for security would get confused. He or she may need to finish a customer sales quote by 8 pm, may have to fly to another country to coordinate a networking project and may have to temporarily leave his or her comfort zone. Here people would need to focus on personal growth not security alone. Clearly autocratic leadership used to be effective, once upon a time, the days of dictators, because employees were looking for job security. However, this type of dominance will conflict with today's employees who are looking for engagement, connect and personal and professional growth. Leaders would need to be inspirational.

For Ben, his staff would need to have an energy level and commitment to persevere, to be adaptable, and to remain focused not only during positive cycles, but also through inevitable disaster periods and must be able to see beyond them!" Ben Van Deputt

Digital Practice 3 - What Are Leadership "Reactions to Critical Incidents and Organizational Crises that impact collaboration"?

Collaboration is not appropriate when: The options are clear-cut. Involving a lot of people requires an investment of time, money, and energy. Time spent in meetings debating options is time away from the business. While involvement up front usually eases the implementation at the back end, sometimes it does not improve the outcome. If the issues are clear and there are few options to consider, it may be best for leadership to make the decisions and involve people in implementation planning rather than analysis or evaluation. The decision should remain with the executive team. Setting the business strategy and direction are executive responsibilities and best not done by consensus. If the organization is small and there are sensitive personnel issues, a participative approach may not be appropriate. For example, if it involves asking people to eliminate their own positions and you have no alternatives for them, it's best to make the decisions yourself. People may be willing to tear down their own house and rebuild it with you; however, asking them to tear down their own house and remain homeless is cruel, not participative. Collaboration is most successful when it is undertaken with clear parameters, when there is equitable representation, and when the process is structured and facilitated. Clear Parameters. Successful participation requires the leader to be absolutely clear about the parameters for decision making, the non-negotiables, and the rules. Many times, the leader communicates the wrong expectations. He intends only to ask for input, but he fails to make explicit that involvement doesn't mean decision making by consensus. People are then disappointed when a decision contrary to their perspective is made.

- Leaders see crisis as an organizational reality. They believe and hope that they have visualized possible scenarios leading to a crisis and would avoid it.
- Crises is an important factor in culture creation
- They handle pressure and believe are competent and confident of handling a crisis.
- They are sure of themselves, at least give an impression of being so.
- Creates new norms, values, working procedures, reveals important underlying assumptions
- Crisis heighten anxiety, which motivates new learning
- A crisis is what is perceived to be a crisis, and as defined by leader
- Crisis about leader, insubordination, tests leader

Digital Practice 4 - What deliberate Role Modeling, Teaching, Mentoring and coaching activities do Leaders perform?

- Personal behavior communicates assumptions and values to others.
- Teaching through workshops
- Coaches in learning implicit knowledge

- Leaders are not shy of show casing themselves as an appropriate role model
- Leaders believe that they need to be extroverts in their leader behavior and should demonstrate what they believe in by practicing it
- Leaders do not indicate concern for people at the cost of performance, while they still like to spend a significant amount of time with people or on people driven issues, challenges, problems and concerns
- Leaders like to show they have something to tell and teach their people. They formally participate in seminars, training programs and communication meetings to share what they know and tech it if required.
- Leaders find enough time to coach high performing people.

Here is an interesting experience from a leadership member of Fragomen Worldwide, Rick Lamanna, espousing the effective connect through role modeling, mentoring and coaching teams.

*"**Become a Chameleon -** I have and continue to manage staff considerably older and now much younger than myself. I made the decision early on to become the managerial version of a chameleon by responding to the needs, styles and nature of the staff members with whom I dealt. It is my belief that the way a manager handles an employee with 30+ years of experience who may be set in their methods should differ from the Millennial who is a relatively new member of the workforce. This is applicable to how a manager motivates, disciplines and interacts with staff.*

My approach has always been to find common ground, and then harness it to the benefit of the team, department, and by extension, the organization as a whole. Whether it is a type of music, a TV show, or a particular sport one follows, my experience has shown it is critical to find something you share in common, and use that as a frequent talking point. If there isn't one, the successful manager will make it his or her job to find or create one, even if it means spending the time outside of work to become knowledgeable about a particular topic. I've learned more about Bollywood, mixed martial arts and South American Telenovelas in the past decade than I care to mention here. Ultimately, understanding and taking an interest in what makes individual staff members "tick" by molding the employer-employee relationship into a slightly different dynamic has many positive benefits, including increased staff engagement, retention, and productivity.

All for One, One for All - One of the potential perils of being a manager is feeling that you are more valuable or important to the organization than the staff you employ. Put another way, everyone on the team serves a purpose, regardless of their title or required duties. My job is to serve the staff; we are interdependent. My experience has been that productivity and employee satisfaction are at their peak when staff see their manager as part of the team. This is not to say that the manager should be seen as a "buddy" but rather a leader who cares about the well-being of the group and will engage appropriately to ensure its continued success. In other words, you can't simply direct from a distance: often times you must get into the boat and paddle alongside your staff.

Additionally, the more a staff member understands the "big picture", and how their role contributes to the goals of the team, department and organization, whether it be a budget target, client satisfaction or otherwise, the more engaged they will be. One approach I have employed at times has been to include certain staff members on email communications late in the evening, knowing they won't see the email until the next day. If staff see their manager being that attentive to client needs, odds are they will follow suit, within the parameters of their role. Another tactic has been to make it clear to all staff that I will always take responsibility for mistakes made. Errors and other similar issues will be dealt with behind closed doors with the staff member responsible, with the focus being on fixing the problem before anything else. This approach builds a lot of loyalty amongst staff.

When employees are loyal, everyone does their part - and many times beyond that which is required of them - to row the boat to the desired destination.

***Don't be a Dinosaur** - The rapid pace of change in technology means having to keep up with internal software upgrades and various social media. A decade ago, Facebook and LinkedIn were in their infancy. Twitter, Instagram, WeChat and other various social media did not even exist, yet each currently boasts hundreds of millions of users worldwide. Younger employees, particularly those of the Millennial generation, have embraced this technology, while those who have not are considered by many to be dinosaurs. Understanding that technology is not only here to stay but also constantly evolving, means having to embrace it. At work, it can come in the form of new software that enhances the client experience. In a social context, it can be a platform that allows users to post photos of what they do in their spare time. In either case, a manager that can be flexible and open-minded enough to embrace new technologies will be more likely to succeed, and better positioned to relate to the new generation of workers who grew up not knowing what a rotary phone was.*

***There is No One Right Way** - Some decisions will be right and some will not be very successful. In all cases, staff members expect at the least that decision-making is based in a reasoned and informed fashion. Being able to explain the basis for a decision builds confidence that the manager is thoughtful and encourages confidence in the manager.*

Stay true to who you are. While being flexible is important, so too is remaining genuine. I try not to take myself too seriously and I find a self-deprecating joke here and there can go a long way in creating open dialogue and making myself more relatable to staff. Knowing that the day-to-day work can lack diversity for stretches, I try to create an atmosphere that people enjoy. We are in the company of our colleagues as much as we are our family, so we are well-served by enjoying each other's presence and the environment in which we operate as much as possible.

We are all unique, staff and managers alike. Finding what works best for you and your group within the scope of your organization's expectations takes critical thinking, emotional intelligence and a willingness and ability to revise your plans over time. Staying humble and accepting that change is inevitable will help with various transitions that are bound to occur. As long as the one constant is that you remain a dedicated, loyal teammate and leader, you may find much of the rest becomes a lot easier to manage" – Rick Lamanna.

Digital Practice 5 - What are the Secondary Articulation and Reinforcement Mechanisms of cultures in young organization design, structure, architecture and goals of an organization are visible?

Structure the architecture primarily around the structure of the business, not around the efficient organization of vendors or technologies; Focus the end users on functional requirements, not on the selection of specific technologies; Allow the business units flexibility in evaluating and selecting their individual risk management and governance approaches; Control the factors of risk that require corporate oversight, consistency, and responsibility; Provide clear requirements for communication of information from the business units (e.g., what information, when, under what circumstances, in what format, for what purpose, through what channels); Create reusable processes and efficient data structures to simplify the architecture; Provide clear requirements for local business unit processing; Keep business unit data stored in the business unit systems; Create new business information records from the information provided by the business units for use in central risk, operations, and financial processing; Drive informational and incident transactions from the business units through layers of risk analysis, coordination, correlation, and assessment on a regular basis; Maintain a central risk management infrastructure that tracks key risk indicators, supports ongoing measurements of relevant performance factors, analyzes risk in various meaningful management categories, and maintains a record of causes, actions taken, and effects.

Facets of Culture

- Rituals, stories, and formal statements cultural re-enforcers, not culture creators.
- On organizational stability these become primary and constrain future leaders.
- These are cultural artifacts that are highly visible but hard to interpret.
- When organization is in developmental stage, the leader is driving force. In maturity stage, these will become the driving forces for next generation.
- Leaders determine organization design and structure
- Leaders influence organizational systems and procedures
- Leaders partake in organizational rites and rituals
- Leaders actively involve themselves in design of physical space, facades, and buildings
- Leaders tell their own stories, legends, and myths about people and events
- Leaders make formal statements of organizational philosophy, values, and creed.

Digital Practice 6 - How do leaders influence Organization Design and Structure?

Link the Design Project to Business Drivers: Explicitly identify the specific strategic business initiatives and KPIs that each project should support; Consider technology-independent design (logical needs) as a step prior to specifying specific technologies or vendors. Many teams make the mistake of choosing technologies too early in the process; Quantify the Measurable Goals: Link business drivers to quantifiable measures of the design to help with prioritization and ongoing benefits tracking; Take a Structured Approach: Consider a structured approach based on one of several current benchmark or industry standard IT design models. ITIL, ISO, BPO and other IT-oriented design frameworks can offer a formal approach based on industry agreed standards; Engage SMPs: Understand that systems design requires a specialized set of skills and design techniques, and do not attempt to overstep your area of expertis; Build Agreement for Requirements: Facilitate formal buy-off on requirements prior to beginning detailed design. Encourage high end-user involvement in early design stages; Ground the Team in the Current Situation: Understand the constraints of current information systems, especially in terms of data available. Understand what has worked or failed in the past. Understand vendor and technology preferences. Observe users in the field to determine their usability requirements. Plan for retirement of replaced systems as part of the design process.; Develop a Migration Plan: Even if a full replacement is suggested, it is likely that data and people will need to migrate to the new environment. Incremental additions to existing systems are usually a cheaper and lower-risk approach, if capacity is available and the systems can perform the work.; Test the Designs: Prototype or test designs, if possible, during the design process.

Facets of Leadership

- Leaders influence structure, roles and responsibilities, many a time decide themselves for their top management
- Organizing organization brings leader's passion than logic
- They worry more on critical jobs and critical players

- How stable structure should be or variable - Some stick to original setup
- Some constantly rework on the same structures hoping to find performance solutions
- Leaders give up good theory for good practice.
- Structure and design reinforces leader assumptions.
- Leaders seek comfort in clarity and avoid ambiguity in defined structures, roles and responsibilities
- Leaders drive performance by pre-determined key performance indicators and implement them through structures
- Leaders ask for flexibility and multi-tasking while they demand performance but seek specialist expertise when they ask for advice.

Digital Practice 7 - What Organizational Technologies, Social Practices, Systems and Procedures do leaders depend upon to influence cultures and organizational models?

The process of aligning IT with business has proven difficult, but it can yield substantial benefits. It involves a transformation of systems, processes, people, and underlying infrastructure. Once this transformation takes place, IT can take on a whole new significance for the business. The image below outlines the steps an organization may take to align IT and business strategies and help ensure continuous process improvement. Security, Privacy, and Continuity Services addresses security issues in enterprise-wide systems and provides for high availability of IT infrastructure, data, and information across the enterprise. Security services help clients design IT architectures that protect information assets and privacy by focusing on the full life cycle model of security, including assessment, design, implementation, and monitoring. In the assessment phase, Services helps clients identify security vulnerabilities, evaluate security controls, and understand the business impact of security and privacy issues. In the design phase, Information Security and Continuity helps build/improve the client's security architecture and align security strategy with business objectives. With security systems designed and in place, continuity services are designed to help organizations deploy business and technology architectures necessary to help ensure continuous availability of systems and data. Architectures are developed on the basis of guiding principles that establish direction and coordination for the design and implementation of all IT initiatives. They serve as an ongoing reminder of the design philosophy embodied in the overall architectural direction of the business.

Facets of Technology

- Leaders ask for performance through formal budgetary, planning and monitoring systems
- Leaders influence organizational systems like appraisals, reward programs, feedback and review
- Some leaders are happy to manage their organization by establishing processes and systems that controls the organizational destiny, figuratively speaking
- Formal leaders believe in systems to replace dynamic decision making
- Some leaders prefer a mechanistic corporation that provides confidence and comfort to systems and processes and consequently streamlined methods and activities.
- They make visible parts of life in organization: daily, weekly, monthly, quarterly, and annually.
- They formalize the process of "paying attention"
- They provide consistency when they choose to and
- Their inconsistency allows for subcultures

"Culture in any organization is a set of shared assumptions which get formed over a period of time. These assumptions primarily help the organization address the issues of external adaptation and internal integration. Culture and leadership are two sides of the same coin. The context of the organizations is undergoing a rapid shift. Among the various forces reshaping the organizational dynamics, the most important and relevant in the current times is digitization. Technology is literally rewriting the rules of the game. To be more specific, confluence of four technologies, namely, SMAC, an acronym which stands for Social, Mobile, Analytics and Cloud is driving the change. SMAC creates an ecosystem that allows the HR function to improve its operations and get closer to the employees, with minimal overhead and maximum reach. None of the four technologies can be an afterthought because it is the synergy created by social, mobile, analytics and cloud working together that creates the wow effect! Employees have also become more receptive to the use of technology". Writes Bhrigu Joshi, KPMG Management Consulting on leading in a Digital era. "This may be attributed to the reduced average age of employees influenced by critical trends and practices:

Explosion in digital participation - If Facebook was a country, it would be third most populous country in the world; and in no time it will become second. In the current era, there is hardly anyone who is left untouched with the increasing reach of the digital platforms. Most notable among these are the social media platforms such as Facebook, Twitter, LinkedIn etc.

Increasing influence of digital citizens - With exponential increase in the two-way data exchange between the customers and the companies happening in the public domain, the power to influence is shifting in the hands of customers. For example, online reviews can inflate or deflate the hotel rates by more than 10%.

Intensifying the war for Tech talent - The demand-supply gap for the Tech talent is more than ever before. With exponential increase in digitization, the supply is not keeping pace with the demand which is causing unsustainable rise in salaries and retention issues.

Blurring lines between personal and professional lives - With most of us connected 24 x 7 through mobile devises such as phones and laptops, the space between our personal and professional lives is fast getting compromised. Also many of our professional relations are part of our personal social networks through tech platforms like Facebook etc.

Shift towards virtual leadership - More than 30% of the global leadership interactions happen over the virtual networks. Capability to effectively conduct such interactions is fast emerging as a key leadership competency. Leaders must significantly invest to be proficient in this competency.

Fluidization of work and workplace - With most of the data exchange happening over cloud, employees can now log-in from their homes or other convenient locations. This is giving rise to trends such as work from home and remote working.

Such trends are redefining the rules of leadership in the current times. Leaders who proactively adapt to this change are the ones who will thrive in the current VUCA environment characterized by digitization. And those who do not, will have to do so in times to come". Bhrigu Joshi

Digital Practice 8 - Do Rites and Rituals actually happen in Organizations and do members believe in them? Do stories pass on from one generation to another? Is there a tech design view about all of this?

Varying approaches may be required to address the needs of each engagement. Designing an organizational structure from scratch will require a different approach than helping to design an existing organizational structure. This section provides high-level guidance for the preferred approach techniques. Below are some high-level points to consider when performing an organization design: Keep the number of levels in the organization to a minimum to avoid unrealistic spans of control; Maintain an alignment between knowledge management and the organizational structure for effective communication and collaboration; Involve the client staff in all organization design work in order to achieve the level of client ownership and commitment desired to help ensure long-term sustainability; Use the organization's business strategy to drive its structure; Establish a flexible structure that is consistent with the environmental change demands; Consider creating economies of scale (reduce redundancies) by leveraging a shared services environment; The management structure, culture, and processes should embrace and support the organization design. Leadership must transform before the organization does; Link skills and desired competencies to a comprehensive model that outlines the skill progression required at each organizational level; Provide employees with development tools and training that help them attain the skills and abilities defined in the competency model; Establish clear roles and responsibilities that help the organization to meet its goals and the individuals to realize their full potential;

Facets of Conventions

- Rites and rituals happen although many deny that traditions are an important part of their culture
- Some unknown actions of organizations tend to be spoken internally as rituals, a rose garden party, founder's day.
- Many leaders seek to project a new outlook from their predecessors. They listen to stories and improvise
- Visible respect to seniors is still a reality in many organizations
- Leaders find influencing or changing rituals more difficult than other aspects of culture comparatively speaking
- Central in deciphering as well as communicating the cultural assumptions
- They articulate stories as powerful re-enforcers

Digital Practice 9 - Does Design of Physical Space, Facades, buildings, and infrastructure including technological infrastructure influence culture and organizational models?

- CEO's see it as an inevitable reality, many try to discourage it only after they have become CEO's.
- Visible features are important to members, although many organizations actively attempt to dissuade its importance
- Symbolic differences in office layout and infrastructure is made
- It conveys a philosophy of the management to differentiate hierarchy
- Dress code has become another signal of difference
- Technology and internet connectivity have gained status signals
- Place of work, office décor, interiors, façade to the client and customer interaction location have made an impact on organizational identity and CEO's mind space.

Digital Practice 10 - How Do Stories, sagas about Important Events and People impact organizational culture and leadership?

- Stories about important people makes way for others to learn from their experience
- Stories of sacrifices mean more to people than successes
- Failure stories are not popular and are not encouraged in many cultures
- That stories happen, exist and continue to be spoken of is very real
- As history develops, stories evolve.
- Stories reinforce assumptions.
- Leaders can't control stories about themselves.
- Using stories to decipher org has its problems: Validity.
- Organizational events make way for story telling time
- There is a thin line between gossip and stories and over time this difference tends to get blurred
- There does not appear to be a formal process to capture and tell stories in an organization

Digital Practice 11 - What formal statements of Organizational Philosophy, Creeds, and Charters exist in the organization and do the leaders influence much of it?

- Leaders are aware that they have to speak of history and values
- Leaders know the merit in articulating vision
- Leaders consciously reinforce HRM thinking to demonstrate his/her concern for people
- Many leaders break hierarchies to connect with people to gain personal credibility and popularity
- Leaders make position statements when they believe that they need, sometime there could be a time lag between expectation and leader behavior
- Leaders speak their mind in regard to organizational soft issues
- Formal statements like mission statement, code of ethics etc. only highlight a small portion of the assumptions
- Picture for public consumption is a reality although internal truths may be different
- Not a complete definition of the organization yet made to make a point.

Digital Practice 12 – How have Digital HR helped build a Performance Oriented Culture?

In, *"Performance Marketing - How Digital HR impact advertising and promotion spends"*, *V Kamath, Partner with Fairwinds Private Equity and Co-founder of a digital marketing company UW Media Ventures, "You cannot manage what you don't measure ~ Dr W Edward Deming, and tell us of an evolving story, "Once upon a time, a glib-talking ad-agency account executive backed by the work of an "expert" creative team and an "expert" media planning team told the client where and how to spend her advertising dollars. There was no way of determining the true ROI on your advertising spends. The memes and jokes on advertisers and advertising that spawned during this 'once upon a time', were second in number only to lawyer jokes. One of the most famous ones, attributed to John Wanamaker, was "Half of advertising works but the problem is I don't know which half." Flip forward to 2002, and you probably remember the scene from the movie Minority Report where a series of advertisements "spoke" to John Anderton, Tom Cruise's character, as he walked past those billboards. By identifying him through his irises and based on his moods and prior shopping habits, the billboards spoke out suggestions.*

Are we there yet?

In 2000, Google launched Adwords, an online advertising solution that in its most rudimentary form would recommend ads to you based on your keyword searches. Flip forward to ten years from Minority Report, in 2012 Facebook started ads in their feeds based on what you were browsing and what your friends liked. And by this time, sufficient technology existed and was constantly evolving, to say which piece of creative worked, where and when. The entire science of digital marketing and performance marketing has brought accountability to the entire ecosystem – a company's marketing manager, the agency, the electronic media platform and research agencies.

In the beginning there was the cookie and the pixel too - This isn't intended to be a primer on digital marketing but necessary to build the context if someone doesn't know how it works. When we browse, websites that we visit leave behind (and there's a way to avoid this, another day's story) a small file on our computers called **cookies**. They help that website and other websites who take a peep at your cookie lists, serve you better on your next visit. All websites who make money through advertising, be they portals, social media sites, news sites etc. have software which manage their entire advertising inventory. These cookies and the technology which reads them, helps "serve" you with ads. So if you were searching for running shoes on google, google will try to sell you shoes and then when you log onto your FB page, you will see leading shoe brands' advertisements. Don't be surprised if you got a lot of spam email from shoe retailers. So the cookie is the culprit that sent you these ads or caused the ad server software to "serve" you. You might act on an ad., you might click on the ad to go to a web page to learn further. You might click on an ad to go to an ecommerce site and buy the product. Each ad is embedded with a **pixel**, a small string of code which captures details of where you were served with the ad and what you eventually did with it – saw, read or bought. And for the last decade or so there has been enough technology to capture millions of such action real-time. So the cookie helped decide what ad you saw and the pixel helped measure what you did with the ad. A performance marketing division within a digital marketing company basically uses these two and builds technology tools to target, re-target, send offers, etc. Just as we say this, you might find articles which already spout headlines such as "digital advertising is broken". And there might be technical arguments about why it already has in such a short time. But this piece is about what and how it has changed the character of the field of marketing and its players.

Accountability - The creative director can no longer hang his hat on a reputation peg. The concept of A/B testing where customers preferences for one particular creative over another can be measured in hours if not in minutes. After all, a successful creative is really about how much it helps sell a client's product rather than the Golden Lion that adds to the agency's bragging rights. Result based media buying such as Cost per Million Impressions (CPM) or Cost per Acquisition (CPA) brings accountability to the advertising budget. So the success of two campaigns is no longer arguable, but can be monitored real-time. And the employees also automatically become accountable. Imagine a performance appraisal where all the boss had to do was pull out a dashboard and tell you the numbers you were supposed to pull in and what you actually did. Wouldn't that be a very SMART performance management? Of course it wouldn't tell you how you would do as a manager, except that the performance bar would ensure that you had ingrained a high level of accountability.

Agility - The basic unit of consumption has become smaller, the default now is the mobile screen. Attention spans have become smaller, the digital generation will not savor a taste for a lifetime. As a result, messages have to be crisp and pointed and campaign lifespans shorter.

When you have a deal or an offer, it has to capture attention in a very short period of time, i.e. go viral. While vitality itself is measurable, its cause isn't. Whether it is an emotional tug at the heartstrings, or a new style of dance, there is no saying what will go viral. So one has to test and be ready to pull unsuccessful campaigns off the shelf very quickly. In video ads where the user has the option of skipping after a mandatory 5 seconds of viewing, the message has to engage in those first five seconds without the luxury of lazy or verbose preambles.

Agility is a key attribute of Digital HR.

Adaptability - If you type "google-algorithm-change" in your browser, your first search result will get you a history of the 150 or so changes Google has made over the last 13 years on how websites are ranked, how email is filtered, and how content is regulated for spam, and many such. If one were to offer an analogue of how it affects a digital marketing company is this. Imagine you had a large hoarding at a prime spot on a busy exit of an inter-state. Then one day, they tore a piece of it and put it in China and the next day, they turned the remainder facing skywards and finally on the third day, the hoarding was teleported to Argentina. And your media plan was to get 200000 views in three months. For employees of this performance marketing company, even the boss isn't necessarily on top of these algorithm changes. One has to learn real-time and adapt all content and marketing plans to these changes. While the analogy might seem exaggerated, trust me when I say it isn't. Say the words, Penguin, Panda, Pigeon and mobilegeddon to a digital marketing professional, watch her roll her eyes. To stay relevant, one has to self-tutor and implement all in real-time. You could take an online class at a MOOC, learning through the night. Dealing with one fundamental change every two months on average, ensures survival of the fittest.

One might now say, half of advertising and advertising professionals are effective and in a digital era we know exactly which half, concludes Kamath, thought leader in his field".

"Media planning determines how the advertiser's media budget should be distributed in order to reach the target market most effectively. From the days, when CAD CAMs used to determine digital thinking through Variant process performance planning, in which process plans are stored in digital form thus allowing the planner to select and modify appropriate plans as needed or Generative process performance planning, in which descriptions of the parts, the manufacturing process, the machine tools and the tooling are entered into the computing system which then develops a new process plan and makes no reference to prior plans requiring more complex decision sequences than variant process planning, today digital thinkers in the world of technology are delivering this value and beyond simply through neural networks, digital simulations, agility thinking, multiple point network interactivity and so on as Kamath points out. An ideal CIM system involves the complete automation of activities with all process planning and control functions under digital control and only digital information tying them together. A designer can construct multi -dimensional models graphically on the screen, or through thus allowing designs to be selected from an operational aspect without the expense of producing working models. This could quite well be about to change". The overall approach is assigned with the challenge of coordinating the specialized component-specific design teams. The techniques used by the design teams may be grouped into two categories: Overall design processes (overall design and integration process); Component-specific design techniques (techniques focused on a specific "design layer"); Overall design processes are characterized by an organizing framework and a high-level process. Component-specific techniques are usually executed by specialized resources who are familiar with the subject area, while the overall design process is facilitated by generalist resources. Common Design components include the following: Digital Strategic Plan; Digital Governance Model and Operational Processes; Digital Standards and Policies;

Budget and Project Portfolio; Digital Systems Architecture (overall blueprint); Digital Presentation Layer (user interface); Business Logic and Applications Portfolio; Data Layer (e.g., models, databases, files); Physical Infrastructure (e.g., servers, routers); Communications and Networking Layer; Support (e.g., help desk and incidents); Service Level Agreements (SLAs) and Vendor Contracts. "A new patent, filed by Xerox Corporation, reimagines the process. The patent — filed under application #20150017271 on January 15th — is for the Digital. Manufacturing System for Printing Three-Dimensional Objects on a Rotating Surface. Invented by Patricia J. Donaldson and Jeffrey J. Folkins for Xerox, who also posted a patent for printing such objects on a rotating core with co-inventor Naveen Chopra, this patent isn't so much reinventing the wheel as simply adding a wheel. Both Donaldson and Folkins appear to have prodigious experience in patenting inventions, and so seem to be just the right team for the job. (3dprint.com) Today capturing digital data is easily done and to record what, when and how much was produced is least of the challenge. The task of enabling a digital culture, capability and nurtures this analysis through big data analytics is the bigger opportunity. Risk analysis techniques such as the calculation of expected values, utility theory, mean variance analysis, game theory, Monte Carlo simulations and decision trees are all used for this purpose. Such models, and simulations of operational situations, assist managers to deal with uncertainty. The right or optimum choice is seldom obvious. But it is all about cultures that help such managers become effective in a digital business.

Digital Practice 13 – How have Cultures specifically impacted the CEO's leadership disrupted style in the context of an organizational model? Are things changing?

Cultures plays an influencing role when confronted with altering organizational models. Therefore, one of the prerequisites for virtual organizational model, for example, is the existence of a techno structural infrastructure to support networks, connections, communication and collaboration. In an ideal virtual organization documents are retained electronically, communication takes place computer mediated, and clear external boundaries of the organization are difficult to establish. A good overview of the different definitions and how employees in such organizations relate to HR applications, self-service portals, networks, joint ventures, strategic alliances, agile enterprises, value adding partnerships or clan organizations is critical to interpret and understand. "HR apps can tell you when employees are thinking about quitting, which employees are the best fit for new assignments, and even the best way to coach a specific employee, according to an article in Fortune by Jennifer Alsever", Theodore Kinni writes in MIT SMR 2016 frontier, "People Management by Algorithm" "It is all about Algorithmic people management: If you're wondering where you'll find the time to tweet encouraging messages to your staff, consider adding people analytics to your digital toolbox. IBM, for instance, uses Blue Matching, which employs Watson technology to analyze thousands of employees and match them to job opportunities". In virtual organizations knowledge processing is inhibited by decentralized structures and geographical distribution. "Cisco is rolling out Team Space, a Web-based app, that assesses employee strengths and recommends how to motivate them. "It's like Moneyball for HR, letting you make better decisions," Josh Bersin of Bersin by Deloitte told Alsever, "and this year it has really peaked." The leaders of companies whose employees perform lots of physical labor should be following the development of robotic assistance devices, especially robotic exoskeletons, which can enhance the performance of employees, as well as protect their health and safety. Warehouse workers, for instance, can don Panasonic's Assist Suit AWN-03, a sort of robotic assistance jacket that lasts eight hours on a charge and can lift up to 33 pounds for them, according to a report by Adario Strange in Mashable. "Linking workforce actions to strategy and results acts as a lead motivator. People cannot execute a strategy if they do not know what it is. One way to broaden the horizons of workers is to get them more closely involved with corporate strategy. In some parts of the world, employee participation on the board has been not only effective but even mandated by law.

A less formal approach, through focus groups or employee forums, may be more appropriate for other kinds of companies. Involving people in strategy development, devices or teaming gives them a higher commitment to their group tasks and a sense of being a part of the overall organization's/unit or functional performance". A new video from Panasonic is "one of the first videos we've seen of an entire team of workers outfitted with exoskeletons," writes Strange. "The team of workers lift boxes and work in unison, evoking images of 'the Borg' from Star Trek … Welcome to the bionic blue collar age." Panasonic is selling a second model, the PLN-01 "Ninja" exoskeleton suit, which is designed for workers who need to negotiate difficult terrain. "This suit features power sensors at the soles of the feet and two motors at the lower back to help people walk more easily," reports Mary-Ann Russon in International Business Times UK. The company is also developing a hospital bed "that splits in two," according to Russon, "and one part of the bed is triggered to convert itself into an armchair while the patient is lying on it, meaning that the caregiver no longer needs to lift the patient at all."

What have been the salient features of a digital culture as it impacts social behaviors.

- *Bridging the technology – management – leadership distance*
- *Exiting from leadership disrupted inertia against social media*
- *Making the social work environment interactive, invigorating and challenging*
- *Culture implies the presence of an approach that is understood, accepted and identified by people*
- *Employees will have more flexible work arrangements*
- *Work hours scheduling will become less important as organizations focus on performance and results*
- *Intelligence through knowledge transfer capability will separate the best employees from the rest*
- *Policies are tuned to needs, company facilities will become "virtual" through work-at-home, telecommuting and outsourcing, the work week will be less structured- employees will still work 40-plus hours, but at varied times and places other than the office and formal rules and policies that will lead to greater portability of health, welfare and retirement benefits. The Virtual Organization is not telecommuting, although it can be made up of telecommuters. Traditional organizations can include Virtual Organizations as components, and indeed are likely to do so as the concept takes hold in the workplace.*
- *When one considers the departmental nature of corporations, with well-delineated areas of responsibility, the corporation is probably one of the best types of organizations to "go virtual". Interaction with administrative support units (e.g. accounting, procurement, or publications) is likely to be transactional in nature. In the old paradigm, completion of a task form and a telephone call or a quick conference, to view catalog information, was all that was needed to send them into action. This translates well to the new paradigm whereby the e-mail takes the place of the form, and a video teleconference, perhaps with some coordinated web page viewing of product offerings, takes the place of the conference.*
- *Free-lance teams of generic problem solvers will market themselves as alternatives to permanent workers or temporary workers would promote collaborative cultures will be the workplace model Society and some degree of materialistic and narcissist values may become prevalent*
- *Customers will expect individual customization of products and services*
- *Family and life interests will play a more prevalent role in people's lives and a greater factor in people's choices about work*

- *Families will return to the center of society and community involvement and social responsibility will become part of an organization's business vision, in fact cocooning will become more popular as workers look to their homes for refuge from the pressures of competitive work place and depersonalized society*
- *Companies will take on responsibility for elder care, long term care and other social needs through cafeteria-style benefits programs*

Physicians and behavioral scientists and, more recently have long recognized the powerful influence of one person's expectations on another's behavior, by teachers. But heretofore the importance of managerial expectations for individual and group performances has not been widely understood. These have been documented as a phenomenon in a number of case studies prepared during the past decade for major industrial concerns. These cases and other evidence available from scientific study now reveal:

What a manager expects of his members and that the way he treats them largely determine their performance and career progress. A unique characteristic of superior managers is their ability to create high performance expectations that his/her team fulfill. Less effective managers fail to develop similar expectations, and, as a consequence, the productivity of their people suffers and colleagues, more often than not, appear to do what they believe they are expected to do.

Chapter 9

Leading an Intellectual Company

An organization's culture doesn't pop out of thin air. Once established, it rarely fades away. What forces influence the creation of a culture? What reinforces and sustains them once they are in place? How do new employees learn their organization's culture? The following summarizes what we've learned about how cultures are created, sustained, and transmitted. And of the crisis of leadership disrupted being the mediocrity, callousness and irresponsibility, and the disdain and contempt that an average citizen have for the men and women in positions of authority and power. Yet in all of this morass lies a small group of men and women who by sheer personal values, beliefs, courage and the desire to make change happen have stridden into the lives of people who they are responsible for. To them dreaming in color and living in black and white is a reality. And they still seek and ask for more as they give and provide more. The chapter focuses on:

A. *Intellectual Maturity*
B. *Interpreting Culture*
C. *Internalizing Culture*
D. *Leading and Managing Culture*
E. *Adaptability to Digital Culture*
F. *Leading Cultural Change:*
G. *Conditions that make Change Happen*
H. *Effecting Cultural Change*
I.   *Effecting Change: If So, how does transformation take place?*
J. *Making Individual Transitions – Digital Directions*

A. Intellectual Maturity

Intellectualized Corporation - Change reflects intellectualization of the corporation. Todays, digital corporations have coped with this changed. Making the organization energized with people, process where the intellect turns into the dominant force in the management process. In all change management efforts current business scenario, strategic positioning of the organization, structure, managerial values, corporate philosophy, the managerial styles and practices, impacted players become relevant for consideration of the facilitator. http://bit.ly/29ncoaM

World Class Firms - Similarly, CEOs, of Apple, IBM, Google, Twitter, Facebook, Amazon, Workday, Oracle, are examples of becoming change agents when they visualized a digital institution of the 21st century – world class firms. And their actions through extra ordinary strategies, products and services, customer connect, cultural insights, diversity programs, in attracting talent, rewarding out of box contribution, offering space for individualized contributions, should make visible the value of intellectual depth and its application in such organizational cultural models. "Adequate communication should constantly take place to make members understand the value of application synthesis in all of their new ideas" has been there common theme. Each communicating group turns into a network and eventually a network of networks. The premium on learning and its use as the only competitive survival strategy should be made known vociferously. See *"Creating Value Through Business Model Innovation" – Using Maturity Analytics.*

Creating Value Through Business Model Innovation - Using Maturity Analytics

	Low to High Quartile Analysis	Financial	Physical	Intangible	Human	Not Measured
		1st Quartile	2nd Quartile	3rd Quartile	4th Quartile	Outlier
	Digital Life Cycle	*Start Up*	*Growth*	*Transforming*	*Evolved*	*Challenged*
Strategic Planning and Change	*Agenda*	Transactional/ Administrative nature, multiple functions working in silos	Focus on administrative efficiency, involvement in few strategic activities	Increased focus on strategic role along with administrative efficiency, function important participant in strategic decisions	Strategically aligned to business with focus on operational efficiency, key driver of business	*Rules and Compliance focused, Ensuring bare minimum requirements*
	Processes Strategy	Intuitive Design of systems based on organization strategy, no established tools/methodologies	Detailed planning for HR processes, partial linkage to org strategy, no concerted effort to link processes with strategy	Development of tools/methodologies to link all systems/processes with business goals	Continuous improvement program to integrate strategy with systems and processes	*Ad hoc processes, no linkages to business goals/strategy*
	Benchmarking Strategy	Minimal benchmarking of some processes, practices and systems to fetch quick results	Due diligence in benchmarking of processes, practices and systems with high strategic value	Development of a framework containing multiple dimensions of performance along with leading practices	Continuous benchmarking of processes and systems against leading practices	*Function focuses on improving processes, practices and systems without benchmarking externally*
	Planning	Minimal planning and budgeting based on high level assessment of priorities; Strategic interventions carried out internally	Annual planning for assessing HR priorities; External sources referred while delivering strategic initiatives	Involvement of functional heads in prioritizing processes; Strategic interventions through external consultants	Continuous revisions in planning process to integrate with business strategy; Continuous scanning of leading industry practices	*No structured planning process - Higher degree of variance - Lack of Consistency - Reliability Suffers*
	Change Management	Change management in isolated projects, generic function works closely with senior management to reach desired state	Functions involves all stakeholders, Communication strategy in place	Functions plays a partnership role in changing the culture of the organization, building business case and vision for change	Function gathers data & analytics & analytics to improve change, function builds a plan based on the annual business plan	*Change Management initiatives are informal in nature, Coalition Based Networks, Freeforms, Individualized Interventions*

Figure 41 - "Creating Value Through Business Model Innovation" – Using Maturity Analytics

Digital Maturity - No Company, like Apple, has generated significant momentum in profound value change efforts without evolving spirited, active, internal networks of practitioners, people sharing progress and helping one another. Critically change in enterprises such as Apple, does not follow a pattern and has strong discontinuous sequences. It can almost be guaranteed that what worked well in the past would probably fail the second time over. So they reinvent themselves constantly. We need to see if we as an organization have learnt to manage this fact up front. As more people involved in change initiatives become part of the extended networks, information about the initiatives spreads more widely, giving rise to more interest, and potentially to more initiatives. Managers do not jump into the change initiative just because it sounds interesting or those key players are all in it. They initially wait for the first cut results, predict, use analytics to pour in and then choose their personal position.

Start with Behavioral Change - Behavioral Change is a starting point in making cultures work and transmit. Typically, informal group houses are created to help each other transit into the knowledge company with limited entry barriers, thereafter meet periodically, share their learning and make each of them enjoy the experience. This would happen as long as it is not position as yet another change management program of the company causing more cynicism. Direct effect of communication and trust has a good example from Unilever. Historical events from Chemicals Division had created the collective assumption that management would always reduce capital funding requests. To offset these reductions, project managers automatically added a "cushion" to their budgets. As the division leaders began to trust their project managers, things changed. Management stopped making these reductions, and project managers stopped adding a cushion. Now people just talk honestly about investments that were needed and the real constraints in funding. This saved a great deal of wasted time and allowing the company to prioritize the investments on a need basis. Trust brings in responsibility.

Intellectual Learning - Learning efforts should focus initially on the thought generation process and thereafter on the practical results that it has commenced to deliver. Results provide a context, a meaning, a method and a reason for experimentation, adaptation, and feedback. Seeing the consequences of team efforts and learning from the experience is critical for the network groups to succeed. Learning fundamentally assumes a time lag between the new thought process creation, establishing the internalizing of learning, bringing connected networks of learning together, application to business processes and attaining concrete business performance and bottom line.

Differentiating Intellectuals - Intellectual corporations prosper in making change happen realistically. It, to our mind, only demonstrates a further application of mind to make the change permanent and effective. Typically, the corporation operates through identification of relevant people to the change process, bringing their values and identity together, network with relevant cross-team players, assess their intellectual compatibility, bring in commitment, define business goals and results and charges the team to move forward. There is a transparent and open communication involving review and feedback including action-oriented goals. Essentially this stage acts as a facilitation step in the intellectualization process. Critically the differentiating factor is that change is neither directed, conceptualized nor delivered by the top management. The change happens by a team of people who feel the need to change without encountering an entry-exit experience. Whirlpool attempted serious management changes while they completed their acquisition processes of other manufacturing plants. While the change by itself could mean an impact on the average employee the process required to help make the transition is definitely not ignored, neglected or derided. Refer - http://on.tcs.com/2a7OLPR

Adaptation Processes - Several intermittent steps are necessary to make this adaptation process real and on line. Pharma Company and its Product development thrust symbolize the need to protect its identity as an innovative company.

- *Intellectual stereotypes (http://bit.ly/2aiCmuv) should be managed across the corporate population. An added element of predictability and behavioral understanding should be brought in while dealing on any people issue. (Drucker)*
- *A detailed start up workshop on Transformation and the creation of the Intellectual Corporation should be a curtain raiser. The entire effort should be fancy free and should mean business with people as the drivers. That the program is eminently capable of being dropped half way through if the concerned people do not want it. No jobs will be lost. The question does not arise either.*
- *Thinkers-doer's distinction should be eliminated in policy, spirit and in action. (Davenport 2000) & http://on.tcs.com/2a7OLPR*
- *The change effort should commence in a small, measurable way and should escalate in intensity logically. (Pfeiffer)*
- *Individuals cannot be subjugated to staid forms and methods outdated in content and spirit while intellectualization efforts are on in an organization. (Andersen – The Renaissance)*
- *Barriers of an intellectual nature describing organization in pockets, creating functional silos, taking positions on right and wrong are all avoidable completely. (KPMG, Andersen, E & Y, PwC, Big 5 Accounting firms that suffer from ill-defined scope of practice as an institutionalized problem on a global basis).*
- *The change envisaged is not a quick fix problem solving initiative. There is an assumed level of intellectual rigor expected of the organizational members and the organizing actors to make the change real to all people. (Quinn)*
- *People encountering change should understand that this is not a yet another corporate HQ driven program with a fix all perspective and that this initiative has come bottom up. That the expectation of the change is only as good as the expectation that they have from it themselves. (Kanter)*
- *First serving a follower, a leader subsequently can best understand his followers. (Hegel 1830/1971)*
- *Top management should know by knowledge and experience when to get off the back of the individual. (Peters and waterman 1982)*
- *Change is not an accident. It is planned and done in a pre-meditated manner if desired results are expected (Shermon 2000 on Lalbhai Group)*
- *Effect of Culture on Organizational Climate (Daftuar C N)*

B. Interpreting Culture

Interpreting Culture: Inherited Cultures

The heroes in Homer's Iliad exemplified Greek concepts of leadership. Ajax symbolized inspirational leadership and law and order. Other qualities that the Greeks admired and thought were needed (and sometimes wanting) in heroic leaders were:

- *Justice and Judgement (Agamemnon)*
- *Wisdom and Counsel (Nestor)*
- *Shrewdness and Cunning (Odysseus)*
- *Valor and Activism (Achilles)*

A scholarly highlight of the Renaissance was Machiavelli's (1513) The prince. Machiavelli's thesis that "there is nothing more difficult to take in hand, more perilous to conduct, or more uncertain in its success, than to take the lead in the introduction of a new order of things". This is still a relevant description of the risks of leadership disrupted and the resistance to it when effecting change, particularly cultural change.

Founders Culture - Understanding organizational processes is a starting point in interpreting organizational culture and following through to its history and founders. An organization's current customs, traditions, and general way of doing things are largely due to what it has done before and the degree of success it had with those endeavors in its context of a culture. This leads us to the ultimate source of an organization's culture: its founders! The founding fathers or mothers of an organization traditionally have a major impact in establishing the early culture. They have a vision or mission of what the organization should be. They are unconstrained by previous customs of doing things or by ideologies. The small size that typically characterizes any new organization further facilitates the founders' imposing their vision on all organizational members. Because the founders have the original idea, they also typically have biases on how to get the idea fulfilled. The organization's culture results from the interaction between the founders' biases and assumptions and what the original members whom the founder initially employs learn subsequently from their own experiences. Once a culture is in place, there are forces within the organization that act to maintain it by giving employees a set of similar experiences. The three forces that play the most important part in sustaining a culture are the organization's selection practices the actions of top management, and the organization's socialization methods. Leaders operate in a context as they determine what culture are they coping with and as they interpret and understand the culture that is encountering. Machiavellian believed that leaders needed steadiness, firmness, and concern for the maintenance of authority, power and order in governance. Leaders deploy styles adaptive to the situation and behave in acceptable forms as the culture asks of them in the initial stages of their roles. Leaders interpret cultures as they perform organizational roles like managing, directing, mentoring or deciding. They realize the organizational culture in each of the circumstance that they experience while performing their roles. And in each of their interventions lies a cultural impact to the organization. As they make their point of view and positions clear the organizations begin to learn and understand the CEO speak. In politics, Aristotle was disturbed by the lack of virtue among those wanted to be leaders. Refer – "Organizational Culture: Creating the Influence Needed for Strategic Success in Health Care Organizations in Nigeria - Dr. Austin O. Oparanma"

Interpreting Culture: Connecting to Strategic Aims

Linkages - The companies have clearly defined corporate culture through which their strategic aims are convincingly promulgated. The new models of corporate organizations retain an entrepreneurial instinct and work hard to stay highly decentralized thereby attaining remarkable properties for coping with change. The organizations are permeated by a restless drive for improvement, an obsessive conviction that a job is never done. To them, no product, service, or function is ever good enough, the search for more, new and better must go on. The long hours of intense work done by organizational team members carry them close their limits. Long hours of close association help them understand and appreciate the difficulties and challenges facing one another. The process of constructive confrontation is encouraged - When employees put their heads together, they cannot only eliminate differences in ideas but strengthen and foster good one. Organizational models make leadership settling down process easier and effective as organizational models are by themselves an amalgamation of actions, decisions, stories and sagas.

Structure and Hierarchy Influence, Management Style, the Role of the CEO in building organization visions. CEO must have a flexibility in developing / evolving Organizational structures and Management style. The needs of organizations will change over time, and so would the challenges and priorities. CEO should not compromise on corporate values but path taken to achieve the results can change over time. The Role of the CEO/leader in regard to strategy processes technology and people actions and leader's influence in the existence of specific types of cultures. Leader must be able to communicate the Corporate Vision and Objectives unequivocally across the organization. However, thereafter he / she must focus on result metrics rather than the process / operating styles of the functional leadership disrupted. Leadership Style as practiced by the management groups influences the culture. And this culture can change as the composition of management groups itself changes. As long as Core Values are held sacrosanct, these cultural changes can actually reflect the vibrancy of the Organization. CEO/leader focus on performance, climate, communication, and HRM practices, on monetary reward programs and influence over high performers, and management attention on retaining high performers. In a fast changing and more competitive world, some of the roles mentioned above have to be shared by the CEO with a few other senior colleagues (e.g. Compensation, Communication, and Motivation leading to retention of high performers). Vision, values, beliefs and his dream drive the Leader as a person. The Leader's emphasizes on the Individual and the Intellect, and a role in building individual and organizational knowledge. Leader definitely emphasizes the corporate recognition of the value of intellectual capital and the individuals having the repository of this capital. However, building the individual and managing storage and retrieval of the knowledge is a key "line" function and should be facilitated by a line manager identified for this purpose (Chief Information Officer – not in the IT sense of the title but on the larger "Information" issue itself). The CEO/leader's has a role in emphasizing on culture aspects pertaining to empowerment, delegation, individual contribution, accountability and responsibility. CEO/leader's has a role in actively participating in attracting, retaining and rewarding star talent and performers. However, this has to be done down the "line", and therefore the CEO also has to encourage such star talent and performers to further develop and reward talent reporting to them. The Leader's has a role in helping the organization retain an open mind to an unknown environment. A. Singhal – CEO – Technopak

Technology Changes Culture - Using "causal maps," a graphical communications method, can help companies spell out exactly what the relationship is between their business strategy and employee behavior. These sorts of approaches are helping management and employees work together toward common goals and for mutual benefit. Focus resources and new techniques on building skills and competencies. Once a company has effectively communicated goals to its employees and vendors, and it has implemented tools and programs for measuring performance, it must resolve any shortcomings in the entire "talent network" of the company, which may include not only its employees but also workers from external consultants, vendors and other companies with which it does business. "A relatively small business-to-business telecommunications company, trying to overcome the challenge of being a fairly small player in a very competitive market, began an initiative that encouraged employees to become brand ambassadors, empowering them to communicate via social media on behalf of the company. To do this, the company provided formal social media training for employee volunteers. It also offered clear, simple guidelines for how employees should communicate about the company on social media employing a "use your best judgment" approach". Gerald C. Kane, Doug Palmer, Anh Nguyen Phillips and David Kiron "Is Your Business Ready for a Digital Future? - MIT SMR 2015, "However, we also found examples where the technology itself began to change the culture of the organization. On all company memos, the company provided preapproved examples of how employees might share the information in various social media channels. The result did not simply accomplish the stated goal of higher recognition in the marketplace for the company. It also had the unanticipated effect of spawning a positive cultural shift in which the employees were more connected to the company, engaged with the brand and aware of the organization's digital strategy. Even if you start a digital initiative in one small part of the division, its effects can begin to creep into other areas of the organization. Such a sentiment was echoed by Carlos Dominguez, president and COO of enterprise social technology provider Sprinklr". Bersin by Deloitte in 2010 (David Mallon) write, while virtually every major HR software company now has products in this market, no vendor seems to have everything we need—forcing us to stitch together multiple systems to create a compelling employee experience. Just as traditional talent management software systems (e.g., recruiting, performance, learning, and compensation) are now combined, a new brand of tools for recognition, engagement, culture assessment, retention analytics, and wellness have emerged. The training industry has exploded with innovation, giving us access to more learning than ever before through MOOCs and online video solutions. Yet companies grapple with actualizing and measuring informal learning, and still cite "building a learning culture" as one of their top challenges".

Interpreting Culture: Striking Mutuality in Values

Mutuality Articulation - The successful organizations strive hard to communicate and interpret a common set of company values that identifies their commitment to serving customers, to attain perfection in quality and to the development of human recourses. The culturally permissive organizations allow the organizational members to do their own things to a remarkable degree. Culture as shared meanings and organizations as ordered behavior, together leading to cooperative result, are not merely planned and commanded, - initiated, created or designed. They are always partially spontaneous, responsive, both self-realized and socially sanctioned and inspired. These values are in turn influenced or imbibed by the leader. There is still not conclusive evidence to prove what factor influence values as much as its articulation to start with. Defined organizational values tend to be a starting point for leaders to speak their perspective of managerial and organizational issues.

And as we go along, organizational culture in the context of leadership serves important functions in organization to:

- *Generate commitment,*
- *Cognitive sense making,*
- *Boundary creation and*
- *Action planning.*

The organizations provide an impetus to exhibit a prolific commitment to long term relationships and ethical understandings.

Founders Culture Example - An analysis of the India Headquartered MNC, Lalbhai Group would tell us: The organizations work towards a climate for openness, mutuality of purpose, trust and fairness. The environment is conducive for self-understanding and development of process skills. The CEO is aware of the environment in which the organization is operating and realistically evaluates the potential for growth. The growth related areas for diversification are also limited to know areas. The organizations achieve internal cohesion by nature of its ability to consolidate and integrate. An area of demarcation that divests people from attaining organizational goals to Individual aggrandizement, are the pretentious organizational lifestyles of the upper echelon of the management. Deceiving job designation, separate `executive' dining halls, larger and luxurious offices separated from the rest of the organization and exclusive parking spaces an individual treatment. All this establishes a 'distance' between the executives and the doers and delays the achievement of the goals of the organization. Dynamic organizations emphasize the need to eliminate such frozen conventions and observance of codes by creating a climate for equality in organizational social status and create a momentum for enhanced pressure of performance. The absence of trust in working relationships is often a symptom of a failure in personal or corporate integrity. There is a definite strong tension between the inability of an organization and its significance and its meaningfulness to its members. Any organization is the product of a mixture of manipulation and participation. The technocratic approach should be complemented by efforts to involve the relevant members of the organization making process in order to find workable solutions. "Participation is a feeling on the part of people, not just the mechanical act of being called in to take part in discussions" – Paul Lawrence in HBR - http://bit.ly/29Xv39d

C. Internalizing Culture

In addition to explicit orientation and training programs, culture is transmitted to employees in a number of other forms – the most potent being through stories, rituals, material symbols, and language.

Internalizing Culture: Role of Stories. As they hear, told and listened and conveyed over time.

All organizations have their fund of stories, myths and legends. The nature and content of these represents and reflects the current state of organizational culture and well-being. In our study we saw this in EY, Apple, Deloitte, Google, LinkedIn, Microsoft, Unilever, KPMG, Andersen, Citibank, Lalbhai Group that they all have stories to tell of what have they done, believed in and died for. Stories doing rounds is reasonably simple to interpret and thereafter internalize. Organizational members are keen to share what they know of the company and this articulation is pretty much done through examples. These examples in time become stories.

Internalizing Culture – Role of Grapevine and Social Networks

All organizations also have their own grapevine; this is the means by which stories, myths and legends become circulated and gain currency. In simple terms, the grapevine is the difference between what people want to know and what they do know. In particular, where communications are bad, a lot of personal time and energy is wasted on informal clusters, talking through particular scenarios and wondering what the future is to hold for them. In the worst cases, this is very destructive of motivation and morale. Grapevine when not managed or understood causes political and insecurity issues within the organization. For example, in Citibank this has been managed well:

Cultural Leaders - "There is a Role of the leader in building work processes, in managing people strategy issues, and organizational emphasis on competing and performing in a complex environment. Leader's emphasizes on building future leaders through mentoring, coaching and teaching, emphasis on teamwork. There is a Role of the CEO/leader in enabling organization to restructure and right size. There is a Role of the CEO/leader in preparing the organization to change as required. Leaders have a role in sponsoring innovation, new ideas, take risks and implementing experiments. CEO/leader's has a role in enabling inters dependencies between functions, businesses, technologies and the organization as a whole not in all circumstances" – Jerry Rao – CEO Citibank NA.

Social Media Influences Culture - The most successful companies make available a wide range of social learning, training and knowledge management programs to their entire talent social network. And because knowledge becomes obsolete more quickly than ever before, companies need to take an enterprise-level approach, continuously refresh their social training and analytics based knowledge management content, capabilities and infrastructure so that people always have access to the most up-to-date information. Because of these needs, which are also felt among a more global workforce population, new e-learning methods are revolutionizing training and development by providing solutions that are both more effective and more efficient. The war for talent may be easing but good people—meaning those who excel at what they do, whether it is crafting corporate strategy, reading an analytics report, work on internet of things, a multi macro enabled spreadsheet, maintaining an aircraft engine, building a robot, work on Watson or interacting with customers—continue to be in demand. In private life, people usually manage the trade-offs between executing their daily routine tasks and preparing for the future—planning their children's schooling, for example, or moving to a new apartment. By pursuing their own perceived interests, they make the right choices because they themselves directly reap the benefits and pay the costs of their actions. Gerald C. Kane in MIT SMR 2016 Social Blogging, "What Companies Should Learn About Social Media From American Politics" further argues, "There are Implications for Decision-Making in a social media driven culture, "While this filtering creates a comfortable personal environment, the larger societal and organizational consequences are more complex. Eli Pariser, in a more stylized version of Sundstein's argument, calls this phenomenon the "filter bubble." "As companies move more toward virtual environments, they may intentionally schedule time to provide these shared experiences. These may take place as weekly "all hands" meetings where all members of an organization can get on the same page. They also may take the place of intentional face-to-face meetings that help people develop and strengthen relationships with people who may be somewhat different from them".

Internalizing Culture: Role of Power and influence bases

Power Coalitions - The analysis at the power and influence base and its interface is primarily focused on documenting and ameliorating the effects of cultural impact on conflict prone decisions on those who remain within the organization. A stream of study, both laboratory and field, has provided documentation of the significant effects of cultural impact on conflict and behavioral modification can have on "survivors". These effects have been described in terms of altered, improved or lower morale (e.g., Armstrong-Stassen, 1993), high stress (e.g., Leana and Feldman, 1992), and a "syndrome" marked by anger, envy, and guilt (e.g., Noer, 1993). The perceived fairness of the downsizing is considered a key mediating variable (e.g., Brockner, 1992), as is the effectiveness of the communication of information (e.g., Bridges, 1987 and http://bit.ly/2a6pG7U)

Key underlying assumptions Internalizing Transitional Culture include:

The pre-eminence of the organization over the individual, accompanied by a strong argument that the organization cannot reach its full potential without maximizing the effective use of human resources; although it is led by the CEO/Leader.

Form a change management perspective, reliance upon the Kurt Lewin's three step approach of unfreezing, moving to a new level, and freezing at a new level; Lewin argued that to "break open the shell of complacency, it is sometimes necessary to bring about a deliberate emotional stir-up" (Lewin, 1951:229) and http://bit.ly/2a6pG7U -

Reliance upon psychological transition models, especially as put forward by Bridges (1991); Bridges theorizes three overlapping phases of transition - the ending of what was, a messy "neutral zone", or limbo, and a new beginning;

The end of the old implicit "psychological contract" assuring lifetime job security as long as the employee "keeps his or her nose clean" and does an adequate job and formulation of a new contract in which employees are more autonomous and self-reliant (e.g., Bridges, 1994).

Downsized Cultures - Brockner (1994) and colleagues have studied the "fairness" of layoffs as a change management issue from a procedural justice perspective and have shown a link between perceived fairness of the layoffs and survivor commitment to the organization (e.g., Brockner et al, 1994). Among the fairness factors, which Brockner examines, is the connection with existing corporate culture and that which is in formation. Some organizations which have traditionally had a policy of averting layoffs are likely to be perceived by employees as violating the psychological contract when they actually conduct a lay off and therefore as more unfair when they do eventually resort to layoffs.

Negative Contracts - Noer (1993) sees letting go of the old employment contract as unfair, insensitive, not so caring, tough but necessary. His view is that implicit lifetime employment guarantees are unhealthy both for individuals and organizations. They result in a sort of "organizational codependency or integrated need" in which individuals invest enormous energy in trying to control the system and at the same time has much of their self-worth tied up in trying to live up to the organization's, not their own, values. In a similar vein, Hecksher (1995) concludes that management loyalty to the organization is no longer needed or is emerging to be a necessary condition; what is needed is more professionalism, an opportunity to display consistent behaviors loyal to as code of conduct, evidenced by creative contributions to the organization. Bridges (1994) goes even further; he sees a secular trend away from the traditional job, with security, roles, job description, goals, exits etc. Like Noer, he sees greater possibility for individuals to achieve autonomy and satisfaction by taking responsibility for their own futures.

Work relationships can become much testier during periods of organizational power challenges. That can take the form of "back stabbing, placing of blame, and overt failure to cooperate" (Mohrman and Mohrman, 1983:459). Hickok (1995) analyzed interview responses at two downsizing military bases and found that mentions of increased conflict in the workplace were significantly greater than the more positive mentions of pulling together. Again a leadership challenge to the commandant on keeping together a team that overtly is charged but covertly is demotivated.

Workplace Power and Barriers - In cultural terms, this refers to the reasons, actions and methods on what and why measures of influence are found in particular places. It also refers to matters of organization politics: the means by which people interact in order to facilitate their own position. Organizational power and its uses have a direct implication to culture as we have seen in the influence of a CEO role and decision making impact. Refer - *Organizational Barriers to Adopting Digital Trends.* "Power is the intentional influences over the beliefs, emotions, and behaviors of people. Potential power is the capacity to do so, but kinetic power is the act of doing so…. One person exerts power over another to the degree that he is able to exact compliance as desired." "A has power over B to the extent that he can get B to do something that B would otherwise not do." Power is "the ability of those who possess power to bring about the outcomes they desire." "Power is defined simply as the capacity to effect (or affect organizational outcomes. The French word 'pouvoir' stands for both the noun 'power' and the verb 'to be able. To have power is to be able to get desired things done, to effect outcomes-actions and the decisions that precede them." Analysis of these definitions shows some common elements: Effectance -getting one's way; the necessity of social interaction between two or more parties; the act or ability of influencing others; and outcomes favoring one party over the other. We therefore define interpersonal power as the ability to get one's way in a social situation. The phenomenon of power is ubiquitous. Without influence (power) there would be no cooperation and no society. Without leadership (power) in medical, political, technological, financial, spiritual, and organizational activities, humankind would not have the standard of living it does today. Without leadership (power) directed toward warfare, confiscation, and repression, humankind would not have much of the misery it does today. Power-in-action may take many forms, both positive and negative. Leading, influencing, selling, persuading-these are examples of positive uses of power. Crushing, forcing, hurting, coercing-these are examples of negative uses of power. Power per se is probably neither good nor bad although Lord Acton observed that "power tends to corrupt; absolute power corrupt absolutely." A moment's reflection, however, suggests that many problems with power stem from some of the goals of persons with power and some of the means they use, not the possession of power as such.

Organizational Barriers to Adopting Digital Trends

Strategic Priorities	Leaders	Managers	Staff	Millennials	Evaluation Scale		
Critical Factors	Resistance Levels				Low	Moderate	High
Competing priorities	H	H	H	L			
Strategic Gaps	M	M	H	H			
Trust on Digital Tech	L	L	M	L			
Tech Competence	H	M	L	L			
Resposiveness	L	L	M	L			
Leadership Understanding	M	L	H	M			
Risk Appetitite	L	L	M	L			
Collaborative Culture	M	M	M	H			
Staff Engagement	H	H	H	L			
Organizational Inertia	M	L	L	L			
Stakeholder Resistance	H	M	L	H			
Job Insecurity	H	M	H	L			

Figure 42 – Organizational Barriers to Adopting Digital Trends

Harold Lasswell, defined politics simply as, "the study of who gets what, when, and how. Organizational politics involve those activities taken within organizations to acquire, develop and use power and other resources to obtain one's preferred outcomes in a situation in which there is uncertainty or dissension about choices. Organizational politics involve intentional acts of influence to enhance or protect the self-interest of individuals or groups. Organizational politics is the management of influence to obtain ends not sanctioned by the organization or to obtain ends through non-sanctioned influence means. We view politics as a subset of power, treating it… as informal power, illegitimate in nature. Likewise, we also treat authority as a subset of power, but in this sense, formal power, the power vested in office, the capacity to get things done by virtue of the position held".

Internalizing Culture: Creating the Ideal culture

Ideal Culture - The ideal culture is one that serves the organization effectively. It may be summarized as the shared patterns of attitudes, values, beliefs and behavior, covering strategy, operations, decision-making, information flow and systems, managerial and supervisory behavior, the nature of leadership disrupted and the general behavior of the staff. It involves setting absolute standards of ensuring that these are achieved. It also requires reference to each of the elements and factors indicated above. The relationship between the ideal and the actual culture should be a matter of constant concern because both develop. Specific attention is paid to those gaps in culture that cause problems where, for example, people follow the leads, values and norms of their work or professional group rather than those of the organization. Technological advances and changes may mean that suddenly the ideal hitherto striven for has to be changed in order to accommodate new visualization, structures, design, patterns of work, retraining, regrouping, and so on. Sub-cultures, parallel cultures and covert cultures are all bound to exist in organizations; the problem is to ensure that they do not damage or detract from total organizational performance. They must be capable of harmonization within the overall standards, and any sub-cultures that do not conform to this should be broken up. The purpose is to arrive at something which is dynamic and which adds value to operations and energizes the people positively. It affects attitudes and values and the ways in which people regard themselves, each other and the organization as a whole. It affects customer relations and relations with the wider community. It contributes to perceptions and images and wider feelings of general confidence. Stories circulate through many organizations. They contain a narrative of events about the organization's founders, key decisions that affect the organization's future course, and the present top management. They anchor the present in the past and provide explanations and legitimacy for current practices.

Honda Ideal Culture - We saw the representation of an ideal culture in Honda: "The leader influences the history and tradition of the organization the leader by his/her actions and enables writing the history of the organization. The actions are determined, thought through, communicated & they also make the traditions of the organization. Having implemented they become a way of life for people as all practice it. The leader not only influences, but is also influenced by the history & traditions of the organization. Thus the leader sees value in respecting what he has inherited from his forefathers. At the same time a strong leader has the capability of changing the culture of the organization provided, he/she is able to take the process of change across levels and functions. Structure and hierarchy influence the management style. The role of the CEO in building organization vision and consequently the organization structure that determines the processes that impact the culture in the organization is an inevitable reality at Honda. Where the individual objectives are aligned towards the organizational goals, the appropriate structures & styles support them.

Digital Maturity - A company can implement portals for use by employees, customers, suppliers, partners and others. From an HR viewpoint, the first of these is obviously the most relevant. Broadly speaking, the content and functionality of the employee (B2E) portal can be divided into four broad categories: employee-to-life, employee-to-organisation, employee-to-employee and employee-to-task. Specific features of the portal include aggregated content, powerful search capabilities, access to communications applications, personalization capabilities and integration with eCommerce applications and workflow. Self-service HR applications are of course a key element in many portal deployments. "Digitally maturing companies behave differently than their less mature peers do. The difference has less to do with technology and more to do with business fundamentals". Say in *"Strategy, not technology drives digital transformation", Gerald C Kane, Doug Palmer, et all, in MIT SMR 2015. Refer - Stages of Maturity and Dimensions.* "Digitally maturing organizations are committed to transformative strategies supported by collaborative cultures that are open to taking risk. Equally important, leaders and employees at digitally maturing organizations have access to the resources they need to develop digital skills and know-how".

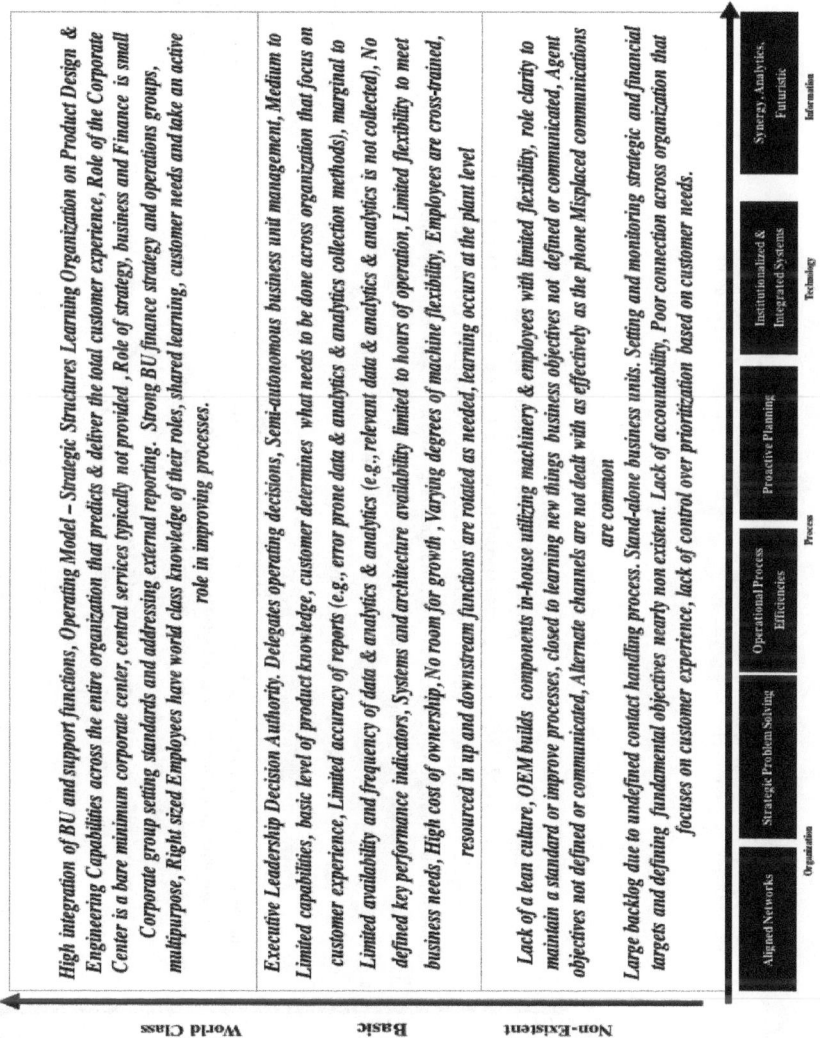

World Class

High integration of BU and support functions, Operating Model – Strategic Structures Learning Organization on Product Design & Engineering Capabilities across the entire organization that predicts & deliver the total customer experience, Role of the Corporate Center is a bare minimum corporate center, central services typically not provided . Role of strategy, business and Finance is small Corporate group setting standards and addressing external reporting. Strong BU finance strategy and operations groups, multipurpose, Right sized Employees have world class knowledge of their roles, shared learning, customer needs and take an active role in improving processes.

Basic

Executive Leadership Decision Authority. Delegates operating decisions, Semi-autonomous business unit management, Medium to Limited capabilities, basic level of product knowledge, customer determines what needs to be done across organization that focus on customer experience, Limited accuracy of reports (e.g., error prone data & analytics & analytics collection methods), marginal to Limited availability and frequency of data & analytics & analytics (e.g., relevant data & analytics & analytics is not collected), No defined key performance indicators, Systems and architecture availability limited to hours of operation, Limited flexibility to meet business needs, High cost of ownership, No room for growth , Varying degrees of machine flexibility, Employees are cross-trained, resourced in up and downstream functions are rotated as needed, learning occurs at the plant level

Non-Existent

Lack of a lean culture, OEM builds components in-house utilizing machinery & employees with limited flexibility, role clarity to maintain a standard or improve processes, closed to learning new things business objectives not defined or communicated, Agent objectives not defined or communicated, Alternate channels are not dealt with as effectively as the phone Misplaced communications are common Large backlog due to undefined contact handling process. Stand-alone business units. Setting and monitoring strategic and financial targets and defining fundamental objectives nearly non existent. Lack of accountability, Poor connection across organization that focuses on customer experience, lack of control over prioritization based on customer needs.

Organization		Process		Technology	Information
Aligned Networks	Strategic Problem Solving	Operational Process Efficiencies	Proactive Planning	Institutionalized & Integrated Systems	Synergy, Analytics, Futuristic

Figure 43 – Stages of Maturity and Dimensions - "Strategy, not technology drives digital transformation", Gerald C Kane, Doug Palmer, et all, in MIT SMR 2015

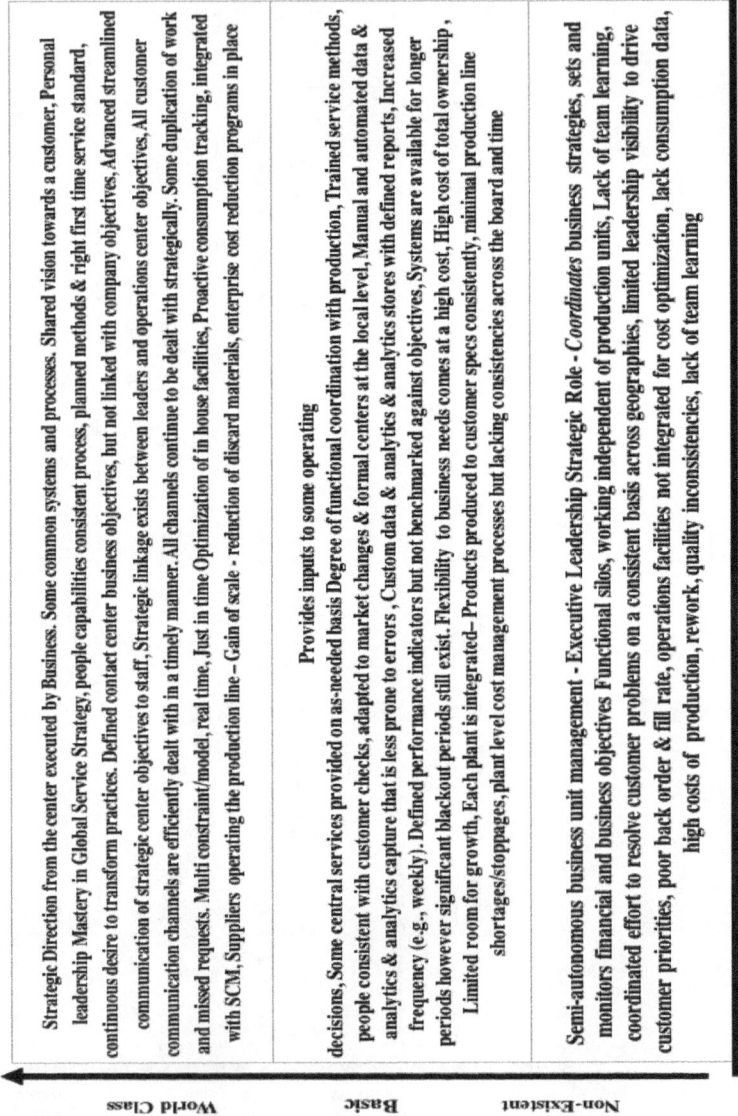

World Class

Strategic Direction from the center executed by Business. Some common systems and processes. Shared vision towards a customer, Personal leadership Mastery in Global Service Strategy, people capabilities consistent process, planned methods & right first time service standard, continuous desire to transform practices. Defined contact center business objectives, but not linked with company objectives, Advanced streamlined communication of strategic center objectives to staff, Strategic linkage exists between leaders and operations center objectives, All customer communication channels are efficiently dealt with in a timely manner. All channels continue to be dealt with strategically. Some duplication of work and missed requests. Multi constraint/model, real time, Just in time Optimization of in house facilities, Proactive consumption tracking, integrated with SCM, Suppliers operating the production line – Gain of scale - reduction of discard materials, enterprise cost reduction programs in place

Basic

Provides inputs to some operating decisions, Some central services provided on as-needed basis Degree of functional coordination with production, Trained service methods, people consistent with customer checks, adapted to market changes & formal centers at the local level, Manual and automated data & analytics & analytics capture that is less prone to errors, Custom data & analytics & analytics stores with defined reports, Increased frequency (e.g., weekly). Defined performance indicators but not benchmarked against objectives, Systems are available for longer periods however significant blackout periods still exist. Flexibility to business needs comes at a high cost, High cost of total ownership, Limited room for growth, Each plant is integrated– Products produced to customer specs consistently, minimal production line shortages/stoppages, plant level cost management processes but lacking consistencies across the board and time

Non-Existent

Semi-autonomous business unit management - Executive Leadership Strategic Role - *Coordinates* business strategies, sets and monitors financial and business objectives Functional silos, working independent of production units, Lack of team learning, coordinated effort to resolve customer problems on a consistent basis across geographies, limited leadership visibility to drive customer priorities, poor back order & fill rate, operations facilities not integrated for cost optimization, lack consumption data, high costs of production, rework, quality inconsistencies, lack of team learning

Figure 43 A – Stages of Maturity and Dimensions - "Strategy, not technology drives digital transformation", Gerald C Kane, Doug Palmer, et all, in MIT SMR 2015

Hierarchical Flow - The CEO plays a very important role as the flow from the top determines the flow down the line in most of the organizations. The role of the CEO/leader in regard to strategy processes technology and people actions and leader's influence in the existence of specific types of cultures. That the processes, technology is woven all around the people and as any systems is as good as people implementing it is but a simple reality of this organization. Various sub-cultures also exist in the organization, which may be in tune or different from the over-riding culture in the organization. The people focus of the organization determines the cultural orientation of the organization. Leadership disrupted style as practiced by the management groups influences the culture. Culture is all-pervasive in an organization, and is determined by the actions of the top management. If the top boss is authoritative & takes all decisions by himself/herself, the culture in the organization cannot be Participative. CEO/leader focus on performance, climate, communication, and HRM practices, on monetary reward programs and influence over high performers, and management attention on retaining high performers. Focus on creating a high-Performing Enterprise is one of the ways of retaining talent in the organization. The systems are thus designed to reward, motivate & recognize high performers. The HR strategy is clearly aligned with the business strategy".

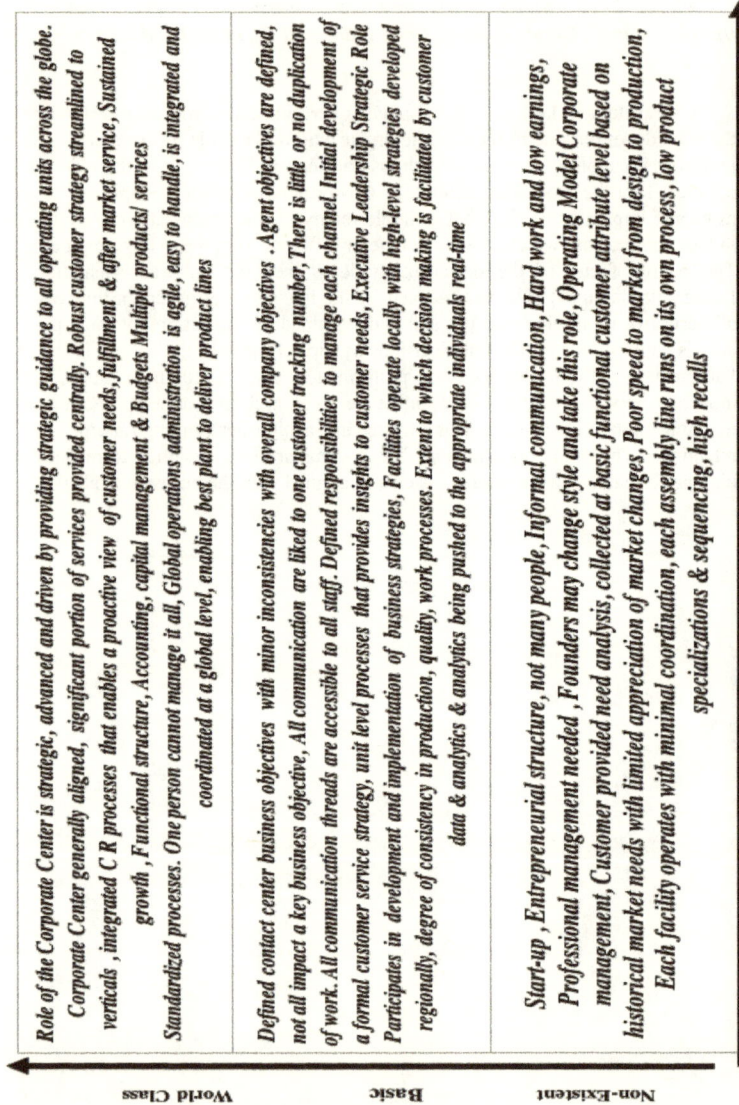

Figure 43 B – Stages of Maturity and Dimensions - "Strategy, not technology drives digital transformation", Gerald C Kane, Doug Palmer, et all, in MIT SMR 2015

Column headers (Dimensions): Aligned Networks | Strategic Problem Solving | Operational Process Efficiencies | Proactive Planning | Institutionalized & Integrated Systems | Synergy, Analytics, Futuristic

Row: **World Class**
Role of the Corporate Center is strategic, advanced and driven by providing strategic guidance to all operating units across the globe. Corporate Center generally aligned, significant portion of services provided centrally. Robust customer strategy streamlined to verticals , integrated C R processes that enables a proactive view of customer needs, fulfillment & after market service, Sustained growth , Functional structure, Accounting, capital management & Budgets Multiple products/ services Standardized processes. One person cannot manage it all, Global operations administration is agile, easy to handle, is integrated and coordinated at a global level, enabling best plant to deliver product lines

Row: **Basic**
Defined contact center business objectives with minor inconsistencies with overall company objectives . Agent objectives are defined, not all impact a key business objective, All communication are liked to one customer tracking number, There is little or no duplication of work. All communication threads are accessible to all staff. Defined responsibilities to manage each channel. Initial development of a formal customer service strategy, unit level processes that provides insights to customer needs, Executive Leadership Strategic Role Participates in development and implementation of business strategies, Facilities operate locally with high-level strategies developed regionally, degree of consistency in production, quality, work processes. Extent to which decision making is facilitated by customer data & analytics and analytics being pushed to the appropriate individuals real-time

Row: **Non-Existent**
Start-up , Entrepreneurial structure, not many people, Informal communication, Hard work and low earnings, Professional management needed , Founders may change style and take this role, Operating Model Corporate management, Customer provided need analysis, collected at basic functional customer attribute level based on historical market needs with limited appreciation of market changes, Poor speed to market from design to production, Each facility operates with minimal coordination, each assembly line runs on its own process, low product specializations & sequencing, high recalls

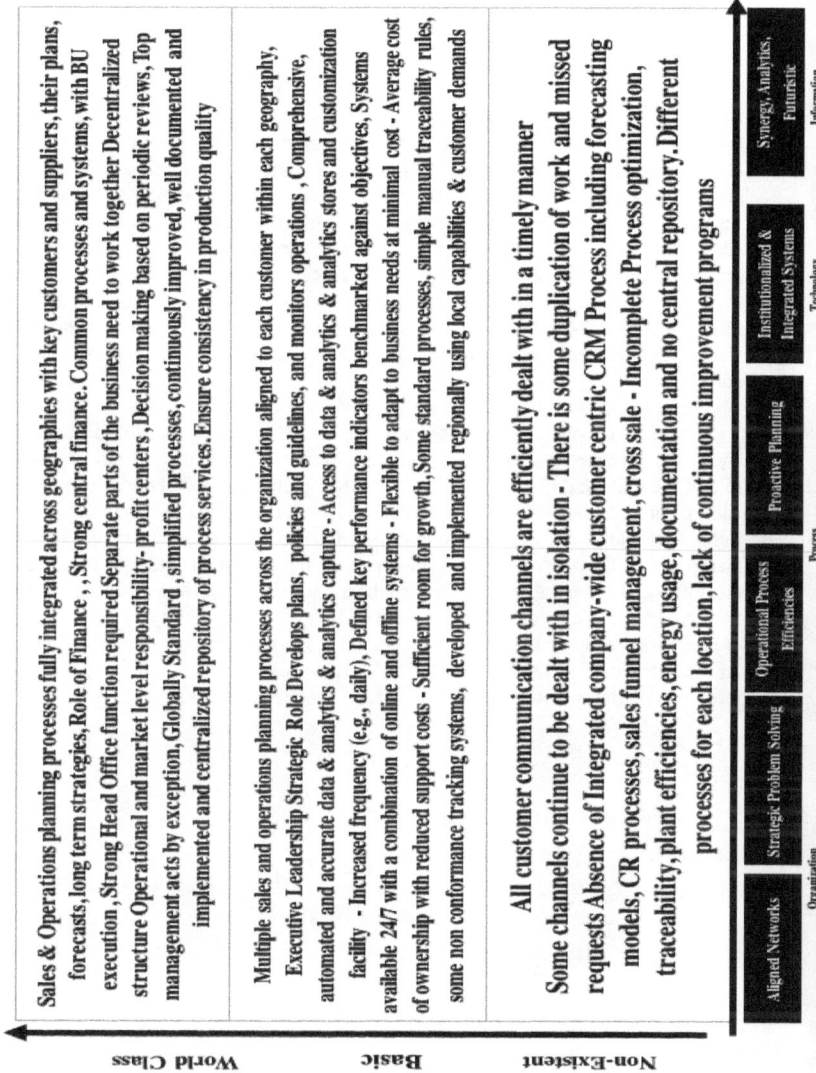

Sales & Operations planning processes fully integrated across geographies with key customers and suppliers, their plans, forecasts, long term strategies, Role of Finance, , Strong central finance. Common processes and systems, with BU execution, Strong Head Office function required Separate parts of the business need to work together Decentralized structure Operational and market level responsibility- profit centers ,Decision making based on periodic reviews, Top management acts by exception, Globally Standard , simplified processes, continuously improved, well documented and implemented and centralized repository of process services. Ensure consistency in production quality

Multiple sales and operations planning processes across the organization aligned to each customer within each geography, Executive Leadership Strategic Role Develops plans, policies and guidelines, and monitors operations , Comprehensive, automated and accurate data & analytics capture - Access to data & analytics & analytics stores and customization facility - Increased frequency (e.g., daily), Defined key performance indicators benchmarked against objectives, Systems available 24/7 with a combination of online and offline systems - Flexible to adapt to business needs at minimal cost - Average cost of ownership with reduced support costs - Sufficient room for growth, Some standard processes, simple manual traceability rules, some non conformance tracking systems, developed and implemented regionally using local capabilities & customer demands

All customer communication channels are efficiently dealt with in a timely manner Some channels continue to be dealt with in isolation - There is some duplication of work and missed requests Absence of Integrated company-wide customer centric CRM Process including forecasting models, CR processes, sales funnel management, cross sale - Incomplete Process optimization, traceability, plant efficiencies, energy usage, documentation and no central repository. Different processes for each location, lack of continuous improvement programs

World Class | Basic | Non-Existent

Figure 43 C – Stages of Maturity and Dimensions - "Strategy, not technology drives digital transformation", Gerald C Kane, Doug Palmer, et all, in MIT SMR 2015

Internalizing Culture: Role of Traditions and Rituals.

Just as rituals are used as a formalization technique, they also are a means for transmitting culture. Activities such as recognition and award ceremonies, weekly Friday afternoon beer bashes, and annual company picnics are rituals that express and reinforce the key values of the organization, what goals are important, which people are important and which are expendable.

Cultural Transformation - In the words of Dr. P Balasubramaniam of I I M Bangalore, "the leader influences the History and Tradition of the Organization. Azim Premji is a case in point: his hands-on leadership disrupted transformed a Vanaspati manufacturer of no great significance into an IT and Software powerhouse, (WIPRO) and an organization of embedded values and integrity. Jack Welch could afford a laid-back life at the already well performing General Electric, but chose his action course that led his company to great heights of excellence in terms of market capitalization and admiration. Structure and Hierarchy Influence, Management Style, the Role of the CEO in building organization visions. Structure comes in different forms: in ownership, in organizational design, in trust and confidence levels, in competencies, and so on. If the company Board has the welfare of its shareholders and stakeholders on a sustainable basis, it would and should empower the executive leadership disrupted team to develop an organizational vision, and provide route maps to achieve set goals".

Cultural Governance - In governance of corporations, the Board of course is responsible to ensure that an appropriate process is in place for strategy formulation and implementation, but it is the role of the CEO and his team to formulate such policies consistent with organizational mandates and values, for endorsement by the Board. The Role of the CEO/leader in regard to strategy processes technology and people actions and leader's influence in the existence of specific types of cultures. If it means, the CEO's role and influence in these matters would be determined by the cultural ambience in the organization (including the corporate board and the controlling owners), one would say only partly true. A charismatic leader should have it in him or her the ability to influence favorable changes in organizational culture itself. Most successful leaders, unable to operate within the framework of an inhospitable culture, often reject such organizations (very much like the body rejecting an incompatible transplant) and move on to more amenable pastures.

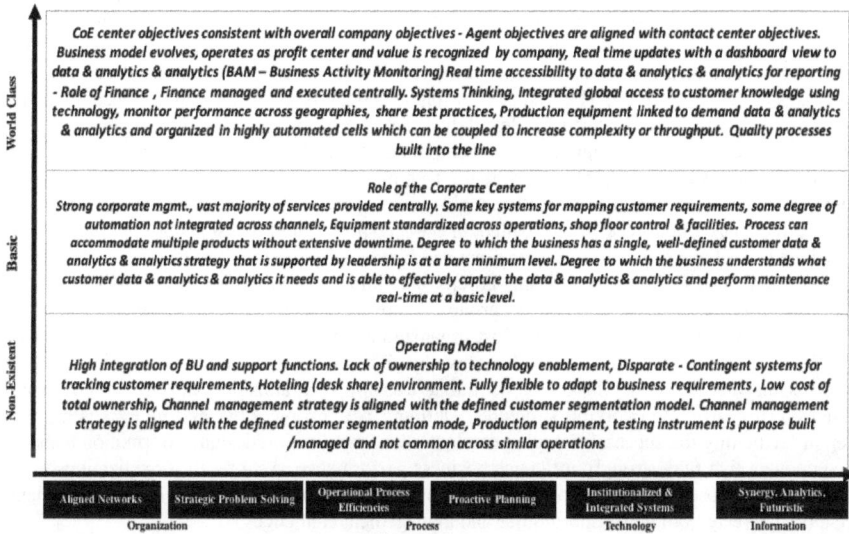

Figure 43 D – Stages of Maturity and Dimensions - "Strategy, not technology drives digital transformation", Gerald C Kane, Doug Palmer, et all, in MIT SMR 2015

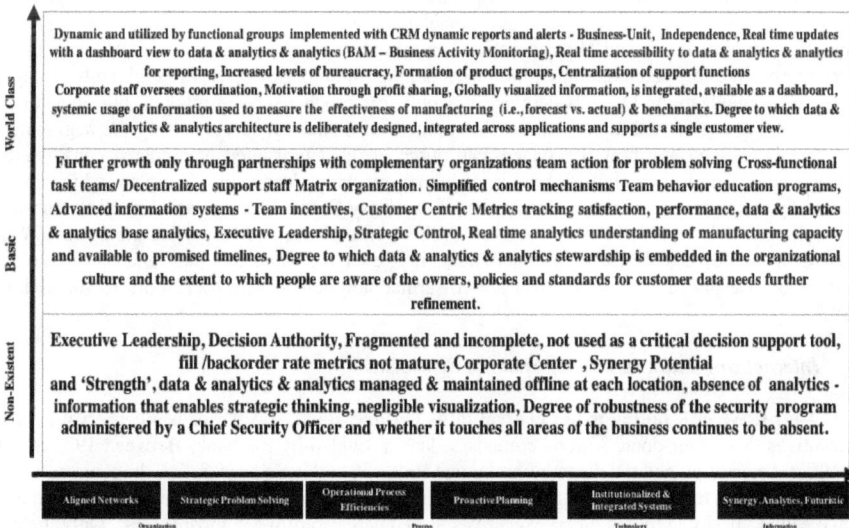

Figure 43 E – Stages of Maturity and Dimensions - "Strategy, not technology drives digital transformation", Gerald C Kane, Doug Palmer, et all, in MIT SMR 2015

Leadership disrupted Style as practiced by the management groups influences the culture. An effective practice would ensure that digital company leadership actively and continuously communicates business goals and performance results throughout the organization. From an organizational structure perspective, the resources should be aligned to support the key business processes in the value chain. The first step of this technique is to perform an organizational structure assessment to determine the "as-is" roles, define the labor pool, and identify the core competencies. This assessment will help highlight key components that should be built into the design of the organizational structure. The objective of the technique is to help develop a number of alternative approaches to determine the basic "strategic groupings" of the organization. Strategic grouping dictates the basic framework within which all organization design decisions are made. The grouping decisions give shape to what work gets done and how. Grouping activities into jobs or teams creates logical "boundaries" between working groups that impacts information processing, economies of scale opportunities, and the behavior of groups. There are a variety of ways to group activities (e.g., by activity, by output, by customer). Most organizations group their activities using a hybrid of the above. It is also important to consider how the different groups can link and interact. Linking mechanisms are the joints in the system that transform organization design models from two-dimensional charts into evolving structures. Defining how people work and interact is an important step in facilitating the successful implementation of an organization design. Information technology is a component that may strongly influence business performance. As a result, organizations seek ways to improve the cost performance of information systems. The complexity and rapid pace of change for technology create both new opportunities and management challenges.

Whether an organization provides enough headroom for its managers to add value depends largely upon managerial styles in place. Authoritarian, arrogant, intolerant, abrasive, credit-snatching, disrespectful leaders are a sure prescription to a self-sustaining mediocrity in organizational performance, managerial succession and societal acceptance. CEO/leader focus on performance, climate, communication, and HRM practices, on monetary reward programs and influence over high performers, and management attention on retaining high performers. In a globally competitive economy, organizations have to compete not only for product/service markets but also for scarce resources like capital and human talent. Recruitment of human resources is only the beginning; how the best is retained and how the system can purge itself of unwanted or outdated constituents will depend upon the motivational calibration of human resources leadership disrupted, which should be driven by the courage and conviction of the CEO. Henry David Thoreau writes, "Whatever your sex or position, life is a battle in which you are to show your pluck, and woe be to the coward. Whether passed on a bed of sickness or a tented field, it is ever the same fair play and admits no foolish distinction. Despair and postponement are cowardice and defeat. Men were born to succeed, not to fail."

Internalizing Culture: Role of Material Symbols.

Aggressive risk taking is not central to its culture. Bank of America is a conservative firm. Its executives drive four-door, American-made sedans, provided by the bank. Between 1983 and 1987, Bank of America owned the discount brokerage firm of Charles Schwab & Co. In contrast to B of A, Schwab built its reputation on aggressiveness. It sought out and hired only outgoing and what some have called "flashy" brokers. Top executives at Schwab also drove company cars. Only theirs were Ferraris, Porsches, and BMWs. The cars" images fit both the people who drove them and the cultural values Schwab sought to maintain. Four-door luxury sedans and Ferraris are material symbols that help to reinforce their organization's culture. The design and physical layout of spaces and buildings, furniture, executive perks, and dress attire are material symbols that convey to employees who is important, the degree of egalitarianism desired by top management, and the kinds of behaviors (i.e., risk taking, conservative, authoritarian, participate, individualistic, social) that are appropriate.

Internalizing Culture: Role of Language.

Language in Cultures - Many organizations and units within organizations use language as a way to identify members of a culture or subculture. By learning this language, members attest to their acceptance of the culture and, in so doing, help to preserve it. Many organizations, over time, develop unique terms to describe equipment, offices, key personnel, suppliers, customers, or products that relate to its business. New employees are frequently overwhelmed with acronyms and jargon that after six months on the job becomes a natural part of their language. The Gujarat ways, customs, rituals and practices were very much a part of the Lalbhai Group culture. Hindu rites were built into the language spoken and understood as a desired way of handling problems and its timing for action. But once assimilated, this terminology acts as a common denominator that unites members of a given culture or subculture.

Internalizing Culture – Data Orientation

"Data-oriented culture will require extra momentum - Organizations on the Collaborative path integrate data from silos and then disseminate the insights across the enterprise. They are almost three times more likely to use analytics to guide future strategies than Specialized organizations, and twice as likely to rely on analytics for day-to-day operations." write David Kiron, Rebecca Shockley, Nina Kruschwitz, Glenn Finch and Dr. Michael Haydock in Analytics: The Widening Divide, MIT SMR 2011, "On the Specialized path, organizations are open to exploring new analytical techniques and applying them liberally within discrete areas of the business. However, when it comes to taking an enterprise approach, most respondents considered the organizational challenges extremely difficult to confront and resolve. Political constraints and a lack of cohesion within the organization can be major barriers to integrating data and using analytics for enterprise wide objectives. Unless these hurdles are overcome, the Specialized path to analytical transformation may reach a point of diminishing returns as siloed programs impede establishment of analytics as a core enabler of business strategy and operations. Either a strong push from senior leaders or grassroots momentum from individuals at many levels will likely be required to create a culture that is open to new ideas and ready to move forward on the basis of fact-based insights. "Some companies see benefits in having a hosted portal. The Cedar survey found that organisations worldwide spent, on average, 17% of their HR self-service/portal budgets on application service provider (ASP) fees and over 50% are transitioning to cloud enabled SaaS solution that includes embedded analytics. According to Pfeifer, the factors leading to outsourcing include a lack of time and resources, a lack of expertise in security and technological development and a desire to focus on the core business. A hosted portal may also be less costly, with a minimal initial investment and reduced costs for ongoing maintenance. Applications and systems are likely to be more secure and more powerful, with a positive impact on employee productivity and on employee, customer and supplier satisfaction. Other benefits, in Pfeifer's view, include ready access to the latest technology and increased flexibility to accommodate rapid growth." Collaborative organizations have cultures where individuals are prepared to challenge current ideas and practices on the basis of new information. To support this culture, they are twice as likely to provide insights to anyone in the organization who needs them. As a result, they've democratized the access to data and insights, empowering employees and executives alike. These organizations enjoy executive-level endorsement for the broad use of analytics to manage day-to-day operations and shape future strategies".

On Analytical insights, continue the authors, "Insights gained through analytics can create a repository of strategic assets as valuable as your databases. But if those insights aren't used, their value is never realized. Does your organization encourage employees to come forward with new ideas? And how likely are any of those ideas to be adopted? What happens when new ideas challenge current assumptions about the market, or how the business operates? And are key executives setting the example by visibly using facts derived from analytics to make key decisions?

Questions to consider for building a data-oriented culture

- *How structured is your process for applying analytics to business strategy?*
- *Are insights about customers, including history and value to the organization, shared with everyone who interacts with them?*
- *Is analytics consistently guiding both strategy and operations?*

The amount you invest in each of these competencies will depend upon your level of sophistication. But mastery of all three is needed to achieve sustainable competitive advantage".

D. Leading and Managing Culture

Leading and Managing Cultures: Are Cultures Manageable? Is there a Leadership Influence?

Sectoral Adoption - Certain types of sectors appear to indicate a faster adoption rate to Digital HR. "Industries born of technology lead the list of sectors with the greatest penetration of digitally maturing organizations — IT, telecom, and media & entertainment. However, this year's digital business study did not find a consistent set of laggards on the opposite end of the spectrum. Companies in each sector have strengths to build on as well as weaknesses to address. The construction and real estate sector, for example, ranks lowest in terms of digital maturity — defined as an organization where digital has transformed processes, talent engagement and business models — but ranks in the top five industries reaping digital gains by improving work with partners and employees. Companies in this sector also lag in the development of digital strategies focused on transforming their businesses. Consumer goods companies sit squarely in the middle of the digital maturity spectrum but fall short on digitally enabling employees. Conversely, the manufacturing sector is providing digital skills to employees but has yet to realize digital gains. The issue may be that executives in the sector need to increase their efforts to encourage employees to use digital technologies to innovate" - *Gerald C Kane, Doug Palmer, et all, in MIT SMR 2015. See Schematic below.*

Stakeholder Maturity Hierarchy

Stakeholder Maturity Hierarchy	SCORE	STAKEHOLDER OPTIONS						STRATEGIC DRIVE					
		CUSTOMERS	PARTNERS	STAFF	VENDORS	SHAREHOLDER	STRATEGIC DRIVE	COMPETITIVE DRIVE	CUSTOMER DRIVE	DISRUPTIVE DRIVE	COST DRIVE	VALUE DRIVE	BEST PRACTICE
High Focus													
Moderate Focus													
No Change													
Moderate Focus													
Low Focus													
Not Applicable													
1 year Plan													
2 Year Plan													
Industry Focus		1	2	3	4	5	6	7	8	9	10	11	12
Financials Banking	A												
Consumer FMCG	A												
Infrastructure	B												
Energy - Oil & Gas	B												
Federal - Provincial	C												
Media Entertainment	C												
IT, Business Services	A												
Manufacturing	C												
Technology	A												
Retail Logistics	A												
Telecom Communications	C												
BPO - KPO, HRPO	A												

Figure 44 – Stakeholder Maturity Hierarchy

Leading and Managing Culture - Are cultures manageable? Can Leadership disrupted be concretely connected to organizations and their cultures?

Dr. Engineer's Managing Cultural Excellence - We would perhaps summarize in the words of Dr. Ferzaan Engineer, the earlier Managing Director of Quintiles, a global clinical study company, an Intellectual Enterprise, "I believe that Leadership disrupted is perhaps the single most important factor for an organization and its culture to achieve sustained excellence in today's environment. Leadership disrupted should be by example and through mentoring and motivation and certainly not by dictate. The days of the hierarchical organization and patriarchal leader are over. Today's knowledge-based industries need a different kind of leadership disrupted that creates an environment of trust, motivation, teamwork and energy in an organization. I also believe that a strong organization will have a strong identifiable culture. It may be pluralistic and does not need to be cult-like. However, a strong organization's culture will stress shared values, shared goals and synergy between Functions and Divisions, thereby creating a seamless, competitive organization which challenges its people, rewards and motivates them and allows them to grow-both individually and collectively. High quality leadership will create, nurture and propagate the organization's culture and ensure that core values are collectively held. However, today's organization needs to allow scope for individual growth, innovation and diversity of views. Managing this paradox is the key to success".

To Dr. Engineer, Leadership disrupted influences cultures in an organizational model:

- *Talks to us about his/her most important values and beliefs*
- *Emphasizes the importance of being committed to our beliefs*
- *Specifies the importance of having a strong sense of purpose*

- *Displays conviction in his/her ideals, beliefs, and values*
- *Clarifies the central purpose underlying our actions*

Clearly an organization's culture and its leadership disrupted has a marked influence on its employees. But should culture be treated as a given, in which case managers would be advised to understand their organization's culture but reminded that there is nothing they can do to change it? As one author put it, "If we take the concept of culture seriously, we may have to face the possibility that cultural assumptions are virtually impossible to change. "Or should culture be taken as a controllable variable that can be adjusted by management, as needed, to align it better with the organization's strategy and environment? As we'll demonstrate, this is the critical issue today underlying organizational culture, and there is a great deal riding on the outcome of the debate. Before we look at this debate in detail, a point of clarification seems appropriate.

Leading and Managing Culture: Managing Cultures mean Changing Cultures

Is Managing Changing? When we discuss managing culture, we mean changing the culture. And social media has a substantive role to play. This has grown to become the prevailing definition. Yet as it has been noted, managing culture need not be the same as changing culture. "Ultimately, the issues of engagement and culture come down to leadership disrupted. If CEOs and business leaders are not talking with employees, examining the work environment carefully, and holding supervisors responsible for engagement, they will likely nd that their organizations suffer, write Bersin by Deloitte in 2015 predictions". In a time of transition, for instance, managing an organization's culture may entail sustaining the present culture rather than inducing any change. So, in a very strict sense, managing a culture could entail stabilizing the status quo as well as inducing a shift to another state. Status quo is easier said than done as we saw in the case of Bank of America that had to struggle back into substantive banking market share after it decided to demerge its retail Banking operations. For our purposes, however, we'll treat managing culture and changing culture as synonymous. We know that the selection process, top management's actions, and the methods chosen for socializing employees sustain a culture. A large bank did just this. Got together people and socialized them into a new bank, one that did not exist before. Similarly, stories, rituals, material symbols, and language are means by which employees learn who and what is important. By changing these factors, we should be able to change the culture. Top management might, for example, fire or demote employees who are rigidly locked into the current culture and replace them with individuals who accept and promote the values that are sought; or they might institute a new set of rituals that will reinforce a different culture milieu". These changes would require transformational agents to Perform an organizational structure assessment that outlines how effective the structure is in supporting the strategy (including any current internal structural issues and operational issues/limitations); Perform high-level "as-is" analysis and process mapping, focusing on role clarity across levels and functions; information and work flows; interfaces – coordination and monitoring; decision making and reporting relationships; Gain understanding of the value chain and "to-be" processes; Gain understanding of current and future Board roles and decision-making powers; Formulate the strategic organization design at an enterprise level; Gain understanding of the core competencies required and Gain understanding of potential or planned changes to the "as-is" situation. "Theodore Kinni writes in MIT SMR 2016 frontier, "People Management by Algorithm" on how digital is reshaping the way leaders behave, "On March 19, Pope Francis began posting on Instagram. He uploaded 8 images in 4 days and attracted 1.9 million followers. It wasn't the Supreme Pontiff's first social media foray. He has been tweeting since he was elected 3 years ago, and he has 8.94 million followers on his English-language Twitter account. In terms of social media savvy, the Pope is running circles around most Fortune 500 CEOs. As of July 28, 2015, 61% of the CEOs had no social media presence at all, according to a study by CEO.com that was released earlier this year. Only 10% of the CEOs were on Twitter, and only 60% of their accounts were active. A new article, by Emily Jane Fox in Vanity Fair, plumbs the state of tweeting among high-profile CEOs and highlights the internal team — led by Nola Weinstein, Twitter's head of executive engagement — that encourages them to join the service. But the article suggests an unexpected reason why CEOs and other execs might want to start thinking in 140 characters. "Interestingly," writes Fox, "the number-one success Weinstein and her team see from executives on Twitter is when they connect with their own colleagues and employees — explaining the reason behind a particular project or campaign, or highlighting a job well done by one of the company's teams or offices. 'If you're a C.M.O. on a global level and you give a global shout-out to a team in Tokyo or Singapore or New York, that goes a long way. The public nature can be very rewarding and gratifying,' Weinstein said."

At the internal pressure level, the interaction between the desired culture and the organization's structures and systems causes stresses. Serious misfit between these leads to stress and frustration and also to customer dissatisfaction and staff demotivation. The expectations and aspirations of staff, and the extent to which these are realistic and can be satisfied within the organization needs to be evaluated and decisions may have to be taken. Unilever used its employee survey to study the changes it had to bring about in a Unilever acquired organization. This becomes a serious issue when the nature of the organization changes and prevailing expectations can no longer be accommodated.

Sub Culture Values - Problems also arise when the organization makes promises that it cannot keep. Concurrently management and supervisory style, and the extent to which this is supportive, suitable to the purpose and generally acceptable to the staff also needs to be considered. The qualities and expertise of the staff, and the extent to which this divides their loyalties has often been an area of concern for organizations attempting to bring people of varying sub cultures together. "Ideas about a person's place in society, his role, lifestyle, and ego qualities will lose their hold as the cohesive forces in society disintegrate. Subculture values will proliferate to such a bewildering extent that a whole new class of professionals will arise to control them. Such a Transmutation Technology will deal in fashions, in ways of being. Lifestyle consultants will become the new priests of our civilizations. They will be the new magicians." Peter J. Carroll, Liber Null and Psychonaut: An Introduction to Chaos Magic. Many staff groups have professional or trade union memberships, continuous professional development requirements and career expectations, as well as a requirement to hold down positions and carry out tasks within organizations. In many cases- and especially when general dissatisfaction is present- people tend to take refuge in their profession or occupation, or their trade union. "In any culture, subculture, or family in which belief is valued above thought, and self-surrender is valued above self-expression, and conformity is valued above integrity, those who preserve their self-esteem are likely to be heroic exceptions" - Nathaniel Branden

Social Media Cultures – "The recruitment process in a social media process can be divided into four steps: define the need; broadcast and attract; collect and qualify; and select and hire. Social Media technology can improve the effectiveness of each of these steps, but the systems designed to automate the processes must offer a wide range of functionality and address the critical issues at each stage. Take needs definition, for instance. This rests on an analysis of the workforce, which requires forecasting capabilities, recruiting metrics, staffing metrics and the ability to assess workforce competencies and link them with the business strategy. Many vendors provide these services in APP mode, but customers should ensure that if they outsource their process, they retain as much data as possible for analysis. Otherwise they will not be able to measure their success. The creation of job requisitions is another important element of needs definition. The critical issues in this area are integration with the HR management system and the need to ensure that the system supports the involvement of all the factors in the recruiting process". Gerald C Kane in "Balancing Tradeoffs in

Social Media", MIT SMR 2016, writes, "Being good at social media is as much about culture as it is about having the right tools. Successful enterprise social media use has less to do with the tools themselves as it does with the climate that the company cultivates. Cultivating the right climate requires managers to balance a number of tradeoffs through carefully crafted social media policies, adapt characteristics of existing organizational culture, and model effective social media practices for their employees. Exploration vs. Exploitation - The first tradeoff is between what Stanford Professor James G. March called exploration and exploitation. Exploration involves the search for and discovery of new knowledge, while exploitation leverages existing knowledge for performance outcomes. Exploration typically results in lower short-term performance but better long-term performance. Searching for new knowledge is inherently inefficient, but often pay dividends down the road. In contrast, exploitation results in better short-term performance, but may produce worse performance over the long term. Leveraging what one knows maximizes performance now, but given that knowledge may not keep up with changing circumstances, this strategy may eventually trap you in increasingly inefficient ways of doing things. The Privacy Calculus - While managers may be tempted to conclude that a more open platform will lead to greater knowledge sharing and information flows across the company, that may not actually be the case. People may be more reluctant to share information if it is made available to everyone in the company by default. In one company I studied, employees were fearful about contributing to the company's social media platform because executives had previously disciplined employees for certain types of posts. In another, employees did most of their posting to private groups, because it was the most effective way to filter out the noise of other activity on the platform. Somewhat paradoxically, providing greater privacy protections for employees on enterprise social media platforms may actually increase the amount of available knowledge, because employees will be more willing to contribute. Effective enterprise social media use actually entails managers surrendering a certain amount of control and trusting employees to organize themselves to address organizational goals. "According to PeopleSoft's Ségolène Finet, director of European HCM product strategy effective recruitment depends not only on embracing a sales and marketing philosophy but also on choosing the right technology. Many technological developments are highly relevant to recruitment. Examples include corporate social networks, video interviews, job portals, recruitment web sites, collaboration tools including company / career oriented email, self-service applications, job boards, video-based interviewing and the use of robots and spiders to search out suitable candidates. Not surprisingly, Internet technologies feature prominently in the list. In the PeopleSoft survey, 83% of HR directors interviewed saw the Internet as key to their recruiting efforts. Yet 82% of interviewees also claimed that they have difficulty integrating recruiting data with core HRMS information in areas such as retention and workforce forecasting. This integration is essential because retention and development become ever more important as the talent pool shrinks and they need to be carefully balanced with recruitment". Herein lies the real power of social media: The ability to allow employees to work together without formal and rigid hierarchies. This loosening of control will likely be a frightening prospect to most managers, yet it creates the possibility of a much more agile and aware organization that less constrained by rigid bureaucracies of more traditional managerial control. Loosened control does not mean eliminating control all together, but it does free up employees to act more on their own initiative to accomplish work goals. Freedom vs. Control - The final, and perhaps most important, tradeoff is one of freedom vs. control, and it is the one with which managers will likely have the most difficulty. Effective enterprise social media use actually entails managers surrendering a certain amount of control and trusting employees to organize themselves to address organizational goals. There is no single "right" solution for adopting social media in companies. Rather, success is about balancing these tradeoffs to create the right mix for your company, its culture, and the goals you have for the platform".

Leading and Managing Culture: The Influence of the Cultural Web

---

The cultural web is an alternative way of looking at the internal pressures upon organization culture. People draw heavily on points of reference which are built up over periods of time and which are especially important at internal organizational level. Nestle and its penchant for focused growth, steady sate management and streamlined work processes. The beliefs and assumptions that comprise this fall within boundaries. The routine ways those members of the organization behave towards each other and that link different parts of the organization, which together comprise 'the way that things are done'. There are organizations where right ways of doing things simply got articulated and followed. All it needed was a dedicated set of top management professionals. These, at their best, lubricate the working of the organization and may provide distinctive and beneficial organizational competency. However, they can also represent a 'take for granted' attitude about how things should happen which can be extremely difficult to change. The rituals of organizational life, such as training programs, promotion and assessment, point out what is important in the organization, reinforce 'the way we do things around here' and signal what is actually valued. Choice of a Chairman of a company over several seniors who were in the pipeline was a clear vindication of taking stances and positions meaning to act as signals to the organization that merit surpasses all other consideration – In Unilever for example. The stories told by members or the organization to each other, to outsiders and to new recruits, embed the present organization in its history and flag up important events and personalities. The more symbolic aspects of organization, such as logos, offices, cars and titles, or the type of language and terminology commonly used.

The control systems, measures and reward systems emphasize what is actually important and focus attention and activity. Power structures are also likely to be associated in so far as the most powerful groupings are likely to be the ones most associated with what is actually valued. The formal organization structure and the informal ways in which the organization works are likely to reflect these power structures and again, to delineate important relationships and emphasize required levels of performance (Johnson and Scholes, 1992)

Leading and Managing Digital Culture: Influence of Leadership disrupted

As stated above, both the actual culture and the perceived ideal are subject to constant development. With this in mind, the best organizations therefore pay this constant attention. There are some basic assumptions here.

Culture can be changed and developed if Leadership disrupted can influence the change.

Nissan UK transformed a population of ex-miner's shipbuilders and steelworkers into the most productive and effective car company in the UK. Toyota and Derby is following suit with former railway staff. British Airways transformed a bureaucratic nationalized monopoly into a customer-orientated multinational corporation. British Steel transformed itself from a loss making National Corporation, riddled with demarcation and restrictive practices, to a profitable, effective and flexible operator. The constant development of operations, technology, markets, customer bases and the capabilities of the human resource also make this inevitable. Current ways of working and equipment, and current skills, knowledge and qualities serve current needs only. The future is based around the developments and innovations that are to take place in each of these areas. Therefore, the culture must itself develop in order that these can be accommodated.

Leaders and Role Models tend to considerably influence behavior and culture. In some cases, the leader is even elevated to the level of an icon and the organization blindly follows his style or culture. The CEO / Leader is constantly watched. His every action (or lack of it) and even idiosyncrasy is observed and influences the organization. He also influences the culture by his expectations even if they are not explicitly stated. While there may be sub-cultures based on geography, functional area etc. most organizations like any other social group tend to have an all-pervasive identifiable culture. The CEO / Leader influences the culture both formally and informally. Often enough different functions have different cultures or different variations of the organizational culture. Some attitudes, roles, behaviors are inherent to some functions and tend to influence the sub-culture. No one style may have greater chance of influence. It needs to be consistent and over a period of time to be able to take root. Often enough there is one style or culture over the organization. There may be some variations for geography or functions but a basic style may still be discernable. All aspects of organizational behavior and even social behavior of the leaders directly and indirectly influence the culture of the organization. While money is necessary it is not the only tool and often enough money does not yield the desired results or the results are short lived. About 50% of top management time would be spent on managing employee retention activities. One would say that the management should perhaps divide time equally between employee satisfaction (including retention), customer satisfaction and planning for the future".

Culture change is long and costly unless it has a Leadership disrupted Impact.

It is certainly true that, where stability has existed for a long while, it is traumatic at first and therefore costly in terms of people's feelings and possibly also in terms of current morale. It is made easier for the future if new qualities and attitudes of flexibility, dynamism and responsiveness are included in the new form and if this is reinforced through ensuring that people understand that the old ways are now neither effective nor viable. Indeed, people who are told that there are to be lengthy periods of turbulence lose interest and motivation. Unilever New Millennium project is a 10-year emphasis to make fundamental changes to the organization. Pfizer – Parke Davis merger integration has been an 18-month long change management process to bring both organizations together into one way of doing things. The reality of change and development can be quickly conveyed through critical incidents: for example, the gain or loss of a major order; the collapse of a large firm in the sector; the entry of a new player into the sector; radical technological advances; and so on. HDFC or YES Bank hired professionals from the banking industry to shorten the leadership disrupted constraints in establishing a new organization. The existence of multiple cultures with professionals from Bank of America, Citibank and ICICI is a reality that CEO Aditya Puri has to reckon with for now. And today when you reflect in 2016, Aditya Puri is now managing the most valuable private sector bank. YES Bank is building upon its ambition aggressively. And ICICI continues its successes established by K V Kamath, Shikha Sharma and Chanda Kochar. Axis Bank is now a critical contender for top spot thanx to its CEO Shikha Sharma. Once this is understood, the attitudes, behavior and orientation of the staff are given emphases in particular direction and the general positioning of their aspirations, hopes and fears is changed.

Leading and Managing Change: Impact on Leadership disrupted

The fact that organization cultures are made up of relatively stable characteristics would imply that they are very difficult for management to change. Cultures take a long time to form. Once established, they tend to become entrenched and resistant to change efforts. Strong cultures are particularly resistant to change because employees become so committed to them. For employees to unlearn years of experiences and memories is a difficult task. That too takes a very long time. So while culture may be theoretically amenable to change, the time frame necessary to unlearn a given set of values and replace them with a new set may be so long as to make the effort realistically impractical. Remember, too, there are a number of forces in an organization that work to maintain its present culture. These would include written statements about the organization's mission and philosophy, the design of physical spaces and buildings, the dominant leadership pattern, past selection practices, entrenched rituals, popular stories about key people and events, the organization's historic performance-evaluation and reward criteria, and the organization's formal structure. To illustrate, past selection practices tend to work against cultural change. Employees chose the organization because they perceived their values to be a "good fit" with the organization. They are comfortable with that fit and will strongly resist efforts that might undermine the predictability and security of the status quo. A final point in the argument against management's ability to change culture is the reality that if culture could be changed, surely management would do so.

Which Culture can be managed? The foregoing discussion suggests that the real question we should be seeking an answer to is not, can culture be managed? But rather, are there conditions under which culture can be managed? This leads us to a situational analysis of conditions that are necessary for, or will facilitate, cultural change. The ideas we offer are based on observation as well as substantive study. However, there seems to be increasing agreement among theorists as to the importance of the leaders call on cultural changes with relevance to a particular organization and management model, be it Competitive Organization or a Performing Enterprise or a Voluntary School.

The Leader's call, impacts cultural changes

"A question that may be running through many minds may be, so all this is fine but What's in it for Me? A large part of the success of any strategy hinges on whether all the people, who must deliver the strategy, connect to the strategy. So let me try and explain how we see all of this coming together. At the broadest level, a strategy is intended to provide a framework to guide our actions and our decisions. We have now clearly defined the market segments that we will seek to address, set out the logic for why we will address these segments, how we will address these segments, who will be responsible, what his / her roles and responsibilities are, and the performance expectations that we have from each person so identified. We have all along been a fairly client focussed organization - however, our client targeting processes have not been well defined resulting in potentially unfocussed targeting. When you worked on a client, or pursued an opportunity, you may not have been able to relate this to the Firm's strategy. Now, with the work that has been done, there is a structure to guide our efforts and imbue them with relevance and coherence - you may be working for Strategic Key Accounts, for Alpha 250 accounts, on industry programs, on our Provincial Government and Capital Funding agency initiatives, or on other client accounts; each has a defined place in our strategy, a reason for being part of our overall client servicing program, and our fee targets have been built bottom up to account for each client within the Firm".

Continues the leader, "A related issue arises from the dictum that we only respect what we measure. Again, historically, our focus has tended to be more on achieving a certain level of growth, across solution segments, across service lines. We have measured a large part of our success on achieving the targeted levels of growth. What we are now seeking to do is to relate our success not only to growth in numbers, but also to the quality of our earnings. By this, what I mean is that we definitely want the growth, but we want it to come from clients that we want to serve, and from solutions that we want to deliver. This is the only way in which we can build a sustainable growth and development platform for the future. We have put in place mechanisms that will help us to track our efforts - these are transparent and are available to the entire Executive Team to view online. Over the coming weeks and months, you should see this translating into a more focussed approach to the market across solution segments, across service lines, and across groups within solution segments where these exist".

"Another key aspect, says the CEO, "on which our strategy is premised is the integrated management of client relationships. We need to have a vastly better coordinated approach to clients in general. Our future success is going to depend critically on how well we are able to work this model. What it will mean is a need for greater coordination across solution segments and service lines, a considerably greater focus on effective teaming. Over the coming weeks and months, many of you will get drawn into Strategic Key Account teams, Alpha 250 teams, industry teams and so on, and you will directly participate in the execution of our strategy. This too will require all of us to work in teams, more so than in the past. Overall, our strategy is intended to provide a significantly sharper focus on bringing the client into the centre of our efforts rather than solution segment or service line driven considerations which somehow do not always end up achieving the client centric approach that we should be adopting".

I could go on, but I will end with a final point. "We have spent over 6 months deliberating our strategy. We have reviewed and re-reviewed every aspect of it. We have challenged ourselves throughout the process, and questioned every aspect, every nuance and every premise. We have discussed it with all the partners, we have shared it with all of you and then discussed it informally with many of you. We are all convinced that this is the right strategy to pursue if we are to continue to grow exponentially. You have the opportunity to participate in this exciting journey on which we have already embarked, and to be the architects as we set about building a Firm of the Future. So what do we need from you? A few things. I have discussed this with all of our partners. I have also discussed it with all of you during our strategy communication meetings. We need commitment to the strategy. You need to understand what we are doing and why we are doing it in the way in which we are. This is the starting point for effective strategy implementation - if all of us are clear on the framework that we are adopting, that's already half the battle won. We need passion and hunger - to work for clients that we have identified as being of strategic significance, to continually find solutions that deliver value to the clients, to continuously deepen our competencies, to consistently strive to delight our clients. We need a deep sense of urgency - we have a challenge on our hands and we have absolutely no time to lose. We need more discipline across the board - whether it is in things like getting time reports in on time, coding jobs correctly or at a more strategic level, in ensuring that we do not allow ourselves to stray from the strategic path that we have set for ourselves. We need much more of One Firm thinking - this is our Firm, the clients we work for are clients of the Firm, the relationships we develop are developed for the benefit of the Firm. We all work first for the Firm; solution segments, service lines, solutions are arrangements to provide a logical pooling of our capabilities, but overall it is the Firm that counts. We will need greater flexibility and changed mindsets - this is what we will need if we are to team more effectively across solution segments, if we are to drive our personal growth based on deepening our competencies, if we are to work in a much more integrated manner. Finally, we need a sense of fun and enjoyment - no challenge is too great if we enjoy what we are doing, enjoy the company of the people with whom we work. Life is too short - we need to live and enjoy every moment of it".

To this leader, Leadership disrupted influence on cultures in an organizational context means:

- *Talking about how trusting each other can help us to overcome our difficulties*
- *Emphasizing the importance of having a collective sense of mission*
- *Considering the moral and ethical consequences of his/her actions*
- *Taking a stand on difficult issues*
- *Behaving in ways that are consistent with his/her expressed values*

Concludes, *"We are embarking on an exciting phase in our development and growth. We have great aspirations for ourselves and our people, we have significant financial targets to achieve. We face an uncertain economic environment ahead of us, but one that is still full of opportunities. We have a rich pool of highly talented partners and professionals, and if we set our minds and hearts to the tasks ahead, I am confident of our success. So let us commit individually and collectively to this strategy, and to a rigour and discipline in our approach as we continue our efforts in building an outstanding professional services organization. I know that I can count on each one of you to deliver. I look forward to receiving your feedback and inputs".* Words that resonate even today as you reflect on what helped visionary leaders such as Elon Musk, Tim Cook, S Nadella, Shikha Sharma, Ben Van Deputt or Rick Lamanna continue to go out and build world class firms.

The conclusion of this is an organization culture for a visionary leader has the following elements:

- *A positive aura, one to which people can subscribe and identify with confidence, pride and feelings of well-being, which in turn encourages positive views of the organization and its work, and positive and harmonious working relationships. Shared values and standards, capable of being adopted and followed by all concerned (this includes attention to high standards of integrity and morality; mutual concern and interest; and equity and equality). High levels of individuality, identity, motivation and commitment; high levels of group identity and mutual respect and regard;*

- *An organization and management style that is supportive of everyone involved (whatever the style, whether autocratic or Participate), and which concentrates on results and output, effectiveness and quality of performance and also on the development and improvement of the people. Regular flows of high-quality information that reflect high levels of respect and esteem for the people on the part of the organization.*

Again, these can provide a useful point of reference for those concerned with the general well-being of the organization, and when it becomes apparent that things are going wrong. Much of this is clearly concerned with setting high standards and creating a positive general environment and background. This is to be seen in the context that where these elements are either not present or not attended to, or where the converse is present- a negative aura, one to which people do not subscribe, lack of shared values, or an unsupported management style, for example- there is no identity or common purpose. People seek refuge in-groups or in their profession or technical expertise. Absenteeism and turnover increases, while performance declines. There becomes an ever-greater concentration on self and on individual performance, often at the expense of that of the organization. Interpersonal and inter group relations also suffer. Both the positive and negative feed off each other. Striving for a positive and ideal culture tends to reinforce the high levels of value placed on the staff and the more general matters of honesty and integrity. Similarly, allowing the negative to persist tends to mean that relationships will get worse, while aims and objectives become ever more frightened or clouded, and the organization purpose ever more obscured.

E. Adaptability to Digital Culture

Adaptability to Cultural Change: Business Case for Change and Employee Resistance

Whenever changes are introduced into an organization, employees will often either resist or resent such changes. This is true when a new system is implemented for the first time and when there is a high percentage of senior staff in the organization who are deeply entrenched and comfortable with the "old" way of working (Low and Goh, 1994). Resistance to change is inevitable. Business case requires, Confirmation of strategic direction; Defining and validating business case - the 'what, why, when, how and who' of the acquisition. For instance, what are our strategic goals and objectives? What are our specific capabilities (i.e.: the skills, technologies, markets and products) that we need to meet these goals and objectives? Is it more beneficial for us to build these capabilities internally or externally through acquisition? What specific value will an acquisition bring to our organization? What are the risks associated with an acquisition? What is the firm's tolerance to the risks associated with an acquisition? The business case should include an evaluation of people, HR and organization alignment issues Where intangible assets such as key individuals and/or skills are being acquired, the business case should employ a mechanism to value these assets. The business case should ensure sufficient attention is paid to determining the potential 'integration effort' as this could significantly influence deal attractiveness The organization's 'track record' at implementing change and/or M&A is a good indicator of the potential success of this M&A Integrating an acquisition can be a significant challenge and can absorb much management time. The existence of other major change efforts could undermine or put at risk the success of the integration (or vice versa). Ability to realize benefits will depend on the scale and nature of the integration challenge. For instance, the higher the degree of overlap of products, customers and operations, the greater the potential integration challenge. The time and cost of the integration effort and the risks involved should be an input to the valuation and should be reflected in early planning around the integration approach Early work on the acquisition is often conducted by people with a financial focus. There is a risk that they may miss some of the change issues resulting from the acquisition and that implementation plans may therefore be inadequate. For example, plans may not include the resources and costs of an effective change plan. The environment for integration or change is determined by the background context of the event e.g. rescue, collaboration, contested, combination or raid and hence the approach to managing the change/integration process is very different. "There is no such thing as a friendly merger". There may be a need to create outline plans for different approaches depending on the likely scenario of the merger.

Define performance measures, success criteria and satisfaction measures. There are a number of reasons why human beings are resistant to changes (Robbins et al., 1994; Certo, 1994):

- *Habit* – *as human beings, life is already complex enough. This becomes a source of resistance. At the Lalbhai Group Diwali meant distribution of sweets.*

- *Security* – *some employees like the comfort and security of doing things the same old way. Thus, people who believe that their security will be threatened by a change are likely to resist the change.*

- *Economic factors* – *another source of individual resistance is the concern that changes will lower one's income, especially when pay is closely tied to productivity.*

- *Fear of the unknown* – *changes substitute ambiguity and uncertainty for the known. Any disruption of familiar patterns may create fear because it can cause delays and the belief that nothing has been accomplished.*

- *Social factors* – *people may resist change for fear of what others may think. For example, others who openly disobey the rules may ridicule an employee who agrees to conform to work rules established by management.*

- *Selective information processing* – *individuals shape their world through their perceptions. They hear what they want to hear and ignore information that challenges the world that they have created.*

- *Manage Resistance* - *Having recognized the reasons why human beings are resistant to change, the manager should identify ways by which employees' resistance towards a new system can be broken. There are a number of ways to break this resistance (Peel, 1993):*

- *Secure top management support* – *the support of top management is essential to the success of any change effort and its support is necessary for addressing control and power problems.*

- *Encourage participation* – *giving employees a say in designing for changes may give them a sense of power and control over their own destinies which may subsequently help win their support during implementation.*

- *Foster open communication* – *open communication is an important factor in managing resistance to change and overcoming information and control problems during transition.*

- *Reward contributors* – *employees, who quickly grasp new work assignments, work hard in the transition or help others adjust to changes deserve special credit.*

In, **Embracing Digital Technology** – Companies need to be prepared by, Assessing history of change and, specifically, understand effectiveness of previous acquisitions, Assessing nature and impact of other significant organizational changes, Assessing change readiness of acquiring organization, Develop potential scenarios of different acquisitions, Assessing risks and issues arising in these different scenarios, Prepare initial assessment of the nature, scale and complexity of the integration effort, If possible, prepare first draft role of integration team, scope and complexity of the task. Determine key skills required. "According to Finet, companies need to develop a broad view of eRecruitment, which is not just about job boards but covers every aspect of managing the relationship with internal and external candidates. As well as costing less than traditional approaches, eRecruitment solutions accelerate the recruitment cycle and enable qualified candidates to be located more quickly from a larger pool. These solutions also enable global companies to implement best practices and adopt a consistent approach to recruitment throughout their operations". "Despite growing acknowledgment of the need for digital transformation, most companies struggle to get clear business benefits from new digital technologies. They lack both the management temperament and relevant experience to know how to effectively drive transformation through technology. There is no one factor that impedes digital transformation. Even companies where leadership has demonstrated it can effectively leverage technology can run into challenges with new digital technologies. Today's emerging technologies, like social media, mobile, analytics and embedded devices, demand different mindsets and skill sets than previous waves of transformative technology. There is no one factor that impedes digital transformation. Lack of vision or sense of urgency plagued many companies, culture at others, and organizational constraints problems at still others. Our research highlighted nine specific hurdles in the broad areas of leadership, institutional obstacles and execution that companies need to overcome to achieve digital transformation". Embracing disruptive technologies could lead to destructive power struggles and battles amongst senior and middle management. The caliber of the top team - having the 'right' type of people running the new organization - is key to transition and sustained success. There is a risk that, in later stages, management will not pay sufficient attention to the effort required to ensure successful integration to drive out synergies. (They may want to move on to the next acquisition or tech innovation, before the benefits from this one are realized). Early education around the success criteria for effective mergers may be appropriate. Early acquisition planning will probably have been conducted by a small, very senior team. However, the acquisition could create uncertainty for many in management positions, especially where roles are duplicated. This will create a risk of resistance by this group. In addition, the success of the integration will depend on their being a common view by leadership disrupted (and subsequently at all levels) on the rationale for and benefits of the implementation/acquisition. "Many managers feel no urgency to achieve digital transformation. This may be because so few leaders offer a vision and a road map for digital transformation, leaving managers with no motivation for achieving it. Complacency affects more companies than any other organizational barrier cited in our survey, with almost 40% of respondents saying that lack of urgency/no sense of burning platform is the biggest single obstacle to digital transformation". A New Strategic Imperative, MIT SMR 2013 research paper, Michael Fitzgerald, Nina Kruschwitz, Didier Bonnet, Michael Welch, writes, "There is always some trouble with digital transformation…. One survey respondent working in higher education continues, "The organization has a long (70 years) history of success ... the need to change is not clear to some members of the old guard." The further down the organizational ladder one goes, the less satisfied workers are with the pace of digital transformation at their organizations. The survey shows a clear split in perception of urgency between the top managers at companies and those below them. In fact, the further down the organizational ladder one goes, the less satisfied workers are with the pace of digital transformation at their organizations. A third of C-level executives and board members think the pace of change is about right, and another 10% think it is fast, or even very fast. CEOs are particularly bullish — 53% think the pace is right, fast, or very fast, the highest of any category. The pace of digital transformation is too slow — unless you're the CEO. CEOs might know something their colleagues don't, of course. " For example, a major consulting firm while implementing a new systems, set up a project office with the following objectives; Understand and assess "top team" effectiveness, caliber, capacity, background, Identify key stakeholders (including Board of Directors, senior executives, HR sponsors), Assess "top team" /leadership disrupted capacity for managing complex change, Assess potential impact of acquisition on management positions, Build and articulate common vision for organization and the need for an acquisition, Engage, educate and gain "buy in" of key stakeholders to the need for specific integration planning, projects and capability and the keys to making this transformation successful". Shared vision (amongst acquiring company stakeholders) of where and how the proposed acquisition will add value through an Initial vision of the future for the combined entity, Assessment of the ability of leadership to make the integration work and to lead the combined entity, understand Initial assessment of likely impact of proposed acquisition on key individuals and establish Initial plans for retention and/or exit of key individuals. They identified a few clear outcomes, understand current culture, management style and HR strategy of client organization, determine critical HR, people and culture enablers and barriers, define target acquisition profile - appropriate organization, culture, management "alignment" criteria and Identify and assess potential target organizations against "alignment" criteria". Or it could be that as one gets into the trenches of transformation, conditions change. Only 25% of managers think the pace is right, and a mere 22% of staff agree. Of these, product development staff are the most positive — just over 40% say the pace is very fast, fast or just right. Management was guilty of "complacency, ignorance of modern technology," said one respondent. "Clueless management," commented another".

Technostress - "Information technology has long been viewed as the power behind a new economic revolution — an evolving set of tools that has made workers much more productive than ever before, powering a step change as dramatic as steam or electricity. According to a report by the World Economic Forum, "digitization boosted world economic output by nearly US$200 billion and created 6 million jobs in 2011." On a company-by-company basis, a number of studies have found that companies that use more IT have higher productivity than their competitors. However, we may be entering an era in which human frailties begin to slow down progress from digital technologies. In a series of studies, we explored the implications of IT-induced technology stress, technology addiction and IT misuse in the workplace. The Effects of "Technostress" - Pervasive and near-continual use of organizational IT systems is now beginning to take a toll on some employees' health. Individuals experience "IT use-induced stress" or "technostress" for a number of reasons. "A Deloitte's global human capital trends research (2015) shows that more than two-thirds of all organizations believe that their employees are "overwhelmed" with too much information, too many projects, too many meetings and phone calls, and an always-on 24x7 work environment. Research shows that, on average, people check their cellphones and email hundreds of times a day, and we know that every stimulus we get at work (even the beep we hear when a new email arrives) creates an addictive reaction that increases peoples' stress. In 2015, as more technology floods the workplace (smart watches, wearable devices, and even smarter phones), HR should take a hard look at the entire work environment—and advise business leaders about steps they can take to make work more humane, rational, and simple". They feel forced to multitask rapidly on simultaneous streams of information from different devices simply because information feeds come at them in real time; remote work and flextime tether them round the clock to their devices and workplaces; and short technology cycles and pressures from IT vendors mean constantly changing interfaces, screens and functionalities, often without sufficient FAQs and help-desk support". Monideepa Tarafdar, John D'Arcy, Ofir Turel and Ashish Gupta writes further in MIT SMR 2014 paper, "The Dark Side of Information Technology", We also found in a survey of about 600 computer-using professionals that 73% worried that refraining from constant connectivity and instantaneous information-feed response would place them at a disadvantage at work.

Up All Night – 24/7 Employees can experience IT-induced stress for a number of reasons. They are bombarded with a flow of information, and remote work and flextime tether them round the clock to their devices and workplaces. There is no denying that disruptions cause stress, a degree of feeling of being quite unsettled. Status quo has now irredeemably changed. Complex user interfaces that do not naturally fit with task workflows are an additional source of stress, because they create work overload when they are used. In studying the use of a health-care IT application in the context of care delivery processes in acute care facilities at two major hospitals, we found that physicians had to juggle between numerous different screens on their monitors to access patient data feeds, test results, clinical notes and treatment notes. Most of the doctors complained that they had to do far more work using IT than they thought reasonable. Often, we find that the more enthusiastically and relentlessly organizations embrace IT, the more technostress their employees suffer. Employee Misuse of IT - Another aspect of the dark side of IT is the threat of employees misusing organizational IT resources and triggering "attacks" of different kinds. Firewalls and other network defenses can potentially stop attacks from the outside. However, no security technology can stop an employee who has authorized access to a computer system from, for example, obtaining confidential company information and selling it to competitors. A number of studies have found that attacks stemming from internal sources are greater in scope and severity and can result in about 10 times as many compromised records as those from external sources. Even more disturbingly, a sizeable percentage of such attacks turn out to be deliberate. Other kinds of insider IT misuse range from truly malicious user behavior (such as stealing sensitive corporate data) to unsanctioned behavior (such as accessing unauthorized parts of a corporate network or knowingly using unlicensed software) to naive user actions such as opening an unknown email attachment. Unsanctioned and naive user behaviors make up the vast majority of IT misuses".

Adaptability to Digital Culture - Change: Kurt Lewin and Managing Cultural Change

Field Theory - One of the methods advocated is the use of 'Field Theory' (sometimes called 'Field Force Theory'). This emanates from the ideas of Kurt Lewin who brings an analogy of vector mechanics to the psychosocial arena. In the simple form usually adopted by change practi-tioners this can involve looking at the factors for and against a particular change, listing them and setting out some sort of weighting. Such an approach can have value in, for example, deciding which of two competing technologies to use Example, staying with Office 365, for use as a word-processing package, or moving to Apple OS 10. Lewin postulated a three-step model of change:

Unfreezing;
Moving;
Re-freezing.
Freezing

This is dependent on the concepts that the old behavior has to be discarded (unfrozen) before moving to the new, and that the new behavior has to be accepted as the norm otherwise there will be regression to old patterns. Compare this with the fifth of the Price Waterhouse paradoxes. Note, however, that in organizational terms regression would often be difficult to accomplish. Unfreezing requires analysis and confrontation of the reasons for change and a develop-mental process to disseminate the need for change. Moving requires the identification of alternative courses of action, evaluation of these and choice of an appropriate route. Re-freezing seeks to rebuild an equilibrium state and may be supported by institutional rewards and benefits or by an educational process, or both. However, change is usually much more complex than this - as is vector mechanics.

Adaptability to Cultural Change: Tom Lupton and Organizational Alternatives for Cultural Change

A less simplistic view put forward by Tom Lupton (1971) comes as a series of injunctions to managers:

* *Set up systematically and in detail the organization alternatives open.*
* *Map out the present organization as a social system, not forgetting its external links.*
* *List the groups affected by each organization alternative.*
* *Examine the issues likely to be raised in each group from the adoption of each alternative.*
* *Assess likely reactions on each issue and score for acceptability.*
* *Test economic feasibility against social acceptability and adopt the course that offers the most adaptive and least costly balance.*
* *Examine the problems this course raises and ask whether existing means of redress of grievance are adequate to cope. If not, take appropriate steps to create such machinery as seems to be required.*

This approach broadens the way in which the change is looked at but is still predicated upon the general idea of listing and choosing. Again, this approach has its value in some straightforward cases but a more general model is required if we are to cope with the variety of change that we have so far discussed.

Adaptability to Cultural Change: Charles Handy and Organizational Change

Charles Handy's (1993) schema for organizational change is:

- *Create an awareness, urgency of the need for change.*
- *Select an appropriate initiating person, sponsor or group.*
- *Articulate Strategy - Be prepared to allow the recipients to adapt the final strategy in a time line that is meaningful.*
- *Accept the fact that the successful doctor gets no credit but must let the patient boast of his or her sound condition.*
- *Be prepared to accept a less than optimum strategy in the interests of achieving some-thing rather than nothing.*

Handy sees this from the manager's perspective, but sometimes change has to be initiated from the grassroots and the above schema can still hold good in such cases.

Adaptability to Cultural Change: Bernard Burnes (1992) on Why changes at all?

Create a vision. Why change? The answer must lie in the need to attain some farther goal or realize a distant vision. The first stage/ argues Burnes, is to construct this vision. In looking at this process/ he suggests four aspects:

- *Mission - a statement of the organization's strategic purpose;*
- *Valued outcomes - specific performance and human outcomes that the organization would like to achieve;*
- *Valued conditions - what the organization should look like to achieve the valued outcomes;*
- *Mid-point goals - intermediate objectives between the current state and the desired future state, usually capable of being more clearly stated than the long-term ambitions.*

A more developed version of this schema is the nine-element model developed by Bernard Burnes (1992):

1. **Develop strategies.** *Having shaped a future vision, the organization' needs to look at the ways of realizing that vision and this is done through a series of strategies. The strategies will relate particularly to those mid-point goals and may be shaped by reference to particular domains - for example finance, human resources or infor-mation systems - or particular geographical regions. Such strategies are destined to change with time and experience even when the vision remains constant.*
2. **Create the conditions for successful change.** *In order to create the right conditions for change it is first necessary to create a readiness for change. Burnes suggests three steps to be taken to create this state of readiness*
3. **Make people aware of the pressures for change -** *the organization not only needs to describe its vision but also to share the vision with its employees. By this means members of the organization come to share common goals and to understand the place of change in safeguarding their future;*
4. **Give regular feedback -** *feedback is essential not only on the performance of the individual within the organization but also of the organization itself. This means that employees become aware of deviations from the strategy and hence are prepared for change;*
5. **Publicize successful change -** *making people aware of successful programmes of change, either within the organization or outside, helps employees see the benefits of the change process. This can also be an important learning tool.*

Burnes (1992) further suggests that other steps need to be taken to deal with causes of resistance:

- *Understand people's fears and concerns - employees' fears may well be groundless but to the individuals concerned they are real and important. Change creates uncer-tainty and failure to get to grips with perceived threats is a major problem in intro-ducing change;*
- *Encourage communication - regular open and effective communication is a basic way in which to promote change and to address uncertainty. Transmission of detail helps to overcome the potential for rumor taking hold;*
- *Involve those affected - not only does involvement create understanding but it can also alert the change-makers to unforeseen difficulties when those concerned with implementing the change are involved in the detail. Create the right culture. Change that is inconsistent with the culture of the organization is doomed to fail, but changing the culture is even more problematic. (Compare this with the third Price Waterhouse paradox.) Desirably, the culture of the organization should foster flexibility and encourage reflection.*
- *Encouragement of what Chris Argyris terms 'double-loop learning' - where underlying paradigms are challenged and changed as well as strategies and assumptions - should provide a fertile seed bed for change. He suggests that 'Model II' theory-in-use is the underlying model for fostering this: his 'theory-in-use' is the implicit values exposed by what people actually do as opposed to their 'espoused' theories which describe what they think they do. Senge suggests that the gap between espoused theory and theory-in-use can present a challenge to the shared vision.*

Assess the need for, and type of, change. Appropriateness of response is also seen as key to the change process - appropriateness not only in the particular change to be under-taken but also in whether to undergo a process of change at all.

Burnes suggests a four-phase approach to the assessment:

The **trigger - organizations** should only investigate change for one of the following reasons for the organization's strategies that highlights the need for change;

- *Performance in attainment of the organization's goals appears seriously impaired;*
- *Opportunities are offered which appear to achieve significant improvement.*
- *The remit - a clear remit must be provided for assessing the process of change. This should include the reasons for carrying out the assessment and should cover all relevant domains.*
- *The assessment team - the team should be led by a senior manager, preferably one who will go on to champion whatever change is necessary, and should include all relevant disciplines. The first task of the team is to clarify its objectives, reviewing the trigger, the remit and the composition of the team itself.*

The assessment - again, Burnes advocates a four-step approach:

1. *first, the problem or opportunity should be clarified or redefined;*
2. *second, alternative proposals should be drawn up and tested against criteria founded on the redefined problem specification;*
3. *third, the proposals meeting the criteria, together with the problem or opportunity statement, should be shared with a wider constituency;*

4. *fourth, recommendations for action should be drawn up, including type of change advocated, timetable for implementation and resource implications, and presented to senior management for decision.*

Plan and implement change. Having gone through the assessment process, management needs to commit to the change and to prepare a detailed plan. This should be based on the work of the assessment team but may be implemented by a different, though equally multidisciplinary, team. This team, or sub-groups for a major project, will need to undertake a number of activities:

- *Activity planning - constructing a detailed list of all the tasks to be undertaken, their sequence and the critical path through them;*
- *Commitment planning- identifying key people and groups whose commitment to the project is essential to success;*
- *Management structures - the team or teams managing the process of change may need new reporting structures with rapid access to top management and to the champions of change;*
- *Training - the obvious aspect of training is the acquisition of new technical skills, but a wider view needs to be taken to ensure that training underpins all aspects of change and targets the appropriate individuals and groups, including middle and senior management;*
- *Review - Burnes calls this 'post audit'. After the changes have taken place the effects should be audited to see how successful the changes have been in meeting their objectives and to learn how the change process can be improved.*
- *Involve everyone - Maintaining the commitment, particularly over a long timescale (remember that even the simplest information technology projects can take years to design, build and implement) requires continuing involvement of all parties.*

Burnes suggests three facets to support this hypothesis:

1. *Information - letting everyone involved know what is happening right from the beginning and reporting honestly on progress or lack of it/ is the key.*
2. *Communication - providing information is only the start. Communication has to be two-way with employees' responses gathered and listened to.*
3. *Actual involvement - responsibility for detailed aspects of change need to be given to those directly affected; this requires the correct identification of those responsible.*

Burnes bring in a perspective on the Elements of Education for Change Management Program

- *Sustain the momentum. Particularly in long-term projects, a failure to maintain the momentum of change can lead to regression on the part of that participating and potentially fatal delay. To bolster the momentum, organizations can:*
- *Provide resources for change - even where a project is looking for down-sizing, the actual pursuit of change is likely to consume resources (note how finance depart-ments expand during periods of retrenchment) and appropriate resources should be allocated from the beginning of the project;*
- *Give support to the change agents - often the change management team has to boost morale and motivate others. They, in their turn, need support and encour-agement lest they become demoralized and pass on their demotivation to others;*
- *Develop new competencies and skills - training has already been mentioned but the momentum has to be borne on a tide of new styles and approaches. This can involve leadership and team working training as well as individual counseling and encouragement;*

- **Reinforce desired behavior** - *behaviors that are consistent with the change can be reinforced not only in financial ways (for example using suggestion schemes or bonuses) but also symbolically (using praise, changing a job title, or awarding prizes).*
- **Commit to continuous improvement.** *Real success should see change as an ongoing process, not a once-and-for-all activity. The prospect of continuing improvement should be built into the project from the outset and a culture of quality enhancement engendered.*

Burnes' method arises from his study of what went well (and badly; two-thirds of the changes he surveyed were unsuccessful) in major reorganizations in substantial firms. However, much of what he has to offer is applicable on a smaller scale. His is one of the more comprehensive approaches to the management of change.

F. Leading Cultural Change:

Geert Hofstede (1980) carried out studies that identified cultural similarities and difference among the several thousands of staff of IBM located in 40 countries. He identified basic dimensions of national culture and the differences in their emphases and importance in the various countries. The dimensions were, as set out below.

At a large European Bank **("EB")** the concept looked at the extent to which managers and supervisors were encouraged or expected to exercise power in the new structure with its authority and responsibility limits and to take it upon themselves to provide order and discipline. Relationships between superior and subordinate were based on low levels of mutual trust and low levels of participation and involvement as the change meant moving from the Bank into shared services center. Employees would accept orders and direction on the understanding that the superior carries full responsibility, authority and accountability. People are expected to be consulted and to participate in decision-making. They expected to be kept regularly and fully informed of progress, and had much greater need for general equality and honesty of approach. They would feel free to question superiors about why particular courses of action were necessary rather than simply accepting that they were. The extent to which power and influence is distributed across the society; The extent to which this is acceptable to the members of the society; access to source of power and influence; and the physical and psychological distance that exists between people and the sources of power and influence. Power distance is the extent to which the less powerful members of organizations within a country expect and accept that power is distributed unequally. This issue was perhaps prominent at "EB" given traditional employee fear of being singled out in the society that they were no longer employees of the parent company, the BANK.

Critical Characteristics of this experiment

In **("EB")** as issues driven by Inequalities among people minimized, decentralization of activities, subordinates expect to be consulted by superiors, privileges and status symbols are less evident. Inequalities are desirable, with greater reliance by the less powerful, Centralization normal, subordinates separated from bosses, Wide differentials in salary, privileges and status symbols etc. all being issues for resolution.

Flexible Centralization and Interdependent Systems: Most professional bureaucracies attempt to provide a decentralized environment to their employees by decentralizing all but the choice aspect of the decision making process. We expect this process to further intensify with all but the strategic decisions restricted to the top. An Information Technology infrastructure can allow decentralization while guaranteeing control through a system of budgeting, maintaining an archive of precedents and the current benchmarks, exception approvals and immediate reporting. This will enable decision making at the customer's doorstep for the empowered customer interface team. The strategic team can be a set of geographically dispersed competent individuals who form a think tank which is in touch with the organizational realities and the external world at the same time while being located where it makes most sense at a point in time.

Stress in Cultures - The extent to which people prefer order and certainty, (Centralized operations preferred to a subsidiary company – **("EB")**) or uncertainty and ambiguity; and the extent to which they feel comfortable or threatened by the presence or absence of each. Uncertainty avoidance is defined as the extent to which the members of a culture feel threatened by uncertain or unknown situations. People with a high propensity for uncertainty avoidance (that is, those that wished for high degrees of certainty) tended to require much greater volumes of rules, regulations and guidance for all aspects of work. They sought stability and conformity, and were intolerant of dissenters. Uncertainty caused stress, strain, conflicts and disputes. Stress could be avoided by working hard, following the company line, and adherence to and compliance with required ways of behavior. Where uncertainty avoidance (Senior management, for example where policy and transfer rules were clear and upfront communicated in some cases – **("EB")** was lower, these forms of stress were less apparent; there was less attention paid to rules and less emphasis placed on conformity and adherence.

Characteristics of the Problem at ("EB") as it was managed

Tolerance - Greater tolerance of ambiguous situations, high risk-taking, hard- working only when they need to be. Precision and punctuality missing, comfortable with deviant and innovative ideas and behavior, motivated by achievement, esteem or belongings, fear of ambiguous situations and unfamiliar tasks, punctual and an emotional need to be, busy, novelty is resisted and motivated by security are some examples of such characteristics. The extent to which individuals are expected or expect to take care of themselves; the extent to which a common good is perceived and the tendency and willingness to work towards this. Individualism/Collectivism pertains to the extent to which individual independence or social cohesion dominant. The concern here was to establish the relative position of individual achievement in terms of that of the organization, and also the wider contribution to society and the community. For example, in the UK and USA overwhelming emphasis was placed on individual performance and achievement. In the **("EB")** context the older seasoned bankers were concerned of their social security benefits, apart from image and respect in the society if the transition were to take place. This has implications for membership of teams and groups and the creation of effective teams and groups in such locations. It also indicates the extent of likelihood of divergence of purpose between the organization and individuals. Where collectivism was higher, there was also a much greater emphasis on harmony, loyalty, support and productive interaction. There was also a much greater attention to organizational performance, as well as the position of the organization and its wider environment, and its contribution to society, in addition to the achievement of its own desired results. Some are as ties between individuals are loose, Individuals look after themselves and their family. Contracts with employers are based on mutual advantage, Hiring and promotion decisions are based on skills and rules, Strong cohesion among people, Contracts with employers on moral terms, Hiring and promotion decisions take employee's working in a group into account are some examples.

The degree to which long-term or short-term is the dominant orientation in life, and is linked to the Confucian concept of 'virtue' that Hofstede contracts with a Western preoccupation with 'truth'. High respect for traditions, emphasize importance of social and status obligations, Demand quick results, concerned with truth, Stress adaptation of traditions to modern context, Limits respect on social and status obligations, Stringent in using resources, tress perseverance, concerned with virtue are typical characteristics of Confucian dynamism.

The distinction between values (the acquisition of money, wealth, fortune, success, ambition, possessions) and the needs (sensitivity, care, concern, attention to the needs of others, quality of life); and the value, importance, mix and prevalence of each. Masculinity/Femininity refers to the degree to which social gender roles are clearly distinct. This considered the value placed on different achievements. Cultures with high degrees of masculinity (Bankers like Citibank and Bank of America) set great store by the achievement of material possessions and rewards. Those with high degrees of femininity saw success in terms of quality of life, general state of the community, individual and collective well-being, the provision of essential services, and the ability to support the whole society and to provide means of social security. The work emphasizes the importance of cultural factors and differences in all areas and aspects of organizational behavior. It indicates both the strength and interaction of cultural pressures. It indicates the source and nature of particular values, particular drives and barriers and blockages, and behavioral issues and problem areas that all organizations need to consider. Above all, it illustrates the relative strength of some of the main cultural and social pressures that are brought to bear on all organizations in all situations. These pressures indicate the context in which organization culture is founded. Culture is present in all organizations. It is either positive (which tends to attract people), or negative (tending to repel people), which people tend to reject; it may also be one of the following as stated in the discussion on Uniform Cultures.

- *Men supposed to be assertive, tough and focused on material success*
- *Women supposed to be more modest, tender and concerned with quality of life*
- *Social gender roles overlap*
- *Both men and women supposed to be modest, tender and concerned with the quality of life*

In effect, for cultures,

- *There is no "right" or wrong about an organization's culture*
- *"It" exists and is observed, commented upon, criticized, or praised*
- *Culture is what the leader and his people choose to adopt*
- *What one sees, hears and feels when encountering a new group*
- *The visible products such as the architecture of its physical environment, language, technology and products, easy to observe - difficult to decipher.*

G. Conditions that make Change Happen

Conditions: A Dramatic Crisis or the Near Death Experience.

The condition that is most universally acknowledged as having to exist before culture can be changed is a dramatic crisis that is widely perceived by the organization's members. This is the shock that undermines the status quo. It calls into question current practices and opens the door toward accepting a different set of values that can respond better to the crisis. Examples of such a crisis would include a surprising financial setback, the hostile takeover of the focal organization by another organization, the loss of a major customer (though such a customer would have to represent a significant proportion of the organization's revenues – typically 25 percent or more), or a dramatic technological breakthrough by a competitor. The crisis, of course, need not be real to be effective. The key is that it is perceived as real by the organization's members.

Conditions: Leadership disrupted Turnover.

Since top management is a major factor in transmitting culture, a change in the organization's key leadership positions facilitates the imposition of new values. But new leadership, per se, is no assurance that employees will accept new values. The new leaders must have a clear alternative vision of what the organization can be; there must be respect for this leadership's ability; and the new leaders must have the power to enact their alternative vision. The result of new leadership disrupted without an alternative set of values is likely to be a response that differs in no way from what had proved successful in the past. Leadership turnover must encompass the organization's Chief executive. But it is not limited to this position. The likelihood of successful cultural change typically increases with a purge of all major management positions. Rather than having previous executives accept the new leader's values, it usually is more effective to replace people with individuals who have no vested interest in the old culture.

- *Sets high standards*
- *Envisions exciting new possibilities*
- *Provides continuous encouragement*
- *Focuses my attention on "what it takes" to be successful*
- *Establish Values*
- *Look beyond your nose despite a sun set industry*

Conditions: Life Cycle Stage Cultural Change Management Process.

Transitory Cultural Change is easier when the organization is in transition from the formation stage to the growth stage, and from maturity into decline. As the organization moves into growth, major changes will be necessary. These changes are more likely to be accepted because the culture is less entrenched. However, other factors will facilitate acceptance of the change. One writer, for instance, has proposed that employees will be more receptive to cultural change if,

1. *The organization's previous success record is modest,*
2. *Employees are generally dissatisfied, and*
3. *The founder's image and reputation are in question.*

The other opportunity for cultural change occurs when the organization enters the decline stage. Decline typically requires cutbacks and other retrenchment strategies. Such actions are likely to dramatize to employees that the organization is experiencing a true crisis, for example:

1. *Drive by energizing the intellect as we are in the Knowledge Business*
2. *Makes me aware of essential work-related issues*
3. *Shows determination to accomplish what he/she sets out to do*
4. *Expresses his/her confidence that we will achieve our goals*
5. *Talks optimistically about the future*
6. *Talks enthusiastically about what needs to be accomplished*
7. *Articulates a compelling vision of the future*

Conditions: Age of the Organization.

Regardless of its life-cycle stage, the younger an organization is, the less entrenched its values will be. We should expect, therefore, that cultural change is more likely to be accepted in an organization that is only five years old than in one that is fifty years old.

- *Encourages us to rethink ideas which had never been questioned*
- *Seeks differing perspectives when solving problems*
- *Suggests new ways of looking at how we do our job*
- *Gets me to look at problems from different angles*
- *Encourages non-traditional thinking to deal with traditional problems*

Conditions: Size of the Organization.

We realize that cultural change is easier to implement in a small organization. Why? In such organization, it's easier for management to reach employees. Communication is clearer, and role models are more visible in a small organization, thus enhancing the opportunity to disseminate new values. Smaller companies implemented programs like BPR, TQM, Customer Satisfaction Programs or JIT effectively and in a shorter time frame given relative small size and geographic spread of these companies. Employees could be connected, processes could be streamlined efficiently and impact maximized. In contrast Arvind Mills took longer time with ab greater lag and loss of momentum and demonstrating conviction across the board.

Conditions: Strength of the Current Culture.

The more widely held a culture is and the higher the agreement among members on its values, the more difficult it will be to change. Conversely, weak cultures should be more amenable to change than strong ones.

The organization's culture or subcultures determine the nature of learning and the way in which it occurs. For example, the entrepreneurial style of Citibank's Global Finance Group results in a learning approach in which information is made available to fund managers and analysts, but its use is at the managers' discretion. In addition, there is a good deal of leeway in how fund managers make their investments; some are intuitive, some rely heavily on past performance, and a few use sophisticated computer programs. Thus the fund managers' use or application of learning is largely informal, not dictated by formal, firm wide programs. Meanwhile, the culture of Citibank's marketing groups is more collaborative; learning is derived more from interaction within and between cross-functional work groups and from improved communication.

In a culture that heavily rewards product group performance, total quality in products and processes that require integrated, inter group action lags behind, particularly in the marketing of systems that cut across divisions.

Conditions: Presence or Absence of Subcultures.

Heterogeneity increases members' concern with protecting their self-interest and resisting change. Therefore, we would expect that the more subcultures there are, the more resistance there will be to changes in the dominant culture. This thesis can also be related to size. Larger organizations will be more resistant to cultural change because they typically tend to have more subcultures.

Conditions: Climate of Openness.

Are the sub cultures around information flow permeable so people can make their own observations? "Joining a sub-culture, any sub-culture, for whatever reason, is as I see it never a legitimate self-expression. It is always a result of sheep mentality; a wish to belong somewhere." Varg Vikernes. Much of cultural learning and dissemination is a function of daily, often unplanned interactions among people. In addition, the opportunity to meet with other groups and see higher levels of management in operation promotes learning. "To acquire the full consciousness of self is to know oneself so different from others that no longer feels allied with men except by purely animal contacts: nevertheless, among souls of this degree, there is an ideal fraternity based on differences, while society fraternity is based on resemblances. The full consciousness of self can be called originality of soul, -and all this is said only to point out the group of rare beings to which Andre Gide belongs. Rémy de Gourmont, writes, "The misfortune of these beings, when they express themselves, is that they do it with such odd gestures that men fear to approach them; their life of social contacts must often revolve in the brief circle of ideal fraternities; or, when the mob consents to admit such souls, it is as curiosities or museum objects. Their glory is, finally, to be loved from afar & almost understood, as parchments are seen & read above sealed cases." The Book of Masks. People need freedom to express their views through legitimate disagreement and debate. Another critical aspect is the extent to which errors are shared and not hidden. Tata Group with its multiple organizations and the units necessitate bringing in openness in its communication and culture. and presence of sub cultures is but an inevitable reality. http://bit.ly/2aiKwTA

Perhaps the most dramatic example of openness is where abnormalities or deviations are publicly reported throughout the entire system of sales branches, manufacturing plants and service stations. The company treats such incidents as study able events to see if the problem exists anywhere else and follows up with learning driven investigation to eliminate it. It then disseminates this knowledge throughout the company. "I'm asked a lot what the best thing about cooking for a living is. And it's this: to be a part of a subculture. To be part of a historical continuum, a secret society with its own language and customs. To enjoy the instant gratification of making something good with one's hands-- using all one's senses. It can be, at times, the purest and most unselfish way of giving pleasure (thought oral sex has to be a close second)." Anthony Bourdain, Kitchen Confidential: Adventures in the Culinary Underbelly. While this openness may be explained by the critical nature of problems in a manufacturing plant, we can only speculate as to what would be gained if any organization functioned as though a mistake is potentially disastrous and also an opportunity to learn.

H. Effecting Cultural Change

Formalized Feedback Process - Some organizations have a quick and formalized method to impact cultural change in a large amorphous organization. This is an upfront development approach, verbal or non-verbal as may be deemed necessary, through which an individual or a group would communicate perceptions, feelings, expectations about actions, behavior and competencies. When soliciting feedback, an individual is asking for a view of others about his behavior. The asking is voluntary and constructive and could break unknown human barriers between people. (Bridges 1996) It is based on a theory of self-development and growth that involves natural stages of identity, orientation to an environment of people, organization of data and information that forms a part of our life experiences and into a path of self-renewal. Leadership disrupted Impacts at the cultural level at the Individual disposition. http://bit.ly/2apQeG0

Articulation - Feedback must be articulated so that the person receiving it can absorb it objectively. It must be stated with limited distortion, understood with an open and honest frame of mind and body, understand it for its use and value, and exercise the choice to use it or not use it. Make known the impact of every episode as they conclude for members to understand the complete implication of what has transpired and bringing all members up the curve. The groups are not exclusively self-directed. The facilitator plays a key role in making the group understand at varying intervals their obligation and responsibility to each other.

Demands & Constraints - This behavior needs to meet with the demands made by the receiver to say it with your feelings. There is a basic need to be emotionally involved and resilient with the problem to deal with it. Values have a lot to do for the process to be effective. It would be impossible and incorrect to deal with an issue where there is a potential value conflict between the group and the member, or the client and the counselor. I cannot believe in abortion and support a religious dilemma of a member., irrespective how dispassionate I could be personally. The issue to bring out in both the sender and the listener a strong reaction of concurrence that we should act upon it, rather than not handle it upfront. Both should exhibit commitment, courage and willingness to the risk of sharing with feelings, as they emanate while the experience is in transaction. For example, withdrawing half way through the episode is not on, we need to go through with and not leave the member half way through the encounter. This implies responsibility. http://bit.ly/2apQeG0

If I cannot I should not participate in "Feedback Process - Tell Me".

Interpersonal Telling - Human communication process involves both the contents of the mind and its usage to communicate to others. The situation created for this communication should be as real as it can get as far as the data and facts beings processed is concerned. The climate is created to carry out a specific task of communication and the tension is released soon after the encounter. Telling happens meaningfully when there is mutual care and concern for each other's well-being. For a start-up state of dominance or submission the gradual process of growth ends with friendly disposition and independence (Polley 1986). Adequate interpersonal space, a form of affiliation spans the climate. Motive to an act is relevant only if data and facts are under investigation. That behavior happens naturally and is manifested externally owing to values, beliefs and experiences. Behavior happens irrespective of the motive or the desired intent. In any event motives or intents are not as important as the behavior itself. In building relationships what you see and feel is what is available for action. Effectively act only on what has been heard or observed and that can be supported by data generated or acquired legitimately. That there is no one behavior for any situation. There is no right or wrong, in fact only interpretation of causes and sources of a problem. That the behavior was rather interpreted as experimentation and exploring new ways of doing. That in my/our behavior I could discover myself for what I am. And interpretation is not a measurement, but a tool for seeking clarification. Logical variations are inevitable and necessary to cause effect in the tell me session although creative contribution by itself is not desirable other than for suggesting hypothetical alternatives. Intensity of the climate determines relevance of creativity. Members could assume triviality of the help being suggested if the alternative is found to be creative and lacking in empathy. Concurrently the communication process should either precede or follow process path flow seen as imperative for the tell me effect. A directional, linear path of the helping transaction. Process path flow is a logical mix of deliverables seen as fundamental to make communication happen. Keeping on to the course, and concluding only when exhausted of alternatives. Congruency in the flow or a linear direction is not necessarily a governing condition. Flow is determined in our judgement by the experience. It could take different turns and make its logical course in and out of the experience. Variations without logic would make members assume bias and an unhelpful attitude. Although sticking to the issue stubbornly until resolution would bring a conclusion. Go for the experience without an expectation. Seek the joy of experience and in it see the learning. Leave the ownership for change with the individual. Bring in spontaneity and energy. Make it a mutual process of learning not excluding any of the players to the episode. Eliminate conditions that appear to determine our way of doing things. Let not rules turn into conditions and in turn into a deep ridge of dissonance. www.rforc.com

Group Feedback Experience - These sessions are planned and a group process is organized. The participants understand the implications of their participation and the responsibility that they would take on for each other. That listening to another person's feedback is voluntary. That the freedom to continually receive information from the environment, to adjust and take corrective action. That the experience brings about growth and a change in perspective, a desire for a new beginning, the creation of a new culture. Impulsive telling could be harmful from process effectiveness as well as the potential scars that it could leave with the participants. Culture Beyond 2020 workshops dealt with this issue upfront and frowned upon any impulsive reaction not substantiated or studied. We are not contradicting with the process of feelings or emotion based sharing that could appear impulsive, but more to do with feedback, that is said without a thought process. At times this could term as devious fun or attitudes to attract attention or impress upon other participants how open a person is. Teams make "Tell Me Effect" simpler to handle. The process is free, un encumbered and not littered with a laundry list of "all that I have to tell you". When Tell Me is given immediately after the event, it is usually group shared, understood and internalized, so that other members can look at the interaction as it occurs, experienced, argued and consolidated. The process of consolidating "Tell Me" adds to the effectiveness of the experience. Consolidation happens when the groups have decided to record the sharing process and work out an action plan. The groups now believe that the transaction has turned beneficial, not competitive and deem it appropriate for risking modified behavior. Events that occur outside the group ("there-and-then") may be known to only one or two group members, and consequently, cannot be reacted to or discussed meaningfully by other participants. If the group members are consistent and clear in their perception of the receiver, and this disagrees with the receiver's view of himself, then he/she needs to look more closely at the validity of his/her self-perceptions. Frequently the fact that people perceive an individual's behavior differently is useful information in itself. Part of each group member's responsibility is to ask for Tell Me from members who refrain from reacting and are not responding to the process in a fair equitable manner so that the receiver will know how everyone sees his behavior. Needless to mention that if one of them simply have nothing to say there is no need to force a response. Participating for the sake of group cohesiveness does not add value to the process. In any event not all members of the group need to play a continuous role of facilitation. Let it be. (Tell Me reference - http://bit.ly/2apQeG0)

Culture rules, norms acceptable to groups could be:

- *Compassionate and Caring telling*
- *Aspiration and Ambitious asking*
- *Challenging and Stretching*
- *Empowering and freedom from inhibitions*
- *Fair, Objective and factual*
- *Concern for the task*
- *Sensitivity to the team and group needs and wants*
- *Mutually Learning and Rewarding*
- *Creative and untested assumptions to be experimented with*
- *A climate of trust and openness.*

Receiver Role - Asking for Tell Me may indicate that the receiver is prepared to listen and wants to know how others perceive his behavior. In asking for tell me, however, it is important to follow some of the same guidelines as for giving a message. A person should be specific, objective, and factual about the subject on which he/she wants behavioral material. Tell Me is a reciprocal process. Both senders and receivers can help each other in soliciting and in giving it. In Tell Me encounter this "give it" and "take it" is fundamental and imposing, as a floor level understanding is critical to ensure success of the experience. Participants should feel the experience as being real, joyful and learning. Several situations may occur when mutual sharing on how do we share "Tell Me" may become important as a basic group norm structuring.

Perceived Behaviors - Many people want to know how others perceive their behavior, their actions, but they fear the consequences of asking for such information. In all such fears the underlying assumption is the suspicion over motives. How easily a person will ask for Tell Me is related to the amount of trust, faith, and mutuality and a gross absence of a motive in the interpersonal relationship. There is nothing in it for me other than your well-being is fundamental to the "feedback" episode. In-groups it is group cohesiveness. However, people fear that the receiver will use "feedback" received (particularly negative) to reinforce negative feelings. In all of "Tell Me" experiences there are clear and potential possibilities of the encounter turning negative, unhappy and sometimes sad. Again, it is sometimes difficult for a person to separate behavior from feelings of self-worth. Helping groups and individuals to cope with this behavioral possibility is critical to implement at the stage setting process. Let not a "Tell Me" session be kicked off without the interacting participants not knowing potential consequences to their current state.

Feedback as a Transaction - Tell Me should be aimed at behavior that is relatively easy to manage, deal with, process and understand and consequently change. Many individual behaviors of habitual and routine nature and could be described as a personal style developed through years of behaving and responding in certain ways may not be the best of situations to start with for the "Tell Me Effect" experience. Tell Me on this kind of behavior is often frustrating because the behavior can be very difficult to change. More importantly it is critical to clarify how relevant is there a need for change on the identified behavior. Tell Me on behaviors that are difficult to change may often make a person self-conscious, moody, encounter fear and anxious about the displayed behavior. Consequences must focus on the effort. Occasionally, in tell me, one must determine whether the behavior represents an individual lifestyle or results from unknown personality factors or issues considerably irrelevant to the transaction in progress. That I hate Banana Milk shake is not relevant to this transaction irrespective of how open minded I am being asked to be through the "Tell Me" session. Sometimes it may be helpful first to ask the receiver whether he/she perceives his/her behavior as modifiable. Whether, secondly, the person wishes a change. Thirdly does the person feel that another behavior pattern is more desirable and acceptable to self and others. Many behaviors can be easily changed through "Tell Me" and the person's conscious desire to change his/her behavior in order to produce a more effective interpersonal style. Obviously the purpose of the episode is not to make people forget how to think, see and feel. Nor is the purpose to make people wonder how would he/she walk out of this experience. In all endeavors involving people and their relationships each group will evolve structures and patterns as the members work together and reach individual or collective assumptions. It is imperative for the primary motivation of membership in growth groups is to help one self and others to believe, learn, grow and evolve as a fully rounded person. Conscious attention to structure, roles, relationship linkages are essential to resolve classical individual and team problems as they arise in everyday life. Meaning, belief and faith are fundamental to make the Tell Me process happen. Dilemmas and paradoxes continue to haunt when tell me effect is in progress. There are occasions of feelings of emptiness on the exercise. There are questions on whether all this worth it? Would people really change? Why should I offer space and time for tell me session? What do I receive in turn? Why? (Tell Me reference - http://bit.ly/2apQeG0)

Goal Setting Feedback - Facilitates employee goals setting and commitment to change towards a desired state of behavior or action. Makes the goal setting standard and mutual expectation ambitious and shared across family/known groups. Synergize individual and group problem and expectation priorities within the overall framework of the organization, identify behavioral competencies that are relevant to make individuals effective. It is possible to create a dream, a shared dream, a vision for the group as it interacts with the organization. That behavioral change would be rewarding in performance enhancement and consequent rewards. And finally, that the change in self make us a happier person.

Experiential Encounter - What are the real encounters that the members feel and experience? Focusing on personal feelings may frequently encourage other group members to help the individual. Anger and conflict are not themselves 'bad'. Angry feelings are as legitimate as any other feelings. Conflict can be growth-producing phenomenon. It is the matter in which conflict or angry feelings are handled that can have negative consequences. Only through surfacing and resolving conflicts can people develop competence and confidence in dealing with feelings and situations. Effectively "Tell Me Effect" happens when there is a bondage to the cause and that we are participating in an act together. The human feeling to help, care, share and love for each other is fundamental to the cause of "Tell Me". The belief in the human spirit, the will and the capability to change is basic for the process. To belong as an individual and as a group individually and collectively should be a reciprocated feeling. That the process makes me feel and do things good should be a cause. That the encounter can happen without fear, anxiety, insecurity, dependence is key to the climate of sharing.

Psychological Contract - We need to get people to take back an experience after the "Tell Me Effect". Experiences do not happen unless we agree on the psychological contract that binds people of varying behaviors together. Each of the "encountered" member should train on recall and goal based follow up. Reinforcement workshops are necessary for periodic up gradation of the behavioral inputs to make the change permanent. Alteration in the post workshop scenario is possible and the facilitator should take upon himself/herself to offer corrections. Active involvement of the same set of participants over time periods would help in the behavioral evolution. In any event if the "Tell Me Effect" has produced adequate fun and laughter the session can be deemed to be a success and mutually rewarding.

To Sanjay Lalbhai, of the Multinational Lalbhai Group, influence of Leadership disrupted on culture in the context of an organization meant:

1. *A culture that performs*
2. *A Vision that works for every one*
3. *Stakes that are shared*
4. *Encourages expression of ideas and opinions*
5. *Encourages addressing problems by using reasoning and evidence, rather than unsupported opinion*
6. *Questions the traditional ways of doing things*
7. *Emphasizes the value of questioning assumptions*
8. *Re-examines critical assumptions to question whether they are appropriate*

I. Effecting Change: If So, how does transformation take place?

We reviewed conditions under which cultural change is likely to be implemented and accepted. Now we ask the question, if conditions are right, how does management go about enacting the cultural change?

Effecting Cultural Change: Unfreeze Current Culture

Unfreeze Feedback Content - The challenge is to unfreeze the current culture. No single action, alone, is likely to have the impact necessary to unfreeze something that is so entrenched and highly valued. Therefore, there needs to be a comprehensive and coordinated strategy for managing culture. Values are the bedrock of any corporate culture and as the essence of a Company's philosophy for achieving success. Work ethos develops as we keep implementing one policy after another and reinforce the work style, method and manner we would basic work to take place.

Feedback Philosophy - A Corporate philosophy states the goals and practices that communities of employees are trying to enact. That philosophy leads over time to the development of a host of smaller practices and modes of conduct that become a corporate culture. Over years of corporate functioning as problems are encountered and solved, as directions are taken or not taken and as crisis are overcome these philosophies take forms through decisions. In this sense, an organizational philosophy underlies the moral philosophy of one or a group of senior management who have shaped the Company through these actions. There is a danger in managing this process that is equally susceptible to human frailties. Strong and consistent fundamentals in the analysis of each of the actions and assumptions facilitates overcoming the human weaknesses built into the system.

Their sense of right from wrong articulated in a particular social and economic setting visibly emerged over the years as a culture and a philosophy. The study would like to present before you four values, we consider as a prerequisite in a philosophy statements: -

- *Openness and Trust in relationships*
- *Collaboration and communicated transactions*
- *Active involvement of people in all aspects which affect them.*
- *Communication and knowledge sharing*
- *Clarity in goals and expectations in performance*
- *Aligned in ways that determine one's way of life*
- *Humility, spirit of service and sacrifice*

Culture Implies Values - There was a preconceived attempt at the unit to convey our philosophy on human resources management. Tradition, history, values, beliefs, norms, managerial styles, leadership, vision, goals and climate make up a Company's culture. Culture implies a Company's values- values that set a pattern for activities, opinions and actions. These patterns are either maintained or in situations dispensed with. Managers instill that pattern in employees by their example and pass it down to succeeding generations of employees. A collaborative work culture assures that any employees life is a whole and suggests that humanized working environment not only increases productivity but also the self-esteem for employees. An increased sense of ease makes everyone function better as people.

Effecting Cultural Change: Make Leadership disrupted Visible in Action

Across the line we have seen the inevitable necessity of the role of a leader in the Organizational building process – a leader with an ability to create and pose a strategic sense of direction with a vision and effort to prod the Organization towards growth. The leader demonstrates traits and habits that demand emulation and becomes a standard. The leader walks the talk.

Reproduced is a leader's exhortation through his vision and plan:

Aspirational, we want to be a leader in the professional services arena - we want to wield significant influence over significant business decisions. We clearly have a global vision statement, and we did not consider it appropriate to articulate a localized version of it. However, the articulation of our aspirations should help us to provide context to our vision statement.

We have tried to dimension the economic environment, possible client needs, the challenges that we will face and our strategic imperatives through discussions with our clients, industry leaders, academics and Government officials.

There is a set of common themes that have emerged:

- *We need deep understanding of the industries in which clients operate and of their particular businesses*
- *We need to build relationships across client organizations*
- *We need to provide clients with a single interface point, and integrate our relationship management and service delivery through this interface*
- *Clients increasingly want their consultants to tell them how the consultants can help them; they want the consultants to bring ideas to them on how they can run their businesses more effectively*

What this means for us is that:

- *We need to be very focussed*
- *We need to improve our client targeting processes*
- *We need to make our client relationship management process more robust*
- *We need to continue to deepen our skills*

We reviewed our industry program and also considered developments that are likely to occur across different industry segments. We propose to expand our industry program to include a few more industries, with the following possibilities being considered:

- *Healthcare*
- *Retailing*
- *Government services*
- *Infrastructure*
- *Real estate and hospitality*

More work is required before we conclude on the specific industries.

We reviewed our existing portfolio of solutions and capabilities, and then debated areas where we needed to build capabilities, areas that we should not operate in, and existing solutions that we should consider dispensing with. Some more work is required in this area.

From a client targeting perspective, we are proposing a framework where we will categorize our existing and target clients into:

CEO Accounts

Lead Partner Accounts
Strategic Apex
Critical key accounts
Super-Fast 250
The Operating Core

Key accounts will represent existing or target clients where we see significant sustained potential over a number of years. This potential should translate into opportunities for two or more solution segments. We will set out financial and other targets in relation to these key accounts and build mechanisms to monitor our performance on these and other accounts on an ongoing basis. We are tentatively looking at around 20 - 25 key account relationships.

Effecting Cultural Change: The story of a Young Professional Experiencing Change

"There is a symbiotic and responsible relationship, apart from a driven identify between the leadership style of the CEO/leader and the culture of the organization. A CEO's personal style often plays a defining role in shaping the culture of the organization. The CEO/Leader has a powerful role to play in the culture of the company. The impact of the CEO's personal style depends on two critical factors, - the life cycle of the organization and the extent of involvement of the CEO. For instance, a new organization or a regenerating organization will be more influenced by the CEO's style than a stable, mature organization. Similarly, a high-touch CEO will shape the culture more than a low-touch CEO. Cultures exist on a mutually exclusive basis in all the companies. I.e. No Company will have one identifiable culture. Culture can at best be described as a heterogeneous and layered iceberg. The layers refer to the artifacts, behaviors, norms & beliefs and values of the organization (from top to bottom). The heterogeneity is defined by individual components comprising each of these layers. Although, no company can have a completely unique culture, as the similarity of culture will be driven by similarity among cultural attributes, the sum total of the parts will almost always be different from other companies. The CEO/leader does not directly influence the existence of any one/all of the three cultures in the company. There is a definite relationship between culture and different functions (Marketing/Production/ Finance/ Personnel/ Study/ IT etc.) of the company. Culture, as defined above, is the composite whole of the artifacts, behaviors, norms & beliefs and values of the organization. The norms, beliefs and values are often shaped as much by individual personal styles as it is by the intrinsic nature of the job. Thus while assertiveness may be a typical characteristic of a sales & marketing department, humility is often a typifying characteristic for an HR function and study orientation may be the defining style of the R&D person. Hence the relationship between different functions and their culture is indeed tangible and linked to the nature of work of and competencies demonstrated by people within that function. There are no definite management style(s) of the top that influences the culture of the organization. Leaders, by virtue of their position within the organizational hierarchy and ability to influence decision-making, can often play a decisive role in shaping the culture of the team/ function/ department / company that they lead. There is no one all-pervasive leadership style that is prevalent across the company. Culture is, as defined before, at best heterogeneous. There may be differences of culture across functions, teams, departments, and even levels. The overall cultural style is defined by the pervasiveness of influence of a particular culture on the whole. Leadership does not always influence and direct the culture of an organization through HRM practices/ processes like hiring, training, performance appraisal, compensation, rewards and communication. The process per se may not influence the culture so much as the people that are filtered by each of these processes. Thus the aggressive, almost domineering culture of investment bankers is often due to the aggressive incentive/ bonus packages that are linked to their performance, which promotes this culture. The CEO/leader would actually significantly focus on monetary reward program for retention of high performers. In today's day and age, a monetary

package is as much retention tool as the roles defined for individuals. Thus a CEO would be foolish if he/ she thinks that without monetarily incentivising employees, he/ she would be able to secure a robust employee contract. About 50% of top management time is not really spent on managing employee retention activities. Unless the organization is embarking on a particularly challenging phase of its existence (e.g. mergers, new businesses, divestment, consolidation, exit from existing business etc.). This often throws employees into a cauldron of insecurity, which top management needs to actively monitor and resolve. However, during normal organizational functioning, employee retention occupies a much lower percentage of the top management time"".

Effecting Cultural Change

1. *Lead from the front, show commitment and action for change*
2. *Practice Values, they in turn help you determine your strategic path and growth objectives*
3. *Implicitly provide a climate in which people trust and collaborate*
4. *Make visible organizational and performance stakes in making change happen*
5. *Create a corporate environment that puts constant pressure on everyone to beat your specific competitors at innovation. http://bit.ly/2aE6S0V*
6. *Structure the organization so that you promote innovation instead of thwarting it.*
7. *Ask for the intellect that would make the organization work.*
8. *Develop a realistic strategic focus to channel innovative efforts.*
9. *Convert every business experience into a knowledge archive. That is the bank of the future.*
10. *Know where to look for good ideas and how to use your business system to leverage them once found.*
11. *Throw the book at good ideas once you've developed them fully. And ask for more.*
12. *Get culture working to make people have fun.*

Refer – HBR – August 2002 - Tough-Minded Ways to Get Innovative - Andrall E. Pearson

Effecting Cultural Change: Cultural Analysis and Learning in the context of Organizations:

Culture Audit - This would include a cultural audit to assess the current culture, a comparison of the present culture against that which is desired, and a gap evaluation to identify what cultural elements needs changing. How much individual initiative is there? Is innovation encouraged? To what degree are rewards contingent on performance rather than seniority or politics? Additionally, three basic questions should be answered in order to tap the content of the culture. First, what is the background of the founders and others who followed them? Second, how did the organization respond to past crises or other critical events, and what was learned from these experiences? Third, who are considered deviants in the culture and how does the organization respond to them? Answers to these questions will reveal how particular values came to be formed, the ordering of these values, and where the culture" boundaries are. The next step in cultural analysis requires that the values sought in the new culture be articulated. What is the preferred culture that is being sought? This desired culture can then be compared against the organization current values.

Effecting Cultural Change: Building Trust

Team Trust - Donald J Bodwell writes on Teaming, "Developing trust among organizational members is at once difficult and essential to becoming High Performance Cultures. Members need to be taught from the start that building trust within the team is critically important to the team's ultimate success. As the culture forms, it is normal that the level of trust is low. Several members or all team members may have worked together before. Or they may know each other by casual acquaintance of interaction. But trust has something to do with loyalties, and at the outset the team will not have developed team loyalty. Rather, each team member's loyalties will be to his or her own organization or manager. As the days and weeks of team building proceed, loyalties will naturally build toward fellow members. This is often a two-step process: one forward, and one step back. During the first few days, it is common for one or more members to respond negatively about the need for the team, its composition, the coaches, the task before them, or whether this is the most important thing they could be spending their time working on. As a result, several complaints before the organization for consideration is an issue. It is best not to name names. This will send a message to the complainers that they are on the verge of being discovered. Invariably the complainers will change their tune, rather than risk a negative reaction from their fellow team members. Members need to be coached to learn that it is important to trust one another. It is not possible, or desirable, for one member to do all the work for the team. Although, someone will almost always try. New members need to learn that to get the job done they have to rely on others to do their part. The analogy to this principle is that each team member needs to be trustworthy. Members need to learn that others are counting on them to do what they said they would do. But personal or business problems outside the team come up that affect individual members' ability to accomplish their agreed tasks. As soon as it becomes clear to members that his or her task cannot be completed in time, the member needs to let the other team members know about the cause of the problem and ask for help. This practice goes a long way to convincing fellow members that one is trustworthy. ("Based on our Forrsights survey data, we are seeing approximately a 12% churn (replacement) rate for these systems" (talking about Replacing legacy systems with SaaS HCM) – Forrester). When a call for help comes from a fellow team member, the others should carefully examine their own responsibilities and available skills or time to see if they can help. It's in the best interest of members to support each other, especially when the organizational performance is judged and rewarded as a whole. The time might come when the team member who has been asked for help, needs help himself. If help cannot be offered, the team should pull together and determine how to be revise the plan or bring in additional resources to get the plan back on track". Refer - http://highperformanceteams.org/combined.htm

Effecting Cultural Change: The Learning Experience

Performance Challenges - Bodwell continues, "Significant performance challenges energize members regardless of where they are in an organization. No team arises without a performance challenge that is meaningful to those involved. A common set of demanding performance goals that a group considers important to achieve will lead, most of the time, to both performance and team. Performance, however, is the primary objective while a process remains the means, not the end. Organizational leaders can foster culturally sensitive performance best by building a strong performance ethic rather than by establishing a culture promoting environment alone. Biases toward individualism exist but need not get in the way of team performance. Real cultures always find ways for each individual to contribute and thereby gain distinction. Indeed, when harnessed to a common team purpose and goals, our need to distinguish ourselves as individuals becomes a powerful engine for team performance". Worldwide, eLearning is the fastest-growing market in the history of education, doubling in size every year and expected to reach a value of more than $30 billion in 2020. Coupled with the core software solutions are a variety of value-added services such as needs assessment, online mentoring, online performance support, reporting and hosting. All these services are in great demand. Russell Harper of Skill Soft defines eLearning as a scalable solution consisting of a combination of learning services and technology that provide high-value integrated learning anywhere at any time. Although it should not and will not replace other forms of learning, it can – when carefully integrated – add an extra dimension to an organisation's training and development strategy. It answers the needs of businesses for faster, better and cheaper solutions that transcend geographical boundaries. It also marks a move towards a more interactive approach to development. "Discipline-both within the team and across the organization-creates the conditions for team performance. For organizational leaders, this entails making clear and consistent demands that reflect the needs of customers, shareholders, and employees, and then holding themselves and the organization relentlessly accountable. **Connect Goals to Plans:** ("Worldwide 80% of all talent management suite deployments are happening in the cloud" – Gartner) Keep the purpose, goals, and approach relevant and meaningful. All members must shape their own common purpose, performance goals and approach. While a leader must be a full working member of the team who can and should contribute to these, he or she also stands apart from the team by virtue of his or her selection as leader. Cultures expect their leader to use that perspective and distance to help the teams clarify and commit to their mission, goals, and approach. **Strengthen institutional framework:** Build commitment and confidence. Leaders should work to build the commitment and confidence of each individual as well as the team as a whole. (It's estimated that **90** percent of **Fortune 1000** companies plan to replace their human resources management software in the next four years." (CIO.com). **Map Competency to Core Capabilities of the organization:** Strengthen the mix and level of skills. Effective leaders are vigilant about skills. Their goal is clear: ultimately, the flexible and top-performing cultures consist of people with all the technical, functional, problem-solving, decision-making, interpersonal, and teamwork skills the team needs to perform. To get there, team leaders encourage people to take the risks needed for growth and development. They also continually challenge team members by shifting assignments and role patterns. **Build Networks:** Manage relationships with outsiders, including removing obstacles".   As part of an integrated solution, eLearning can be used effectively before, during or after a programme of instructor-led training (ILT). It is also important for "just-in-time" learning support to address specific needs. A recent survey conducted by Taylor Nelson Sofres on behalf of Skill Soft showed that 46% of UK organisations & 85% in the US, Fortune 1000 companies have already implemented some form of eLearning – an increase of 12% over the previous year. Within two years, 78% of the sample expect to be using eLearning for staff development. Among the organisations interviewed, IT and telecoms companies stood out as early adopters. The most widely quoted reasons for implementing eLearning were its cost-effectiveness and its ability to be implemented across multiple sites. IT, compliance, safety, OSHA, diversity and customer service skills were some of most popular applications of eLearning. Bodwell says, "Leaders are expected, by people outside as well as inside the team to manage much of the team's contacts and relationships with the rest of the organization. This calls on team leaders to communicate effectively the team's purpose, goals, and approach to anyone who might help or hinder it. They also must have the courage to intercede on the team's behalf when obstacles that might cripple or demoralize the team get placed in their way". **Make people Grow.** Create opportunities for others. High Performance Culture is not possible if the leader grabs all the best opportunities, assignments, and credit. Indeed, the crux of the leader's challenge is to provide performance opportunities to the team and the people on it. **Do real work.** Everyone on a real organization, including the leader, does real work in roughly equivalent amounts. Leaders do have a certain distance from the team by virtue of their position, but they do not use that distance "just to sit back and make decision." "Leaders must contribute in whatever way the team needs", says Bodwell in Team effectiveness, "just like any other member. Moreover, team leaders do not delegate the nasty jobs to others. Where personal risks are high or "dirty work" is required, the team leader should step forward. **Small enough in number.** Can convene and communicate easily and frequently. Discussions are open and interactive for all members. Each member understands the other's roles and skills. All three categories of skills are either actually or potentially represented across the membership (functional/technical, problem-solving/decision-making, and interpersonal). Each member has the potential in all three categories to advance his or her skills to the level required by the team's purpose and goals. For example, as per Deloitte, "every part of HR touches everything else. Performance management impacts development planning, career progression, and selection. Talent acquisition is impacted by employment brand, talent mobility, and varying internal demands for skills. Once independent, programs like diversity, inclusion, engagement, and employee communications are now part of everything we do". The member's purpose constitutes a broader, deeper aspiration than just near term goals. All members understand and articulate the purpose the same way. Members define the purpose vigorously in discussion with outsiders. Members frequently refer to the purpose and explore its implications. The purpose contains themes that are particularly meaningful and memorable. Members feel the purpose is important, if not exciting. There are goals versus broader organizational goals versus just one individual's goals. **Goals are clear, simple, and measurable.** If they are not measurable, can their achievement be determined? **Goals are realistic as well as ambitious.** The approach is concrete, clear, and really understood and agreed to by everybody. It requires all **members** to contribute equivalent amounts of real work. It provides for open interaction, fact-based problem solving, and result-based evaluation. The approach provides for modification and improvement over time. Fresh input and perspective is systematically sought and added, for example, through information and analysis, new members, and sponsors. There is sense of mutual accountability".

Effecting Cultural Change: Making cultural change happen is fraught with consequences and some critical learning in this area would be:

Unintended consequences. Unintended consequences are of two types. First there is that under or over estimation of the effects of change; typical here is the construction of a new motorway producing more traffic than predicted by the highway engineers. Metro plans have often been challenged as causing greater congestion than release of space. Business failure of Enron Corporation led to the break-up of Andersen, the Big 5 firm. The second type is where there are unexpected consequences, usually in a domain situation not been considered. An example of this is where one section of a department moved out of a building to a more remote site and social and communicator problems arise within the department because people are no longer in informal contact. Technical collaboration with a product development group leads to the resignation of the current R and D head who visualizes his lowering importance in the new scenario. For example, Diversity and inclusion, unconscious bias, and gender issues are on a similar trend. This year, Facebook, Google, Twitter, and Apple Inc. each disclosed that the bulk of their engineering and technical professionals are male. While the CEOs of these companies are now talking about the issue openly, it begs the question of why the pipeline of candidates is not more diverse and why only 4.8 percent of all *FORTUNE* 500 CEOs are women. Inclusion and diversity are business problems. Deloitte *Simply Irresistible* engagement research shows that diversity and inclusion directly impact employee engagement; Deloitte Australia research shows that highly diverse teams outperform non-diverse teams by as much as 80 percent. (Research by Catalyst validates this at a board and senior executive level.) So, in 2015, inclusion and diversity should be high on your agenda, concludes Bersin.

- *Self-fulfilling fear of failure. This reflects on the fourth Price Waterhouse paradox - the true empowerment needs a forceful leader. Sometimes change requires a bold leap forward and a half-hearted attempt will lead to a fall into the chasm of failure. Sanjay Lalbhai, the Denim King (Arvind Inc.) took upon himself to do what no third world country promoter would do. Take on the world textile players. Markets dipped, he took his challenge on, forcefully retained his faith in the vision that he had carefully constructed. This company is now strongly on its way to being a world class leader. A brand name to be proud of. It took 10 strong years for this leader to turnaround and build back a strong, resilient organization. And to the non-believer here is a true story of an organization built on vision and values.*

- *Lack of preparation.* The process of change needs to be supported by appropriate human resource development efforts at all stages. Often training and development needs are recognized as an afterthought so that new technology may be introduced. At times without operators being given any grounding. More subtly, the less tangible areas like support may be neglected, for example training in leadership disrupted or teamwork. Pepsi's in its initial years in the market acquired organizations and were growing, but did not focus on bringing their new people into their organizational culture, systems and processes.

- *Ill-conceived change process.* Considerable forethought is one of the keys to successive; change. Causes of failure can include inadequate attention to any of the stages in the change management process but particularly with regard to inappropriate time scales going for the quick fix - or to a lack of clear dissemination of ideas and processes. Recall the devastating Power Sector Privatization or the Telecom Regulatory Commission work. All of their interventions had to be re done.

- *Inadequate consultation.* Nothing can sink a project faster than poorly motivated staff: (except, perhaps, a catastrophic computer failure!). An imposed change will only attain grudging acceptance and adherence to the letter rather than the spirit of the transforming nation. Equally a pragmatic shop floor change of practice can induce alarm and antagonism in management if they have not been consulted. Perhaps a special case like VRS for PSU employees is a classic example. Unions were not consulted and the employees were unwilling to accept the program. Again PSU Banks VRS program accomplished officer level resignations but miserably failed on subordinate staff who were not convinced of the need to accept the program and leave their employment.

- *'Not invented here' syndrome.* Sometimes the strongest resistance to change is shown as response to what is seen as importing the ideas of an alien culture. In university circle we often find this voiced as 'It might work in industry but it's different in a university or 'The American (Australian, India, Dutch, Scandinavian, etc.) system is not the same as ours, it would never work here', Or even 'Well, that's Mechanical Engineering; in Sri Lanka, we have to do everything on the blackboard!' Arvind Inc. encountered this problem when attempting to introduce their Knowledge Management and Benchmarking for Best Practices initiative. The traditional managers were quite reluctant to learn from any practices or people brought in from non-textile businesses.

Effecting Cultural Change: The Critical Leadership disrupted Question?

Is leadership disrupted at every organizational level engaged in hands-on implementation of the vision? This includes eliminating management layers, being visible in the bowels of the organization, and being an active, early participant in any learning effort. Only through direct involvement that reflects coordination, vision, and integration can leaders obtain important data and provide powerful role models.

At Motorola, the CEO not only drove the quality vision, he was a student in the first seminars on quality and made it the first item on the agenda at monthly meetings with his division executives. Much-admired Wal-Mart CEO spends two or three days each week at stores and warehouse; employees can call him at home and are often transferred to his hotel when he is in the field.

J. *Making Individual Transitions – Digital Directions*

435

The basic approach is not to allow culture to emerge and to form itself at the whim of the staff, but rather to create that which is desired by means of predetermined and targeted interventions.

Making Individual Transitions - Enable Plans for Change - Strategy and direction, to ensure that everyone understands that their place is in the pursuit of the organizations purpose whatever job they are carrying out. For example, a janitor at a factory, when asked what his job was, replied 'I am helping to place the first car on the floor'. Reorganization, to ensure that old ways, procedures and practices are confined to history. Induction, to ensure that the required attitudes, values, beliefs and standards are understood by all at the outset. Reinduction, socialization, reorientation is required where the prevailing standards are no longer satisfactory. Anything may act as a lever for this: new technology, new premises, work and job redesign, skills up gradation, training and development. For each new store that it opens at out-of-town sites, for example, the Tesco super Market Company provides extensive job training for all the staff who are to work there, whether or not they have worked for the company in the past. Use of dramas and crises to get people to think. Where necessary this may involve overstating the case. For example, the entry of the Virgin Group into the cola market had business analysts and pundits wondering publicly if this was to be the beginning of the end for Pepsi and Coca Cola. This plainly was a vast exaggeration. However, the volume of attention given was quite sufficient to ensure that everyone at both Pepsi and Coca Cola continued to pay positive attention to their own activities.

Making Individual Transitions - Establish Standards - This is to ensure that they know the new and absolute standards to which they are required to conform. Other human resource activities targeted to give impetus to the new. This includes everything: rewriting job descriptions (and the retraining that is then required for new job holders); changing recruitment advertising; attention to qualities and capabilities of new and existing staff; repositioning and reorientation of performance appraisal, industrial relations and staff management activities. Use of fashions and fads such as total quality management, customer service training and business process re-engineering as the means of doing that which is required.

Making Individual Transitions - Challenge Assumptions - The main service of these to all organizations is to challenge existing thinking and to act as the means by which desired developments can be introduced. Use of new language, which is ideally both more direct and also sufficiently different from the old. This drives and reinforces development. It also reinforces understanding and Acceptance as long as the language is more direct. It is also a general underlining of the fact that there is a general new way in existence. Use of project work and cross-functional teams to break down existing barriers and fiefdoms, as well as generating expertise and potential among employees, and also raising their sights and expectations. Furthermore, this enables positive relationships to be built between departments and individuals with different expertise and profession including transition from approved ways and means of doing things turning into unanticipated influences over people, systems and process would happen unknowingly. Employees are directly influencing through direct involvement in decisions affecting their work and their departments. Business school graduates prefer to exercise a choice of their roles and responsibilities. Practical mechanisms like open door policy, open communication sessions, grievance management system, and representative groups for unionized staff, task forces on special issues, problem solving work forces have time and again served their utility. Increased collaboration between union and management through employee relations executive forums and participate work groups like Quality Circles, quality of work life programs, safety, health and welfare committees have been used for bringing in a sense of involvement. Obviously all this is just not enough. A natural process of asking individuals before we act upon them is inevitable if we desire their wholesome commitment to their roles and the company.

Making Individual Transitions - Establish urgency and direction. All members need to believe the team has urgent and worthwhile purpose, and they want to know what the expectations are. Indeed, the more urgent and meaningful the rationale, the more likely it is that a real team will emerge. The best cultural charters are clear enough to indicate performance expectations, but Reinforcing folklore flexible enough to allow teams to shape their own purpose, goals, and approach. Select members based on skill and skill potential, not personalities.

Cultures must have the complementary skills needed to do their job. Three categories of skills are relevant: **1) technical and functional, 2) problem solving, and 3) interpersonal**. Refer – Bodwell. "The key issue for potential teams is striking the right balance between members who already possess the needed skill levels versus developing the skill levels after the team gets started. Pay particular attention to first meetings and actions. Initial impressions always mean a great deal. When potential teams first gather, everyone alertly monitors the signals given by other to confirm, suspend, or dispel going-in assumptions and concerns. They particularly pay attention to those in authority: The team leader and any executives who set up, oversee, or otherwise influence the team. And, as always, what such leaders do is more important than what they say".

Making Individual Transitions - Set some clear rules of behavior. Quoting works by Bodwell, http://bit.ly/2akTwJc -"All real cultures in performance orientation develop rules of conduct to help them achieve their purpose and performance goals. The most critical early rules pertain to attendance (for example: "no interruptions to take phone calls"), discussion-"no sacred cows", confidentiality, analytic approach-facts are friendly, end-product orientations-everyone gets assignments and does them, constructive confrontation-no finger pointing, and often the most important-everyone does real work. Set and seize upon a few immediate performance-oriented tasks and goals. Most cultures trace their advancement to key performance-oriented events that forge them together. Potential cultures can set such events in motion by immediately establishing a few challenging yet achievable goals that can be reached early on".

Making Individual Transitions - Performance Feedback - "Challenge the group regularly with fresh facts and information. New information causes a potential team to redefine and enrich its understanding of the performance challenge, thereby helping the organization shape a common purpose, set clearer goals, and improve on its common approach. Spending a lots of time together. Common sense tells us that members must spend a lot of time together, especially as the beginning. Yet potential teams often fail to do so. The time spent together must be both scheduled and unscheduled. Indeed, creative insights as well as personal bonding require customers, competitor, or fellow employees, and constantly debating issues. Exploit the power of positive feedback, recognition, and reward. Positive reinforcement works as well in team context as elsewhere. "Giving out gold stars" helps to shape new behaviors critical to high performance cultures. If people in the group, for example, are alert to a shy person's initial efforts to speak up and contribute, they can give him or her the positive reinforcement that encourages continued contributions".

Making Individual Transitions - Learning Experiences - Culture to perform to culture to learn, contribute, add value and enhance shareholder value is an organizational expectation for the individuals of the future. Individuals in doing their learning and contribution would seek fundamental and basic experiences. Not rocket science demands. A place to work, a working infrastructure, learn as they go along and spend time, an opportunity to create, feel a sense of identity on what they have created and eventually believe that all that they have done has impacted the shareholder. People centric ways in treating people for their potential and human nature to help them feel a sense of belonging, a feeling of achievement and an opportunity to bring out the best in them is essential to this process of attempted transition. The culture provides for failure as much as enjoying its share of success. "Outsiders think Silicon Valley as a success story," writes Silicon Valley commentator Mike Malone, "but in truth, it is a graveyard. Failure is Silicon Valley's greatest strength. Every initial product or enterprise is a lesson stored in the collective memory of the country". Venture capitalist Don Valentine says, "The world of technology is complex, fast changing and unstructured and it thrives best when individuals are left alone to be different, creative and disobedient".

Making Individual Transitions - Career – Succession Pathing Mechanisms - Psychometric Testing Canada's research on career employees indicate, "Organizations see the need for institutionalizing learning and teaching systems for people to learn, develop and intellectually grow as a responsibility, "self-imposed", on them. While people are doing their jobs and getting things done there is a group of facilitators, coaches and trainers who perform the role of institutionalizing learning. They are the leaders of tomorrow. They make education happen naturally without elaborate systemic processes or planned classroom training. Electronic learning methods, long distance teaching modules, state of art knowledge programs, behavioral modification and cultural adaptation modules, unlearning in preparedness for the next set of concepts to absorb all become a laundry list of required facilitator's role. Individuals in turn are demanding corporate commitment and willingness to make employees employable over time. The process of reciprocity is essential in making knowledge managers work for others. For the individual's knowledge is their core competency and they would like to share, display and contribute depending on their constant state of upgradation. While it is not being presupposed that this becomes a corporate responsibility a learning culture perhaps is an inescapable responsibility of the corporate management. Organizational learning forums would multiply several folds with members demanding time and opportunity to participate physically or electronically. As the learning centers proliferate cultural influences just occurs. Corporations view culture management as a competitive weapon to fight unprecedented economic wars. In a scenario where easy finance, adequate raw material, cheap labor and growing market is a real life scenario, knowledge becomes the true competitive source. In the individual intellect lie the competitive edge and the push factor against competition. When individuals are prodded to perform against intellectual odds they are likely to be at their best. Good work comes out of the human minds' defiance to doing it the proven way. Firms need to capitalize on this potential of the human mind to take on challenges that a product or a service cannot offer consistently over time". Refer - http://bit.ly/2aiCmuv

Making Individual Transitions - Digital Skill Building - Decision-making, an important aspect of the changing cultural dimension, has moved to the point of impact. Seniority of people and their experiences are no longer the governing principles for vesting of authority and power. As organizations employ managers with the power to think and do, there would arise a need for empowerment. There would also be the scope demanded of the individuals to do their job holistically being responsible for what they are accountable for. The operating front line manager is equipped with the capability to decide and act upon his/her problems. An empowered sales manager in the field talking and dealing with the customer best services customers. Getting back to the head office to seek an answer is not a workable proposition to customers demanding on time all the time service. Decisions, as a consequence, have moved to the point of impact. The shop floor supervisor answers the employee on his/her questions. First line managers ask for the freedom to do their job independently. Organizations cannot work through a long and an expanded hierarchy of seasoned managers who apparently know the one best answer. In any event we do not visualize adequate time in the hands of managers to manage a "ladder of references" before they could get their job done.

Making Individual Transitions - Digital Change - Change has become a way of life for corporate managers whose ability to reckon with and manage change as a day to day issue has become a necessary competency for effectiveness. If we presuppose an organization that is expected to operate on a flexible basis at a strategic level, with structures happening on an impromptu basis, with people processes depending on the current situation meeting with change head on is but a minimum. CEO's of corporations see change management, building people preparedness to face change, bringing in change adept internal practices in managerial actions, making change facilitators create and nurture the risk taking factor amongst employees as their single largest priority in the management of the enterprise. Intellectual Corporation rarely is change shy, as their coping mechanism happens to be their mind that understands rationally the purpose and goals aimed through the planned change. The users rather than the supervisory managers initiate Many times change. Individuals of well-managed Intellectual Companies do not like to be told to change. They would rather identify the change, plan for its execution, and cover the impacted people by themselves instead of waiting for the systemic influences to announce and manage the change. Motorola would be one corporation where the ownership for change rests with the impacted people. Motorola University focuses their training attention to managing the turbulent environment with managers taking charge of their change needs and actions.

Making Individual Transitions - Digital Careers - Work role professionals see organizational life no longer as an extension of their real world full time life. Many would like it to be independent of each other, family and work, with adequate quality space available for leading a life of fulfillment. Seeking joy is but one phenomenon that is very real for high performing individuals. It is in this context that flexible working, own time scheduler, self-goal prioritization, including variable bonuses and pay linked to targets achieved and virtual offices become real and inevitable. Apart from significant advantages in terms of office space, support staff, nearness to the customer, delivery based pay systems and virtual speed of response. Individuals would also demand more time for their learning and knowledge updating efforts. Working spouse, care for parents, off line work and hobbies, mid-career education and planning, and choice of school for children, geographic location preference and more importantly the employee would like to work at a location where his/her contribution is maximized. It is possible to receive a higher number of applications for part time employment just to help the applicant have more time to do other things. While this is perhaps a loss to the corporation for the increasing amount of limited time availability of their effective performers the upside would be the opportunity for organizations to have half as many more people and their creative minds.

Making Individual Transitions - Diversity in Digital HR - Corporations see the real need to integrate diversity issues as a basic management challenge and are creating culture facilitation strategies to make diverse people live and work well with each other. Cross culture studies have revealed that over 50% of the work force of the 21st century would consist of people of diverse background, demographics, varying personal preferences and cultural milieu. Diversity preparation becomes an important organizational action point to have people not just tolerate each other but actually enjoy working and sharing with their colleagues. The emergence of the third world in the global business scenario makes diversity management extremely crucial immediately in the short run. Workplace management demands would need to be reckoned with to allow for minds of several types and dispositions would work together. They could be physically together or could be working miles apart but attitudinal congruence and tolerance towards diverse people sets is essential and inevitable. Concurrently it is critical to see the validity of a set of competencies in a multi-cultural environment. The success of a transformation of this magnitude is predicated on the ability of the people in the organization to accept, enact and sustain the changes to technology, process and strategic direction. In the paper, Cross-cultural social intelligence: An assessment for employees working in cross-national contexts, Ma. Evelina Ascalon, Deidra J. Schleicher, Marise Ph. Born, "Cross Cultural Management: An International Journal Volume: 15 Issue: 2 2008 discuss the concept of cross-cultural social intelligence (CCSI), its relevance for both selecting and developing expatriates and other employees working in cross-cultural contexts, the development of a situational judgment test to assess CCSI, and practical "lessons learned" in each of these areas. The four phases of the development and validation of the CCSI measure (using a total of 184 cross-cultural SMEs) were developing the scenarios and the response alternatives, the content analysis, and establishing construct validity".

Transformational tools and methods focus on delivering results. They are built to:
- **Accelerate** results by leveraging our access our portfolio of proven templates and tools
- **Focus** on an integrated process for executing the strategy by understanding the disciplines that need immediate attention through systematic prioritization
- **Support** the development of process for evaluating and monitoring internal initiatives
- **Educate** the organization on its current capabilities, new capabilities, and a roadmap for improvement
- **Promote** the alignment and acceptance of performance measures and business goals through clear measures.

"The results from the content analysis and construct validation provide support for the use of the CCSI in cross-cultural situations. The CCSI has not yet been validated in a criterion-related way (i.e. based on relations to job performance). This should be done before using for selection. Possible uses for the CCSI in organizations include selection and/or promotion of expatriates and other employees in cross-cultural contexts and several types of training and development initiatives. This instrument is offered (free of charge) to any interested managers or HR practitioners. Despite the expressed need for instruments of this sort, nothing similar currently exists (especially not a theoretically grounded and empirically sound instrument). In addition, the "lessons learned" provide practical advice to others engaged in similar undertakings".

Making Individual Transitions - Changing Digital Roles - Teams performances could be influenced by the role played by the intellectual manager depending upon the method used by the group to make participating members learn, share and co-exist. It is ironical to argue for team performance in an individualized Intellectual Company. Yet we do not see a contradiction. Teams will always be there with individuals participating in it working towards a common objective. The issues on team working could substantially be different with team norms including aspects of individual contribution based on areas of expertise, seasoning of managers to the task in hand, working out of physically dispersed locations and an element of competitive spirit bordering on individual excellence. Team leadership could vary based on expertise, client requirement and the attitudinal vagaries of the team members. Teams would exercise considerable influence over their choice of team members. Effectively teams would turn into clusters and coalition groups with similar and dissimilar purposes and goals. Formal creations may turn into a challenge for the management as the clusters would have a unique internal management style for leading, participating, sharing, working norms, for example, long hour working, helping a colleague through a personal problem and substituting him/her on the job etc. Many organizational norms of discipline and rules of work ethic traditionally understood and practiced in the organization may undergo a change given the cluster desire to achieve their goals in their own way. In our opinion managers, in managing their independent work force whose demands for autonomy may border on laissez faire, would face considerable degree of difficulty.

Making Individual Transitions - Propensity for Conflicts - "Intellectual culture could sometimes, in fact many times be conflict prone given occasional polarized and strong views on individual positions and perspectives. Participating members typically have a point of view on issues confronting him or herself or the organization and feel their role to be critical enough to substantiate their argument. Large-scale differences are eminently possible. When two minds that think are put together there would a point of difference. Organizations and individuals should be aware of this possibility and seek out acceptable and pre-determined means of conflict resolution and due process. The corporate would become responsible to create confrontation forums and stress release mechanisms to make people of intellectual intensity work together. The dispersion possibility of people flying off the handle owing to combination of work role pressures and an inability to sell their idea across is high. Study and development departments interfacing closely with manufacturing or marketing departments would need careful monitoring and coaching, counseling to manage themselves in their new context. A software development pocket with people rushing to advance their knowledge is another area of concern. Similarly, HR professionals who have become responsible for HR services and people counseling roles would need considerable adaptation and focus maintenance training. Making people emotionally resilient to what affects them while on the job is a critical role to be performed. Defining the changed context and their meaning or adaptation to the context is relevant to eliminate identity loss and frustration amongst people in "high think" jobs". Refer - http://bit.ly/2aiCmuv

Making Individual Transitions - Attrition - Clearly the participating managers impact the culture in several ways both in the short and long run. The organization tends to be perceived as being excessively skewed in favor of meritocracy albeit at the cost of loyal long-term employees. Some overtly aggressive individuals who would make normal circumstance appear conflict and confrontation prone could vitiate the culture. Some amount of survival of the fittest tendency may creep in. Placement and hiring decisions would lean in favor of college degrees, professional education, organizational skills and competencies and knowledge that is application and growth based. A natural process of attrition of those who do not "fit in" would emerge for a natural process of elimination. Employees would consider the organizational career plan to consist of a successive set of hurdles to be crossed at every stage of their career with no letting go at any time. People will simply have to be at the top of their performance graphs to move up hierarchically. Who knows more, how much more do people know, know more and more of less and less, (know what, know why), gross focus on issues, a quality of mind that is inquiring, investigating, challenging, considerable skills of creativity, deep and powerful analytical insights, sharpened process skills, critical understanding of organizational knowledge linkages and many such factors would become relevant. The employees would simply have to think more before they act. Employees would be expected to be at their best at literally all times. Speed would mean a combination of responsiveness and superior quality of input. Effective service at acceptable quality would not be good enough.

Making Individual Transitions - Digital Performance – People Systems - "Creation of a performing culture where people would sense the common goal of customer service, satisfaction, adding to shareholder's wealth and bottom line orientation is key to the Intellectual Corporation. A culture where "people – systems" would replace "systems – people" with the original contribution of the people as the critical input" - http://bit.ly/2aiCmuv . The human school linked with the systems approach to make the human mind superior to the machine with the caveat that they are now inter dependent. There would be a premium on doing it different every time. Task orientation would create a new sort of peer group competitiveness with competent minds chasing self-imposed goals and deadlines. The organizational performance would emerge into one of spontaneous discovery process where people would cherish the task of achieving yet another milestone.

Making Individual Transitions - Digital Hiring - Theodore Kinni in MIT SMR 2016, "The $105 Billion Enterprise Market for Pokémon Go" writes, Automating the hiring process: Being a nontraditional employee (to put it mildly), I've yet to encounter an automated hiring process that doesn't cut me off long before I get to a human being. But maybe chatbots will be my salvation. Khari Johnson reports in VentureBeat that a "millennial search company" (are millennials hard to find in their parent's basements?) named FirstJob has launched a recruitment automation bot named Mya. Mya adds some smarts to the hiring process, while automating three-quarters of it. What's cool about "Mya" is its ability to question the applicant when it appears that some qualification or another is missing on his or her application. The chatbot identifies the missing qualification and asks the applicant to explain the gap. Then, instead of getting kicked out of contention for the job, the applicant gets a chance to respond. "The application assistant uses artificial intelligence and natural language processing to ask a few questions, verify qualifications, and answer questions from job applicants about things like company culture, policy, and benefits," reports Johnson. "At the end of the application process, Mya ranks candidates top to bottom based on weighted factors like qualifications, recent activity, engagement, and other metrics. FirstJob, which works with companies like Fitbit and Evernote, says that candidates who apply for jobs through Mya are more than three times more likely to hear back from a real, live person. Moreover, it enhances the productivity of recruiters by 38%".

Making Individual Transitions - "Crowd Sourcing"— tapping into the collective intelligence of the public or one's peer group—has become particularly popular. The reach and accessibility of social media have amplified the voice of individual consumers. Now anyone can become an expert. Messages that resonate are quickly spread and reinforced through user reviews and other online forums". In, a BCG Research Report of 2012, "The Millennial Consumer Debunking Stereotypes" authors Christine Barton (BCG), Jeff Fromm (Share Like Buy), Chris Egan (Service Management Group), continue, "Given this new reality, companies must monitor what is being said about their brands and participate in the conversation, especially since Millennials are much more likely than non-Millennials to explore brands on social networks (53 percent versus 37 percent). It may also be time to reevaluate whether current brand endorsers are credible and effective with this audience, because while the right brand advocates can be very influential, the wrong ones can be detrimental". Gerald C. Kane in MIT SMR 2016 Social Blogging, writes, "Awareness of this tendency for social media to result in filter bubbles is important for executives and companies using social media for communication, innovation, and decision making. First, executives should be aware of this filter-bubble tendency when using social media data for decision making, recognizing that the voices that come through on social media are not necessarily representative of the majority of customers or stakeholders — they may only represent the views of a small but vocal online community. For example, when Dell Inc. decided to use social media to launch Linux laptops, the effort yielded lackluster results, partly because Dell failed to recognize that the online voices were not representative of a larger customer base. Even if a particular view is representative of all users of a specific platform such as Twitter, those users may not reflect the overall views of the population at large. As an example, Twitter sentiment nearly unanimously supported Scotland's independence from the United Kingdom during a 2014 referendum, but the measure failed at the polls, with slightly more than 55% of Scots voters rejecting the measure. Social media data can result in an invaluable source of insight for companies, but only when used correctly. Executives should always augment that social media data with other sources of information before using it for important decisions. Second, companies should also be aware of this tendency toward filter bubbles when using social media for internal communication and collaboration purposes. The same filter bubble dynamics can occur among employees just as easily as it does in politics, or in their personal life, but Sundstein's analysis offers some helpful guidance for how to avoid them. He notes that shared experiences are important for developing the types of connections and information exchange that break down filter bubbles"

Making Individual Transitions - Creative Managerial Actions - Managerial actions by itself would no longer determine company priorities on an exclusive basis in this dynamic culture. The managerial act would be either preceded or succeeded by individual or collective intellect providing information based knowledge, sensitivity analysis with "go – no go" options, scenario planning and scoping etc. The responsibility of managing the company would cut across lines of control and power and would depend on groups of people vested with the correct knowledge of the issue in question. Every function and activity of the company would turn knowledge and intellect driven. Manufacturing teams would be driven by their knowledge of technology, process, standards and methods. Marketing would make brands, study, and customer data knowledge intensive. Study and development would focus on new products, inventions and innovations. Finance and HR functions would attempt making every policy and system intellect friendly and knowledge sensitive. Everybody knows everything. Knowledge sharing would be the power that people would exercise. Routine would considerably give way to creative new.

Making Individual Transitions - Changing Vision in Digital Enterprises - Darius Ghandhi, a career HRM professional from the C Suite, says, "Vision, values, beliefs and his dream drive the Leader as a person. Yes, it is the power and intensity of the vision, and the strength of values & beliefs that is the hallmark of a leader. Effective leaders have the ability to translate their vision, beliefs, and values into actionable goals for their people and the organization. The often reach out beyond the boundaries of their own organizations and seek out ways to positively impact the society and other stakeholders, at large. The leader becomes the fountainhead of inspiration and guides his people towards desired outcomes. The Leader's emphasizes on the Individual and the Intellect, and a role in building individual and organizational knowledge. A leader displays the ability to motivate and encourage others to strive for greater professional achievement. He sets a climate of high performance and positive reinforcement. He builds in his people an insatiable appetite for accomplishment and results. This is the Personal Leadership disrupted style whereby he takes complete and personal responsibility for the team's results. The CEO/leader's has a role in emphasizing on culture aspects pertaining to empowerment, delegation, individual contribution, accountability and responsibility. This is an example of Operational Leadership disrupted. He serves as a positive role model and articulates and practices the cultural values of the organization. He creates a sense of openness and inclusion that values differing perspectives and fosters innovation. Speaks up for what he/she believes while also voicing and respecting minority opinions. CEO/leader's has a role in actively participating in attracting, retaining and rewarding star talent and performers. The leader taps into the capabilities of his people and provides everyone with appropriate development opportunities. And this responsibility extends beyond those who are recognized as Star performers. He has to build in his people a 'passion for excellence' and help them find new ways of improving their individual and team performance. All this then goes into creating an environment that promotes meritocracy and a culture based on results. These are the characteristics of a being a true People Leader. The Leader's has a role in helping the organization retain an open mind to an unknown environment. A leader has the ability to anticipate and deals proactively with resistance to change. It is his responsibility to challenge status quo and champion new initiatives; to act as a catalyst of change and stimulate others to change. And to manage the implementation of change effectively by creating the necessary environment for a more purposeful buy-in to change and involving those who are affected by it to embrace and internalize the change."

The Paradox of High Performance Culture - *'Creating a high-performance culture' is a phrase that adorns many a corporate presentation, made by both business and Human Resources leaders. Once you have spoken about whatever else you wanted to say about your business strategy, adding this magic phrase, 'creating a high-performance culture', gives it a nice 'human touch' and demonstrates your commitment to facilitating the unfolding of human potential in your organization! Says Prasad Kurian who leads Talent Management & Organization Development at Coca-Cola.*

"So, what is the problem? He asks. "Just because something looks good on PowerPoint slides, we can't assume that it won't work in real life. The problem begins when we start asking questions. Is there really something like a high-performance culture? Does it remain constant across organizations? Is it a naturally occurring phenomenon or is it something that can be created? If it can be created, what kind of creation is required? Once created, can it be sustained? It is when we try to answer these questions we come to the paradox mentioned in the title of this discussion.

An issue becomes a paradox when there are multiple opinions the issue, each of which appears to be true, but they seem to be in conflict with one another. In this discussion, we will look at the various perspectives that exist regarding high-performance cultures and try to make some sense out of them. Let's start with some of the perspectives:

- *High-performance culture is the ultimate source of competitive advantage and hence developing a high-performance culture should be given the highest priority*
- *High-performance culture is just a fad. It sounds good. But it is very difficult to bring it down to specifics and impossible to implement. It is just something that has been invented in retrospect to explain the success of some high-performing groups*
- *Culture is a characteristic of a group whereas high-performance is an outcome that depends on multiple factors. So it is misleading to speak about high-performance work cultures. One should instead speak about high-performance work systems*
- *There is no one culture that leads to high-performance*
- *There are cultural traits leading to high-performance that hold good across organizations*
- *We can define a target high-performance culture and create it in a short period of time*
- *Culture is something that evolves over a period of time and deepest levels of culture consist of unconscious assumptions. It is not something that be 'copied and pasted' on a group*

To make sense out of this we need to clarify what is 'culture' and what is 'high-performance'. While there are multiple perspectives here also, let us use the following as working definitions. A group is said to be high-performing when it consistently achieves its goals. Culture is the 'way we do things around here' – the recurring patterns of behavior in a group. If we put these two definitions together, we can define a 'high-performance culture' as those recurring patterns of behavior in a group that enables the group to consistently achieve its goals. So, the real question becomes 'is there really a set of such of behaviors that by itself lead to high performance of the group'?

If we have to understand the functioning of groups, we have to look at both its hardware and software. Hardware is the structure, policies, processes etc. Software is the people and the culture. Often, problems at the hardware level get conveniently misdiagnosed as software problems, because it is much easier to train people and to run culture-building sessions as compared to making significant changes in structure, policies and processes. So, if we have to have a high performing group, both the hardware and the software have to be good and also in sync with each other.

Most of the studies in the domain of high-performance cultures list a set of characteristics and factors associated with high-performance cultures. These characteristics and factors and their relative importance vary across the different studies, Yes, sometimes they do look like wish-lists and not like proven causal factors for high-performance cultures. Nevertheless, it is instructive to take a look at them.

Some of the popular characteristics listed are passion for excellence, shared understanding and buy-in to the organization purpose, vision and goals, outward focus, decisiveness, sense of urgency, speed and agility, sense of ownership and personal accountability on the part of all the employees, discipline, diversity and inclusion, innovation and risk taking, passion for learning and renewal etc. All these do seem reasonable. What is not proved is whether these characteristics are causally linked to high-performance or if they are just correlated with some of the high-performance situations.

Now let us look at the factors that the studies on high-performance culture list as the ones responsible for high-performance. They include high performance standards and benchmarks, alignment of goals, high person-job fit, clarity of individual performance goals coupled with real-time feedback, review and coaching mechanisms, streamlined, and simplified processes and procedures, policies that enable and not hinder performance, flatter organization structures, realigned competency frameworks and incentive schemes to reinforce appropriate behaviors, high degree of performance based differentiation in rewards, role modeling by the leaders etc. Here again all these factors seem reasonable. But, they seem to be part of any good performance management system and not something unique to high-performance cultures.

May be, that exactly is the crux of the issue. If these factors corresponding to good performance management are coherently and consistently implemented, it will lead to high-performance. That is, when these gets consistently done and get role modeled by the leaders, it becomes 'the way things get done' and that is exactly the definition of culture that we have been using! When these are also structurally reinforced by appropriate structures, processes and policies they become sustainable. This helps us to realize the true power and importance of performance management. The performance management system, when properly designed and implemented, can be the most effective culture building tool instead of being a collection of annoying forms and formats!

Yes, spelling out what exactly is high performance and what exactly is the target culture required in their particular context would be helpful for a group to work towards high performance. High-performance need not necessarily be relative. It is with respect to whatever goals a group sets for itself though the group might refer to external performance benchmarks before arriving at the its goals. Similarly, there is no one right blueprint for culture as the culture that will lead to high-performance for a group will depend on the group's strategy, context and stage of evolution.

The most important thing here is to go beyond broad statements of intent and empty platitudes. To make things we work, we have to identify the few most important cultural characteristics that needs to be changed and reinforced. We also need to keep in mind the interrelationships, structural reinforcements and alignments. We must ensure that the new cultural characteristics that we are trying to build is in alignment with the core values of the organization. Another important enabler is to remove impediments to high performance like 'passive resistance'. All these, when done consistently, becomes the way of life and hence fit to be called 'culture'!

So where does this leave us? Yes, groups vary in terms of performance levels and some of that variations in performance can be attributed to differences in the patterns of behavior (culture) in the group. Since these groups function in different contexts and with different goals, we can't identify a single blueprint for high-performance culture that will be valid across groups though there could be some common characteristics and factors. Yes, in any group we can examine the hardware and software of the group to see if they are optimized and aligned for the achievement of the goals that the group has set for itself. When we detect gaps in the same, steps can be taken to address the same. However, these will often require fundamental changes in the functioning of the group and that requires commitment and investment from the leaders for an extended period of time. We must remember that what often differentiates a high-performance culture is the intensity and rigor of the *implementation and not content of the culture! Unless the group is fully committed to the change, in both letter and spirit, the changes can't be implemented and sustained. After all, culture becomes real only when it is experienced! concludes, Prasad Kurian.*

Chapter 10

Digital Building Blocks

And now we commence our conclusions on culture, leadership disrupted, organization and management models. ***Digital Linkages in Culture*** - *Effectively organizations by themselves or for that matter culture and leadership in isolation cannot manage without effective integration. They strongly need inter connections and linkages to gain a meaningful appreciation of an organization, particularly its culture. in our opinion it is very desirable to understand these linkages to help understand each of the three aspects of this study, namely, Leadership, Culture and Organization and Management Model in its totality and that studying one without a relevance to the other two would perhaps be a little myopic, although this statement would over time need empirical validation in all fairness.*

A. *Digital Vision & Values*
B. *Digital Strategy, Governance & Risk*
C. *Digital Demystified*
D. *Digital Social Networks*
E. *Digital Processes*
F. *Digital Leadership disrupted & Teams*
G. *Digital People Processes*
H. *Digital Data is Evidential*
I. *Digital Disruptions*

"Momentum can become dysfunctional for many reasons. In the first half of a transformation, no organization has the momentum, power, or time to get rid of all obstacles. But the big ones must be confronted and removed. If the blocker is a person, it is important that he or she be treated fairly and in a way that is consistent with the new vision. But action is essential, both to empower others and to maintain the credibility of the change effort as a whole. For example, Action orientation to start with. Our culture values action and decisiveness; we get rewarded for making progress and getting things done, especially in hypercompetitive business environments". In SMR 2009, Michelle A. Barton and Kathleen M. Sutcliffe in Learning When to Stop Momentum, write, "but when people are under pressure to perform and produce, the last thing they want is someone pointing out irksome problems that imply things may be going awry. (Culture is best influenced in a staff – talent management context, when enterprises focus on implementation of an HCM – talent Management system. Workforce Management, Performance Management and Learning continue to be the growth foundation for Talent Management Solutions accounting for more than 75% of the market – These are the focus modules of Talent Management Solution. North America (US and Canada) continues to demonstrate market adoption of SaaS HR solutions in line with global average. " Talent Management (SaaS + On premise) market stands at \$3.5Bn in 2015 to grow to \$4.5 Bn in 2018" IDC). Moreover, managers may feel that they don't have the time to stop, reconsider, re-evaluate and slow things down — that they just can't afford to waffle. When Carly Fiorina came to power at Hewlett-Packard Co., she was thought by some to be just the kind of decisive and forceful leader HP needed; the bursting technology bubble and rising competitive threats at the time seemed to be a call to action. Yet her merger with Compaq Computer Corp., among other things, eventually led to her downfall and her portrayal as a leader too focused on action and not enough on evaluation. or inflexible planning as another momentum challenge. But she rose again to fight for Republican nomination while standing tall to protect American values. The implementation of strategy, plans and is critical to organizational success, as important as the plan itself and is one of the key ways in which managers display competence, a sense of purpose and a strong set of home grown values. But planning often locks business organizations into courses of action because the repercussions of going off-plan are so serious. We evaluate people, processes and outcomes against plans rather than re-evaluate the plans themselves. When situations are complex and volatile, however, any course of action is likely to require adjustments; organizations that make a plan and stick with it, even in the face of shifting requirements, will eventually find themselves in crisis".

Samuel Tilden said "It is said that it is far more difficult to hold and maintain leadership (liberty) than it is to attain it. Success is a ruthless competitor for it flatters and nourishes our weaknesses and lulls us into complacency. We bask in the sunshine of accomplishment and lose the spirit of humility which helps us visualize all the factors which have contributed to our success. We are apt to forget that we are only one of a team, that in unity there is strength and that we are strong only as long as each unit in our organization functions with precision".

George Mathew Adams (Goodman 1997) said of organizations as the only institutions that lasts a long time, do good and useful work, and are profitable, are those that are, and have been well organized. You get to feel of this immediately, when you visit such a place.

Digital Linkages in Culture - *Effectively organizations by themselves or for that matter culture and leadership in isolation cannot manage without effective integration. They strongly need inter connections and linkages to gain a meaningful appreciation of an organization, particularly its culture. in our opinion it is very desirable to understand these linkages to help understand each of the three aspects of this study, namely, Leadership, Culture and Organization and Management Model in its totality and that studying one without a relevance to the other two would perhaps be a little myopic, although this statement would over time need empirical validation in all fairness.*

A. Digital Vision & Values

Digital Culture and Vision: Without a leader committed to learning, an organization will never approach its potential success. Such a leader must have a clear vision, deeply held and consistently communicated. The new vision should energize those striving to turn it into reality, despite the skepticism of those who holds on to old visions, old habits and old ways of doing things. The vision should enable members of the organization to anticipate what they can contribute to help achieve important results. A clear vision also helps an organization focus on those things/ideas that are central to their goals. The best visions are usually direct and uncomplicated, like that of Boeing's newest project, the 777 long-range twin-jet. One vision is "working together to produce the preferred new airplane family." The leader also needs to fire his team with the spirit of "what more we can do." For this the leader needs insights, strength and perseverance. Builder initiatives present special challenges to culture change projects. Individual initiative is sometimes viewed as competing with culture change. The most effective building programs engage people in developing their own individual initiative while finding or building supportive environments. The organization believes in creating effective structures and hierarchies that provides clarity to roles, responsibilities, tasks and actions. The knowledge emphasis in the institution is driven by systems that override individual initiative as long as the institutional norms are met. The atmosphere and interpersonal relations in the work group are friendly and co-operative. The members of the work group encourage one another's best efforts, reinforcing successful behavior. The work group organizes and problem-solves effectively. The members of the group maintain adequate standards of performance. The group communicates well within and outside our work unit. The members provide group input and may participate in the management process as appropriate. Developing trust among organizational members is at once difficult and essential to becoming High Performance Cultures. Members need to be taught from the start that building trust within the team is critically important to the team's ultimate success. As the culture forms, it is normal that the level of trust is low. Several members or all team members may have worked together before. Or they may know each other by casual acquaintance of interaction. But trust has something to do with loyalties, and at the outset the team will not have developed team loyalty. Rather, each team member's loyalties will be to his or her own organization or manager.

Digital Culture Value Alignment - People are well aware of the organization goals, objectives and the strategic direction/mission of the business. The company standards of performance, productivity and growth are higher than those of similar organizations. The organization rewards correctly that who/ what should be rewarded only. Today given the realities of global work force it is critical to structure organizations which can offer combination of high pay and high value at work. The group makes effective use of available equipment and resources. The members generally demonstrate pride in themselves and their work. The group actively seeks to utilize the skills and abilities of its members. The members do not feel constrained by rules, regulations and unnecessary bottlenecks in accomplishing their work. The group is excited about its work activities. The group has a record of consistent accomplishment.

B. Digital Strategy, Governance & Risk

Digital Business Inevitability – GE Take - Real transformation takes time, and a renewal effort risks losing momentum if there are no short-term goals to meet and celebrate. Most people won't go on the long march unless they see compelling evidence within 12 to 24 months that the journey is producing expected results. Without short-term wins, too many people give up or actively join the ranks of those people who have been resisting change. Jeffrey R. Immelt has been the chairman and

CEO of General Electric since 2001 and explains why industrial companies are now in the information business—whether they like it or not. Rik Kirkland is the senior managing editor of McKinsey Publishing and is based in McKinsey's New York office. On Changing company culture, "When you think about internal change—culture, people, leadership development—again, here's a time where multiple things happened at the same time. We started our digital initiative maybe five or six years ago. We've also, as a company—and I don't think GE's unique—lived through the financial crisis. And we're an old company. We live in highly regulated industries. What we found was our culture was too complicated to get the work done the way we needed to get our work done, both in terms of how we were trying to digitize and how we were trying to survive in terms of a more highly regulated world. And just think about our footprint and the complexity of running a global operation: even since I was CEO, GE has gone from 70 percent inside the United States to 70 percent outside the United States".

Digital HR focuses on Strategic Priorities - Even when management provides simple instructions such as a desire to reduce cost, many questions remain cost reductions at the expense of sales? Reduce our own costs, but push costs off on some other organization or a supplier? Or the customer? Larger objectives quickly come into play, and the team is going to also have to be given the strategic objectives of the organization so it can detail out whether what is trying to do will contribute to the organizations strategy. A leadership disrupted and management that pays attention to high performance lead the organization. Unfortunately, the organization's strategy may be only in one person's head, or it seems to change with the wind, or is not followed at all by anyone in the organization. When an organization discovers that it doesn't understand the organization's strategy, it must stop progress and get briefed by someone who does understand it. In the sad event that there is no clear organizational strategy, the team will have to presume a strategy and run it past the sponsoring manager for confirmation. Once the strategy is set or understood by the team members, work can proceed on refining performance measures. High Performance cultures is chartered to improve performance in some way. Performance is associated with speed, quality, cost, and effectiveness. Finding good measures on these variables is not always easy.

Digital HR helps Strategic Focus - "Hire, Rally, Live are the principles followed by Slack Technologies, say Gerald C Kane, Doug Palmer, Anh Nguyen Phillips, David Kiron, Natasha Buckley et all, in MIT SMR 2016 in Aligning the Organization For Its Digital Future, "When it comes to building a culture for a digital environment, Slack Technologies Inc., the messaging software platform based in San Francisco, doubles down on the effort to make sure it can keep pace. In a fast-moving environment, company culture is what Slack's chief marketing officer Bill Macaitis says keeps him up at night. To fortify the company's culture, Macaitis relies on three principles:

- *Hire for it: Slack's hiring process screens for all its core values. "When we hire people, we look at how empathic and courteous they are, along with evidence of their craftsmanship," he says. "When we make an offer, we are confident that the candidate aligns with our values."*
- *Rally around it: Slack reinforces the culture of empathy by embracing an "everyone does support" ethos. Designers, developers, and product managers work alongside customer support agents to answer support tickets. This helps build empathy as the people building the product hear firsthand about the problems existing customers have.*
- *Live it: "We've written our values on the walls," says Macaitis. "But as the old saying goes, it's not just what you write, it's what you do. You have to lead by example and provide ample training. That is what we are trying to do."*

"Culture eats strategy for breakfast." For an organization, revitalization involves creating and managing its purpose, identity, values, beliefs and core mission and culture with renewed vigor and vitality. Reinventing the culture that performs is revitalization. In its consistency lies renewal. Renewal would necessitate understanding the people interaction processes, the shared meanings, beliefs, language, customs, traditions and rituals of the corporation. It would seek to redefine the pattern of shared assumptions that the group has learned as it solved its problems. It would prescribe the ways new members would join in and assimilate themselves into the work environment and learn the correct way to think, perceive and feel in relation to others and the problems. But he (Drucker) certainly recognized the influential role that culture plays in corporate success and failure. The problem is that nobody really knows how to measure culture's effects, let alone what levers to pull and how hard to pull them to get a great one". In, SMR 2016 issues, "Using Predictive Analytics to Enhance Your Company Culture" Theodore Kinni, writes, simulate your organizational culture: I don't think Peter Drucker ever actually said that! "Enter predictive analytics and a company called Icosystem. "[Icosystem's] software simulates the complex workings of any given organization by mimicking the behaviors and interactions of individual employees, like a custom-built Sims universe, in order to predict how slight changes in one area, like a call operator's time on the phone, might impact another, like customer satisfaction," writes Stephanie Russell-Kraft in Motherboard. If you can simulate the effect a call operator's behavior has on customer satisfaction, why can't you measure the effect of, say, a better gender balance in your company? Icosystem CTO Paolo Gaudiano thinks you can. He tells Russell-Kraft that Icosystem is now developing software can be used to model changes to the organizational culture, simulating, for example "typically 'female' and 'male' attributes to see how putting women in leadership positions might help firms lower HR costs or boost sales." In new organizations the original founder often imposes his or her personal values and beliefs on the people that they hire and, if the organization thrives, these beliefs become seen as correct and adopted. If there is no strong leader at inception then the original group members bring in their existing values and try to impose them, with the values of those that are perceived as successful becoming accepted. We can begin to see that it is success that incubates cultural values and it is not possible to say whether any particular type of culture is 'right'. It is only 'right' if it helps the organization succeed in its primary task and only 'wrong' if it hinders. Add software to your value proposition: Vijay Gurbaxani, director of the Center for Digital Transformation at UC Irvine's Paul Merage School of Business, says that no matter what business you're in these days, you're in the software business. "That doesn't mean that you should stop delivering your current products or services. And it certainly doesn't mean that you should suddenly start selling something labeled 'software,'" he writes in Harvard Business Review. "Rather, this approach recognizes a fundamental shift in the sources of value creation and competitive advantage toward software." That means incorporating software into your company's strategic thinking by asking how it can contribute to competitive differentiation, help surmount barriers that keep customers from realizing value, and bolster your value proposition. Look to Disney World, says the business professor. Its $1 billion investment in the RFID-enabled Magic Band created a better, more seamless customer experience and provided the data needed to better manage its parks — enabling the company to "accommodate an additional 5,000 daily visitors."

"**Technology Skills – Appreciation of Digital Trends** are only one of many categories of leadership skills rated as most important by respondents. Managerial skills like understanding the market and/or having a sound strategy are most valued for enabling success in a digital workplace" See image below: (Refer - *Leadership Competencies in a Digital Age)...*

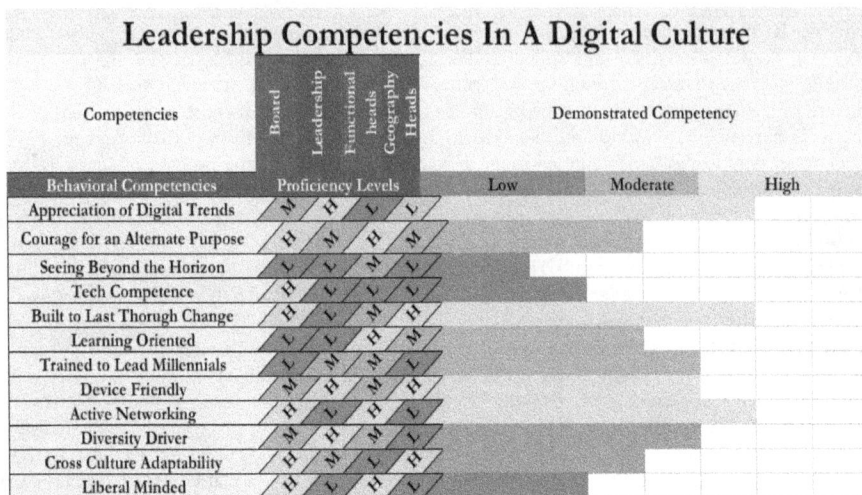

Leadership Competencies In A Digital Culture

Competencies	Board	Leadership	Functional heads	Geography Heads	Demonstrated Competency		
Behavioral Competencies	Proficiency Levels				Low	Moderate	High
Appreciation of Digital Trends	M	H	L	L			
Courage for an Alternate Purpose	H	M	H	M			
Seeing Beyond the Horizon	L	L	M	L			
Tech Competence	H	L	L	L			
Built to Last Thorugh Change	H	L	M	H			
Learning Oriented	L	L	H	M			
Trained to Lead Millennials	L	M	M	L			
Device Friendly	M	H	M	H			
Active Networking	H	L	H	L			
Diversity Driver	M	H	M	L			
Cross Culture Adaptability	H	M	L	H			
Liberal Minded	H	L	H	L			

Figure 45 – Leadership disrupted Competencies in a Digital Age

Digital Culture Nurtures Governance - Under our old system of governance, one could lead by mandate. If you had the ability to climb the ladder, gain power, and then control that power, you could enforce these changes in attributes. But the forthcoming kind of company is going to require voluntary follower ship. Most of our leaders don't think in terms of getting voluntary followers; they think in terms of control. Generally, everyone here is mainly concerned about one's own affairs. People do not have time to think of future needs; they are too busy completing their assigned tasks and making revenues. People here are more individualistic; they complete assigned tasks for which they expect to be compensated. Pleasant behavior is preferred here to telling an unpleasant truth. People here are treated according to their working assignments and not on the basis of kinship, cast, language, etc." Governance should play the role of managing the quality of collective thinking and knowledge of the corporation. Their role is to help maximize the organization's intelligence, ownership to contribution and identity with content changes. Such a culture now moves into the role of nurturing inquiry, reflection, dialog, sensitivity, and knowledge enhancement in their training and development work. Here training – learning - engagement is not a confined to policy papers, trite communication or traditional class room activity. It is essentially an experience and these experiences make learning happen. Yet another factor is the true sharing of knowledge, expertise and invention. Pfizer has created competence models for recruiting treasury executives. This goes beyond access to data and re circulating hoarded data from control managers. "Work responsibility here is given more importance than demands of the family. Driven by a performance system that overrides all other considerations and makes individual targets an important element achieving results. Nurturing and helping subordinates is encouraged here. This executive worldview is built around the necessity to maintain the financial health of the organization and is fed by the pre-occupations of boards, of investors, and of the capital markets. Whatever other pre-occupations executives may have, they cannot get away from having to worry about and manage the financial issues of the survival and growth of their organization Achievement and competence is not always more important than hierarchical status. Christine Bader (SMR 2014) writes, "Hold users accountable" she says. "Microsoft suspends the accounts of XBox Live Users for violating their Code of Conduct". The benefits of a robust internal controls program are evident. With these controls in place, transformations can:

- **Reduce** the potential for fraud, misdemeanor and inconsistencies around financial – shareholder – market reporting
- **Comply** with applicable laws and regulations, including those relating to corporate governance, internal controls, risk management and privacy, among many others
- **Reduce** the risk of asset or resource losses
- **Optimize – Obtain Feedback** on business decisions with higher quality, more timely information
- **Improve** operating inefficiencies, tech enable
- **Instil** trust in the system, benchmark for best practices and the standardized processes it enables, eliminating unnecessary workarounds (i.e. reduce the proliferation of 'spreadsheet processing').

"Google should make it clear that they do not condone unsafe behavior with Glass and will participate in users' prosecution when they've violated the law. Companies must manage the social risks that they cause or contribute to, no matter where they occur and at whose hands". These are governance driven actions that establishes an ethical framework for all stakeholders. "As they develop technology that aims to transform how we live; it is even more critical that they acknowledge this responsibility".

Digital Culture has to manage commercial Risk - Change methodology enables the organization to be ready and able to work with a new or changed set of processes enabled by new technology and business processes, thereby realizing the benefits of the transformation. The approach helps the impacted organization to clearly understand the need for change and the outcomes of the change, and ultimately ensures that the organization possesses the capabilities and motivation to make and sustain the change. Additionally, there is a large focus on transferring knowledge to the organization, as well as developing methods and content for ongoing support of job performance. The activities in this thread can help accelerate stakeholder adoption of the changes and reduce the performance dip typically seen on large-scale business transformations of the size and complexity to drive management of commercial risk. "Today, the costs of inaction almost always exceed the costs of action." Making a culture less risk averse is by no means an insurmountable task. To boost risk taking in their companies, executives need to change their mindsets. Dr. John Halamka, chief information officer of the Boston health care provider Beth Israel Deaconess Medical Center, says that leaders must acknowledge failure as a prerequisite for success. "Failure is a valid outcome," he says. "Wearable computing is great, but Google Glass wearable computing devices turned out not to be for us right now. We may discover that patients love the Apple Watch wrist-wearable device and it becomes a platform. It's hard to know. But even if it doesn't, it's OK." In the research paper, "Strategy, not technology drives digital transformation", Gerald C Kane, Doug Palmer, et all, in MIT SMR 2015, write, "Phil Simon, author of several books on how technology impacts business, sees risk aversion as a serious impediment that plagues many established companies. "For every Google, Amazon or Facebook taking major risks, hundreds of large companies are still playing it safe," he says. "Cisco CEO John Chambers echoes the sentiment. "We began working on the Internet of everything more than seven years ago," he comments. "The market wasn't ready for it. In that instance, we had the courage to keep going without overinvesting to the point where we were betting the company on it." But it would be a mistake to suggest that only the mindset of leaders drives aversion to risk. Employees may fear taking risks as much as their managers do. Encouraging employees to be bolder is especially important in digital business transformations. To draw employees into the fold, businesses may have to take deliberate actions".

Digital Culture Emphasizes Risks & Responsibilities - The organization emphasizes co-operation and co-ordination on a regular basis, the organization demonstrates commitment to providing high quality service to its clients/customers. The work environment is highly motivating. The work climate encourages us to do our best and to perform as well as we can. The organization treats all employees equally and fairly. Generally, employees here are warm and friendly. Employees have a lot of freedom to do their work, to plan and set their work pace, style and methods. Employees trust top management. There is frank and open discussion with top management, providing authentic feedback. Employees usually are open and authentic in their work relations among each other. If there is a conflict or disagreement with top management, it is usually worked out directly. The organization is more concerned about the needs of its people over simply getting the task done. The organization places a lot of faith and relies on the individual sense of responsibility. The leader believes in competing in challenging environments by preparing the organization in advance, sets meaningful goals and targets and competes to conquer.

C. Digital Demystified

Digital Simplification - Effective management of simplification, buy in from middle management and support from leaders across operating units will work towards a successful roll out of new technology and processes. Simplification to increase visibility into operations (at the article level and overall volume) will enable operational planning for all the facilities through planning tools. This will help improve employee productivity through better manpower planning. The advent of internet, mobiles and alternative means of communication has led to a serious set of challenges for the "So what we've tried to do inside the company is really just drive what we call a "culture of simplification": fewer layers, fewer processes, fewer decision points, says Immelt. We've adapted the lean tools in what I would call a Silicon Valley approach, what we call "Fast Works." We've embraced some of the Silicon Valley tools in terms of putting everything on the clock, bringing commercial intensity into the company. The way I describe that is, like biggest companies, we're willing to take all kinds of market risk so that we don't have to take internal risk, right? We try to say, "Look, let's actually be aggressive in the markets, and let's count on our own execution to risk reduce inside the company." And broadly, getting to digitization, we're democratizing information inside the company; getting IT tools that were contemporary in a mobile setting, and we call these things the culture of simplification". Simplification includes a high-level mapping of the business's future architecture, the Target Operating Model (TOM) represents the future state of the business, based on an evolution across the enterprise and in vital areas including technology and operations. Integrated design tools are used to manage the complexity of large organizations from architecture through to detailed design and requirements management. Multiple iterations are necessary to develop an optimal TOM. This step addresses the creation of the initial TOM, which is updated and refined as part of detailed design activities. In the Interview with John D. Sterman - Professor of Management Science Director, System Dynamics Group Massachusetts Institute of Technology, "Jay Forrester frequently likens this problem to solving in your head a hundredth-order nonlinear differential equation system, but, frankly, that's an underestimate, because a hundredth-order system would actually be quite a considerable simplification from the real-life systems people have to deal with. Evolution did not equip us with the capability to simulate intuitively the type of complex, dynamic systems we have created for ourselves. The result is an interesting dilemma. The better job you do with the conceptual modeling tools the better your mental map of how a system works, the less able you are to use that map to make reliable inferences about the consequences of new policies or new structures you may want to put into place. The solution is to test the models, to test your hypotheses about the consequences of new policies. In most of the social systems we are concerned with, experiments in the real world are, prohibitively costly, unethical, or simply impossible. Simulation then becomes the only means to determine the consequences of policies you might want to try".

Complexity Drives Digital Simplicity - Martin Mocker, Peter Weill and Stephanie L. Woerner in MIT SMR 2014, "Revisiting Complexity in the Digital Age" write, "With a clear vision and a simple set of metrics identified, we suggest companies seeking their complexity sweet spot consider the following steps: **Assess your company's current complexity position.**

"The first step, the authors state, "is to determine where your company is now on product complexity and process simplification. The best place to start is by assessing your customers' needs against your product and service offerings. Are your key customers satisfied with your level of product variety and linking? To find the answer, we suggest asking three questions:

- *Do your best customers buy from companies similar to yours? Why?*
- *Is your customer satisfaction rating (such as a Net Promoter Score or similar measure) lower than those of competitors that offer more product variety and linking?*
- *Is there work your customers do that you could do for them? For example, the USAA service to purchase a car includes negotiating with the car dealer for the best price".*

Digital Acceleration - "Companies such as Amazon, Facebook, and Google actively control the tempo of their IT infrastructure and have aligned their technology and production systems with their business goals. They think differently about how they are organized at all levels. They limit the size of their application-development teams. They encourage product managers to think about digital experiences rather than discrete applications or components—a product manager may be accountable for the entire checkout process, for instance, rather than for the payment application alone. These companies engage in frequent testing and experimentation. They pursue hyper-targeted marketing strategies. "If your organization is geographically dispersed, you may have created something that looks like a headquarters with "field" digital locations that accelerates. Activities needed by everyone are located in headquarters. In this way scale is achieved, duplication is avoided, and a broad enterprise wide view is maintained. However, you can anticipate conflicts that are likely to arise when these centralized activities are perceived as too far removed from the realities and concerns of the operating units. HR is frequently configured in this way. HR generalists are aligned with the specific sites or businesses. Specialized functions such as compensation, benefits, and training are located in the headquarters. Predictable tension occurs regarding who works for whom. Are the generalists there to roll out programs from headquarters, or are the specialized staffs in place to support the generalists? In addition, field units generally feel that the services and products provided by headquarters aren't customized enough for them. As a result, they begin to re-create the activities in their local organization. The next step is often a move to decentralize to divide up an activity and give autonomy back to the local organization. This swing of the pendulum toward decentralization, while moving decision making closer to the customer, results in duplication that centralization and shared services are intended to avoid. An alternative to consider is a distributed structure. Distribution gives a whole activity to a local unit to serve its own needs as well as other units. Responsibility is placed where the competence is located. The function or service is centralized but not necessarily in a headquarters or corporate location. Large consulting firms are typically organized in this way. The center of power and knowledge for a practice is located close to customers, rather than centralized in a headquarters. The financial practice may be in New York, automotive in Detroit, entertainment in Los Angeles, and energy in Dallas. The distributed structure is less hierarchical than the traditional headquarters model. Local units gain enterprise wide responsibility that ties them more closely to the overall direction of the organization. When different units each have responsibilities, mutual interest is created to ensure that local interests don't supersede broader needs. One unit may provide training, another may provide project management services, and a third may provide application development. Each then has an interest in providing excellent service to the other units. The distributed organization relies on a set of senior players who can work well together peer to peer". They collect and learn from consumer data. And they are not afraid to fail. Traditional companies are challenged to achieve similar levels of alignment and internal accountability. They typically rely on legacy enterprise resource planning and other transaction-oriented IT systems for security and reliability. Major changes to these systems can often take months of development and testing". Oliver Bossert, Martin Harrysson, and Roger Roberts, in McKinsey Quarterly 2015, "Organizing for digital acceleration: Making a two-speed IT operating model work", writes further, "At the outset, many brick-and-mortar companies will probably lack the tools, governance models, and skill sets required to pursue the same agile approaches and test-and-learn strategies their digital competitors are using. How can traditional consumer-facing organizations get up to speed? The first step, which addresses the need for alignment, is adopting a two-speed IT architecture—one that decouples the management of customer-centric front-end systems and applications from the management of existing transaction-oriented back-end systems. The second step, which addresses the need for accountability, is adopting the same focus on digital product management that digital companies demonstrate—that is, empowering managers to incorporate users' feedback into product-development efforts actively and systematically and holding managers accountable for results. Traditional companies therefore need to emulate online companies' best practices in governance and talent development".

D. *Digital Social Networks*

Digital Culture Social Media Influences Behavior - "When social media tools provide the ability to find the content we most want to read; we are most likely to search out content that confirms our existing views. Algorithmic search tools like Facebook's newsfeed exacerbates this tendency by automatically recognizing which content we have sought out in the past and then showing users other content that is most like that which we have previously viewed". Gerald C. Kane in MIT SMR 2016 Social Blogging, "What Companies Should Learn About Social Media from American Politics" writes further, "We no longer need to seek out the content that confirms our own views — Facebook finds it for us. As a result, we rarely engage with content that represents viewpoints different from our own. The same characteristic also extends to those with whom we connect using social media tools".

Digital Culture Social is Beyond Internet – An organisation which has the capability to adapt to changes in its external environment, continually enhance its capability to change/adapt and innovate, develop collective as well as individual learning and use the results of learning to achieve better results. A Socio learning organisation is one that learns and encourages learning among its people. It promotes exchange of information between employees hence creating a more knowledgeable workforce. Hence, this produces a very flexible organisation where people will accept and adapt to new ideas and changes through a shared vision. For example, Royal Dutch / Shell institutionalised and internalised the Scenario Planning process in all its businesses. This gave the company the collective ability to envision scenarios in every area of its operation, create strategies for coping with environmental scenarios such as oil shocks. "The Internet provides a nearly limitless ability to connect with almost anyone online, and research has long shown that the types of "weak ties" we establish on these platforms can be very valuable for finding information, continues Kane on Influence of Social Media. On the other hand, we are also likely to use this unparalleled networking ability to connect mostly with people who are most like ourselves, which compounds the effects of content filtering. Social media allows us to connect only with people who are most like us and only listen when we like what they say, resulting in merely the illusion of broad and diverse weak-tie networks for information sharing on social media platforms. This tendency for social media to support our existing views and preferences is no accident. It is what users want. People want to spend time in environments where they are supported and liked. The more we are supported and liked, the more time we spend on social media sites, and the more content we share through it. It is this innate preference upon which the business model of social media is built. The more time we spend on social media, the more advertisements they can show us, and the more data they can collect to more effectively tailor the environment to our established preferences. Social media succeeds by creating a comfortable environment that continually reassures us that most people are like us, that our own views are the "right" ones, and that they are shared by a greater number of people than they actually are".

Digital Culture Manages Social Risks – Management of Social Risks in a digital transformation context necessitates the following; Need to gear up for Greater Scale of Operations to make the transition efficient and smooth. Need to deal with more diverse set of customers, some of whom may ask for digital solutions now and some may ask at a later date, while certain business models may choose to continue to do business as usual. There will be a need and requirement of Behavioural Change. Probable linking of Customer Satisfaction / Complaints to Performance, to imbibe new knowledge, i.e., conceptual, operational processes etc. while planning for redundancy of some of existing activities. Additional elements would include a need to acquire system skills, need for re-skilling, re-deployment of employees in some cases. A California woman charged with distracted driving last fall for wearing Google Glass behind the wheel was acquitted because police couldn't prove the device was on; even so, a spokesman for the American Automobile Association noted, "Just looking at this and using common sense, it would seem to be something someone should not be doing while they're behind the wheel." Individuals must drive safely. But does Google also bear responsibility for potential harm caused by Glass users? Google's design, manufacture, and distribution of Glass clearly constitute Google's "own activities"; therefore, if Glass distracts drivers and thereby causes traffic accidents, Google has a responsibility to address this issue". As indicated above, impact on employees is an inevitable reality of any change in extant business objectives. Hence, to ensure successful achievement of business objectives, not only does one need to identify those organization aspects which can adversely impact the transformation process, these aspects should be treated such that those business aspects, which have triggered the transformation process, get addressed. This way, the organization can ensure that addressing of Change imperatives do not run the risk of become distinct from achievement of business objectives, but act as catalyst to the entire transformation process. "Do companies bear responsibility for the social risks of how consumers or buyers use their products? ask further, Christine Bader in MIT SMR 2014, "The Risks and Responsibilities of Tech Innovation". "Companies clearly have a responsibility for working conditions in their supply chain. But what are companies' responsibilities in the "demand chain"? This question has been less explored, but is no less important, particularly in light of one of the most talked-about tech products now hitting the market: Google Glass. Google Glass is prompting concern among lawmakers and advocates for safe driving, worried about what drivers will do with the Internet at their eyeballs".

Digital Culture Analytics - Documenting and understanding stakeholder perspectives and requirements as well as key performance indicators is instrumental to executing an effective business transformation. Robust stakeholder management guidance and benchmarks comparing performance metrics against similar sector organizations offer critical support to these activities. The ability to rapidly and objectively assess an organization's current-state activities against known and/or applicable benchmarks, supported by comprehensive comparator data to maximize opportunities, is critical to an effectiveness business transformation. "In last year's social business report, we found that socially mature organizations integrate social data into decisions and operations. Twitter is meeting a similar need by expanding its scope from being just a social media platform to being a social and mobile analytics provider. In 2014, Twitter acquired the social data aggregator GNIP as part of Twitter's strategy to create a new service offering that integrates social and mobile data with analytics to provide real-time business intelligence. Data is also changing the delivery of health care. "We can identify pathogens and chronic diseases quickly with rapid, low-cost diagnostic tools," says John Brownstein, an associate professor at Harvard Medical School". "Organizational cultures must be primed to embrace analytics and the use of data in decision making and processes. These must include activities in support of overall value management also include the set-up of a **management monitoring dashboard**, providing client leadership with a snapshot of **how people are responding to the change**, at a given point in time, and enabling them to attain a sense of the current success and impact of change, on chosen people-related dimensions (using people related KPIs). This information should feed into ongoing value management activities and program reporting, e.g., data of the management monitoring dashboard can be used to initiate, adjust or review project functional streams and related change management activities. Says, Kane, Palmer Et all, "Strategy, not technology drives digital transformation", in MIT SMR 2015, he continues to write, "These tools can be connected directly to individuals and create an aggregated view of the population's health." As Harvard chief digital officer Hewitt points out: "We are at the cusp of really interesting and valuable predictive analytics for the enterprise. Many organizations will have to change their cultural mindsets to increase collaboration and encourage risk taking. Business leaders should also address whether different digital technologies or approaches can help bring about that change. They must also understand what aspects of the current culture could spur greater digital transformation progress. Although leaders don't need to be technology wizards, they must understand what can be accomplished at the intersection of business and technology. They should also be prepared to lead the way in conceptualizing how technology can transform the business."

Digital Networks and Games - "It's safe to say that when one out of every two working-age adults in the United States has registered for a certain website—LinkedIn, for example, boasts more than 122 million US members—it has achieved critical mass. In fact, LinkedIn and sites like Careerbuilder and Monster.com have changed the way employers and employees connect, and digital marketplaces such as Freelancer.com, Toptal, and Upwork have transformed the sourcing of contractors' services around the world. Digital labor platforms have also created a more transparent job market". Establishing an approach to documenting and tracking the realization of value derived from a platforms are key steps in completing an organization's roadmap and are the means of tracking the realization of benefits documented as part of the transformation business case. High-level benefits may include: Alignment of the activities with the overall business strategy and objectives; Optimal balance of efficiency, effectiveness, and controls; An informed and empowered leadership disrupted team; Rational allocation of resources and capability development and Objective understanding and measurement of current and targeted performance. "Top performers know their value and are growing more footloose as a result; many are going online to find new opportunities and to evaluate potential employers. What's more, a lot of people now scour platforms such as Glassdoor to learn what current employees have to say about their job satisfaction, company culture, and lifestyle. Companies that don't manage their workplace reputations carefully or engage their employees appropriately will find themselves on the losing side of an increasingly digital war for talent". Susan Lund, James Manyika, Kelsey Robinson from McKinsey Consulting and McKinsey Global Institute, McKinsey Quarterly - March 2016, continue on their research, "A new wave of digital tools can help companies to focus not only on hiring but also on managing, retaining, and developing employees. Digital labor platforms can pull these tools into an integrated whole as companies widen their labor pools, refine their recruiting and screening methods, and deploy their employees more effectively. Such tools, and the platforms that include them, can put the right person in the right job, identify gaps in skills, help employees as they gain new capabilities, chart career paths, and nurture the development of the next generation of leaders. "One way to move the design work forward and begin planning for implementation is to create a governance structure. A governance structure is a set of roles and processes used to ensure that plans progress, activities are coordinated, and the change process is not overwhelmed by current business demands. It acts as a planning group for the organization that provides both consistency during the transition process and models the new behaviors (teamwork, cross-functional cooperation, etc.) that demonstrate visible and tangible evidence of the commitment to change. It is used to gain ownership, participation, and involvement across the organization. The governance structure combats the inertia that is likely to set in after the initial enthusiasm of the design off-site and of the whole creative process of the design stage wears off. As much as the intensity and excitement of an off-site can focus and accelerate change, there is a danger that as soon as people return to their jobs, the momentum is lost. Follow-up plans get pushed to the side while everyone catches up on the work he or she missed and deals with immediate business needs. The hard labor of working through the details is given low priority. The positive experiences of working together across organizational lines gives way to old patterns of behavior. The governance structure comprises a parallel set of roles outside of the current hierarchy that is responsible for the day-to-day business. This parallel structure brings together a subset of people in the organization to take ownership of the design process and push the work forward. Involvement in the process is usually in addition to job duties, although you may want to excuse some people from some of their job responsibilities or provide them with extra support so that participation doesn't become perceived as punishment". Digital tools can also help companies recruit candidates who are not actively job hunting. For instance, they can search GitHub, which hosts the largest repository of open-source code on the Internet, for examples of excellent coding and then contact its authors for recruiting purposes. TopCoder conducts regular online competitions that allow users, even those without formal training or experience, to showcase their technical skills to the companies that post challenges and award prize money. Codility, HackerRank, HireIQ, and TRUE Talent are additional examples of this emerging data-driven ecosystem, where the range of talent grows wider as subjective hiring biases fall. Online tests, games, and analytics also improve the recruiting process. Good&Co uses online psychometric tests to assess whether a potential employee would be a good fit with a company's culture and an effective match for a given job. And instituting a 30-minute online screening test comparing an applicant's profile with those of top performers helped one leading company to reduce attrition among new hires and to raise productivity by 3 to 4 percent".

Digital Testing - The penetration of sociological and anthropological conceptions into psychology and the growth of social psychology exposed psychologists to a whole range of new concepts and research methods. Although concepts like social role, status, social class, reference groups, culture, and social system were developed outside of traditional psychology, they have become increasingly important in psychological analysis. New research methods – such as surveys by large-scale questionnaire or interview, the use of participant observation, and field experiments – have stimulated psychologists to go beyond introspection and laboratory experiments. It is these concepts and these methods which made it possible to tackle organizational problems, and which have shifted the focus of analysis from the individual per se to the individual as a member of a group or to larger units like groups and organizations. The rapid and tremendous changes in technology and organization that have occurred within the last several decades have forced scientist and practitioner alike to recognize the interdependency of human and technological factors and the need to develop theories and concepts which can encompass such interdependencies. For example, we have seen the growth of man-machine systems within industry and military operations where it no longer makes scientific or practical sense to ask where the man leaves off and the computer or machine begins. Practitioners themselves have come to recognize the complex world in which they must operate and have been increasingly willing to have social scientists help with organizational problems. Thus, psychologists have become more involved in higher management decisions and have been brought into organizational positions from which they could more easily see the complexities of organizations.

Digital Skilling (Using Psychometric Testing) - A corollary trend has been the increasing Professionalization of management, with the result that mangers are now technically more qualified than they were and, by the same token, more prepared to accept help from other professions. Thus, managers have become not only more aware of their needs for help from psychologists, but have also become more willing to use this help. This development, in turn, has made organizations more accessible to researchers. Psychologists themselves have become more skilled in dealing with problems of complex systems. They have, therefore, been able to help organizations to a greater degree; in return organizations have supported the efforts of those psychologists willing to tackle the more nebulous and difficult systems problems. Out of this increased interaction have come better theory and new research techniques.

For example, Problems of recruiting, selecting, training, and allocating human resources; Problems deriving from the psychological contract between individuals and organizations, involving the nature of authority within the organization and the nature of influence which the individual can exert on the organization; Problems of integrating the various units of a complex organization, which means to extent the improvement of communication and relations among the various informal organizations which arise in the formal structure; and Problems stemming from the needs of the organization to survive, grow, and develop the capacity to adapt to and manage change in a rapidly changing world.

It can be argued that the selection and engineering approach rest on certain assumptions, including predictions, about people that are communicated to new employees of organizations through the practices of recruitment, selection, and job placement. Some of these assumptions deny certain emotional and social needs which an employee brings with him, leaving him in the situation of having to find satisfactions either in informal organizations or, if this is impossible, outside the organizations; the consequence is that he becomes either alienated from the organization or passively resistant to it. This is not to say that selection methods and industrial engineering should therefore be abolished and replaced by other methods that may be less efficient. One can says that organizations should recognize the consequences of their own approaches and practices, and decide whether to use them partly on the basis of their willingness to accept these consequences.

Digital Prediction (Using Psychometric Testing) commonly connotes a temporal estimate – for example, individual's future performance on a job being forecast from their present test performance. In a broader sense, however, even the *diagnosis* of present condition, such as mental retardation or emotional disorder, implies a prediction of what the individual will do in situations other than the present test. It is logically simpler to regard all tests as behavior samples from which predictions regarding other behavior can be made. Different types of tests can then be characterized as variants of this basic pattern.

E. *Digital Processes*

Digital Cultural Delivers Effectiveness - Effectiveness is very elusive and in the service industry. Quality may be difficult to define as well. To top all this off, most of us are blinded by the current set of performance measures we maintain. Most organizations count what can be easily counted, without regard to whether these counts define the organization's performance: Number of telephone calls answered, number of orders processed, number of thing made, or shipped, or serviced, are only the starting point for understanding performance. A fresh start on measurement may be needed. Getting a better handle on performance usually means starting with your customer's point of view about your performance. Finding out what is important to your customers and building a set of measures around these variables is usually much more effective than counting what can be easily counted. Sometimes discovering who your customers are is a challenge by itself. Governmental organizations usually correctly assume their customers are the taxpayers. But even this simple distinction blurs when you look at public school systems that have students, parents, teacher organizations, and state legislative mandates as well.

Digital Delivers Customer Delight - The CEO/leader's has a role in emphasizing on culture aspects pertaining to empowerment, delegation, individual contribution, accountability and responsibility. Great Leaders lead by example. They have the power to transform organizations and inculcate a culture that is fully supportive of the organizational strategy. For example, the Ritz Carlton has a culture of Service Orientation where each employee, even a cleaner (I am told), is empowered to commit an on the spot refund to a grieved customer. This can only be done if the organization, right from the top, leads by example and not only empowers each employee but actively supports him or her in the quest of this goal. CEO/leader's has a role in actively participating in attracting, retaining and rewarding star talent and performers. While the CEO has a role in this aspect, this is not an activity that a CEO in a large organization will himself spend too much time on. However, most organizations do claim that people are their best asset and to that extent work with HR to put in place compensation policies that not only attract but also retain their best performers. The Leader has a role in helping the organization retain an open mind to an unknown environment. The Leader is supposed to have the vision to look ahead, to constantly scan the environment, not only for blue skies but also for dark clouds. Great industries (like the Steel industry in the US) have perished simply because they failed to keep track of changes in the Business environment. In these times of rapid change, the one thing that will distinguish the dynamos from the dinosaurs is a forward-looking approach and nimble-footed responses.

Digital Managerial Discovery - As managers rise higher and higher in the hierarchy, as their level of responsibility and accountability grows, they not only have to become more pre-occupied with financial matters, but they also discover that it becomes harder and harder to observe and influence the basic work of the organization. Other managers who think like they do, thus making it not only possible but likely that their thought patterns and world view will increasingly diverge from the world view of the operators. The most straightforward approach is to trace the money flow. Someone is paying someone else money for something. The one who is paying is the customer. One caution is that in large corporations, this rule might not be true. Corporations sometimes pay for services at one place in the organization and receive the services at another. When this occurs the provider can quickly become confused about which place is the customer.

F. Digital Leadership disrupted & Teams

Digital Culture has a Leadership disrupted Orientation - The leader's orientation to retain competitive advantages by providing profitability through consistent intervals and prefers revenue to growth. Most members of this organization feel helpless in relation to vital matters as it is strictly driven from the top. People feel pressure to have and express opinions and ideas that are different from their partners. Bottom line paramount, financial focus primary objective, rigors of feedback high, low tolerance for failures, political climate, survival driven beyond values, inability to work in team's evident, non-negotiable goals. People are proud and happy to be acknowledged as a member of this organization when tasks have been accomplished. Problems are not smoothened out, not avoided but faced. Rules are applied uniformly here, without any consideration to special circumstances in special cases. In this organization every department/group is concerned only about itself. This organization can be described as fire-fighting organization, dealing with the issues as they emerge. Have known such a leader for over 18 years, who, as a senior partner at RSM to Arthur Andersen to today as the

CEO at KPMG LLP – Richard Rekhy made a difference. These 18 years, I have watched him up close. Playing roles such as a leader, follower, team member, client relationship manager, functional specialist, auditor, peer, risk and compliance head, a friend, a boss, now a CEO and so on. And in all of these roles I noticed just a simple pattern – courage to do, character, credibility, competence, compassion, commitment, care and concern. In every role, his purpose was clear – what can I contribute? People mattered to him. Just that; he will do anything for people to help them, no matter what may be the constraint, how unpopular may that make him. He was not into a popularity contest. In the history of KPMG, no other CEO has institutionalized so many radical, creative, path breaking and contemporary people best practices as Richard has managed to do so. Equally matched with high energy, volatility, and the determination – integrity to win and build an institution – an extra ordinary fire in the belly. For his direct reports working with him was just one minimal challenge – keeping pace with his energy and passion was completely another ball game. (How can I do all in one life when it is meant for two?) And prone to being values based, ethical, emotional, sensitive, loyal, passionate with a strong personality, his desire to rule with one's heart and lead with your team and mind to get things done as another, and go after what matters has been his core purpose of leadership style. Simply that! Every random interview (stratified across the chain) that I conducted while writing this book resonated with this view. and was so enlightening. I was quite amazed how across the pyramid an average KPMG staff member's understanding of Richard as a leader was as good as a discerning behavioral scientist. Simply shows how transparent, approachable Richard is and has been, a decent person to his people. Even his die hard detractors would grudgingly give him credit for pioneering KPMG successes and for leading from the front. A firm that has exponentially grown, has now become the envy of the Big 4, not to forget now becoming a convenient target for attacks. No other leader could have positioned KPMG as competitively as Richard has done so, for KPMG, to push it fast and as a favorite into the digital world.

Digital Culture has a Leadership disrupted Risk Agenda – "Taking risks becomes a cultural norm. Digitally maturing organizations are more comfortable taking risks than their less digitally mature peers. To make their organizations less risk averse, business leaders have to embrace failure as a prerequisite for success. They must also address the likelihood that employees may be just as risk averse as their managers and will need support to become bolder. **The digital agenda is led from the top while coping with risk.** Maturing organizations are nearly twice as likely as less digitally mature entities to have a single person or group leading the effort. In addition, employees in digitally maturing organizations are highly confident in their leaders' digital fluency", Figure: "Strategy, not technology drives digital transformation", Gerald C Kane, Doug Palmer, et all, in MIT SMR 2015 continue, "Digital fluency, however, doesn't demand mastery of the technologies. Instead, it requires the ability to articulate the value of digital technologies to the organization's future".

Digital Team Dynamics - As the days and weeks of team building proceed, loyalties will naturally build toward fellow members. The organization has effective communication channels, with and without boundaries, people enjoy communicating in relation to business and tasks to be accomplished. This is often a two-step process: one forward, and one step back. During the first few days, it is common for one or more members to respond negatively about the need for the team, its composition, the coaches, the task before them, or whether this is the most important thing they could be spending their time working on. As a result, several complaints before the organization for consideration is an issue. It is best not to name names. This will send a message to the complainers that they are on the verge of being discovered. Invariably the complainers will change their tune, rather than risk a negative reaction from their fellow team members. Members need to be coached to learn that it is important to trust one another. It is not possible, or desirable, for one member to do all the work for the team. Although, someone will almost always try. New members need to learn that to get the job done they have to rely on others to do their part. The analogy to this principle is that each team member needs to be trustworthy. Members need to learn that others are counting on them to do what they said they would do. But personal or business problems outside the team come up that affect individual members' ability to accomplish their agreed tasks. As soon as it becomes clear to members that his or her task cannot be completed in time, the member needs to let the other team members know about the cause of the problem and ask for help. This practice goes a long way to convincing fellow members that one is trustworthy. When a call for help comes from a fellow team member, the others should carefully examine their own responsibilities and available skills or time to see if they can help. It's in the best interest of members to support each other, especially when the organizational performance is judged and rewarded as a whole. The time might come when the team member who has been asked for help, needs help himself. If help cannot be offered, the team should pull together and determine how to be revise the plan or bring in additional resources to get the plan back on track. This organization places a lot of faith and relief on the individual sense of responsibility.

"What defines great talent within your organization? Qualifications matter of course, but there are other factors that are just as important and often overlooked. As a Recruitment Consultant and Advisor, I spend many hours with hiring managers. They pitch me on the products and services they are selling and why they are the best in the marketplace, or how they should have bigger market share if only they could hire the right people. I always listen intently regarding this information as important but not key to my search. My question is, "what kind of person do you want to work with?" They often look at me perplexed. "What do you mean?" says Linda Garneau, a Canadian HR Transformational Specialist. "The number one reason employees leave a company", she says "is that they do not like their boss or coworkers, whatever that may mean to them. As well, lack of productivity in employees is often related to lack of respect or admiration or even a sense of relatability for the people they report to. Relationships matter. When hiring, consider the collective personality of your existing team, how you relate to them, engage, challenge and reward them. Hire based on how the candidate fits in and can thrive and contribute positively to your team".

Humanize Digital Culture – "Humanyze, a people-analytics company headquartered in Boston that is a spinoff of the MIT Media Lab. Humanyze integrates wearables, sensors, digital data and analytics to identify who talks to whom, where they spend time and how they talk to each other. The analysis identifies patterns of collaboration that correlate with high employee productivity. Humanyze analyzed the travel company's workforce and discovered that people eating lunch together shared important insights that made them more productive. In addition, the analysis showed that productivity went up based on the number of people at the same table. At the company being analyzed, Humanyze found that employees typically lunched with either four or 12 people". In the research paper, "Strategy, not technology drives digital transformation", Gerald C Kane, Doug Palmer, et all, in MIT SMR 2015 continues further to this, "One wouldn't expect that changing the size of tables in an employee cafeteria could be emblematic of the digital transformation of a business. But consider this example: The tables in question were in the offices of a large, online travel company working with "A quick inspection of the cafeteria solved the puzzle — all the tables were for either four or 12 people. The integration of digital technologies pointed the way to increasing table sizes, which had a direct and measurable impact on employees' ability to produce".

Digital Culture in Fashion - If conflicting parties accept a part of each other's demands; conflicts can be resolved. An impartial arbitrator who finds solutions acceptable to both the conflicting parties can solve difficult conflicts. It is better to buy peace for some time even by acceding to some demands of the conflicting group, so that conflicts can be effectively resolved later. Waiting for some time to let emotions subside helps in solving the major problems. The culture involves a strong human interaction, team working and passion to work to a vision. This culture is the most difficult to describe because it evolves locally in organizations and within operational units.

Thus one can identify an operator culture in the manufacturing plant, in the textile complex, in the appliance manufacturing plant, in the garments factory in the retail outlet, and in the office. Long Term desire to make lasting organizations that can stream through economic and business life cycles and does not have the pressure to retain performance under all circumstance.

Digital Culture – Small is Beautiful - Can convene and communicate easily and frequently. Discussions are open and interactive for all members. Each member understands the other's roles and skills. All three categories of skills are either actually or potentially represented across the membership (functional, technical, problem-solving, decision-making, and interpersonal). Each member has the potential in all three categories to advance his or her skills to the level required by the team's purpose and goals. The member's purpose constitutes a broader, deeper aspiration than just near term goals. All members understand and articulate the purpose the same way. Members define the purpose vigorously in discussion with outsiders. Members frequently refer to the purpose and explore its implications. The purpose contains themes that are particularly meaningful and memorable. Members feel the purpose is important, if not exciting. There are goals versus broader organizational goals versus just one individual's goals. Goals are clear, simple, and measurable. If they are not measurable, can their achievement be determined? Goals are realistic as well as ambitious. The approach is concrete, clear, and really understood and agreed to by everybody. It requires all members to contribute equivalent amounts of real work. It provides for open interaction, fact-based problem solving, and result-based evaluation. The approach provides for modification and improvement over time. Fresh input and perspective is systematically sought and added, for example, through information and analysis, new members, and sponsors. There is sense of mutual accountability.

Digital Communication - Once the boundaries for the digital communication process are determined and the highest-priority actions are identified, work groups can be used to generate options, research best practices, and make recommendations. The work groups focus on the details. They flesh out the design framework and decisions developed by the leadership disrupted teams. If the work is complex, it may be organized into work streams with multiple work groups within each stream. The leader of each work group is usually appointed. The work group leaders should not simply mirror the leadership team. Leading a work group is a great opportunity for high potentials in the organization to get visibility. Depending on the size of your organization, companies will probably want to choose people two or three levels down from the incumbent. One issue companies may encounter when setting up work groups is that the work will overlap with the mandate of a functional group. "We issue social communications challenges for our employees, and in return those employees who publish via social or complete a challenge get points," says a telecom company's former chief marketing officer and chief of staff". In the research paper, "Strategy, not technology drives digital transformation", Gerald C Kane, Doug Palmer, et all, in MIT SMR 2015, writes, "To encourage employee buy-in, one telecommunications company uses gamification. When the company made its first forays into social marketing, many employees were reluctant to communicate directly with the market. To encourage staff to participate, the company created contests, (reward mechanisms, compensation, identity, loyalty programs) and leaderboards. "Those points get higher the more important the message or challenge is. We publish leaderboards, and every month we have an award for the winner for that month. And guess what? Everyone wants to be on the top of the list." For example, an area of work identified in the design process could be creating a new compensation plan for teams that are being introduced into the design. Clearly, if you have compensation experts in your organization, they should be involved in this work along with representatives from other parts of the organization. The work should also become part of the compensation group's work plan. By creating a work group around the issue, however, you ensure that a topic that is essential for the success of the new teams, roles, and structure doesn't get neglected. "As **Disney's Milovich** has pointed out, most employees use sophisticated social media platforms and interact with companies using seamless digital technologies in their personal life, but things become more difficult at work: "When we started this journey, we had a gap that existed between how someone interacted with relative ease in their personal life — to tap on an app and do his online banking or to quickly look up the weather where they lived — and how they interacted at work." A good size for a work group is eight to ten members. Although a smaller group is easier to manage, the reality is that day-to-day business needs will vary the level of time that participants can devote to the work group. A larger size ensures that there are enough people available for meetings and to keep the work going. The members of the work group should reflect a range of views in the organization. Disney is making great strides in closing the gap. The company is identifying early adopters and rallying them. These employees buoy risk taking by encouraging Disney employees who are not yet actively involved in the company's digital efforts to join the ranks. "We are moving with as much speed and nimbleness with our efforts as we do on the consumer side, so that the appropriate level of risk taking and speed is balanced," Milovich says. "You can tap into small but growing virtual communities to keep things moving along."

G. Digital People Processes

Digital Culture Does Talent Branding – "The tactic of culture-jacking (also, news jacking) can be employed to personify a brand as current, topical and in tune with the times. If executed seamlessly, as Oreo did during the power outage on the 2013 Super Bowl, a company may connect its brand with the trending topic of the day, appear clever and witty, and have the message become viral. But it can also backfire quite easily and bring unwanted negative attention toward the brand. This is what happened when Gap sought to drive traffic to its website through an indiscreet tweet during Hurricane Sandy. Clearly, tactics such as these are potentially risky and need to be conducted with extreme caution and sensitivity". What do smart talent of the digital enterprise do to build their profile? Jay I. Sinha in "The Risks and Rewards of Brand Personification Using Social Media" in MIT SMR 2015, write of three ways,

1. *Use social media to articulate your brand's personality and core values (its DNA), which are often most effective in influencing prospective customers and converting them from casual to loyal buyers.*
2. *Create attention-grabbing content using visuals, wit and humor to engage brand followers, but be careful about treading the boundary between what seems clever and funny and what can be deemed as controversial and insensitive.*
3. *Understand that even on social media, less is more. Too much content and too-frequent updating can be off-putting and devolve into noise, so it is best to strike a balance and develop a positive and engaging image for the brand".*

Digital HR Fosters Goal Setting - The organization drives action through its orientation and emphasis to competition, performance and goals focused energies. These organizations ask a price for their actions. Nothing comes for free is the basic belief and they charge for all their actions, intended or otherwise. The organization believes in swift and effective communication, work long hours to conclude tasks, people live at work, identify with winning and use all resources at one's disposal to accomplish tasks. There is a Role of the leader in building work processes, in managing people strategy issues, and organizational emphasis on competing and performing in a complex environment. Leader's emphasizes on building future leaders through mentoring, coaching and teaching, emphasis on teamwork. There is a Role of the CEO/leader in enabling organization to restructure and right size. Driven by sharing strategic goals, communicates, shares values, distinctive concern for individual sensitivity, empowerment, delegation, clear accountability and demonstrated by examples. There is a Role of the CEO/leader in preparing the organization to change as required. Leader's has a role in sponsoring innovation, new ideas, take risks and implementing experiments. CEO/leader's has a role only partly in enabling inters dependencies between functions, businesses, technologies and the organization as a whole. High Performance Cultures are established to accomplish something within a timeframe. A clear understanding of the organizational objectives is a very important element of creating successful effective cultures. When what needs to be done and how we will know we have done it is known, life is simple. Their outlook towards commerce is simply driven by shareholder wealth and to a considerable degree personal gains and benefits.

Digital Culture Talent – The New Maturity Game – "Developing Digitally Savvy Talent - Another factor distinguishing the most digitally mature companies from the least is the development and training of digitally savvy talent. Respondents from companies across all maturity levels reported a lack of certain key skills. The major difference, however, is in what the companies are doing about it. Only about 19% of surveyed employees from companies that are in the early stage of digital maturity agreed or strongly agreed that their organizations provide them with the resources or opportunities to obtain the right skills to take advantage of digital trends. This contrasts with 76% of employees from maturing digital companies. Consistent with the results seen elsewhere in our research, the skills and abilities that respondents indicated are most important for leveraging digital technologies are not purely technical. Respondents — regardless of company maturity level — indicated that the most important ability necessary for taking advantage of digital trends is "knowing the business and being able to conceptualize how new digital technologies can impact current business processes/models." Gerald C. Kane, Doug Palmer, Anh Nguyen Phillips and David Kiron "Is Your Business Ready for a Digital Future? - MIT SMR 2015, further continue, "This ability was also identified by the highest percentage of respondents as lacking in their organizations. Hiring managers are beginning to recognize and respond to these changes. For example, when asked what types of skills she looks for in new hires, Perry Hewitt, chief digital officer of Harvard University, said, "We often seek agility over specific skills. And interest and aptitude in addition to demonstrated track record. We look for people who are 'data informed and mission driven' — striking a balance between serving the mission of the institution and having robust digital skills."

Designing the lateral digital organization ensures that the efforts of each role add up to more than the sum of the parts. It is also critical for creating a dynamic and reconfigurable organization. Since the lateral organization is more flexible and easily changed than the vertical structure, a focus on its design will allow the company to respond quickly to shifts in strategy, skills, competencies without having to restructure the entire organization. The vertical structure provides the clarity and sense of stability that people need in order to function in large organizations. It provides the "home base" for skill building, goal setting, reporting, and performance management. However, the vertical structure doesn't necessarily provide flexibility. Each structural option brings a defined group of people together into departments focused by function, customer, product, or some other dimension. Yet, most organizations must be skill – focus, customer-centric and a product leader and operationally excellent. Companies struggle to build global product design capability while delivering those products in different local markets. There is pressure to grow in order to gain the advantages of scale yet remain nimble and entrepreneurial to compete with digital start-ups. The reality is that most digital savvy organizations operate in a complex, multidimensional world. The dilemma is that by improving the organization's ability to respond to one constituency or market force, it is easy to fragment its ability to deal with others. It is the lateral organization that allows you to get the "and" by optimizing multiple capabilities.

"Many survey respondents, in the Digitally Savvy Organizations, also questioned whether their company's leadership has the skills and abilities to lead the organizations in a digital environment. In fact, only 44% of respondents said that their organization's leadership disrupted has sufficient skills and experience to lead their organization's digital strategy. These responses varied substantially by digital maturity levels — with only 15% of employees from early-stage organizations and 76% from maturing organizations believing their leaders have sufficient skills and expertise to lead their organization's digital strategy. Even in the developing maturity group, the numbers are unsettlingly low, with less than 40% of respondents indicating that they believe their organization's leaders have sufficient skills and expertise for the task". For example, Matrix Structures create dual reporting relationships in order to manage the conflicting needs of functional, customer, product, or geographic forces. Teams, many integrative roles, and matrix structures are elective mechanisms. "What's more, these leaders may not recognize their own deficiencies (in a structural context too): Our survey found that the higher in the organization respondents work, the greater their confidence in the ability of the organization's executives to lead its digital strategy. While this could have to do with senior executives knowing their own skill and ability levels better than their employees know them, it still raises the likelihood that these capabilities aren't being clearly demonstrated or communicated to the broader networked organization". Networks are the interpersonal relationships and communities of practice that underlie all other types of lateral capability and serve to coordinate work informally. Lateral Processes move decisions and information through the organization in a formalized flow. "One way of overcoming this lack of skills at the leadership level is to hire executives from technology companies. David Mathison, founder and CEO of the CDO Club, a global professional community of digital executives, noted that many organizations are recruiting from the technology sector to obtain the requisite skills to lead in the digital age. He said: What we're seeing now is that a majority of chief digital officers are coming up through general management ranks, particularly from technology companies. The new, first-ever CDO at McDonald's, Atif Rafiq, was most recently general manager of Kindle Direct at Amazon. Before that he was general manager at Yahoo! and founding member of the corporate strategy and business development groups at AOL". Teams are cross-business structures that bring people together to work interdependently and share collective responsibility for outcomes. Integrative Roles are managerial, coordinator, or boundary-spanning positions charged with orchestrating work across units. "Individuals working at digital native organizations, maybe as a GM, somebody who has P&L responsibility, are being pulled into a variety of sectors … to figure out how to digitally transform a company".

Digital Culture Builds Performance - From the sponsoring manager's point of view, the objectives may not be all that clear. The sponsor may "feel" that significant improvement in overall organizational performance (new business or reduced costs, or improve service) is needed. In this more common instance team has some serious work to do defining and refining performance measures. A High Performance culture can and should be expected to develop and refine its objectives and measures of performance. Vision, values, beliefs and his dream drive the Leader as a person. The Leader must be able to communicate the shared vision and create a meaningful goal to strive for. I think this is absolutely correct. The Leader must be a visionary, fired up with enthusiasm and able to translate this vision to his team, right from the soldiers in the trenches to the Generals leading the battle. He must dream yet be practical. The vision he communicates must be meaningful and strike a chord with his troops, only then will they really be committed to it. The Leader's emphasizes on the Individual and the Intellect, and a role in building individual and organizational knowledge. I see the Leader as a facilitator. Smart Leaders realize that they cannot do everything on their own. The best Leaders hire people who they believe are smarter than them, energize them, empower them and equip them with the tools that they believe are needed for them to achieve superlative performance.

Digital Culture Performance Consistencies - Significant performance challenges energize members regardless of where they are in an organization. No team arises without a performance challenge that is meaningful to those involved. A common set of demanding performance goals that a group considers important to achieve will lead, most of the time, to both performance and team. Performance, however, is the primary objective while a process remains the means, not the end. Organizational leaders can foster culturally sensitive performance best by building a strong performance ethic rather than by establishing a culture promoting environment alone. Biases toward individualism exist but need not get in the way of team performance. Real cultures always find ways for each individual to contribute and thereby gain distinction. Indeed, when harnessed to a common team purpose and goals, our need to distinguish ourselves as individuals becomes a powerful engine for team performance. Discipline-both within the team and across the organization-creates the conditions for team performance. For organizational leaders, this entails making clear and consistent demands that reflect the needs of customers, shareholders, and employees, and then holding themselves and the organization relentlessly accountable.

Digital Learning - The organization emphasizes an appropriate management style that foster learning. Driven by organizational energy to learn, self-develop, perpetuate individualization as they grow to compete. Experts and experienced creative practitioners are invited to share their ideas with members of the organization. Employees are encouraged to attend external programs. Experience and concerns of the organization are shared with other organizations. Employees are encouraged to experiment. Innovations are rewarded. Periodic meeting is held for sharing result of experiments. Periodic meeting is held for sharing on going experiments. Focus on people productivity through learning drivers on what can be done should be done. Employee seminars on new developments are organized. The organization focuses on learning environments that involves brings together intellect, knowledge, systemic processes, personal mastery and role models. Task groups are created for implementing and monitoring new projects and experiments. Detailed plans reflecting contingency approaches are prepared. Task groups are created to examine common elements between old practices and innovations. Newly proposed practices are linked with known practices. Records of experiences are maintained. Periodic meeting, chaired by top or senior management, are held to review innovations. Relevant existing skills are utilized in implementing change. Task groups are created for data based critiquing of the innovations. The climate is conducive and non-threatening to share successes and failures and is not a performance consideration. Periodic meetings are held to review and share experiences. Task groups are created to evaluate and report on plus and minus aspects of innovations. Task groups are created to follow up on experiments. Widespread debates are held on experiences of implementation. Realistic appraisals are made of team support needed for continued use of innovation. Implementation plans are modified when experience indicates that modification is needed. Various groups are encouraged to prepare alternative forms of implementation.

Digital HR Enhances Engagement - They exist to respond to complexity in the business environment, but when used, each also introduces a degree of internal complexity that must be managed. They require more management time and employee skills to make full use of their potential and to avoid introducing dysfunctional behaviors and relationships. Lateral capability is cumulative. You can't have effective teams or cultural engagement if your organization doesn't have strong networks and well-designed processes. "The first thing we did was disrupt the way that we traditionally reviewed people's performance (structurally or informally). We adopted what we call Check-in, which is an ongoing mechanism for ensuring that all our employees are aligned with the overall goals of the organization. It's also a mechanism for providing them with **real-time feedback**. Gone are the days of annual **performance reviews and ratings**. That was one very big change. Next week, we're launching what we call "Experience-a-thons," which will be an opportunity for our **employees not only to engage directly** with the technology we use for our products and services but also to provide immediate feedback to our customer organization and product teams before we go live with them. Another thing we did was reassess our locations". Many business leaders, as per Jay

Galbraith, are trying to get their employees to think like owners, to make decisions as though it was their own money on the line. Integrating mechanisms help employees to think more broadly and to understand and incorporate other perspectives into their own decisions and actions. "Engaged employees ensure personalized customer experience. Moving to the Cloud was a bold strategy, and it clearly has had all kinds of cultural ramifications" say, Donna Morris (Adobe), interviewed by Gerald (Jerry) C. Kane in MIT SMR 2016, "Adobe Reinvents its Customer Experience" writes further, "We were a pretty dispersed as a company with more than 80 locations in 41 countries. Looking at the size of our company, you would say that growth requires that, but we contended that growth in so many locations added another layer of complexity. So, we reinvested in some locations and we pulled out of others. Today we're down to around 68 locations. That was a very deliberate decision to ensure that our employees had the opportunity to work together in close proximity. We also felt that doing that would help scale the business more effectively".

H. Digital Data is Evidential

Digital Culture Builds Intellectual Loyalty - Great value is given here to good relationships and loyalty to the organization. Attempts are not always made here to resolve conflicts without loss of face by a party involved in the conflict. People feel comfortable in-groups of their own affinity. Managers generally spend more times on their jobs, even at the cost of personal needs. Competitiveness and smartness are highly valued here. Seniors exercise their authority in most matters and their juniors accept theirs. Employees feel they can influence many important issues here. All matters are worked out meticulously, including course of action, and deviations are not liked. Although rules are worked out in detail, these are applied according to the background of a case. People care for the total organization and not only about their own groups or teams in some situations. Importance is given to long-term planning and working for the future. Employees enjoy freedom to do their work, to plan and set their work pace, style and methods, but are severally accountable for their goals and targets. Generally, employees here are warm, friendly, forth coming with a clear agenda on performance orientation. Maintaining harmony is highly valued here. Confrontation and frank communication are generally avoided here. Leaders here nurture and protect the interests of those who belong to them. Managers care a great deal about their personal time and do not like business to Intrude on it. Importance is given to compassion and caring. Hierarchical relationships are seen as necessary for running the organization. There is a general feeling of indifference among employees because they feel that they cannot influence critical matters here. Different ways of solving problems are encouraged here. Decisions are objective and clear-cut, and are not influenced by the context.

Digital Culture is Evidence Based - In some cultures there is a premium to learn as much if not more from failure as success (evidence, data, experiential, factual) and it supports "incremental improvements all the time based on such dynamic feedback". They assume that the front line knows the best while actively encouraging knowledge movement to the point of deployment apart from extensively look outside their boundaries for knowledge. "In a *data-oriented culture*, behaviors, practices and beliefs are consistent with the principle that business decisions at every level are based on analysis of data. Leaders within organizations that have mastered this competency set an expectation that decisions must be arrived at analytically, and explain how analytics is needed to achieve their long-term vision" write authors, David Kiron, Rebecca Shockley, Nina Kruschwitz, Glenn Finch and Dr. Michael Haydock in Analytics: The Widening Divide, MIT SMR 2011, "Organizations with this culture are likely to excel at innovation and strategies that differentiate them from their peers (BAE Systems: A New Business Model Takes Flight). They typically benefit from a top-down mandate, and leaders clearly articulate an expectation for analytical decision making aligned to business objectives. Transformed organizations, in fact, are nearly five times more likely to do this than Aspirational organizations. A pattern of behaviors and practices by a group of people who share a belief that having, understanding and using certain kinds of data and information plays a critical role in the success of their organization. In these data-driven cultures, expectations are high. Before "giving the green light" to a new service offering or operational approach, for example, leaders ask for the analytics to support it. They express their conviction in the value of faster and more precise decisions by using analytics to guide to day-to-day operations. Employees are confident they have the information to make data-based decisions. They are encouraged to challenge the *status quo*, and follow the facts in order to innovate. Transformed organizations are more than twice as likely as Aspirational groups to be receptive to new insights".

I. *Digital Disruptions*

Digital HR Have Disruptors - "First, incumbents must think carefully about the strategy available to them. The number of companies that can operate as pure-play disrupters at global scale—such as Spotify, Square, and Uber—are few in number. Rarer still are the ecosystem shapers that set de facto standards and gain command of the universal control points created by hyper scaling digital platforms". A transformation initiative involves a significant investment of management and financial resources and appurtenant risk. By involving a consultant, you are placing substantial trust on an external agency. A transactional approach is antithetical to this. An organizational transformation is a long term process and not a 3 or 4-month project. It is a partner who will bring the commitment and drive to see it through successfully. The scope of such a program can neither be exhaustively articulated nor can it be delivered through deliverables alone. A partner recognizes that ambiguity will exist, both in scope and delivery and will invest in the relationship and understand the organization to manage it. This exercise, even if constructed in a modular manner, would demand a variety of deep skill sets all of which cannot be foreseen. Larger organizations drive knowledge, beyond the assigned project team that is mandated to make this change that includes disruptors. Risk sharing in key to partnership. As your partner in this transformation, we can and will link our success to that of yours. Organizational success is not measured as much by what we achieve when we work with you as against what we leave behind to sustain the gains achieved through an intervention. Our approach is therefore inclusive with a thrust on strengthening client capabilities to receive the benefits of an external intervention and a commitment to transferring knowledge and capabilities to achieve sustainability. In McKinsey Quarterly 2015, "Raising your Digital Quotient", Tangly Catlin, Jay Scanlan, and Paul Willmott continue, "Following the leader is a dangerous game. It's better to focus on building an organization and culture that can realize the strategy that's right for you. Ninety-five to 99 percent of incumbent companies must choose a different path, not by "doing digital" on the margin of their established businesses but by wholeheartedly committing themselves to a clear strategy. Second, success depends on the ability to invest in relevant digital capabilities that are well aligned with strategy—and to do so at scale. The right capabilities help you keep pace with your customers as digitization transforms the way they research and consider products and services, interact, and make purchases on the digital consumer decision journey. Third, while technical capabilities—such as big data analytics, digital content management, and search-engine optimization—are crucial, a strong and adaptive culture can help make up for a lack of them. Fourth, companies need to align their organizational structures, talent development, funding mechanisms, and key performance indicators (KPIs) with the digital strategy they've chosen. Collectively, these lessons represent a high-level road map for the executive teams of established companies seeking to keep pace in the digital age. Much else is required, of course. But in our experience, without the right road map and the management mind-set needed to follow it, there's a real danger of traveling in the wrong direction, traveling too slowly in the right one, or not moving forward at all".

Digital Culture has a Confrontational Tone – Not all aspects of businesses are managed without debates, differences and decisions. Cultures that provides staff an opportunity to think and contribute also means confrontation and challenges. "All problems, personal, national, or combat, become smaller if you don't dodge them, but confront them" declares, G Bromley Oxnam (Goodman 1997) as he defined culture as to "what is left after everything we have learned is forgotten. It consists of deepened understanding, a breadth of outlook, an unbiased approach and a heart that has deep sympathy and strength of courage. " Admiral William "Bull" Halsey "Admiral Nelson's counsel" guided me time and again. On the eve of the critical battle of Santa Cruz, in which the Japanese ships outnumbered ours more than two to one, I sent my task force commanders this dispatch: ATTACK REPEAT ATTACK. They did attack, heroically, and when the battle was done, the enemy turned away. Touch a thistle timidly, and it pricks you; grasp it boldly, and its spines crumble. Carry the battle to the enemy! Lay your ship alongside his"! http://bit.ly/2apRRUf

Digital Culture Conflicts - Conflicts are inevitable in organizations and nothing can be done about them. The best strategy is to avoid conflict situations. A conflict is like a problem; we have to find the causes and take steps to find solutions. Conflict can be solved only if one shows one's strength to the other party. In a conflict situation both the parties have to give up something in order to reach a solution. A third party should be asked to give a solution to a difficult conflict. It is better to give some concessions to the opponent group to win their confidence. The best way to deal with conflicts is to withdraw from the scene for some time. It is better to lie low and live with the conflict. In a conflict situation, one party should get away to avert unpleasantness. Conflict management needs an involved process of joint exploration for solution(s). In most conflicts, one should fight out the solution. Compromise is the best strategy for managing conflict. When two parties are deeply involved in conflict, arbitration by an acceptable outside party may be very helpful. Accepting a few demands of the opponent group may help in resolving conflicts. If we wait for some time and don't attempt to solve problems, conflicts will get defused and resolved in due course of time. It is foolish to be bothered by conflict; they are there and we may as well live with them. If a group interacts with other groups only on necessary and limited dimensions, conflicts can be managed. Conflicts can be solved if the parties understand each other, and jointly search alternative solutions. The more powerful you are, the more effectively you can resolve conflicts.

Chapter 11

The Intellectual Company – Discover

The Intellectual Corporation personifies the human being and makes the human mind the foundation of the corporation. Intellect seen in its purest form is propaedeutic in its conceptual state. It is primarily elementary and forms the core of the enterprise. Individuals seek freedom of expression, in an environment where learning, teaching, technology and understanding is available and is in a position to adapt, contribute and improve as they learn. The intellectual corporation deals below the surface of overt relationships, seeks psychological contract built on trust, collaboration and mutuality of purpose and provides an environment that offers respect and dignity to the individual. The Corporation has an undebatable, unalterable diktat on the faith in the human mind, the spirit and power of the intellect. All other facets of the corporation described through the knowledge organization succeed in the management of the enterprise. Managing the corporate of the future leaves us with a limited choice option. There simply aren't enough proven ways to manage uncertainty and a period of constant change despite proven past track records of high performance. The past is neither a winning condition for future success nor a panacea for all evils that an institution is likely to face and reckon with.

A. *Altered Reality of the New World of Business*
B. *The Intellectual Company Organizational Models*
C. *Changing Organizational Assumptions*
D. *Changing Paradigms*
E. *Intellectual Realities*
F. *Managing Intellect*
G. *Digital Business Models - Characteristics*
H. *Achieving Synthesis*
I. *Are Organizations Intelligent?*
J. *Adapt and Internalize Intelligence*
K. *Social Interactions and Intellect*
L. *Strategic Revitalization*
M. *Platforms*
N. *Defining Digital Culture and Building Characteristics*
O. *Human Capital – Knowledge – Learning - Intellect Interface - Context for work level Intellect*
P. *So What Now?*

"Of course the work of Nostradamus continues to be a part of our life as a possible work of hypothesis and reality. While work would engulf our lives, as individuals, and we would go on as one human kind, I am unable to see the continuance of the corporation with 20th century as model for the future. It is not a conjecture to make a point but more summation and learning out of the last two decades of pace of change, particularly, in the commercial sciences and its consequence to the business enterprise". New systems also exact a psychological cost on employees, which has to be anticipated and managed. Putting a higher percentage of reward mechanisms for intellect at risk is good for companies. It allows them to move dollars out of the fixed-cost category and into the variable-cost category, and it provides tangible evidence that things must change. For employees, however, it means trading something that is sure—base pay tied to time and seniority—for an incentive that may or may not be paid out. Keeping values at the core of their thinking, Continue, Grenny et all, "When leaders want to influence people to make significant changes, they need to help them connect the changes to their deeply held values, those beliefs and practices that has held them to their behaviors over their life time. It is the moral compass that helps people see right from wrong or can do versus cannot do. This establishes a moral framework that shifts people's experience of the new behaviors. If leaders fail to engage people's values, it means a conspicuous evidence of lack of commitment, they must compensate for a lack of personal motivation, drive with less profound and sustainable, retained sources of motivation, such as carrots – sticks and intrinsic or extrinsic rewards or punishment". Without clear measures, decisions made by supervisors and managers can seem arbitrary and create resentment between business units if some managers are perceived as easier than others. Are socio technical aspects of work for changes in behavior built into the system? In, "How to Have Influence, 2008 SMR, Joseph Grenny, David Maxfield and Andrew Shimberg write further of their attempt to focus on, the challenges they wanted to explore in regard to bureaucratic infighting, silo thinking and lack of accountability. Nothing is less motivating than for a person to work as hard or harder than before, meet their personal goals, and find out there is no upside because of factors out of their control. "In fact, their study showed, they say, (believing that learning is a bridge to fill gaps) that a robust training initiative is at the heart of almost all successful influence strategies. Mike Miller, vice president of business customer billing at AT&T Inc., succeeded in turning around a 3,000-person IT function by creating a culture where everyone spoke up early (no one can walk out without saying something) and honestly about the risks they saw affecting project goals. Early in the change initiative, Miller saw that people needed more than the motivation to speak up. He realized people also needed the ability to step up (skill or competency gaps or process and knowledge fillers) to crucial conversations. In the heat of the moment, speaking up about emotionally risky issues requires as much skill as motivation. So Miller made sure people got the right kind of training". There are a few things to consider when contemplating introducing new structures: Is there agreement on what is important and is there a way to measure it? Any rewards given for meeting specific production, quality, or service goals need to have clear criteria. Some work needs to be done as part of the planning process to identify the behaviors that people need to do more of—and less of—to impact the culture and business results. Although the management team can determine these behaviors, involving a representative sample of the people impacted will improve the result. They will identify the management behaviors that need to change in addition to what they and their peers need to do differently. They will also ensure the language is direct and descriptive. Finally, the involvement process will increase buy-in to the overall plan. Are people enabled and empowered to control the variables? It is impossible to ask people to excel if they are not enabled to achieve excellence. Whether it is pay for performance, skill-based pay, or some team incentive plan, it will only work when the people participating have some control over the outcome. These could include: Another business division not making their goals, Lack of reasonable authority to make decisions and solve problems, Lack of tools and resources to do the job well. The 20th century, when looking back, were possibly the most eventful and impacting in all spheres of life. From entry into space, several global wars, mass destruction weapons, the advent of biotechnology, emergence of the third world economy, death of socialism and communism, the consequent rise of capitalism, globalization, and domination of the service sector and finally the entry of Internet, E Commerce and its opportunities. These are but a few of the radical changes that have impacted literally the human kind from all walks of life. One would never know how much of all of this at a minimum was predicted at the beginning of the 20th century or how many organized activities were undertaken by the thinkers of yesteryears to forecast for themselves their future.

Influence of Culture to Digital Thinking Organizations

		State of Readiness	Degree of Motivation	Mastery of Competencies
Personal	Mastery of Self	Alignment to Values	Practicing Engagement	Clear Behavioral Learnings
Dyads	Team Effectiveness	See Beyond Self. Status Seekers Mutual Persuasive, Conviction	Lower Focus on Hierarchies, Pyramid Climbers	Multiple Competencies, Organizational Leaders Demonstrated Experiences
Groups		Well qualified and trained team members Trained for Contingency Management	Team Goals, Rewards, Incentives Programs for Peer Equivalencies	Application of Learning, Variety of Situations Group Problem Solving Inter Group Functional Deals
Social	Socio Structural	Harness Peer Pressure	Create Social Collaborative Support	Simulate Live Working Conditions
Organization Structural		Benchmarked to Performance Orientation Flexible Speedy	Seek Role Confluence Manage Ambiguity Align Rewards Demonstrate Accountability	Influence Situation Confirm Business Competencies Focus on Financials Measure Outcomes

Figure 46 – Influence of Culture to Digital Thinking Organizations

A. Altered Reality of the New World of Business

The way we do business has changed irrevocably be it in human attitudes and disposition towards work itself, the diminishing business and geographic boundaries, technology – product – market-innovations on customer service and satisfaction, changing patterns of product life cycles, liberalized economies of many a third world countries, abundant capital resources, economy of plenty in many countries, IT, Internet usage and domination and several other macro and micro factors affecting the firm. In this period, we have seen the rise and fall of many organizations, entrepreneurial outfit, visionary leaders, successful task masters, legendary family enterprise with long years of substantive work experience, organizational champions and many more. Refer - *Influence of Culture to Digital Thinking Organizations.* Since organizations can absorb only a limited amount of change in a given period of time, attempting to develop or seek an altered reality quickly will cause much of the new investments to be wasted. Surveys show that 70 percent of organizations that introduce expensive, comprehensive CRM software packages cannot show results, primarily because the software investments were not linked to change management initiatives. Spending on new information capital applications reflects two underlying phenomena: the replacement of obsolete systems with state-of-the-art technology (such as ERP systems), and the application of totally new technology to new applications (such as e-commerce).

Meaningless Market Cap - Fortune 500 list of every year appears to be undergoing radical changes. Market capitalization of IT firms simply has no holds barred while peaking to hit the circuit barrier on day's limits. The business enterprise, for what it is worth, is today considered to be a knowledge organization poised competitively to face the new millennium. The knowledge organization, as currently defined, represents services, value additions, use of data and information, collection, storage, synthesis, assimilation and transmission to relevant sectors of competitive information. The organization encompasses basic sources of data and information origin and converts it into usable knowledge base for effective organizational performance. At a point, Microsoft and Cisco enjoyed stock market capitalizations that are hundreds of billions of dollars higher than the book value of their tangible assets, largely because their complex software and hardware have become standards for the industry, are difficult for rivals to replicate, and are costly for customers to switch from. Today while Microsoft has retained its value, CISCO's place has been taken up by Apple, Google and other digital companies.

Digital World Has Changed - Conventional wisdom states that companies in a mature industry try to maintain profitability and deter new entrants in three ways. Product proliferation which involves moving from a narrow to a wide range of products to cater for various market niches; Price-cutting, to maintain and build market share, and the excess production capacity to threaten increased output if new competitors enter the industry. He goes on to say that a company, as well as finding ways of keeping out new entrants, must manage its existing rivals in a number of ways so as to maximize its profitability and Price signaling to inform competitors of pricing intentions, price leadership to attain the lowest delivered cost in the industry and non-price competition, based on product characteristics, are all recommended by Porter. A key strategic variable in this environment is investment in intellectual – smart capacity as companies that can meet increases in demand have a considerable advantage over their rivals. However, there is risk, as large investments in implementing a generic strategy are required before the environmental change occurs. Amazon has avoided this risk through innovation in supply chain, information processing and logistics design. Hence mere capacity investment and generic business strategies are not adequate tools for managers involved in digital industries. At a simplistic level software organization, consulting, advisory firms, research, new product development and generic knowledge based value-adding companies (advertising, financial services, communication, entertainment, education) are treated as knowledge firms given their role in development of raw data, creation of unknown into known and the utilization of people as the primary state of creators. These organizations position themselves competitively depending on their availability of quality human resource and their contributions to the business bottom line achieved through their knowledge contribution. The knowledge is commercialized as a product or service to begin with and thereafter converted into a system for its effective storage, retrieval and application. While organizations treat knowledge as its sustainable competitive advantage and make systemic contributions to make effective its application the corporate intent in managing knowledge makes the role of intellect subservient to the cause and consequent process. Eventually corporations turn knowledge creators into knowledge merchants contributing for a price. To my mind there is a definitive dissonance, when seen in isolation, between the knowledge and Intellectual Corporation.

Personifies Human Being - The Intellectual Corporation personifies the human being and makes the human mind the foundation of the corporation. Intellect seen in its purest form is propaedeutic in its conceptual state. It is primarily elementary and forms the core of the enterprise. Individuals seek freedom of expression, in an environment where learning, teaching and understanding is available and is in a position to adapt, contribute and improve as they learn. The intellectual corporation deals below the surface of overt relationships, seeks psychological contract built on trust, collaboration and mutuality of purpose and provides an environment that offers respect and dignity to the individual. The Corporation has an undebatable, unalterable diktat on the faith in the human mind, the spirit and power of the intellect. All other facets of the corporation described above through the knowledge organization succeed the management of the enterprise. A schematic model is presented below as a case for demonstrating the inevitability of The Intellectual Corporation and its inter dependence between Organization/Management, Culture and Leadership disrupted.

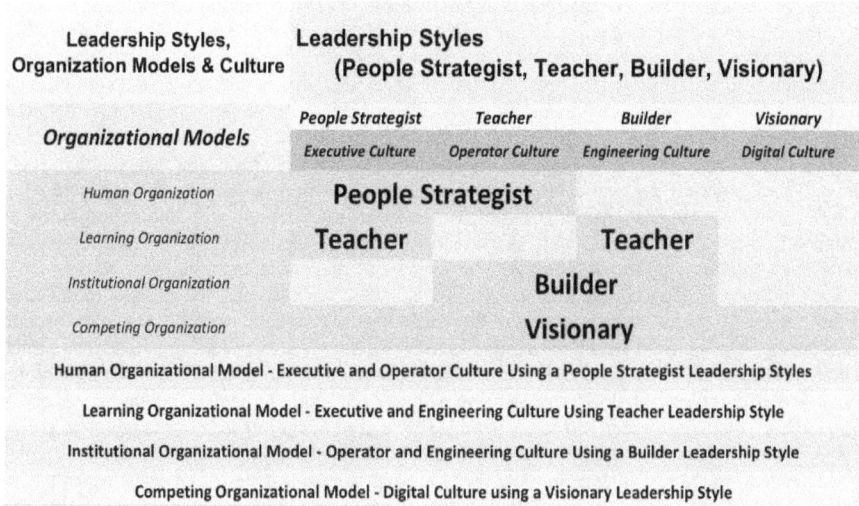

Leadership Styles, Organization Models & Culture	Leadership Styles (People Strategist, Teacher, Builder, Visionary)			
Organizational Models	People Strategist	Teacher	Builder	Visionary
	Executive Culture	Operator Culture	Engineering Culture	Digital Culture
Human Organization	**People Strategist**			
Learning Organization	**Teacher**		**Teacher**	
Institutional Organization			**Builder**	
Competing Organization			**Visionary**	

Human Organizational Model - Executive and Operator Culture Using a People Strategist Leadership Styles

Learning Organizational Model - Executive and Engineering Culture Using Teacher Leadership Style

Institutional Organizational Model - Operator and Engineering Culture Using a Builder Leadership Style

Competing Organizational Model - Digital Culture using a Visionary Leadership Style

Figure 47 – Leadership disrupted Organization Culture – The Intellectual Company

B. The Intellectual Company Organizational Models

Several structural interventions have been attempted in large and small organizations. The vertically integrated structure demanded management intensiveness, competencies to perform the job and the ability to integrate roles, functions and activities together. The functional model with a simple structure offering specialization as a means of organization the company. While this form continues to be effective for some type of organizations, increasing complexity in the management of the environment has changed the rules of managing through a structured outfit. The divisional, strategic business unit structure meant matrix management, focused businesses, and strategic goal orientation and leveraging company potential for growth.

Performance - Effective organizations were defined as those with a performance orientation of doing what is right for business. In doing so businesses attempted models that were appropriate at a point in time. Models included structural interventions, long range planning, environment scanning, management accounting and systems, management by objectives, performance planning, managerial effectiveness etc. these models continue to be of relevance to organizations experiencing various stages of their life cycles. Its application and usefulness has varied depending on the usage and manner in which they were implemented. While some of the models have outlived their usefulness there are several other concepts and applications that continue to serve their time. To overcome market constraints, there must be value creation and innovation in both strategy and organization. Benetton achieves this by creating value for all those who deal with it. This includes, first and foremost, the customer. In parallel with this the company satisfies suppliers and distributors who are often neglected. The rationale behind this is that increasing the overall value of the firm will be beneficial for all interested groups.

Design - Organizations moved vertically from strategy, to structure and process. In the knowledge generation role, content has a distinctive role to play in making corporations effective. In fact, content and process to a considerable extent go logically together. One at the cost of another has long since been way laid. Nevertheless, for corporations into intense knowledge management roles content tends to be an important area, no doubt. At another conceptual plane one could debate on structure and content preceding strategy given that people who contribute through their intellect have done so without either the strategy or the structure in mind. They have simply made a difference through their thought process. Innovative organizations do not have tight rope structures with clearly defined boundaries of roles and responsibilities. Benetton, for example, used to prepare multiple ranges of product designs a year. The sample collection was a result of collaboration between the design office and the marketing staff. A non- hierarchical system seemed to have developed which allowed a continuous informal exchange of information. If an acceptable garment was devised that was not in the sample collection, then a 'fashion flash' was issued to bring the garment to the attention of all relevant parties. In some cases, the 'fashion flash' article may be put into production immediately. This showed Benetton's responsiveness to the market's needs. Organizational structures started reflecting this change and roles modified. Reorders occur to take into account unforeseen demand and purchases of articles which were launched after the sample collection. These were produced in smaller numbers and were intended as a contingency if trends change. The collection requires rapid revision three months after the launch of the sample collection. This allowed Benetton's producers to work in real time as much as possible and to take account of changes in fashion which may take place. This limited revision of the product range was very important in completing design strategy. Consulting companies (McKinsey, KPMG, Bain and Company, Price Waterhouse Coopers, Boston Consulting Group) have long since used the Adhocracy Model (Henry Mintzberg) with team based structures constructed on the basis of competence, client needs and delivery schedules. Their industry and functional specialization matrix structure offers them the unique advantage of providing more than a plain vanilla service. Research labs of large pharmaceutical companies (Glaxo/ Rhone Poulenc, Merck, Smith Klein Beecham, Novartis) have depended on a structure that allows flexibility in roles, areas of contribution and the best person is right there doing what he/she knows best. "Workday" is an appropriate example. The recognition by Fortune (100 Best Companies to Work for) follows other honors Workday has received as a top workplace in the U.S. and Europe in the past year:

- *Ranked #1 in the large company's category by the Great Place to Work Institute on its "People's Picks: 20 Top Workplaces in Technology" list*
- *Named the #1 top workplace in the Bay Area for large companies for the fourth consecutive year by the Bay Area News Group*
- *Named the #2 best place to work in the Bay Area for large companies by the San Francisco Business Times / San Jose Business Journal. Workday has been named to this list for the past seven years*
- *Selected as one of the top companies to work for in Utah by the Deseret News*
- *Named a best workplace in Ireland by the Great Place to Work Institute for medium-sized companies*

Bottom Line Basics - Organizations evaluated their state of business presence through growth and bottom line orientation. The worth of the shareholder was meant to be a long-term proposition. Dominance continues to be an effective strategy. In competitive environment organizations need a combination of hardware and software resources, apart from sustainable advantages in technology, product dominance, market shares and a financial muscle. As more firms begin concurrent strategy to dominate demand-supply equilibrium significant oversupply and narrow penetration strategies are deployed making either the market base grow or cause abundance. Eventually the firm has to either turn cost effective to remain competitive or create winning marketing tactics to sustain. Dominance through mergers or strategic alliance help in managing this process where equitable partners align to make the market. While the reward system will provide some incentive for managers to prepare effective strategic plans. If the reward system is based solely on the short-range bottom line, the CEO cannot expect top quality strategic planning. If a manager is evaluated solely on the basis of the short-term bottom line there will be little or no long-range strategic thinking.

Dependence on Tools - Successful corporations have used several tools, systems and methods managerially acceptable acts to keep their competitive positioning fast paced and contemporary. Reengineering, delayering, financial restructuring, outsourcing, sub-contracting, forming alliances and many other methods and tools have been of use. When looking back some of the tools have simply been there available as a promised solution with limited delivery history. Some of course have done their share of time and success and the companies have moved on. Managerial process methods have also had its share of creating excessiveness in approaches deployed by the top management. There have been instances wherein the process and methods have long dominated strategic focus, speed and pace of action required to handle a dynamic environment. On the other hand, innovative corporations like for example Bose Corporation has spearheaded the concept of JIT II with complete partnership with their suppliers who locate themselves in the office of Bose and offer service.

Economic Impact - In business the fundamental criteria for determining the rationality of decisions usually are specific economic measures such as return on investment, market share, profits, sales, and margin. Yet despite usage of modern management tools or state of art practices several corporations have not emerged out of the woods in difficult economic downturns. Economic impact of the firm, obviously, is more than internal management approaches alone. Best of organizations have encountered failures for want of strategic differentiators. For example, Michael E. Porter defined five basic forces as the basic state of "barriers to competition" for a firm: Economies of scale, Product Differentiation, Capital Requirements, Cost disadvantages independent of size, Access to distribution channels and Government Policy. At any given point in time firms are at varying stages of advantage on this five-stated entry barriers. It makes vulnerability that much more relevant in the context of a going concern. GE has consistently stated dominance, economies of scale and size as their competitive positioning.

Turbulence - Organizations have seen turbulent recessions and their impact on business. Yet their ability to cope with the crisis has not necessary been enhanced on an exponential basis. Not a difficult task to decipher logically. Firms create internal coping mechanisms and are at different stages of preparedness against negative forces impacting business. It could range from environmental exposure to product status, market dominance, competitive positioning including external mergers and acquisitions, demand-supply scenario or macro-economic factors including war, run-away inflation etc. Reeling under pressure should not be treated as poor management practices and punished summarily. Several inevitable factors plague organizations, as firms grow larger and significant in the market place. Commodity industries form a classical example of being impacted by recessionary cycles, steel, textiles, and cement form a part of this segment.

Chasing Numbers - Well managed management's meant attaining bottom line targets and growth curves as promised to the shareholders. The goal of meeting quarterly budgets has been dealt with before. When balance sheets are squeezed to show profits in an area where there are none firms do push the balance sheet to its precipice. It is while making the balance sheet look good do corporate managements miss the wood from trees. Several short term strategies to prop up performance make the firm go belly up as the organization does not possess the sustenance power to hang out there with cash flows and customer loyalties for long. Although achievement of the targeted goals has not secured the corporation from destruction and decay as we have seen it happen to large companies.

Revival - Traditional organizations did not see the need for continuous renewal to remain competitive and vibrant. In fact in contrast organizational mediocrity was its best when large corporations did not see the need to rapidly change their strategic and structural orientation and its consequent linkages to performance. Large corporate, perhaps, is more at fault than small vibrant companies. As organizations grow in size it is but natural for complexity and distances to emerge between front line realities and decision making power sources. The front line could mean employees, suppliers, governments, society and more importantly and sadly the customer itself. When this distance becomes more than manageable companies commence reeling under pressure of performance. Somewhere along the line of business we have lost touch. A process of renewal, an act involving "involvement" on a continuous basis, needs to be established and new ways of thinking becomes essential. Thinking differently from initial concept to actual implementation should become an organizational rigor where translation of ideas into workable ideas and that in turn into action plans make the organization vibrant and energized at more than one plane.

Systems Thinking in Business - Organizations with dominant systems thinking have possibly made people orientation second to the systemic orientation. The information era brings in the inevitability of systems, data management and systemic approaches to management problem solving. While the 90's saw the systems dominance to make business performance advanced and electronic the 21st century possibly has a modified version of the system story. A situation where system creators no longer turn subservient to what they have created but have actually built in adequate flexibility and innovation modules to grab the attention of every individual who is working with the system and see the potential to add value and make a difference to the system. The suggestion may sound preposterous to organizations that have spent millions of dollars to make their data and process systems beyond the tinkering capability of the individual. After all the logical fear could be the unleashing of anarchy with every working individual tampering with the system as they are working. Well, perhaps, it is this or may something significantly more meaningful.

Systems in Structures - Organizations in preparedness of tomorrow, the model organization, as well as those that are right there today have created working effective system to manage a corporation of today for tomorrow. The question before us whether they have created systems flexible and dynamic enough to adapt to the thinking individuals of tomorrow? It is not as if maintenance or the production, planning functional system is expected to be dabbled with and thereby the production schedule has all but come to a near stop. The stated positioning is that people would no longer accept systems just because they because production runs in an efficient form. There would exploiting questions asked on could not the following changes be made to make this system more user friendly, more effective and more dynamic. Do we as a consequence have adequate checks, balances and flexibility built into a system to make it versatile, high performing and dynamic?

Culture Goes Beyond - "While culture is a strong driver of effective capability building, companies that focus on certain capabilities for competitive reasons rather than just cultural ones gain a stronger competitive advantage". This is not to take away the critical element culture has to play but to emphasize the need for business strengths which not be forgotten. Contributors to the development and analysis of this survey (McKinsey Global Survey results) include Liz Gryger, Tom Saar and Patti Schaar (McKinsey Consulting), write on "Building organizational capabilities. "Most companies focus on the capability executives say is most important to business performance because it's a part of the companies' culture, not for any competitive reason. It's notable that the majority of companies don't focus on a specific priority capability for purely competitive reasons; most often, the reason is that the capability is part of their culture". Strategic Communication helps establish a 2-way Communication mechanism within the organization, in this cultural change context, .e. to 'communicate' with the stakeholders and also 'listen' to their needs for communication . This is enabled through mechanisms to ensure stakeholder feedback and response, including communication audit, benchmarking and establishing feedback and measurement systems. Change was an unavoidable evil and if it could organizations would rather try to adapt reality than the other way round. Several corporate suffered the same fate as that which befell the dinosaurs of yesterday; those which evolved and adapted survived. Some even made the elephant dance. Isn't it timed that organizations are now built with this perspective rather than encounter with it as one would with a thorn in the little finger. You can afford to ignore it only thus far. Gryger continues, "Further, some three-quarters of respondents don't think their companies are good at building the capability that is most important. When senior executives are involved in setting the capabilities agenda, companies are more successful at aligning those agendas with the capability most important to performance and more effective at building the needed skills. Notably, however, the most common reason respondents give for their companies' focus on the capability identified as most important to business performance is that the skill is a part of their companies' culture, rather than any competitive reason".

Change Propensity and Perpetual Modesty - Organizations like accounting entities are conceptualized to be enduring in time. Like the accountants who make a balance sheet that captures a fleeting moment in the life of an enduring organization. Organization designers of our generation and that of the previous one have always thought of them as being built for eternity. The Knowledge Bureaucracy of tomorrow will have a propensity to expect, adapt and be "ready for next" change to an extent much greater than that found in any of the contemporary organizations. Take a look at the number of organizations that are undergoing restructuring at any point in time and the truth will be readily apparent. To that extent therefore, there will always be a sense of impermanence about the organization. While to those who build a home for a lifetime, leaving the old home for a new one may be painful, for those who expect to change houses every five years it may be the excitement of doing something new.

Red Tape - Organizational bureaucracies and policy orientation can turn into milestones around one's neck and needs appropriate management. Basic concepts that determined a well-run corporation of the current era are likely to be discarded as those that are outdated and no longer in fashion. We would classify working bureaucracy and rigid policy framework management style and two of the critical aspects to make a point. The bureaucracy that helped structure, plan, process, style and staff work together through forms, procedures and approval mechanisms has turned into a liability of today's managerial effectiveness. Bureaucracies at its best cause delay in action and decisiveness although for a stated valid reason. Where customer satisfaction is crucial for corporate credibility "time" and "speed" is an important strategic intent. Similarly, policy dependence with everybody knows about everything approach has its limitation with individuals feeling considerably confined to the closed quarters of corporate bondage. It is significantly unlikely that high dependence on bureaucracies or policies would ever have its usefulness in a wholesome sense ever again. It has done its time for both the corporation and the individual. Individuals seeking space to contribute would ask for an environment where their opportunity to think, feel and act is uninhibited and a constraint free work place is but a minimum that would be asked of the organization.

C. Changing Organizational Assumptions

Non Negotiable Mindset - Re-emergence of strategic revitalization, more as a process of renewal, as a means to propel directional orientation is inevitable. Strategic management would need to reorient itself towards renewal and revitalization. The basics of the formulation process should be revamped to provide for revisiting vision, mission, values and key goals and objectives. The company philosophy towards how should the business be managed and run needs revitalization. An analysis of SWO (P) T should be redone to modify the last stated positions in the analysis. There has to be a synthesis between the strategic intent and the intellectual orientation of the organization. The firm has to position itself again in the market place in terms of its products, customer service charters, contracts of employment and ways of managing the commercial enterprise. Directions perceived, as right as of yesterday may need a relook not for any dramatic reason but to take stock of the company in the context of an emerging economy. Companies that saw growth as a strategic direction have revised their view to consolidation as of today. Similarly, corporations that confined themselves to their known areas of competence are looking at alliances and acquisitions to get into industries of the 21st century. To our mind any non-negotiable mind set on company strategy or its business opportunities bends to an ostrich like attitude. India Based Global Multi National, Wipro Inc. that kicked off as a consumer marketing company is now a dominant software player. All in a span of 2 decades. Their corporate outlook shifted as radically as the changes itself. They had the mindset to transit from current sober state to a radical dynamic state.

Behaviors Need to Change – "Clear Vision - Large Scale transformations, to be successful, require that not only the senior management, **all** internal stakeholders in the organization possess a common and shared understanding of: What the organization desires to achieve, how to achieve, where it wants to be, when it wants to be where it wants to be. Hence, while the institution may have has defined its vision clearly, its success in achieving that vision is strongly contingent on its internal stakeholders, especially its employees to understand the larger vision, Why is a change required now when an organizational has already been providing substantive client service or has appropriate products and services? How will the organization and equally critically, how will they benefit if the Vision were to be achieved? How will their work be impacted, i.e., what would be the end state, for them? What changes would need to be brought in their current work-style and work profile to achieve the Vision? How would a transformed digital organization help them in collectively realising this Vision and; How are the employees required to contribute while on the journey towards achieving the vision? A well-defined change journey can be charted only when one is aware of the existing state of the organization in transition. Only when both the 'As-is' and 'To-be' states are clearly articulated can a company identify gaps which need to be plugged / improvements which need to be made / changes which need to be incorporated. Additionally, a comprehensive As-is Analysis will allow it to prepare a strong business case for change.

Communication - Like any other initiative which impacts lives of employees, effective and impactful communication will play a pivotal role for the entire lifecycle of this initiative. While the importance of continuous communication cannot be understated, its role becomes all the more critical on account of the following factors: IT modernisation project directly impacts the work of people and by implication, their role in the value chain and their own self-worth, Diverse nature of stakeholders involved, i.e., from operating heads and operations, customer facing roles to the Head of Functions and above, Large number of employees, wide customer base, Geographical dispersion of the target change audience, i.e., Limited channels of communication, i.e., very large number employees may not be connected to official emails and hence, their only mode of knowledge of what is happening at the company or the multiple geographies or functions, may be limited to official circulars, instructions of their seniors and grapevine of (Electronic channels not very pervasive). Weak communication may in turn result in the following: Intended message not getting through rumours and misconceptions may spread among employees; both in turn impacting the change management process. Equally critically, ineffective communication has the potential to augment all the 4 risks, i.e., Culture Risk, Organization Risk, Know-How Risk and Stakeholder Risk, mentioned above. Hence, the institution will need to identify means of effective and continuous communication to its employees, taking into account its infrastructural and cultural realities

Leading Change - Over the years, it has been observed that large scale transformation is successfully brought about only when the top leadership team is supported by intermediary leaders and opinion makers across levels. While organizations may have steadily expanded its scale of operations with times, i.e., For example, introduction of digital products and Service, Computerization etc, the current initiative is even more critical as it has the potential to redefine the way general public/customers/shareholder looks at Digital Products and Services. Hence, it is imperative that the change initiative being driven by the Leadership, in addition to support from stakeholders, supported by Change Leaders across levels, who would act as ambassadors of the need to change, to the larger group of employees. These change leaders not only are at various levels but are working in a synchronised manner to achieve their objectives, i.e., sending the right messages to employees and leading change initiatives supported by interconnected leaders.

- **Network Leaders:** These leaders act on the interfaces between project groups, functions and teams. These are the guides, advisors, active helpers and assessors, working in partnership with line leaders. Formal – informal leaders would form the major share of Network leaders.

- **Local Line Leaders:** These are the front line managers who make the core processes work for the company. Without the commitment of these people, no significant change will happen. They rely on the network leaders to link them with other parts of the organization, and on executive leaders to create the right infrastructure for change to get institutionalized. Product heads, digital specialists, among others, would be a critical component of local line leadership.

- **Executive Leaders:** These leaders exist at the board - directorate level and provide the overall guidance and direction to the change initiative. One of their key responsibilities is to create the right infrastructure for change to get institutionalized. Top Management would form the Executive Leadership for this initiative". There is a state of perpetual modesty in coping with change as it affects individuals and organizations. We do not wish to draw an analogy to the nomadic dwellings which have no permanency at all but rather to way in which the dialects change every ten miles in England, while the language remains the same, till you cross the Channel. "It is neither easy nor straightforward to improve a company's performance through a comprehensive program to change the behavior of employees by changing their mind-sets. No company should try to do so without first exhausting less disruptive alternatives for attaining the business outcome it desires. Incremental and Strategic is self-evident and includes changes of work methods and processes, new product launches etc where most people see a continuity between the old state to the new. It is progress by evolution rather than revolution and though over a long period an observer can see the difference between how the organization was and how it is no one change makes the organization feel very different. Sometimes tactical moves will be enough; sometimes new practices can be introduced without completely rethinking the corporate culture". Emily Lawson and Colin Price in a McKinsey's Quarterly paper, "The psychology of change management", write, "A few years ago, this CEO took the helm of a large European retail bank that employed more than 30,000 people. He set several targets: doubling the economic profit of the bank, reducing its cost-to-income ratio to 49 percent (from 56), and increasing its annual revenue growth from the current 1 to 2 percent to 5 to 7 percent—all within four years. Fundamental or tactical change is quite a contrast to incremental strategic change. This kind of change may be termed visionary and transformational. Such changes make a noticeable impact on the organization and if successful can make a visible difference to the organization's standing. Such changes usually involve a major upheaval. And affect the future operations of the company. But retail banking is almost a commodity business so it is not easy to usher in fundamental changes. No financial-engineering shortcuts or superficial changes in practice could win a competitive edge for the bank. It could meet these performance goals, the CEO realized, only by galvanizing its people to deliver far better customer outcomes at a much lower cost. That meant changing the culture of the bank by transforming it from a bureaucracy into a federation of entrepreneurs: managers would be rewarded for taking charge of problems and deciding, quickly, how to fix them. But if the only way for a company to reach a higher plane of performance is to alter the way its people think and act, it will need to create the four conditions for achieving sustained change".

Technology - Technological superiority and strong asset base is not a necessary competitive advantage. Technology, as in plant and machinery, will become available to any manufacturer if it is their strategic intent to increase their asset base. Organizations of tomorrow are unlikely to enhance the weight of their balance sheet. It is possible to contract out manufacturing or the technology necessary to perform the manufacturing activity for a price. Venture capitalists are available to pay for purchase of technology if that makes commercial sense. Whereas organizational direction is likely to be creating capital value out of their intellectual and human assets. If all of competition is likely to possess similar technology, there is hardly a possibility of the customer not receiving a product quality of choice that the technology can provide. The differentiators would move into the realm of enhanced quality, superior processes, new product development, innovative designs, shopping experience, value for money, new brands and customer delight opportunities like service charters and so on. All that is possible with the human mind and with the technology taken for granted and assumed as available and performing. Amazon.com is an example of a virtual million-dollar enterprise that can compete with an established Nobles and Barnes in the distribution business.

Markets - Local market dominance is no longer the recipe' global competitiveness for sustaining long term developmental growth. Several examples are now available be it fashion brands, telecommunication networks, financial institutions where being a large US firm is not guarantee that their entry into a new market will be successful. Pepsi Cola and Coca-Cola have planned their paybacks well beyond 10 years in developing Asian markets. AT &T is still not a dominant player in their new entry Asian markets. Although each of these brands would eventually dominate the market but with an altered strategy after adapting themselves to the new market and creating conditions of success. A proven strategy for firms have been dominance in the local market that has significantly helped their entry strategies into the new market given their learning by fire experience. The transitions for these firms have been their early globalization and early bird advantages. Globalization turning into an inevitable growth route for national players is a minimum for strategy managers.

Products - Conglomerate and widely diversified corporations of multi product menagerie are not a panacea for global growth. This again has been on account of several factors:

- *Corporate with significant product features and value tend to specialize and offer a center of plate quality and service.*
- *Organizations with a product focus and expertise in sales, distribution, variety and dominance possess a strategic advantage versus organizations that have a large portfolio of products but with limited market share and customer base.*
- *Organizations with several products (not brands) of diametrically opposite features tend to generalize the marketing mix and are unable to position for themselves as a large enough corporation with the mass scale advantages.*

- *Firms need to look at size as an important strategic advantage to dominate the market.*
- *Multi brand companies should have the financial muscle, global experience, and staying power, people and reach to penetrate significantly.*
- *Or alternatively focus on a single product and turn into the best supplier of any comparable benchmark.*
- *Large-scale mergers and acquisitions have focused on size to grow. Eventually mid-sized organizations without strategic advantages are unlikely to survive.*
- *Effectively conglomerate corporations with a wide portfolio of product offering will not be at an advantage. One Coke is sufficient to take on an industry of soft drink manufacturers.*
- *Large single product and small multi brand portfolio appears to be coexisting in markets that are similar in nature but varying in size.*

Product life cycles simply do not have a long shelf life. They would come and go, as fast, yet corporations would have to continuously supply a new range of brands, products to keep the customer satisfied. While looking at the changing customer needs and the level of specialist research being undertaken by competition it is critical for organizations to float a range of consumer products to retain shelf space. This is largely on account of in-depth knowledge work being undertaken by specialist staff to study changing consumer preferences and creating products that fit the needs of as many as possible. The growth in the economy in an overall sense together with enhanced purchasing power, choice of value for money products offers the consumer an opportunity to choose. While competencies, competition and economic factors change, markets have shown its inability to buy unacceptable products. The key is in realizing this as an issue and creating alternate strategies.

Corporate structure and strategy linkages are increasingly turning blurred and lacking in positional clarity owing to closer change dynamics as it impacts the firm. As companies face change and the need to renew itself and get fighting fit, limited time will be available to work close strategy-structure work outs. Change may become necessary, for example, to fix remuneration to hold on to critical individuals. The traditional course followed through a process of consultation, market data, involvement of appropriate peers, impact on the top and bottom line may all become relatively irrelevant given the square need to fix the issue promptly. Launch of a product depending on the personal expertise of an officer of a firm may become immediate and necessary to pre-empt competition. The product is out in the market before a structure has been put in place. Unilever launched Wheel detergent washing powder to compete with a potential threat in the most dynamic manner. Very limited time was spent between strategy-structure interfaces while this launch was planned and executed. Trivial as the example might sound this is the reality of tomorrow's corporation. Getting on with the business would mean flexibility in all our actions with limited recourse to proven practices of the managerial past.

Corporate goals focus would be dependent on a performance cycle rather than the traditional quarterly reviews. Publicly quoted companies have the obligation of reporting monthly, quarterly results to the investing public. Organizations have long since been lost to this requirement and have trapped themselves into managing the last quarter performance to help show an acceptable balance sheet. Income and expenditures are booked just around the quarter corner to position it for public consumption. Government sectors and government run companies are notorious for maximizing their expense budgets in the last quarter of the year just in case the budget for a similar expense is not approved the next year. An emerging practice would be to work goal cycles that are not monthly or quarterly or a traditional Roman calendar based. Organizations should evaluate performance cycles in terms of the work content, targets to be met and the optimum time required to achieve it. The balance sheet as a consequence would reflect a true performance of the tasks completed, tasks on hand and the pending work content. A management accounting balance sheet should be the norm for presentation, rather than an accounting balance sheet. Corporations would then be forced to evaluate their performance on a virtual cycle.

Financial leverage as a critical success factor of new business horizon is not dealt with as comprehensively in high value, margin, and low asset and less management intensive business ventures as it is in low value/margin, financially intensive capital structuring and management intensive businesses. This is the reality of tomorrow. Few takers would be available for low knowledge intensive businesses with a heavy capital outlay. More so if the knowledge is confined only towards the running of a fully automated process industry. Where machines can do the job as efficiently why waste an intellectual manpower. Arguably there would still be businesses and promoters for heavy industries, commodity based products and so on, nevertheless, their orientation would move from ownership to management where their managerial expertise would be of value to the enterprise rather than their ability to invest.

Competitive Situations - To face competition over time and retaining a winning condition, organizational competencies have to be identified and changed dynamically. This is inevitable realistically. Identification of what we can do best and having them implemented expeditiously are both equally important. Organizations of tomorrow have to be in touch with their organizational members and their individual competencies to realize what can they do best and at a given point of time. Summation of individual competencies determines the organizational competencies. Making a five-year plan with current state of competencies is a true reflection of a company's suicidal tendency. Knowledge of the business as we ran it yesterday makes no meaning for tomorrow. Competencies would radically shift from one stage of development to another depending upon the stated position of the organization at a point in time. What was evaluated as our source of strength may emerge to be our single largest weakness? There are examples of the buggy whip syndrome where the company has lived on its cash cow of yesterday.

Environmental and socio-political factors continue to be critical success factors for global organizations. Large corporations have consistently seen the need to evaluate and work with their environments systemically. Environment managers perform the role of knowledge gathering, analysis and evaluation of its impact on the business of the corporation. Enron Corporation is an example of managing a whimsical political scenario and their CEO Rebecca Mark's role in bringing about a rapprochement between the corporation and the wily politicians was a classical case study of environment management. The information generated could be from socio political changes, to local community acceptance of the presence of the company, ecology laws governing the company, the financial institution perception of the company, media influence or the talent pool receptivity to join the firm and make a career.

Scale - Downsized organizations continue to feel the pain of separations dealt over time on its people owing to absence of a clear prescriptive formula of success post the restructuring exercise. People restructuring have seen its time to a considerable degree as organizations continue to reel under the negative impact of their actions. As we stated earlier there are instances of quarterly balance sheet management issues where corporate management chooses the people departure route to show action in a non-Performing Enterprise . Post restructuring the promised results simply did not happen, obviously given the reasons for non-performance being other factors beyond people alone. Again the science of rationalizing manpower needs considerable refinement with methods of identifying surplus people, redundancies, strategic realignment of people and abolished jobs requiring an accredited method. Structural weight traditionally seen in large corporate are now decreasing as companies see the emergence of individuals who can substitute large numbers with their agile mind. Although in the

Intellectual Corporate headcount is less likely to ever be an issue. Individuals would pay for their compensation several times over through the application of their mind. It is in the bureaucratic hierarchies that we apprehend a continuous act of purging and that to our mind, if not managed well, could lead to an organizational freeze.

Role stresses and work load loop encountered by middle level managers would increase given pressure to perform owing to a push factor from below from managers wanting early and substantive space to contribute and grow. And a pull factor from the top where the top management is demanding on time innovative performance. There is an emerging value conflict between the large-scale number of middle and senior managers who have spent large years in the corporate but have retained some amount of their competitive competencies. They may not be as ready and would be ideally expected but they are somewhere there close enough. This is a potential area of current knowledge and expected knowledge competencies. Where an organization has not kept pace with training and development a significant portion of managers would turn knowledge redundant periodically and would come up for the retention review.

Active Control - People do not wish to be told, controlled, directed, guided or led, irrespective of our noble intentions. They would fundamentally like to be left to themselves to show initiative, make new products, redesign, change, create, add value, learn, reflect and make their impact on the company bottom line. They would basically like to be liberated from the corporate bureaucratic shackles. In fact important shifts and specified emphatic changes are increasing on freedom, autonomy, responsibility, and the influence of employees at all levels are happening across select organizations showing a clear trend. In some ways I can think of the characters in the classic "Drifters" by James Michener or the Hare Krishna movement in a positive sense, Of course.

D. Changing Paradigms

Paradigm on Defining Cultures - Everyone in the organization shares the culture. Culture has among its central components "values (what is important) and beliefs (how things work). Culture "encompasses norms and expectations that influence the way members of organizations think and behave. The culture of an organization is reflected in its norms and values, its traditions and what is expected from its people. The organization culture inventory (OCI) provides an assessment of an organization's operating culture in terms of the behaviours that members believe are required to "fit in and meet expectations" within their organization. Such analysis reveals a person's individual normative beliefs (when the perspective of only one person is plotted) or the shared behavioural expectations that operate within the organization (when the perspectives of different people are combined). The results reveal any counterproductive behaviours that the organization may be inadvertently reinforcing, as well as the negative impact these behaviours may be having on both individual and organizational performance.

Constructive orientation reflects a healthy balance of task and people related concerns. The emphasis is on non-defensive behavior that is aimed at achieving 'higher-order' needs. The styles associated with this orientation are directed aa Achievement - setting of personal standards and the attainment of goals, Self -actualizing - the value of personal learning and a sense of 'perspective', Humanistic - a belief in the value of others and a supportive/encouraging interpersonal approach and Affiliate – a desire to build personal relationships and interact with others.

Passive/Defensive orientation reflects a dependence upon others for a sense of personal security. This results in defensive behavior, designed to self-protect. The styles associated with this orientation are directed at Approval - the need to be liked and the seeking of approval from others , Conventional - an approach to others that relies doing what they think others want of them and maintaining the status quo, Dependence - a need to rely on others, with low personal confidence , Avoidance - the need to avoid any issues seen as personally threatening and become absorbed in one's own problems.

Aggressive/Defensive orientation reflects an emphasis on seeking personal security through task activity, emphasizing task over people, often in fact at the expense of people. The styles associated with this orientation are directed at Oppositional - the need to seek attention through being cynical and critical and aggressively disagreeing with others, Power - the tendency to associate one's self-worth with the degree to which one can dominate and control others, Competitive - the need to build self-esteem through competing with others and comparing self to others and Perfectionist - the driven need to be seen by others as 'perfect' and avoid any form of 'failure'

Culture definitions have undergone a shift from culture inheritance, management and absorption to cultural creation, assimilation, influencing and impacting for change. There was a time, as we would like say now, "when culture was told to the new recruit. This is your organization and this is the way we do things out here. These are the stories of the past and we guess having understood our past your ability to adapt to the future is quite possible". Alas this is unlikely to succeed as a method of socialization. Even traditional methods of induction and socialization would need to be modified. If an organization consists of people, who work out of several locations, hired and placed in countries many miles away, process of induction may have to be electronic. But as they interact and deal with people, issues, organizational values and practices the induction process has definitely begun. More importantly people begin influencing culture the long distance way. The process of discovery would radically change for the new recruits. They would perhaps get in and do what they want to start with and would object if somebody protests or resists. Individuals would seek their space irrespective of whether we have it to offer or not. In any event if that space was not available the individual would seek the next possible station to alight. Culture, perceptibly, would turn significantly more dynamic in its understanding to people. Individuals would see the organization changing and unchanging periodically given the critical mass of people who are influencing it. As more and more people experience the changing circumstance more cultural exchanges would become real and necessary. It is our hypothesis that never would a day come when the organizational members can sit back and define their company culture in a constant, consistent sort of way. At best that by itself would become the culture, in ambiguity there would be clarity.

Paradigm on Transitions - Transition from approved ways and means of doing things turning into unanticipated influences over people, systems and process would happen unknowingly. Employees are directly influencing through direct involvement in decisions affecting their work and their departments. Business school graduates prefer to exercise a choice of their roles and responsibilities. Practical mechanisms like open door policy, open communication sessions, grievance management system, and representative groups for unionized staff, task forces on special issues, problem solving work forces have time and again served their utility. Increased collaboration between union and management through employee relations executive forums and participate work groups like Quality Circles, quality of work life programs, safety, health and welfare committees have been used for bringing in a sense of involvement. Obviously all this is just not enough. A natural process of asking individuals before we act upon them is inevitable if we desire their wholesome commitment to their roles and the company.

Paradigm on Dynamics of Culture - Culture to perform to culture to learn, contribute, add value and enhance shareholder value is an organizational expectation for the individuals of the future. Individuals in doing their learning and contribution would seek fundamental and basic experiences.

Not rocket science demands. A place to work, a working infrastructure, learn as they go along and spend time, an opportunity to create, feel a sense of identity on what they have created and eventually believe that all that they have done has impacted the shareholder. People centric ways in treating people for their potential and human nature to help them feel a sense of belonging, a feeling of achievement and an opportunity to bring out the best in them is essential to this process of attempted transition. The culture provides for failure as much as enjoying its share of success. "Outsiders think Silicon Valley as a success story," writes Silicon Valley commentator Mike Malone, "but in truth, it is a graveyard. Failure is Silicon Valley's greatest strength. Every initial product or enterprise is a lesson stored in the collective memory of the country". Venture capitalist Don Valentine says, "The world of technology is complex, fast changing and unstructured and it thrives best when individuals are left alone to be different, creative and disobedient".

Paradigm on Institutional Emphasis - Organizations see the need for institutionalizing learning and teaching systems for people to learn, develop and intellectually grow as a responsibility, "self-imposed", on them. While people are doing their jobs and getting things done there is a group of facilitators, coaches and trainers who perform the role of institutionalizing learning. They are the leaders of tomorrow. They make education happen naturally without elaborate systemic processes or planned classroom training. Electronic learning methods, long distance teaching modules, state of art knowledge programs, behavioral modification and cultural adaptation modules, unlearning in preparedness for the next set of concepts to absorb all become a laundry list of required facilitator's role. Individuals in turn are demanding corporate commitment and willingness to make employees employable over time. The process of reciprocity is essential in making knowledge managers work for others. For the individual's knowledge is their core competency and they would like to share, display and contribute depending on their constant state of upgradation. While it is not being presupposed that this becomes a corporate responsibility a learning culture perhaps is an inescapable responsibility of the corporate management. Organizational learning forums would multiply several folds with members demanding time and opportunity to participate physically or electronically. As the learning centers proliferate cultural influences just occurs.

Paradigm on Knowledge – Intellect - Corporations view knowledge management as a competitive weapon to fight unprecedented economic wars. In a scenario where easy finance, adequate raw material, cheap labor and growing market is a real life scenario, knowledge becomes the true competitive source. In the individual intellect lie the competitive edge and the push factor against competition. When individuals are prodded to perform against intellectual odds they are likely to be at their best. Good work comes out of the human minds' defiance to doing it the proven way. Firms need to capitalize on this potential of the human mind to take on challenges that a product or a service cannot offer consistently over time.

Paradigm on Digital Skills – Socially compatible Decision-making, an important aspect of the changing cultural dimension, has moved to the point of impact. Seniority of people and their experiences are no longer the governing principles for vesting of authority and power. As organizations employ managers with the power to think and do, there would arise a need for empowerment. There would also be the scope demanded of the individuals to do their job holistically being responsible for what they are accountable for. The operating front line manager is equipped with the capability to decide and act upon his/her problems. An empowered sales manager in the field talking and dealing with the customer best services customers. Getting back to the head office to seek an answer is not a workable proposition to customers demanding on time all the time service. Decisions, as a consequence, have moved to the point of impact. The shop floor supervisor answers the employee on his/her questions. First line managers ask for the freedom to do their job independently. Organizations cannot work through a long and an expanded hierarchy of seasoned managers who apparently know the one best answer. In any event we do not visualize adequate time in the hands of managers to manage a "ladder of references" before they could get their job done.

Paradigm on Mastering Change - Change has become a way of life for corporate managers whose ability to reckon with and manage change as a day to day issue has become a necessary competency for effectiveness. If we presuppose an organization that is expected to operate on a flexible basis at a strategic level, with structures happening on an impromptu basis, with people processes depending on the current situation meeting with change head on is but a minimum. CEO's of corporations see change management, building people preparedness to face change, bringing in change adept internal practices in managerial actions, making change facilitators create and nurture the risk taking factor amongst employees as their single largest priority in the management of the enterprise. Intellectual Corporation rarely is change shy, as their coping mechanism happens to be their mind that understands rationally the purpose and goals aimed through the planned change. The users rather than the supervisory managers initiate Many times change. Individuals of well-managed intellectual companies do not like to be told to change. They would rather identify the change, plan for its execution, and cover the impacted people by themselves instead of waiting for the systemic influencers to announce and manage the change. Motorola would be one corporation where the ownership for change rests with the impacted people. Motorola University focuses their training attention to managing the turbulent environment with managers taking charge of their change needs and actions.

Paradigm on Professionalization - Work role professionals see organizational life no longer as an extension of their real world full time life. Many would like it to be independent of each other, family and work, with adequate quality space available for leading a life of fulfillment. Seeking joy is but one phenomenon that is very real for high performing individuals. It is in this context that flexible working, own time scheduler, self-goal prioritization, including variable bonuses and pay linked to targets achieved and virtual offices become real and inevitable. Apart from significant advantages in terms of office space, support staff, nearness to the customer, delivery based pay systems and virtual speed of response. Individuals would also demand more time for their learning and knowledge updating efforts. Working spouse, care for parents, off line work and hobbies, mid-career education and planning, and choice of school for children, geographic location preference and more importantly the employee would like to work at a location where his/her contribution is maximized. It is possible to receive a higher number of applications for part time employment just to help the applicant have more time to do other things. While this is perhaps a loss to the corporation for the increasing amount of limited time availability of their effective performers the upside would be the opportunity for organizations to have half as many more people and their creative minds.

Paradigm on Diversity - Corporations see the real need to integrate diversity issues as a basic management challenge and are creating culture facilitation strategies to make diverse people live and work well with each other. Cross culture studies have revealed that over 50% of the work force of the 21st century would consist of people of diverse background, demographics, varying personal preferences and cultural milieu. Diversity preparation becomes an important organizational action point to have people not just tolerate each other but actually enjoy working and sharing with their colleagues. The emergence of the third world in the global business scenario makes diversity management extremely crucial immediately in the short run. Workplace management demands would need to be reckoned with to allow for minds of several types and dispositions would work together. They could be physically together or could be working miles apart but attitudinal congruence and tolerance towards diverse people sets is essential and inevitable.

Paradigm on Group Dynamics - Teams performances could be influenced by the role played by the intellectual manager depending upon the method used by the group to make participating members learn, share and co-exist. It is ironical to argue for team performance in an individualized Intellectual Company. Yet we do not see a contradiction. Teams will always be there with individuals participating in it working towards a common objective. The issues on team working could substantially be different with team norms including aspects of individual contribution based on areas of expertise, seasoning of managers to the task in hand, working out of physically dispersed locations and an element of competitive spirit bordering on individual excellence. Team leadership could vary based on expertise, client requirement and the attitudinal vagaries of the team members. Teams would exercise considerable influence over their choice of team members. Effectively teams would turn into clusters and coalition groups with similar and dissimilar purposes and goals. Formal creations may turn into a challenge for the management as the clusters would have a unique internal management style for leading, participating, sharing, working norms, for example, long hour working, helping a colleague through a personal problem and substituting him/her on the job etc. Many organizational norms of discipline and rules of work ethic traditionally understood and practiced in the organization may undergo a change given the cluster desire to achieve their goals in their own way. In our opinion managers, in managing their independent work force whose demands for autonomy may border on laissez faire, would face considerable degree of difficulty.

Paradigm on Intellectual culture could sometimes, in fact many times be conflict prone given occasional polarized and strong views on individual positions and perspectives. Participating members typically have a point of view on issues confronting him or herself or the organization and feel their role to be critical enough to substantiate their argument. Large-scale differences are eminently possible. When two minds that think are put together there would a point of difference. Organizations and individuals should be aware of this possibility and seek out acceptable and pre-determined means of conflict resolution and due process. The corporate would become responsible to create confrontation forums and stress release mechanisms to make people of intellectual intensity work together. The dispersion possibility of people flying off the handle owing to combination of work role pressures and an inability to sell their idea across is high. Research and development departments interfacing closely with manufacturing or marketing departments would need careful monitoring and coaching, counseling to manage themselves in their new context. A software development pocket with people rushing to advance their knowledge is another area of concern. Similarly, HR professionals who have become responsible for HR services and people counseling roles would need considerable adaptation and focus maintenance training. Making people emotionally resilient to what affects them while on the job is a critical role to be performed. Defining the changed context and their meaning or adaptation to the context is relevant to eliminate identity loss and frustration amongst people in "high think" jobs.

Paradigm on Collaboration - Clearly the participating managers impact the culture in several ways both in the short and long run. The organization tends to be perceived as being excessively skewed in favor of meritocracy albeit at the cost of loyal long-term employees. Some overtly aggressive individuals who would make normal circumstance appear conflict and confrontation prone could vitiate the culture. Some amount of survival of the fittest tendency may creep in. Placement and hiring decisions would lean in favor of college degrees, professional education, organizational skills and competencies and knowledge that is application and growth based. A natural process of attrition of those who do not "fit in" would emerge for a natural process of elimination. Employees would consider the organizational career plan to consist of a successive set of hurdles to be crossed at every stage of their career with no letting go at any time. People will simply have to be at the top of their performance graphs to move up hierarchically. Who knows more, how much more do people know,

know more and more of less and less, (know what, know why), gross focus on issues, a quality of mind that is inquiring, investigating, challenging, considerable skills of creativity, deep and powerful analytical insights, sharpened process skills, critical understanding of organizational knowledge linkages and many such factors would become relevant. The employees would simply have to think more before they act. Employees would be expected to be at their best at literally all times. Speed would mean a combination of responsiveness and superior quality of input. Effective service at acceptable quality would not be good enough.

Paradigm on Creation of a performing culture where people would sense the common goal of customer service, satisfaction, adding to shareholder's wealth and bottom line orientation is key to the Intellectual Corporation. A culture where "people – systems" would replace "systems – people" with the original contribution of the people as the critical input. The human school linked with the systems approach to make the human mind superior to the machine with the caveat that they are now inter dependent. There would be a premium on doing it different every time. Task orientation would create a new sort of peer group competitiveness with competent minds chasing self-imposed goals and deadlines. The organizational performance would emerge into one of spontaneous discovery process where people would cherish the task of achieving yet another milestone.

Paradigm on Managerial actions by itself would no longer determine company priorities on an exclusive basis in this dynamic culture. The managerial act would be either preceded or succeeded by individual or collective intellect providing information based knowledge, sensitivity analysis with "go – no go" options, scenario planning and scoping etc. The responsibility of managing the company would cut across lines of control and power and would depend on groups of people vested with the correct knowledge of the issue in question. Every function and activity of the company would turn knowledge and intellect driven. Manufacturing teams would be driven by their knowledge of technology, process, standards and methods. Marketing would make brands, research, and customer data knowledge intensive. Research and development would focus on new products, inventions and innovations. Finance and HR functions would attempt making every policy and system intellect friendly and knowledge sensitive. Everybody knows everything. Knowledge sharing would be the power that people would exercise. Routine would considerably give way to creative new.

E. Intellectual Realities

Talent Realities - Quality of hiring talent into the corporation has undergone a radical shift. Firms now bring in people with special expertise to the job, people with proven academic depth and potential to pursue intellectually stimulating assignments. Best of organizations compete to obtain preferred employer status in engineering and business management institutions. The race is to gain access to the student to help sell the organization. Corporations today have a choice of talent to pick and choose from depending on their demonstrated college degree, proven academic performance and other performance attributes relevant to organizations. An increasing supply of professionally qualified employees is available to the organizations for employment in their organizations. Many teaching institutions are focusing on academic and on the job performance simulated excellence to prepare students to face work life.

Knowledge Realities - Generalist studies as seen in last few decades with a focus on arts and humanities have given way to accounting, technology, behavioral sciences and psychology, environment and business management specialization. The quality of education has significantly increased in the professional institutions where the premium on excellence is not being under estimated. Large number of academic faculty from professional course universities and institutes are actively pursuing business consulting and organizational interventions. Case methodology has come to stay with the students being prepared for their life in business organizations by seeing, learning and experiencing real life class room drama. Academic focus is increasingly knowledge driven with a greater emphasis on teaching and helping students learn depth of the subjects being taught in preparation of their future of functional specializations. Computer studies with a knowledge emphasis are very real. A unique phenomenon is the usage of the World Wide Web for advancing people knowledge and learning capabilities. If knowledge is available at the fingertips of learners, there is but limited chance that the opportunity will be passed over by the knowledge seekers. The web now has students and the teaching community talking across borders on issues that are of common interest and those that affect business organizations in any part of the globe. Faculty, students and working professionals are now actively making their presence felt through the web through their intellectual contribution. For example, the reluctant writer of the past has today a medium where sharing is easy and simple to handle and an opportunity to show their work to the world at large. Seeking recognition is no longer confined to own circle of friends, peers, superiors and mutual admirers. The posting of one's work on the Web ensures that it has the potential of being seen perhaps by the best in the world and a response including recognition being received from a strange but important visitor to your site.

360 Perspective of Enterprises Realities - Organizations have a large number of employees who understand and know what have they visited the corporation for and what do they have to receive in return for their contribution. Corporations too have made learning and development as a necessary condition for employee development and systemic interventions at periodic intervals are provided to make employees employable. Training function and its focus on development has undergone a significant shift and moving away from staid forms of development routes. Substantive amount of quality managerial time is currently spent on managerial competencies, performance goals and action report charts to evaluate performance against set work plans. Added to this phenomenon is the issue of employees asking for substantive job content that includes thinking and doing. There is urgency on the part of the new employee to demand active involvement in management thinking and decision making process. People would like to be involved in all aspects of business that affects them first of all and in all aspects of the business where they believe they can contribute. Lines of control, hierarchy is no longer emerging to be relevant need to know information is in question.

Realities of Internet of Things - What was in yesteryears treated as "none of my business" is today made into "everything is my business" by the thinking employee group? Employees would rather not be left behind in a decisive situation. And there are many and many that would like this level of active involvement. As a consequence, there is a need for offering intellectual equity for people with personal commitments to make their contribution real and meaningful to organizational performance. Intellectual equity is available through many internal mechanisms for those who desire challenges. Special group should be created and exposed to cross functional and cross business interfacing with accountability for results, not a one large familiarization program. Intellectually stimulated individuals should be offered high-risk assignments involving new product launches, financial market management, union settlement, meeting aggressive project deadlines. Special assignments should mark for people with the potential who can think beyond their job and who are keen to spare time beyond their work hours to do something more meaningful. While creating worth and equity for individual's adequate steps should be taken to make people work consistently through time. Irregular and spurts of workloads would cause thinking disarray. More importantly it is not always essential for all assignments to the thinking individuals be only driven by practical application. Several project works involving strategies not attempted before should be a part of their curriculum. Involving individuals in activities beyond their defined scope of work is fundamental a form of offering intellectual equity to people.

Realities of Complexity - Employees view the emerging business complexity as an inevitable feature of the modern economy. In it they see an opportunity for individual capabilities, skills, competencies and most of all their intellect to be put to use considerably. Employees like to make clean, clear, connection with organizational bottom-line orientation/result and the intellect that has been utilized to make it happen. Application of the intellect too versatile and barrier breaking episodes offers the intrinsic motivation to the intellectually bored set of corporate citizens. They are looking for an avenue to articulate their mind and see its impact on the company. In a sense they are like chess players making one move, predicting the next few moves of the opponent and yet looking forward to the surprise element that stretches their mind. Every idea thought plan generated, created, nurtured and consolidated by the thinking population is seeking contribution space and medium.

That the organization is managed with data, information and consequent knowledge is undebated. Yet the integrating function is the intellect in the individual that helps process, analyze, synthesize, store and make a coherent meaning to all pieces of connected and dispersed set of factors. It is the intellect again that brings in the recall, create relevant connections, make a method to the plan, provides scope for development of competencies and provides the employee with the capabilities to manage, decide, judge and make a meaning to all actions. In fact, it is the intellect that makes learning happen to the individual.

F. Managing Intellect

I as Intellect - Existence of a culture that facilitates the continuing presence of people who bring in quality of thinking not normally experienced by the corporation is but a minimum expectation of the intellectual corporation. As we stated earlier this process of culture creation is likely to be influenced by the intellect to a considerable extent. The culture creation effort is more through a loop wherein both the internal players as well as the new entrants react to the environment based on their experience. The trigger is when the issue is in conflict with their personal disposition and attitudes that they have brought into the company. The new entrant, who displays a severe sense of rebound, experiences a heightened level of intensity. It is essential for the recruiters to be aware of this emotion and help the new recruit make the transition into the culture. The organization in addition should make intellectual interaction a formal management process in resolving organizational problem solving scenarios. Creating and fostering a work culture where the best of people have the opportunity to work and give their best is critical to make the culture work for all. Where they seek excellence in all their actions is when intensity is managed.

- *Essentially the intellectual employee also arrives with a baggage of imponderables behaviorally and intellectually.*
- *To our mind this cultural mix confusion is eminently possible at the first few stages of the interactive processes:*
- *Make knowledge intensive tasks routine to the work groups and is in fact a way of life to reach out to enduring goals.*
- *Make scenario-setting agendas to make intellectually superior people to come together and work on organizational challenges.*
- *Make group cross-functional where required, and make the encounter mutually beneficial.*
- *Create crucial interdependencies amongst employees who need to make their target only through a formal process of transaction.*
- *Create "Techno Chat Groups" that has been created to discuss on issues on a periodic basis in a formal setting. Have the group inundated with employees seeking space to say what they have to say.*

Intellect has an untold, unseen intensity to break apart and come out into the open irrespective of behavioral consequences on themselves or those they are dealing with. This needs management and a system of fast-cycle feedback is essential to make the interactive process work at the ground. Organizational charisma needs to capture the minds and the imagination of the intellectual population and channelize their energies and goals towards organizational effectiveness. Empowerment at a minimum is essential for hanging on the very bright and bubbly. One can hardly see any conflict in the management of the very bright Vs the not so up and tidy lot of managerial population surrounding the organization. Intellectual initiatives should not go unrewarded or unrecognized. Every step in providing identity and visibility to the corporate intellect there is a greater scope for legitimizing their contributory presence and making change sustain.

Intellect as Freedom of Choice - To the average corporation this added complexity of managing the intellect is an unwanted friend. Knowledge intensive people come into organizations with the untiring urge to contribute as against an emphasis on money as a motivator. To their sense of identity, working in or out of a commercial world is irrelevant but contributing is more self-actualizing. Many intellectually bright people left to them would rather learn, teach, consult and operate out of value adding knowledge organizations given their predisposition to learning oriented environments. But for them an opportunity to work in real life organizations where the output is measurable and implementable is not substitutable. Nevertheless, this is unlikely to turn real unless corporations create adequate space.

However, there are some imponderables to reckon with on the intellectual individual:

- *Individuals of this corporation have rarely worked in teams and show reluctance in doing things together. Individual excellence and team excellence should be dealt with up front.*
- *Large number of intellectually inclined individuals shows deep sensitivity and care towards organizational processes that may appear to be so rigorous and meaningless traditional managers. What may appear to be a loss of quality time would appear to these thinkers that without a fair process change in any event does not internalize or happen.*
- *It would but become inevitable for organizations to create and manage institutions on an ethical basis in their policies and practices.*
- *For the intellectual managers this is a path of realism, a journey necessary for organizations to transit from current state to a desired state of performance and effectiveness.*
- *Rarely do organizations encounter counter insurgency measures from the intellectual managers who believe by nature of their work ethic and value that corporations have been created to generate wealth and all members should do whatever necessary to make this happen.*
- *The purpose of an organization rarely needs to be told to an intellectual manager. They know what they in business for and for what purpose have they been hired. An organizational mercenary, perhaps, if it explains our position.*
- *As complex set of human minds, these people in real life organizations evolve, grow and contribute to their own limits, stretch and challenges. They become a set of organizational benchmarks and are at it themselves to break it for their next standard. Their actions are symbolic to the Chinese notion of "crisis": two symbols meaning "danger" and "opportunity".*
- *An intellectual manager asks of organizations to create organic systems and processes that facilitate freedom of expression, democracy and the right to do what is right. They are at several instances unconventional and would border on the maverick.*

- *The challenges of redesigning, rethinking and initiating change at various intervals would become necessary to sustain a performing culture. Organizations with comparatively static policy measures and change approaches would need to radically shift their stylet to turn compatible.*
- *Over time intellectually intensive organizations and consequently teams would eliminate through natural competitive positioning peers, superiors or subordinates not comparable to their current averages. In time the eliminators in turn get eliminated when new entrants bring in a fresh insight into a past, present or future processes.*
- *Organizational survival to the intellectual manager is relative to his/her current level of contribution and making change happen. They're relative in performance standards and stand out loud when compared on a peer basis. So would their non-performance become that much more visible? After effect is inevitable:*
- *Several after effect issues on hiring and retaining high think performers become real for operating managers to consider.*
- *Many untold, unseen human conflicts emerge when the culture is plastered with an emphasis on "think and do" as against traditional management methods of "follow the system and do".*

Intellect as Limited or Limiting Options - Managing the corporate of the future leaves us with a limited choice option. There simply aren't enough proven ways to manage uncertainty and a period of constant change despite proven past track records of high performance. The past is neither a winning condition for future success nor a panacea for all evils that an institution is likely to face and reckon with. Several organizational models experimented with including one stop shop recipes on quality, restructuring, total management theories have all but provided a permanent solution. They have provided an additional critical input to improve the management process but have not resolved the management dilemma conclusively. Perhaps they were not meant to resolve them either. After all theories and concepts have their usage, time relevance and application intent. What possibly could then be an option but to nurture and grow the in house intellect and use their native brilliance to resolve home grown problems and fix oneself to cope with and resolve the market challenges.

The individuals on their part need to relook at their learning and educating styles and see its applicability to an organizational setting on a dynamic and sustaining basis. Organizations have a double loop syndrome to hold forth and meet the unexpected head on. Neither is the theoretical solutions appearing to be effective nor are in house time tested providers working. The new millennium managers bring in diversity and cross culture influences in the organizational circumstance not dealt with before. They would need a reorientation to understanding current state before embarking upon the change program or its consequent intervention.

G. Digital Business Models - Characteristics

Digital Business Drivers - The modern day organization methods would no longer apply itself as yet another firm attempting to survive in the new age. This is not being stated dramatically but with a deep sense of purpose and seriousness necessitated by the roots of the hypothesis presented in this article. Traditional advantages be it financial resources, state of art technological competitiveness, raw material funding and source connection, in house capabilities to manufacture, market, buy and sell all appear to be disappearing into the oblivion all for want of a strategically perceptible advantage. The implications of an effective model when a change situation is faced are: Does each aspect in the model contribute to the implementation of change? If not which part requires changes in-order to enable the change to be effective? Is it possible for the person managing change to bring about the changes that are necessary? If not possible should the proposed change be abandoned? Firms have historically, sometimes conventionally, been at its best when its strategies have been applied across borders and the organizational boundaries making each of the core processes and tactics relevant and successful to the applied situation. The strategic planning process and the management of the firm through a formalized SWO(P)T analysis did work the right chords in the minds of the CEO who had the fundamental responsibility to the make the organization work.

Market Scan as a Business Model Driver - A quick scan of the environment would make clear that strategic advantages normally available to companies be it financial resources, technology, strategic partners, specific raw material all are available for a competitive price. Yet the human capital, the software, needed to make the hardware produce effectively has increasingly become scarce and sometimes completely unavailable. An added disdainful dimension would be when the human capital is available but not to our firm in any case.

Agility Volatility in Business Model - Again the firm and its capacity to face challenges had drastically under gone a permanent shift given unexpected volatility and never could endure or keep in existence while the markets were being lifted off the ground by seismic trauma. Corporations attempted to fortify lost ground by bringing in strategic reorientation's in areas not seen as the realm of strategic thinking (people process, system dynamics, development interventions, management morale, learning). Their ability to perennially sustain competitiveness without understanding the root cause of the problem turned finally into the problem itself.

Strategic reorientation as a Business Model Driver - meant a sort of capitulation, in a seeming state of conditional surrender and resignation that what now has to happen would happen for sure. This is indeed the beginning of an effective change program to make intellectual capital happen in organization. Firms need to position themselves competitively in the game of human capital orientation. Very limited options become available when firms do not have the built in advantages of the Knowledge Corporation. People, knowledge, process and systems. Yet there is a need for those corporate to identify the human capital requirements and plan for recruitment. Large corporations would now see the human capital planning integrated with the corporate plan. In fact, a significant portion of the people plan and their costing is now a part of the capital investment plan and not a part of the operating cost or the revenue expense.

Human capital as the Business Model Driver - is the relevant factor for firms who wish to position themselves logically with people attuned, with a mind set and trained to face a difficult set of actuality and materiality not been reckoned with earlier by the corporate planning function of the firm. More often than not such adept people profiles become the corporate fire fighters that understand the current state of affairs and would smoothly and efficiently into the problem and would evaluate the alternatives in a constrained circumstance and resolve. They bring in an undetected sensibility, solidity and perceptibility, a fact that is so very necessary for the corporate involved in intricate problem solving. Human capital management needs a firm absoluteness and verity in making the change over from current to desired state of management style, approach, and thinking and action orientation. It is a change for the good as people come in and take charge. The new breed of talent operates on the basis of the reality principle and would effectively adjust to meet the unavoidable demands of the environment by postponing a current priority.

Strategic prioritization as a Business Model Driver - is also in the realm of the intellectual managers of the modern era. It is possible to differentiate prioritization and planning where there is an application of the mind. Formal plans would sustain periodic reviews and dynamic shifts from stated plans and goals set at the beginning of the year. No firm unadulterated plan would survive through the year unchanged. The CEO's priority would be to be in touch with the environment and make changes as and when they are called for. Strategic management would no longer be a one-time formal activity but would on the contrary become yet another specialization wherein consistent shift formalizations are programmed and implemented.

Environmental scanning as Business Model Driver - would emerge to be a growing and contributing field of science. Management specialists would be forced with understanding the global economy, the market influencer, and the political scenario affecting the corporation and the impact of its growth and performance. Organizations with a quality people focus, a determination to demonstrate mind over matter, making systemic interventions where the human mind is not subservient to the system would eventually compete in the contemporary market place.

Systemic Mind Set as Business Model Driver - For quality human mind to work for the organization a systematic mind set change is essential across the cultural milieu of the company. The CEO should lead the way in bringing a set of direct reports who are known and have demonstrated exceptional intellectual talent in managing their business or function. Programs and policies should favor knowledge management activities as being business priorities and that all-organizational members should adhere to it. Organization work role activities should manacle and shackle the players from doing anything but intellectually focused value adding work. Their delivery schedules should under pin the criticality of getting things done in a "people-systems" way. Daily schedules should reflect time for thought and planning with organizational members receiving consistent signals that original, untested ideas are most welcome. Tactful treatment should be meted out to people who are unable or unwilling to make the transition into the fundamentally necessary way of getting things done. Consistent hiring pattern should exist across the organization. Selection managers across the company should be trained to identify and nurture talent for the new corporation. Middle managers should be put through an Assessment Center to help them understand their capabilities and the need for improvement/development, as the case may be.

H. Achieving Synthesis

Intellectual depth and Application Synthesis - Hired quality talent does not mean or imply automatic intellectual application and consequent benefit to the corporation through an impacting bottom line performance. Employees bring in their native talent combined with their learning, experiences and value into the business organization on a Greenfield basis. In other words, on a "not tried before" basis. Large-scale assumptions are relevant in usage of past experiences in a new organizational setting. Willingness to mirror past learnings does not mean a successful usage of the experience. It is now possible for untested assumptions, but those led by a quality of the thought to receive experimental space to try out. It is paramount that culture is conducive towards this application of mind on problems encountered while performing a job and not be rebuffed that we have done it before and do not reinvent the wheel- the not invented here syndrome.

Programs Synthesis - The performance programs involving goal setting and objective achievement systems need relevant interpretation to make way for goals involving unique contribution, methodology used while solving a problem, changes from the past that has proven successful, usage of past documentation and data while solving the current problem and its relevance etc. Goal setting programs need a radical reorientation to make them application oriented. Considerable change in the type and make of goals would become inescapable. Several objectives would come up the manager's work plan with new ideas and original work as goal for the year. They may to some extent appear irrelevant to the current state of the organization or the priorities it is pursuing. Yet the corporate would have to create coping mechanisms to bring in a reasonable number of original contribution goals and have them applied to the real life setting. An element of complexity in what is being stated is not being under estimated.

Opportunities Synthesis - Effective organizations would do well to create avenues for intellectual satisfaction and contributory space for individuals who have an urge to keep creating new ideas and activities. The organizational setting should convert itself into one large laboratory with concurrent experiments, inventions and approaches being debated, attempted, succeeded and failed.

Team Synthesis - Team orientation approaches should be welcomed as a part of the management structure and style. Thinking minds should be placed along with application tigers for the thinkers to learn the art of getting things done. Team goals should involve generation of new ideas to be put to work while performing a set of activities. Members and their roles should be continuously exchanged and role reversals should be enacted regularly and systemically.

Mechanisms Synthesis - Organizational reward system should consciously identify groups of individuals who have contributed to the thinking of the organization. A set of people who have done nothing through the year but only generated brilliant thoughts out of their drawing boards for implementation should be isolated for recognition. The task of the managerial group would be to get the original thinkers to apply their ideas in a test laboratory organizational setting, learn from the experience through formal systems of feedback and "tell me" experiences. Recognizing the importance of personal results does not mean obsessing about us. If that happens, innovative teams could get isolated from business purposes.

I. Are Organizations Intelligent?

Intelligence as Product of Ways - Organizations are products of the ways that people in them think and interact in differing situations, exploit the opportunities provided to them like the 3M program and actively engage and manage themselves in management dynamics. People in turn become products of experiences, interactions, connections and collaborations in such organizations. Experiences and connections are made possible by the processes deployed by organizations. Janette Batten, Director HR at 3 M Canada, in the HR Professional, November/December 2013 issue wrote a story on Developing Innovative Leaders and quoted 3M Canada focusing on the need to keep employees engaged, feeling relevant and in return how they will continue to contribute, feel identified, perform roles that are stretching and continue to do best in class work. Sarah Tattersall's of 3M Canada had stated, "3M recognizes that millennial want to be engaged in the workforce. They want to see a clear career path in front of them and understand what they need to do to get there. The emerging leaders program given them the leadership skills that are beyond what they would be learning at their career level. It pushes the employees out of their comfort zone and forces them to look at and work on their leadership skills".

Intelligence as Par for Course - "The second perspective to culture - performance relationship is named as strategically appropriate culture. This theory states the direction that culture must align and motivate employees. It talks about "fit" between culture and strategies. No culture is fit everywhere. A culture must fit to objective conditions of industry, segment of its industry as specified by firm's strategy and business strategy in totality". In, "Corporate Cultures and Performance" 1992, By John Kotter and James Heskett, write on Strategically appropriate culture, a culture may lead to good performance under one condition and strategy while it may be detrimental in another. A stable culture may be working only in slow moving environment.

The research studied a dozen large and well known US companies. The study revealed following

- *The strategically appropriate culture helps managers deal with making complex decision easier, consistent and better in light of industry conditions.*
- *Strong founders are important in establishing cultures that are internally consistent as well as sensible in light of industry conditions.*
- *In case of minor changes in environment, a firm can continue for long with minor modifications"*

In all situations risk has been a common thread.

- **Risk Mitigation -** In any change management initiative, risks associated with the change management process need to be identified and steps taken for their mitigation. With the complexities involving these type of changes, i.e., the risks associated with the change process can only get magnified on account of the geographical and cultural variety. Since any risk, left unaddressed, has the potential to negatively impact or even derail the change management process, it is vital that the company identifies and takes steps to mitigate the following risks associated with its overall tech modernisation – digital transformation project.

- **Culture Risk:** Unsupportive/hostile organizational culture may prove to be a huge deterrent for the company to implement large scale organization. As indicated earlier, large number of units, spread across the country, quite a few of which have distinctive style of working, magnifies this risk.

- **Organization Risk:** Process change and automation will require modification in the way people usually do their work. New roles, competencies and structure may need to be introduced in the right places to institutionalize process change and automation. Additionally, existing people processes need to be in alignment with the direction of the change. Not only does a large number of units pose significant infrastructural challenges, a large number of employees, across age-profiles, spread across jobs which are both managerial and operational in nature, makes identification and mitigation of organizational risk critical.

- **Know-How Risk:** Large scale automation and IT implementation will mandate timely know-how up-gradation for employees to appreciate and accept the changes. Companies will need to undertake a skill gap assessment of its employees, quite a large number of which may be involved in manual or relatively simple work on computers. This know-how risk will need to be assessed employee group wise for more effective mitigation strategy, i.e., It is probable that employees over 50 years of age might display a greater need to required skill enhancement and at the same time, might require more intensive and sustained skill development effort.

- **Stakeholder Risk:** The project will have variable impact on multiple stakeholder groups as the existing work level relationships between them might undergo a significant change. In a scenario where teams are working for a common objective but not necessarily with a shared understanding of their role in the changed dispensation, there is a risk of running the project into internal conflicts, with work groups trying to gain more power over the others. In large scale transformation initiatives, not only is the managerial group worried about loss of or reduction in their powers, the clerical group may equally be worried of their activities being rendered redundant post the exercise.

While the institution being a change seeking service has clearly defined hierarchical norms and offers a greater degree of employment security as compared to other organizations, stakeholder risk identification and mitigation remains critical to the effectiveness of its initiative. "This theory, continue Professor Kotter, propounds that a culture has to be dynamic at the pace of environmental dynamism. As per earlier theory, a singular culture can produce good performances in changing conditions. This is not true. If a company does not change its culture, then the performance may start deteriorating. And a stable culture can make an organization resistant to change. However, there are criticism even to this "fit" theory. The critics say that it is not easy for an organization to have culture - strategic fit and changing culture to fit conditions can bring in instability and insecurity within the organization. Northwest Airlines had a culture fit to its cost cutting financially oriented strategies and regulated industry. It paid rich dividends. However, as soon as the market was deregulated and the industry became very competitive, its poor customer service hit their performance. Their traditional labor relations practices made it difficult to implement a new customer-service strategy. As seen in the above example, firms with sacrosanct culture may produce results in one particular condition but the performance may start deteriorating as the condition change. The pace at which the environment changes and need for change in appropriate strategy may vary. However, change is inevitable".

Intelligence as Stakeholders' Resistance - Unawareness, risk averseness, unknown future - Proactive, regular and comprehensive communication define some of the critical aspects of this resistance. These are specific to different audiences (senior management, mid management & masses) and may include issues pertaining to capturing the business case, individual impact, benefits at business & individual levels; and showcasing external benchmarks. Alleviating concerns through leadership commitment, role-modeling & change-agents while leadership asks for 'emotional commitment' from their key people is a start. 'Apprehension' of Technology- Skill gap (conscious or unconscious incompetence of the incumbents), regular training to develop skills – upskilling to 'conscious competence' level, capturing training effectiveness and fine-tuning content/ plan as may be required. While sustaining the change during the 2 years of this project the company's leaders need to continue supporting the change managing the momentum going down due to lack of visible success, lack of clarity or an inability to visualize the benefits, etc. Applying the vision to all aspects of operations – from training to performance reviews, demonstrating and celebrating 'quick-wins' at short & regular frequency, setting up change-support systems (like 'change-helpdesk', etc.) to ensure ready answers to the masses' clarifications (in order to openly & honestly address peoples' concerns and/ or anxieties). Further, avoiding/ not allowing employees to go back to the 'pre-IT' era work practices, helping to replace barriers to change in a positive and quick manner is another aspect of managing this inherent desire to resist. Non-synchronization in Change Management plan against Technology changes introduced often has been seen a trigger. To mitigate such occurrences, change management leadership needs to continuously be in sync with the new business processes and technology changes released. There are situations when technology program plan is unknown at detailed level. All change management initiatives need to be fine-tuned rigorously with any advancements, delays and change in direction of the Technology changes. Sustaining the change post implementation, demonstrating 'artifacts' that will show-case the change across the organization – for example, 'Anchor the Changes in the company's Corporate Culture'. Change not becoming part of the organization culture is best managed by encouraging 'change-agents' to evolve into role models/ leaders for this change by publicly recognizing key members of the original change coalition, and ensuring that the rest of the staff – new and old – remembers their contributions. Creating plans to replace key leaders of change as they 'move on' will help ensure that their legacy is not lost or forgotten.

Intelligence as Fit - "So a corporate culture needs to change for an appropriate fit. The pace of change is determined by pace of environmental changes. However, this theory has no concept to explain differential success at adapting to change and hence the differences in long term performance. Only an adaptive culture will help an organization to sustain for longer period and be associated with long term performance. A non-adaptive culture is very bureaucratic. Key questions to be considered while handling an effective fit; What are the skills and abilities of those affected? Are people motivated to participate? Does the suggested approach fit the organizations culture? How critical is this expected to be? Why is fit an important consideration for intelligence and firms? How important is it to retain the loyalty and sustain the motivation of the affected people? People in such firms are reactive, risk averse and not very creative. There is more emphasis on control. At the same time adaptive firms are proactive, creative and risk taking. These firms emphasize more on innovation. Adaptive firms are learning continuously and people have confidence of managing any kind of new problem faced. 3M is a best example for an adaptive culture. 3M has made certain minimum percentage of sales come from relatively new products as a practice. It has a cultural norm to fund good development initiatives though they may be originating from lower ranks. So the culture of 3M is to grow through innovation and encourage initiatives. This culture itself helps employees to anticipate changes and adapt accordingly, adds Kotter". People, who work in such organizations must receive an opportunity to change the ways they think, feel and act in relation to the problems, issues or challenges on hand. The growth of learning capabilities and self-renewal attitudes brings in team congruence, candor and transparency in communication.

Intelligence as Networks - "Organizations are webs of participation", says Xerox Vice President John Seely Brown, "Change the participation and you change the organization". It is this mix of the population affecting the organization and we change the way we do things. Informal networks turn into superior forms of channelizing the organizational intellectual energies into productive efforts. The information transmission becomes credible as it goes from the rank and file of grass root managers and not a corporate HQ chief with gross lack of credibility. When people talk of the new that they are experimenting with people listen, as they are initially curious and later attentive to learn.

Intelligence as Entrepreneurship – Always starts with building a entrepreneurial culture. For example, Is the performance management system adequate? Performance management processes are closely linked to compensation and reward systems. No matter how solid the metrics or innovative the compensation system, if managers don't set goals, coach their people, and give candid feedback, the entrepreneurial outcome will be compromised. There's no one best system among the all the performance management systems available. The scales, forms, and process are less important than the consistency and honesty with which they are applied. "Entrepreneurship actually is perceived as more a secure path than traditional career paths. In terms of skill sets, in the remix era, my skills are going to be different. I need to be able to break things apart and put them together, put them together in new ways. Traditional skills are going to be less important than an ability mix and remix". In a conversation with Gerald C. (Jerry) Kane, for MIT Sloan Management Review's Social Business Big Idea Initiative (and a one-time student of Konsynski's at Emory), Benn Konsynski describes, "how he sees work for the average employee changing? What skills are they going to need? First of all, we know the assumptions they make are very different. Recent surveys show that many of the Millennials find higher security in entrepreneurship than in corporate work. That would be shocking to a member of the Boomer generation, who has always expected that the corporation is the secure path. And yet the Millennial experience is that they saw their parents failing to receive promised pension or being misled on job longevity. They no longer find that a secure pathway. I think you see that in the successful Millennials as well, that willingness to not take things as permanent, to break them up and reconfigure them in new ways rather than looking for operational efficiency or improvement along the historic lines. That is a new kind of skill to many. Is there a plan for when times are bad? Alfred Lord

Tennyson said, 'Tis better to have loved and lost than to never have loved at all." The same may not be true of variable compensation. It is hard to have it one year and lose it the next. Some people are comfortable with wide fluctuations in their pay, but a lot of people join corporations for the predictability. They will be unhappy if a down business cycle means they make less for the same amount of work. Many start-up companies that gave stock instead of salary or bonuses found that people were all too ready to jump ship when their stock options became worthless, no matter how exciting the work environment. The certainty of unknown, one would call it. They emerge in a market, absolutely certain that the job that they will have five years from now doesn't exist today. And so, how does one prepare for that? Do I prepare for it by being prepared at the time it arrives, or even helping it to arrive or making it arrive — inventing it myself".

Intelligence as Networks - Change this mix of the human capital affecting the organization and we change the way we do things. Informal networks turn into superior forms of channelizing the organizational intellectual energies into productive efforts. The information transmission becomes credible as it goes from the rank and file of grass root managers and not a corporate HQ chief with gross lack of credibility. When people talk of the new that they are experimenting with, people listen, as they are initially curious and later attentive to learn. For 3 M Canada Janette, 3Mers are constantly on the pursuit of discovering the next innovation and solving the next big problem for the industries that matter most to us Canadians. People are bound together by a common sense of purpose and a real need to know what each other knows. John Seely Brown of Xerox calls this "the critical building block of a knowledge-based company".

J. Adapt and Internalize Intelligence

Adapt – Internalize Change - Reflect Intellectualization of the corporation. Making the organization energized with people, process where the intellect turns into the dominant force in the management process. In all change management efforts current business scenario, strategic positioning of the organization, structure, managerial values, corporate philosophy, the managerial styles and practices, impacted players become relevant for consideration of the facilitator. Similarly, in this program too change agents should make visible the value of intellectual depth and its application. Adequate communication should constantly take place to make members understand the value of application synthesis in all of their new ideas. Each communicating group turns into a network and eventually a network of networks. The premium on learning and its use as the only competitive survival strategy should be made known vociferously. No Company has generated significant momentum in profound change efforts without evolving spirited, active, internal networks of practitioners, people sharing progress and helping one another.

"CEOs can't lead from ivory towers disconnected physically and emotionally from their teams. To lead today, you need to be a man/woman of the people. Leaders need to be relatable, real, fallible – human!" Peter Aceto CEO of ING Direct, Canada, speaks with absolute clarity on what can cultures do to make smart people work well. "People are too smart to actually believe that their leaders are perfect. So demonstrating who you are is fundamental. This is not something you haven't heard from me before. But I bring it up again in this context because who you are as a leader is of the utmost importance in leading – and succeeding".

Adapt – Internalize Pattern Disruptions - Critically change does not follow a pattern and has strong discontinuous sequences. It can almost be guaranteed that what worked well in the past would probably fail the second time over. We need to see if we as an organization have learnt to manage this fact up front. As more people involved in change initiatives become part of the extended networks, information about the initiatives spreads more widely, giving rise to more interest, and potentially to more initiatives. Managers do not jump into the change initiative just because it sounds interesting or those key players are all in it. They initially wait for the first cut results to pour in and then choose their personal position. The informal group houses are created to help each other transit into the knowledge company with limited entry barriers, thereafter meet periodically, share their learnings and make each of them enjoy the experience. This would happen as long as it is not position as yet another change management program of the company causing more cynicism.

Adapt – Internalize Intelligence as Building Trust - Direct effect of communication and trust has a good example from Ford. Historical events from Electrical and Fuel Handling Division (EFHD) had created the collective assumption that management would always reduce capital funding requests. To offset these reductions, project managers automatically added a "cushion" to their budgets. As the division leaders began to trust their project managers, things changed. Management stopped making these reductions, and project managers stopped adding a cushion. Now people just talk honestly about investments that were needed and the real constraints in funding. This saved a great deal of wasted time and allowing the company to prioritize the investments on a need basis. Trust brings in responsibility.

Adapt – Internalize as Learning efforts should focus initially on the thought generation process and thereafter on the practical results that it has commenced to deliver. Results provide a context, a meaning, a method and a reason for experimentation, adaptation, and feedback. Seeing the consequences of team efforts and learning from the experience is critical for the network groups to succeed. Learning fundamentally assumes a time lag between the new thought process creation, establishing the internalizing of learnings, bringing connected networks of learning together, application to business processes and attaining concrete business performance and bottom line.

Adapt – Internalize as Engage Realism - Intellectual corporations prosper in making change happen realistically. It, to our mind, only demonstrates a further application of mind to make the change permanent and effective. Typically, the corporation operates through identification of relevant people to the change process, bringing their values and identity together, network with relevant cross-team players, assess their intellectual compatibility, bring in commitment, define business goals and results and charges the team to move forward. There is a transparent and open communication involving review and feedback including action-oriented goals. Essentially this stage acts as a facilitation step in the intellectualization process.

Critically the differentiating factor is that change is neither directed, conceptualized nor delivered by the top management. The change happens by a team of people who feel the need to change without encountering an entry-exit experience. While the change by itself could mean an impact on the average employee the process required to help make the transition is definitely not ignored, neglected or derided.

Adapt – Internalize Adaptation

- *Intellectual stereotypes should be managed across the corporate population. An added element of predictability and behavioral understanding should be brought in while dealing on any people issue.*
- *A detailed start up workshop on Transformation and the creation of the Intellectual Corporation should be a curtain raiser. The entire effort should be fancy free and should mean business with people as the drivers. That the program is eminently capable of being dropped*

half way through if the concerned people do not want it. No jobs will be lost. The question does not arise either.

- *Thinkers-doer's distinction should be eliminated in policy, spirit and in action.*
- *The change effort should commence in a small, measurable way and should escalate in intensity logically.*
- *Individuals cannot be subjugated to staid forms and methods outdated in content and spirit while intellectualization efforts are on in an organization.*
- *Barriers of an intellectual nature describing organization in pockets, creating functional silos, taking positions on right and wrong are all avoidable completely.*
- *The change envisaged is not a quick fix problem solving initiative. There is an assumed level of intellectual rigor expected of the organizational members and the organizing actors to make the change real to all people.*
- *People encountering change should understand that this is not a yet another corporate HQ driven program with a fix all perspective and that this initiative has come bottom up. That the expectation of the change is only as good as the expectation that they have from it themselves.*
- *Top management should know by knowledge and experience when to get off the back of the individual.*

K. Social Interactions and Intellect

Social Technology - The globalizing economy, technological upheavals, shortened life cycles of both organizations and products, cross border transactions, diminishing boundaries, unprecedented opening up of economies all have contributed to the face of the new Intellectual Company. A major transformational change with people operating in a flexible, dynamic environment, with skill and competencies changed from past paradigms, radical shift in approaches to learning and development of people, empowerment at the grass root levels of management have become a basic survival means for the corporation. While managerial problem solving adhesives were available for every organizational, strategic and functional, systemic problems none could conclusively and sufficiently resolve the pending dilemmas.

Social Benchmarking - Benchmarking is only as good as the standards set do not turn into a self-fulfilling limitation or reengineering does not stop at processes for going concern and lacks the inputs for start-ups or a comprehensive overhauling. Not because the new methods or approaches were bad in concepts or application but were simply not holistic for the company as a whole. Transformation needs a combination of a radical positioning while understanding the organizational issues comprehensively and a revolutionary approach while using managerial skills and style appropriate to make the change happen. Benchmark leading practice design principles, structures, models, and performance measures; Determine how organization design impacts business results; Analyze industry trends to identify the business implications of organizational trends; Assist the client to develop criteria "statements," which describe those functions the organization design should accomplish; e.g., the design should facilitate fast reaction to market changes (strategic focus), the design should reduce the amount of paperwork (diagnostic focus), and the design should foster the effective information exchange between institutional sales and trading. Gain understanding of operating principles, philosophy, and business ethics; Assist the client to develop a communications and involvement plan; Perform a preliminary high-level change-readiness assessment; Assess the management capability in terms of skills, knowledge, and experience for delivering a new organization structure.

Social Influence - Corporations would be influenced by the changes in the socio-economic, cultural and political arena. The approaches taken up by the educational institutions would impact the student products available to the companies, the remuneration systems followed by comparable organizations and its consequent life style issues would play upon the people of the company, the growth rates of one industry Vs another would make demand-supply of people arguable. Entry of global soft drinks or the presence of global consumer brands would make life style changes real to the average consumer. At differing points in the life of the corporation there would arise business interfaced with the environment conflict.

L. Strategic Revitalization

Digital is here to stay. Organizational need to generate priorities that supports digital strategies would become a core necessity. Organizations have developed beyond strategic planning, the capital budgeting systems, operating plans and a culture wherein policy and procedures determined organizational form and practices. The management strategy and structural processes of most of today's enterprises were designed for a period that has perhaps gone past us. The systems need to be thoroughly revamped, interventions created to focus on the desired structure and appropriate replacements planned. More jobs need to be radically revised, content modified to include the changed expectation, positions defined more open ended, so that the individual can add more value. The redesign effort has to synchronize with the corporate changed outlook, with mechanisms to facilitate radical transformation. Strategic alternatives have meant doing sometimes just the opposite. Alliances with yesterday's enemies. Apple computers and Microsoft or the pharma majors or the large banks. Conventional forms of strategies and structures have to be conclusively eliminated to provide space for the new era of management. A structure where the individual is the fulcrum of action. The orderly hierarchies and strategic structures of the 1980's have long since disappeared.

Need for Digital Strategy Revitalization - Creative Complexity and Constructive Clusters: How does organizational transformation differ from organizational growth? In the case of growth, the focus within the organization is far more on the 'outside', i.e. on markets, customers, segments and so on. A great part of the discussion within the organization is on how it can address the existing or emerging needs-for example, on what product/market facilities to set up, joint ventures, certification, and approvals and so on for making the product/company acceptable and credible. On the other hand, in cases of transformation, the focus appears to be more on the 'inside'. The 'unlearning' challenge is a big one-there is a great deal of concern with what would happen to existing relationships, people, systems, departmental positions, power structures, information sharing and so on. The cultural issues are felt much more strongly in the cases of transformation. Another difference lies in the age of the organization. Growing organizations are typically younger. The average age of the members may be lower; even when the employee may be older; the person may be new to the organization and may have come for a fresh start. In cases of transformation, there are more likely to be established relationship patterns, and 'branding' of individuals is more likely to have taken place, which makes it so much more difficult to initiate new patterns of behavior. In the case of growth, people see themselves as being 'on the move'; their arena of action is more 'outside'. There seems to be greater apprehension of loss of status in the case of transformation, and greater feeling that the reward systems need to be made commensurate with efforts and appropriately designed. Large organizations operating in widely diversified businesses spread over several geographical locations managed through a long hierarchy are high on complexity. Since digital is likely to see highly focused organizations operating over a wide range of locations the overall complexity index is not likely to be higher than that found in the most widely diversified organizations like GE. On the contrary since the spread will be a function of the IT and with advances in IT the overall index of complexity may actually come down. If we further factor in the greater sector / business focus that we are likely to see, the digital organization is likely to be a disciplined entity than most of the contemporary diversified dinosaurs. For example, **Auto Dealers.** Automobile dealers would be significantly impacted by the widespread adoption of self-driving cars. When cars can drive themselves, they don't need to wait for their owners to pilot them. Passengers can subscribe to an Uber-like service that will be dispatched to pick up passengers on demand. This shift means that individual people won't necessarily need to own their own self-driving cars personally. If so, it could undermine the current value of the network of automobile dealers who sell these cars to individuals". "Gerald C Kane in MIT SMR 2016, "Predicting the Future: How to Engage in Really Long-Term Strategic Digital Planning", writes further, "Ubiquitous self-driving cars would have a number of impacts on a variety of industries. "**Auto Manufacturers.** If the auto industry no longer sells primarily to individuals, it also changes the design options available to the industry. It can potentially shift design more toward utility than customer preference. It raises the possibility for designing cars that are not optimized for passenger loads composed of individuals or family units and their cargo. **Government.** The shift toward self-driving cars has implication for government services. Self-driving cars can collect data through their sensors and this data can be uploaded to the cloud and sent back to the cars to optimize routing and traffic flows. It could challenge the dependence on public transportation, as larger self-driving busses can develop customized routes to pick up passengers as needed and in response to current weather and traffic conditions. If executives don't think through some of these possible implications, their companies are virtually guaranteed to get caught flat-footed when they do become reality. It also could mean that optimizing for short-term strategies may lead the organization in exactly the opposite direction of these longer-term digital trends. Can the system be manipulated? Time is easy to measure. Jobs can be compared externally and their value set. Once you get into valuing skills, rewarding learning, and creating complex incentive plans based on softer performance measures, you introduce opportunity to manipulate outcomes. **Time Structuring.** Create pay plans that are simple, valid, and transparent so that the outcomes can be neither debated nor perceived as unfair. What is the time orientation? The closer rewards and compensation are given to the time when the goal is met, the more motivating and reinforcing it will be. A mix of short-term and longer-term rewards will ensure that while current actions are rewarded, it is not done at the expense of long-term goals. **Retail and Restaurants.** Retail stores could begin to use self-driving cars as a delivery infrastructure. The restaurant ordering platform **Olo** has recently gotten $40M in funding to expand their Dispatch platform, which integrates restaurants' software with Uber's platforms to enable on-demand delivery drivers. **Real Estate.** Self-driving cars will also have implications for real estate valuations. More urban locations may become more valuable in certain situations, because parking no longer becomes a constraint to access. Conversely, more suburban locations may also become more valuable as traffic is reduced and people can use the commuting time for tasks other than driving. These shifts have implications for where companies choose to build office locations.".

Strategic revitalization consolidates the all-pervasive strategic planning process involving formulation, activation, control and implementation. The modified version brings in limited control factors to the Intellectual Company and substitutes it with strategic influence, a process by which people formulate, edit and revitalize the strategy as periodically as deemed appropriate for the organization. The time horizon for the strategic use becomes dynamic enough to allow for frequent changes and adaptation.

Globalasticity - Again the impact of globalasticity, meaning globalization and economic theories of elasticity needs to be juxtaposed and seen concurrently. Economies and product lifelines need close interaction and linkages. Companies attempting to fly with limited emphasis on the economic scenario affecting the business scenario would be fated to doom and destruction. There is an undeniable proximity of businesses and economics. Macro-economic factors be it trade policies, money markets, interest rates, capital markets, governmental financing or the conditions that facilitate exports and imports all have to be a part of the strategic power play involving globalasticity. Globalization has meant several things to several people. But in effect some basics continue to be essential, be it global awareness, diversity skills, in depth knowledge of the worldwide scene in more ways than social or economic, cultural sensitivity, multicultural attitudes, flexible schedules, friendly telecommunicating and so on. Globalasticity would involve creating structures to manage geography, create products that is locally made and delivered to the palate of the local consumer, market the products from a low cost manufacturing location to a high value consumer consumption base, manufacture from locations that offer the most cost effective production facilities, source raw materials from the cheapest location and hire and train people for competencies and skills that would make them a flexible, elastic global manager.

M. Platforms

Intellectual Corporation is not bullet proof to the vagaries of the people, their idiosyncrasies, and the complication they could behaviorally bring in to the organization. Yet there is an opportunity to bring together like-minded individuals who share a common vision, a passion for Orgxcellence, for performing roles and endeavors that bring in a path towards the new and the unknown. There is still a group of people of the future generations who would not give up circumstances that would offer enabling advantages to remain competitive in a volatile business environment. More importantly their experience of time and space that is scarce while people wish to be at their creative best. If an organizational climate exists that is conducive to sharp shoot they would grab and go for the kill.

What makes platforms effective? Activating - This is the task of ensuring that others in the organization understand, support and eventually share the vision that transitioning from infrastructure dominant individual disparate systems, the organization is now embarking on an integrated platform that is digital. Commitment to the vision is a prerequisite for success, particularly among the people who have a key role in turning the vision into reality. **Supporting** - Good leadership is not just about telling people what to do. It is as much about inspiring them to do more than they might otherwise achieve and providing the necessary moral and practical support to enable this to happen. The leader must have a strong empathy with the people he is trying to inspire and the imagination to see things from their point of view. Support works when it is built on respect, trust and integrity. **Implementing** - This is about detailed plans and schedules that have to be executed to turn any vision into reality. The instruments may vary depending on time available and the nature of the change. It is vital to take into account the consequences of the change, identify actions to be taken the priorities the teams and structures needed to implement and setting goals for the change program. **Ensuring** - This includes monitoring and controlling processes to ensure that all actions are taken on time, there is a good reason when they are changed and there is re-planning for the new circumstances. **Recognizing** - The last step involves recognizing those involved in the process. This may be positive or negative and should be used to reinforce the change and to ensure that obstacles to progress are removed. Financial rewards, public recognition, promotions may be some ways of doing. George Westerman, Didier Bonnet and Andrew McAfee, "The Digital Capabilities Your Company Needs" in MIT SMR 2012, "A Unified Digital Platform - The most fundamental technology enabler (or inhibitor) of transformation is a digital platform of appropriately integrated data and processes. Many large successful companies have historically operated in silos, each with their own systems, data definitions and business processes. Generating a common view of customers or products can be very difficult. Without a common view, advanced approaches to customer engagement or process optimization cannot occur. Unfortunately, many executives blame their CIOs for problems with a disconnected legacy of systems; fifty percent of our interviewees cited ineffective IT as a challenge. Solution Delivery - Companies also need the ability to modify their processes or build new methods onto the data and process platform. Such solution delivery requires effective methods and strong skills. Most IT departments have solid development methods in place. However, those methods are often geared to well-defined requirements and mature technologies but not to emerging digital technologies and practices. Mobile and social media, for example, often require iterative approaches to learn about what will work in the market or workplace. Such initiatives also use technology that may not be commonly available in enterprises. Analytics activities often require specific knowledge and temperaments that typical IT developers do not possess”.

Platforms Reward Transformation - A well-designed reward and recognition program can: Support business goals by reinforcing desired values, behaviors, and results. Build a high-performance organization by creating an environment in which people want to perform to the best of their abilities. Increase retention by communicating each employee's importance to the success of the organization, and by building a sense of belonging and pride. Values and behaviors are the basis of the organizational culture, influencing not only employee morale, commitment, and satisfaction, but ultimately the customer experience as well. The behaviors that are rewarded need to balance improving internal interactions (e.g., between managers and employees or between business units) as well as those that more directly influence customers. Rewarding only values and behaviors can result in people losing sight of business results. For example, in one company a program intended to promote teamwork encouraged people to increase the number of meetings held, memos circulated, and people involved in projects. Without any measure of outcomes, however, there was no way to ensure that all of this activity produced a better business result.

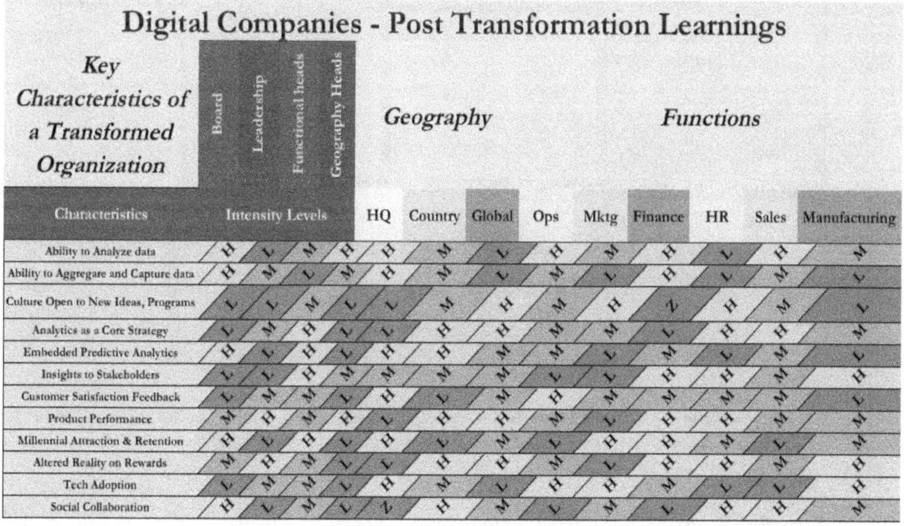

Digital Companies - Post Transformation Learnings

Key Characteristics of a Transformed Organization	Board	Leadership	Functional heads	Geography Heads	*Geography*			*Functions*					
Characteristics	Intensity Levels				HQ	Country	Global	Ops	Mktg	Finance	HR	Sales	Manufacturing
Ability to Analyze data	H	L	M	H	H	M	L	H	M	H	L	H	M
Ability to Aggregare and Capture data	H	M	L	M	H	M	L	M	L	H	L	M	L
Culture Open to New Ideas, Programs	L	L	M	L	L	M	H	M	H	L	H	M	L
Analytics as a Core Strategy	L	M	H	L	L	H	H	M	M	L	H	H	M
Embedded Predictive Analytics	H	L	H	L	H	H	M	M	L	M	L	M	L
Insights to Stakeholders	L	L	H	M	M	M	M	L	L	H	H	M	H
Customer Satisfaction Feedback	L	M	M	L	H	L	M	H	M	M	M	M	L
Product Performance	M	H	M	H	L	H	H	M	L	H	H	M	M
Millennial Attraction & Retention	H	L	H	L	H	L	M	L	H	H	M	L	M
Altered Reality on Rewards	M	H	M	L	L	H	H	M	L	H	H	M	H
Tech Adoption	L	M	M	L	H	M	L	H	H	M	L	L	H
Social Collaboration	H	L	M	L	L	H	M	L	M	L	H	H	M

Figure 48 - Key Characteristics Of A Transformed Organization - David Kiron, Rebecca Shockley, Nina Kruschwitz, Glenn Finch and Dr. Michael Haydock in Analytics: The Widening Divide, MIT SMR 2011

"For organizations seeking to **emulate Transformed organizations,** it is useful to know which actions have the biggest impact on their level of sophistication. Analysis showed that of all the characteristics exhibited by Transformed organizations, their proficiency (represented by the percentages) in six characteristics distinguished them the most. The breadth of these leading characteristics suggests that excellence in all three analytics competencies noted in our study is fundamental to the competitive use of analytics". Nina Kruschwitz and Rebecca Shockley in "The Second Annual New Intelligent Enterprise Survey" in MIT SMR Survey 2011, continues "An organization may be able to capture, integrate and analyze its data, but it will not likely be able to act on what it finds unless it has a culture that is ready to embrace ideas that depart from intuition or experience. For example, a leading global bank transformed its operations when it decided to analyze the impact of debit and credit card purchases on mortgage default settlements. The bank was able to use this new customer information effectively because it developed a culture that encouraged multiple departments to collaborate on managing, understanding and acting quickly on data and ideas that went above and beyond traditional approaches to lending decisions".

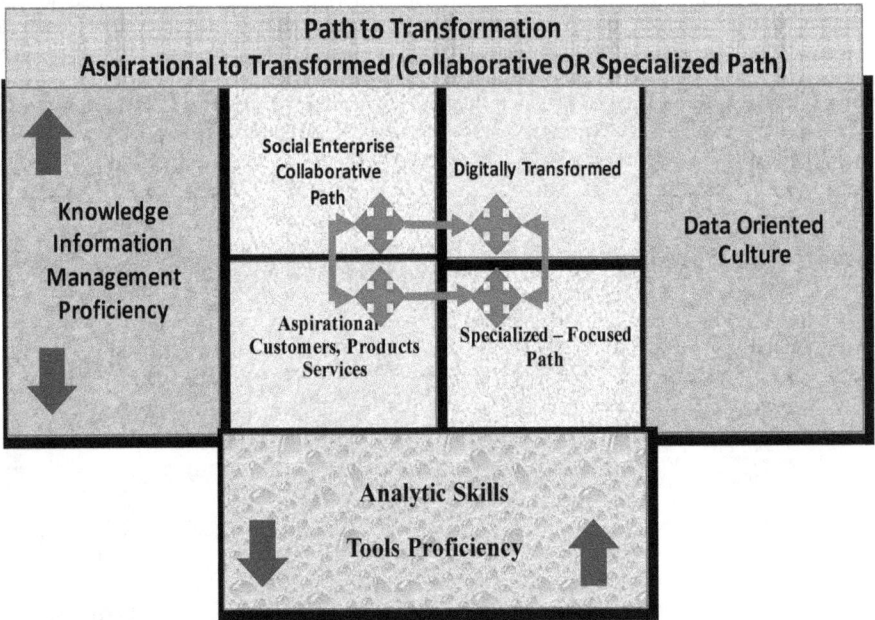

Figure 49 – Path to Transformation – Adapted from "Analytics: The Widening Divide" David Kiron, Rebecca Shockley, Nina Kruschwitz, Glenn Finch and Dr. Michael Haydock, MIT SMR 2011

Why do Platforms make Digital companies successful? Michael Schrage in MIT SMR 2016 frontiers blog, "Rethinking the Value of Customers in a Digital Economy" writes, "Successful platform companies and competitors see their customers and clients as assets worthy of innovative investment. Yes, treat customers very, very well, but invest smartly to make them even better. In Uber's business model, for example, smart apps make both the company's customers and drivers more valuable to both Uber and each other. In fact, the ability to creatively invest in one's customers as a result of digital networks is central to our new research, Rethinking Networks: Exploring Strategies for Making Users More Valuable. As platform companies like Google, Apple, Facebook, Uber, Amazon, Airbnb, and LinkedIn relentlessly disrupt — and redefine — mainstream industries, we see network effects as their "secret sauce" for success. For example, Values and Behaviors – These companies recognize people at all levels who demonstrate desired values and behaviors. Is especially important in an environment of change when reinforcing the behavior (e.g., risk taking) is as important as getting the right outcome. They help sustain interest when time frames for outcomes are long term or if outcomes may not materialize (e.g., an information technology project gets canceled because business priorities change). And reinforce borderline performers who are improving. Shows appreciation for day-to-day contributions and service to the organization. Identifies service to the company and communicates that everyone is valued. Often includes families to recognize their contribution and sacrifices. Doesn't differentiate based on performance (e.g., events to which everyone is invited or service awards based on anniversary date). Special Achievement (largely social and collaborative effort is another digital differentiator. Celebrates peer innovation success, creative innovation, disruptive learning, and smart effort. Allows recognition of unique events/contributions and those that occur irregularly, such as: Completion of special projects, Successful passing of work-related classes and exams, or completion of degrees, Extraordinary overtime, perfect attendance, (24/7 – 365 day attitude) innovative ideas, creates role models for others though conventional continue to be of value).

"Network effects increasingly determine innovation opportunity, value creation, and growth in digital markets. This holds true for Netflix, Twitter, Github and Alibaba — as well as the so-called Internet of Things — that all rely heavily upon network effects as a competitive edge and innovation resource. Technically, economists say network effects — known also as network externalities — exist when the value of a product or service to users increases as the number of users grows. But this traditional definition is woefully incomplete. Quality of use — and users — matters as much or more to value creation as quantity. In other words, how networks are used is as important as how much they are used. Amazon, for example, may have hundreds of millions of customers shopping for goods, but the fact that tens of millions of those customers actively browse through recommendation engine suggestions and customer reviews, sample book and video content, and write comments and reviews themselves, contributes enormously to the company's value. Amazon's network facilitates the creation and capture of data proffering insights into customers and products alike. These qualitative insights have quantitative impact for both Amazon and its customers, concludes Michael Schrage".

Platforms help allocate resources - Legendary Percy Barnevik, CEO of Asea Brown Boveri (ABB) said," there is tremendous unused potential in our people. Our organizations ensure they only use 5 to 10 percent of their abilities to work. Outside of work they engage the other 90 – 95 percent of their time, energy and work. We have to learn how to recognize and employ that untapped ability that each individual brings to work every day". People from all areas should be moved to contribute with their expertise, convert their knowledge base into a commercial proposition and make their intellectual presence felt in appropriate roles, positions and platforms. The earlier Chairman of ITT had said, "Once the system had selected for and reinforced conformity and obedience, no amount of top management exhortation about individual initiative or encouragement of personal risk taking could change the dominant pattern".

Platform in a Sharing Economy – Empowerment research can give us clear signals and create "morale indices" for tracking over time, can allow us to measure progress against cultural goals, and enable us to benchmark key indicators with other organizations. How often should they be done? This depends on the pace of change in the organization. Employees can get fed up with filling in questionnaires, and excess quantity reduces quality. But surveys definitely become an integral part of building change factors. "Before we end, I'd like to hear your thoughts about the role of culture in the sharing economy. How is it different and how do those differences manifest? Asks in MIT SMR 2016, Arun Sundararajan (New York University Stern School of Business), who was interviewed by Gerald C. Kane on "Crowd-Based Capitalism? Empowering Entrepreneurs in the Sharing Economy" the author continues, "Here are some excerpts. Companies need to be thinking about how the changes associated with a sharing economy are going to affect their business models. The sharing economy, which is sometimes called the collaborative economy or the on-demand economy, started out as a way for consumers to pay to temporarily access or share products and services rather than buying or owning them. Today, it's really a broad and emerging economic system with five characteristics. One is that it's market-based, meaning that there is some sort of digitally enabled market that enables the exchange of goods and the emergence of new services. Uber and Airbnb are good examples. One is a peer-to-peer marketplace providing transportation, and the other is a marketplace for short-term accommodation. A second characteristic associated with the sharing economy is that there is an increase in the impact of capital, which means that a range of things, from physical assets to people's time to people's money, begin to get used at levels close to their full capacity. (In building a platform, specific culture change program surveys might be done before the change, during, and after. One company example is the Individual Dignity Entitlement survey. This produces an index, which affects managers' bonuses. Six questions are tracked every quarter: Have you considered opportunities in the macro economic environment before taking this role? Do you have a substantive meaningful job that contributes to the success? Do you have on-the-job behaviors and the knowledge base to be successful? Does your role require you to be inter dependent with other role holders, functions or geographies? Do you feel comfortable to work in environments where the degree of uncertainty is high? Has training been identified and made available to continuously upgrade your skills? Do you have a platform dedicated career plan and is it exciting, achievable, and being acted on? Have you received candid positive or negative feedback within the last 30 days that has been helpful in improving your performance or achieving your career plan? Is there appropriate sensitivity to your personal circumstances, gender, and cultural heritage so that such issues do not distract from your success?) The emergence of crowd-based networks that compete with centralized institutions is another characteristic. These networks thrive when the supply of capital, the supply of assets, and the supply of labor originates from decentralized crowds of individuals rather than from aggregates assembled centrally by corporations or governments. The sharing economy is also characterized by the blurring of lines between what used to be personal and what used to be professional. In scaling and commercializing peer-to-peer activities — giving someone a place to stay, lending someone money, giving someone a ride — many activities that used to be considered personal are now entering the commercial realm. Hosting an Airbnb part-time or driving a Lyft part-time or becoming a banker through funding circles are all examples of personal activities that are blurring these lines. The fifth characteristic is the blurring of lines between a fully employed workforce and casual labor. What used to be a full-time job is now supplanted partially by contract work".

Relevance of Organization and Platform Culture - Organizations exist to coordinate the exchange of survey results between companies, and firms also create their own clubs for this purpose. Ideally, the questions we would want to benchmark would be those that we see as fundamental to our value-management strategy. They will be about innovation, learning, knowledge and information sharing, personal development, and overall satisfaction. On Cultures. "I think there are two different forms of culture here: an organizational culture and a platform culture. Organizational culture is familiar. But there's a much broader platform culture among the distributed group of people who are your suppliers of labor and capital, analogous to organizational culture, but more fluid". Arun Sundararajan continues, "Uber has over 1 million drivers and Airbnb has more than 1.5 million hosts who are an integral part of delivering a consistent, high-quality experience — the crux of a brand —

but who aren't under an organizational umbrella in the same way full-time employees are. I think establishing a platform culture is hugely important for a distributed workforce because the options for managing a distributed workforce are more limited. Culture is such a complex issue. What are the main takeaways?" "People who are highly motivated by their work have less time off than those who find their work unfulfilling or where there is a general malaise concerning morale. Similar organizations or units can vary significantly in their absentee rates. We should set a target that we believe we should be able to expect from a highly motivated workforce, and regard the difference between this and our actual rate as a gap to be closed." "Two thoughts here. One is that it's too early to generalize about how culture develops in a generic platform. In the two cases I've talked about, I think the culture at Airbnb was a designed culture. The prescription I would give is don't let culture emerge organically, but think of it the way Brian Chesky, the CEO of Airbnb does: As a design problem that needs to be solved right because if you don't design it in a particular way, it may evolve in a way you don't like. The other takeaway is that I think a platform should make a conscious effort to create a particular platform culture among its providers just as a large organization might create a particular culture among its employees. Buckingham and Coffman ask, "Do I know what is expected of me at work? Do I have the materials and equipment I need to do my work right? At work, do I have the opportunity to do what I do best every day? In the last seven days have I received recognition or praise for good work? Does my supervisor, or someone at work, seem to care about me as a person? Is there someone at work who encourages my development? At work, do my opinions count? Does the mission/purpose of my company make me feel that my work is important? Are my co-workers committed to doing quality work? Do I have a best friend at work? In the last six months have I talked to someone about my progress? At work, have I had opportunities to learn and grow?" I think it's easier for a large corporation to figure out how to extend its culture to a distributed, on-demand workforce because it's already aware of the importance of establishing the right one, but it's certainly something new that a smart manager of an on-demand workforce should pay very careful attention to".

Platforms Proliferate Intellect - Intellect is not the prerogative of a select few, at least not in the business organization. At best this should be a minimum assumption to make the organization vibrant intellectually. Traditionally, organizations would create blinds between the thinkers and the doer's and would bring up Chinese walls affecting relationships and working advantages. For corporations to reap the benefits of an intellectual performance mix it is essential, if not critical, those performing players are put together and demanded work output. Intellectually stimulated people seek a demanding work environment where they are stretched to produce results, are expected to be at their best at all times. It is fostering a culture where performance orientation is simply a way of life.

Beyond Intellect - We do not attempt to position intellect as the final panacea for all corporate evils. In fact, managing the intellect will perhaps be the single most important HR challenge of the 21st century. But their empirical trends demonstrating the distinctiveness of the human mind as a competitive weapon for the corporate of the future. And some discontinuities, continue:

- *Digital makes for competitive advantage*
- *Big Data and Analytics forms the basis for analysis*
- *Artificial Intelligence and Machine Learning become the new norm*
- *Each year more than a half-million good jobs are eliminated by the US companies alone.*
- *Statistics indicate that by the early 21st century less than 50% of the industrial world's workforce will hold conventional full time jobs.*
- *Even the physical work place is no longer designed for mass production and conventional schedules.*

- *The decline in manufacturing jobs has been accompanied by growth in service, intellectual and knowledge functions and industries.*
- *Two-third of the current industrial workforce in the US are already in service jobs.*
- *Yesterday's vertical management is being replaced by horizontal networking among clusters of small functions and firms.*
- *Small firms are generating disproportionate number of jobs and tend to be more innovative than large enterprises.*
- *More and more people want less routine, boring job contents and more control and freedom over their work content, schedules and manner of doing the job.*
- *According to the Bureau of Labor Statistics, 18% of US firms are estimated to have work-at-home programs.*
- *Technology and business management has integrated as never before, with technical staff gaining knowledge that they cannot survive without business knowledge.*
- *There are jobs for both generalists and specialists. People need to find their niche and move on into becoming specialists as generalists.*
- *Hiring of large numbers would become inevitable, but each would several times over their costs and contribution. The age of downsizing in knowledge intensive industries is over.*
- *Companies would either grow or diminish and there would be no half way measures*

Platform Analytics – Involvement Strategies - What is our overarching strategy to prepare the organization build an analytics platform. To develop a thorough roadmap in close collaboration with the Project Management Office (PMO) which synthesizes various change inputs into an integrated roadmap containing not only all change Management dimensions but also all interdependent initiatives in play. In addition, the governance infrastructure of a Change Agent network is set up as the execution arm. "Governance often begins by establishing specific roles to help ensure data quality for analytics initiatives. A collaborative group of business leaders needs to be convened to provide sustained governance with key responsibilities that include setting enterprise wide data standards, prioritizing and selecting analytics projects, and monitoring measurements", write David Kiron, Rebecca Shockley, Nina Kruschwitz, Glenn Finch and Dr. Michael Haydock in Analytics: The Widening Divide, MIT SMR 2011, "The contest between Watson and previous *Jeopardy!* champions was more than a game. Contestants also had opportunities to wager their "earnings" based on confidence in their own capabilities, and their assessment of the competition. In the real world, too, competitors have everything to gain or lose". For example, Watson-based clinical decision support system will have very different requirements than the Watson system that competed in Jeopardy! Watson's task in Jeopardy! was to generate a single correct answer in response to a question and to buzz in with that answer if the answers confidence estimate exceeded a dynamically computed threshold. Watson did this by generating a set of candidate answers (hypotheses) and then collecting and scoring evidence for each answer. The hypothesis with the most compelling evidence was selected as the best answer. In effect, the hypotheses competed within the evidence space. "In today's world, lack of an adequate analytics strategy is increasingly likely to put their future in jeopardy. A previous study showed the emerging gap between organizations that use analytics for competitive advantage and those that do not. This year, we see a divide that is even larger, and is rapidly widening. Taking advantage of new business models and new data, unexpected competitors are emerging and familiar customers are demanding unprecedented attention. Disruptions like these create a widening set of opportunities for players at every level". Organizational Integration is a critical component in a platform execution - Is the operating model and organization structure aligned to the strategy and does it create an environment that positions the workforce to be successful? To develop a future state organization at both the macro and micro levels that aligns the workforce to adopt and execute effectively in the changed environment. "With a full range of analytics capabilities governed by an integrated analytics strategy, organizations are better positioned to widen, or narrow, the distance between themselves and competitors to their own best advantage. Rigorous review of project delivery progress and business contribution is paramount. In addition to an aligned business and IT plan, having a business-driven enterprise governance of data, information and analytic tools is an essential component of the information agenda. Most importantly, an information agenda is essential for providing benchmarks and outcomes to evaluate progress in developing competencies at each step along the way. It helps determine whether IT is supporting the business strategy effectively, and whether that strategy is understandable to those who must implement it. It identifies the analytical techniques needed to implement specific programs and defines metrics for assessing the outcome of those efforts. Just as importantly, it encompasses governance structures — business rules and standards — that support, rather than hinder, the ability to manage information in its various forms. By tying these elements together, the information agenda can provide a solid organizational foundation for achieving enduring competitive advantage with analytics".

Platforms Focus on an Urgency to Change – Psychological factors-these cover unwritten and subconscious elements and cause feelings of resentment and resistance when taken away. **Actual threats**-things that are perceived as affecting personal standing or prestige, or as altering the things we value most about our jobs. **Imposed change**-When reasons for the change must be unclear or when benefits from the change are hard to see. **Lack of faith in making the change** -Resistance increases when there is little respect for the abilities of those who are causing the change. This may imply a lack of faith in the leadership. **Gaps in the area** -Due to an expertise in an area some people may feel important aspects have been overlooked and this may cause them to oppose change. **Emotional barriers**- Sentiments, loyalty and desire for continuity can prompt a person to resist change. Is it desirable in the circumstances; Are there circumstances which prevent participation, can they be removed? Who should participate: key people or all concerned? What is the scope for participation: decision making, post-decision implementation? How should participation be achieved: individual discussions, group meetings, working parties? How different will the job of each person be after the change in terms of content and style? Do their skills, knowledge and abilities match these requirements? How confident are the people concerned that they know and understand the new requirements and possess the required competencies? Would a training initiative provide a mechanism to enable wide participation in the change processor as a minimum enable concerns to be expressed and dealt with? Who are the target groups who should receive communication? What should be communicated? What mix of one/two-way communication should be planned? What style of communication should be planned? What mode of communication should be used?

Platforms Enable Resource Mobility - All organizations must manage the flow of people in, through, and out of the company so as to make available the new breed of intellect and talent for the varying needs of the organization. To start with employees, need to take charge of their learning and their careers. The corporate responsibility should be providing avenues where learning can occur. The rest is up to the individual. Where the employee and the employer feels that the career is stagnating on account of stifled intellectual stimulation the employee should be encouraged to seek out other internal or external positions. Selections again could be significantly more participate. Selections workshop and a career counseling session could be conducted for potential employees to help them make up their mind whether the wish to pursue a career in the environment with the company. The views of the current employees critically explaining the strengths and weaknesses of the company should be shared with candor and uprightness. Intellectual corporations create reward systems that go beyond the guaranteed base pay or position driven compensation. The remuneration is paid for the competencies that the employee brings in to the company and the variable bonus of a substantial value is a function of the intellectual contribution. Pay is closely linked to individual performance.

Compensation systems are a basic part of the command and control system of an organization. It is important to create open approaches to pay design, remuneration planning for individuals, equity participation for ownership and sense of belonging that the reward is available when job is done and the individual could calculate prior to the completion of the task the bonus available if the job is done.

N. Defining Digital Culture and Building Characteristics

Digital Culture Defined – A Digital Organization values history and tradition. The organization is built upon stories that lasts over time and that is believed and revered by people as important learning of the past. In the organization time is not an important consideration, as it is perceived to be relative to the tasks and is managed appropriately as long as basic human processes are followed. The organization emphasizes an appropriate management style that foster learning. The organization focuses on learning environments that involves brings together intellect, knowledge, systemic processes, personal mastery and role models. The climate is conducive and non-threatening to share successes and failures and is not a performance consideration. The organization believes in creating effective structures and hierarchies that provides clarity to roles, responsibilities, tasks and actions. The organization has effective communication channels, with and without boundaries, people enjoy communicating in relation to business and tasks to be accomplished. A leadership and management that pays attention to high performance lead the organization. The organization believes in swift and effective communication, work long hours to conclude tasks, people live at work, identify with winning and use all resources at one's disposal to accomplish tasks. The organization emphasizes an appropriate management style that foster learning. The organization focuses on learning environments that involves brings together intellect, knowledge, systemic processes, personal mastery and role models.

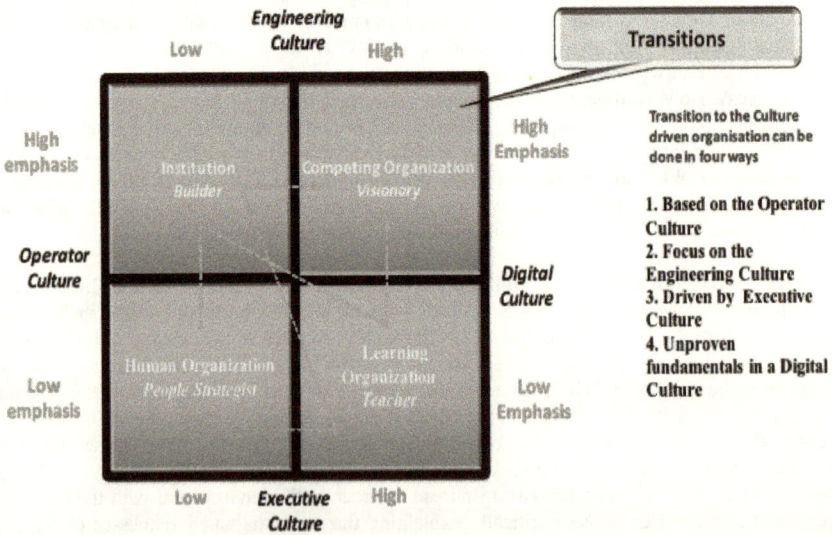

Figure 50 – Defining Digital Culture - Integrating Organizations with Culture & Leadership disrupted

Digital Data - Ongoing systemic flow of data, information and consequent knowledge is vital to make the organization responsive to the new organizational type. The smooth flow of data becomes essential for making ideas and learning cut across departmental boundaries and traditional locations of specialist conflicts. While people experience more and more information at their door steps the urge to make comprehensive decisions become paramount. Communication accelerates processes essential to link the factors that make the intellect work together. In making process effective wide band networking, an act of bringing in diverse sets of connected and unconnected people is important for execution effectiveness. As people network across channels not done before the quality of information exchanged crosses traditional shoptalk. The content of communication ranges between current priorities, problems encountered or solved, people met with and understood successes and disasters. Inter departmental barriers disappear as people learn to laugh at each other including at their goof ups and booboo's. Making chatting up with your colleagues as a part of the day's routine is not necessarily an idea to be thrown to the wolves a' la the discipline managers. In the process of chatting up people derive relationships bonds and working styles and learn to work in a competitive team environment. Alienating people from each other and expecting high output has long since been discarded as a useful theory.

Digital Styles - An interactive, challenging management styles where people experience their real life virtual role in building and shaping the future of the organization is a part of the process synthesizing effort. Typically, in such organizations styles are neither consistent nor permanent. People employ styles depending on the situation and emerge transformational given the compelling or facilitating circumstance. The style will be based on consent, an approach involving asking, listening, and understanding, absorbing and giving. The process of "consent" needs elaboration. In the "Intellectual Corporation" people dynamics and inter relationships is dependent on how far have we transacted, networked with each other on issues confronting each other, the team or the organization as a whole. Concurrently the task of setting working norms on how would the hierarchical superior behave with the colleague also needs elaboration. Typically, the superior is a coach, an on line trainer supporting the task effectiveness of his/her colleague and does this by communicating "consent" with each other on the varying subjects dealt with. Essentially this is possibly the one best management style where colleagues learn to work around each other by talking and concretely communicating. What has to be told will be told no hidden agendas or circumspections in communication?

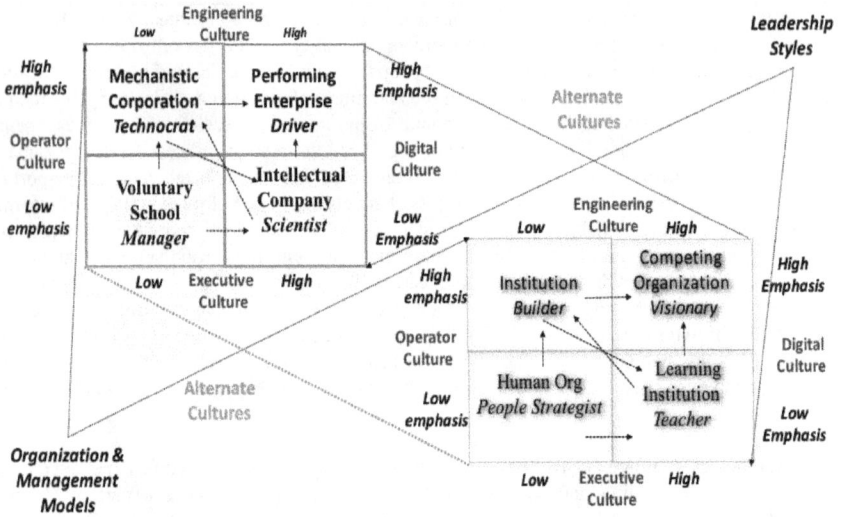

Figure 51 – Defining Digital Culture - Integrating Organizations with Culture & Leadership disrupted

Digital Competencies - To help build behavioral competencies that brings down the inherent human inhibitions, the odd behavioral eccentric, make communication and "tell me sessions" meaningful. "Tell Me Effect" is a concept written by the author explaining the method and advantages of communicating and helping each other through an encounter process where the transacting parties feel a mutual need and obligation to speak and help each other in an honest up front approach. Personality mix matches are sometimes inevitable despite best of selection approaches or training sessions dealt with on people. Organizations have to make behaviorally inclined learning, feedback, change techniques as a normal form of building people programs. Without an exception people should have periodically experienced developmental workshops that takes them back to learning as a key competency.

Digital Accuracy - It is essential for the company to make honest, above board corporate statements and thereafter practice openness to ideas, warring on conflicting positions, embolden people to kickback on points of significant difference, deviate from the norm at will. Effectively the final countdown is based on the quality of the idea. Input, system or suggestion. People should be in a position to take risks without feeling threatened of their job. Motive to add value to the corporation is a fundamental assumption and in which case quality or the dimension of the risk is irrelevant.

Digital Learning - Learning environment, amongst other things, insists on sharing of experiences, learnings, insights, experimental outcomes etc. This has to be a mandate across the company. As in 3M products belong to the division, the technology belongs to the company. There will be compulsory sharing eliminating time consuming management processes that make organizations and teams work together.

Digital Technology - Organizations are not devoid of their conflicting variables. Environment, strategies deployed by competition, manufacturing – marketing optimization goals, source availability of critical, data management, systemic influences, changes in trade regulations, management of barriers, tech influence that influence internal processes. After all companies do not work in isolation of the external variables although process integration efforts, enterprise software's, tech infrastructure should attempt minimal confusing positions.

Digital Teamgruence has been consciously coined to convey the power of congruence and team working when put together. While team working by itself has its built in advantages, congruence in thought, sense of purpose, a climate of trust, availability of mutual perspectives and styles, assimilation of attitudes, similarity of goals, seeking coherent conclusions and common concern for each other's well-being and security is essential to an Intellectual Corporation. Creating clusters of people who have been brought together to achieve something of a mutual benefit has been an organizational practice over time. Several situations have arisen when the team effectiveness has appeared to be low, if not non-performing, largely because of an absence of commonly agreed and internalized sense of purpose and togetherness. And in these failure experiences arise the management need for direction, control and command to make it work.

Digital Team Goals - Teamgruence - Getting like-minded people together is one simple solution to achieve Teamgruence. Concrete congruence and team orientation. However, this is not likely to be a possible scenario at all times. It would also be difficult to keep creating clusters that appear to be tailor made for each situation. Corporate have the unenviable task of putting together teams with the best despite their stated conflicting personalities or positions. There probably on the surface appears no solution other than to create and instill in people the common intellectual goal. One possible way is to get clusters form by themselves depending upon the goals to be achieved. The individuals then have the choice of leveraging their competencies with others and producing results that demonstrate achievements beyond the capabilities of one person or let them experience for themselves the shortfall of an isolated approach.

Digital Intellect Seeks Partnership - In the organization of the future where several inter departmental linkages have become real and a way of life, the intellectual mind would seek partnerships where maximization of effort is possible, albeit as long as there exists a choice to the individual with whom should he/she participate and team up. This approach is perhaps inevitable going forward. Individuals would ask for an environment that includes peer groups that are intellectually comparable and over which learning and teaching becomes easy and interesting. Individuals would seek opportunities to learn from anyone, could have been their ex-boyfriend or the neighbor with whom they disagreed last week. The learning need comprises both the opportunity and a fear of obsolescence. It is this attitude that would bring antithetical poles together. Again in creating teamgruence a mindset that crosses personality stereotypes become important for the corporate to think upon while approaching hiring decisions.

Digital Talent Mindset - Performing climate of the future would allow limited interpersonal conflicts or personality differences. There should be no time to harangue over a lost cow. Hiring specialists need a comprehensive orientation of the manager of the future. A comprehensive wish list of what makes an intellect and an intellect that culturally and schematically fits in with our organizational purpose and goals. The list could range from personality mix, to competencies, to cross cultural orientation, socio-political views, knowledge competencies, advanced specialization needs, mobility etc. These factors may have to be reinvented periodically as organizations learn and grow. To succeed considerable time and effort should be spent in identifying, recruiting, socializing and training people to adapt to the Intellectual Corporation. Retention is, of course, a function of whether we are really an Intellectual Corporation and they perceive it to be so.

Digital Groups - Work groups form an important part of the teamgruence activity. Work groups are assigned complete tasks that involve planning, scheduling, tasking, mutual workload sharing, deadlines, costs and profitability. The self-managed empowered teams bring in opportunities for work role enrichment, self-determined powers and the firm view of being in control over their own lives. Supervision does not exist in any traditional form and the reporting lines are with superiors who are coaches and trainers and are available at call to add value. In getting the work groups effective structural and managerial changes are essential to make delegation and decentralization real. Authority matrix on a self-created basis should become available.

Digital Excellence - The **Digital thinking** is the foundation of the HR Platform. This organization embodies potential and competencies beyond the realm of staid corporations. These organizations stand by a set of visions, values, beliefs and actions that are consistent over time and offer the opportunity for managerial members to see their work life as an extension of their life as a whole. Here vision, values and actions does what it is intended to create and keep and is not left to itself as espoused statements and exhortation. People find security not in holding on what they know but in sharing, interacting and letting go what they know in quest of learning more of what they do not know. Learning Companies need a commitment and environment to develop, learn, teach, communicate and train. Imagine an organization where people are only expected to do a job but are never let out to train. Like a tennis player who never has the time to practice. Over time their performance capabilities will substantially diminish as their ability to think and do innovative actions will subjugate and beaten down to a path of obsolescence and personal boredom.

Digital Orgxcellence - While seeking to create an organization of the future very little chance would we have from escaping from the temptation to seek the ideal and the utopia? We would rather that we do not take shelter in this escape and avoid the act of thinking the utopia. In utopia lies unlimited opportunities never explored before. In it lies the vast, unexplored potential of the individual and the organization and in utopia do we have dreamers. Utopist are indeed dreamers, idealists and romanticists. And all of them form the organization of tomorrow. In a narrow perspective world of today where utilitarianism is key to organizational survival seeking the utopia may mean considerable hardship to the to those who are not dogged by dogmas and stereotypes of why, why not, how and what not. Yet there possibly lies no domain beyond utopia for the corporation willing to go the extra mile in sponsoring the intellect and the individual and are willing to let go of today's utility for tomorrow's stability.

Digital Learn to Excel - Basically we define "Orgxcellence" as. "Digital Corporations created by individuals who wish to learn and contribute in an environment that fosters value for the human dignity and spirit, where people can come and give their best, where merit and human mind is at a premium, where a culture that fosters nurturing originality, where the corporation cherishes experimentation, where the human mind is set free from inhibitions, where intellect is treated and dealt with as a superior form of value addition and contribution, where individuals individually and collectively focus on results and where people attempt flying despite aero dynamic limitation".

Digital Orgxcellence and Utopia are dealt together in building a culture that performs. In organization building-seeking excellence is but the minimum that the members could do while performing a job role. And in doing so dreaming of an unknown future and working towards it is but utopia. The essence of Orgxcellence is competitiveness and intellectualism combined to form a lethal mix of mind that matters to real life companies. In nurturing such an organization people, process, knowledge and learning form the core of the enterprise. Organizations experience competitive pressures through competition, economic upheavals, entry of strong dominant players but more importantly the power of another through the intellect to innovate, substitute and replace all that your organization stands for in business.

Digital Intellect is Lethal - The intellect of one firm can wipe out another firm, not any other singular factor. In pursuit of the utopia, firms create in house processes where dreaming and footloose actions and creations gain legitimacy in the corridors of corporate power. The youth in the old is the intellect that sponsors activities that stretch firms beyond their conventional borders. Every successful software firm has in it the youth of the young and old. They bounce with knowledge and create unseen opportunities. Walk into the product development or the research center of Walt Disney and we see the walking dreamers. They enact their dreams through the imagination of their customers and make business sense. If there is a power available to exploit free of cost and business entertainment expenses, we have the dreams and imagination of people who work for the firm. It is their captive soul searching endeavors that bring to bay ships that were anchored and forgotten many years ago.

O. Human Capital – Knowledge – Learning - Intellect Interface - Context for work level Intellect

Dynamic modeling frameworks, says Jeffrey Schmidt, managing director of innovation at consulting firm Towers Perrin, seek to establish links between human capital drivers (compensation, training), human capital capabilities (leadership, employee engagement), intermediate key performance indicators (productivity, customer satisfaction), and, ultimately, financial performance measures such as stock performance or revenue growth. ("Tying Your People Strategy to the Bottom Line," Harvard Management Update, Vol.8, No. 8, August 2003. Loren Gary can be reached at lgary@hbsp.harvard.edu).

"Work level Intellect' is what we believe people know and know how to use it. To manage this work level Intellect, we must first recognize that it operates on four levels or clusters within the modern organization:

Substantive Cognitive Knowledge: Know-what is the basic mastery of knowledge-based disciplines that professionals achieve through extensive education, training and certification. Sustained education and training enables learning as a critical element of knowledge creation.

Competency Mastery: Know-how is the translation of "book learning" into effective execution. It evidences the ability to apply a discipline to complex real-world problems. Applicability of competencies, skills and capabilities to deliver value to roles.

Institutionalized Interpretation: Know-why is the knowledge of cause-and-effect relationships underlying a discipline? Experience is stated to provide this wisdom of know why there is a cause and effect to every organizational action. It allows knowledge-holders to apply professional intuition, informed judgment to solving complex problems and creating new value. Applied experience is treated as performance.

Power of Expansion: Special intellect, Innovation, expanding from known and unknown sources spins knowledge in unsuspected ways to eventuate new and exciting contributions. The cultivation of this level resides in an organization's culture. Nurturing this talent helps build organizational potential.

Knowledge	Learning	Intellect
Acquisition	Buy Knowledge	Experience Factor
Inheritance	Left By Ancestors & Predecessors	Qualification factor
Creation	Invention / Discovery	Special Intellect & Potential
Expansion	Innovation / Build Up	Training & Learning
Institutionalization	Permeate / Vertical / Across / Horizontal	Behavioral Competencies
Commercialization	Market	Performance
Digital Culture Continuum		

Figure 52 - Knowledge - Learning – Intellect Interface

Significantly, the value of Professional Intellect increases exponentially as one moves up the scale of knowledge, reaching its pinnacle in creative mastery and the innovation and discovery most valued within an enterprise. Identified capability that is predictable is treated as the potential in people to apply work level intellect in business organizations. Essentially these eight factors identified in bold above deals with our work in this paper on human capital or the formation of a professional intellect.

"The value of intellect increases markedly as one moves up the intellectual scale from cognitive knowledge to innovation and invention". And Keith Rosen in HBR paper continues, http://bit.ly/2akUTI0, "Intellect clearly resides in the brains of professionals. The first three levels can also exist in the organization's systems, databases, or operat-ing technologies, whereas the fourth is often found in its culture. Yet most enterprises focus virtually all their training attention on developing basic (rather than advanced) skills and little or none on systems or creative skills".

Knowledge	Learning	Intellect
Knowledge can be learnt through acquisition and for which you need Experience Factor		
Inheritance of knowledge is learnt through Ancestors & Predecessors helps us be qualified		
Creation, Invention and Discovery of knowledge is learnt through special intellect demonstrating Potential		
Expansion of Knowledge is learnt through Innovation - Build Up and enhances intellect by Training & Learning		
Institutionalization of knowledge is learnt through Permeate / Vertical / Across / Horizontal by utilization Behavioral Competencies intellect		
Commercialization of knowledge is learnt through market understanding and Performance is an intellectual driver		
Digital Culture Continuum		

Figure 53 – Understanding How Does Knowledge Data Learning Drives Intellect

Is Intellect Seeking Perfection? Most of a typical professional's activity is directed at perfection, not creativity. People rarely want surgeons, accountants, pilots, maintenance personnel, or nuclear plant operators to be very creative. Managers clearly must prepare their professionals for the few emergencies or other special circum-stances that require creativity, but they should focus the bulk of their attention on delivering consistent, high-quality intellectual output. Organizations are made up of individuals each of who attempt to satisfy their personal wishes and aspirations in a group context. The context is influenced by the individual intellect and what it leaves behind for others to absorb as knowledge and react.

Must Leaders walk the talk, ask, Nina Kruschwitz and Rebecca Shockley in "The Second Annual New Intelligent Enterprise Survey" in MIT SMR Survey 2011, "Organizations are concerned that the quality of the data they use in decision making is consistent. It may be more important to have uniformly consistent data quality across the organization, rather than perfect data from one business unit and poor quality data from another. Survey respondents want leaders to practice what they preach. If the organization's leaders make fact-based decisions themselves, in service of the organization's long-term vision, and demonstrate a willingness to share data across silos, will the rest of the organization be more willing to do the same? For example, climate includes all the local influences that coexist with the wider culture; and there may be many variations. It is particularly affected by the people—their geography and history—and by local leadership. The combination of culture and climate includes the following kinds of characteristics: Norms of behavior—what is expected, what is OK and not OK. The amount of "fun" that goes along with the work, The Human Value of the Enterprise. What gets rewarded. Degrees of freedom and empowerment as opposed to bureaucracy and restraint. The match between authority and responsibility. The extent and effectiveness of communication. The amount of trust in the organization. The level of respect and flexibility regarding the individual.

Must Leaders Walk The Talk

Key Characteristics of a Leaders who make Digital Organizations work	Board	Leadership	Function at heads	Geograp by Heads	Geography			Functions					
Characteristics	Intensity Levels				HQ	Country	Global	Ops	Mktg	Finance	HR	Sales	Manufacturing
Evidence & Behaviors Based Decision making	H	L	M	H	H	M	L	H	M	H	L	H	M
Sponsoring a Long Term Purpose - Assymetrical	H	M	L	M	H	M	L	M	L	H	L	M	L
Sharing of Data Across Traditional Silos - Challenge	L	L	M	L	M	H	M	L	H	L	M	L
Distributed & Altered Reality Decision Making	L	M	H	L	M	H	H	M	L	H	L	M
Deep Tech Understanding as it impacts Customers based on Broad Access to Data & Insights	H	M	H	H	M	L	L	L	L	L	M	L
Articulation of the Value of Scorecard, Metrics, KPIs, Analytics	L	L	H	M	H	L	M	L	M	L	H	L	H
Evaluation of data for enterprise implications - Quality Checks	L	M	H	H	M	L	H	H	M	H	M	L	H
Reward and Promote Successful Projects	M	H	H	H	L	L	M	H	L	M	L	M
Invest in Education & Training (Learning Technologies)	M	H	H	M	L	M	L	M	H	M	L	M
Bias towards experimentation, Active Orientation to Unknown	M	H	M	L	L	H	M	H	L	H	L	H
Respect for Beyond Diversity - LGBT, Specially Abled - Gifted	M	H	H	L	H	M	H	M	H	L	H
Aligments with Millennials - Contrast Boomers - Build for Both	L	M	H	H	M	L	H	M	H	L	H
Friendly State with conflicting values	H	L	M	H	H	M	L	H	M	H	L	M

Figure 54 – Adapted from "Must Leaders Walk the Talk"? Nina Kruschwitz and Rebecca Shockley in "The Second Annual New Intelligent Enterprise Survey" in MIT SMR Survey 2011 Evaluated as H – High, M – Medium and L – Low.

Beyond Knowledge - Organizational knowledge creation is defined as the capability of a company as a whole to create new knowledge, disseminate it through the Organization, and embody it in products, services and systems. It is these capabilities developed through intellect, knowledge and learning that forms the core of Intellectual Capital" - http://bit.ly/2aiCmuv

To paraphrase from June 1998 Hirotaka Takeuchi, (http://bit.ly/2anWTh3) in the last five to seven years, managers focused their attention on cutting costs to the bone through downsizing and re-engineering. Recently, however, they discovered that the removal of all slack from a worker's day runs counter to creativity and innovation, which are the engines of growth. Nonaka and Takeuchi argue that Japanese companies have advanced their position in international competition because of their skills and expertise at organizational knowledge creation, which is the key to the distinctive way that Japanese companies innovate. Japanese companies, which have shunned downsizing and re-engineering for the most part, even during the recent recession, are especially good at utilizing this process to bring about innovation continuously and incrementally. Andersen Consulting set up Knowledge Xchange; KPMG set up Knowledge World, Booz Allen & Hamilton developed Knowledge On-Line; Ernst & Young created their Center for Business Knowledge, KPMG established A Knowledge Manager; and Price Waterhouse has Knowledge View, an Andersen Knowledge Space & Saratoga Institute through PwC. Organizations like Booz Allen & Hamilton have built a knowledge management infrastructure that Includes specialized positions for people who organize and summarize the know- ledge contributions of others

Collective Individual Intelligences Build Organizational Intelligence - "Although the distinction between intelligences has been set out in great detail, Howard Gardner (http://bit.ly/2aE8Uyb) opposes the idea of labeling learners to a specific intelligence. Each individual possesses a unique blend of all the intelligences. Gardner firmly maintains that his theory of multiple intelligences should "empower learners", not restrict them to one modality of learning. Gardner (Dec 1, 2015) - argues intelligence is categorized into three primary or overarching categories, those of which are formulated by the abilities. According to Gardner, intelligence is: The ability to create an effective product or offer a service that is valued in a culture, a set of skills that make it possible for a person to solve problems in life, the potential for finding or creating solutions for problems, which involves gathering new knowledge. Many of Gardner's "intelligences" correlate with the g factor, supporting the idea of a single dominant type of intelligence. According to a 2006 study, each of the domains proposed by Gardner (http://bit.ly/2a3Ot1O) involved a blend of g, cognitive abilities other than g, and, in some cases, non-cognitive abilities or personality characteristics. All too often, company policy determines what is "good for you" in the work environment. Standardization of where and how people work comes from seeing people as cost-based human resources. Empirical support for non-g intelligences is lacking or very poor. Despite this lack of evidence, the ideas of multiple non-g intelligences are attractive to many due to the suggestion that everyone can be smart in some way. Cognitive neuroscience research does not support the theory of multiple intelligences." In, Making of Intelligence: Maps of the Mind – Oct 1999, by Ken Richardson summarizes Gardner, H. (1984)

Frames of Mind - "The Theory of Multiple Intelligences comprehensively, Ken Richardson continues. "A representative account has been expressed by "Howard Gardner" in a series of works from Multiple Intelligences (1984) to Extraordinary Minds (1997). Gardner says that there are biologically specified modules that differ in strength or prominence from person to person. They each have their peculiar computational mechanisms, defining the function of the particular 'intelligence', and each is based on a distinct neural architecture. He says that the plan for these in the genome, and that the specified structure will develop even in widely varying circumstances or environmental experiences". In a value-creating organization these are the behaviors we want to see: Providing clear direction and vision, enabling people to take decisions themselves, ensuring that people are clearly accountable, being a visible role model for the organization's values, showing an overriding and balanced concern for stakeholder value, supporting the growth of people's capability through coaching and work assignments, building and maintaining a learning and sharing environment, providing recognition for achievement, empowering people to innovate and take decisions, outlawing a "blame" culture, continually being open to feedback, keeping people fully informed of what is happening and regularly listening to their input.

Biological – "Gardner has appealed to a range of biological sources of evidence to support his thesis. Among these is the fact that brain damage sometimes appears to knock out or disrupt specific intelligences. For example, it has long been known that injury to parts of the left hemisphere of the cerebral cortex can damage language ability, suggesting that cognitive loci are really neurological loci". How can we track intellectual capability and understand whether the balance of its impact is positive or negative? First of all, it is the application of intellects job to produce results. The productivity or added value of the unit is the ultimate output measure and this is a fair reflection of a leader's ability to gain results through people. The best people to judge how effectively a leader is leading are the followers, hence the strong emphasis on behavioral assessments, based on capability frameworks, mental models and 360° feedbacks. The resulting summary of perceptions is also an output measure of leadership effectiveness, since the style and behavior of leaders will affect morale and motivation. Good systems, processes, systems of multi-input feedback mechanisms will give more than a mere numeric or quantitative evaluation, but through open comments offer illustrative and visual examples that enable individuals to relate to the perceptual reality of how they are seen. However, some of the instruments in use are extremely complex, and delve into such detail of perfection that they risk being demotivating to the leader concerned. "Gardner claims that neuroscientists have identified neurological units corresponding with distinct cognitive functions. He argues that all children (and especially many with learning disabilities) excel in one or two domains, yet remain mediocre or downright backward in others, is also evidence of a modular view. He claims that these forms of evidence suggest a biological basis for specialized intelligence, such as linguistic intelligence, logico-mathematical intelligence, spatial intelligence, musical intelligence, and so on. In his more recent work."

Seven Intelligences – "Gardner has extended his original list of seven intelligences, and suggests that the list will grow as further identifications are made. We should be clear right away that there is nothing really new about these views. We believe that thinking as a kind of computation was an idea proposed in the seventeenth century, and the idea of 'mental (intellectual) faculties' was popular for a time in the early nineteenth century. What is new is the assumed theoretical underpinning for them provided by evolutionary biology. As in the past, though, there are serious problems with it. We get a strong whiff of the nature of these problems from the admissions of Gardner himself". Are there any inputs to intellectual effectiveness other than the intellect itself? Clearly, one is our ability to select— and promote, and the criteria and processes we use have a significant influence. A measure would be the percentage of appointments made that are successful. We adapt our criteria based on experience, problem solving and analytical experiences, climatic presence and in order of contribution to increase the success rate. Another input is the extent to which we invest in leadership development, programs aimed at self-awareness, personal change, and people management skill improvement. Not all such natural programs achieve very much in terms of the outcomes we have mentioned, however, and this is often due a lack of clarity on the desired outcome. "In his book Multiple Intelligences, he suggests that 'findings from neurobiology' provide us 'with a powerful hint about the possible "natural kinds" of intelligence'. At the same time, he warns that we must not think of these intelligences as physically verifiable entities, but only as 'potentially useful scientific constructs'. We are told of the neurological evidence for modules, but warned that 'even the most informed scholars of the nervous system differ about the level of modules that are most useful for various scientific or practical purposes'. He is keen to stress how innate knowledge 'has been internalized through evolution so that it is now "pre-wired" in individuals', yet claims that 'an intelligence' is a set of problem-solving skills valued by a particular culture".

Modules are Products – "Gardner notes how modules are products of the imagination rather than empirical demonstration. He candidly admits that the selection (or rejection) of a candidate intelligence 'is more reminiscent of an artistic judgement than of a scientific assessment', thereby acknowledging the dangers of reification (or attributing real existence to something that doesn't actually exist): 'Sympathetic readers, will be likely to think – and fall in the habit of saying – that here we behold the "linguistic intelligence", the "interpersonal intelligence", or the "spatial intelligence" at work, and that's that. But it's not. These intelligences are fictions.' "Flexibility of time and place for many roles has led to "intellectual hot-desking," where it is assumed that desks are products and are only required for part of the time and you take the nearest desk available. Some people value the freedom inherent in the arrangement; because it is an imagination of the utility value of a product, others become very demotivated by an absence of personal space and having their established environment turned upset down. Personal productivity is reduced until a person feels stabilized. We need to avoid general rules for all without taking the trouble to understand the needs and concerns of each person individually. Space is one thing, but equipment and facilities are another. Too often, company policy determines what is "good for you" in the work environment. Standardization of where and how people work comes from seeing people as cost-based human resources. Case studies of highly innovative companies show how freedom for people to define their own working space, facilities, and equipment can be very significant. So one input measure here would be the degree of freedom that people have to "do their own thing." This wishing to have things both ways by appeals to reified or mystical entities as products of genes is not untypical of evolutionary psychologists. Thus, although the idea of genetic constraints is now very popular, not one such constraint has yet been identified (beyond, that is, hypothetical attentional tendencies or other predispositions). Many will agree with the view of Frank Keil that such constraints act as core principles or structural skeletons of abilities, which still permit considerable development flexibility. But this doesn't explain how the historically and contemporary huge variety of forms of intelligence among humans can arise from the same 'skeleton'. Substantial differences in animal bodies, for example, are not found without underlying differences in the skeleton".

Science of Restructure - Restructured organizations continue to feel the pain of conflicts, departures, exits dealt over time on its people owing to absence of a clear prescriptive formula of success post the restructuring exercise. People restructuring have seen its time to a considerable degree as organizations continue to reel under the negative impact of their actions. As we stated earlier there are instances of quarterly balance sheet management issues where corporate management chooses the people departure route to show action in a non-Performing Enterprise. Post restructuring the promised results simply did not happen, obviously given the reasons for non-performance being other factors beyond people alone. Again the science of rationalizing manpower needs considerable refinement with methods of identifying surplus people, redundancies, strategic realignment of people and abolished jobs requiring an accredited method. Structural weight traditionally seen in large corporate are now decreasing as companies see the emergence of individuals who can substitute large numbers with their agile mind. Although in the Intellectual Corporate headcount is less likely to ever be an issue. Individuals would pay for their compensation several times over through the application of their mind. It is in the bureaucratic hierarchies that we apprehend a continuous act of purging and that to our mind, if not managed well, could lead to an organizational freeze.

Networks Challenges Resistance – Some questions need an urgent perspective in the digital market place. Are the controls and incentives driving the organization in the same direction? Are the personal aims of the key people in the market place and the organizational goals in harmony? How far can self-control be used as a driving force in this market? Give constant recognition to the parts others play as the market place moves forward. Take opportunities to acknowledge the achievements of others in public. Use opportunities to reinforce the behavior you want from others. Do not indulge in empty praise and insincere comments. Have regular performance reviews. Thought processes and relationship dynamics are fundamental if change has to be successful. Change only happens when each person makes a decision to implement the change. People fear change it happens to them. Given the freedom to do so, people will build quality into their work as a matter of personal pride. Traditional organizational systems treat people like children and expect them to act like adults. Truth is more important during periods of change and uncertainty than good news. Trust is earned by those who demonstrate consistent behavior and clearly defined values. People who work are capable of doing much more than they are doing. The intrinsic rewards of a market place project are often more important than the material rewards and recognition. A clearly defined vision of the end result enables all the people to define the most efficient path for accomplishing the results. The more input people have into defining the changes that will affect their work, the more they will take ownership of the results. To change the individual, change the system. At the heart of change management lies the change problem i.e. some *future state* to be realized. At a conceptual level the change problem is a matter *of moving from one state to another. Change can therefore be seen as a **How**, **What** and **Why** problem.*

Networks helps build talent market place - Organizations exist to create value for people, either individually or collectively. Very few organizations can say that they know how to balance the talent needs of organizations with their respective replacement value. They may have lists of people with their respective value (built around historical output etc). They may have lists of people with potential, perhaps also of key players who make a special contribution. Most are conscious of their significant talent and where it resides. What is lacking is a systematic, rigorous approach to understanding the value of people. McKinsey Consultants Lowell Bryan, Claudia Joyce, Leigh Weiss make a business case for Talent marketplaces. "Law firms and other professional-services groups, academia, and R&D units often have informal talent marketplaces where senior people try to find the best junior employees and the best junior employees can choose the most attractive assignments. These marketplaces generally follow informal rules of conduct and work best when the market members are fewer than 100 and know one another". And the the availability of qualified leaders at all levels to mobilize the organizations toward their strategies.

Figure 55 – Digital and Market Place - "Strategy, not technology drives digital transformation"

Market Place - A market based workgroup is often unjustifiably called a "team," which should be defined as a group with one common goal and yet interdependence. Good leaders seek to maximize team spirit, on the assumption that this is a positive input to motivation in its own right. But many work on their own personal accountabilities, with some dependence, either psychologically or workflow-wise, on other colleagues. Sometimes the dependence is critical, and an input or output from other group members determines the person's effectiveness. "In the complex corporate world, which involves thousands of professionals and managers, the best approach is formalizing the talent marketplace—that is, a managed marketplace created to bind the interests of individuals to the interests of the company", continue Bryan, Joyce and Weiss. "A formal talent marketplace doesn't

---

528

come into existence naturally; a company must invest in it to ensure that it makes a fair exchange of value to both parties in a transaction—otherwise, it will fail. Formal talent marketplaces can develop around functional areas or managerial roles. Large companies with a formal talent marketplace include American Express and IBM. They believe there are sure shot conditions for success. For example, "A talent marketplace isn't for all types of employees. The majority of those at most companies are workers in the traditional sense: individuals who have skills that are largely interchangeable and can be managed adequately through line supervision. (The problem is that people do not fit the strict market definition of an "asset." They cannot be transacted at will; their contribution is individual and variable (and subject to motivation and environment), and they cannot be valued according to traditional financial principles. And yet, organizations today are as much concerned about the "war for talent" as any other business issue. Why is this so? It is very simple. The valuation of companies has changed progressively since about 1990, putting a much higher value on "intangible – human capital assets" such as knowledge, skills, special contribution, innovation, competence, brands, and systems. These assets are also known as the "intellectual capital", as we have seen earlier, of the organization. And it is people, and alone-the "human capital"-who build the value.) These employees might operate a large bank's call center, work in a big-box retailer, or drive a truck for a logistics provider—jobs where the work is tightly managed to specified processes. For such employees, the traditional line-driven approaches still work. Talent marketplaces also may not be necessary for smaller companies and for companies that are less global and have fewer organizational silos, because these types of organizations find it easier to allocate talent effectively".

Digital Market Place Transformational Drivers		
Technology – Applications Pressure	Regulatory – Compliance Pressure	Customer (Demand - Supply) Pressure

Measures   **Indicators**

Measures	Technology	Regulatory	Customer	Indicators
Competitive	✓	✓	✓	CAGR Herfindahl Index
Market Size	✓	✓	✓	CAGR Market Size
Profitable Growth	✓	✓	✓	CAGR Growth
Investments	✓	✓	✓	CAGR Gross Assets

* Herfindahl Index is a measure of the 'concentration' in an industry. Computed as the sum of the of market shares of the players in the market. The value of the index, H, is the sum of the squares of the market shares of all firms in an industry:
H = 1 implies a monopoly where 100% of the market share is held by a single player
H = 0 implies a situation where the number of players is very high and each holds a very small fraction of the total market.
Differential Rate of Return (DRR) as the primary measure of performance - DRR = Return on Capital Employed - Cost of Capital

Figure 56 – Industry Pressure for Change - Three drivers identified for Industry pressure for change are best measured through a combination of surrogate indicators

Role Stresses - Where an organization has not kept pace with training and development a significant portion of managers would turn knowledge redundant periodically and would come up for the retention review. Role stresses and work load loop encountered by middle level managers would increase given pressure to perform owing to a push factor from below from managers wanting early and substantive space to contribute and grow. And a pull factor from the top where the top management is demanding on time innovative performance. There is an emerging value conflict between the large-scale number of middle and senior managers who have spent large years in the corporate but have retained some amount of their competitive competencies. They may not be as ready and would be ideally expected but they are somewhere there close enough. This is a potential area of current knowledge and expected knowledge competencies.

Choice - People do not wish to be told, controlled, directed, guided or led, irrespective of our noble intentions. They would fundamentally like to be left to themselves to show initiative, make new products, redesign, change, create, add value, learn, reflect and make their impact on the company bottom line. They would basically like to be liberated from the corporate bureaucratic shackles. In fact, important shifts and specified emphatic changes are increasing on freedom, autonomy, responsibility, and the influence of employees at all levels are happening across select organizations showing a clear trend. In some ways one can think of the characters in the classic "**Drifters**" by James Michener or the Hare Krishna Movement, of course.

Talent Rules - The relative value of teams and departments is best determined on the basis of distribution of talent across the unit (horizontal/vertical/performance ranking). Our efforts on the retention of talent can be focused through seeing the relative value of different groups of people. This value may then be compared with the contribution that the group is making—and, indeed, their costs. Arguably, there should be a more or less linear relationship between "asset value" and "value added" for most groups. The distribution of potential. We can get an understanding of how potential is distributed and where we may have continuity problems. The extent of values alignment. We can look at the factors that have been judged and get a feel of how values alignment is distributed, in functions and in areas. This may lead to some action to shift the culture more toward the espoused values. The flexibility of our workforce. The higher the average factor for "capability," the more flexible our people are. In times of restructuring this may save unnecessary redundancies and it also gives us more options in career management. "It's time to tear up your recruitment rule book. the recruitment industry is in the early stages of digital disruption. Job boards are being replaced by social networks. software algorithms are challenging headhunters. the power is in the hands of candidates, and there's no shortage of jobs for top talent to choose from. As an eBusiness leader, it's time you engaged your HR and recruitment team to truly build your brand as a digital employer of choice. In a Forrester research paper, 2015, "Recruit And Retain Top Digital Talent" visionary analyst Martin Gill writes, "Build your Digital employer Brand to attract the Best People", Many digital agencies and pure plays are already doing a great job of highlighting why their firm is the destination of choice for digital talent, so it's no accident that many of the brightest minds in digital gravitate to such rms. to follow the lead of these firms:

› *Go large on highlighting your firm's digital credentials. eBusiness leaders must collaborate with their HR colleagues to build digital into their firm's employer branding. try things like entering key digital projects, like an e-commerce offering, into industry awards. Build a modern work environment that encourages collaboration and innovation — this means giving employees the tools, the physical environment, and the freedom to challenge organizational norms to innovate. then use YouTube videos, press releases, or blog posts to show potential candidates what it's like to work at your rm. Build and maintain a proactive candidate network on key social platforms like LinkedIn. Don't think that this is a one-off exercise. it's an ongoing process with multiple candidate touchpoints.*

Holistic Digital Performance Measure	Performance	Explanation
Differential Rate of Return (Return on Capital Employed - Cost of Capital)	Good - Average	5-10%
Market Capitalization compared to industry average	Good - Excellent	Above
Industry Leadership	Good	Top 20%
Investment / expenditure towards customer education / welfare as a % of turnover	Excellent	1-3%
Investment in environmental development / preservation	Average - Good	Accepts and abides by regulation
Contribution to national development / calamity management	Poor - Good	Some contribution by company apart significant staff contribution
Investment in employee welfare(health, education & development) beyond statutory obligations	Good	Some benefits for all categories
Investment in Vendor Development beyond that needed for own interest as a % of turnover	Average – Poor	Only for reducing own costs
Net Global Income FX Exchange earned as a % of turnover	Very Poor – Poor	Negative Outflow
Overall Performance	**Good**	

Figure 57 – Digital and Market Place - "Strategy, not technology drives digital transformation"

Should we assume that our human capital is only those people with an exclusive contract to us, an institution as those we would regard as employees? Boundaries are breaking down in many ways: Previous competitors collaborate, customers and suppliers interact electronically and share knowledge databases, and individuals work for a variety of organizations. Former employee departments become outsourced suppliers. Are they still part of our human capital? Or is our asset value confined to the management activity of them as a supplier?

› ***Don't let "authenticity" become a dirty word.*** *transparency is vital in how you engage candidates and employees. social sites like Glassdoor open up a window into your organization, giving candidates a view of what it's really like to work there. to attract the right candidates, based on competencies and keep them for the long haul, you can't fake your employer brand. it must be genuine. But don't think that your firm must be a digital master to attract talent. eBusiness leaders in firms at lower levels of digital maturity should highlight the longer-term potential for candidates to play a leading role in transforming a traditional business. show candidates how they will make a demonstrable difference in their roles.*

Many frameworks that concentrate on competences combine everything a person knows about the business into one competence called "business awareness" or "technical knowledge." The test of any framework must be its perceived usefulness in the eyes of managers and employees. In interviewing, managers generally are at least equally concerned about what and who a person knows, and what experience they have, as they are about personal behaviors. A framework for understanding and measuring capability is the most fundamental tool we can have in facilitating all those processes that require comparison between a person and a job profile.

› *Link employee measurement and reward to digital strategy.* *eBusiness leaders must do more than just challenging existing pay scales to attract the right skills. overall compensation, including a flexible work environment and freedom to grow and develop, are just as important — as is helping employees measure the impact they have. For instance, digital agency Rosetta measures three key aspects of employee performance: how employees deliver benefit to their clients, how they collaborate with other colleagues, and how they deliver value back to the agency in terms of driving revenue. this framework supports employee performance appraisals and talent development, with clear requirements for roles at each level of the organization, from associate to SVP".*

This area covers personal traits, attitudes, and behaviors that are demanded by a role, or that generally characterize "high performance." They are undoubtedly important and very individual. In many job roles, aspects of personal behavior can be extremely pertinent to the likelihood of success. As one goes up the management ladder, these behaviors gain increasing importance and can outweigh the technical knowledge that might have been more important in junior jobs. Paul Dobson of City University Business School writes, Personal competencies alone are unlikely to deliver superior performance outcomes. This is because of the influence of the environment in which people work, and the fact that they are only one component of capability. There are severe limitations in the way that competencies are chosen, validated and assessed, and they lack the flexibility needed to cope with change and diversity. Results can be achieved successfully in many different ways. Moreover, each area of adding value demands its own set of behaviors for success.

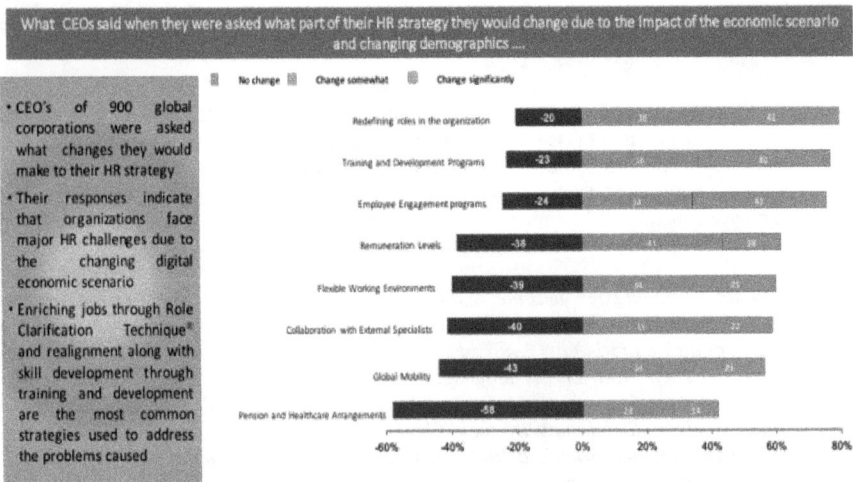

Figure 58 – Adapted People Implications of the Economic Scenario - CEO Perspective HR Strategy

P. So What Now?

The Intellectual Worker brings in

To face competition over time and retaining a winning condition, organizational competencies have to be identified and changed dynamically - This is inevitable realistically. Identification of what we can do best and having them implemented expeditiously are both equally important. Organizations of tomorrow have to be in touch with their organizational members and their individual competencies to realize what can they do best and at a given point of time. Summation of individual competencies determines the organizational competencies. Making a five-year plan with current state of competencies is a true reflection of a company's suicidal tendency. Knowledge of the business as we ran it yesterday makes no meaning for tomorrow. Competencies would radically shift from one stage of development to another depending upon the stated position of the organization at a point in time. What was evaluated as our source of strength may emerge to be our single largest weakness? There are examples of the buggy whip syndrome where the company has lived on its cash cow of yesterday. ICIM Computers, IBM Business Machines or ICIL large frames are examples of once upon a time successful competency. Go back in history. The launch of MSOffice in 1999 is an example of Microsoft answer to its competition on the future of the office products in the windows range.

A Psychometric Testing Canada Research indicates, "Individuals of this corporation have rarely worked in teams and show reluctance in doing things together. Individual excellence and team excellence should be dealt with up front. Key challenges included Accountability / Ownership on key decisions diffused due to over dependence on committees or non-productive group processes. There is a tendency to take accountability for personal actions instead of position actions. Compensation and incentive structure governed by public sector environment / pay commissions including a lack of alignment between function performance and corporate strategy. Promotion policies not driven by individual performance or capability-strategy alignment including a rigid process of exams, interviews, transfers for promotions. Focus only on near term performance including monitoring through dashboards / sophisticated IT tools absent – difficulty in training & assessing competence of employees and excessive focus on lag performance indicators.

Sensitivity - Large number of intellectually inclined individuals shows deep sensitivity and care towards organizational processes that may appear to be so rigorous and meaningless traditional managers. What may appear to be a loss of quality time would appear to these thinkers that without a fair process change in any event does not internalize or happen. It would but become inevitable for organizations to create and manage institutions on an ethical basis in their policies and practices.

Realism - For the intellectual managers this is a path of realism, a journey necessary for organizations to transit from current state to a desired state of performance and effectiveness. An intellectual manager asks of organizations to create organic systems and processes that facilitate freedom of expression, democracy and the right to do what is right. They are at several instances unconventional and would border on the maverick. Many intellectually bright people, left to themselves would rather learn, teach, consult and operate out of value adding knowledge organizations given their predisposition to learning oriented environments

Articulate Minds - Employees view the emerging business complexity as an inevitable feature of the modern economy. In it they see an opportunity for individual capabilities, skills, competencies and most of all their intellect to be put to use considerably. Employees like to make clean, clear, connection with organizational bottom line orientation/result and the intellect that has been utilized to make it happen. Application of the intellect too versatile and barrier breaking episodes offers the intrinsic motivation to the intellectually bored set of corporate citizens. They are looking for an avenue to articulate their mind and see its impact on the company. In a sense they are like chess players making one move, predicting the next few moves of the opponent and yet looking forward to the surprise element that stretches their mind. Every idea thought plan generated, created, nurtured and consolidated by the thinking population is seeking contribution space and medium.

Mindtree Ltd, A Global Digital Leader write of their (Digital) journey so far and its future,

"In the context of technology evolving at an incredible speed, businesses have no choice but to go digital in order to stay relevant. We believe that companies that are prepared for this disruption are building their strategies to gain an advantage. Mindtree is at the forefront of this disruptive odyssey and continuously evolves with an aim to be the Digital Leaders of the industry. Mindtree delivers digital transformation, technology services and accelerates growth for Global 1000 companies by solving complex business challenges with technical innovations.

"Born Digital", Mindtree takes an agile and collaborative approach to creating customized solutions across the digital value chain. This is permeated in every aspect of the organization; be it onboarding Campus Minds fresh from campus, our Leadership Journeys, engaging with our clients or our overall approach to learning.

Our investment in Digital is infused in some of these areas:

- *Young Graduates, Campus Minds, undergo a 90-day assimilation in our new state of the art Learning Center and come out with confidence to take on the challenges of tomorrow's world; they are The Engineers of Tomorrow.*
- *Our leadership development focusses on the challenges of convergence of mobile, social, data & cloud technologies and continuously seek new digital strategies to satisfy our customer needs.*
- *Assessing the ever changing demands of the organization and needs of learners, the learning platform (developed in-house) was designed to be simpler, more agile, flexible and social.*
- *The Digital Pumpkin is where all the magic happens. We work with our clients to accelerate their innovation funnel. It is an innovation hub where clients are invited to co create cutting edge digital solutions.*

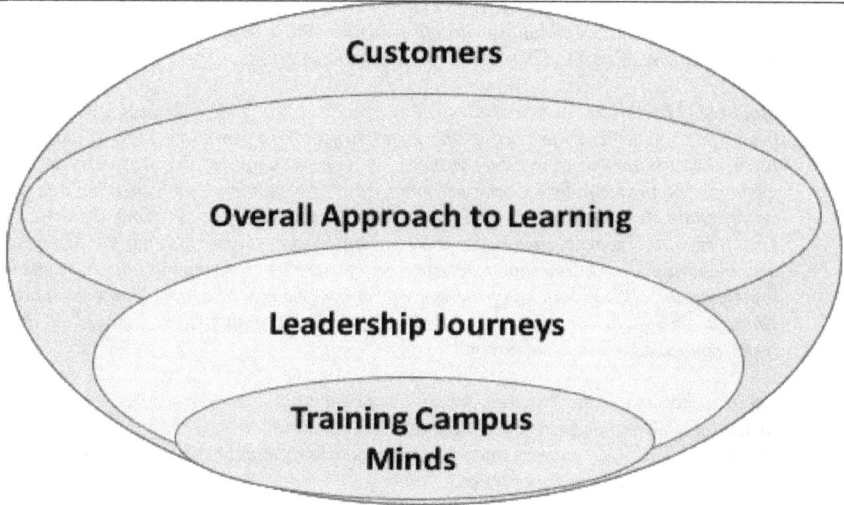

Figure 59 - Mindtree Digital Spectrum

Developing Talent for Tomorrow; Today

Since the company's founding in 1999, Mindtree has recognized its people as its greatest asset and refers to them as 'Mindtree Minds'. We have invested in their future with our new state of the art Global Learning Center called Mindtree Kalinga, in Bhubaneshwar, India. This facility introduces new hires from universities to our corporate culture and values with the aim of nurturing the Engineers of Tomorrow. This 90-day program has been designed to mold in each Campus Mind, an engineering mindset backed with a social conscience, and not just another programmer. Campus Minds are made to appreciate the fact that we are running a business, with the additional goal of helping communities flourish as a result of our actions. We help our talent develop the right mindset by focusing on the engineering, business and social aspects of thinking.

Kalinga's mission is to encourage curiosity, ignite courage and foster responsibility. We instill and encourage these values from the very beginning because these are what differentiate us as a company. We believe that curiosity should be nurtured throughout one's career. Curiosity inspires Mindtree Minds to continuously seek knowledge and to question status quo. New Mindtree Minds are encouraged to stand up for their values, challenge belief systems and even risk failure. Courage requires the integrity to take responsibility for one's actions.

At Kalinga, Mindtree's fully sustainable campus, there are no classrooms, departments, curriculums or faculty and no new content is created. The focus is solely on real time problem solving, which demands inter-disciplinary thinking. The young hires interact with experts and collaborate to solve real life problems. The experts are present there to work with them and to empower them. Midlevel and senior Mindtree Minds can give back by sharing their knowledge and time through teaching at Kalinga. The center has no permanent faculty; experienced Mindtree Minds take sabbaticals to lead and learn from new Mindtree Minds while improving their own skills. Even the physical and virtual infrastructure has been designed to support the learning methods. Sustainability practices within the campus are an integral part of the learning course to develop healthy habits and eco-awareness.

Mindtree Minds are encouraged to turn solutions to real life problems into working prototypes, implement them using the same structure or workflow they would follow in a professional setting in their future projects. A recent example of this was solving the laundry management problem for a campus comprising 500 residents and effectively learning the supply chain elements. The environment at Kalinga has an impact on group dynamics, self and Group regulated learning methods. During their 90-day stay at Kalinga the Mindtree Minds are encouraged to do one good deed everyday such as watering the plants in the campus, arranging the chairs, managing the library on campus etc. Mindtree Minds graduating from Kalinga emerge focused, confident, collaborative, and equipped to succeed in the global, hyper connected world of tomorrow.

On the other end of the spectrum where our Leadership Journeys are concerned, Mindtree is fueling growth and preparing for the future by providing a transformational development path for our leaders. Our leaders must have the agility to manage change in the way digital is shaping our business at hyper speed.

Our Leadership Journey

We started this journey by asking how we could best equip ourselves for change while honoring our deep belief that leadership is critical to the direction of our company and how we serve our clients, Mindtree Minds and society at large.

Our leadership model helps us identify and nurture the kind of talent we need at all levels across the organization. Mindtree Minds are measured for development and engagement using several factors like Aspirations, Performance as value champions & Attributes that support the Mindtree leadership model.

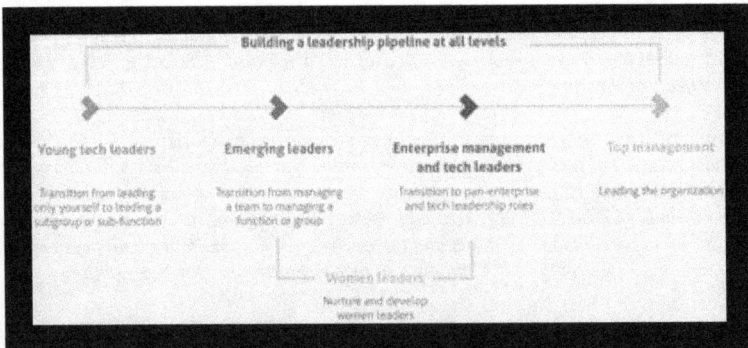

Building a leadership pipeline at all levels

Young tech leaders	Emerging leaders	Enterprise management and tech leaders	Top management
Transition from leading only yourself to leading a subgroup or sub-function	Transition from managing a team to managing a function or group	Transition to pan-enterprise and tech leadership roles	Leading the organization

Women leaders
Nurture and develop women leaders

Figure 60 – Mindtree's Leadership Journey

Digital Leadership - Digital Water Walkers Leadership Journey

The digital economy is transforming every industry. *Consumers have become more connected and engaged. They want rich experiences tailored to their needs. And the* *convergence of mobile technology, social media, data analytics and cloud computing requires organizations to seek new digital strategies to satisfy evolving customer needs. Faced with these challenges, along with the tremendous opportunity that comes with getting the solution right, companies have rushed to reimagine and reinvent the way to do business.*

At Mindtree, we Make Digital Real *– To turn web, collaboration, social, mobile, cloud, analytics and smart device technologies into effective customer experiences, organizations need creative talent, deep technology and domain expertise. Digital is a Key focus area for Mindtree. The Leadership Development program is specifically curated for high potential mid-management Minds in the Digital Unit. The learning journey of about 6 months has been highly personalized for each individual and will enable them to leverage the power of peer network.*

The journey enhances their:

1. ***Leadership*** *– There will be focus on building perspectives on key Leadership skills, Consultative Skills, Trusted Advisorship and a need to mold the mindsets of the future.*
2. ***Technology*** *– Each participant will be assigned, after careful consideration, one technology or domain area to build expertise during the program journey leading to adjacency and breadth with depth.*
3. ***Mentoring*** *– Core to the program is the time and mindshare given to each participant from a Mindtree Leader. The Mentor shall work closely with the participant on their individual development plan and share key experiences with the participants through shadowing or accompanying a leader when he or she visits a client, meets a prospect, etc.*

Exuberance: Developing and nurturing women talent

Exuberance is a leadership development program that focuses exclusively on developing and nurturing women talent in the organization. It was born from the realization that it is critical for organizations, in the digital era, to invest in the growth of their women leaders to achieve optimal business outcomes. The program focuses primarily on women leaders in mid-management roles, and aims at enabling them to perform better in their current roles and scale up to the next level. Exuberance anchors on the philosophy that, an innate aspiration is the key driver to success.

While the needs of the Campus Minds who start their careers in Mindtree, as well as the needs of our Leaders are addressed, we have taken a transformative step towards disrupting the learning process across Mindtree. Our new learning platform breaks the barriers of space and time and allows users to access virtual training from anywhere. It allows Mindtree Minds to set their own learning pace and based on their needs.

Digital Learning Journey – Need based & self-paced

The knowledge era as we call our times, have brought with it interesting differences in the way information has been made available, and in the way information has been perceived. Though, in this era we come across concepts of information overload and knowledge explosion, it is interesting to observe that it has always been this way. We have always been surrounded by enormous amount of information and we have been continuously learning and assimilating it. This becomes very clear when you observe an infant from the time it is born, it is continuously assimilating the enormous amount of information around it, the languages, actions, colors, emotions, relationships and movement.

As we grow, education presents to us curated information from these vast sources packaged to meet a certain need in a certain context. Slowly we get tuned to learning and assimilating information in this form. Today, with the Digital boom, learning is breaking into a new dimension. The information sources have exploded and we tend to look for packaged relevant content, the absence of which results in a feeling of information overload. Hence organizations and individuals need to find a way to harnessing the existing knowledge resources to their advantage.

As an organization that has always been proud of its rich learning culture some of the steps we took in this direction are:

1. **Realizing that there is massive content out there** - *The learning needs are continuously changing and the learning content is continuously getting upgraded. It would be a humongous task and probably waste of resources if each one of us were to create our own content when we are already overload with the information around us. The best option for us was to pick and leverage the best content that is already available at our disposal. The learner's quest of "what-to-learn" gets addressed with this.*

2. **Create a platform to offer this information in a structured way** - *Going back to our earlier thought on how learners are used to receiving capsules of information, the platform was built to channelize the massive amount of available content in the context of the individual and the organization. Small learning packages are curated from the open world outside to cater to the needs of the learner. This provided the solution to "how-to-learn" problem of the learner.*

3. **Bring about process and organizational alignment** - *Organizations look at continuous growth which links to individuals getting better at what they do which in turn links to learning. As we provide an infrastructure of "what-to-learn" and "how-to-learn", it is equally important to let learners know "why-to-learn". Organizational policies enable this or sometimes mandate this.*

4. **Delving a little deeper into the digital learning platform,** *we had to ensure few points to make this transformation successful. Assessing the changing demands of the organization and needs of learners, the learning platform was designed with the following attributes:*

   - *Simple and light weight – Ease of access, intuitive, what you need is what you see*
   - *Agile – Ability to adapt to continuously changing learning demands*
   - *Flexible – Various learning enablers and learner needs are catered to*
   - *Social – Needless to mention, the trend of the times*

In our effort of 'Making Digital (Learning) Real', it was but imperative to study learner behaviors to be able to build a platform that would support these behaviors, thus make the changing digital culture an implicit process. Few learner behaviors that are supported by the platform are:

   - *Learners want to choose what they want to learn.*
   - *Learners want to customize standard learning packages*
   - *Learning can happen anytime and anywhere.*
   - *Small bytes of learning based in the context of the learner is more effective*
   - *Seek expert support*
   - *Group learning*

We as an organization are seeing employee skilling as a critical factor in the growth of the organization and the spotlight is moving towards the learning platform as one of the means to achieve skilling. The move towards a digital learning platform has made multi-skilling, re-skilling and up-skilling of our work force an easier process. The digital wave is hitting every sector and like our earlier experiences, we are not sure if it is a momentary one but the learning wave is here to stay and progress. Our endeavor to onboard all our stakeholders digitally can be seen in the following section. Through this we help our biggest stakeholders, our customers, devise the perfect cross channel experiences that take advantage of digitization to provide just-in-time product or service information effectively.

Mindtree - The Digital Pumpkin – where we work with clients to accelerate their innovation funnel The Digital Pumpkin is an innovation hub that invites clients to a collaborative environment to create cutting edge digital solutions. At The Digital Pumpkin, we work with our clients to help ideate, experience and create a meaningful digital experience. Most business have smart business and technical people who have a lot of innovative ideas. To be able to innovate you need to build many, fail fast and learn quickly. Many of our successful clients often throw us a challenge, be it about solving the problem of queuing at one of their outlets, or simply visualizing what the future would look like. We take these problems and a multi-functional team researches, ideates and designs. We come back with a working prototype. These prototypes work much better when presenting to customers and seek feedback. Businesses cannot afford to focus only on operational or performance improvements but, should actively focus on customer delight. And that's what we help our customer do at *"The Mindtree Digital Pumpkin"*.

How the Digital Pumpkin is different from the traditional IT development center –

Mindtree Digital Pumpkin	Traditional IT contract
More Right Brain	More Left Brain
The primary task is defining "What?", therefore it is more exploratory and requires lateral thinking hence the team is more designed focused.	There is clarity in "What?" is to be built. Therefore the effort is towards realizing the need therefore the team is engineering focused.
Difficult to earmark the effort required, as work is based on the paradigm of learn and build	Scope binds contract therefore any change results in cost, time and product variation
Small sprints of learn and build-only-required	As functional and non-functional needs have to be addressed, the lifecycle is longer and non-negotiable
Short development cycles can address more ideas in a given time	Longer development cycle can address limited number of ideas in a given time

Through the use of digital technologies companies are creating new value for customers. Brands are shaping the journeys customers take rather than just helping them along the path. We believe that we will evolve to be stronger and become Digital Leaders of the industry by being better prepared for this disruption".

MindTree Ltd. Case led by Vidya Santhanam, supported by P Bhosle, D Shekar, J Reddy, A Singh & R S Mathew from Mindtree Ltd.

*The author had the privilege of closely following the co-founder and current Executive Chairman, of Mindtree Ltd, **KrishnaKumar Natarajan, (KK)**, what many in the industry circles call as a Digital Icon. A leading authority in the global IT sector, Krishnakumar Natarajan co-founded Mindtree in 1999 and has played key roles in building the company's innovative approach to delivering IT services and solutions to global 2000 enterprises. A leader who is known by genial nature, disarming smile and the attitude to make things happen retaining sensitivity, care and concern for all his stakeholders. His contribution to building an institution with world class leadership practices is legendary. Natarajan was instrumental in setting up Mindtree's U.S. operations, driving expansion in Europe and Asia Pacific regions, and transforming Mindtree's IT services business. Today, his mission as Executive Chairman is to focus on leadership development and ensure a high quality of governance. He also actively mentors different business groups within the company and works closely with the start-up ecosystem to bring in innovative models of business transformation for clients. In his prior role as CEO and Managing Director, KK was responsible for making Mindtree a global IT player. Natarajan's efforts as a business leader have been recognized worldwide, winning him several laurels. He was ranked amongst the most valuable CEOs in India by Business World & Forbes in 2016. He won Bloomberg UTV's award as the CEO of the Year in 2010, Business Today CEO of the year award in 2014 and was recognized by Chief Executive Magazine's as one of the twelve global leaders of tomorrow. EY honored him with Entrepreneur of the year 2015 in Services. A 35-year IT industry veteran, Natarajan held several key positions at Wipro before co-founding Mindtree. During this time, he launched and grew the ecommerce division of Wipro, served as Group Vice President of human resources, and was Chief Marketing Officer for Wipro's IT business. In 2013, Natarajan served as Chairman of the National Association of Software and Services Companies (NASSCOM), where he worked to strengthen the Indian IT industry to be a globally competitive ecosystem comprised of both established and emerging companies.*

Chapter 12

Leadership Disrupted

This chapter covers the following:

A. You have NO Rules
B. You have Freedom
C. You have Dignity
D. You are Relevant
E. You Know
F. You are Aligned
G. You see and set examples
H. You are not wanted
I. You are the Best
J. When you Let Go Legacy You Embrace Change

You can't learn surgery by watching! But if you are consumed by self-think and working in a digital culture that barely recognizes who you are, that precisely will be your capability!

What makes organizations develop a DNA that is not replaceable. What makes cultures so unique to organizations that staff who change jobs and see new cultures either like it or don't? What makes for some the world to go around and for them to integrate seamlessly while for others there are many jerks and potholes?

The wishes and expectations of talent differ, and also change over time. - Some people are looking for a career in one organization;

- *Some people are looking for a couple of years' experience, and their plan is to move on afterwards (although they might not express this when you interview them);*
- *Some people are not looking forward to be employed by a big employer, but they like to be involved in challenging complex projects;*
- *Organizations that define talent too narrow might miss opportunities to connect talent to their organization". Organizations that build a talent management platform into their strategy find avenues for talent to identify world class opportunities to build their careers.*

But a common thread bringing all such talent together is their aspiration. Their dream to build world class careers by learning and contributing. They would like to fly despite aerodynamic disadvantages. And they cannot be managed without aligning them to global talent technologies that captures their dream.

A. *You have No Rules*

The best of work places do not have rules. Best of people don't operate through rules. Nothing that binds them in a conventional way. They only have a vision; for themselves, make their people and for their companies! They practice that vision, they practice what they can, by believing, trusting, enabling & doing.

These are firms in which & where things happen because people act on what they believe is right, act with courage, stand up for they believe in and achieve together out of alignment. It is aligned when people tell you stories about their company, its people, anecdotes from last night's party, share water cooler tips, of people who can be jibed for their eccentricities, quirks and idiosyncrasies, all for the fun of it & of course, of those who visibly show excitement at any news about their company. You can be called a nerd in a nice way!

They would now go beyond and introduce their company to people they care for & known as their own. They would have friends at work who go beyond work. These people take their company home every day, not just work. They don't have a problem taking a phone call at 7 pm just as much as they can enjoy their personal space when they want. There are no boundaries for these staff. They can't differentiate work and pleasure, and they are not called workaholics too!

After all people seek identity, pride, responsiveness & belonging wherever they may be & whatever they may be doing. These people communicate and connect. If you write to them, be guaranteed that they will write back, respond with the warmth and affection that you will only see in world class enterprises. You don't need to follow up. Don't need to send apologetic E mails reminding people that they are overdue in their response. That they have not had the courtesy to reply. They don't follow rules!

Rules are explicit statements that tell an employee what he or she ought or ought not to do. Procedures are a series of interrelated sequential steps that employees follow in the accomplishment of their job tasks policies are guide- lines that set constraints on decisions that employees make. Each of these represents techniques that organizations use to regulate the behavior of members.

When you don't have rules people make their own rules. And the best of them comply with their self-imposed rules of good behaviors. Work environments in which people have dignity, beliefs, and those that binds people to a common cause, in whatever profit motive context may it be, there is only an environment of joy, not rules. You are ruling!

B. You have Freedom

And, in cultures where people come to give their best, there is only an open canvas for people to paint a picture of their choice. They are aware of the freedom that they have, enjoy and know how to use it responsibly. There are no episodes of friction for people to endure & plan mitigate steps to escape from the wrath of the folks who lead, manage and are titled boss. They don't fear a conspiracy around them. They don't imagine the worst. And they are not gossiping about their bosses or speaking ill of their cultures too.

Role expectations may be explicit and defined narrowly. In such cases, the degree of formalization is high. Of course, the role expectations attributed to a given job by management and members of a role set can traverse the spectrum from explicit and narrow to very loose. The latter, for instance, allows employees freedom to react to situations in unique ways. It puts minimum constraints on the role incumbent. So organizations that develop exacting and complicated job descriptions go a long way toward undoing the expectations of how a particular role is to be played. By loosening or tightening role expectations, organizations are actually loosening or tightening the degree of formalization.

Fun - In places where you see visible fun you find people who are engaged. This is not about events, parties, gala dinners, founder's day, celebrating survival, anniversaries, diversity, men's day, women's day etc. There are no rituals. Nothing because we "have" to do that and appear to have done so. It is about energy & experiences of people who connect while at work or elsewhere, where there is real respect for diversity and women, where the HR function is not playing event management, resource optimization or actively distributing "Don't Do" policies, but HR & people celebrate as if they are all in it together and on what excites them. It is not about an organized activity or symbols, it is about living life, creative chaos in which all let their hair down without fear of reprimand. Every day is a party. Not an office party and the politics that go with it!

C. You have Dignity

Sometimes, where you can hear people, but cannot see them or where you see people but cannot hear, it tells you about whether, the voice of people exists or not in that organization. Work places in which people have a voice, speak in public; they are neither shy nor fearful. To be heard is a critical aspect of human expectation, imbibed in us from early stages of personality development. When you understand the social needs of individuals by trusting their quality of thinking, their point of view, their decision making maturity and their usage of resources you begin to convey a message of, "Your decisions matter in this scheme of things".

Respect - In work situations, where you see people respect their boss you know that Generation Y and the stereotypes of their disrespect for the hierarchy or the powerful is bull! You will know that respect is not hierarchically demanded but commanded, gained and earned. When you find organizations with people clamoring to be tutored or mentored by someone in particular you know the popularity quotient of that boss. And they are not an exception. Organizational expertise is after all a summation of individual competencies. There are very many who are role models because of what they are and do, not what they speak or project to the outside world. The very young too, have no qualms in acknowledging the value of a wise old man with integrity, than an articulate pony tailed boss, who pretends to vibe with you and chill out at all the most happening places, yet cannot be trusted even to walk your dog!

Trust - In companies where employees feel they are not treated with respect, or where, what they think and feel is quite inconsequential, you know that the place has a distinctive stench. Such odor is not easy to remove like mold & mildew. Chilled out work places, thrive on dignity, trust and have people who stand by what they consider as a commitment. These are environments where, whether at an individual or institutional level, if a promise has been made then it is expected that they are honored. No matter what may be in store in an unknown future? Do you remember an industrialist who had once said, "A promise is a promise that I had made to my customer, and I will do it". And that automobile has made global strides.

D. You are Relevant

It is interesting to note that in environments where people ask - what keeps you going, you know that someone, somewhere, somehow is keen to know of your well-being. Why do we ask or why do we convey our deep disenchantment at exiting employees with masterful dialogues such as, "I wish you had spoken to me earlier", "Give me a few suggestions on how do we ensure this is not repeated again", or "Do you wish to reconsider", "Let us have a meal together and talk about it" and so on, when we could have conveyed such care or concern, in fact done all of the above, while they were slogging at work, hoping to make one eye contact with you once in a while? Why do we deliver with utmost seriousness sincere questions in exit interviews but neglect asking early enough to make a difference? It may not be a bad idea to seek a feedback from your people on what binds them to the company and what might cause them to leave. Don't leave this conversation until the exit interview.

E. You Know

At another level, in fact, where you are communicated the organizational strategy you know that you are in a safe & secure place, where you are trusted for your intelligence, judgment and perspective. You are not stuck in a pigeon hole where you are barely aware of the small picture, forget about knowing strategy or the long term thinking of your institution. Organizations where employees understand what managements consider as big picture, the long term future, the method that leaders follow while exercising strategic options, employees see quite vividly where they fit in and how they are making a difference to the organization. It is silly to ask how can this be possible to execute with a call center operator, some hourly minimum wage blue collar staff, hotel chef or a doorperson given that each of them are working in their own small worlds. Try it and figure it out for yourself. In fact, if you were to not give people an opportunity to think, an advance notice about key decisions affecting their jobs, the company's overall direction or if the employees do not feel informed about what is happening, they will not feel as though they are a part of the company. They will not want to stay in the long run. In addition, let your folk know when they're doing good work. Don't wait until the formal review ritual to say "thank you" or "job well done."

F. You are Aligned

For some incomprehensible reason, if you are unable to differentiate between what you personally like and what you like about your job, you know that your interests have been aligned with your role. When you proactively know your people including their likes & dislikes, you also get to know what makes them tick; you are now, not cross referencing books on motivation, but checking your assumptions about that person and recalibrating your leadership disrupted style to adapt to each of your people's expectations. Don't work for a reason; let the reason be work!

Loyalty to Profession - Where you hear sordid stories of the economic meltdown and overbearing tales of death, decay and doom, and in contrast, when you hear an honest evaluation of the situation and its likely consequences on you, or your job, whether you realize now or not, you, your colleagues, and your family in the long run would know that this was an honest, upright work place. They did not play games, despite the gravity of the situation, to them employees were not to be used for another bigger political objective. In turbulent times, not all employees are safe, after all many jobs are saved, when some lose them. The target opportunity in clean business environments is to focus on getting employees to understand that the inevitable exit option is not exercisable until such time other cost management options have been exhausted.

G. You see and set examples

If communication, hearing, listening, understanding and knowing is so essential to you for your own effectiveness, why is that you do not practice it with your colleagues? Why do you, as a leader find it so easy to expect more, ask more and demand more from your boss and find it so easy to give less to your subordinates? What gives you the right to take more than what you are willing to give? But, in contrast, imagine your discovering in a very short period of time from the date of your joining that for some reason your boss, your organization, your colleagues, your human resources and lots of people around you are visibly in touch with you - not in a remote electronic way, are staying connected with you, are showing a great keenness to know and understand you, you know that this organization wishes to actively exist in your life.

Show Action - People don't wish to stay away from you. You are not feeling lonely and isolated. Or strangely, you suddenly discover that some aspect of your long forgotten past, where you had held leadership disrupted positions, has suddenly been discovered because someone had remembered this from your interview with them or had kept a dossier on you through your CV scanning, web search, references, you know for sure that your strengths will be nurtured; you are remembered by this company. It matters to your new employer to have you contribute to their growth. They did not hire you for your past, but for their future. Self-Discovery (SD) is process, an experience, an encounter enabled to facilitate face to face exchange, focus on here and now and encourage openness, honesty, interpersonal communication, constructive confrontation, self-disclosure and strong emotional expression. Self-discovery strives to enhance self and social awareness and helps change behavior.

Nobody washes a rental car. Unless of course you are on a contract to do so!

Stretch - HBR states that, "People will go the extra mile only if they feel they have ownership. Ownership & Belonging in a way that is best defined by the one who feels it, not by those who are articulating or expecting it. It's much the same in the workplace. Employees who take ownership of their work — and who feel that what they are doing matters — are far more likely than others to feel engaged on the job.

Display Skills - You can have great talent that is appropriately brought together with a common agenda and teamed. You can demonstrate capability, display skills when it is recognized. You can eliminate structural barriers to effective collaboration, and you can design meetings, opportunities to coexist and other interactions so that people can actually get things done. But if your company's employees don't have a sense of ownership and engagement, all the other steps won't make much difference. By the same token, if you can increase the average level of engagement in your organization, you will likely see the productivity of your entire workforce increase."

H. You are not wanted

Look back and reflect. You form an impression of a leader when you know the leader, based on his or her visibility, you hear, see, listen, observe, analyze, conclude, and after which you make a choice to admire or dislike such a leader and his or her institution. Leaders set the threshold for organizational dignity. Leaders form the bedrock of institutional identify, form, substance, character and functionality. When you see institutions that are Centered around one leader you then wonder what could have happened to the remaining folks? When you find such leaders more often than not is playing popularity policies, plays favorites, to attract a crowd to the gallery, you know that the leader lacks substance in his or her ability to make fundamental changes to their institutions.

Sycophants - When leaders take new positions after ousting a predecessor and finds her dominant need is to belittle the last role incumbent rather than focus on the future you know that the leader is struggling with establishing an identity, purpose, goals, meaning to their life to steer their company forward. When leaders surround themselves with a cheering squad, incompetence, dethroning mature incumbents and surrounding themselves with a coterie of failed managers, playing politics through fads, you can be assured that the leader is not waiting to improve the institution for long term growth and benefit but is chasing an unfortunate personal agenda that is only detrimental to ethical demands & governance required in such a role. Wanting to be the center of attention, showing eccentric behaviors, running fiefdoms, having private advisors beyond organizational structures are sure signs of a melodramatic leaders.

Animal Instincts - As we turn more competitive, as we see human nature seeking basic survival instincts there is a case for relook at our maliciousness, a core viperish tendency to demand what we want as staff, supervisor or as a CEO and the desire and urge to seek it at any cost, any circumstance or situation and for any price. It is possible and we can learn to "see ourselves as others see us". What makes a leader a bully, so megalomaniacal manipulative to see so much of herself in whatever that happens in the firm? What makes them deprive others of their rightful space? If you see this behavior in yourself, you need a fresh start!

I. You are the Best

Best of organizations have an old fashioned character - These organizations are leader free, jargon free, structure free, have no quick fix techniques being deployed, have no surveys to tell them about employee engagement and do things in a deliberate thought through style, as if it is in a pre-ordained way. These organizations are not prone to chasing metrics that are meaninglessly imposed without reason, but goals that have been established to bond people towards a common outcome. Leaders in these organizations work as Partners without being called a "Partner". Not the charade, but the real McCoy. These organizations focus on customer, health, fitness, purpose and active employee commitment.

A Journey Beyond - They look at all programs as a life long journey. They look at results as just another outcome. Everything that they do has a "life" attached to it. For them an employee is there for life. So let the programs be organized for life too. Why not? They act on issues after substantive deliberation. They are slow, steady and distinctive in all of their significant activities. Their people know that too. It takes time in this organization, but when done, it is done well. Speed is not as important as quality, care and customer - employee alignment. They make distinctive difference between theory & practice, they reflect on risks, cost & consequences; they belabor & agonize over impact of their decisions on values, culture, long term implications. Their outlook towards future is about holding on to a strong present, preparing for a stable future and building a foundation that holds on a many do's and many don'ts in behaviors. People in such companies feel that they are led by responsible leaders and in whose hands their life is safe!

J. When you Let Go Legacy You Embrace Change

Intellectual Honesty Performance - Unfortunate but true is the fact that organizations tend to cling to systems and practices that were successful for them in their formative years, but are now no longer appropriate. But legacy has an uncanny ability to cling on. And legacy comes in multiple forms including a set of leaders who have not moved from their age old jobs and are now wanting to maintain their status quo. The environment that created and nurtured most of our older organizations was breathtakingly simple compared to that we now face. They emerged at a time when our population was growing rapidly and our economy successfully supported by primitive HR policies, programs and employee management practices. Under these conditions, an affluent and acquiescent employee group accepted processes, policies and services they were given to them, with no questions asked, employee policies were either highly protective, patronizing or tightly regulated, controlled by leaders and efficiency, engagement, dignity and respect was simply not demanded. Performance in appropriating capital – the management must have a willingness to commit oneself to expectations, when the decision is being made and the intellectual honesty to face up to the actual results by measuring actual results against expectations. Performance in people decisions – there is a need to assess the performance of decisions made about people compared to the expectations underlying them. Performance in innovation – research results can be measured, or at least appraised, and then projected backward on the promises and expectations at the time the research effort was started. Strategies versus performance – the strategies have to be judged against performance. This is necessary so that the management at least knows when it strikes out or makes a hit so that they know what they do well and what they need to improve upon.

Eliminate Political Leaders - There used to be a prevailing notion. "In larger organizations, tall hierarchical cultures developed in which "employee management practices" was determined at the top and divided into tasks to be fed down as management directives, in ways that no employee can every piece them together. In smaller, leaner and flatter structural organizations employee focus was either non-existent or resided only in the head of the "chief human resources officer" or at its worst in power hungry business leaders. This simplistic approach is no longer appropriate because it ignores the real purpose of employee development achieved through a formal talent management system and the proven fact that flatter organizations are mastering the art of pushing employee engagement to the operating management. That is, to explain how objectives will be achieved. Nevertheless, its influence remains and has contributed to a failure to acquire real skills in employee management as it is significantly depending on the culture in which talent management is emphasized.

Intellectual Sensitivity - To successfully lead an organization through a transformation, leaders need to adopt a focused, systematic and a sensitive approach. Too many leaders have been pressured into an "act now, think later" mentality, especially when the transformation is to be accomplished under difficult circumstances, with boards and shareholders clamoring for immediate results. Leaders will be more effective when they launch a transformation by conducting an assessment of the existing corporate culture—a "snapshot" and see how it might affect or interact with initiatives that need to be put into place. And in the process learn on what is the best timing for acting on a decision just as much as cultures impact quality and timing of a decision. A certain amount of trust must pervade the organizational structure of a company that wants to drive acting upon any change and only honest and open communication channels can bring this about. To many organizations, action oriented communication implies the periodic and dry feedback processes, town halls, performance reviews or a suggestion box, that is hardly dusted if ever even considered by management.

Social Image - And today there is a danger that employees make take to Glassdoor or social networks to voice their opinion. The kinds of window dressing that these organizations indulge in are detrimental to their development of a culture of change and success. Openness and communication are linked in that the degree of one determines the extent of another, i.e. the communicative strength of the organization determines how open the organization will be.

Do it Now Urgency - Establishing a Sense of Urgency as defined by Dan Cohen and John P Kotter is a good starting point. Examine market and competition realities without acting upon it until such time there is state of readiness. Identify and discuss crises, potential crises, or major opportunities. Eliminate obvious examples of corporate excess (i.e., company planes, catered lunches). Change won't occur where there is complacency in appreciating a CEOs priority, unless of course those priorities are whimsical. Role Requirements. Individuals in organizations fulfill roles. Every job carries with it expectations on how the role incumbent is sup- posed to behave. Job analysis, for instance, defines the jobs that need to be done in the organization and outlines what employee behaviors are necessary to perform the jobs. This analysis develops the information from which job descriptions are created. The fact that organizations identify jobs to be done and the desirable role behaviors that go with those jobs means that role expectations playa major part in regulating employee behavior.

Intellect Rules - Culture supports sharing or otherwise. Strategy enables it. Command and control cultures discourage interactions other than those that create tangible and measurable benefit for the customer immediately. Learning, sharing and teaching, all means for increasing knowledge and talent productivity, are looked down upon as a waste of time given organizational inability to capture systemically learning and contribution. Over a period, these natural human tendencies to learn and engage with talent die so that when the need arises to share available knowledge, a Herculean effort is needed to build back a system that in any case was absent to start with. Unless corporate cultures explicitly support knowledge generation and dissemination that influences business performance through an effective talent management process, it is unwise to expect that people will have exhilarating employee experience and effusive knowledge sharing.

Epilogue

People Factor - A Digital Mind Set

This is an Epilogue because we don't know the answers to a lot of questions pertaining to Digital HR in Digital Business Organizations, as they emerge, evolve, internalize and institutionalize. We don't know how many more companies will want to and actually become digitally savvy companies (From "Wannabe to Actuallybe"). We don't know (but know for sure there are many) how many companies not in (our) public domain but are into path breaking digital thinking and research outcomes. We don't have answers to the interplay between digital business models and what drives these smart - intellectually inclined talent to continue to do what they do best in creating, innovating, breaking rules - paths and challenging assumptions, hypothesis, mindsets, perhaps existence. We don't know what will happen if there are more hacks, WIKIs, Snowden - Assange syndrome, inter country spying swoops, internet wars, cyber-crimes – terror, privacy issues, identity thefts, utility power grid threats, China factor, Trump factor, and the New Republicans, India (Boom or Bust), Wars for Peace, Surgical Strikes, New Allies and Coalitions, oil and shale or war against it evolves. We don't know the way in which technology, neural, machines, robots, artificial intelligence, internet of things, 3D, cloud, devices, Big Data, crowd sourcing, crowd funding, crowd talent market places, predictive analytics and other smart programs are evolving to influence organizational models, structures, leadership disrupted styles and people engagement. And we definitely don't know how all of these in a geo political security challenged environment will play out. So we have tried to bring in many of these aspects as they only relate to corporate talent management environment and presented research based material as trends, practices, thinking, hypothesis and assumptions – "World class work by thought leaders and researchers and practitioners while we have been messengers". And finally, we for sure don't know, after all of these 600 pages on what actually drives, continues to inspire "The Leadership Disrupted", because that is one domain that is beyond our comprehension - capability or our intellect to interpret, conclusively understand and have a firm prescriptive answer. We have tried very hard but this is "Not Possible" by us. We cannot compete against the human mind. The more we have researched for this book there is more we just simply don't seem to know at all. Rather than giving up we have tried to write this book – In some parts the contents may have sounded complex and confusing. We have tried to simplify it as much as possible. But there is a very long way to go. You be the judge of what more insights are needed.

A. *Digital HR! The Eventual Goal*
B. *Developing Trends and Perspectives to a Digital Mind Set*
C. *Managing Risk*
D. *Knowledge Infrastructure*
E. *Learning - The Differentiator*
F. *What does Behavioral Intelligence do?*
G. *Emergence of Neural Networks and Machine Learning Models*
H. *Neural Digital Business Models reflect Learning Capability*
I. *Leadership Disrupted or Machine? The Debate!*
J. *Structure is Strategy is Process*
K. *Intellectual Commercial Differentiators*
L. *Intellectual Proximity to Advantage*
M. *Systems Thinking has its roots in Behavioral Intelligence*
N. *Knowledge Intellect Strategic Synthesis*
O. *Behavioral Drainers*

P. *The World is Engaging with Intellectual Learners*
Q. *Way forward*

A. Digital HR! The Eventual Goal!

"Keep focus on individual development, not the past" Mark Spears, Global Lead for people & change practice at KPMG LLP to ET, "KPMG recently got rid of the bell curve performance evaluation system. Scrapping it was an overnight decision. Our attrition rates were high and we had issues with employee engagement. We had to deal with it quickly." Traditional use of a forced ranking process prioritized remuneration changes, bonus payouts and incentive schemes and pay grade change but rarely feedback, performance improvement or learning. But those uses that dealt with monetary drivers are surely passé. Josh Bersin Deloitte says, "The present day organizations are highly networked. Employees work in teams, while projects and goals change quite frequently. Therefore, leading companies are now reinventing the way they manage and measure performance. From a traditional approach of developing aligned goals from the top down, conducting annual performance reviews on those goals and ranking and rating people based on that performance, organizations are now creating a more agile approach. The new model is built around periodic check-ins; shared goals developed from the bottom up, and transparent to the entire team; regular developmental conversations; and feedback that goes from employee to employee, employee to manager, and manager to employee. Owing to the shift in performance management requirements of the organizations and employees, the old forms-based performance and goal-management tools now seem archaic and unproductive. Some of the new tools look like games; some resemble personality assessments; and others look like online check-in systems".

Simplification – An Employee Experience – Decoding complexity to simple structures is the art of wisdom! Spears speaks of the need to simplify how they work. "Yes", Spears, says, "Some companies were forced to rethink their performance management. In a study we did, we found only 40 per cent of employees were satisfied with the bell curve system and thought it fair. Another 98 per cent of HR managers thought the yearly evaluation process wasn't useful and were considering simplification and new ways of doing the evaluations. Companies are experimenting with different ways of doing things. For instance, they're saying, 'Let's have a guided distribution instead of a forced distribution of reward'. Some organizations didn't want any rating system". When John Humble wrote on the management by objectives system (MBO), his emphasis was on organizational need to focus on key result areas for performance focus. Similarly, when Kaplan and Norton identified the balanced scorecard (BSC) as a strategic performance management tool, their primary aim was to link strategy to performance measures, targets, linkages, lewd and lag indicators, cause and effect. Today the distribution curve defeats the purpose of these contemporary theories. Neither MBO nor the BSC can achieve employee engagement unless there is a solution to this forced ranking challenge. Clearly normal distribution curve in itself is not the problem. The end use and outcomes derived from the curve has become the problem. Talent Management Platforms that brings the best of a distribution curve in its solution derived from a formal performance management system with employee experience as a stated outcome clearly achieve this purpose, that of an effective end state outcome - a la employee engagement. Process simplification, integration and commonality is an additional aspect - The utilization of a common set of processes is inherent in the adoption of the Target Operating model. Companies will challenge the business to adopt a simplified approach to back office processing wherever viable. Integration is critical to achieve management visibility and reduce disparate data and system proliferation. This will include, System consolidation - The Consolidations of systems is best view in a wide context. The consolidation of systems infers the achievement of a single set of Policies, Business Rules, Procedures, Key Performance Measures, Reports and Data Structures. Establishing within Client X, a single uniformed way of doing business would provide the desired results of a consolidated system. The actual systems architecture and instance environment is subject to another set of parameters and will be the remit of IT to facilitate and optimize. Reporting and Key Performance Measures standardization and Decision Support is a key improvement process for the implementation. Driving a common approach across is part of the implementation strategy. Headcount optimization is a real possibility. Reducing the portfolio will create opportunities to reduce work and headcount. Simplifying processes and systems will likely reduce volumes of work and supporting resources once fully implemented. Redistribution of work and labor- Consolidating or eliminating volumes of work through simplification will enable reorganization of work for higher efficiency. Standardization of work and supporting infrastructure should drive a further concentration of work and workforce. Product substitution by new businesses is achieved through simplification through substitution may be possible. New offers may replace several old offers by changing customer's perception of need.

HR for Digital Reinvention – "How does digiglobalization (digitalization + globalization) impact organizational culture" asks Srinath Sridharan, Member, GMC, Wadhawan Global Capital the promoters of DHFL, "Who is the custodian of organizational culture? Once upon a time, it was the HR head who was the custodian. Well, this was in the time of the industrial era. This was the time when information was arbitrage. Currently we live in the knowledge era, which Rewards speed of access to information and accuracy of information as the key to success. Today all of us as employees / entrepreneurs live in times of digital democracy. Here, decision-making or polling ability is literally at our fingertips and that too not even necessarily glued to physical workspace but even on our mobile telephones.

Let's look at how the world of alphabets has changed. I am using this as an example of how infants of today learn their basic English language! We have moved from A for apple, B for ball to A for artificial intelligence, B for Boolean logic, C for cloud, D for data, E for e-commerce and so on. And these very infants when they get into Workspace are (and will be) true digital citizens who use digital way of living as their second skin! So the conventional methods of managing their careers, aspirations and then work output may not necessarily be the ideal HR methodology in the 21st-century.

For Srinath, current methods of recruitment are simply outdated while looking at some of the challenges & implications of the digital era on HR space. "The old logic that people stayed on their entire career with a single or two organizations is no more valid. There is not really much credence to phrases such as organizational brand loyalty. The current generation pays much heed to personal loyalties/professional loyalties to individual reporting managers/individual business leaders. This is a serious implication the way organizations are built. The way people are recruited. The way people are trained, reskilled, trained for next successive faces in their career. It is severe implications on talent attrition and retention challenges. It also gives raise to the fundamental question of how do you assess performance and who assesses performance? In short, what is the role of HR function? Do they really understand aspirations and needs of employs? Or can we simply use computing power in today's times along with the analytical tools, map out the career path, based on each individual employee's aspirations, actions and inputs on various psychometric tools available. And so forth .... Time won't tell. It's a tough taskmaster"! concludes Srinath.

B. Developing Trends and Perspectives to a Digital Mind Set

Social Media Links: Organizations can take advantage of new communication channels and mobile devices to better enable the use of cloud computing collaboration, e.g. global social networks, blogs, real-time communication via video conferencing & chats, internal and external networking platforms (Facebook, Tumblr, Instagram, Twitter, LinkedIn, Yammer, Skype etc.). External communication with customers, suppliers, potential employees, stakeholders etc. via new communication means that influences branding and marketing activities for better understanding of resources and tools. These cultures enable IT updates provided in real time and communicated by leadership. Technical training and use of multimedia devices and systems will be more frequent and available with a greater accessibility to workers using their own devices: IT platforms become more accessible to workers using their own devices. As part of their employee value propositions, some firms may seek to make it easier for employees to use their own computing device of choice (tablets, iPad, laptops, smartphones). Significant Speed of access to computer-based training will increase due to real-time capability for Cloud computing and become an expectation by employees and consistent training contents can be developed and provided nationally and globally (pooled training resources). Learning processes can support a virtual learning and knowledge management platform and Risk, procedure and policy training will become prevalent in order to ensure that the cloud and misinformation is being used and published accordingly.

Social is Cloud Enabled - Cloud computing has evolved quickly from being an innovative approach to IT to being a mainstream business technology. It is changing the way people and organizations work—and the HR department is no exception. In essence, cloud-based solutions mean that HR can purchase software as a service (SaaS), rather than run and maintain it in-house. This approach began finding its way into HR as organizations, looking for broader functionality to keep up with their changing needs, adopted niche cloud-based applications to address specific areas such as performance management. That gave HR groups access to these emerging tools. But it also brought the challenges associated with fragmented, standalone systems, such as islands of data and processes that create inefficiency and ineffectiveness. That disjointed approach is no longer necessary, however. The market has evolved to the point where some providers now offer comprehensive cloud-based solutions that are strategic, encompass multiple perspectives and the full spectrum of integrated HR deliverables and applications. As a result, HR can easily access the software capabilities it needs, and deliver them to business and HR users across locations and devices. The cloud is opening up new ways for HR to tap into the power of today's technology—and HR executives need to understand how to exploit it to benefit both HR and the business. The cloud provides a cost-effective approach to technology in other ways, as well. Companies often turn to the cloud and SaaS for a better user experience. Vendors may provide easy-to-use, up-to-date user interfaces, and some deliver services based on the user's role, so that content is relevant and streamlined. In addition, cloud services can often be accessed on mobile devices, making them a good t with on-the- move employees. The improved user experience is more than just a nice-to-have feature. The cloud gives HR an alternative approach to accessing and using applications that can help address a number of key issues—starting with costs. It lets HR get up to speed with new technology without the need for upfront capital expenditures for new software or hardware. In addition, pricing plans often provide both clarity and exitability, with a pay-as-you-go approach. The Oracle HCM Cloud applications, for example, are offered through a monthly subscription based on the number of users accessing the various software modules. A cloud-based approach also reduces the need for operational expenses for in- house application maintenance and adoption, which is key to getting the most business bene t out of technology. And it can enable a shift to more employee self-service and manager-controlled processes, helping to reduce the burden on—and the costs to—HR. In some cloud arrangements, HR can add new features, functions and applications on an as-needed basis, calls it SaaS or On Demand service. A company may want to use only recruiting or learning or a specialist tools, but later need to add, say, compensation, benefits, self-service or talent-review tools: That's a fairly simple change when a provider has a comprehensive set of HR functionalities - capabilities.

Social Enabling the Agile Business - Perhaps more important, the cloud can do much to make HR more flexible and responsive in support of the business. "As the world becomes increasingly unpredictable, organizations that can adapt to changing business conditions will outperform the competition," Accenture Future of HR researchers note. "HR will reshape itself so that the function becomes the critical driver of agility." Cloud-based HR applications can support agility in several ways. For example, the cloud vendor is usually in position to refresh technology more frequently, compared to in- house IT staff. With traditional on-premises technology, an application is typically upgraded every two to three years. With the cloud, on the other hand, "the vendor may provide three updates a year, plus patches," says Cara Capretta. And from HR's perspective, "those happen instantaneously, and the customer can pick and choose or simply adopt and you don't have to do all the planning, costs, change management, process changes (Not always) and work to do the upgrade. That's a big change from the past." On another level, some cloud-based applications can be tailored by HR professionals and business people, without the need for IT specialists. With Oracle's cloud-based offerings, HR professionals can adjust the look, feel and behavior of different screens, customize them, make it thematic, add new fields, run custom reports, circulate analytics, enable new roles, introduce new languages, modify standard reports and create new process flows. In short, HR can adapt the technology to changing circumstances quickly, without waiting for changes to work their way through IT—a level of flexibility and independence that is good for both HR and IT". http://bit.ly/2b1jfqj.

Social SaaS sees the biggest spending increase both as an investment and as a technological innovation (infrastructure optimization, speed, ease of adoption, collaboration, upgrade advantages etc.). Transformational thinkers within organizations are increasing their spending for cloud-based services, with the biggest increases coming for SaaS offerings. SaaS offerings in the area of collaboration, learning, e recruitment, analytics and email have seen significant increase in the respondents that have either implemented or will implement solutions in this space. The term of a SaaS agreement is typically three to five years, and will provide IT organizations opportunities to at least evaluate the ITSSM market. SaaS licensing is currently offered by more than half of ITSSM tool vendors, presenting more choices for IT organizations. Gartner predicts, "Business users are becoming increasingly frustrated with the long deployment cycles, high costs, complicated upgrade processes and IT infrastructures demanded by traditional BA solutions. SaaS-based BA offers a quick, low-cost and easy-to-deploy alternative that has proved popular, particularly in SMBs and in the individual departments of large enterprises that lack or do not want to support internal BA resources". Nearly every software-as-a-service (SaaS) application has a mobile client now, which is proof of the model as well. As Forrester Analyst Glenn O'Donnell puts it, cloud plus mobile is a classic 'more than the sum of its parts' combination.

Social is human and physical collaboration - Robert Owen (1771-1858) Human Relations Pioneer was one of the first to emphasize treatment of employees as "human beings" and give best attention to "human needs" of the employees. He taught his workers cleanliness and temperance; abolished child labor; established nursery schools in his factories; stressed on the welfare consideration of employees; reduced working hours; introduced health and sanitary facilities; brought about changes and improvements in the environmental conditions of factories; and paid adequate attention to the housing needs of the workers by building modern communities. This was the period, as already stated, when machines were replacing home sewing and weaving in factories and were constantly increasing in size, and the lot of the workers was miserable. It may be added here that child labor was common in the factories.

This has an element of touch. Wearables touch people every day as they use and be continually excited with their new devices, its functionality etc. Morgan from Chess Media Says, "With wearables and enterprise-level social network platforms, HR teams are able to collect an enormous amount of information on employees. These technologies will provide HR professionals with insights into where skill gaps might exist, when employees are most productive and much more". In most cases video conferencing is part of the overall communication and collaboration strategy of organizations. Especially now when all services are cloud-based and therefore implementation costs became more affordable. The long term vision for video conferencing lies in the correct usage of computer processing power, data storage or mobile bandwidth speeds to further decrease the obstacles of collaboration. One should ask, can "Fitbit" become an integral part of a talent management solution? After all which enterprise would not like to invest in a staff welfare program that focuses on employee health, wellness and care? These allied skills and competencies in turn influence enterprise wide employee concern, training team focus, group collaboration and self-learning opportunities. Innovation would be a digital advantage. Flexible composition of teams, information and systems favor an innovative culture and contribute to the establishment of a learning organization. Promote innovation through collaboration and real-time data access for virtual and diverse teams. The cloud may provide a migration path for employers and functional departments seeking to maximize this value proposition, particularly for Gen Y and Z, who as digital natives have grown up with the latest technology at their fingertips, and may not wish to endure the corporate 5-year laptop update lifecycle. In many ways this demonstrates the need of employees to be in control of their own learning destined to help them qualify and be continuously employable is a critical 2020 driver. Morgan continues, "Organizations will be able to anticipate employee needs and more effectively plan how work gets done," says Morgan, who authored "The Future of Work". "Ultimately all these things boil down to data that can be collected and shared."

Social Platforms - In 1813, Robert Owen, referred to his employees as "Vital Machines". He showed the insight and understanding of human behavior and work that earned him the title of the "Father of Personnel Management". Owen's studies, their applications and practices convinced him that the behavior of human beings was motivated and influenced not by economic things alone, but by other things as well. He believed that physical environments of individuals influenced their physical, mental and psychological conditions, which in turn, directly had an important bearing on the performance and productivity of employees. He tried to humanize the work environments of his employees. Workers could complain and had a say in the rules and regulations as affecting them. General quality of the workers was improved. All this resulted in the bringing about of a change in the attitudes and behaviors of both the workers and the management, towards each other, and the development of harmonious relationships between the employer and the employees, and in the added profitability for his factories. So to say, this ushered in the beginnings of "Human Relations" considerations in industry. Then came management expert and writer Andrew Ure, who incorporated human factors into his philosophy of manufactures, published in 1835. Soon after came the recognition of mechanical and commercial aspects of manufacturing, to which was added 'the human factor'.

Also, when employees use these enterprise-level social network platforms to share ideas, passions and feedback, they can help shape their own career paths. "Employees can attain leadership positions the same way so many people have through public social channels," says Morgan. "If you're an employee who gets hired in sales but is passionate about creative design, you can participate in those creative design groups and discussions via your company internal network, says Morgan. "There is such a trend towards mobile technology that many payroll providers are building their applications from the ground up based on it," says Jamie Hawkins, president and CEO of Benefit Technology Resources, an HR technology-consulting firm. "It's an acknowledgement that employees and managers will only access data in that fashion. In terms of how an employee digital experience should feel, Morgan cites the consumer-website model. "You want to make sure that the experience you created for your online customers is easy, modern and rich," Morgan says, referring to desktop and mobile apps. "In this case we're talking about employees who are interacting with your organization, so the same logic applies. Their interactions need to be rich, easy and modern".

Social Planning Schedules – With geographically dispersed personnel, offering a single data footprint for calendars, emails, documents and projects, person-to-person collaboration becomes easier. Accessibility to up-to-date data becomes much more feasible. New processes will emerge that will enable cross functionality globally and better customer centricity and higher response rates from service providers. Due to the mobile and global access to data and systems true global collaboration is possible paving the way for a 'globalized' organization sourcing team members according to specific topics, markets and industries, local regulations, etc. Work life balance follows. Hours of work will be based on individual schedules and the expectation will be that employees will get the work done by the deadline regardless of where and how it gets completed as they will have 24/7 access to self-service web-based applications, networks and technologies. Family commitments, health and stress levels are dealt with ease and flexibility as individuals can work from anywhere at a time that is convenient to them. Organizational cultures that support work life balance will have Leadership that support new expectations/attitudes of ways of working. "Through group calendars meetings (shared, mutual, trusting, access – controlled or otherwise) can be scheduled, projects managed and people coordinated. It is a great tool to help you overlook your deliverables and deadlines. A group calendar includes functions such as the detection of conflicting schedules with other people in your team or organization or coordination of meeting times that suit everybody in your team. Calendars bring to bear an important sharing attitude. For some executive's calendar, email etc is a private matter (what they meet, what do they do, how do they spend time etc). E Mail servers are sensitive as we have only seen up close in the 2016 elections. Besides the positive effects of group calendar there is also controversy about privacy and control that might influence your productivity", says Morgan continuing, "With workflow systems files or documents can be communicated (access provided, drop box advantages, good drives, apple cloud etc.) to the organization by following a strict and organized process. They provide services for routing, development of forms and support for roles. As current workflow systems are controlled from one point, individuals within an organization normally do not have the permission to manage their own processes so far - this should be changed by implementing collaborative planning tools to current workflow systems. Shared whiteboards, discussion e boards, blog shares, story boards give its users the capability to work efficiently on a task through a web-based or a shared device platform. They can be used for informal discussions, casual off the cuff conversation encrypted and confidential despite its simple format and also for communications that need structure, involve drawing or are in general more sophisticated. This might also be very useful in to realize virtual classrooms".

Social Connectivity is Collaboration - Collaboration on documents and presentations, finances etc. will have to use sharing platforms where more than one individual can manipulate the document and someone can lead a meeting were everyone globally is following as if they were in the same room. "Seventy-three percent of respondents use tablets to access the Internet and 69 percent to check e-mail. KPMG research indicates the need for multiple devices to make it user friendly for consultants in a client environment. Quick and speedy access depending upon whether the client meeting is in a board room, a bar or at the ball game. However, rather more interesting are the 46 percent of people who use iPads to provide "sales support," and the 45 percent who use them for "customer presentations". Device connected LCDs or a TV is no longer new! (PC World). With geographically dispersed personnel, offering a single data footprint for calendars, emails, documents and projects, person-to-person collaboration becomes easier accessibility to up-to-date data becomes much more feasible. New processes will emerge that will enable cross functionality globally and better customer centricity and higher response rates from service providers. Global Collaboration will become a reality in digitally savvy connected enterprises. Due to the mobile and global access to data and systems true global collaboration is possible paving the way for a 'globalized' organization sourcing team members according to specific topics, markets and industries, local regulations, etc. Empowering individual to create a culture of excellence leads to another important function — building up of teams. Teams are created in an organization for a specific purpose and are usually temporary. As such, individuals with high performance and those that are sharp be chosen as team members. While the teams ensure high performance, it often proves to be highly difficult to manage them. Each team is an organization in itself. Since the team members are highly equipped in interpersonal and managerial skills, the team management should be left to them. Self-managed teams are the best teams. To build up effective teams, highly motivated individuals with good performance should be chosen. Once the individuals are chosen, they should be trained in cross — functional areas, and also complete information should be supplied with regard to the given task objectives, functions and process of achieving these objectives. Further to avoid any ego clashes and conflicts within the group, clear rules and code of behavior should be established even before the team starts functioning.

Multimedia solutions will have to be easily accessible to allow employees to collaborate in a global framework. Face to face (skype), real time document and data sharing applications and various other infrastructures will be required to support global collaboration to get the most out of cloud computing to become effective.

Diverse Virtuality a critical differentiator. Diverse and location independent team structures allow differentiated perspectives and tailored expertise to increase speed of responding to market developments and Virtual roles and new roles will be established. Virtual global leadership meeting and messaging should take place to address ways of working and expectations that coincide. The focus of various roles within certain functions will change and will open up more options to reorganize the business. Reallocate more administrative positions to work on higher value project including providing autonomy will become an expectation that will come with working on individualized schedules. New opportunities open up for functions that certain services have been located to the cloud. These changes will impact the environment in a more positive light, as we are consuming less gas and not clogging the highways. Innovation would be a digital advantage. Flexible composition of teams, information and systems favor an innovative culture and will contribute to the establishment of a Learning Company. Promoting innovation through collaboration and real-time data access for virtual and diverse teams and cloud may provide a migration path for employers and IT departments seeking to maximize this value proposition, particularly for Gen Y and Z, who as digital natives have grown up with the latest technology at their fingertips, and may not wish to endure the corporate 5-year laptop update lifecycle.

When On Line roles lack clarity - leadership is not transparent, without time spent identifying and clarifying roles, responsibilities and accountabilities and individuals will find it difficult to navigate their way through their tasks and complete work as a collaborative group and teams unless established role clarity processes are conducted. Communication pathways from leadership can be broken when dealing on a global, even national scale and would need to be managed.

Work life balance – Hygiene Condition - Employees will have to learn to set 'different than used to' expectation with customers, clients and superiors in terms of scheduling around their personal affairs to ensure that work is complete and on time if the organization takes on a virtual way of working. Independent / self-organized ways of working result in potential **adaption of working hour models** considering work-life balance. Employees will begin working more and more from anywhere and anytime that is convenient for them as organizations move to a move virtual world.

Employers/leaders will have to walk the walk if there are going to talk to providing and supporting work life balance in their culture.

Flexibility - including hours of work will be based on individual schedules and the expectation will be that employees will get the work done by the deadline regardless of where and how it gets completed as they will have 24/7 access to self-service web-based applications, networks and technologies. Family commitments, health and stress levels are dealt with ease and flexibility as individuals can work from anywhere at a time that is convenient to them. Organizational cultures that support work life balance will have leadership that support new expectations/attitudes of ways of working. Competency realignment and performance management changed to reflect strategy can help alleviate anxiety about new ways of working and expectations. Employers can test drive giving people freedom to try out and master knew knowledge and skills without the pressure of producing real work. There are a number of remote management training courses that help supervisors learn how to effectively manage in a virtual team. Managers who know their employees are able to optimize individual skills sets and styles, and are able to identify 'the right' person for the job. Managers who understand the policies and requirements for working remotely can better communicate expectations, set performance goals with their employees and better support the overall process.

Work distribution policies require addressing - Formal work distribution policies have not been created or its being done ad hoc and in a highly inconsistent manner creating unawareness or jealousy between employees who are able to benefit from informal "work from home" programs. Informal programs and ad hoc arrangements leave companies open to legal liability for workmen's compensation, and potential violation of the employee's standards act.

Performance and Rewards will be more heavily focused on competency achievement as related to working in a cloud environment. Individuals that demonstrate the ability to work independently and collaboratively across the spectrum can be recognized a high potential employee. Meeting customer demands, new productivity and collaboration levels at a faster rate will enhance organizational performance. When norms, attitudes and expectations are clearly defined, trust is enables with relationships. Employees will become more 'contactable' in a cloud environment and should be capable of setting expectations with their customer base. Performance management and reward frameworks that have been redeveloped to align with working remotely and enabling cloud computing will reap the benefits from such change. Such individuals will learn how to be productive when alone and learn the etiquette of communicating with remote colleagues, staff, clients, customers, etc. Potential to build a high Performing Enterprise through creating a distributed work plan and a performance metrics that align with the ways of working in a remote workforce. Employee attraction and retention increases when working from home becomes an option and performance is based on quality of work produced, not time taken to produce. Organizations with a formal distributed work program and policy are finding that geographic expansion becomes much easier to manage.

The annual/bi-annual process of reviewing performance and setting goals will become difficult - Managers and leaders looking to provide feedback and review performance will run into issues if tracking of employee efforts is not maintained. Employees will become the owners of their performance reviews and require constant tracking of all accomplishments, reports and feedback provided throughout the year. Tracking systems that are not available or easily accessible will hinder the process.

Performance Management in the Digital Culture - Potential impacts on the organization's performance management and Reward strategy. Addressing what should be recognized by the organization as high performance will change based on new roles and ways of working. The key performance areas would be identified in the light of changing business environment. People performance metrics will change and require reconsideration in order to align to new organizational strategies. The metrics require to be cascaded to all levels till an individual level hence providing clarity and direction at all levels. Performance Management and Compensation strategies will change and require that leadership encourage and drive the change. Expectations and high performance will revolve around how efficient and effective one is at being autonomous and getting the work done as opposed to 'showing face' and being present in the office. Incentive Plans: Performance linked incentive plans need to be revised based on the changes in the business environment. Cloud computing has developed into a business enabler and related performance levers need to be built into the incentive plan design.

Pay-out gates: Pay-out gates need to be developed and linked to minimum expected performance by the organization on the cloud computing front. The gates would have to be developed at Organization level and department/functional level. Individual pay-outs need to be linked to the achievement of cloud computing goals. **Capabilities and expectations require alignment to cloud strategy.** The capabilities of cloud computing have to be analysed and utilized effectively to enable achievement of organization goals. The metrics need to be designed to ensure organization utilizes cloud computing effectively so that the goals can be achieved. The change would start at a fundamental level by introducing appropriate changes to the role expectations and hence Job Descriptions. Overview on how the metrics would shape up for organization, functions and individuals on all dimensions of performance will involve consideration of Financial, Customer, Process and Capability. Performance Management and expectations will have to set the stage in terms of executing new roles. In order to embed a cloud computing framework, performance management practices will have to be addressed in a way that will support collaboration, promote autonomy and clarify roles and expectations.

Business HR versus Tech HR - The business leaders also emphasized on the development of a genuine attitude, or a social responsibility on the part of, labor, staff, technicians and management, which as likely to go a long way in lessening the conflict between capital and labor. Trusteeship, in its broader meanings they opined, will emphasize on economic interest (business aspects of HR) and responsibility, not merely mutual differences. Such a spirit, they believed, would bring in new health to the business world. Analyst reports are indicating that our appreciation of Business HR has to be greater than Tech Software driven approach to acquiring a talent solution. The disappearance of IT identification of a talent solution is fast on the horizon. Unlike traditional enterprise software's, HR and talent systems no longer boast of complex IT software's, but speak more of functions, features and HR value add. Admin control now rests with the employee and human resources. The sales speak today is about human resources transformation not technology change, gadgets, devices or jargons from IT whiz kids. Human resources professionals responsible for people engagement are seeking solutions that can speak their language and the language that their staff can relate, beyond gadgets and toys, to understand and use seamlessly, by bringing internet of things closer home. A contra research report (TCS.com) on Internet of Things, states, "Gadget trends come and go, with only a few starting real tech revolutions. Thus, it is natural to be skeptical about the latest gadgets-gone-gaga trend: The Internet of Things (IoT). By this broad phrase, technology companies mean the digital hardware and software that is being embedded in items ranging from cameras and coffee makers to mattresses and multimillion-dollar aircraft engines and are skeptical of their end use. For what purpose would there be the use of a digital revolution in a situation that one can have bed and mattress turn 15%. This is a facetious argument. Every major digital device connect appears to have grown in its usage and popularity. (Watches, Machines, Robotic uses, AI devices, Phones, Lights, Security, Cars, Video, Pens etc). The technology also includes the communications networks (the Internet, fiber, satellite, laser and wireless) that let such digitally endowed 'things' report their condition to businesses and consumers. Technology researcher Gartner projects that there will be 4.9 billion 'connected things' (or 'smart-connected products', as Harvard Business School Professor Michael Porter refers to them) this year. Gartner is unfazed. "And we haven't seen anything yet, according to Gartner. It predicts the number will grow five times by the end of the decade, to 25 billion connected things, including a quarter billion vehicles". Technology, then, is driving change and at the same time enabling HR to keep up with that change—and ultimately bring order to a dynamic, fast-changing environment. But the technology itself is multifaceted, and it can be hard to know how to proceed. In developing strategies for using technology, HR executives need to think about "technology imperatives" as they chart a course for their organizations. Take an integrated approach to talent management that fits in beyond hire to retire and should include learning, career and succession. Use analytics to power people decision making including predictive models. Extend people function and talent management integration out to the workforce. Take advantage of advanced recruiting processes, tools, machines, systems. Leverage the cloud, social and collaboration tools for efficiency and agility.

Building Trust in Digital Technologies - This opened up a new whole vista of goodwill, mutual trust, confidence, understanding and relationships, between the employees, the supervisors and the management. There came about a wonderful change and adjustment in the attitudes and behavior of the employees, who no longer felt emotionally upset. The supervisors and their superiors were more than happy, felt at ease and no longer there was any baffling problem left, which was beyond solution. The management too responded readily to the feelings of the workers, which persuaded them in formulating personnel policies and resorting to such practices, so much, conducive to the maintenance of good employee-management relations. Complexity and lack of trust in new technologies might cause resistance to the adoption of cloud services. Providing adequate information about cloud related changes to daily business and security issues, give targeted guidance to users and supporting units would be a critical step to mitigate this fear. Virtual team setup implies little time for relationship building and bonding and diverse cultural backgrounds might cause conflicts and block benefits of diverse teams. Achieving openness and sensitivity to national characteristics and business habits, fostering intercultural competence, building up leadership skills in a virtual environment, establishing adequate infrastructures to overcome lack of personal presence, using social media to support interpersonal relationship building, face time and networking would help manage these inter personal dynamics. **People Transition and Workforce Effectiveness** - Once we understand the impacts, how do we help position the workforce to successfully adopt the future state business model? How do we create a workforce transition strategy which takes into account job role impact and training, as well as navigating the knowledge, skill and ability gaps? We ask questions pertaining to **Benefit Realization and Sustainable Performance**. How do we measure and monitor progress to help ensure sustainable benefits? To develop a set of tools to drive sustainable organizational adoption and measure potential benefits realization. **Communication.** How do I increase awareness, understanding, buy-in and ownership amongst stakeholders to drive the change process? To plan and execute an effective communications campaign which delivers compelling and relevant messages to all impacted audiences as a way to drive organizational readiness and adoption.

C. Managing Risk

Resistance to share knowledge - Silo-thinking might inhibit cloud triggered collaboration: Knowledge sharing attitude is to be anchored in organizational culture. Language translation will be required at a global level and data and Knowledge Management that is eventually placed on the cloud may require multiple language translations. Productivity and collaboration breakdown possibility exists and individuals may lack motivation to complete work on schedule under the circumstances of working in a cloud environment. Time zone differences can interfere with collaboration and sharing of documents in real-time, affecting productivity levels and efficiency. Performance measures, competencies and expectations may not be clearly defined, therefore affecting the way people are motivated to manage their time and development. Individuals may be expected to do more when productivity is already suffering.

Internet Risk Management - Potential demographic divide due to increased relevance of multimedia in a multi-generation environment. Generation Y characterized by experienced multimedia users favors the implementation of new technologies just as well as past generations have their own distinct ways of interaction. Understanding values, motivation and behaviors of each generation, applying adequate communication, training and teaching techniques, support and closing the generation gaps e.g. by mentoring / buddy programs while training programs must consider all age groups and their capabilities with training tools, social media usage expectations and current technology (Ipads, smartphones).

Risks and Mitigation Thinking - Behaviours and Attitudes may require shifting. Desired behaviours and attitudes are not present, therefore hindering the drive for an innovative and information sharing culture. Management and leadership may lack the vision and understanding required to promote working remotely.

Intellectual property ownership as a risk - A key risk with all cloud technologies is the ownership of the intellectual property, copyrights contained within the 'cloud', both for commercial and sovereign risk (e.g., US based physical servers, Canadian Law on Privacy or the Patriot act). Risk of identity theft and 'employees finding ways around the lock down' when employees use their own devices. "A survey by Proofpoint and Osterman Research, 2011 Consumerized IT Security Survey, found that 16 percent of companies totally lock down their networks (Backups, downloads of IP) to access from any personal devices and prohibits access to any non-approved web sites writes David Knight". The debate on Intellectual property has proved that what gives a cutting edge is not the knowledge of the process (which is readily replicable once the product is known) but the product development capability. This ability is a function of the competence that the organization has acquired and developed and nurtured over the years. In the knowledge environment, these competence centers will be the other major independent variable in the design of tomorrow's organization. The Fine Art of Management will lie in recognizing the key customers for today and tomorrow, creating competence centers and configuring the organization structure around them. "But even among those companies with locked down access, 64 percent of IT staff fear that employees are finding ways to get around the lock down". This is similar to hacking or jail break. For every secure system lies an outlier of break ins. The task here is the need for continually retaining a level of high security. But from a culture perspective it is also about nurturing greater degree of integrity, trust and honesty in work places. "At the other end of the spectrum, 12 percent of companies secure their networks by trusting that their employees to use their "good judgement" in avoiding security vulnerabilities." (http://www.formtek.com/blog/?p=2281). David Knight, executive vice president of product management and marketing at Proofpoint, said "Companies that have no strategy for managing consumer-driven technologies on their network are in serious peril". The need for securing and establishing a policy for disruptive technologies is now. "Sooner or later, an unprotected device, social media or IM platform is going to provide unauthorized access to sensitive or regulated information". To us this is a reality and organizations would do well to be aware and find preventive mechanisms. "Enterprises that stick their heads in the sand when it comes to consumerized IT are increasing risk at an unquantifiable rate." (http://www.formtek.com/blog/?p=2281).

Knowledge Infrastructure

Managing Knowledge - New tools and processes will require implementation. Cloud technologies may require greater uptake of formal KM tools to enhance exchange of information, and this will require organizations to continue pursuing KM tools, and the supporting ways of working needed to deliver enhanced KM. Processes and policies that support controls, address risks and enable the employee to upload, share and ensure security and privacy is not breached is imperative to successfully implement cloud. **Business requirements will need to be understood.** Employee engagement in the development of these policies and processes will have to be considered, as their input will provide large benefits to understanding the ins and outs of their departmental businesses and operational requirements. **Strategy will be imperative to proper execution.** There needs to be a strategy to secure data exchanges and retrieval to ensure privacy for newsletters, announcements, files, etc. and enable exchange of information.

Store Knowledge - Identifying the resource where knowledge is stored will prove to be difficult. Many jurisdictions have detailed legislation about the physical location of customer, and in particular customer financial information. This traditional offshoring issue is potentially accelerated by exposure to cloud based solutions where the end user is less able to identify the physical location of the 'cloud'. For Knowledge Management, this issue is exacerbated by the pervasive nature of storing knowledge across the organization.

Digital Knowledge Computing Policies - Policies around digital computing and sharing information remains a constant subject of discussion, however, with the right platform, policies and processes addressed a database could be shared without concern given that controls and risks will have been addressed during training and communication from leadership. Policies that address the what, where and how of placing information on the cloud will help employees understand what their role is and how they can mitigate risks and support controls. Processes that automatically enable a push of data to either a knowledge management or risk employee will prove beneficial, in that the organization will have one point of contact for review and acceptance of information being pushed to the cloud.

Digital Knowledge Structure Questions - Will there be a structure at all, the radicals would ask. However, the way that structure is defined, there cannot be a state of "no structure". Organizations cannot be made infinitely flat with innumerable outposts guided by one central "rules based" or computer controlled inquiry system. Absence of a structure is an anarchical structure and any other form will still be definable in some way. Our hypothesis is that the structure of tomorrow will be both similar and different from the structural forms that we are accustomed to seeing today.

- *Knowledge Hierarchy and Pattern Maintenance: The hierarchy will be that of increasing levels of knowledge as relevant. An organization operating at the higher levels of knowledge will have higher average knowledge levels. A person coming into this organization from outside will be placed not on the basis of his rank and authority in his previous role but on the basis of where does his knowledge level fit into in the new situation. Rising up the hierarchy will therefore be a function of acquiring additional knowledge and demonstrating it through competencies.*

- *Specialist Focus for knowing more and more of less and less: We see an emergence of the specialist, with greater gusto than was ever thought possible. Deep functional knowledge acquired through education and lifelong learning would be a hallmark of the knowledge worker. The generalist roles would die a natural death and the coordination roles currently performed by scores of middle managers would be replaced by effective and efficient coordination systems. Designing such systems will be a task performed by functional specialists. We visualize a complete and total elimination of the "process managers" where the only role is to create forums to manage individual "sensitivities". Such "processes" will be consciously 'not' managed.*

- ***Team based Network Relationships****: While hierarchies of deep functional skills will exist and perpetuate a knowledge culture, the predominant relationships will be a network of crisscross interactions. Each position will be defined in terms of membership of several teams and it is this team relationship which will take precedence over other relationships. The top management will constitute a Strategy team whose task is to give strategic leadership to the organization and not behave as factional chiefs fighting turf wars. Similarly, specialists of various types will operate through teams dedicated to managing the customer, managing the environment, managing the culture, creating and percolating vision and practicing Common values[3]. The best performers possess personal competence, motivation to deliver, the organizational empowerment, and the psychological motivation to deliver the service in its most effective form. Structures and hierarchies interact and form the team integration.*

- ***Customer and Supplier Focus:*** *The customer continues to be the focus of the organization and the endeavor of the members will be to create and deliver value to the customer and in so doing create knowledge for the organization. Constant utilization of the knowledge resources for customer delight and organization development will be the other foci.*

- ***Environment and Ecology Focus****: A clear understanding of the open system model will define the organization in relation to its environment and teams located at the boundary will constantly give and take feedback from the environment and convert this feedback into actionable decisions. This will be necessitated because the new millennium will call for a heightened environment consciousness.*

Private Cloud provides piece of mind. A SAAS private cloud may give firms the opportunity to take advantage of best in class sharing tools with minimum investment in infrastructure and IT development. For knowledge based organizations this may allow them to experiment with a variety of knowledge management platforms to find one which best suits the organization. Once selected, a cloud approach may assist in reducing the total cost of ownership. As always, a KM tool must be supported by appropriate controls, rewards and leadership to ensure sustainable adoption. For example, removing access to laptop and USB hard drives may force staff to use the KM solution, while pull factors such as linking performance review and remuneration to KM tool use, as well as controls to monitor compliance may be required.

Employee wide understanding of controls are not currently understood. Organizations may need to adopt closer controls on use of KM and classification of data by sensitivity. Establishing and addressing controls and processed need to be considered. **Hesitation to fully utilize the cloud remains an ongoing issue.** Individuals are afraid to share information and data, which interferes with the culture and behaviours some organizations are trying to achieve.

Organizational Impact - Significant education and awareness campaigns about the Cloud within the organization is required: Ensuring that employees understand the benefits and challenges of moving to the cloud, Educating the organization on organizational process changes to adapt to cloud standardization. Communication on the "how to" in regard to security and privacy, data retrieval and storage. Communicate where and when training programs will take place. Communicating where employees can go for support and how moving to the cloud is going to change the organization. Clear message from the management on what are the new expectations and what would be recognized. Intentional and structured communications between user company and Cloud vendor/implementer around Service-Level agreements and performance expectations to avoid "under-delivery of services". There needs to be a strategy to communicate policies and processes to help employees understand how to they can secure data to enable exchanges and retrieval and ensure privacy for newsletters, announcements, files, etc. and enable exchange of information.

Virtuality- Potential for more time spent on ongoing user training and retraining due to integrating with legacy systems. Training organization may need to grow in structure and resources, and be flexible to meet the growing requirements for training as a result of Cloud. This includes strategizing about a learning and development platform that can meet the needs of the training organization. Availability of virtual and cross-national organizations/teams training including opportunities for Virtual management/leadership skills will become a requirement and have high impact on productivity and innovation and understanding security and privacy policies.

Digital Culture Strategy - Without a sound strategy and clearly identified goals and expectations, shifting to a cloud environment will fail. Individuals working in a cloud environment will require clearly outlined responsibilities, tools and practices in place to properly support a remote working environment that strives off collaboration, data sharing and innovation. Remote projects will suffer without clear instruction and support from leadership. In building a cloud based culture strategy, there is a need to assess the maturity of the organization and its change readiness in order to define the change management appropriate approach and understand level and methods of communication necessary to educate/secure commitment and buy-in on the Cloud. There is a need to establish tailored communication and involvement of employees to reduce uncertainty and resistance and support cultural transformation by articulating the strategy regarding performance management and rewards systems including assisting in establishing new communication technology triggered by cloud technology (link to social media). Helping the transforming company around communication planning and execution to help with key messages going across the company amidst competing priorities and IT implementations including proposing new ways of branding/marketing Cloud to the organization and implementation support for the new rewards system for the organization. Change management for the organization to enable the organization to transition smoothly into the new rewards system and business environment and support for the new performance management and rewards system. Help clients around training strategy reassessment and development to ensure that training activities remain strategic given the impact of Cloud in the organization. Align and coach top leadership to achieve buy in and enable the successful implementation of organizational changes (link to training). There would be support the development of a new talent management framework that will support the new ways of working re: use of technology, independence, data management and help identify leadership that will address changes and communication.

D. Learning - The Differentiator

Attitudinal Discontinuities - The way we do business has changed irrevocably be it in human attitudes and disposition towards work itself, the diminishing business and geographic boundaries, technology – product – market- innovations – learning on customer service and satisfaction, changing patterns of product life cycles, liberalized economies of many a third world countries, abundant capital resources, economy of plenty in many countries, social media, analytics, technology interfaces, IT, Internet of Things and so on. From realm of change we now move on into building organizational intelligence through learnings from neural networks, behavioral psychology and machine learning. The learning management system (LMS), learning processes, learning styles, learning members and learning tools are fast emerging as key disruptors for organizations as the technology morphs and dominates to serve corporate learning, technology, psychology, agility, content and collaboration needs. Bersin and associates point out that the LMS is now moving past its content storing/accessing/modular access practices/ testing – certification methods - capabilities and moving to: engage staff through reskilling, employment ready, continued education programs, on boarding, socialization, affiliation teams, leadership development and performance success.

Learning Experience Gap is a reality that talent management solution companies are not focusing sufficiently enough. Bersin, predicts. "The problem many companies face now is that all this content is unintegrated; it exists on many different platforms, and there is no real "middleware" to bring it all together into an integrated content experience". These could be costs, integration, application conflicts, lack of compatibility, outdated codes etc. Continues Bersin, "One would have expected the LMS – content providers and delivery specialist vendors to address this issue, but most of them have focused on talent management software (Hire to retire HR engagement functionalities) instead. Their "learning experience" products have not kept up. Although it is as much a fact that many LMS vendors have ben specialist providers for a period longer than many new age talent software's. The new job for CLOs or training leaders is likely to make it easy for learners to find good content, discerning knowledge banks, curate the best content available, and create a dynamic procurement process to endorse new content as it becomes obtainable – usable and administrable". Online MOOC providers claim to have trained more than 2 million people over the last two years and provided 160,000 completion certificates. For example, Coursera from University of Michigan, Ann Arbor.

Proliferation Possibilities in Learning – Scaling, Adapting, Dissemination is the new game. "A digital renovation of the corporate university: A lot of technology has passed under the bridge since the 1980s, when Jack Welch revamped GE's sleepy Crotonville (New Jersey) leadership center in order to produce the scores of hard-driving leaders needed to mount a do-or-die effort to push the company's business units to the top of their markets" - in, "$127 Billion in Drone-Powered Business Applications", (MIT SMR 2016) writes Theodore Kinni. "Now a new phase (unchartered waters) is unfolding at [corporate learning, knowledge dissemination, dialogue forums] organizations, which must grapple with tools (enable, voice, choice, delivery, Virtuality, device agnostic, certify, feedback, review, performance) and platforms that facilitate knowledge sharing and employee interactions on an almost limitless scale, challenging — and sometimes appearing to sweep away — the old brick-and-mortar model," write McKinsey consultants Richard Benson-Armer, Arne Gast, and Nick van Dam. On the other hand, the article notes, a large number of the CLOs also believe that their organizations are not properly equipped to meet the learning challenge. (For example, in our view, costs, content conflicts, degree of customizations, personalizations, digitization, learning style variations, language barriers, duplicated platforms, scalability issues, no remote access, not across chain of command, feedback could range from readiness, appropriateness, adoption, culture sensitization, content audits, risk recognized). What enterprise learning needs is a digital update. The authors recommend that companies adopt cloud-based learning platforms capable of hosting and running "such personalized applications as MOOCs (massive open online courses), SPOCs (small private online courses), instructional videos, learning games, e-coaching, virtual classrooms, online performance support, and online simulations. "Ultimately, we believe, the future of corporate academies lies in blended learning, which combines classroom forums, in-field applications, (technology gamification), personal and results-oriented feedback, and online engagement," conclude the consultants. "There is no magic number for allocating time between digital and in-person learning; different industries, geographies,

---

functions, roles, competencies and different companies within them, must determine the mix that makes the most sense for their circumstances and capability-development priorities."

Flexible Learning - Being a **Learning Company** becomes even more important due to fast and flexible availability of cloud services/technologies - pace of change increases. Cultural Impact on Digital Organizations - **Global' mindset' will gain importance Re: a virtual world**. Customer service, communication, training and development, learning styles, operations and delivery roles will all be affected at some level and require revisiting in terms of approach and expectations. Developing a 'cloud vision' will support buy-in and engagement in cloud related changes and support a better transition to a virtual way of working. **Expert-on-demand' mentality,** global sourcing, melting team structures. **Shifting focus on war for talents** to emerging economies as distance becomes less of an issue because of potential future lack of qualified personnel in Western economies leveraging human capital outside of our landscape.

LMS - Bersin Continues to See Further - With real-time communication, contact and employee sensing being built into internal HR systems, HR and business managers are benefiting from real-time and immediate feedback on workplace learning, education and management issues. Another example Bersin highlights is the evolution and establishment of the learning management system (LMS). Originally a place to create, consume, store, distribute and access course content, the LMS is now a place for employees to learn via social skills, build relationships, collaborate, identify, build competencies and content matching applications. This means that employees, learners as virtual – colleagues as peers, bosses as equals, are able to consume learning content in Facebook-like ways— say by taking the same courses as your supervisor, mentor or peers.

Diverse change management teams become part of daily life: various cultural backgrounds, values, experience, languages, business habits require openness, intercultural competence and consideration. **Responsibility will lay heavily with Leadership to push the strategy and be change agents.** Leaders throughout the organization will have to understand their role and how it can impact the change. Leaders will have to be transparent, present and easily accessible. Management culture: leadership styles will need to be adapted to 'virtual workforce' (role as a connector increases due to less face-to-face time).

E. What does Behavioral Intelligence do?

Intelligent Organizations personifies the human being and makes the human mind the foundation of the corporation. Intellect seen in its purest form is propaedeutic in its conceptual state. It is primarily elementary and forms the core of the enterprise. Individuals seek freedom of expression, in an environment where learning, teaching and understanding is available and is in a position to adapt, contribute and improve as they learn. The intellectual corporation deals below the surface of overt relationships, seeks psychological contract built on trust, collaboration and mutuality of purpose and provides an environment that offers respect and dignity to the individual. The Corporation has an undebatable, unalterable diktat on the faith in the human mind, the spirit and power of the intellect. Quintiles the Clinical Trial and Data Management Company focus on identifying human potential as the foundation for professional contribution.

Multiple Intelligences - The theory of multiple intelligences is a theory of intelligence that differentiates it into specific (primarily sensory) "modalities", rather than seeing intelligence as dominated by a single general ability. This model was proposed by Howard Gardner in his 1983 book Frames of Mind: The Theory of Multiple Intelligences. Gardner articulated eight criteria for a behavior to be considered an intelligence. These were that the intelligences showed: potential for brain isolation by brain damage, place in evolutionary history, presence of core operations, susceptibility to encoding (symbolic expression), a distinct developmental progression, the existence of savants, prodigies and other exceptional people, and support from experimental psychology and psychometric findings.

Gardner Unplugged - Gardner chose eight abilities that he held to meet these criteria: musical–rhythmic, visual–spatial, verbal–linguistic, logical–mathematical, bodily–kinesthetic, interpersonal, intrapersonal, and naturalistic. He later suggested that existential and moral intelligence may also be worthy of inclusion. Built this thought with psychology, behavioral implications to business organizations combined with machine learning, we have a motley of ideas that integrates to a new Behavioral intelligence model.

F. Emergence of Neural Networks and Machine Learning Models

Neural Networks - Neural networks are similar to biological neural networks in the performing of functions collectively and in parallel by the units, rather than there being a clear delineation of subtasks to which individual units are assigned. The term "neural network" usually refers to models employed in quantitative methods, applied statistics, cognitive psychology, behavioral modification theory and artificial intelligence. Neural network models which emulate the central nervous system are part of theoretical neuroscience and computational neuroscience. In "Neural Networks and deep learning" Michael Nielsen, calls it "Perceptrons, A way you can think about the perceptron is that it's a device that makes decisions, asks and answers questions, offers choices evaluate alternatives, find intrinsic connections, apply logic by weighing up evidence. Margaret Rouse in TECH Target defines it as ""In information technology, a neural network is a system of programs, applications, experiences and data, storage, retrieval structures that approximates the operation of the human brain. It is evidence based generated by data stored and analyzed at periodic intervals to provide for changes, updates etc. A neural network usually involves a large number of processors operating in parallel, each with its own small sphere of knowledge and access to data in its local memory. Typically, a neural network is initially "trained" or fed large amounts of data and rules about data relationships (for example, "A grandfather is older than a person's father"). These networks helps organizations, for example, predict attrition or staffing patterns or global meltdowns impacting stock programs.

Perceptron Programs - A program can then tell the network how to behave in response to an external stimulus (for example, to input from a computer user who is interacting with the network) or can initiate activity on its own (within the limits of its access to the external world)". In this network, Michael Nielsen says, "the first column or layer of perceptrons - is making very simple decisions, by weighing the input evidence. What about the perceptrons in the second layer? Each of those perceptrons is making a decision by weighing up the results from the first layer of decision-making. In this way a perceptron in the second layer can make a decision at a more complex and more abstract level than perceptrons in the first layer. And even more complex decisions can be made by the perceptron in the third layer. In this way, a many-layer network of perceptrons can engage in sophisticated decision making". These programs become available for dynamic learning, competency gap management, individualized problem solving and customizing engagement expectations.

Neural Impacts Sales Culture in Digital Companies - "Our research shows large companies are applying machine learning to sales – outcome processes (recruiting numbers, sales targets, learning person days, performance ranking, engagement across borders) along three dimensions, each of which adds algorithmic rigor to human intelligence and intuition, creating a dynamic new formula they hope will boost sales. The first dimension allows for a scientific approach — with data, information and clarity of process — in customer – dealers, wholesalers, retail sales interactions. The second enables more data-driven experimentation within a sales and marketing environment. The third uses science to create more time to sell, that is, by automating the administrative tasks that get in the way of managing accounts, finding leads, and closing deals or finding campuses of hire, identify skill shortages or see patterns on students from which school has the highest probability of success". In, Sales Gets a Machine-Learning Makeover, H. James Wilson, Narendra Mulani, Allan Alter, MITSMR 2016, write, "Taken across these three dimensions, machine learning is creating speedier, more scientific processes for generating sales revenue or hiring numbers. Before machine learning came along, static databases, lag indicators, analytics from historical data, and experience and instinct steered execution — with performance improvements coming in set increments over time".

Real Cycle Time - "With machine learning, real-time data can drive actions, real time data facilitates information analysis, enables simplification, and process change along a continuous path. Hypotheses can be quickly formed, tested, and revised, enabling a new kind of workflow process that can dramatically outperform previous ones, continue, Wilson, Mulani, Alter - (MIT SMR 2016)". "In our survey, they continue, 38% of respondents credited machine learning for improvements in their key performance indicators for sales — such as new leads, upsells, and sales cycle times — by a factor of 2 or more, while another 41% created improvements by a factor of 5 or more. Whether machine learning facilitates analysis, experimentation or automation, it provides real value for sales and marketing teams. In some cases, salespeople and marketers gain confidence and clarity in processes that were previously opaque, enabling a more systematic and consistent approach to client interaction. In others, machine learning runs the experiments behind the scenes by pruning processes and allowing salespeople to attend to higher-value tasks. While we remain in the early stages of bringing the full value of machine learning to bear in sales (and elsewhere in the organization), what's clear already is that machine learning holds the potential to find significant hidden revenue where there were previously only marginal gains".

Artificial Intelligence brings in additional complexity to the Digital HR. AI can be applied in the following ways: *Expert systems,* which aim to emulate the reasoning process of an expert in a particular domain (area of expertise). *Natural language processing (NLP),* which aims to enable people and computers to communicate in a 'natural' (human) language, such as English, rather than in a computer language. *Speech or voice recognition,* which enables computers to understand and react to human speech. *Computer or machine vision,* which aims to build machines capable of simulating human vision. *Robotics,* which use AI techniques to develop a sensory apparatus allowing the robot to respond to changes in its environment. *Decision support* to collect, analyse and manipulate data in order to model alternatives and explore the consequences of different courses of action. In, $127 Billion in Drone-Powered Business Applications, (MIT SMR 2016), Theodore Kinni writes, "Many of the experiences and interactions people have on Facebook today are made possible with AI," wrote Facebook software engineer Jeffrey Dunn in a post on the company's blog last week. In it, he called AI out as the mechanism behind ranking and personalizing news feed stories, blocking offensive content, identifying trending topics, and ranking search results. "There are numerous other experiences on Facebook that could benefit from machine learning models, but until recently it's been challenging for engineers without a strong machine learning background to take advantage of our ML infrastructure," Dunn explained. "In late 2014, we set out to redefine machine learning platforms at Facebook from the ground up, and to put state-of-the-art algorithms in AI and ML at the fingertips of every Facebook engineer." The result is FBLearner Flow, which Dunn calls "Facebook's AI backbone." He reports that more than 25% of the company's engineering team is using the software. "Since its inception, more than a million models have been trained," he writes, "and our prediction service has grown to make more than 6 million predictions per second. Eliminating manual work required for experimentation allows machine learning engineers to spend more time on feature engineering, which in turn can produce greater accuracy improvements … FBLearner Flow provides the platform and tools to enable engineers to run thousands of experiments every day."

G. *Neural Digital Business Models reflect Learning Capabilities*

Machine Learning a reality – Intelligent or sensor-controlled robots which use artificial intelligence techniques to enable them to take appropriate actions in response to various external situations or stimuli. Intelligent robots plan and monitor their own operation on the basis of contact sensing (physically touching another object), non-contact sensing (using computer or robot vision to recognize items or aspects of the environment to which it is required to respond) or environmental sensing (which enable the robot to respond to external stimuli such as temperature). 2013 McKinsey Institute research, says, "Advances in artificial intelligence, machine learning, and natural user interfaces (e.g., voice recognition) are making it possible to automate many knowledge worker tasks that have long been regarded as impossible or impractical for machines to perform. For instance, some computers can answer "unstructured" questions (i.e., those posed in ordinary language, rather than precisely written as software queries), so employees or customers without specialized training can get information on their own. This opens up possibilities for sweeping change in how knowledge work is organized and performed. Sophisticated analytics tools can be used to augment the talents of highly skilled employees, and as more knowledge worker tasks can be done by machine, it is also possible that some types of jobs could become fully automated". Why is machine learning a reality? Natural language processing (NLP) allows computers to understand natural language, ie, human language. The term NLP generally refers to language that is typed or printed rather than spoken. The acceptance by computers of spoken language is covered by the associated artificial intelligence activities of speech recognition and understanding. NLP involves the acceptance of natural language inputs, their interpretation and understanding and the production of natural language outputs. NLP programs are applications of artificial intelligence (AI) and are made up of a knowledge and an inferencing program like all AI systems. The knowledge base essentially consists of a dictionary of words and methods of analyzing relationships between them which the computer understands. When a natural language statement is typed into the computer, the inferencing program examines it to determine whether the words within the input are understood. If they are, the appropriate response is initiated. An NLP system will enable users to ask questions or issue commands in their natural language rather than computer language. If the NLP program does not understand the question it will ask the user to define the term or spell it correctly.

Deep learning (deep machine learning, or deep structured learning, or hierarchical learning, or sometimes DL) is a branch of machine learning based on a set of algorithms that attempt to model high-level abstractions in data by using model architectures, with complex structures or otherwise, composed of multiple non-linear transformations. Deep learning is part of a broader family of machine learning methods based on learning representations of data. An observation (e.g., an image) can be represented in many ways such as a vector of intensity values per pixel, or in a more abstract way as a set of edges, regions of particular shape, etc. Some representations make it easier to learn tasks (e.g., face recognition or facial expression recognition, from examples. The inference engine, also known as the control structure or the rule interpreter, runs the expert system. It obtains input from the expert system user and searches the knowledge base looking for rules which match the input. It decides what rules are to be invoked, accesses them and compares the input data to either the *if or then* portion of rules in the knowledge base. It continues its search until an acceptable solution is found. The rule interpreter within the inference engine determines the sequence in which it examines rules and asks for additional input information if it cannot make a decision on the available facts and rules. One of the promises of deep learning is replacing handcrafted features with efficient algorithms for unsupervised or semi-supervised feature learning and hierarchical feature extraction. McKinsey recently published, how the institution had tested the ability of three algorithms developed by external vendors and one built internally to forecast, solely by examining scanned résumés, which of more than 10,000 potential recruits the firm would have accepted. The predictions strongly correlated with the real-world results. Interestingly, the machines accepted a slightly higher percentage of female candidates, which holds promise for using analytics to unlock a more diverse range of profiles and counter hidden human bias. The arrival of neural networks and machine learning is now becoming a way of life. Natural language generation is concerned with the computer's output when carrying out NLP. The aim is to ensure that the computer knows what to say and how and when to say it in a way that can be easily understood by the user. A natural language interface program translates natural language typed on to the screen into a form which the computer can understand and, after the computer has generated information in its own language, translates it back into ordinary English as information on the screen. In theory, a natural language interface should allow any users who know what information is available on a database to find out what they want and display it in a form they can understand and use without knowing anything about the internal structure of the database or having to learn a set of special commands. Natural language processing can be used wherever people want access to information recorded on a database and where it will make life easier for them if they can use natural language commands rather than use an instruction which has to be entered precisely in the language which the computer has been programmed to understand. NLP can also be used for machine translation or for enabling text to be *understood* as well as recognized. But these applications are still at a relatively early stage of development. NLP can enable people to obtain information for problem-solving, decision-making and analytical purposes by communicating with the computer in their own words, thus saving them the time and trouble to learn a special computer language. Potentially this provides for a considerable extension to the 'user friendliness' of computers.

Neural Identities - The use of intelligence by people requires more than simply processing information, which basically is what computers do. People *understand* information. The goal of AI is to develop an intelligent computer which emulates this type of intelligent behavior in human beings. The intelligence possessed by the computer, however, is given to it by humans. AI therefore attempts to simulate intelligent behavior. This means that it is necessary to explain the workings of human intelligence by using cognitive science - the science of understanding human intelligence. One of the problems is programming this understanding into a computer. It is relatively easy to program a sequence of procedures or steps in processing data by the use of algorithms (a step-by-step procedure with well-defined starting and ending points, which is guaranteed to reach a solution to a specific problem). It is much more difficult to represent or program intelligent behavior, simply because it is very hard to define the mental processes involved which come naturally to people and which cannot be reproduced in a,.1inear or step-by-step way. Dorian Pyle is a data expert in McKinsey & Cristina San Jose a Principal, state that "In 2007 Fei-Fei Li, the head of Stanford's Artificial Intelligence Lab, gave up trying to program computers to recognize objects and began labeling the millions of raw images that a child might encounter by age three and feeding them to computers. By being shown thousands and thousands of labeled data sets with instances of, say, a cat, the machine could shape its own rules for deciding whether a particular set of digital pixels was, in fact, Last November, Li's team unveiled a program that identifies the visual elements of any picture with a high degree of accuracy. IBM's Watson machine relied on a similar self-generated scoring system among hundreds of potential answers to crush the world's best Jeopardy! players in 2011. Machine learning is based on a number of earlier building blocks, starting with classical statistics. Statistical inference does form an important foundation for the current implementations of artificial intelligence. But it's important to recognize that classical statistical techniques were developed between the 18th and early 20th centuries for much smaller data sets than the ones we now have at our disposal".

Neural & Digital Algorithm – Neural is for real – Neural integrates with Artificial intelligence (AI) and is the process of developing computer systems which exhibit the characteristics associated with intelligence in human behavior. Artificial intelligence (machine intelligence) represents knowledge by using symbols rather than numbers and by employing heuristic methods of processing information. A heuristic is a rule-of-thumb which, when applied to a situation, suggests how it should be dealt with. AI also uses pattern-matching methods which enable relationships to be established between different things, and explain how the various items are linked to one another. Intelligence is the ability to think and reason. AI aims to reproduce intelligent behavior in human beings. Such behavior involves: recognizing the importance of different elements in a situation; finding similarities in situations despite the differences which may separate them; drawing distinctions between situations despite the similarities which may link them; responding to a situation flexibly; and making sense out of ambiguous or contradictory messages. There is now a need to provide a common foundation for key items that leaders say and do related to the transformation process in the context of complex technological change requirements. A process that enables individuals in the organization to begin answering the question "What will all this mean for me and my job?" By helping to focus stakeholders on the change effort and build a momentum across the organization. Change of this magnitude includes initiating support for change and helps employees overcome resistance. Is an input to the formation of a change strategy and architecture. Provides a foundation for communications program. A case for change, not only articulates the answer to following questions: "Where are we going?", "Why do we have to go?", and "Why would I want to go along?" But, also unveils the tangible value of the change for all levels of the organization by: Moving beyond the economic business case behind initiatives, Translating the change into practical terms that are meaningful and relevant to stakeholders and the workforce, Uncovering the specific facets of the change relevant to individual user groups. "Machine learning is unconstrained by the preset assumptions of statistics", says Pyle. "As a result, it can yield insights that human analysts do not see on their own and make predictions with ever-higher degrees of accuracy. Machine learning is based on algorithms that can learn from data without relying on rules-based programming. It came into its own as a scientific discipline in the late 1990s as steady advances in digitization and cheap computing power enabled data scientists to stop building finished models and instead train computers to do so. The unmanageable volume and complexity of the big data that the world is now swimming in have increased the potential of machine learning—and the need for it" Organizations willing to implement any type of neural intervention, machine based change, For example, simplification of IT maintenance, should consider the following before and during implementation. Organizations should be looking to change to keep up with the pace of technology and be competitive within their industries

- Invest in revisiting the corporate strategy and those of the departments
- Align programs, policies, processes and tools to the organization's strategy
- Outline performance measures and competencies
- Clearly articulate roles and accountabilities during every task and assignment
- Have a transparent and present leadership team and a communication strategy that enables a cloud environment
- Outline strict policy and guidelines around usage of personal devices when connected to a corporate cloud
- Invest in security technology that inhibits employees for accessing sites that may harm the database or inhibit their productivity and consider paying for a portion of the bill for personalized devices in which the organization wishes to have some level of control over

·

- Utilize mentors and superiors that are close in proximity, while using other social media devices to connect globally and learn
- Provide training when moving from a non-cloud environment to a cloud environment in order to provide employees with 'transferable skills' that will support them through the transition.
- Extensive training and acceptance of the changed way of working including bringing up a degree of excitement at the possibility of improved productivity, performance, customer engagement owing to these new technologies.

In, Not All Digital Threats Are Disruptions, Theodore Kinni, in MITSMR 2016 writes, "There's a mismatch between human and machine processing, with machines outrunning us by many orders of magnitude. "This mismatch becomes even more pronounced as machines get more sophisticated. So much so, several roboticists told me, that a failure to improve existing interfaces will ultimately stop advances in fields like machine learning and artificial intelligence until there are changes," explains LaFrance. The ultimate solution is direct communication between the human brain and machine, which LaFrance spends the bulk of article exploring. The man, who controls drones with his mind, is Panagiotis Artemiadis, and he runs Arizona State University's Human-Oriented Robotics and Control Lab. Artemiadis has developed, writes Overly, "what looks like a high-tech swimmer's cap, equipped with 128 electrodes that detect brainwaves. The electrodes identify where thoughts originate in the brain and determine the pilot's intended commands, and then those commands are communicated to the robots via Bluetooth." Currently, the cap's wearer can control four drones in a lab".

Prescription Learners - AI systems try to model human performance on a computer driving the benfits oif prescription learners. To do this it is necessary to use cognitive science to determine the process used by humans to produce a particular type of intelligent behavior and then create a model of that behavior so that an attempt can be made to simulate it on a computer. As explained cognitive scientists develop theories of human intelligence which are programmed into computer models by AI researchers. The computer models are then used to test the validity of those theories. The feedback from the computer models allows the cognitive scientists to refine their theories, which can be used to develop better models, and so on. McKinsey's, Dorian Pyle and Cristina San Jose, state, it as - Description, Prediction and Prescription. "Today's cutting-edge technology already allows businesses not only to look at their historical data, collecting data in databases but also to predict behavior or outcomes in the future—for example, by helping credit-risk officers at banks to assess which customers are most likely to default or by enabling telcos to anticipate which customers are especially prone to "churn" in the near term and Prescription, "the third and most advanced stage of machine learning is the opportunity of the future and must therefore command strong C-suite attention. It is, after all, not enough just to predict what customers are going to do; only by understanding why they are going to do it can companies encourage or deter that behavior in the future.

Technically, today's machine-learning algorithms, aided by human translators, can already do this. Natural language understanding interprets natural language by the use of the following techniques: *Lexical analysis* - a program which allows access to a lexicon (dictionary) containing symbolic definitions of the words and phrases it is likely to encounter. *Keyword analysis* - a pattern-making technique which scans the text, looking for keywords which the program has been designed to recognize. When a keyword is identified the program responds by manipulating the text in a predetermined fashion. *Syntactic analysis* enables the computer to understand the function of each word in a sentence as well as its relationship to each of the other words. Syntactic analysis uses a parsing technique to separate sentences into their component parts. *Semantic analysis*, which interprets a sentence according to its meaning rather than simply deploying the syntactic analysis technique of interpreting the form of a sentence. Semantic analysis makes use of various types of grammars - formal systems of rules which describe the ways in which sentences can be constructed. *Dialogue analysis* clarifies ambiguous sentences by overcoming the linguistic difficulties of ellipsis (the omission of a word or words from a sentence) or anaphora (the abbreviation of a previous word or phrase) and *Pragmatic analysis*, which relates sentences to one another and their context, and which attempts the difficult task of analyzing what a sentence really means. This requires a considerable amount of information about the domain (area) under discussion but also about the perceptions of communicators about the situations in which they find themselves. For example, an international bank concerned about the scale of defaults in its retail business recently identified a group of customers who had suddenly switched from using credit cards during the day to using them in the middle of the night. That pattern was accompanied by a steep decrease in their savings rate. After consulting branch managers, the bank further discovered that the people behaving in this way were also coping with some recent stressful event. As a result, all customers tagged by the algorithm as members of that micro-segment were automatically given a new limit on their credit cards and offered financial advice, says Pyle and Jose".

H. Leadership Disrupted or Machine? The Debate!

Leadership Disrupted or Machine? "IBM Watson was the first tool capable of ingesting, analyzing, and "understanding" text well enough to respond to detailed questions. However, it doesn't deal with structured numerical data, nor can it understand relationships between variables or make predictions. It's also not well suited for applying rules or analyzing options on decision trees. However, IBM is rapidly adding new capabilities included in our matrix, including image analysis. "Let us understand Watson's value proposition. How Watson answers questions. Watson first needs to learn a new subject before it can answer questions about it, first Watson learns a new subject, then all related materials are loaded into Watson, such as word documents, pages, PDFs and web pages, questions and answers pairs are added to train Watson on the subject and Watson is automatically updated as new information is published. Then Watson answers a question. Here, Watson searches millions of documents to find thousands of possible answers, collects evidence and uses a scoring algorithm to rate the quality of this evidence and ranks all possible answers based on the score of its supporting evidence. Watson analyzes unstructured data **80% of all data today is unstructured**. This includes news articles, research reports, social media posts and enterprise system data. How Watson reveals insights? Analyzes unstructured data - Uses natural language processing to understand grammar and context. Understands complex questions. Evaluates all possible meanings and determines what is being asked. Presents answers and solutions. Based on supporting evidence and quality of information found. Analyzes information to reveal insights and Interprets information with Watson API.

IPsoft, Digital Reasoning, and the original Watson all use similar components, including the ability to classify parts of speech, to identify key entities and facts in text, to show the relationships among entities and facts in a graphical diagram, and to relate entities and relationships with objectives. This category of application is best suited for situations with much more — and more rapidly changing — codified textual information than any human could possibly absorb and retain. Image identification and classification are hardly new. "Machine vision" based on geometric pattern matching, interface technology has been used for decades to locate parts in production lines and read bar codes. The user interface provides a means of producing two-way communications between the user and the computer. The expert system asks questions to which the user replies by typing in answers. The system may request additional information from the user and the user can ask the system to explain its reasoning. The expert system displays an output result to the user which may take the form of a firm conclusion or may indicate that either no conclusion can be reached or that it has to qualify its conclusion with a certainty factor. Today, many companies want to perform more sensitive vision tasks such as facial recognition, classification of photos on the Internet, or assessment of auto collision damage. Such tasks are based on machine learning and neural network analysis that can match particular patterns of pixels to recognizable images. The most capable machine learning systems have the ability to "learn" — their decisions get better with more data, and they "remember" previously ingested information. For example, as Watson is introduced to new information, its reservoir of information expands. Other systems in this category get better at their cognitive task by having more data for training purposes". In, Just How Smart Are Smart Machines? authors, Thomas H. Davenport and Julia Kirby in MIT SMR 2016 write, "If popular culture is an accurate gauge of what's on the public's mind, it seems everyone has suddenly awakened to the threat of smart machines. Several recent films have featured robots with scary abilities to outthink and manipulate humans."

The basic approach to expert system development is to identify heuristic (practical) knowledge, extract it from the expert, and represent it in the computer. Expert systems are developed by knowledge engineers who develop the system on the basis of domain experts who have expertise in the particular subject area or domain to be covered by the system. "In the economics literature, too, there has been a surge of concern about the potential for soaring unemployment as software becomes increasingly capable of decision making. Yet managers we talk to don't expect to see machines displacing knowledge workers anytime soon — they expect computing technology to augment rather than replace the work of humans. In the face of a sprawling and fast-evolving set of opportunities, their challenge is figuring out what forms the augmentation should take. Given the kinds of work managers oversee, what cognitive technologies should they be applying now, monitoring closely, or helping to build? "But as Mike Rhodin, senior vice president of business development for IBM Watson, noted, "Watson doesn't have the ability to think on its own," and neither does any other intelligent system thus far created. IBM, for example, has disaggregated Watson into a set of services — a "cognitive platform," if you will — available by subscription in the cloud. Watson's original question-and-answer services have been expanded to include more than 30 other types, including "personality insights" to gauge human behavior, "visual recognition" for image identification, and so forth. Other vendors of cognitive technologies, such as Cognitive Scale Inc., based in Austin, Texas, are also integrating multiple cognitive capabilities into a "cognitive cloud." Robots have varying degrees of autonomy". Today, Watson is an IBM supercomputer that combines artificial intelligence (AI) and sophisticated analytical software for optimal performance as a "question answering" machine. The supercomputer is named for IBM founder, Thomas J. Watson. The Watson supercomputer processes at a rate of 80 teraflops (trillion floating-point operations per second). To replicate (or surpass) a high-functioning human's ability to answer questions, Watson accesses 90 servers with a combined data store of over 200 million pages of information, which it processes against six million logic rules. The device and its data are self-contained in a space that could accommodate 10 refrigerators. "Some, such as remotely piloted drone aircraft and robotic surgical instruments and mining equipment, are designed to be manipulated by humans. Slowly but surely, the worlds of artificially intelligent software and robots seem to be converging, and the boundaries between different cognitive technologies are blurring. In the future, robots will be able to learn and sense context, robotic process automation and other digital task tools will improve, and smart software will be able to analyze more intricate combinations of numbers, text, and images. Clearly, smart machines are advancing at the things they do well at a much faster rate than we humans are. And granted, many workers will need to call on and cultivate different capabilities than the ones they have relied on in the past. But for the foreseeable future, there are still unlimited ways for humans to contribute tremendous value. To the extent that wise managers leverage their talents with advanced technology, we can all stop dreading the rise of smart machines".

Intelligent Machines Meets the Intellect – A study says that now, Google is less likely to show 10 organic blue links. Instead, Google shows only 8.5 blue links on average but supplements those links with featured snippets, app packs, knowledge panels, images, videos and more. The Google user interface has exactly number of words. Google understand the value of speed. If they add more words to our webpage, their dial-up customers will find the website too slow. Google Labs allows Google customers to experiment, critique and provide valuable feedback on how and what to improve in their applications/ services. It is perhaps the only organization whose stated goal is to get the customer to leave their website at the earliest possible. Google will know more about the customer because it benefits the customer if we know more about them. We want to have a little bit of Google in every transaction on the internet. Google believes that artificial intelligence (A.I.) virtual assistants (VA) and the conversational user interface (CUI) will largely supplant search engines and mobile apps for many users. We're moving into an "A.I.-first world," according to Google CEO Sundar Pichai. Simply put, all that means is you talk to a computer. It "understands" what you say no matter how you say it. Then the computer does things for you based on those conversations. Google Now can be safely categorized as a non-A.I. virtual assistant. It's like Siri, Cortana, Alexa and other virtual assistants. "Two questions that managers of intelligent machines should ask: It's been a couple of years since Stephen Hawking warned that artificial intelligence could "spell the end of the human race", continue Theodore Kinni, "The terminators aren't here yet and unless they come very soon, the managers of AI-based technology have a couple of more immediate issues to address, according to Vasant Dhar of NYU's Stern School of Business and Center for Data Science. The first, which Dhar takes up in a new article on TechCrunch, is how to "design intelligent learning machines that minimize undesirable behavior." Pointing to two high-profile juvenile delinquents, Microsoft's Tay and Google's Lexus, he reminds us that it's very hard to control AI machines in complex settings. "There is no clear answer to this vexing issue," says Dhar. But he does offer some guidance: Analyze the machine's training errors; use an "adversary" — through means such as crowdsourcing — to try to trip up the machine; and estimate the cost of error scenarios to better manage risks. The second question, which Dhar explores in an article for HBR.org, is when and when not to allow AI machines to make decisions. "We don't have any framework for evaluating which decisions we should be comfortable delegating to algorithms and which one's humans should retain," he writes. "That's surprising, given the high stakes involved." Dhar suggests addressing this issue with a risk-oriented framework that he calls a Decision Automation Map. The map plots decisions in two independent dimensions — predictability and cost per error — and suggest whether it would be better made by human or machine".

I. Structure is Strategy is Process

Organizations moved vertically from strategy, to structure and process. In the knowledge generation role, content has a distinctive role to play in making corporations effective. In fact content and process to a considerable extent go logically together. One at the cost of another has long since been way laid. Nevertheless, for corporations into intense knowledge management roles content tends to be an important area, no doubt. At another conceptual plane one could debate on structure and content preceding strategy given that people who contribute through their intellect have done so without either the strategy or the structure in mind. They have simply made a difference through their thought process. Innovative organizations do not have tight rope structures with clearly defined boundaries of roles and responsibilities. Consulting companies (McKinsey, Andersen, Bain and Company, Price Waterhouse Coopers, Boston Consulting Group) have long since used the Adhocracy Model (Henry Mintzberg) with team based structures constructed on the basis of competence, client needs and delivery schedules. Their industry and functional specialization matrix structure offers them the unique advantage of providing more than a plain vanilla service. Research labs of large pharmaceutical companies (Glaxo – GSK, Sanofi, Merck, SmithKline Beecham, Novartis) have depended on a structure that allows flexibility in roles, areas of contribution and the best person is right there doing what he/she knows best.

Changing Organizational Models - Effective organizations were defined as those with a performance orientation of doing what is right for business. In doing so businesses attempted models that were appropriate at a point in time. Models included structural interventions (GE), long range planning (MIT), environment scanning (Google), management accounting and systems, management by objectives (Apple), leadership pipeline, performance planning, managerial effectiveness (Unilever) etc. these models continue to be of relevance to organizations experiencing various stages of their life cycles. Its application and usefulness has varied depending on the usage and manner in which they were implemented. While some of the models have outlived their usefulness there are several other concepts and applications that continue to serve their time.

Organizational structures and stakeholder management will change. Specific functions where cloud computing is introduced will change the eexpertise from technical and administrative to rather strategic skills (CIO's become designers/architects, IT experts become service provider). Roles will shift from 'in office' to virtual and individuals will require an understanding of the competencies and behavioural expectations that will be required of them. Creating a culture that favors **innovation** will be supported by new technologies. Stakeholders can be defined as any person / group of individuals, internal or external to the organization who will be impacted by the changes, or who could have an impact on the success of the project. A Stakeholder Analysis identifies who the stakeholders are and evaluates their current commitment and what level of commitment is required from them in order for the project to succeed. The results of the analysis provide information to support development and/or implementation of: Stakeholder Management Plan; Communication Assessment and Strategy; Communication Plan; Change Leadership Behaviors Diagnostic; Leadership disrupted Action Plan Framework; People and Organization Issues Log. Each of these in turn detail the actions required to strengthen stakeholder support and/or to overcome resistance. A Stakeholder Analysis helps our clients and the program team by identifying and understanding who are the most powerful/ influential stakeholders and where the change team needs to spend time managing stakeholders to achieve effective support for the project. Achieving this insight early on in the project enables active stakeholder management to achieve sustainable commitment, using a range of interventions to explore barriers, build commitment and trust, and leverage their organizational influence. Use a standard format for collating and presenting information. Together with the client, develop a clear and consistent understanding of where the stakeholder analysis data and outputs will be held, who will have access to the information and who will be accountable for maintaining it. The outputs contain sensitive, arguably subjective, information and must be controlled. Refresh the analysis at regular intervals and apply the new insights to stakeholder management initiatives. A Stakeholder analysis is a snapshot, point-in-time representation of available information. Impact/Influence and Support/Commitment change throughout the program lifecycle. Re-visit your prioritization of stakeholder management activities in response to the refreshed analysis.

J. Intellectual Commercial Differentiators

Economic impact of the firm, obviously, is more than internal management approaches alone. Best of organizations have encountered failures for want of strategic differentiators. For example, Michael E. Porter defined five basic forces as the basic state of "barriers to competition" for a firm: Economies of scale, Product Differentiation, Capital Requirements, Cost disadvantages independent of size, Access to distribution channels and Government Policy. At any given point in time firms are at varying stages of advantage on this five-stated entry barriers. It makes vulnerability that much more relevant in the context of a going concern. GE has consistently stated dominance, economies of scale and size as their competitive positioning. Well-managed management's meant attaining bottom line targets and growth curves as promised to the shareholders. Citicorp evaluates countries for its human potential. The goal of meeting quarterly budgets has been dealt with before".

Fixing Balance Sheets for Value – "When balance sheets are squeezed to show profits in an area where there are none firms do push the balance sheet to its precipice. It is while making the balance sheet look good do corporate managements miss the wood from trees. Several short-term strategies to prop up performance make the firm go belly up as the organization does not possess the sustenance power to hang out there with cash flows and customer loyalties for long. Although achievement of the targeted goals has not secured the corporation from destruction and decay as we have seen it happen to large companies. Pierre Nanterme (Accenture), interviewed by Paul Michelman, who asked, You have said that "businesses could be more incentivized to assess the social impact of their digital investments." You believe that digitization and social impact have kind of a special relationship that is different from business activities in the pre-digital age" in a Conversation with the CEO: Pierre Nanterme, Chairman and CEO, Accenture, in MITSMR 2016, Pierre Nanterme says, "Absolutely. The latest wave of the digital revolution will change people's lives. Life is not about productivity gains or privacy issues, two of the issues we've associated with technology advancements over the past 10 or 20 years. But with artificial intelligence, cognitive computing, machine learning, we are talking about things that can enhance humanity. And that's a different game".

Flourishing Networks - McKinsey Consultants Lowell Bryan, Eric Matson, Leigh Weiss, say, "In any professional setting, networks flourish spontaneously: human nature, including mutual self-interest, leads people to share ideas and work together even when no one requires them to do so. As they connect around shared interests and knowledge, they may build networks that can range in size from fewer than a dozen colleagues and acquaintances to hundreds. Research scientists working in related fields, for example, or investment bankers serving clients in the same industry frequently create informal—and often socially based—networks to collaborate". What has attracted the most interest in neural networks is the possibility of learning. Given a specific task to solve, and a class of functions learning means using a set of observations to find which solves the task in some optimal sense".

Device Obsolescence – "Most large corporations have dozens if not hundreds of informal networks, which go by the name of peer groups, communities of practice, or functional councils—or have no title at all, continue, Lowell Bryan, Eric Matson, Leigh Weiss. "These networks organize and reorganize themselves and extend their reach via cell phones, Blackberries, community Web sites, and other accessories of the digital age. As networks widen and deepen, they can mobilize talent and knowledge across the enterprise. They also help to explain why some intangible-rich companies, such as ExxonMobil and GE, have increased in scale and scope and boast superior performance". For example, in neural networks, Knowledge' is thus represented by the network itself, which is quite literally more than the sum of its individual components.

K. Intellectual Proximity to Advantage

Bring Down Complexity - As organizations grow in size it is but natural for complexity and distances to emerge between front line realities and decision-making power sources. The front line could mean employees, suppliers, governments, society and more importantly and sadly the customer itself. When this distance becomes more than manageable companies commence reeling under pressure of performance. Somewhere along the line of business we have lost touch. A process of renewal, an act involving "involvement" on a continuous basis, needs to be established and new ways of thinking becomes essential. Thinking differently from initial concept to actual implementation should become an organizational rigor where translation of ideas into workable ideas and that in turn into action plans make the organization vibrant and energized at more than one plane. Every flat structure supports this finding.

Unique Intellect - Sustaining a competitive advantage through management of people has become an inevitable management paradigm. While we evaluate the impact of the factors that make the hardware of the firm we do see the inevitability of turbulence. Yet the people factors, the much-publicized area, deserve the final go signal. "As we move towards the chaos of the future," Bob Buckman of Buckman Labs had once said, " the progress of Buckman Labs relative to other companies will be determined by the growth in the value of knowledge that exists within the company. The acceleration of knowledge transfer is how we will grow this collection of individuals we call into what it can be. Our strategic advantage lies in the leverage of knowledge".

Dopamine Squirt - In a McKinsey paper, Derek Dean and Caroline Webb, stated, "Recovering from information overload, "Nonetheless, evidence is emerging that humans can become quite addicted to multitasking. Edward Hallowell and John Ratey from Harvard, for instance, have written about people for whom feeling connected provides something like a "dopamine squirt" the neural effects follow the same pathways used by addictive drugs. This effect is familiar too: who hasn't struggled against the urge to check the smart phone when it vibrates, even when we're in the middle of doing something else?"

Intellectual Change Risk Analysis - There is a need to demonstrate change risk analysis - Identifying potential risks which might impact the change process is critical to any change management initiative. An effective Change Management Approach not only identifies such risk elements, but also helps the organization define a strategy by which such identified risks can be mitigated. In order to develop a good case for change, the team must: Engage key leaders beyond the project team in case development; Make sure that client leadership disrupted owns the Business Case for Change deliverable; Tie to the strategic, financial and operational goals of the organization and business units; Understand what else is going on at the enterprise and business unit level; Link the initiative to other active or planned initiatives; Understand the history of change; Identify appropriate resources; Ensure you are spending adequate time to socialize and validate the Business Case for Change with the organization. Key elements of a Case for Change should answer the following questions: What is the need for change? Why is your organization driving to the change? Where are the driving forces coming from? What are the changes? Are the changes process related? Are customers bringing about change? Are the changes internal or external? What is the impact? What is the impact on your organization, business unit, customers? What will this mean to People, Process and Technology? What are the positive and negative impacts? What are the internal and external impacts? How does this translate? What does this mean from the day to day running of the business? How does this change benefit me? What are the tangible performance improvements that will be realized?

L. Systems Thinking has its roots in Behavioral Intelligence

Dominance - Organizations with dominant systems thinking have possibly made people orientation second to the systemic orientation. The information era brings in the inevitability of systems, data management and systemic approaches to management problem solving. While the 90's saw the systems dominance to make business performance advanced and electronic the 21st century possibly has a modified version of the system story. A situation where system creators no longer turn subservient to what they have created but have actually built in adequate flexibility and innovation modules to grab the attention of every individual who is working with the system and see the potential to add value and make a difference to the system. The suggestion may sound preposterous to organizations that have spent millions of dollars to make their data and process systems beyond the tinkering capability of the individual. After all the logical fear could be the unleashing of anarchy with every working individual tampering with the system as they are working. Well, perhaps, it is this or may something significantly more meaningful. Organizations in preparedness of tomorrow, the model organization, as well as those that are right there today have created working effective system to manage a corporation of today for tomorrow. Do we as a consequence have adequate checks, balances and flexibility built into a system to make it versatile, high performing and dynamic?

M. Knowledge Intellect Strategic Synthesis

Strategic readiness gets converted into tangible value only when internal processes create increased levels of revenue and profit. An organization cannot possibly assign a meaningful financial value to an intangible factor like a "motivated and prepared workforce" because tangible value can be derived only in the context of the strategy. It is possible from the financial perspective of the strategy to state that successful execution of the strategy is worth some amount in revenue growth and another amount in shareholder value. A workforce that has achieved satisfactory levels of strategic readiness is one, but only one, of the factors that enable such revenue growth or shareholder value creation to be achieved. Thus, the readiness of the human capital intangible asset is a necessary but not sufficient condition for strategic success. But when knowledge – intellect converges with learning and strategy the synthesis becomes possible. The general background knowledge required to perform the job is a starting point in enhancing value. This includes job-specific knowledge (for example, a "subject matter expert"), as well as surrounding knowledge (for example, "know the customer") that tailors the job-specific knowledge to the environment and context of the job. Value includes the set of characteristics or behaviors that produce outstanding performance in a given job. Some jobs require teamwork, while others are built around a customer focus. Matching, the values to the job is essential.

3 D KM Matrix - Consequently, knowledge, learning and intellect form the three-dimensional matrix. Intellect drives its creation and expansion. Knowledge is derived through six variants, be it acquisition when a product, service or a company is purchased and consequently the knowledge. In the context of buying knowledge, involves learning to acquire, purchase, and negotiate knowledge sourcing. Building upon the experience of knowing and learning how and what to buy, when, at what price and through whom or the to buy or not are decisions taken through an experience ridden path. This deployment of intellect titled experience enables acquisition and buying right.

Inheritance of knowledge occurs when it is passed down from one person to another or when a system or processes is an established norm in the organization. What is left by predecessor's needs to be managed maintained and should be learnt to not destroy value. Intellectual contribution arises only when inheritance as a value symbol can be upgraded for its value and for assembling its properties to make business profitability. This combination of managing inheritance and helping advance its value arises when deploying an educational intellect. That of knowing through substantive academic or training work on how to maintain what has been inherited. Here the intellectual contribution is limited to utilizing what has been learnt has been put to substantive use. Facilitating creation of knowledge necessitates learning and teaching to discover and seek the unknown and becomes essential competency development in a research or thinking organization. Intellectually this can be managed only if it is supported by special, spatial capabilities, seeking the unknown, experimenting and utilizing the innate potential in the human mind.

Special Intellect - This deployment of the special intellect is a necessary condition for expanding knowledge or making learning for seeking the unknown an incentive to the human mind. Enabling expansion of any type of knowledge would mean that the individual or the organization has to learn the art of innovation, expanding upon ideas and building upon a thought. Innovation arises when knowledge is meant to be learnt or trained depending upon the skills and competencies necessary to be administered in performing an expanding role in a context.

Expanding knowledge intellectually necessitates incumbents of human minds to substantively deploy their learning capabilities and the skills and capabilities that they have been trained in. Similarly, knowledge has now got to be internalized by its members and a significant degree of learning to absorb, share becomes essential. Internalization has meant communication, coverage of information and data, enabling communities of practice, and pulling together into a meaningful whole aspects pertaining to the knowledge that needs to be absorbed and applied. Intellectually this would mean utilization of behavioral competencies that are effectively programmed to help individuals to develop in them capabilities that enables understanding and application of what has been learnt to a larger mass of population.

Commerce - Finally, knowledge has its commercial compulsions and the learning required is to train and help people learn how to market, create a selling strategy, agree on pricing and the pre requisites necessary to commercially make viable the knowledge now converted into a product or a service. This effectively connects knowledge and learning and demonstrates its unequivocal linkages. Performance factors at an intellectual level provide the framework for enabling commercialization of knowledge and implementing measurable and tangible goals and targets make achievement of results pertaining to commercialization of such assets.

Knowledge	Intellect	Digital Strategy
Acquisition	*Experience Factor*	**BUY COMPETITIVE**
Inheritance	*Qualification factor*	**DOMINATE DOMAIN EXPERTISE**
Creation	*Special Intellect & Potential*	**FIRST MOVER**
Expansion	*Training & Learning*	**CANNABALIZE**
Institutionalization	*Behavioral Competencies*	**EXECUTION**
Commercialization	*Performance*	**BUILD ON FIRM RESOURCES**
Digital Culture Continuum		

Figure 61 - Knowledge – Intellect - Strategy Interface

N. Behavioral Drainers

Bureaucracy - Organizational bureaucracies and policy orientation can turn into millstones around ones' neck and needs appropriate management. Basic concepts that determined a well-run corporation of the current era are likely to be discarded as those that are outdated and no longer in fashion. Commodity companies need to reshape to survive. Successful telecom companies Reliance, Bharati, Tata Indicom, would have to reinvent itself in the next 5 years, as their costs would become difficult to bear. We would classify working bureaucracy and rigid policy framework management style and two of the critical aspects to make a point. The bureaucracy that helped structure, plan, process, style and staff work together through forms, procedures and approval mechanisms has turned into a liability of today's managerial effectiveness.

Employee Disruptions -'From an employee experience perspective, Stacey Harris from Sierra-Cedar, says, "there are three areas they need to examine closely. *First* is workforce composition, which encompasses skills inventory. The entrepreneurial spirit of millennials has resulted in non-traditional engagements. Many of them are seeking to engage with employers as freelancers or contingent workers, putting pressure on traditional employment models. While this variable labor force represents potential cost-savings, they can just as easily walk out the door, taking valuable skills and knowledge with them. Digital enterprises need to analyze which roles need to be on staff and which roles can be outsourced. And, since misclassification of workers can result in hefty fines, HR needs to ensure regulations are being met locally". "There is a need to leverage HR portal technology. Further leverage employee and manager self-service portal offerings across businesses and regions. Eliminate any manual operational HR tasks that can be moved to self-service without significant reduction in service quality. Also eliminate any opportunities for manual workarounds. Ensure system stability and usability for highest possible user acceptance'.

Second, "people functions need to embrace technology, and it's not always their fault that they cannot. Many technology providers have designed their solutions for HR instead of the entire workforce with a social digital slant. Given the consumerism of technology, workers expect to access flexible systems that can accommodate business change. Mobile has accentuated this gap – it literally puts HR applications in the hands of the employees; however, if the user or candidate experience isn't positive, the outcomes aren't positive either. If the user or candidate experience isn't positive, the outcomes aren't positive either".

Third and Last – "and many would argue, most importantly – to support the future of work, HR needs to build its own bench strength in the area of data interpretation. We've seen some progress made in terms of data collection, yet without the ability to predict and forecast based on the data, it's not actionable. Business wins are created by those organizations that can make strategic decisions, quickly. Given what a valuable asset one's workforce is; HR's insights are indispensable to the business".

Bersin by Deloitte Just Not Talent Anymore - Establish the new talent service delivery model based on three key building blocks. HR Business Partners, exclusively providing commercially-driven resourcing staffing services and support to the senior business management by converging technology, service and processes. HR Centers of Expertise, performing product design and specialist expert services to the Business Partners, Shared Service Centers, and within HR. HR Shared Service Centers, executing product and service administration and the day to day HR-client interaction (primarily focused on serving employees and line managers in general). There is a need to focus high-touch Business Partner interactions on strategic services for senior business management. The Business Partner organizations interface with senior business management only, serving senior leadership of the business and line managers with significant people responsibility (amounting to no more than 10% of the organization) to jointly ensure successful people operations in the business. With the exception of specific business-related needs, the remaining business managers will be served through Service Centers / Self Service portals. "Technology and processes will continue to adapt to the Millennials, says, Josh Bersin, (top thinker and visionary in HR) principal at Bersin by Deloitte, Deloitte Consulting LLP, "By now it's no secret that the younger generation has its own way of doing things. Millennial employees and managers are extremely tech-savvy. They spend a lot of time online and on mobile devices. They expect to interact with technology and be engaged by it. They adapt quickly to changing business conditions and are good at thinking outside the box. But it's hard to recruit them and even harder to keep them; according to a new survey by Elance/oDesk, 58% of Millennials plan to leave their jobs in three years or less. Whatever you think of Millennial workers, this much is certain: they are having a huge impact on the workforce. In 2015, Millennials will make up the largest portion of the workforce for the first time, according to the U.S. Bureau of Labor Statistics. There are several ways that you'll see HR technology (and indeed all business technology) continue to adapt to an increasingly Millennial workforce, including:

- *Mobility will dominate all new business technology as Millennials expect to be able to utilize mobile devices and mobile apps to work anytime, anywhere.*
- *Gamification will be built into more business systems to engage Millennial employees.*
- *Greater emphasis on learning management will increase as Millennials demand more on the job training for advancement opportunities.*
- *HRMS will play a big role in "big data"*

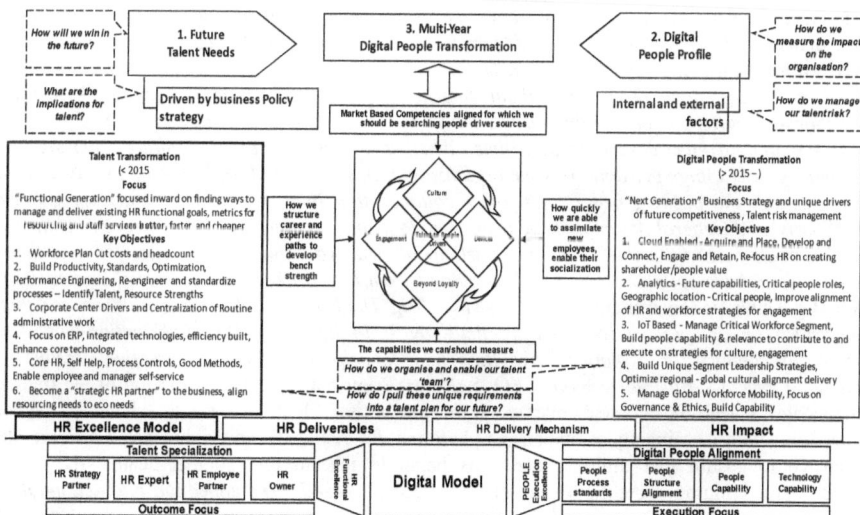

Figure 62 – From Talent to People Management

As companies refine their use of big data for business decision-making, HRMS and talent management systems contain a trove of information about workforce costs, productivity, skills needed for business objectives, and much more. The goal is to move from backward-looking reports to real-time decision-making and even predictive analytics. When you can study labor activities in real-time, you can make adjustments today before inefficient processes or poor worker performance affects your organization's bottom-line. Moreover, if your HR analytics solution helps you take what you learned yesterday, last month, and last year and apply it to forward-looking decisions about employee schedules, hiring needs, benefits costs, training programs, and a myriad of other human capital decisions, how much more strategic could planning become?"

O. The World is Engaging with Intellectual Learners

Work with Vendor Eco System - By 2025, says, McKinsey, "it is possible that productivity gains of 30 to 40 percent could be achieved for the 50 million knowledge workers in this category, which would lead to economic impact of $0.8 trillion to $1.1 trillion per year". Vendors such as Grovo (Lenny DeFranco - *Make people feel special. Jeff told a story about when the company was throwing a party back in the early days. "Nick looks at me and says, 'We have four thousand dollars left. Maybe we shouldn't be spending $750 on this party.'" Jeff insisted that they did. "You need to make people feel special," he reasoned. Consequently, we all do feel special. Between Grovo Clubs, rec league sports, and departmental and inter-departmental outings)*, Floqq, Vodeclic (fast, video-based online learning), as well as marketplaces including Udemy (*Culture at Udemy - We're a small but growing team with hopes of building a truly great culture. We know we're only at the beginning, but we try to live our values in the way we work and find people who share our ideals. It all starts with the phrase - LET'S GO. Let's go help 100 million people learn anything they can imagine. Let's go get 100,000 instructors to share their knowledge with the world. Let's go get 10,000 organizations to change the way their employees learn. Let's go make it so that one day, anyone can truly learn anything*), Pluralsight (*Keith Sparkjoy (Culture Coach) - Is the CEO a humble person? CEOs who focus on their own greatness are often limited by their own imaginations. A humble CEO will hire smart people and focus on helping them succeed. A humble CEO's goal is to make the company great rather than being self-serving. It'll be an exciting day when I get a pitch that includes not just financial details, but also details about the health of the company!*), General Assembly (*A collaborative culture is one of the hardest things to maintain as a company grows and scales. It is also essential to ensure success over time. Whether you are shaping a culture from scratch or revamping how things get done in your organization, this event will explore how to shake up those silos, disrupt the pecking order, and foster collaboration internally to drive success. CultureIQ, ZogSports, and General Assembly have teamed up to bring you a memorable, interactive gathering of professionals faced with this challenge. Participants will walk away with tactics for how they can authentically bake collaboration into their culture from the speakers, the exercises, and each other*) and Big Think (video content expert – SAP - *"Big Think is an outstanding platform for thought leadership, diverse perspectives, and practical advice. In the 21st century information environment, people are hungry for a platform like Big Think to help them focus on practical lessons in an engaging format." Bill McDermott, CEO, SAP*), are contributing to the disruption of the traditional knowledge - learning content market. It is integrative, delivery friendly, language agnostic, compatible with learning styles, expansive platforms, futuristic, stylish, sophisticated and knowledge intensive to ensure that multiple platforms begin to talk to one another seamlessly. Learning middleware (bridging content software's) – Degreed (*Degreed turns education into actionable data predictive of success - Dave Ulrich HR Magazine's #1 most influential thought leader worldwide in HR*), Pathgather, Intrepid Learning – (*"To support our cloud-first mobile-first business transformation, we developed a course for our global sales professionals leveraging Intrepid's platform in a Corporate MOOC model, and have been running it for nearly a year now. This sales enablement program delivered on Intrepid Learning's technology is one of the highest rated and most engaging our Sales and Marketing Readiness Group (SMSGR) has ever seen. Period. I've never seen so much buzz at the senior levels about a learning technology. The mobile-first, contemporary design, deeply integrated social discussions and real-world assignments have led to absolutely thrilling levels of seller engagement — all of which is directly supporting our transformation. And the Intrepid* *platform has allowed us to move at the speed of modern business." - Chris Pirie, General Manager Microsoft SMSG Readiness, former ATD Chair)*, Xyleme *(When you create a high-performance learning culture in your organization, your learning and development function is much more likely to be seen as a strategic business partner — instead of a cost center. The best Learning Companies have a deeper understanding of their learning culture, analytics, and content capabilities)*, Fuze, Wisetail – *(To ensure our own path as a company is aligned with our overall goal of helping our clients be great places to work we focus on three areas: Purpose, Path and Play. **Purpose** is our shared mission, the direction of our company. **Path** is how each individual can grow and develop in parallel to company growth. **Play** is making sure the ride is fun and enriching)*, Integrator box by TCS, and OpenSesame are trying to address this need by bringing a wide range of affordable, easy to use learning programs. hiQ Labs *(We created a team of top data scientists and engineers, human resources experts, and people analytics leaders from the most respected technology and scientific firms. We worked for over four years to solve for these questions)* can predict attrition based on external data using open jobs, social media activity, questions pertaining to exit formalities, engagement score etc. KPMG conceptualized a *"Predictive Analytics Index"* (Shermon 2008) for their clients using quantitative, Psychometrics and behavioral sciences, an ability to predict performance and attrition. Psychotesting Canada uses a *"Strategic Scan Score"* and *"Strategic Scan Zone"* (Shermon 2008) to predict employee' readiness for career programs, transfers, mobility and job preferences.

Digital Strategy, Organizational Model, Shareholder Value & Speed of Response		
Digital Workforce Effectiveness	Digital Leadership	Business Model Driver
Digital Millennials & Founders Talent View & Pipeline	Value, Productivity, Costs & Budgets	National – Regional - Globalization
Pre & Post Merger Play Book	Organization Charting	Digital Technology
Predict, Plan, Organize, Acquire and place		
Exec & One on One Search & Selection	Succession Planning template	Workforce Optimisation
Dynamic Boarding	Pre & On Line Testing	Campus Connect
Goodwill Alumni Network	Rehire & Re Recruit	Analytics, Predictors Projections
Personalization My Page	School Connect Offers	Placement Choice
Pre Joining Skill Development	Retained Reskilled Rehire	Analytical Projections
Diversity – Frat Clubs - Greek life	Electronic & Beyond Accessibility	Self Regulated Private Forums
Forensic / Security Background Check	Global Mobility	Optimise Recruitment (HiPo)
Critical Role Cover	Leadership Development Assessment Centres	Job Role Analysis Rotation
100 Day Socialization	180 day Evaluation Resettlement Processes	360 day Engagement
Culture, Eco System, Risk management, Compliance, Community & Governance		
LMS & L&D Technology Governance	Resourcing & Talent Systems	New HCM Talent Technologies
Leadership Assessments Appointments	Compliance Networks and Adherence	Job Value Rewards & Compensation Choices
Community Networks Neural Networks	Games, EST, T Group, Group Dynamics Social Collaboration	High Risk Skill Development
Technology, Infrastructure, Communication & Change Management		
Knowledge Letters Mails Document Management	Collaboration Tools	Outcomes Reports Communication Processes	Gamification Cloud

Figure 63 – People Management Best Practices

Market Dynamics – While Google continues to grow at a frenetic pace, it has also massively expanded in size over the years. With the increase in scale it is going to become even more challenging to maintain the current Entrepreneurial Spirit and Social Culture, in the organization. Microsoft & Apple are currently the biggest competitors to Google. While Bing (Microsoft) has managed to create some impact in the Search space, Apple continues to precede Google in launching new products. Facebook and Twitter are also a significant threat, since Facebook practically dominates the Social Networking space today. This competitor threat is even more severe in terms of the talent flight and attrition levels Google could face going forward. While Google's decision to suspend operations in China has been met positively, it is not favorable for Google to be forced to repeat the same elsewhere. Privacy concerns over Google Buzz have led to more questions over Google's increasing dominance and ability to intrude on the privacy of their customer. Sustaining the leadership at the top level, in its new avatar is another prime concern for the organization.

Predictive Analytics - "Wells Fargo has developed a predictive model to select the most qualified candidates for positions as tellers and personal bankers. Working with Kiran Analytics, the company identified the qualities that characterize engaged, high-performing employees in client-facing positions and then screened for those attributes in new candidates. By the end of the program's first year, the retention of tellers and personal bankers rose by 15 and 12 percent, respectively". Susan Lund, James Manyika, Kelsey Robinson from McKinsey Consulting and McKinsey Global Institute, McKinsey Quarterly - March 2016, write further, "What's more, predictive analytics can identify employees likely to depart, flagging the need for mentoring, new jobs, or advancement to improve their satisfaction and engagement and thus decreasing employee turnover and raising productivity. Bank of America, for instance, has made its employees more engaged by using Humanyze's Sociometric Badges (ID cards with embedded sensors that monitor interpersonal interactions) to gauge and improve the cohesion of call-center teams whose turnover dropped sharply as a result.".

Mobile Apps Versus Talking Mobility is no longer a differentiator. It is a new normal. One of the most demanded APP today is the emergence of mobile apps as the primary technology platform we use. Try using an application on an IPAD. If it doesn't work the solution has a problem. Vendors are no longer making mobile app as a web enabled application. "It is all about APPification", says Bersin. Market is speaking of a unique way by which DEVICE uniqueness should be maintained. "Organizations will be able to anticipate employee needs and more effectively plan how work gets done," says Morgan, who authored "The Future of Work". "Ultimately all these things boil down to data that can be collected and shared. Also, when employees use these enterprise-level social network platforms through their devices to share ideas, passions and feedback, using special Apps, they can help shape their own learning and consequently their career paths. Employees can attain leadership positions the same way so many people have through public social channels, says, Morgan, "If you're an employee who gets hired in sales but is passionate about creative design, you can participate in those creative design groups and discussions via your company internal network".

Digital Strategy, Organizational Model, Shareholder Value & Speed of Response		
Intellectual Value Proposition		Digital Millennials Key Roles
Digital Value Employee - Employer Branding		Supervisory Structure Board Management
Human Capital Valuation		Learning Knowledge Management
Develop, Energize, Connect, Redeploy, Re Engineer		
Technical/Functional Development	L&D LMS Maturity model	Academies, L&D Budgets/spend
Mentor/Buddy/Cohorts Self Help Friend	Succession Potential PMS - PIP	Dyadic Learning
Technical, Functional, Leaderial Dev	Leadership Competencies	On Line Virtual University
Mentor/Buddy/ Cohorts	Self Portal,	Special Skills
Learning help desk	Creative Reports & Presentations	Predictive Charts
Learning Style Inventory	Self Help Tests Real Time Assess	Private Feedback Learning
Simulations Evaluations Development	Capability Framework Development	Coaching/Leadership Development
Operationalize 70:20:10	Team Group Development	Mobile - learning
CEO - Leadership Connect	Team Connect , Rotate & Projects	Recertification & Re Skilling
Culture, Eco System, Risk management, Compliance, Community & Governance		
Digital Talent Risk Management		
Demographic Diversity Mix		
SOX/IFRS Compliance		
Technology, Infrastructure, Communication & Change Management		
Business Case for Digital Change	Internet of Things	Influencing Stakeholder Management

Figure 63A – People Management Best Practices

Changing Nature of Work - Management Structure at Google is structured around the social architecture of the Internet – open, flat, malleable and non-hierarchical. Hierarchical layers were experimented with but they interfered with the innovative spirit of the organization and were done away with. From a decision making perspective most ideas/proposals/ plans are discussed with the employees at length, before being formalized and implemented and Control is more peer-driven than managerial. Innovation is the cornerstone of Google. Every Googler is to spend their time as 70-20-10 (70% on Google core business, 20% on adjacent products and 10% on highly experimental products). Google is painstakingly cautious about who enters the organization and the focus is to weed out the average and hire only the best. There is no non-performer at Google. In case a Googler does not perform as per expectations he/she is not being utilized well….it is regarded as Google's fault, not the employee's. Google drives behavior through incentives. Engineers working on important projects are, on average, rewarded more than those on less-important projects. Google Founders' Awards are special awards given as recognition for extraordinary entrepreneurial achievement and is the highest employee award at Google Inc. Concurring with Morgan, McKinsey research by James Manyika and team predicts, "The nature of work will change, and millions of people will require new skills. It is not surprising that new technologies make certain forms of human labor unnecessary or economically uncompetitive and create demand for new skills. This has been a repeated phenomenon since the Industrial Revolution: the mechanical loom marginalized home weaving while creating jobs for mill workers. However, the extent to which today's emerging technologies could affect the nature of work is striking. Automated knowledge work tools will almost certainly extend the powers of many types of workers and help drive top-line improvements with innovations and better decision making, but they could also automate some jobs entirely. Advanced robotics could make more manual tasks subject to automation, including in services where automation has had less impact until now. Business leaders and policy makers will need to find ways to realize the benefits of these technologies while creating new, innovative ways of working and providing new skills to the workforce".

Devices Management - Employees are increasingly using their personal devices that are link to corporate email and intranet site to visit consumer websites. Privacy and security is affected when employees that are using personal devices that are linked to corporate applications visit consumer websites. (link to communication – data security/protection). A study by Snapshot Spy reflects employee admissions that the Internet is used for personal purposes up to three hours per day).Productivity, performance metrics can be negatively affected, as findings suggest that individuals are using 18 hours of their time per week on consumer, social websites(http://www.minitrax.com/bw/whitepapers/AIWhitePaper.pdf). Nielsen studies show more than 18 hours per week is spent by workers visiting websites during working hours. Individuals may run into technical difficulties and security issues when using personal 'gadgets' that have been approved by the organization. This can prove to affect productivity, customer service and data security. HR processes must support cloud triggered developments towards global sourcing. The selection process becomes more complex and networking more important and would require alignment and tailoring HR activities to organizational cloud strategy.

People Leadership disrupted Versus Managing People is another changing dimension. Feedback, feedback management, self-discovery, assessments, culture tools, (TINYPulse, Glint, CultureIQ, Culture Amp (employee engagement), all forms of testing and certification (psychometric, personality, aptitude, managerial effectiveness, career - vocational inventories, skill gap, conflict management), learning. Testing, assessments and Feedback are fast growing employee experience areas. Vendors are tying up with global psychometric testing companies as a talent management functional differentiator. "**Feedback** is the Killer App" says, Bersin. "The traditional annual engagement survey, testing, employee pulse is going the way of the dinosaur (slowly however) and a new breed of pulse tools, feedback apps, and anonymous social networking tools has arrived. If you aren't exploring this space, you are missing a huge opportunity to make your company better. I won't list the vendors here, but every one of them is growing and I see this as a whole new segment".

Digital Strategy, Organizational Model, Shareholder Value & Speed of Response		
Intellectual Talent Scanner		Global Talent Analytics
Social and Talent Track		Compliance Dashboard
Self Reports Play Book		Geographic Needs
Optimize, Engage, Retain, Grow, Succeed, Eliminate		
Mobile engagement app	Employee engagement (commercial)	Generic roles/Career paths
Fun @ Workplace	Problem Solving help desk	HR Ombudsman
Personal Brand	Productivity	Team Competitiveness
Fun @ Workplace	Best Practices Benchmarking	360 View of Performance
Sales / Performance Incentives	Internal Job Hopping	Internal Talent Exchange
Outcome Feedback	Re On Boarding/Re Orientation	Benchmarking Big data (External)
HiPo Tool - Selection	Performance Management maturity curve	Exec Compensation, Fringes, Perquisites
Virtual Teaming Programs	Middle Retention	Monitor Variety, Unique Contributions
Social Network Behavioural Evaluation	Ethics & Discipline	Special Intellect
Culture, Eco System, Risk management, Compliance, Community & Governance		
Digital Nomination Committee		Talent Team Infrastructure
Ethics, Values & Governance Testing		Market Risk Maps
Benefits, Wealth Management		360 Feedback
Technology, Infrastructure, Communication & Change Management		
Devices Wearables	Sensitivity Management	AI/Robots	External Communication

Figure 63 B – People Management Best Practices

Digital Solutions to speak Employee Experience to build cultures - We live in 2015, but we work in 1975," says Jacob Morgan, co-founder of Chess Media Group, a management-consulting firm. Corner offices, pompous bosses, cubicle-based, 9-to-5 work culture of the past is fast receding", so execs need to help close that gap between traditionalists and the needs of the millennial. Employees seek engagement through active participation and control over their own issues and challenges. Careers are not built by bosses but by a staff engaging with a mentor and designing a career path for herself. The transformation of the HR organization will take time and requires discipline and support of all stakeholders. As the philosophy of the HR talent delivery model will change, not all stakeholders, especially within the businesses, will necessarily experience an improvement of services. The support of some processes/functions today might be more comfortable than it will be in the future, as service levels will be adopted to equal standards wherever possible. HR transformation programs are ambitious and more so when it has to be digitally renewed. Challenges can only partially be foreseen. The reaction to those challenges requires flexibility and adoption in the approach. The need to realize quick wins should not jeopardize the overall transformation program. Transforming organizations have to accept that a certain investment in resources, technology and time has to be undertaken to transform the HR organization. It will be essential to identify the key players for the future HR Organization as soon as possible to allow sustainability of services and successful implementation of the New Talent Service Delivery Model. For example, Skillsoft and Saba can recommend which courses employees should take if they want to mimic the experiences of their career idols. Talent Management Solutions can provide a cause and effect linkage to competencies, performance and employee experience. A PwC, 2013 report asks, "Technology is in a state of disruptive innovation. Multiple significant market forces are keeping HR technology departments on their toes; at the same time, these market shifts are providing great opportunities for functional departments to deliver more value. The question is: Will people functions departments position themselves to take advantage?" Monolithic large companies that believes that size mattered are rethinking their cultural disadvantages, to connecting with people, given their loss of agility, speed, employee experiences, responsiveness, customer care and appropriate platform".

Figure 64 – Key People Priorities

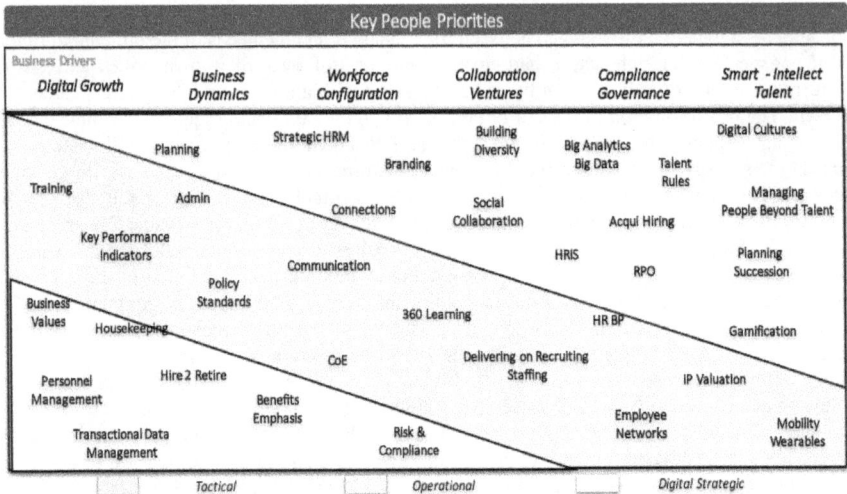

Key People Priorities					
Business Drivers *Digital Growth*	*Business Dynamics*	*Workforce Configuration*	*Collaboration Ventures*	*Compliance Governance*	*Smart - Intellect Talent*

Content within figure (positioned diagonally, tactical to digital strategic):

- Planning
- Strategic HRM
- Building Diversity
- Big Analytics / Big Data
- Digital Cultures
- Training
- Admin
- Branding
- Talent Rules
- Connections
- Social Collaboration
- Acqui Hiring
- Managing People Beyond Talent
- Key Performance Indicators
- Communication
- HRIS
- RPO
- Planning Succession
- Business Values
- Policy Standards
- 360 Learning
- HR BP
- Gamification
- Housekeeping
- CoE
- Delivering on Recruiting Staffing
- IP Valuation
- Personnel Management
- Hire 2 Retire
- Benefits Emphasis
- Employee Networks
- Mobility Wearables
- Transactional Data Management
- Risk & Compliance

| | Tactical | | Operational | | Digital Strategic |

Figure 64 – Key People Priorities - Digital Solutions to speak Employee Experience to build cultures

Platform Culture Fit - Effectively Intellectual Companies are those that have derived an intellectual compatibility and a fit between the intellectual individuals who make up the organization and the processes, variables and systems that are available to make the individual work effectively. The organization assumes that people are capable of growth individually and collectively provided the environment, the climate and system is right with legitimacy accorded to people and their prowess. The system is non-evaluative or judgmental while the task is in progress and evaluates only at the final stages on both the processes and the results. HR processes and systems have to be revitalized to bring in a new sense of ownership and commitment to the ways and means being articulated through the HR system. A revamped, rearticulated model breaking away from the traditional policy, power, process, people syndrome to people, process, content alternative. Every act of HR should be revisited to allow for dissonance and prefabrication to suit the individuals who form the core of the organization. If there are systems that are systems friendly and needs modification to make it people friendly it has to be done. This round of modification would impact the organizational functioning considerably given some amount of inevitable confusion in the medium term.

However, as things settle down and people realize the impact of their own HR decisions processes would become easy and reliable to handle.

P. Way forward

"Dazzling as such feats are", the Dorian Pyle from McKinsey's caution, "machine learning is nothing like learning in the human sense (yet). But what it already does extraordinarily well—and will get better at—is relentlessly chewing through any amount of data and every combination of variables. Because machine learning's emergence as a mainstream management tool is relatively recent, it often raises questions. In this book, we've posed some that we often hear and answered them in a way we hope will be useful for any executive. Now is the time to grapple with these issues, because the competitive significance of business models turbocharged by machine learning is poised to surge. Indeed, Ram Charan suggests that "any organization that is not a math house now or is unable to become one soon is already a legacy company." C level executives have a big role to play.

But, Dorian Pyle continues, **"Behavioral change will be critical,** and one of top management's key roles will be to influence and encourage it. Traditional managers, for example, will have to get comfortable with their own variations on A/B testing, the technique digital companies use to see what will and will not appeal to online consumers. Frontline managers, armed with insights from increasingly powerful computers, must learn to make more decisions on their own, with top management setting the overall direction and zeroing in only when exceptions surface".

"Democratizing the use of analytic, providing the front line with the necessary skills and setting appropriate incentives to encourage data sharing, will require time".

The lack of strategic direction and dysfunctional activities undertaken at enormous cost in terms of wasted human resources and money by organizations should provide sobering lessons in terms of organizational learning and business performance. Never before have so many employees had formal business education and management qualifications. How then could the past decade show evidence of so many managers clearly having little strategic appreciation of how to manage an organization in order to achieve long-term sustainable competitive advantage? Individuals seek freedom of expression, in an environment where learning, teaching and understanding is available and is in a position to adapt, contribute and improve as they learn. Intelligent Organizations deals below the surface of overt relationships, seeks psychological contract built on trust, collaboration and mutuality of purpose and provides an environment that offers respect and dignity to the individual. The Corporation that has an undebatable, unalterable dictate on the faith in the human mind, the spirit and power of the intellect.

Culture - Business Process facets of the corporation through the intelligent organization succeeds the management of the enterprise.

Behavioral change will be critical, http://bit.ly/24h5OoQ and one of top management's key roles will be to influence and encourage it. Traditional managers, for example, will have to get comfortable with their own variations on A/B testing, the technique digital companies use to see what will and will not appeal to online consumers. Frontline managers, armed with insights from increasingly powerful computers, must learn to make more decisions on their own, with top management setting the overall direction and zeroing in only when exceptions surface.

Democratizing the use of analytic, providing the front line with the necessary skills and setting appropriate incentives to encourage data sharing, will require time.

Talent Seeks Digital HR - Creating & sustaining an optimized high Performing Enterprise is best achieved when business strategy effectively converges with Human resources strategy, a talent management goal, to achieve fundamental objectives that pertain to talent management, performance, productivity for enhancement of shareholder value. In many organizations workforce challenges need to deal with cost escalation, regulatory compliance, effective workforce planning, leadership pipeline, diversity, KPIs and bringing the elements of people forces together objectively and the need to integrate these objectives together with business outcomes is an inevitable & perhaps an overarching objective of a CEO. Microsoft recognizes that the US and global diverse markets represent tremendous source of value in workplace and marketplace. By the year 2050, 85% of the entrant into the U.S. workforce will be color and women. Developing regions like China, Brazil, India and Africa make up for the increasing share of world population. Economically, the diverse markets represent a growing source of market consumption and buying power. They are important customer group for Microsoft. By increasing the diversity of workforce, the company can create a team effortlessly designs products with the needs of these growing customers in mind. Microsoft promotes behaviors that encourage new ways of solving problem- solving and reward diversity of thought. Focus on providing leaders with cultural competency training and best practices management strategies. Microsoft supports Employee Resource Groups and Employee Networks which provide cultural awareness and social networking. Microsoft focuses on building employee leadership pipeline, by recruiting and hiring the world's top talent from all group within the society. Microsoft offers several programs that provide students in grades K-12 with opportunities with today's technology and conduct workshops. Microsoft believes in incorporating the talents of varied workforce and recognizing the needs of diverse customers, supplier and partner base. Microsoft partners with top diversity related organizations and participates in several community events to bring technology innovation to diverse communities.

Thus, it is imperative that dimensions of organizational framework- structure, planning, workforce, processes and technology be aligned to the overall objective of managing people towards establishment of a high value enterprise. Culture weaves these elements into a uniform thread, thus strengthening the alignment. While it is important to explore individual dimensions of the organizational framework to identify avenues of People performance optimization, it may be observed that the real opportunity for talent management is locked in the way these dimensions interact with one another in a HCM systemic context.

Talent Transaction	Talent Transformation
Transactional Program - People Management is about standard hire to retire practices. Dependence of manual processes	Focus on Digital Talent - Management is about understanding and developing the unique critical skills and capabilities you need to win in the future
No visibility of either quantum or focus of investment in Talent. Poor top management commitment to social collaboration	High Social Skills. Clear visibility and control of spend; clear alignment of spend to unique skills and capabilities.
Limited ability to understand, identify, track, deploy and develop global talent. Low emphasis on value.	Identify Talent Analytics - Clear view on where the talent lies, where the future needs lie, and how to align the two
Narrow, traditional, permanent, inflexible view of the workforce and sources of capability.	Intellectual Workforce is viewed as more open, distributed, diverse, entrepreneurial, flexible, contract, managed accordingly
Narrow set of talent tools - focused on traditional recruitment, development, satisfaction applications and processes	Broader business perspective on sources of capability – to include M&A, JVs, partnerships, alumni, communities, customers, the crowd. High on value realization
Absence of line management – supervisor being accountable for managing talent – Greater focus on rules driven management	Provide Digital Infrastructure - Executive team being accountable for engagement. Proliferation of wearables.
Talent risks continue to be HR domain and low on the Boardroom agenda	Transformational Partnership - Business Partners determine Talent risks- Boardroom agenda, Embedded in enterprise risk management

Figure 65 – Digital Culture - Talent Transitions in The Intellectual Company

Organizations are consequently leveraging advances in technologies, data proliferation, newer delivery models and commercials options to manage their global and diverse talent base to help mitigate an overriding competitive and business trauma in a global business environment.

People Tech Way to Go - From a business perspective, these aspects are converging to bring together a commitment to offer clients a comprehensive digital talent management platform, those that bring in a combination of functionality, UI, collaboration and digital competitiveness. Investments in Digital People Solutions is strategized to offer a globally benchmarked HCM functionality on a cloud enabled digital platform with all of best in class capabilities including offering functional best practices, Wearables, AI, Analytics, Mobility, Social & Cloud, with the opportunity for the Chief Human Resources Officer to drive business performance by effective utilization of resources. New features are quickly being ushered into a standard talent management system. Social and informal learning, Integrated network recruiting, Candidate relationship management, Social recognition, Real-time employee feedback, engagement sensing, learning agility, on line testing, Culture assessment, Fit gap analysis, succession sensitivity, competency cultures and socially connected person.

Disruptions Continue and Business Models Change- Writes, Martin Gill of Forrester Research (2015) in "Recruit and Retain Top Digital Talent, "it's time to Disrupt your Firm's talent Management strategy "if eBusiness leaders are serious about Branding, recruiting, and retaining today's top digital talent, they need to rattle some cages and challenge their organization's preconceptions of talent management. This means a fundamental rethink of where you look to find candidates, which firms you compete against, and your working environment and practices. For instance, when Infosys wanted to create its edgeVerve platform business, senior leadership realized that they needed a new set of business and technology skills. they found themselves competing for talent with firms like Google and Facebook, not other systems integrators, and the traditional software engineering culture of the organization presented a challenge. Infosys made the tough choice to spin the organization off as a separate business unit to foster a new digital culture. to begin with, senior management didn't de ne any job descriptions. they embraced a flexible, startup-like culture and allowed people to define their own roles. eBusiness leaders must challenge their organization's status quo and lead a rethink in how they find, recruit, and retain digital talent".

Life Cycle Business Model Development In Digital Cultures					
Low to High Quartile Analysis	**1st Quartile**	**2nd Quartile**	**3rd Quartile**	**4th Quartile**	**Outlier**
Digital Life Cycle	*Start Up*	*Growth*	*Transforming*	*Evolved*	*Challenged*
Operator Culture	Entrepreneurial Performance Talent Focus	Retention Thinking (Product, Process)	Inter-dependencies between separate elements of the process - New Talent Profiles	Work Ethic Mindset (Right First Time, Efficiencies)	Significant faults, Teaming Challenge, Small Mindset
Executive Culture	Business Strategy - Policy Focus, intrinsically hierarchical	Execution Drive, financial survival and growth	Group Think - willingness to experiment and take risks	Value Building - Personal relationships are a means to the end of motivation and control	Structural Conflicts
Engineering Culture	Emphasis on Quality, Productivity, Tech Builder	Design, Detail, Product Competencies, New Product emphasis, lower service orientation higher product	Quantitative, Scientific, Precision data Performance Focus	Technology enabled Best Practices, Safety, Back Ups, Reliability	Lack Digital Thinking
Digital Culture	Aligned to Innovations, Empowered Pro Active	Symbiotic Identities - gradual, systematic, flexible, adaptive and appropriate.	Knowledge Intensive, Perceptive - Focus on Self	Collaborative & Dynamic Virtual Reality, across geographies, clients and stakeholders	Pedantic

Figure 66 - Life Cycle Business Model Development in Digital HR

Deliver Intellect - Organizations deploy combinations of different delivery models to realize the benefits of building structure that synergize fundamentally and significantly redefines the nature of interactions among the structure, workforce, processes and technology. This challenge to our mind will now been fixed with an appropriate Social Management System. HR technologies, programs and policies have to become adaptable, flexible and customer friendly. In an environment of shifting economic circumstances, organizations are striving to achieve the ability, flexibility and capacity to manage change in a way that maintains profitability and performance, and protects competitiveness. Public and private sector organizations are also striving to respond to the challenges of supporting national competitiveness and the demands of users for services of higher quality and greater accessibility. Increased globalization, the rapid pace of change and the requirement for organizations to foster creativity and innovation has highlighted the role of human resources as an enduring source of improved organizational capacity and competitive advantage.

Converge Social & Intellect - An effective system that can engage with employees at an intellectual and social level is a discovery & a one stop HCM platform for answering questions that pertain to talent management in a way that helps a company deal with their business strategy for collaborating effectively with their people strategy. But more importantly, establishing employee experience.

If you can meet with triumph and disaster with equal contempt and yet keep your peace, you are perhaps better placed to lead.

While people realize their objectives of self-fulfillment, self-respect and dignity and see for themselves their Intellectual Corporation standing for its values and beliefs, the company in turn realizes its vision, dream and objectives, adding wealth to the shareholders, its purpose of being in business.

We must ask, are we ready to build upon organizational intelligence while building an intellectual company?

Annexure 1

The Intellectual Corporation of the 21st Century

- *Defining the attributes of the 21st Century Intellectual Corporation in terms of Organization, Systems, Culture, People, Organizational Processes, People Processes, Knowledge Management, and Environment Management.*
- *This can be a survey conducted amongst four demographic sections, Executive Managers, Managers, Academics and Students.*
- *The outcome will be a perceptual image of a 21st Century Intellectual Corporation*
- *Administer a questionnaire to Executives and Managers of a company to assess the organization on the attributes measured above.*
- *This can be correlated with the organization's performance within its industry*

For each of the statements below indicate on a six-point scale your agreement or disagreement with the statement. 1 indicates strong disagreement while 6 indicates strong agreement.

The ideal 21st Century Intellectual Corporation will

1. Have a high physical asset base
2. Physical size will not be of significance
3. Invest in organizational learning
4. People retention will be a priority
5. Not have a high dependence on bureaucracies & policies in a wholesome sense
6. Invest in creating new policies & systems
7. Have formal processes for knowledge sharing
8. Leave knowledge sharing to individual abilities
9. Knowledge management gains priority over individual intellect
10. The human mind is the foundation of the corporation
11. Growth through people contribution is organic without the foundation of a formal structure and strategy
12. Have clearly defined role & responsibility boundaries.
13. Have people competencies as the basis for organization
14. Growth in size of the organization necessitates complexity and distances to emerge between front-line and decision-making.
15. Systems thinking will be dominant and defined systems will dominate and guide all actions
16. Individuals will create and identify flexibilities in the systems to add value and make a difference to the system
17. Company strategy and business opportunities will evolve based on the context of the emerging economy.
18. Technological superiority and strong asset base is not necessarily a competitive advantage
19. Local market dominance will not sustain long-term developmental growth
20. Global growth will be achievable by conglomerates and widely diversified corporations
21. Blurred strategy & structure linkages owing to change dynamics
22. Dynamic identification and changing of competencies will be an inevitability

23. Organizations with dominant systems thinking have possibly made people orientation second to the systemic orientation.
24. The question before us is whether they have created systems flexible and dynamic enough to adapt to the thinking individuals of tomorrow?
25. Do we as a consequence have adequate checks, balances and flexibility built into a system to make it versatile, high performing and dynamic?
26. Directions perceived, as right as of yesterday may need a relook not for any dramatic reason but to take stock of the company in the context of an emerging economy.
27. Companies that saw growth as a strategic direction have revised their view to consolidation as of today.
28. Corporations that confined themselves to their known areas of competence are looking at alliances and acquisitions to get into industries of the 21st century.
29. Organizational direction is likely to be creating capital value out of their intellectual and human assets.
30. Organizations with a product focus and expertise in sales, distribution, variety and dominance possess a strategic advantage versus organizations that have a large portfolio of products but with limited market share and customer base.
31. Organizations with several products (not brands) of diametrically opposite features tend to generalize the marketing mix and are unable to position for themselves as a large enough corporation with the mass scale advantages.
32. Firms need to look at size as an important strategic advantage to dominate the market.
33. Multi brand companies should have the financial muscle, global experience, and staying power, people and reach to penetrate significantly.
34. Or alternatively focus on a single product and turn into the best supplier of any comparable benchmark.
35. Eventually mid-sized organizations without strategic advantages are unlikely to survive.
36. Effectively conglomerate corporations with a wide portfolio of product offering will not be at an advantage.
37. Large single product and small multi brand portfolio appears to be coexisting in markets that are similar in nature but varying in size.
38. Product life cycles simply do not have a long shelf life.
39. The product is out in the market before a structure has been put in place.
40. Very limited time was spent between strategy-structure interfaces while this launch was planned and executed.
41. Getting on with the business would mean flexibility in all our actions with limited recourse to proven practices of the managerial past.
42. Corporate goals focus would be dependent on a performance cycle rather than the traditional quarterly reviews.
43. Organizations should evaluate performance cycles in terms of the work content, targets to be met and the optimum time required to achieve it.
44. The balance sheet as a consequence would reflect a true performance of the tasks completed, tasks on hand and the pending work content.
45. A management accounting balance sheet should be the norm for presentation, rather than an accounting balance sheet.
46. Corporations would then be forced to evaluate their performance on a virtual cycle.
47. Financial leverage as a critical success factor of new business horizon is not dealt with as comprehensively in high value, margin, and low asset and less management intensive business ventures as it is in low value/margin, financially intensive capital structuring and management intensive businesses.
48. Few takers would be available for low knowledge intensive businesses with a heavy capital outlay.

49. To face competition over time and retaining a winning condition, organizational competencies have to be identified and changed dynamically.
50. Identification of what we can do best and having them implemented expeditiously are both equally important.
51. Summation of individual competencies determines the organizational competencies.
52. Knowledge of the business as we ran it yesterday makes no meaning for tomorrow.
53. Competencies would radically shift from one stage of development to another depending upon the stated position of the organization at a point in time.
54. Environmental and socio-political factors continue to be critical success factors for global organizations.
55. Large corporations have consistently seen the need to evaluate and work with their environments systemically.
56. Downsized organizations continue to feel the pain of separations dealt over time on its people owing to absence of a clear prescriptive formula of success post the restructuring exercise
57. Structural weight traditionally seen in large corporate are now decreasing as companies see the emergence of individuals who can substitute large numbers with their agile mind.
58. In the Intellectual Corporate headcount is less likely to ever be an issue.
59. Where an organization has not kept pace with training and development a significant portion of managers would turn knowledge redundant periodically and would come up for the retention review.
60. People do not wish to be told, controlled, directed, guided or led, irrespective of our noble intentions.
61. They would fundamentally like to be left to themselves to show initiative, make new products, redesign, change, create, add value, learn, reflect and make their impact on the company bottom line.
62. Culture definitions have undergone a shift from culture inheritance, management and absorption to cultural creation, assimilation, influencing and impacting for change.
63. Individuals would see the organization changing and unchanging periodically given the critical mass of people who are influencing it.
64. Never would a day come when the organizational members can sit back and define their company culture in a constant, consistent sort of way.
65. Transition from approved ways and means of doing things turning into unanticipated influences over people, systems and process would happen unknowingly.
66. The world of technology is complex, fast changing and unstructured and it thrives best when individuals are left alone to be different, creative and disobedient
67. Organizations see the need for institutionalizing learning and teaching systems for people to learn, develop and intellectually grow as a responsibility, "self-imposed", on them.
68. While it is not being presupposed that this becomes a corporate responsibility a learning culture perhaps is an inescapable responsibility of the corporate management.
69. Organizational learning forums would multiply several folds with members demanding time and opportunity to participate physically or electronically.
70. Decision-making, an important aspect of the changing cultural dimension, has moved to the point of impact.
71. Intellectual Corporation rarely is change shy, as their coping mechanism happens to be their mind that understands rationally the purpose and goals aimed through the planned change.
72. Individuals of well-managed intellectual companies do not like to be told to change.
73. Work role professionals see organizational life no longer as an extension of their real world full time life.

74. It is possible to receive a higher number of applications for part time employment just to help the applicant have more time to do other things.
75. While this is perhaps a loss to the corporation for the increasing amount of limited time availability of their effective performers the upside would be the opportunity for organizations to have half as many more people and their creative minds.
76. Corporations see the real need to integrate diversity issues as a basic management challenge
77. Diversity preparation becomes an important organizational action point to have people not just tolerate each other but actually enjoy working and sharing with their colleagues.
78. Teams would exercise considerable influence over their choice of team members.
79. Effectively teams would turn into clusters and coalition groups with similar and dissimilar purposes and goals.
80. Many organizational norms of discipline and rules of work ethic traditionally understood and practiced in the organization may undergo a change given the cluster desire to achieve their goals in their own way.
81. Intellectual culture could be conflict prone given occasional polarized and strong views on individual positions and perspectives.
82. The corporate would become responsible to create confrontation forums and stress release mechanisms to make people of intellectual intensity work together.
83. The dispersion possibility of people flying off the handle owing to combination of work role pressures and an inability to sell their idea across is high.
84. Similarly, HR professionals who have become responsible for HR services and people counseling roles would need considerable adaptation and focus maintenance training.
85. The organization tends to be perceived as being excessively skewed in favor of meritocracy albeit at the cost of loyal long-term employees.
86. A natural process of attrition of those who do not "fit in" would emerge for a natural process of elimination.
87. Employees would consider the organizational career plan to consist of a successive set of hurdles to be crossed at every stage of their career with no letting go at any time.
88. Creation of a performing culture where people would sense the common goal of customer service, satisfaction, adding to shareholder's wealth and bottom line orientation is key to the Intellectual Corporation.
89. A culture where "people – systems" would replace "systems – people" with the original contribution of the people as the critical input.
90. Managerial actions by itself would no longer determine company priorities on an exclusive basis in this dynamic culture.
91. Firms now bring in people with special expertise to the job, people with proven academic depth and potential to pursue intellectually stimulating assignments.
92. Generalist studies as seen in last few decades with a focus on arts and humanities have given way to accounting, technology, behavioral sciences and psychology, environment and business management specialization.
93. Substantive amount of quality managerial time is currently spent on managerial competencies, performance goals and action report charts to evaluate performance against set work plans.
94. There is urgency on the part of the new employee to demand active involvement in management thinking and decision making process.
95. What was in yesteryears treated as "none of my business" is today made into "everything is my business" by the thinking employee group?
96. Intellectually stimulated individuals should be offered high-risk assignments involving new product launches, financial market management, union settlement, meeting aggressive project deadlines.

97. Involving individuals in activities beyond their defined scope of work is fundamental a form of offering intellectual equity to people.

98. Employees view the emerging business complexity as an inevitable feature of the modern economy. In it they see an opportunity for individual capabilities, skills, competencies and most of all their intellect to be put to use considerably.

99. The integrating function is the intellect in the individual that helps process, analyze, synthesize, store and make a coherent meaning to all pieces of connected and dispersed set of factors.

100. It is the intellect again that brings in the recall, create relevant connections, make a method to the plan, provides scope for development of competencies and provides the employee with the capabilities to manage, decide, judge and make a meaning to all actions.

101. In fact, it is the intellect that makes learning happen to the individual.

102. As we stated earlier this process of culture creation is likely to be influenced by the intellect to a considerable extent.

103. The organization in addition should make intellectual interaction a formal management process in resolving organizational problem solving scenarios.

104. Essentially the intellectual employee also arrives with a baggage of imponderables behaviorally and intellectually.

105. Make knowledge intensive tasks routine to the work groups and is in fact a way of life to reach out to enduring goals.

106. Make scenario-setting agendas to make intellectually superior people to come together and work on organizational challenges.

107. Make group cross-functional where required, and make the encounter mutually beneficial.

108. Create crucial interdependencies amongst employees who need to make their target only through a formal process of transaction.

109. Intellect has an untold, unseen intensity to break apart and come out into the open irrespective of behavioral consequences on themselves or those they are dealing with.

110. For the intellectual, an opportunity to work in real life organizations where the output is measurable and implementable is substitutable or not.

111. Large number of intellectually inclined individuals shows deep sensitivity and care towards organizational processes that may appear to be so rigorous and meaningless traditional managers.

112. The purpose of an organization rarely needs to be told to an intellectual manager. They know what they in business for and for what purpose have they been hired.

113. Intellectuals can be organizational mercenaries, these people in real life organizations evolve, grow and contribute to their own limits, stretch and challenges.

114. They are at several instances unconventional and would border on the maverick.

115. Over time intellectually intensive organizations and consequently teams would eliminate through natural competitive positioning peers, superiors or subordinates not comparable to their current averages.

116. In time the eliminators in turn get eliminated when new entrants bring in a fresh insight into a past, present or future processes.

117. Many untold, unseen human conflicts emerge when the culture is plastered with an emphasis on "think and do" as against traditional management methods of "follow the system and do".

118. What possibly could then be an option but to nurture and grow the in house intellect and use their native brilliance to resolve home grown problems and fix oneself to cope with and resolve the market challenges.

119. The individuals on their part need to relook at their learning and educating styles and see its applicability to an organizational setting on a dynamic and sustaining basis.

120. The intellectual talent would demand remuneration and a life style commensurate with their competency and knowledge depth that they bring in to the organization and would not be

governed by equitable and peer group factors traditionally used by compensation specialists for salary and equivalencies.

121. Their ability to perennially sustain competitiveness without understanding the root cause of the problem turned finally into the problem itself.

122. Strategic reorientation meant a sort of capitulation, in a seeming state of conditional surrender and resignation that what now has to happen would happen for sure.

123. In fact a significant portion of the people plan and their costing is now a part of the capital investment plan and not a part of the operating cost or the revenue expense.

124. They bring in an undetected sensibility, solidity and perceptibility, a fact that is so very necessary for the corporate involved in intricate problem solving.

125. The new breed of talent operates on the basis of the reality principle and would effectively adjust to meet the unavoidable demands of the environment by postponing a current priority.

126. Programs and policies should favor knowledge management activities as being business priorities and that all-organizational members should adhere to it.

127. Their delivery schedules should under pin the criticality of getting things done in a "people-systems" way.

128. Daily schedules should reflect time for thought and planning with organizational members receiving consistent signals that original, untested ideas are most welcome.

129. Hired quality talent does not mean or imply automatic intellectual application and consequent benefit to the corporation through an impacting bottom line performance.

130. Employees bring in their native talent combined with their learning, experiences and value into the business organization on a Greenfield basis.

131. Willingness to mirror past learning does not mean a successful usage of the experience.

132. Yet the corporate would have to create coping mechanisms to bring in a reasonable number of original contribution goals and have them applied to the real life setting.

133. The organizational setting should convert itself into one large laboratory with concurrent experiments, inventions and approaches being debated, attempted, succeeded and failed.

134. A set of people who have done nothing through the year but only generated brilliant thoughts out of their drawing boards for implementation should be isolated for recognition.

135. The task of the managerial group would be to get the original thinkers to apply their ideas in a test laboratory organizational setting, learn from the experience through formal systems of feedback and "tell me" experiences.

136. Organizations are products of the ways that people in them think and interact in differing situations and management dynamics.

137. Organizations are webs of participation. Change the participation and you change the organization.

138. Learning efforts should focus initially on the thought generation process and thereafter on the practical results that it has commenced to deliver.

139. Critically the differentiating factor is that change is neither directed, conceptualized nor delivered by the top management. The change happens by a team of people who feel the need to change without encountering an entry-exit experience.

140. Thinkers-doer's distinction should be eliminated in policy, spirit and in action.

141. Individuals cannot be subjugated to staid forms and methods outdated in content and spirit while intellectualization efforts are on in an organization.

142. A structure where the individual is the fulcrum of action.

143. In the process of chatting up people derive relationships bonds and working styles and learn to work in a competitive team environment. Alienating people from each other and expecting high output has long since been discarded as a useful theory.

144. Typically, in such organizations styles are neither consistent nor permanent. People employ styles depending on the situation and emerge transformational given the compelling or facilitating circumstance.

145. In the "Intellectual Corporation" people dynamics and their inter relationships is dependent on how far have we transacted, networked with each other on issues confronting each other, the team or the organization as a whole.

146. Concurrently the task of setting working norms on how would the hierarchical superior behave with the colleague also needs elaboration.

147. People should be in a position to take risks without feeling threatened of their job. Motive to add value to the corporation is a fundamental assumption and in which case quality or the dimension of the risk is irrelevant.

148. Learning environment, amongst other things, insists on sharing of experiences, learning, insights, experimental outcomes etc. This has to be a mandate across the company.

149. While team working by itself has its built in advantages, congruence in thought, sense of purpose, a climate of trust, availability of mutual perspectives and styles, assimilation of attitudes, similarity of goals, seeking coherent conclusions and common concern for each other's well-being and security is essential to an Intellectual Corporation.

150. Getting like-minded people together is one simple solution to achieve Teamgruence.

151. One possible way is to get clusters form by themselves depending upon the goals to be achieved.

152. The individuals then have the choice of leveraging their competencies with others and producing results that demonstrate achievements beyond the capabilities of one person or let them experience for themselves the shortfall of an isolated approach.

153. The learning need comprises both the opportunity and a fear of obsolescence. It is this attitude that would bring antithetical poles together.

154. In a Learning Company, people find security not in holding on what they know but in sharing, interacting and letting go what they know in quest of learning more of what they do not know.

155. Utopist are indeed dreamers, idealists and romanticists. And all of them form the organization of tomorrow.

156. Corporations created by individuals who wish to learn and contribute in an environment that fosters value for the human dignity and spirit, where people can come and give their best, where merit and human mind is at a premium, where a culture that fosters nurturing originality, where the corporation cherishes experimentation, where the human mind is set free from inhibitions, where intellect is treated and dealt with as a superior form of value addition and contribution, where individuals individually and collectively focus on results and where people attempt flying despite aero dynamic limitation

157. Current organizations ensure they only use 5 to 10 percent of people's abilities to work. Outside of work they engage the other 90 – 95 percent of their time, energy and work.

158. Intellect is not the prerogative of a select few, at least not in the business organization. At best this should be a minimum assumption to make the organization vibrant intellectually.

159. Intellectually stimulated people seek a demanding work environment where they are stretched to produce results, are expected to be at their best at all times.

160. Intellect does not guarantee success.

161. In fact, managing the intellect will perhaps be the single most important HR challenge of the 21st century.

162. Small firms are generating disproportionate number of jobs and tend to be more innovative than large enterprises.

163. There are jobs for both generalists and specialists. People need to find their niche and move on into becoming specialists as generalists.

164. Hiring of large numbers would become inevitable, but each would several times over their costs and contribution. The age of downsizing in knowledge intensive industries is over.

165. Companies would either grow or diminish and there would be no mid-way.

166. To start with employees, need to take charge of their learning and their careers. The corporate responsibility should be providing avenues where learning can occur. The rest is up to the individual.

167. Intellectual corporations create reward systems that go beyond the guaranteed base pay or position driven compensation.

168. Effectively Intellectual Corporations is those that have derived an intellectual compatibility and a fit between the intellectual individuals who make up the organization and the processes, variables and systems that are available to make the individual work effectively.

169. While people realize their objectives of self-fulfillment, self-respect and dignity and see for themselves their Intellectual Corporation standing for its values and beliefs, the company in turn realizes its vision, dream and objectives, adding wealth to the shareholders, its purpose of being in business.

Annexure 2

Defining Organizational Cultures, Leadership disrupted Styles,

Organizational Models

Definitions

Part A - Defining Organizational Culture

Type 1 – Operator Culture

Based on human interaction and most line units learn those high levels of communication, trust and teamwork as essential to getting the work done efficiently. Learn that no matter how clearly the rules are specified of what is supposed to be done under different operational conditions, the world is to some degree unpredictable and one must be prepared to use one's own innovative skills to deal with them. The action of any organization is ultimately the action of people. The success of the enterprise therefore depends on people's knowledge, skill, learning ability and commitment. Rules and hierarchy often get in the way under unpredicted conditions. People become highly sensitive to the degree to which the production process is a system of interdependent functions all of which must work together in order to be efficient and effective. These points apply to all kinds of "production processes" whether we are talking about a sales function, a clerical group, a cockpit, or a service unit. The knowledge and skill required are "local" and are based on the Organization's core technology. No matter how carefully engineered the production process is or how carefully Rules and routines are specified, operators will have to deal with Unpredictable contingencies. Therefore, operators have to have the capacity to learn and to deal with Surprises. Most operations involve inter-dependencies between separate elements of the Process hence operators must be able to work as a collaborative team in which Communication, openness, mutual trust and commitment are highly valued.

Type 2 – Engineering Culture

People of all persuasions are attracted in the first place because as it is abstract and impersonal. Their education reinforces the view that problems have abstract solutions and those solutions can, in principle, be implemented in the real world with products and systems that are free of human foibles and errors. In the broadest sense, they are designers of products and systems that have utility, elegance, permanence, efficiency, safety, and maybe, as in the case of architecture, even aesthetic appeal. They are basically designed to require standard responses from their human operators, or, ideally, to have no human operators at all. Pro-actively optimistic, nature can and should be mastered: "that which is Possible should be done". Based on science and available technology. Stimulated by puzzles and problems to be overcome. Pragmatic oriented towards useful products and outcomes. Perfectionist oriented toward elegance, simplicity, and precision: "keep it Neat and simple". Preference for "people free" solutions, for working with "things". The ideal world is one of elegant machines and processes working in perfect Precision and harmony without human intervention. Preference for linear, simple cause and effect, quantitative thinking. absolutes view of reality. Attractive to people whose careers are oriented in "technical/functional Competence." and "pure challenge"

Type 3 – Executive Culture Global Community

Absolute focus on finances – without financial survival and growth there Are No returns to shareholders or to society. Financial survival is equivalent to perpetual war with one's Competitors. One cannot get reliable data from below because subordinates will tell one What they think one wants to hear: therefore, as CEO one must trust one's own Judgement more and more (i.e. Lack of accurate feedback increases own sense of Rightness and omniscience). Organization and management are intrinsically hierarchical: the hierarchy Is the measure of status and success and the primary means of maintaining Control. Therefore, the willingness to experiment and take risks extends only to those Things that permit one to stay in control. Because the organization is very large it becomes depersonalized and Abstract, and, therefore, has to be run by rules, routines (systems), and Rituals ("machine bureaucracy"). Personal relationships are a means to the end of motivation and control, they Are not ends in themselves (the inherent value of relationships and community Becomes lost as one rises in the hierarchy). The ideal world is one in which the organization performs like a well-oiled Machine, needing only occasional maintenance and repair.

Type 4 – Digital Culture

The organization values history and tradition. The organization is built upon stories that lasts over time and that is believed and revered by people as important learning of the past. In the organization time is not an important consideration, as it is perceived to be relative to the tasks and is managed appropriately as long as basic human processes are followed. The organization emphasizes an appropriate management style that foster learning. The organization focuses on learning environments that involves brings together intellect, knowledge, systemic processes, personal mastery and role models. The climate is conducive and non-threatening to share successes and failures and is not a performance consideration. The organization believes in creating effective structures and hierarchies that provides clarity to roles, responsibilities, tasks and actions. The organization has effective communication channels, with and without boundaries, people enjoy communicating in relation to business and tasks to be accomplished. A leadership disrupted and management that pays attention to high performance lead the organization. The organization believes in swift and effective communication, work long hours to conclude tasks, people live at work, identify with winning and use all resources at one's disposal to accomplish tasks. The organization emphasizes an appropriate management style that foster learning. The organization focuses on learning environments that involves brings together intellect, knowledge, systemic processes, personal mastery and role models.

Part B – Defining Organizational Model – 1

Human Organization Culture - Driven by orientation to people, their actions, beliefs in the value of human good and concerns. Focus on making people productive through internal drivers with or without clarity on final goals and tasks. Action through policies, rewards, interactive processes, job design making people an important consideration in organizational issues. Long term organization growth, meaning profits, shareholder value meant people growth.

Learning Company Culture - Driven by organizational energy to learn, self-develop, perpetuate individualization as they grow to compete. Focus on people productivity through learning drivers on what can be done should be done. Action through making knowledge an important performance parameter. Long term competitive advantage through focus on performance empowerment.

Institutional Organizational Culture - Driven by structural effectiveness, procedural clarity, defined end states and eventual success of people and the systems that lasts over time. Focus on institutional success on a holistic basis and dependent on people expertise. Action through making systems the critical consideration for organizational effectiveness. Long term orientation to building an enterprise that works through economics cycles without a major emphasis on revitalization or renewal.

Competing Organization Culture - Driven by the need for internal and external energy to compete and focus on results. To make people work to plan and have targets achieved as per plan. Focus on organizational vision, values, philosophy and performance and establish concrete direction and make all people, systems and processes work together. Action through making people subservient to systems and external stimuli. Long Term competitive advantage seen as dominance and measures that sustain organizational competitiveness.

Part C – Defining Organizational Model – 2

Voluntary School Culture - Driven by conscious endeavor to support a cause that extends beyond commercial perspective in many situations. Focus through driving synergies of the people and process systems that integrate organizational goals to an end objective. Action orientation measured by appropriates planning, measured steps, building consensus and reasonable task orientation. Long term goals to build sustainable business models that can seamlessly move from one situation to another without a strong immediate task and performance pressure.

Intellectual Company Culture - Driven by the need to promote and perpetuate intellect as it determines individual and organizational means and tasks. Focus on delivery through advancement of learning, knowledge, skills but lacks need for attitudes and appropriate behavior to make things happen. Action driven by merciless meritocracy and rewards to processes and systems that goes beyond human dependence. Long Term sustainability only based on enhanced intellectual capital, innovation and newness of things done within and without the organization.

Mechanistic Corporation Culture - Driven by the successes, stories, rituals and processes that have proved in time that it works and should be followed mechanically. Focus on building internal architectures, systems and processes that drives individual and team performance. Action orientation is expected to be more an outcome given smooth working methods and competitive pressures built within the organizational framework. Long Term need to make teams work together to achieve group goals that achieves today's performance and tomorrow's systems.

Performing Enterprise Culture - Driven by business bottom line, performance, financial focus and the need to achieve tasks and goals established to be accomplished under any circumstance. Focus on driving results through structure, style, roles, and benchmarks as it impacts organizational effectiveness. Action to demonstrate what finally matters in the organization, the stakes involved and reward and punishment that follows post action. Long Term destination treated as an end in itself and pursuit of the goals set as non-negotiable and that it should be accepted and achieved by all internal stakeholders.

Part D – Leadership disrupted Style Model – 1

People Strategist - Driven need to motivate and keep people in the right frame of mind to be productive and happy. Focus on creating people oriented systems that enable a culture that brings individuals, teams and organizations together. Action oriented to demonstrate by action that concern for people enables organizations to perform above expectation. Long Term orientation to delivering

---

value through people development, individualized tasks, creating an environment that is self-exhilarating.

Teacher - Driven by the need to make people, processes and systems learn from one another, interact to make a meaningful whole and are constantly seeking holistic behavior from organizational systems. Focus through clear policy perspectives and on delivering intellectual and performance value that sponsors native instincts, creative pursuits, feedback and review processes and encourages actions that facilitates results. Action oriented towards developing people competencies, ensures organizational competitiveness is appropriately managed by right people and makes organizational goals subservient to competency development. Long Term vision to build an organizational that can culturally sustain itself to teach, renew, learn, contribute in varying life cycles and has adequate organizational energy to grow with momentum.

Builder - Driven by encouraging things to be worked out, provides job clarity, coaches and rewards for performance. Focus on building for the future through institutional processes, demanding systems that connect organizational functions and works through structures that are streamlined, regulated and planned. Action oriented through appropriateness of actions driven by circumstance, enabling learning to be documented, creates knowledge sharing atmosphere, drives decisions through consensus and takes meaningful time to accomplish tasks. Long Term desire to make lasting organizations that can stream through economic and business life cycles and does not have the pressure to retain performance under all circumstance.

Visionary - Driven by vision, sharing strategic goals, communicates, shares values, distinctive concern for individual sensitivity and demonstrated by examples. Focus on competitiveness, some collaboration, business models that are appropriate and accepted by people and goals that have been worked to individual and organizational advantage. Action oriented to make people accept the overall good, establishes concreteness to tasks to be accomplished, yet merciless in search of meritocracy. Long Term priority to build organizational wealth, individual intellect, collective wisdom, sustainable business model and overall organizational effectiveness parameters.

Part E – Leadership disrupted Style Model – 2

Manager - Driven by institutionalizing policies that provide clarity to goals, tasks and manages a team through maintaining status quo through conflicting circumstance and taking decisions that involve retaining established norms and practices. Focus on building loyalty through establishing people oriented systems that enable handling tasks that are individually focused. Action oriented to enable easy and smooth management of the organization, streamlines administrative processes, establishes a string back office operations organization and manages customer oriented roles through follow procedure route. Long Term desire to make organizational working built on strong fundamentals of bureaucracy, frameworks and management styles.

Scientist - Driven by the urge to create, make actions intellectually dominant, treats developmental processes a predominant organizational factor and is willing to compromise for nothing other than intellectual superiority in actions. Focus on attracting and nurturing talent, systems and processes that are of utility today and tomorrow, more tomorrow, and is willing to absorb the costs of human and organizational process costs as a necessary condition of managing the human mind. Action oriented to demonstrate merit and results supersedes all other performance factors, does not believe in means as an important consideration while acting upon information and manages rewards as a necessary evil in people management processes. Long Term desire to create a self-propelling organization that has internal renewal capability to prod organizational performance, individual effectiveness and shareholder satisfaction.

Technocrat - Driven by engineering sciences, that technology provides solutions to complex organizational problems and believes in logic and rationality as desired attitudes. Focus on adding technical and functional values to business situations enables competency development that is vertical and incisive and promotes organizations to drive business through technological excellence. Action through individualized working, avoiding teams and consequent inefficiencies, meets deadlines under all circumstance and seeks the best. Long Term desire to make people processes subservient to technological processes and works towards eliminating elaborate actions that involve meetings, group work, communication forums and large scale explanation to actions.

Driver - Driven by a performance system that overrides all other considerations and makes individual targets an important element achieving results. Focus on priorities that are determined quickly, followed through decisively and ensure that different parts of the organization are focused on their own deliverables. Action oriented to provide criteria for success and failures and ensures it is adequately communicated and holds accountability on streamlined systemic norms. Long Term orientation to retain competitive advantage by providing profitability through consistent intervals and prefers revenue to growth.

Part F – Defining Organizational Models on an Absolute Basis for the corporation	
ORGANIZATION TYPES	
Type 1	**Competing Organization**
	High Performance, Swift and Effective Communication, concludes tasks, market focused, dominated by systems, high value for money orientation, ambitious, aggressive goal setting, directive and task oriented
Type 2	**Learning Company**
	Fosters learning, intellectually stimulating environments, high internal energy, and adaptability to individuals high, freedom to act, fair play in targets, time to develop, opportunity to apply, experiment, enabling the unknown
Type 3	**Human Organization**
	Values history and tradition, builds upon its people strengths, acts through clarity in all its orientation, philosophy to make people productive, high resilience, mutual expectations matched, long lasting relationships, mutual respect in work cultures, work ethic
Type 4	**Institutional Corporate**
	Effective Structures, roles and responsibilities, elaborate communication channels, slow to react, defined end states, moderate goal setting, long lasting organization, ability to bounce back high
Type 5	**Performing Enterprise**
	Bottom line paramount, financial focus primary objective, rigors of feedback high, low tolerance for failures, political climate, survival driven beyond values, inability to work in teams evident, non-negotiable goals
Type 6	**Intellectual Company**
	Promotes and perpetuates intellect as an end in itself, limited space to learn as organizations evolve, best in class focus, content than process delivery mechanisms, organizational purpose beyond bottom line
Type 7	**Voluntary School**
	Supports a purpose and cause beyond commercial purposes, drives people and process synergies, high resilience to economic up and down turns, long range planning, organizational strategy differentiates businesses and other purposes
Type 8	**Mechanistic corporation**
	Conglomerate, multi business, geographic organizations, thick internal architectures, long hierarchies, open to change although long in time, stable goals, consistent methods, predictive approaches, systemic and role driven.

Author's Profile

Dr. Ganesh Shermon, Oakville, Ontario, Canada, is a Managing Partner & Lead for Talent Solutions, for America's. A 35-year experience - Global Steercom Leadership - P & L Head for People & Change Practice, Consulting & Industry work, (KPMG LLP, Andersen LLP), specializing in Strategy, Organization & People, Personality Profiling, Talent, HCM & HR Tech Advisory work. Currently engaged in researching digital organizations and disruptions.

Research and Thought Paper publications of over 300 articles in journals (Columnist for Business Manager, Business World and Human Capital) and books (McGraw Hill, UnivCanada Himalaya, LULU) include

1. **"Digital Cultures** – Age of the Intellect",
2. **"Business of Staffing** - A Talent Agenda",
3. **"Talent Assessments** – A Manual of Competency Based Assessment Development Tools",
4. "**Competency Based HRM** – Competency Mapping, Assessment & Development Centers",
5. "**Knowledge HRM** – A Strategy – Structure Perspective",
6. **"Star Track 100** – A Century 21 Leadership Model",
7. **"Strategic Business Balanced Scorecard** - Tool Book",
8. **"Turning Star Talent into Careers"** (Play Book),
9. **"Psychometric Testing & Assessment Tools & Techniques"** (Tool Book)",
10. **"Business of Strategy** - Keeping Scores",
11. **"Business of Leaders** – Axis of Influence",
12. **"Pinewood Global Inc.",**
13. **"Ripla Motors Global Inc.",**
14. "**Disruptive Human Resources** - The People Organization",
15. "**Digital Human Resources Management** – Leadership Disrupted",
16. **"Digital Organizations** – Leadership Disrupted",
17. **"Disrupting Human Resources** – Talent Rules",
18. **"Handbook of Assessments** – Tools, Games, Simulations, Cases & Role Plays"

A Private Pilot & a recipient of the Award "500 Leaders of Influence in the 20th Century" from American Biographical Association, Washington DC, US, is listed in the World Directory of "International Who is Who of Professionals" & "Heritage Who is Who" USA. Also received the title "Lifetime Deputy Governor" of the ABI-USA, Research association as a member of the Board of Governors. Has a PGDM from XLRI, India and a Ph. D – Organizational Theory & Structure – MSU/AMP MIT Sloan School of Management, Cambridge, MA. Can be reached at GRShermon@ICloud.Com

Comments by Global Thought Leaders on "Business of Staffing – A Talent Agenda"

"Your section on how HR needs to change in a digital context is spot on with those 20 points" - *M.S. Krishnan, Associate Dean, Global Initiatives, Accenture Professor of Computer Information Systems, Professor of Technology & Operations, Ross School of Business, University of Michigan, Ann Arbor, MI.*

"Ganesh Shermon has really nailed it. He really knows this area well. Well worth reading for anyone interested in this field." **Mark Smith**, *National Industry Leader, Financial Services, KPMG LLP & earlier Global Head of People & Change Practice.*

"In a digital world, there is no greater asset than talent. The ability to meet the challenge of staffing is a strategic advantage - the companies that are creative, agile, innovative will harness the power of the millennial workforce, setting themselves apart to become a global workforce". **Andy Manko** – *Digital Tech Transformation Specialist, Canada*

"Ganesh and Kavita share a detailed and pragmatic look at the full spectrum of attracting and retaining talent. It is a must read for today's HR professionals as they seek to learn evidence based practices as they transform their talent management performance." **Laura Croucher**, *Americas Leader, KPMG HR Transformation Centre of Excellence.*

"Managing Talent is now about inspiring, empowering and enriching your employee's learnings. Challenge your talent and watch them thrive and be happy in their work day. **Jimmy Diamantakis** – *Digital Tech Evangelist & IT Executive Management - Canada*

" The core purpose of any Talent Agenda, has to be enhancing the Value of Human Capital as an enabler to increase the overall Value of the Enterprise. A unique thesis encompassing " Why " & " How "of different globally proven approaches. Truly a practitioner's manual- deep insights - proven methods" **Wilton Henriques** – *Member of the Board – Avantha Group*

" A comprehensive examination of long-term staffing strategies and the changes - A fantastic look into evolving models and policies with insight from global leaders in the field." **Rick Lamanna** – *Leadership Canada – Fragomen Worldwide*

"A comprehensive resource for HR professionals trying to sync Talent Agenda with Business Strategy!" **R Sridhar** – *CHRO – ITC Limited*

"This book is a road map to select the best candidate for your firm. Also, many real life examples and case studies, …an excellent read". **Benjamin Van de Putte** - *President APCI Communications Inc.*

"…Yet another practical prose; yet again, sets him apart from theory-spouting, seminar-chasing "experts"- **Srinath Sridharan** – *Member, GMC, Wadhawan Global Capital*

"is one of the most thoughtful books I have come across in the recent times for the industry where talent is gold - it's real, shows the mirror and gives implementable strategies to follow." **Pradeep Udhas**, *Senior Partner, MD and Global Leader – KPMG LLP – USA.*

www.ingramcontent.com/pod-product-compliance
Lightning Source LLC
Chambersburg PA
CBHW021022210326
41598CB00016B/888